TO THE STUDENT: Study Guides for the textbook are available through your college bookstore under the titles Study Guide I (Chapters 1–14) and Study Guide II (Chapters 14–28) to accompany *Principles of Accounting,* Second Edition by Helmkamp, Imdieke, and Smith, prepared by Bruce Baldwin. The Study Guides can help you with course material by acting as a tutorial, review and study aid. If one of the Study Guides is not in stock, ask the bookstore manager to order a copy for you.

S0-AFF-387

PRINCIPLES OF ACCOUNTING

SECOND EDITION

Tissues

JOHN G. HELMKAMP
Indiana University

LEROY F. IMDIEKE
Arizona State University

RALPH E. SMITH
Arizona State University

JOHN WILEY & SONS
New York Chichester Brisbane Toronto Singapore

Cover photo: Peter Miller/Image Bank.
Cover and text designed by Ann Marie Renzi.
Production supervised by Jan M. Lavin
Copyedited by Regina Weiss
Copyediting supervised by Barbara Heaney

Part Opening Photographs:

Part 1: New York
Part 2: St. Louis
Part 3: Atlanta
Part 4: Chicago
Part 5: Boston
Part 6: Denver
Part 7: Dallas
Part 8: San Francisco

Copyright © 1983, 1986 by John Wiley & Sons, Inc.

All rights reserved. Published simultaneously in Canada.

Reproduction or translation of any part of
this work beyond that permitted by Sections
107 and 108 of the 1976 United States Copyright
Act without the permission of the copyright
owner is unlawful. Requests for permission
or further information should be addressed to
the Permissions Department, John Wiley & Sons.

Library of Congress Cataloging in Publication Data:

Helmkamp, John G.
  Principles of accounting.

  Includes indexes.
  1. Accounting. I. Imdieke, Leroy F. II. Smith,
Ralph Eugene, 1941–. III. Title.
HF5635.H453 1985   657   85-26357
ISBN 0-471-82018-0
Printed in the United States of America
10 9 8 7 6 5 4 3 2

TO OUR FAMILIES

Sheri, Eric, John, and Kevin Helmkamp
Lorraine, Arlene, Brian, Gary, Julie, Lynda, and Marla Imdieke
Mary, Alison, and Tucker Smith

PREFACE

This textbook presents a comprehensive, straightforward description of modern-day principles of accounting. It is a blend of the preparation and use of accounting information, designed primarily for students who have not previously studied accounting or other business subjects. We have taken special care to achieve a realistic balance between the procedures used in accounting and the concepts on which they are based. As such, we have attempted to describe in a logical and understandable way the "how it is done" aspect of accounting as well as the "why it is done" phase.

Our primary objective has been to describe accounting fundamentals as they relate to today's business world because we believe that this textbook is almost as much an introduction to business as it is to accounting. We have carefully selected the subject matter, its organization, and its description to ensure that the book will fit the needs of all beginning accounting students. Consequently, the coverage is relevant for students interested in any type of business career, whether it is accounting oriented or not. The book is intended for use in the traditional two-semester and two- or three-quarter sequences.

WHY STUDY ACCOUNTING?

Virtually every business administration program requires principles of accounting as an important prerequisite to other business courses and as an integral part of preparation for a business career. During the twentieth century, accounting has become essential to the needs of our society. Every person and organization uses accounting information to make decisions. Many times, we use accounting concepts and procedures without even realizing it. On a personal level, individuals maintain bank accounts, prepare budgets, account for their income, and file tax returns. Examples of the many other areas in which accounting information is crucial are:

- Investors evaluate alternative investments such as bonds, stocks, money market funds, and real estate to decide how to invest their money.
- Individuals must often prepare personal financial information that will support an application for an automobile loan or a home mortgage.
- A small business needs accounting information to determine if it is financially successful.

- Large corporations must have detailed records to decide how to allocate scarce resources among their various activities and to report financial results to their owners.
- Boards of directors, partners, and owners use accounting information to evaluate management's performance.
- Creditors rely on accounting information to determine whether to lend money or extend credit to a business.
- Charitable organizations rely on accounting information to determine their sources and uses of funds.
- Governments use accounting procedures to plan and control the receipts and expenditures of public funds.

Accounting is often described as the "language of business" because so much business communication takes place with accounting information. Like any form of communication, accounting has its own specialized terminology, concepts, procedures, and standards. Because of its essential role in our society, accounting as a means of communication must be continually modified and updated to satisfy the changing needs of the business world. For example, inflationary pressures in the past have raised questions about certain traditional accounting fundamentals and have forced the accounting profession to seek a better means of accounting. In addition, the severe squeeze on business profits in today's competitive economy has created the need for more effective managerial accounting techniques.

ORGANIZATION OF THE BOOK

The textbook is organized into eight parts as a logical development of both financial and managerial accounting principles. Part 1 includes Chapters 1 through 5 and covers the Basic Accounting Process. Chapters 6 and 7 constitute Part 2 and describe Accounting Systems and Controls. Part 3 discusses Accounting for Assets and Liabilities in Chapters 8 through 13. Partnerships and Corporations are described in Part 4, consisting of Chapters 14 through 16. The final coverage of financial accounting topics is presented in Part 5 (Chapters 17 through 20) where Additional Financial Reporting Issues are discussed.

A transition is made from financial accounting to managerial accounting in Chapter 21 as an introduction to Part 6, Managerial Accounting Fundamentals (Chapters 21 through 23). Financial Planning and Controlling Operations makes up Part 7 and is discussed in Chapters 24 and 25. The final segment of the textbook (Part 8, Chapters 26 through 28) is directed toward Business Decision Making. The 28 chapters represent a comprehensive, modern version of the principles of accounting.

BASIC FEATURES OF THE BOOK

1. Each chapter begins with a concise description (overview) of the coverage of the chapter and a list of the learning objectives involved. The learning objectives are also repeated in the margins of the text next to the relevant subject material to assist the students through the chapters.

2. A glossary of key terms is presented at the end of each chapter. Each definition is keyed to a page within the chapter where the term is identified in boldface color. In addition, the index at the back of the text uses boldface type to refer students to the end-of-chapter glossary definitions.

3. Demonstration problems are used in Chapters 2–5 to reinforce understanding of the basic concepts and procedures.

4. Discussion questions are included in every chapter to emphasize major points.

5. Exercises pertaining to the most important topics of the chapters are presented in compact form.

6. Problems and alternate problems are included for more comprehensive homework assignments.

7. Each exercise and problem has a brief description of the topic(s) covered. The intent is to focus the students' attention on the main consideration being addressed.

8. Cases are included as thought-provoking applications of accounting topics. Many of these cases require the students to refer to the annual reports of Chrysler Corporation, Holiday Inns, Inc., and Kmart, Inc., located in Appendix A at the end of the text.

9. Illustrations of and references to real-world accounting applications are presented throughout the text to show the students how accounting is used.

10. Authoritative and informative references are made in nontechnical language throughout the text to such sources as the Accounting Principles Board, Financial Accounting Standards Board, Accounting Trends and Techniques, and specific firms' financial statements.

11. A comprehensive discussion of the time value of money is presented in Appendix B at the end of the text.

CHANGES IN THE SECOND EDITION

We sincerely appreciate the very positive response to the first edition of this textbook. At the same time, we fully realize that any book has room for improvement to meet the different and ever-changing needs of the classroom. We have listened carefully and responded to comments and suggestions made by adopters, reviewers, and students. As a result, the second edition contains many adjustments and refinements recommended to us as well as some we have chosen on the basis of our own experience in using the book. The following is a partial list of those changes we feel are most important from a teaching perspective:

1. We have added a brief coverage of the historical development of accounting in Chapter 1 to assist the students in seeing how accounting evolves over time.

2. We have substantially reduced the coverage of perpetual inventory in

Chapter 5. It is now a brief illustration at the end of the chapter, and the worksheet presentation covers only the periodic method. The perpetual inventory material in Chapter 9 has been moved to an appendix at the end of the chapter.

3. The discussion of internal control has been moved to Chapter 6 to align it more closely with the coverage of accounting systems.

4. Temporary investments are now included in Chapter 7, which also covers accounting for cash, to differentiate them more clearly from long term investments.

5. We have added material on international accounting to Chapter 18, from the perspective of foreign currency transactions, foreign currency translation, and international accounting standards.

6. Additional material covering the FIFO method of process costing is included in Chapter 23 to show the effect on the computation of equivalent units and inventory costing.

7. Contribution margin variance analysis has been moved to Chapter 26 to align it more closely with other topics related to the contribution margin form of the income statement.

8. A significant increase in the coverage of capital budgeting is presented in Chapter 27, including the internal rate of return, cost of capital, profitability index, and tax shield effects. ,

9. Chapter 28 has been divided into two parts: Part 1 deals with individual income taxes and Part 2 covers corporate taxation. The subject of deferred taxes has been moved to Chapter 17 to align it more closely with liabilities.

10. Throughout the book, all exercises and problems have been updated and revised. A significant number of new exercises and problems has been added to illustrate major points in the chapters. Comprehensive problems have been included in Chapters 6 and 12 to assist students in developing a total perspective of accounting systems and payroll systems.

11. We have generally increased the use of flowcharts, graphs, and real-world examples throughout the text in order to enhance student understanding and interest.

12. Learning objectives, previously listed only at the beginning of each chapter, are also now floated in chapter margins and act as ''road maps'' for the students.

13. The package of supporting materials has been polished and enhanced. We have worked hard to increase the integration of the supplemental package so that it is more than ever a total teaching approach. In addition, we have added a number of computerized supplements that have their roots in real-world software used by businesses every day.

14. We have attempted to improve our writing style, the description of accounting principles, and the relevancy of the end-of-chapter material wherever users of the first edition have pointed out the need for them.

15. We have moved the discussion of the time value of money to an appendix at the end of the book and added problems to illustrate its application in the business world.

SUPPLEMENTARY MATERIALS

FOR THE STUDENT

Study Guide

Written by Bruce Baldwin of Portland State University, the Study Guide contains learning objectives, study tips, and chapter reviews organized by learning objectives, as well as matching questions, true-false questions, completion questions, multiple choice questions, short answer exercises, and crossword puzzles. A major new feature is the addition of explanations of why answers to multiple choice questions contained in the Study Guide are correct. Volume I covers Chapters 1–14; Volume II, Chapters 14–28.

Practice Sets

Practice sets related to specific chapters in the text are available to provide the student with opportunities to apply accounting concepts and procedures to specific situations.

Practice Set IA—Narrative of Transaction and

Practice Set IB—Business Papers Version by Leroy Imdieke & Ralph Smith. For use after Chapter 6

Practice Set IIA—Narrative of Transactions: Written by Sandra F. Knecht and Thomas A. Warren, Florida Junior College at Jacksonville, this practice set covers a small merchandising and repair business and is intended for use after Chapter 12.

Practice Set IIB—Business Papers Version: The business papers version of Practice Set IIA is intended for those instructors who want their students to organize and work with facsimiles of original documents.

Practice Set III: Corporate practice set for use after Chapter 16.

Computerized Materials

Computerized materials in practice set and template forms are available with the book to enable students to experience how a microcomputer can be used to process accounting data and solve accounting problems using real-world software.

Workpapers I and II

Workpapers designed to minimize the "pencil-pushing" aspect of accounting for the student are available for Chapters 1–14 and Chapters 14–28. The workpapers should assist students in learning proper formats and procedures.

Problem and Demonstration Book

Written by Jay Gelbein and Andre Montero of Kingsborough Community College, this workbook is intended for use in class. It is particularly useful for instructors who like to teach accounting by working exercises and problems.

FOR THE INSTRUCTOR

Solutions Manual

The Solutions Manual, prepared by the authors, provides answers and the procedures used to determine them for all discussion questions, exercises, and problems in the textbook. We have significantly increased the computations that support the solutions. For instructional convenience, it has been divided into two volumes covering Chapters 1–14 and 14–28 in the textbook.

Instructor's Manual

This manual, prepared by Robert Hines of Humboldt State University, identifies chapter learning objectives; keys discussion questions, exercises, and problems to the learning objectives; gives time for completion and difficulty level of the problems; and contains chapter outlines with detailed teaching hints and examples.

Test Bank/Microtest

Available in traditional and computerized formats, the Test Bank consists of multiple choice questions, true-false questions, completion questions, and problems and exercises for each chapter. It contains approximately 1,800 items.

Achievement Tests IA, IB, IIA, and IIB

Written by Ron Burrows of the University of Dayton, the achievement tests are preprinted, 50-minute examinations containing matching questions, true-false questions, multiple choice questions, and exercises/problems. IA and IB cover Chapters 1–14, whereas IIA and IIB relate to Chapters 14–28. There is one test for every two chapters plus a final examination in each packet. Each test is bundled separately for ease of use. All materials are free in quantity for adopters.

Checklist of Key Figures

These are available in quantity for instructors to distribute as learning aids to students.

Overhead Transparencies

The transparency package contains hundreds of transparencies related to all exercises and problems as well as certain text material.

Solutions to Practice Sets

Solutions are available for Practice Sets IA/IB and IIA/IIB, both the narrative transactions and business papers versions; and Practice Set III, corporate.

Solutions to Computerized Materials

Solutions manuals are available for all computerized materials that accompany the text.

Instructor's Manual for Problem and Demonstration Book

This is the instructor's version of the Problem and Demonstration Book. It contains fully worked answers to all exercises and problems and acts as a lecture guide.

ACKNOWLEDGMENTS

As we move from a first edition to a second edition, the list of people who have been instrumental to the book has grown dramatically. We sincerely thank them for all their help. The following faculty members have assisted us in many ways during the development of the first and/or second edition of the book:

Hobart Adams
University of Akron

Toby Atkinson
Brevard Community College

Gerald Axel
Nassau Community College

Bruce Baldwin
Portland State University

Robert Barnes
National College

Henry Beck
Danville Community College

Jane Burns
Indiana University

Frances Carroll
Frances H. Carroll & Co.

Edward Corcoran
Philadelphia Community College

Pauline Corn
Virginia Polytechnic Institute

William Donahue, Jr.
University of Maryland

Alfred Emerson
Northern Essex Community College

Inez Gross
Youngstown State University

David Hansen
David T. Hansen CPA & Associates

Robert Holtfreter
Fort Hays State University

Bonnie Lambert
Chaffey Community College

Arthur LaPorte
Salem State College

Bill Magers
Tarrant County Junior College

Gary Maydew
Iowa State University

Lois McClean
California State University, Los Angeles

Alice Nichols
Florida State University

David Oliver
Edison Community College

John Otto
Grove City College

Lynn Paluska
Nassau Community College

Gordon Pirrong
Boise State University

Earl Purkhiser
Mt. San Antonio College

Robert Schesser
Chaffey Community College

David Schmedel
Amarillo College

Dorothy Sloan
Fresno City College

Charles Thompson
University of Lowell

Steven Tuttle
University of New Hampshire

Herbert Wakeford
Watts, Scobie, Wakeford & McGuirt, Inc.

William Welke
Western Michigan University

A special note of thanks is due to all those people who adopted the first edition and shared their suggestions and criticisms with us. Without them, the second edition would not have been possible. In particular, we would like to thank Arthur J. LaPorte of Salem State College who gave so much of his time and whose comments were so helpful for the completion of the second edition. Also, our special thanks go to Inez Gross of Youngstown State University for a particularly thorough review of the first edition. Finally, we want to recognize David Schmedel of Amarillo College for his outstanding work on the Solutions Manual for the second edition and his many contributions to the overall project.

We would be remiss not to express a special thanks to the many people on the John Wiley & Sons' staff who gave so much of themselves to this book. Don Ford started the project, Lucille Sutton provided the necessary editorial support, and Wayne Anderson put the finishing touches on the second edition. Jan M. Lavin was particularly effective in guiding the book through the production process. As always, any errors or omissions are the responsibility of the authors.

John G. Helmkamp
Leroy F. Imdieke
Ralph E. Smith

ABOUT THE AUTHORS

John G. Helmkamp, DBA, CPA, is Chairperson/Professor of Accounting at Indiana University. He received his doctorate in accounting from Indiana University and has published articles in *The Accounting Review, Journal of Information Science, Managerial Planning,* and other professional journals. He has taught undergraduate and graduate accounting courses at Arizona State University, Purdue University, and Indiana University during an eighteen-year academic career. In addition, Professor Helmkamp has developed and taught a variety of managerial accounting courses offered both nationally and internationally in executive development programs. He is a member of the American Institute of Certified Public Accountants, American Accounting Association, Financial Executives Institute, and Indiana CPA Society. Professor Helmkamp is also active as a consulting CPA and is listed in *Who's Who in America.*

Leroy F. Imdieke, PhD, CPA, is Professor of Accounting at Arizona State University. He received his PhD in accounting from the University of Illinois. He has instructed graduate and undergraduate courses in financial accounting and reporting and has conducted many professional development seminars during his twenty-year career. Professor Imdieke's articles on financial accounting and reporting topics have appeared in *The Accounting Review,* the *Journal of Accountancy,* and other professional journals. He is a member of the American Accounting Association and the Arizona State Society of Certified Public Accountants. He has served on several committees of the American Accounting Association and is currently a member of the Financial Accounting Standards Committee of the Arizona Society of Certified Public Accountants. He has served as a consultant to a number of business firms and state agencies.

Ralph E. Smith, PhD, CPA, is Professor of Accounting at Arizona State University. He has instructed graduate and undergraduate courses and seminars in financial accounting theory and problems. He has also been active in developing and conducting a number of professional development seminars. Professor Smith received his PhD in accounting from the University of Kansas. He is a CPA in the state of Kansas and is a member of the American Accounting Association and the American Institute of Certified Public Accountants. He has served on several committees of the American Accounting Association and also holds membership in Beta Gamma Sigma and Beta Alpha Psi. He has written a number of articles that have appeared in *The Accounting Review,* the *Journal of Accountancy,* the *Journal of Financial and Quantitative Analysis,* and other professional and academic journals.

CONTENTS

CHAPTER 15
CORPORATIONS: ORGANIZATION AND OPERATION

CHAPTER 16
CORPORATIONS: OTHER TRANSACTIONS, INCOME AND RETAINED EARNINGS

PART 5
ADDITIONAL FINANCIAL REPORTING ISSUES

CHAPTER 17
ACCOUNTING FOR LONG-TERM LIABILITIES

PRINCIPLES OF ACCOUNTING

PART 1

THE BASIC ACCOUNTING PROCESS

1

AN INTRODUCTION TO ACCOUNTING AND ITS CONCEPTS

CHAPTER OVERVIEW AND OBJECTIVES

This chapter presents an overview of the purpose and nature of accounting. When you have completed the chapter, you should understand:

1. The historical development of accounting.
2. The purpose of accounting.
3. What accounting information is.
4. The difference between recording and reporting accounting information.
5. Uses of accounting information.
6. The main fields of accounting and the type of work involved in each.
7. The purpose of the balance sheet, income statement, and statement of changes in owner's equity.
8. The meaning of the terms *asset, liability, owner's equity, revenue,* and *expense.*
9. Some of the basic accounting principles.
10. The effect of transactions on the accounting equation.

ACCOUNTING—ITS HISTORICAL DEVELOPMENT

Objective 1: Historical development of accounting

Accounting, as a recordkeeping process, has evolved over many centuries to serve the changing social and economic needs of society. As early as 3600 B.C., clay tablets were used in the Babylonian empire to record various facts. Many of these records contained lists of events as they occurred or lists of goods belonging to an individual, estate, or temple. Similar types of records have also been discovered describing business activities in ancient Greece, Egypt, and Rome. While these early records contained mostly inventories of goods and debts, later records began to reflect a concern for computing profit and loss from different ventures. Some additional advances in recordkeeping were made by church officials and governments during the Middle Ages. Although these early records are interesting, they add little insight into the development of modern-day accounting, which is based on a double-entry method.

Modern-day accounting has its origins in the double-entry bookkeeping method developed by Italian merchants during the twelfth and thirteenth centuries. Probably the most important condition giving rise to this development was the rise of trade between medieval Italian cities and the East. The crusaders of the eleventh and twelfth centuries used ships to carry them and their supplies to the East and brought back spices, satins, and other riches that served to increase demand for such items. As trade expanded, large amounts of capital were needed, so traders often formed partnerships to share the risks involved in relatively long voyages and other ventures. These ventures and partnerships were influential in creating the need for the concept of a business entity as well as a method of determining profits and losses, and double-entry bookkeeping was developed in response to these needs.

The first complete description of the double-entry system was included in a book called *Summa de Arithmetica, Geometria, Proportioni et Proportionalita,* published in 1494 by a Franciscan monk named Luca Pacioli. Although the *Summa* was essentially a treatise on mathematics, it contained a complete description of a way of keeping business records that had developed gradually over the preceding two or three centuries. Pacioli's description of the double-entry process was included in other books and was used widely throughout Europe during the fifteenth, sixteenth, and seventeenth centuries. This double-entry process, which will be described later in this book, became the basis for modern accounting procedures.

The Industrial Revolution in Europe during the eighteenth and nineteenth centuries produced many significant social and economic changes, including a change from the handicraft production system to the factory system. The factory system was based on the use of machinery and equipment to produce many identical products at low costs. Relatively large industrial and commercial enterprises developed, requiring large investments of capital. Many of these enterprises were incorporated, which meant that they were given separate legal status by the appropriate governmental body. These corporations were owned by individuals called shareholders, who demanded regular, detailed reports concerning the financial condition and operating results of the firms. As a result, accounting gradually began to serve as a communication process as well as a means of keeping records.

During the nineteenth and twentieth centuries, corporations have become a dominant force in financing, producing, and distributing goods and services. These corporations are often large, complex organizations whose owners demand accounting systems that can provide relevant and reliable information for use in evaluating the efficiency of operations. Governmental regulation and income tax legislation have resulted in increased demands on accounting systems in both their recordkeeping and communication functions. The double-entry system developed by the early Italian merchants is essentially the same system used today to satisfy the increased demands for accounting information.

THE PURPOSE OF ACCOUNTING

**Objective 2:
Purpose of accounting**

Accounting is a service activity. It provides financial information about economic activity that is intended to be useful in making economic decisions.[1] Business firms, governmental agencies, charitable foundations and nonprofit organizations, families, and individuals are all economic units engaged in economic activity. Most economic activity involves decisions about how to allocate available resources effectively among alternative needs. People need relevant information for making sound decisions. In our complex society, decision makers rely on data supplied by specialists in various fields. Lawyers, for example, provide information about the effects of existing and changing legislation, medical professionals offer advice about the possible effects of different health-care decisions, and accountants provide information about the effects of business activities.

A five-step process is generally followed in making and executing decisions. Thus, decision makers:

1. Establish goals.
2. Consider various alternatives for reaching the goals.
3. Make decisions.
4. Implement the decisions.
5. Evaluate the results and revise goals if necessary.

Thus, the decision-making process may be illustrated by the following system

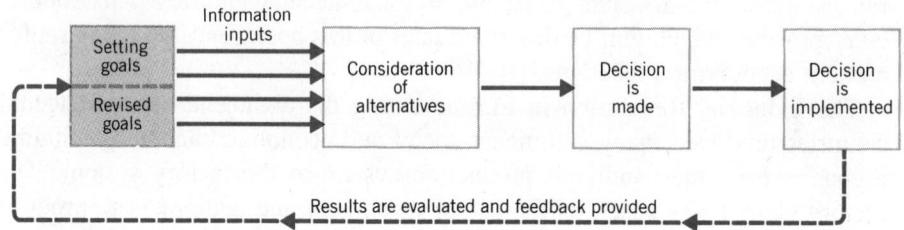

ACCOUNTING—AN INFORMATION PROCESSING SYSTEM

Accounting is a means of social communication and involves a flow of information. To be effective, the recipient of the information must understand the message that is being conveyed. Accounting uses words and symbols to communicate financial information to managers, investors, creditors, and other decision makers. As you study accounting, you must learn the meanings of the words and symbols used by accountants, so that you can understand the messages contained in financial summaries and reports. Everyone involved in

---

[1]Accounting Principles Board, "Basic Concepts and Accounting Principles Underlying Financial Statements of Business Enterprises," APB Statement No. 4 (New York: AICPA, October, 1970), par. 9.

business, from the new employee to the top manager, eventually uses some accounting information.

The importance of understanding accounting information is not limited to those directly engaged in business. Lawyers, for example, must often understand the meaning of accounting information if they are to represent their business clients effectively, and engineers and architects must consider cost data in their work. In fact, daily living requires all adults to deal with their finances. Limited resources must be carefully budgeted; excess resources must be wisely invested. Thus, accounting plays a significant role in society.

Although accounting procedures and techniques can be used in accounting for all types of economic units, such as cities, universities, and businesses, this book will concentrate on accounting for businesses. Business managers need information provided by the accounting system in order to plan and control their business activities. In addition, investors, creditors, and governmental agencies need financial information to make investing, lending, regulatory, and tax-related decisions.

CHARACTERISTICS OF ACCOUNTING INFORMATION

Accounting is the process of measuring, recording, classifying, and summarizing financial information that is used in making economic decisions. Accounting information is financial data about business transactions expressed in monetary terms. **Business transactions** are the economic activities of a business. Accountants classify these business transactions into two types, external and internal. *External transactions* (often called *exchange transactions*) are those involving economic events between two or more independent firms. When a business purchases merchandise from a supplier, borrows money from a bank, or sells merchandise to customers, it participates in economic events that constitute external or exchange transactions. *Internal transactions* are those economic events that take place entirely within one firm. Converting wheat into flour or using machinery and equipment are examples of internal transactions. Accountants use the term *transaction* to refer to all internal and external transactions, which constitute the input of the accounting information system. Recording these historical events is an important function of accounting.

Before the effects of transactions can be recorded, however, they must be *measured.* To be useful, accounting data must be expressed in terms of a common denominator, so that the effects of transactions can be combined. Dissimilar items, such as apples and oranges, cannot be combined unless we express them in terms of a common measuring unit. In our economy, business activity is measured by prices expressed in monetary terms. *Money* serves as both a medium of exchange and a measure of value, allowing us to compare the value or worth of diverse objects and to add and subtract the economic effects of various transactions.

However, simply measuring and recording transactions would provide information of only limited use. To be useful in making decisions the recorded data must be classified and summarized. *Classification* reduces the effects of

Objective 3:
Nature of accounting information

thousands of transactions into useful groups or categories. For example, all transactions involving the sale of merchandise can be grouped into one sales total and all transactions involving cash grouped to report a single net cash figure. *Summarization* of financial data is achieved by preparing reports and financial statements, which are then provided for use to both internal management and outside users of accounting information. These reports usually summarize the effects of all business transactions occurring during some time period such as a month, a quarter, or a year.

RECORDING AND REPORTING ACCOUNTING INFORMATION

Objective 4: Recording vs. reporting accounting information

Accounting is often viewed as being limited to the recording process. No distinction is perceived between the recording and the reporting of accounting data. The *recording* or *bookkeeping* process involves measuring and recording business transactions. This process may take the form of handwritten records, records produced by mechanical or electronic devices, or records produced by magnetic marks on cards or magnetic tape in a computerized system.

The *reporting* function is much broader. It consists of classifying and summarizing accounting data into financial statements, as well as preparing any other interpretive disclosures necessary to make the data understandable. The process is highly technical, and requires an accountant with extensive training, experience, and professional judgment. In addition to recording and reporting, accounting also includes the design of accounting systems, the audit of financial statements, cost studies, and the preparation of various tax returns.

USING ACCOUNTING INFORMATION

Objective 5: Uses of accounting information

As stated earlier, accounting provides techniques and procedures for accumulating and reporting financial data. Although accountants are sometimes involved in the analysis and interpretation of accounting data when they serve as advisors to users of accounting information, the ultimate objective of accounting is to provide information usable to internal and external decision makers. Business managers (internal decision makers) must have financial data for planning and controlling business operations. Managers must answer questions like: What resources are available to the firm? How much does the company owe to outsiders? How much income is being earned? What products should be produced? What is the most efficient production process? What will be the effect of increasing or decreasing selling prices? Will cash be available to pay debts as they come due? What is the comparative effect of owning or leasing facilities? Providing data to help answer these and similar questions is an accounting function, generally called *managerial accounting*. Chapters 21 through 27 are devoted to the preparation of reports and analyses for use by management.

External decision makers such as creditors, stockholders, and governmental agencies need accounting information to make decisions concerning the granting of credit, the purchase of shares of stock, and compliance with tax laws and other regulatory standards. Questions raised by external users include:

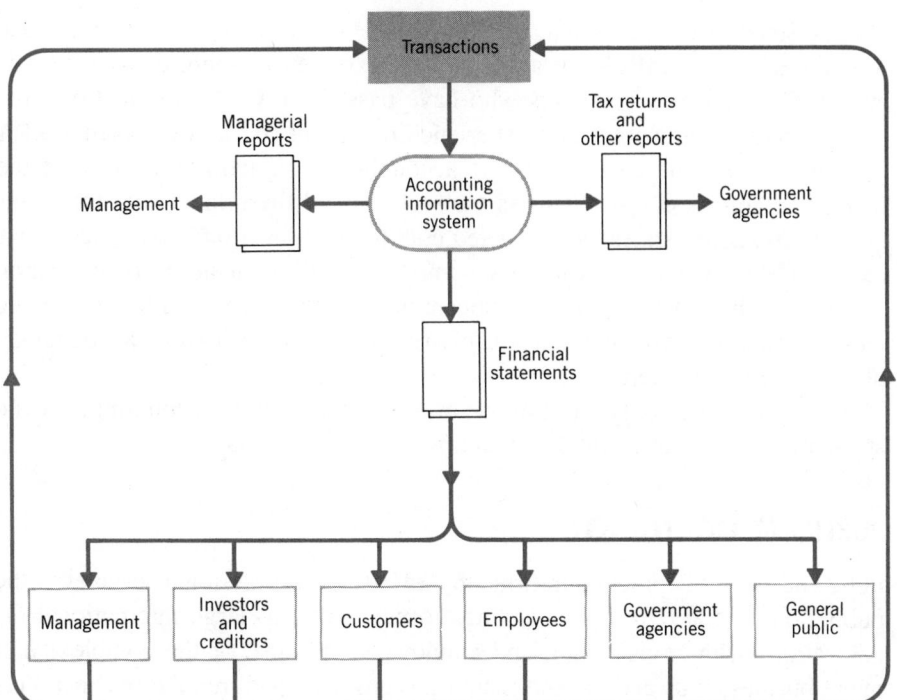

Figure 1–1
Accounting Reports
and Users

Will the business be able to repay money lent to it? What are the company's earning prospects? Is the business financially sound?

Reports prepared for external users are called *financial statements* and generally consist of a balance sheet (sometimes called a statement of financial position), an income statement, a statement of changes in owner's equity, and a statement of changes in financial position. These statements are often called *general purpose financial statements* because they provide general information for use by all external users. General purpose financial statements are also used by management, along with the various internal reports. Figure 1–1 illustrates the relationship between accounting reports and users of accounting information.

ACCOUNTING AS A PROFESSION

Accounting has developed as a profession over the past century, attaining a status equivalent to the practice of law and medicine. Individual states license **certified public accountants** (CPAs) just as they license lawyers and doctors.

State requirements for the CPA license vary. Most states require a college degree with a specified minimum number of college credits in accounting and business. All states require the candidate to pass a nationally uniform examination. The exam, prepared and graded by the American Institute of Certified Public Accountants (AICPA), is a rigorous, two-and-a-half-day examination covering accounting theory, accounting practice, auditing, and business law. A minimum grade of 75 is required on each part of the examination. The test is administered by each state on the same dates in May and November.

Most states also require that a candidate have one or two years of experience working in a CPA office—or an equivalent experience—before the license is issued. Only those accountants who have passed the CPA examination, met certain state-set education and experience requirements, and received a CPA license may use the certified public accountant designation. Because of the increasing complexity of business transactions and the related accounting requirements, many states have enacted continuing-education laws. These laws require CPAs to take a minimum number of additional hours of education periodically in order to retain their licenses. Students interested in the specific requirements of individual states can write to the state board of accountancy of the state in question.

Objective 6:
Fields of accounting and types of work

Accountants generally work in one of three areas: public accounting, private accounting, or governmental accounting.

PUBLIC ACCOUNTING

Public accountants practice in firms that offer their professional services to the public. These vary from small, single-office firms, to large international organizations with several thousand employees. Because of the complexity of many business transactions and increasing governmental regulation, members of public accounting firms tend to specialize in either auditing, taxation, or management advisory services, as shown in Figure 1–2.

Figure 1–2
Public Accounting
Specialties

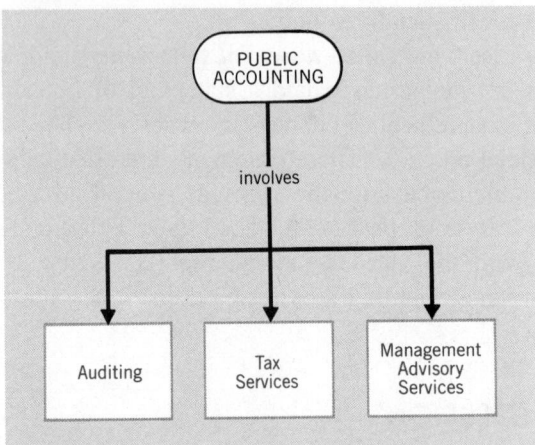

Auditing

Auditing is the primary service offered by most public accounting firms. An **audit** is an independent examination of a firm's financial statements, supporting documents, and records, undertaken in order to give an opinion about the fairness and general reliability of the financial statements. Independent CPA audits are often required by banks and other lending agencies before making business loans. Companies intending to offer their securities for public sale through a national securities market or exchange must have independent

CPA audits. Creditors and investors who use financial statements in decision making place considerable reliance on the CPA's audit report.

Tax Services

Another service offered by public accountants is advice concerning the tax consequences of business decisions. Few business decisions are made without considering such consequences. To offer tax advice, accountants must be thoroughly familiar with federal and state tax laws and regulations. They must also keep up-to-date on court decisions and changes in tax law. Accountants are often hired to aid in tax planning in order to minimize the tax liability of the business, consistent with the rules and regulations established by taxing agencies. Accountants are also often called upon to prepare the state and federal tax returns required by law.

Management Advisory Services

Although audit and tax services have traditionally been the mainstay of public accountants, another area, generally called *management advisory services,* has experienced rapid growth in recent years. While performing audits accountants often discover defects or problems in the client's accounting system. It is natural for the accountant to advise the client on means of correcting defects and improving procedures for the purpose of producing more efficient operations and related cost savings. Clients expect these recommendations and often engage the accountant to undertake additional investigations to improve operations. Public accountants offer a wide range of advisory services, some with little relationship to accounting. Services provided include advice on such things as mergers with other companies, installation or modification of accounting systems, design or modification of pension plans, and advice regarding budgeting, forecasting, and general financial planning.

PRIVATE ACCOUNTING

An accountant working for a single industrial company is employed in private accounting. The firm's chief accounting officer, the **controller,** has overall responsibility for directing the activities of the accounting personnel. In a large company the controller may have several assistant controllers, each with assigned responsibility for various accounting functions, such as cost accounting, tax accounting, or internal auditing. As illustrated in Figure 1–3, private accountants, who do not have to be CPAs, often specialize in a single phase of the accounting process.

General Accounting

Private accounting functions include recording the company's transactions, preparing reports for management, and classifying and summarizing transaction data for the preparation of financial statements. It is difficult to clearly

Figure 1–3
Private Accounting
Specialties

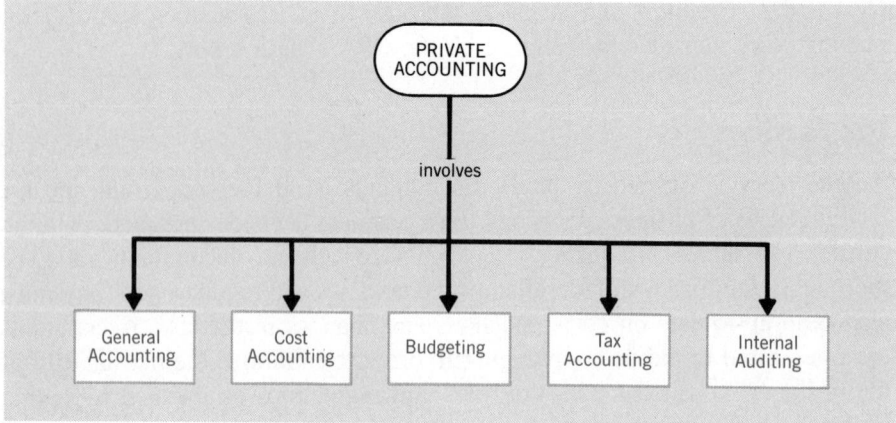

distinguish between general accounting and other private accounting activities because the accounting data recorded from transactions form the basic data base from which other phases draw relevant information.

Cost Accounting

Cost accounting deals with the collection, allocation, and control of the cost of producing specific products and services. It is important to know the cost of each business operation and manufacturing process in order to make sound business decisions. For example, if management wants to determine whether a particular product is profitable, it must first know that product's production and sales costs. Large manufacturing companies employ many accountants in their cost accounting departments.

Budgeting

Budgeting is the phase of accounting that deals with the preparation of a plan or forecast of future operations. Its primary function is to provide management with a projection of the activities necessary to reach established goals. Budgets are generally prepared for the business as a whole, as well as for subunits, such as individual departments. Budgets also serve as control devices and as a means of measuring the efficiency of operations. This is discussed further in Chapter 24.

Tax Accounting

Businesses are assessed a variety of taxes—including income tax, payroll tax, and excise tax—all of which require the preparation of periodic reports to taxing agencies. Management must consider the tax effects of every investment and financing decision. Although many businesses rely on public accountants for some tax-planning advice and tax-return preparation, most large companies also maintain a tax accounting department to deal with the day-to-day tax problems encountered in operating a business.

Internal Auditing

The primary function of **internal auditing** is to conduct ongoing reviews to make certain that established procedures and policies are being followed. Any deficiencies can be identified and corrected quickly. Many companies also maintain an internal audit staff because an internal audit process can reduce the time required by the CPA firm conducting the annual audit. Often, significant cost savings are realized.

GOVERNMENTAL ACCOUNTING

Many accountants are also employed in governmental accounting. Cities, counties, states, and the federal government collect and spend huge amounts of money annually. Governmental accounting is concerned with the identification of the sources and uses of resources, consistent with the provisions of city, county, state, and federal laws. Other nonprofit organizations (churches, hospitals, charities, public educational institutions) follow accounting procedures similar to those used in governmental accounting. Many of the problems and decisions faced by government officials are the same as those encountered in private industry, but governmental accounting requires a different approach in some respects because of the absence of a profit motive.

As indicated earlier, accounting is applicable to all types of economic entities, including governmental and nonprofit units. The rest of this book, however, will concentrate on methods used in accounting for business entities that have a profit motive.

THE SOURCE OF ACCOUNTING PRINCIPLES AND PRACTICES

Accounting has changed along with society's needs. As new types of transactions occur in trade and commerce, accountants develop rules and practices for recording them. These accounting practices have come to be known as *generally accepted accounting principles (GAAP),* and consist of the rules, practices, and procedures used in the preparation of financial statements. Their authority stems from their general acceptance by the accounting profession. Three main formal organizations—the American Institute of Certified Public Accountants (AICPA), the Financial Accounting Standards Board (FASB), and the Securities and Exchange Commission (SEC)—predominate in the development of accounting practices and procedures. Knowing their historical and continuing roles in the development of accounting practices will help in understanding the overall accounting process. In addition, there are other U.S. and international organizations that affect accounting practices.

THE AICPA

The AICPA is a national professional organization of certified public accountants that has been particularly active in describing and defining GAAP. The AICPA publishes a monthly journal, *The Journal of Accountancy,* which serves as a medium by which accountants share their experiences and research results. Between 1939 and 1959, the AICPA's Committee on Accounting Procedure issued fifty-one *Accounting Research Bulletins* (ARBs) containing recommendations on a wide variety of accounting problems. These recommendations, however, were not mandatory in accounting. As a result, different companies often developed different practices for accounting and reporting identical transactions.

Recognizing the need for a more formal process in the development of GAAP, the AICPA replaced the Committee on Accounting Procedure in 1959 with the Accounting Principles Board (APB). The APB was asked to establish principles that would narrow the areas of difference and inconsistency in accounting. The Accounting Principles Board consisted of 18 part-time, non-salaried members from accounting firms, industry, and universities. These individuals maintained their affiliations with their respective firms or educational institutions. As a result, the APB was frequently charged with being unduly influenced by the wishes of clients and management.

Because of the part-time nature of its members' appointments, the APB was also attacked for moving too slowly in solving accounting problems. To avoid such criticism as well as to avoid the possibility of having a governmental body take over accounting rule-making activities, the APB was terminated in 1973, and a new board, the **Financial Accounting Standards Board** (FASB), was created. Between 1959 and 1973, the APB issued thirty-one *APB Opinions* dealing with specific accounting problems.

THE FASB

The FASB has seven members, all of whom are full-time employees, receive substantial salaries, and have severed their relationships with prior employers. The FASB is an independent, autonomous body whose members are appointed by the Financial Accounting Foundation. Appointments are for five-year terms with a maximum of two terms. The foundation receives its financial support from the private sector, that is, from public accounting and industrial firms.

The FASB is responsible for establishing accounting standards that will be responsive to the needs of the entire business community, not just the accounting profession. It provides a forum in open hearings, discussion memoranda, and exposure drafts through which all interested parties may express their views concerning proposed accounting standards. After considering the views of all parties, the FASB issues *Statements of Financial Accounting Standards* which, like APB Opinions, must be followed by accountants. By the end of 1984, the FASB had issued eighty accounting standards. Both APB Opinions and FASB Statements will be referred to frequently in this book.

THE SEC

The Securities and Exchange Commission (SEC) is a regulatory agency established by Congress through the Securities Acts of 1933 and 1934. The commission has the authority to establish accounting standards for the financial reports required of companies that list their securities for sale through one of the national securities exchanges. It has published accounting guidelines, particularly Regulation S–X, which contain specific reporting standards for the financial statements that must be filed annually with the SEC.

The SEC has played a significant role in setting accounting standards since its inception. It has accomplished this through both its published regulations and by working closely with the FASB in the development of accounting standards.

OTHER U.S. ORGANIZATIONS

Three other U.S. organizations, the American Accounting Association (AAA), the National Association of Accountants (NAA), and the Government Accounting Standards Board (GASB), also contribute to the development of accounting standards. The AAA membership consists mainly of accounting educators. It encourages the improvement of accounting instruction and sponsors various types of accounting research, the results of which are often published in its quarterly publication, *The Accounting Review*. Its committees work with the FASB on various accounting problems. Several of its members have served on the APB and FASB.

The NAA consists primarily of accountants working in industrial firms and educators whose interests are cost and managerial accounting. It supports research in various cost and managerial accounting areas and publishes *Management Accounting,* a monthly publication.

The GASB is the formal body responsible for establishing financial accounting and reporting standards for state and local governmental units. Formed in 1984, it consists of five members appointed by the Financial Accounting Foundation for five-year terms.

INTERNATIONAL ORGANIZATIONS

Two international organizations, the International Accounting Standards Committee (IASC) and the International Federation of Accountants (IFAC) encourage worldwide cooperation in the development of accounting practices. The IASC was formed in 1973 through an agreement among the leading accounting organizations of Australia, Canada, France, Germany, Japan, Mexico, the Netherlands, the United Kingdom and Ireland, and the United States. The IASC issues *Statements of International Accounting Standards*. Although they do not replace local practices, the hope is that local practices will eventually conform to the international standards, thereby harmonizing accounting standards at the international level.

The IFAC consists of a federation of ninety-nine professional accounting organizations from seventy-one countries. It was established in 1977 to promote international agreement on accounting issues. The primary objectives of the IFAC are: (1) to aid the development of international guidelines for auditing, ethics, education, and management accounting, and (2) promote research and close relationships among all accountants.

FORMS OF BUSINESS ORGANIZATION

As illustrated in Figure 1–4, business organizations may be in the form of *proprietorships, partnerships,* or *corporations.*

A **proprietorship** is a business owned by one person. Many small service enterprises, retail stores, and professional practices are operated as proprietorships. The owner of a proprietorship is the legal owner of its assets, is legally liable for its debts, and is entitled to the proprietorship's earnings. From an accounting standpoint, however, the business is treated as an entity separate from its owner.

A **partnership** is a business owned by two or more people who generally share profits and management responsibilities. No special legal requirements need to be met in order to form a partnership. All that is necessary is an agreement among the persons joining together as partners. Although the partnership agreement may be oral, a written agreement is preferred in order to minimize partnership disagreements.

Partnerships are not separate legal entities. Consequently, in a general partnership each partner is personally liable for partnership debts. From an accounting viewpoint, however, partnerships are treated as entities separate from their owners. Like proprietorships, partnerships are widely used for small service firms, retail stores, and professional practices. For example, many CPA firms are operated as partnerships.

A **corporation** is a separate legal entity formed under the incorporation laws of individual states or the federal government. Its owners are called **stockholders** or **shareholders** because their ownership interests are represented by shares of the corporation's stock. Since a corporation is a separate legal entity, its stockholders are not personally liable for the corporation's debts; that is, each stockholder is liable for the debts of the corporation only to the extent of his or her investment therein. Separate legal entity status enables a corporation to conduct its business affairs in its own name as a legal person. Thus, a corporation can: (1) buy, own, and sell property, (2) sue and be sued in its own name, and (3) enter into contracts with others. In essence, a corporation is treated as a legal person with all the rights, duties, and responsibilities of a person.

Figure 1–4
Forms of Business
Organization

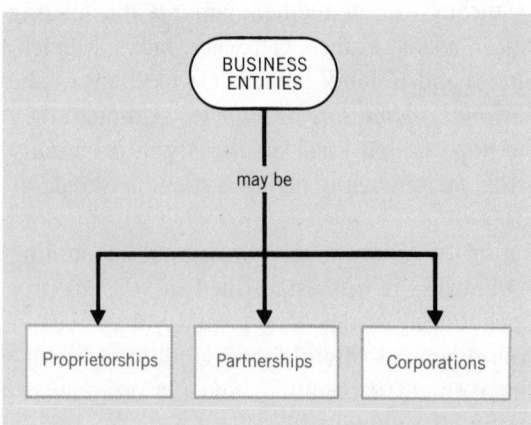

Corporate stockholders are free to sell all or part of their shares at any time. The ease of transferability of ownership, coupled with the lack of personal liability for corporate debts, generally adds to the attractiveness of investing in corporate stock. Although corporations conduct the majority of business activity in the United States, proprietorships are more numerous. Because of the relatively simple nature of the proprietorship form, it will be used as the basis for the early discussion and illustrations in this book. Partnerships and corporations and their special accounting problems will be discussed in Chapters 14, 15, and 16.

FINANCIAL STATEMENTS

As we have seen, accounting is an information system that provides financial data to interested parties for decision-making purposes. The final result of the accounting process is the preparation of various financial statements that serve as important communication devices. Some knowledge of the content of financial statements and the types of information they are designed to communicate will help you better understand the underlying concepts and measurement processes followed in accounting.

The purpose of financial statements is to communicate to users the effect of operating activities during a specified time period and the financial position at the end of the period for a specific business. The types of financial statements most generally prepared are balance sheets, income statements, statements of changes in owner's equity, and statements of changes in financial position. The balance sheet, income statement, and statement of changes in owner's equity will be discussed briefly here. The statement of changes in financial position, which is somewhat more complex, will be discussed in detail in Chapter 19.

Objective 7: Purpose of financial statements

THE BALANCE SHEET

The **balance sheet** reports the financial position of a business at a specific point in time. It is sometimes called a statement of financial position. Financial position is reflected by the amount of the business's assets (resources), the amount of its liabilities or debts owed, and the amount of its owner's equity. Figure 1–5 shows a balance sheet for Acme Repair Company as of December 31, 1987.

The balance sheet heading indicates the name of the business, the name of the statement, and the statement's date. The balance sheet is divided into three main sections: assets, liabilities, and owner's equity. The assets of the business are listed on the left side and the liabilities and owner's equity are listed on the right side. Note that the totals of each side of the balance sheet are equal. This equality must exist because the left side lists the assets of the business and the right side shows the sources of the assets. Of the total assets of $169,480 owned by the business, $73,920 was provided by creditors and the remainder of $95,560 was provided by the owner, Mary Brady, by direct investment or by retaining part of the earnings of the business.

Figure 1–5
Balance Sheet

ACME REPAIR COMPANY
Balance Sheet
December 31, 1987

Assets		Liabilities	
Cash	$ 16,780	Accounts payable	$ 6,920
Accounts		Mortgage payable	67,000
receivable	5,930	Total liabilities	73,920
Repair supplies	4,870		
Repair equipment	36,900	Owner's Equity	
Land	20,000	Mary Brady, capital	95,560
Building	85,000		
		Total liabilities and	
Total assets	$169,480	owner's equity	$169,480

The basic accounting model (**accounting equation**) for the balance sheet is:

Assets = Liabilities + Owner's Equity

All transactions of a business could be analyzed using this basic model, although we will see later that better analysis can be made by expanding the equation to include the effect of the income statement.

Assets

Objective 8: Meaning of asset, liability, owner's equity, revenue, and expense

Assets are the cash and noncash resources owned by a business. They may be tangible assets (for example, land, buildings, and equipment) or intangible assets (e.g. legal claims or rights, such as accounts receivable, patent rights, or rights to use leased assets). Assets have economic value because they contain service benefits that can be used in future operations or sold to another entity.

Liabilities

Liabilities are the debts owed by a business to outside parties (called **creditors**). Liabilities include such things as amounts owed to suppliers for goods or services purchased on credit (accounts payable), amounts borrowed from banks or other lenders (notes payable), amounts owed to employees for salaries and wages, and amounts owed to tax agencies for taxes incurred but not yet paid. Cancellation of liabilities requires either an outlay of assets (generally cash) or the performance of future services. Liabilities may also be thought of as creditors' claims against the assets of the business.

Owner's Equity

Owner's equity is the owner's interest in the assets of the business. It may be thought of as the owner's claims against those assets. The basic accounting model introduced earlier (Assets = Liabilities + Owner's Equity) indicates that the total assets of the business equal the total claims against those assets by creditors and owners. Creditors' claims take legal precedence over owner's claims; if the assets are sold, creditors must be paid before the claims of the owners are recognized. Thus, owner's equity is considered a residual claim, and the basic accounting model is sometimes expressed as:

$$\text{Assets} - \text{Liabilities} = \text{Owner's Equity}$$

Other terms used for owner's equity are **proprietorship,** and **capital.** Preferred terminology, however, is: (1) owner's equity for a proprietorship, (2) partners' equity for a partnership, and (3) stockholders' equity for a corporation. In summary, the two sides of the balance sheet are always equal because they simply reflect two views of the same thing. The list of assets shows the resources owned by the business. The list of liabilities and the list of owner's equity show the amounts of the resources provided to the business by the creditors and the owner(s). Thus, all of the firm's assets are provided to it by its creditors or its owner(s). Because creditor's claims take legal precedence, a business with a relatively large ratio of liabilities to owner's equity is considered financially weaker than a business with a relatively large ratio of owner's equity to liabilities.

THE INCOME STATEMENT

The **income statement** reports the results of earning activities for a specific time period, such as a month, quarter, or year. **Net income** for the period is the excess of revenues over expenses for that time. If expenses for the period exceed revenues, a **net loss** is incurred.

Figure 1–6 shows an income statement for the Acme Repair Company. The heading of the income statement indicates the name of the business, the name

Figure 1–6
Income Statement

```
ACME REPAIR COMPANY
Income Statement
For the Year Ended December 31, 1987


Revenues
Repair revenue                                      $147,500

Expenses
Advertising                        $ 6,750
Repair supplies used                30,570
Salaries and wages                  42,600
Rent expense                        13,420
Telephone expense                    6,730
Utilities expense                   15,980
   Total expenses                                    116,050
Net income                                          $ 31,450
```

of the statement, and the time period covered by the statement. Identification of the time period covered is particularly important because it indicates the length of time it took to earn the reported net income. (In Figure 1–6 the period is one year.) Without a clear indication of the period covered, the data in the income statement would have little if any meaning to a user of the statement.

Revenues

Revenues are increases in owner's equity from the sale of goods or the performance of services. They are measured by the amount of cash or other assets received. Although revenue often consists of cash, it may consist of any asset received, such as a customer's promise to pay in the future (an account receivable) or the receipt of property from a customer. Regardless of the type of asset, to represent revenue it must reflect compensation for the sale of goods or the performance of services. Other types of revenue are interest, dividends received on stock owned, and rent received.

Expenses

Expenses are decreases in owner's equity resulting from the costs incurred in order to earn revenue. Expenses are measured by the amount of assets consumed or the amount of liabilities incurred. They may be immediate cash payments, such as current wages and salaries, or promises to pay cash in the future for services received, such as advertising. In some cases, cash may be paid out before the expense is incurred, as, for example, in payment for next month's or next year's rent. These prepayments represent assets in the balance sheet until they are used. The total of all expenses incurred during 1987 by Acme Repair Company was $116,050. Subtracting these expenses from revenues produces a net income of $31,450. It is important to understand that the net income earned represents an increase in owner's equity. Because revenues result in an increase in owner's equity and expenses result in a decrease in owner's equity, the difference between the two—net income—must represent a net increase in owner's equity. Similarly, a net loss represents a decrease in owner's equity.

THE STATEMENT OF CHANGES IN OWNER'S EQUITY

The statement of changes in owner's equity (Figure 1–7) serves as a connecting link between the balance sheet and the income statement by explaining the changes that took place in owner's equity during the period covered. For example, assuming that Mary Brady's capital balance on January 1, 1987, was $79,110 and that she withdrew $15,000 from the business for personal use during 1987, the statement of changes in owner's equity for 1987 would be:

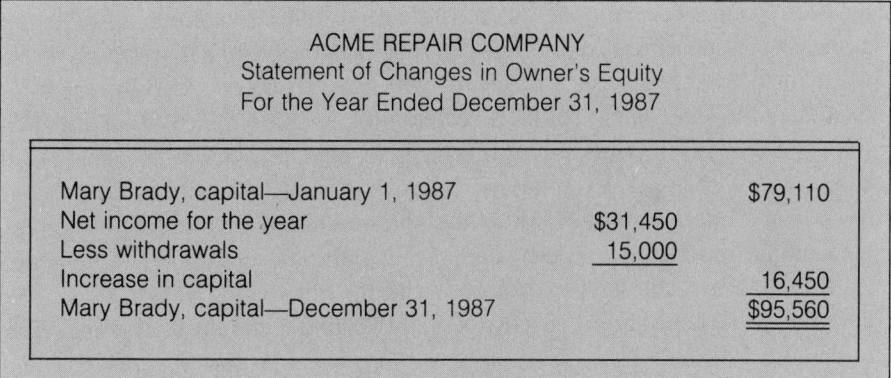

Figure 1–7
Statement of
Changes in Owner's
Equity

SOME UNDERLYING ACCOUNTING CONCEPTS, PRINCIPLES, AND ASSUMPTIONS

We have described accounting as a service activity designed to accumulate, classify, and summarize financial data of a business for use in making economic decisions. As accounting evolved, questions arose concerning the nature of the unit to be accounted for, the measurement principles to be used, and the general guidelines to be followed in order to make the financial data useful in decision making. Accountants gradually produced responses to these questions and developed underlying accounting concepts, principles, and assumptions that are followed in present-day accounting.

Objective 9: Some basic accounting principles

THE BUSINESS ENTITY CONCEPT

If the transactions of a business are to be recorded, classified, and summarized into financial statements, the accountant must be able to identify clearly the boundaries of the unit being accounted for. Under the **business entity concept,** the business (Acme Repair Company, for example) is considered a separate entity distinguishable from its owners and from all other entities. Each entity is assumed to own its assets and incur its liabilities. The assets, liabilities, and business activities of the business are kept completely separate from those of the owner of the business, and from the assets, liabilities, and activities of other businesses. For example, the personal assets, debts, and activities of Mary Brady are not included in the records of Acme Repair Company because they do not constitute part of the business. A separate set of accounting records is maintained for each business, and the prepared financial statements represent the financial position and results of operations of that business alone.

THE COST PRINCIPLE

Resources of a business are recorded initially at their cost under the **cost principle.** Cost is determined by the exchange price agreed upon by the parties to the exchange and is measured by the amount of cash to be given in exchange for the resource received. If the consideration given is something other than cash, cost is measured by the fair (market) value of what is given or the fair value of the asset or service received, whichever is more clearly evident. For example, the land entry in the asset column of the balance sheet for Acme Repair Company reflects the $20,000 price paid to acquire the land on the date it was purchased. Even though Mary Brady may have considered the land to be worth more than $20,000 when she purchased it, the cost principle in accounting limits the recorded value of the land to the $20,000 paid to acquire it. And although the land may have a current sales value of $40,000, it will continue to be reported at its cost of $20,000 under the cost principle. Thus, in reading a balance sheet, *it is important to remember that the dollar amounts reported do not show the amounts that would be received if the assets were sold, but the cost of the assets on the date that they were acquired.*

THE OBJECTIVITY PRINCIPLE

It is appropriate to ask why accountants do not record changes in the values of assets to reflect their current market values. One explanation is the **objectivity principle** in accounting, which holds that accounting data should be reported on a factual basis that is free from personal bias. Cost of the resource acquired is determined objectively on the basis of the exchange price negotiated by the independent parties to the exchange. The recording of current market values requires use of estimates, appraisals, or opinions, all of which are much more subjective. Users of accounting information should be given the most objective, factual data available.

THE GOING CONCERN ASSUMPTION

Another reason for the use of historical cost rather than current market value is that many assets are acquired for use rather than for resale. In fact, some assets, like land, buildings, and equipment, cannot be sold without disrupting ongoing business operations. Financial statements are prepared on the assumption that the existing business will continue to operate in the future—the **going concern assumption.** It is assumed that the business will not be sold in the near future but will continue to use its resources in operating activities. Therefore, the current market values of the assets are of little importance to decision makers.

In the event that management is planning the sale or liquidation of the business, the going concern assumption and the cost principle are set aside and financial statements are prepared on the basis of estimated sales or liquidation values. When this is the case, the statements should identify clearly the basis upon which the values are determined.

THE STABLE DOLLAR ASSUMPTION

Another underlying assumption of accounting is the **stable dollar assumption,** under which changes in the purchasing power of money are ignored. In our country, accounting transactions are recorded and reported in terms of dollars that are assumed to have a constant value. As a result, 1987 dollars are intermingled with 1980 and 1970 dollars as though they all represented the same purchasing power. Unfortunately, this is not realistic. When the general purchasing power of the dollar changes, the value of money also changes. As inflation occurs, for instance, the purchasing power of money declines. Although accountants recognize this fact, changes in the value of the measuring unit are ignored. As a result, gains are often reported on the disposal of assets when there has, in fact, been little or no gain in purchasing power.

To illustrate, assume that a business purchased a piece of land for $50,000 when the general price level (the average of prices in our economy) was 100, and later sold it for $100,000 when the general price level had increased to 200. The doubling of the general price level reflects a decrease in the purchasing power of the dollar from 100 cents to 50 cents. Current accounting practice reports a $50,000 gain on the sale of the land even though the company is no better off from a purchasing-power standpoint since it would take $100,000 on the date of sale to buy the same amount of goods and services that could have been purchased for $50,000 on the date the land was purchased.

When inflation rates are high, serious doubts are raised about the wisdom of following the stable dollar assumption. Methods have been devised to convert the dollar amounts in financial statements into dollars of current purchasing power. These restated financial statements are called ***constant-dollar financial statements.*** Accounting standards require that large companies disclose the effects of inflation on certain assets and net income. However, these are only supplemental disclosures; the primary financial statements are still prepared following the stable dollar assumption. If high inflation rates return, we might reasonably expect a shift away from the stable dollar assumption—and possibly away from the cost principle—to some other valuation basis for financial statements. A detailed discussion of this topic will be found in Chapter 13.

THE EFFECT OF TRANSACTIONS ON THE ACCOUNTING EQUATION

Before looking at the effect of transactions on the accounting equation, let's review the nature of business transactions. Business transactions are the economic activities or events that affect the financial position of a business. They may be external (exchange) transactions involving economic events between one firm and another independent firm. Buying assets from another firm or selling assets to another firm are examples of external transactions. On the other hand, some transactions are internal ones, involving economic events entirely within one firm, such as using machinery or equipment over a period of time.

Objective 10: Effect of transactions on accounting equation

The basic accounting model or accounting equation was expressed earlier as:

Assets = Liabilities + Owner's Equity

The sum of the assets of a business will always be equal to the total sources from which those assets came—liabilities plus owner's equity. Business transactions result in changes in assets, liabilities, and owner's equity. Even though the elements of the accounting equation change as a result of transactions, its basic equality remains unchanged, as may be demonstrated by illustrating some transactions undertaken by Sam's Cleaners.

Transaction 1. Assume that Sam Drew decided to open Sam's Cleaners on January 2 by taking $30,000 from his personal savings account and depositing it in a checking account he opened for Sam's Cleaners. This investment by Sam Drew represents the first transaction of Sam's Cleaners (1). After this initial investment, the new business has one asset (cash) and no liabilities. Thus, the equation for Sam's Cleaners would be:

Assets	=	Liabilities	+	Owner's Equity	Owner's Equity Explanation
Cash				Sam Drew, Capital	
(1) $30,000	=			$30,000	Investment

The effect of this transaction was to increase assets by $30,000, with an equal increase in owner's equity on the other side of the equation. (Remember that the equation relates only to the business entity.) Following the business entity concept, Sam Drew's personal assets and debts are not part of the business endeavor and therefore, are excluded from the equation.

Transaction 2. After making the initial investment, Sam Drew, who manages the business himself, engaged in his next transaction by purchasing some cleaning equipment. The list price of the equipment was $16,000, but after some hard negotiation, the supplier agreed to sell the equipment to Sam's Cleaners for $14,000 cash. The equation before this transaction (2), the effect of the transaction on the equation, and the equation after the transaction are:

	Assets		=	Liabilities	+	Owner's Equity	Owner's Equity Explanation
	Cash	+ Cleaning Equipment	=			Sam Drew, Capital	
(1)	$30,000		=			30,000	Investment
(2)	− 14,000	+ 14,000					
	16,000 +	14,000	=			30,000	

This transaction resulted in an exchange of one asset (cash) for another asset (cleaning equipment). No liabilities were incurred and Sam Drew's equity remained unchanged. Note that, following the ***cost principle,*** the cleaning equipment was recorded at its cost of $14,000; the list price of the equipment is irrelevant.

Transaction 3. Sam Drew then purchased $4,500 worth of cleaning supplies from Adam Supply Company on account, with an agreement to pay for the supplies later. The effect of this transaction (3) is an increase in assets of $4,500, and an increase in liabilities, (accounts payable) of $4,500:

	Cash	+	Cleaning Equipment	+	Cleaning Supplies	=	Accounts Payable	+	Sam Drew, Capital	Owner's Equity Explanation
			Assets			=	**Liabilities**	+	Owner's **Equity**	Owner's Equity Explanation
(1)	$30,000					=			30,000	Investment
(2)	−14,000		+14,000							
	16,000	+	14,000			=			30,000	
(3)					+4,500		+4,500			
	16,000	+	14,000	+	4,500	=	4,500	+	30,000	
			34,500						34,500	

Sam Drew's equity in the business did not change, because assets and liabilities increased by equal amounts. The accounting equation is still in balance, with $34,500 in total assets and $34,500 of liabilities and owner's equity.

Transactions 4 and 5. One of the prime objectives of a business is to engage in operating activities that will result in net income to its owners. As explained earlier, net income is the excess of revenues over expenses for a specific time period. Revenues for Sam's Cleaners are earned by charging a fee for the performance of cleaning and laundry services for its customers. Because the assets received as revenues belong to the owner, revenues increase owner's equity. Expenses for Sam's Cleaners consist of such things as wages and salaries paid to employees, newspaper advertising, and cleaning supplies used. Just as revenues increase owner's equity, expenses decrease owner's equity. Therefore, the excess of revenues over expenses results in an increase in the net assets of the business and a net increase in owner's equity. Of course, an excess of expenses over revenues (net loss) has the opposite effect.

To illustrate the effect of revenues on the accounting equation, assume that Sam's Cleaners performed cleaning and laundry services for customers in the amount of $1,200, which was received in cash. In addition, Sam's Cleaners completed the cleaning of draperies for a local hotel and sent the customer a bill for $550. The effects of these transactions on the accounting equation are indicated in (4) and (5):

	Cash	+	Cleaning Equipment	+	Cleaning Supplies	+	Accounts Receivable	=	Accounts Payable	+	Sam Drew, Capital	Owner's Equity Explanation
				Assets				=	**Liabilities**	+	Owner's **Equity**	Owner's Equity Explanation
(1)	$30,000							=			30,000	Investment
(2)	−14,000		+14,000									
	16,000	+	14,000					=			30,000	
(3)					+4,500				+4,500			
	16,000	+	14,000	+	4,500			=	4,500	+	30,000	
(4)	+ 1,200										+ 1,200	Service Revenue
	17,200	+	14,000	+	4,500			=	4,500	+	31,200	
(5)							+550				+550	Service Revenue
	17,200	+	14,000	+	4,500	+	550	=	4,500	+	31,750	
				36,250						36,250		

Observe that the effect of transaction (4) is to increase the asset cash and, because it represents a receipt for the performance of services (revenue), to increase owner's equity by an equal amount. Transaction (5) introduces another important principle in accounting, the **revenue principle** (sometimes called the *realization principle*), which requires the recognition of revenue when the earning process is completed rather than when cash is received. The revenue is represented by the receipt of an asset, in this case an account receivable, which represents the right to collect cash in the future.

Transactions 6 and 7. To see the effect of expenses on the accounting equation, assume that Sam's Cleaners paid cash in the amount of $450 for employee wages. In addition, a count of the cleaning supplies showed that cleaning supplies on hand amounted to $3,700. The other $800 ($4,500 − $3,700) of cleaning supplies had been used. The effects of these transactions on the accounting equation are shown in (6) and (7):

	Cash	+	Cleaning Equipment	+	Cleaning Supplies	+	Accounts Receivable	=	Accounts Payable	+	Sam Drew, Capital	Owner's Equity Explanation
(1)	$30,000							=			30,000	Investment
(2)	−14,000		+14,000									
	16,000	+	14,000					=			30,000	
(3)					+4,500				+4,500			
	16,000	+	14,000	+	4,500			=	4,500	+	30,000	
(4)	+1,200										+ 1,200	Service Revenue
	17,200	+	14,000	+	4,500			=	4,500	+	31,200	
(5)							+550				+550	Service Revenue
	17,200	+	14,000	+	4,500	+	550	=	4,500	+	31,750	
(6)	−450										−450	Wage Expense
	16,750	+	14,000	+	4,500	+	550	=	4,500	+	31,300	
(7)					−800						−800	Cleaning
	16,750	+	14,000	+	3,700	+	550	=	4,500	+	30,500	Supplies Used

35,000   35,000

Note that expenses have an effect opposite the recognition of revenue, with a decrease in assets and a decrease in owner's equity. The basic **expense recognition principle** in accounting requires that, in general, expenses should be recognized in the period in which the asset or benefit is used in the process of earning revenue. In transaction (6), the benefits received from employees had been used at the time payment was made. Thus, the payment represents expenses that reduced the asset cash as well as the owner's equity by equal amounts of $450. The initial purchase of cleaning supplies in transaction (3) resulted in the acquisition of an asset that will benefit several accounting periods. The counting of cleaning supplies at the end of the period indicated that $800 of the supplies had been used during the period and, therefore, are treated as an expense by decreasing cleaning supplies and decreasing owner's equity.

The combination of the principle of recognizing revenue when it is earned rather than when it is collected and the principle of recognizing expenses when assets or benefits are used rather than when they are paid for, is referred to as *accrual accounting.* We will have more to say about this important concept later.

Transactions 8, 9, and 10.   As one last illustration of the effect of transactions on the accounting equation, assume that Sam's Cleaners collected the account receivable recognized in transaction (5) and paid the amount due to Adam Supply Company for the purchase of cleaning supplies in transaction (3). In addition, Sam Drew withdrew $200 from the business for his personal use. The effects of these transactions on the accounting equation are demonstrated in (8), (9), and (10):

	Cash	+	Cleaning Equipment	+	Cleaning Supplies	+	Accounts Receivable	=	Accounts Payable	+	Sam Drew, Capital	Owner's Equity Explanation
(1)	$30,000							=			30,000	Investment
(2)	−14,000		+14,000									
	16,000	+	14,000					=			30,000	
(3)					+4,500				+4,500			
	16,000	+	14,000	+	4,500			=	4,500	+	30,000	
(4)	+1,200										+ 1,200	Service Revenue
	17,200	+	14,000	+	4,500			=	4,500	+	31,200	
(5)							+550				+550	Service Revenue
	17,200	+	14,000	+	4,500	+	550	=	4,500	+	31,750	
(6)	−450										−450	Wage Expense
	16,750	+	14,000	+	4,500	+	550	=	4,500	+	31,300	
(7)					−800						−800	Cleaning Supplies Used
	16,750	+	14,000	+	3,700	+	550	=	4,500	+	30,500	
(8)	+550						−550					
	17,300	+	14,000	+	3,700			=	4,500	+	30,500	
(9)	−4,500								−4,500			
	12,800	+	14,000	+	3,700			=			30,500	
(10)	−200										−200	Withdrawal
	12,600	+	14,000	+	3,700			=			30,300	
			30,300								30,300	

The effect of the collection of the account receivable in transaction (8) is to increase one asset (cash) and decrease another asset (accounts receivable). There is no effect on total assets and none on liabilities or owner's equity. The payment of the account payable in transaction (9) results in a decrease in cash and an equal decrease in liabilities, with no effect on owner's equity. The withdrawal by Sam Drew in transaction (10) decreases cash and owner's equity by equal amounts.

A review of this illustration brings out two important facts. First, every transaction recorded affected at least two items in the equation. This dual recording process, known as **double-entry accounting,** is the method followed in the vast majority of accounting systems. Second, after the effects of each transaction were recorded, the equation remained in balance, with the sum of the assets equal to the sum of the liabilities plus owner's equity.

Observe that, after all transactions have been recorded, Sam Drew's equity (or capital) is $30,300, composed of the $30,000 he invested at the inception of the business, plus $500 net income representing the excess of revenues ($1,750) over expenses ($1,250) for the period, minus the $200 withdrawal. In addition, total assets of Sam's Cleaners are $30,300 and the business owes no liabilities. Therefore, assets have increased by $300 during the period.

After taking the effects of the above transactions into account, we would arrive at the financial statements for Sam's Cleaners shown in Figure 1–8.

Figure 1–8
Financial Statements

SAM'S CLEANERS
Income Statement
For the Month Ended January 31, 1987

Cleaning revenue		$ 1,750
Operating expenses:		
Cleaning supplies used	$800	
Employee wages	300	
Advertising	150	
Total operating expenses		1,250
Net income		$ 500

SAM'S CLEANERS
Statement of Changes in Owner's Equity
For the Month Ended January 31, 1987

Sam Drew, capital—January 2, 1987		$30,000
Net income for the month	$500	
Less withdrawals	200	
Increase in capital		300
Sam Drew, capital—January 31, 1987		$30,300

SAM'S CLEANERS
Balance Sheet
January 31, 1987

Assets		Owner's Equity	
Cash	$12,600	Sam Drew, capital	$30,300
Cleaning supplies	3,700		
Cleaning equipment	14,000		
Total assets	$30,300	Total owner's equity	$30,300

GLOSSARY

ACCOUNTING. The process of recording, classifying, and summarizing the financial data of a business that will be used to make decisions (p. 5).

ACCOUNTING EQUATION. An algebraic expression of the equality of assets to liabilities and owner's equity: Assets = Liabilities + Owner's Equity (p. 16).

ASSET. A resource owned by a business (p. 16).

AUDIT. An examination by an independent CPA of the financial statements and supporting documents of a business (p. 8).

BALANCE SHEET. A report listing the assets, liabilities, and owner's equity of a business as of a specific date (p. 15).

BUDGETING. Preparation of a plan for the operating activities of a business (p. 10).

BUSINESS ENTITY CONCEPT. The assumption that a business entity is separate and distinct from its owners and from other business entities (p. 19).

BUSINESS TRANSACTIONS. The events that make up the economic activity of a business (p. 5).

CERTIFIED PUBLIC ACCOUNTANT (CPA). An accountant who has met the qualifications and received a license to practice public accounting (p. 7).

CONTROLLER. The chief accounting officer of a business (p. 9).

CORPORATION. A form of business organization licensed to operate as a business by state or federal laws (p. 14).

COST ACCOUNTING. The phase of accounting that deals with the collection, allocation, and control of the cost of producing a product or service (p. 10).

COST PRINCIPLE. The rule behind the accounting practice of recording resources and services acquired by a business at cost (p. 19).

CREDITOR. A person or business to whom a debt is owed (p. 16).

DOUBLE ENTRY ACCOUNTING. The concept that every transaction affects two or more items in the accounting equation (p. 26).

EXPENSE. Resources consumed in the process of earning revenues (p. 18).

EXPENSE RECOGNITION PRINCIPLE. The rule that expenses should be recognized when an asset is used to produce revenue, rather than when it is paid for (p. 24).

FINANCIAL ACCOUNTING STANDARDS BOARD. The current rule-making body of the accounting profession (p. 12).

GOING CONCERN (CONTINUITY) ASSUMPTION. The assumption that a business will continue in the future and use its assets in operations, rather than sell them (p. 20).

INCOME STATEMENT. A financial report listing the revenues, expenses, and net income or net loss of a business for some time period (p. 17).

INTERNAL AUDITING. The ongoing investigation of compliance with established procedures and policies of a business by its internal audit staff (p. 11).

LIABILITIES. Debts owed by a business (p. 16).

NET INCOME. The excess of revenues over expenses (p. 17).

NET LOSS. The excess of expenses over revenues (p. 17).

OBJECTIVITY PRINCIPLE. The rule that accounting data should be reported on a factual basis (p. 20).

OWNER'S EQUITY. The owner's interest in the assets of a business (p. 16).

PARTNERSHIP. A form of business organization under which the business is owned by two or more people as partners (p. 14).

PROPRIETORSHIP. A form of business organization in which the business is owned by an individual (p. 14).

REVENUE. The inflow of assets into a business from the sale of goods or the performance of services (p. 18).

REVENUE PRINCIPLE. The rule that revenue should be recognized when it is earned rather than when cash is received (p. 24).

SHAREHOLDER (STOCKHOLDER). A person or entity owning shares of stock in a corporation (p. 14).

STABLE DOLLAR ASSUMPTION. The assumption in accounting that the purchasing power of the dollar does not change (p. 20).

DISCUSSION QUESTIONS

1. What is the purpose of accounting?
2. Who are the primary users of accounting information?
3. Explain and give an example of each of the two types of business transactions: external transactions and internal transactions.
4. What is the purpose of classifying and summarizing accounting data?
5. Accounting data is useful in decision making. List six examples of business decisions requiring the use of accounting information.
6. Distinguish between recording and reporting accounting information.
7. What are the main services offered by public accountants?
8. What is the purpose of an audit?
9. Private accounting includes a number of phases. List four of them.
10. What is the Financial Accounting Standards Board? What is its function?
11. What is the Securities and Exchange Commission? What is its function?
12. A business may take one of three forms. What are they?
13. What is the general purpose of a balance sheet?
14. Define assets and give five examples.
15. Define liabilities and give three examples.
16. State two forms of the accounting equation.
17. Define revenue and expense.
18. Explain what is meant by the business entity concept.
19. If an asset is appraised at $12,000 but a company pays $10,000 for it with full knowledge of its appraised value, at what amount should the asset be recorded? Why?
20. Explain what is meant by the stable dollar assumption.
21. If a company has assets of $30,000 and owner's equity of $17,000, how much are its liabilities?
22. What is meant by double-entry accounting?
23. Why are the two sides of a balance sheet always equal?
24. Give an example of a transaction that will
    (a) Increase an asset and decrease another asset.
    (b) Increase an asset and increase a liability.
    (c) Increase an asset and increase owner's equity.

(d) Decrease an asset and decrease a liability.
(e) Decrease an asset and decrease owner's equity.
25. What are the two sources of owner's equity?
26. The term accrual accounting encompasses two fundamental accounting principles. What are they?

EXERCISES

Exercise 1-1 **Preparing a Balance Sheet**
Balance sheet items for Beverly's Copy Shop on May 31, 1987, are presented below in alphabetical order.

Accounts payable	$ 4,600	Land	$13,000
Accounts receivable	1,600	Mortgage payable	58,000
Building	75,500	Beverly Jones, capital	42,170
Cash	1,620	Supplies	750
Equipment	12,300		

Required:
Prepare a balance sheet similar to the one in Figure 1–5.

Exercise 1-2 **Effects of Transactions on Total Assets**
The following transactions were completed by Oulette Company.

1. Invested cash in the business.
2. Purchased office equipment for cash.
3. Sold land for an amount equal to its cost.
4. Paid a liability.
5. Collected an account receivable.
6. Sold land for an amount in excess of its cost.
7. Borrowed money from a bank.
8. Sold land for an amount less than its cost.
9. Purchased equipment at a total cost of $3,000; paid $1,000 cash with the balance due in 90 days.

Required:
Indicate the effect of each transaction on total assets of Oulette Company. Use the following terms: increase total assets, decrease total assets, and no effect on total assets.

Exercise 1-3 **Effect of Transactions on Accounting Equations**
Set up headings accross a piece of paper as follows.

Transaction	Assets = Liabilities + Owner's Equity

For each of the following transactions, indicate its effect on the accounting equation by placing a + (increase), − (decrease), or 0 (no effect) below the elements of the accounting equation. Transaction (a) is given as an example.

Transaction	Assets	=	Liabilities	+	Owner's Equity
(a)	+	=	0	+	+

The owner

(a) Invested cash in the business.
(b) Purchased supplies on account.
(c) Purchased equipment for cash.
(d) Sent a bill to a customer for services performed.
(e) Paid rent for a month.
(f) Collected the amount billed in (d).
(g) Purchased equipment, paying half of the purchase price in cash and agreeing to pay the remainder in three months.
(h) Paid for the supplies purchased in (b).

Exercise 1-4 Explaining Accounting Transactions

The following schedule shows the effect of several transactions on the accounting equation of Sun Audio Company and the balance of each item in the equation after each transaction. Write a sentence to explain the nature of each transaction.

	Cash	+	Accounts Receivable	+	Equipment	+	Supplies	=	Accounts Payable	+	Karen Moore Capital
(1)	+ 15,000										+ 15,000
(2)	− 8,000				+ 8,000						
	7,000	+			8,000			=			15,000
(3)	+ 3,000										+ 3,000
	10,000	+			8,000			=			18,000
(4)			+ 5,000								+ 5,000
	10,000	+	5,000	+	8,000			=			23,000
(5)							+4,000		+4,000		
	10,000	+	5,000	+	8,000	+	4,000	=	4,000	+	23,000
(6)	+2,000		−2,000								
	12,000	+	3,000	+	8,000	+	4,000	=	4,000	+	23,000
(7)	−5,500										− 5,500
	6,500	+	3,000	+	8,000	+	4,000	=	4,000	+	17,500
(8)							−2,000				− 2,000
	6,500	+	3,000	+	8,000	+	2,000	=	4,000	+	15,500
(9)	−4,000								−4,000		
	2,500	+	3,000	+	8,000	+	2,000	=	—0—	+	15,500

Exercise 1-5 Preparation of a Balance Sheet

Month-end balance sheet amounts for the legal practice of Mike Wilson, a local attorney, for three consecutive months are presented below. The information is complete except for the balance in the capital account.

	October 31	November 30	December 31
Cash	$ 8,000	$ 7,000	$ 5,000
Accounts receivable	14,000	14,500	10,000
Prepaid insurance	800	.400	1,200
Office equipment	24,000	25,000	24,500
Building	56,000	55,800	55,700
Land	8,000	8,000	8,000
Accounts payable	12,000	7,000	500
Wages payable	7,000	7,000	6,000
Note payable	43,000	42,900	42,800
Mike Wilson, capital	?	?	?

Required:

A. Determine the balance in Mike Wilson's capital account at the end of each month.

B. Assuming that Mr. Wilson made no additional investments and did not withdraw any money from the business during the three months, determine net income for November and for December.

C. Prepare a balance sheet for the business at December 31, 1986. (The heading should read: Mike Wilson, Attorney.)

Exercise 1-6 Examples of Business Transactions

For each of the following, describe a transaction that would have the stated effect on the accounting equation.

1. Increase an asset and increase a liability. *Reciept from customer.*
2. Increase an asset and decrease another asset.
3. Decrease an asset and decrease owner's equity.
4. Increase an asset and increase owner's equity.
5. Decrease a liability and decrease an asset.

Exercise 1-7 Recording Transactions

Dana's Electronic Repair began operations on August 1 and completed the following transactions during the first month.

1. Dana Milne deposited $13,000 of his personal funds in a checking account opened in the name of the business.
2. Electronic repair equipment was purchased at a cost of $8,000, of which $4,000 was paid in cash. A note payable was given for the remainder of $4,000.
3. Dana collected $1,500 from customers for repair services performed.
4. Rent was paid for the month of August, in the amount of $700.
5. Supplies amounting to $600 were purchased on account.
6. Wages of $300 were paid, as well as a utility bill for electricity and water, amounting to $150.
7. Dana paid for the supplies purchased in (5) above.
8. Supplies used during August amounted to $150.

Required:

A. Prepare a schedule similar to that on page 25. List the following assets, liabilities, and owner's equity as column headings: Cash, Supplies, Equipment, Notes Payable, Accounts Payable, D. Milne, Capital.

B. Show the effects of each of the transactions on the accounts listed. Indicate totals after each transaction and complete the schedule as shown on page 25.

C. Prepare an income statement, balance sheet, and statement of changes in owner's equity.

PROBLEMS

Problem 1-1 Preparation of Income Statement and Balance Sheet

Asset, liability, owner's equity, revenue, and expense amounts for Cave Creek Stitchery at December 31, 1987, are presented below.

Cash	$ 3,000
Accounts receivable	10,000
Supplies	6,000
Equipment	21,500
Accounts payable	4,000
Alicia Jones, capital	?
Design revenue	47,000
Advertising expense	3,000
Insurance expense	1,500
Rent expense	6,000
Supplies expense	2,500
Telephone expense	700
Utilities expense	2,000
Wage expense	15,000

Required:

A. Prepare an income statement for the business for the year ended December 31, 1987.

B. Prepare a balance sheet at December 31, 1987.

✗ Problem 1-2 Determining Missing Elements in Accounting Equation

Compute the two missing amounts for each independent case below.

Case	Total Assets	Total Liabilities	Owner's Equity	Total Revenue	Total Expenses	Net Income (Loss)
A	$ 86,000	$70,000	$16? 000	$43,200	$ 3? 0700	$ 12,500
B	36? 000	16,000	20,000	47,000	5? 9 000	(12,000)
C	103,000	20? 000	83,000	75,000	36,000	3? 000
D	68 ? 500	27,000	41,500	47? 000	27,000	20,000
E	104,000	44? 000	60,000	15? 000	23,000	(8,000)

Problem 1-3 Preparation of Income Statement and Balance Sheet

Data for the Bellview Company as of December 31, 1987, follow.

Accounts receivable	$ 21,000	Wage expense	$58,000
Revenue	125,000	Advertising expense	10,000
Accounts payable	12,000	Land	12,000
Joe Bellview, capital	?	Equipment	23,000
Cash	15,000	Notes payable	15,000
Mortgage payable	22,000	Utilities expense	5,000
Building	50,000	Telephone expense	850

Required:
Prepare an income statement and balance sheet for Bellview Company.

Problem 1-4 Recording Transactions and Preparing Financial Statements

Balance sheet item balances for Milton Company on April 30 are given below in accounting equation form similar to the chapter illustrations.

Assets				=	Liabilities		+	Owner's Equity
Cash	+ Accounts Receivable	+ Supplies	+ Equipment	=	Accounts Payable	+ Notes Payable	+	Mark Milton, Capital
Bal. $8,500	$12,400	$1,000	$21,000		$2,300	$10,000		$30,600

During May, Milton Company entered into the following transactions.

1. Collected $8,400 of accounts receivable.
2. Paid $1,000 on accounts payable.
3. Billed customers for services performed, in the amount of $6,000.
4. Purchased equipment for $4,100. Paid $2,100 in cash, and signed a note payable for $2,000.
5. Paid expenses in cash $3,100. (Employee wages, $2,000; utilities, $600; advertising, $500)
6. Purchased supplies on account, $300.
7. Used $500 worth of supplies during the period.
8. Mark Milton withdrew $1,000 for personal use.

Required:
A. List the April 30 balances for assets, liabilities, and owner's equity in table form as shown in the example.
B. Record the effects of each transaction. Show the total of each column after recording each transaction.
C. Prepare an income statement, statement of changes in owner's equity, and balance sheet for Milton Company.

Problem 1-5 Identifying Transactions from Balance Sheet Changes

During the month of June 1987, Aaron Haynes was in the process of organizing a new business, Aaron's Cafe. After each transaction he entered into, Aaron prepared a balance sheet. During June, the following balance sheets were prepared.

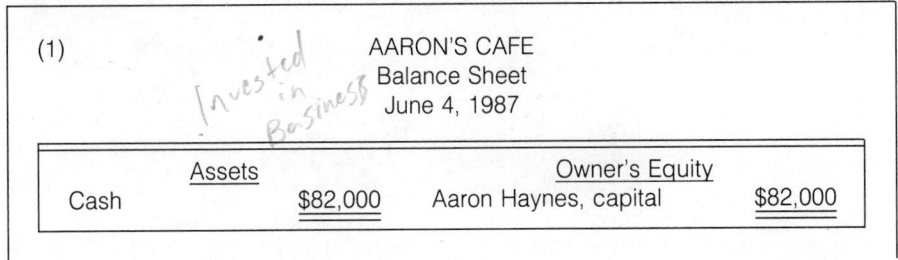

(1)   AARON'S CAFE
                             Balance Sheet
                             June 4, 1987

Assets		Owner's Equity	
Cash	$82,000	Aaron Haynes, capital	$82,000

(2)

Bought Equipment for Cash

AARON'S CAFE
Balance Sheet
June 13, 1987

Assets		Owner's Equity	
Cash	$42,000	Aaron Haynes, capital	$82,000
Equipment	40,000		
Total	$82,000	Total	$82,000

(3)

Land 9,000
Building 65,000
45,000 - Notes
20,000 Cash

AARON'S CAFE
Balance Sheet
June 18, 1987

Assets		Liabilities and Owner's Equity	
Cash	$ 22,000	Note payable	$ 45,000
Equipment	40,000	Aaron Haynes, capital	82,000
Land	9,000		
Building	56,000		
Total	$127,000	Total	$127,000

(4)

Food Supplies 12,000 on Account

AARON'S CAFE
Balance Sheet
June 26, 1987

Assets		Liabilities and Owner's Equity	
Cash	$ 22,000	Accounts payable	$ 12,000
Food supplies	12,000	Note payable	45,000
Equipment	40,000	Total liabilities	57,000
Land	9,000	Aaron Haynes, capital	82,000
Building	56,000		
Total	$139,000	Total	$139,000

Required:
Describe the nature of each of the four transactions that took place during June.

ALTERNATE PROBLEMS

Problem 1-1A Preparation of Financial Statements

Avon Industries began operations in early January 1987. On December 31, 1987, the company's records showed the following asset, liability, owner's equity, revenue, and expense amounts.

Accounts receivable	$ 18,600
Rent expense	12,000
Cash	13,300
Supplies expense	3,600
Accounts payable	11,200
Service revenue	87,500

Supplies	17,000
Equipment	43,000
Kent Avon, capital	?
Utilities expense	5,000
Telephone expense	2,200
Advertising expense	7,000
Insurance expense	1,500
Wages expense	32,000
Withdrawals	20,000

Required:

A. Prepare an income statement for Avon Industries for the year ended December 31, 1987.

B. Prepare a statement of changes in owner's equity for 1987.

C. Prepare a balance sheet as of December 31, 1987.

Problem 1-2A Determining Missing Elements in Accounting Equation

Compute the two missing elements for each independent case below.

Case	Total Assets	Total Liabilities	Owner's Equity	Total Revenue	Total Expenses	Net Income (Loss)
1	$140,000	$ 46,000	$94,?000	$ 94,000	$ 6?8000	$26,000
2	4?2	14,000	28,000	105,000	9?9500	5,500
3	47,000	1?000	30,000	65,000	48,000	1?000
4	20?000	86,000	118,000	15?000	100,000	52,000
5	350,000	1?0000	210,000	6?0000	80,000	(20,000)

Problem 1-3A Preparation of Income Statement and Balance Sheet

Data for East Company as of December 31, 1987, follows.

Accounts receivable	$ 49,000	Wages expense	$ 86,000
Revenue	147,000	Advertising expense	25,000
Accounts payable	30,000	Land	21,000
Gary Toliver, capital	?	Equipment	107,500
Cash	39,000	Notes payable	50,000
Mortgage payable	185,000	Utilities expense	12,500
Building	230,000	Telephone expense	3,000

Required:

Prepare an income statement for 1987 and a balance sheet for East Company as of December 31, 1987.

Problem 1-4A Recording Transactions and Preparing Financial Statements

Balance-sheet item balances for Young Company on June 30 are given below in accounting equation form similar to the chapter illustrations.

Assets				=	Liabilities		+	Owner's Equity
Cash +	Accounts Receivable +	Supplies +	Equipment =		Accounts Payable +	Notes Payable +		Roy Young, Capital
Bal. $8,900	$28,000	$17,000	$41,000		$6,500	$22,000		$66,400

During July 1987, Young Company entered into the following transactions.

1. Collected $21,000 of accounts receivable.
2. Paid $5,000 on accounts payable.
3. Billed customers for services performed, in the amount of $8,200.
4. Purchased equipment for $3,000. Paid $2,000 in cash and signed a note payable for $1,000.
5. Paid expenses of $8,000 in cash (advertising, $1,000; rent, $3,000; employees' wages, $4,000).
6. Paid $3,000 on notes payable.
7. Used $2,000 worth of supplies during the period.
8. Collected $10,000 of accounts receivable.
9. Roy Young withdrew $10,000 for his personal use.

Required:
A. List the June 30 balances for assets, liabilities, and owner's equity in table form as shown in the example.
B. Record the effects of each transaction. Show the total of each column after recording each transaction.
C. Prepare an income statement and statement of changes in owner's equity for July, and a balance sheet for Young Company as of July 31, 1987.

Problem 1-5A Identifying Transactions from Balance Sheet Changes

After obtaining her real estate broker's license, Melissa Davis spent the month of May organizing her own business, Melissa's Realty. Melissa prepared a new balance sheet after each transaction she entered into. During May, the following balance sheets were prepared.

(1)

MELISSA'S REALTY
Balance Sheet
May 5, 1987

Assets		Owner's Equity	
Cash	$100,000	Melissa Davis, capital	$100,000

(2)

MELISSA'S REALTY
Balance Sheet
May 11, 1987

Assets		Liabilities and Owner's Equity	
Cash	$ 60,000	Note payable	$ 48,000
Land	18,000	Melissa Davis, capital	100,000
Building	70,000		
Total	$148,000	Total	$148,000

(3)

MELISSA'S REALTY
Balance Sheet
May 22, 1987

Assets		Liabilities and Owner's Equity	
Cash	$ 60,000	Accounts payable	$ 3,000
Office supplies	3,000	Note payable	48,000
Land	18,000	Total liabilities	51,000
Building	70,000	Melissa Davis, capital	100,000
Total	$151,000	Total	$151,000

(4)

MELISSA'S REALTY
Balance Sheet
May 25, 1987

Assets		Liabilities and Owner's Equity	
Cash	$ 55,000	Accounts payable	$ 3,000
Office supplies	3,000	Note payable	43,000
Land	18,000	Total liabilities	46,000
Building	70,000	Melissa Davis, capital	100,000
Total	$146,000	Total	$146,000

(5)

MELISSA'S REALTY
Balance Sheet
May 30, 1987

Assets		Liabilities and Owner's Equity	
Cash	$ 53,000	Accounts payable	$ 3,000
Office supplies	3,000	Note payable	43,000
Land	18,000	Total liabilities	46,000
Building	70,000	Melissa Davis, capital	98,000
Total	$144,000	Total	$144,000

Required:
Describe the nature of each of the five transactions that took place during May.

CASES

CASE 1-1:   Discussion Case   Preparation of Financial Statements

Paul Michaels was raised on a farm in the southwest. While in high school, he was an active member of the local 4H club and grew several ornamental plants that he sold at auction at state and local fairs. He saved his earnings and by the time he graduated from high school in 1987, Paul had nearly $8,500 in a savings account.

He was undecided on whether to go to college to continue his education or use his savings in a business venture. Because of his love for plants, he believed he could successfully operate a landscaping business and decided to use the summer months as a trial.

During the month of April, Paul located a small building that he could rent for $200 per month. After transferring $6,500 from his savings account to a business checking account in the name of Paul's Landscaping Service, he wrote checks for rent and for the purchase of landscaping equipment and gardening supplies. Although he would not keep a full set of accounting records, he decided to deposit all receipts from services performed into the checking account and to make all payments by check. In this way he would have a relatively complete record of his business activities. Paul also kept a daily workbook in which he recorded all services performed for customers.

On May 1, Paul opened his business to the public. During the first three months, he was unusually busy. Early in August he needed to make a decision on whether to continue the operation of his business or to enroll for the fall semester of college. To aid him in making this important decision, Paul reviewed his checking account and daily workbook to determine how well he had done. The review disclosed the following.

1. Total cash deposited in the checking account (including the initial $6,500 deposit) was $11,300.
2. The daily workbook showed that on July 31 customers owed him $700 for services performed, which he expected to collect during August.
3. Checks were written for
   a. Rent payments, totaling $800 for the months of May through August.
   b. The purchase of landscaping equipment, totaling $1,500. The equipment cost $2,000 and Paul still owed the supplier $500 on the purchase.
   c. Gardening supplies, totaling $200. Paul estimated that the cost of gardening supplies on hand on July 31 was $80.
   d. The payment of gasoline bills for the months of May and June, totaling $190. He had just received his bill from Exxon for the month of July in the amount of $91, but had not yet paid it.
   e. Advertising, totaling $400.
   f. Withdrawals made by Paul to pay for personal expenses, totaling $1,800.

Required:
A. Prepare an income statement for Paul's Landscaping Service for the three-month period from May 1 to July 31, 1987.
B. Prepare a statement of changes in owner's equity for the three-month period, and a balance sheet on July 31, 1987.
C. What other information would you need to determine how well Paul had done during the three-month period?

2

RECORDING BUSINESS TRANSACTIONS

Handwritten margin notes:

Debits | Credits
Dr | Cr.

Assets = Lia + OE
increased by Debits | Increased by Credits

OE
+ Invest cr.
+ Revenues cr.
- Expenses drs
- Withdrawals drs

Normal Balance = Side increases recorded on.

CHAPTER OVERVIEW AND OBJECTIVES

This chapter describes the basic procedures used to record the effects of transactions on a firm's financial position. When you have completed the chapter, you should understand:

1. The nature of accounting transactions.
2. The time period assumption.
3. A basic accounting model used to record, classify, and summarize transactions.
4. The use of source documents.
5. The purpose and basic formats of accounts.
6. The rules of debit and credit and how to apply these rules in analyzing transactions.
7. How to record transactions in the journal.
8. How to transfer data from the journal into the ledger.
9. How to verify the equality of debit and credit account balances by preparing a trial balance.
10. How to correct errors made in the journal or ledger.

This chapter contains a discussion of the basic procedures used in a manual accounting system to record and summarize the effects of transactions. In many firms, the recording and summarizing functions are performed by machines, as we shall see in Chapter 6, but the data gathered and stored in an automated system are based on an analysis quite similar to the one in this chapter. You must have an understanding of the underlying accounting framework to be an effective user of financial reports. Knowledge of the accounting system is most easily acquired by studying the procedures used in a manually operated system.

This chapter focuses on a business that performs a service for its customers. Accounting for businesses that engage in merchandising operations will be examined in Chapter 5 and accounting for businesses that manufacture products will be covered in Chapters 22 through 25.

TRANSACTIONS

TYPES OF TRANSACTIONS

**Objective 1:
Nature of trans-
actions**

A firm may enter into transactions with outside parties that affect the firm's financial statements. Examples include the purchase of office supplies, the performance of a service for others, the performance of a service by others for the firm, borrowing cash from a bank, and the purchase of equipment. These transactions are recorded by the accountant and (as we saw in Chapter 1) are called *external transactions* because there is an exchange of economic resources and/or obligations between two independent firms. In other words, in an extenal transaction the firm gives up something and receives something in return. For example, when a business purchases inventory for cash it gives up one resource (cash) in exchange for another resource (inventory). When the goods are purchased on credit, the firm is obligated to pay cash in the future.

Other business activities that do not involve a transaction with outside parties are recorded because they affect the relationship between the firm's assets, liabilities, and owner's equity. The use of office supplies by an employee, the conversion of wheat into flour, and the use of equipment to perform a service are examples of internal transactions. *Internal transactions* are those events that take place entirely within one firm.

Some events of importance to the firm are not recorded because there has not been an exchange of goods or services—for example, receiving an order from a customer, entering into a commitment to purchase an asset in the future, the hiring or retiring of an employee, or changes in market interest rates. In other words, such events do not initially affect the firm's recorded assets, liabilities, or owner's equity. Such events will be given accounting recognition in the future if an exchange takes place—for example, when goods are delivered to customers, an asset is received that was ordered, an employee is paid for services performed, and money is borrowed at the market rate of interest.

Other events that do not involve an exchange of resources, such as the destruction of an office building by fire or the city's donation of land to a company, are also given accounting recognition because assets and owner's equity are either decreased or increased. As noted in Chapter 1, the term *transaction* is often used to refer to all events that are given accounting recognition.

Financial accounting is based on a framework of rules for determining which events constitute accounting transactions. Two of the difficulties you will encounter in the study of accounting are determining which events to record and deciding at what stage an event should be given accounting recognition. Unfortunately, there are no simple rules.

TYPICAL TRANSACTIONS OF A BUSINESS ENTITY

Assets were defined in Chapter 1 as resources owned by the business. A firm acquires its assets from investment by the owners, from a variety of lending sources, such as commercial banks and finance companies, or from operations. The initial source of assets is an investment by the owners. Although investments by the owners may take various forms (such as cash, land, or equipment), the initial investment is frequently cash. To record this initial transaction, both assets and owner's equity are increased by an equal amount. Individuals invest in a business in anticipation of eventually being able to withdraw assets in excess of those invested. In other words, they expect that the firm will operate at a profit and that they will receive a return on their investment.

The mere holding of cash invested by the owners will not provide a return. Cash is useful as a medium of exchange or as a measure of value, but it is essentially a nonproductive asset. In order to generate revenue, the firm enters into external transactions with other firms to acquire productive assets, such as machinery, equipment, buildings, and inventory for sale to its customers. Such productive assets may be purchased for cash or financed on credit. The noncash assets are used (internal transactions) to provide goods or services for customers. The company then engages in transactions with customers to exchange goods or services for cash or for the customer's promise to pay cash in the future. Cash received from customers is then used to pay the operating expenses and obligations of the business. Such transactions may include payments to employees, to utility companies, to local governments for property taxes, and to landlords for rent. Any remaining cash may be used to pay obligations, retained in the business to finance future expansion, or distributed to owners as a return on their investment.

ACCOUNTING PERIODS

Most businesses engage in a continuous series of transactions for an indefinite period of time that may span many years. The most complete and accurate measure of a firm's success is achieved when the firm discontinues its operations and goes out of existence. At that time, the firm's life cycle is complete and all facts concerning its performance are known. However, financial statement users must make current decisions regarding the firm and cannot wait for an indefinite period for information. Thus, financial statement users must be provided with timely information. In order to report on the periodic progress of the firm, its life is divided into artificial time periods of equal length called **accounting periods.** Dividing the economic activity of a firm into various time periods for financial reporting purposes is called the **time period assumption.**

Accounting periods of approximately equal length are established to enable

Objective 2:
Time period assumption

the statement user to make meaningful comparisons of operating results of the current period with those of prior periods. A complete set of financial statements is issued to interested parties once a year as part of the firm's **annual report.**[1] In addition to the financial statements, annual reports contain comments from management about the year's events, the auditor's report, detailed notes related to information presented in the statements, and other information, such as financial highlights and historical summaries.

A firm may select any 12 consecutive months for reporting—the **fiscal year.** Many firms select a natural business year as a reporting period such as February 1 to January 31. A **natural business year** is a 12-month period that ends when business activities are at their lowest level during the year. If a firm's annual period ends on December 31, it is referred to as a **calendar year firm.**

Annual reports are used by creditors, investors, and other interested parties to assess the firm's progress from year to year. Although the basic accounting period for which financial statements are presented is one year, quarterly statements are also commonly issued to external parties to provide timely information on the operation of the firm. Generally, quarterly statements are not as detailed as annual reports. Many firms also prepare monthly or weekly statements for internal use by management. Statements prepared before the end of the annual period are called **interim statements.**

THE ACCOUNTING CYCLE

**Objective 3:
Accounting
model**

During each fiscal period, a sequence of accounting procedures called the **accounting cycle** is completed. The occurrence of a business transaction is the initial step in the accounting cycle, the end product of which is the firm's year-end financial statements. The first three steps of the accounting cycle, as shown here, are carried out continuously during the period as transactions occur. A trial balance may be prepared (Step 4) at any time during the period to verify the equality of the account balances. These four steps of the cycle are described in detail in this chapter in the following order.

The First Four Steps in the Accounting Cycle

Step 1.   Transactions occur and information is collected through use of source documents.

Step 2.   Transactions are analyzed on the basis of the source documents and are recorded in a journal.

Step 3.   Information is transferred (posted) from the journal to ledger accounts.

Step 4.   A trial balance is prepared from the account balances in the ledger to prove the equality of debits and credits.

The remaining part of the accounting cycle, completed at the end of the accounting period, is discussed in Chapters 3 and 4.

---

[1]Examples of annual reports for three companies are presented in an appendix to the text. One quarterly report is also presented so that you can compare the information contained in the two types of statements.

STEP 1: PREPARATION OF SOURCE DOCUMENTS

For most transactions that are recorded in the accounting system, a business record called a **source document** is prepared to provide written evidence that a transaction has occurred. A source document contains information about the nature of the transaction and the dollar amounts involved. Source documents, which are generally prepared for external transactions, may take the form of sales invoices for credit sales, purchase invoices for purchases of supplies, and cash register tapes for cash sales. An example of a sales invoice is shown in Figure 2–1. The recording of internal transactions such as depreciation on equipment used, supplies used by employees, and the conversion of raw materials into a finished product, is based on special schedules or other supporting documentation prepared internally.

Objective 4:
Use of source documents

The arrival of a source document in the accounting department generally initiates the recording process. Once received, the source document is analyzed to determine the amount and the effect of the transaction on the firm's financial position. Thus, it is important that a firm establish procedures to ensure that the effects of all transactions are recorded.

Source documents are also an important element in the audit of a firm. If the firm's financial statements are audited by an independent CPA (see Chapter 1), the source documents are examined because they provide evidence of the underlying transaction that was processed by the accounting department.

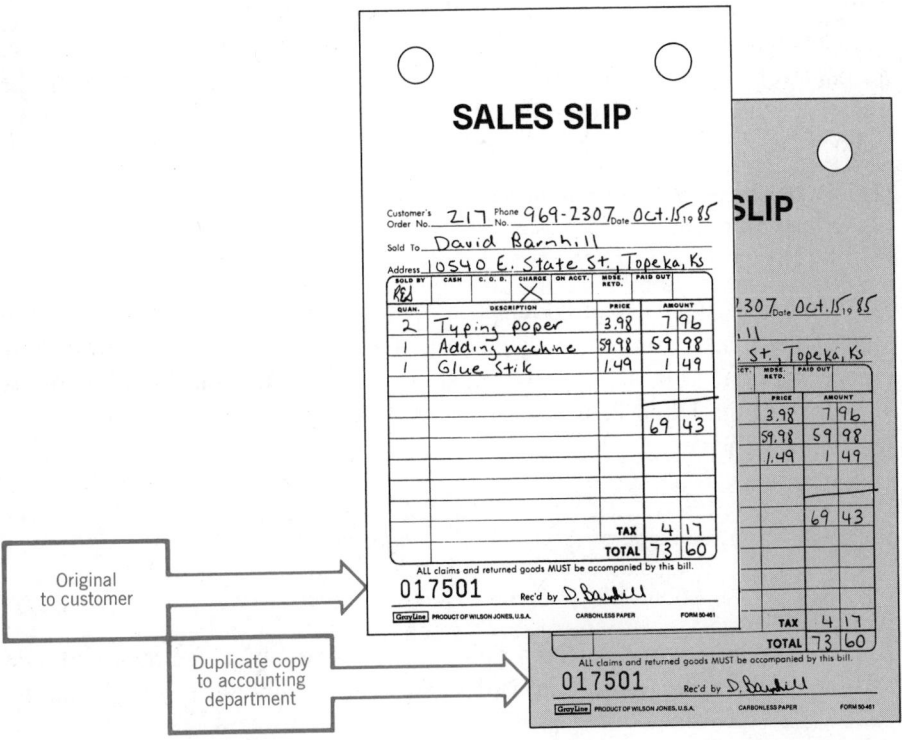

Figure 2–1
Example of a Source Document—Sales Invoice

STEP 2: TRANSACTIONS ARE
ANALYZED AND RECORDED IN A JOURNAL

In Chapter 1, a columnar format was used to record transactions and accumulate data in a form from which the firm's financial statements were prepared. In such a system, a separate column was used for each kind of asset and liability. All owner's equity transactions were summarized in one column and identified as to capital investment, withdrawal, revenue, or expense. Although the columnar accounting system is useful for illustrating double-entry accounting and the fact that the accounting equation must always remain in balance, it is not practical for most firms that engage in a large number of transactions. A better accounting system must be devised that is capable of processing a large number of transactions.

THE USE OF ACCOUNTS

**Objective 5:
The use of accounts**

Each transaction recorded results in an increase or decrease in one or more assets, liabilities, owner's equity, revenues, or expenses. A part of the accounting function is to classify the effects of transactions into meaningful categories and to summarize the results in the firm's financial statements. To facilitate accumulating financial statement data, transactions are recorded in accounts. An **account** is a device used to provide a record of increases and decreases in each item that appears in a firm's financial statements. Thus, as a part of its accounting system, a firm will typically maintain an account for each kind of asset, liability, owner's equity, revenue, and expense item. For example, a firm will maintain a separate account to record increases and decreases in cash, a separate account to record increases and decreases in accounts receivable, a separate account for accounts payable, and still another account for capital investment. The **general ledger** is a collection of the complete set of accounts established by a specific firm.

Each account has three basic parts.

(1) A title that is descriptive of the nature of the items being recorded in the account.
(2) A place for recording increases.
(3) A place for recording decreases.

Also, accounts typically provide space for recording an account number, the date of the transaction, an explanation of the transaction, and a posting reference column. One simplified format, called a **T account** because of its similarity to the letter T, is shown below. Two other formats are illustrated later in this chapter.

Account Title	
Left side or debit side (Abbreviation—Dr.)	Right side or credit side (Abbreviation—Cr.)

A T account has a left side and a right side, respectively called the **debit** side and the **credit** side. An account is debited when an amount is entered on the left side and credited when an amount is entered on the right side. A debit is also called a **charge** to the account.

To illustrate the mechanics involved, assume that a general ledger contained the following *Cash* account after certain transactions had been recorded.

Cash

Debit (Dr.)	Credit (Cr.)
10,000	6,200
7,200	4,000
3,000	10,200
20,200	
Balance 10,000	

Cash receipts (increases) are recorded on the debit side of the account and cash payments (decreases) are entered on the credit side.

Recording the receipts and payments separately facilitates the determination of the account balance. The **account balance** is the difference between the sum of its debits and the sum of its credits. If the sum of the debits exceeds the sum of the credits, the account has a debit balance. A credit balance results when the sum of the credits is greater than the sum of the debits. An account will have a zero balance if the sum of the debits equals the sum of the credits. In the *Cash* account above, the cash receipts of $20,200 exceeded the payments of $10,200, resulting in a debit balance of $10,000.

In a T account format the totals, called **footings,** are sometimes written smaller or in a different color than the postings so that the totals will not be interpreted as additional debits and credits. The debit balance of $10,000 in the *Cash* account is inserted on the debit side of the account. A balance sheet prepared at this time would report $10,000 in cash as an asset.

STANDARD ACCOUNT FORMS

The T account format described above is a convenient way to show the effects of transactions on individual accounts and is used primarily in accounting textbooks and in classroom illustrations. In practice, however, ledger accounts generally take one of the formats shown in Figure 2–2.

INDIVIDUAL ACCOUNTS COMMONLY USED

As mentioned previously, the accountant establishes an account for each type of asset, liability, owner's equity, revenue, and expense reported in the financial statements. The number of accounts and specific account titles will vary, depending on the nature and complexity of the business operation. For example, the accounts used to record transactions of a real estate sales office will differ significantly from those of a manufacturing firm. You will also find that the same type of account will be given different titles by different firms. In addition, the number of accounts can reflect the amount of information desired by the statement users. For example, although one account could be

Figure 2–2
Examples of Two
Account Forms

Balance-column or three-column format

ACCOUNT   Cash   ACCOUNT NO. 100

Date		Explanation	Post* Ref.	Debit	Credit	Balance
1987 Nov.	6		1	10,000		10,000
			1	7,200		17,200
			1		6,200	11,000
	7		2	3,000		14,000
			2		4,000	10,000

Four-column format

ACCOUNT   Cash   ACCOUNT NO. 100

Date		Explanation	Post. Ref.	Debit	Credit	Balance Debit	Credit
1987 Nov.	6		1	10,000		10,000	
			1	7,200		17,200	
			1		6,200	11,000	
	7		2	3,000		14,000	
			2		4,000	10,000	

*The numbers in the Posting Reference column refer to the page in the general journal on which the transaction was recorded. The purpose of the column is discussed later in this chapter.

used for recording all expenses, it would generally not provide sufficient detail to monitor and control the firm's operations.

The title or name given to a specific account should be descriptive of the items recorded in the account. Because some account titles consist of terms new to you, or with special technical meaning in accounting, it will be helpful to look first at the nature of the accounts normally used by a service organization before discussing the recording of transactions. Additional accounts are introduced in later chapters.

BALANCE SHEET ACCOUNTS

Asset Accounts

Cash.   The cash account is used to record receipts and payments of cash. The cash balance includes cash on hand and the balance on deposit in a bank.

Notes Receivable.   This account is used to record claims against another party that are evidenced by signed legal documents called ***promissory notes.*** A note is signed by the maker and contains, among other things, a promise to pay a definite sum of money at a specified time. Typically, a note receivable is requested by the firm when an account receivable from a customer is to be extended beyond the normal due date. Notes receivable are usually interest-bearing.

Accounts Receivable. Accounts receivable are amounts owed to a firm by customers who have purchased goods or received services on credit. An account receivable, less formal than a note, is generally based on an oral agreement to pay. Parties outside the firm that owe the firm are called **debtors.**

Other Receivables. At the end of the period, the firm may have receivables resulting from a variety of other transactions. For example, cash advances may have been made to employees, deposits may have been made with another firm for goods or services to be received in the future, utilities frequently require a deposit before service is provided, interest revenue may have accumulated on an outstanding note receivable, or a tenant may owe the firm rent. A firm will normally establish an individual account for each type of receivable.

Prepaid Expenses. Prepaid expenses are goods or services that have been paid for but not yet used or received. At the time of payment, an asset is recorded and subsequently expensed as the asset is used to produce revenue. Included in this category are advance payments of rent and insurance premiums. Each type of prepaid expense may be recorded in a separate account.

Land. The land account is used to record land owned by the firm. Land is recorded in an account separate from the building.

Buildings. The buildings account, sometimes called the plant account, is used to record purchases of buildings to be used by a firm to carry out its normal operations.

Equipment. Physical items used in the business for a relatively long period of time are recorded in the equipment account. In general, this account includes any item not permanently attached to the land or building. The account is used to record acquisitions of transportation equipment, office furniture and machines, factory equipment, store and office fixtures, and store furniture. Greater detail may be obtained by establishing a separate account for each major type of equipment owned.

Land, buildings, and equipment accounts are used for items to be used in the operations of the firm. Assets held for resale are reported in separate accounts.

Liability Accounts

Notes Payable. A note payable is a written promise to pay a specified amount to an outside party—a creditor—at a specified time. A note may be issued to a lending institution in exchange for cash, or the purchase of other assets may be made on credit by issuing a note payable. Notes payable are normally interest-bearing.

Accounts Payable. An account payable is an obligation to pay an amount to a creditor for the purchase of goods, supplies, or services on account.

Unearned Revenues. Customers often pay in advance for goods to be delivered or services to be performed in the future. Such advances are liabilities to the firm receiving the advance until the goods are delivered or the services performed. For example, magazine publishers require subscribers to pay for subscriptions in advance. The receipt of cash for a 24-month subscription is not recognized as revenue because the service has not been provided. Instead a liability, called unearned revenue, is recorded, because the firm has an obligation to deliver goods in the future. As the magazines are mailed to the subscriber, the amount earned is transferred from the unearned revenue account, a liability, to a revenue account. Rent collected in advance from a tenant and cash received for an airline ticket in advance of the flight are other examples of unearned revenue.

Other Short-Term Liabilities. At any given time, firms generally owe employees, taxing authorities, or other parties for services that have been received by the firm but that have not been paid. Generally a separate account is used for each type of liability.

Mortgage Notes Payable. This account is used to record a note for which the creditor has a secured claim against one or more of the firm's assets. A *secured claim* means that if the firm is unable to pay the obligation when due, the creditor may force the sale of the asset(s) pledged as security to recover the debt.

OWNER'S EQUITY ACCOUNTS

Four main types of transactions affect the owner's interest in the firm: (1) investment of assets in the firm by the owner, (2) withdrawals of assets by the owner, (3) earning of revenue, and (4) incurring of expenses to produce revenue. Thus the owner's equity part of the accounting equation may be expanded as follows.

Assets = Liabilities + Owner's equity

Owner's equity = Investment by the owner—Withdrawals by the owner + Revenue earned − Expenses incurred

In Chapter 1, transactions affecting the owner's equity in the business were recorded in a single column under the owner's name. However, separate accounts are maintained for each of these four categories as a convenient means for preparing a report of the changes in owner's equity that occurred during the period.

Capital.   Assets invested in the firm by the owner are recorded as an increase in assets and an increase in the capital account established in the name of the owner.

Withdrawals or Drawing.   The withdrawals account (sometimes called the *drawing account*) is used to record the withdrawals of assets, usually cash, from the business by the owner. Thus, withdrawals are recorded as a reduction in both assets and owner's equity. An owner of a proprietorship will often establish a fixed amount to be withdrawn at specific intervals for personal living expenses. Although the owner may think of these withdrawals as a salary, neither accounting practice nor tax codes recognize a proprietor as an employee of the firm, because the owner cannot hire himself. Consequently, withdrawals made in anticipation of earning income are not considered a salary nor an expense of the business.

Occasionally, personal expenses of the owner may be paid directly from the cash of the firm. Such payments are withdrawals and not expenses of doing business, since they are not associated with producing revenue.

INCOME STATEMENT ACCOUNTS

Revenue and expense accounts are subclassifications of owner's equity. Because of the variety and volume of revenue and expense transactions, it is helpful in the preparation of the income statement to maintain accounts separate from other owner's equity accounts. In addition, a separate account is maintained for each major type of revenue and expense item so that statement users will know the amount and source of revenue and the expenses used to produce revenue. Relatively insignificant amounts are normally recorded in a *Miscellaneous Revenue* or a *Miscellaneous Expense* account.

Revenue Accounts

Revenues are increases in owner's equity from the performance of services or the sale of goods. They are measured by the fair value of assets received. The asset received as payment for the goods or services is normally cash or a receivable. In a double-entry accounting system, revenue is recorded as both an increase in an asset and an increase in owner's equity. Each major source of revenue is recorded in a separate revenue account in order to disclose a particular source of assets.

Some businesses perform services for their clients and charge a fee or commission for the services rendered. Examples are a real estate office, a barber or beauty salon, a law office, an accounting firm, or an investment advisory service. Various account titles are used to describe the major sources of revenue. The account titles used should be descriptive of the nature of the revenue. For example, *Management Service Fees Earned* and *Tax Service Fees Earned* may be used by an accounting firm to account for major categories of revenue. Other firms, called merchandising firms, earn revenue by selling a finished product. An account entitled *Sales* is commonly used by merchandising firms to record revenue from the sale of merchandise.

Expense Accounts

The costs of assets consumed to produce revenue are called expenses. Expenses are recorded by decreasing an asset account and increasing the appropriate expense account (a decrease in the owner's equity in the firm). If an expense has not yet been paid for, a liability is recorded, rather than decreasing an asset. A number of expense accounts are normally needed to report the wide variety of expense items.

Although expenses decrease owner's equity, not all decreases in owner's equity are expenses. For example, a withdrawal of an asset by the owner decreases owner's equity but is not an expense of the business. Remember also that not all cash payments are expenses. Examples are the repayment of a loan, the cash purchase of office equipment (the cost will be expensed in future periods as the asset is used), and cash withdrawals by the owners.

When revenues exceed expenses, the difference is called *net income, earnings,* or *profit.* When expenses exceed revenue, the firm is said to be operating at a *net loss.* The earning of net income is obviously a major objective of a business, and one important function of accounting is to measure a firm's net income or net loss.

GENERAL LEDGER

In a manual system, each account is maintained on a separate card or on a separate sheet in a loose-leaf binder. The card file or the loose-leaf binder with all of its pages is, collectively, the general ledger.

Chart of Accounts—Sequence and Numbering of Accounts

Accounts are normally contained in the ledger in the order they appear in the balance sheet and the income statement, making them easier to find when preparing financial statements. Each account has an identification number that is useful for reference and as a means for cross-referencing the transactions entered in a specific account. A chart of accounts is a listing of the complete account titles and their related numbers.

When analyzing transactions, one refers to the chart of accounts to identify specific accounts to be increased or decreased. A flexible numbering system permits the addition of accounts as necessary. For example, all assets could be assigned a three-digit number from 100 to 199, liabilities could be 200 to 299, owner's equity 300 to 399, revenues 400 to 499, and expenses 500 to 599. Some numbers would not be assigned within each classification of accounts to permit the insertion of new accounts as they are needed.

A chart of accounts is used in this and later chapters to illustrate the accounting for the Starbuck Real Estate Office, as shown in Figure 2–3.

STARBUCK REAL ESTATE OFFICE
Chart of Accounts

Figure 2–3
Chart of Accounts

| **Balance Sheet Accounts** | | **Income Statement Accounts** | |
Account Title	Acct. No.	Account Title	Acct. No.
Assets		*Revenue*	
Cash	100	Commissions Revenue	400
Accounts Receivable	104	Appraisal Fees Revenue	401
Prepaid Insurance	110	Service Fees Revenue	402
Office Supplies Inventory	111	*Expenses*	
Land	150	Salaries Expense	500
Building	160	Commissions Expense	505
Accumulated Depreciation—		Utilities Expense	510
Building	161	Advertising Expense	520
Office Equipment	170	Insurance Expense	521
Accumulated Depreciation—		Office Supplies	
Office Equipment	171	Expense	530
Liabilities		Depreciation Expense—	
Accounts Payable	200	Building	540
Salaries Payable	210	Depreciation Expense—	
Commissions Payable	211	Office Equipment	541
Interest Payable	215	Interest Expense	560
Utilities Payable	216		
Unearned Appraisal Fees	220		
Mortgage Notes Payable	230		
Owner's Equity			
Mike Starbuck, Capital	300		
Mike Starbuck, Drawing	310		
Income Summary	350		

Debit and Credit Rules in Transaction Analysis

In Chapter 1, the analysis of transactions consisted of determining which items were affected and the amount that each item was increased or decreased. We emphasized that after every transaction the accounting equation had to be in balance. Each transaction affected at least two financial statement items, a system called double-entry accounting.

   When accounts are used in the accounting process, each transaction must also be analyzed to determine which accounts are affected, and whether each account is increased or decreased so as to determine whether they are to be debited or credited.

Objective 6: Debit and credit rules

Balance Sheet Accounts

As noted earlier, the left side of a T account is called the debit side and the right side is called the credit side. When accounts are maintained in the formats shown on page 46 and in the general journal, which is discussed later in this chapter, "debit" simply means the left column and "credit" means the right column. Whether a debit or a credit is an increase or a decrease to the account balance depends on whether the account is an asset, a liability, or an owner's equity account. Increases and decreases are recorded in the three categories of balance sheet accounts as shown in the T account format, as follows.

Assets		=	Liabilities		+	Owner's Equity	
Debit to increase +	Credit to decrease −		Debit to decrease −	Credit to increase +		Debit to decrease −	Credit to increase +

An increase to an asset account is recorded as a debit; an increase in a liability or owner's equity account is recorded as a credit. Note the relationship of the debit/credit rules to the accounting equation. Assets are on the left side of the equation and are increased on the left side of the T account (the debit side); liabilities and owner's equity accounts are on the right side of the equation and are increased on the right side of the account (the credit side). Decreases are recorded opposite of increases. Thus, a decrease in an asset is recorded as a credit; a decrease in a liability or an owner's equity account is recorded as a debit.

The recording of increases to liability and owner's equity accounts on the credit side and decreases on the debit side, a procedure that is opposite that of assets, permits an additional check for accuracy. Not only must the accounting equation be in balance, but the dollar amounts of the debits must equal the dollar amounts of the credits for each transaction. Since each transaction must balance, the sum of the accounts with debit balances must equal the sum of the accounts with credit balances.

Income Statement Accounts

The debit/credit rules for revenues and expenses can be developed by examining the relationship of revenue and expense accounts to the owner's equity account. As explained in Chapter 1, owner's equity is increased by revenues and decreased by expenses. Thus, increases in revenues are recorded as credits consistent with the recording of increases in owner's equity. Increases in expenses are recorded as debits, because they decrease owner's equity. A debit to an expense account is both a reduction in owner's equity and an increase in an expense account.

Debit and credit rules for income statement accounts are shown below in T account format.

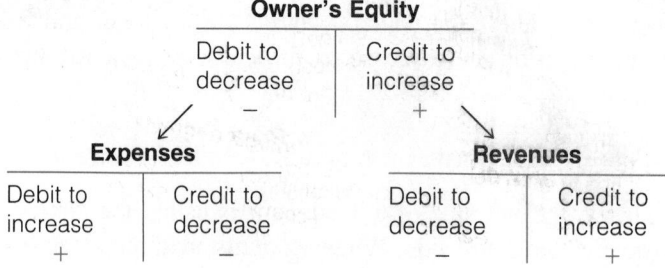

Note: A debit increases an expense account balance but is a decrease in owner's equity.

Normal Account Balances

The **normal balance** of an account is the side on which increases to the account are recorded. Knowing the normal account balance can help find errors. In particular, if the balance-column format illustrated on page 46 is used, the balance does not indicate whether it is a debit or credit.

Account	Side Increases Recorded on	Normal Balance
Assets	Debit	Debit
Liabilities	Credit	Credit
Owner's Equity		
Investment	Credit	Credit
Withdrawals	Debit	Debit
Revenues	Credit	Credit
Expenses	Debit	Debit

If an account has a balance different from its normal balance, it is likely that an error has been made. For example, the land account should never have a credit balance, nor should a revenue account have a debit balance. However, if a bank account has been overdrawn, the cash account will have a credit balance.

Understanding the rules of debit and credit is fundamental to understanding the material in the rest of this book. Because of the importance of understanding these rules, they should be mastered now. Here are some easy rules to help.

Remember that to debit an account simply means to enter the amount on the left side of the account.

To credit an account simply means to enter the amount on the right side of the account.

A debit may increase or decrease the account balance, depending on whether the account is on the left or right side of the accounting equation. The same is true for a credit.

Don't think of a debit or credit as an increase or decrease, but simply as an entry on the left or right side.

When analyzing a transaction, think in terms of which accounts are affected by the transaction. Given the type of account, should it be debited or credited to properly reflect the change in the account?

The debit and credit rules, their relationship to the types of accounts, and the normal balance of each type of account are summarized in Figure 2–4.

RECORDING TRANSACTIONS IN THE GENERAL JOURNAL

In the typical manual accounting system, a transaction is analyzed, and recorded in a book called a **journal,** before the effects of the transaction are entered in the individual accounts in the ledger. Since this is the initial recording of a transaction, journals are referred to as **books of original entry.** Although transactions could be entered directly to the accounts in the ledger, it is more convenient in a manual system to record them first in a journal. The debit and

Objective 7: Recording transactions in the general journal

Figure 2–4
Summary of Debit/
Credit Rules and
Normal Balance

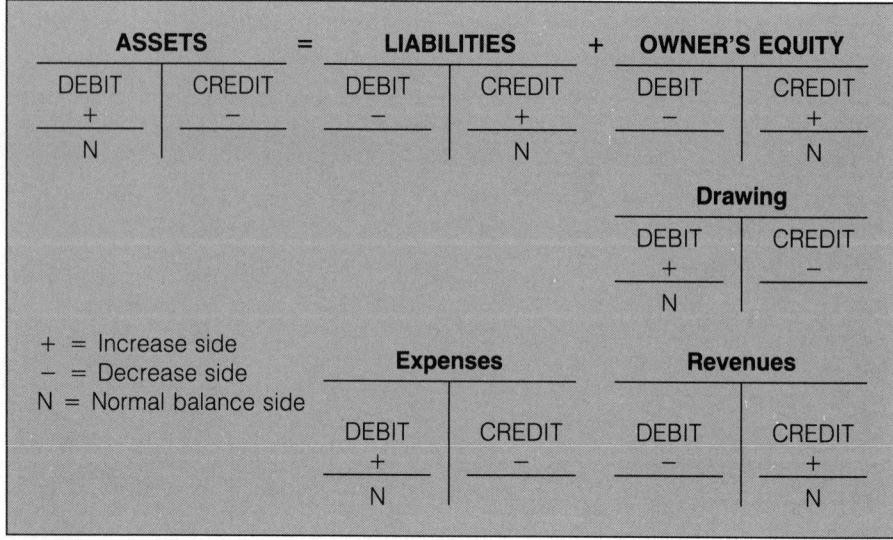

credit amounts can then be transferred to the proper ledger accounts at a convenient time.

The journal provides a complete record of all transactions in one place, by date, as they occur in chronological order. That is, in the journal, the title and dollar amounts of each account to be debited or credited are listed for each transaction. Since each individual transaction is recorded in two or more accounts in the ledger, no single account will contain a complete record of a transaction. However, the journal makes it possible to review the full effect of a particular transaction on the business.

In additon to providing a complete record of every transaction, the journal is a useful device for reducing and locating errors. If a transaction is recorded directly in the ledger accounts, the effect of the transaction may inadvertently be recorded initially as two debits or two credits, or one side of a transaction may be omitted entirely. Such errors would be difficult to locate. However, in the journal, the debit and credit information for each transaction is shown together in one place. For instance, the omission of a debit or a credit or the inclusion of two debits without an offsetting credit would be evident (although errors may still be made when transferring the effects of the transaction from the journal to the ledger). With a complete record of each transaction in the journal, some errors can be isolated by retracing the debits and credits to ledger accounts to ensure that the correct amounts were transferred to the proper accounts.

Recording Transactions in a Journal—Illustration

The number of journals used and the design of each journal varies from firm to firm, depending on the nature of the firm's operations and the frequency of a particular type of transaction. This chapter is concerned with the **general journal** or **two-column journal,** so called because it contains two columns for entering dollar amounts. Often, when large numbers of transactions of the same type occur, a firm establishes *special journals* to reduce the clerical work involved in recording and posting the transactions. Special journals are discussed in Chapter 6.

The standard form of a general journal and the steps followed in recording a journal entry are shown in Figure 2–5. Recording transactions in a journal is called **journalizing.** Each transaction recorded is a separate **journal entry.** Two transactions are illustrated in Figure 2–5. The first journal entry records the receipt of cash in exchange for services performed for a customer. The second entry records the purchase of office equipment with a partial payment in cash and the issuance of a note payable for the balance. The second entry is called a **compound journal entry** because it involves more than two accounts.

Before a journal entry is prepared, it is necessary to analyze the transaction to determine which accounts are affected and the amount by which each account is to be changed. Note that the rules of double-entry accounting are observed for each transaction. First, two or more accounts are affected by each transaction; second, the sum of the debit amount(s) for every transaction equals the sum of the credit amount(s); third, the equality of the accounting equation is maintained.

Every page in the journal is numbered for easy reference. Before an entry is made in the journal, the year and month are written at the top of the first column. The year and month are not repeated until the start of a new page or a new month. The process for journalizing transactions is described below. The steps in the process are keyed to the first entry in Figure 2–5.

GENERAL JOURNAL				Page 64	
Date	Accounts and Explanation	Post Ref.	Debit	Credit	
1987	②				
①July 5	Cash	⑧	③14,000		
	④Service Fee Revenue			⑤14,000	
	⑥To record services performed in exchange for cash.				
	⑦				
10	Office Equipment		62,000		
	Cash			22,000	
	Notes Payable			40,000	
	Purchased equipment for cash and issued a short-term note.				

Figure 2–5
Example of a General Journal

1. The date that each transaction occurred is entered in the first two columns.
2. The title of the account to be debited is entered against the left margin of the *Accounts and Explanation* column.
3. The amount to be debited to the account identified is entered in the debit-amount column on the same line as the account name.
4. The title of the account to be credited is entered on the line immediately

below the account to be debited. It is indented to set it apart from the account to be debited.

5. The amount to be credited to the account identified is entered in the credit-amount column on the same line as the account name.

6. An explanation of the transaction may be entered on the line immediately below the journal entry. Unless a transaction is unusual, this step is often omitted because the nature of the transaction is obvious from the accounts debited and credited.

7. A single line is sometimes skipped between each transaction.

8. At the time that the journal entry is made, the posting reference column (discussed in the next section) is left blank.

In the analysis of transactions, the chart of accounts should be referred to in order to ensure that proper account titles are used. If an appropriate account title is not listed in the chart of accounts, an additional account may be added.

STEP 3: JOURNAL ENTRIES ARE POSTED TO THE GENERAL LEDGER

Objective 8: Posting to the general ledger

The process of transferring amounts entered in the journal to the proper ledger accounts is called **posting**. The objective is to classify the effects of transactions on each individual asset, liability, owner's equity, revenue, and expense account. Posting is done periodically, such as at the end of each day or week.

The posting of one journal entry from Figure 2–5 with one debit and one credit is shown in Figure 2–6. The debit is posted in the top half of the figure and the credit is posted in the bottom half.

The steps involved in the posting process are:

1. Locate in the ledger the account to be debited.
2. Enter the date that the transaction occurred, as shown in the journal.
3. Enter the debit amount in the debit column of the ledger account.
4. Enter in the posting reference column of the ledger account the page number of the journal from which the entry is being posted.
5. Enter in the posting reference column of the journal the account number to which the debit amount was posted.

6–10. Repeat steps 1 through 5 for the credit part of the entry.

In Step 4, the posting reference in the general ledger indicates the journal and page number from which the transaction was taken. This provides a convenient means for tracing an amount recorded in an individual account back to the general journal when additional information is needed about the posting. The account number, entered in the posting reference column of the general journal in Step 5, tells the account number to which the amount was posted in the general ledger. A number in this column indicates that the amount has been posted.

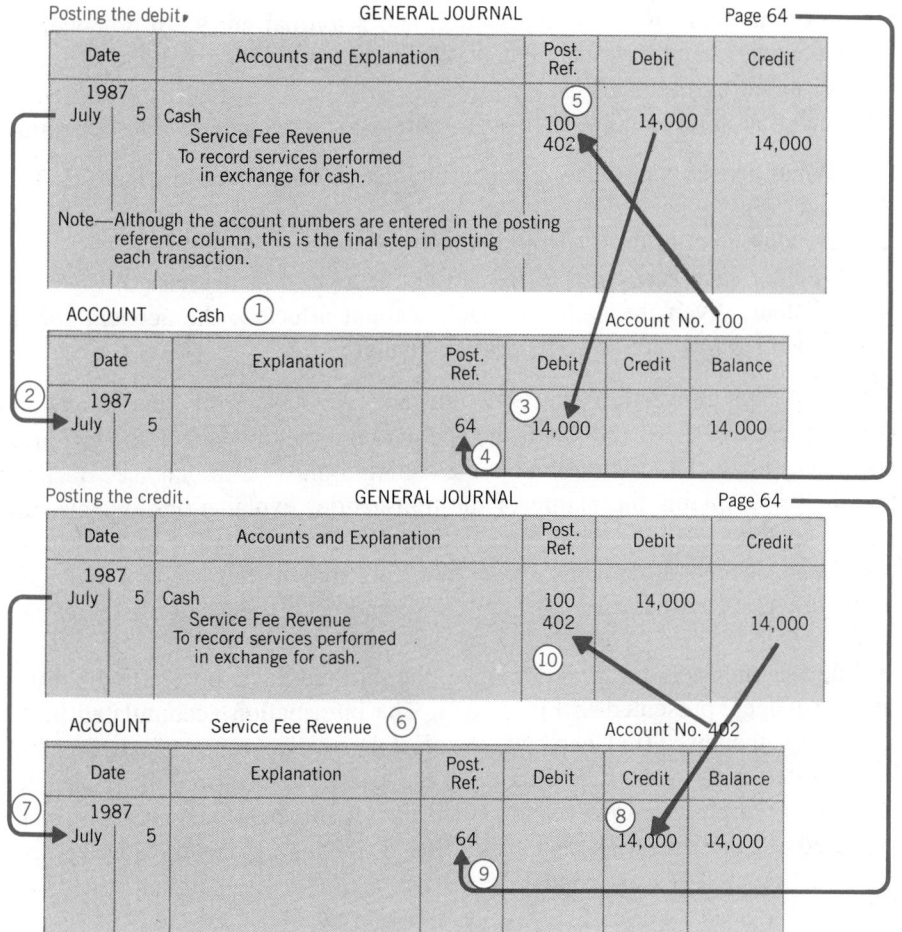

Figure 2–6
Posting from the
General Ledger to
the General Ledger

STEP 4: PREPARATION OF A TRIAL BALANCE

One aspect of a double-entry accounting system is that for every transaction there must be equal dollar amounts of debits and credits recorded in the accounts. The equality of debits and credits posted to the ledger accounts is verified by preparing a **trial balance**—a list of all the general ledger accounts in the order in which they appear in the ledger with their current balances. The dollar amounts of accounts with debit balances are listed in one column, and the dollar amounts of accounts with credit balances are listed in a second column. The sum of the two columns should be equal. When this occurs, the ledger is said to be "in balance." A trial balance may be prepared at any time to test the equality of debits and credits in the ledger.

**Objective 9:
Preparing a
trial balance**

ILLUSTRATIVE PROBLEM OF ACCOUNTING FOR A SERVICE FIRM

The June transactions for the Starbuck Real Estate Office are used to illustrate the analysis of transactions and the sequence of steps to be followed in recording and summarizing the transactions. Each transaction is stated below, followed by an analysis of the transaction and a journal entry. In practice, the journal entries would appear sequentially in the general journal and would be uninterrupted by the analysis.

Recall that in transaction analysis each transaction is analyzed to determine:

1. Which accounts are affected (see the chart of accounts in Figure 2–3 on page 51).
2. By what amount each account is changed.
3. Whether each account affected is to be increased or decreased.
4. Whether, given the nature of each account affected, the account should be debited or credited to record the change.

Note that each transaction affects two or more accounts with equal debits and credits recorded. Also, although the accounting equation is not shown, after each entry is posted to the accounts the equation must be in balance. Because the analysis explains the nature of the transaction, explanations, which may appear in the general journal after each entry, are omitted. For illustrative purposes, accounts affected by a transaction are shown after each journal entry using the T account format for simplicity, and each transaction is shown in color.

After the transactions are journalized, the information is posted to the firm's general ledger, presented in Figure 2–7. The information accumulated in the accounts is then used (in Chapter 3) to adjust the accounts and prepare financial statements for the month of June. A time period of one month is used for illustrative purposes. However, as noted earlier, financial statements may be prepared at other intervals desired by management (e.g., every quarter), but must be prepared at least annually.

June   1   Mike Starbuck deposited $60,000 cash in a checking account opened for the real estate business.

Analysis   The asset cash is increased by a debit. At the same time the investment by the owner increases his equity in the firm and is recorded by a credit to his *Capital* account.

GENERAL JOURNAL					Page 1
Date		Accounts and Explanation	Post. Ref.	Debit	Credit
1987 June	1	Cash	100	60,000	
		Mike Starbuck, Capital	300		60,000

Cash	100		Mike Starbuck, Capital	300
6/1 60,000			6/1 60,000

June   1   Signed an agreement for the firm to manage an apartment complex for a monthly fee of $400, to be paid on the fifth day of the following month.

Analysis Initially, signing the agreement does not create a recordable asset or revenue and, therefore, is not given accounting recognition. That is, the signing of the agreement does not constitute an accounting transaction. In the future, as the service is performed, the fee is earned by the firm and becomes recordable.

June   1   Purchased land and office building for $72,000. The terms of the agreement provided for a cash payment of $12,000, the remainder to be financed with a 20-year mortgage, bearing interest at 12% per year. The purchase price is allocated $10,000 to land and $62,000 to the building.

Analysis The land and building are both assets that are increased by debits. The decrease in cash is recorded by a credit. The unpaid portion of the purchase price is a liability called a *Mortgage Notes Payable*. A liability is increased by a credit. Although this transaction involves more than two accounts (a compound entry), the sum of the dollar amounts of the accounts debited equals the sum of the dollar amounts of the accounts credited.

June	1	Land	150	10,000	
		Building	160	62,000	
		Cash	100		12,000
		Mortgage Notes Payable	230		60,000

	Cash		100		Land		150
6/1	60,000	6/1	12,000	6/1	10,000		

	Building		160		Mortgage Notes Payable		230
6/1	62,000					6/1	60,000

June   3   Cash payment of $960 was made for a 24-month fire and business liability insurance policy.

Analysis The advance cash payment is recorded as a debit to an asset account, *Prepaid Insurance*. The asset acquired is insurance protection for 24-months, which will subsequently be expensed at some regular interval as insurance protection benefits are received and as a portion of the premium expires. Entries needed to adjust asset and liability accounts are covered in Chapter 3. The payment of cash decreases the *Cash* account and is recorded as a credit.

June	3	Prepaid Insurance	110	960	
		Cash	100		960

Cash			100		Prepaid Insurance		110
6/1	60,000	6/1	12,000	6/3	960		
		6/3	960				

June   5   Purchased office supplies for the amount of $620 on credit.

Analysis   This transaction increases both an asset and a liability by the same amount. Increases in assets are recorded by debits and increases in liabilities are recorded by credits. As the supplies are consumed, their cost will be transferred to an expense account, as discussed in Chapter 3.

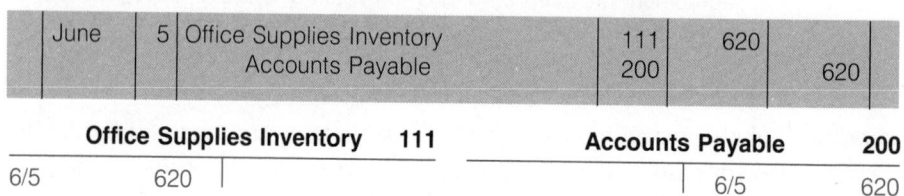

June	5	Office Supplies Inventory	111	620	
		Accounts Payable	200		620

Office Supplies Inventory		111		Accounts Payable		200
6/5	620				6/5	620

June   5   Purchased office furniture and equipment for a total price of $9,600. Paid $5,000 in cash, with the balance due in 60 days.

Analysis   The account *Office Equipment* is debited for $9,600 to record the purchase of the asset. At the same time, *Cash* is decreased by a credit of $5,000 and *Accounts Payable,* a liability, is increased by a credit of $4,600 to recognize a claim against the firm.

June	5	Office Equipment	170	9,600	
		Cash	100		5,000
		Accounts Payable	200		4,600

Cash			100	Office Equipment		170	Accounts Payable		200
6/1	60,000	6/1	12,000	6/5	9,600			6/5	620
		6/3	960					6/5	4,600
		6/5	5,000						

June   5   Hired two sales agents and an office secretary.

Analysis   The hiring of employees is an important event but is not given accounting recognition since there are no effects at this time on the firm's accounting equation.

June   6   Paid $120 for radio commercials aired on June 3 and 4.

Analysis   Advertising is an operating expense. The benefits were considered to be received when the commercial announcements were made. The *Advertising Expense* account is increased by a debit. Expenses decrease owner's equity (a debit), but a separate account, *Advertising Expense,* is established to facilitate preparation of the income statement. The *Cash* account is decreased by a credit.

June	6	Advertising Expense	520	120	
		Cash	100		120

Cash		**100**			**Advertising Expense**	**520**	
6/1	60,000	6/1	12,000	6/6	120		
		6/3	960				
		6/5	5,000				
		6/6	120				

June 15 Sold a residence that had been listed with the firm. A commission of $4,200 was earned on the sale, to be received when the loan is closed.

Analysis Under accrual accounting, this is a revenue transaction, even though no cash was received. *Accounts Receivable* is increased (a debit) to recognize the right to receive cash in the future. When the cash is received, *Cash* will be debited and *Accounts Receivable* credited. Revenues increase owner's equity (a credit), but a separate account, *Commissions Revenue,* is established to facilitate preparation of the income statement.

June	15	Accounts Receivable	104	4,200	
		Commissions Revenue	400		4,200

Accounts Receivable	**104**		**Commissions Revenue**	**400**
6/15	4,200		6/15	4,200

June 19 Sold a residence that had been listed with the firm. A commission of $5,400 was earned on the sale, to be received when the loan is closed.

Analysis Same as for the revenue transaction on June 15.

GENERAL JOURNAL					Page 2
Date		Accounts and Explanation	Post. Ref.	Debit	Credit
1987 June	19	Accounts Receivable	104	5,400	
		Commissions Revenue	400		5,400

Accounts Receivable	**104**		**Commissions Revenue**	**400**
6/15	4,200		6/15	4,200
6/19	5,400		6/19	5,400

June   22   Paid salaries of $1,800 to the secretary, part-time employees, and sales staff for services rendered during the last two weeks.[2] Withholdings from the employees' salaries for taxes are ignored for now.

Analysis   Analysis is similar to the advertising expense transaction on June 6. However, the transactions differ as to the kind of expense involved. A separate expense account is established for each significant expense category.

| June | 22 | Salaries Expense | 500 | 1,800 | |
| | | Cash | 100 | | 1,800 |

	Cash		**100**		**Salaries Expense**		**500**
6/1	60,000	6/1	12,000	6/22	1,800		
		6/3	960				
		6/5	5,000				
		6/6	120				
		6/22	1,800				

June   23   Conducted a real estate appraisal for a customer and received a fee of $250 in cash.

Analysis   The performance of the service is a revenue transaction and the receipt of cash increases both assets (debited) and owner's equity (credited). A separate revenue account is established to recognize the kind of revenue earned.

| June | 23 | Cash | 100 | 250 | |
| | | Appraisal Fees Revenue | 401 | | 250 |

	Cash		**100**	**Appraisal Fees Revenue**		**401**
6/1	60,000	6/1	12,000		6/23	250
6/23	250	6/3	960			
		6/5	5,000			
		6/6	120			
		6/22	1,800			

June   23   Starbuck withdrew $600 cash from the business for his personal use.

Analysis   This transaction is a withdrawal of assets by the owner and is not an expense related to the production of revenue. A debit is made to the *Drawing* account to record the decrease in capital, and the decrease in the *Cash* account is recorded by a credit.

| June | 23 | Mike Starbuck, Drawing | 310 | 600 | |
| | | Cash | 100 | | 600 |

[2]The term *salary* is usually used to refer to fixed compensation paid on a regular basis for services received from employees. The term *wage* is commonly used to refer to compensation stated in terms of an hourly rate or a similar basis. Here, for convenience, the term salary applies to both.

	Cash	**100**		**Mike Starbuck, Drawing**	**310**
6/1	60,000	6/1 12,000	6/23	600	
6/23	250	6/3 960			
		6/5 5,000			
		6/6 120			
		6/22 1,800			
		6/23 600			

June   27   Paid $620 to creditors for office supplies purchased on credit.

Analysis The payment reduced a creditor's claim against the assets of the firm. A decrease in liabilities is recorded by a debit and the asset *Cash* is decreased by a credit.

June	27	Accounts Payable	200	620	
		Cash	100		620

	Cash	**100**		**Accounts Payable**	**200**
6/1	60,000	6/1 12,000	6/27 620	6/5	620
6/23	250	6/3 960		6/5	4,600
		6/5 5,000			
		6/6 120			
		6/22 1,800			
		6/23 600			
		6/27 620			

June   29   Received a check for $280 for an appraisal to be performed in July.

Analysis Cash is increased by a debit. Since the service has not yet been performed, the revenue has not been earned. Therefore a liability, *Unearned Appraisal Fees,* is recorded to reflect the obligation of the firm to perform the appraisal at some future date.

June	29	Cash	100	280	
		Unearned Appraisal Fees	220		280

	Cash	**100**		**Unearned Appraisal Fees**	**220**
6/1	60,000	6/1 12,000		6/29	280
6/23	250	6/3 960			
6/29	280	6/5 5,000			
		6/6 120			
		6/22 1,800			
		6/23 600			
		6/27 620			

June   30   Paid telephone bill in the amount of $72.

Analysis Analysis is similar to the advertising expense transaction on June 6.

June	30	Utilities Expense		510	72	
		Cash		100		72

Cash			**100**	**Utilities Expense**			**510**
6/1	60,000	6/1	12,000	6/30	72		
6/23	250	6/3	960				
6/29	280	6/5	5,000				
		6/6	120				
		6/22	1,800				
		6/23	600				
		6/27	620				
		6/30	72				

June 30 The loan closed and a check for $4,200 was received for commissions earned on the residence sold on June 15.

Analysis The increase in cash is recorded by a debit. The receipt also reduced the firm's claims against a debtor. A decrease in the asset *Accounts Receivable* is recorded by a credit. Note that this transaction increases one asset and decreases another. Recall that revenue was recorded on June 15 when it was earned. That is, the revenue was earned when the residence was sold for the client, rather than when the cash was collected.

June	30	Cash		100	4,200	
		Accounts Receivable		104		4,200

Cash			**100**	**Accounts Receivable**			**104**
6/1	60,000	6/1	12,000	6/15	4,200	6/30	4,200
6/23	250	6/3	960	6/19	5,400		
6/29	280	6/5	5,000				
6/30	4,200	6/6	120				
		6/22	1,800				
		6/23	600				
		6/27	620				
		6/30	72				

The general ledger for the Starbuck Real Estate Office showing the effects of the above transactions on the accounts maintained by the firm is presented in Figure 2–7. In an actual accounting system, each account would be a separate page in the ledger. The three-column account format is used to replace the simpler T account form, which was used previously to illustrate the effects of the transactions on the accounts.

Figure 2–7
General Ledger

ACCOUNT: Cash   Account No.   100

Date		Explanation	Post. Ref.	Debit	Credit	Balance
1987						
June	1		1	60,000		60,000
	1		1		12,000	48,000
	3		1		960	47,040
	5		1		5,000	42,040
	6		1		120	41,920
	22		2		1,800	40,120
	23		2	250		40,370
	23		2		600	39,770
	27		2		620	39,150
	29		2	280		39,430
	30		2		72	39,358
	30		2	4,200		43,558

ACCOUNT: Accounts Receivable   Account No.   104

Date		Explanation	Post. Ref.	Debit	Credit	Balance
1987						
June	15		1	4,200		4,200
	19		2	5,400		9,600
	30		2		4,200	5,400

ACCOUNT: Prepaid Insurance   Account No.   110

Date		Explanation	Post. Ref.	Debit	Credit	Balance
1987						
June	3		1	960		960

ACCOUNT: Office Supplies Inventory   Account No.   111

Date		Explanation	Post. Ref.	Debit	Credit	Balance
1987						
June	5		1	620		620

ACCOUNT: Land   Account No.   150

Date		Explanation	Post. Ref.	Debit	Credit	Balance
1987						
June	1		1	10,000		10,000

ACCOUNT: Building   Account No.   160

Date		Explanation	Post. Ref.	Debit	Credit	Balance
1987 June	1		1	62,000		62,000

ACCOUNT: Office Equipment   Account No.   170

Date		Explanation	Post. Ref.	Debit	Credit	Balance
1987 June	5		1	9,600		9,600

ACCOUNT: Accounts Payable   Account No.   200

Date		Explanation	Post. Ref.	Debit	Credit	Balance
1987 June	5		1		620	620
	5		1		4,600	5,220
	27		2	620		4,600

ACCOUNT: Unearned Appraisal Fees   Account No.   220

Date		Explanation	Post. Ref.	Debit	Credit	Balance
1987 June	29		2		280	280

ACCOUNT: Mortgage Notes Payable   Account No.   230

Date		Explanation	Post. Ref.	Debit	Credit	Balance
1987 June	1		1		60,000	60,000

ACCOUNT: Mike Starbuck, Capital   Account No.   300

Date		Explanation	Post. Ref.	Debit	Credit	Balance
1987 June	1		1		60,000	60,000

ACCOUNT: Mike Starbuck, Drawing   Account No.   310

Date		Explanation	Post. Ref.	Debit	Credit	Balance
1987						
June	23		2	600		600

ACCOUNT: Commissions Revenue   Account No.   400

Date		Explanation	Post. Ref.	Debit	Credit	Balance
1987						
June	15		1		4,200	4,200
	19		2		5,400	9,600

ACCOUNT: Appraisal Fees Revenue   Account No.   401

Date		Explanation	Post. Ref.	Debit	Credit	Balance
1987						
June	23		2		250	250

ACCOUNT: Salaries Expense   Account 500

Date		Explanation	Post. Ref.	Debit	Credit	Balance
1987						
June	22		2	1,800		1,800

ACCOUNT: Utilities Expense   Account No.   510

Date		Explanation	Post. Ref.	Debit	Credit	Balance
1987						
June	30		2	72		72

ACCOUNT: Advertising Expense   Account No.   520

Date		Explanation	Post. Ref.	Debit	Credit	Balance
1987						
June	6		1	120		120

Figure 2–8
Trial Balance

STARBUCK REAL ESTATE OFFICE Trial Balance June 30, 1987		
Account Title	Debit	Credit
Cash	$ 43,558	
Accounts Receivable	5,400	
Prepaid Insurance	960	
Office Supplies Inventory	620	
Land	10,000	
Building	62,000	
Office Equipment	9,600	
Accounts Payable		$ 4,600
Unearned Appraisal Fees		280
Mortgage Notes Payable		60,000
Mike Starbuck, Capital		60,000
Mike Starbuck, Drawing	600	
Commissions Revenue		9,600
Appraisal Fees Revenue		250
Salaries Expense	1,800	
Utilities Expense	72	
Advertising Expense	120	
Totals	$134,730	$134,730

Figure 2–8 is a trial balance taken directly from the ledger of Starbuck Real Estate Office (see Figure 2–7).

DISCOVERY AND CORRECTION OF ERRORS

The fact that the sum of the debit column equals the sum of the credit column in the trial balance does not guarantee that errors have not been made. The trial balance is simply a verificaton that (1) equal debits and credits have been recorded in the accounts; and (2) the account balances were computed correctly, based on the recorded data. However, errors can be made that do not affect the equality of debits and credits. For example, a correct amount can be posted to the wrong account, a journal entry may be omitted, or an incorrect amount can be posted to both accounts. The possibility of making such errors should serve to emphasize the need to exercise due care in journalizing and posting transactions.

DISCOVERY OF ERRORS

Some errors are discovered by chance or during normal operations. For example, if an account receivable is overstated, the customer will usually inform the firm when the monthly billings are made. Other errors may be identified through procedures established by the firm to check on the accuracy of its records. For example, as will be discussed in Chapter 7, a firm performs a bank reconciliation each month to verify the balance in the cash account.

A trial balance that does not balance is a clear indication either that there are one or more errors in the accounts or that there was an error in preparing the trial balance. Although there is no one correct procedure for locating all types of errors, the following systematic approach is helpful.

1. Check the accuracy of the trial balance totals by adding the columns again.
2. Certain types of error may be identified by performing a couple of simple computations. First, compute the difference between the totals and divide the difference by two. Next, review the trial balance and the journal for each of these amounts. The amount of the difference may be equal to a debit or credit that was omitted or, if a debit or credit was recorded twice, the erroneous posting will be equal to one-half of the difference. This is also true if a debit account balance is listed accidentally in the trial balance as a credit or vice versa.

    If the difference between the two trial balance totals is evenly divisible by nine, it may be an indication of two common errors called transpositions and slides. To illustrate, assume that an expense account should have been debited for $460. If the error is a **transposition,** the order of the digits in a number is altered, as in posting the amount of $640 instead of $460. In a **slide,** the decimal point is shifted to the left or the right, as by writing $46 instead of $460. In both types of error, the difference between the correct number and the incorrect number can be evenly divided by nine.
3. Compare the account balances listed in the trial balance with the ledger accounts, to verify that all account balances were included and copied correctly.
4. Recompute the account balances.
5. Verify that the debits equal the credits for each entry in the journal.
6. Trace the entries as recorded in the journal to the ledger accounts, and place a small check mark by each amount in the journal and ledger as each posting is verified. Be alert for the posting of wrong amounts and for debits posted as credits or vice versa. If the error is not found before this process is completed, review the journal and ledger, looking for amounts without a check mark.

CORRECTING ERRORS

Once an error is located, it must be corrected. An error in a journal entry discovered before the amount is posted is corrected by crossing out the wrong amount with a single line and inserting the correct amount immediately above it. An error in an amount posted to a correct ledger account is corrected in the same way. Errors should never be erased because erasures may give the impression that something is being concealed.

Objective 10: Correction of errors

Journal entries that have been posted in the wrong accounts should be corrected by a journal entry. For example, assume that the following entry was made in the journal to record the receipt of cash for the performance of a service for a customer and was posted in the ledger.

Feb.	14	Accounts Receivable	862	
		Service Revenue		862
		To record the performance of service on account		

A correcting entry is needed to cancel the incorrect debit to *Accounts Receivable* and to record a correct debit to the *Cash* account.

Mar.	10	Cash	862	
		Accounts Receivable		862
		To correct an entry recorded on Feb. 14 in which a cash receipt was debited to Accounts Receivable.		

USE OF DOLLAR AMOUNTS, COMMAS, AND PERIODS

Note that in the figures in this chapter, dollar signs are not used in the journal or the ledger. Dollar signs *are* used, however, in the financial statements and other financial reports. A common practice in formal reports is to place a dollar sign before the first amount in a column of figures, and also before the total amount. Also, a single ruled line is placed under a column of figures to indicate that the amounts above the line are added or subtracted. A double line is placed after a total.

When dollar amounts are entered in the journal or ledger and the columns are ruled, commas and periods are not necessary. For the convenience of the statement reader, commas and periods should be used if the paper is unruled.

DEMONSTRATION PROBLEM

At the end of Chapters 2, 3, 4, and 5, a demonstration problem and suggested solution are presented for your use as a tool to test your comprehension of the chapter material. To make the best use of this material, you should attempt to solve the problem before studying the suggested solution.

Mary Johnson established an interior decorating service, to be operated out of her home, called the Johnson Decorating Service. During the first month of operation, she completed the following transactions.

1987
July
- 1 Deposited $4,000 in the business checking account.
- 1 Purchased office equipment on credit for $1,200.
- 2 Purchased a used automobile for $4,200, paying $1,200 cash and signing a 12% note for the balance.
- 2 Paid $180 cash for a one-year insurance policy on the automobile.
- 8 Purchased office supplies on account for a total of $140.
- 15 Completed a decorating assignment for a client and received $280 cash.

17 Received a deposit from a customer for services to be performed in August, in the amount of $80.

28 Billed a client for $240 for services completed in July.

30 Withdrew $400 from the business for personal use.

31 Paid $20 for advertising, which appeared in the newspaper last week.

Required:

A. Set up a general ledger in T account format using the following account titles and numbers:

Cash	100	Unearned Service Fees	220
Accounts Receivable	105	Notes Payable	250
Office Supplies Inventory	120	Mary Johnson, Capital	300
Prepaid Insurance	131	Mary Johnson, Drawing	320
Automobile	160	Service Fees Revenue	400
Office Equipment	180	Advertising Expense	510
Accounts Payable	200		

B. 1. Journalize the above transactions.
  2. Post the entries to the T accounts.
  3. Prepare a trial balance as of July 31.

ANSWER TO DEMONSTRATION PROBLEM

B. 1. Recording transactions in the general journal. The posting reference column of the journal would be completed as the entries are posted in part B.2.

GENERAL JOURNAL					Page 1
Date		Accounts and Explanation	Post. Ref.	Debit	Credit
1987					
July	1	Cash	100	4,000	
		Mary Johnson, Capital	300		4,000
		The owner invested cash in the business.			
	1	Office Equipment	180	1,200	
		Accounts Payable	200		1,200
		Purchased office equipment on account.			
	2	Automobile	160	4,200	
		Cash	100		1,200
		Notes Payable	250		3,000
		Purchased an automobile for $1,200 cash and signed a $3,000 note.			
	2	Prepaid Insurance	131	180	
		Cash	100		180
		Purchased a one-year insurance policy on the automobile.			

	8	Office Supplies Inventory	120	140	
		Accounts Payable	200		140
		Purchased office supplies on account.			
	15	Cash	100	280	
		Service Fees Revenue	400		280
		Earned revenue by completing an assignment.			
	17	Cash	100	80	
		Unearned Service Fees	220		80
		Received an advance payment for services.			
	28	Accounts Receivable	105	240	
		Service Fees Revenue	400		240
		Billed customers for services performed.			
	30	Mary Johnson, Drawing	320	400	
		Cash	100		400
		Withdrew cash from business for personal use.			
	31	Advertising Expense	510	20	
		Cash	100		20
		Paid advertising expense.			

A. and B. 2

Johnson Decorating Service General Ledger

Cash			100		Prepaid Insurance	131
7/1	4,000	7/2	1,200	7/2	180	
7/15	280	7/2	180			
7/17	80	7/30	400			
		7/31	20			
Bal.	2,560					

Accounts Receivable		105		Automobile	160
7/28	240		7/2	4,200	

Office Supplies Inventory		120		Office Equipment	180
7/8	140		7/1	1,200	

Accounts Payable			200		Unearned Service Fees	220
		7/1	1,200		7/17	80
		7/8	140			
		Bal.	1,340			

Notes Payable	250
	7/2 3,000

Service Fees Revenue	400
	7/15 280
	7/28 240
	Bal. 520

Mary Johnson, Capital	300
	7/1 4,000

Advertising Expense	510
7/31 20	

Mary Johnson, Drawing	320
7/30 400	

B. 3. Preparation of trial balance on July 31.

JOHNSON DECORATING SERVICE
Trial Balance
July 31, 1987

Account Title	Debit	Credit
Cash	$2,560	
Accounts Receivable	240	
Office Supplies Inventory	140	
Prepaid Insurance	180	
Automobile	4,200	
Office Equipment	1,200	
Accounts Payable		$1,340
Unearned Service Fees		80
Notes Payable		3,000
Mary Johnson, Capital		4,000
Mary Johnson, Drawing	400	
Service Fees Revenue		520
Advertising Expense	20	
Totals	$8,940	$8,940

GLOSSARY

ACCOUNT.   A device used to record increases and decreases for each item that appears in a financial statement (p. 44).

ACCOUNT BALANCE.   The difference between the dollar amounts of debits and credits recorded in a particular account (p. 45).

ACCOUNTING CYCLE.   The sequence of accounting procedures that take place during each accounting period (p. 42).

ACCOUNTING PERIOD.   A period of time covered by a set of financial statements (p. 41).

ANNUAL REPORT.　A document issued to interested parties at the end of a firm's fiscal period containing the firm's financial statements and other data, such as historical summaries, notes regarding the financial statements, and highlights of the year's operations (p. 42).

CALENDAR YEAR FIRM.　A firm whose annual period begins on January 1 and ends on December 31 (p. 42).

CHARGE.　A debit to an account (p. 45).

CHART OF ACCOUNTS.　A schedule listing the titles of all accounts contained in the ledger (p. 50).

COMPOUND JOURNAL ENTRY.　A journal entry involving three or more accounts (p. 55).

CREDIT.　An amount entered on the right side of an account (p. 44).

DEBIT.　An amount entered on the left side of an account (p. 44).

DEBTORS.　Parties that have an obligation to the firm (p. 47).

FISCAL YEAR.　An accounting or reporting period of any 12 consecutive months (p. 42).

FOOTING.　Computing the total of a column of figures (p. 45).

GENERAL JOURNAL (TWO-COLUMN JOURNAL).　A book containing a chronological listing of transactions (p. 54).

GENERAL LEDGER.　A collection of a group of accounts, with each account appearing on a separate page (p. 44).

INTERIM STATEMENTS.　Financial statements prepared between annual reports (p. 42).

JOURNAL (BOOKS OF ORIGINAL ENTRY).　A book in which transactions are first recorded (p. 53).

JOURNAL ENTRY.　The format in which a transaction is entered in the general journal (p. 55).

JOURNALIZING.　The process of recording a transaction in the journal (p. 55).

NATURAL BUSINESS YEAR.　A 12-month period that ends when business activities are at their lowest level (p. 42).

NORMAL ACCOUNT BALANCE.　The side of the account on which increases are recorded (p. 52).

POSTING.　The process of transferring information recorded in the journal to the individual accounts in the ledger (p. 56).

SLIDE.　An error in which the decimal point is shifted to the left or right (p. 69).

SOURCE DOCUMENT.　A paper or form that provides evidence that a transaction has occurred (p. 43).

T ACCOUNT.　An account format shaped like the letter T, in which the left side of the account is the debit side and the right side is the credit side (p. 44).

TIME PERIOD ASSUMPTION.　The assumption that the operating life of a firm can be divided into specific time periods of equal length (p. 41).

TRANSPOSITION.　An error in which the order of the digits of a number is altered (p. 69).

TRIAL BALANCE.　A statement listing all of the accounts in the general ledger and their debit or credit balances. A trial balance is prepared to verify the equality of debits and credits made to the accounts (p. 57).

DISCUSSION QUESTIONS

1. Indicate whether each of the following events is an internal transaction, an external transaction, or not a recordable business transaction.
   (a) Purchased equipment for cash.
   (b) Received payment from a customer on account.
   (c) Equipment is used to provide a service for a customer.
   (d) Land owned by the firm increased in value.
   (e) Money is borrowed from the First National Bank.
   (f) Supplies are used by an employee.
   (g) Hired an employee at a monthly salary of $1,800.
   (h) Paid monthly salary to employee.
2. What is the accounting cycle?
3. List the following steps in their proper sequence.
   (a) The journal entry is posted to the ledger.
   (b) A source document is prepared.
   (c) Analysis of the transaction is performed.
   (d) A business transaction occurs.
   (e) A trial balance is prepared.
   (f) An entry is made in the general journal.
4. Explain the purpose of an account. Explain the purpose of a ledger.
5. Explain the following terms as they pertain to a T account.
   (a) Debit side.
   (b) Credit side.
   (c) To debit.
   (d) To credit.
6. What are the four types of transactions that affect the owner's equity in the firm?
7. Define the term *revenues* and indicate how revenues affect owner's equity.
8. What is net income? What is net loss?
9. One sometimes hears the statement: ''Debits are bad and credits are good for the business.'' Do you agree with this statement? Why or why not?
10. How are the accounts usually ordered in the general ledger?
11. On what side of the account are increases recorded for the following?
    (a) Assets.
    (b) Liabilities.
    (c) Owner's equity.
    (d) Revenues.
    (e) Expenses.
12. Identify the normal balance of the following accounts.
    (a) Equipment.
    (b) Rental Revenue.
    (c) Accounts Payable.
    (d) H. R. Wicks, Drawing.
    (e) Salaries Expense.
    (f) H. R. Wicks, Capital.
    (g) Accounts Receivable.
    (h) Cash.
    (i) Prepaid Rent.
    (j) Rent Expense.
13. Why do expense accounts have a normal balance (debit) opposite the normal balance of owner's equity accounts?
14. What is the purpose of the journal?
15. What is the purpose of posting references?

16. Give an example of a transaction that results in
    (a) An increase in an asset and an increase in a liability.
    (b) A decrease in one asset but no change in total assets.
    (c) An increase in an asset and an increase in owner's equity.
    (d) A decrease in an asset and a decrease in a liability.
    (e) A decrease in an asset and a decrease in owner's equity.
    (f) One asset is increased, one asset is decreased, and one liability is increased.
17. What is the purpose of taking a trial balance?
18. Explain the fact that errors can exist even though the sum of the debit account balances may equal the sum of the credit account balances in the trial balance.
19. Identify the transposition and the slide in the following two examples.
    (a) An account that should have been debited for $9,840 is debited for $9,480.
    (b) A credit of $570 is listed as $57.

EXERCISES

Exercise 2-1 Identification of Type of Account

For each of the accounts listed, indicate whether it is an asset, a liability, an owner's equity, a revenue, or an expense.

1. Unearned Revenue.
2. Accounts Receivable.
3. Prepaid Insurance.
4. Rent Expense.
5. Service Fees Revenue.
6. Cash.
7. Lynn Harris, Capital.
8. Taxes Payable.
9. Wages Expense.
10. Interest Revenue.
11. Lynn Harris, Drawing. Contra A
12. Land.
13. Building.
14. Note Payable.

Exercise 2-2 Debits and Credits and Normal Balance

For each of the accounts listed in Exercise 2-1
    (1) Indicate whether increases are recorded as debits or credits.
    (2) Indicate whether the normal balance is a debit or a credit.

Exercise 2-3 Transaction Analysis

Analyze each of the following transactions. Indicate whether each of the accounts affected is an asset, a liability, an owner's equity, a revenue, or an expense. Also indicate whether the account is being increased or decreased and whether the increase or decrease is a debit or credit.

> Example: Paid the rent
> Increase an expense (debit), decrease an asset (credit)

1. Purchased supplies on account.
2. Owner invested cash.

3. Sold equipment for cash.
4. Billed customer for a service performed.
5. Purchased land for cash and a note payable.
6. Paid cash to a creditor.
7. Owner withdrew cash.
8. Cash payment made for a 36-month insurance policy.
9. Received and paid an advertising bill for an ad that appeared in last week's newspaper.
10. Received payment on an account receivable.

Exercise 2-4 Normal Balance and Classification in Financial Statements

For each of the following accounts, indicate whether the normal balance is a debit or a credit and whether the account would appear in the balance sheet or in the income statement.

1. Mortgage Notes Payable.
2. Office Supplies Inventory.
3. Service Revenue.
4. Repair Expense.
5. Accounts Receivable.
6. Cash.
7. Unearned Service Fees.
8. Interest Revenue.
9. James Olson, Capital.
10. Accounts Payable.
11. Telephone Expense.
12. Equipment.
13. Rent Revenue.
14. Prepaid Advertising.

Exercise 2-5 Type of Accounts Affected by Transactions

For each transaction given, indicate what type of account (asset, liability, owner's equity, revenue, or expense) would be debited and what type would be credited. The first transaction is done for you as an example.

	Debit	Credit
1. Owner invested $1,000 in business	Asset	Owner's Equity
2. Purchased $500 of equipment and signed a $500 note payable.		
3. Paid wages.		
4. Received cash from customers in payment on account.		
5. Purchased office supplies on account.		
6. Owner withdrew $100 from business for personal use.		

Exercise 2-6 Effect of Transactions on Account Balances

For each of the following transactions, indicate its effect on the proper account by writing the account names in the proper columns (shown below). Transaction 1 is given as an example.

Transaction	Account(s) Increased	Account(s) Decreased	Account(s) Debited	Account(s) Credited
1	Cash Owner, Capital		Cash	Owner, Capital

1. Owner transferred cash to business.
2. Paid rent for the current month.
3. Mailed bills to customers for services performed.

4. Purchased land; paid 50% of the purchase price in cash; gave a note payable for the unpaid amount.
5. Paid for office supplies previously purchased on account.
6. Purchased a 12-month insurance policy.
7. Received payment from customers on account.
8. Performed services for cash.
9. Borrowed money from the bank for 90 days at 12% interest.
10. Received and recorded first month's utility bill. The bill *was not paid.*

Exercise 2-7 Recording Transactions in General Journal

Prepare the general journal entries that are needed to record the following transactions of Polchinski Distributing.

1. G. P. Polchinski, owner, invested $3,000 in cash to the business.
2. Polchinski hired a new employee at an annual salary of $14,400.
3. The company completed a service order and billed the customer $600.
4. Polchinski purchased office equipment for $10,590. The company paid $1,600 in cash and signed a one-year, 15% note payable for the remainder.
5. Polchinski Distributing signed an agreement with a grocery store to deliver goods next month for $500.
6. Polchinski paid $300 to a creditor for supplies purchased on account.
7. The company paid $500 for the current year's property taxes.
8. G. P. Polchinski withdrew $360 from the business for personal use.
9. The company will no longer be open on Sunday. The business will lose approximately $275 in revenue per week because of this decision.

Exercise 2-8 Recording Transactions in General Journal

Prepare the general journal entries needed to record the following transactions of Dan's Photo World.

1. Paid the telephone bill of $115.
2. Purchased office supplies totaling $200 on credit.
3. Daniel Bush, the owner, invested an additional $3,575 in the business.
4. Received $185 in cash from a customer as advance payment for photography work to be done.
5. Paid $200 for supplies purchased on credit.
6. Billed a customer $500 for photography services performed.
7. Daniel Bush withdrew $575 from the business for living expenses.

Exercise 2-9 Preparation of Corrected Trial Balance

The trial balance of the Johnson Company presented here does not balance. In examining the general journal and the general ledger you discover the following information.

1. A purchase of supplies for $300 in cash was erroneously recorded as a purchase of equipment.
2. The debits and credits to *Accounts Receivable* totaled $10,400 and $7,900, respectively.
3. The balance in the *Salaries Payable* account is $310.
4. A $500 payment received from a customer on his account was not posted to the cash account.
5. The debit to record the withdrawal of $500 in cash by the owner was not posted.

Prepare a corrected trial balance.

Account Title	Debit	Credit
Cash	$ 900	
Accounts Receivable		$ 2,480
Supplies Inventory	90	
Equipment	7,000	
Accounts Payable		2,400
Salaries Payable	130	
Taxes Payable		2,300
E. Johnson, Capital		7,200
E. Johnson, Drawing	3,920	
Service Revenues		13,800
Salary Expense	5,100	
Rent Expense	3,200	
Tax Expense	2,300	
Totals	$22,640	$28,180

JOHNSON COMPANY
Trial Balance
June 30, 1987

Exercise 2-10 Effect of Errors on Trial Balance
A. For each of the following errors
   (1) Indicate if the error would cause the trial balance to have unequal totals.
   (2) Determine the amount by which the trial balance totals would differ.
   (3) Determine if the error would cause the debit total or the credit total to be larger.

1. A $24 debit to *Cash* was posted as a credit.
2. Receipt of a payment on account from a customer was recorded as a debit to *Cash* for $135 and a credit to *Accounts Payable* for $135.
3. A purchase of supplies for $89 on account was recorded as a debit to *Supplies* for $89 and a credit to *Accounts Payable* for $98.
4. A $250 credit to *Service Revenue* was not posted.
5. A $432 debit to the *Drawing* account was debited to the *Capital* account.
6. A $570 debit to *Insurance Expense* was posted as a $57 debit.

B. How would each error be corrected? Give the correcting journal entry where appropriate.

PROBLEMS

Problem 2-1 Identification of Type of Account, Debit/Credit Analysis, and Normal Balance
Listed here are the ledger accounts of Casey Real Estate.

1. Cash.
2. Land.
3. Salary Expense.
4. Interest Revenue.
5. Miscellaneous Revenue.
6. Building.

7. Mortgage Notes Payable.
8. Christine Casey, Drawing.
9. Accounts Receivable.
10. Sales Tax Payable.
11. Supplies Inventory.
12. Insurance Expense.
13. Notes Payable to Bank.
14. Deposits with Utility Company.
15. Service Fee Revenue.
16. Interest Receivable.

17. Salaries Payable.
18. Prepaid Insurance.
19. Accounts Payable.
20. Maintenance Equipment.
21. Unearned Revenue.
22. Christine Casey, Capital.
23. Interest Expense.
24. Property Taxes Payable.
25. Notes Receivable.
26. Rent Revenue.

Required:

For each account just listed, complete the following solution form by placing a check mark in the proper columns to indicate the type of account, the side of a T account the item increases on, and the normal balance of the account.

Suggested solution form:

Account	Type of Account			Increases		Normal Balance	
	Asset	Liability	Owner's Equity (includes revenues and expenses)	Debit	Credit	Debit	Credit
1. Cash (List remaining 25 accounts.)	✓			✓		✓	

Problem 2-2 Journal Entries, Posting to Three-Column Ledger, and Trial Balance

Brian Marr opened Marr's Advertising in September of 1987. The following transactions occurred during the first month of the business.

Sept.		
	2	Marr invested $2,500 cash in the business.
	2	Paid rent of $500 for the first month.
	3	Purchased equipment for $1,000 cash and a $2,300 note.
	3	Purchased supplies for $400 cash.
	5	Paid advertising expense of $25.
	15	Recorded advertising revenue for the first half of the month of $600 in cash and $30 on account.
	20	Paid insurance expense for September of $192.
	24	Received a $24 payment from customers on account.
	27	Withdrew $130 for personal living expenses.
	30	Recorded advertising revenue for the second half of the month of $625 in cash and $25 on account.
	30	Paid utilities expense of $126.

Use the following account titles and numbers: *Cash*, 100; *Accounts Receivable*, 101; *Supplies Inventory*, 102; *Equipment*, 103; *Note Payable*, 200; *Brian Marr—Capital*,

300; *Brian Marr—Drawing*, 301; *Advertising Revenue*, 400; *Rent Expense*, 500; *Advertising Expense*, 501; *Insurance Expense*, 502; *Utilities Expense*, 503.

Required:
A. Prepare the general journal entries to record each transaction.
B. Post the entries from the general journal to the general ledger (three-column format) and enter the posting references in the general journal.
C. Prepare a trial balance as of September 30.

Problem 2-3 Journal Entries, Entering Beginning Account Balances, Posting to T Accounts, and Trial Balance

The April 30 trial balance of Jesse Greer Architectural Services is shown here.

JESSE GREER ARCHITECTURAL SERVICES
Trial Balance
April 30, 1987

Account Title	Debit	Credit
Cash	$ 260	
Accounts Receivable	1,205	
Supplies Inventory	310	
Prepaid Insurance	205	
Furniture and Equipment	6,580	
Accounts Payable		$ 245
Utilities Payable		360
Unearned Revenue		104
Jesse Greer, Capital		7,950
Jesse Greer, Drawing	4,070	
Revenue		9,231
Salary Expense	4,300	
Utilities Expense	360	
Rent Expense	600	
Totals	$17,890	$17,890

when you PAID you credit cash

The following transactions were completed during May.

May 1 Purchased supplies on account for $175.
4 Received $480 from clients as payment on account.
5 Paid the April utility expense of $360, previously recorded.
11 Performed services to earn revenue of $90, which was previously recorded as unearned revenue.
14 Recorded revenue earned of $6,450 in cash and $465 on account. *Add together*
15 Paid salaries of $2,850.
21 Purchased furniture for $270 in cash.
23 Paid creditors $240.
24 Withdrew $3,000 from the business for personal use.
28 Purchased 36-month insurance policy for $300.
30 Received $595 from clients as payment on account.
31 Recorded revenue earned of $5,775 in cash and $700 on account. *Add together 6,475 Revenue*
31 Paid rent of $600.

Required:

A. Prepare journal entries to record each transaction.

B. 1. Open T accounts for the accounts shown in the trial balance.

   2. Enter the April 30 balance in each account.

   3. Post the May journal entries to the T accounts.

C. Prepare a trial balance as of May 31.

Problem 2-4 Journal Entries, Posting to Three-Column Ledger, and Trial Balance for Two Consecutive Months

Carmen Shands opened Carmen's Sundae Shoppe in July of 1987, and completed the following transactions during the month.

July	1	Invested $9,750 in the business.
	2	Paid the July rent of $378.
	4	Purchased ice cream cases for $2,000 in cash and a $3,000 note payable.
	5	Paid $144 for a 12-month insurance policy.
	6	Purchased supplies totaling $175 on account.
	15	Paid salaries expense of $322.
	31	Recorded cash revenue earned for July of $1,050.
	31	Paid advertising expense of $125.

Chart of Accounts:

Account Title	Number	Account Title	Number
Cash	10	C. Shands, Capital	30
Supplies Inventory	11	C. Shands, Drawing	31
Prepaid Insurance	12	Revenue	40
Shop Equipment	13	Rent Expense	50
Accounts Payable	20	Salaries Expense	51
Notes Payable	21	Advertising Expense	52

Required:

A. Prepare general journal entries to record the July transactions.

B. Post the entries from the journal to three-column ledger accounts and enter the posting references in the journal.

C. Prepare a trial balance as of July 31.

The following transactions were completed during August.

Aug.	1	Paid salaries expense of $370.
	1	Paid $55 on account for supplies purchased in July.
	9	Withdrew $195 from the business for personal use.
	16	Paid salaries expense of $380.
	16	Recorded cash revenue earned for the first half of August of $740.
	19	Paid $80 for radio advertisements.
	23	Purchased supplies for $72 on account.
	31	Recorded cash revenue earned for the second half of August of $880.

Required:

D. Prepare general journal entries to record the August transactions.

E. Post the entries from the general journal to the general ledger.

F. Prepare a trial balance as of August 31.

Problem 2-5 **Preparation of Trial Balance**

The ledger account balances for the Farnsworth Computer Consulting as of December 31, 1987, are shown below. Each of the accounts contained a normal balance. The *Cash* account balance has been intentionally omitted.

Accounts Payable	$ 5,950	Equipment	$ 21,250
Accounts Receivable	1,700	Computer Instruction Revenue	18,700
Curt Farnsworth, Capital	122,400	Consulting Fees Revenue	157,250
Curt Farnsworth Drawing	34,000	Insurance Expense	535
Building	123,250	Land	54,000
Cash	?	Mortgage Note Payable	62,500
Unearned Consulting Fees	2,635	Prepaid Insurance	400
Utilities Expense	49,300	Salary Expense	76,500

Required:

Prepare a trial balance inserting the correct *Cash* account balance. The accounts should be listed in the sequence in which they would normally appear in the ledger.

Problem 2-6 **Correction of Errors**

Your first assignment on your new job was to determine why the December 31, 1987, trial balance did not balance. In your review of the records you uncovered a number of errors described here.

1. A $2,178 debit to *Cash* was posted as $2,718.
2. A $298 credit to be made to the *Sales* account was credited to the *Accounts Receivable* account instead.
3. A cash collection of $1,600 from customers in partial settlement of their accounts was posted twice to the *Cash* account and the *Accounts Receivable* account.
4. The *Accounts Payable* account balance of $36,894 was listed in the trial balance as $36,849.
5. A $940 credit to *Sales* was posted as a $94 credit. The debit to *Cash* was for the correct amount.
6. A purchase of office supplies totaling $150 on account was not recorded.
7. A purchase of a delivery truck for $5,663 cash was posted as a debit to the *Cash* account and a debit to the *Equipment* account.
8. The *Drawing* account balance of $24,900 was listed as a credit balance in the trial balance.
9. A $450 payment to employees for their weekly salaries was posted twice to the expense account. The credit to *Cash* was made only once.
10. The *Miscellaneous Expense* account with a balance of $870 was omitted from the trial balance.
11. A payment of $575 on a note payable was posted correctly to the *Cash* account, but was not posted to the *Note Payable* account.

Required:

A. Indicate, in the solution format shown on page 84, how each error would affect the trial balance totals. If the error does not cause the trial balance to be out of balance and you check "no" in the third column, write "equal" in the Difference Between Trial Balance Totals column. Each error is to be considered independent of the others.

	Would the error cause the trial balance to be out of balance?		Difference Between Trial Balance Totals	Column having largest total	
Error	Yes	No		Debit	Credit
1.			$		
2. . . .					
through					
11.					

B. Prepare the journal entries necessary to correct errors number 2, 3, and 6.

Problem 2-7 Comprehensive Review Problem to be worked before Problem 3-9.

On January 2, 1987, Curtis Archer began a new business called Archer TV and Radio Repair. The fiscal year of the business is January 1 to December 31. The purpose of the business is to provide TV and radio repair services.

Following are the first year's transactions in summary form. When accounting for an actual business, these transactions would have consisted of numerous individual transactions.

1. Curtis Archer invested $30,000 in the business.
2. A van was purchased for the business, and paid for in cash at a cost of $11,700.
3. Various tools and equipment were purchased for cash at a cost of $4,500.
4. One-year's building rent, totaling $7,200, was paid.
5. Office supplies costing $800 and repair supplies costing $18,500 were purchased on account.
6. On July 1, 1987, $20,000 was borrowed from the First National Bank. The note was for one year at an annual interest rate of 12%. The note for $20,000 and the interest are due on July 1, 1988. 1200 ½   2400 yr
7. Insurance policies costing $1,800 were purchased.
8. Repair revenue for the year totaled $95,000, of which $16,000 was done on credit.
9. All of the office supplies purchased and $12,000 of the repair supplies were paid for during the year, (item 5).
10. The following expenses were incurred and paid in cash.

Salaries	$43,600	Utilities	3,230
Auto	5,540	Telephone	2,800
Advertising	4,800		

11. On December 31, 1987, land and a building were purchased at a total cost of $40,000. The land is valued at $5,000 and the building is valued at $35,000. A down payment of $15,000 was given, with the remaining $25,000 financed by a 20-year, 14% mortgage.
12. $8,500 was collected on the credit extended for services during the year, (item 8).
13. Archer received $1,200 from Good Samaritan Hospital. The payment was for a six-month service contract in which Archer is to perform repairs on the hospital's television sets. The contract period is from November 1, 1987 to May 1, 1988.
14. Curtis Archer withdrew $7,000 from the business for personal expenses.

The chart of accounts for Archer TV and Radio Repair is given here.

Account Number	Account Title	Account Number	Account Title
	Assets		**Owner's Equity**
100	Cash	300	Curtis Archer, Capital
104	Accounts Receivable	310	Curtis Archer, Drawing
110	Office Supplies Inventory		**Revenues**
111	Repair Supplies Inventory	400	Repair Revenues
120	Prepaid Insurance		**Expenses**
121	Prepaid Rent	500	Salaries Expense
150	Land	501	Auto Expense
151	Building	502	Advertising Expense
152	Accumulated Depr.—Bldg.	503	Utilities Expense
153	Vans	504	Telephone Expense
154	Accumulated Depr.—Vans	506	Rent Expense
155	Tools and Equipment	507	Insurance Expense
156	Accumulated Depr.—Tools and Equipment	508	Office Supplies Expense
		509	Repair Supplies Expense
	Liabilities	510	Interest Expense
200	Accounts Payable	552	Depreciation Expense—Building
201	Salaries Payable		
202	Utilities Payable	554	Depreciation Expense—Vans
205	Interest Payable	556	Depreciation Expense—Tools and Equipment
209	Unearned Repair Revenues		
210	Notes Payable		
220	Mortgage Notes Payable		

Required:

A. Prepare a T account for each account listed in the chart of accounts.

B. Prepare general journal entries to record transactions 1 through 14. Because these are summary transactions, identify each transaction by its respective number in the date column of the general journal.

C. Post the journal entries to the T accounts.

D. Prepare a trial balance as of December 31, 1987.

ALTERNATE PROBLEMS

Problem 2-1A Journal Entries, Posting to Three-Column Ledger, and Trial Balance

Larry Newman opened a travel agency in September of 1987. The following transactions occurred during the first month of the business.

Sept.	1	Newman invested $8,000 cash in the business.
	2	Paid $590 for the first month's rent.
	3	Purchased equipment costing $7,250 for $3,500 cash and a $3,750 note.
	3	Purchased supplies costing $421 on account.
	15	Recorded revenue for the first half of the month of $1,560 in cash and $250 on account.
	17	Paid $421 to a creditor on account.
	19	Paid insurance expense for September of $203.

23 Received payment from customers due on account of $95.
27 Purchased supplies costing $75 on account.
30 Recorded revenue for the second half of the month of $1,950 in cash and $50 on account.
30 Paid telephone expense of $96.

Use the following account titles and numbers.

Cash, 101   Larry Newman, Capital, 301
Accounts Receivable, 102   Service Revenue, 401
Supplies Inventory, 103   Rent Expense, 501
Equipment, 104   Insurance Expense, 502
Accounts Payable, 201   Telephone Expense, 503
Note Payable, 202

Required:
A. Prepare the general journal entries to record each transaction.
B. Post the entries from the general journal to a three-column general ledger and enter the posting references in the general journal.
C. Prepare a trial balance as of September 30, 1987.

Problem 2-2A Journal Entries, Entering Beginning Account Balances, Posting to T Accounts, and Trial Balance
David Jackson, Attorney, recently started his own practice. The trial balance as of October 31 is shown here.

DAVID JACKSON, ATTORNEY
Trial Balance
October 31, 1987

Account Title	Debit	Credit
Cash	$ 994	
Accounts Receivable	1,498	
Supplies Inventory	294	
Prepaid Insurance	218	
Equipment	6,265	
Accounts Payable		$ 427
Notes Payable		2,100
D. Jackson, Capital		6,440
D. Jackson, Drawing	4,956	
Legal Fees Revenue		9,521
Salaries Expense	2,940	
Rent Expense	1,036	
Interest Expense	67	
Cleaning Expense	220	
Totals	$18,488	$18,488

The following is a list of transactins completed during November.

Nov. 2 Paid the rent for November of $500.
3 Received $950 from clients as payment due on account.
6 Purchased supplies on account totaling $154.
8 Billed clients $2,273.

Acc. Rec.
   Revenue

13   Withdrew $533 from the business for personal use.
15   Paid salaries of $662.
17   Received $1,390 from clients as payment on account.
20   Paid maintenance service $85 for cleaning the office.
23   Paid creditors $140.
25   Paid $350 on the note, plus interest of $30.
29   Purchased a typewriter for $325 on account.
30   Paid $60 for a three-month insurance policy.

Required:
A. Prepare general journal entries to record the transactions.
B. 1. Open T accounts for the accounts shown in the trial balance.
    2. Enter the October 31 balance in each account.
    3. Post the November journal entries to the T accounts.
C. Prepare a trial balance at November 30.

Problem 2-3A Journal Entries, Posting to Three-Column Ledger, and Trial Balance for Two Consecutive Months

Mike Sanders opened Sanders' Theater during June of 1987 and completed the following transactions during the month.

June   1   Invested $9,000 of his own money in the business.
       1   Paid rent for June of $450.
       2   Purchased projectors and other equipment for $8,000 in cash and a $16,000 note.
       4   Paid $103 for advertising.
       6   Purchased supplies on account for $175.
      15   Recorded cash revenue for the first half of the month of $600.
      24   Withdrew $350 from the business for personal use.
      30   Recorded cash revenue for the second half of the month of $885.
      30   Paid wages of $235.

Use the following account titles and numbers.

Cash, 110   Mike Sanders, Capital, 310
Supplies Inventory, 111   Mike Sanders, Drawing, 311
Equipment, 112   Ticket Revenue, 410
Accounts Payable, 210   Rent Expense, 510
Notes Payable, 211   Advertising Expense, 511
                                 Wages Expense, 512

Required:
A. Prepare general journal entries to record the June transactions.
B. Post the entries from the general journal to three-column general ledger accounts and enter the posting references in the journal.
C. Prepare a trial balance as of June 30.

The following transactions took place in July.

July   1   Paid rent for July of $450.
       3   Paid $116 of the amount owed for supplies.
       8   Paid $70 for newspaper advertisements.
      13   Withdrew $417 from the business.
      15   Recorded cash revenue for the first half of July of $895.
      15   Paid wages of $310.
      19   Purchased supplies on account for $113.
      31   Recorded cash revenue for the second half of July of $875.

Required:
D. Prepare journal entries to record the July transactions.
E. Post the entries to the ledger.
F. Prepare a trial balance as of July 31.

Problem 2-4A Journal Entries, Posting to T Accounts, and Trial Balance
Alice Jennings decided to open her own mobile bicycle repair business. She completed the following transactions during May of 1987.

May	1	Invested $5,000 cash and equipment valued at $175 in the business.
	2	Purchased a truck for $3,250 cash and a $1,750 note.
	2	Purchased additional equipment for $185 cash.
	7	Paid $136 for a 12-month insurance policy on the truck.
	12	Recorded revenue earned of $200 cash and $25 on account.
	13	Paid assistant $67 for 20 hours of work.
	13	Paid $20 to have fliers printed advertising her business.
	14	Paid $20 for gas for the truck.
	15	Paid $32 for a 12-month insurance policy on the equipment.
	18	Received $15 from customers previously billed.
	27	Paid assistant $57 for 17 hours of work.
	28	Recorded revenue earned of $240 cash and $30 on account.
	31	Paid $118 on the note signed for the truck consisting of $100 principal and $18 interest.
	31	Paid $23 for gas for the truck.

Required:
A. Open the following T accounts: *Cash*, 1; *Accounts Receivable*, 2; *Prepaid Insurance*, 3; *Equipment*, 4; *Truck*, 5; *Notes Payable*, 10; *Alice Jennings, Capital*, 20; *Revenue*, 30; *Wages Expense*, 40; *Advertising Expense*, 41; *Truck Expense*, 42; *Interest Expense*, 43.
B. Enter the transactions in the general journal.
C. Post the entries from the general journal to the general ledger.
D. Prepare a trial balance as of May 31.

Problem 2-5A Preparation of Trial Balance
The ledger of the Park Lane Arcade contains the following account titles and balances as of December 31, 1987. Each account has a normal balance. The balance in the cash account has been intentionally omitted.

Accounts Payable	$ 1,080	Video Revenue	$88,750
Accounts Receivable	720	Z. Best, Capital	31,000
Pool Revenue	14,580	Z. Best, Drawing	16,500
Cash	?	Note Payable	18,000
Pool Tables	14,400	Prepaid Rent	990
Interest Expense	540	Rent Expense	23,150
Interest Payable	540	Salary Expense	38,500
Utilities Expense	4,320	Supplies Inventory	380
Video Game Machines	32,950	Supplies Expense	2,700

Required:
Prepare a trial balance as of December 31, 1987. Include the correct balance in the *Cash* account. List the accounts in the proper order.

3

ADJUSTING ACCOUNTS AND PREPARING FINANCIAL STATEMENTS

CHAPTER OVERVIEW AND OBJECTIVES

This chapter describes the preparation of adjusting entries and financial statements, two of the steps in the accounting cycle, which are completed at the end of the accounting period. When you have completed the chapter, you should understand:

1. The difference between cash basis accounting and accrual basis accounting.
2. The need for adjusting entries.
3. How to classify adjusting entries into the two broad categories of deferrals and accruals.
4. How to analyze and prepare adjusting entries.
5. How to prepare an adjusted trial balance.
6. How to prepare financial statements from the adjusted trial balance.
7. The major categories commonly used to classify accounts in the balance sheet.
8. The meaning of the normal operating cycle.

In the last chapter, the first four steps in the accounting cycle were covered. These steps, which are carried out during an accounting period are:

1. Preparing source documents.
2. Recording transactions in a general journal.
3. Posting transactions to the general ledger.
4. Preparing a trial balance.

Many transactions recorded during a period affect the current period's financial statements as well as those prepared in future periods. For example, the cost of a 24-month insurance policy purchased in the current period should be allocated as an expense to all accounting periods receiving the protection. There are other events, such as the increase in interest revenue earned on notes receivable, which are often unrecorded at the end of the current period. Thus, as part of the accounting cycle completed at the end of the period, the accounts and source documents must be analyzed, and entries must be made to adjust the accounts before the financial statements are prepared. Failure to make the entries, (called *adjusting entries*), will result in a misstatement of both income and the balance sheet accounts. For example, failure to adjust the *Prepaid Insurance* account for the expired portion of the cost will result in the asset account being overstated and the *Insurance Expense* account being understated.

This chapter deals with the concept of measuring net income. Both the cash basis and the accrual basis of accounting are discussed. To comprehend the income statement and adjusting entries, the concept of net income, as it is measured by accountants, must be understood. Next, the need for making adjusting entries is related to the use of the accrual basis of accounting. The account balances developed in the last chapter for the Starbuck Real Estate Office are used as a basis for illustrating the analysis and preparation of adjusting entries. The adjusting entries are recorded in the general journal and posted to the ledger. A trial balance, called an *adjusted trial balance,* is then taken from the general ledger to verify the equality of debits and credits after the adjusting entries are posted to the accounts. In this chapter, the financial statements are prepared from an adjusted trial balance.

Two additional steps in the end of period process are discussed in the next chapter. These are the preparation of the closing entries and a post-closing trial balance. As we shall see in the next chapter, accountants often use a special form, called a *worksheet,* to accumulate the information needed to complete the accounting cycle.

MEASURING NET INCOME

Objective 1: Cash basis and accrual basis accounting

A major objective of a business is to earn a profit (called net income). As discussed in Chapter 2, in order to provide timely information to statement users, the operating life of a business is divided into relatively short intervals of equal length called accounting periods. One important accounting function is measuring the net income earned or the net loss incurred during an accounting period. The amount of net income or loss is the difference between revenues and expenses. Revenues and expenses may be measured either on a cash basis or on an accrual basis.

CASH BASIS METHOD OF MEASURING NET INCOME

Under the cash basis of accounting, revenues are recorded in the period in which cash is received and expenses are recorded in the period in which cash is paid. In this system, net income is the excess of cash inflow from revenues over cash outflow for expenses. This method does not recognize revenue from the sale of goods or the performance of a service on credit. In addition, the costs of goods and services used to produce revenue during the current period are recognized as expenses in the period they are paid for.

Thus, as shown on page 94, a cash basis system does not properly match the efforts of the firm to produce revenues with revenues earned. Furthermore, although the cash basis approach is used by small businesses and professional people who conduct most of their activities in cash, it is not generally accepted for use by businesses that conduct a significant portion of their business on credit. The cash basis system can be justified only because it is simple to operate and, when transactions are primarily in cash, will produce results essentially the same as those produced by accrual accounting.

ACCRUAL BASIS METHOD OF MEASURING NET INCOME

Under the accrual basis of accounting, revenues are recognized in the period in which they are earned, that is, usually in the period in which a business sells goods or performs services, rather than when cash is received. Expenses are recognized when incurred, that is, when goods are used or services are received, rather than in the period they are paid for. The accrual basis net income for an accounting period is determined by subtracting expenses incurred during the period from revenues reported earned, in accordance with the revenue principle. The process of associating expenses with revenues generated during the period is called **matching.**

Thus, the process of determining periodic net income involves identifying and measuring the revenues earned during a specific accounting period. Next, expenses associated with producing those revenues are identified and measured. As a result, both revenues earned and the cost of assets consumed in the process of producing those revenues (i.e., expenses) are reported in the same income statement. In order to fully understand accrual accounting, the important concepts of revenue and expense must be fully understood.

Accrual Basis Revenues

Revenues are inflows of assets resulting from the sale of goods or the performance of services. As noted in Chapter 1, revenues for a period are determined by applying the revenue principle. Essentially, the revenue principle asserts that revenue should be recognized under accrual accounting when it is earned, rather than when the actual cash is received. Consequently, it is important to understand what is meant by ''earning revenue.''

Some revenue, such as interest revenue and rent revenue, is earned with the passage of time and, therefore, is not difficult to associate with specific time periods. However, revenue such as sales revenue is earned in a continuous process as the operating activities that give rise to revenue take place. For example, the earning process (or earning cycle) for a manufacturing firm involves the acquisition of goods and services, the production of a product, the sale of the finished product, and collection of payment from customers. Each of these steps contributes to the earning process, but it is difficult to objectively determine how much revenue is earned at each step.

To provide a practical guide, accountants have adopted the revenue principle, which provides that revenue should be recognized when (1) the earning process is complete or essentially complete; and (2) an exchange has taken place. Following this principle, most revenue is recognized when goods are sold (which normally means when they are delivered) or when services are rendered and thus, can be billed for.

At this point, the earning process is considered essentially complete. The only remaining part of the earning cycle is the collection of the sales price, which is considered relatively assured in today's credit-oriented society. The exchange price provides the necessary objective evidence of the amount of revenue to recognize.

The exchange price is normally received in cash or as a customer's promise of cash at a set time in the future (an account receivable). Occasionally, however, a firm may receive either property or services in payment. In such cases, the amount of revenue recorded is the fair value (market value) of the asset or services received.

Thus, for a given accounting period, revenue earned is the sum of cash, accounts receivable, and the fair value of other assets received from customers for the sale of goods or the performance of services during that period. However, there are exceptions to the revenue principle which are discussed in Chapter 13.

Accrual Basis Expenses

Costs are incurred as a necessary part of the revenue-generating process. The portion of the cost that is expected to be used in the production of revenue in the future is reported as an asset and is called an **unexpired cost.** The purchase price (cost) of a delivery truck is an example of an unexpired cost. The cost of the truck is debited to an asset account. The asset account is then reduced when the cost of the asset can be identified (i.e., matched) with the revenue earned during each period. The amount of the reduction is reported in the income statement as an expense (sometimes called an **expired cost**). Expired costs are deducted from revenue in the determination of net income.

These important concepts are diagrammed below, assuming that a firm paid $6,000 for equipment to be used for 10 years.

ASSET	ACTIVITY	EXPENSE
Unexpired costs—Cost incurred to acquire economic resources. ($6,000)	Equipment is used during the period to produce revenue.	Expired costs— Associate cost of asset used with revenue earned. ($600)

The firm computed the cost of the asset to be matched against revenues of the current period to be $600. The remaining unexpired cost of $5,400 is a measure of the costs of future economic services, an asset. Put another way, the $5,400 is an asset to be utilized in future periods to earn revenue. Thus, assets are the resources owned by the firm, and expenses are the dollar amount of these resources consumed during the period to produce revenue.

Matching Expenses Incurred With Revenues Earned

As noted in the preceding paragraph, the cost of assets must be allocated to both the current period and future periods, in order to provide proper matching of expenses incurred with revenues earned. Some costs, such as the cost of a refrigerator sold by an appliance store, can be directly associated with the revenues of a specific accounting period. In contrast, other costs cannot be as directly associated with revenue, or they can be associated with revenue of more than one accounting period. Two examples are the costs incurred in advertising a firm's product and the cost of buying an office building.

Just as the revenue principle has been developed by accountants to serve as a guide in the timing of revenues, the matching principle has been developed to guide the timing of expense recognition. A hierarchy of three basic rules—associating cause and effect, systematic and rational allocation, and immediate recognition—specify the bases for recognizing expenses.

Associating Cause and Effect.   Some expenses—such as the cost of a computer sold by a computer store and the commission earned by the person making the sale—are recognized as having a relatively direct cause and effect association with revenues earned. Therefore, these expenses are recorded in the same period in which the revenues associated with them are recognized. For example, the sale of the computer that produced the revenue, the cost of the computer, and the sales commission are all recorded in the same period.

Systematic and Rational Allocation.   Many expenses cannot be associated directly with revenue-producing transactions but *can* be associated with specific accounting periods. For example, the cost of purchasing a building should be allocated to each period that the building is used. Although there is no direct association between the specific revenues produced and the use of the building, a portion of its cost should be expensed because the building contributes to revenue.

Accounting principles require that the method used to allocate costs to specific accounting periods must be systematic and rational. Systematic means that the allocation is based on a prescribed method or formula. Rational means that there is some logical relationship between the cost allocated and the benefits received in the current period. For example, a building that is expected to produce equal benefits each year should have an equal amount of its cost expensed each year.

Immediate Recognition. Some expenses are associated with the current accounting period because:

1. They cannot be directly associated with revenue transactions.
2. They have no discernible benefits for future accounting periods, or.
3. Their allocation among several accounting periods serves no useful purpose.

According to this rule, costs, such as officers' salaries, advertising expenses, and research and development expenditures, are charged as expenses in the period in which payment is made or in which a liability is incurred. In addition, items carried as assets that are determined to have no discernible benefit for future periods are charged as expenses. One example of such an item is equipment that has become obsolete before the end of its original useful life.

CASH BASIS VERSUS THE ACCRUAL BASIS

To contrast cash basis and accrual basis accounting, assume the following situation.

1. Systems Company contracted for $60,000 to install a management information system for Scotch Company.
2. Systems started the project in October, 1987, and completed it by December 31, 1987, its fiscal year-end.
3. The fees for the services were received in January, 1988.
4. Expenses of $36,000 were incurred in 1987; $24,000 were paid in 1987 and $12,000 in 1988.

Net income is measured below for each of the two periods under both the cash basis and the accrual basis.

Cash Basis	1987	1988	Total
Cash receipts	$ -0-	$60,000	$60,000
Cash payments for expenses	24,000	12,000	36,000
Net income (loss)	$(24,000)	$48,000	$24,000
Accrual Basis			
Service revenue	$ 60,000	$ -0-	$60,000
Expenses	36,000	-0-	36,000
Net income	$ 24,000	$ -0-	$24,000

This illustration clearly shows the failure of the cash basis method to associate the firm's economic activity with a given accounting period. Although the efforts of the firm to earn the revenue were made in 1987, under the cash basis method, revenue is not reported until cash is received. The cash basis method also fails to properly match expenses with revenues. Expenses of $24,000 are reported in 1987 even though none of the revenue is reported in that period. In contrast, the accrual basis recognizes revenue in the period when the economic activity occurs. Expenses are then associated with the revenue earned. This approach is much more useful for evaluating the performance of a firm.

As we shall see throughout the remainder of the book, some aspects of applying the accrual basis of accounting involve the use of estimates, professional judgment, and assumptions. For example, allocating the cost of a building must be based on estimates because accountants are simply unable to predict with certainty the length of time the building will be used. However, the need for timely information (the *time period assumption*) takes precedence over the lack of precision involved in preparing accrual basis financial statements. Although the estimates should be made as accurately as possible, the *financial statements are only tentative,* and the actual results can be determined only when the firm ends operations. That is, although the information reported in the financial statements appears to be precise, it can only be considered reasonably accurate. An effective user of financial statements should be aware of the limits of the statements and understand the basis on which they are prepared. Additional explanation to make them more meaningful are presented in notes immediately following the statements.

WHY ADJUSTING ENTRIES ARE NEEDED?

During the accounting period, the accountant records many external trans-actions relative to the receipt or payment of cash. In some cases, the period in which the cash flow is recorded coincides with the period in which the revenue is earned or the expense is incurred. However, some cash receipts or payments that are recorded in the current period will affect the firm's net income and financial position for two or more accounting periods. For example, a firm that purchases a 36-month insurance policy pays for the policy in advance of receiving the protection. Although the protection expires on a daily basis over several accounting periods, the accountant does not make a series of daily entries to expense the cost of the protection. Such a procedure requires too much clerical effort and is unnecessary because expiration of the asset is an internal transaction that does not affect external parties. Instead, before the financial statements are issued, one entry is made to expense the cumulative total cost of the protection that has expired during the current period.

There are also cases in which revenues and expenses are reported in the current period, even though the cash for them may not be received or paid until the next period. For example, interest on notes receivable is earned on a daily basis but is not recorded during the period until cash is received. The growth in interest since the last cash receipt is properly reported as revenue of the current period. Whatever the situation, it is important to recognize that under the accrual basis of accounting, the recognition of revenues and expenses often do not occur in the same accounting period as the cash flow.

The types of events mentioned above happen relatively often in business. At the end of the period, the account balances may include neither the proper

Objective 2: Need for adjusting entries

amount of revenues earned and expenses incurred during the period nor an accurate measure of the asset and liability balances on the last day of the accounting period. Before the financial statements are issued, journal entries are prepared to record the internal transactions and the additional events that are unrecorded as of the last day of the accounting period. The journal entries made at the end of the period in order to change the account balances are called **adjusting entries.**

The adjusting process involves an analysis of the accounts and supporting source documents to determine whether entries are needed to adjust account balances to their proper amounts for financial statements. Once this analysis is completed, adjusting entries are recorded in the journal and posted to the accounts.

CLASSIFICATION OF ADJUSTING ENTRIES

Objective 3: Classification of adjusting entries

Adjusting entries are normally classified into two major categories with two types of adjustments within each category. The two major categories of adjusting entries are usually referred to as deferrals and accruals. A **deferral** is either (1) the prepayment for goods or services in advance of their use; or (2) the receipt of revenue in advance of the related earning activities. An **accrual** is the recognition of either (1) an expense for benefits received before the cash payment is made; or (2) a revenue that has been earned but for which cash has not yet been received. Thus, in the case of a deferral, the cash flow precedes the recognition of an expense or a revenue. The payment or receipt of cash necessitates the recording of a deferral. Conversely, in the case of an accrual, the recognition of a revenue or an expense precedes the receipt or payment of cash, and thus, the transactions have not been recorded.

DEFERRALS (PREPAYMENTS OR PRECOLLECTED ITEMS)

Prepaid expenses are the costs of resources acquired by a firm before they are used to produce revenue. Prepaid expenses are assets until they are used or consumed in the earning process. They must be allocated to the periods in which they are used to properly match expenses with revenues. Examples include rent expenses paid by a firm in advance of occupancy and insurance premiums paid for protection to be received in the future. At the end of the period, an adjusting entry is needed to allocate the cost of the resource between an asset and an expense account.

Unearned revenues are cash receipts for the sale of goods or the performance of a service before the goods are delivered or the services performed. Advance receipts of revenues are liabilities until they are earned by the firm. Examples include the receipt of cash by a publishing company for a two-year magazine subscription and a rent payment received from a tenant before the occupancy period occurs. At the end of an accounting period, an adjusting entry is needed to allocate the advance receipt between a liability and a revenue account.

ACCRUALS (UNRECORDED ITEMS)

Accrued expenses are expenses that have been incurred before being paid for by the firm. To properly match expenses with revenues, expenses should be recognized in the period incurred, regardless of when the cash payment is made. Examples include unpaid wages earned by the firm's employees and interest expense that has accumulated on an outstanding note payable. Because the goods or services received have not been paid for, an adjusting entry is made at the end of the period to record a liability and an expense.

Accrued revenues are revenues earned for services that have been performed or for goods that have been delivered in advance of collecting the payment from the customers. Under the accrual basis of accounting, revenues should be reported in the period earned, even though the cash has not been received. Examples include sales commissions earned but not yet received and interest revenue accumulated on a note receivable. An adjusting entry is made at the end of the accounting period to record a receivable from the customer and earned revenue.

ADJUSTING ENTRIES ILLUSTRATED

To demonstrate each of these four types of adjusting entries, the illustration of the Starbuck Real Estate Office will be continued from the previous chapter. Adjusting entries are illustrated first assuming that deferrals are initially recorded in an asset or a liability account. An alternative approach is to record deferrals in income statement accounts. The latter approach is discussed in a later section of this chapter. Note that each adjusting entry in the illustration changes the balance of one balance sheet account and one income statement account.

Objective 4: Preparing adjusting entries

In determining whether an adjusting entry is needed, the accountant examines the appropriate source document. For example, an insurance policy or the billing from the insurance company is examined to verify the cost of the policy and its term. The account balances listed in a trial balance are reviewed to compute the amount of the adjustment needed. The trial balance prepared on June 30 (Figure 2–8) for Starbuck Real Estate Office is shown again in Figure 3–1 for convenience. Such a trial balance is called an **unadjusted trial balance** because it is prepared from the general ledger before the adjusting entries are posted.

For illustrative purposes, it is assumed that monthly financial statements are to be prepared and that monthly adjusting entries are made in the general journal. However, it is common accounting practice to prepare formal adjusting journal entries only at the end of the fiscal period. If more frequent reports are prepared, the adjusting entries are entered only on a worksheet, as illustrated in Figure 4–3 in Chapter 4.

PREPAID EXPENSES

A business often pays for some expense items (such as rent, insurance, and supplies) in advance of the items' use. Goods and services, such as office

Figure 3–1
Unadjusted Trial
Balance

STARBUCK REAL ESTATE OFFICE Unadjusted Trial Balance June 30, 1987		
Account Title	Debit	Credit
Cash	$ 43,558	
Accounts Receivable	5,400	
Prepaid Insurance	960	
Office Supplies Inventory	620	
Land	10,000	
Building	62,000	
Office Equipment	9,600	
Accounts Payable		$ 4,600
Unearned Appraisal Fees		280
Mortgage Notes Payable		60,000
Mike Starbuck, Capital		60,000
Mike Starbuck, Drawing	600	
Commissions Revenue		9,600
Appraisal Fees Revenue		250
Salaries Expense	1,800	
Utilities Expense	72	
Advertising Expense	120	
Totals	$134,730	$134,730

supplies, which are paid for in advance and are expected to benefit several periods, are *normally* recorded as assets (unexpired costs) at the time of payment. At the end of the accounting period, adjusting entries are made to transfer the portion of the costs associated with the goods that have been used or with the services that have been received to expense accounts (expired costs). The remaining unexpired or unused portion of each cost is reported as an asset on the balance sheet. Thus, before the financial statements are prepared, the balance in each asset account is analyzed and allocated between an asset and an expense.

In many cases, however, the prepayment and expiration of the asset occurs in the same accounting period. While the costs of such goods and services are considered assets at the time of payment, such payments are charged directly to an expense account if the item will be consumed only in the current period. For example, the payment of one month's rent in advance on the first of the month is debited to *Rent Expense*.

Prepaid Insurance

On June 3 a 24-month fire and insurance policy was purchased by Starbuck Real Estate Office for $960. Insurance coverage began on June 1. The transaction was recorded as follows.

June	3	Prepaid Insurance	960	
		Cash		960

The balance in the *Prepaid Insurance* account remains the same until the end of the month, at which time the cost of the insurance protection for the month of June is computed. The cost of the insurance protection per month is $40 ($960/24 months). The following adjusting entry is made on June 30 to record *Insurance Expense* and to reduce the *Prepaid Insurance* account.

a.	June	30	Insurance Expense	40	
			Prepaid Insurance		40
			(The adjusting entries are identified by letters in this illustration for reference purposes only.)		

After the adjusting entry is posted, the account balances are:

Prepaid Insurance				Insurance Expense	
6/3	960	6/30	40	6/30	40
6/30 Bal.	920				

The adjusting entry reduced the *Prepaid Insurance* account balance to $920, which is the unexpired portion of the cost applicable to future periods and which is reported as an asset. The portion of the cost that expired in this period ($40) is properly matched as an expense with the revenue reported in June. If the adjusting entry were not made, net income, assets, and owner's equity would all be overstated.

In future periods, the $920 balance is reduced by $40 each month as insurance protection is received by the firm. The insurance expense is $40 per month. The costs of additional policies purchased are debited to the *Prepaid Insurance* account and allocated to expense by following similar procedures.

Office Supplies Inventory

Starbuck Real Estate Office made the following journal entry on June 5 to record the purchase of office supplies.

June	5	Office Supplies Inventory	620	
		Accounts Payable		620

The cost of unused office supplies is reported as an asset in the balance sheet. As the office supplies are used, their cost is transferred to an expense account. The recognition of the expense is normally deferred until the end of the accounting period. In other words, no journal entry is made during the period to record the cost of supplies consumed because this information is not needed on a day-to-day basis. Before financial statements are prepared, an adjusting entry is made to remove the cost of the supplies used from the asset account and increase an expense account.

For control purposes, firms generally keep supplies in a central location. Employees may be required to fill out a form, called a requisition, which identifies the supplies they have taken or used. For each requisition form, the total cost of the supplies is determined. The total of these requisitions is the cost of supplies used during the period. If a requisition system is not used, the original cost of the supplies on hand is determined at the end of the period by counting and pricing them, which, in turn, allows for computation of the cost of supplies used during the period.

Assume that the cost of the supplies that Starbuck Real Estate had on hand at the end of June was determined to be $540. Therefore, the cost of supplies used during this period was $80 ($620 − $540). The following adjusting entry is made to record the supplies used.

b.	June	30	Office Supplies Expense	80	
			Office Supplies Inventory		80

After this entry is posted, the accounts will appear as follows.

Office Supplies Inventory				**Office Supplies Expense**	
6/5	620	6/30	80	6/30	80
6/30 Bal.	540				

The $540 balance left in the *Office Supplies Inventory* account is the cost of supplies available for use in future periods (an asset). The $80 balance in the *Office Supplies Expense* account is the cost of supplies used during June, which is matched with revenue earned during June in the income statement.

In future periods, the cost of additional purchases of supplies is debited to the *Office Supplies Inventory* account. The same analysis and process described above is performed at the end of each subsequent accounting period.

Depreciation of Equipment and Building

Included in the June transactions entered into by the Starbuck Real Estate Office were the purchases of a building for $62,000 and office equipment for $9,600. These assets were acquired and held by the firm for use in performing operating activities. To provide proper matching, the cost of each asset, less its estimated residual value, is allocated as an expense in the accounting periods in which the asset is expected to be used to produce revenue. The **residual value** of a plant asset is its estimated value at the end of its useful life. The amount of time that the asset is expected to be used is called its **estimated useful life.** The portion of the asset's cost assigned to expense is referred to as **depreciation.**

The adjusting entry to record depreciation is similar in concept to the entries described previously for the allocation of the cost of the insurance policy and office supplies. That is, an expense account is debited for the portion of the cost allocated to the current period and an asset is decreased for the same amount. However, unlike the insurance policy and the office supplies, which are generally consumed during one or two fiscal periods, items of equipment and buildings are frequently used for extended periods of time, sometimes up to 30 years or longer. Since it is often impossible for the accountant to know either the exact useful life of such an asset or the residual value at the end of its useful life, the depreciated value must be recognized as being only an estimate.

In making the adjusting entry for depreciation, a separate account, entitled *Accumulated Depreciation* is credited for the cost associated with the period. This is done instead of making a direct credit to the asset account. The balance in the **Accumulated Depreciation** account is the portion of the cost that has been assigned to expense since the item was purchased.

The *Accumulated Depreciation* account is called a **contra account.** A contra account is reported as an offset to or a deduction from a related account. Thus, in the balance sheet, the *Accumulated Depreciation* account is reported as a deduction from the original cost reported in the related asset account. Reporting both the original cost and the accumulated depreciation of the asset provides useful information about the age of the asset to statement users.

To illustrate, assume that the building has an estimated useful life of 25 years, at which time it is expected to have a residual value of $2,000. The office equipment has an eight-year estimated useful life and a zero residual value at the end of eight years. The monthly depreciation expense for each asset, assuming an equal charge per month, is computed as follows.

Building	Office Equipment
$\dfrac{\$62,000 - \$2,000}{300 \text{ months}} = \$200 \text{ per month}$	$\dfrac{\$9,600}{96 \text{ months}} = \$100 \text{ per month}$

The adjusting entries to record depreciation for the month of June are:

c.	June	30	Depreciation Expense-Building	200	
			Accumulated Depreciation-Building		200
d.		30	Depreciation Expense-Office Equipment	100	
			Accumulated Depreciation-Office Equipment		100

The depreciation expense is reported as an expense in the income statement. The *Building* and *Office Equipment* accounts will be shown in the balance sheet, as follows.

Building	$62,000	
Less: Accumulated depreciation	200	$61,800
Office equipment	9,600	
Less: Accumulated depreciation	100	9,500

The difference between the original cost of the asset and its accumulated depreciation is called the **book value** of the asset and represents the unexpired cost of the asset.

As long as the assets are in use, the same adjusting entries are made for every accounting period until the cost, less estimated residual value, is fully assigned to expense. Thus, in successive balance sheets the *Accumulated Depreciation–Building* account will increase $200 each month and the *Accumulated Depreciation–Office Equipment* account will increase $100 each month. The original cost of the two assets remains in the *Office Equipment* and *Building* accounts and does not change. A more complete discussion of depreciation is included in Chapter 10.

UNEARNED REVENUE (PRECOLLECTED REVENUE)

A firm may receive payment in advance for services that are to be performed in the future. Until the service is performed, a liability equal to the amount of the advance payment is reported in the balance sheet. Thus, the firm's obligation to perform future services is reported. That is, recognition of the revenue is postponed until the earning cycle is completed by performance of the services.

Unearned Appraisal Fees

For example, on June 29 Starbuck Real Estate Office received a $280 advance payment for an appraisal to be completed in July. The following entry was made to record the receipt of cash.

June	29	Cash	280	
		Unearned Appraisal Fees		280

Since the appraisal will not be performed by June 30, the credit is made to an ***unearned revenue*** account (a liability) at the time the cash is received. The revenue will be earned in July when the appraisal is performed for the client. Assuming that the appraisal was completed in July, an entry to transfer the earned portion of the advance payment to revenue is made either at the time the revenue is earned or at the end of the period when the accounts are reviewed.

July	16	Unearned Appraisal Fees	280	
		Appraisal Fees Revenue		280

Note that the revenue is recognized in July, when the service is performed, rather than in June, when the cash is received.

Another Illustration of Unearned Revenue

The Starbuck Real Estate Office illustration contains one example of adjusting an unearned revenue account. Some other common unearned revenue items include rent received in advance, magazine subscriptions and advertising fees received in advance, and deposits received from customers before merchandise is delivered.

To further illustrate the accounting for unearned revenue, another example *unrelated to Starbuck's operations* will be used. Assume that on September 8, People of the World, publishers of a monthly magazine, received $24 for a one-year subscription beginning with the October issue. The company made the following entry upon receipt of the cash.

Sept.	8	Cash	24	
		Unearned Subscriptions Revenue		24

On December 31, the fiscal year-end, the balance in the *Unearned Subscriptions Revenue* account includes three months (3/12) of the revenue that was earned in the current period and nine months (9/12) that will be earned and reported as revenue in the next period. Therefore, the following entry must be made to remove $6 (3/12 × $24) from the liability account and record the revenue earned in the current period.

Dec.	31	Unearned Subscriptions Revenue	6	
		Earned Subscriptions Revenue		6

After the two journal entries are posted the accounts will appear as follows.

Unearned Subscriptions Revenue				**Earned Subscriptions Revenue**	
12/31	6	9/8	24	12/31	6
		12/31 Bal.	18		

The adjusting entry leaves a balance of $18, which is reported as a liability in the balance sheet, in the *Unearned Subscriptions Revenue* account; the $6 of subscription revenue earned will appear as revenue in the income statement. In the next period, an adjusting entry of $18 will be made to transfer the liability balance to a revenue account.

ACCRUED (UNRECORDED) EXPENSES

Most operating expenses are recorded during the period in which they are paid. However, at the end of the accounting period there are usually some expenses that have been incurred but not recorded because payment has not been made. Such expenses might include unpaid employee salaries, utilities, and interest on notes payable.

An adjusting entry is needed to assign the expense to the period in which it is incurred, rather than to the period of payment. A credit is made to a liability account to record the firm's obligation to pay for the goods or services that were received. These items are called accrued expenses or accrued liabilities. A separate liability account, such as *Salaries Payable* or *Utilities Payable,* may be established for each type of accrued expense.

Accrued Payroll Expense (Liability)

Employees normally are not paid until they perform a service for the firm. Although an expense is incurred each hour that they work, the expense is not recognized until it is paid. Starbuck follows the practice of paying employees every two weeks for the preceding two weeks of service. On Friday, June 22, the employee payroll for the service period of June 8 through June 22 totaled $1,800. No particular problem was encountered when salaries were paid on June 22 because both the payment and the expense occurred in the same period. The following entry was made to record the payment.

June	22	Salaries Expense		1,800	
		Cash			1,800
		(Withholdings from the employees'			
		salaries for taxes are ignored for now.)			

A diagram of the salaries earned up to June 30 and the payment made on July 6 is presented in Figure 3–2. This pay period *does* have special problems, because the end of the period (June 30) occurred before the next salary payment date (July 6). An adjusting entry is required (1) to provide a proper matching of expenses incurred in June with revenues earned in June; and (2) to provide a record of the firm's liabilities at the end of June. Even though the employees are not paid until July 6, a portion of the $1,700 payment is for employee services that were received in June. The entry to accrue the unpaid wages up to June 30 is:

e.	June	30	Salaries Expense	990	
			Salaries Payable		990

The accounts after the adjusting entry is posted are as follows.

Salaries Payable		Salaries Expense	
	6/30 990	6/22 1,800	
		6/30 990	
		6/30 Bal. 2,790	

Figure 3–2
Diagram of Salaries Paid and Accrued

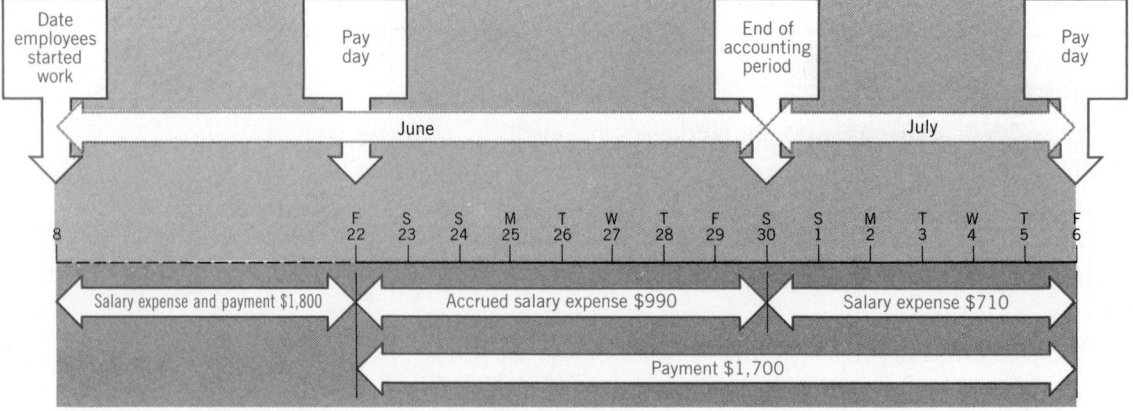

The total salaries vary each pay period because some employees work part-time.

The adjusting entry records an expense of $990 for the services received in June and reported in the June income statement, along with the salaries previously paid for totaling $1,800. The credit of $990 in the *Salaries Payable* account discloses *the amount owed* to the employees for services performed up to June 30. It is reported as a liability in the balance sheet. Failure to make the June 30 adjusting entry will result in an understatement of expenses and an overstatement of net income for June. In the balance sheet, liabilities would be understated and owner's equity would be overstated.

The $990 liability is eliminated on July 6, when the $1,700 employee payroll is paid. The $710 earned by the employees in July is recorded as an expense, as shown in the following entry.

July	6	Salaries Payable		990	
		Salaries Expense		710	
		Cash			1,700

The effect of the above entries is to recognize the expense and liability during the period in which the expense was incurred, rather than during the period when payment is made to the employees.

Accrued Commissions Expense (Liability)

Employees on the sales staff of Starbuck Real Estate Office are paid their commissions on the tenth day of the month following the month in which a sale is made. At the end of June, $4,800 in sales commissions were owed on the two residences that had been sold. Since this expense is directly associated with the revenue earned in June, the following adjusting entry is needed to provide proper matching.

f.	June	30	Commissions Expense	4,800	
			Commissions Payable		4,800

The expense is reported as a deduction from revenues in the income statement, and the payable is shown as a liability in the balance sheet.

Accrued Interest Expense (Liability)

On June 1, the Starbuck Real Estate Office financed a portion of the land and building purchase with a 20-year, $60,000, 12% mortgage. An annual payment of $3,000, plus accrued interest, is to be made on June 1 of each subsequent year. As with accrued salaries, interest accumulates daily. Therefore, Starbuck must prepare an adjusting entry on June 30 to record the interest expense incurred in June and to recognize a liability for the unpaid interest. The amount of the accrued interest is computed using the following formula.

$$\text{Principal} \times \text{Rate} \times \text{Time} = \text{Interest}$$
$$\$60,000 \times 12\% \times 1/12 = \$600$$

The entry is:

| g. | June | 30 | Interest Expense | 600 | |
| | | | Interest Payable | | 600 |

Notice that only the $600 additional liability for the accrued interest is recorded on June 30. The *Mortgage Notes Payable* account is already on the books as a result of making the June 1 entry to record the asset purchase. Interest is shown as an expense in the income statement for June, and interest payable is reported as a liability on the June 30 balance sheet.

Accrued Utilities Expense (Liability)

A utility company usually bills its customers after the service has been provided. Assume that on July 5 Starbuck Real Estate Office received a bill in the amount of $210 for electricity used in June. The adjusting entry to record the expense in June is:

| h. | June | 30 | Utilities Expense | 210 | |
| | | | Utilities Payable | | 210 |

This entry increases expenses and liabilities by equal amounts. Note that although the bill was not received until July 5, the journal entry is dated June 30 so that the expense and liability are properly reflected in the June financial statements. However, in practice, when the amounts are immaterial, service companies often follow the cash basis for utility expenses and recognize the expense in the period in which the cash is paid.

ACCRUED (UNRECORDED) REVENUE

In most cases when a service is performed by the firm, an entry is made to recognize the transaction when the job is completed. Even if cash is not immediately received, an account receivable is established in order to maintain a record of amounts owed to the firm and to recognize revenue earned. No entry is required at the end of a period since the receivable and revenue have been recorded.

There are occasions in most firms, however, when revenue has been earned but not recorded. Examples of this include the portion of revenue earned on a partially completed service contract, and interest accrued on notes receivable. Earned revenue that is unrecorded at the end of the period must be included in the accounting records by debiting a receivable and crediting a revenue account.

Accrued Service Fee Revenue

Consider the following illustration. Starbuck Real Estate Office signed an agreement on June 1 to manage an apartment complex for a monthly fee of $400. Although the service fee is earned by the firm in one month, the agreement provides for payment to be made on the fifth day of the following month. No entry was made on June 1, when the agreement was made, because there was no exchange of goods or services and none of the fee was earned at that time. However, as services are performed, a portion of the fee is earned from day-to-day. By June 30, the full monthly fee of $400 is earned and is recorded by the following entry.

i.	June	30	Accounts Receivable	400	
			Service Fees Revenue		400

Receivables for partially completed service contracts are generally recorded in an *Accounts Receivable* account. Separate receivable accounts, such as *Interest Receivable,* may be established for other types of accrued revenues. The *Accounts Receivable* account is shown in the balance sheet as an asset; the revenue account is reported in the income statement.

AN ALTERNATIVE METHOD OF RECORDING DEFERRALS

In the preceding illustration, revenue collected in advance was initially recorded in an unearned revenue account, a liability account. Likewise, an expense paid for in advance was initially recorded in an asset account. In the case of unearned revenue, an adjusting entry was made to transfer earned revenue from the liability account to a revenue account. Similarly, an adjusting entry was made at the end of the period to transfer the portion of the asset consumed during the period to an expense account.

However, it is possible to use another approach in recording prepaid items. Some businesses find it more convenient to initially record all payments for goods or services in expense accounts, regardless of whether a particular cost will benefit only the current period or several accounting periods. Consistent with this approach, the receipt of cash for services to be performed in the future is recorded directly in a revenue account, not a liability account, as in the prior methods discussed. If this procedure is used, the unused portion of the prepaid expense must be transferred at the end of the period to an asset account from an expense account. Similarly, at the end of the period an adjusting entry is prepared to transfer the unearned revenue from the revenue account to a liability account in the balance sheet.

Prepaid Expenses Initially Recorded in an Expense Account

On June 3, Starbuck paid $960 for a 24-month insurance policy. If the policy of the company is to record payments for insurance policies in an expense account, the entry on June 3 is:

	June	3	Insurance Expense	960	
			Cash		960

The monthly cost for the insurance protection is $40 ($960 ÷ 24 months). One month of the coverage expired during June, leaving 23 months prepaid.

The unexpired portion at June 30 is:

$$\text{Prepaid insurance} = 23 \text{ months} \times \$40$$
$$= \$920$$

At the end of the period, an adjusting entry is needed to remove the unexpired portion of the insurance coverage from the expense account and transfer it to an asset account.

a.	June	30	Prepaid Insurance	920	
			Insurance Expense		920

After these entries are posted, the two accounts appear as follows.

Prepaid Insurance			Insurance Expense		
6/30	920		6/3	960	6/30 920
			6/30 Bal.	40	

Note that the June 30 balances are the same (*Prepaid Insurance,* $920; *Insurance Expense,* $40) as when the insurance premium payment was initially made to the *Prepaid Insurance* account (see page 99).

Prepaid Revenue Initially Recorded in a Revenue Account

On September 8, the publishers of *People of the World* monthly magazine received $24 for a one-year subscription that is to begin with the October issue. The company records prepayments in a revenue account. The entry to record the receipt is:

Sept.	8	Cash	24	
		Earned Subscriptions Revenue		24

Beginning with the October issue, $2 of revenue is earned each month. At December 31, three months of revenue ($6) is earned, leaving nine months unearned ($18). Thus, an adjusting entry must be made to transfer the unearned portion of the prepayment from the revenue account to a liability account. The adjusting entry is:

Dec.	31	Earned Subscriptions Revenue	18	
		Unearned Subscriptions Revenue		18

Note again that the entry results in balances that are the same as those that existed when the cash receipt was recorded initially in the liability account (see page 103).

SUMMARY OF ADJUSTING ENTRIES

The various types of adjusting entries that have been illustrated are summarized in Figure 3–3. Failure to make an adjusting entry will affect a balance sheet account and an income statement account. For example, failure to adjust a

Type of Adjustment	Initial Entry	Adjusting Entry	Income Statement			Balance Sheet		
			Revenue	Expense	Net Income	Asset	Liability	Owner's Equity
DEFERRALS Prepaid Expense— expense paid in advance; e.g., rent paid in advance of occupancy.								
1. Recorded initially in an asset account.	Asset Cash	Expense Asset For the amount used.	0	−	+	+	0	+
2. Recorded initially in an expense account.	Expense Cash	Asset Expense For the amount unused.	0	+	−	−	0	−
Unearned Revenue— revenue received before earned; e.g., rent received from a tenant before occupancy occurs.								
1. Recorded initially in a liability account.	Cash Liability	Liability Revenue For the amount earned.	−	0	−	0	+	−
2. Recorded initially in a revenue account.	Cash Revenue	Revenue Liability For the amount unearned.	+	0	+	0	−	+
ACCRUALS Accrued Expense— expense incurred but not paid for; e.g., salaries earned by employees but not paid for.	None	Expense Liability For the amount incurred.	0	−	+	0	−	+
Accrued revenue— revenue earned but not yet received; e.g., interest earned on notes receivable but not yet received.	None	Asset Revenue For the amount earned.	−	0	−	−	0	−

Figure 3–3
Summary of Adjusting Entries

prepaid expense will result in an understatement in expenses, which results in an overstatement in net income, total assets, and owner's equity. The effects on the financial statements of failure to make adjusting entries are also shown in Figure 3–3.

ADJUSTED TRIAL BALANCE

Objective 5: Preparing an adjusted trial balance

As stated above, adjusting entries must be journalized and posted to the ledger accounts. The ledger accounts for Starbuck Real Estate Office are shown, after the adjusting entries were posted, in T account form in Figure 3–4. A trial balance is then taken from the general ledger to verify the equality of debits and credits in the accounts. This trial balance is called an **adjusted trial balance** because it is taken from the ledger after the adjusting entries have been posted. An adjusted trial balance for the Starbuck Real Estate Office as of June 30 is presented in Figure 3–5.

Figure 3–4
General Ledger After Adjusting Entries Were Posted

Assets

Cash   100

6/1	60,000	6/1	12,000
6/23	250	6/3	960
6/29	280	6/5	5,000
6/30	4,200	6/6	120
		6/22	1,800
		6/23	600
		6/27	620
		6/30	72
6/30 Bal.	43,558		

Accounts Receivable   104

6/15	4,200	6/30	4,200
6/19	5,400		
6/30 (i)	400		
6/30 Bal.	5,800		

Prepaid Insurance   110

| 6/3 | 960 | 6/30 (a) | 40 |
| 6/30 Bal. | 920 | | |

Office Supplies Inventory   111

| 6/5 | 620 | 6/30 (b) | 80 |
| 6/30 Bal. | 540 | | |

Land   150

| 6/1 | 10,000 | | |

Building   160

| 6/1 | 62,000 | | |

Accumulated Depr.—Bldg.   161

| | | 6/30 (c) | 200 |

Office Equipment   170

| 6/5 | 9,600 | | |

Accumulated Depr.—Off. Equip.   171

| | | 6/30 (d) | 100 |

Liabilities

Accounts Payable   200

6/27	620	6/5	620
		6/5	4,600
		6/30 Bal.	4,600

Salaries Payable   210

| | | 6/30 (e) | 990 |

Commissions Payable   211

| | | 6/30 (f) | 4,800 |

Interest Payable   215

| | | 6/30 (g) | 600 |

Utilities Payable   216

| | | 6/30 (h) | 210 |

Unearned Appraisal Fees		220
	6/29	280

Commissions Expense		505
6/30 (f)	4,800	

Mortgage Notes Payable		230
	6/1	60,000

Utilities Expense		510
6/30	72	
6/30 (h)	210	
6/30 Bal.	282	

Owner's Equity

Mike Starbuck, Capital		300
	6/1	60,000

Advertising Expense		520
6/6	120	

Mike Starbuck, Drawing		310
6/23	600	

Insurance Expense		521
6/30 (a)	40	

Commissions Revenue		400
	6/15	4,200
	6/19	5,400
	6/30 Bal.	9,600

Office Supplies Expense		530
6/30 (b)	80	

Appraisal Fees Revenue		401
	6/23	250

Depreciation Expense—Bldg.		540
6/30 (c)	200	
6/30 Bal.	200	

Service Fees Revenue		402
	6/30 (i)	400

Depreciation Expense—Off. Equip.		541
6/30 (d)	100	
6/30 Bal.	100	

Salaries Expense		500
6/22	1,800	
6/30 (e)	990	
6/30 Bal.	2,790	

Interest Expense		560
6/30 (g)	600	

PREPARATION OF FINANCIAL STATEMENTS

After the adjusting process is completed, the financial statements can be prepared directly from the adjusted trial balance. The income statement is normally prepared before the balance sheet, because the net income or net loss is needed to complete the owner's equity section of the balance sheet.

Objective 6: Preparation of financial statements

INCOME STATEMENT

An income statement for the Starbuck Real Estate Office may be prepared from the adjusted trial balance as shown in Figure 3–6. Note that the heading

Figure 3–5
Adjusted Trial
Balance

STARBUCK REAL ESTATE OFFICE
Adjusted Trial Balance
June 30, 1987

Account Title	Debit	Credit
Cash	$ 43,558	
Accounts Receivable	5,800	
Prepaid Insurance	920	
Office Supplies Inventory	540	
Land	10,000	
Building	62,000	
Accumulated Depreciation—Building		$ 200
Office Equipment	9,600	
Accumulated Depreciation—Office Equipment		100
Accounts Payable		4,600
Salaries Payable		990
Commissions Payable		4,800
Interest Payable		600
Utilities Payable		210
Unearned Appraisal Fees		280
Mortgage Notes Payable		60,000
Mike Starbuck, Capital		60,000
Mike Starbuck, Drawing	600	
Commissions Revenue		9,600
Appraisal Fees Revenue		250
Service Fees Revenue		400
Salaries Expense	2,790	
Commissions Expense	4,800	
Utilities Expense	282	
Advertising Expense	120	
Insurance Expense	40	
Office Supplies Expense	80	
Depreciation Expense—Building	200	
Depreciation Expense—Office Equipment	100	
Interest Expense	600	
Totals	$142,030	$142,030

contains the name of the company, the type of financial statement, and the length of time it took to earn the reported income. In formal statements, revenues and expenses are often listed either in order of size, with the biggest dollar amounts first, or alphabetically. For a service firm, the accounts are commonly classified into two major categories, revenues and expenses. Such a format is called a *single-step* income statement. The difference between revenues and expenses is the net income or net loss for the period.

In this illustration, a net income of $1,238 is reported. This means that the sum of the credit balances in the revenue accounts ($10,250) exceeded the

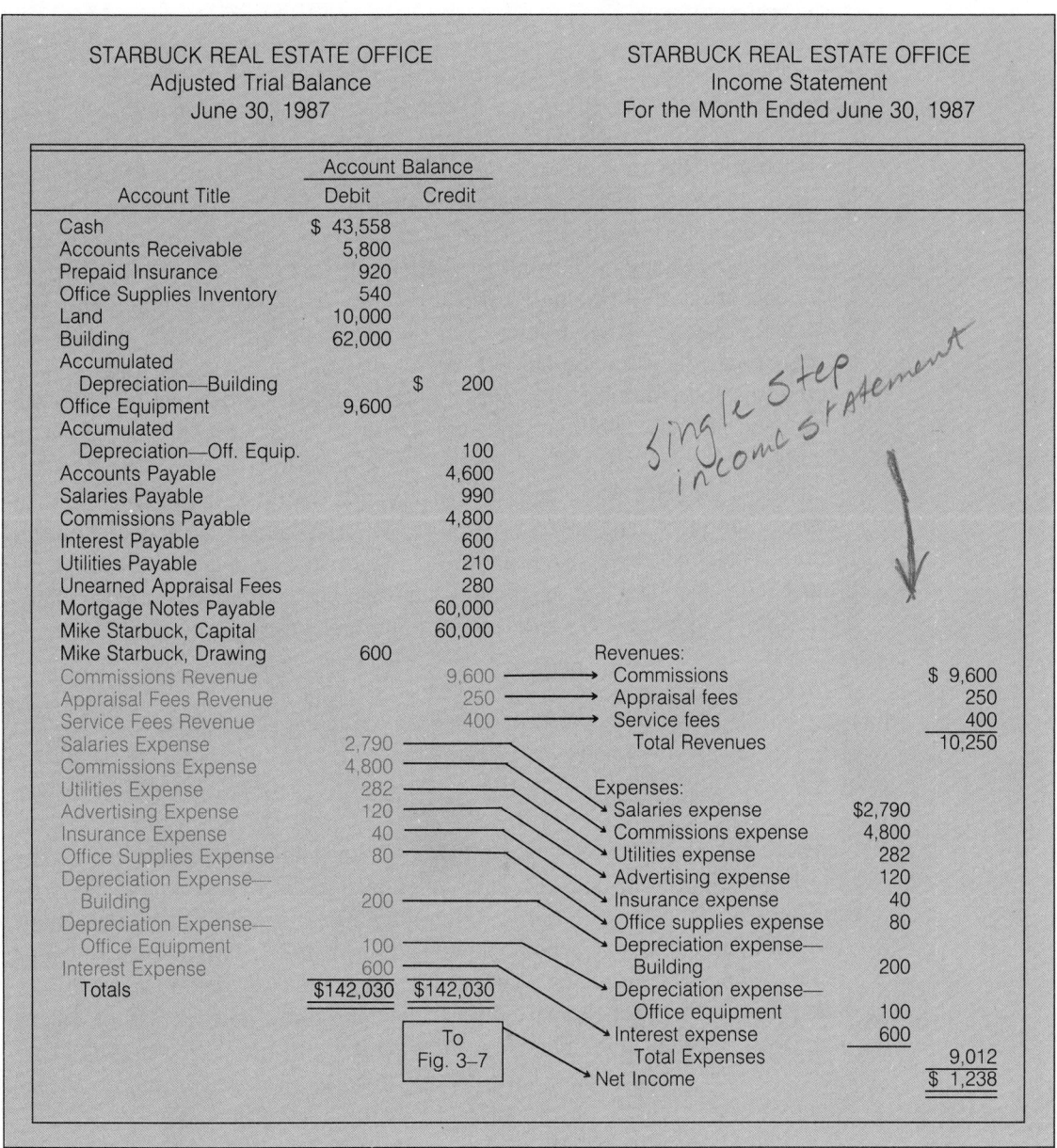

STARBUCK REAL ESTATE OFFICE
Adjusted Trial Balance
June 30, 1987

STARBUCK REAL ESTATE OFFICE
Income Statement
For the Month Ended June 30, 1987

| Account Title | Account Balance | |
	Debit	Credit
Cash	$ 43,558	
Accounts Receivable	5,800	
Prepaid Insurance	920	
Office Supplies Inventory	540	
Land	10,000	
Building	62,000	
Accumulated		
Depreciation—Building		$ 200
Office Equipment	9,600	
Accumulated		
Depreciation—Off. Equip.		100
Accounts Payable		4,600
Salaries Payable		990
Commissions Payable		4,800
Interest Payable		600
Utilities Payable		210
Unearned Appraisal Fees		280
Mortgage Notes Payable		60,000
Mike Starbuck, Capital		60,000
Mike Starbuck, Drawing	600	
Commissions Revenue		9,600
Appraisal Fees Revenue		250
Service Fees Revenue		400
Salaries Expense	2,790	
Commissions Expense	4,800	
Utilities Expense	282	
Advertising Expense	120	
Insurance Expense	40	
Office Supplies Expense	80	
Depreciation Expense—		
Building	200	
Depreciation Expense—		
Office Equipment	100	
Interest Expense	600	
Totals	$142,030	$142,030

Single step income statement

Revenues:
Commissions → $ 9,600
Appraisal fees → 250
Service fees → 400
Total Revenues → 10,250

Expenses:
Salaries expense $2,790
Commissions expense 4,800
Utilities expense 282
Advertising expense 120
Insurance expense 40
Office supplies expense 80
Depreciation expense—
Building 200
Depreciation expense—
Office equipment 100
Interest expense 600
Total Expenses 9,012
Net Income $ 1,238

To
Fig. 3–7

Figure 3–6
Preparation of Income Statement from Adjusted Trial Balance

sum of the debit balances in the expense accounts ($9,012) by $1,238. The net income of $1,238 must be added to owner's equity to equalize the total liabilities and owner's equity with the total assets. In other words, during the period there was an increase in net assets from earning a net income. This increase in net assets (assets minus liabilities) belongs to the owner and should be added to the owner's capital balance in the balance sheet.

BALANCE SHEET

Objective 7:
Classification
of accounts

A balance sheet for Starbuck Real Estate Office is prepared in Figure 3–7 from the adjusted trial balance. The heading indicates the name of the company, the title of the statement, and the statement date. Recall that the balance sheet reports the financial position on a specified date (June 30 in this illustration), whereas the income statement reports the flow of revenues and expenses during a period (the month of June). The form of the balance sheet presented in Figure 3–7 is called the **report form.** In the report form, the accounts are listed in a single vertical column. This format is commonly used when the balance sheet is presented on one page. In contrast, the **account form** shows the assets on the left side of the page and liabilities and owner's equity on the right side. In annual reports, the assets are sometimes listed on one page and the liabilities and owner's equity accounts are placed on the facing page.

There are three major categories of accounts reported in the balance sheet: assets, liabilities, and owner's equity. When a number of accounts are reported, statement users have found the information contained in the balance sheet more useful if the assets and liabilities are further classified (called a **classified balance sheet**) into several important subcategories.

Assets	**Liabilities**
Current assets	Current liabilities
Long-term investments	Long-term liabilities
Property, plant, and equipment	
Intangible assets	
Other assets	

These categories facilitate the evaluation of financial data and are arranged in the balance sheet so that important relationships between two subcategories are shown. For example, the **liquidity** of a firm—its ability to satisfy short-term obligations as they become due—is of primary concern to most statement readers. To facilitate the evaluation of a firm's liquidity, assets and liabilities are classified as short-term (current) and long-term. The excess of current assets over current liabilities is called **working capital.** The use of the categories to perform analyses and interpretations is discussed in more detail in Chapter 20.

In Figure 3–7 only two of the asset categories are shown: current assets and property, plant, and equipment. Transactions involving accounts classified in the other categories were not experienced by the firm. A detailed discussion of these accounts is deferred to later chapters.

Current Assets

Objective 8:
Normal operating cycle

Current assets are cash and other types of assets that are reasonably expected to be converted into cash, sold, or consumed, either during the normal operating cycle of the firm or within one year after the balance sheet date, whichever is longer. For a merchandising firm, the **normal operating cycle** is the average length of time it takes a firm to acquire inventory, sell the inventory

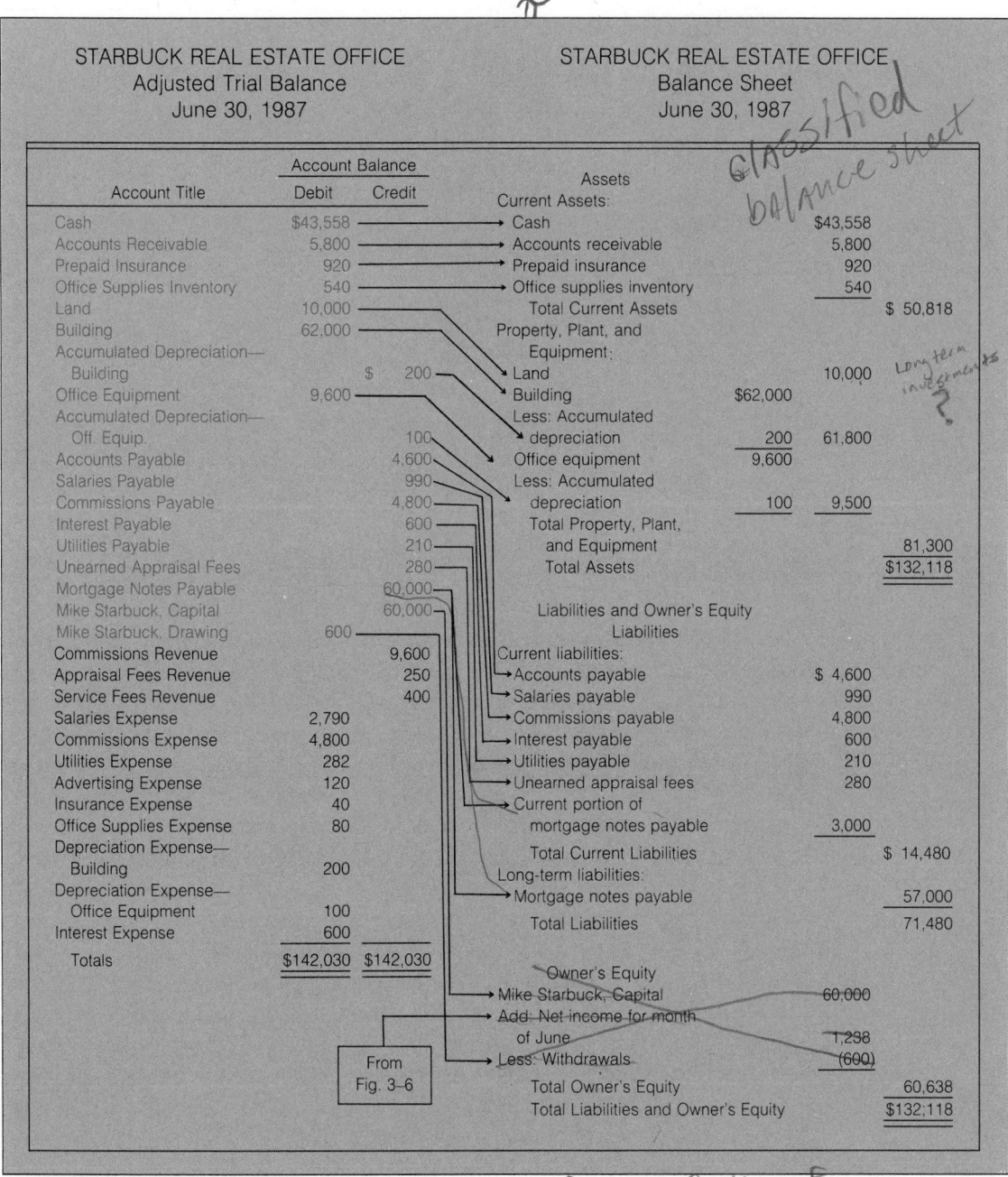

Figure 3–7
Preparation of Balance Sheet from Adjusted Trial Balance

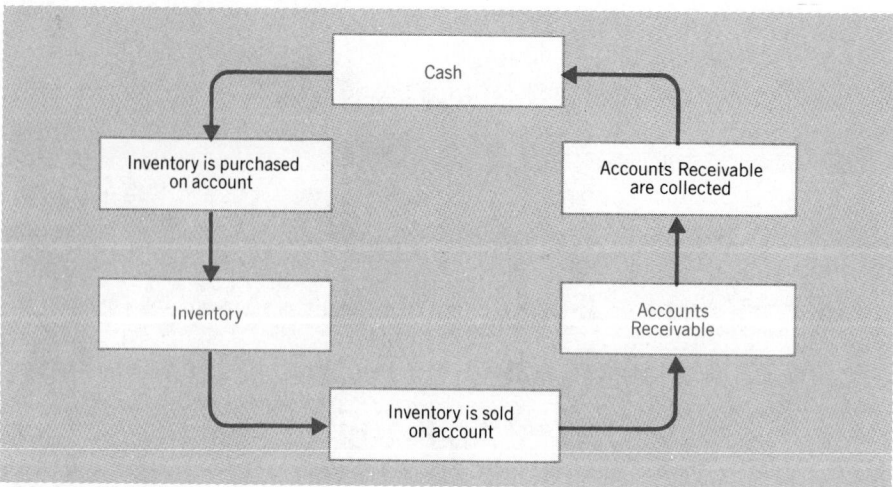

to its customers, and ultimately collect cash from the sale. The cycle is diagrammed above. The cash collected from customers is used to pay for the inventory purchased and the other operating activities of the firm, and then the cycle starts over.

The length of the operating cycle tends to vary for different businesses and is dependent on a number of factors. Obviously, the length is affected by certain management policies, such as the length of the credit period granted to customers. The type of inventory involved and the nature of the firm's operations will also affect the cycle. For example, a grocery store should have a shorter operating cycle than a jewelry store, because it sells its inventory faster. Of course, service organizations will not purchase and hold inventory. An operating cycle for a service organization involves using cash to acquire supplies and services, using the supplies and services acquired to perform a service for a customer, and then collecting cash from the customer. For many merchandising or service firms the operating cycle is less than one year. For those firms, the one-year rule is applied in classifying current assets. However, many firms have an operating cycle that is longer than 12 months. Examples include firms involved with large construction projects, distilled products, and lumber operations. For these firms, the operating cycle, rather than the one-year period, is used to classify current assets. Unless indicated otherwise, it will be assumed in the remainder of this text that a one-year time period is to be used as the basis for classifying current assets.

Current assets are listed in the order of their liquidity. Here the term *liquidity* refers to the average length of time it takes to convert a non-cash asset into cash. The following major items, listed in their order of liquidity, are commonly found in a current asset section of a balance sheet.

1. Cash.
2. Marketable securities.
3. Notes receivable.
4. Accounts receivable.
5. Inventory.
6. Prepaid assets.

These items are discussed individually in more detail in later chapters. For now, note that marketable securities (discussed in Chapter 7) are investments that can be converted back into cash for use in conducting the normal operations of the firm. The inclusion of prepaid assets, some of which may expire or be consumed over a period of years, is supported on the grounds that if an advance payment had not been made, a cash outflow would be required in the next period to acquire the items. For reporting purposes, it is common practice to combine the balances in the prepaid assets accounts into a single dollar amount, rather than list them separately in the balance sheet.

Long-term Investments

Assets that are held for investment purposes, rather than for use in normal operations are classified in the **long-term investment** section. Investments normally consist of stocks and bonds of other companies, land held for speculation, and cash or other assets set aside for specific long-term purposes, such as a retirement fund for the firm's employees.

Property, Plant, and Equipment (Plant Assets)

The property, plant, and equipment category consists of assets of a physical nature (tangible) that are used in the normal operations of the firm to produce goods, sell goods, or perform services for customers. Other terms used for this classification are plant assets and operational assets. **Plant assets** are expected to be used by the business for a number of years and are not held for resale. Examples include land, building, equipment, furniture, fixtures, patterns, dies, and tools used in operating the business.

Plant assets have limited useful lives, and their cost is depreciated over their estimated useful life. The depreciation recorded to date on an asset is shown in the *Accumulated Depreciation* account, which is deducted from the cost of the asset in the balance sheet to show the asset's book value. Because land has an unlimited life, it is not depreciated.

Intangible Assets

An **intangible asset** is one that does not have a physical substance but is expected to provide future benefits to the firm. Intangibles derive their value from the rights that possession and use confer to their owner. Like plant assets, intangibles are initially recorded at cost, which is allocated to future periods over the asset's estimated useful life. Examples are patents, trademarks, copyrights, franchise fees, secret processes, and trade names.

Other Assets

The other assets category is used to report those assets that do not readily fit into one of the categories described above. Some examples are plant and equipment no longer being used in operations but held for future disposal and costs incurred to rearrange equipment for a more efficient operation.

Current Liabilities

Current liabilities are obligations of the firm that are reasonably expected to be paid or settled in the next 12 months or within the normal operating cycle, whichever is longer. Most current liabilities will require the payment of cash in the short term. Examples include short-term notes payable (notes that are *not* due within 12 months or within the normal operating cycle are reported as long-term liabilities), accounts payable, interest payable, and other accrued liabilities. However, some current liabilities, such as cash advances received from customers, do not require the payment of cash, but are settled by the delivery of goods or the performance of services. Also included as a current liability is the portion of long-term debt that is due within one year. To illustrate, recall that the Starbuck Real Estate Office issued $60,000 in mortgage notes payable to partially finance the purchase of certain assets. The contract provided for Starbuck to make a $3,000 payment, plus accrued interest, on each June 1 for the next 20 years. In Figure 3–7, the $3,000 due within the next year is reported with the current liabilities of the firm. The remaining $57,000 due beyond 12 months of the balance sheet date is reported as a long-term liability.

Within the current liability section there is no agreed-upon uniform order of presenting accounts. One approach is to list the accounts from the largest amount due to the smallest amount due. Another approach commonly used is to list the notes payable first, followed by accounts payable, accrued liabilities, and the current portion of the long-term debt.

Long-term Liabilities

Long-term liabilities are those obligations of the firm that do not require payment within the next year or the normal operating cycle, whichever is longer. In other words, liabilities not classified as current are reported in this section of the balance sheet. Thus, if a firm's normal operating cycle is less than one year, obligations that mature more than one year beyond the balance sheet date are reported as long term. If the normal operating cycle is longer than 12 months, obligations due beyond the next operating cycle are reported as long-term liabilities.

In the case of the Starbuck Real Estate Office, the only long-term debt is that portion of the mortgage notes due after one year. Note, in Figure 3–7, that only the interest that has accrued up to June 30 on the $60,000 outstanding debt is reported as interest payable. In other words, the total interest that will be paid over the life of the notes is not recognized as a liability at this time. Interest accrues with the passage of time and is not reported as a liability until it is accrued. The interest accrued on both the long-term and the short-term portion of the debt is reported as a current liability, because the interest payment is due on June 1, which is 11 months after the balance sheet date.

Owner's Equity

The owner's equity section of the balance sheet reports the equity of the owner in the assets of the firm. Owner's equity is increased by the investment of assets by the owner and the earning of a net income. It is decreased by the withdrawal of assets and by operating at a net loss for the period. Normally, the changes in owner's equity during the period are disclosed as follows in a schedule called a statement of changes in owner's equity.

STARBUCK REAL ESTATE OFFICE
Statement of Changes in Owner's Equity
For the Month Ended June 30, 1987

Mike Starbuck, Capital, June 1, 1987	$60,000
Add: Net income for the month of June	1,238
Sub-Total	61,238
Less: Withdrawals during June	600
Mike Starbuck, Capital, June 30, 1987	$60,638

The statement illustrated is a supplemental schedule to the balance sheet. When the statement of changes in owner's equity is prepared, the total owner's equity on June 30 of $60,638 is reported as a single amount in the balance sheet, rather than showing the detailed information as presented in Figure 3–7.

DEMONSTRATION PROBLEM

The unadjusted trial balance prepared for the Johnson Decorating Service on July 31 is as follows.

JOHNSON DECORATING SERVICE
Unadjusted Trial Balance
July 31, 1987

Account Title	Debit	Credit
Cash	$2,560	
Accounts Receivable	240	
Office Supplies Inventory	140	
Prepaid Insurance	180	
Automobile	4,200	
Office Equipment	1,200	
Accounts Payable		$1,340
Unearned Service Fees		80
Notes Payable		3,000
Mary Johnson, Capital		4,000
Mary Johnson, Drawing	400	
Service Fees Revenue		520
Advertising Expense	20	
Totals	$8,940	$8,940

Other information available at the end of July is as follows.

a. Depreciation for one month is $100 on the automobile and $20 on the office equipment.

b. Interest accrued on the notes payable is $30.

c. Received a $48 invoice from Jayhawk Oil Company for gasoline used in the business and charged on a credit card.

d. Office supplies in stock, valued at $85, were determined by a physical count.

e. The balance in the *Prepaid Insurance* account is the cost of a 12-month policy purchased on July 1.

f. Utilities used in July but not paid for total $165.

Required:

A. Journalize the required adjusting entries.

The following account titles are to be added to those listed in the trial balance.

Depreciation Expense—Automobile
Depreciation Expense—Office Equipment
Automobile Expense
Insurance Expense
Office Supplies Expense
Utilities Expense
Interest Expense
Interest Payable
Accrued Expenses Payable
Accumulated Depreciation—Automobile
Accumulated Depreciation—Office Equipment

B. Prepare an adjusted trial balance.

ANSWER TO THE DEMONSTRATION PROBLEM

A. Adjusting Entries

Date		Accounts and Explanation	Post. Ref.	Debit	Credit
July	31	Depreciation Expense—Automobile		100	
		Accumulated Deprec.—Auto.			100
		To record depreciation on the			
		automobile for the month of July.			
	31	Depreciation Expense—Off. Equip.		20	
		Accumulated Deprec.—Off.			
		Equip.			20
		To record depreciation on the office			
		equipment for the month of July.			
	31	Interest Expense		30	
		Interest Payable			30
		To record interest on notes			
		payable.			

			Debit	Credit
31	Automobile Expense		48	
	Accrued Expenses Payable			48
	To record unpaid gasoline bills.			
31	Office Supplies Expense		55	
	Office Supplies Inventory			55
	To record office supplies used in July.			
31	Insurance Expense		15	
	Prepaid Insurance			15
	To record expired insurance.			
31	Utilities Expense		165	
	Accrued Expenses Payable			165
	To record accrued expense.			

B. Adjusted Trial Balance

JOHNSON DECORATING SERVICE
Adjusted Trial Balance
July 31, 1987

Account Title	Debit	Credit
Cash	$2,560	
Accounts Receivable	240	
Office Supplies Inventory	85	
Prepaid Insurance	165	
Automobile	4,200	
Accumulated Depreciation—Automobile		$ 100
Office Equipment	1,200	
Accumulated Depreciation—Office Equipment		20
Accounts Payable		1,340
Unearned Service Fees		80
Notes Payable		3,000
Interest Payable		30
Accrued Expenses Payable		213
Mary Johnson, Capital		4,000
Mary Johnson, Drawing	400	
Service Fees Revenue		520
Depreciation Expense—Automobile	100	
Depreciation Expense—Office Equipment	20	
Automobile Expense	48	
Insurance Expense	15	
Office Supplies Expense	55	
Utilities Expense	165	
Advertising Expense	20	
Interest Expense	30	
Totals	$9,303	$9,303

GLOSSARY

ACCOUNT FORM. A balance sheet format in which the assets are listed on the left side of the statement and the liabilities and owner's equity accounts are listed on the right side (p. 114).

ACCRUALS. Expenses that have been incurred but not paid, or revenues that have been earned but not received (p. 96).

ACCUMULATED DEPRECIATION. The amount of depreciation that has been recorded on an asset since it was acquired (p. 101).

ADJUSTED TRIAL BALANCE. A trial balance taken from the ledger after the adjusting entries have been posted (p. 110).

ADJUSTING ENTRIES. Journal entries made at the end of an accounting period to update the balance sheet account balances and to record income effects in the proper period (p. 96).

BOOK VALUE. The original cost of an asset less its accumulated depreciation (p. 101).

CLASSIFIED BALANCE SHEET. A balance sheet with assets and liabilities arranged into significant groups that have some common basis (p. 114).

CONTRA ACCOUNT. An account that is deducted from a related account (p. 101).

CURRENT ASSETS. Cash and other forms of assets that are reasonably expected to be converted to cash, sold, or consumed, either during the normal operating cycle of the firm or within one year of the balance sheet date, whichever is longer (p. 114).

CURRENT LIABILITIES. Obligations of the firm that are reasonably expected to be paid or satisfied within one year of the balance sheet date or the normal operating cycle, whichever is longer (p. 118).

DEFERRALS. The postponement of the recognition of expenses that have been paid for or of revenues received during the period (p. 96).

DEPRECIATION. The practice of assigning a portion of the cost of a plant asset to current expense over its estimated useful life, in a systematic and rational manner (p. 100).

ESTIMATED USEFUL LIFE. The period of time during which a plant asset is expected to be used by the firm owning it (p. 100).

EXPIRED COST. The cost of an asset used to produce revenue; an expense (p. 92).

INTANGIBLE ASSETS. Assets that do not have a physical existence and that derive value from the rights that their possession confer to their owners (p. 117).

LIQUIDITY. The ability of a firm to satisfy its short-term obligations. Also refers to the average length of time that it takes to convert a noncash asset into cash (p. 114).

LONG-TERM INVESTMENTS. Investments that are restricted for use to other than current operations (p. 117).

LONG-TERM LIABILITIES. Obligations of the firm that do not require payment within one year of the balance sheet date or the normal operating cycle, whichever is longer (p. 118).

MATCHING PRINCIPLE. The process of associating expenses with revenues earned during the period (p. 91).

NORMAL OPERATING CYCLE. The average period of time it takes for a company to purchase inventory and then receive cash from its sale (p. 114).

PLANT ASSETS. Resources of the firm that are tangible in nature, have a relatively long useful life, and are used in the normal operations of the firm (p. 117).

REPORT FORM. A balance-sheet format in which the accounts are listed in a single vertical column (p. 114).

RESIDUAL VALUE. The estimated value of an operating asset at the end of its useful life (p. 100).

UNADJUSTED TRIAL BALANCE. A trial balance prepared before the adjusting entries are posted to the general ledger (p. 97).

UNEXPIRED COST. A cost that has not been used to produce revenue; this represents future economic benefit to the firm. Unexpired costs are reported as assets (p. 92).

WORKING CAPITAL. The excess of current assets over current liabilities (p. 114).

DISCUSSION QUESTIONS

1. How is net income determined under: (a) the cash basis of accounting; and (b) the accrual basis of accounting?

2. A company receives a machine as payment in full for services rendered. The machine has a book value of $1,250 on the books of the customer and a fair value of $1,400. How much revenue should the company record?

3. What generally accepted accounting principles are the bases for accrual accounting?

4. What accounting principle is defined by the phrase, "associating cause and effect"?

5. The withdrawal of cash by the owner is not an expense. Explain.

6. The owner of a business reviews the income statement you prepared and asks: "Why do you show a net income of only $30,000 when cash collections of $100,000 were received and cash payments of $50,000 were made for expenses during the year?" How would you respond to this question?

7. What are the objectives of making adjusting entries?

8. Define the following terms.
   (a) Prepaid expense.
   (b) Unearned revenue.
   (c) Accrued expense.
   (d) Accrued revenue.
   What is generally the balance-sheet classification of each item?

9. Explain the difference between prepaid expenses and expenses incurred.

10. Explain why the purchase of supplies is usually recorded in an asset account, rather than in an expense account.

11. If a company debits *Supplies Expense* when supplies are purchased, which account should be debited and which credited at the end of the period to reflect the amount of supplies on hand?

12. What is a contra account? Give an example of one contra account used in the adjusting process.

13. During the year, *Aerobics for Women,* a monthly magazine, received cash for a three-year magazine subscription. A credit was made to the *Unearned Subscription Revenue* account.
   (a) Is the required adjusting entry made at the end of the period an example of an accrual or a deferral?
   (b) What types of accounts will be affected by the required adjusting entry?

(c) What effect will omission of the adjusting entry have on net income and the balance sheet?

14. What would be the effect on the financial statements if an adjusting entry was not made to record revenue earned but not yet received?

15. Which financial statement is usually prepared first? Why?

16. What is a classified balance sheet?

17. What is the normal operating cycle?

18. Define current assets. In what order are current assets listed in the balance sheet?

19. Define current liabilities. Define long-term liabilities.

20. In what section of the balance sheet should the following items appear, if at all?
    (a) Cash.
    (b) Notes payable due in six months.
    (c) Bond investment to be disposed of in the near future to finance operations.
    (d) Land held for speculation.
    (e) Patent.
    (f) Prepaid insurance.
    (g) Equipment.
    (h) Merchandise inventory.
    (i) Land on which the office is located.
    (j) Trademark.
    (k) Mortgage note due in five years.
    (l) Salary expense.
    (m) Current portion due on long-term debt.
    (n) Accumulated depreciation on office building.

EXERCISES

Exercise 3-1 Cash Versus Accrual Basis of Accounting

At the end of the first year of operations, Scott Miller, owner of the Paper Dolls Modeling Agency, contracted with you to prepare 1987 financial statements using both the cash basis and the accrual basis. The firm's fiscal year-end is December 31. Following is a summary of selected transactions that occurred during the year.

1. Fees of $78,000 were collected for services rendered during the year.
2. There were $6,500 in receivables at the end of 1987 for services performed on credit.
3. Cash payments of $48,500 were made for salaries, utilities, rent, insurance, and other operating expenses *incurred* during the year.
4. On December 10, 1987, a client had paid $3,000 in advance for services to be rendered in 1988.
5. Expenses of $8,000 were prepaid (not included in the $48,500) as of December 31.

Required:

A. Calculate net income using both the cash basis and the accrual basis.

B. Indicate how the following items would be reported in the firm's balance sheet under the accrual basis.
   1. The $6,500 receivable.

2. The $3,000 advance received on December 10.
3. The prepaid expense of $8,000.

Exercise 3-2 Accrual Basis Income Statement

After graduating from medical school in 1985, Dr. Art Taylor established a family medical practice in Atlanta. An income statement for the current period is presented here.

Dr. Art Taylor, Family Medical Practice
Income Statement
For the Year Ended December 31, 1987

Office fees revenue	$210,000
Less: Operating expenses	135,000
Net income	$ 75,000

Additional data:
1. Services performed in 1986 in the amount of $7,000 were collected in 1987 and are included in the 1987 revenue figure.
2. Services performed in 1987 in the amount of $9,000 are expected to be collected in 1988 and were not included in 1987 revenues.
3. Depreciation expense of $20,000 is not included in the operating expenses.
4. Accrued salaries at the end of 1986 and 1987 were $5,000 and $6,000, respectively. Expenses were recognized when cash payment was made.

Required:
A. Prepare a condensed income statement using the accrual basis. Show all computations in good form.
B. Briefly explain why the statement you prepared is considered a better measure of net income than the one presented.
C. Dr. Taylor withdrew $1,000 per week as a salary to cover his personal living expenses. The withdrawals were not included with the operating expenses. Is this a correct accounting procedure? Explain.

Exercise 3-3 Adjusting Entry for Accrued Salaries

Delta Company pays its employees every Friday for a five-day work week, which begins on Monday and ends on Friday. The weekly payroll amounts to $2,500.

Required:
A. Assuming that December 31 falls on a Tuesday, give the year-end adjusting entry. What type of adjusting entry is this?
B. If no adjusting entry were made on December 31, by how much would net income be overstated or understated? What would be the errors in the balance sheet?
C. Assuming that January 1 is a paid holiday, give the entry to pay the employees on January 3.

Exercise 3-4 Adjusting Entry for Unearned Rent

A printing firm owns the building it occupies. The firm rents one office to a tenant who paid six months' rent in advance on August 1. The firm credited *Unearned Rental Revenue* to record the $2,700 received.

Required:

A. Prepare the December 31 adjusting entry. What type of adjusting entry is this?

B. What are the effects on the firm's financial statements from omitting the adjusting entry?

C. Prepare the entry to be made in the next period to recognize the remaining portion of the rent earned.

Exercise 3-5 Adjusting Entry for Prepaid Insurance

Anderson Company purchased a three-year insurance policy on June 1. The entire premium of $5,400 was recorded by debiting *Prepaid Insurance*.

Required:

A. Give the December 31 adjusting entry. What type of adjusting entry is this?

B. What amount should be reported in the December 31 balance sheet for *Prepaid Insurance*?

C. If no adjusting entry were made on December 31, by how much would net income be overstated or understated? Would assets be overstated or understated, and by how much?

D. Give the adjusting entry for December 31 of the following year.

Exercise 3-6 Adjusting Entry for Accrued Revenue

Club Company sells service contracts on office machines. Its clients are billed a fixed fee per machine at the end of each month, payable by the fifteenth of the following month. On December 31, the end of the current fiscal year, billings for services performed in December in the amount of $9,400 were prepared and mailed to clients, but no entry was made to reflect the revenue earned.

Required:

A. Prepare the adjusting entry needed as of December 31.

B. Indicate the financial statement classification of each account affected by the adjusting entry.

C. Give the journal entry on January 15, assuming that the full $9,400 was collected.

Exercise 3-7 Adjusting Entries

The annual accounting period for Brennan Dental ends on June 30.

1. Brennan Dental performed services in the amount of $2,250 during June, which were not collected or recorded on the books.

2. The telephone expense for June amounted to $95. This amount has not been recorded because it will not be paid until July.

3. The *Office Supplies* account had a $65 debit balance on July 1 of the preceding year. Supplies in the amount of $235 were purchased during the year and $50 worth of supplies are on hand on June 30.

4. The secretary's salary of $230 for the five-day work week ending July 2 will be paid on July 2.

Required:

Prepare the June 30 adjusting entries for each transaction, and, in each case, indicate the type of adjusting entry prepared.

Exercise 3-8 Adjusting Entries and Effect on Financial Statements

The following information pertains to the P. K. Perkins firm at the end of the current fiscal year.

1. Interest revenue of $580 has been earned but has not been received or recorded.
2. Property taxes of $630 have accrued but have not been recorded.
3. The balance of $1,400 in the *Prepaid Insurance* account includes $1,050 paid for insurance for the next year.

Required:

A. Prepare the necessary adjusting entries.

B. If no adjusting entries are made, will net income be overstated or understated, and by how much?

C. If none of the adjusting entries are made, will the asset section of the balance sheet be overstated or understated, and by how much? What about the liability section and the owner's equity section?

Exercise 3-9 Adjusting Entries—Missing Data

Selected T accounts for the Western Horizons Company are shown here. Adjusting entries for the period have been posted.

Prepaid Insurance		Insurance Expense	
12/31 Bal. 540		12/31 Adj. Ent. 380	

Supplies Inventory		Supplies Expense	
12/31 Bal. 270		12/31 Adj. Ent. 320	

Rental Revenue Receivable		Unearned Rental Revenue	
1/1 Bal. -0-			12/31 Bal. 400
12/31 Bal. -0-			

Earned Rental Revenue	
	12/31 Bal. 8,000

Required:

A. The balance in the *Prepaid Insurance* account on January 1 was $450. Compute the total cash payment made during the year for insurance premiums.

B. Supplies totaling $340 were purchased during the year. Compute the January 1 balance in the *Supplies Inventory* account.

C. No balance existed in the *Unearned Rental Revenue* account on January 1. Compute the total amount of rental fees that were received in cash during the period.

Exercise 3-10 Adjusting Entries—Missing Data

Selected T accounts for the Sunshine Solar Repair Company are shown here. Adjusting entries for the period have been posted.

Accumulated Depreciation		Depreciation Expense	
	12/31 Bal. 3,430	12/31 Adj. Ent. 670	

Salaries Expense		Salaries Payable	
12/31 Bal. 47,480			12/31 Adj. Ent. 860

Prepaid Rent		**Rent Expense**	
12/31 Bal. 450		12/31 Adj. Ent. 900	

Required:

A. Compute the January 1 balance in the *Accumulated Depreciation* account.

B. The balance in the *Salaries Expense* account on June 30 was $18,990. The balance in the *Salaries Payable* account on June 30 was $740. All salaries due are paid on the last day of each work week. Compute the amount of salary payments during the last half of the year.

C. The balance in the *Prepaid Rent* account on January 1 was $800. Compute the total cash payment made during the year for rent.

Exercise 3-11 Recording Deferrals in Income Statement Accounts

Part I

Anderson Company purchased a three-year insurance policy on June 1. The premium of $5,400 was recorded by debiting *Insurance Expense*.

Required:

A. Give the December 31 adjusting entry.

B. What amount should be reported in the December 31 balance sheet for *Prepaid Insurance*?

C. What amount should be reported in the current year's income statement for *Insurance Expense*?

Part II

A printing firm owns the building that it occupies. The firm rents an office to a tenant who paid six months' rent in advance on August 1. The firm credited *Earned Rental Revenue* to record the $2,700 received.

Required:

A. Prepare the December 31 adjusting entry.

B. What are the effects on the firm's financial statements from omitting the adjusting entry?

Exercise 3-12 Classified Balance Sheet

Presented here are the captions of a balance sheet.

A. Current assets
B. Long-term investments
C. Property, plant, and equipment
D. Intangible assets
E. Other assets

F. Current liabilities
G. Long-term liabilities
H. Owner's equity
I. Not reported on the balance sheet

Required:

Indicate by letter where each of the following items would be classified:

_____ 1. Land held for speculation
_____ 2. Cash held for operations
_____ 3. Accounts receivable
_____ 4. Copyright
_____ 5. Accrued wages payable
_____ 6. Earned revenue
_____ 7. Unearned revenue

_____ 8. Stock in other companies held in employees' retirement fund
_____ 9. Furniture and fixtures
_____ 10. Notes payable due in two months
_____ 11. Mortgage note payable due in 20 years

_____ 12. Interest receivable
_____ 13. Depreciation expense
_____ 14. Merchandise inventory

_____ 15. Ron Heck, Capital
_____ 16. Land and building held for
       sale

Exercise 3-13 **Preparing the Current Assets and Current Liabilities Sections of a Balance Sheet**

From the following list of accounts, prepare the current assets and current liabilities sections of a balance sheet and calculate the working capital.

Prepaid Insurance	$370	Land	$10,000
Salaries Payable	210	Earned Rent Revenue	950
Rent Expense	300	Cash Held in Employee's	
Office Supplies Inventory	95	Retirement Fund	22,480
Unearned Revenue	250	Copyright	5,480
Equipment	675	Notes Payable—due in	
Cash	385	5 years	1,700

Exercise 3-14 **Adjusting Entries—Type of Accounts Affected**

Complete the chart presented here by filling in the combinations of accounts debited and credited in preparing adjusting entries.

	Type of Account Debited	Type of Account Credited
Deferrals:		
Originally recorded as asset or liability:		
Prepaid Expenses	_____	_____
Unearned Revenues	_____	_____
Originally recorded as expenses or revenues:		
Prepaid Expenses	_____	_____
Unearned Revenues	_____	_____
Accruals:		
Accrued Revenues	_____	_____
Accrued Expenses	_____	_____

Exercise 3-15 **Multiple-Choice—Adjusting Entry Concepts**

1. An item that represents services that have been paid for by a firm, but which have not yet been received by that firm is called an
   (a) Accrued expense.
   (b) Accrued revenue.
   (c) Prepaid expense.
   (d) Unearned revenue.
2. An item that represents services received by the firm that it will pay for in the future is called an
   (a) Accrued expense.
   (b) Accrued revenue.
   (c) Prepaid expense.
   (d) Unearned revenue.

3. An item that represents services provided by a firm for which it will receive payment in the future is called an
    (a) Accrued expense.
    (b) Accrued revenue.
    (c) Prepaid expense.
    (d) Unearned revenue.
4. Accrued revenues
    (a) Decrease assets.
    (b) Increase liabilities.
    (c) Decrease liabilities.
    (d) Increase assets.
5. Accrued expenses
    (a) Decrease assets.
    (b) Increase liabilities.
    (c) Decrease liabilities.
    (d) Increase assets.
6. Adjusting entries are necessary to
    (a) Update and correct the accounts at the end of the fiscal period.
    (b) Balance the books at the end of the fiscal period.
    (c) Record the sales for the period.
    (d) Ensure the equality of the debits and credits.

PROBLEMS

Problem 3-1 Correction of Income Statement

Tropical Island Cruises completed its third year of operations. The income statement prepared by the firm's bookkeeper is shown here.

TROPICAL ISLAND CRUISES
Income Statement
For the Year Ended December 31, 1987

Revenues—Cruise tickets	$342,000	
Miscellaneous revenues	3,000	
Total revenues		$345,000
Operating Expenses:		
Salaries and wages expense	82,000	
Depreciation expense	64,000	
Dock rental fees expense	45,000	
Gas and oil expense	35,000	
Maintenance expense	21,000	
Insurance expense	18,000	
Miscellaneous expense	7,000	
Total operating expenses		272,000
Net Income		$ 73,000

This is the first year the company has shown a profit. Concerned that the new and inexperienced bookkeeper may have made some errors, the owner of the firm asked your firm to review the records and financial statements. In conducting your review, you uncover the following.

1. Depreciation of $14,000 on a new ship purchased during the year had not been recorded.
2. Advance ticket sales of $8,000 were included in the $342,000 revenue figure. This revenue will be earned next year.
3. Employees' salaries and wages earned during the last week of December in the amount of $3,000 were unpaid and unrecorded.
4. A dock rental fee of $6,000, paid on December 1 for a three-month period, was debited to *Prepaid Rent*. An entry had not been made to adjust the account at year-end.
5. Tropical Island Cruises has a contract to sail members of the Sun Valley Social Club. Sun Valley is billed at the end of each quarter and makes payment by the fifteenth of the following month. Revenues of $10,000 earned for the quarter ending December 31 had not been collected or recorded. *Acc. Rev / Cr. Rev.*

Required:

A. Prepare the entries necessary to correct the accounts of Tropical Island Cruise Line.
B. Prepare a revised income statement incorporating the corrections made in requirement A.
C. The owner of the company could not understand why you excluded the advance ticket sales of $8,000 from revenues, since the cash was received during the year. How would you respond to the concern of the owner?

Problem 3-2   Adjusting Entries

The following transactions pertaining to the business of Judy Newman, CPA, occurred during December.

1. December 1. Paid $2,160 for office furniture. The furniture will be depreciated on a straight-line basis over a useful life of three years at which time it is expected to have no resale value.
2. December 1. Paid $1,104 for a 24-month fire insurance policy.
3. December 1. Borrowed $9,000 from State Bank by signing a promissory note. The principal, plus 16% annual intrest, will be repaid in three months. Interest of $120 accrued on the note during December.
4. December 11. Paid $138 for office supplies. On December 31, supplies worth $83 remained in inventory.
5. December 15. Paid $470 for one month's rent for the period December 15 to January 15. The payment was recorded in a *Prepaid Rent* account.
6. December 18. Received a check from a client for $780 as an advance payment for services to be performed. Only 10% of the work was completed by December 31.
7. December 28. Received a bill for $255 for accrued property taxes.

Required:

Prepare the journal entries to record each transaction and prepare the adjusting entries for December 31, the end of the fiscal year.

Problem 3-3   Adjusting Entries and Effect on Financial Statements

A. The fiscal year for Daisy Dry Cleaning Company ends on December 31. Using the following information, make the necessary adjusting entries at year-end.

(a) On October 15, Daisy Company borrowed $5,300 from Southern Bank at 14% interest. The principal and interest are payable on April 15. Interest of $155 had accrued on the loan by December 31.

(b) Property taxes of $870 for the six-month period ending January 31 are due in February.

(c) The annual depreciation on equipment is estimated to be $6,700. The January 1 balance in the *Accumulated Depreciation* account was $19,400.

(d) Daisy Company purchased a one-year insurance policy on October 1 of the previous year for $288. A three-year policy was purchased on May 1 of the current year for $684. Both purchases were recorded by debiting *Prepaid Insurance*.

(e) Daisy Company has two employees who each earn $50 a day. They both worked the last four days in December, for which they have not yet been paid.

(f) On November 1, the Uptown Hotel paid Daisy Company $750 in advance for doing their dry cleaning for the next three months. This was recorded by a credit to *Unearned Dry Cleaning Revenue*.

(g) Utilities for December, totaling $365, are unpaid and unrecorded.

(h) The *Supplies Inventory* account had a $145 debit balance on January 1. Supplies in the amount of $650 were purchased during the year and $105 worth of supplies are in the inventory as of December 31.

B. As you know, all adjusting entries affect one balance sheet account and one income statement account. Based on your adjusting entries

1. Complete the following schedule.

2. Compute the increase or decrease in net income.

3. Compute the increase or decrease in total assets, total liabilities, and total owner's equity.

Entry	Account	Balance in the Account Before Adjustment	Dollar Effect of Adjusting Entries	Balance Reported in 12/31 Balance Sheet	Balance Sheet Classification*	Type of Adj. Entry
(a)	Interest Payable	$742	$ —	$587	L	
(b)	Property Tax Payable	870	=	145	L	
(c)	Accumulated Depreciation	19400	+	26100	L	
(d)	Prepaid Insurance	972	—	604	A	
(e)	Salaries Payable	400	—	400	L	
(f)	Unearned Dry Cleaning Revenue	750	—	250	OE	
(g)	Utilities Payable	365	—	365		
(h)	Supplies Inventory					

*For each account, indicate whether it is an asset, liability, or owner's equity, and whether it is classified as a current asset or liability.

Problem 3-4 Adjusting Entries, Posting to T Accounts, and Effect on Net Income

At the end of the fiscal year, the trial balance of the M. L. Sullivan Law Firm appeared as follows.

M. L. SULLIVAN LAW FIRM
Unadjusted Trial Balance
December 31, 1987

Account Title	Debit	Credit
Cash	$ 2,045	
Accounts Receivable	3,315	
Notes Receivable	4,000	
Prepaid Rent	1,050	
Prepaid Insurance	1,300	
Office Supplies Inventory	1,600	
Office Equipment	4,700	
Accumulated Depreciation—Office Equipment		$ 950
Accounts Payable		125
Unearned Legal Fees		420
Notes Payable—Due 1990		3,500
M. L. Sullivan, Capital		12,000
M. L. Sullivan, Withdrawals	24,000	
Legal Fees Earned		56,215
Salaries Expense	22,000	
Utilities Expense	2,720	
Rent Expense	6,480	
Totals	$73,210	$73,210

Required:

A. Using the following information, prepare adjusting entries. Use the accounts shown in the trial balance and these additional accounts: *Interest Payable, Utilities Payable, Salaries Payable, Interest Expense, Depreciation Expense, Office Supplies Expense, Insurance Expense.*

   (a) A physical inventory of office supplies on December 31 showed $140 of unused supplies on hand.

   (b) One-half of the amount in the *Unearned Legal Fees* account had been earned by the end of the year.

   (c) Interest expense of $175 has accrued on the note payable.

   (d) The utilities expense of $260 for December has not been recorded or paid.

   (e) Salaries expense accrued for the last four days in December amounts to $440.

   (f) Twenty-five percent of the prepaid insurance expired this period.

   (g) The amount in the *Prepaid Rent* account consists of rent for this December, plus January of the following year.

   (h) Depreciation on the office equipment this year is estimated to be $425.

B. Open T accounts for the accounts shown in the trial balance and enter the December 31 balance in each account. Post the adjusting entries to the T accounts.

C. Prepare an adjusted trial balance, an income statement, and a classified balance sheet.

D. Compute the amount of net income that would be reported, assuming that the adjusting entries were not made. Compare this amount to the net income derived in requirement C. What is the difference between the two figures?

Problem 3-5 Impact of Errors in the Adjusting Entry Process on the Income Statement and Balance Sheet

Following are listed nine errors that were made during the adjusting entry process for a firm. For each situation, indicate the effect of the error on: total revenues, total expenses, net income, total assets, total liabilities, and owner's equity by placing a "−" for understate, "+" for overstate, and "0" for no effect. Use the format shown.

ERROR	Total Revenues	Total Expenses	Net Income	Total Assets	Total Liabilities	Total Owner's Equity
1. Did not record depreciation for the period.	_____	_____	_____	_____	_____	_____
2. Did not record cost of supplies used during the period.	_____	_____	_____	_____	_____	_____
3. Failed to accrue interest on note payable.	_____	_____	_____	_____	_____	_____
4. Did not accrue salaries owed to employees at year-end.	_____	_____	_____	_____	_____	_____
5. Failed to recognize portion of unearned revenue earned during the period.	_____	_____	_____	_____	_____	_____
6. Debited cash instead of interest receivable when recording accrued interest on notes receivable.	_____	_____	_____	_____	_____	_____
7. Did not record the expired portion of prepaid insurance.	_____	_____	_____	_____	_____	_____
8. Utilities expense included amounts paid for previous year.	_____	_____	_____	_____	_____	_____

Problem 3-6 Determination of Adjusting Entries from Changes in two Balance Sheets

Tom Peters, owner of the On Time Watch and Clock Repair Shop, prepared the first of the following balance sheets. He then realized that he had not made the adjusting entries, so he prepared the second, correct balance sheet.

ON TIME WATCH AND CLOCK REPAIR SHOP
Balance Sheet
December 31, 1987

	Before Adjustments		After Adjustments	
Assets				
Cash		$ 1,745		$1,745
Accounts Receivable		820		820
Supplies Inventory		965		75
Prepaid Rent		1,260		840
Prepaid Insurance		870		340
Spare Parts Inventory		675		675
Shop Fixtures	$5,670		$5,670	
Accumulated Depreciation	1,980	3,690	3,040	2,630
Total Assets		$10,025		$7,125
Liabilities and Owner's Equity				
Accounts Payable		$ 1,635		$1,635
Salaries Payable		-0-		170
Utilities Payable		-0-		115
Unearned Service Fees		350		125
T. Peters, Capital		10,215		7,255
T. Peters, Withdrawals		(2,175)		(2,175)
Total Liabilities and Owner's Equity		$10,025		$7,125

Required:

A. Give the adjusting entries that caused the differences between the two balance sheets.

You may find the following format helpful in solving these types of problems.

	Original Balances		Adjustments		Revised Balance	
Account	Debit	Credit	Debit	Credit	Debit	Credit

B. Compute the amount of increase or decrease in net income resulting from the adjusting entries.

Problem 3-7 Adjusting Entries for Prepaid Insurance, Unearned Revenue, and Prepaid Rent

The ledger of the Prestige Publishing Company includes these accounts: *Prepaid Insurance, Insurance Expense, Unearned Subscriptions Revenue, Subscriptions Revenue, Prepaid Rent,* and *Rent Expense*.

Required:

Set up T accounts for each ledger account. For each of the following situations, enter the beginning balance and record the transactions in the proper asset or liability T account. Then, record the necessary adjusting entry as of June 30, 1987, the end of the fiscal year. The company has not made any adjustments to the accounts during the period.

Insurance:

July 1, 1986.   The *Prepaid Insurance* account contained a debit balance of $2,430, which is allocable to the period July 1 through March 31.

October 15, 1986.   Prestige Publishing Company paid $3,840 for a 12-month policy beginning coverage on October 15.

Subscriptions:

July 1, 1986.   The *Unearned Subscriptions Revenue* account contained a credit balance of $12,350. Of this balance, $3,350 is for subscriptions expiring at the end of September and $9,000 is for subscriptions expiring at the end of April.

October 1, 1986.   Prestige received $2,100 for subscriptions lasting six months.

February 1, 1987.   Prestige received $5,040 for subscriptions lasting 24 months.

May 1, 1987.   Prestige received $2,850 for subscriptions lasting six months.

Rent:

July 1, 1986.   The *Prepaid Rent* account contained a debit balance of $2,750, which is allocable to July through November.

December 1, 1986.   Prestige paid $5,085 for nine months' rent.

Problem 3-8 Opening T Accounts, Adjusting Entries, and Preparation of Financial Statements

The unadjusted trial balance of the Ace Answering Service is shown here.

ACE ANSWERING SERVICE
Unadjusted Trial Balance
December 31, 1987

Account Title	Debit	Credit
Cash	$ 6,780	
Accounts Receivable	2,130	
Office Supplies Inventory	320	
Furniture and Equipment	6,790	
Accumulated Depreciation—Furniture and Equipment		$ 1,360
Accounts Payable		460
Unearned Fees		1,210
Note Payable (Due 6/30/1988)		3,000
Dennis McKeever, Capital		11,190
Dennis McKeever, Drawing	12,400	
Service Fees Revenue		39,000
Rent Expense	5,720	
Salaries Expense	21,480	
Miscellaneous Expenses	600	
Totals	$56,220	$56,220

The following adjustment information is given.
(a) Depreciation expense is $930.
(b) The *Rent Expense* account was debited for $880 on December 1, for two months' rent paid in advance.
(c) Office supplies on hand as of December 31 total $90.
(d) Accrued interest on the note payable is $350.
(e) Salaries earned, but not paid, amount to $340.
(f) The balance in the *Unearned Fees* account includes $180 received for services rendered during December.
(g) A $120 payment for salaries was inadvertently recorded as a miscellaneous expense.

Required:
A. Set up T accounts for the accounts listed in the trial balance and for these additional accounts: *Depreciation Expense, Interest Expense, Interest Payable, Office Supplies Expense, Prepaid Rent, Salaries Payable.*
   1. Post the balances shown in the trial balance to the T accounts.
   2. Post the adjustments directly to the T accounts.
B. Prepare an adjusted trial balance.
C. Prepare an income statement for the year ended December 31, 1987.
D. Prepare a classified balance sheet as of December 31, 1987.

Problem 3-9 Comprehensive Review Problem to be Worked after Problem 2-7

Refer to Problem 2-7. The following information relates to adjusting entries needed on December 31, 1987.

(a) Depreciation on the van for 1987 is $2,340.
(b) Depreciation on the tools and equipment for 1987 is $750.
(c) The building rent prepayment was made on February 1, 1987, and the building was occupied on that date. The payment was for the period of February 1, 1987 through January 31, 1988.
(d) Office supplies worth $150 were on hand on December 31, 1987.
(e) Repair supplies worth $2,200 were on hand on December 31, 1987.
(f) Insurance costing $1,300 expired by December 31, 1987.
(g) Accrued interest on the First National Bank loan is $1,200.
(h) Salaries owed to employees on December 31, 1987, were $1,300.
(i) The utilities bill of $315 had been received by December 31, 1987 but was unrecorded and unpaid.
(j) Two months of the service contract with Good Samaritan Hospital was earned.

Required:
A. Prepare the required adjusting entries on December 31, 1987. Identify each adjusting entry by letter.
B. Post the adjusting entries to the T accounts.
C. Prepare an adjusted trial balance as of December 31, 1987.
D. Prepare an
   1. Income statement.
   2. Statement of changes in owners' equity.
   3. Balance sheet. (Assume that $1,250 of the mortgage is to be paid during 1988.)

ALTERNATE PROBLEMS

Problem 3-1A Conversion from Cash to Accrual Basis of Accounting

Steve Pearson established the Pearson Accounting Service in 1985. The accounting records were maintained on a cash basis. During 1987, Steve decided to switch to using the accrual basis and has asked you to assist in converting the 1985 and 1986 financial statements to the accrual basis. Your analysis of the accounting records reveals the following data.

	1985	1986
Accounting Fees Revenue		
Cash collected for services performed during the year	$72,000	$75,000
Charged customers for services performed during the year, but cash was not received until the following year	9,000	11,000
Revenue collected in 1985 for services performed in 1986	1,500	
Operating Expenses		
Cash paid for services received	16,000	17,000
Accrued expenses at end of the year paid for in the following year	4,000	4,100
Prepaid expenses		
Cash paid during the year	5,000	7,200
Amount prepaid at the end of the year	3,400	7,500

Required:

A. Using the data just given, you are to complete abbreviated income statements in the following form for the years 1985 and 1986, for both the cash basis and accrual basis of accounting.

	Cash Basis		Accrual Basis	
	1985	1986	1985	1986
Accounting fees revenue				
Operating expenses	___	___	___	___
Net income	===	===	===	===

Show supporting computations in good form.

B. Show the differences that would result in the December 31, 1986, balance sheet accounts from using the accrual basis, as compared to the cash basis.

Problem 3-2A **Adjusting Entries**

The following transactions of the Four Corners Travel Agency occurred during June.

1. June 1.   Purchased a 36-month insurance policy for $2,160.
2. June 1.   Borrowed $6,000 from American Bank. The principal, plus 14% annual interest, is due in six months. A note was signed as evidence of the loan. Accrued interest on the note will amount to $70 on June 30.
3. June 1.   Purchased three typewriters for $2,016. The typewriters will be depreciated on a straight-line basis over their estimated useful life of four years, at which time they are expected to have no resale value.
4. June 6.   Purchased supplies for $78. On June 30, supplies costing $17 remained in inventory.
5. June 15.   Prepaid $820 in rent for the period ending August 15. The payment was recorded in the *Prepaid Rent* account.
6. June 29.   Earned a commission of $460, which will be received in July.

Required:

Give the journal entries to record each transaction and give the adjusting entries for June 30, the end of the fiscal year.

Problem 3-3A **Adjusting Entries and Effect on Financial Statements**

Uptown Realty ends its fiscal year on June 30.

Required:

A. Using the following information, make the necessary adjusting entries.

   (a) Property taxes of $495 for the three-month period ending July 31 are due in August.
   (b) The June telephone expense of $112 is unpaid and unrecorded.
   (c) The supplies account had a $145 debit balance on July 1 of the preceding year. Supplies costing $1,280 were purchased during the year, and $160 of supplies are in inventory as of June 30.
   (d) Uptown Realty borrowed $7,400 from Metropolitan Bank on March 15. The principal, plus 14% annual interest, is payable on September 15. Accrued interest on June 30 was $302.
   (e) The annual depreciation on equipment is estimated to be $4,935. The balance in the *Accumulated Depreciation* account at the beginning of the fiscal year was $7,410.
   (f) The secretary earns $48 a day. She will be paid in July for the five-day period ending July 3.
   (g) On June 1, Uptown Realty received two-months' rental income in advance, totaling $720. This was recorded by a credit to *Unearned Rental Revenue*.
   (h) Uptown Realty purchased a 6-month insurance policy for $425 on November 1. A 24-month policy was purchased on April 30 for $1,344. Both purchases were recorded by debiting *Prepaid Insurance*.

B. As you know, all adjusting entries affect one balance sheet account and one income statement account. Based on your adjusting entries prepared in requirement A

   1. Complete the following schedule.
   2. Compute the increase or decrease in net income.
   3. Compute the increase or decrease in total assets, total liabilities, and total owner's equity.

Entry	Account	Balance in the Account Before Adjustment	Dollar Effect of Adjusting Entries	Balance Reported in 6/30 Balance Sheet	Balance Sheet Classification*
(a)	Property Tax Payable	$____	$____	$____	____
(b)	Telephone Exp. Payable	____	____	____	____
(c)	Supplies Inventory	____	____	____	____
(d)	Interest Payable	____	____	____	____
(e)	Accumulated Depreciation	____	____	____	____
(f)	Salaries Payable	____	____	____	____
(g)	Unearned Rental Revenue	____	____	____	____
(h)	Prepaid Insurance	____	____	____	____

*For each account, indicate whether it is an asset, liability, or owner's equity, and whether it is classified as a current asset or liability.

Problem 3-4A Adjusting Entries, Posting to T Accounts, and Preparation of Financial Statements

The trial balance of Speedy Print Shop at the end of the fiscal year appeared as follows.

SPEEDY PRINT SHOP
Unadjusted Trial Balance
December 31, 1987

Account Title	Debit	Credit
Cash	$ 1,640	
Accounts Receivable	295	
Supplies Inventory	1,780	
Prepaid Insurance	1,790	
Equipment	13,770	
Accumulated Depreciation		$ 2,015
Accounts Payable		205
Unearned Printing Revenue		420
Dave Case, Capital		12,080
Dave Case, Drawing	10,200	
Printing Revenue		28,610
Wages Expense	9,640	
Rent Expense	3,020	
Utilities Expense	1,195	
Totals	$43,330	$43,330

Required:

A. Using the following information, prepare adjusting entries. Use the accounts shown in the trial balance and these additional accounts: *Supplies Expense, Wages Payable, Insurance Expense, Utilities Payable, Depreciation Expense.*

   (a) Insurance expense is $144 per month.

   (b) Depreciation on the equipment this year is estimated to be $1,485.

   (c) Supplies costing $245 remained in inventory on December 31.

   (d) The December utilities expense of $107 has not been paid or recorded.

   (e) Wages accrued but not paid amounted to $115.

   (f) The balance in the *Unearned Printing Revenue* account includes $105 received as payment in advance for an order to be started in January.

B. Open T accounts for the accounts shown in the trial balance and enter the December 31 balance in each account. Post the adjusting entries to the T accounts.

C. Prepare an adjusted trial balance, an income statement, and a classified balance sheet.

D. Compute the difference between the net income that would be reported, assuming that the adjusting entries were not made and assuming the net income derived in requirement C.

Problem 3-5A Determination of Adjusting Entries from Changes in Two Trial Balances

The following accounts are taken from the ledger of MPD Enterprises. Account balances are shown both before and after the year-end adjustments were made.

	Before Adjustments	After Adjustments
Service Fees Receivable	$ -0-	$ 425
Supplies Inventory	430	265
Prepaid Insurance	1,525	610
Prepaid Rent	840	420
Accumulated Depreciation	815	1,230
Salaries Payable	-0-	290
Utilities Expense Payable	-0-	245
Service Fees Revenue	29,700	30,125
Interest Revenue	2,460	2,460
Supplies Expense	1,270	1,435
Insurance Expense	-0-	915
Rent Expense	4,620	5,040
Depreciation Expense	-0-	415
Salaries Expense	11,340	11,630
Utilities Expense	2,365	2,610

Required:

Give the adjusting entries in journal entry form that resulted in the balances found in the column labeled "After Adjustments."

Problem 3-6A Determination of Adjusting Entries from Changes in Two Balance Sheets

The first of the following balance sheets of the D. D. Wright Company was inadvertently prepared before the year-end adjusting entries had been made. The second balance sheet is correct.

D. D. WRIGHT COMPANY
Balance Sheet
December 31, 1987

	Before Adjustments		After Adjustments	
Assets				
Cash		$ 2,490		$ 2,490
Accounts Receivable		1,650		1,650
Interest Receivable		-0-		270
Note Receivable		4,500		4,500
Supplies Inventory		1,630		105
Prepaid Insurance		740		475
Machinery and Equipment	$14,900		$14,900	
Accumulated Depreciation	6,130	8,770	8,020	6,880
Total Assets		$19,780		$16,370
Liabilities and Owner's Equity				
Accounts Payable		$ 4,570		$ 4,570
Telephone Expense Payable		-0-		95
Wages Payable		-0-		305
Unearned Revenue		2,445		420
D. D. Wright, Capital		24,390		22,605
D. D. Wright, Withdrawals		(11,625)		(11,625)
Total Liabilities and Owner's Equity		$19,780		$16,370

Required:

A. Give the adjusting entries that caused the differences between the two balance sheets. You may find the following format helpful in developing your solution.

	Unadjusted Balances		Adjustments		Adjusted Balance	
Account	Debit	Credit	Debit	Credit	Debit	Credit

B. Compute the amount of increase or decrease in net income resulting from the adjusting entries.

Problem 3-7A Adjusting Entries for Supplies Inventory, Unearned Rent, and Prepaid Interest

The ledger of the R. H. Klein Company includes these accounts: *Supplies Inventory, Unearned Rent,* and *Prepaid Interest.* The accounts are adjusted only at December 31, the end of the fiscal year.

Required:

For each situation, enter the information directly in the accounts just listed. The company records prepayments in asset and liability accounts. Also record the December 31 adjusting entries directly to the accounts. No adjustments have been made to the accounts during the period. The chart of accounts also includes these accounts: *Supplies Expense, Rent Revenue,* and *Interest Expense*.

Supplies:
Jan. 1 The supplies account contained a $75 balance.
3 Supplies costing $290 were purchased.
Aug. 22 Supplies costing $410 were purchased.
Dec. 31 A physical inventory count shows $105 of supplies on hand.

Rent:
Jan. 1 The *Unearned Rent* account contained a credit balance of $3,900. The balance represents $1,250 for the period of January through April and $2,650 for the period of January through August.
Sept. 1 Rent of $1,650 is received for the six-month period ending February 28.
Nov. 15 Rent of $868 is received for a two-month period ending January 15.

Interest:
Jan. 1 The *Prepaid Interest* account contained a debit balance of $150, which is allocable to the period of January through March.
May 7 Interest of $210 was paid in advance on a three-month loan.
Oct. 15 Interest of $300 was paid in advance on a six-month loan.

Problem 3-8A Opening T Accounts, Adjusting Entries, and Preparation of Financial Statements

United Rentals rents appliances and furniture. The unadjusted trial balance of the company appears below.

UNITED RENTALS
Unadjusted Trial Balance
December 31, 1987

Account Title	Debit	Credit
Cash	$ 3,860	
Accounts Receivable	2,460	
Prepaid Insurance	1,500	
Appliances	33,670	
Accumulated Depreciation—Appliances		$ 18,340
Furniture	49,100	
Accumulated Depreciation—Furniture		23,370
Accounts Payable		6,940
P. L. Pearson, Capital		29,030
P. L. Pearson, Drawing	24,370	
Rental Fees Earned		75,340
Salaries Expense	26,950	
Rent Expense	6,890	
Maintenance Expense	2,750	
Utilities Expense	1,470	
Totals	$153,020	$153,020

The following information pertains to adjustments.
(a) Expired insurance amounts to $600.
(b) The December utilities bill for $130 has not been paid or recorded.

(c) Depreciation on the appliances is $5,990. Depreciation on the furniture is $9,600.
(d) Rental fees of $1,470 were received in advance and have not yet been earned. The receipt was recorded in the *Rental Fees Earned* account.
(e) The *Rent Expense* account contains $530 paid for January 1988 rent.
(f) A cash receipt of $140 for rental fees was recorded by debiting *Accounts Receivable*.
(g) Salaries earned amounting to $240 will be paid in January and have not been recorded.

Required:
A. Set up T accounts for the accounts listed in the trial balance and the following accounts: *Depreciation Expense, Insurance Expense, Prepaid Rent, Salaries Payable, Unearned Rental Fees, Utilities Payable.*
  1. Post the account balances from the trial balance to the T accounts.
  2. Post the adjusting information directly to the T accounts.
B. Prepare an adjusted trial balance.
C. Prepare an income statement for the year ended December 31, 1987.
D. Prepare a classified balance sheet as of December 31, 1987.

CASE

CASE 3-1 Discussion Case Accrual Basis of Accounting

A friend of yours, Mike Dunham, started a business with a $20,000 investment. Business has been better than Mike had expected and on June 1 he hired an assistant so that he could spend more time soliciting new business. Anxious to determine whether his business had been profitable during the first year of operation, Mike prepared the financial statements shown here from the account balances contained in the general ledger. The ledger had been maintained by a bookkeeping service, which he had contracted with to keep the firm's records.

DUNHAM DRYWALL
Income Statement
For the Year Ended December 31, 1987

Drywall fees revenue (includes $4,000 received in advance)		$48,500
Expenses:		
Salary expense	$ 9,000	
Mike Dunham, Withdrawals	36,000	45,000
Net income		$ 3,500

DUNHAM DRYWALL
Balance Sheet
December 31, 1987

Cash	$10,700	Notes payable	$14,000
Office supplies inventory	800	Mike Dunham, Capital	20,000
Prepaid rent	6,000	Net income	3,500
Furniture and equipment	20,000		
Total	$37,500	Total	$37,500

Mike was quite disturbed with the level of income and was unable to reconcile a declining cash position with a net income for the year. Knowing that you were enrolled in an accounting course, he showed you the results and asked you to review them and confirm his computations.

In discussing the results of operations, Mike states: "The furniture and equipment were purchased on January 1 for $20,000. I paid cash of $6,000 and signed a 16% note for the balance. Due to my meticulous care, the items are just as useful today as when I bought them. I expect to use these items for five years, after which they will probably be obsolete and will be worth approximately $2,000. The interest on the note, along with a $700 principal payment, are not due until January 1, 1988." He adds that if he is successful, he plans to buy a building after he uses the office space he has rented for two years. Rent for the two years was prepaid in the amount of $6,000 on January 1, 1987.

Confidently, he tells you that hiring the assistant has permitted him to obtain new customers, and that he has received $4,000 in advance for services to be performed in 1988. He adds that at the end of the year, customers owed him $2,200, but that because of his persistent efforts these accounts had all been collected by January 10, 1988. Asking about the employee, you are told that her monthly salary of $1,500 is paid on the fifth of the following month. Mike then says: "I know that the office supplies account shows a balance of $800, but when I counted them on December 31 to see if I needed to place an order, there was only $270 in the supply closet. What happened to the difference?"

Required:
A. Following the accrual basis of accounting, prepare a revised income statement and an unclassified balance sheet for the fiscal year.
B. Explain to Mike how a company with profits could have a reduction in cash during the year.

4

THE PREPARATION OF A WORKSHEET AND COMPLETION OF THE ACCOUNTING CYCLE

CHAPTER OVERVIEW AND OBJECTIVES

This chapter completes the accounting cycle. It also introduces a worksheet that is used to accumulate the information needed to complete the accounting cycle at the end of the accounting period. When you have completed the chapter, you should understand:

1. How to prepare a worksheet.
2. How to prepare financial statements from the worksheet.
3. How to journalize adjusting entries using information from the worksheet.
4. The closing process, and how to prepare closing entries using information from the worksheet.
5. How to prepare a post-closing trial balance.
6. The purpose of reversing entries.
7. The difference in the owner's equity section of a balance sheet prepared for a partnership or a corporation.

The data developed in Chapters 2 and 3 for the Starbuck Real Estate Office will be used in this chapter to illustrate (1) the preparation of a worksheet; and (2) the use of a worksheet to complete the steps in the accounting cycle. The worksheet is a business form designed to gather in one place the account balances needed to complete the accounting cycle at the end of the period.

An optional step in the accounting process, the preparation of reversing entries, is discussed after the use of the worksheet is illustrated. Reversing entries are optional entries made at the beginning of the next period to simplify the recording of transactions in that period.

The operation of a proprietorship was used in the early chapters to illustrate the accounting cycle. Partnerships and corporations are two other common forms of business organizations. The accounting for such organizations is introduced in the last section of this chapter. They are covered in more detail in Chapters 14 through 16.

COMPLETION OF THE ACCOUNTING CYCLE

The accounting cycle, which is diagrammed in Figure 4–1, is completed at least once each fiscal year. In Chapter 2, we discussed the steps in the cycle that are carried out during an accounting period (Steps 1–3). An unadjusted trial balance (Step 4) may be prepared at any time during the period to see if the ledger accounts are in balance.

The remaining steps in the cycle (Steps 5–9) are completed at the end of the accounting period. Two of these steps—preparation of financial statements

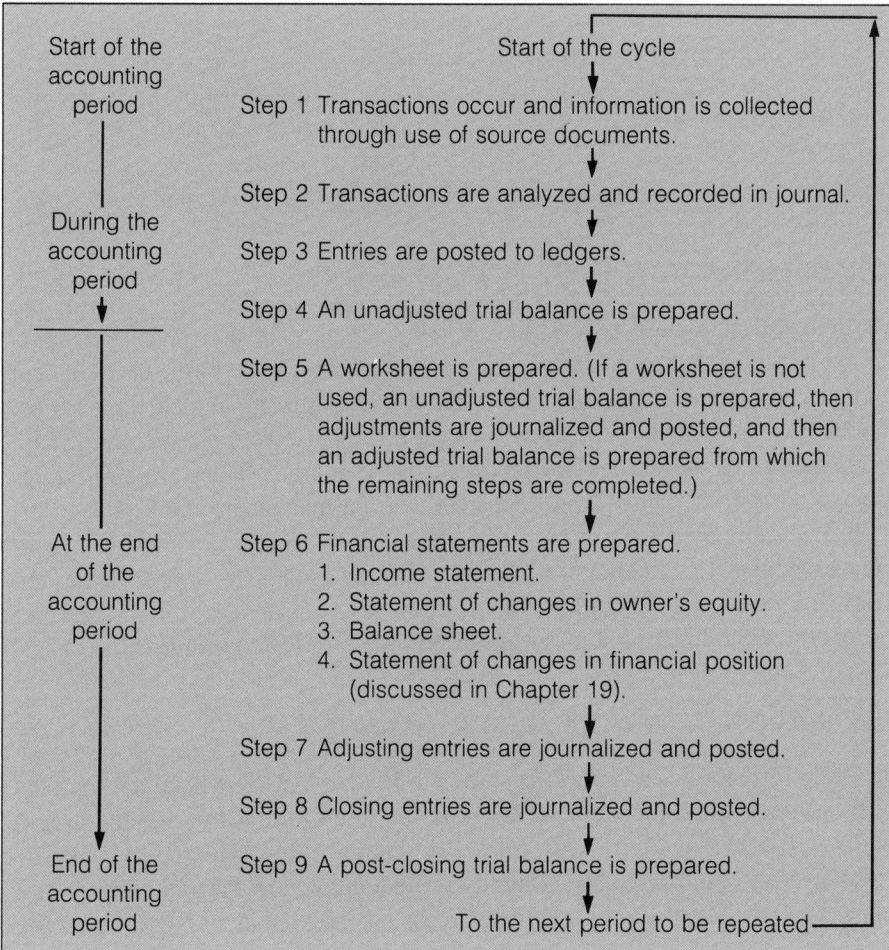

Figure 4–1

Diagram of the Accounting Cycle

(Step 6) and adjusting entries (Step 7)—were covered in detail in Chapter 3. In Chapter 3: (1) an unadjusted trial balance was prepared; (2) account balances were analyzed and adjusting entries were made directly in the journal and posted to the ledger; (3) an adjusted trial balance was prepared; and (4) the financial statements were prepared directly from the adjusted trial balance. An adjusted trial balance can be used to complete the closing process (Step 8) which is discussed in this chapter. A post-closing trial balance (Step 9) is taken from the ledger to verify that the accounts are in balance after the adjusting and closing entries are posted.

Thus, preparation of a worksheet (Step 5) is an optional step in the sequence. However, because of the volume of work and the amount of detail involved in completing the accounting cycle, accountants for most firms prepare a worksheet to help organize their work and minimize errors. When a worksheet is used, an unadjusted trial balance is prepared as part of the worksheet, adjusting entries are first entered in the worksheet before they are recorded in the journal, and an adjusted trial balance is developed as part of the worksheet. In this chapter, the worksheet will be used as a tool to assist in completion of the accounting cycle. Each of the steps in the cycle completed at the end of the period will be examined.

Some companies make reversing entries after the steps in the cycle diagrammed in Figure 4–1 have been completed. A *reversing entry,* which is dated as of the first day of the next accounting period, is a journal entry that is the opposite of a related adjusting entry that was made at the end of the current period. The term "reverse" simply means that the debit and credit in the reversing entry are the opposite of those in the adjusting entry.

STEP 5: PREPARATION OF A WORKSHEET

Objective 1: Preparation of a worksheet

A **worksheet** is a device designed to bring together in one place the information needed to prepare formal financial statements, except for the statement of changes in financial position, and to record the adjusting and closing entries. Worksheets are generally prepared in pencil so that errors can be erased and corrected before the entries are recorded in the journal. Here are some facts about a worksheet: (1) it is not a part of the permanent accounting records; (2) it is not prepared for use by the owners or management of the firm; (3) it replaces neither the financial statements nor the necessity to journalize and post the adjusting and closing entries; and (4) it is simply a tool used to gather and organize the information needed to complete the accounting cycle.

PREPARATION OF A WORKSHEET ILLUSTRATED

The basic format of a worksheet is shown in Figure 4–2. The heading contains the usual three parts: the name of the firm, the title of the form, and the period covered. The first column is used for the account titles. This column is followed by five sets of money columns provided for: (1) the unadjusted trial balance; (2) adjusting entries; (3) the adjusted trial balance; (4) the income

	STARBUCK REAL ESTATE OFFICE Worksheet For the Month Ended June 30, 1987									
	Unadjusted Trial Balance		Adjustments		Adjusted Trial Balance		Income Statement		Balance Sheet	
Account Title	Debit	Credit	Debit	Credit	Debit	Credit	Debit	Credit	Debit	Credit
Cash	43,558									
Accounts Receivable	5,400									
Prepaid Insurance	960									
Office Supplies Inventory	620									
Land	10,000									
Building	62,000									
Accumulated Depr.— Building										
Office Equipment	9,600									
Accumulated Depr.— Office Equipment										
Accounts Payable		4,600								
Unearned Appraisal Fees		280								
Mortgage Notes Payable		60,000								
Mike Starbuck, Capital		60,000								
Mike Starbuck, Drawing	600									
Commissions Revenue		9,600								
Appraisal Fees Revenue		250								
Salaries Expense	1,800									
Utilities Expense	72									
Advertising Expense	120									
Totals	134,730	134,730								

Figure 4–2
Worksheet Format With Unadjusted Trial Balance Entered (Step 1 in the preparation of a worksheet).

statement; and (5) the balance sheet. Each set consists of a debit column and a credit column, making a total of 10 columns for entering dollar amounts.

The steps followed in preparing a worksheet will be illustrated and described by using the information developed in Chapters 2 and 3 for the Starbuck Real Estate Office.

Step 1. **Enter the ledger account titles and balances in the Account Title and Unadjusted Trial Balance columns.** After all of the transactions that occurred during the period have been posted, an unadjusted trial balance is prepared to verify the equality of debit and credit account balances, as shown in Figure 4–2. The trial balance is taken directly from the general ledger.

Note that every account with a balance at the end of the period is listed. Also listed are the two accumulated depreciation accounts that currently have zero balances at this stage in the cycle. Since these accounts normally report a balance in all periods except the first, they are listed here to illustrate how they are extended in the worksheet. In the next period, these zero-balance accounts will carry forward a credit balance as a result of the adjusting process.

Step 2. **Enter the necessary adjusting entries in the Adjustments columns.** The adjusting entries are entered first in the worksheet in the Adjustments columns. After the worksheet is completed, the adjusting entries are recorded in the journal. To aid in journalizing the entries and in locating errors, each adjusting entry is identified by a separate letter so that the debit part of the entry can be cross-referenced to the credit part of the entry. The adjustments made in Figure 4–3 are the same as those explained in detail in Chapter 3. Adjustments were required for the following items.

Entry (a) Prepaid insurance expired, $40.
Entry (b) Office supplies used, $80.

Figure 4–3
Adjusting Entries are Entered in Adjustments Column and Account Balances Extended to the Adjusted Trial Balance Column (Steps 2 and 3 in the preparation of a worksheet).

STARBUCK REAL ESTATE OFFICE
Worksheet
For the Month Ended June 30, 1987

Account Title	Unadjusted Trial Balance Debit	Unadjusted Trial Balance Credit	Adjustments Debit	Adjustments Credit	Adjusted Trial Balance Debit	Adjusted Trial Balance Credit	Income Statement Debit	Income Statement Credit	Balance Sheet Debit	Balance Sheet Credit
Cash	43,558				43,558					
Accounts Receivable	5,400		(i) 400		5,800					
Prepaid Insurance	960			(a) 40	920					
Office Supplies Inventory	620			(b) 80	540					
Land	10,000				10,000					
Building	62,000				62,000					
Accumulated Depr.— Building				(c) 200		200				
Office Equipment	9,600				9,600					
Accumulated Depr.— Office Equipment				(d) 100		100				
Accounts Payable		4,600				4,600				
Unearned Appraisal Fees		280				280				
Mortgage Notes Payable		60,000				60,000				
Mike Starbuck, Capital		60,000				60,000				
Mike Starbuck, Drawing	600				600					
Commissions Revenue		9,600				9,600				
Appraisal Fees Revenue		250				250				
Salaries Expense	1,800		(e) 990		2,790					
Utilities Expense	72		(h) 210		282					
Advertising Expense	120				120					
Totals	134,730	134,730								
Insurance Expense			(a) 40		40					
Office Supplies Expense			(b) 80		80					
Depreciation Expense— Building			(c) 200		200					
Depreciation Expense— Office Equipment			(d) 100		100					
Salaries Payable				(e) 990		990				
Commissions Expense			(f) 4,800		4,800					
Commissions Payable				(f) 4,800		4,800				
Interest Expense			(g) 600		600					
Interest Payable				(g) 600		600				
Utilities Payable				(h) 210		210				
Service Fees Revenue				(i) 400		400				
Totals			7,420	7,420	142,030	142,030				

Entry (c) Depreciation on the building, $200.
Entry (d) Depreciation on the office equipment, $100.
Entry (e) Salaries earned by employees but not yet paid, $990.
Entry (f) Commissions earned by employees but not yet paid, $4,800.
Entry (g) Accrued interest on mortgage notes payable, $600.
Entry (h) Utilities used but not yet paid for, $210.
Entry (i) Revenue earned from management of apartment complex but not yet
           received, $400.

When entering the adjustments, if an account already has a balance in the Unadjusted Trial Balance columns, the adjusting amount is entered on the same line. The account titles required by adjusting entries that were not listed in the Unadjusted Trial Balance columns are added on lines immediately below the trial balance.

For example, in adjusting entry (a) the *Insurance Expense* account is debited and the *Prepaid Insurance* account is credited for $40. To enter the debit amount of this entry, it is necessary to add an *Insurance Expense* account on the line below the trial balance, because the account had a zero balance before the adjusting entry and consequently was not included in the unadjusted trial balance. The $40 credit is entered in the Adjustments credit column on the same line as the *Prepaid Insurance* account balance of $960. Thus, in this entry it is necessary to add only one new account. However, in adjusting entry (f), observe that both accounts affected by the entry must be entered below the unadjusted trial balance. The appropriate account titles were selected from the chart of accounts presented in Chapter 2 on page 51.

After all of the adjustments are entered, the two Adjustments columns are totaled to prove that the total debit adjustments equal the total credit adjustments. Adding the amount entered in a vertical column is called footing the column.

Step 3. **Prepare an adjusted trial balance.** In this step, each account

balance in the Unadjusted Trial Balance columns is combined with the corresponding adjustments, if any, in the Adjustments columns and the resulting balance is extended on the same line to the proper Adjusted Trial Balance column, as shown in Figure 4–3. The combined amounts entered in these two columns will be the same as the ledger account balances after the adjusting entries are recorded in the journal and posted to the ledger. (To confirm this, refer back to the adjusted trial balance of Starbuck Real Estate Office in Figure 3–5 on page 112.) Combining the amounts entered on each line—that is, adding or subtracting across the worksheet horizontally—is called **crossfooting.** The crossfooting must be done very carefully, because it is easy to make an error.

For those accounts unaffected by the adjustments, such as *Cash, Accounts Payable,* and *Commissions Revenue,* the balance is simply extended directly to the appropriate debit or credit column in the Adjusted Trial Balance columns. If an account has a debit balance in the Unadjusted Trial Balance column, a debit adjustment will increase the balance (see the *Salaries Expense* account), whereas a credit adjustment will decrease the balance (see the *Prepaid Insurance* account). An account with a credit balance is increased by a credit adjustment and decreased by a debit adjustment. In some cases, an account may not have a balance in the Unadjusted Trial Balance columns, but an adjustment is made to the account. In such cases, the amount of the adjustment is extended directly to the Adjusted Trial Balance columns. Examples are those accounts added below the unadjusted trial balance. After all adjusted account balances have been determined, the equality of debits and credits is verified by footing the two columns.

Step 4. Extend every account balance listed in the Adjusted Trial Balance columns to its proper financial statement column. Every account balance listed in the Adjusted Trial Balance columns is extended to either the Balance Sheet columns or the Income Statement columns, as shown in Figure 4–4. Asset, liability, and owner's equity accounts are extended to the proper Balance Sheet debit or credit column. Revenue accounts are extended to the Income Statement credit column, and expense accounts are extended to the Income Statement debit column. In other words, in this part of the process accounts are sorted on the basis of their financial statement classification.

Note that the *Drawing* account is extended to the Balance Sheet debit column, rather than to the Income Statement debit column, because it is not an expense. To avoid leaving out an account, the process should start by extending the first account listed, which is usually *Cash,* and then proceeding down the worksheet line by line. As a word of caution, the accounts listed in the Unadjusted Trial Balance are in Balance Sheet and Income Statement order. However, the accounts added below the unadjusted trial balance must be analyzed to determine whether the balance is extended to the Balance Sheet or Income Statement columns. The balance sheet columns will eventually contain all data needed to prepare both the statement of changes in owner's equity and the balance sheet.

Step 5. Add the two Income Statement and the two Balance Sheet columns. Compute the difference between the totals of the two Income Statement columns and enter this as a balancing amount in both the Income Statement and Balance Sheet columns. Add the four column totals again with the balancing amount included. After all the amounts have been extended to either the Income Statement or the Balance Sheet columns, the four columns are added and their totals entered at the bottom of each column. The net income or net loss for the period is determined by computing the difference between the totals of the two Income Statement columns as shown in Figure 4–4. The computation in this illustration is:

Total of the credit column	$10,250
Total of the debit column	9,012
Difference	$ 1,238

In this illustration, the revenues earned ($10,250) exceeded the expenses incurred ($9,012), resulting in a net income of $1,238. This difference is entered in the Income Statement debit column to balance the two columns. On the same line in the Account Title column, a caption, "Net income for the period," is entered to identify the nature of the item being entered in the two sets of columns.

STARBUCK REAL ESTATE OFFICE
Worksheet
For the Month Ended June 30, 1987

Account Title	Unadjusted Trial Balance		Adjustments		Adjusted Trial Balance		Income Statement		Balance Sheet	
	Debit	Credit	Debit	Credit	Debit	Credit	Debit	Credit	Debit	Credit
Cash	43,558				43,558				43,558	
Accounts Receivable	5,400		(i) 400		5,800				5,800	
Prepaid Insurance	960			(a) 40	920				920	
Office Supplies Inventory	620			(b) 80	540				540	
Land	10,000				10,000				10,000	
Building	62,000				62,000				62,000	
Accumulated Depr.— Building				(c) 200		200				200
Office Equipment	9,600				9,600				9,600	
Accumulated Depr.— Office Equipment				(d) 100		100				100
Accounts Payable		4,600				4,600				4,600
Unearned Appraisal Fees		280				280				280
Mortgage Notes Payable		60,000				60,000				60,000
Mike Starbuck, Capital		60,000				60,000				60,000
Mike Starbuck, Drawing	600				600				600	
Commissions Revenue		9,600				9,600		9,600		
Appraisal Fees Revenue		250				250		250		
Salaries Expense	1,800		(e) 990		2,790		2,790			
Utilities Expense	72		(h) 210		282		282			
Advertising Expense	120				120		120			
Totals	134,730	134,730								
Insurance Expense			(a) 40		40		40			
Office Supplies Expense			(b) 80		80		80			
Depreciation Expense— Building			(c) 200		200		200			
Depreciation Expense— Office Equipment			(d) 100		100		100			
Salaries Payable				(e) 990		990				990
Commissions Expense			(f) 4,800		4,800		4,800			
Commissions Payable				(f) 4,800		4,800				4,800
Interest Expense			(g) 600		600		600			
Interest Payable				(g) 600		600				600
Utilities Payable				(h) 210		210				210
Service Fees Revenue				(i) 400		400		400		
Totals			7,420	7,420	142,030	142,030	9,012	10,250	133,018	131,780
Net income for the period							1,238			1,238
Totals							10,250	10,250	133,018	133,018

Figure 4–4
Account Balances Extended to Financial Statement Columns and Totals Computed (Steps 4 and 5 in the preparation of a worksheet).

The net income is also entered on the same line in the Balance Sheet credit column to balance the debit and credit subtotals. The balance sheet subtotals are not equal because the revenues and expenses are changes in owner's equity extended to the Income Statement columns to determine the net income for the period. Stated another way, all of the account balances extended to the Balance Sheet columns from the Adjusted Trial Balance columns are end-of-period balances, except for the owner's *Capital* account of $60,000. The excess of revenues over expenses for the period represents an increase in owner's equity. The other change in the owner's equity, a decrease due to the cash withdrawal of $600, is reported in the balance sheet debit column. Therefore, extending the net income of $1,238 to the Balance Sheet credit column updates the owner's equity in the business to the end of the period.

The four columns are added again with the net income of $1,238 included as a balancing amount in the columns. If the debit and credit columns under Balance Sheet are not equal, there is an error in extending the amounts from the Adjusted Trial Balance columns.

If the Income Statement debit column had exceeded the Income Statement credit column, a net loss for the period would be indicated. In this case, the difference between the two columns would be captioned "Net loss for the period," and that difference entered in the Income Statement credit column and the Balance Sheet debit column.

Adding the debit and credit columns as work proceeds across the worksheet does not ensure that an error has not been made. For example, as discussed in Chapter 2, not all errors in the accounts are uncovered by the trial balance. Needed adjustments may have been omitted entirely, or the wrong adjusting amounts may have been entered in the worksheet. In Step 4, an amount may be extended to the wrong column—as in extending the credit balance in the *Unearned Appraisal Fees* account, a liability, to the Income Statement credit column. This will not destroy the equality of debits and credits, but it *will* result in an overstatement of revenues in the income statement, an understatement of liabilities, and an overstatement of owner's equity in the balance sheet.

Once the worksheet is completed, it is used to prepare the financial statements and to journalize adjusting and closing entries.

STEP 6: PREPARATION OF FINANCIAL STATEMENTS

Objective 2: Preparation of financial statements

Because the worksheet format provides for sorting account balances between the income statement and the balance sheet, preparation of the formal financial statements—such as the income statement in Figure 4–5, the statement of changes in owner's equity in Figure 4–6, and the balance sheet in Figure 4–7—is a relatively easy step.

The income statement in Figure 4–5 is prepared from account balances listed in the two Income Statement columns in Figure 4–4. The statement of changes in owner's equity, illustrated by Figure 4–6, and the balance sheet, illustrated by Figure 4–7, are prepared from data contained in the Balance Sheet columns in Figure 4–4.

STEP 7: RECORDING ADJUSTING ENTRIES

Objective 3: Recording adjusting entries

After the financial statements have been prepared, the adjusting entries are entered in the general journal, as shown in Figure 4–8. The necessary information is available directly from the Adjustments columns of the worksheet. Note that the entries are dated on the last day of the accounting period and, generally, the caption "Adjusting Entries" is written in the general journal to separate these entries from other transactions. After the adjusting entries are

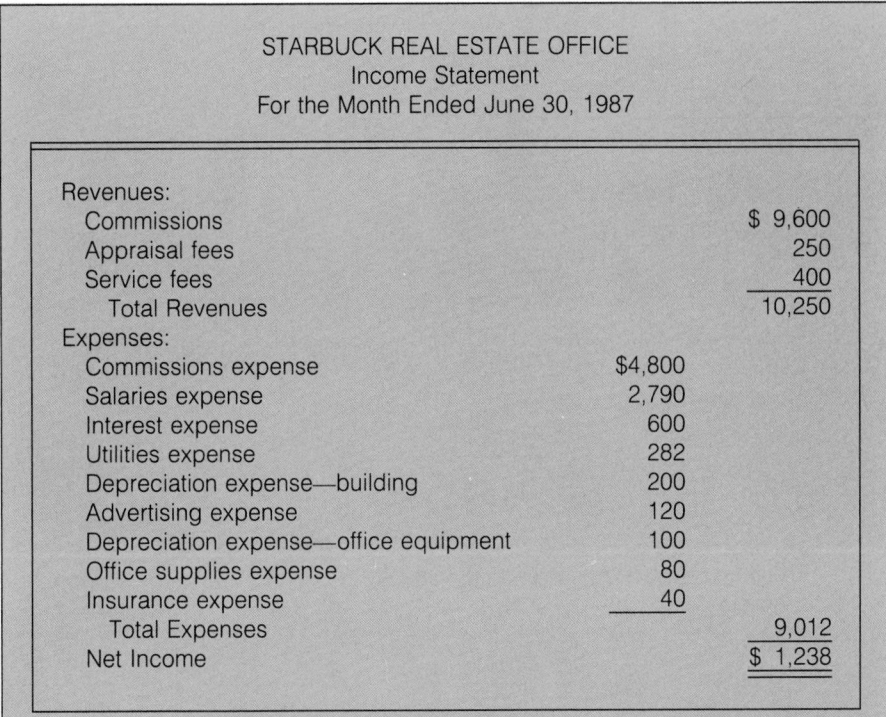

Figure 4–5
Income Statement

STARBUCK REAL ESTATE OFFICE
Income Statement
For the Month Ended June 30, 1987

Revenues:		
Commissions		$ 9,600
Appraisal fees		250
Service fees		400
Total Revenues		10,250
Expenses:		
Commissions expense	$4,800	
Salaries expense	2,790	
Interest expense	600	
Utilities expense	282	
Depreciation expense—building	200	
Advertising expense	120	
Depreciation expense—office equipment	100	
Office supplies expense	80	
Insurance expense	40	
Total Expenses		9,012
Net Income		$ 1,238

Figure 4–6
Statement of
Changes in Owner's
Equity

STARBUCK REAL ESTATE OFFICE
Statement of Changes in Owner's Equity
For the Month Ended June 30, 1987

Mike Starbuck, Original investment, June 1, 1987	$60,000
Add: Net income for the month of June	1,238
Total	61,238
Less: Withdrawals during the month of June	600
Mike Starbuck, Capital, June 30, 1987	$60,638

posted, the ledger account balances should agree with the balances reported in the worksheet.

STEP 8: CLOSING THE ACCOUNTS

The income statement reports revenues earned and expenses incurred to earn those revenues during a single accounting period. Data needed to prepare the income statement are accumulated in the individual revenue and expense accounts. Once the income statement has been prepared for the current period, the revenue and expense accounts have served their intended purpose, and they are closed or cleared (reduced to a zero balance) by transferring their

**Objective 4:
Preparation of
closing entries**

Figure 4–7
Balance Sheet

STARBUCK REAL ESTATE OFFICE
Balance Sheet
June 30, 1987

Assets

Current Assets:

Cash	$43,558	
Accounts receivable	5,800	
Prepaid insurance	920	
Office supplies inventory	540	
Total Current Assets		$ 50,818

Property, Plant, and Equipment:

Land		$10,000	
Building	$62,000		
Less: Accumulated depreciation	200	61,800	
Office equipment	9,600		
Less: Accumulated depreciation	100	9,500	
Total Property, Plant, and Equipment			81,300
Total Assets			$132,118

Liabilities and Owner's Equity
Liabilities

Current Liabilities:

Accounts payable	$4,600	
Commissions payable	4,800	
Salaries payable	990	
Interest payable	600	
Unearned appraisal fees	280	
Utilities payable	210	
Current portion of mortgage notes payable	3,000	
Total Current Liabilities		$ 14,480

Long-term Liabilities:

Mortgage notes payable		57,000
Total Liabilities		71,480

Owner's Equity

Mike Starbuck, Capital, June 30, 1987		60,638
Total Liabilities and Owner's Equity		$132,118

balances to the *Income Summary* account, as will now be discussed. This step in the accounting cycle is referred to as the closing process, and journal entries made to close the accounts are called **closing entries.** The closing process results in each revenue and expense account beginning the next period with a zero balance. Because revenue and expense accounts are closed each period, they are called **temporary accounts** or **nominal** accounts. Balance sheet accounts are not closed; their ending balances of one period are carried forward and become the beginning balances of the next period. Thus, balance sheet accounts are called **permanent accounts** or **real accounts.**

As emphasized before, owner's equity is increased by revenues and de-

GENERAL JOURNAL				Page 3
Date	Accounts and Explanation	Post Ref.	Debit	Credit
	Adjusting Entries			
June 30	Insurance Expense	521	40	
	Prepaid Insurance	110		40
	To record insurance expense for June.			
30	Office Supplies Expense	530	80	
	Office Supplies Inventory	111		80
	To record office supplies used in June.			
30	Depreciation Expense—Building	540	200	
	Accumulated Depreciation— Building	161		200
	To record depreciation for June on the building.			
30	Depreciation Expense—Off. Equip.	541	100	
	Accumulated Depreciation— Office Equipment	171		100
	To record depreciation for June on office equipment.			
30	Salaries Expense	500	990	
	Salaries Payable	210		990
	To record unpaid salaries at the end of June.			
30	Commissions Expense	505	4,800	
	Commissions Payable	211		4,800
	To record unpaid commissions at the end of June			
30	Interest Expense	560	600	
	Interest Payable	215		600
	To record accrued interest on mortgage notes payable at the end of June.			
30	Utilities Expense	510	210	
	Utilities Payable	216		210
	To record unpaid utilities at the end of June.			
30	Accounts Receivable	104	400	
	Service Fees Revenue	402		400
	To record revenue earned from management of apartment complex during June.			

Figure 4–8
Recording of Adjusting Entries

creased by expenses. Such changes are recorded in separate temporary accounts, but are really changes in the owner's *Capital* account. Therefore, journal entries are needed to transfer the net change in owner's equity, from revenues and expenses during the period, to the owner's *Capital* account. When the closing entries are entered in the journal, the individual revenue and expense accounts are debited or credited as will be shown.

A new temporary account, called the *Income Summary* account, is normally established to summarize the balances in the revenue and expense accounts. For a service firm, this is the only time in the accounting process when this account is used. Closing entries are generally made in the following sequence.

1. Each revenue account is reduced to zero by transferring its balance to the *Income Summary* account.
2. Each expense account is reduced to zero by transferring its balance to the *Income Summary* account.
3. The balance in the *Income Summary* account is transferred to the owner's *Capital* account.
4. The balance in the owner's *Drawing* account is transferred to the owner's *Capital* account.

The information needed to prepare the closing entries is conveniently available from the Income Statement columns of the worksheet. The process is diagrammed in Figure 4–9 in T account format, using the totals from the Income Statement columns in the worksheet presented in Figure 4–4.

Closing Entries Illustrated

The owner's equity and income statement account balances after the adjusting entries were posted are shown in Figure 4–10 for the Starbuck Real Estate Office.

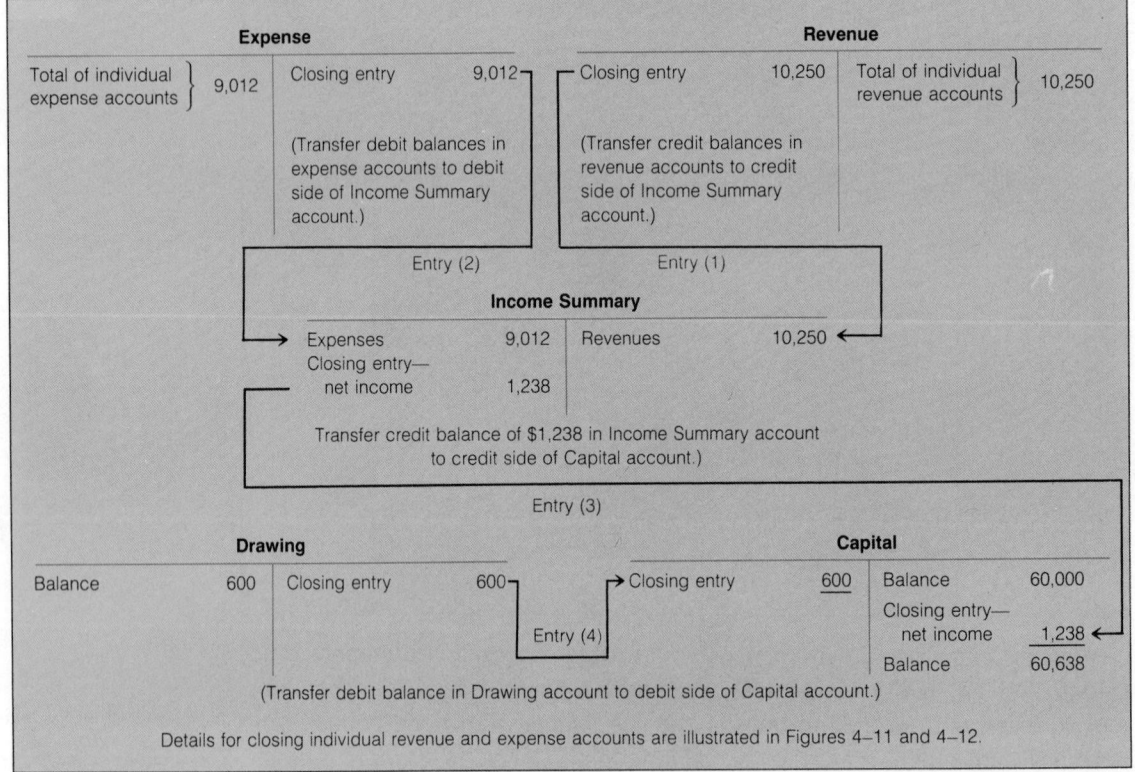

Figure 4–9
Diagram of Closing Process

The Capital and Temporary Accounts of
STARBUCK REAL ESTATE OFFICE
After Adjusting Entries and Before Closing Entries Are Posted

Figure 4–10
Partial General
Ledger

Account   Mike Starbuck, Capital   Account No.   300

Date		Explanation	Post. Ref.	Debit	Credit	Balance
1987 June	1		1		60,000	60,000

Account   Mike Starbuck, Drawing   Account No.   310

Date		Explanation	Post. Ref.	Debit	Credit	Balance
1987 June	23		2	600		600

Account   Income Summary   Account No.   350

Date		Explanation	Post. Ref.	Debit	Credit	Balance

Account   Commissions Revenue   Account No.   400

Date		Explanation	Post. Ref.	Debit	Credit	Balance
1987 June	15		1		4,200	4,200
	19		2		5,400	9,600

Account   Appraisal Fees Revenue   Account No.   401

Date		Explanation	Post. Ref.	Debit	Credit	Balance
1987 June	23		2		250	250

Account   Service Fees Revenue   Account No.   402

Date		Explanation	Post. Ref.	Debit	Credit	Balance
1987 June	30	Adj. ent (i)	3		400	400

Figure 4–10
Continued

Account   Salaries Expense   Account No.   500

Date		Explanation	Post. Ref.	Debit	Credit	Balance
1987 June	22		2	1,800		1,800
	30	Adj. ent. (e)	3	990		2,790

Account   Commissions Expense   Account No.   505

Date		Explanation	Post. Ref.	Debit	Credit	Balance
1987 June	30	Adj. ent. (f)	3	4,800		4,800

Account   Utilities Expense   Account No.   510

Date		Explanation	Post. Ref.	Debit	Credit	Balance
1987 June	30		2	72		72
	30	Adj. ent. (h)	3	210		282

Account   Advertising Expense   Account No.   520

Date		Explanation	Post. Ref.	Debit	Credit	Balance
1987 June	6		1	120		120

Account   Insurance Expense   Account No.   521

Date		Explanation	Post. Ref.	Debit	Credit	Balance
1987 June	30	Adj. ent. (a)	3	40		40

Account   Office Supplies Expense   Account No.   530

Date		Explanation	Post. Ref.	Debit	Credit	Balance
1987 June	30	Adj. ent. (b)	3	80		80

Figure 4–10
Continued

Account   Depreciation Expense—Building   Account No.   540

Date		Explanation	Post. Ref.	Debit	Credit	Balance
1987 June	30	Adj. ent. (c)	3	200		200

Account   Depreciation Expense—Office Equipment   Account No.   541

Date		Explanation	Post. Ref.	Debit	Credit	Balance
1987 June	30	Adj. ent. (d)	3	100		100

Account   Interest Expense   Account No.   560

Date		Explanation	Post. Ref.	Debit	Credit	Balance
1987 June	30	Adj. ent. (g)	3	600		600

Closing the Revenue Accounts

A revenue account normally contains a credit balance. Therefore, to close the account requires debiting it for an amount equal to its credit balance. The offsetting credit is made to the *Income Summary* account. The compound journal entry needed to close the revenue accounts is:

GENERAL JOURNAL					Page 4
Date		Accounts and Explanation	Post Ref.	Debit	Credit
		Closing Entries			
June	30	Commissions Revenue	400	9,600	
		Appraisal Fees Revenue	401	250	
		Service Fees Revenue	402	400	
		Income Summary	350		10,250
		To close the revenue accounts.			

In the journal, the adjusting entries are separated from the closing entries by the caption "Closing Entries." For posting purposes, it is assumed that the closing entries are entered on page four of the general journal. Also, account numbers are entered in the posting reference column to indicate that the amounts have been posted.

The effect of this entry is to transfer the sum of the credit balances in the revenue accounts to the credit side of the *Income Summary* account and reduce the revenue accounts to a zero balance for the start of the next period, as

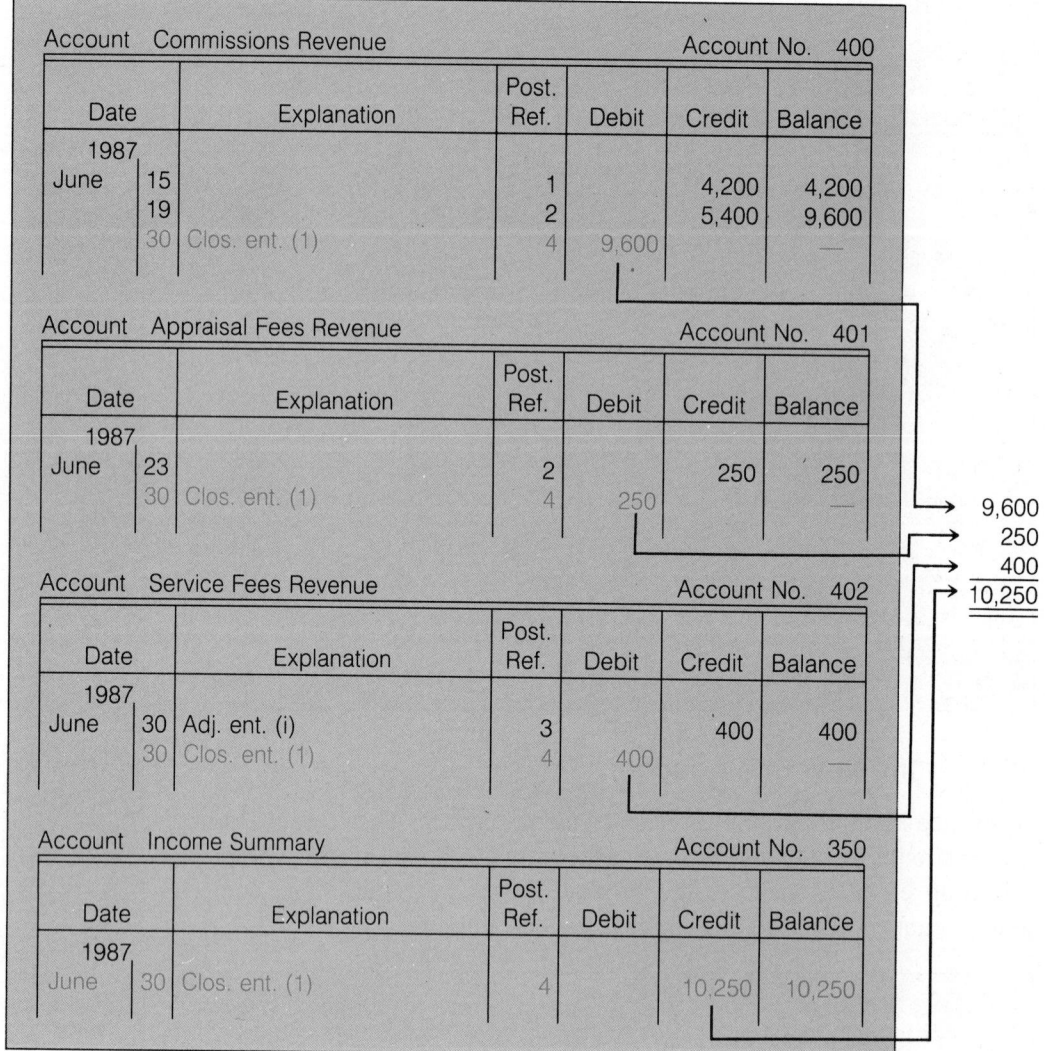

Figure 4–11
Closing the Revenue Accounts to the Income Summary

shown in Figure 4–11. The closing entries are shown in the ledger accounts in color for illustrative purposes only.

Closing the Expense Accounts

Expense accounts normally have debit balances. Each expense account is therefore credited for an amount equal to its balance, and the *Income Summary* account is debited for the sum of the individual balances. The compound journal entry is:

June	30	Income Summary	350	9,012	
		Salaries Expense	500		2,790
		Commissions Expense	505		4,800
		Utilities Expense	510		282
		Advertising Expense	520		120
		Insurance Expense	521		40

	Office Supplies Expense	530			80
	Depreciation Expense—Building	540			200
	Depreciation Expense—				
	Office Equipment	541			100
	Interest Expense	560			600
	To close the expense accounts.				

As shown in Figure 4–12 on pages 164–165, the entry transfers the sum of the debit balances of $9,012 as a debit to the *Income Summary* account and reduces each expense account to a zero balance.

Closing the Income Summary Account

After the first two closing entries are posted, the balances formerly reported in the individual revenue and expense accounts are summarized in the *Income Summary* account. If revenues exceed expenses, a net income is earned and the *Income Summary* account will contain a credit balance. If expenses exceed revenues, a net loss is indicated and the account will have a debit balance. In either case, the balance is transferred to the owner's *Capital* account.

The Starbuck Real Estate Office earned a net income during June. The credit balance of $1,238 in the *Income Summary* account is closed as follows.

June	30	Income Summary	350	1,238	
		Mike Starbuck, Capital	300		1,238
		To close the Income Summary			
		account.			

This entry is posted to the accounts as shown in Figure 4–13 on page 166.

The effect of this entry is to recognize that the net assets (i.e., assets minus liabilities) of Starbuck Real Estate Office increased this period due to profitable operations. This increase in net assets adds to the owner's interest in the firm. Conversely, if a net loss is reported, the *Income Summary* account is credited to reduce the account to a zero balance and the *Capital* account is debited to reflect a decrease in owner's equity from operations.

Closing the Drawing Account

The debit balance in the *Drawing* account reflects the decrease in the owner's interest during the period from the withdrawal of cash and/or other assets for personal use. The balance in the account is transferred directly to the owner's *Capital* account by the following entry.

June	30	Mike Starbuck, Capital	300	600	
		Mike Starbuck, Drawing	310		600
		To close the Drawing account.			

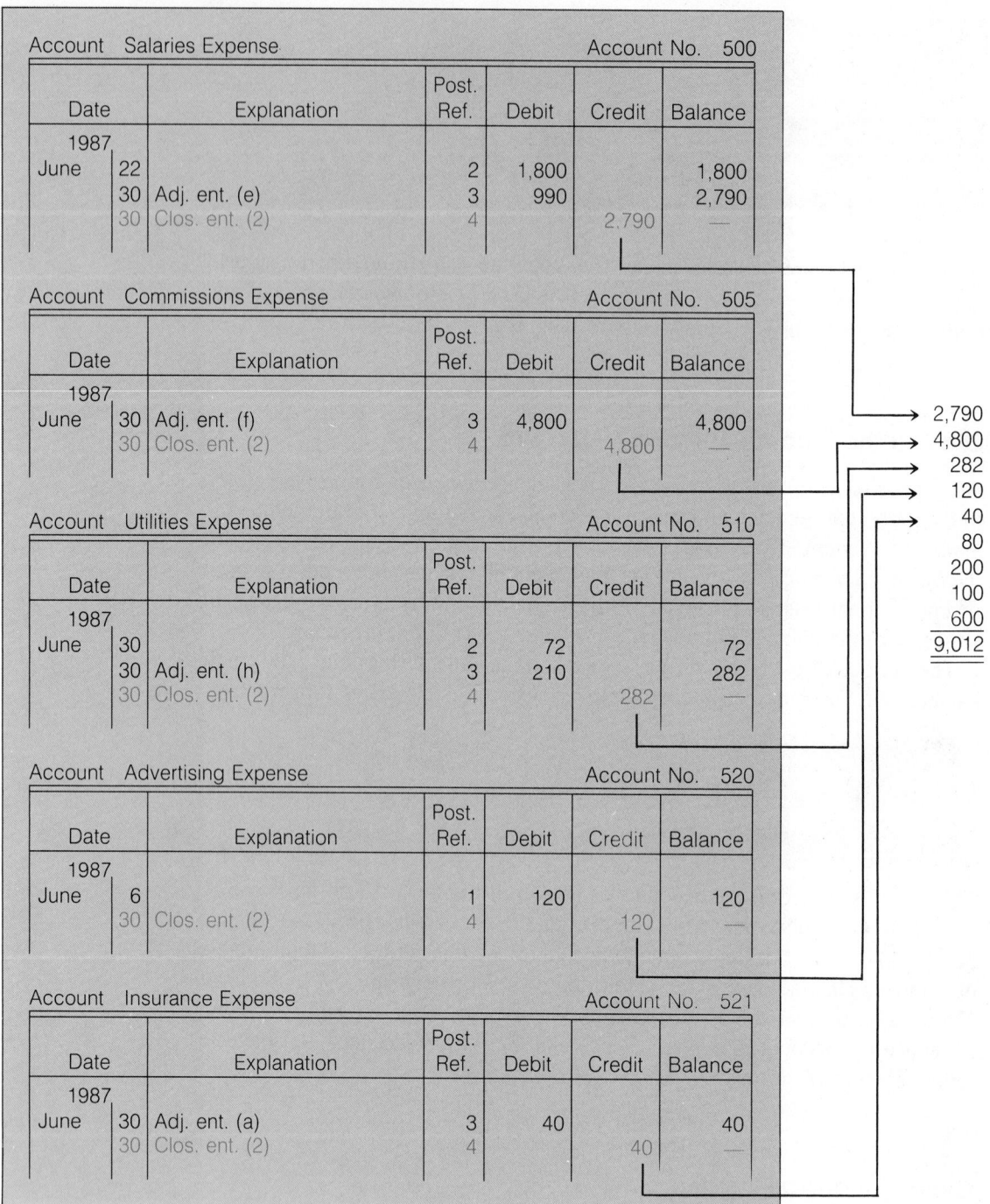

Figure 4–12
Closing the Expense Accounts to the Income Summary

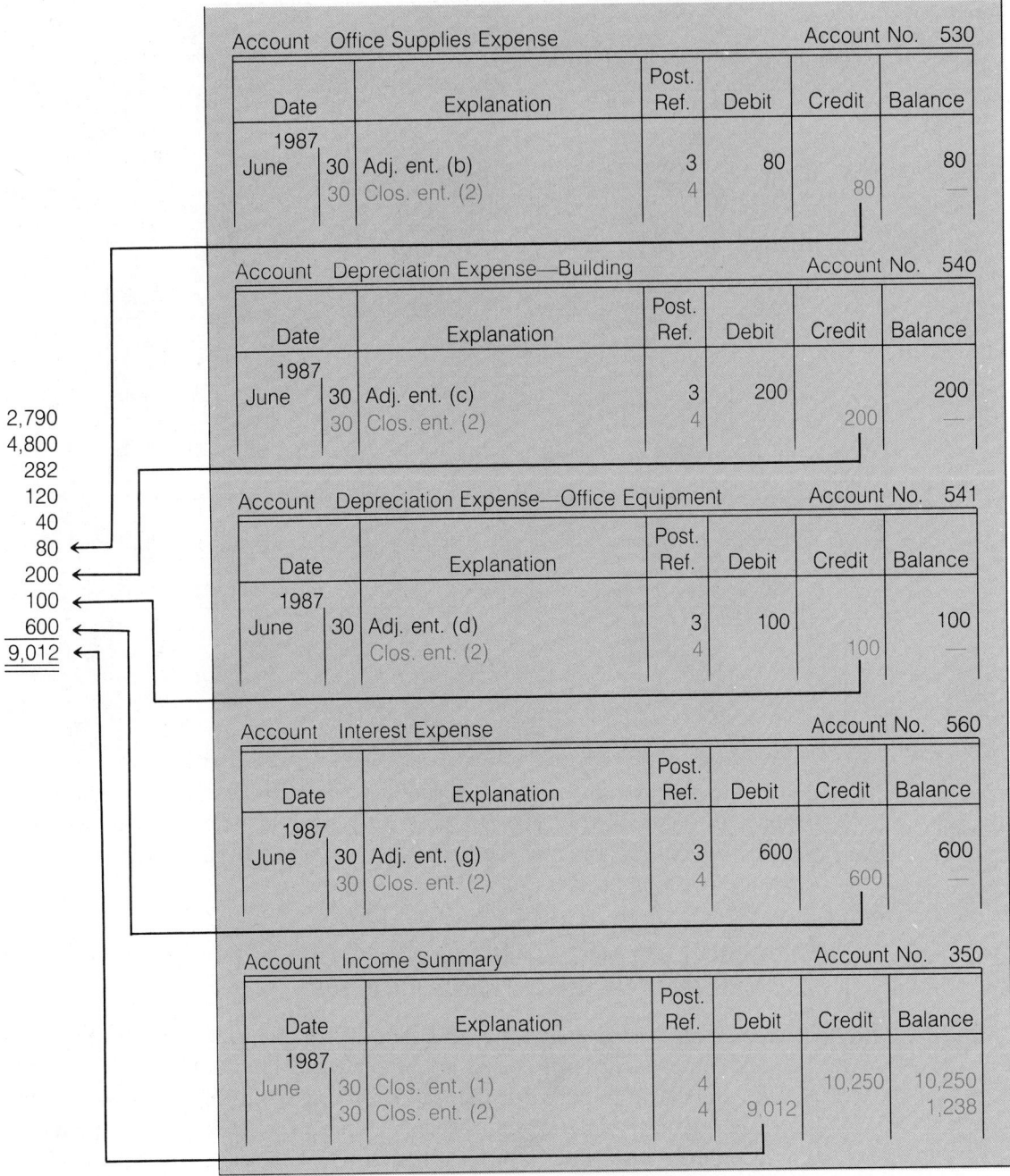

Figure 4–12
Continued

Figure 4–13
Closing the Income
Summary and Draw-
ing Account

Account Income Summary						Account No. 350
Date		Explanation	Post. Ref.	Debit	Credit	Balance
1987 June	30	Clos. ent. (1)	4		10,250	10,250
	30	Clos. ent. (2)	4	9,012		1,238
	30	Clos. ent. (3)	4	1,238		—

Account Mike Starbuck, Drawing						Account No. 310
Date		Explanation	Post. Ref.	Debit	Credit	Balance
1987 June	23		2	600		600
	30	Clos. ent. (4)	4		600	—

Account Mike Starbuck, Capital						Account No. 300
Date		Explanation	Post. Ref.	Debit	Credit	Balance
1987 June	1		1		60,000	60,000
	30	Clos. ent. (3)	4		1,238	61,238
	30	Clos. ent. (4)	4	600		60,638

After the entry is posted, the *Drawing* account will have a zero balance, as shown in Figure 4–13. The *Drawing* account is not closed to the *Income Summary* account, because the withdrawal of assets by the owner is not an expense of doing business.

ACCOUNT BALANCES AFTER COMPLETION OF THE CLOSING PROCESS

The accounts for the Starbuck Real Estate Office after both the adjusting and closing entries have been posted are presented in Figure 4–14. The closing entries are shown in color for illustration only. Note in Figure 4–14 that the revenue, expense, and drawing accounts all have zero balances and are ready for recording transactions of the next period. The balances in the balance sheet accounts are carried forward to the next period and are the only accounts that have a balance.

STEP 9: THE POST-CLOSING TRIAL BALANCE

Objective 5: Preparing a post-closing trial balance

After the closing entries have been posted, a trial balance is prepared to verify the equality of debits and credits in the ledger. Because the trial balance is taken from the ledger after the revenue and expense accounts have been closed, it is called a **post-closing trial balance.** At this point, only the balance sheet

Figure 4–14
General Ledger after
Completion of the
Closing Process

Account   Cash   Account No.   100

Date		Explanation	Post. Ref.	Debit	Credit	Balance
1987						
June	1		1	60,000		60,000
	1		1		12,000	48,000
	3		1		960	47,040
	5		1		5,000	42,040
	6		1		120	41,920
	22		2		1,800	40,120
	23		2	250		40,370
	23		2		600	39,770
	27		2		620	39,150
	29		2	280		39,430
	30		2		72	39,358
	30		2	4,200		43,558

Account   Accounts Receivable   Account No.   104

Date		Explanation	Post. Ref.	Debit	Credit	Balance
1987						
June	15		1	4,200		4,200
	19		2	5,400		9,600
	30		2		4,200	5,400
	30	Adj. ent. (i)	3	400		5,800

Account   Prepaid Insurance   Account No.   110

Date		Explanation	Post. Ref.	Debit	Credit	Balance
1987						
June	3		1	960		960
	30	Adj. ent. (a)	3		40	920

Account   Office Supplies Inventory   Account No. 111

Date		Explanation	Post. Ref.	Debit	Credit	Balance
1987						
June	5		1	620		620
	30	Adj. ent. (b)	3		80	540

Account   Land   Account No.   150

Date		Explanation	Post. Ref.	Debit	Credit	Balance
1987						
June	1		1	10,000		10,000

Figure 4–14
Continued

Account   Building   Account No.   160

Date		Explanation	Post. Ref.	Debit	Credit	Balance
1987 June	1		1	62,000		62,000

Account   Accumulated Depreciation—Building   Account No.   161

Date		Explanation	Post. Ref.	Debit	Credit	Balance
1987 June	30	Adj. ent. (c)	3		200	200

Account   Office Equipment   Account No.   170

Date		Explanation	Post. Ref.	Debit	Credit	Balance
1987 June	5		1	9,600		9,600

Account   Accumulated Depreciation—Office Equipment   Account No.   171

Date		Explanation	Post. Ref.	Debit	Credit	Balance
1987 June	30	Adj. ent. (d)	3		100	100

Account   Accounts Payable   Account No.   200

Date		Explanation	Post. Ref.	Debit	Credit	Balance
1987 June	5		1		620	620
	5		1		4,600	5,220
	27		2	620		4,600

Account   Salaries Payable   Account No.   210

Date		Explanation	Post. Ref.	Debit	Credit	Balance
1987 June	30	Adj. ent. (e)	3		990	990

Figure 4–14
Continued

Account   Commissions Payable   Account No.   211

Date		Explanation	Post. Ref.	Debit	Credit	Balance
1987 June	30	Adj. ent. (f)	3		4,800	4,800

Account   Interest Payable   Account No.   215

Date		Explanation	Post. Ref.	Debit	Credit	Balance
1987 June	30	Adj. ent. (g)	3		600	600

Account   Utilities Payable   Account No.   216

Date		Explanation	Post. Ref.	Debit	Credit	Balance
1987 June	30	Adj. ent. (h)	3		210	210

Account   Unearned Appraisal Fees   Account No.   220

Date		Explanation	Post. Ref.	Debit	Credit	Balance
1987 June	29		2		280	280

Account   Mortgage Notes Payable   Account No.   230

Date		Explanation	Post. Ref.	Debit	Credit	Balance
1987 June	1		1		60,000	60,000

Account   Mike Starbuck, Capital   Account No.   300

Date		Explanation	Post. Ref.	Debit	Credit	Balance
1987 June	1		1		60,000	60,000
	30	Clos. ent. (3)	4		1,238	61,238
	30	Clos. ent. (4)	4	600		60,638

Figure 4–14
Continued

Account   Mike Starbuck, Drawing   Account No.   350

Date		Explanation	Post. Ref.	Debit	Credit	Balance
1987 June	23		2	600		600
	30	Clos. ent. (4)	4		600	—

Account   Income Summary   Account No.   350

Date		Explanation	Post. Ref.	Debit	Credit	Balance
1987 June	30	Clos. ent. (1)	4		10,250	10,250
	30	Clos. ent. (2)	4	9,012		1,238
	30	Clos. ent. (3)	4	1,238		—

Account   Commissions Revenue   Account No.   400

Date		Explanation	Post. Ref.	Debit	Credit	Balance
1987 June	15		1		4,200	4,200
	19		2		5,400	9,600
	30	Clos. ent. (1)	4	9,600		—

Account   Appraisal Fees Revenue   Account No.   401

Date		Explanation	Post. Ref.	Debit	Credit	Balance
1987 June	23		2		250	250
	30	Clos. ent. (1)	4	250		—

Account   Service Fees Revenue   Account No.   402

Date		Explanation	Post. Ref.	Debit	Credit	Balance
1987 June	30	Adj. ent. (i)	3		400	400
	30	Clos. ent. (1)	4	400		—

Figure 4–14
Continued

Account   Salaries Expense   Account No.   500

Date	Explanation	Post. Ref.	Debit	Credit	Balance
1987 June 22		2	1,800		1,800
30	Adj. ent. (e)	3	990		2,790
30	Clos. ent. (2)	4		2,790	—

Account   Commissions Expense   Account No.   505

Date	Explanation	Post. Ref.	Debit	Credit	Balance
1987 June 30	Adj. ent. (f)	3	4,800		4,800
30	Clos. ent. (2)	4		4,800	—

Account   Utilities Expense   Account No.   510

Date	Explanation	Post. Ref.	Debit	Credit	Balance
1987 June 30		2	72		72
30	Adj. ent. (h)	3	210		282
30	Clos. ent. (2)	4		282	—

Account   Advertising Expense   Account No.   520

Date	Explanation	Post. Ref.	Debit	Credit	Balance
1987 June 6		1	120		120
30	Clos. ent. (2)	4		120	—

Account   Insurance Expense   Account No.   521

Date	Explanation	Post. Ref.	Debit	Credit	Balance
1987 June 30	Adj. ent. (a)	3	40		40
30	Clos. ent. (2)	4		40	—

Figure 4–14
Continued

Account	Office Supplies Expense				Account No.	530
Date	Explanation	Post. Ref.	Debit	Credit	Balance	
1987 June 30	Adj. ent. (b)	3	80		80	
30	Clos. ent. (2)	4		80	—	

Account	Depreciation Expense—Building				Account No.	540
Date	Explanation	Post. Ref.	Debit	Credit	Balance	
1987 June 30	Adj. ent. (c)	3	200		200	
30	Clos. ent. (2)	4		200	—	

Account	Depreciation Expense—Office Equipment				Account No.	541
Date	Explanation	Post. Ref.	Debit	Credit	Balance	
1987 June 30	Adj. ent. (d)	3	100		100	
30	Clos. ent. (2)	4		100	—	

Account	Interest Expense				Account No.	560
Date	Explanation	Post. Ref.	Debit	Credit	Balance	
1987 June 30	Adj. ent. (g)	3	600		600	
30	Clos. ent. (2)	4		600	—	

accounts (i.e., the permanent accounts) should have balances. A post-closing trial balance for the Starbuck Real Estate Office is presented in Figure 4–15.

PREPARING INTERIM STATEMENTS WITHOUT CLOSING THE ACCOUNTS

It is common practice for a firm to prepare monthly financial statements for use by management. In addition, most large firms issue quarterly statements to external statement users. Such statements are called interim statements because they are prepared between the annual reports issued at the fiscal year-end. The preceding illustration assumed that (1) monthly financial statements were to be prepared; and (2) the accounting cycle, including journalizing and posting both adjusting and closing entries, was completed at the end of the month. However, most firms adjust and close their accounts at the end of the fiscal period only. Information needed to prepare interim financial statements is accumulated on the worksheet only. In other words, most accountants make

Figure 4–15
Post-closing Trial
Balance

STARBUCK REAL ESTATE OFFICE
Post-closing Trial Balance
June 30, 1987

Account Title	Debit	Credit
Cash	$ 43,558	
Accounts Receivable	5,800	
Prepaid Insurance	920	
Office Supplies Inventory	540	
Land	10,000	
Building	62,000	
Accumulated Depreciation—Building		$ 200
Office Equipment	9,600	
Accumulated Depreciation—Office Equipment		100
Accounts Payable		4,600
Salaries Payable		990
Commissions Payable		4,800
Interest Payable		600
Utilities Payable		210
Unearned Appraisal Fees		280
Mortgage Notes Payable		60,000
Mike Starbuck, Capital		60,638
Totals	$132,418	$132,418

adjustments on the worksheet, but do not enter them in the accounting records or close the accounts until the end of the fiscal period.

REVERSING ENTRIES

In the Starbuck Real Estate Office illustration, the closing process was the last step in the accounting cycle. After this step is completed, the records are ready for entering the transactions of the next period. However, some firms prepare reversing entries as a bridge between the last step in the accounting cycle of one year and the first step in the next period. A **reversing entry** is a journal entry that is the opposite of a related adjusting entry that was made at the end of the current period. It is dated as of the first day of the next accounting period. The reversing process *is a bookkeeping technique made to simplify the recording of regular transactions in the next period*.

Objective 6: Purpose of reversing entries

REVERSING ENTRIES ILLUSTRATED

To illustrate reversing entries, we will continue the same accrued salaries adjustment that was used in Chapter 3: salaries paid during June were $1,800 and $990 of unpaid salaries were accrued on June 30; salaries earned for the period June 23 to July 6 in the amount of $1,700 are to be paid on July 6.

Throughout an accounting period, the normal entry to record the payment of salaries is a debit to *Salaries Expense* and a credit to *Cash*.

At the end of June, accrued salaries were recorded by the following *adjusting entry.*

June	30	Salaries Expense	990	
		Salaries Payable		990
		To record unpaid salaries at the end of June.		

At the end of the period, the balance of $2,790 in the *Salaries Expense* account is closed to the *Income Summary* account and the *Salaries Payable* balance of $990 is reported as a liability in the balance sheet.

If the adjusting entry is not reversed, the following entry is made on July 6 to record payment.

July	6	Salaries Payable	990	
		Salaries Expense	710	
		Cash		1,700
		To record payment of salaries for the period June 23 to July 6.		

Because the $1,700 payment is for salaries earned during two different accounting periods, the payment must be divided into two elements. First, the $990 debit settles the liability for the salaries earned by employees in June that were reported as an expense in June. The $710 debit to the expense account properly recognizes as an expense that portion of the payment made for salaries incurred in July.

After posting the entry, the *Salaries Payable* and *Salaries Expense* accounts appear as follows.

Salaries Payable

		6/30 Adj. ent.	990
7/6	990	7/1 Bal.	990
		Bal.	-0-

Salaries Expense

6/22	1,800	6/30 Clos. ent.	2,790
6/30 Adj. ent.	990		
	2,790		2,790
7/1 Bal.	-0-		
7/6	710		

Note that the July 6 entry requires two debits—a variation from the normal entry of one debit to the *Salaries Expense* account. Thus, a change from the normal procedures is necessary. The accountant or bookkeeper is required to refer to the adjusting entry or the *Salaries Payable* account in the general ledger in order to divide the payment between the two accounts. To simplify the July 6 entry, a ***reversing entry*** may be made to reverse the effects of the adjusting entry as follows.

July	1	Salaries Payable	990	
		Salaries Expense		990
		To reverse the adjusting entry to accrue		
		unpaid salaries.		

Compare this reversing entry to the adjusting entry on June 30. Observe that the debit and credit amounts are the same in both entries, but the account debited (*Salaries Expense*) in the adjusting entry is credited in the reversing entry, while the account credited (*Salaries Payable*) in the adjusting entry is debited in the reversing entry. In other words, the reversal is the opposite of the adjusting entry.

The reversing entry transfers the liability to the expense account. This produces a temporary credit balance (a liability) of $990 in the expense account on July 1, since it had a zero balance before the reversing entry as a result of the closing process. This permits making the normal entry to record the payment on July 6 as follows.

July	6	Salaries Expense	1,700	
		Cash		1,700
		To record payment of salaries for the		
		period June 23 to July 6.		

After this entry is posted the accounts are as follows.

Salaries Payable

7/1 Rev. Ent.	990	6/30 Adj. ent.	990
		Bal.	-0-

Salaries Expense

6/22	1,800	6/30 Clos. ent.	2,790
6/30 Adj. ent.	990		
	2,790		2,790
7/6	1,700	7/1 Rev. ent.	990
7/6 Bal.	710		

The debit of $1,700 to the expense account is partially offset by the credit of $990 made in the reversing entry. This leaves a balance of $710 in the *Salaries Expense* account, which is the expense for July.

A comparison of the account balances will reveal that the two approaches produce identical results. Salaries expense for June and July are $2,790 and $710, respectively, and a liability for $990 is reported in the June 30 balance sheet.

Reversing entries are also useful when many similar transactions involve the computation of accruals. For example, a bank may have thousands of outstanding notes receivable. At the end of the period, interest earned but not received must be accrued in order to properly report interest revenue and interest receivable in the financial statements. If a reversing entry is not made, then each time that an interest payment is received in the next period, an employee must refer back to the list of accruals. This is necessary in order to divide the amount of the payment between the reduction in the receivable balance accrued with the adjusting entry and the interest earned in the current period. If the adjusting entry is reversed, the receipt of cash for interest is simply recorded as a debit to *Cash* and a credit to *Interest Revenue*. In this case, reversals will result in saving a great deal of time, since an employee will not have to allocate each interest payment between two periods. An illustration of a reversing entry related to a revenue transaction is presented in Figure 4–16.

A discussion of reversing entries is presented here because they are used in practice by many companies. It should be emphasized that reversing entries are optional and are made only to facilitate the recording of routine transactions in future periods. Furthermore, *all* accruals, but only deferrals initially recorded in income statement accounts, are reversed if it is beneficial to do so. A general rule is that a *reversing entry should be made for any adjusting entry that increased an asset or liability account*. Thus, adjusting entries for accruals of unrecorded revenues and expenses can be reversed. The prepayment of expenses and the advance receipt of revenues (deferrals) are normally initially recorded in a permanent account. An adjusting entry made to adjust a deferral will decrease an asset or a liability account, and is not reversed. However, reversing is appropriate if these prepayments were first made to a temporary account.

ACCOUNTING PROCEDURES APPLICABLE TO A PARTNERSHIP OR A CORPORATION

Objective 7: Owners' equity section for a partnership and a corporation

In the preceding illustration, Starbuck Real Estate Office was owned by one person, who had elected to operate the firm as a proprietorship. Although proprietorships are the most numerous form of business organization in the United States, the majority of business activity in terms of dollar volume is conducted by corporations. A *corporation* is a separate legal entity incorporated under the laws of a particular state or the laws of the federal government. A third form of business organization is the *partnership,* which is a business owned by two or more persons acting as partners. Accounting and reporting for partnerships and corporations are similar in most respects to accounting and reporting for proprietorships. The income statement and the balance sheet are essentially the same for all three forms of business organization, except for transactions that directly affect the owner's equity accounts. Accounting problems associated with partnerships and corporations are discussed in detail in Chapters 14 through 16. However, there will be some references to owners' equity in terms of corporations and partnerships prior to Chapters 14 through 16. Therefore the differences in owner's equity are discussed briefly here.

ACCOUNTING FOR A PARTNERSHIP

In accounting for a partnership, separate capital and withdrawal accounts are maintained for each partner. An investment by a partner is credited to his or her capital account, and a withdrawal of cash or other assets from the part-

To illustrate the reversal of the accrual of revenue, assume that a company loaned a client $100,000 on May 1, 1987, and that at December 31, the fiscal year-end, unpaid interest of $2,000 had accrued on the note.

WITHOUT REVERSING ENTRIES   WITH REVERSING ENTRIES

1. November 1, 1987   Entry to record the receipt of $6,000 interest payment.
Nov.   1 Cash   6,000   Cash   6,000
              Interest Revenue   6,000   Interest Revenue   6,000

2. December 31, 1987   Adjusting entry to accrue interest revenue and interest receivable.
Dec. 31 Interest Receivable   2,000   Interest Receivable   2,000
              Interest Revenue   2,000   Interest Revenue   2,000

3. December 31, 1987   Closing entry assuming that the Interest Revenue account contained a
                       $6,000 balance before the adjusting entry.
Dec. 31 Interest Revenue   8,000   Interest Revenue   8,000
              Income Summary   8,000   Income Summary   8,000

4. January 1, 1988   Entry to reverse the effects of the adjusting entry.
Jan.   1 No entry is made.   Interest Revenue   2,000
                                                      Interest Receivable   2,000

5. May 1, 1988   Record the receipt of the interest payment in the amount of $6,000.
May   1 Cash   6,000   Cash   6,000
              Interest Receivable   2,000   Interest Revenue   6,000
              Interest Revenue   4,000

WITHOUT REVERSING ENTRIES

Interest Receivable			Interest Revenue			Cash		
12/31	2,000	5/1	2,000	12/31	8,000	11/1	6,000	11/1	6,000
						12/31	2,000	5/1	6,000
					8,000		8,000		
						5/1	4,000		

WITH REVERSING ENTRIES

Interest Receivable			Interest Revenue			Cash		
12/31	2,000	1/1	2,000	12/31	8,000	11/1	6,000	11/1	6,000
						12/31	2,000	5/1	6,000
					8,000		8,000		
		1/1	2,000	5/1	6,000			
				Bal.	4,000			

Figure 4–16
Illustration of Reversing Entries–Revenue Transaction.

nership is debited to his or her withdrawal account. At the end of the period, the *Income Summary* account is closed by making a compound journal entry that allocates the balance in the account to each partner's capital account in accordance with the partners' profit- and loss-sharing agreement.

ACCOUNTING FOR A CORPORATION

An individual or individuals who want to organize and start a business as a corporation in a particular state must submit an application and pay a specified fee to the appropriate state official, usually the secretary of state. If the application is approved, the state authorizes the corporation to conduct business. The first transaction for a corporation is the issue of stock in exchange for cash, property, or services. That is, ownership interests in a corporation are represented by shares of the corporation's stock. For this reason, the owners are called stockholders or shareholders. As an owner of the firm, a shareholder has certain rights and privileges. Two of the basic rights are the right to vote in the election of directors and in the development of certain corporate policies, and the right to share in income by receiving dividends. Stockholders are not directly involved in daily management of the corporation, but instead elect a board of directors who formulate the major business policies and appoint the administrative officers.

In a corporate balance sheet, the total interest of the owners in the assets of the corporation is called stockholders' equity. State incorporation laws generally require that the stockholders' equity section must be separated into two categories or sources of capital: (1) **paid-in capital** represents the amount of assets invested in the corporation by the stockholders; (2) **retained earnings** reflect the accumulated income earned by the corporation and retained in the business.

The investment of assets in a corporation is recorded by debits to the asset accounts and a credit to a paid-in capital account, such as *Common Stock*. When an investment is made in the corporation, the investors are given shares of the corporation's stock as evidence of their ownership. For example, assume that Starbuck Real Estate Office was organized on January 1, 1987, as a corporation, and initially issued 10,000 shares of its common stock for a total of $100,000. The entry to record the issue is as follows.

	1987				
Jan.	1	Cash		100,000	
		Common Stock			100,000

Just as the owner of a proprietorship may periodically withdraw cash from the business in anticipation of profits, cash distributions, called **dividends,** may be made to the owners of a corporation. Because corporate stockholders are free to sell their shares at any time, most corporations follow the procedures outlined in this section to assure that the dividends are paid to the rightful owners of the shares. There are three dates associated with the payment of a dividend, as explained here.

1. The *declaration date* is the date on which the board of directors declare that a dividend is going to be paid. On this date, the dividend becomes a liability of the corporation.

2. The *date of record* is the date on which the corporation prepares a list of those stockholders eligible to receive the declared dividend. The date of

record is between the declaration date and the payment date, in order to enable investors to get the ownership of their shares recorded with the corporation before the payment is made.

3. The **payment date** is the date on which the dividend payment is mailed to the stockholders of record.

To illustrate, assume that on December 1 Starbuck's board of directors declared a cash dividend of $1.00 per share on the 10,000 shares issued. The dividend is to be paid on December 31 to the stockholders of record as of December 21. Entries to record the declaration and payment are:

Dec.	1	Dividends Declared	10,000	
		Cash Dividends Payable		10,000
		Declared a cash dividend of $1 per share on the 10,000 common shares outstanding.		
Dec.	31	Cash Dividends Payable	10,000	
		Cash		10,000
		To record payment of the dividend declared.		

The first entry recognizes a current liability on the declaration date and the second entry records the payment of the dividend. No entry is required on the date of record, since that date is used ony to determine the owners of the stock who are to receive the dividend.

The *Dividends Declared* account is a temporary *Retained Earnings* account, rather than an expense account, because dividends are considered a distribution of income and are not a cost incurred for the purpose of producing revenue. At the end of the period, the *Dividends Declared* account is closed to the *Retained Earnings* account.

If net income for the year is $25,000, the *Income Summary* account will have a credit balance and will be closed by the following entry.

| Dec. | 31 | Income Summary | 25,000 | |
| | | Retained Earnings | | 25,000 |

At the end of the period, a corporation will normally prepare a statement of retained earnings similar to the following.

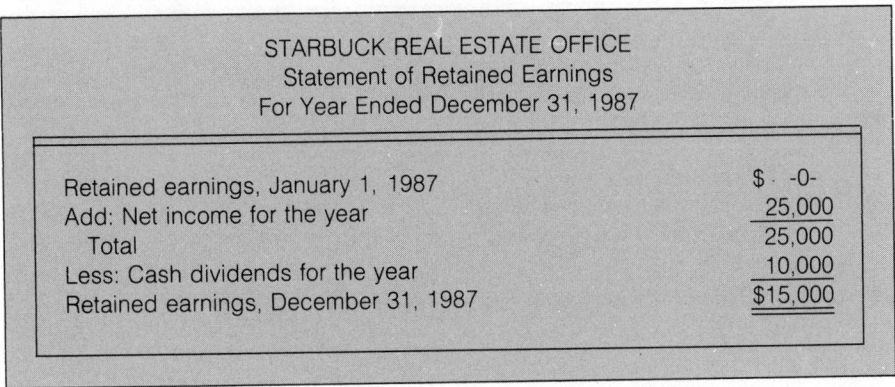

STARBUCK REAL ESTATE OFFICE
Statement of Retained Earnings
For Year Ended December 31, 1987

Retained earnings, January 1, 1987	$ -0-
Add: Net income for the year	25,000
Total	25,000
Less: Cash dividends for the year	10,000
Retained earnings, December 31, 1987	$15,000

Based on the above entries, the stockholders' equity section of the balance sheet will appear as follows:

Stockholders' Equity	
Common stock, 10,000 shares issued	$100,000
Retained earnings, December 31, 1987	15,000
Total Stockholders' Equity	$115,000

The balance of $115,000 reports the interest of the stockholders in the assets of the firm. Of this balance, $100,000 was invested by the owners and the other $15,000 was an increase in assets from operations.

One important difference between the three forms of business organization (proprietorship, partnership, corporation) is in the way that income taxes are computed. Although all three forms are recognized as separate business entities for accounting purposes, proprietorships and partnerships are nontaxpaying entities. Proprietors or partners must include their share of business income or loss in their individual tax returns. Thus, income tax expense will not appear in the income statement of a proprietorship or partnership. Except for the S Corporations described in Chapter 28, corporations are separate taxable entities that must file tax returns and pay a state and federal tax on their taxable income. Therefore, in its financial statements, a corporation must show the amount of income tax expense incurred for the period, and record any unpaid portion of the tax as a liability. The amount of income tax to be paid each period is computed in accordance with the Internal Revenue Code. Some provisions of the code are discussed in more detail in Chapter 28. Until then, we will assume a simplified tax computation for illustrative purposes.

DEMONSTRATION PROBLEM

The unadjusted trial balance for Meadows Law Office at the end of the current fiscal year is presented on page 181. Additional information needed to adjust the accounts is:

(a) The office supplies inventory determined by physical count was $620.

(b) The balance in the *Prepaid Rent* account is for three months' rent paid on November 1.

(c) Unpaid salaries earned by employees amount to $1,300.

(d) Insurance expired during the period totals $600.
(e) The balance in the *Unearned Fees* account consists of advance payments of $700 for law services to be performed next year. The remaining advance payments were earned this period.
(f) Estimated depreciation on office equipment totals $800.
(g) Accrued interest on notes payable due on January 15 is $210.
(h) Travel expenses incurred by employees but not yet paid total $220.

The following account titles are included in the chart of accounts, in addition to those listed in the trial balance.

Salaries Payable   Insurance Expense
Interest Payable   Depreciation Expense
Travel Expense Payable   Interest Expense
Office Supplies Expense

Required:
A. Prepare a 10-column worksheet.
B. Prepare closing entries.

MEADOWS LAW OFFICE
Unadjusted Trial Balance
December 31, 1987

Account Title	Debit	Credit
Cash	$ 9,880	
Accounts Receivable	4,310	
Prepaid Rent	1,500	
Prepaid Insurance	1,320	
Office Supplies Inventory	1,280	
Office Equipment	4,000	
Accumulated Depreciation—Office Equipment		$ 2,400
Accounts Payable		630
Unearned Fees		1,800
Notes Payable		3,000
Jane Meadows, Capital		10,000
Jane Meadows, Drawing	36,000	
Fees Earned		79,320
Salaries Expense	25,200	
Rent Expense	5,000	
Utilities Expense	2,490	
Research Expense	4,310	
Travel Expense	1,860	
Totals	$97,150	$97,150

ANSWER TO DEMONSTRATION PROBLEM

A. 10-column Worksheet

MEADOWS LAW OFFICE
Worksheet
For Year Ended December 31, 1987

Account Titles	Unadjusted Trial Balance		Adjustments		Adjusted Trial Balance		Income Statement		Balance Sheet	
	Debit	Credit	Debit	Credit	Debit	Credit	Debit	Credit	Debit	Credit
Cash	9,880				9,880				9,880	
Accounts Receivable	4,310				4,310				4,310	
Prepaid Rent	1,500			(b) 1,000	500				500	
Prepaid Insurance	1,320			(d) 600	720				720	
Office Supplies Inv.	1,280			(a) 660	620				620	
Office Equipment	4,000				4,000				4,000	
Accumulated Deprec.— Office Equipment		2,400		(f) 800		3,200				3,200
Accounts Payable		630				630				630
Unearned Fees		1,800	(e) 1,100			700				700
Notes Payable		3,000				3,000				3,000
Jane Meadows, Capital		10,000				10,000				10,000
Jane Meadows, Drawing	36,000				36,000				36,000	
Fees Earned		79,320		(e) 1,100		80,420		80,420		
Salaries Expense	25,200		(c) 1,300		26,500		26,500			
Rent Expense	5,000		(b) 1,000		6,000		6,000			
Utilities Expense	2,490				2,490		2,490			
Research Expense	4,310				4,310		4,310			
Travel Expense	1,860		(h) 220		2,080		2,080			
Totals	97,150	97,150								
Office Supplies Expense			(a) 660		660		660			
Salaries Payable				(c) 1,300		1,300				1,300
Insurance Expense			(d) 600		600		600			
Depreciation Expense			(f) 800		800		800			
Interest Expense			(g) 210		210		210			
Interest Payable				(g) 210		210				210
Travel Expense Payable				(h) 220		220				220
Totals			5,890	5,890	99,680	99,680	43,650	80,420	56,030	19,260
Net income for the period							36,770			36,770
Totals							80,420	80,420	56,030	56,030

(net loss)

Completed worksheet

B. Closing Entries

Dec.	31	Fees Earned	80,420	
		Income Summary		80,420
		To close the revenue account.		
	31	Income Summary	43,650	
		Salaries Expense		26,500
		Rent Expense		6,000
		Utilities Expense		2,490
		Research Expense		4,310
		Travel Expense		2,080
		Office Supplies Expense		660
		Insurance Expense		600
		Depreciation Expense		800
		Interest Expense		210
		To close the expense accounts.		
	31	Income Summary	36,770	
		Jane Meadows, Capital		36,770
		To close the Income Summary account.		
	31	Jane Meadows, Capital	36,000	
		Jane Meadows, Drawing		36,000
		To close the Drawing account.		

[Handwritten margin note: Do not close out capital]

[Handwritten margin note: reasons! capital up to date start rev. out fresh & exp. out fresh]

GLOSSARY

CLOSING ENTRIES.   Journal entries made at the end of an accounting period to reduce temporary accounts to a zero balance and transfer the net balance to the owner's capital account (p. 156).

CROSSFOOTING.   Adding or subtracting horizontally across a worksheet (p. 151).

DIVIDEND.   A distribution of cash by a corporation to its stockholders (p. 178).

PAID-IN CAPITAL.   The capital invested in the corporation by its stockholders (p. 178).

PERMANENT ACCOUNTS (REAL ACCOUNTS).   Balance sheet accounts are called permanent accounts because they are not closed at the end of the period (p. 156).

POST-CLOSING TRIAL BALANCE.   A trial balance taken after the adjusting and closing entries have been posted to the accounts (p. 166).

RETAINED EARNINGS.   Earnings of a corporation that have been retained in the business, rather than distributed to stockholders (p. 178).

REVERSING ENTRIES.   Entries made to record the opposite effects of certain adjusting entries (p. 173).

TEMPORARY ACCOUNTS (NOMINAL ACCOUNTS).   The revenue, expense, and drawing accounts are called temporary accounts, because they are reduced to a zero balance at the end of an accounting period (p. 156).

WORKSHEET.   A form used by accountants to gather and organize the information needed to complete the accounting cycle (p. 148).

DISCUSSION QUESTIONS

1. Why do accountants prepare a worksheet?
2. Which one of the following steps in the accounting cycle may be omitted?
   (a) Posting the entries to the ledger.
   (b) Preparing a worksheet.
   (c) Journalizing the adjusting entries.
   (d) Posting the closing entries to the ledger.
3. Why are the entries in the Adjustments column of the worksheet identified by either letters or numbers?
4. Define the terms *footing* and *crossfooting*.
5. In which columns of the worksheet is the net income for the period entered?
6. Will the columns of the worksheet balance if an expense is accidentally entered in the debit column of the Balance Sheet, rather than the Income Statement? What will be the effect on the reported net income?
7. In a proprietorship, which accounts are involved in closing entries? Why are the revenue and expense accounts closed?
8. What is the purpose of the *Income Summary* account?
9. List the four steps in closing the accounts of a proprietorship.
10. Why is a post-closing trial balance prepared?
11. Which accounts appear on the post-closing trial balance?
12. Which steps in the accounting cycle are performed in order to prepare interim financial statements?
13. Why are reversing entries so named?
14. What is the purpose of reversing entries? Which adjusting entries may be reversed?
15. At the end of the preceding period, the company accrued salaries payable of $1,500. On January 2, the company debited *Salary Expense* and credited *Cash* for $2,000.
    (a) If a reversing entry had not been made on January 1, would the financial statements be in error for the month of January? Explain.
    (b) What entry should have been made on January 2, given that a reversing entry was not made?
    (c) If the company made reversing entries, what reversing entry should have been made on January 1?
16. Describe the owners' equity section of a corporation's balance sheet and compare it to the owners' equity section of a partnership.
17. Explain the difference between the payment of cash dividends and the withdrawal of cash by a proprietor. What is the effect of each on assets, owners' equity, and net income?

EXERCISES

Exercise 4-1 Extension of Account Balances to Proper Worksheet Columns

Ledger accounts that appear in the Adjusted Trial Balance columns of a worksheet are listed here. You are to complete the tabulation shown, by entering a check mark in the proper worksheet column in which the amount in each account would be extended in completing the worksheet.

1. Cash
2. Building
3. Service Revenue
4. Wages Expense
5. Sam Holly, Capital
6. Accumulated Depreciation
7. Depreciation Expense
8. Accounts Receivable
9. Wages Payable

10. Sam Holly, Drawing
11. Prepaid Insurance
12. Equipment
13. Office Supplies Inventory
14. Office Supplies Expense
15. Interest Revenue
16. Interest Expense
17. Interest Receivable
18. Interest Payable

Solution Format

	Income Statement		Balance Sheet	
Account	Debit	Credit	Debit	Credit
1. Cash	_____	_____	_✓_	_____

Exercise 4-2 Completion of Worksheet, Preparation of Financial Statements, and Closing Entries

The following unadjusted trial balance was taken from the ledger of Johnson Company on December 31, 1987.

Account Title	Debit	Credit
Cash	$12	
Accounts Receivable	8	
Prepaid Insurance	4	
Equipment	30	
Accumulated Depreciation		$10
Accounts Payable		4
Charles Johnson, Capital		37
Charles Johnson, Drawing	5	
Service Revenue		34
Wages Expense	17	
Utility Expense	6	
Miscellaneous Expense	3	
Totals	$85	$85

Required:

A. Prepare a 10-column worksheet using the following additional information on December 31, 1987 (000 omitted). Add the following account titles to those listed in the trial balance: *Insurance Expense, Accrued Wages Payable, Depreciation Expense.*

   (a) Expired insurance, $2.
   (b) Accrued wages, $2.
   (c) Depreciation on equipment, $5.

B. Prepare an income statement, a statement of changes in owner's equity, and an unclassified balance sheet.

C. Record the adjusting and closing entries in the general journal.

Exercise 4-3 Closing Entries

The following accounts and account balances were taken from the Adjusted Trial Balance columns of the worksheet of the Knight Company for the year ended December 31, 1987.

Jay Knight, Capital	$12,300
Jay Knight, Drawing	15,730
Fees Earned	47,230
Interest Revenue	7,300
Salaries Expense	19,700
Rent Expense	6,200
Advertising Expense	3,970
Depreciation Expense	5,340
Utilities Expense	2,100

Required:

Prepare the closing entries.

Exercise 4-4 Reversing Entries—Accrued Expense

On December 31, 1987, the accountant for Szabo Plumbing determined that one month's interest of $36 had accrued on a note payable. An interest payment of $144 was made on March 31, 1988.

Required:

A. Give the adjusting entry needed on December 31, 1987.

B. Give the closing entry.

C. Give the reversing entry that could be made and the subsequent entry to record the payment on March 31, 1988.

D. Assuming no reversing entry, give the entry to record the interest payment.

Exercise 4-5 Closing Entries

The year-end income statement of Cross Country Rental Unlimited is presented here.

CROSS COUNTRY RENTAL UNLIMITED
Income Statement
For the Year Ended June 30, 1987

Revenues:		
Car rental fees		$47,910
Truck rental fees		15,420
Total Revenues		63,330
Expenses:		
Salaries expense	$18,990	
Depreciation expense	7,870	
Maintenance expense	2,650	
Insurance expense	1,970	
Supplies expense	1,460	
Advertising expense	830	
Total Expenses		33,770
Net Income		$29,560

Required:
Given that the owner, Kyle Davis, withdrew $25,200 from the business during the year, prepare the closing entries.

Exercise 4-6 Reversing Entries—Accrued Revenue

Paula Larson operates a telephone answering service. Her clients are charged $75 a month for the service and are billed four times a year on January 31, April 30, July 31, and October 31. Quarterly payments are due by the fifteenth of the month following the end of a quarter. The balance in the *Answering Service Fees Revenue* account was $45,900 on December 31, 1987, the end of the fiscal period. Service fees earned in November and December, but not yet recorded, were $7,650.

Required:

A. Prepare the adjusting entry in the general journal to record the earned fees.
B. Assuming that reversing entries were not made, record the receipt of a $225 quarterly payment from a client on February 12 for three months' service, and the receipt of $150 on February 13 from a new client who had contracted for the service to start on December 1. Revenue was last accrued on December 31.
C. Assuming that reversing entries were made to facilitate the bookkeeping process, prepare the appropriate reversing entry, if any, and the receipt of cash on February 12 and 13.

Exercise 4-7 Determination of Cash Paid—Missing Data

Selected accounts of the Sells Company contain the following balances at the beginning and the end of the year. The year-end adjusting entries have been made.

	Jan. 1	Dec. 31
Prepaid Insurance	$ 300	$620
Supplies Inventory	690	430
Salaries Payable	1,250	915

The following items appear on the income statement for the year ended December 31.

Insurance Expense	$ 650
Supplies Expense	900
Salaries Expense	27,370

Required:
Determine how much cash was used during the year
A. To purchase insurance.
B. To purchase supplies.
C. For salaries.

Exercise 4-8 Reversing Entries—Unearned Revenue

During the 1987 fiscal year, Mystery Publishing Company received $82,500 for magazine subscriptions. The bookkeeper credits *Unearned Subscriptions,* a liability account, for the full amount when cash is received. At December 31, 1987, it is determined that $27,500 of the subscriptions relate to magazines that are to be published and delivered in future periods.

Required:

A. What amount should be reported in the 1987 income statement for earned subscriptions revenue?
B. What amount should be reported in the December 31, 1987, balance sheet for unearned subscriptions?
C. Prepare the adjusting entry needed as of December 31, 1987.
D. What reversing entry, if any, would you make on January 1, 1988?
E. The bookkeeper could have initially recorded the receipt of cash in a revenue

account. Prepare the adjusting entry, assuming that the *Earned Subscriptions Revenue* account contains a credit balance of $82,500 as of December 31.

F. Compare the balances in the *Unearned Subscriptions* account and the *Earned Subscriptions Revenue* account derived in requirement E, with those computed in requirements A and B.

G. What reversing entry, if any, would you make on January 1, 1988, to reverse the adjusting entry made in requirement E?

Exercise 4-9 Preparation of Statement of Changes in Owner's Equity

The adjusted trial balance of the J. M. Sholin Company is shown here.

J. M. SHOLIN COMPANY
Adjusted Trial Balance
December 31, 1987

Account Title	Debit	Credit
Cash	$ 2,430	
Accounts Receivable	1,710	
Supplies on Hand	240	
Accounts Payable		$ 2,790
J. M. Sholin, Capital		3,560
J. M. Sholin, Drawing	6,850	
Fees Earned		17,760
Wages Expense	9,250	
Supplies Expense	770	
Advertising Expense	2,860	
Totals	$24,110	$24,110

Required:

Prepare a statement of changes in owner's equity for the year ended December 31, 1987. Assume that J. M. Sholin did not invest any additional capital during 1987.

Exercise 4-10 Preparation of Statement of Changes in Owner's Equity

The following accounts are taken from the ledger of the Rowan Company on December 31, 1987, the end of the current fiscal year.

W. Rowan, Capital					**W. Rowan, Drawing**			
12/31	17,370	1/1	9,840	2/15	2,800	12/31	17,370
		12/31	37,510	4/29	5,270		
				5/17	3,950		
				9/4	5,350		

Income Summary			
12/31	24,390	12/31	61,900
12/31	37,510		

Required:

Prepare a statement of changes in owner's equity.

Exercise 4-11 Recording Capital Transactions of a Corporation

Prepare the general journal entries that are needed to record the transactions of Miser Corporation.

1. Issued 1,000 shares of common stock for $5,000.
2. The board of directors declared a cash dividend of $1 per share.
3. The cash dividend declared in (2) was paid.
4. Closed a $7,800 credit balance in the *Income Summary* account.

Exercise 4-12 Closing Accounts and Preparation of Statement of Retained Earnings for a Corporation

On January 1, 1987, the owners' equity of the Todd Corporation consisted of common stock of $100,000 and retained earnings of $650,000. During the period, the company declared and paid a cash dividend of $90,000. The general ledger contains only two income statement accounts—*Revenues Earned* and *Operating Expenses*. On December 31, the balance in the *Revenues Earned* account was $730,000 and the balance in the *Operating Expenses* account was $625,000.

Required:
A. Prepare closing entries.
B. Prepare a statement of retained earnings at the end of 1987.
C. Compute the total owners' equity in the assets of the firm at the end of 1987.

PROBLEMS

Problem 4-1 Preparation of Worksheet

The unadjusted trial balance of Ambassador Taxi Cab Service is shown here.

AMBASSADOR TAXI CAB SERVICE
Unadjusted Trial Balance
December 31, 1987

Account Title	Debit	Credit
Cash	$ 10,300	
Accounts Receivable	4,610	
Prepaid Insurance	3,790	
Taxi Cabs	91,000	
Accumulated Depreciation—Taxi Cabs		$ 42,000
Office Equipment	2,100	
Accumulated Depreciation—Office Equipment		890
Accounts Payable		10,930
Note Payable		25,000
Unearned Taxi Cab Fares		840
Cherry Jones, Capital		32,160
Cherry Jones, Drawing	9,300	
Taxi Fares Earned		37,270
Salaries Expense	15,200	
Rent Expense	1,630	
Taxi Maintenance and Repair Expense	2,960	
Gas and Oil Expense	6,800	
Telephone Expense	1,400	
Totals	$149,090	$149,090

The following additional information is available at the end of December.

(a) Expired insurance amounted to $2,400.
(b) Depreciation on the taxi cabs for one year is $7,000.
(c) Depreciation on the office equipment is $390.
(d) Accrued interest on the note payable is $3,340.
(e) The balance in the *Unearned Taxi Cab Fares* account includes $125 received for services rendered on December 27. 715
(f) Cab driver salaries earned, but not paid, amounted to $840.
(g) Taxi repair work done in December for $470 has not been paid for or recorded.
(h) The December telephone bill of $250 was received during January and has not been recorded.

Required:

A. Prepare a 10-column worksheet for the year ended December 31, 1987.
B. Add the following account titles to those listed in the trial balance: *Depreciation Expense—Cabs, Depreciation Expense—Office Equipment, Telephone Expense Payable, Interest Payable, Interest Expense, Insurance Expense, Salaries Payable.*

Problem 4-2 Preparation of Worksheet, Financial Statements, and Closing Entries

The ledger of Bill Forbes, Chiropractor, contains the following accounts and account balances on December 31, 1987.

Account Title	Debit	Credit
Cash	$ 2,410	
Accounts Receivable	2,950	
Prepaid Insurance	770	
Land	15,300	
Building	49,000	
Accumulated Depreciation—Building		$ 28,220
Equipment	5,030	
Accumulated Depreciation—Equipment		2,200
Accounts Payable		3,010
Mortgage Note Payable		5,130
B. Forbes, Capital		23,960
B. Forbes, Drawing	30,840	
Fees Earned		55,980
Rent Revenue		3,600
Salaries Expense	13,900	
Utilities Expense	1,130	
Interest Expense	770	
Totals	$122,100	$122,100

The following additional account titles are included in the chart of accounts.

Interest Payable	Unearned Fees
Property Tax Payable	Insurance Expense
Salaries Payable	Property Tax Expense
	Depreciation Expense—Building
	Depreciation Expense—Equipment

The following information was not reflected in the December 31, 1987 account balances.

(a) Property tax for 1987 is $430.
(b) Depreciation on the equipment is $910.
(c) Depreciation on the building is $4,420.
(d) An advance fee payment of $100 for therapy to be performed in January was credited to *Fees Earned*.
(e) The mortgage contract provides for a monthly payment of $250, plus accrued interest. The December payment was not made. Interest of $170 is accrued on the mortgage note.
(f) Prepaid insurance of $310 has expired.
(g) Salaries earned but not paid amount to $690.

Required:
A. Prepare a 10-column worksheet for the year ended December 31, 1987.
B. Prepare an income statement, a statement of changes in owner's equity, and a balance sheet. (Hint: A portion of the mortgage note payable should be classified as a current liability.)
C. Journalize the adjusting entries.
D. Journalize the closing entries.

2750

Problem 4-3 Preparation of Worksheet, Financial Statements, and Closing Entries

Marie Townley owns Prudential Employment Agency. Her accountant prepared the following unadjusted trial balance on June 30, 1987, the end of the fiscal year.

PRUDENTIAL EMPLOYMENT AGENCY
Unadjusted Trial Balance
June 30, 1987

Account Title	Debit	Credit
Cash	$ 3,035	
Accounts Receivable	6,540	
Prepaid Advertising	940	
Office Supplies Inventory	205	
Office Equipment	7,790	
Accumulated Depreciation—Office Equipment		$ 1,040
Accounts Payable		6,835
Unearned Fees		1,190
M. Townley, Capital		4,000
M. Townley, Drawing	10,830	
Placement Fees Earned		43,890
Rent Expense	5,440	
Salaries Expense	21,115	
Telephone Expense	1,060	
Totals	$56,955	$56,955

The following additional information is available as of June 30.

(a) Advertising costing $500 expired during the year.
(b) Unused supplies on hand on June 30 totaled $85. Supplies Expense 120
　　　　　　　　　　　　　　　　　　　　　　　　　Supplie Inventory   120

(c) Estimated depreciation on the office equipment is $935.

(d) The *Unearned Fees* account includes $200 received for fees earned during June.

Required:

A. Prepare a 10-column worksheet for the year ended June 30, 1987.

B. Prepare an income statement, a statement of changes in owner's equity and a balance sheet.

C. Journalize the closing entries.

Problem 4-4 The Complete Accounting Cycle

Marie Cook owns Cook Piano Tuning and Repairs. The post-closing trial balance as of December 31, 1987, is as follows.

Account Title	Account Number	Debit	Credit
Cash	100	$ 2,640	
Accounts Receivable	101	3,440	
Prepaid Insurance	105	80	
Supplies Inventory	110	105	
Truck	116	10,700	
Accumulated Depreciation—Truck	117		$ 4,013
Accounts Payable	200		955
Interest Payable	204		220
Note Payable	210		6,000
M. Cook, Capital	300		5,777
Totals		$16,965	$16,965

Transactions completed during 1988 are summarized here.

1. Piano tuning fees of $13,000 were earned during the year; $10,500 of this total was received in cash. The remainder consisted of transactions on account.

2. Revenue from piano repairs was $11,900. Cash received totaled $10,400, and accounts receivable increased by $1,500.

3. Supplies costing $170 were purchased during the year on account.

4. On June 29, the company paid $2,750 on the note payable, plus interest of $430. The interest payment consisted of $220 accrued during 1987 and $210 accrued during the first half of 1988. The balance of the note is due in 1989.

5. Gas and oil for the truck, purchased on account, totaled $2,340.

6. Insurance on the truck, paid in advance, was $250.

7. Telephone expense of $1,100 was paid.

8. Accounts receivable of $4,950 were collected.

9. Marie Cook withdrew $16,000 in cash from the business.

10. Paid $2,595 on accounts payable.

The following information relating to adjusting entries is available at the end of 1988.

(a) A physical count of the supplies showed supplies costing $90 on hand as of December 31, 1988.

(b) Accrued interest on the note payable is $120.

(c) Insurance costing $110 expired during the year.

(d) Depreciation on the truck is $1,675.

(e) The December telephone bill of $90 has not been paid or recorded.

Required:

A. Open T accounts for each of the accounts listed in the post-closing trial balance and the accounts listed here. Insert beginning balances in the accounts, as shown in the post-closing trial balance.

Account Title	Account Number
Telephone Expense Payable	205
M. Cook, Drawing	301
Income Summary	305
Piano Tuning Fees	400
Piano Repair Fees	401
Gas and Oil Expense	500
Telephone Expense	501
Supplies Expense	502
Insurance Expense	503
Depreciation Expense	504
Interest Expense	505

B. Prepare journal entries to record the transactions completed in 1988.
C. Post the entries to the T accounts.
D. Prepare a 10-column worksheet.
E. Prepare an income statement, a statement of changes in owner's equity, and a balance sheet.
F. Journalize and post the adjusting entries.
G. Journalize and post the closing entries.
H. Prepare a post-closing trial balance.

Problem 4-5 Adjusting and Reversing Entries

The records of the Tillis Company contain the following information as of December 31, the end of the fiscal year.

1. Interest of $210 has accrued on a note payable.
2. Wages earned, but not paid, total $600.
3. Depreciation on the office equipment is $3,345.
4. On September 1 the company paid $1,080 for a six-month advertising campaign beginning on that date. This transaction was recorded by debiting *Prepaid Advertising*. At the end of the year, advertising costing $720 had expired.

Required:

A. Prepare an adjusting entry for each transaction.
B. Prepare reversing entries where appropriate.

Problem 4-6 Adjusting Entries, Posting to T Accounts, Reversing Entries, and Entries in Subsequent Period

Selected accounts taken from the general ledger of Baker Company showed the following balances at December 31, the fiscal year-end.

Prepaid Insurance		Insurance Expense	
12/31 Bal. 2,220		12/31 Bal. -0-	

Accrued Interest Receivable		Interest Revenue	
12/31 Bal. -0-			12/31 Bal. 4,200

Accrued Wages Payable		Wages Expense	
	12/31 Bal. -0-	12/31 Bal. 77,800	

Required:

A. Prepare adjusting entries for the above accounts, based on the following data, which is not yet recorded.

  (a) Insurance expired during the year totals $520.

  (b) Wages earned by employees, but not paid, at year-end total $1,300.

  (c) Interest accrued, but not yet received, on notes receivable totals $290.

B. Open T accounts for each of the accounts just listed. Enter the December 31 balances and the adjusting entries.

C. In the appropriate accounts, enter the effects of the closing entries that would be made at year end.

D. Complete the following tabulation.

Account	Balance Before Adjustment	Effects of Adjusting Entries	Balance After Adjustment	Effect of Closing Entries	Balance After Closing Entries
Prepaid Insurance	$2,220	−$520	$1,700	-0-	$1,700
Insurance Expense	___	___	___	___	___
Accrued Interest Receivable	___	___	___	___	___
Interest Revenue	___	___	___	___	___
Accrued Wages Payable	___	___	___	___	___
Wages Expense	___	___	___	___	___

E. The Baker Company follows the practice of making reversing entries. Prepare the reversing entries that would be made on January 1 of the next period. In a balance sheet prepared on January 1, how would the balance in the *Interest Revenue* and *Wages Expense* accounts be reported?

F. Record the payment of $3,240 in weekly wages on January 3 and the collection of $350 in interest on January 18. What are the balances in the *Wages Expense* and *Interest Revenue* accounts after these entries are posted?

G. Prepare the two entries given in requirement F, assuming that the company did not prepare reversing entries.

ALTERNATE PROBLEMS

Problem 4-1A Preparation of Worksheet

The unadjusted trial balance of the U-Movit Moving Company is presented here.

U-MOVIT MOVING COMPANY
Unadjusted Trial Balance
December 31, 1987

Account Title	Debit	Credit
Cash	$ 4,200	
Accounts Receivable	6,430	
Prepaid Insurance	4,090	
Prepaid Advertising	1,940	
Office Supplies Inventory	320	
Moving Vans	46,800	
Accumulated Depreciation—Moving Vans		$ 20,700
Office Equipment	4,200	
Accumulated Depreciation—Office Equipment		2,230
Accounts Payable		6,020
Unearned Transporting Fees		1,130
Paula Starr, Capital		38,300
Paula Starr, Drawing	10,300	
Transporting Fees Earned		45,350
Wages Expense	27,310	
Maintenance Expense	2,800	
Gas Expense	5,340	
Totals	$113,730	$113,730

The following additional information should be considered for adjusting entries.

(a) A physical inventory showed office supplies totaling $130 on hand as of December 31.

(b) Depreciation for one year on the moving vans is $2,260.

(c) Depreciation on the office equipment is $1,760.

(d) The balance in the *Unearned Transporting Fees* account includes $340 received in November for moving done in December.

(e) Wages earned but not paid amounted to $1,030.

(f) Gas purchased on account for $220 and used during the last week in December has not been paid for or recorded.

(g) Prepaid insurance of $250 is expired.

(h) Prepaid advertising of $1,740 is expired.

Required:

Prepare a 10-column worksheet for the year ended December 31, 1987. Add the following account titles to those listed in the trial balance: *Advertising Expense, Depreciation Expense—Vans, Depreciation Expense—Equipment, Office Supplies Expense, Wages Payable, Insurance Expense.*

Problem 4-2A Preparation of Worksheet, Financial Statements, and Closing Entries

The ledger of Kate Cavity, Dentist, contains the following accounts and account balances on December 31, 1987.

Account Title	Debit	Credit
Cash	$ 1,400	
Accounts Receivable	4,030	
Prepaid Insurance	1,092	
Supplies Inventory	570	
Land	11,500	
Building	73,000	
Accumulated Depreciation—Building		$ 21,162
Dental Equipment	6,750	
Accumulated Depreciation—Equipment		3,210
Accounts Payable		3,380
Unearned Dental Fees		780
Mortgage Notes Payable		43,000
K. Cavity, Capital		21,035
K. Cavity, Drawing	23,890	
Dental Fees Earned		76,130
Salaries Expense	43,970	
Advertising Expense	380	
Interest Expense	1,045	
Telephone Expense	1,070	
Totals	$168,697	$168,697

The following account titles are included in the chart of accounts.

Interest Payable   Supplies Expense
Telephone Expense Payable   Depreciation Expense—Building
Insurance Expense   Depreciation Expense—Equipment

The following additional information is also available.

(a) According to a physical inventory count, supplies totaling $155 are on hand at December 31.
(b) The balance in the *Unearned Dental Fees* account includes $100 earned for services rendered the last week of December.
(c) Estimated depreciation on the dental equipment is $1,240.
(d) Depreciation on the building is $3,650.
(e) The balance in the *Prepaid Insurance* account represents a six-month insurance policy which was purchased on September 1 for $1,092.
(f) The December monthly mortgage payment of $900 has not been paid or recorded. In each payment, $190 is attributable to interest.
(g) The December telephone bill for $258 is unrecorded.

Required:
A. Prepare a 10-column worksheet for the year ended December 31, 1987.
B. Prepare an income statement, a statement of changes in owner's equity, and a balance sheet. (Hint: A portion of the mortgage note payable should be classified as a current liability.)
C. Journalize the adjusting entries.
D. Journalize the closing entries.

Problem 4-3A Preparation of Worksheet, Financial Statements, and Closing Entries

Tom's Travel Agency had the following unadjusted trial balance prepared on September 30, 1987, the end of the fiscal year.

TOM'S TRAVEL AGENCY
Unadjusted Trial Balance
September 30, 1987

Account Title	Debit	Credit
Cash	$ 2,450	
Accounts Receivable	2,670	
Prepaid Rent	1,400	
Office Supplies Inventory	505	
Office Equipment	8,640	
Accumulated Depreciation—Office Equipment		$ 2,105
Accounts Payable		1,970
Note Payable (Due 3/31/1988.)		7,100
Tom Jenkins, Capital		3,940
Tom Jenkins, Drawing	13,155	
Fees Earned		30,340
Rent Expense	3,500	
Wages Expense	11,840	
Utilities Expense	1,295	
Totals	$45,455	$45,455

Consider the following information for making year-end adjustments.

(a) Rent of $1,400 for the four-month period beginning August 1 was paid in advance.
(b) A physical inventory count showed supplies totaling $145 on hand as of September 30.
(c) Depreciation on the office equipment is $580.
(d) Interest accrued on the note payable amounts to $535.

Required:
A. Prepare a 10-column worksheet for the year ended September 30, 1987.
B. Prepare an income statement, a statement of changes in owner's equity, and a balance sheet.
C. Journalize the closing entries.

Problem 4-4A The Complete Accounting Cycle

The post-closing trial balance of the Student Counseling Service is shown here.

STUDENT COUNSELING SERVICE
Post-closing Trial Balance
December 31, 1987

Account Title	Account Number	Debit	Credit
Cash	100	$ 2,720	
Accounts Receivable	101	2,950	
Prepaid Rent	102	480	
Office Supplies Inventory	106	410	
Furniture and Equipment	110	9,875	
Accumulated Depreciation—Furniture and Equipment	111		$ 2,040
Accounts Payable	200		1,700
Salaries Payable	201		130
James Short, Capital	300		12,565
Totals		$16,435	$16,435

Transactions completed during 1988 are summarized here.

1. Counseling fees of $28,860 were earned during the year. Clients are billed after their appointments and are given 30 days in which to pay.
2. Collections on accounts receivable totaled $26,910.
3. $4,560 was spent to pay the rent in advance.
4. Office supplies were purchased during the year for $90 in cash and $130 on account.
5. Salary payments amounted to $9,980, of which $130 was for salaries accrued in 1987.
6. Utilities expense of $2,075 was paid.
7. Advertising totaling $1,500 was purchased on account.
8. Accounts payable of $1,830 were paid.
9. James Short withdrew $7,000.

The following additional information should be considered for adjusting entries.

(a) Depreciation on the furniture and equipment is $840.
(b) Rent for six months of $2,280 was paid in advance on February 1 and August 1.
(c) Unused office supplies on hand at the end of the year totaled $210.
(d) Salaries earned but not paid amount to $270.

Required:
A. Prepare the company's ledger by opening T accounts for the accounts listed in the post-closing trial balance and for the accounts listed here. Post the December 31, 1987, balances.

Account Title	Account Number
James Short, Drawing	301
Income Summary	320
Counseling Fees Revenue	400
Salaries Expense	500
Utilities Expense	503
Advertising Expense	504
Depreciation Expense	505
Rent Expense	512
Office Supplies Expense	513

B. Prepare journal entries to record the transactions completed during 1988.

C. Post the entries to the T accounts.

D. Prepare a 10-column worksheet for the year ended December 31, 1988.

E. Prepare an income statement, a statement of changes in owner's equity, and a balance sheet.

F. Journalize and post the adjusting entries.

G. Journalize and post the closing entries.

H. Prepare a post-closing trial balance.

Problem 4-5A Adjusting and Reversing Entries

The following information concerning Smith and Sons Company is available on June 30, the end of the fiscal year.

1. Smith and Sons received $1,050 rental revenue on May 1 for the three-month period beginning on that date. The transaction was recorded by a credit to *Unearned Rental Revenue*.

2. The June utilities bill for $215 has not been paid or recorded.

3. Interest earned but not received totals $1,015.

4. *Prepaid Insurance* was debited for $420 on February 28 to record the cost of a six-month policy beginning March 1.

Required:

A. Prepare an adjusting entry for each item.

B. Prepare reversing entries where appropriate.

5

ACCOUNTING FOR MERCHANDISING OPERATIONS

CHAPTER OVERVIEW AND OBJECTIVES

This chapter describes accounting procedures for businesses that buy and sell merchandise inventory. When you have completed the chapter, you should understand:

1. The nature of merchandise inventory.
2. The basic format of an income statement prepared for a merchandising firm.
3. How to record transactions related to the sale of inventory.
4. The various credit terms related to the sale of inventory.
5. How to record inventory transactions for a firm using a periodic inventory system.
6. How to prepare a worksheet and complete the accounting cycle for a firm using a periodic inventory system.
7. The nature of a perpetual inventory system.
8. How to record the purchase of inventory using the net invoice method.

In preceding chapters, a business organized to render personal services was used to illustrate the accounting cycle. Service firms make up a significant part of our economy and provide a wide range of important services. Service firms include law firms, accounting firms, management consulting firms, equipment repair firms, motels, barber and beauty shops, airlines, advertising agencies, golf courses, theatres, and photography studios. The primary business activity of many other firms centers on selling merchandise rather than services. Manufacturing firms (accounting for which is covered in Chapters

22–25) purchase raw materials and component parts for conversion into finished products. Merchandising or trading firms, which often distribute at both the wholesale and retail levels, purchase goods in substantially the same form in which they are sold.

In this chapter, we will consider the accounting problems associated with the operations of a merchandising firm. Although the accounting principles and methods described in earlier chapters apply to merchandising firms, a number of additional accounts and procedures are used to record inventory transactions. The chapter begins with a discussion of the operations of a merchandising firm with an emphasis on the accounting concepts involved in recording the operations. This is followed by an examination of an income statement prepared for a merchandising firm. Next, accounting for the sale of inventory is described, along with two inventory systems, periodic and perpetual, that are used to account for inventory costs.

MERCHANDISE INVENTORY

The term **merchandise inventory**, or simply **inventory**, is used in a merchandising operation to designate tangible assets held for sale in the normal course of business. Other assets held for future disposition but not normally sold as part of the regular business activities, such as an item of used office equipment that is no longer needed, are not included in the inventory category.

Objective 1:
The nature of
merchandise in-
ventory

MERCHANDISING FIRM OPERATIONS

As described in Chapter 3, the normal operating cycle for a merchandising firm is the average length of time it takes for the firm to acquire inventory, sell that inventory to its customers, and collect cash from the sale. At the time of purchase, inventory is recorded at its acquisition cost in accordance with the cost principle described in Chapter 1. Cost is defined as all costs that are related to the acquisition and preparation of the inventory for sale to customers. Thus, inventory cost should include the invoice price, plus such costs as freight charges paid on the goods purchased and costs incurred to assemble the product. The cost of inventory available for future sale is reported in the balance sheet as a current asset, because it is expected to be sold within the normal operating cycle, or one year, whichever is longer. Inventories are usually listed after receivables because they are one step further removed from cash.

When a sale is made, both an asset account and a revenue account are increased in an amount equal to the sales price. In the income statement, the cost of inventory sold during the current period is matched with revenue received from selling it. Proper *matching* of costs and revenues is, in fact, a major objective of accounting for inventory. It involves determining the amount of the total inventory cost to be deducted from sales in the current period's income statement, and the amount to be carried forward as an asset to be expensed in some future period.

Inventory is one of the most active assets in a merchandising firm. It is continually being acquired, sold, and replaced. Inventory also makes up a significant part of a firm's total assets. The cost of goods sold for a given period is frequently the firm's largest expense, sometimes exceeding the sum of all operating expenses. For these reasons, the control and safeguarding of inventory is essential for efficient and profitable operations. The establishment of such controls is discussed in Chapter 6.

INCOME STATEMENT FOR A MERCHANDISING FIRM

Objective 2: Income statement for a merchandising firm

A condensed income statement for Sunrise Hi-Fi Sales, a merchandising firm, is shown in Figure 5–1.

A comparison of this income statement with the one prepared for Starbuck Real Estate Office on page 155 reveals several differences. First, revenue earned is the first item reported in both cases but, for a merchandising firm, revenue is called **sales.** Second, the income statement of Sunrise Hi-Fi Sales contains a **cost of goods sold** section that shows the total cost of the inventory that was sold during the period. The cost of goods sold is subtracted from sales to arrive at an intermediate income amount called **gross profit** or **gross margin on sales.** The gross profit is calculated to show the amount of markup on the goods sold during this period. The relationship between gross profit and sales is of interest to statement users because companies must sell their inventory at an adequate markup if they are to cover operating expenses and produce a desirable profit.

Third, operating expenses are subtracted from gross profit on sales to determine the net income (or net loss) for the period. Operating expenses are those expenses incurred in operating a business during the period. Although many of the operating expenses incurred by a service firm are also incurred by a merchandising firm, additional expenses that relate to buying and selling inventory are incurred by a merchandising firm. Operating expenses are normally separated by function. **Selling expenses** result from efforts to sell the inventory and include storage costs, advertising, sales salaries and commissions, and the cost of delivering goods to customers. **Administrative expenses**

Figure 5–1
Income Statement

SUNRISE HI-FI SALES Income Statement For Year Ended December 31, 1987		
Net sales		$172,000
Less: Cost of goods sold		103,000
Gross profit on sales		69,000
Less: Operating expenses		
Selling expenses	$26,000	
Administrative expenses	18,000	
Total operating expenses		44,000
Net income		$ 25,000

are management costs associated with the general administration of the company's operations. These expenses include those incurred to operate such subdivisions of the firm as the general office, accounting, personnel, and credit and collection departments. Net income for a merchandising firm results if the revenue from sales exceeds the cost of the goods sold and the operating expenses incurred.

ACCOUNTING FOR SALES TRANSACTIONS

A sales transaction is generally recorded by the seller when the ownership of the inventory is transferred from the firm to the customer. To record the sale, an asset account is debited and the *Sales* account is credited for an amount equal to the fair value of the asset received. Usually, the asset recorded in exchange for the inventory is cash or accounts receivable. The entry to record a credit sale is:

Objective 3: Recording the sale of inventory

Aug.	5	Accounts Receivable*	180	
		Sales		180
		Sold merchandise to Ray Stevens on account.		

*Cash account is debited if a cash sale.

At year's end, the balance in the *Sales* account shows the total amount of cash and credit sales made during the accounting period. When a sale is made on account, the cash may be received in a subsequent period. As a result, there may be a significant difference between cash collections from sales and the balance accumulated in the *Sales* account.

SALES RETURNS AND ALLOWANCES

In order to maintain good customer relations and honor warranty agreements, most businesses permit a customer to return unsatisfactory goods. Alternatively, the customer may agree to keep the goods in exchange for a reduction in the sales price. The return of goods (sales return), or an adjustment to the sales price (sales allowance), is a reduction in the amount of recorded sales, and either a cash refund is made to the customer or the customer's account receivable is credited. In either case, once a return or allowance is authorized, the seller issues a source document, called a **credit memorandum** (or **credit memo**), to the customer, and forwards a copy to the accounting department so that the transaction can be properly recorded. The document is called a credit memorandum because the seller is informing the customer that the customer's account is being reduced (credited) on the seller's books.

Handling returned merchandise is time-consuming and results in increased costs. For these reasons, management must look for the cause of excessive returns and correct the problem whenever possible. To provide information on the volume of returns and allowances, a contra sales account called *Sales Returns and Allowances* is debited, as follows.

Aug.	8	Sales Returns and Allowances	30	
		Accounts Receivable*		30
		Ray Stevens returned unsatisfactory		
		merchandise sold on Aug. 5 for credit.		
		(Making only one entry at this time		
		assumes use of the periodic inventory		
		system discussed in a later section of		
		this chapter.)		

*Cash is credited if the original sale had been a cash sale.

As shown on page 206, sales returns and allowances are subtracted from sales in the income statement.

CREDIT TERMS

Objective 4:
Credit terms

The parties involved in an inventory transaction may agree that payment is to be made immediately upon transfer of the goods (a cash sale). Sometimes the sale is made on credit and payment is delayed for a specific length of time called the **credit period.** The length of the credit period varies among firms, but 30 to 60 days is typical.

When inventory is sold on credit, the terms of payment, called the **credit terms,** agreed to by the buyer and seller should be clear as to the amount due and the credit period. The terms of payment normally appear in a source document called the **sales invoice** by the seller and the **purchase invoice** by the buyer. The credit period is usually abbreviated in the following form: ''n/10 EOM'' or ''n/30.'' In the first case, the invoice price is due 10 days after the end of the month in which the sale occurred. In the second case, the invoice price is due within 30 days after the invoice date.

CASH DISCOUNTS

To provide an incentive for the buyer to make payment before the end of the credit period, the seller may grant a cash discount, called a **sales discount** by the seller and a **purchases discount** by the buyer. A **cash discount** entitles the buyer to deduct a specified percentage of the net sales price if payment is received within a given time span, called the **discount period.** The terms are normally quoted in a format such as: ''2/10,n/30'' (the terms are read ''two ten, net thirty''). This notation means that the buyer has two payment options. If payment is made within 10 days of the invoice date, the buyer may deduct 2% from the amount of the invoice. If payment is not made within the 10-day discount period, the full price is due 30 days from the invoice date.

To illustrate, assume that the credit terms were 2/10, n/30 on the $180 sale to Ray Stevens shown previously. The entry to record the collection within the discount period, net of the $30 return, is:

				147	
Aug.	15	Cash		3	
		Sales Discounts			
		Accounts Receivable			150
		Received payment from Ray Stevens			
		within the discount period.			

Note that the sales discount of $3 is computed on the sales price less the merchandise returned by the customer [($180 − $30) × 2%].

These entries are based on use of the **gross invoice method** under which sales and accounts receivable are recorded at gross invoice price. In other words, under this method, sales discounts are not recorded unless the customer takes advantage of the cash discount. If the customer pays within the discount period, the sales discount is recorded in a separate account in order to provide information to management on the amount of sales discount taken. A sales discount is considered a reduction in the sales price of the goods. It is reported as a subtraction from sales revenue (i.e., a contra revenue account) in the income statement as shown on page 206.

From the seller's point of view, the purpose of granting cash discounts is to induce the customer to pay the receivable earlier. Hence, the firm will have the cash available for use before the end of the credit period. The earlier payment may also tend to reduce losses from uncollectible accounts receivable.

When a cash discount is included in the credit terms, the buyer must decide whether or not to pay the account payable within the discount period. Usually, the annual cost of forgoing cash discounts is quite high, which can be shown by converting the discount rate to an annual rate. For example, assume that an agreement for the purchase of $300 in goods contained the terms of 2/10, n/30. To obtain the maximum benefit of the credit terms granted by the seller, the buyer should pay the invoice on the last possible date. Thus, the buyer will either (1) pay $294 ten days from the invoice date; or (2) pay the full invoice price of $300 thirty days from the invoice date. By not paying within the ten-day discount period, the buyer has the use of $294 for an additional 20 days. The additional $6 that must be paid in 30 days is an interest charge for extending the credit period 20 days. The effective annual yield is computed as follows.

$$\text{Effective rate for the 20 day period} = \frac{\$6}{\$294}$$
$$= 2.04\%$$
$$\text{Effective annual rate} = \frac{360 \text{ days}}{20} \times 2.04\%$$
$$= 36.7\%$$

The effective rate of 36.7% is quite high. A company should compare this rate to the rate it would have to pay to other sources of credit such as banks, savings and loans, or other lending institutions.

NET SALES

Sales returns and allowances and sales discounts are subtracted from sales to arrive at net sales in the income statement as illustrated here.

Revenue from sales:		
Gross sales		$177,600
Less: Sales returns & allowances	$3,400	
Sales discounts	2,200	5,600
Net sales		$172,000

TRADE DISCOUNTS

A **trade discount** is a percentage reduction granted to a customer from the suggested list price. In contrast to a cash discount, a trade discount is not related to early payment. Instead, it is used to compute the actual invoice price to a particular class of customer. Trade discounts enable the firm to print one price list or catalog but still vary prices for different customer groups, such as retailers or wholesalers, or to grant quantity discounts.

Trade discounts are not normally recorded in the accounts by either the buyer or the seller. For example, assume that a wholesaler quotes a list price of $200 per item but grants retailers a trade discount of 30% on the purchase of five or more units. The entry to record the sale of 10 units is:

July	10	Accounts Receivable	1,400	
		Sales		1,400
		To record the sale of inventory on credit subject to a 30% quantity discount.		

The amount of the entry is computed as follows.

List price—10 units × $200	$2,000
Less: 30% quantity discount	600
Invoice price	$1,400

The buyer records a purchase of inventory in the amount of $1,400.

If included in the terms of the sale, a cash discount is computed on the $1,400 sales price less any subsequent returns or allowances. For example, if three of the ten items are later returned, then the cash discount is computed on $980 (7 units × $140).

FREIGHT-OUT

The sales invoice normally indicates which party to the transaction must pay the cost of shipping the goods. If the goods are sold **FOB (free on board) shipping point,** the buyer takes title at the seller's shipping dock. Therefore, freight costs incurred from the point of shipment are paid by the buyer. Conversely, the term **FOB destination** indicates that the title changes when the goods reach the buyer's receiving dock. Hence, the seller is responsible for paying the freight cost. The party responsible for the freight cost is summarized as follows.

Shipping Terms	Point Title Transfers	Party Responsible for Freight Costs
FOB shipping point	At shipping dock of seller	Buyer
FOB destination	At receiving dock of buyer	Seller

When terms of the sale are FOB destination, the seller will normally record the payment of freight costs as a debit to a **Freight-Out** or **Delivery Expense** account. The entry to record a $35 freight payment on goods sold is:

Aug.	10	Freight-out	35	
		Cash		35

Freight-out is an expense that should be reported in the selling expense category of the income statement. Freight charges *paid by the seller on goods sold* should not be confused with freight charges *paid on goods purchased,* which is discussed later in the chapter.

ACCOUNTING FOR INVENTORY AND COST OF GOODS SOLD

As noted earlier, the cost of inventory sold during the year is matched against sales revenues earned from selling the inventory. The cost of unsold inventory is reported as a current asset in the balance sheet. Two distinctly different inventory systems, perpetual and periodic, are used to determine the amounts reported for the ending inventory and the cost of goods sold. The system adopted by a firm is largely determined by the type of inventory held.

PERPETUAL INVENTORY SYSTEM

When a **perpetual inventory system** is used, a current and continuous record of the goods on hand is maintained and the cost of goods sold is recorded at the time of each sale. To record the cost of each item sold, a firm must refer to its inventory records to determine the cost. Because the maintenance of perpetual inventory records involves more clerical work than the periodic system, the system is usually used by firms that sell a limited number of items with a high unit cost, such as automobiles, heating and air-conditioning units, works of art, computers, pianos, television sets, stereo equipment, and home appliances.

PERIODIC INVENTORY SYSTEM

Firms that sell a large number of items with a low cost per unit—such firms include drug stores, variety stores, hardware stores, and grocery stores—may find the maintenance of perpetual inventory records too costly and time-consuming. This type of business often uses the **periodic inventory system,** in which the cost of goods sold for the period is determined at the end of the

Objective 5: Using a periodic inventory system

accounting period. A store operating with a high volume of sales may conveniently record the amount of each sale, but would find it difficult to trace the cost of each item sold back to the inventory records. Thus, a day-to-day record of goods on hand or cost of goods sold is not maintained. Because the periodic inventory system is used by many merchandising firms, it is illustrated in detail in the next section.

ILLUSTRATION OF A PERIODIC INVENTORY SYSTEM

In a periodic inventory system, the cost of the merchandise on hand at the beginning of the period, called the **beginning inventory,** is reported in the *Merchandise Inventory* account. The balance in the account is not changed, except to correct errors, until the end of the accounting period.

The costs of inventory purchases made during a period are recorded in a **Purchases** account. When inventory is sold, an entry is made to record only the sale. No records of the goods on hand or the goods sold are maintained during the period. To determine the cost of goods on hand at the end of the period, (called the **ending inventory**) it is necessary to take a physical inventory. A **physical inventory** involves first counting all inventory units on hand. Next, the unit cost of each type of item in stock is determined from purchase invoices and multiplied by the appropriate number of units on hand to determine the dollar cost of that particular item. The dollar cost of the ending inventory is the sum of the costs determined for each type of item held in stock. Once this is completed, the cost of goods sold is computed as follows.

Cost of beginning merchandise inventory	$2,600
Add: Cost of goods purchased during the current period	6,159
Cost of goods available for sale	8,759
Less: Cost of ending merchandise inventory (per physical count)	2,950
Cost of goods sold	$5,809

The cost of ending inventory for the current period of $2,950 will become the beginning inventory amount for the following period. The process of adjusting the inventory account to its end of year balance is discussed later in this chapter.

To illustrate a periodic inventory system, assume that the *Merchandise Inventory* account at the beginning of the period for the Campus Bookstore was:

Merchandise Inventory

1/1 Beg. Bal.	2,600	

The beginning inventory of $2,600 is the ending inventory determined by a physical inventory conducted on the last day of the preceding period.

Transaction 1 Purchased merchandise on account.

Jan.	15	Purchases	6,500	
		Accounts Payable		6,500
		Purchased merchandise inventory on		
		account from Hansen Office Supply.		
		Terms: 2/10, n/30; Invoice date, Jan. 15;		
		FOB Shipping Point.		

The *Purchases* account is a temporary account used to accumulate the cost of all merchandise acquired for resale during the period. This account is used to record inventory purchases only. Acquisitions of other assets are recorded in appropriate asset accounts. Because the balance is closed at the end of each accounting period, the accumulated account balance reflects the purchases for the current period only.

Transaction 2 Paid freight cost of $426 on goods purchased FOB shipping point.

Conceptually, the cost of an asset, in this case inventory, includes the invoice price plus freight charges and other costs directly related to acquiring merchandise. This means that freight costs incurred on a shipment of merchandise should be allocated to each unit and recorded as a cost of the inventory. Under the periodic system, such cost should be included in the cost of goods available for sale, and, at the end of the period should be allocated between the units on hand and the units sold during the period. In other words, the invoice price plus the freight cost should be expensed as each unit is sold to be matched against revenue as part of the cost of goods sold.

In practice, however, freight costs are normally not allocated between the units on hand and the units sold because of the practical problem of allocating them to individual units when several types of inventory are acquired in one shipment. Furthermore, in most cases the allocation of freight costs would not significantly change the firm's financial statements. As a result, freight costs are expensed in the period incurred.

If the seller includes the freight charges in the list price, it is not separated on the invoice and becomes a part of the inventory cost when the entry is made to record the purchase transaction. If the seller pays the freight and charges the buyer, it will normally be listed separately on the invoice and is generally debited to an account called **Freight-in** or **Transportation-in.** For example, assume that the invoice for the purchase on January 15 contained a separate charge for freight in the amount of $426. The entry is:

Jan.	15	Purchases	6,500	
		Freight-in	426	
		Accounts Payable		6,926
		Purchased merchandise on account for		
		$6,500 plus freight charges of $426.		

The *Freight-in* account is also used to record freight cost paid by the buyer directly to the freight company when the terms of the sale are FOB shipping point. The entry in this case is as follows.

Jan.	17	Freight-in	426	
		Cash		426
		Paid freight cost on merchandise purchased FOB shipping point.		

Freight-in is reported as an addition to purchases in the income statement.

Transaction 3   Sold merchandise inventory to customers on account.

Jan.	21	Accounts Receivable	10,400	
		Sales		10,400
		Sold merchandise inventory on account.		

At the time of sale, one entry is made to record the revenue earned from the sale of merchandise.

Transaction 4   Returned defective merchandise to Hansen Office Supply for credit on account.

The buyer and seller may agree that an item is to be returned or that the item is to be kept and an adjustment made to the purchase price for a number of reasons, such as that the goods were damaged when received by the buyer. A source document that contains the information needed to record the transaction, called a **debit memorandum** (or **debit memo**), is prepared. The document is called a debit memorandum because the supplier's account payable is debited on the buyer's books. The return of goods to Hansen Office Supply is recorded as follows.

Jan.	23	Accounts Payable	650	
		Purchases Returns and Allowances		650
		Returned merchandise to Hansen Office Supply for credit on account.		

There is a cost to the firm to order merchandise, receive and inspect the merchandise, and to repack it for return to the manufacturer. To provide relevant information to management concerning the total amount of goods returned, the return is recorded in a contra purchases account, **Purchases Returns and Allowances,** rather than directly as a credit to the *Purchases* account. The entry is the same if the goods are kept by the buyer and an adjustment is made to the invoice price.

Transaction 5   Paid within the discount period for the purchase made on January 15.

Accounting for cash discounts by the seller, and the notation 2/10, n/30, have already been discussed. Recall that a cash discount entitles the buyer to deduct a specified amount from the invoice price if payment is made within the discount period. When payment is made within the discount period, a purchase discount is recorded by the buyer. The entry to record the payment is:

Jan.	25	Accounts Payable	5,850	
		Purchases Discounts		117
		Cash		5,733
		Paid for inventory purchased on Jan. 15.		

The amount of the cash payment and discount are computed as follows.

Total cost of goods purchased	$6,500
Less: Cost of goods returned on Jan. 23	650
Cost of goods being paid for	5,850
Less: Cash discount—$5,850 × 2%	117
Cash payment	$5,733

The *Purchases Discounts* account is reported as a contra account to *Purchases* in the buyer's income statement.

Transaction 6 Merchandise inventory is returned by a customer for credit.

Jan.	26	Sales Returns and Allowances	720	
		Accounts Receivable		720
		A customer returned merchandise inventory.		

COMPUTATION OF COST OF GOODS SOLD

Based on these six transactions, a partial income statement is prepared in Figure 5–2. It is assumed that a physical inventory count taken at the end of the period determined the cost of inventory on hand to be $2,950.

Some relationships shown in statement format for the periodic inventory system are summarized as follows.

1. Gross profit on sales = net sales − cost of goods sold; or net sales = cost of goods sold + gross profit on sales.
2. Cost of goods purchased = purchases − purchases returns and allowances − purchases discounts + freight-in.
3. Cost of goods available for sale = cost of beginning inventory + cost of goods purchased.
4. Cost of goods sold = cost of goods available for sale − cost of ending inventory; or cost of goods sold = cost of beginning inventory + cost of goods purchased − cost of ending inventory.

Familiarity with these relationships will aid in understanding the characteristics of the periodic inventory system and make it easier to determine the effect of inventory errors.

Note that under the periodic inventory system, the cost of goods sold is a residual amount that is left after deducting the ending inventory from the cost

CAMPUS BOOKSTORE
Income Statement
For Month Ended January 1987

Sales				$10,400
Less: Sales returns and allowances				720
Net Sales				9,680
Cost of Goods Sold:				
Beginning merchandise inventory			$2,600	
Add: Purchases		$6,500		
Less: Purchases returns and allowances	$650			
Purchases discounts	117	767		
Cost of net purchases		5,733		
Add: Freight-in		426		
Cost of goods purchased			6,159	
Cost of goods available for sale			8,759	
Less: Cost of ending merchandise inventory			2,950	
Cost of Goods Sold				5,809
Gross Profit on Sales				$3,871

Figure 5–2

Partial Income Statement with a Periodic Inventory System Worksheet for a Merchandising Firm Using the Periodic Inventory System

of goods available for sale. As a result, losses of inventory from causes such as theft, shrinkage, breakage, and clerical error are difficult to identify. Techniques used to determine any large inventory losses are examined in Chapter 9.

END-OF-PERIOD PROCESS—PERIODIC INVENTORY SYSTEM

Illustration of a Worksheet for a Merchandising Firm

Objective 6: Completing the accounting cycle

At the end of the accounting period, a worksheet can be used to organize the information needed to prepare financial statements and closing entries. Except for the new accounts introduced in this chapter, the preparation of a worksheet and the closing process for a merchandising business are similar to those illustrated for a service firm in Chapter 4.

A worksheet for Sunrise Hi-Fi Sales, a firm that has adopted the periodic inventory system, is presented in Figure 5–3. In Figure 5–3, the Unadjusted Trial Balance columns contain a listing of the account balances taken from the general ledger of the company. The next two columns are for the end-of-year adjustments based on the following information.

a. Accrued salaries:	Sales	$2,200
	Administrative	1,050
b. Depreciation:	Store equipment	7,600
c.	Office equipment	3,200
d. Prepaid insurance expired during the year		610
e. Accrued interest at the end of the period		1,470

SUNRISE HI-FI SALES
Worksheet
For Year Ended December 31, 1985

Account Title	Unadjusted Trial Balance Debit	Unadjusted Trial Balance Credit	Adjustments Debit	Adjustments Credit	Adjusted Trial Balance Debit	Adjusted Trial Balance Credit	Income Statement Debit	Income Statement Credit	Balance Sheet Debit	Balance Sheet Credit
Cash	41,170				41,170				41,170	
Accounts Receivable	98,710				98,710				98,710	
Merchandise Inv.—1/1	58,400				58,400		58,400	53,260	53,260	
Prepaid Insurance	1,910			(d) 610	1,300				1,300	
Store Equipment	72,000				72,000				72,000	
Accumulated Depr.— Store Equipment		46,600		(b) 7,600		54,200				54,200
Office Equipment	26,400				26,400				26,400	
Accumulated Depr.— Office Equipment		13,300		(c) 3,200		16,500				16,500
Notes Payable		36,000				36,000				36,000
Accounts Payable		107,610				107,610				107,610
Anne Clark, Capital		50,000				50,000				50,000
Anne Clark, Drawing	10,000				10,000				10,000	
Sales		713,280				713,280		713,280		
Sales Returns & Allowances	21,390				21,390		21,390			
Sales Discount	3,260				3,260		3,260			
Purchases	472,620				472,620		472,620			
Freight-in	6,210				6,210		6,210			
Purchases Returns & Allowances		13,480				13,480		13,480		
Purchases Discounts		2,860				2,860		2,860		
Sales Salaries and Commissions	58,840		(a) 2,200		61,040		61,040			
Delivery Expense	15,210				15,210		15,210			
Advertising Expense	22,620				22,620		22,620			
Rent Expense	29,000				29,000		29,000			
Office Salaries Exp.	47,790		(a) 1,050		48,840		48,840			
Interest Expense	1,000		(e) 1,470		2,470		2,470			
Rent Revenue		3,400				3,400		3,400		
Totals	986,530	986,530								
Salaries Payable				(a) 3,250		3,250				3,250
Depr. Exp.—Store Equipment			(b) 7,600		7,600		7,600			
Depr. Exp.—Office Equipment			(c) 3,200		3,200		3,200			
Insurance Expense			(d) 610		610		610			
Interest Payable				(e) 1,470		1,470				1,470
Totals			16,130	16,130	1,002,050	1,002,050	752,470	786,280	302,840	269,030
Net income for the period							33,810			33,810
Totals							786,280	786,280	302,840	302,840

Figure 5–3
Worksheet for a Merchandising Firm Using the Periodic Inventory System

Based on a physical inventory taken December 31 of each year, the ending merchandise inventory was determined to be $53,260 at the end of the current period and was $58,400 at the end of the prior period.

Merchandise Inventory in the Worksheet

Under a periodic inventory system, the merchandise inventory balance of $58,400 listed in the Unadjusted Trial Balance debit column is the beginning inventory amount. This amount is extended to the Income Statement debit column because it is added to the cost of goods purchased to determine the cost of goods available for sale. The accounts that enter into the cost of goods purchased—*Purchases* (debit), *Freight-in* (debit), *Purchases Returns and Allowances* (credit), and *Purchases Discounts* (credit)—are also extended to the appropriate Income Statement columns.

The ending merchandise inventory of $53,260 does not appear in the accounts, but is entered directly in the Income Statement credit column, since it is a deduction from the cost of goods available for sale when computing the cost of goods sold. That amount is also entered in the Balance Sheet debit column, because the ending inventory is an asset to the firm, and because it is necessary to enter an equal debit to maintain the equality of debits and credits in the worksheet. Journal entries made to enter the balances in the general ledger *Merchandise Inventory* account are discussed in the next section. The inventory balances, purchases, and purchase-related accounts enter into the computation of cost of goods sold, as shown in Figure 5–4.

CLOSING ENTRIES

Information needed to prepare the closing entries is available in the Income Statement columns of the worksheet. The process is similar to that illustrated in Chapter 4 for a service firm. Closing entries are made (1) to close the temporary accounts with debit balances; (2) to close the temporary accounts with credit balances; (3) to close the balance in the *Income* Summary account; and (4) to close the balance in the *Drawing* account. In addition, it is necessary to remove the beginning inventory balance and record the ending inventory in the *Merchandise Inventory* account. Although there are several ways to accomplish this, each method produces the same cost of goods sold amount. One approach is to adjust the *Merchandise Inventory* account during the closing process at the time the other income statement accounts are closed. This approach is illustrated here because it requires making fewer journal entries than the other methods.

		Closing Entries		
Dec.	31	Income Summary	752,470	
		Merchandise Inventory		58,400
		Sales Returns and Allowances		21,390
		Sales Discounts		3,260

		Purchases		472,620
		Freight-in		6,210
		Sales Salaries & Commissions		61,040
		Delivery Expense		15,210
		Advertising Expense		22,620
		Rent Expense		29,000
		Office Salaries Expense		48,840
		Interest Expense		2,470
		Depreciation Expense—Store Equip.		7,600
		Depreciation Expense—Office Equip.		3,200
		Insurance Expense		610
		To remove the beginning balance from the inventory account, close all temporary accounts with debit balances, and record the total in the Income Summary account.		
	31	Merchandise Inventory	53,260	
		Sales	713,280	
		Purchases Returns and Allowances	13,480	
		Purchases Discounts	2,860	
		Rent Revenue	3,400	
		Income Summary		786,280
		To record the ending inventory balance, close all temporary accounts with credit balances, and record the total in the Income Summary account.		
	31	Income Summary	33,810	
		Anne Clark, Capital		33,810
		To close the net income to the Capital account.		
	31	Anne Clark, Capital	10,000	
		Anne Clark, Drawing		10,000
		To close the Drawing account.		

The credit of $58,400 to the *Merchandise Inventory* account in the first closing entry removes the beginning balance from the account and transfers it to the *Income Summary* account. The ending inventory balance of $53,260 is recorded in the second closing entry as shown here.

ACCOUNT: Merchandise Inventory					Account No. 130
Date	Explanation	Post Ref.	Debit	Credit	Balance
1/1	Beginning balance		58,400		58,400
12/31	Closing entry	22		58,400	-0-
12/31	Closing entry	22	53,260		53,260

Before the second entry is made and posted, the ending inventory is not reported in any ledger accounts.

INCOME STATEMENT FOR A MERCHANDISING FIRM

An income statement for Hi-Fi Sales is presented in Figure 5–4 to show how a merchandiser's income statement accounts are reported. The company uses a periodic inventory system and reports a detailed cost of goods sold section. In practice, there is considerable variation in income statement formats. As a general rule, only the net sales and cost of goods sold amounts are reported in annual reports.

The format shown in Figure 5–4 is called a **multiple-step income statement** because it shows several subtotals to highlight significant relationships, such as gross profit on sales. Note that in this format, income is divided into income from operations and other revenues and expenses. Income from operations includes revenues earned and expenses incurred that pertain to the company's principal operations. Other revenues and expenses are items that are not directly related to the principal operations of the firm. In other words, other revenues and expenses result from transactions related to secondary or miscellaneous activities of the firm. Included in this category are items such as interest expense, dividend revenue, interest revenue, miscellaneous earnings from rentals, and gains and losses from the sale of nonmerchandise assets. Also note that in this format, the expenses are classified by function, such as cost of goods sold, selling expenses, and administrative expenses.

Operating expenses are often separated into two categories: selling expenses and administrative expenses. Operating expenses exclude cost of goods sold and other expenses. Some expenses, such as the rent expense of $29,000, may need to be allocated between selling expenses ($17,000) and administrative expenses ($12,000). Several methods can be used to allocate an expense. The allocation should be based on a logical relationship between the expense to be allocated and the benefits from the expense. For example, rent could be allocated based on the number of square feet occupied by each department. Allocation methods are covered in more detail in Chapter 21. Although not illustrated here, the worksheet prepared in Figure 5–3 is used to prepare the adjusting entries.

PERPETUAL INVENTORY SYSTEM

Objective 7: Using a perpetual inventory system

As noted earlier, firms that sell inventory of high unit cost often use a perpetual inventory system, rather than a periodic inventory system, to account for inventory cost. A perpetual inventory system involves keeping a current and continuous record of all increases and decreases in each item of inventory.

When the perpetual inventory method is used in a merchandising firm, a single *Merchandise Inventory* account is maintained in the general ledger to record all inventory transactions. Supporting details are entered on individual inventory cards. One card is maintained for each type of inventory item held. Each inventory card shows the units, unit cost, and total cost for each purchase, each sale, and the balance on hand. When each item is different, as with automobiles where each item has different options and cost, a separate inventory card is maintained for each item. The balance in the general ledger

SUNRISE HI-FI SALES
Income Statement
For the Year Ended December 31, 1987

Mult. step

Gross Sales			$713,280
Less: Sales returns and allowances		$ 21,390	
Sales discounts		3,260	24,650
Net sales			688,630
Cost of goods sold:			
Merchandise inventory—1/1		58,400	
Purchases	$472,620		
Less: Purchases returns and allowances	$13,480		
Purchases discounts	2,860	16,340	
Cost of net purchases		456,280	
Add: Freight-in		6,210	
Cost of goods purchased		462,490	
Cost of goods available for sale		520,890	
Less: Merchandise inventory—12/31 *Ending Inventory*		53,260	
Cost of goods sold			467,630
Gross profit on sales			221,000
Operating expenses:			
Selling expenses:			
Sales salaries and commissions expense	61,040		
Advertising expense	22,620		
Rent expense–store space	17,000		
Delivery expense	15,210		
Depreciation expense–store equipment	7,600		
Total selling expenses		123,470	
Administrative expenses:			
Office salaries expense	48,840		
Rent expense–office space	12,000		
Depreciation expense–office equipment	3,200		
Insurance expense	610		
Total administrative expenses		64,650	
Total operating expenses			188,120
Income from operations			32,880
Other revenues and expenses:			
Add: Rent revenue		3,400	
Less: Interest expense		2,470	
Net other revenues and expenses			930
Net income for the year			$ 33,810

Figure 5–4
Income Statement for a Merchandising Firm Using the Periodic Inventory System

account (*Merchandise Inventory*) should equal the sum of the dollar amounts shown on all of the individual inventory cards.

When the perpetual system is used, purchases are added to both the beginning inventory balance in the *Merchandise Inventory* account and the appropriate inventory cards. As goods are sold, an entry for the cost of goods sold is made to reduce the *Merchandise Inventory* account and increase the *Cost of Goods Sold* account. To determine the dollar cost of each unit sold, the accountant refers to the individual inventory card of the item sold. Therefore, an item sold must be identified so that the unit and related cost may be removed from the proper inventory card and the cost removed from the inventory account in the general ledger.

Note that these procedures are essentially consistent with the accounting procedures illustrated in earlier chapters for other asset accounts (such as supplies inventory, prepaid rent, and prepaid insurance). That is, the cost of inventory purchased is accounted for as an asset until it is sold to produce revenue, at which time the cost of the asset is transferred to an expense account to be matched against earned revenue.

In recent years, with the introduction of computers and other electronic business machines, many firms dealing in low-unit-cost items have found it feasible to use a perpetual inventory system in order to better plan and control their investment in inventory. The development of on-site computers, in particular, has been a real breakthrough for the perpetual inventory system. For example, many grocery stores now use optical-scan cash registers that not only record the sales price of the item, but also enter the item sold for inventory purposes. Firms that adopt the perpetual inventory system do so because they believe the benefits of improved managerial planning and control obtained from detailed inventory records outweigh the additional costs of maintaining the system.

ILLUSTRATION OF A PERPETUAL INVENTORY SYSTEM

Figure 5–5 is an example of an inventory card kept for a Model HE 1120 personal computer. The beginning inventory consisted of four units at a unit cost of $650. The other data entered on the card are based on the following transactions.

Jan. 15 Purchased 10 units for $650 per unit on account from Horn Electronics.
21 Sold three units on account for $1,050 per unit; cost $650 per unit.
23 Returned to Horn Electronics a defective unit which cost $650.
24 A unit sold on January 21 is returned by a customer for credit on account. Because the unit was suitable for resale, it was returned to stock.

The entries to record the transactions above and the postings to the inventory related accounts for a perpetual inventory system are shown in Figure 5–6 on page 220. The operations of the system may be summarized as follows.

		Purchases			Cost of Goods Sold			Balance		
			Unit	Total		Unit	Total		Unit	Total
Date	Explanation	Units	Cost	Cost	Units	Cost	Cost	Units	Cost	Cost
1/1	Beginning balance							4	650	2,600
1/15	Purchase	10	650	6,500				14	650	9,100
1/21	Sales				3	650	1,950	11	650	7,150
1/23	Purchase returns	(1)	650	(650)				10	650	6,500
1/24	Sales returns				(1)	650	(650)	11	650	7,150

Item Personal Computer — *Code* HE1120 — *Location* 1 unit showroom, Remainder—Warehouse — *Minimum Stock* 4 — *Maximum Stock* 15

Figure 5–5
Inventory Card

1. The inventory on hand at the beginning of the period is reported in the inventory account.
2. Purchases of inventory are added to the beginning inventory balance in the inventory account.
3. When goods are sold, an entry is made to record the sale (the revenue aspect of the transaction) and another entry is made to reduce the inventory account and increase the *Cost of Goods Sold* account (the expense aspect of the transaction).
4. To provide a continuous record of inventory on hand, units returned to the manufacturer and units suitable for resale that are returned by customers are recorded in the inventory account.
5. Assuming that this is the only item of inventory held, the cost of the ending inventory is the balance in the inventory account ($7,150); the cost of goods sold for the period ($1,300), to be matched against revenues in the income statement is the balance in the *Cost of Goods Sold* account. The inventory balance is an asset and, accordingly, it is extended to the Balance Sheet debit column in the preparation of a worksheet. The balance in the *Cost of Goods Sold* account is extended to the Income Statement debit column and is closed, along with the other expense accounts.

Note that in Figure 5–6, the entry to record the sale and return of the merchandise is based on the sales price, whereas the amount of the inventory entry is based on the cost of the units sold, as shown in the inventory card. Also, every entry made to the *Merchandise Inventory* account requires that an entry be made to an inventory card. Thus, the balance in the inventory account agrees with the ending balance shown on the inventory card (see Figure 5–5). By maintaining a continuous inventory record, it is not necessary to take a physical count of the inventory on hand to determine the ending balance. Firms using a perpetual inventory system should nevertheless take a physical inventory once a year to verify the accuracy of the inventory records.

FIGURE 5–6
Illustration of a Perpetual Inventory System

Merchandise Inventory

1/1 Beg. Bal. (4 units @ $650)	2,600		

(In actuality, the balance in this account would be much larger and would show the total cost of all types of computers held at the beginning of the period rather than the cost of these computers only.)

1. Purchased ten computers on account from Horn Electronics.

Jan. 15	Merchandise Inventory	6,500	
	Accounts Payable		6,500

2. Sold three computers on account.

21	Accounts Receivable	3,150	
	Sales		3,150
21	Cost of Goods Sold	1,950	
	Merchandise Inventory		1,950

3. Returned one computer for credit on account.

23	Accounts Payable	650	
	Merchandise Inventory		650

4. Customer returned one computer for credit on account.

24	Sales Returns and Allowances	1,050	
	Accounts Receivable		1,050
24	Merchandise Inventory	650	
	Cost of Goods Sold		650

General ledger account balances at the end of the period.

Merchandise Inventory				Cost of Goods Sold			
1/1 Bal.	2,600	1/21	1,950	1/21	1,950	1/24	650
1/15	6,500	1/23	650	1/31 Bal.	1,300		
1/24	650						
1/31 Bal.	7,150						

ALTERNATIVE METHODS OF ACCOUNTING FOR CASH DISCOUNTS WITH A PERIODIC SYSTEM

Recall from our previous discussion that a cash discount entitles the buyer to deduct a specified amount from the invoice price if payment is made within a specified discount period. In the preceding illustrations, purchases were recorded at the gross invoice price. An alternative approach is to record the purchase at the net invoice amount (invoice price − sales discount).

GROSS INVOICE METHOD

When the gross invoice method is used, the cost of the inventory and account payable are recorded at the full invoice price and purchase discounts are not recorded unless payment is made within the discount period. To illustrate the gross invoice method, assume the purchase of goods for $5,850 on terms of 2/10, n/30, and the settlement of the account balance within the discount period. The entries, assuming the use of the periodic inventory system, are as follows.

Purchase transaction

Jan.	15	Purchases	5,850	
		Accounts Payable		5,850

Payment made within the discount period

	25	Accounts Payable	5,850	
		Purchases Discounts		117
		Cash		5,733

When payment is made within the discount period, a purchase discount is recorded by the buyer. Although the account has a credit balance, it is not revenue to the firm. A firm does not realize revenue by purchasing goods; it realizes revenue from selling them. In a periodic inventory system, purchases discounts are reported as a contra account to purchases in the firm's income statement.

The payment is recorded as follows if payment is not made within the discount period.

Payment not made within the discount period

Feb.	15	Accounts Payable	5,850	
		Cash		5,850

As can be seen from these entries, the amount of the cash discount is included in the cost of the inventory. Conceptually, however, a purchase discount reduces the unit cost of the inventory purchased; if the payment is not made within the discount period, the discount lost should be reported as an interest expense. Sometimes it is reported as an administrative expense on the basis that it is poor cash management to miss taking a discount. Thus, use of the gross method overstates inventory costs and understates interest expense if the discount is not taken.

NET INVOICE METHOD

**Objective 8:
Net invoice
method**

Another procedure used by some firms, called the **net invoice method,** is to record the purchase for the net invoice amount. The same set of facts used for the gross invoice method are used here to illustrate the net invoice method.

Purchase transaction

Jan.	15	Purchases		5,733	
		Accounts Payable			5,733
		Invoice price	$5,850		
		Less: 2% discount	117		
		Net invoice price	$5,733		

Payment made within the discount period

	25	Accounts Payable	5,733	
		Cash		5,733

If the payment is not made within the discount period, the full invoice price of $5,850 must be paid, since the cash discount is lost. The entry is as follows.

Payment is not made within the discount period

Feb.	15	Accounts Payable	5,733	
		Purchases Discounts Loss	117	
		Cash		5,850

Note that the Accounts Payable account must be reduced by $5,733 to offset the initial credit of $5,733 made to the account on January 15, even though cash in the amount of $5,850 was eventually paid. The difference of $117 is the discount. Purchase discounts lost are a financing expense that results from delaying payment and should either be reported along with interest expense in the other expense section of the income statement or included with the administrative expenses as a cost of inefficient cash management.

The net method is conceptually preferable to the gross method because (1) the cost of the inventory purchased is recorded in terms of the cash price; (2) the account payable is reported at the amount expected to be paid; and (3) the amount of purchase discounts lost is reported as a separate item to management. Nevertheless, in practice, the gross method is commonly used because it avoids the problem of allocating the discount to individual units when a physical inventory is taken.

DEMONSTRATION PROBLEM

Plaza Business Equipment opened for business on May 1, 1987. The transactions shown here were completed during May. Credit terms are 2/15, n/30 for purchases on account, and 3/10, n/30 for sales on account. Plaza uses a periodic inventory system, and the gross invoice method of recording purchases.

May 1 Purchased merchandise inventory on account for $8,000.
     3 Made sales on account, $2,200.
     5 Returned $500 of inventory purchased on May 1.
     8 Made sales on account, $1,150.
    14 Customer returned items sold for $150 on May 8.
    15 Purchased merchandise inventory on account for $6,000.
    18 Received payment for sales made on May 8.
    20 Purchased merchandise inventory on account for $800.
    22 Paid freight bill for inventory purchased, $230.
    23 Made sales on account, $3,400.
    25 Paid for inventory purchased on May 15.
    30 Paid for inventory purchased on May 1.
    31 Made sales on account, $12,620.
    31 Received payment for sales made on May 3.

Required:
A. Prepare journal entries for the May transactions.
B. Set up T accounts for the following accounts.

Cash	Sales Returns and Allowances
Accounts Receivable	Purchases
Accounts Payable	Purchases Discounts
P. Mason, Capital	Purchases Returns and Allowances
Sales	Freight-in
Sales Discounts	

Cash and *P. Mason, Capital* should have a beginning balance of $15,000 each. All other accounts have a zero beginning balance.

C. Post the May journal entries to the T accounts.
D. Prepare a partial income statement for May. The statement should begin with gross sales and end with gross profit on sales. (Additional information: the value of inventory on hand at May 31 was $2,500.)

Answer to Demonstration Problem

A.

May	1	Purchases	8,000	
		Accounts Payable		8,000
	3	Accounts Receivable	2,200	
		Sales		2,200
	5	Accounts Payable	500	
		Purchases Returns and Allowances		500
	8	Accounts Receivable	1,150	
		Sales		1,150
	14	Sales Returns and Allowances	150	
		Accounts Receivable		150
	15	Purchases	6,000	
		Accounts Payable		6,000
	18	Cash	970	
		Sales Discounts	30	
		Accounts Receivable		1,000

20	Purchases		800	
		Accounts Payable		800
22	Freight-in		230	
		Cash		230
23	Accounts Receivable		3,400	
		Sales		3,400
25	Accounts Payable		6,000	
		Purchases Discounts		120
		Cash		5,880
30	Accounts Payable		7,500	
		Cash		7,500
31	Accounts Receivable		12,620	
		Sales		12,620
31	Cash		2,200	
		Accounts Receivable		2,200

B. and C.

Cash

5/1	Bal.	15,000	5/22	230
5/18		970	5/25	5,880
5/31		2,200	5/30	7,500
5/31	Bal.	4,560		

Accounts Receivable

5/3	2,200	5/14		150
5/8	1,150	5/18		1,000
5/23	3,400	5/31		2,200
5/31	12,620			
5/31	Bal. 16,020			

Accounts Payable

5/5	500	5/1		8,000
5/25	6,000	5/15		6,000
5/30	7,500	5/20		800
		5/31	Bal.	800

P. Mason, Capital

5/1	Bal.	15,000

Sales

5/3		2,200
5/8		1,150
5/23		3,400
5/31		12,620
5/31	Bal.	19,370

Purchases

5/1	8,000	
5/15	6,000	
5/20	800	
5/31	Bal. 14,800	

Sales Discounts

5/18	30

Purchases Discounts

5/25	120

Sales Returns and Allowances

5/14	150

Purchases Returns and Allowances

5/5	500

Freight-in

5/22	230

D.

```
                    PLAZA BUSINESS EQUIPMENT
                      Partial Income Statement
                   For the Month Ended May 31, 1987


  Gross Sales                                                    $19,370
  Less: Sales returns and allowances            $    150
        Sales discounts                               30             180
  Net Sales                                                       19,190
  Cost of goods sold:
    Merchandise inventory—5/1                             -0-
    Purchases                          $14,800
    Less: Purchases returns and
          allowances         $500
          Purchases discounts  120         620
    Cost of net purchases              14,180
    Add: Freight-in                       230
    Cost of goods purchased                           14,410
    Cost of goods available for sale                  14,410
    Less: Merchandise inventory—5/31                   2,500
  Cost of goods sold                                             11,910
  Gross profit on sales                                        $ 7,280
```

GLOSSARY

ADMINISTRATIVE EXPENSES. Expenses associated with the management of the business, such as operations of the general, accounting, personnel, and credit offices (p. 202).

BEGINNING INVENTORY. Merchandise on hand at the start of an accounting period that is available for sale to customers in the normal course of business (p. 208).

CASH DISCOUNT. An incentive offered to the buyer to induce early payment of a credit sale. Cash discounts are a reduction in the invoice price (p. 204).

COST OF GOODS SOLD. An amount that is deducted from sales in the income statement and is a measure of the cost of the inventory sold during the accounting period (p. 202).

CREDIT MEMORANDUM. A business form prepared by the seller that contains information related to the receipt of returned goods or an adjustment to the sales price. Its purpose is to inform customers that their accounts are being credited on the books of the firm preparing the credit memo (p. 203).

CREDIT PERIOD. The period of time granted for the payment of an account (p. 204).

CREDIT TERMS. The agreement made between buyer and seller concerning the sale of goods on credit (p. 204).

DEBIT MEMORANDUM. A business form prepared by the buyer that contains information relating to the return of goods or an adjustment to the purchase price. Its purpose is to inform suppliers that their accounts are being debited on the books of the firm preparing the debit memo (p. 210).

DISCOUNT PERIOD. The period of time during which a cash discount may be taken if payment is made. The discount is subtracted from the invoice price (p. 204).

ENDING INVENTORY. Merchandise on hand at the end of an accounting period that is available for sale to customers in the normal course of the business (p. 208).

FOB DESTINATION. Shipping terms in which freight is paid by the seller and transfer of title to the buyer occurs when the goods arrive at the buyer's firm (p. 206).

FOB SHIPPING POINT. Shipping terms in which freight is paid by the buyer and transfer of title to the buyer occurs when the goods have left the seller's firm (p. 206).

FREIGHT-IN (TRANSPORTATION-IN). An account used to accumulate the expense incurred by the buyer in transporting inventory purchases (p. 209).

FREIGHT-OUT (DELIVERY EXPENSE). Transportation expenses incurred by the seller to deliver goods to customers (p. 207).

GOODS AVAILABLE FOR SALE. The cost of beginning inventory plus the cost of purchases (p. 208).

GROSS INVOICE METHOD. A procedure in which sales revenue and purchases of inventory are recorded at the gross or full invoice price (p. 205).

GROSS PROFIT OR GROSS MARGIN ON SALES. Net sales less the cost of goods sold (p. 202).

MERCHANDISE INVENTORY (INVENTORY). Goods acquired by a merchandising firm for the purpose of resale in the normal course of business (p. 201).

MULTIPLE-STEP INCOME STATEMENT. An income statement format in which operating and nonoperating items are separated and expenses are classified by function (p. 217).

NET INVOICE METHOD. A procedure in which sales revenue and purchases of inventory are recorded at the net invoice amount, invoice price less the available cash discount (p. 221).

PERIODIC INVENTORY SYSTEM. A system of accounting for inventory in which the goods on hand are determined by a physical count. Cost of goods sold is determined at the end of the period and is equal to the beginning inventory plus purchases less ending inventory (p. 207).

PERPETUAL INVENTORY SYSTEM. A system of accounting for inventory that provides a continuous and detailed record of the goods on hand and the costs of goods sold (p. 207).

PHYSICAL INVENTORY. The process of counting and pricing the goods on hand (p. 208).

PURCHASES. An account used in a periodic inventory system to record the cost of goods acquired for resale to customers (p. 208).

PURCHASES DISCOUNTS. An account used to record cash discounts taken by a firm on goods purchased for resale (p. 204).

PURCHASE INVOICE. A business form that contains the terms of a purchase transaction (p. 204).

PURCHASES RETURNS AND ALLOWANCES. An account used to record the return by a firm of inventory or adjustments made to the purchase price (p. 210).

SALES. A revenue account used by a merchandising firm to record the sales price of goods sold (p. 202).

SALES DISCOUNT.   An account used to record cash discounts taken by customers on the sale of inventory (p. 204).

SALES INVOICE.   A business form prepared by the seller that contains the information relating to a sale (p. 204).

SALES RETURNS AND ALLOWANCES.   An account used to record the receipt of inventory returned by customers or adjustments made to the sales price (p. 203).

SELLING EXPENSES.   Expenses incurred in storing the inventory, promoting the inventory for sale, selling the inventory, and delivering the inventory to customers (p. 202).

TRADE DISCOUNTS.   A reduction in the suggested list or catalog price granted to various classes of customers. Trade discounts are not normally recorded in the accounts (p. 206).

DISCUSSION QUESTIONS

1. Define "merchandise inventory" as the term is used in a merchandising operation.
2. What is the normal operating cycle for a merchandising firm?
3. How is the gross profit on sales computed?
4. Differentiate between selling expenses and administrative expenses.
5. What is the purpose of recording sales returns and allowances in a contra sales account, rather than debiting a return or allowance directly to the *Sales* account?
6. What is a cash discount? What are the benefits to the seller of granting cash discounts?
7. For the credit terms, 1/15, n/45, what is the length of the discount period? What is the length of the credit period? Prepare the journal entry to record a $300 sale, assuming that the firm uses the gross method to record sales. Also, record the collection within the discount period.
8. At what amount would a seller record merchandise sold for a list price of $180 and a 25% trade discount?
9. Five accounts are shown here in T account format. Prepare, in general journal form, the entries to record the transactions reflected in the accounts. Include an explanation with each entry.

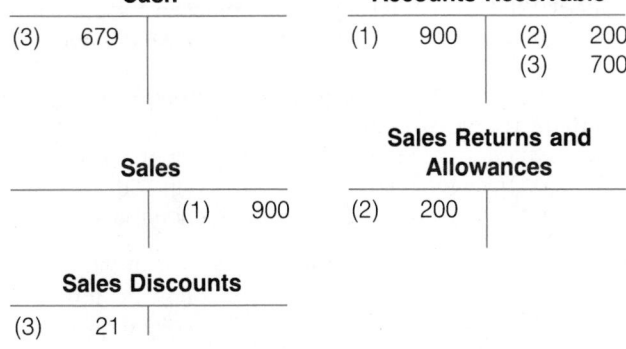

10. What does the term "FOB shipping point" mean, when included in the terms

of a sale? Why is freight-in considered a part of the cost of purchasing merchandise?

11. Why do high volume merchandisers, such as grocery stores, tend to use a periodic inventory system?

12. When a periodic inventory system is used, what does the balance in the *Inventory* account during the period represent?

13. Davis Hardware purchased $190,000 in merchandise during the year. Compute the cost of goods sold for each of the following independent situations.

	Beginning Inventory	Ending Inventory
(a)	-0-	-0-
(b)	$20,000	-0-
(c)	-0-	$30,000
(d)	$20,000	$30,000

14. Where on the income statement do losses from inventory theft, shrinkage, and breakage appear when a periodic inventory system is used?

15. Under the periodic inventory system, in which columns of the worksheet does the beginning inventory appear? In which columns does ending inventory appear?

16. Where do the following items appear on the income statement: sales discounts, purchases discounts, and purchases discounts lost? What is the normal balance of each account?

17. Why is there no *Purchases* account when a perpetual inventory system is used? How is the return of purchases to the supplier recorded under a perpetual inventory system?

18. Why do firms that use a perpetual inventory system take a physical count of the inventory at least once a year?

19. Distinguish between the gross invoice method and the net invoice method of recording cash discounts.

EXERCISES

Exercise 5-1   Journal Entries for Both Buyer and Seller—Periodic Inventory System

A. Prepare general journal entries to record the following transactions for both the Jay Company and the Kay Company. Both companies use a periodic inventory system and the gross invoice method of recording cash discounts.

May 2 Jay Company sold merchandise to Kay Company for $550 with terms 2/10, n/30, FOB shipping point.

6 Kay Company paid the transportation cost of $30.

8 Kay Company returned merchandise worth $50.

11 Kay Company paid Jay Company the amount due.

B. Indicate how each account balance should be reported in the financial statements of Jay Company and Kay Company. Use the following format (examples are given).

Account Name	Financial Statement	Shown as
Cash	Balance Sheet	Current Asset
Purchases	Income Statement	Addition to Beginning Inventory

Exercise 5-2 Journal Entries—Periodic Inventory System

Using a periodic inventory system, prepare general journal entries for the following transactions.

1. Purchased merchandise on account for $7,500.
2. Sold merchandise for $5,200 in cash and $2,000 on credit.
3. A customer returned merchandise he had bought on credit for $525.
4. Purchased a typewriter to be used in the business for $425 cash.
5. Returned merchandise for credit that was previously purchased for $235.
6. Purchased merchandise on account with $4,100 list price and a 20% trade discount.
7. Sold merchandise for $282 on credit.

Exercise 5-3 Income Statement—Periodic Inventory System

Use the following information from the books of Quality Company to prepare a multiple-step income statement.

Purchases	$120,500
Merchandise Inventory, January 1, 1987	9,200
Merchandise Inventory, December 31, 1987	12,390
Selling Expenses	22,980
Sales	163,740
Purchases Returns and Allowances	2,690
Sales Returns and Allowances	3,140
Administrative Expenses	9,800
Sales Discounts	976
Freight-in	2,246
Purchases Discounts	1,710

Exercise 5-4 Completion of Worksheet—Periodic Inventory System

Select accounts and a partial worksheet are shown here.

Account Title	Adjusted Trial Balance		Income Statement		Balance Sheet	
	Debit	Credit	Debit	Credit	Debit	Credit
Merchandise Inventory	?					
Sales		93,000				
Sales Returns and Allowances	3,200					
Sales Discounts	2,400					
Purchases	70,000					
Purchases Returns and Allowances		1,500				
Purchases Discounts		900				
Freight-in	500					

Required:

The beginning and ending merchandise inventory were $16,000 and $18,000, respectively. You are to enter the beginning and ending inventory amounts in the proper columns and extend the other account balances listed to their proper columns.

Exercise 5-5 Computing Missing Data in Income Statement

For each of the following independent cases, compute the missing amounts.

	Cases		
	1	2	3
Sales	$65,200	$42,160	$ g
Beginning Inventory	a	23,700	34,000
Purchases	36,500	d	34,000
Ending Inventory	17,230	24,600	h
Cost of Goods Sold	b	34,700	35,300
Gross Profit on Sales	37,760	e	i
Operating Expenses	c	27,460	20,100
Net Income (loss)	15,890	f	7,300

Exercise 5-6 Closing Entries—Periodic Inventory System

The following information is taken from the trial balance of Barbara's Health Food Store.

	Debit	Credit
Merchandise Inventory, January 1, 1987	$ 19,600	
Barbara Bran, Drawing	10,200	
Sales		$515,320
Sales Returns and Allowances	5,091	
Sales Discounts	1,380	
Purchases	331,176	
Purchases Returns and Allowances		2,422
Purchases Discounts		1,000
Freight-in	6,278	
Selling Expenses	77,900	
Administrative Expenses	48,340	

Given that the cost of the inventory on December 31, 1987 is $25,760, prepare the closing entries.

Exercise 5-7 Journal Entries—Perpetual Inventory System

Using a perpetual inventory system, record the following transactions in the general journal.

1. Purchased 40 units for $60 each on account. 2400
2. Returned 5 units to the manufacturer. 300
3. Sold 22 units for $95 each, on credit. 2090 -1320
4. Purchased office supplies for $108 cash. 108
5. Customer returned 3 of the units sold in (3). 285
6. Sold 10 units for $98 each, on credit. 940

Exercise 5-8 Completion of Worksheet—Perpetual Inventory System

Select accounts and a partial worksheet are shown here.

Account Title	Adjusted Trial Balance		Income Statement		Balance Sheet	
	Debit	Credit	Debit	Credit	Debit	Credit
Merchandise Inventory	?					
Sales		75,000				
Sales Returns and Allowances	2,500					
Cost of Goods Sold	52,200					
Selling Expenses	8,000					
Administrative Expenses	8,000					

Required:
The beginning and ending merchandise inventory were $6,500 and $8,500, respectively. You are to enter the proper inventory amount in the trial balance column and extend the other account balances to the proper columns.

Exercise 5-9 Closing Entries—Perpetual Inventory System

The trial balance of Barbara's Health Food Store contains the following account balances as of December 31, 1987.

	Debit	Credit
Merchandise Inventory	$ 25,760	
Barbara Bran, Drawing	10,200	
Sales		$515,320
Sales Returns and Allowances	5,091	
Sales Discounts	1,380	
Cost of Goods Sold	322,594	
Selling Expenses	77,900	
Administrative Expenses	48,340	

Required:
Prepare the closing entries.

Exercise 5-10 Net Invoice Method to Record Purchases

A. Prepare general journal entries to record the following transactions for Connie's Corner Store. Assume that Connie's Corner Store uses a periodic inventory system and uses the net invoice method to record purchases.

Nov. 2 Dave's Outlet sold merchandise to Connie's Corner Store for $1,300, with terms of 1/10, n/30.
  11 Connie's Corner Store paid for the merchandise.
  15 Dave's Outlet sold merchandise to Connie's Corner Store for $500, with terms of 1/10, n/30.
Dec. 14 Connie's Corner Store paid for the merchandise.

B. Indicate how purchases discounts lost would be reported in the financial statements of Connie's Corner Store.

Exercise 5-11 Net Invoice Method to Record Purchases

A. Slick Comics purchased merchandise for $800 on April 10. The credit terms were 2/15, n/45, and the goods were shipped FOB destination. Slick Comics uses a periodic inventory system and the net invoice method is used to record purchases.

1. Give the general journal entry to record the $800 purchase.

2. Assume that Slick paid for the goods in full on April 24. Give the entry to record the cash payment.

3. Assume that Slick paid for the goods in full on May 25. Give the entry to record the cash payment.

4. Determine the effective annual interest rate of forgoing the cash discount.

B. Indicate how purchases discounts lost would be reported in the firm's financial statements.

PROBLEMS

Problem 5-1 Journal Entries for Both Buyer and Seller—Periodic Inventory System

Prepare general journal entries to record the following transactions for Dave's Outlet and for Connie's Corner Store. Assume that both companies use a periodic inventory system and use the gross invoice method to record purchases and sales.

Nov.	2	Dave's Outlet sold merchandise to Connie's Corner Store for $1,300, with terms of 1/10, n/30.
	11	Connie's Corner Store paid for the merchandise.
	15	Dave's Outlet sold merchandise to Connie's Corner Store for $500, with terms of 1/10, n/30.
Dec.	14	Connie's Corner Store paid for the merchandise.

Problem 5-2 Journal Entries—Periodic Inventory System

The following transactions related to product S-2 occurred in August. Prepare journal entries to record the transactions, assuming that a periodic inventory system is used. The beginning inventory on August 1 consisted of 120 units at $8 each.

Aug.	1	Purchased 405 units for $8 each on credit.
	7	Returned 10 units, which were defective.
	12	Sold 200 units on account for $14 each.
	24	A customer returned 3 units.
	25	Sold 68 units on account for $14 each.
	31	A physical inventory count shows 250 units at a total cost of $2,000. The company, owned by S. Jackson, closes its books each month. Prepare entries to close the income statement accounts for August, based on the data just given, and assuming that operating expenses for August were $1,580.

Problem 5-3 Journal Entries Involving Purchases and Sales Discounts, Closing Entries, and Income Statement—Periodic Inventory System

The Brandon Company buys tables for $30 each and sells them for $50 each. The company uses the gross invoice method to record purchases and sales, and the periodic inventory system. On April 1, 24 tables were in inventory. Credit terms are 2/10, n/30 for all purchases on account, and 3/10, n/30 for all sales on account. Brandon Company completed the following transactions during April of 1987.

April   3   Purchased 50 tables on account. FOB shipping point.
             4   Paid freight cost of $65 on April 3 purchase.
             5   Sold 25 tables on account. FOB destination. Paid freight cost of $30.
          13   Returned 10 of the tables purchased on April 3, and paid the amount due on the tables retained.
          13   A customer returned 5 of the tables sold on April 5. The tables were not defective and were returned to stock.
          13   Purchased 15 tables on account. FOB shipping point.
          14   Received payment from customer for the amount due on April 5 sale.
          19   Sold 40 tables on account.
          20   Two of the tables sold on April 19 were returned by the customer for credit on account. The tables were not defective.
          23   Paid the supplier the amount owed for the April 13 purchase.

A physical inventory taken on April 30 shows 21 tables in stock.

Required:
A. Prepare general journal entries to record the April transactions.
B. Assuming that Brandon Company closes its books every month, prepare entries to close the accounts that enter into the determination of net sales and cost of goods sold.
C. Prepare an income statement through gross profit on sales for April, 1987.

**Problem 5-4 Worksheet and Completion of Accounting Cycle—
Periodic Inventory System**
A trial balance for Decker's Sporting Goods is shown here.

DECKER'S SPORTING GOODS
Unadjusted Trial Balance
December 31, 1987

Account Title	Debit	Credit
Cash	$ 4,800	
Accounts Receivable	10,500	
Merchandise Inventory	26,050	
Prepaid Rent	3,900	
Office Equipment	42,600	
Accumulated Depreciation—Office Equipment		$ 7,400
Accounts Payable		9,950
M. Decker, Capital		80,170
M. Decker, Drawing	27,360	
Sales		221,040
Purchases	128,560	
Salary Expense—Sales	36,430	
Salary Expense—Administrative	11,400	
Utilities Expense—Store	9,360	
Rent Expense—Store	17,600	
Totals	$318,560	$318,560

Required:

A. Prepare a worksheet using the following information to make adjusting entries.
   (a) Depreciation on the office equipment, $2,300.
   (b) Expired prepaid rent, $1,600.
   (c) Accrued utilities expense, $310.
   Add *Utilities Payable* and *Depreciation Expense* to the account titles listed in the trial balance. The ending inventory was valued at $25,300.

B. Prepare an income statement, a statement of changes in owner's equity, and a classified balance sheet for the year ended December 31, 1987.

C. Prepare adjusting and closing entries.

Problem 5-5 **Worksheet and Completion of Accounting Cycle—Periodic Inventory System**

The unadjusted trial balance of Walton Furniture is shown here.

WALTON FURNITURE
Unadjusted Trial Balance
December 31, 1987

Account Title	Debit	Credit
Cash	$ 26,800	
Accounts Receivable	31,210	
Merchandise Inventory (January 1)	63,780	
Prepaid Insurance	3,400	
Office Equipment	42,800	
Accumulated Depreciation—Office Equipment		$ 12,600
Delivery Truck	11,950	
Accumulated Depreciation—Delivery Truck		5,300
Accounts Payable		16,725
Note Payable (Due June 30, 1988)		18,000
J. B. Walton, Capital		112,590
J. B. Walton, Drawing	30,200	
Sales		364,495
Sales Returns and Allowances	8,900	
Sales Discounts	1,920	
Purchases	202,510	
Purchases Returns and Allowances		11,600
Purchases Discounts		860
Freight-in	5,750	
Freight-out	2,000	
Sales Dept. Salary Expense	26,000	
Sales Commissions Expense	11,000	
Rent Expense—Store	48,000	
Administrative Salary Expense	22,850	
Interest Expense	3,100	
Totals	$542,170	$542,170

Required:

A. Prepare a worksheet for Walton Furniture. Use the following information to make the year-end adjustments.

(a) Prepaid insurance expired during the year, $2,000.
(b) Depreciation on the office equipment, $4,200.
(c) Depreciation on the delivery truck, $2,100.
(d) Accrued interest on the note payable, $500.
In making the adjustments, *Interest Payable, Depreciation Expense—Office Equipment, Depreciation Expense—Delivery Truck,* and *Insurance Expense* are to be added to the accounts in the trial balance. The ending merchandise inventory determined by physical count was $52,150.

B. Prepare an income statement, a statement of changes in owner's equity, and a classified balance sheet for the year ended December 31, 1987. Expired insurance is reported as an administrative expense.

C. Prepare adjusting and closing entries.

Problem 5-6 Journal Entries, Worksheet and Completion of Accounting Cycle—Periodic Inventory System

The trial balance of Broadway Office Supplies as of November 30, 1987 is shown here.

BROADWAY OFFICE SUPPLIES
Trial Balance
November 30, 1987

Account Title	Debit	Credit
Cash	$ 15,230	
Accounts Receivable	36,870	
Merchandise Inventory (1/1)	23,620	
Prepaid Advertising	1,100	
Office Equipment	12,000	
Accumulated Depreciation—Office Equipment		$ 6,000
Accounts Payable		10,160
Note Payable		12,000
M. West, Capital		28,730
M. West, Drawing	70,640	
Sales		495,000
Sales Returns and Allowances	1,650	
Sales Discounts	2,280	
Purchases	315,650	
Purchases Returns and Allowances		2,900
Purchases Discounts		3,100
Freight-in	3,870	
Salary Expense—Sales	32,000	
Rent Expense—Store	28,800	
Salary Expense—Administrative	10,200	
Rent Expense—Administrative	2,880	
Interest Expense	1,100	
Totals	$557,890	$557,890

Additional information:

The credit terms of all sales on account are 2/10, n/30. The credit terms of all purchases on account are 1/15, n/45. No discounts are allowed for sales or purchases in cash.

Required:

A. Prepare journal entries to record the following transactions.

Dec. 2 Purchased inventory on account, gross price $10,000.
5 Received a $1,470 payment within the discount period from customers, for sales made on November 25.
7 Paid $1,500 on account for inventory purchased on Oct. 22.
15 Recorded cash sales for first half of month, total $16,750.
16 Paid for inventory purchased on Dec. 2.
18 Made sales on account of $8,600.
21 Customer returned $300 of merchandise purchased on Dec. 18.
30 Paid salaries of $5,000 to sales staff, and $1,200 to office staff.
31 Recorded cash sales for second half of month, total $9,840.
31 Paid rent of $2,700. Approximately 90% relates to store space and 10% is for office space.

B. Set up T accounts for the accounts listed on the trial balance, entering the November 30 balances, and post the journal entries to the T accounts.

C. Prepare a worksheet for Broadway Office Supplies as of Demcember 31, 1987. Use the following information to make year-end adjustments.

(a) Depreciation on office equipment, $2,000.

(b) Prepaid advertising expired, $600.

(c) Accrued interest on the note payable, $100. (Both the interest and the note are due January 1, 1988.)

In making the adjustments, add the following accounts to the trial balance: *Depreciation Expense, Advertising Expense,* and *Interest Payable.* The ending merchandise inventory on Dec. 31, 1987 was $22,580.

D. Prepare an income statement, a statement of changes in owner's equity, and a classified balance sheet for the year ended December 31, 1987.

E. Prepare adjusting and closing entries.

Problem 5-7 Journal Entries—Perpetual Inventory System

The following transactions related to product S-2 occurred in August. Prepare journal entries to record the transactions, assuming that a perpetual inventory system is used. The beginning inventory on August 1 consisted of 120 units at $8 each.

Aug. 1 Purchased 405 units for $8 each on credit.
7 Returned 10 units, which were defective.
12 Sold 200 units for $14 each, on account.
24 A customer returned 3 units.
25 Sold 68 units for $14 each, on account.
31 A physical inventory count shows 250 units at a total cost of $2,000. The company, owned by S. Jackson, closes its books each month. Prepare entries to close the income statement accounts for August, based on the data provided, and assuming that operating expenses for August were $1,580.

ALTERNATE PROBLEMS

Inventory
Acc Payable

Acc. Payable
cash

Problem 5-1A   Journal Entries for Both Buyer and Seller—Periodic Inventory System

Prepare general journal entries to record the following transactions for AAA Paper and for James Stationery. Both companies use a periodic inventory system and both use the gross invoice method to record purchases and sales.

Sept. 14   AAA Paper sold merchandise to James Stationery for $1,800. Terms were 2/15, n/30.
28   James Stationery paid AAA Paper the net amount due.
29   AAA Paper sold merchandise to James Stationery for $2,300. Terms were 2/15, n/30.

Oct.   29   James Stationery paid for the merchandise.

Problem 5-2A   Journal Entries—Periodic Inventory System

The following transactions related to product item 4P-Y occurred in June. Prepare journal entries to record the transactions, assuming that a periodic inventory system is used. The beginning inventory on June 1 consisted of 40 units at $12 each.

June   2   Purchased 62 units for $12 each on credit.
11   Returned 3 units to the manufacturer for credit on account.
13   Sold 30 units for $20 each, on account.
17   The customer returned 5 units.
28   Sold 43 units for $20 each, on account.
30   According to a physical inventory count, 31 units are on hand at a total cost of $372. The company, owned by J. Peterson, closes its books each month. Prepare entries to close the income statement accounts for June, based on the data provided and operating expenses of $300.

Problem 5-3A   Journal Entries Involving Purchases and Sales Discounts, Closing Entries, and Income Statement—Periodic Inventory System

The Taylor Company sells calculator model number SC5 for $20 each. It buys the calculators for $10 each. Taylor uses the gross invoice method to record purchases and sales, and the periodic inventory system. On November 1, 50 calculators are in inventory. Credit terms are 2/10, n/30 for all purchases and sales on account. Taylor Company completed the following transactions during November of 1987.

Nov.   3   Sold 6 calculators on account.
4   Paid the supplier for 15 calculators purchased on October 5.
5   Purchased 30 calculators on account. FOB shipping point.
6   A customer returned 3 of the calculators sold on November 3 for credit on account. The calculators were not defective in any way.
9   Paid $35 in freight charges on the November 5 purchase.
12   Returned 5 of the calculators purchased on November 5 for credit.
13   Sold 15 calculators on account.
14   Paid the supplier the amount due on the November 5 purchase.
20   Purchased 20 calculators on account, FOB shipping point.
22   A customer returned 5 calculators sold on November 13 and included a check for the amount due on the other 10 calculators. The calculators were not defective and were returned to inventory.
30   Paid the supplier for the November 20 purchase.

A physical inventory count taken on November 30 verified that 82 calculators were on hand.

Required:

A. Prepare general journal entries to record the November transactions.

B. Assuming that Taylor Company completes the closing process each month, prepare entries to close the accounts that enter into the determination of net sales and cost of goods sold.

C. Prepare an income statement through gross profit on sales for November.

Problem 5-4A Worksheet and Completion of Accounting Cycle—Periodic Inventory System

A trial balance for Sew Pretty Fabrics Store is shown here.

SEW PRETTY FABRICS STORE
Unadjusted Trial Balance
December 31, 1987

Account Title	Debit	Credit
Cash	$ 16,700	
Accounts Receivable	18,210	
Merchandise Inventory	20,890	
Office Supplies	450	
Store Equipment	32,630	
Accumulated Depreciation—Store Equipment		$ 6,900
Accounts Payable		3,870
Note Payable (Due Oct. 15, 1988)		10,000
S. D. Riche, Capital		69,670
S. D. Riche, Drawing	28,000	
Sales		125,910
Purchases	72,970	
Salary Expense—Sales	12,000	
Rent Expense—Sales	10,000	
Salary Expense—Office	4,500	
Totals	$216,350	$216,350

Required:

A. Prepare a worksheet for Sew Pretty Fabrics Store. Use the following information to make adjusting entries.

(a) Office supplies on hand as of December 31, $200.

(b) Depreciation on store equipment, $2,850.

(c) Interest accrued on the note payable, $1,200.

Add the following account titles to those listed in the trial balance: *Interest Payable, Depreciation Expense, Interest Expense, Supplies Expense.* The inventory as of December 31, 1987 was valued at $17,800.

B. Prepare an income statement, a statement of changes in owner's equity, and a classified balance sheet for the year ended December 31, 1987.

C. Prepare closing entries.

Problem 5-5A Worksheet and Completion of Accounting Cycle—Periodic Inventory System

The unadjusted trial balance of the Midtown Bicycle Shop appears here.

MIDTOWN BICYCLE SHOP
Unadjusted Trial Balance
December 31, 1987

Account Title	Debit	Credit
Cash	$ 12,620	
Accounts Receivable	17,230	
Merchandise Inventory (January 1)	9,780	
Prepaid Rent	1,400	
Store Equipment	8,675	
Accumulated Depreciation—Store Equipment		$ 3,280
Accounts Payable		4,750
S. Wheeler, Capital		41,585
S. Wheeler, Drawing	12,000	
Sales		84,650
Sales Returns and Allowances	1,340	
Sales Discounts	220	
Purchases	43,970	
Purchases Returns and Allowances		810
Purchases Discounts		315
Freight-in	1,600	
Freight-out	335	
Rent Expense—Sales	6,100	
Salaries Expense—Sales	12,700	
Salaries Expense—Office	6,200	
Accounting Fees	500	
Telephone Expense—Office	120	
Interest Expense	600	
Totals	$135,390	$135,390

The following accounts listed in the chart of accounts contained a zero balance: *Salaries Payable, Telephone Expense Payable,* and *Depreciation Expense.*

Required:
A. Prepare a worksheet. The ending inventory was determined to be $15,010. Use the following information to make the year-end adjustments.
   (a) Prepaid rent expired during the year, $700.
   (b) Depreciation on the shop equipment, $2,130.
   (c) Accrued salaries expense for sales staff, $800.
   (d) Accrued telephone expense, $30.
B. Prepare an income statement, a statement of changes in owner's equity and a classified balance sheet for the year ended December 31, 1987.
C. Prepare closing entries.

Problem 5-6A **Journal Entries, Worksheet, and Completion of Accounting Cycle—Periodic Inventory System**

The trial balance of Executive Stationery as of November 30, 1987, is shown here.

EXECUTIVE STATIONERY
Trial Balance
November 30, 1987

Account Title	Debit	Credit
Cash	$ 17,250	
Accounts Receivable	35,650	
Merchandise Inventory (1/1)	22,890	
Prepaid Advertising	2,200	
Office Equipment	15,000	
Accumulated Depreciation—Office Equipment		$ 7,500
Accounts Payable		11,800
Note Payable		10,000
W. Stephens, Capital		29,480
W. Stephens, Drawing	97,045	
Sales		529,650
Sales Returns and Allowances	2,320	
Sales Discounts	3,900	
Purchases	318,650	
Purchases Returns and Allowances		2,575
Purchases Discounts		3,245
Freight-in	2,940	
Salary Expense—Sales	34,500	
Rent Expense—Store	26,550	
Salary Expense—Administrative	11,800	
Rent Expense—Administrative	2,655	
Interest Expense	900	
Totals	$594,250	$594,250

Additional information:

The credit terms of all sales on account are 2/10, n/30. The credit terms of all purchases on account are 1/15, n/45. No discounts are allowed for sales or purchases in cash.

Required:

A. Make journal entries to record the following transactions.

Dec. 2 Purchased inventory on account, gross price $12,000.

5 Received a $1,960 payment within the discount period from customers, for sales made on Nov. 25.

7 Paid $1,800 on account for inventory purchased on Oct. 22.

15 Recorded cash sales for first half of month, total $15,830.

16 Paid for inventory purchased on Dec. 2.

18 Made sales on account, totaling $9,200.

21 Customer returned $400 worth of merchandise purchased on Dec. 18.

30 Paid salaries of $6,000 to sales staff, and $1,000 to office staff.

31 Recorded cash sales for second half of month, total $9,720.

31 Paid rent of $2,500. Approximately 90% relates to store space and 10% is for office space.

B. Set up T accounts for the accounts listed on the trial balance and post the journal entries shown to the T accounts.

C. Prepare a worksheet for Executive as of December 31, 1987. Use the following information to make year-end adjustments.

(a) Depreciation on office equipment, $2,500.

(b) Prepaid advertising expired, $1,800.

(c) Interest on the note payable accrued, $100. Both the interest and the note are due Jan. 1, 1988.

In making the adjustments, add the following accounts to the trial balance: *Depreciation Expense, Advertising Expense,* and *Interest Payable.* The ending merchandise inventory on December 31, 1987 was $18,780.

D. Prepare an income statement, a statement of changes in owner's equity, and a classified balance sheet for the year ended December 31, 1987.

E. Prepare adjusting and closing entries.

Problem 5-7A Journal Entries—Perpetual Inventory System

The following transactions related to product item 4P-Y occurred in June. Prepare journal entries to record the transactions, assuming that a perpetual inventory system is used. The beginning inventory on June 1 consisted of 40 units at $12 each.

June	2	Purchased 62 units for $12 each, on credit.
	11	Returned 3 units to the manufacturer for credit on account.
	13	Sold 30 units for $20 each, on account.
	17	The customer returned 5 units.
	28	Sold 43 units for $20 each, on account.
	30	According to a physical inventory count, 31 units are on hand at a total cost of $372. The company, owned by J. Peterson, closes its books each month. Prepare entries to close the income statement accounts for June, based on the data provided and operating expenses of $300.

CASE

CASE 5-1 Discussion Case Perpetual versus the Periodic Inventory System

The Grand Forks Discount Office Furniture is a retailer for office furniture and equipment. The firm stocks about 70 different items ranging in retail price from $60 to $1,200 per unit. Throughout the fiscal year, the inventory balance at cost is maintained at approximately $90,000. This requires that the company make 15 to 20 purchases a month from 20 manufacturers. Approximately 70% of the sales are on terms n/30, and 70 to 100 sales are made on a typical day. The dollar sales volume is not seasonal, but is sensitive to the general economic conditions of the area.

Required:

Management has been using the periodic inventory system, but is considering changing to the perpetual inventory system to ascertain the information needed to prepare monthly statements, and for placing orders with their suppliers. Management has asked you to explain the advantages and disadvantages of each system and to recommend one for them to use.

ACCOUNTING SYSTEMS AND CONTROLS

6

ACCOUNTING SYSTEMS AND INTERNAL CONTROL

CHAPTER OVERVIEW AND OBJECTIVES

This chapter describes accounting systems and general internal control concepts. When you have completed the chapter, you should understand:

1. The basic structure of an accounting system.
2. How data are transformed into information within an accounting system.
3. General internal control concepts.
4. The distinction between administrative controls and accounting controls.
5. The impact of the Foreign Corrupt Practices Act on an accounting system.
6. The key features of any good internal control system.
7. The development of an accounting system with systems analysis, systems design, and systems implementation.
8. How control accounts and subsidiary ledgers are used in a manual accounting system.
9. The advantages of special journals.
10. The formats of and procedures used with a sales journal, purchases journal, cash receipts journal, and cash disbursements journal.
11. The use of a general journal when special journals are utilized.
12. The need for electronic data processing.
13. The basic components of a digital computer.
14. How a computer can be used in an accounting system.

In earlier chapters, we have seen that the effects of various business transactions are **collected, processed,** and **reported** with a firm's accounting system. An **accounting system** is a collection of business forms (also called source documents), records, procedures, management policies, and data-processing methods used to transform economic data into useful information. Accounting systems can take many forms, ranging from simple manual systems to sophisticated computerized systems.

We have limited the consideration of an accounting system in earlier chapters to one that is both *simple* and *manually operated* in order to introduce basic accounting procedures. Such a system may be satisfactory for a small business with a limited number of transactions. In most cases, however, even relatively small businesses require a more sophisticated accounting system for two reasons. First, the procedures described earlier may be too time-consuming for rapid data processing and timely reporting. The volume of transactions may be so great that the accounting staff cannot process the data manually at a reasonable cost and on a sufficiently prompt basis. Second, many of the transactions will be so repetitive that they can be handled more efficiently with more specialized treatment, than with the general procedures so far discussed. Special journals can be used for such repetitive transactions as sales, purchases, cash receipts, and cash disbursements, instead of the less efficient general journal. This chapter describes accounting systems as they are designed and installed for efficient and dependable processing of financial data. We will begin by considering the fundamental concepts associated with any accounting system.

OPERATION OF AN ACCOUNTING SYSTEM

The operation of an accounting system consists of three basic phases: *input, processing,* and *output.* Transactions are recorded as they occur on numerous business forms, such as sales invoices, purchases invoices, checks, bank deposit tickets, and payroll cards. These documents serve as input that is entered into some type of journal as a chronological record of the transactions. Periodically, the debits and credits in the journal are posted to a general ledger, which represents a permanent file classified as assets, liabilities, owner's equity, revenues, and expenses. Financial reports, such as an income statement, a balance sheet, and other special reports, are prepared from the data in the general ledger as output from the system. These reports provide useful information concerning the operating results and financial position of the firm for a variety of interested parties. Some of the parties are outside the firm (such as creditors and taxing authorities), while others are insiders as members of the management team. Consequently, both financial accounting information (externally oriented) and managerial accounting information (internally oriented) are produced by the same accounting system.

Objective 1:
Basic structure
of an accounting system

In the conversion of input to output, data are transformed into information. While the two terms *data* and *information* are often used synonymously, a useful distinction between them can be made. *Data* are recorded facts; *information* is data that have been processed in some prescribed manner so that they are more useful to a potential user. For example, sales data are collected chronologically on invoices, processed through the accounting system, and

Objective 2:
Comparing
data and information

reported as sales information (revenue) on the income statement. The development of information from data in an accounting system can be diagrammed as:

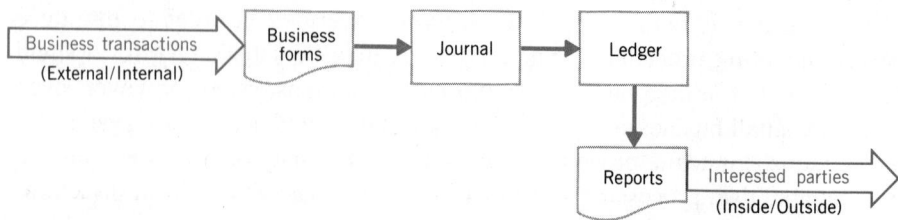

INTERNAL CONTROL

**Objective 3:
General internal control concepts**

Assets have value to a firm because they represent resources that will be utilized by the business in future operations. The efficient use and protection of these resources are primary management functions. As a business grows, its owners must place increasing reliance on employees to help control the various operations. The procedures adopted by a business to control its operations are defined collectively as an **internal control system.** This type of system consists of all measures used by a business to safeguard its resources against waste, fraud, and inefficiency; to promote the reliability of accounting information; and to encourage compliance with company policies and governmental regulations.

ADMINISTRATIVE CONTROLS AND ACCOUNTING CONTROLS

**Objective 4:
Distinguishing between administrative controls and accounting controls**

Two types of internal control measures are used by a business: administrative controls and accounting controls. **Administrative controls** are used to maintain an efficient operation and ensure adherence to prescribed company policies. An example of an administrative control is a written statement describing the employment standards to be followed by a firm's personnel department in hiring new employees. Other examples of administrative controls are manuals specifying the purchasing and sales procedures to be followed, and various performance reports that may be required from employees.

Accounting controls are the methods used to protect assets and ensure that accounting information is reliable. They include procedures used to authorize various business transactions and to separate recordkeeping duties from the custody of a firm's assets. Accounting controls are designed to provide reasonable assurance that:

1. Transactions are executed in accordance with management's general or specific authorization.
2. Transactions are recorded as necessary to: (a) permit preparation of financial statements in conformity with generally accepted accounting principles; and (b) maintain accountability for assets.
3. Access to assets is permitted only in accordance with management's authorization.

4. The recorded accountability for assets is compared with the existing assets at reasonable intervals and appropriate action is taken with respect to any discrepancies.[1]

THE FOREIGN CORRUPT PRACTICES ACT

During the 1970s, several large corporations admitted making payments to foreign officials in order to obtain or retain business. Although these payments were not necessarily illegal under the laws of the countries in which the payments were made, they were considered illegal, or at least unethical, in the United States. Payments were often made from secret funds that did not appear in the company's records, and top executives of some companies maintained that they were not even aware that the payments were being made.

In an effort to halt these practices, the U.S. Congress passed the Foreign Corrupt Practices Act in 1977. The act contains two types of provisions: antibribery provisions and accounting standards provisions. The *antibribery provisions* apply to all American businesses and individuals. They prohibit the offer, payment, promise to pay, or authorization of a payment of anything of value to a foreign official or foreign political party for the purpose of obtaining or retaining business. They also make it illegal to make such a payment to any person while knowing or having reason to believe that the person will offer, give, or promise the item of value to a foreign official.

The *accounting standards provisions* require that all publicly owned corporations keep reasonably detailed and accurate accounting records. Under these provisions, such corporations must also maintain internal controls sufficient to provide reasonable assurance that transactions are properly authorized, that transactions are recorded in accordance with generally accepted accounting principles, and that assets are used only in compliance with management's authorization. These accounting standards provisions apply to all companies that must file annual reports with the Securities and Exchange Commission, even if they are not operating in a foreign country. Violators are subject to severe penalties, including prison terms and fines.

A major impact of the Foreign Corrupt Practices Act is the recognition that management is solely responsible both for maintaining an adequate internal control system and for the accuracy of financial statements. As a result, top corporate managers have directed much more attention to strengthening internal control systems than they did before the act. Corporate boards of directors now regularly assure compliance with the act by obtaining written evidence of management's primary responsibility for the content of financial statements, as well as the adequacy of internal controls. An example of this involvement taken from an annual report of Smith International, Inc., is presented in Figure 6–1.

Although each business must design its own internal control system to meet its specific needs, several general elements of internal control can be identified, as will now be discussed.

Objective 5: Foreign Corrupt Practices Act

[1]*Professional Standards No. 1,* ''Auditing, Management Advisory Services, Tax Practice, and Accounting and Review Services,'' (Commerce Clearing House, Inc.: Chicago, June, 1980), Sec. AU 320.28.

Figure 6–1
Management Report

Report of Management

The accompanying consolidated financial statements have been prepared in conformity with generally accepted accounting principles and, as such, include amounts that are based on our best estimates and judgments, giving due consideration to materiality. Financial information included elsewhere in this Annual Report is consistent with that in the financial statements.

The integrity and objectivity of data in these financial statements are the responsibility of management. To this end management maintains a system of accounting and controls, which includes an internal audit function. The system of controls includes a careful selection of people, a division of responsibilities, and the application of formal policies and procedures that are consistent with high standards of accounting and administrative practices. Management is continually reviewing, modifying and improving its system of accounting and controls in response to changes in business conditions and operations. We believe our controls provide reasonable assurance that assets are safeguarded against loss from unauthorized use or disposition and that accounting records are reliable for preparing financial statements.

The independent public accountants, recommended by the Audit Committee of the Board of Directors and selected by the Board of Directors and the shareholders at the annual meeting, are engaged to express an opinion on our financial statements. Their opinion is based on procedures performed in accordance with generally accepted auditing standards, including tests of the accounting records and such other auditing procedures as they considered necessary in the circumstances.

The Board of Directors, acting through the Audit Committee composed solely of outside directors, is responsible for determining that management fulfills its responsibilities in the financial control of operations and preparation of financial statements. The Committee meets regularly with management, the internal auditors and the independent public accountants to discuss the Company's system of accounting and controls and financial reporting matters. The independent public accountants have full and free access to the Audit Committee.

Management has long recognized its responsibility for conducting the Company's affairs in a manner which is responsive to the ever increasing complexities of the business environment. The responsibility is reflected in key Company policies regarding, among other things, potential conflicting outside business interests of Company employees, proper conduct of domestic and international business activities and compliance with anti-trust laws.

JERRY W. NEELY
Chairman of the Board,
President and Chief Executive Officer

FRED J. BARNES
Group Vice President and
Chief Financial Officer

CLEARLY ESTABLISHED LINES OF RESPONSIBILITY

**Objective 6:
Key features of
a good internal
control system**

Control ultimately involves people. Individuals initiate business transactions, record the transactions, and handle the assets resulting from transactions. Thus, the cornerstone of a good internal control system is the employment of competent personnel and the appropriate assignment of responsibilities to them. Responsibility should be commensurate with ability and authority. If employees are to operate effectively, they must have a clear understanding of their responsibilities. In addition, responsibility must be assigned in a way that avoids both overlapping and uncovered areas. If two or more employees share a specific area of responsibility and something goes wrong in that area, it is very difficult to determine who is at fault. This can impede the taking of corrective action. Responsibilities and duties should be rotated among employees periodically, so that they can become familiar with an entire operation. Rotation of duties also tends to discourage deviation from prescribed procedures, because employees know that other workers may soon be taking over their duties and reviewing their performance.

SEPARATION OF RECORDKEEPING AND CUSTODIANSHIP

To help avoid the misappropriation or misuse of assets, responsibility for initiating business transactions and for custody of the firm's assets should be separated from the responsibility for maintaining the accounting records whenever possible. Under these circumstances, the person assigned custody of an asset is unlikely to misappropriate or misuse it, because a record of the asset is kept by another employee. The employee maintaining the records has no reason to falsify them because he or she has no access to the asset. A theft of assets and falsification of records to cover up the theft would, therefore, require collusion between the two employees.

To minimize the possibility of errors, fraud, and theft, responsibility for a series of related transactions should be divided among two or more employees or departments, so that the work of one employee acts as a check on the work of another. For example, if one employee is permitted to order inventory, receive the goods, and pay the supplier, that person might be tempted to order items for personal use, have them delivered at home, and make the related payment from business funds. Or an employee might be tempted to place orders with personal friends, rather than to seek the best quality item at the lowest price. To avoid such abuses, authority for ordering inventory should be assigned to a purchasing department, the goods should be physically received by a receiving department, and payment for the order should be made by a third department or employee. Business forms (e.g., purchase orders, receiving reports, and invoices) showing the work done by each department or employee are then sent to the accounting department for recording purposes. In this way, the work of each employee serves as a check on the work performed by others.

MECHANICAL AND ELECTRONIC DEVICES

Mechanical and electronic devices designed to protect assets and to improve the accuracy of the accounting process should be used wherever feasible. Cash registers are used to provide an accurate record of cash sales, produce a receipt for the customer, and protect the cash received. A safe or vault may be provided for the protection of cash on hand and important documents. Measuring devices, such as those used to measure yards of cloth sold, and check protectors, which perforate the amount of a check on its face, thereby making alteration of the amount difficult, are other examples of devices utilized to strengthen internal control.

ADEQUATE INSURANCE AND BONDING OF EMPLOYEES

Another element of good internal control is the provision of adequate insurance on business assets to protect against loss, theft, or casualty. In addition, employees having access to cash or other negotiable assets should be bonded by coverage with fidelity insurance to insure against losses by fraud on the part of those employees. Bonding companies generally investigate an employee's background before issuing a bond on the person. Consequently, bonding also serves as a deterrent to misappropriation of funds because employees are aware that they are bonded and that they will have to deal with the insurance company if a shortage is discovered. Bonding companies generally will not cover a loss unless the employer is willing to prosecute employees accused of misappropriating funds.

INTERNAL AUDITING

Many companies have internal auditors who are responsible for a continuous review and analysis of the internal control system. Both administrative controls and accounting controls are studied by the internal auditors to identify weaknesses in internal control that can develop over time. Deviations from established procedures and suggestions for improving the system are reported to top management. Internal auditors also often aid the independent CPA who conducts the annual audit.

DEVELOPMENT OF AN ACCOUNTING SYSTEM

Objective 7: Developing an accounting system

When a new business is started, one of the first steps taken is the development of a dependable accounting system. In many instances, the system is designed and installed by a member or members of the firm's own accounting department, although the system may be developed by an outside source, such as a CPA firm. With either approach, the development of an accounting system must be based on a thorough *understanding* of the business and the industry in which it operates.

As the business grows and engages in different activities, the accounting system must be revised frequently to accommodate a larger volume of transactions and changes in the nature of those transactions. Therefore, the design of an accounting system is not a one-time endeavor; rather, it requires continuous development in order to ensure that the capability of the system is compatible with the changing needs of the business it serves. Many large firms have a systems department, which is responsible for continuously reviewing the accounting system to determine whether portions or all of it require revision. The installation or revision of an accounting system consists of three phases: systems analysis, systems design, and systems implementation.

SYSTEMS ANALYSIS

The objective of systems analysis is to gather facts that provide a thorough understanding of a business's information requirements and the sources of the required information. Systems analysis is performed in the installation of a new system or the evaluation of an existing system. A study of the organization and how it functions is performed to determine the best combination of personnel, forms, records, procedures, and equipment. Such questions as these must be considered.

How is the business organized?

What is its history?

What type of business is involved?

What activities are performed?

Who is responsible for the activities?

What decisions must be made to properly manage the business?

What needs to be reported, to whom, and for what purposes?

How often is information required?

How much money will be devoted to the development and operation of the system?

What is the projected growth and direction of the firm?

What are the strengths and weaknesses of the business?

What are management's plans for future changes in operations?

What business forms, records, procedures, reports, and equipment are currently being used?

In existing systems, much of the information required for systems analysis may be available in the form of an operating manual—a detailed description of how the system should function. A major consideration in such cases is an evaluation of how closely the instructions in the manual are followed in the actual operation of the accounting system. Any deficiencies in procedures and data-processing methods currently in use should be corrected with the analysis. In the installation of a new system, many of the facts gathered during systems analysis are later used in the preparation of an operating manual.

SYSTEMS DESIGN

A new system is developed or improvements are made to an existing system in the systems design phase, based on the facts gathered through systems analysis. A team approach using accountants, managers, engineers, computer experts, and other specialists is often required in the design of an accounting system. The specific means to be used for input, processing, and output must be selected in light of the information requirements of the business.

The design must include a consideration of the *personnel* required to operate the system, the *business forms* needed to document transactions, the *accounting records* and *procedures* to be used to process data, the *reports* to be prepared for interested parties, and any *automated features* of the system. The basic concern in the design phase is to develop an accounting system with the most efficient flow of information possible, given the funds committed to the system and the information requirements involved. A fundamental part of the design phase is the development of reliable internal control. The guiding principle in the choice of output in the form of reports is that the benefits from each must exceed the costs. Some reports, such as financial statements and tax returns, are mandatory, but should still be produced at a reasonable cost. The value of other reports, such as those prepared for management, must be compared continuously with the preparation cost. The information in these reports must be accurate, timely, and relevant to be beneficial to users. In most cases, the ultimate measure of the benefits of information is the quality of the decision making based on it. Cost/benefit analysis of accounting information is particularly important when a large investment of funds is required for a computer and other electronic equipment.

SYSTEMS IMPLEMENTATION

Systems implementation is the final phase in the development or revision of an accounting system. This step involves the implementation of the decisions made during the design stage. The business forms, records, and equipment chosen must be purchased. The personnel needed to operate the system must be selected, trained, and closely supervised to assure that they understand how the system should function. An operating manual should be prepared as a formalized description of the procedures required to transform economic data into useful information. When an existing system is being revised, the old system is often operated parallel to the new one until management is certain that the new system is reliable. Major revisions are usually accomplished gradually, rather than all at once, to aid in ensuring reliable data flows. Any new accounting system should be tested thoroughly to be certain that its output is compatible with the desired results. Modifications should be made whenever necessary.

MANUAL ACCOUNTING SYSTEMS

As its name suggests, a manual accounting system is operated by human effort. Clerical personnel or bookkeepers prepare business forms, make journal entries, post to ledger accounts, and prepare financial reports. Many small businesses are able to satisfy their information requirements with a manual system, although this has decreased significantly in recent years because of the increasing popularity and decreasing cost of the computer. In earlier chapters, we illustrated basic accounting procedures by recording each transaction with an entry in a general journal and later posting each debit and credit to an appropriate account in the general ledger. We now can extend this basic version of a manual accounting system to one that is more streamlined and efficient by introducing subsidiary ledgers and special journals. Similar subsidiary ledgers and special journals are used in a computer accounting system; therefore, it is important that you learn how they function in a manual system, where it is easier to visualize them.

CONTROL ACCOUNTS AND SUBSIDIARY LEDGERS

So far, discussion of a ledger as an essential part of an accounting system has been limited to a general ledger. For more timely and efficient processing, we need to examine the use of control accounts and subsidiary ledgers. Before doing so, assume that a business sells merchandise on credit to 5,000 customers. If the firm used only one *Accounts Receivable* account—as we have done for illustrative purposes so far—it would not provide adequate detail concerning the amount of merchandise sold to individual customers, the amount of money received from them, and the amount still owed by them. Consequently, the firm will want to establish a separate *Accounts Receivable* account for each customer. If this were done in the general ledger, 5,000 accounts would have to be established and combined with the other assets, liabilities, owner's equity, revenues, and expenses. As a result, the general ledger would be unwieldy, and the likelihood of errors would be high. The trial balance prepared from such a large general ledger would also be very long and difficult to work with. This situation is complicated further by the fact that other general ledger accounts, such as *Accounts Payable* and *Inventory*, require the same detailed information.

Objective 8:
Use of control
accounts and
subsidiary
ledgers

When a large amount of detailed information must be kept about a certain general ledger account, a separate record, called a **subsidiary ledger,** is used. Thus, the detailed information is recorded outside the general ledger. For example, one *Accounts Receivable* account can be used in the general ledger and a separate *Accounts Receivable* account can be established for each customer (5,000 in the case being discussed) in the subsidiary ledger. The *Accounts Receivable* account in the general ledger is called a **control account,** a general ledger account supported by the detail of a subsidiary ledger. A subsidiary ledger consists of a group of individual accounts, the total of which should equal the balance of the related control account in the general ledger after all accounting is finished. Control accounts and subsidiary ledgers are used for a number of general ledger accounts such as *Accounts Receivable, Accounts Payable, Inventory,* and *Plant Assets.*

To illustrate the relationship between *Accounts Receivable* as a control account and its subsidiary ledger, consider the following simplified illustration that summarizes the November sales and cash receipts activities of a firm with three customers, given their beginning-of-the-month account balances.

General Ledger Accounts Receivable					Subsidiary Ledger P. Able			
Date	Debit	Credit	Balance		Date	Debit	Credit	Balance
Nov. 1			6,500		Nov. 1			3,200
30	5,100	6,900	4,700		8	1,800		5,000
					16		3,200	1,800

Proof of Agreement Between Control Account and Subsidiary Ledger

Beginning balances:
$6,500 = $3,200 + $1,100 + $2,200

Ending balances:
$4,700 = $1,800 + $2,400 + $500

R. Baker			
Date	Debit	Credit	Balance
Nov. 1			1,100
3		1,100	
20	2,400		2,400

D. Cane			
Date	Debit	Credit	Balance
Nov. 1			2,200
12	900		3,100
28		2,600	500

The accounts receivable subsidiary ledger is an alphabetical file with a separate account for each customer. Note that at the beginning and end of November, the totals of the subsidiary ledger accounts are in agreement with the *Accounts Receivable* control account in the general ledger. The use of a subsidiary ledger has three major advantages: it relieves the general ledger of a mass of detail; it allows a division of labor in maintaining the ledgers; and it provides effective internal control.

SPECIAL JOURNALS

Objective 9: Advantages of special journals

The general journal described in earlier chapters can be used to record all types of transactions: sales, purchases, cash receipts, cash disbursements, sales returns and allowances, and purchase returns and allowances. The universal nature of the general journal imposes some limitations that will adversely affect the efficiency of processing data. Each debit and credit recorded in the general journal must be posted individually, requiring a large amount of posting time. As the number of transactions increases, this inefficiency can make it difficult to provide accounting information on a timely basis. Also, only one person at a time can record the effects of transactions and post debits and credits to the ledger accounts, since all of the entries are recorded in one journal.

To avoid the limitations of using only a general journal, *transactions* are grouped into like categories and a **special journal** is set up for each category. Most of a typical firm's transactions fall into four categories, which in turn require four special journals.

Category of Transaction	Special Journal
Sales of merchandise on credit	Sales journal
Purchases of merchandise on credit	Purchases journal
Receipts of cash	Cash receipts journal
Disbursements of cash	Cash disbursements journal

The general journal is retained for recording transactions other than those in these four categories. For example, sales returns and allowances, purchase returns and allowances, adjusting entries, and closing entries are recorded in the general journal. If the sales returns and allowances or the purchase returns and allowances occur frequently, special journals may also be established for them. The combination of the five journals represents a much more efficient way to process data than the use of a general journal alone. As will be shown later, under this system the time required to journalize entries will be less, and totals, rather than individual entries, can be posted to ledger accounts in many cases, thus reducing the cost of accounting labor. Also, an efficient division of labor can be achieved by assigning different journals to different employees so that work can be performed concurrently. Several selected transactions during the month of January, involving the Baldwin Video Equipment Store, illustrate the four special journals in the next section. The formats used for the four special journals are typical and not unique. The nature of a given business determines the exact formats required.

Sales Journal

A **sales journal,** such as the one shown in Figure 6–2, is used solely for recording sales of merchandise on credit (cash sales are recorded in the cash receipts journal, as will be shown later). As each credit sale occurs, several copies of a sales invoice are prepared to document the transaction. The information shown on a sales invoice includes the customer's name, date of sale, invoice number (usually prenumbered), amount of sale, and the credit terms. One copy of the sales invoice is used by the seller to record the sale in the sales journal. In Figure 6–2, eight sales to five different customers have been recorded. All credit sales are made on the basis of 2/10, n/30 terms. Other columns can be added to the sales journal to satisfy the needs of a specific business. If credit terms vary among customers, an additional column can be added to the sales journal to identify the terms of each sale. In addition, a sales tax payable column can be used to record the amount of sales tax to be collected from customers when a business is required to do so for state or local taxing authorities.

Objective 10:
Formats of and procedures used with special journals

Advantages of a Sales Journal. The sales journal shown in Figure 6–2 has these time-saving advantages.

1. Each sales transaction is recorded on a *single line*. All credit sales are alike in that they result in a debit to *Accounts Receivable* and a credit to *Sales*. Recordkeeping efficiency is achieved by simply identifying the customer who is the debtor instead of entering the account titles—*Accounts Receivable* and *Sales*—for each transaction.

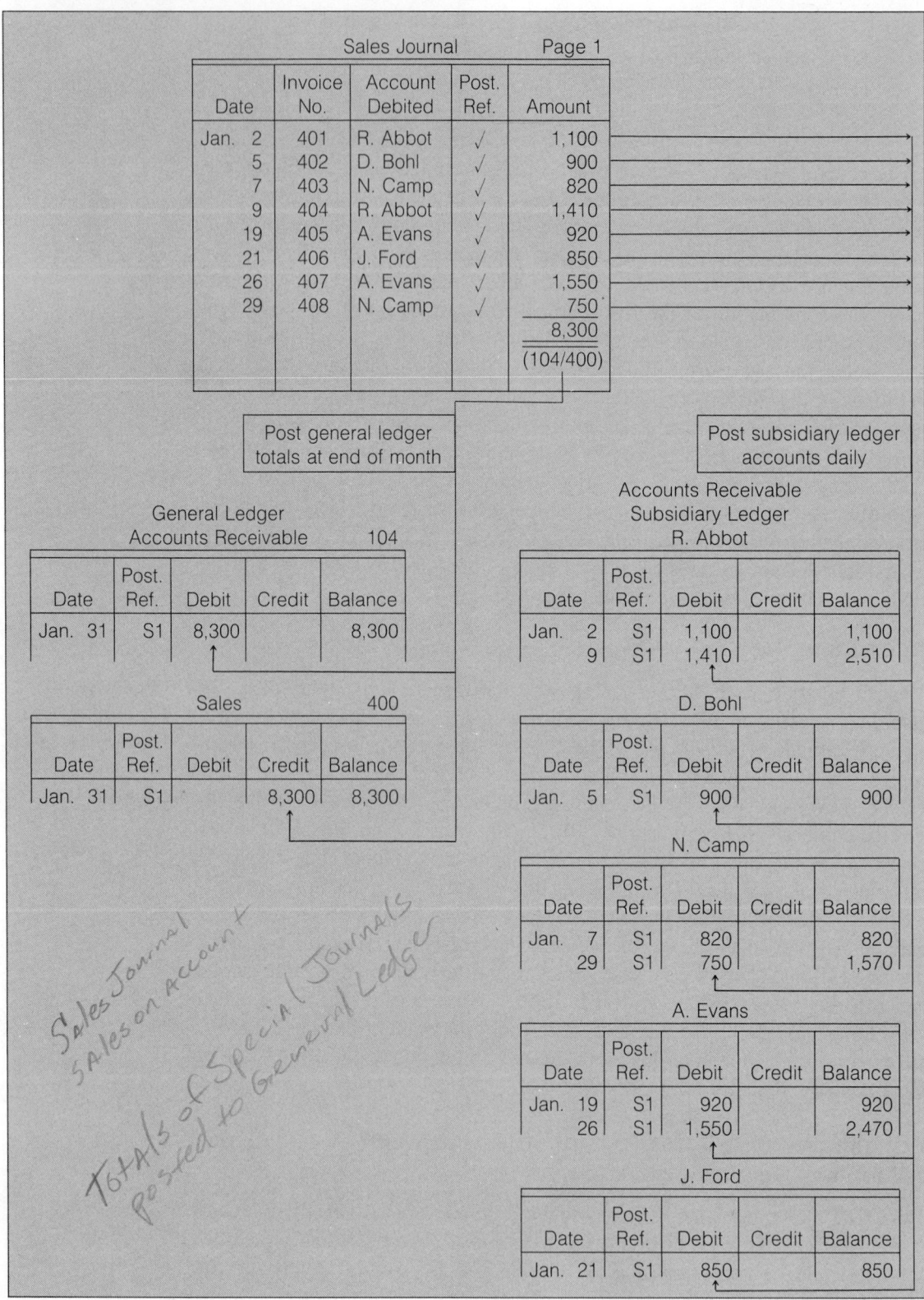

Figure 6–2
Relationship of Sales Journal and Ledger Accounts

2. The entries in the sales journal do not require an explanation for two reasons. First, all the transactions involved are the same, as previously discussed. Second, the detailed information related to each sale is documented on a sales invoice that is referenced in the second column of the sales journal. If additional information concerning a particular sale is required, the interested party can simply identify the invoice number and refer to the details of the sales invoice.

3. Posting efficiency is achieved with the sales journal since only one amount, the total of credit sales for the month, is posted to the general ledger. Note in Figure 6–2 that the total credit sales of $8,300 are posted twice—once to the *Accounts Receivable* control account and once to the *Sales* account. This procedure eliminates posting separate debits and credits during the month. In addition, the sales information needed for each customer in the accounts receivable subsidiary ledger is posted daily from the line items of the sales journal. A checkmark is recorded in the Post. Ref. (posting reference) column to indicate that each sale has been posted to the subsidiary ledger. The account numbers for *Accounts Receivable* (104) and *Sales* (400) are entered below the total credit sales for the month, to show that the general ledger accounts have been posted. A posting reference column is also included in the ledger accounts to indicate the source of the entries posted for cross-referencing purposes. S1 refers to the first page of the sales journal. Note that we can use the posting reference columns of the journal and the ledger to go back and forth easily between the two accounting records.

Summary of Sales Journal Procedures.   The procedures used with the sales journal illustrated in Figure 6–2 can be summarized as follows.

1. From each sales invoice, enter the date of sale, invoice number, customer's name, and amount of sale on a line of the sales journal.
2. *At the end of each day,* post each sale to the related customer's account in the subsidiary ledger. Place a checkmark in the posting reference column of the sales journal and S1 in the posting reference column of the customer's account.
3. *At the end of each month,* total the amount column of the sales journal and post the total amount as a debit and credit to the two general ledger accounts, *Accounts Receivable* and *Sales,* respectively. Place the general ledger account numbers involved (104/400) below the amount column total and S1 in the posting reference columns of the two general ledger accounts.
4. Add the account balances of the accounts receivable subsidiary ledger to verify that the total is equal to the *Accounts Receivable* control account balance in the general ledger. In Figure 6–2, the amount involved is $8,300 (the same as the balance of the *Accounts Receivable* control account), as shown in the following accounts receivable schedule.

Accounts Receivable Schedule

Customer	Amount
R. Abbot	$2,510
D. Bohl	900
N. Camp	1,570
A. Evans	2,470
J. Ford	850
Total	$8,300

Purchases Journal

The **purchases journal** can be set up as either a single-column or a multi-column journal. In either case, the purchases of merchandise must be recorded separately from the acquisition of other assets because, as we have seen earlier, the total purchases of merchandise for a period are used to compute cost of goods sold. A single-column purchases journal, such as that shown in Figure 6–3, is used solely for recording the purchases of merchandise on credit with a periodic inventory system. Cash purchases of merchandise are recorded in the cash disbursements journal, as will be discussed later. Other purchases, such as the acquisition of an automobile or an office machine, will be recorded in some other journal, determined by the means of payment involved. If such assets are acquired for cash, the transactions are recorded in the cash disbursements journal; if purchased on credit, they are recorded in the general journal.

The advantages of and procedures required for a single-column purchases journal are similar to those described earlier for a sales journal. Recall from the discussion in Chapter 5 that the purchase of merchandise on credit with a periodic inventory system is recorded with a debit to *Purchases* and a credit to *Accounts Payable* (as we are assuming here). If a perpetual inventory system is used, the debit is entered to the *Inventory* account. The account credited on each line item of a purchases journal is an account payable with a particular creditor to whom the business has an obligation. A subsidiary ledger is maintained to provide the detailed information concerning each individual account payable. An *Accounts Payable* control account is also established in the general ledger. The procedures used with a single-column purchases journal, as illustrated in Figure 6–3, can be summarized as follows.

1. Enter the recording date, invoice date, supplier's name, credit terms if applicable, and the dollar amount of the purchase on a single line of the journal from each purchase invoice.
2. *At the end of each day,* post each purchase to the related supplier's account in the subsidiary ledger. Place a checkmark in the posting reference column of the purchases journal and P1 (indicating page one of the purchases journal) in the posting reference column of the creditor's account. These posting reference marks indicate that the journal entry has been posted and identify the source of the entry.
3. *At the end of each month,* total the amount column of the purchases journal and post the total amount as a debit and a credit to the two general ledger accounts, *Purchases* and *Accounts Payable,* respectively. Place the general

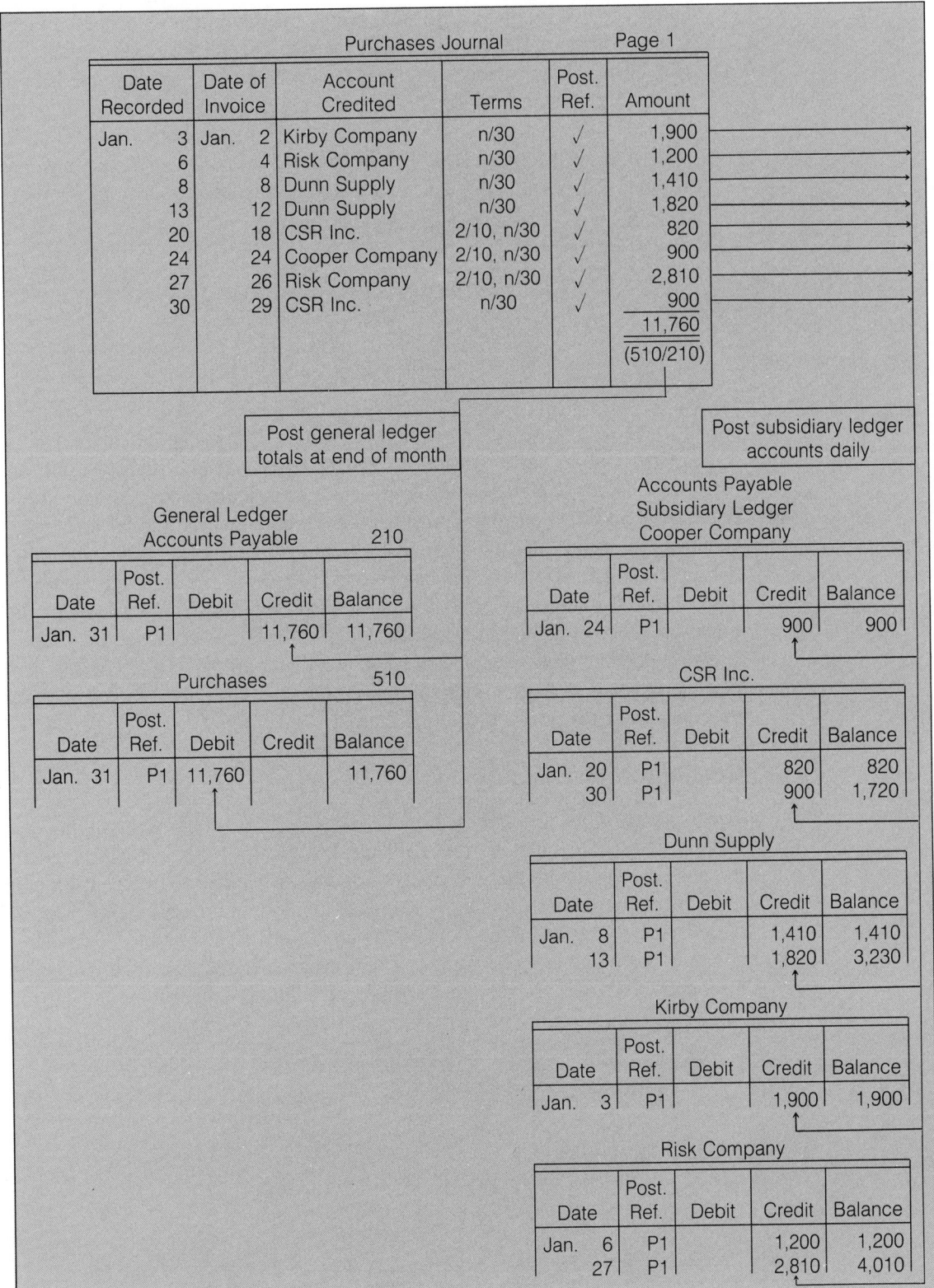

Figure 6–3
Relationship of Purchases Journal and Ledger Accounts

ledger account numbers (510/210) below the amount column total and P1 in the posting reference columns of the two general ledger accounts.

4. Add the account balances of the accounts payable subsidiary ledger to verify that the total is equal to the *Accounts Payable* control account balance in the general ledger. In Figure 6–3, the total amount is $11,760 (the same as the balance of the *Accounts Payable* control account), as verified by the following accounts payable schedule.

Accounts Payable Schedule

Supplier	Amount
Cooper Company	$ 900
CSR Inc.	1,720
Dunn Supply	3,230
Kirby Company	1,900
Risk Company	4,010
Total	$11,760

A single-column purchases journal can be expanded to a multicolumn format, such as the one shown in Figure 6–4. This journal has a single credit column for accounts payable and several debit columns for purchases of merchandise, purchases of store supplies, purchases of office supplies, and other debits. The other debits column can be used to record such transactions as the acquisition of equipment or the incurrence of freight-in charges. All of the transactions recorded in this journal will involve credit, rather than cash, because of the single accounts payable credit column. The recording and posting procedures with a multicolumn purchases journal are similar to those described next for the cash receipts journal.

Cash Receipts Journal

The **cash receipts journal** is used to record all transactions involving the receipt of cash (a debit to cash). Typical sources of cash are the sale of merchandise for cash, the collection of accounts receivable from customers, investments by owners, and bank loans. A multicolumn cash receipts journal is necessary because of the numerous sources of cash possible. Two debit columns are required—one for the actual cash collected, the other for sales discounts. To keep the required number of columns manageable and at the

Date	Account	Post. Ref.	Purchases Debit	Stores Supplies Debit	Office Supplies Debit	Other Debits Account	Post. Ref.	Amount	Accounts Payable Credit
Jan. 3	Hull Co.	✓	1,900						1,900
10	Kirk, Inc.	✓	2,800						2,800
14	Deckers, Inc.	✓		810					810
19	Short Co.	✓			465				465
24	Zinn Co.	✓				Office Equipment	170	1,155	1,155

Figure 6–4
Multicolumn Purchases Journal

same time achieve efficient processing, three credit columns are often used to separate the sources of cash in the journal. The headings on the three credit columns, as shown in Figure 6–5, are sales, accounts receivable, and other accounts. The first two credit columns are used to record collections from cash sales and accounts receivable. All other sources of cash are entered in the third credit column.

These cash receipts transactions for the Baldwin Video Equipment Store provide the basis for the entries in Figure 6–5.

1. The owner of the business, Betty Baldwin, invested $10,000 of her own cash on January 3.
2. Video equipment was sold for $285 cash on January 8.
3. Received payment from Robert Abbot for an eight-day-old account receivable of $1,100 less a 2% sales discount of $22 on January 10. Therefore, $1,078 cash was received. Credit terms are 2/10, n/30 and the cash was received within 10 days.
4. Received payment from Don Bohl for a 15-day-old account receivable of $900 on January 20. No discount was involved since the cash was not received within 10 days.
5. Video equipment was sold for $220 cash on January 21.
6. A bank loan of $2,500 was received on January 31.

The two debit columns and three credit columns of the cash receipts journal shown in Figure 6–5 are used as follows.

Debits

Cash. The cash column is used in *every* entry, because only cash receipt transactions are recorded in the cash receipts journal.

Sales Discounts. This column is used to record all sales discounts allowed customers for prompt payment. Note that on January 10 the 2% discount ($.02 \times \$1,100 = \$22$) given to R. Abbot was recorded because the payment was made within 10 days. The total debits to Cash ($1,078) and Sales Discounts ($22) are equal to the $1,100 credit to Accounts Receivable, all of which are recorded on one line.

Credits

Sales. All cash sales are recorded in the sales column. Most firms use cash registers to account for daily cash sales. At the end of a day, a sales tape showing the total cash sales is removed from the cash register and used to make the entry in the sales column.

Accounts Receivable. This column is used to record the collections on accounts from customers. The name of the customer is written in the account credited column to identify the proper account to be credited in the subsidiary ledger.

Other Accounts. This column is used for all cash collections other than those from cash sales and accounts receivable. The title of the specific account to be credited is identified in the account credited column. For

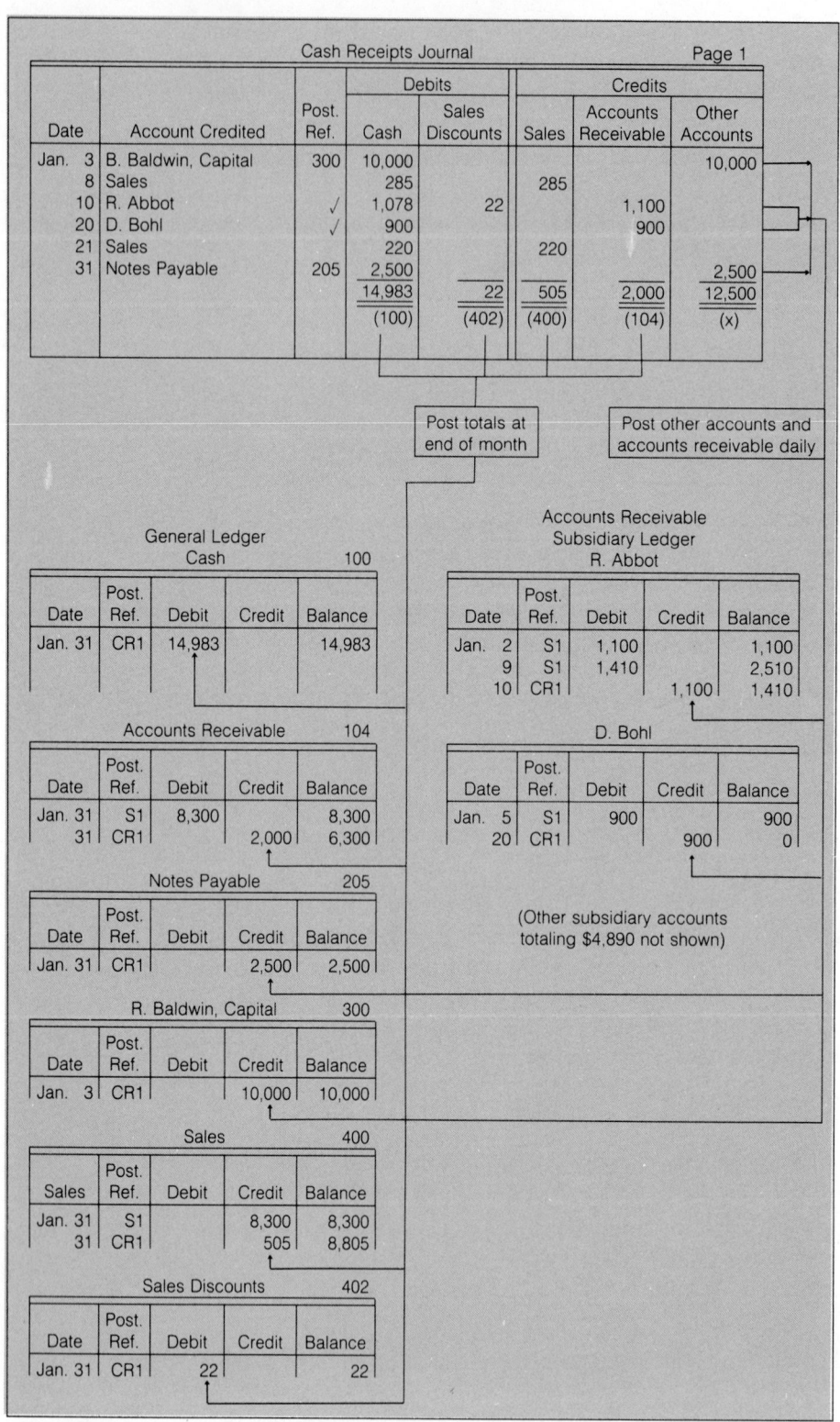

Figure 6–5

Relationship of Cash Receipts and Ledger Accounts

example, Betty Baldwin's *Capital* account is credited on January 3 for the $10,000 investment.

Summary of Posting Procedures for Cash Receipts Journal. The procedures required to post the entries in the cash receipts journal can be summarized as follows.

1. The entries in the accounts receivable column should be *posted daily* to the subsidiary ledger. A checkmark is placed in the posting reference column of the cash receipts journal, and CR1 (indicating page one of the cash receipts journal) is entered in the posting reference columns of the subsidiary ledger accounts. Note that by posting the receipts daily (along with the accounts receivable recorded in the sales journal), we have up-to-date balances in the customers' subsidiary *Accounts Receivable* accounts.

2. The credits in the other accounts column should be posted *when it is convenient but no later than at the end of the month*. The number of the account involved is recorded in the posting reference column as the entries are posted to show that the posting has been accomplished. In addition, CR1 is entered in the posting reference column of each account to indicate the source of each entry.

3. *At the end of the month,* the entries in each column should be totaled. The sum of the debit columns should be compared with the sum of the credit columns to verify that the debits and credits are equal. This procedure is called crossfooting, and gives the following results, using the totals of the journal columns.

Debit Columns		**Credit Columns**	
Cash	$14,983	Sales	$ 505
Sales discounts	22	Accounts receivable	2,000
		Other accounts	12,500
Total debits	$15,005		$15,005

Crossfooted

After the totals have been crossfooted, the following four column totals are posted.

Cash debit column. Posted as a debit to the *Cash* account. The account number (100) is entered below the total to indicate that the posting has been done, and CR1 is recorded in the posting reference column of the *Cash* account.

Sales discounts debit column. Posted as a debit to the *Sales Discounts* account. The account number (402) is placed below the total to show that the posting has been accomplished, and CR1 is entered in the *Sales Discounts* account.

Sales credit column. Posted as a credit to the *Sales* account. The account number (400) is entered below the total as an indication that the posting has taken place, and CR1 is recorded in the *Sales* account.

Accounts receivable credit column. Posted as a credit to the *Accounts*

Receivable control account. The account number (104) is recorded below the total, and CR1 is entered in the control account.

The total of the other accounts column *is not posted at the end of the month* because each entry is posted individually. Some accountants use a special symbol—such as (x)—at the bottom of the column to indicate that it is not posted as a total.

Cash Disbursements Journal

The **cash disbursements journal,** also called the cash payments journal, is used to record all transactions involving payments of cash: cash purchases of merchandise, payment of accounts payable to creditors, disbursements for operating expenses, and payment of bank loans. The multicolumn format of the cash disbursements journal is similar to the one described earlier for the cash receipts journal. Three debit columns (purchases, accounts payable, and other accounts) are used along with two credit columns (cash and purchase discounts), as illustrated in Figure 6–6. These transactions for Baldwin Video Equipment Store illustrate the cash disbursements journal.

1. Merchandise costing $680 was purchased for cash on January 4.
2. Store rent of $325 was paid on January 7.
3. Store equipment costing $410 was purchased for cash on January 14.
4. Merchandise costing $840 was purchased for cash on January 28.
5. A one-year premium for an insurance policy amounting to $510 was paid on January 29.
6. The $1,900 account payable to the Kirby Company was paid on January 30.
7. The $900 account payable to the Cooper Company was paid, less a 2% discount of $18 on January 30. Therefore, $882 cash was paid.

The three debit columns and two credit columns of the cash disbursements journal shown in Figure 6–6 are used as follows.

Debits

Purchases. The purchases column is used to record all cash purchases of merchandise. The total of this column is posted to the *Purchases* account in the general ledger. When posted, the amount is added to the credit purchases posted from the purchases journal to determine the total purchases for the period.

Accounts Payable. Payments of accounts payable are entered in this column. The name of the supplier is written in the account debited column, so that the entry can be posted to the appropriate subsidiary ledger account.

Other Accounts. This column is used for all cash disbursements except cash purchases and payments of accounts payable. The title of the account to be debited is entered in the account debited column to identify a specific type of cash disbursement. In Figure 6–6, rent expense and prepaid insurance were paid for, along with store equipment.

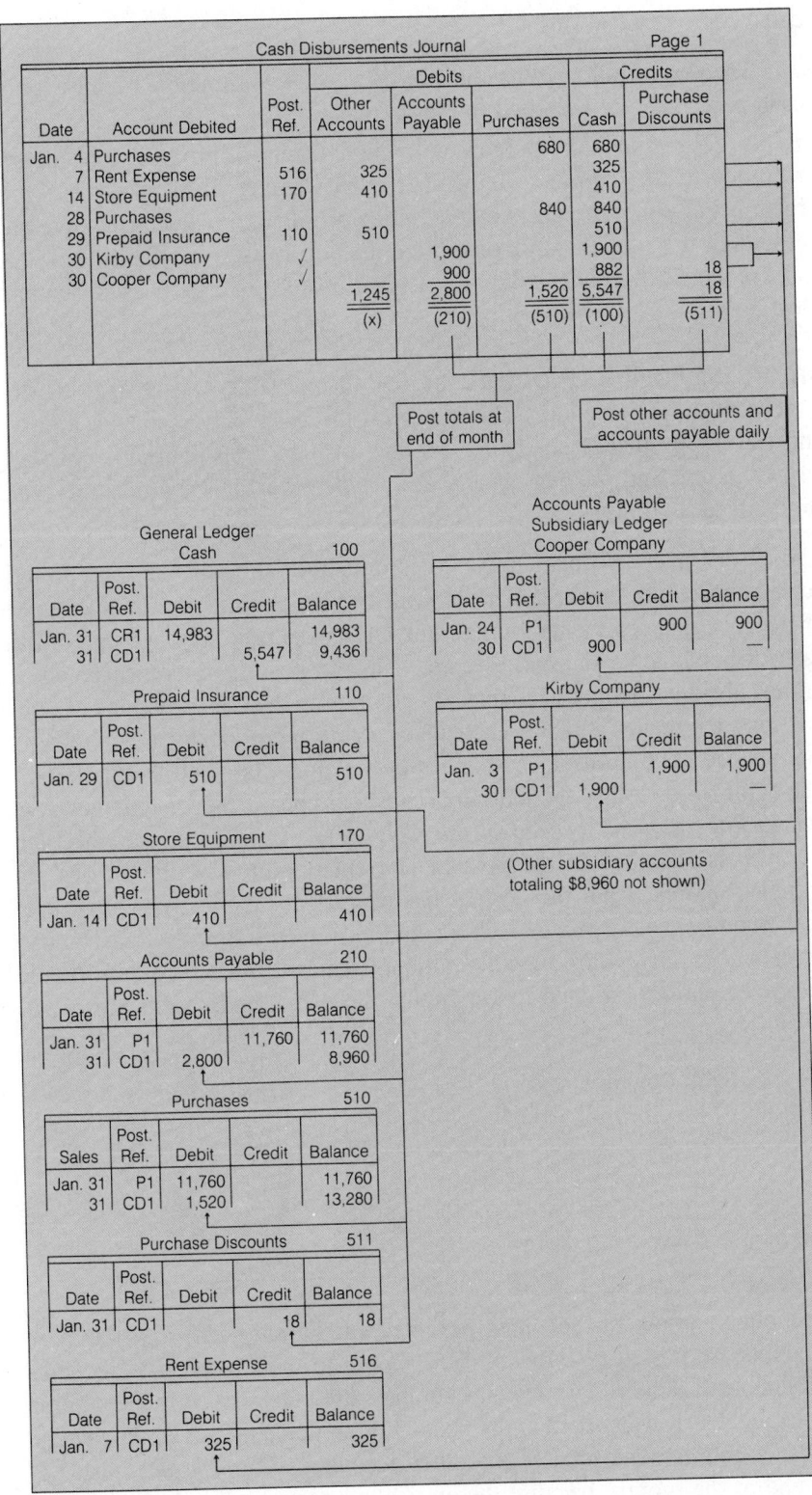

Figure 6–6
Relationship of Cash Disbursements Journal and Ledger Accounts

Credits

Cash. The cash column must be used for *each* transaction because *only* cash payments are recorded in the journal.

Purchase Discounts. Any purchase discounts taken for prompt payment are recorded in this column. Remember from Chapter 5 that purchases are recorded at either the gross invoice price or the net invoice price. We are assuming that the gross invoice price method is used in this illustration, so a purchase discounts column is needed, instead of a purchase discounts lost column.

Summary of Posting Procedures for Cash Disbursements Journal.
The posting procedures required with the cash disbursements journal are the two types discussed earlier for the cash receipts journal—*postings during the month* and *postings at the end of the month*. The procedures can be summarized as follows.

1. The entries in the accounts payable column should be posted *daily* to the subsidiary ledger. A checkmark is placed in the posting reference column of the cash disbursements journal, and CD1 (representing page one of the cash disbursements journal) is entered in the posting reference columns of the subsidiary ledger accounts. By combining the daily postings of both the cash payments and the accounts payable recorded in the purchases journal, we have up-to-date balances of the amounts owed to suppliers.
2. The debits in the other accounts column should be posted *when convenient but no later than at the end of the month.* The number of each account involved is recorded in the posting reference column as the entries are posted to indicate that the posting has been done. CD1 is entered in the posting reference column of each account to show the source of each entry.
3. *At the end of the month,* the dollar amounts entered in each column should be totaled and crossfooted to verify that the debits and credits are equal, as follows.

Debit Columns		**Credit Columns**	
Other accounts	$1,245	Cash	$5,547
Accounts payable	2,800	Purchase discounts	18
Purchases	1,520		
Total debits	$5,565	Total credits	$5,565

Crossfooted

4. The column totals for accounts payable, purchases, cash, and purchase discounts are posted *at the end of the month* to their respective accounts in the general ledger. The account numbers are entered below the column totals, and CD1 is recorded in the posting reference columns of the general ledger accounts. The total of the other accounts column is *not* posted at the end of the month, because the entries are posted individually. An (x) can be placed below the column total to indicate that it is not posted at the end of the month.

THE USE OF A GENERAL JOURNAL

Despite the inefficiency of a general journal for repetitive transactions such as sales, purchases, cash receipts, and cash disbursements, it is an essential part of every accounting system. A *limited number* of transactions (such as sales returns and allowances, purchase returns and allowances, and the purchase or sale of equipment on credit) are recorded in the general journal *during* an accounting period. If a particular transaction cannot be recorded efficiently in one of the special journals, it should be entered in the general journal. The general journal is also used for all *adjusting* and *closing entries* at the end of the accounting period. The procedures used to record entries in the general journal and to post them to ledger accounts have already been described. As we have seen in the description of special journals, the ledger accounts should indicate the journal from which each debit and credit is posted. The symbol GJ typically is used in the ledger accounts for postings from the general journal; GJ1 would refer to page one of the general journal. The following symbols can be used to identify the sources of entries posted from the five journals discussed so far.

Objective 11:
Using a general
journal with
special journals

S1: page 1 of the sales journal

P2: page 2 of the purchases journal

CR3: page 3 of the cash receipts journal

CD4: page 4 of the cash disbursements journal

GJ5: page 5 of the general journal

To illustrate the use of the general journal, assume that Betty Baldwin agreed to give A. Evans a $72 allowance on his account because of a faulty component on video equipment sold to him on January 19. The sales allowance would be recorded in the general journal as shown in Figure 6–7. Both the *Accounts Receivable* control account and the customer's subsidiary ledger account must be credited; otherwise the control account will not be in balance with the subsidiary ledger. The number of the *Accounts Receivable* account (104) and a checkmark are recorded in the posting reference column to indicate that both postings are made.

REFINEMENTS OF AN ACCOUNTING SYSTEM

We have emphasized that a business will often refine the general accounting records of a manual system to provide more efficient data processing and to satisfy its own information requirements. Two means of refinement are worthy of noting at this point because of their popularity: *direct posting from invoices* and a *one-write system.* Many businesses maintain a numerical file of sales invoices from which sales and accounts receivable information is posted to ledger accounts. The sales invoices are numbered serially and filed as they are prepared in a binder of some sort, so that, in effect, the binder takes the place of the sales journal (this is often called journaless accounting). Each sales invoice total is posted directly to the related customer's account in the accounts receivable subsidiary ledger on a daily basis. At the end of the month, all invoices for that month are totaled, and a general journal entry is made,

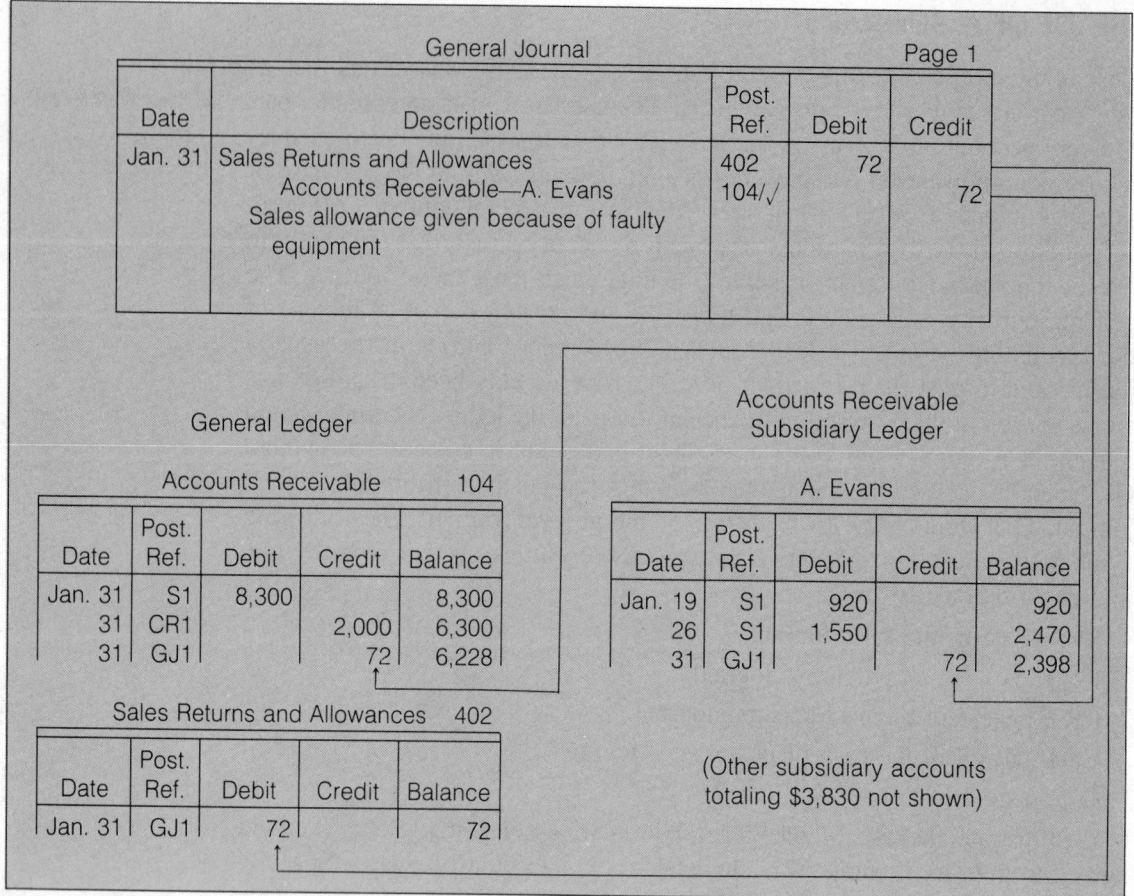

Figure 6–7
Relationship of General Journal and Ledger Accounts

debiting the *Accounts Receivable* control account and crediting the *Sales* account for the total monthly sales. These same procedures can be used in recording purchase invoices, in lieu of maintaining a purchases journal.

As the name suggests, a one-write system eliminates the need to enter the same data more than once. Several business forms for different recording functions can be held in alignment on some type of writing board so that a single entry on the top form produces the same entries on the forms beneath it. Since only the one entry is made, repetitive copying is avoided, reducing clerical costs. For example, a one-write approach can be used with a cash disbursements journal. When a check is written, the information is also recorded in the appropriate column of the cash disbursements journal and in the accounts payable subsidiary ledger whenever applicable. This is accomplished by using special paper that reproduces what is written on the check on the other records.

DATA-PROCESSING EQUIPMENT

To process data accurately and rapidly, most businesses use some type of equipment. Even in the manual accounting applications discussed earlier, such equipment as calculators, typewriters, cash registers, and copy machines are used to reduce the workload and to reduce errors. A wide range of additional equipment is available and can be adopted to satisfy the information requirements and operating conditions of a firm. The most modern and sophisticated type of automated accounting system involves an electronic computer. While a detailed description of a computer accounting system is beyond the scope of this book, we should develop a fundamental understanding of how a computer operates and the importance of its role in the accounting function.

ELECTRONIC DATA PROCESSING

The terms **electronic data processing (EDP)** and computer data processing are often used interchangeably. They refer to the use of electronic equipment, consisting of a computer and its peripheral equipment, to process data. The primary advantages of a computer as a data-processing device are its *accuracy, speed, storage capacity,* and *versatility* for performing analytical operations. As a firm grows in size and complexity, the volume of paperwork from transactions to be processed increases significantly. At some point the cost, inaccuracy, and time delays of a manual system force a business to consider using a computer. For example, think about the data-processing requirements of a medium-sized commercial bank with assets of $150,000,000. The bank must have an accounting system to process data related to revenue and expense transactions, as well as its balance-sheet accounts. It must also maintain detailed records of functions such as credit card activity, installment loans, business loans, real estate loans, check processing, customer deposits, and savings accounts. Hundreds of thousands of transactions are involved, and a computerized operation of some sort is required to cope with the volume of data. A similar situation confronts a variety of other operations, such as an airline, a retail store chain, a stockbrokerage firm, a hospital, a hotel chain, or a manufacturing company.

Today, the increasing popularity of minicomputers, microcomputers, and time-sharing services have made EDP affordable even for small businesses. As its name suggests, a *minicomputer* is a small, low-cost machine, capable of performing many of the operations of a large computer, although on a more limited scale. A *microcomputer* is even smaller than a minicomputer; it can have most of its essential components on a single silicon chip that is smaller than a key on a pocket calculator. A *time-sharing application* exists when a business shares a computer's time with other users, as happens when time is rented from a service bureau specializing in data processing.

USE OF A COMPUTER

A computer is a high-speed electronic machine that receives data and instructions, processes the data into information, and reports the results in a form readable by a human being or another machine. The type of computer used in an accounting system is a **digital computer,** a machine that processes discrete numbers in accordance with a sequence of internally stored instructions. The other type of computer is an analog computer, which manipulates

*Objective 12:
Importance of
EDP*

*Objective 13:
Basic features
of a computer*

some physical quantity, such as voltage or temperature change, and is used in engineering applications. Today's large digital computers can execute an instruction in a nanosecond—one billionth of a second—and can process a large volume of data in a fraction of the time required to do so by human effort. For example, a large company with thousands of employees can process its payroll in a *few hours* with a computer, instead of it taking the *several days* required to do so with manual processing. Today, millions of digital computers are being used in the United States. In particular, the microcomputer explosion we have been experiencing in recent years has contributed significantly to the number of computers in use.

A digital computer has five basic components, which are illustrated in Figure 6–8.

1. **Input.** This component receives data and instructions from the computer operator or an electronic device. Many different means can be used for the input process: *punched cards, disks, paper tape, magnetic cards, magnetic tape,* or a *keyboard.*
2. **Memory unit.** This is the primary storage component of the computer, where data and instructions are stored and from which data are obtained when needed.
3. **Arithmetic-logic unit.** This performs arithmetical and logical operations, such as addition, subtraction, multiplication, division, and comparison of two values. Data in the memory section are manipulated according to instructions from the control unit and the arithmetic-logic unit.
4. **Control unit.** This directs the sequencing of operations that process input data according to well-defined instructions fed into the memory unit.
5. **Output.** This component translates the results of processed data into such usable form as *printed copy, punched cards, disks, paper tape, magnetic cards, magnetic tape, or lines on a display screen.*

The central processing unit (CPU) of a computer consists of its memory, arithmetic-logic, and control components. The CPU determines the operating

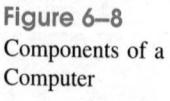

Figure 6–8
Components of a Computer

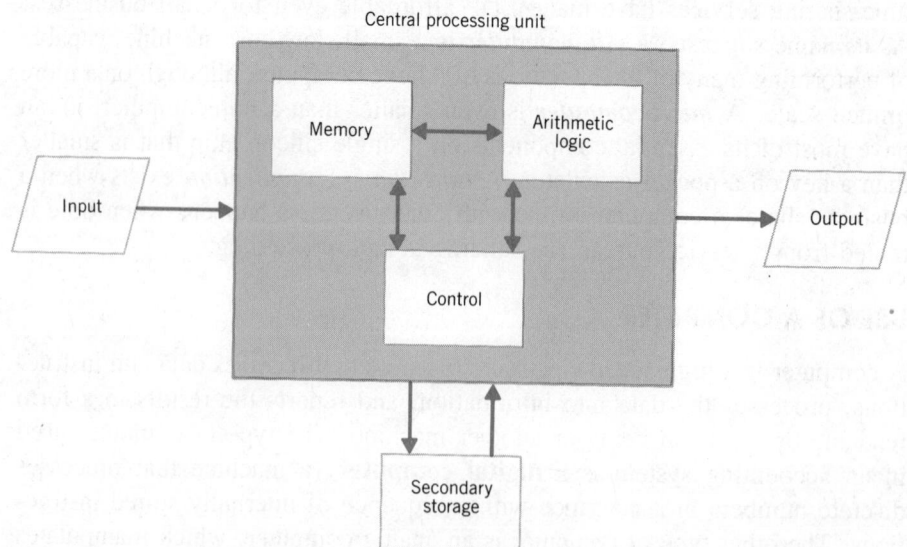

capacity of the computer, because it controls the flow of data into the system, performs calculations and other manipulations on the data, and regulates the flow of output. In addition to the primary storage of the memory component, a computer is usually supported with secondary storage external to the computer, which allows the storage of a larger volume of data than permitted in the memory of the computer itself. The secondary-storage capacity is normally less expensive than the computer memory.

OPERATION OF A COMPUTER

A computer must be told exactly *where to find data input, how to process the data, and what to do with the output.* These instructions are given to the CPU in the form of **computer programs,** a series of precise instructions that tell the computer what it is to do step by step. Programs are read into the memory of the computer to provide these instructions. Whereas the term **hardware** is used to denote the components of the computer and its peripheral equipment, **software** refers to the programs that will make the equipment function along with documentation and instructions for using the programs.

A **computer programmer** is a person who writes computer programs. These programs are usually written in a language that people can work with, such as BASIC, FORTRAN, or COBOL. They are later translated into a machine-readable form through the use of special programs called compilers. Common Business Oriented Language (COBOL), is particularly useful for such accounting applications as updating ledgers, processing payrolls, preparing financial statements, and maintaining inventories. In a computerized accounting system, a computer program must be written to tell the computer how to proceed through each accounting application. To do so, the programmer must know whether the data processing will be performed with batch processing or online processing. In **batch processing,** transaction data are accumulated until a large volume is processed at one time. This method is often used for such routine procedures as payroll, customer billing, and general ledger accounting. For example, payroll data can be collected at the end of each pay period, then batched, and processed by the computer. **Online processing** involves processing transactions as they occur, so that a user can obtain current information at any time. An example of online processing is the system used for airline reservations. Each ticket counter has a terminal with which an agent can instantly communicate with a computer concerning flight information and available space. Online processing can be applied to such accounting activities as accounts receivable, accounts payable, and inventory.

THE IMPACT OF THE MICROCOMPUTER ON ACCOUNTING

The microcomputer explosion has been well recognized because of the publicity it has received, the number of microcomputers sold, their use in education, and the versatility of microcomputer applications. The field of accounting has been widely affected by the dramatic impact of the microcomputer, which has permitted computerized accounting in businesses that previously

Objective 14: Using a computer in an accounting system

could not have afforded the cost of larger computers or the employees needed to make the computers work. Popular models of microcomputers are the IBM Personal Computer (which is being used to write this book), the Apple Macintosh, the Hewlett Packard Touchscreen Personal Computer, the TRS-80, and the COMPAC Portable Computer.

A microcomputer can be used to perform virtually every accounting function, including accounts receivable, accounts payable, payroll, inventory control, and general ledger. Software is readily available for these accounting functions, and, therefore, the need for specialized programming is avoided. In addition, electronic spreadsheet programs are sold that support many important accounting applications. An **electronic spreadsheet** is a versatile computer program that can be utilized to perform numerous types of financial analysis on a microcomputer. Electronic spreadsheets are similar to the worksheets you have been exposed to in manual form in this book, in that they consist of a matrix display of cells organized into rows and columns. These can be used to electronically manipulate accounting data.

A spreadsheet program permits a business to perform calculations that would be impossible using a manual system because of the time involved. For example, using a computer, the impact on net income over the next ten years of an annual sales increase of eight percent combined with an annual manufacturing cost increase of six percent can be quickly evaluated during a management meeting. Names of popular electronic spreadsheets used today are VisiCalc, SuperCalc, and Lotus 1-2-3. These spreadsheets provide the means of electronically applying many of the accounting topics developed in this book. Software called a **database management system** is also available to efficiently create and maintain files of accounting data (defined in the next section) that can easily be converted into a variety of financial reports with the microcomputer. Names of some database management systems are dbase III, PC/FOCUS, and REVELATION.

COMPUTER ACCOUNTING SYSTEMS

It is important to note the similarities between a basic accounting system and a computer. Each involves three essential phases: *input, processing,* and *output.* The integration of a computer into an accounting system is, therefore, a relatively simple task. Remember that a manual accounting system consists of business forms, journals, ledgers, and reports. In a computer accounting system, the same basic business forms can be used as those used in a manual system, but they must be converted into a machine-readable format to be accepted as input to the computer. Business transactions are recorded on coding forms similar to the special journals discussed earlier. The data are then put into the computer through some device, such as a keyboard, which is similar to the keyboard on an ordinary typewriter.

The programs supporting a particular accounting application are moved into the primary storage area of the computer, the work area of the CPU. Input, programs, and output are moved in and out of the primary storage area as the computer processes data according to well defined instructions. **Files,** which are ordered sets of accessible records, are used to process the accounting data. For example, the accounts receivable master file (consisting of a record for each customer) at the beginning of an accounting period can be updated by the computer to record credit sales billed to customers, as follows.

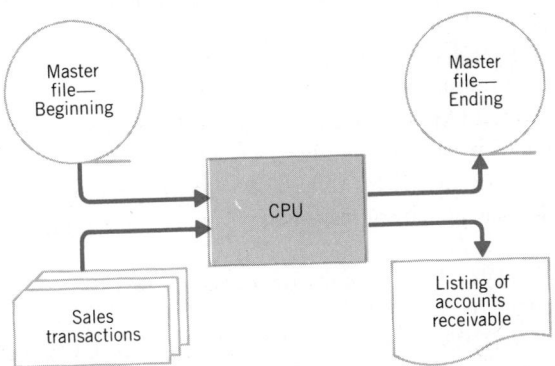

Note the similarities between this updating of the accounts receivable file and the manual procedures discussed earlier regarding the sales journal.

In this simple case, there are two sources of input and output. The input consists of the accounts receivable file (a master file) at the beginning of the period and the sales transactions (called a transactions file) required to update the beginning balances. On the output side, an updated accounts receivable master file and a listing of accounts receivable billed are produced through the computer processing. In general, the transformation of data into information with a computer accounting system can be diagrammed as.

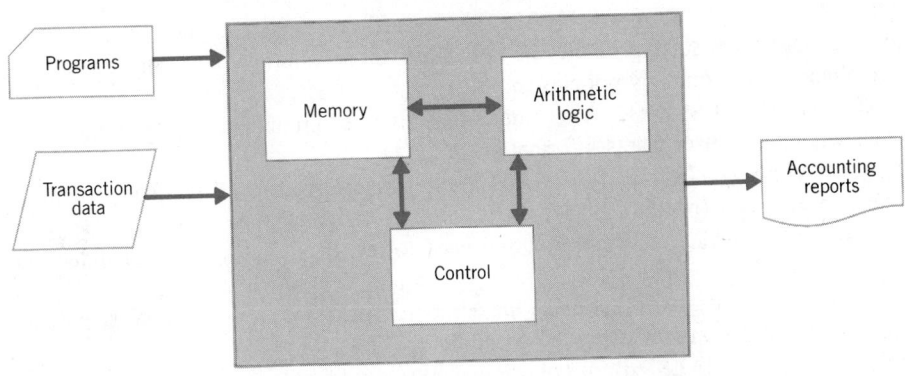

GLOSSARY

ACCOUNTING CONTROLS. Internal controls used to protect assets and ensure reliability of accounting records (p. 246).

ACCOUNTING SYSTEM. A collection of business forms, records, procedures, management policies, and data-processing methods used to transform economic data into useful information (p. 244).

ADMINISTRATIVE CONTROLS. Internal controls used to provide operating efficiency and adherence to prescribed company policies (p. 246).

BATCH PROCESSING. Accumulating a volume of data and processing it at one time (p. 271).

CASH DISBURSEMENTS JOURNAL. A special journal used to record all cash payments (p. 264).

CASH RECEIPTS JOURNAL. A special journal used to record transactions involving the receipt of cash (p. 260).

COMPUTER PROGRAM. A sequence of instructions stored in a computer's memory that tell the computer what to do and when to do it (p. 271).

COMPUTER PROGRAMMER. A person who writes computer programs, usually in a language understandable by humans that is later converted into a machine-readable form by a compiler (p. 271).

CONTROL ACCOUNT. A general ledger account that is supported by the details of a subsidiary ledger (p. 253).

DATABASE MANAGEMENT SYSTEM. A program developed for a computer that enables a business to efficiently develop data files and prepare financial reports (p. 272).

DIGITAL COMPUTER. An electronic machine that processes discrete values and consists of input, a memory unit, an arithmetic-logic unit, a control unit, and output (p. 269).

ELECTRONIC DATA PROCESSING (EDP). The use of a digital computer and its peripheral equipment to process data (p. 269).

ELECTRONIC SPREADSHEET. A versatile computer program that can be used to perform numerous types of financial analysis (p. 272).

FILE. An ordered set of records used to process data (p. 272).

HARDWARE. The components of the computer and its peripheral equipment (p. 271).

INTERNAL CONTROL SYSTEM. The overall procedures adopted by a business to safeguard its assets, promote the reliability of accounting data, and encourage compliance with company policies (p. 246).

ONLINE PROCESSING. A technique that involves immediate access to the computer whenever a user wants information (p. 271).

PURCHASES JOURNAL. A special journal used to record all purchases of merchandise on credit (p. 258).

SALES JOURNAL. A special journal used to record all sales of merchandise on credit (p. 255).

SOFTWARE. Programs that make the computer function, along with the documentation and instructions for using the programs (p. 271).

SPECIAL JOURNALS. Books of original entry used for such repetitive transactions as sales, purchases, cash receipts, and cash disbursements (p. 254).

SUBSIDIARY LEDGER. A group of individual accounts, the total of which should equal the balance of a related control account in the general ledger (p. 253).

SYSTEMS ANALYSIS. The initial stage in the development of an accounting system through which an understanding of a business's information requirements and sources of information is provided. (p. 251).

SYSTEMS DESIGN. The second stage in the development of an accounting system through which the specific means to be used for input, processing, and output are determined (p. 251).

SYSTEMS IMPLEMENTATION. The final stage in the development of an accounting system through which the system is made operational (p. 252).

DISCUSSION QUESTIONS

1. What are the three phases of an accounting system? Explain each one.
2. Distinguish between *data* and *information* as the two terms apply to an accounting system.
3. Why is internal control important in the operation of an accounting system?
4. Distinguish between administrative controls and accounting controls. Give an example of each.
5. What was the most significant accomplishment of the Foreign Corrupt Practices Act, as far as accounting is concerned?
6. Why are clearly defined lines of responsibility an important element of internal accounting controls?
7. How does the policy of rotating duties among employees aid in strengthening internal control?
8. If a firm's cashier has the responsibility of determining the specific accounts receivable to be written off as uncollectible, what general element of internal control is lacking?
9. If an employee is responsible for ordering inventory, receiving goods, and paying the supplier, what general element of internal control is lacking?
10. Why is it important that the employee designated to approve invoices for payment not have checkwriting or accounting responsibilities?
11. What are the three phases of the installation of an accounting system? Explain each one.
12. What is the basic limitation of a manual accounting system?
13. How are control accounts and subsidiary ledgers used? What are their major advantages?
14. What are the advantages of using special journals? Why is the general journal needed, even when special journals are used?
15. How often are sales transactions posted from the sales journal to the general ledger? How often are they posted to the subsidiary ledger?
16. What are the advantages of the sales journal?
17. How often are purchase transactions posted from the purchases journal to the general ledger? How often are they posted to the subsidiary ledger?
18. Why is it necessary to crossfoot both the cash receipts journal and the cash disbursements journal?
19. Why is a multicolumn journal used for cash receipts and cash disbursements?
20. Identify the major sources of cash receipts recorded in the cash receipts journal. Identify the major transactions involving cash payments recorded in the cash disbursements journal.
21. Explain how copies of sales invoices can be used as a sales journal.
22. What is meant by the term *one-write system* as it is applied to an accounting system?
23. What are the primary advantages of computerized data processing?
24. What are the five basic components of a computer?
25. Distinguish between the terms *hardware* and *software* as they apply to electronic data processing.
26. What is a computer program and why is it important in data processing?
27. Differentiate batch processing from online processing.
28. Why has the microcomputer had such a major impact on accounting?

29. Differentiate between an electronic spreadsheet and a database management system. How are each used in accounting?
30. What is a *file* in the application of electronic data processing?

EXERCISES

Exercise 6-1 Evaluating Internal Control Procedures

John Rigner, the owner of a hardware store, has asked for your advice concerning the internal control of his business. In order to keep procedures simple, Rigner has assigned one employee the responsibility for ordering inventory, receiving goods, and paying suppliers. Another employee maintains the accounting records, collects cash from customers, and makes all bank deposits. Rigner notes that his system is not only simple, but that it also takes full advantage of specialization, because the two employees have been with the business for 15 years performing the same jobs.

Required:
Evaluate the internal control procedures of the hardware store.

Exercise 6-2 True/False Analysis of Internal Control and Accounting Systems

Indicate whether each of the following statements is true or false.

1. An accounting system consists of processing procedures and the output from them.
2. A fidelity bond would be a waste of money where a strong internal control system is in place.
3. Management's primary attention should be with accounting controls, because the administrative controls will take care of themselves.
4. A major impact of the Foreign Corrupt Practices Act has been an increased concern for sound internal control.
5. According to the Foreign Corrupt Practices Act, the CPA performing the audit for a publicly held company has the primary responsibility for sound internal control.
6. Custodianship of assets and recordkeeping should be combined in assigning responsibilities to employees in an efficient manner.
7. A major benefit of a subsidiary ledger is sound internal control.
8. The use of special journals is helpful in maintaining current balances in general ledger accounts and subsidiary ledgers during the month.
9. It is possible to eliminate certain special journals and still have a good accounting system.
10. All column totals in a cash receipts journal must be posted at the end of the month.

Exercise 6-3 True/False Analysis of Computerized Accounting

Indicate whether each of the following statements is true or false.

1. The major factor in the feasibility of adding a computer to an accounting system is the number of business transactions involved.
2. An analog computer is the type used for electronic data processing.

3. The CPU of a computer consists of its memory.
4. Computer programs are referred to as software.
5. When batch processing is used, a business can access current account balances at any time.
6. A record is an ordered set of files in an accounting system.
7. When computerized accounting is utilized, the basic steps involved are input, processing, and output.
8. A major advantage of a microcomputer is its affordability.
9. Electronic spreadsheets have revolutionized accounting to the point that it is no longer necessary to master the principles of accounting.
10. A database management system is an important accounting tool because it enables a business to efficiently develop files of data without employing an experienced computer programmer.

Exercise 6-4 Reconciling a Control Account and a Subsidiary Ledger

Assume that a retail store sold merchandise to three customers during March, as shown in the following *Accounts Receivable* account. Explain why the control account and related subsidiary ledger are not in balance, and what must be done to correct the situation.

General Ledger
Accounts Receivable

Date	Explanation	Post. Ref.	Debit	Credit	Balance
Mar. 1	Bal.				4,200
6		GJ9		400	3,800
30		S6	4,580		8,380
30		CR5		3,900	4,480

Subsidiary Ledger

Customer A

| 3/1 Bal. | 1,400 | 3/6 GJ9 | 300 |
| 3/9 S6 | 1,800 | 3/10 CR5 | 1,400 |

Customer B

| 3/1 Bal. | 1,500 | 3/17 CR5 | 1,500 |
| 3/15 S6 | 1,900 | | |

Customer C

| 3/1 Bal. | 1,300 | 3/24 CR5 | 1,300 |
| 3/27 S6 | 1,150 | | |

Exercise 6-5 Identifying the Correct Journal

Indicate which of the following five journals would be used to record each of the business transactions listed on the next page. Use the proper journal symbol to identify the correct answer.

Journal	Symbol
Sales	S
Purchases	P
Cash Receipts	CR
Cash Disbursements	CD
General	GJ

1. Cash sales
2. Purchase of inventory on credit
3. Payment for insurance
4. Year-end accruals
5. Collection of accounts receivable

6. Purchase of inventory for cash
7. Credit sales
8. Sales returns
9. Payment of accounts payable
10. Purchase returns

Exercise 6-6 Matching Transactions with Journals

The Grover Company uses a purchases journal, a cash receipts journal, a cash disbursements journal, a sales journal, and a general journal. Indicate in which journal each of the following transactions would most likely be recorded.

1. Sales of merchandise on credit.
2. Payment of rent on a building.
3. Received payment on a customer's account.
4. Purchased merchandise on account.
5. Cash purchase of merchandise.
6. Year-end closing entries.
7. Sale of equipment no longer used in the business for cash.
8. Received credit for defective merchandise, which was purchased on account and returned to the supplier.
9. Cash invested in the business by an owner as capital.
10. Cash refunded to a customer who returned merchandise.

Exercise 6-7 Matching Ledger Accounts with Journals

The Wright Company has an accounting system that uses sales, purchases, cash receipts, cash disbursements, and general journals. Identify the journal that was most likely used for each posting to the following accounts.

Cash		Sales	Purchases	Accounts Payable	
(a) 11,900	(g) 8,740	(b) 21,000 (d) 2,000	(h) 900 (k) 12,000	(j) 8,000	(l) 12,000

Accounts Receivable		Sales Discounts	Purchase Discounts	Purchase Allowances
(c) 21,000	(e) 10,000 (f) 100		(i) 160	(m) 150

Exercise 6-8 Relating Special Journals to the Subsidiary Ledger

The sales and cash receipts journals of the Beta Company for the month of July are presented on the next page. The company maintains an accounts receivable subsidiary ledger, which is balanced with the general ledger account each month. On July 1, the subsidiary ledger was comprised of four accounts: B. Allen—$180; J. Kline—$240; M. Feldman—$360; B. Lang—$150.

Sales Journal			P. 15
Date	Invoice	Account	Amount
7/2	503	R. Raman	130
7/6	504	B. Allen	60
7/7	505	J. Kline	125
7/15	506	M. Feldman	100
7/25	507	K. Light	95

Cash Receipts			P. 11
Date	Account	Cash	Accounts Receivable
7/5	B. Allen	75	75
7/10	J. Kline	200	200
7/23	M. Feldman	190	190
7/27	B. Lang	125	125

Required:
A. Establish a T account for each customer's account in the subsidiary ledger and an *Accounts Receivable* control account. Post the amounts to the accounts receivable subsidiary ledger and the general ledger using the information in the journals shown.
B. Prepare a schedule of the accounts in the subsidiary ledger and compare its total to the balance in the control account.

Exercise 6-9 Accounting with Several Journals
The Moore Company uses sales, purchases, cash receipts, cash disbursements, and general journals. The following column totals were taken from the company's journals at the end of October.

1. Sales journal	$1,800
2. Purchases journal	960
3. Cash receipts journal:	
(a) Cash	1,488
(b) Accounts receivable	1,248
(c) Sales	252
(d) Sales discounts	12
4. Cash disbursements journal:	
(a) Cash	1,416
(b) Accounts payable	1,200
(c) Purchase discounts	24
(d) Purchases	240

The balance in the *Accounts Receivable* control account on October 1 was $720 and the *Accounts Payable* control account balance was $1,020.

Required:
A. At the end of October, the total amount from the sales journal should be posted to what account or accounts?
B. At the end of October, the total amount from the purchases journal should be posted to what account or accounts?
C. For each column total in the cash receipts and the cash disbursements journals, specify whether it would be posted to the general ledger as a debit or a credit.
D. After the amounts in the journals have been posted to the general ledger for October, what would the balances be in the *Accounts Receivable* and the *Accounts Payable* control accounts?

Exercise 6-10 Detecting Errors in an Accounting System

The James Company has an accounting system that uses sales, purchases, cash receipts, cash disbursements, and general journals. At various times during the year, the following errors have occurred. Specify a procedure that would detect each error.

1. An error was made in totaling the cash column in the cash receipts journal.
2. A customer's check, net of the applicable sales discount, was correctly entered in the cash column at the net amount and in the accounts receivable column at the gross amount. No entry was made in the sales discounts column.
3. The amount column in the purchases journal was incorrectly totaled.
4. A subtraction error was made on a customer's account in the accounts receivable subsidiary ledger.
5. The amount of a bank loan entered in the other column of the cash receipts journal was posted as a debit to notes payable.
6. A sales return, journalized in the general journal, was posted to the *Accounts Receivable* control account and to the *Sales Return and Allowances* account but was not posted to the accounts receivable subsidiary ledger.
7. A credit sale for $850 was posted as $85 in the accounts receivable subsidiary ledger.
8. A purchase discount was not entered in the cash disbursements journal. The gross amount of supplier's invoice was entered in the accounts payable column and the net amount of the check was entered in the cash column.
9. A purchase allowance for merchandise purchased on account was entered in the general journal. The entry was posted to only two accounts—the Accounts Payable subsidiary account and to Purchase Returns and Allowances.
10. The sales journal was incorrectly totaled.

PROBLEMS

Problem 6-1 Relating Journals to Accounts Receivable Control Account

The William Company uses sales, cash receipts, and general journals in its accounting system. The company also maintains an accounts receivable subsidiary ledger, which contained the following five accounts on August 31.

B. Albright

Date	Explanation	Post. Ref.	Debit	Credit	Balance
8/1	Balance				1,800
8/7		CR3		1,440	360

E. Dewey

Date	Explanation	Post. Ref.	Debit	Credit	Balance
8/5		S7	840		840
8/15		S7	720		1,560
8/21		CR3		600	960

E. Khan

Date	Explanation	Post. Ref.	Debit	Credit	Balance
8/10		S7	600		600
8/19		CR3		240	360

J. Parker

Date	Explanation	Post. Ref.	Debit	Credit	Balance
8/1	Balance				1,080
8/11		CR3		480	600
8/21		S7	240		840

T. Sanders

Date	Explanation	Post. Ref.	Debit	Credit	Balance
8/1	Balance				1,500
8/19		GJ4		240	1,260
8/30		CR4		1,260	—0—

Required:

Establish an *Accounts Receivable* control account and post all entries for the month of August in chronological order with the necessary posting references.

Problem 6-2 Accounting with Sales and Purchases Journals

The Dabbs Company uses sales and purchases journals in its accounting system. The following transactions occurred during March, 1987. (Sales discounts are not given by Dabbs Company.)

March 3 Purchased merchandise on account from the James Co., Invoice 307, $600, terms 2/10, n/30.

7 Purchased merchandise on account from the Weiner Co., Invoice 737, $420, terms 2/10, n/30.

10 Sold merchandise on account to the Blander Co., Invoice 126, $1,140.

15 Sold merchandise on account to the Duton Co., Invoice 127, $990.

17 Purchased merchandise on account from the Dale Co., Invoice 328, $294, terms, 2/10, n/30.

25 Sold merchandise on account to the Giles Co., Invoice 128, $780.

27 Sold merchandise on account to the Duton Co., Invoice 129, $600.

Required:

A. Establish all necessary general ledger accounts, accounts receivable subsidiary ledger accounts, and accounts payable subsidiary ledger accounts. Use the following account numbers *Accounts Receivable*—105; *Accounts Payable*—200; *Sales*—400; *Purchases*—500.

B. Journalize the March transactions in the appropriate journals.

C. Post the data from the journals to the correct general ledger and subsidiary accounts.

D. Prepare a schedule of the accounts receivable subsidiary ledger and the accounts payable subsidiary ledger as of March 31, to prove that their totals are equal to the balances of the control accounts.

Problem 6-3 Accounting with Sales, Cash Receipts, and General Journals

The Bearden Company maintains a sales journal, a cash receipts journal, a general journal, and an accounts receivable subsidiary ledger. The terms of all credit sales are 2/10, n/30, and all account receivable balances as of December 1, 1987, arose from transactions prior to November 20, 1987. The trial balance as of December 1 included the following accounts, among others.

Acct. No.	Acct. Title	Acct. Balance
100	Cash	$ 8,400
150	Accounts Receivable	6,000
400	Sales	96,000
410	Sales Discounts	960
420	Sales Returns and Allowances	1,200

The accounts receivable subsidiary ledger balances were as follows.

L. Alton	$ 900
M. Carr	1,500
N. Fawset	360
P. Kline	1,800
S. Sweet	1,440
V. Wright	0

The following transactions in December involved the sales, cash receipts, and general journals.

December 1 Issued a credit of $90 to L. Alton for defective merchandise sold on account during November.

3 Sold merchandise on account to V. Wright, $1,000, Invoice 254.

6 Received a check from N. Fawset for payment of a November purchase, $360.

7 Sold merchandise on account to M. Carr, $120, Invoice 255.

8 Sold merchandise on account to P. Kline, $216, Invoice 256.

10 Received payment from V. Wright for Invoice 254, less 2% discount.

11 Received payment in full from L. Alton.

13 Borrowed $6,000 cash from the bank.

14 Sold merchandise for cash, $150.

25 Received a check from P. Kline, $1,800, for payment of his account.

27 Sold merchandise on account to N. Fawset, $400, Invoice 257.

30 Received payment from N. Fawset for Invoice 257, less 2% discount.

Required:

Record the December transactions in the appropriate journals. Set up all ledger accounts needed and make all postings to the proper general ledger accounts and to the accounts receivable subsidiary ledgers.

Problem 6-4 Accounting for Transactions with Several Journals

The Mayfield Company started operations March 1. Its accounting system includes a sales journal, a purchases journal, a cash receipts journal, a cash disbursements journal, and a general journal. During March, the following accounts were used.

100 Cash	405 Sales Discounts
110 Accounts Receivable	410 Sales Allowances
115 Prepaid Insurance	500 Purchases
150 Office Equipment	503 Purchase Returns
201 Accounts Payable	505 Purchase Discounts
210 Notes Payable	550 Rent Expense
300 J. Mayfield, Capital	560 Insurance Expense
301 J. Mayfield, Drawing	570 Utilities Expense
400 Sales	

During March, the transactions were as follows.

March 1 E. Mayfield invested $12,000 in the business.
3 Borrowed $8,000 from a local bank.
3 Paid rent for March, $1,200.
5 Purchased merchandise on account from the Gibson Co., $2,400, Invoice 433, terms 2/10, n/60.
6 Purchased merchandise on account from Murray Co., $900, Invoice 220, terms 1/10, n/30.
7 Purchased office equipment for cash, $600.
8 Sold merchandise on account to McHenry Co., $900, terms 2/10, n/30, Invoice 301.
10 Paid for merchandise purchased from the Gibson Co., Invoice 433.
11 Received credit from the Murray Co. for merchandise returned, $50.
12 Paid Murray Co. in full for balance of Invoice 220.
13 Sold merchandise for cash, $252.
17 Paid for a 12-month insurance policy, $600. The effective date of the policy was March 1.
19 Purchased merchandise on account from the Abell Co., $1,440, Invoice 760, terms n/60.
20 Purchased merchandise on account from the Croydon Co., $800, Invoice 760, terms 2/10, n/30.
25 Sold merchandise on account to the Beresford Co., $700, Invoice 302, terms 2/10, n/30.
26 Received payment from the McHenry Co. in full settlement of Invoice 301.
27 Sold merchandise on account to the Palm Co., Invoice 303, $1,200, terms 2/10, n/30.
28 Paid the Croydon Co. in full for merchandise purchased March 20.
30 Paid the electric bill, $108.
30 Issued credit to the Palm Co. for defective merchandise sold March 27, $36.
30 Received payment from the Beresford Co. in full settlement of Invoice 302.

Required:
Record the transactions in the proper journals. Indicate how the postings would be made from the journals by entering the appropriate posting references.

Problem 6-5 Journalizing Transactions and Completing the Accounting

The Clifton Company uses sales, purchases, cash receipts, cash disbursements, and general journals along with subsidiary ledgers for accounts receivable and accounts payable. The post-closing trial balance as of April 30, 1987, and the trial balances of the subsidiary ledgers are presented next.

CLIFTON COMPANY
Post-Closing Trial Balance
April 30, 1987

Acct. No.	Account Title	Debit	Credit
100	Cash	$ 7,200	
110	Accounts Receivable	3,600	
150	Inventory	6,000	
170	Equipment	12,000	
175	Accumulated Depreciation		$ 1,200
200	Accounts Payable		4,800
300	Clifton, Capital		22,800
400	Sales		
405	Sales Returns		
410	Sales Discounts		
500	Purchases		
510	Purchase Discounts		
515	Purchase Returns		
530	Rent Expense		
540	Utilities Expense		
550	Commissions Expense		
	Totals	$28,800	$28,800

Accounts Receivable Subsidiary Ledger

Carter Co.	$ 840
High Co.	1,680
Stance Co.	1,080
Total	$3,600

Accounts Payable Subsidiary Ledger

Poole Co.	$1,200
Rogers Co.	1,920
Thomas Co.	1,680
Total	$4,800

The following transactions occurred in May, 1987.

May 1 Received a check from Carter Co. for payment of account, $840.
3 Sold merchandise to the Bloom Co. on account, Invoice 502, $1,200, terms 2/10, n/30.
4 Paid rent for May, $900.
5 Purchased merchandise on account from the West Co., $1,360, Invoice 123, terms 2/10, n/30.
6 Paid Poole Co. for merchandise purchased previously, $1,200.
8 Received payment from Bloom Co. for full settlement of Invoice 502.
9 Received credit from the West Co. for merchandise returned, $60.
11 Paid the West Co. in full, Invoice 123.
12 Paid sales commissions, $2,460.

13 Received a check from the High Co. in partial payment of the account, $840.
17 Paid $3,600 for new office equipment.
18 Cash sales, $672.
19 Sold merchandise on account to the Carter Co., $1,000, Invoice 503, terms 2/10, n/30.
21 Sold merchandise on account to the Davon Co., $500, Invoice 504, terms 2/10, n/30.
23 Paid the Rogers Co. for merchandise purchased in April, $1,920.
25 Cash sales, $750.
30 Received a check from Stance Co., $1,080, for payment on account.
30 Received a check from Davon Co. for full payment of account.

Required:
A. Journalize the transactions in the appropriate journals.
B. Set up all ledger accounts needed and make all necessary postings for the month.
C. Prepare a trial balance of the general ledger and schedules of the subsidiary ledgers on May 31.

Problem 6-6 Comprehensive Accounting System Problem

The Sun Diver Company uses a sales journal, purchases journal, cash receipts journal, cash disbursements journal, and a general journal. The firm also maintains subsidiary accounts receivable and accounts payable ledgers, in addition to the control accounts. The relevant account balances as of January 1, 1987, were as follows.

		Account Balance	
Acct. No.	Account Title	Debit	Credit
100	Cash	$ 4,500	
110	Accounts Receivable	6,000	
130	Beginning Inventory	10,000	
200	Plant and Equipment	110,000	
300	Accounts Payable		$ 5,000
330	Notes Payable		50,000
400	Capital		75,500
500	Sales		
510	Sales Discounts		
520	Sales Returns & Allowances		
600	Purchases		
610	Purchase Discounts		
		$130,500	$130,500

The accounts receivable and accounts payable subsidiary ledger balances were as follows.

Accounts Receivable		Accounts Payable	
J. Dickson	$1,200	C. J. Inc.	$1,000
M. Moreau	800	Design Concepts	1,000
A. Piccioli	2,000	Williams Wholesale	3,000
L. Robbins	1,500	Total	$5,000
D. Roberge	500		
Total	$6,000		

The following transactions occurred during the first quarter.

Jan. 5 M. Moreau took advantage of the 2% sales discount and paid off her account with $784.
10 Sold a $1,000 couch to D. Roberge on account, Invoice no. 401.
15 Purchased $3,000 in inventory from Design Concepts on account. The terms were 2/10, n/30.
18 Received $500 from J. Dickson on his account. He has passed the discount period without paying.
20 Paid $1,000 to Design Concepts on its previous account balance. No discount was taken.
24 Paid $2,940 to Design Concepts, taking advantage of the 2% discount. This reduced the balance on this account to zero.
Feb. 10 A cash sale of $2,000 was made to a new customer.
13 A. Piccioli paid $1,000 on his account. He missed the discount period.
23 Sold a $500 painting to D. Roberge on account, Invoice no. 402.
28 Paid $2,000 on the Williams Wholesale account. No discount was taken.
Mar. 4 Purchased $4,000 in inventory from C. J. Inc. on account. Terms were n/30.
16 Sold a $50 lamp to L. Robbins on account, Invoice no. 403.
22 Paid $2,000 on the C. J. Inc. account.
27 A $50 sales allowance was given to L. Robbins, due to a defective product.

Required:
A. Journalize the first quarter's transactions in the appropriate journals.
B. Open the necessary general ledger accounts, the accounts receivable subsidiary ledger accounts and the accounts payable subsidiary ledger accounts.
C. Post the data from the journals to the appropriate general ledger and subsidiary ledger accounts.
D. Prepare a schedule of accounts receivable and accounts payable as of March 31, 1987, to confirm the balance in the control accounts.
E. Prepare a trial balance like the one given in the problem, as of March 31, 1987.

ALTERNATE PROBLEMS

Problem 6-1A Relating Journals to Accounts Receivable Control Account
The Weir Company uses sales, cash receipts, and general journals in its accounting system. The company also maintains an accounts receivable subsidiary ledger that contained the following five accounts on July 31.

	D. Ford					
Date	Explanation		Post. Ref.	Debit	Credit	Balance
7/1	Balance					2,160
7/10			CR4		1,728	432

J. Jones

Date	Explanation	Post. Ref.	Debit	Credit	Balance
7/6		S9	1,008		1,008
7/16		S9	864		1,872
7/22		CR4		720	1,152

A. Kliner

Date	Explanation	Post. Ref.	Debit	Credit	Balance
7/9		S9	720		720
7/18		CR4		288	432

R. Kohn

Date	Explanation	Post. Ref.	Debit	Credit	Balance
7/1	Balance				1,296
7/11		CR4		576	720
7/22		S9	288		1,008

C. Plant

Date	Explanation	Post. Ref.	Debit	Credit	Balance
7/1	Balance				1,800
7/20		GJ5		288	1,512
7/29		CR4		1,512	0

Required:
Establish an *Accounts Receivable* control account. Then, post all entries for the month of July in chronological order and show the necessary posting references.

Problem 6-2A Accounting with Sales and Purchases Journals

The Hansen Company uses sales and purchases journals in its accounting system. The following transactions took place during March. (Sales discounts are not given by the Hansen Company.)

March 2 Purchased merchandise on account from the Rye Co., Invoice 408, $504, terms 2/10, n/30.
6 Purchased merchandise on account from the Pannell Co., Invoice 606, $720, terms 2/10, n/30.
11 Sold merchandise on account to the Smith Co., Invoice 228, $1,368.
14 Sold merchandise on account to the Dooley Co., Invoice 229, $1,188.
19 Purchased merchandise on account from the Brooks Co., Invoice 1614, $612, 2/10, n/30.
23 Sold merchandise on account to the Chester Co., Invoice 230, $936.
28 Sold merchandise on account to the Walter Co., Invoice 231, $720.

Required:

A. Establish all the necessary general ledger accounts, accounts receivable subsidiary ledger accounts, and accounts payable subsidiary ledger accounts. Use the following account numbers: *Accounts Receivable*—104; *Accounts Payable*—201; *Sales*—400; *Purchases*—500.

B. Journalize the March transactions in the appropriate journals.

C. Post the data from the journals to the appropriate general ledger and subsidiary ledger accounts.

D. Develop a schedule of the accounts receivable subsidiary ledger and the accounts payable subsidiary ledger, as of March 31, to prove that the subsidiary ledger balances are equal to the control accounts.

Problem 6-3A Accounting with Sales, Cash Receipts, and General Journals

The Blackwell Company uses a sales journal, a cash receipts journal, a general journal, and an accounts receivable subsidiary ledger. The terms of all credit sales are 2/10, n/30 and all account receivable balances as of October 1, 1987, were the result of transactions prior to September 15, 1987. The trial balance as of October 1 included the following accounts, among others.

Acct. No.	Acct. Title	Acct. Balance
100	Cash	$ 9,600
150	Accounts Receivable	7,200
400	Sales	96,000
410	Sales Discounts	960
420	Sales Returns	1,200

The accounts receivable subsidiary ledger balances were:

P. Dickens	$ 0
D. Fields	2,160
S. Lamb	432
R. Roberts	1,800
S. Sheets	1,728
J. Tinker	1,080
Total	$7,200

The following October transactions were recorded in the sales, cash receipts, or general journals.

October 1 Issued credit to J. Tinker for defective merchandise sold on account during September, $108.
4 Sold merchandise on account to P. Dickens, $1,150. Invoice 324.
8 Received a check from S. Lamb for payment of a September purchase, $432.
9 Sold merchandise on account to R. Roberts, $144, Invoice 325.
10 Sold merchandise on account to D. Fields, $260, Invoice 326.
13 Received payment from P. Dickens for Invoice 324, less 2% discount.
17 Received payment in full from J. Tinker.
20 Borrowed $6,000 cash from the bank.
21 Sold merchandise for cash, $180.

27 Received a check from D. Fields, $2,420, for payment on his account.
27 Sold merchandise on account to S. Lamb, $500, Invoice 327.
30 Received payment from S. Lamb for Invoice 327 less 2% discount.

Required:
Record the October transactions in the appropriate journals. Establish all ledger accounts needed and make all postings to the proper general ledger accounts and to the accounts receivable subsidiary ledgers.

Problem 6-4A Accounting for Transactions with Several Journals
The Pong Company started operations on August 1 with an accounting system that includes a sales journal, a purchases journal, a cash receipts journal, a cash disbursement journal, and a general journal. During August, the following accounts were used.

100 Cash	405 Sales Discounts
110 Accounts Receivable	410 Sales Allowances
115 Prepaid Insurance	500 Purchases
150 Office Equipment	503 Purchase Returns
201 Accounts Payable	505 Purchase Discounts
210 Notes Payable	550 Rent Expense
300 J. Pong, Capital	560 Insurance Expense
301 J. Pong, Drawing	570 Utilities Expense
400 Sales	

The following transactions took place during August.

August 1 J. Pong invested $14,400 cash as capital in the business.
3 Borrowed $7,200 from a local bank.
3 Paid rent for August, $1,440.
5 Purchased merchandise on account from the Rolley Co., $2,400, Invoice 483, terms 2/10, n/60.
6 Purchased merchandise on account from the Dickens Co., $900, Invoice 284, terms 1/10, n/30.
7 Purchased office equipment for cash, $720.
8 Sold merchandise on account to the Rogers Co., $900, Invoice 101, terms 2/10, n/30.
10 Paid for merchandise purchased from the Rolley Co., Invoice 483.
11 Received credit from the Dickens Co. for merchandise returned, $100.
12 Paid Dickens Co. in full for the balance of Invoice 284.
13 Sold merchandise for cash, $302.
17 Paid for a 12-month insurance policy, $864. The effective date of the policy was August 1.
19 Purchased merchandise on account from the Ace Co., $1,728, Invoice 980, terms, n/60.
20 Purchased merchandise on account from the Keri Co., $700, Invoice 1012, terms 2/10, n/30.
25 Sold merchandise on account to the Richards Co., $756, Invoice 102, terms 2/10, n/30.
26 Received payment from the Rogers Co., in full settlement of Invoice 101.
27 Sold merchandise on account to the Hines Co., Invoice 103, $1,260, terms 2/10, n/30.

28 Paid the Keri Co. in full for merchandise purchased August 20.
29 Paid the electric bill, $108.
30 Issued a credit memo to the River Co. for defective merchandise sold April 27, $36.

Required:

Record the transactions in the appropriate journals. Indicate how the postings would be made from the journals by entering the posting references involved.

Problem 6-5A **Journalizing Transactions and Completing the Accounting**

The Schwarz Company uses sales, purchases, cash receipts, cash disbursements, and general journals, along with subsidiary ledgers for accounts receivable and accounts payable. The post-closing trial balance as of May 31, 1987, and the schedules of accounts in the subsidiary ledgers are presented here.

SCHWARZ COMPANY
Post-Closing Trial Balance
May 31, 1987

Acct. No.	Account Title	Debit	Credit
100	Cash	$ 8,640	
110	Accounts Receivable	4,320	
115	Inventory	7,200	
170	Equipment	14,400	
175	Accumulated Depreciation		$ 1,440
200	Accounts Payable		5,760
300	R. Schwarz, Capital		27,360
400	Sales		
405	Sales Returns		
410	Sales Discounts		
500	Purchases		
505	Purchase Returns		
510	Purchase Discounts		
530	Rent Expense		
540	Utilities Expense		
550	Commissions Expense		
	Totals	$34,560	$34,560

Accounts Receivable Subsidiary Ledger

Fall Co.	$1,008
George Co.	2,016
Monroe Co.	1,296
Total	$4,320

Accounts Payable Subsidiary Ledger

Bruce Co.	$1,440
Carter Co.	2,304
Linden Co.	2,016
Total	$5,760

The following transactions took place during June, 1987.

June 1 Received a check from the Fall Co. for payment on account, $1,008.
      3 Sold merchandise to the Bluer Co. on account, Invoice 602, $1,200, terms 2/10, n/30.
      4 Paid rent for June, $1,080.
      5 Purchased merchandise on account from the West Co., $1,272, Invoice 383, terms 2/10, n/30.
      6 Paid the Bruce Co., for merchandise purchased previously, $1,440.
      8 Received payment from the Bluer Co. for full settlement of Invoice 602.
      9 Received credit from the West Co. for merchandise returned, $72.
     11 Paid the West Co. the amount due on Invoice 383.
     12 Paid sales commissions, $2,952.
     13 Received a check from the George Co. in partial payment of the account, $1,008.
     17 Paid $3,600 for new office equipment.
     18 Cash sales, $672.
     19 Sold merchandise on account to the Fall Co., $1,600, Invoice 603, terms 2/10, n/30.
     21 Sold merchandise on account to the Garner Co., $600, Invoice 604, terms 2/10, n/30.
     23 Paid the Carter Co. for merchandise purchased in May, $2,304.
     25 Cash sales, $750.
     30 Received a check from Monroe Co., $1,296, for payment of account.
     30 Received a check from Garner Co. for payment of account.

Required:
A. Journalize the transactions in the appropriate journals.
B. Establish all ledger accounts required and make all necessary postings for the month.
C. Prepare a trial balance of the general ledger and schedules of the subsidiary ledgers on June 30.

Problem 6-6A Comprehensive Accounting System Problem
The New River Company uses a sales journal, purchases journal, cash receipts journal, cash disbursements journal, and a general journal. The firm also maintains subsidiary accounts receivable and accounts payable ledgers in addition to the control accounts. The relevant account balances as of August 1, 1986, were as follows.

Acct. No.	Account Title	Account Balance Debit	Account Balance Credit
100	Cash	$ 9,300	
110	Accounts Receivable	4,700	
135	Beginning Inventory	25,000	
210	Plant and Equipment	78,000	
300	Accounts Payable		$ 6,200
320	Notes Payable		45,000
400	Capital		63,300
500	Sales		10,500
510	Sales Discounts	200	
520	Sales Returns and Allowances	100	
600	Purchases	8,000	
610	Purchase Discounts		300
		$125,300	$125,300

The accounts receivable and accounts payable subsidiary ledger balances were as follows.

Accounts Receivable		Accounts Payable	
C. Clark	$1,800	Miller Company	$1,200
P. Hills	600	Royal Inc.	4,000
R. Kennison	1,300	Sterling Co.	1,000
B. Murry	1,000	Total	$6,200
Total	$4,700		

The following transactions occurred during August.

Aug.
2   Purchased merchandise from Sterling Co. for $2,000 on account. The terms were 2/10, n/30.
3   Received $600 from P. Hills on his account.
6   Paid $1,000 to Sterling Co. on its previous balance. No discount was taken.
9   Sold merchandise to B. Murry on account for $500, Invoice no. 201.
11   Paid $1,960 to Sterling Co., taking advantage of the 2% discount.
13   Sold $1,500 in merchandise to P. Hills on account. The terms were 1/10, n/60. Invoice no. 202.
14   Received $300 from R. Kennison on his account.
15   Paid $2,000 on the Royal Inc. Account.
17   Purchased inventory for $1,000 from Miller Company on account. Terms were n/30.
19   Sold merchandise for $500 in cash.
23   Received $1,000 from C. Clark on her account. There was no discount.
29   Purchased merchandise for $100 in cash.

Required:
A. Journalize August's transactions in the appropriate journals.
B. Open the necessary general ledger accounts, the accounts receivable subsidiary ledger accounts and the accounts payable subsidiary ledger accounts.
C. Post the data from the journals to the appropriate general ledger and subsidiary ledger accounts.
D. Prepare a schedule of accounts receivable and accounts payable as of August 31, 1986, to confirm the balance in the control accounts.
E. Prepare a trial balance like the one given in the problem, as of August 31, 1986.

CASE

CASE 6-1   Discussion Case   Internal Control Procedures

John Brown took over the management of his family's successful retail store upon graduation from college where he majored in foreign languages. Since he had little knowledge of business practices and internal control procedures, he relied heavily on the company's new accountant, Tom Krieder, to establish appropriate inventory control. Tom decided that the best way to operate was for him to have complete responsibility for ordering inventory, inspecting the goods when received, and making payments to the suppliers. Tom convinced John that this was the best approach because he knew all the suppliers personally and could get good service from them.

When inventory is purchased, Tom prepares a purchase order and sends it to the supplier. Frequently, he phones an order into a supplier to save time and does not prepare a purchase order, since the supplier does not require one. When the inventory is received by the store, it is left on the receiving dock until Tom has a chance to inspect it and record it in the accounting system. Usually, the inspection is done at night after the store is closed so that Tom does not interfere with the regular business of the store while performing inspection. After inspecting the goods received, Tom initials the supplier invoice involved, attaches it to the purchase order (if one exists), and journalizes the transaction. On the due date, Tom prepares a check for payment to the supplier and mails it himself.

After several months, John Brown has become very concerned about the store's gross profits, which have steadily declined from their historical levels. When he mentioned his concern to Tom Krieder, the reply was "you should either raise prices or sell more inventory."

Required:
Evaluate the internal control procedures currently used by the store. What suggestions would you recommend to improve the situation?

CASE 6-2 Financial Report Analysis Case Accounting System Considerations

Refer to the 1984 annual report of Chrysler Corporation in Appendix A at the end of the book.

Required:
A. The management of Chrysler Corporation must take the responsibility for preparing the financial statements. Where is this disclosed in the annual report? What are the ramifications of these responsibilities for the firm's accounting system? Has the Foreign Corrupt Practices Act affected these responsibilities?
B. What steps would be continuously taken to revise an accounting system as large as the one operated by this company?
C. What balance sheet accounts of the firm would be maintained as control accounts with subsidiary ledgers supporting them?

7

CASH AND TEMPORARY INVESTMENTS

CHAPTER OVERVIEW AND OBJECTIVES

This chapter discusses the nature of cash, cash controls, and temporary investments in marketable securities. When you have finished the chapter, you should understand:

1. What cash consists of.
2. The procedures used to control cash receipts and cash disbursements.
3. The purpose and operation of a petty cash fund.
4. The purpose and preparation of a bank reconciliation.
5. How to account for temporary investments in marketable securities.
6. The purpose and operation of a voucher system in controlling cash disbursements (Appendix).

Cash and temporary investments in marketable securities are often called liquid assets because they are either in the form of cash or are easily convertible into cash in the near future. Because of their nature, they are classified as current assets in the balance sheet. Knowledge of the amount and composition of these liquid assets is helpful to users of financial statements in evaluating the ability of the company to meet currently maturing obligations.

CASH

**Objective 1:
Nature of cash**

Cash is a term used in accounting to identify money and any other instrument, such as a check or money order, that a bank normally accepts as a deposit to the depositor's bank account. Cash does not include accounts or notes receivable, post-dated checks, IOUs, or postage stamps (which represent prepaid postage expense). Cash is a medium of exchange, as well as a measure of value in our economy. Although companies may have several bank accounts, as well as cash on hand, the sum of all of the cash items is reported as a single item in the current asset section of the balance sheet. Users of financial statements are interested in the current cash position of a company because it aids them in evaluating the ability of the company to pay short-term cash expenses and to meet currently maturing obligations. Practically every business transaction eventually results in an inflow or outflow of cash.

The control and proper use of cash is an important management function. Cash is an unproductive asset because it produces no revenue directly. Thus, any cash accumulated in excess of that needed for current use should be invested, even temporarily, in some type of revenue-producing investment.

Perhaps most importantly, cash is the asset that is most easily subject to misappropriation. Therefore, it must be adequately protected by controlling access to and use of it. Several techniques have been developed to aid in cash management, the most important of which is the establishment of an *internal control system for cash*. Other techniques are the preparation of cash forecasts and cash investment planning.

CONTROL OF CASH

A good internal control system for handling cash and cash transactions is vital. Such a system must contain procedures for protecting cash on hand as well as for handling both cash receipts and cash disbursements. Three particularly important elements of the internal control system for cash are:

Objective 2:
Cash control
procedures

1. The separation of the responsibility for handling and custodianship of cash from responsibility for maintaining cash records. This prevents the misappropriation of cash and the corresponding falsification of accounting records without collusion among employees.
2. The deposit of each day's cash receipts intact, which prevents the cash custodian from "borrowing" the funds until the next deposit date.
3. Making all cash payments by check. This element, in combination with the deposit of each day's cash receipts intact, allows the business to use the bank's record of cash transactions as a cross check of its internal records.

Because the details of a system of internal control over cash varies with the size and type of business, only a general system will be considered here. Procedures used to build an internal system of cash control can be illustrated best by considering cash receipts and cash disbursements separately.

Control of Cash Receipts

Cash receipts normally consist of two types: (1) over-the-counter receipts from cash sales; and (2) cash received through the mail from customers making payments on charge accounts. Different control procedures are established for each type.

Receipts from Cash Sales. Cash received over the counter from cash sales should be rung up on a cash register. The register should be located in a position that permits the customer to see the amount recorded. The receipt printed by the register should be given to the customer. Each register also has a locked-in tape on which each cash sale is recorded, thus keeping an accurate running total of cash sales.

The basis for internal cash control is the principle of separation of record-keeping from custodianship. The salesclerk who collects the cash should not have access to the tape in the register. At the end of each business day, the salesclerk should be required to count the cash in the register and to record the amount on a memorandum form that is sent to the accounting department. An employee other than the salesclerk should be responsible for removing the tape and cash from the register, counting the cash, comparing the count with that of the salesclerk, and noting any discrepancies. The cash is then forwarded to the cashier (the employee responsible for accumulating and depositing cash) for deposit. The tape, along with any discrepancy noted, is sent to the accounting department, where it is used to prepare appropriate accounting entries. In this way, neither the salesclerk nor the cashier has access to the accounting records, and the accounting department personnel have no access to cash.

Prenumbered Sales Tickets. Additional internal control of cash receipts can be obtained by using prenumbered sales tickets, prepared in duplicate for each cash sale. The sale is recorded on the cash register, the original copy of the sales ticket is given to the customer, and the carbon copy of the sales ticket is retained. At the end of the day, an employee other than the salesclerk should total the sales tickets and verify that none of the tickets are missing. The total of the sales tickets then should be compared with the total sales recorded on the cash register tape.

Cash Received Through the Mail. Procedures for the control of mail receipts are also based on the separation of recordkeeping and custodianship. The employee who opens the mail prepares a list of the amounts received. One copy is sent to the cashier along with the receipts (usually checks or money orders). The receipts are combined with those from the cash registers in preparing the daily bank deposit. Another copy of the list is forwarded to the accounting department for use in preparing entries in the cash receipts journal and the individual customers' accounts. Again, neither the mail clerk nor the cashier has access to the accounting records, and accounting department personnel have no access to cash. Thus, fraud is generally avoided unless there is collusion.

Cash Short and Over

When numerous individual cash sales are recorded, it is inevitable that some errors will be made (for example, some customers might be given the wrong change). As a result, when the actual cash in the cash register is compared with the register tape, there will be a cash shortage or overage.

For example, assume that the cash register tape shows that total sales recorded were $1,272, and the cash in the register amounted to $1,264. The cash shortage is recorded as follows when the daily sales are recorded.

April	4	Cash	1,264	
		Cash Short and Over	8	
		Sales		1,272
		To record the day's cash sales.		

If short Debit CASH Short & Over

If the cash count exceeds the amount of sales recorded, the *Cash Short and Over* account is credited for the difference. The *Cash Short and Over* account is closed to the *Income Summary* account at year end as part of the normal closing process. If the account has a debit balance (that is, shortages exceed overages), it is reported as miscellaneous expense on the income statement. If the account has a credit balance (that is, overages exceed shortages), it is normally reported as an item of other revenue on the income statement.

The entry shown is presented in general journal form for illustration purposes. If special journals are used, the entry is recorded in the cash receipts journal. Throughout the remainder of this book, entries will be illustrated in general journal form, but the reader should remember that the entry would be made in the appropriate special journal if such journals are used.

Control of Cash Disbursements

Just as an adequate system of internal control must contain procedures for controlling cash receipts, it must also provide for the protection of cash balances and procedures for the control of cash disbursements. A safe or vault should be provided for the protection of cash on hand. The daily deposit of cash receipts provides additional protection for cash balances.

Control over cash disbursements centers on the policy of making all cash disbursements by check. Checks should be prenumbered so that they can be easily accounted for. These procedures should be supported by a division of responsibility for the approval and payment of invoices. The employee designated to approve invoices for payment should have no check-writing or accounting responsibility. Before authorizing payment, the employee should be required to verify that the goods or services represented by the invoice were properly ordered and actually received. Approval of the invoice for payment is generally indicated by placing an approval stamp on its face.

The employee responsible for signing checks should have no invoice-approval or accounting responsibilities. Checks presented for signature should be signed only upon receipt of a properly approved invoice indicating that payment is justified. At the time that the check is signed, the related invoice should be cancelled either by perforating it or by stamping it *paid*. Either of these approaches prevent the possibility of having the invoice presented for payment a second time. The approved invoice and a copy of the check should be forwarded to the accounting department, where the appropriate entry is made to record the payment.

The combination of these procedures makes it difficult for a fraudulent disbursement to be made without collusion by two or more employees. Internal control of cash disbursements can be further strengthened by use of a voucher system. A detailed description of a voucher system and its use is presented in the appendix to this chapter.

THE PETTY CASH FUND

Objective 3:
Petty cash fund

As emphasized earlier, a basic principle of internal control is that all disbursements should be made by check. However, to avoid the expense and inconvenience of writing many small checks for minor expenditures, such as for postage stamps and miscellaneous supplies, a petty cash fund is usually established. A **petty cash fund,** which is a specified amount of cash, placed under the control of a particular employee (the petty cash fund cashier) for use in making small payments, generally should be the only exception to the policy of making all cash disbursements by check.

Establishing the Fund

The petty cash fund is established by writing a check to the petty cash fund cashier. The amount is generally an even amount such as $100 or $200. The amount should only be expected to handle petty cash payments for a relatively short period, such as a month. The petty cash fund cashier cashes the check and places the money in a locked box to which only he or she has access.

The check is recorded by a debit to a *Petty Cash* account and a credit to the *Cash* account. For example, assuming a fund of $100 is established on January 2, the journal entry is:

Jan.	2	Petty Cash	100	
		Cash		100
		To establish a petty cash fund.		

Making Disbursements from the Fund

As cash payments are made from the fund, the recipient should be required to sign a **petty cash receipt** prepared by the petty cash fund cashier. The receipt should show the amount paid, the purpose of the payment, and the date paid. A receipt should be prepared for every payment made from the fund. Each receipt should be stamped *paid* and placed in the petty cash fund box. Thus, the total of the receipts plus the cash in the fund should always be equal to the amount originally placed in the fund ($100 in our illustration). Figure 7–1 shows an example of a petty cash receipt.

Replenishing the Fund

The petty cash fund must be replenished periodically. Every paid receipt in the fund should be sent to the accounting department to serve as a basis for the entry needed to record the replenishment. A check should then be issued in an amount sufficient to restore the fund to its original amount ($100). The

Figure 7–1
Petty Cash Receipt

PETTY CASH RECEIPT

No. ___2___   Date ___January 4, 1987___   Amount ___$12.35___

Purpose ___Miscellaneous Office Supplies___

Debit to ___Office Supplies Expense___

Approved by ___MPn___   ___J. B. Small___

Signature

---

check should be cashed by the petty cash fund cashier and the money placed in the petty cash box.

The petty cash fund is always replenished at the end of an accounting period, even when the fund is not running low on cash, so that the expenses represented by the receipts in the fund can be recorded during the current accounting period. If the fund is not replenished at the end of each period, cash will be overstated on the balance sheet and expenses will be understated on the income statement.

On occasion, the custodian of the fund may forget to obtain a signed receipt for a payment from the fund, in which case the fund will be short. When this occurs, the *Cash Short and Over* account is debited for the shortage when the fund is replenished.

Various expense accounts are debited as indicated by the petty cash receipts, and cash is credited for the amount needed to replenish the fund. For example, assume that the petty cash box contained the following receipts and cash at the end of the first month of operations.

Receipt No.	Purpose	Amount
1, 3	Postage Stamps	$ 56.47
2, 5	Office Supplies	12.35
4	Gasoline	15.22
	Cash in Box	13.40
	Cash Shortage	2.56
		$100.00

Because the cash in the fund is low, the fund is replenished and the following journal entry is prepared.

Jan.	31	Postage Expense		56.47	
		Office Supplies Expense		12.35	
		Auto Expense		15.22	
		Cash Short and Over		2.56	
		Cash			86.60
		To replenish the petty cash fund.			

Since the petty cash receipts are supplementary records, this entry is needed so that the expenses are properly recorded in the journal and general ledger accounts. Thus, expense accounts are debited when the fund is replenished.

Note that the *Petty Cash* account is not affected by the replenishing entry. The *Petty Cash* account is debited only when the fund is initially established, and no other entries are made to the *Petty Cash* account unless a decision is made to increase or decrease the size of the fund. The petty cash fund is normally included with other cash amounts and reported as a single amount on the balance sheet.

BANK CHECKING ACCOUNTS

As mentioned earlier, an important element of internal control of cash is the requirement that each day's cash receipts be deposited intact into a bank checking account and that all disbursements be made by check. Internal control is strengthened by doing this because the bank record of deposits received and checks paid provides a cross-check on the internal cash records of the business.

Deposits of cash receipts are made by preparing a deposit ticket (Figure 7–2) that includes the amount of paper currency and coin and a list of the checks included with the deposit. Each check deposited is identified by the

Figure 7–2
A Deposit Ticket

DEPOSIT TICKET
United Bank
Akron, Ohio

Date Sept. 4, 1987

Depositor: Calhoun, Inc.
4214 Stemmer Avenue
Akron, Ohio

CASH	Currency		126	00
	Coin		7	80
CHECKS:	18-122		86	23
	45-41		214	25
	19-162		74	56
	18-113		316	31
Total			825	15
Less Cash Received			–0–	
Net Deposit			825	15

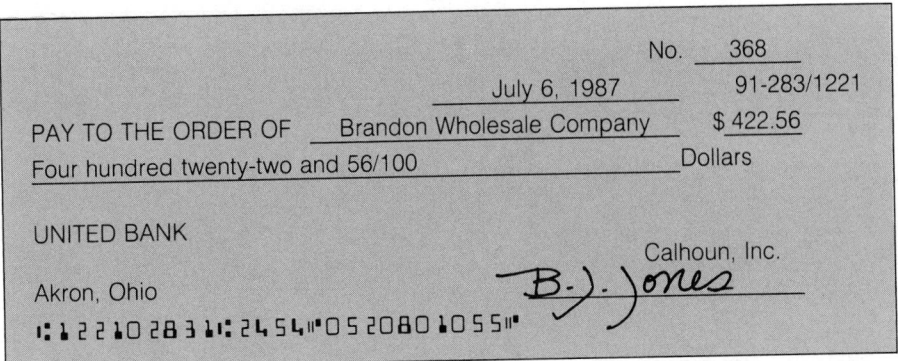

Figure 7–3
A Check

code number of the bank on which the check is drawn. The deposit ticket is prepared in duplicate; one copy is sent to the bank with the deposit and the other copy is retained by the depositor.

Disbursements from the checking account are authorized by checks written by the depositor. Checks are legal instruments signed by the depositor, ordering the bank to pay a specified amount of money to the person or company identified on the check. Figure 7–3 shows a copy of a typical check.

THE BANK STATEMENT

Each month the bank sends the depositor a **bank statement**. The bank statement is a monthly report detailing the activity that has taken place in the depositor's account. The statement contains the following information.

1. The balance in the account at the beginning of the month.
2. Each deposit received during the month.
3. A list of all checks written by the depositor and paid by the bank during the month (**cancelled checks**). If the depositor elects not to leave his cancelled checks on file at the bank, the bank statement will also include the depositor's cancelled checks.
4. Debit and credit memoranda identifying miscellaneous charges (e.g., bank service charges) and credits (e.g., amounts collected by the bank for the depositor) made to the account.
5. The account balance at month's end.

The depositor's cash balance in the account represents a liability on the bank's part. Therefore, it is shown on the bank's books by a credit balance. An example of a bank statement is shown in Figure 7–4.

Debit and Credit Memos

Debit memos identify charges (debits or decreases) in the depositor's account during the month. Things such as bank service charges, check-printing charges, and **nonsufficient funds (NSF) checks**—checks that were included in a depositor's deposit and recorded by the bank but were not paid by the check writer's bank because of the lack of sufficient funds to cover the check—are

Figure 7–4
A Bank Statement

| UNITED BANK |
| New York, New York |

STATEMENT OF ACCOUNT WITH
   DATA COMPANY
    1842 Elm Street
    New York, New York 10160

Account No.
052181059

Period Covered
9/1/87 to 9/30/87

Page
1

Date	Check No.	Amount	Deposits/Credits	Balance
	Checks/Debits			
8/31				4,260.82
9/2	1016	326.50		
	1017	219.18		
	1018	182.96	972.85	4,505.03
9/5	1019	494.22		
	1020	384.60	618.42	4,244.63
9/9	1021	66.43		
	1022	198.39		
	1023	764.80	866.34	4,081.35
9/15	1024	36.72		
	1025	117.81		
		89.78 DM	544.54	4,381.58
9/22	1026	127.94		4,253.64
9/27	1028	313.30		
	1030	123.65	614.88	4,431.57
9/29	1033	197.54		4,234.03
9/30		8.50 SC	1,200.00 CM	5,425.53

Beginning Balance	Debits		Credits		Current Balance
	No.	Amount	No.	Amount	
4,260.82	16	3,652.32	6	4,817.03	5,425.53

SYMBOLS: DM = Debit Memo   CM = Credit Memo
          NSF = Nonsufficient Funds   SC = Service Charge

debit memo items. NSF checks and other charges are subtracted from the depositor's account and the depositor is notified by debit memos.

Credit memos identify credits (i.e., increases) made to the depositor's account by the bank. For example, the depositor may request that notes receivable be paid directly to the depositor's bank. When collected, the bank puts the proceeds in the depositor's account and notifies the depositor by a credit memo. Debit and credit memos may also be used by the bank to correct errors made by the bank in previous months.

Reconciling the Bank Account

Objective 4:
Bank reconcili-
ation

The cash balance reported on the closing date of the bank statement seldom agrees with the balance shown in the depositor's general ledger *Cash* account. As a result, a **bank reconciliation** is prepared for each bank account. The purpose of the reconciliation is to reconcile the cash balance reported on the bank statement with the balance according to the depositor's records. The purpose is to prove the accuracy of both records.

The bank statement balance may differ from the depositor's records for several reasons.

1. Cash shown as deposited in the depositor's books has not yet been added to the bank account by the bank. Such deposits generally reflect what are called "deposits in transit," (that is, deposits that were either deposited late in the day on the last day of the month or were mailed to the bank, and which were not recorded by the bank at the time that the bank statement was prepared).

2. Amounts deducted from cash on the depositor's books have not yet been deducted from the bank account balance by the bank. The most common example is **outstanding checks**, that is, checks written by the depositor that have not yet cleared the bank.

3. Amounts added to the depositor's bank account by the bank and not yet recorded on the depositor's books, for example a note or other receivable collected by the bank on behalf of the depositor and credited directly to the bank account.

4. Amounts deducted from the depositor's account by the bank but not yet recorded on the depositor's books—service charges, check-printing charges, and NSF checks.

The form of bank reconciliation generally followed consists of the four parts shown here. The numbers in parentheses refer to the four reasons for differences between the bank statement balance and the cash balance per the depositor's books.

Balance per Bank Statement	$2,000
Add: (1) Amounts added to the books that have not yet been added to the bank account; for example, deposits in transit.	500
	2,500
Deduct: (2) Amounts deducted from the books that have not yet been deducted from the bank account; for example, outstanding checks.	900
Adjusted Bank Balance	$1,600
Balance per Books	$1,310
Add: (3) Amounts added to the bank account by the bank that have not yet been recorded on the depositor's books; for example, a note collected by the bank on behalf of the depositor.	300
	1,610
Deduct: (4) Amounts deducted from the bank account by the bank that have not yet been recorded on the depositor's books; for example, bank service charges.	10
Adjusted Book Balance	$1,600

The objective of the bank reconciliation is to reconcile both the cash balance on the depositor's records and the bank cash balance to the correct amount that would be included on a balance sheet prepared at the end of the period.

Procedures for Locating Reconciling Items.

The following steps are generally taken in order to locate reconciling items and determine the correct cash balance.

1. The individual deposits listed on the bank statement are compared with those recorded on the depositor's books. Any discrepancies are identified. Any deposits unrecorded by the bank are added to the bank statement balance on the reconciliation.

2. The amounts of the individual checks paid by the bank as listed on the bank statement are compared with the amounts listed on the depositor's records. (If the canceled checks are returned to the depositor, they may be placed in numerical order and their amounts compared with the amounts listed on the depositor's records.) Any errors are identified for later correction. Issued checks that have not yet cleared the bank are deducted from the bank balance on the reconciliation as outstanding checks.

3. Any debit or credit memos included with the bank statement are separated so that they can be deducted from or added to the book balance as reconciling items. The depositor must also prepare adjusting journal entries that correspond to these items.

4. Errors discovered in steps 1 through 3 are listed separately as reconciling items. The bank is notified of errors in its records so that bank employees can make appropriate adjustments to the bank account. Errors discovered in the depositor's own records are corrected by appropriate journal entries.

To illustrate the bank reconciliation process, assume that Data Company received the bank statement presented in Figure 7–4. The bank statement shows a bank balance of $5,425.53 on September 30, 1987. Assume that the cash balance shown on Data Company's books is $4,215.51. The following differences between the bank statement and Data Company's cash records were identified in applying the reconciliation steps described above.

1. A deposit in the amount of $546.87 was placed in the night depository at the bank by Data Company's cashier on the evening of September 30. (This was not shown on the bank statement because it was received too late.)

2. Checks issued and recorded by Data Company that were not returned with the bank statement were:

Check No.	Amount
1027	$ 94.67
1029	174.83
1031	102.62
1032	39.58
1034	216.47
Total	$628.17

(These checks were not returned with the bank statement because the bank had not yet received them.)

3. Two debit memos were included with the bank statement.
   (a) One debit memo, in the amount of $89.78, represented a check received from a customer (Mary Jonas) and deposited by Data Company that was returned for lack of sufficient funds in Mary Jonas's account.
   (b) The second debit memo, amounting to $8.50, represented bank service charges for the month of September.
4. A credit memo included with the bank statement indicated that the bank had collected a noninterest-bearing note receivable for Data Company in the amount of $1,225. The bank charged a collection fee of $25 and credited the remaining $1,200 to Data Company's account.
5. Comparison of the canceled checks with the accounting records showed that check number 1024 in the amount of $36.72, in payment for the purchase of office supplies, had been incorrectly entered in the cash disbursements journal as $63.72, thereby producing an understatement of the cash account of $27.

The bank reconciliation for Data Company as of September 30 is shown in Figure 7–5.

Notice that the correct cash balance of $5,344.23 is different from both the balance on the bank statement and the balance in Data Company's general ledger *Cash* account. After the bank records the deposit in transit and the outstanding checks clear, the bank records will show the correct balance of $5,344.23. In order to adjust Data Company's cash balance to the correct amount, either several individual adjusting journal entries or one composite entry must be prepared *for those reconciling items made to the book balance* on the bank reconciliation.

Figure 7–5
Bank Reconciliation

DATA COMPANY
Bank Reconciliation as of September 30, 1987

Balance per Bank Statement		$5,425.53
Add: Deposit in transit		546.87
Subtotal		5,972.40
Deduct: Outstanding checks		628.17
Adjusted Bank Balance		$5,344.23
Balance per Books		$4,215.51
Add: Proceeds from note collected, less collection		
fee ($1,225 − $25)	$1,200.00	
Error in recording check No. 1024	27.00	1,227.00
Subtotal		5,442.51
Deduct: NSF Check—Mary Jonas	89.78	
Bank service charge	8.50	98.28
Adjusted Book Balance		$5,344.23

Individual adjusting entries might be made as follows.

Sept.	30	Cash	1,200.00	
		Miscellaneous Expense	25.00	
		Notes Receivable		1,225.00
		To record the collection of a note receivable by the bank, less collection fee.		

The entry records the collection of the note receivable by increasing cash, recording the collection fee as miscellaneous expense, and reducing notes receivable.

Sept.	30	Cash	27.00	
		Office Supplies Inventory		27.00
		To record correction of Check No. 1024.		

The purchase of office supplies was recorded as a debit to *Office Supplies Inventory* and a credit to *Cash* in the incorrect amount of $63.72. The actual amount of the purchase and check was $36.72. The entry above corrects the error by increasing the *Cash* account and decreasing the *Office Supplies Inventory* account by the amount of the error, $27.

Sept.	30	Accounts Receivable—Mary Jonas	89.78	
		Cash		89.78
		To set up NSF check as a receivable from Mary Jonas.		

This entry establishes an account receivable from Mary Jonas for the amount of the NSF check. As with other accounts receivable, an attempt will be made to collect from Ms. Jonas.

Sept.	30	Miscellaneous Expense	8.50	
		Cash		8.50
		To record bank service charges for September.		

This entry charges the bank service charge to *Miscellaneous Expense* so that it will be included on the income statement for the month of September, if one is prepared.

However, the adjustments to the accounting records are generally accomplished by one combined entry such as the following.

Sept.	30	Cash	1,128.72	
		Miscellaneous Expense	33.50	
		Accounts Receivable—Mary Jonas	89.78	
		Notes Receivable		1,225.00
		Office Supplies Inventory		27.00
		To record bank reconciliation items for September.		

After the combined adjusting entry has been posted, the *Cash* account will have a balance of $5,344.23 as indicated here.

Cash

Balance before adjustment	4,215.51
Adjustment	1,128.72
9/30 Balance	5,344.23

The account balance now agrees with the adjusted book balance on the bank reconciliation. The balance should equal the amount of cash—including any cash on hand—that should be included in the September 30, 1987, balance sheet.

TEMPORARY INVESTMENTS IN MARKETABLE SECURITIES

Companies often have cash that is not needed immediately but may be needed later for current operating purposes. To obtain revenue from interest, dividends, and market appreciation, this excess cash may be invested in marketable securities such as U.S. Government securities (U.S. treasury bonds or treasury bills), stocks and bonds of corporations, or bank certificates of deposit.

Marketable securities held as investments are classified as either temporary (short-term) investments or as long-term investments. Classification is determined on the basis of marketability and the length of time management intends to hold the securities. To be classified as temporary investments, the securities must be readily marketable and intended to be held for a short time.

Marketability means that the security is traded regularly on an organized market, such as the New York Stock Exchange, so that there is a continuous market available. The holding period is short-term if management intends to convert the securities into cash within the normal operating cycle or one year, whichever is longer. If management intends to hold the securities for a long period, then the securities are considered long-term investments. Long-term investments are discussed in Chapter 18.

Securities may be purchased directly from the issuer, for example, when an investor purchases a new issue of treasury bills from the U.S. Government. However, many securities are purchased from other investors through brokers who charge a commission (generally some percentage of the value of the transaction) for their services. Brokers are normally employees of brokerage firms such as Merrill Lynch or E. F. Hutton. Brokers act as agents, since they buy and sell stocks and bonds for their clients through securities exchanges such as the New York or American Stock Exchange.

Millions of securities are traded each weekday. A record of these transactions is reported daily in the financial pages of many newspapers. Stock prices are quoted in terms of dollars and fractions of dollars, with ⅛ of a dollar normally being the minimum fraction. Thus, a quote of 42⅜ means that the security has a value of $42.375 per share and a stock quoted at 107½ means that the security has a price of $107.50. Bond prices are quoted as a

Objective 5: Temporary investments in marketable securities

Debt
Bonds
Notes

Equity
Stocks

percentage of the bond's par value. Therefore, a quote of 97¼ means that a $1,000 par value bond has a market value of $972.50 ($1,000 × 97.25%).

REPORTING TEMPORARY INVESTMENTS IN MARKETABLE SECURITIES

Since temporary securities are readily marketable, they can be converted to cash on short notice and are generally considered to be as liquid as cash itself. Consequently, they are reported on the balance sheet as current assets included with cash or immediately after cash. For example, the 1984 annual report for U.S. Steel Corporation shows temporary investments as follows:

	(Millions of Dollars)
Current Assets:	
Cash and marketable securities	$ 355.0

In contrast, General Motors reports its temporary investments separately in its 1984 annual report as:

	(Millions of Dollars)
Current Assets:	
Cash	$ 467.5
U.S. Government and Other Marketable Securities and Time Deposits—at Cost, Which Approximates Market of $8,108.7	8,099.9

ACCOUNTING FOR MARKETABLE SECURITIES PORTFOLIOS

As mentioned earlier, marketable securities may consist of debt securities (bonds and notes payable of other companies or governmental bodies) or equity securities (preferred and common stock of other corporations). When a company holds debt securities or shares of stock in several companies, the group of debt securities is called a *debt securities portfolio* and the group of equity securities is called an *equity securities portfolio.*

Temporary Investments in Debt Securities

Temporary investments in debt securities are recorded initially at their cost, including brokers' fees, in accordance with the *cost principle.* Since interest on debt securities accrues over time, the purchaser must also pay interest accrued between the date of the last interest payment and the purchase date. The amount paid for accrued interest is normally debited to *Interest Revenue* so that it will be offset against the credit to *Interest Revenue* when interest payments are received.

On subsequent balance sheets, normal increases and decreases in the market value of the debt securities are ignored and the portfolio is reported at its acquisition cost. However, if the market value of the securities is substantially less than cost and the decline in market value is not due to a temporary condition, an exception is made and the securities should be reported at their lower market value.[1]

The write-down to market value is recorded by a debit to a *Loss on Temporary Investments* account, which is reported as a loss in the ''Other expense'' section of the income statement. Because the decline in market value is other than temporary, the *Temporary Investment in Debt Securities* account is credited directly; later recoveries in market value are not recognized. Since temporary investments in debt securities generally consist of U.S. Government securities that are held for relatively short periods, substantial and permanent declines in market value are rare.

The following journal entries, with explanations, illustrate the normal accounting for investments in temporary debt securities.

Jan.	31	Temporary Investment in Debt Securities	87,000	
		Interest Revenue	1,087	
		Cash		88,087
		To record the purchase of U.S. Government bonds for $87,000 (including brokers' fees) plus accrued interest of $1,087.		
July	3	Cash	6,525	
		Interest Revenue		6,525
		To record the receipt of six months' interest.		
Nov.	1	Cash	92,650	
		Temporary Investment in Debt Securities		87,000
		Interest Revenue		4,350
		Gain on Sale of Investments		1,300
		To record the sale of temporary investments for $88,300 (net of brokers' fees) plus accrued interest of $4,350.		

(handwritten note: Bonds Always pay 6 months Interest)

Note that the gain on sale of investments is the difference between the selling price of the securities ($88,300) and their original cost ($87,000).

Temporary Investments in Equity Securities

Like temporary investments in debt securities, temporary investments in equity securities are also recorded initially at their cost. For example, if 8,000 shares of Dix Company common stock were purchased for $94,000, including brokers' fees, the purchase would be recorded as follows.

Jan.	18	Temporary Investment in Equity Securities	94,000	
		Cash		94,000
		To record the purchase of 8,000 shares of Dix Company common stock for $94,000, including brokers' fees.		

[1]Accounting Research Bulletin No. 43, ''Restatement and Revision of Accounting Research Bulletins'' (New York: AICPA, 1953), Ch. 3A, par. 9.

Dividends are recorded as revenue when declared. For example, if Dix Company declared a $1.50 per share cash dividend on June 18, the entry would be:

June	18	Dividends Receivable	12,000	
		Dividend Revenue		12,000
		To record dividends receivable on 8,000 shares at $1.50 per share.		

When the cash is received, the following entry is made.

July	6	Cash	12,000	
		Dividends Receivable		12,000
		To record the receipt of cash dividends.		

When all or part of the investment is sold, the cost of the shares sold is removed from the *Temporary Investment in Equity Securities* account and the difference between this cost and the selling price of the securities is recognized as a gain or loss. For example, if one-half of the Dix Company shares were sold for $50,000, net of brokers' fees, the entry would be:

Nov.	14	Cash	50,000	
		Temporary Investment in Equity Securities		47,000
		Gain on Sale of Investments		3,000
		To record the sale of 4,000 shares of Dix Company stock for $50,000, net of brokers' fees.		

Lower of Cost or Market Method

The temporary equity securities portfolio is reported on the balance sheet at the lower of its total cost or total market value at the balance sheet date.[2] For example, assume that Flank Corporation purchased equity securities during 1987 and had a portfolio of temporary equity securities on December 31, 1987 as shown here.

Temporary Portfolio of Equity Securities	Cost	Market
Brad Company—Preferred Stock	$ 22,000	$ 18,000
Crance Company—Common Stock	46,000	49,000
Ever Company—Common Stock	35,000	35,000
Hulto Company—Common Stock	81,000	70,000
Total	$184,000	$172,000

[2]Statement of Financial Accounting Standards No. 12, "Accounting for Certain Marketable Securities" (Stamford, Conn.: FASB, 1975), par. 8.

Assuming that the securities were all purchased on January 15, the purchase would be recorded as follows.

Jan.	15	Temporary Investment in Equity Securities	184,000	
		Cash		184,000
		To record the purchase of temporary equity securities.		

Because the December 31 market value of the portfolio is $12,000 less than its cost, a $12,000 unrealized loss has been incurred and the portfolio should be reported in the balance sheet at its lower market value of $172,000. To record the loss and reduce the temporary equity securities portfolio to its market value, an entry is made as follows.

Dec.	31	Unrealized Loss on Equity Securities	12,000	
		Allowance to Reduce Equity Securities to Market Value		12,000
		To reduce investment in temporary equity securities to the lower of cost or market.		

Note that the lower of cost or market method is applied using the portfolio's total cost and total market value, rather than on an item-by-item basis. Although the loss is unrealized because the securities have not been sold, it must be deducted on the income statement. These losses normally are reported in the "Other expense" category. The *Allowance to Reduce Equity Securities to Market Value* is a contra asset account and is deducted from the cost of the equity securities on the balance sheet as follows.

Current Assets:		
Cash		$ 78,000
Temporary investment in equity securities	$184,000	
Less: Allowance to reduce equity		
securities to market value	12,000	172,000

Reporting in this way discloses to statement users both the cost of the equity securities and their current market value.

If the market value of the portfolio is greater than its cost, the unrealized gain is not recorded and the equity securities are reported at their cost with market value disclosed parenthetically or in a footnote. This treatment is consistent with the accounting convention of **conservatism,** under which gains are not recognized until realized by a sale but losses are recognized when they are incurred.

If the portfolio's total market value in a subsequent period is higher than its carrying value (cost minus allowance account), an unrealized loss recovery is recognized up to the amount in the *Allowance* account and included in net income for that period. Thus, when the temporary equity securities portfolio has been written down to its market value, it may be written back up only to its original cost. In other words, the *Allowance* account is adjusted downward and upward so that the *Allowance* account balance equals the excess of cost over market value of the portfolio on the balance sheet date. For example, if the market value of the portfolio was $180,000 as of December 31, 1988, the following entry would be made.

Dec.	31	Allowance to Reduce Equity Securities to Market Value	8,000	
		Recovery of Unrealized Loss on Temporary Equity Securities		8,000
		To record a reduction in the allowance account due to the increase in market value of temporary equity securities.		

The temporary equity securities portfolio would be reported on the December 31, 1988 balance sheet, as follows.

Current Assets		
Cash		$ 97,000
Temporary investment in equity securities	$184,000	
Less: Allowance to reduce equity securities to market value	4,000	180,000

If the December 31, 1988 market value of the portfolio was $184,000 or more, the entire balance of $12,000 would be removed from the allowance account and reported as an unrealized loss recovery. Remember, however, that the portfolio may be written up to its original cost only. Thus, even if the market value of the portfolio was $200,000 on December 31, 1988, the maximum amount that is reported as an unrealized loss recovery is the $12,000 balance in the allowance account. The *Recovery of Unrealized Loss on Temporary Equity Securities* account is reported on the income statement as "Other revenue."

It is also important to understand that a portfolio of temporary equity securities may be on hand at the end of every fiscal period. However, the individual securities in the portfolio change over time as some are sold to obtain cash and others are purchased later as temporary cash investments.

When temporary equity securities are sold that previously were part of a portfolio written down to a lower market value, the gain or loss recognized is the difference between the selling price and the original purchase cost, regardless of the balance in the *Allowance* account. The balance in the *Allowance* account is adjusted up or down to reflect the difference between total portfolio cost and a lower total portfolio market value of the equity securities held at the end of the period.

To illustrate the sale of securities, assume that the Crance Company common stock was sold on February 4, 1988 for $53,000, net of brokers' fees. The entry would be:

Feb.	4	Cash	53,000	
		Temporary Investment in Equity Securities		46,000
		Gain on Sale of Investments		7,000
		To record the sale of Crance Company common stock.		

APPENDIX: CASH DISBURSEMENTS AND THE VOUCHER SYSTEM

A **voucher system** consists of the procedures followed to accumulate, verify, and record all cash disbursements made for the acquisition of goods or services. Four relatively distinct steps make up the cycle involved in the ordering, receipt, and payment for goods and services.

Objective 6:
Using voucher system to control cash disbursements

1. Orders are placed.
2. Goods or services are received.
3. The accuracy of invoices is verified and the invoices are approved for payment.
4. Checks are written in payment of approved invoices.

In a small business, the steps are often controlled and performed entirely by the owner or manager. In a large business, control is achieved by assigning the various steps to specific individuals or departments. One or more source documents are prepared at each step to provide verification that the step was completed properly. Although the same general procedures are followed for the acquisition of both goods and services, the following description concentrates on the acquisition of goods—inventory and other physical assets.

PLACING ORDERS

Operating department managers are normally prohibited from placing orders directly with suppliers; to permit them to do so would prohibit effective centralization of the control of the total goods ordered and the resulting liabilities. Operating managers, who have responsibility for determining the goods needed by their departments, prepare a form called a **purchase requisition** (Figure 7–6) that lists the items needed by the department. The purchase requisition is sent to a central purchasing department that has responsibility for placing orders, and a copy is forwarded to the accounting department. Purchasing department personnel determine the appropriate source of supply, negotiate the terms of the purchase with the supplier, and place the order by preparing a **purchase order**—a business form that authorizes a supplier to ship specific goods (Figure 7–7). The original of the purchase order is sent to the supplier, a copy is sent to the requisitioning department to inform the manager that the order has been placed, and a copy is forwarded to the accounting department, which will eventually approve payment for the order.

RECEIPT OF GOODS

When goods are shipped, the supplier prepares a document called an **invoice** or bill (Figure 7–8) that itemizes the goods shipped, the price charged for each item, and the total amount of the invoice. A copy of the invoice is mailed to the purchaser. The invoice represents a sales invoice to the supplier and a purchase invoice to the buyer. When the invoice is received, it is sent to the

Figure 7–6
A Purchase Requisition

PURCHASE REQUISITION

Data Company

No. 269

Date August 6, 1987

From: Assembly Department
To: Purchasing Department

Please place the following order:

Quantity	Number	Description
200	142 JX	J-type Gear Boxes
400	142 JY	Gear Box Brackets

For Purchasing Department Use:
Date Ordered   August 9, 1987

Betty Wallace
Approved

Purchase Order No.   348

Figure 7–7
A Purchase Order

PURCHASE ORDER

No.   348

Data Company
1842 Elm Street
New York, New York 10160

To: Croyden Gear Supply Company
    1478 Sundown Avenue
    Los Angeles, California 94412

Date   August 9, 1987
Ship Via   Acme Trucking
Terms   2/10, n/30

Please ship the following:

Quantity	Description	Price	Total
200	142 JX J-type Gear Boxes	$ 4.95	$990.00
400	142 JY Gear Box Brackets	.78	312.00

Data Company
By *P. Schneider*

accounting department, where it is held until the goods are received and inspected. Most large companies maintain a separate department responsible for receiving and inspecting the goods as they are received. The receiving department prepares a **receiving report** (Figure 7–9), which lists the type and quantity of goods received. Copies are sent to the requisitioning department and the purchasing department to serve as notification that the goods have been received, and a copy is sent to the accounting department for comparison with the purchase requisition, purchase order, and purchase invoice.

Figure 7–8
An Invoice

INVOICE

No.   2416

Croyden Gear Supply Company
1478 Sundown Avenue
Los Angeles, California 94412

Sold to	Data Company	Invoice Date	8/15/87
	1842 Elm Street	Your Order No.	348
	New York, New York 10160	Date Shipped	8/15/87
		Terms	2/10, n/30

Quantity	Description	Price	Amount
200	142 JX J-type Gear Boxes	$ 4.95	$ 990.00
400	142 JY Gear Box Brackets	.78	312.00
			$1,302.00

Figure 7–9
A Receiving Report

RECEIVING REPORT

No.   694

Data Company
New York, New York

To: Accounting Department   Date Received   8/19/87
From: Receiving Department   Purchase Order No.   348
                              Supplier   Croyden Gear Supply Co.

The following items have been received:

Description	Quantity	Condition
142 JX J-type Gear Boxes	200	Good
142 JY Gear Box Brackets	400	Good

SB.Frandin
Signed

The flow of documents in the acquisition of goods can be depicted as follows:

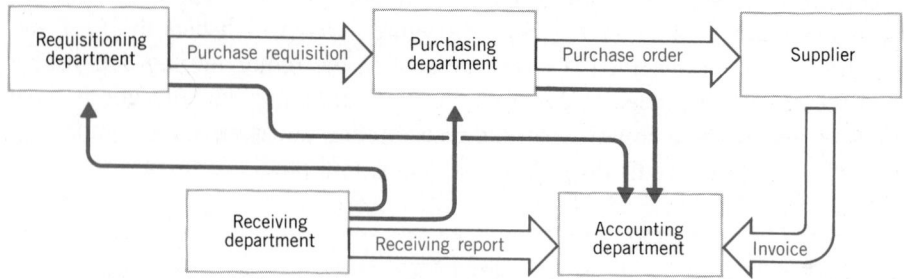

The large arrows represent the transfer of the original documents; the single lines show the transfer of copies of the various documents.

VERIFICATION OF THE ACCURACY OF INVOICES AND APPROVAL OF PAYMENT

Upon receipt of the receiving report, the accounting department will possess copies of the purchase requisition, purchase order, purchase invoice, and receiving report, all of which relate to a specific purchase from a specific supplier. Accounting department personnel then perform several important verification procedures, after which the invoice is approved for entry into the accounting records and for payment. Verification procedures generally followed are:

1. Items on the purchase invoice are compared with those listed on the purchase requisition to verify that the goods shipped by the supplier were properly requisitioned.
2. Items on the purchase invoice are compared with those listed on the purchase order to verify that the goods shipped are the same as those ordered.
3. Items listed on the purchase invoice are compared with those listed on the receiving report to verify that the goods billed by the supplier were actually received.
4. Additional verification is performed on the purchase invoice to assure that prices charged and credit terms are those agreed upon and that computations and price extensions are accurate.

THE VOUCHER

As each purchase invoice is received by the accounting department, a document called a voucher (Figure 7–10) is attached to the invoice. The other related documents (requisition, purchase order, and receiving report) will also be attached to the voucher as they are received so that they can be used by the accounting department employee who will perform the verification process.

Figure 7–10
A Voucher

Voucher No. ___341___

DATA COMPANY
New York, New York

Pay to ___Reardon Wholesale___   Date ___Sept. 1, 1987___
___224 W. Oak___
___Phoenix, Arizona 85042___   Due Date ___Sept. 10, 1987___

Date of Invoice	Sept. 1, 1987	Invoice Amount $2,147.80
Invoice Number	2163	Cash Discount 42.97
Payment Terms	2/10,n/30	Net Amount 2,104.83

Verification of: Approved by

Proper Purchase Requisition   B.Y.
Quantities on Purchase Order with Invoice   B.Y.
Quantities on Receiving Report with Invoice   B.Y.
Prices on Purchase Order with Invoice   B.Y.
Credit Terms in Agreement with Purchase Order   B.Y.
Invoice Extensions and Footings   B.Y.
Approved for Payment   Don Artem

Account Distribution	Amount
Advertising	
Freight-in	
Office Salaries	
Office Supplies	
Purchases	$2,147.80
Sales Salaries	
Utilities	
Miscellaneous Expense	
Total Vouchers Payable Credit	$2,147.80

Payment Record:
Date Paid ___9/10/87___ Check No. ___260___ Amount ___$2,104.83___

The voucher contains five sections, used to record various information.

1. The name of the creditor, the date the voucher is prepared, and the last date on which payment can be made to obtain cash discounts or the date on which payment is otherwise due.
2. General invoice data, such as the date of the invoice, payment terms, the amount of the invoice, and the net amount due after allowing for cash discounts, if any.
3. The initials of the person performing the verification steps and of the employee authorized to approve payment of the invoice.
4. Amounts to be debited to identified general ledger accounts by the accounting department and the total amount to be credited to vouchers payable.

5. Payment data identifying the date paid, the check number, and the amount of the check.

Every cash payment, including reimbursement of the petty cash fund, requires a voucher, regardless of whether the payment is for services, merchandise, equipment, dividends, or a mortgage payment. Even the receipt of a bill (such as a utility bill) that is to be paid immediately must first be vouchered. Probably the greatest benefit received from use of a voucher system is the assurance that every cash expenditure has been thoroughly reviewed and amounts verified before payment is made. If there is no collusion among employees, management is assured that all expenditures were made for valid business purposes.

The Voucher Register

After the voucher is prepared it is recorded in a **voucher register,** a book of original entry which, in combination with a check register under the voucher system, takes the place of the cash disbursements journal described in Chapter 6. The function of a check register is described in a later section of this appendix, and a voucher register is shown in Figure 7–11.

Under the voucher system, a *Vouchers Payable* account takes the place of the *Accounts Payable* account. Every voucher is entered in the voucher register with a debit to various asset, expense, or liability accounts and a credit to vouchers payable. All information in the voucher register is entered from the voucher at the time that it is approved for recording with the exception of the payment information, which is entered as each voucher is paid.

The posting of the voucher register follows the same general procedures used to post the cash disbursements journal. Columns are totaled and cross-footed at month's end to verify the equality of debits and credits. The total of

Voucher Register													Page 17		
			Payment		Vouchers Payable Credit	Pur-chases Debit	Freight In Debit	Adver-tising Debit	Sales Salaries Debit	Office Salaries Debit	Other Debits				
Date 1987	Voucher No.	Payee	Date	Chk. No.							Account	P/R	Amt.		
9/1	341	Reardon Wholesale	9/10	260	2,147 80	2,147 80									
9/1	342	Daly Freight Co.	9/3	251	122 50		122 50								
9/4	343	Haried Insurance Co.	9/5	253	347 80						Prepaid Insurance	136	347 80		
9/6	344	Acme Office Supply	9/12	263	89 40						Office Supplies	124	89 40		
9/6	345	The Leader	9/11	261	138 00			138 00							
9/7	346	Doug Johnson	9/7	256	236 50				236 50						
9/7	347	Rick Burdick	9/7	257	149 30					149 30					
9/7	348	Charles Myler	9/7	258	220 00				220 00						
9/8	349	Zylon Equipment Co.	9/20	284	370 00						Office Equipment	158	370 00		
9/30	382	United Bank	9/30	349	2,060 00						Notes Payable	210	2,000 00		
											Interest Expense	535	60 00		
9/30	383	Turner Supply Co.			896 22	896 22									
9/30	384	Adventure Travel	9/30	350	384 50						Travel Expense	574	384 50		
9/30	385	The Leader			74 90			74 90							
					18,249 24	6,483 94	286 89	399 40	1,839 42	597 20			8,642 39		
					(202)	(533)	(520)	(504)	(562)	(572)			(X)		

Figure 7–11
A Voucher Register

all debit columns, including the "Other Debits" column, must equal the total of the Vouchers Payable column. The total of each column, with the exception of the "Other Debits" column, is posted as a debit or credit to the appropriate account listed in the column heading. Evidence of the posting is indicated by placing the general ledger account number in parentheses just below the column total. Entries in the "Other Debits" column are posted individually as debits to the account listed and the account number is entered in the posting reference column.

Unpaid Vouchers File

Some vouchers—particularly those prepared for the payment of ongoing expenses, such as sales salaries, office salaries, and utilities—are often paid on the date they are recorded in the voucher register. With other payments, however, there may be a time lag between the receipt of an invoice and its due date. In these cases, the voucher is prepared and filed in an **unpaid vouchers file**. To protect the company's credit rating and to assure the payment of invoices in time to obtain cash discounts, the vouchers are filed under the dates on which payment is due. The unpaid vouchers file constitutes a subsidiary ledger of vouchers payable and, under a voucher system, takes the place of the accounts payable subsidiary ledger described in Chapter 6. The elimination of the accounts payable subsidiary ledger often results in a considerable cost savings to the business. At the end of the month, after month-end posting has taken place, the total of all vouchers in the unpaid voucher file should be equal to the balance in the *Vouchers Payable* account in the general ledger. A reconciliation should be prepared at month-end to verify that the total of unpaid vouchers in the voucher register agrees with the total of all vouchers in the unpaid vouchers file and the balance of the *Vouchers Payable* general ledger account.

The Check Register

On each business day, the vouchers in the unpaid vouchers file under that date are removed and sent to the employee authorized to approve vouchers for payment. The employee reviews the voucher to assure that all verification steps have been completed; initials the voucher to signify approval for payment; fills in the payment-record section of the voucher indicating the date paid, check number, and amount; prepares a check; and forwards the check and voucher to the person authorized to sign checks, usually the company's treasurer. The treasurer then reviews the voucher for proper authorization of payment, signs the check, mails it to the payee, and sends the voucher to the accounting department.

When the voucher is received by the accounting department, an entry is made in the payment column of the voucher register to indicate that the voucher has been paid. The check is then recorded in a **check register** (Figure 7–12), which serves as a record of all cash disbursements, and the paid voucher is filed in numerical order in a **paid vouchers file**.

Check Register							Page 12	
Date 1987	Check No.	Payee	Voucher No.	Vouchers Payable Debit		Purchase Discounts Credit	Cash Credit	
Sept. 1	251	Daly Freight Co.	342	122	50		122	50
3	252	Haried Insurance	343	347	80		347	80
5	254	Reardon Wholesale	335	1,246	00	24 92	1,221	08
6	255	Batho Company	334	1,322	80	26 46	1,296	34
7	256	Doug Johnson	346	236	50		236	50
7	257	Rick Burdick	347	149	30		149	30
7	258	Charles Myler	348	220	00		220	00
30	349	United Bank	382	2,060	00		2,060	00
30	350	Adventure Travel	384	384	50		384	50
				18,629	90	193 48	18,436	42
				(202)		(534)	(101)	

Figure 7–12
A Check Register

Because checks are written only in payment of specific vouchers, every check drawn results in a debit to *Vouchers Payable* and a credit to *Cash,* with the exception of cases where a check is drawn in payment of a voucher on which a cash discount is involved. In those cases, the entry in the check register results in a debit to *Vouchers Payable* for the gross amount, a credit to *Purchase Discounts,* and a credit to *Cash* for the net amount paid. At the end of the month, the columns of the check register are footed and crossfooted, and the column totals are posted to the general ledger accounts specified in the column headings. As with the posting of other special journals, the general account ledger numbers are written in parentheses at the bottom of each column to indicate that the total has been posted.

After the voucher register and check register have been posted, the general ledger *Vouchers Payable* account has a balance of $971.12 as shown here.

Vouchers Payable			202
9/30 CR12	18,629.90	9/1 Balance (assumed)	1,351.78
		9/30 VR17	18,249.24
		9/30 Balance	971.12

Reference to the voucher register shows that there are two unpaid vouchers on September 30, as follows.

Payee	Amount
Turner Supply Co.	$896.22
The Leader	74.90
Total	$971.12

Thus, the list of unpaid vouchers reconciles with the balance in the *Vouchers Payable* account as of September 30.

MAKING PARTIAL PAYMENTS

If an invoice is to be paid in installments, a separate voucher is prepared for each installment when the invoice is received. However, if installment payments are decided upon after the invoice has been vouchered, the original voucher is cancelled and new vouchers prepared, one for each installment.

RECORDING PURCHASE RETURNS AND ALLOWANCES

On occasion a defective item is returned to a supplier or an allowance is received from a supplier. If this occurs prior to the preparation of the voucher, the voucher is prepared for the amount of the corrected invoice. If returns are made or allowances received after the voucher has been prepared and entered in the voucher register, a general journal entry is prepared debiting *Vouchers Payable* and crediting *Purchase Returns and Allowances* for the appropriate amount. A reference to this general journal entry is then made on the appropriate line in the voucher register and the amount of the return or allowance is deducted on the voucher. A copy of the credit memorandum or other document verifying the return is attached to the voucher. The check drawn in payment of the voucher is then written for the corrected amount.

GLOSSARY

BANK RECONCILIATION. A form prepared to reconcile the cash balance reported on the bank statement with the balance per the depositor's records (p. 302).

BANK STATEMENT. A statement prepared by the bank that provides the details of activity that has taken place in a checking account for a specific period of time (p. 301).

CANCELLED CHECKS. Checks written by the depositor and paid by the bank (p. 301).

CASH. Money, and any instrument, such as a check or money order, that a bank will accept for immediate deposit in a bank account (p. 294).

CHECK REGISTER. A book in which all checks written are recorded in numerical order (p. 319).

INVOICE. A business form prepared by a supplier that itemizes the goods shipped, prices charged, and total amount due. To the buyer it is a purchase invoice; to the seller it is a sales invoice (p. 313).

NONSUFFICIENT FUNDS (NSF) CHECK. A check that was included in a depositor's deposit, but was not paid by the maker's bank because of insufficient funds (p. 301).

OUTSTANDING CHECKS. Checks written by a depositor that have not yet cleared the bank (p. 303).

PAID VOUCHERS FILE. A file in which vouchers are placed in numerical order after they have been paid (p. 319).

PETTY CASH FUND. A specified amount of cash placed under the control of an employee for use in making small cash payments (p. 298).

PETTY CASH RECEIPT. A form used as a receipt for payments from a petty cash fund (p. 298).

PURCHASE ORDER. A business form prepared by the buyer that authorizes a supplier to ship specific goods (p. 313).

PURCHASE REQUISITION. A business form used by operating managers to request the purchasing department to place orders for goods and services (p. 313).

RECEIVING REPORT. A business form prepared by the receiving department that lists the type and quantity of goods received (p. 315).

UNPAID VOUCHERS FILE. A file in which unpaid vouchers are stored under the date on which they must be paid (p. 319).

VOUCHER REGISTER. A book of original entry in which all vouchers prepared are listed in numerical order (p. 318).

VOUCHER SYSTEM. An accounting system used to control all cash disbursements (p. 313).

DISCUSSION QUESTIONS

1. What items are included as cash on the balance sheet?
2. Procedures for the control of receipts from cash sales and for the control of mail receipts are based on the same general principle of internal control. What is this principle? Why is the possibility of fraud decreased when this principle is followed?
3. Why is it important that the employee designated to approve invoices for payment not have check-writing or accounting responsibilities?
4. What account(s) are debited when (a) establishing a petty cash fund, and (b) replenishing a petty cash fund?
5. Why is the petty cash fund replenished at the end of an accounting period, even if the amount of cash in the fund is not running low?
6. What document serves as the basis for the entry needed to record the replenishment of a petty cash fund? Who makes such an entry?
7. Why is internal control strengthened by requiring that each day's cash receipts be deposited intact and by further requiring that all disbursements be made by check?
8. Define the terms *debit memo* and *credit memo*. Give an example of each.
9. Identify each of the following bank reconciliation items as (a) an addition to the bank statement balance, (b) a deduction from the bank statement balance, (c) an addition to the book balance, or (d) a deduction from the book balance.
   (a) Bank service charges.
   (b) Outstanding checks.
   (c) Deposit in transit.
   (d) Check of a customer returned by the bank because of insufficient funds.
   (e) A note collected for the depositor by the bank.
   (f) A depositor's check written for $200 but charged by the bank as $20.
10. In reconciling a bank statement, what items require a journal entry on the depositor's books?
11. What entry should be made when a customer's check is deposited and returned later by the bank marked ''NSF''?
12. Contrast the accounting for a temporary debt securities portfolio with the accounting for a temporary equity securities portfolio.
13. Are unrealized gains on a temporary equity securities portfolio ever reported on the income statement? If so, when and how?

14A. What documents are used in the verification procedures performed by the accounting department prior to approving an invoice for payment?

15A. What account(s) are debited in the voucher register? What account is credited?

16A. What accounts are debited and credited in the check register?

EXERCISES

Exercise 7-1 Composition of Cash

On June 30 the safe of Zam Company contained the following items.

1. Currency and coin, $4,048.64.
2. A $75 IOU from an employee, representing a temporary loan, which is to be deducted from the employee's next paycheck.
3. Checks dated June 30 in the total amount of $3,838.52 received from customers on June 30.
4. A check for $530 received from a customer on June 30, but dated July 3.

Required:

A. What dollar amount should be included in "cash" on the June 30 balance sheet?

B. Explain how any items not included in "cash" should be reported in the June 30 balance sheet.

Exercise 7-2 Cash Internal Control Procedures

Janet Stine, owner of Stine Equipment Sales, is troubled by the fact that her business consistently shows good earnings but is often short of cash. She explains to you that she has made a serious effort to establish good internal control procedures for cash transactions. She says "I have made one employee responsible for keeping the accounting records, making cash collections, and making bank deposits. I have assigned to another employee the responsibility for ordering merchandise, receiving and counting the goods when they arrive, and writing checks to pay for the merchandise. I want to be sure that we are actually getting what we're paying for."

Required:

Evaluate Stine's internal control procedures and explain the reasoning behind any criticism you have.

Exercise 7-3 Petty Cash and Cash Receipts

Prepare journal entries for the following transactions of Ade Company. If an entry is not required, indicate so and explain why.

1. A petty cash fund was established in the amount of $100.
2. Cash sales for Monday recorded on the cash register tape amounted to $913.06. A count of the cash in the register showed a total of $958.96. The cash register contained a $50.00 change fund at the beginning of the day.
3. An employee paid $5.29 postage to mail a package and was reimbursed from the petty cash fund.
4. Cash sales for Tuesday recorded on the cash register tape amounted to $850.30. A count of the cash in the register showed a total of $903.10. The register contained a $50.00 change fund at the beginning of the day.

Exercise 7-4 Petty Cash Fund Transactions

On July 1, Dino Company established a $150 petty cash fund. On July 31, the petty cash box contained the following cash and expense receipts.

Cash $20.71

Expense Receipts		
Receipt No.	**Purpose**	**Amount**
1	Postage	$48.11
2	Office supplies	32.35
3	Taxi fares	15.75
4	Gasoline	22.54
5	Newspapers	7.00

Required:

A. Prepare the entry that was made to establish the petty cash fund.

B. Prepare the entry needed to replenish the petty cash fund. (Taxi and newspaper expenditures should be charged to *Miscellaneous Expense*.)

C. Assume that a decision was made to increase the petty cash fund to $200. Prepare the journal entry to do so.

Exercise 7-5 Petty Cash

Custer Company's petty cash box contained the following items on December 31, the end of the fiscal year.

Cash	$51.46
Expense Receipts	
Office supplies	33.06
Postage	53.14
Freight-in	34.50
Taxi fares (Miscellaneous Expense)	27.84

Required:

A. Explain why the petty cash fund should be replenished on December 31, even if there is a substantial amount of cash in the fund.

B. Prepare the entry to replenish the petty cash fund.

Exercise 7-6 Bank Reconciliation

Woods Company received its bank statement for the month of July, which showed a bank balance of $1,235.27. The cash balance on the company's books on July 31 was $1,092.77. The following reconciling items were identified.

1. Outstanding checks amounted to $205.
2. The bank statement included an $8.00 debit memorandum for bank service charges for the month and a $12.50 debit memorandum for printing checks.
3. Cash receipts of $350 for July 31 were placed in the bank's night depository and were unrecorded by the bank at the time that the July bank statement was prepared.
4. A credit memorandum received with the bank statement indicated that a noninterest-bearing note receivable in the amount of $300 was collected for Woods Company by the bank. The bank charged a collection fee of $10 and credited the remaining $290 to Woods' account.
5. Woods Company's bookkeeper discovered that check No. 410 in the amount of $46.20, in payment of office supplies purchased, had been incorrectly recorded as $64.20.

Required:
Prepare a bank reconciliation for Woods Company as of July 31.

Exercise 7-7 Adjusting Entries from Bank Reconciliation
Prepare the journal entries needed on Woods Company's books as a result of the bank reconciliation in Exercise 7-6.

Exercise 7-8 Temporary Investments in Debt Securities
Burden Barter Company decided to purchase some debt securities as a temporary investment of excess cash. During the year, the following transactions took place.

1. On March 1, Burden Baxter Company purchased U.S. Government bonds for $93,000, plus accrued interest of $3,333, and brokers' fees of $1,620.
2. Interest of $4,000 was received on the U.S. Government bonds on April 1.
3. On May 1, Burden Baxter purchased Rico Company bonds for $16,000, plus brokers' fees of $550.
4. On June 1, Burden Baxter sold its investment in U.S. Government bonds for $97,000, plus accrued interest of $1,333.

Required:
Prepare journal entries to record Burden Baxter's transactions.

Exercise 7-9 Temporary Equity Securities Portfolio
A corporation had the following temporary equity securities portfolio on December 31, 1987.

Stock	Cost	Market Value
St. John Corporation—Preferred	$122,000	$130,000
McGregor Company—Common	67,500	60,000
Dumbald Company—Common	85,000	80,000
Total	$274,500	$270,000

Required:
A. Prepare the journal entry to reduce the temporary equity securities portfolio to the lower of cost or market.
B. Explain how the accounts debited and credited in requirement (A) should be reported in the financial statements for 1987.

Exercise 7A-10 Recording Transactions Using a Voucher System
Evans Company uses a voucher system. Selected transactions during June are as follows.

June	2	Voucher No. 540 was prepared, for the purchase of merchandise from Franklin Retailers, $3,720; terms, 2/10, n/30.
	5	Voucher No. 546 was prepared, for an advertising bill received from Urbanco, $1,680; terms, n/20.
	7	Voucher No. 549 was prepared, for the purchase of office equipment from Jake & Company, $2,700; terms, 2/10, n/30.
	11	Issued check No. 1242 to Franklin Retailers in payment of voucher No. 540.
	16	Issued check No. 1245 to Jake & Company in payment of voucher No. 549.
	25	Issued check No. 1248 to Urbanco in payment of voucher No. 546.

Required:
Record each of the transactions in general journal form.

PROBLEMS

Problem 7-1 Petty Cash Transactions

Transactions and events affecting the petty cash fund of Lane Company are as follows.

1. Paid $28 for the repair of an office typewriter.
2. Paid $60 for postage.
3. Purchased office supplies for $39.
4. Paid $12 for newspapers and magazines.
5. Paid $42 C.O.D. charges on merchandise purchased.
6. The custodian of the fund exchanged the receipts in the petty cash box for a check to reimburse the fund and to increase the size of the fund from $200 to $300.
7. Paid Speedy Express $72 for overnight delivery of some important machinery replacement parts.
8. Paid $12 to have the office windows washed.
9. Paid $8 for coffee and supplies for the employee lounge.
10. Reimbursed an employee $20 for taxi fares.
11. Paid $26 to a dry cleaner for office drapes cleaned.
12. Paid $40.50 to the driver of the company's delivery truck for gasoline purchased.

Required:
Prepare general journal entries to:

A. Establish the petty cash fund in the amount of $200.
B. Replenish the fund after transaction (5) and increase its size to $300. (C.O.D. charges and express payments may be debited to *Freight-in*. Expenses unrelated to autos, office supplies, and postage should be debited to *Miscellaneous Expense*.)
C. Replenish the fund after transaction (12).

Problem 7-2 Bank Reconciliation

Marchem Company received its bank statement for the month of April, showing a bank balance of $8,794.51. The cash balance on Marchem Company's books on April 30 was $8,642.02. The following reconciling items were identified.

1. Outstanding checks amounted to $990.79.
2. Debit memos were included with the bank statement, as follows.
   (a) A $796.95 check received from a customer (S. Shudde) and deposited by Marchem Company was returned for lack of sufficient funds in S. Shudde's account.
   (b) Service charges for the month were $30.
3. A credit memo received with the bank statement indicated that a note receivable in the amount of $1,200, plus interest of $130, had been collected by the bank. The bank charged a collection fee of $70 and credited the remaining $1,260 to Marchem Company's account.
4. A deposit of $1,298.35 was in transit on April 30.
5. The bookkeeper discovered that check No. 462 in the amount of $714.75, in payment of insurance expense, had been incorrectly recorded as $741.75.

Required:

A. Prepare a bank reconciliation as of April 30.

B. Prepare any adjusting general journal entries required.

Problem 7-3   Bank Reconciliation

The following information was taken from the bank statement of Roger Inc., dated June 30.

May 31 Balance				$8,777.05
	Checks/Debits			
Date	Check No.	Amount	Deposits/Credits	
June 1	488	121.00	718.80	
	480	469.08		
2	489	483.33		
4	490	581.90	678.50	
6	491	635.13	823.70	
	494	82.50		
7	493	508.75		
10	492	1,007.50	948.98	
12	499	648.80	628.68	
16	495	773.40	670.60	
21	496	405.15	555.75	
	497	498.45		
	498	480.10		
23	500	120.60	743.58	
	501	138.70		
	503	165.00		
26			758.10	
28			818.30	
29	504	500.10		
30		118.00 DM		
		6.00 SC	545.00 CM	
Totals		7,743.49	7,889.99	
June 30 Balance				$8,923.55

On June 30, the bank debited Roger's account for $118 for a check returned because of insufficient funds, and for $6.00 for bank service charges. The NSF check was written by Tom Jones, a customer. On June 30, the bank also credited the company's account for $545 for the net proceeds ($555 less $10 collection fee) of a noninterest-bearing note receivable that it had collected on behalf of the company.

The number and amount of each check written during the month were recorded in the cash disbursements journal, as follows.

Check No.	Amount	Check No.	Amount	Check No.	Amount
489	$ 483.33	495	$773.40	501	$138.70
490	581.90	496	504.15	502	201.40
491	635.13	497	498.45	503	165.00
492	1,007.50	498	480.10	504	500.10
493	508.75	499	648.80	505	174.00
494	82.50	500	120.60		

The date and the amount of each deposit as recorded in Roger's books during June were as follows.

Date	Amount	Date	Amount
June 4	$678.50	June 21	$555.75
6	823.70	23	743.58
10	948.98	26	758.10
12	628.68	28	818.30
16	670.60	30	642.90

The bookkeeper discovered that check No. 496 (in payment for the purchase of office equipment) was correctly issued for $405.15 but incorrectly recorded in the cash disbursements journal as $504.15.

Outstanding checks at the last statement date, May 31, were: No. 480 for $469.08; No. 488 for $121.00; and No. 486 for $406.50.

The balance in the cash account on the company's books on June 30 was $8,264.55.

Required:
A. Prepare a bank reconciliation for Roger Inc., as of June 30.
B. Prepare the general journal entries needed to reconcile the company's cash account with the correct balance.

Problem 7-4 Bank Reconciliation

Information about cash transactions and cash balances for Jules Company for the month of September is presented here.

1. The general ledger *Cash* account had a balance of $6,231.03 on August 31.
2. The cash receipts journal showed total cash receipts of $20,458.50 for September.
3. The cash disbursements journal showed total cash payments of $22,400.60 for September.
4. The September bank statement reported a bank balance of $3,912.96 on September 30.
5. Cash receipts of $960.20 for September 30 were placed in the bank's night depository on September 30 and were not included in the September bank statement.
6. Outstanding checks at the end of September were: No. 764, $50.00; No. 766, $75.30; and No. 770, $119.89.
7. Included with the bank statement were:
   (a) A debit memo for service charges, $8.00.
   (b) A check written by Loud Bros., a customer, for $286.46 marked NSF.
   (c) A credit memo for $642.50, indicating the collection of a note receivable of $600 plus interest, which the bank had credited to Jules Company's account.
8. Comparison of the canceled checks with the entries in the cash disbursements journal disclosed that check No. 742 for $643, written in payment of rent expense, had been incorrectly recorded as $634.

Required:
A. Prepare a bank reconciliation for September.
B. Prepare general journal entries to adjust the accounts.
C. What is the amount of cash that should be reported on the September 30 balance sheet?

Problem 7-5 Temporary Equity Securities Portfolio

On January 2, 1987, Firmco purchased the following securities as temporary investments.

Investment	Cost
Window Company Common Stock	$25,000
Ocean Incorp. Common Stock	42,000
Marilyn Company Preferred Stock	19,000
Total	$86,000

During 1987, Firmco received $5,250 in dividends from these investments. On December 31, 1987, the market values of the investments were:

Investment	Market Value
Window Company Common Stock	$28,000
Ocean Incorp. Common Stock	37,000
Marilyn Company Preferred Stock	16,000
Total	$81,000

Required:

A. Prepare journal entries to
   1. Record the receipt of dividends.
   2. Adjust the temporary equity securities portfolio as of December 31, 1987.
B. Explain where the accounts used in requirement (A.2.) should be reported in the financial statements on December 31, 1987.
C. Assume that the Window Company stock was sold on February 8, 1988, for $33,000, less a broker's fee of $1,000. Prepare the entry to record the sale.
D. If the total market value of the portfolio had been $106,000 on December 31, 1987, what entry would have been made? Explain.

Problem 7A-6 Recording Transactions Using a Voucher System

Gem Retailers completed the following transactions affecting vouchers payable during May.

May	1	Prepared voucher No. 531, payable to Sam Company for merchandise purchased, $975.60; invoice dated April 29; terms, 2/10, n/30.
	7	Prepared voucher No. 532, payable to Canyon Insurance for one year's insurance premiums, $370.
	8	Issued check No. 876, in payment of voucher No. 531.
	10	Prepared voucher No. 533 for sales salaries, $802.60, and administrative salaries, $1,010.40.
	10	Issued check No. 877, in payment of voucher No. 533. Cashed the check and distributed cash to employees.
	11	Issued check No. 878, in payment of voucher No. 532.
	18	Prepared voucher No. 534, payable to Safe Wholesalers for merchandise purchased, $1,426.82; invoice dated May 17; terms, 2/10, n/30.
	20	Prepared voucher No. 535, payable to Med Company for office furniture, $822.19; invoice dated May 18; terms, n/30.

22 Prepared voucher No. 536, payable to Electric Company, $526.87, for monthly utility bill.
23 Issued check No. 879, in payment of voucher No. 536.
24 Prepared voucher No. 537 for sales salaries, $892.80, and administrative salaries, $1,422.40.
24 Issued check No. 880, in payment of voucher No. 537. Cashed the check and distributed cash to employees.
26 Issued check No. 881, in payment of voucher No. 534.
28 Prepared voucher No. 538, payable to Bell Telephone Company for telephone bill, $90.30.
29 Prepared voucher No. 539, payable to Sam Company for merchandise purchased, $860.40; invoice dated May 27; terms, 2/10, n/30.

Required:

A. Prepare a voucher register and check register similar to those illustrated in this chapter and record the transactions in these registers. Set up separate debit columns for Purchases, Sales Salaries, Administrative Salaries, and Utilities Expense.

B. Post the appropriate amounts to a *Vouchers Payable* account (No. 516).

C. Prove the balance in the *Vouchers Payable* account by preparing a list of unpaid vouchers.

ALTERNATE PROBLEMS

Problem 7-1A Petty Cash Transactions

Carol Gordon set up a petty cash fund for her business and appointed an office secretary custodian of the fund. The following transactions and events affecting the petty cash fund were then completed.

1. Wrote a $100 check payable to the petty cash fund custodian to establish the petty cash fund.
2. Paid $17 for postage *(Postage Expense)*.
3. Paid $12 C.O.D. charges on merchandise purchased *(Delivery Expense)*.
4. Paid for janitorial supplies purchased, $14 *(Miscellaneous Expense)*.
5. Paid $15 for the repair of an office machine *(Repairs Expense)*.
6. Paid $5.50 for newspapers and magazines *(Miscellaneous Expense)*.
7. The custodian of the fund exchanged the receipts in the petty cash box for a check to reimburse the fund and to increase the size of the fund from $100 to $200.
8. Paid Statewide Delivery Service for the overnight delivery of an important contract, $21 *(Delivery Expense)*.
9. Paid $30.50 for the installation of a new regulator in the company's automobile *(Repairs Expense)*.
10. Paid $17.30 to have the office windows washed and carpet cleaned *(Miscellaneous Expense)*.
11. Paid $11.75 for coffee and supplies for the employee lounge *(Miscellaneous Expense)*.

Required:

Prepare general journal entries to

A. Establish the petty cash fund.
B. Replenish the fund after transaction (6) and increase its size to $200.
C. Replenish the fund after transaction (11).

Problem 7-2A Bank Reconciliation

Wales Company received its bank statement for the month of September, showing a bank balance of $4,188.30. The cash balance on Wales Company's books on September 30 was $4,029.30. The following reconciling items were identified.

1. Outstanding checks amounted to $489.11.
2. Debit memos were included with the bank statement as follows.
   (a) A $225.00 check received from a customer (Nuber Company) and deposited by Wales Company was returned marked "NSF."
   (b) Service charges for the month were $12.
   (c) Check printing charge, $15.
3. A credit memo received with the bank statement indicated that a note receivable in the amount of $500 plus interest of $63 had been collected by the bank. The bank charged a collection fee of $20 and credited the remaining $543 to Wales Company's account.
4. A deposit of $641.11 was in transit on September 30.
5. The bookkeeper discovered that check No. 103 in the amount of $311, in payment of insurance expense, had been incorrectly recorded on the books as $331.

Required:
A. Prepare a bank reconciliation as of September 30.
B. Prepare any adjusting general journal entries required.

Problem 7-3A Bank Reconciliation with Errors

The March bank statement and general ledger cash accounts of Harrison Company are given below.

Bank Statement			
	Debits	Credits	Balance
Balance, March 1			$ 4,555
Deposits recorded during March		$26,000	30,555
Checks paid during March	$23,700		6,855
NSF check—M. L. Douglas	290		6,665
Bank service charges	20		6,645
Balance, March 31			6,645

Cash

March 1 balance	4,855	March checks written	25,750
March deposits	27,500		

Petty Cash

March 31 balance	150		

Cash on hand for making change (included in the *Cash* account) on March 1 and March 31 was $300.

Required:
A. Prepare a bank reconciliation. (*Hint:* You might find an error made either by the bank or by the company.)

B. Prepare any adjusting general journal entries necessary.

C. What total amount of cash should be reported on the March 31 balance sheet?

Problem 7-4A Bank Reconciliation

The accountant for Ollie Company gathered the following information concerning cash transactions and cash balances for the month of August.

1. The general ledger cash account had a balance of $4,660.50 on August 1.
2. Total cash receipts and cash disbursements during August were: cash receipts, $16,382.45; cash disbursements, $14,008.90.
3. The August bank statement showed a cash balance of $6,866.55 on August 31.
4. Outstanding checks at the end of August were: No. 230, $56.70; No. 233, $211.20; and No. 248, $370.50.
5. Included with the bank statement were:
   (a) A check written by Chin Company (a customer) for $530.75 marked NSF.
   (b) A debit memo for service charges, $9.
   (c) A credit memo for $563 indicating the collection of a note receivable of $500, plus interest which the bank had credited to Ollie Company's account.
6. Cash receipts for the last day of August amounting to $848.15 were placed in the bank's night depository on August 31 and were not included in the August bank statement.
7. Comparison of the cancelled checks with the entries in the cash disbursements journal disclosed that check No. 241 for $635, written in payment of utilities expense, had been incorrectly recorded as $654.

Required:

A. Prepare a bank reconciliation as of August 31.

B. Prepare general journal entries to adjust the accounts.

C. What is the amount of cash that should be reported on the August 31 balance sheet?

Problem 7-5A Temporary Investments Portfolios

During 1987, Choiseul Company's transactions in temporary marketable securities were as follows.

1. On March 2, Choiseul Company purchased 2,500 shares of Flander Inc. common stock for $75,000 and 1,000 shares of Top Chemical Company common stock for $28,000, including brokers' fees.
2. On April 7, Choiseul Company purchased U.S. government bonds for $90,000 plus $1,800 for accrued interest and $500 for the broker's fee.
3. On May 23, Choiseul Company purchased 148 shares of Yellow Aircraft preferred stock for $6,660, plus brokers' fees of $700.
4. On July 1, interest of $3,600 was received on the U.S. government bonds.
5. On July 6, Choiseul Company received a $1.50 per share dividend on its Top Chemical common stock.
6. On August 15, Choiseul Company sold 1,500 shares of its Flander Inc. common stock for $31 per share.
7. On September 10, Choiseul Company purchased additional U.S. government bonds for $30,500 (including brokers' fees) plus $534 for accrued interest.

December 31, 1987 market values of Choiseul Company's temporary investments were:

Flander Inc. common stock	$14,000
Top Chemical common stock	30,000
U.S. government bonds, first purchase	90,000
Yellow Aircraft preferred stock	5,624
U.S. government bonds, second purchase	31,500

Accrued interest on all U.S. government bonds on December 31 amounted to $4,668. Choiseul Company separates its debt and equity investments in its balance sheet.

Required:

A. Prepare all journal entries needed to record these transactions.

B. Prepare the descriptions and amounts to be reported on Choiseul Company's income statement and balance sheet on December 31, 1987.

Problem 7A-6A Recording Transactions Using a Voucher System

Peters, Moro, and Company began operations on November 1 and decided to use a voucher system to aid control of cash disbursements. During November, Peters, Moro, and Company completed the following transactions affecting vouchers payable.

Nov.	4	Prepared voucher No. 1, payable to Washington Company for merchandise purchased. $189.80; invoice dated November 2; terms, 3/10, n/60.
	6	Prepared voucher No. 2, payable to Treetop Realtors for November rent, $621.50.
	10	Prepared voucher No. 3, payable to Able Company for office equipment, $344.00; invoice dated November 9; terms, n/20.
	10	Prepared voucher No. 4 for employee wages, $822.60.
	11	Issued check No. 100, in payment of voucher No. 4. Cashed the check and distributed cash to employees.
	14	Issued check No. 101, in payment of voucher No. 1.
	15	Issued check No. 102, in payment of voucher No. 2.
	17	Prepared voucher No. 5, payable to Republic Company for merchandise purchased, $1,580.88; invoice dated November 17; terms, 2/10, n/30.
	20	Prepared voucher No. 6, payable to Ronnie Graphics for advertising, $336.71; invoice dated November 18; terms, n/30.
	21	Prepared voucher No. 7, payable to Mountain Power Company, $205.10 for monthly utility bill.
	23	Issued check No. 103, in payment of voucher No. 7.
	24	Prepared voucher No. 8 for employee wages, $2,100.40.
	24	Issued check No. 104, in payment of voucher No. 8. Cashed the check and distributed cash to employees.
	26	Issued check No. 105, in payment of voucher No. 5.
	29	Prepared voucher No. 9, payable to Two's Company for merchandise purchased, $89.90; invoice dated November 27; terms, 2/10, n/30.
	30	Issued check No. 106, in payment of voucher No. 3.

Required:

A. Prepare a voucher register and check register similar to those illustrated in this chapter and record the transactions in these registers. Set up separate debit columns for Purchases, Wages, and Utilities Expense.

B. Post the appropriate amounts to a *Vouchers Payable* account (No. 403).

C. Prove the November 30 balance in the *Vouchers Payable* account by preparing a list of unpaid vouchers.

CASE

CASE 7-1 Discussion Case   Internal Control Procedures

Jerry Barnes took over the management of his family's successful retail business shortly after graduating from Westwood University with a degree in economics. Because Jerry had little knowledge of internal control procedures, he relied heavily upon the company's new bookkeeper, Ted Crawford. Ted, with the help of an assistant bookkeeper, had full responsibility for keeping the company's accounting records, preparing financial statements, making bank deposits, preparing checks for payment for purchases and expenses, maintaining the petty cash fund, and preparing the monthly bank reconciliation.

The monthly income statements received by Jerry Barnes from Ted Crawford reported a highly satisfactory net income. However, Jerry noticed that the amount of cash in the bank was steadily declining. After several months he was forced to apply for a bank loan in order to meet his current obligations. The bank loan officer reviewed the company's financial statements and, expressing his belief that "there must be something wrong," recommended that Jerry review his operating procedures for cash receipts and disbursements. Upon return to the company's premises, Jerry announced that he intended to begin a review of operating procedures the next morning. On the following morning Ted Crawford did not report for work and telephone calls to his home went unanswered. With the help of a friend with some experience in accounting, Jerry began his review of cash procedures and discovered the following.

1. At the close of each business day, Ted Crawford removed the cash and the tape from the two cash registers, prepared a cash deposit ticket, and made the bank deposit in the night depository at the company's bank. He also prepared the daily cash receipts summary that was given to the assistant bookkeeper for the preparation of accounting entries. A comparison of daily cash register tapes with daily bank deposits showed that deposits were often much smaller than cash receipts.

2. Ted Crawford was custodian of the petty cash fund. For each payment from the fund, Ted prepared a petty cash receipt that he signed to verify the disbursement. Investigation showed that the $500 fund had been replenished frequently during the past several months.

3. Ted Crawford relieved the salesclerks and recorded cash sales on their registers during the salesclerks' lunch hours.

4. Ted Crawford prepared all purchase orders. He also approved payment of all purchase invoices, wrote and properly signed the check in payment, and mailed the payment to the vendor. Investigation revealed that payment was made to one company for several large purchases of store equipment that could not be located on the premises.

Required:

For each of the numbered paragraphs above, describe the internal control procedures that should be established to help prevent the occurrence of fraudulent events.

PART 3

ACCOUNTING FOR ASSETS AND LIABILITIES

8

ACCOUNTING FOR RECEIVABLES AND PAYABLES

CHAPTER OVERVIEW AND OBJECTIVES

This chapter describes the accounting treatment of short-term receivables and payables—those classified as current assets and current liabilities. When you have completed the chapter, you should understand:

1. The different types of short-term receivables and payables and how to account for them.
2. The nature of uncollectible accounts.
3. The difference between the income statement and balance sheet approaches to estimating bad debts expense.
4. How to compute and account for interest.
5. What is meant by discounting notes receivable and notes payable.

Today's U.S. economy is essentially a credit economy. Manufacturers, wholesalers, and retailers regularly extend credit to buyers of their goods and services as a means of increasing sales. The willingness of businesses to extend credit is an important factor in the significant growth of our economy. Most businesses not only extend credit to customers, which results in receivables, but also receive credit from suppliers, resulting in payables.

RECEIVABLES

Objective 1: Types of short-term receivables and payables

Receivables are amounts due from other persons or businesses. Although arising from various business transactions, receivables most often result from the sale of goods or services on credit. There are two common kinds of receivables.

Accounts Receivable When credit is extended to customers on open account, the buyer has a specified length of time, such as 30 or 60 days, before payment is due. These open accounts are called **accounts receivable** by the business granting credit.

Notes Receivable   Sometimes credit is granted only upon receipt of a formal legal instrument, such as a promissory note. A promissory note is a negotiable instrument. A **negotiable instrument** is a legal document that can be transferred to a third party by **endorsement.** An endorsement is a signature on the back of the instrument that assigns the rights therein to another party. To the grantor of credit a promissory note is a **note receivable.** Creditors often favor promissory notes because (1) they are generally interest-bearing (thereby producing interest revenue); and (2) they are easily converted into cash before their maturity dates because they can be transferred by endorsement to a bank or finance company. Promissory notes are generally used for transactions that have a long payment period, such as sales on an installment plan or sales of large items like machinery or equipment. A promissory note is also often demanded by the creditor when a customer requests an extension of payment of an open account.

Other types of receivables include amounts receivable from officers and employees for loans or salary advances, amounts receivable from the sale of assets other than inventory, and amounts receivable from lending money to affiliated companies or outside parties.

CLASSIFICATION OF RECEIVABLES

Accounts and notes receivable that arise from the sale of merchandise or services in the normal course of business are sometimes called **trade receivables.** They are normally classified as current assets on the balance sheet because they are scheduled for collection in cash within the operating cycle. Other receivables, such as those from officers and employees and from the sale of nonmerchandise assets, are called *nontrade receivables.* They are considered current assets if they are to be collected within one year or within the operating cycle, whichever is longer; otherwise, they are classified as noncurrent assets under the caption ''Other assets.'' Receivables from officers and employees generally must be reported separately.

To facilitate the proper classification and reporting of receivables, a general ledger account should be used for each type. Subsidiary ledgers should be provided where necessary.

ACCOUNTS RECEIVABLE

Accounts receivable arise from the sale of goods or services on open account. Although businesses would prefer to collect the sales price at the time of sale, experience has shown that extending credit can sometimes increase revenue and net income significantly by major increases in sales volume. However, to accomplish an increase in net income, the additional gross profit generated by credit sales must exceed the additional expenses incurred in extending credit. These expenses include investigation of the creditworthiness of prospective customers, additional recordkeeping, and provision for uncollectible accounts. The lack of adequate control of receivables is often a major cause of business failures.

No business wants to extend credit to a customer who is unlikely to pay the account when due. Therefore, most large companies maintain a credit department. The credit department has responsibility for investigating the credit history and determining the debt-paying ability of customers who apply for credit. If the customer is a business, the credit department normally requests a set of its audited financial statements for use in judging its ability to pay. If the customer is an individual, the credit department will ask for information about current earnings, current expenses, outstanding debts, and general financial position. In addition, the credit department normally obtains a credit report from a local or national credit-rating agency that accumulates data on the credit history of individuals and businesses.

Uncollectible Accounts

Objective 2: Nature of uncollectible accounts

Regardless of the diligence and care exercised in extending credit, there are always some customers who do not pay their accounts. Credit department personnel may have misjudged a customer's ability to pay, or financial reverses may result in an inability to pay. A downturn in general economic conditions often results in an increase in business failures and personal bankruptcies, resulting in uncollectible accounts to those who have extended credit. Business managers know that some of the accounts receivable will eventually prove to be uncollectible when they make the decision to sell goods and services on credit. These uncollectible accounts, called **bad debts**, are considered an expense of doing business on a credit basis.

The matching principle requires that the expense of uncollectible accounts be deducted in the same accounting period in which the credit sales were recognized. There is no general rule for determining the time at which a receivable actually becomes uncollectible. The fact that the debtor fails to pay the receivable on its due date does not by itself establish uncollectibility. The debtor may simply have forgotten to pay or may be temporarily short of cash and cannot pay until later.

The creditor normally will make a continued effort to collect past-due accounts through oral or written communication with the debtor, and may eventually turn the receivable over to a collection agency or begin legal action. This process may take several months or years to complete, with receivables arising in one accounting period being collected or written off in the following accounting period or later. Because there is no way of telling in advance which accounts will become uncollectible, bad debts expense is estimated at the end of the accounting period by the allowance method of accounting for uncollectible accounts.

Allowance Method of Accounting for Uncollectible Accounts

At the end of the accounting period, before the books are closed and the financial statements prepared, an estimate is made of the amount of accounts receivable expected to become uncollectible. An adjusting entry is prepared with a debit to *Bad Debts Expense* and a credit to an account called **Allowance for Uncollectible Accounts.**

To illustrate, assume that Cardon Company began operations in January, 1987, made credit sales in the amount of $400,000 during 1987, and collected $300,000 of these accounts during the year. The balance in the *Accounts Receivable* account at the end of the year is therefore $100,000. After a careful review of the accounts receivable, the management of Cardon Company estimated that $6,000 of the accounts will be uncollectible. An adjusting entry is made on December 31, 1987, the end of the fiscal year for Cardon Company, as follows.

Dec.	31	Bad Debts Expense	6,000	
		Allowance for Uncollectible Accounts		6,000
		To record estimated bad debts expense.		

The entry serves two important purposes. First, it records the estimated bad debts of $6,000 as an expense of the period in which the revenue from credit sales is recognized, thereby properly matching expenses and revenues. Thus, bad debts expense is deducted as an administrative expense on the income statement for 1987. Second, the entry establishes an allowance account that is deducted from accounts receivable (i.e., a contra account) on the balance sheet in order to report accounts receivable at the estimated amount expected to be collected (the expected realizable value of accounts receivable).

The Allowance for Uncollectible Accounts.   Rather than crediting *Accounts Receivable* directly when recording the entry for estimated bad debts, the allowance account is credited. This is because the general ledger *Accounts Receivable* account is a control account supported by a subsidiary ledger that identifies the amounts owed by individual customers. Any debit or credit to the *Accounts Receivable* control account requires a like debit or credit to one or more of the subsidiary-ledger accounts. However, it is impossible to determine in advance which specific accounts will prove uncollectible. A direct credit to the *Accounts Receivable* control account would produce an imbalance between it and the accounts receivable subsidiary ledger, thereby destroying an important element of internal control. The alternative is to credit an *Allowance* account. When the allowance account is subtracted from accounts receivable on the balance sheet, accounts receivable are reported at their realizable value as shown in Figure 8–1.

Estimating the Amount of Bad Debts Expense

The estimate of the amount of bad debts is generally based on a combination of past experience and best-guess forecasts of future economic and business conditions. Considerable personal judgment is involved. The goal is to produce a reasonable estimate of the amount of accounts receivable that eventually will be collected in cash. However, the practice of conservatism in accounting often comes into play, and accountants may have a tendency to estimate the

Figure 8–1
Allowance for Uncollectible Accounts

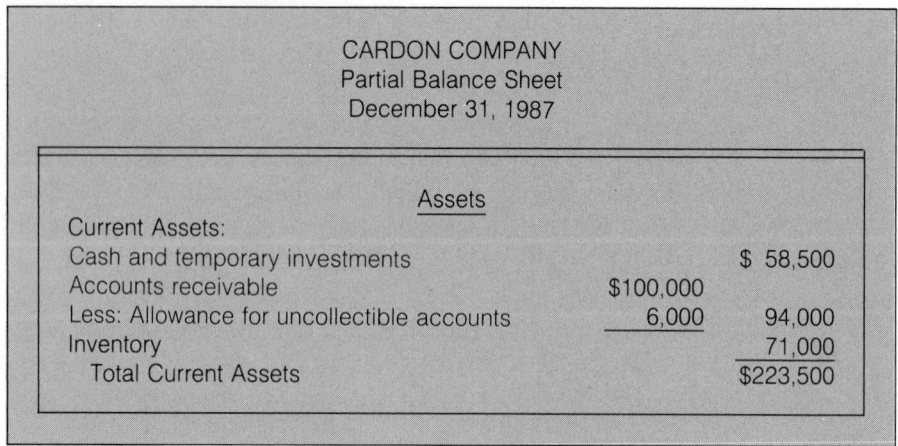

CARDON COMPANY
Partial Balance Sheet
December 31, 1987

Assets

Current Assets:

Cash and temporary investments		$ 58,500
Accounts receivable	$100,000	
Less: Allowance for uncollectible accounts	6,000	94,000
Inventory		71,000
Total Current Assets		$223,500

Objective 3: Income statement vs. balance sheet approaches to estimating bad debts expense

uncollectible amount at the upper end of the "reasonable" range, to produce a relatively low asset value for accounts receivable, as well as a conservative net income figure.

Two methods are widely used to estimate bad debts expense. One method determines the amount as a percentage of net credit sales for the period. Because this method uses net credit sales (credit sales less credit sales returns and allowances, and discounts on credit sales) as a base, it is sometimes called the *income statement method.* This method places emphasis on the relationship between credit sales and uncollectible accounts and, therefore, is more in accordance with the matching principle.

The second method analyzes the age and probability of collection of the individual accounts receivable and is called **aging the accounts receivable** Since this method bases bad debts expense on an analysis of accounts receivable, it is often called the *balance sheet method.* Emphasis is placed on the estimated realizable value of accounts receivable on the balance sheet. Most firms will use either of these two methods, but not both.

Estimate Based on the Income Statement Method. An analysis of past accounting data usually shows some predictable percentage relationship between the amount of bad debts and the amount of net credit sales. This percentage is then applied to net credit sales for the period to estimate the amount of bad debts expense. The logic of this method is that credit sales produce the accounts receivable that may become uncollectible in the future. As an example, assume that past experience shows that about 1% of net credit sales each year have been uncollectible and that net credit sales for the year amounted to $847,000. The year-end adjustment to recognize bad debts expense would be:

Dec.	31	Bad Debts Expense	8,470	
		Allowance for Uncollectible Accounts		8,470
		To record bad debts expense for the year in the amount of 1% × $847,000.		

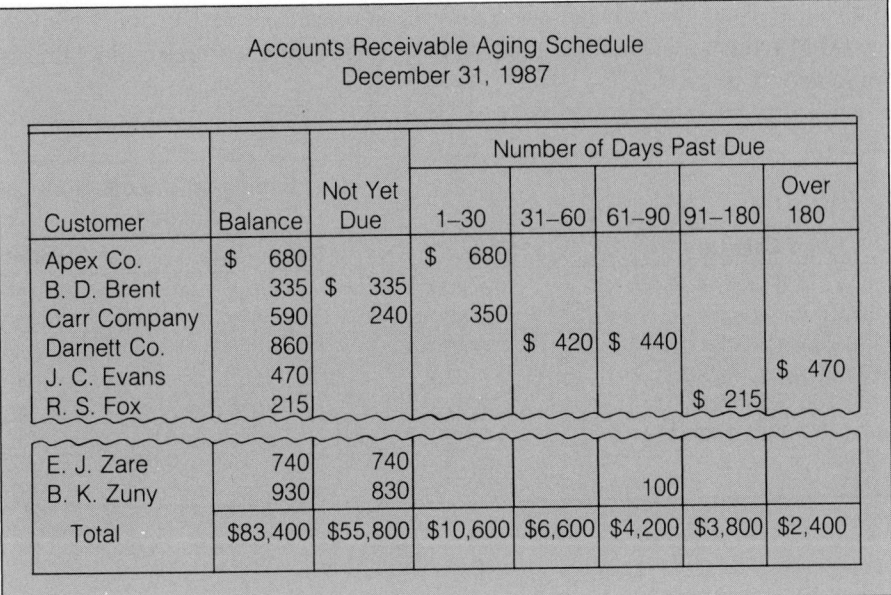

Figure 8–2
Accounts Receivable
Aging Schedule

Under this method, any existing balance in the *Allowance for Uncollectible Accounts* is ignored in computing the amount of bad debts expense. Basically, this method answers the question, "How much of this year's net credit sales is expected to be uncollectible?" The *Allowance for Uncollectible Accounts* is then adjusted by that amount.

Estimate Based on the Balance Sheet Method. If the estimate of bad debts expense is based on an analysis of the individual accounts receivable in the subsidiary ledger, the estimate is normally derived from a schedule on which the accounts receivable have been classified and analyzed by age. As already mentioned, the preparation of the schedule is called *aging the accounts receivable,* and generally takes the form shown in Figure 8–2.

The older an account receivable, the greater the probability that it will be uncollectible. Therefore, past accounting records are analyzed to determine the approximate percentage of each age group that will be uncollectible. For example, assume that an analysis of past accounting records shows the following percentages of accounts receivable that were written off as uncollectible.

Age Category	Percent
Not yet due	1%
1 to 30 days past due	5%
31 to 60 days past due	10%
61 to 90 days past due	20%
91 to 180 days past due	30%
Over 180 days past due	60%

With these data, the balance needed in the *Allowance For Uncollectible Accounts* to reduce the accounts receivable to their estimated realizable value is computed as follows:

Age Category	Amount	Estimated Uncollectible Accounts	
		Percentage	Amount
Not yet due	$55,800	1	$ 558
1 to 30 days past due	10,600	5	530
31 to 60 days past due	6,600	10	660
61 to 90 days past due	4,200	20	840
91 to 180 days past due	3,800	30	1,140
Over 180 days past due	2,400	60	1,440
Total	$83,400		$5,168

The total determined, $5,168, is the balance needed in the *Allowance for Uncollectible Accounts*. Consequently, any existing balance in the *Allowance* account must be taken into consideration in determining the amount of the year-end adjustment. For example, if the *Allowance for Uncollectible Accounts* has a $1,540 credit balance before adjustment, bad debts expense must be charged for the difference of $3,628 ($5,168 − $1,540) and the following adjusting entry prepared.

Dec.	31	Bad Debts Expense	3,628	
		Allowance for Uncollectible Accounts		3,628
		To record bad debts expense for the year.		

After this entry is posted, the *Accounts Receivable* and *Allowance for Uncollectible Accounts* will appear as follows.

Accounts Receivable

12/31 Balance	83,400	

Allowance for Uncollectible Accounts

	12/31 Balance before adjusting	1,540
	12/31 Adjustment	3,628
	12/31 Balance	5,168

Although the *Allowance for Uncollectible Accounts* will normally have a credit balance before the year-end adjustment, it may sometimes have a debit balance because more accounts than estimated in prior years actually became uncollectible. If write-offs during the period are less than the opening balance in the account, the account will have a credit balance at the end of the period before adjustment. If write-offs during the period exceed the opening balance, the account will have a debit balance at the end of the period before adjustment.

If the *Allowance for Uncollectible Accounts* has a debit balance (for example $260) before adjustment, that balance is added to the $5,168 and the total of $5,428 is debited to *Bad Debts Expense* and credited to the *Allowance for Uncollectible Accounts* to produce the desired balance of $5,168 in the allowance account. After the year-end adjustment to record bad debts expense, the *Allowance for Uncollectible Accounts* will always have a credit balance.

Rather than preparing an aging schedule, some companies simply analyze past data to determine a percentage relationship between uncollectible accounts and accounts receivable. This percentage is multiplied by the balance in accounts receivable at the end of the year to determine the balance needed in the *Allowance for Uncollectible Accounts*. The allowance account is then adjusted to that balance.

For example, rather than aging the accounts, assume that the company in the previous example observed from past experience that about 6% of the year-end balance of accounts receivable eventually was uncollectible. Thus, the balance needed in the *Allowance* account is $5,004 (6% × $83,400). Since there is a balance of $1,540 in the *Allowance* account before adjustment, an adjusting entry for $3,464 ($5,004 − $1,540) is needed and the following entry is prepared.

Dec.	31	Bad Debts Expense	3,464	
		Allowance for Uncollectible Accounts		3,464
		To record bad debts expense for the year.		

Writing Off an Uncollectible Account

When an account receivable is determined to be uncollectible, it is written off against the *Allowance for Uncollectible Accounts* by debiting the *Allowance* account and crediting *Accounts Receivable*. The related account in the accounts receivable subsidiary ledger is also credited. For example, assume that after an extended effort to collect, the $470 account of J. C. Evans is determined to be uncollectible. The following entry is made.

Dec.	31	Allowance for Uncollectible Accounts	470	
		Accounts Receivable—J. C. Evans		470
		To write off the account receivable as uncollectible.		

After the write-off entry is posted, the general ledger accounts appear as follows.

Accounts Receivable

12/31 Balance before write-off	83,400	12/31 Write-off	470
12/31 Balance	82,930		

Allowance for Uncollectible Accounts

12/31 Write-off	470	12/31 Balance before write-off	5,168
		12/31 Balance	4,698

Two important things should be noted concerning the write-off entry. First, the write-off is debited to the *Allowance for Uncollectible Accounts*, rather than to *Bad Debts Expense*. Expense was recognized on an estimated basis at the end of the year in which the sale was made. To charge an expense account again at the time the account is written off would result in a double recording of expense with a resulting understatement of net income. Second, the *net amount* of accounts receivable (the estimated realizable value) is unchanged by the entry to write off an uncollectible account, as shown below.

	Before Write-off	After Write-off
Accounts Receivable	$83,400	$82,930
Less: Allowance for Uncollectible Accounts	5,168	4,698
Estimated Realizable Value	$78,232	$78,232

The fact that the write-off did not change the net amount of accounts receivable clearly demonstrates the notion that no expense results from the write-off of an account receivable. The expense from uncollectible accounts is properly charged to the period in which the credit sale was made, rather than to the period in which the account is written off.

Recovery of an Account Written Off

In some cases, an account that has been written off will be collected in part or in full at a later date. If this occurs, the account receivable should be reestablished in the accounts, in order to maintain a complete history of the customer's activity. Assume, for example, that J. C. Evans underwent bankruptcy proceedings and that a final settlement of his account was received on May 4 in the amount of $250. The entry to reinstate the account receivable is:

May	4	Accounts Receivable—J. C. Evans	250	
		Allowance for Uncollectible Accounts		250
		To reestablish part of the account		
		receivable written off as uncollectible on		
		December 31.		

After the account is reestablished, the cash collection is recorded as usual by a debit to *Cash* and a credit to *Accounts Receivable—J. C. Evans*, as follows.

May	4	Cash	250	
		Accounts Receivable—J. C. Evans		250

Notice that the recovery of an account previously written off has no effect on net income—no revenue or expense account is involved.

Direct Write-Off Method

Although the allowance method is the one that properly matches expenses and revenues and is the method most widely used, some companies use the **direct**

write-off method. With this method, uncollectible accounts are charged to expense at the time an account is determined to be uncollectible. This is done by debiting *Bad Debts Expense* and crediting *Accounts Receivable.* No attempt is made to match expense with related revenue. The direct write-off method is, therefore, not generally accepted, and its use can be justified only on the basis of immateriality. Some companies sell goods and services primarily on a cash basis and make only occasional, small sales on account. Any uncollectible accounts written off will be small and, therefore, immaterial in relation to total revenue and net income.

In the event that an account previously written off is collected later, the collection is normally recorded by a debit to *Cash* and a credit to either *Bad Debts Expense,* if that account has a debit balance large enough to absorb it, or a credit to an appropriately titled miscellaneous revenue account, such as *Bad Debts Recovered.* The direct write-off method is often used for income tax purposes and, therefore, is sometimes called the ''income tax approach.''

NOTES RECEIVABLE

Sometimes credit is extended only upon receipt of a promissory note, often referred to simply as a *note.* A **promissory note** is an unconditional written promise to pay a sum, certain in money, on demand or at a future determinable date. The person making the promise to pay by signing the note is called the **maker** of the note. The person to whom payment is to be made is called the **payee.** In the note illustrated in Figure 8–3, DMF Corporation is the maker and Baker Wholesale Company is the payee. To Baker Wholesale, the note is a *note receivable,* and to DMF Corporation it is a *note payable.*

If the note bears interest, it is called an *interest-bearing note.* The interest rate must be specified and is usually expressed as a rate (such as 10%) per year. If no interest rate is specified, the note is called a *noninterest-bearing note.* **Interest** is a charge made for the use of money. To the payee, interest is revenue; to the maker of the note it is an expense.

The dollar amount printed on the note is called its **face value,** or **principal.** The amount due on the maturity date of the note is called the **maturity value.**

Figure 8–3
A Promissory Note

$3,000		Los Angeles, Calif. _February 12_ 19 _87_
90 days	after date	_we_
promise to pay to the order of		_Baker Wholesale Company_
three thousand and 00/100--- dollars
payable at	_United Bank of Los Angeles_
for value received with interest at	_10%_
		DMF Corporation
		Jake Smith
		Treasurer

The maturity value of an interest-bearing note is the sum of its face value plus interest. The maturity value of a noninterest-bearing note is its face value.

Computing Interest

**Objective 4:
Computing and
accounting for
interest**

The formula for computing interest is:

$$\text{Principal} \times \text{Rate} \times \text{Time} = \text{Interest}$$

Interest rates are normally stated in terms of an annual rate. Thus the interest rate of 10% on the note illustrated is an annual interest rate. If the term of the note is expressed in days, the exact number of days should be used to compute interest. For convenience, however, it is generally assumed that a year contains 360 days. Therefore, interest on the note illustrated is computed as follows.

$$\text{Principal} \times \text{Rate} \times \frac{\text{days}}{360} = \text{Interest}$$

or

$$\$3,000 \times 10\% \times \frac{90}{360} = \$75$$

On the maturity date of the note, DMF Corporation must pay the maturity value of $3,075 ($3,000 principal plus $75 interest).

Determining Due Date

The period of time from the issue date of a note to its due date is generally expressed in days or months, and the date on which the note is due is called the **maturity date.** If expressed in months, the note is due in the month of its maturity on the day of the month it was issued. Thus a four-month note issued on February 14 has a due date of June 14; a two-month note issued on December 30 is due on February 28, since February does not have 30 days. In computing interest, each month is considered to be $\frac{1}{12}$ of a year; therefore, interest on the four-month note would be computed by taking $\frac{4}{12}$ of the annual interest amount.

If a note is expressed in days, the maturity date is computed as follows, assuming a 90-day note dated February 14.

Term of the note in days		90
Number of days in February	28	
Date of Note	14	
Number of days outstanding in February		14
Number of days remaining		76
Number of days in March		31
Number of days remaining		45
Number of days in April		30
Due date in May		15

Accounting for Receipt and Collection of a Note

A single *Notes Receivable* account is normally maintained in the general ledger. The *Notes Receivable* account is a control account, with a subsidiary ledger consisting of a file of the actual notes received, arranged in order of due date.

No other record is necessary because the notes themselves contain all the information needed—the maker, maturity date, and interest rate.

To illustrate the accounting for a note receivable, assume that Cardon Company has an account receivable from Dennis Mead in the amount of $1,500, which is past due. Mead requested a 90-day extension of the payment date, and Cardon Company agreed by accepting a 90-day, 10% note in exchange for the account receivable. Upon receipt of the note, Cardon Company would make the following entry.

July	9	Notes Receivable	1,500	
		Accounts Receivable—Dennis Mead		1,500
		To record the receipt of a note in		
		settlement of an account receivable.		

This entry simply substitutes a note receivable for the account receivable. If a note had been received at the time of the original sale, the entry just shown would be the same, except that the credit would be to *Sales* rather than to *Accounts Receivable*.

On October 7, when Mead pays the note, the entry in general journal form is:

Oct.	7	Cash	1,537.50	
		Notes Receivable		1,500.00
		Interest Revenue		37.50
		To record collection of a note receivable		
		from Dennis Mead. ($1,500 × 10% ×		
		90/360)		

Dishonored Notes Receivable

If a maker of a note fails to pay on the maturity date, the note is said to have been **dishonored** and the maker is said to have *defaulted* on the note. Because the maturity date has passed, the note is no longer negotiable and cannot be sold. However, the maker is not relieved from legal responsibility for the debt, and the payee will make the normal effort to collect. For these reasons, the payee generally transfers the claim, including any interest due, to an *Accounts Receivable* account.

To illustrate, assume that in the previous illustration Dennis Mead failed to pay the note on its maturity date. Cardon Company would make the following entry.

Oct.	8	Accounts Receivable—Dennis Mead	1,537.50	
		Notes Receivable		1,500.00
		Interest Revenue		37.50
		To record Dennis Mead's dishonored		
		note.		

This entry removes the note from the *Notes Receivable* account and reinstates an account receivable from Mead, thereby maintaining a complete history concerning his payment activities. The *Notes Receivable* account will then contain only those notes that have not yet matured and, therefore, represent collectible items.

Notice that the account receivable includes the interest on the note, which was credited to *Interest Revenue* even though it has not yet been collected. Mr. Mead's legal obligation to Cardon Company is for the maturity value of the note—principal and interest—and his account should contain the full amount owed. In addition, since interest is earned over time, the accrued interest on the note is revenue of the current period.

Discounting Notes Receivable

**Objective 5:
Discounting
notes receivable
and notes payable**

One of the positive features of a note receivable is its relative ease of conversion to cash before its maturity date. The note may be endorsed by the holder and sold to a bank in exchange for cash. The bank then holds the note until its maturity date, when it expects to collect the maturity value from its maker.

This process is called *discounting notes receivable* because the bank will deduct in advance an interest charge, called a **discount.** The discount is based on the maturity value of the note for the period the bank will hold the note (called the **discount period**). The discount period is the time between the date the note is transferred to the bank and its due date. The maturity value of the note less the discount deducted is called the **proceeds.** The proceeds are paid to the endorser by the bank.

To illustrate, assume that Cardon Company received a $2,000, 90-day, 10% note dated March 16 from Frank Morgan, a customer. Cardon Company held the note until April 15, when it discounted it at a bank at a discount rate of 12%. Since the maturity date of the note is June 14 (15 days in March, 30 days in April, 31 days in May, and 14 days in June total 90 days), the bank will hold the note for 60 days (15 days in April, 31 days in May, and 14 days in June total 60 days). The period of time that the bank holds the note before its collection is the discount period, for which the bank will charge interest (discount) at 12%. The bank will deduct from the maturity value of the note 60 days' interest at 12%, and give Cardon Company the proceeds as follows.

Face Value of the Note	$2,000
Interest at 10% for 90 days ($2,000 × 10% × 90/360)	50
Maturity Value	2,050
Less: Discount at 12% for 60 days ($2,050 × 12% × 60/360)	41
Proceeds	$2,009

The entry to record the discounting of the note by Cardon Company would be:

Apr.	15	Cash	2,009	
		Notes Receivable		2,000
		Interest Revenue		9
		Discounted Frank Morgan's note at the bank at 12%.		

The excess of the proceeds received over the face value of the note is recorded as interest revenue. It represents the amount of interest that Cardon Company would have earned if it had held the note to maturity ($50), less the amount of interest deducted as discount by the bank when it purchased the note ($41). In this case, the proceeds exceed the face value of the note, resulting in interest revenue. If the proceeds are less than the face value, the difference is debited to *Interest Expense*. For example, if the note had been discounted by Cardon Company on March 31 at 18%, the proceeds would be:

Maturity value of the note	$2,050
Less: Discount at 18% for 75 days	
($2,050 × 18% × 75/360)	77 (rounded)
Proceeds	$1,973

The entry to record the discounting would be:

Apr.	1	Cash	1,973	
		Interest Expense	27	
		Notes Receivable		2,000
		Discounted Frank Morgan's note at the bank at 18%.		

Contingent Liability. A discounted note must be endorsed by the payee. The payee then becomes contingently liable for payment of the note, unless the endorsement is made without recourse, that is, unless it contains the words "without recourse" as part of the endorsement. *Without recourse* means that the endorser cannot be held liable if the maker of the note defaults. Because banks will seldom accept notes without recourse, the payee of most discounted notes has a contingent liability.

Contingent liability means that the endorser (Cardon Company in our illustration) must pay the maturity value of the note ($2,050) on its maturity date if the maker (Frank Morgan) fails to do so. Therefore, the discounting of the note creates a contingent liability for Cardon Company that continues until the due date of the note. If the maker pays the note on its due date, the contingent liability ceases. If the maker defaults, the contingent liability becomes an actual, that is, a real liability for Cardon Company, and Cardon Company must pay the note.

The nature and amount of any contingent liability must be disclosed in the financial statements. Consequently, the contingent liability for discounted notes receivable must be disclosed if a balance sheet is prepared earlier than the maturity date of the notes. Disclosure is normally made by a footnote to the financial statements that explains the nature and amount of the contingent liability. For example, White Consolidated Industries, Inc. included the following footnote in its 1984 annual report.

Note M—Contingencies
The Corporation is contingently liable at December 31, 1984, for certain notes receivable . . . sold with recourse ($11,870,000), for dealer finance

repurchase agreements ($26,310,000) and other obligations, all aggregating approximately $44,200,000. In the opinion of management, losses, if any, will be insignificant.

Dishonor of a Discounted Note

Normally, the bank collects a discounted note directly from the maker, so that no further obligation remains for the endorser. If a maker fails to pay on the maturity date, however, the note has been *dishonored* and the bank is required by law to notify the endorser promptly that it intends to collect from the endorser. To accomplish this, the bank normally protests the dishonored note by sending the endorser a notarized statement called a *notice of protest.* A fee called a **protest fee** is often assessed by the bank when a dishonored note is protested, and the endorser is legally obligated to pay the maturity value of the note, plus the protest fee. When the endorser pays the bank, the amount paid is recorded as a receivable from the maker of the note.

As an example, assume in the previous illustration that instead of paying the $2,050 due on the note on its maturity date, Frank Morgan dishonored it and the bank sent Cardon Company a notice of protest and assessed a protest fee of $20. Cardon Company will pay the bank and make the following entry.

June	15	Accounts Receivable—Frank Morgan	2,070	
		Cash		2,070
		To establish a receivable for a dishonored note.		

The amount of the account receivable is computed as follows.

Note Receivable	$2,000
Interest	50
Protest Fee	20
Total	$2,070

Cardon Company will make the normal effort to collect the receivable from Frank Morgan. If this fails, the receivable will be written off against the *Allowance for Uncollectible Accounts.*

End-of-period Adjustment for Interest Revenue

Interest is a function of time, that is, interest is earned as time passes. When an interest-bearing note receivable is held at the end of the accounting period, accrued interest should be computed and recorded to recognize the interest earned, as well as interest receivable. For example, assume that Cardon Company received a $4,000, 75-day, 12% note on November 1. On December 31, the end of the fiscal year for Cardon Company, the following adjusting entry will be made to accrue interest for 60 days on the note.

Dec.	31	Interest Receivable	80	
		Interest Revenue		80
		To accrue interest on a note receivable.		
		($4,000 × 12% × 60/360)		

This entry results in the recognition of interest revenue during the period when it was earned and establishes a receivable for interest to be reported as a current asset on the December 31 balance sheet.

When the note is collected on January 15, the collection is recorded as follows, assuming that reversing entries are not made.

Jan.	15	Cash	4,100	
		Notes Receivable		4,000
		Interest Receivable		80
		Interest Revenue		20
		To record collection of a note receivable.		

This entry eliminates the note and the interest receivable, and recognizes $20 of interest revenue for the 15 days the note was held during the current accounting period.

PAYABLES

Payables are the opposite of receivables, representing amounts due to creditors of the business. They result from various transactions, such as the purchase of merchandise or other assets on credit and from borrowing money from banks or finance companies. The business also may owe amounts for accrued expenses, such as salaries and wages due to employees, interest accrued on loans, and taxes due to governmental agencies. Payables are also called liabilities.

CLASSIFICATION OF PAYABLES

Payables are classified into two broad groups, current liabilities and long-term liabilities, based on the time they are due. *Current liabilities* are those obligations that must be settled within one year or within the operating cycle, whichever is longer. They require the use of current assets (or the incurring of other current liabilities) to eliminate them. Among the common current liabilities are accounts payable, short-term notes payable, unearned revenue, and accrued expenses. *Long-term liabilities* are those whose settlement date is beyond one year or the operating cycle, and generally include mortgage notes payable, bonds payable, and obligations for employee pensions. Accounting for current liabilities is discussed here. Payroll liabilities are discussed in Chapter 12, and long-term liabilities in Chapter 17.

Objective 1: Types of short-term receivables and payables

Accounts Payable

Accounts payable designates amounts owed to creditors for the purchase of merchandise, supplies, and services in the normal course of business. Because they are not evidenced by a formal debt instrument, such as a note, they often are referred to as *open accounts* or *payables*. Each time merchandise, supplies, or services are acquired on open account, the appropriate asset or expense account is debited and *Accounts Payable* is credited.

Short-term Notes Payable

Notes payable differ from accounts payable in that the liability is evidenced by a promissory note. They are often issued when a business borrows money from a bank. In some industries it is normal practice for the purchaser of merchandise to give a note payable to the seller at the time of purchase, as we have seen. Other transactions that result in notes payable are purchases of relatively high-cost items of machinery or equipment, and the substitution of a note payable for a past-due open account payable.

Note Issued for a Bank Loan. When money is borrowed from a bank, the borrower may issue an interest-bearing note payable to the bank, under which the borrower agrees to repay the amount of the note plus interest on its maturity date. For example, assume that Cardon Company borrowed $20,000 from a bank on June 1, and signed a six-month note for $20,000 at an interest rate of 12%. The journal entry on Cardon Company's books to record the note would be:

June	1	Cash	20,000	
		Notes Payable		20,000
		Borrowed $20,000 for 6 months at 12%.		

No interest is recorded on the note until it is paid on December 1, when the entry would be:

Dec.	1	Notes Payable	20,000	
		Interest Expense	1,200	
		Cash		21,200
		Paid a note payable plus interest		
		($20,000 × 12% × 6/12 = $1,200).		

Objective 5: Discounting notes receivable and notes payable

In this illustration, the note provided for the payment of its face value, plus interest at a stipulated rate. The borrower received the face amount of the note at the time that it was given to the bank, and repaid the amount plus interest on the maturity date. As an alternative, banks sometimes have the borrower sign a note for the amount to be repaid at maturity. Interest is deducted in advance, and the borrower receives the difference between the face value of the note and the amount of interest deducted, the proceeds. This practice is called discounting a note payable. Using this practice, the note in the preceding illustration would be recorded by Cardon Company as follows.

June	1	Cash	18,800	
		Discount on Notes Payable	1,200	
		Notes Payable		20,000
		Discounted a 6-month, $20,000 note at		
		12%.		

The discount on notes payable is deducted from notes payable as a contra liability in the current liability section of the balance sheet as shown here.

Current Liabilities

Accounts payable		$46,500
Notes payable	$20,000	
Less: Discount on notes payable	1,200	18,800
Accrued expenses		6,700
Total Current Liabilities		$72,000

Because the discount on notes payable represents interest deducted in advance, it will be transferred to interest expense over the term of the note. In our illustration, the maturity date of the note falls within the same year as the issue date. Thus, the discount will be charged to interest expense when the note is paid on December 1, as follows.

Dec.	1	Notes Payable	20,000	
		Interest Expense	1,200	
		Discount on Notes Payable		1,200
		Cash		20,000
		Paid a $20,000 note payable.		

Discounting a noninterest-bearing note increases the effective annual interest rate on the loan, as compared to borrowing on an interest-bearing note. This results because the same amount of interest is paid under either method, but the borrower has the use of less money under the discounting method. If the effective interest rate on a $20,000, one-year, 12% interest-bearing note is compared with the effective interest rate on a $20,000, one-year note discounted at 12%, we obtain the following results.

	Annual Interest Amount	Amount Borrowed	Effective Interest Rate
Interest-bearing Note	$2,400	$20,000	12.00%*
Discounted Note	2,400	17,600	13.64%**

*$2,400/$20,000
**$2,400/$17,600

End-of-period Adjustments for Interest

When a note payable is issued in one accounting period and matures in another, an adjusting entry must be made at the end of the first period to allocate interest expense properly. For example, assume that the $20,000, six-month, 12% note of Cardon Company in the previous illustration was issued on November 1, rather than on June 1. Since the note is interest-bearing, an adjusting entry is needed on December 31 to accrue interest expense for two months, as follows.

Dec.	31	Interest Expense	400	
		Interest Payable		400
		To accrue interest at 12% for two months		
		on a $20,000 note. ($20,000 × 12% ×		
		2/12)		

When the note is paid on May 1, the following entry is prepared.

May	1	Notes Payable	20,000	
		Interest Payable	400	
		Interest Expense	800	
		Cash		21,200
		To record payment of a note plus interest.		

The adjustment process would be slightly different if the note had been discounted at 12% on November 1. The year-end adjustment would then be:

Dec.	31	Interest Expense	400	
		Discount on Notes Payable		400
		To record interest for two months on		
		discounted note.		

The entry to record payment of the note on May 1 is:

May	1	Notes Payable	20,000	
		Interest Expense	800	
		Discount on Notes Payable		800
		Cash		20,000
		Paid a $20,000 discounted note.		

In either case, the amount of interest expense allocated to each accounting period is the same; $400 to the period in which the note was issued and $800 to the following period.

Other Current Liabilities

In addition to accounts payable and short-term notes payable, other payables are reported as current liabilities because they will require the use of current assets or the incurring of other current liabilities to settle the obligation. Expenses incurred but unpaid at the end of the period are accrued for such items as interest on notes payable, rent, and wages due employees in order to include them in the accounting period in which they were incurred. Any portion of long-term debt that matures within one year is also reported as a current liability. In addition, cash received for goods or services before it is earned, such as rent received in advance and magazine subscriptions received by a publishing company, is classified as a current liability. These cash advances are often called *deferred revenue* or *unearned revenue* such as unearned subscription revenue. They are classified as current liabilities because they will normally be earned within the operating cycle or a period of one year, whichever is longer.

GLOSSARY

ACCOUNTS PAYABLE. Amounts owed to creditors for the purchase of merchandise, supplies, and services in the normal course of business (p. 353).

ACCOUNTS RECEIVABLE. Amounts due from customers for sales or services performed on credit (p. 339).

AGING OF ACCOUNTS RECEIVABLE. The process of classifying accounts receivable on the basis of the length of time they have been outstanding (p. 342).

ALLOWANCE FOR UNCOLLECTIBLE ACCOUNTS. The estimated amount of accounts receivable expected to be uncollectible (p. 341).

BAD DEBTS. The estimated amount of expense resulting from accounts receivable that are expected to be uncollectible (p. 340).

CONTINGENT LIABILITY. A possible liability that may become actual if certain future events occur (p. 351).

DIRECT WRITE-OFF METHOD. The recognition of a bad debt expense at the time an account receivable is deemed to be uncollectible (p. 346).

DISCOUNT. Interest deducted in advance (p. 350).

DISCOUNT PERIOD. The period of time for which a bank will charge interest on a discounted note (p. 350).

DISHONORED NOTE. A note that the maker has failed to pay on its maturity date (p. 349).

ENDORSEMENT. A signature on the back of a negotiable instrument that assigns the rights therein to another party (p. 339).

INTEREST. A charge made for the use of money, computed as principal $\times$ rate $\times$ time (p. 347).

MAKER. The person who promises to pay a note on its maturity date (p. 347).

MATURITY DATE. The date on which the maturity value of a note is due (p. 348).

MATURITY VALUE. The amount of a note due on its maturity date; it includes principal as well as interest (p. 347).

NEGOTIABLE INSTRUMENT. A legal document that can be transferred to another party by an endorsement (p. 339).

NOTE PAYABLE. An obligation evidenced by a formal written promise to pay (p. 354).

NOTE RECEIVABLE. A receivable evidenced by a formal written promise to pay (p. 339).

PAYEE. The person to whom a promissory note is made payable (p. 347).

PRINCIPAL (FACE VALUE). The face amount of a note (p. 347).

PROCEEDS. The maturity value of a note less discount (p. 350).

PROMISSORY NOTE. An unconditional written promise to pay a sum certain in money on demand or at a future determinable date (p. 347).

PROTEST FEE. A fee assessed by a bank when a note is dishonored (p. 352).

TRADE RECEIVABLES. Accounts and notes receivable that arise from the sale of merchandise or services in the normal course of business (p. 339).

DISCUSSION QUESTIONS

1. What is a note receivable? Why do creditors favor promissory notes over accounts receivable?
2. Where are accounts and notes receivable reported on the balance sheet?
3. Explain briefly how the allowance method of accounting for uncollectible accounts works.
4. Two methods are widely used to estimate bad debts expense. Name them and explain how each works.

5. What is the direct write-off method of accounting for uncollectible accounts? What is its main shortcoming?

6. What type of account is the *Allowance for Uncollectible Accounts*?

7. Explain how the *Allowance for Uncollectible Accounts* might have a debit balance before the end-of-period adjustment is made.

8. After the accounts are adjusted at the end of the fiscal year, *Accounts Receivable* has a balance of $135,000 and *Allowance for Uncollectible Accounts* has a balance of $7,000.
   (a) What is the realizable value of accounts receivable?
   (b) If a $1,000 account receivable is written off as uncollectible, what effect will the write-off have on the realizable value of accounts receivable?

9. A $700 account receivable is considered to be uncollectible and is to be written off. Give the journal entry to record the write-off, assuming that (a) the allowance method is used; and (b) the direct write-off method is used.

10. What entry is made when an account receivable that has been written off is collected in part or in full at a later date? Why?

For questions 11 through 17, assume a fiscal year-end of December 31.

11. A note dated June 8 provides for payment after 90 days of $1,000 plus interest at 10%. What is the face value, maturity value, and maturity date of the note?

12. On March 6, a company accepts a 90-day, 10% note with a face value of $5,000. Give the journal entry to record collection of the note at its maturity date.

13. Assume that the maker of the note in Question 12 defaulted on the note. Give the entry to record the default.

14. X Company received a $5,000, 90-day, 10% note dated July 9 from a customer and discounted it at a bank at 11% after holding the note for 30 days. How much will X Company receive from the bank? Give the journal entry to record the discounting of the note.

15. Brad Company issued a 120-day, 15% note payable dated February 16, to replace an account payable to Cleve Company in the amount of $10,000. Give the journal entries to record the issuance of the note payable and the payment of the note on its maturity date.

16. A company borrowed $5,000 from a bank and signed a six-month note payable dated May 1 for $5,000 at an interest rate of 15%. Give the entry to record payment of the note on its maturity date.

17. Assume the note in Question 16 was issued on October 1, rather than on May 1. What entry should be made on December 31 concerning the note?

18. What would the effective interest rate on the note in Question 16 be if the company had discounted the $5,000 note at a discount rate of 15%?

EXERCISES

XExercise 8-1 Accounting for Bad Debts

Marshall Company completed the following transactions.

Dec.	31	Based on past experience, Marshall Company estimates that 1% of the year's credit sales of $146,000 will be uncollectible.
Mar.	10	After a concerted effort to collect, an account receivable of $216 from Harmon Company was written off as uncollectible.

May   28   Harmon Company unexpectedly paid the amount written off on March 10.

Required:
Prepare journal entries.   *[handwritten: PartA. Debit balance in AUA 200   Part B Credit balance AUA 450]*

X Exercise 8-2 Accounting for Bad Debts

At the end of its fiscal year, December 31, Newby Company aged its accounts receivable and determined that an allowance for uncollectible accounts of $1,690 was needed to report accounts receivable at their realizable value.   *[handwritten: 1740]*

Required:
A. Prepare the entry to record *Bad Debts Expense,* assuming that the *Allowance For Uncollectible Accounts* currently has an $870 credit balance.
B. Prepare the entry to record *Bad Debts Expense,* assuming that the *Allowance For Uncollectible Accounts* currently has a $175 debit balance.
C. Prepare the entry to write off as uncollectible an $86 account receivable from R. D. Pinson.
D. Assume that before the entry recorded in C, the net amount of accounts receivable on Newby Company's books was $21,050. What is the net amount of accounts receivable after recording the write-off of the Pinson account? Why?

Exercise 8-3 Note Received in Exchange for Account Receivable

Flynn Company has an account receivable from Dave Roberts in the amount of $1,500 that is past-due. On March 3, Mr. Roberts requested a 90-day extension of the payment date, and Flynn Company agreed to accept a 90-day, 14% note in exchange for the account receivable.

[handwritten: 210]

Required:
A. Prepare a journal entry to record the receipt of the note.
B. Prepare a journal entry to record the receipt of payment of the note on its maturity date, assuming the fiscal year ends on December 31.
C. Assume that Mr. Roberts defaulted on the note on its maturity date. Prepare the journal entry that Flynn Company would make to record the default.

[handwritten: $1500 \times 14\% \times \frac{90}{360} =$ 52.50]

Exercise 8-4 Note Received in Exchange for Account Receivable

On December 1, Brooks Company accepted a $4,500, 90-day, 12% note from Jill Morgan in exchange for a $4,500 account receivable that was past due.

Required:
Prepare all entries that should be made for this note from the time of its receipt to the time of its collection. Brooks Company's fiscal year ends on December 31.

Exercise 8-5 Discounting a Note Receivable

Jorgen Company sold merchandise to Bailor Company and accepted a $6,000, 90-day, 10% note dated July 24 in payment. On September 22, Jorgen Company discounted the note at its bank at a discount rate of 14%. Bailor Company dishonored the note on its maturity date and the bank sent Jorgen Company a notice of protest, including a protest fee of $26. Jorgen Company paid the bank for the maturity value of the note, plus the protest fee. Jorgen Company's fiscal year ends on December 31.

Required:
A. Prepare the journal entry to record the receipt of the note.
B. Prepare the journal entry to record the discounting of the note by Jorgen Company.

C. Prepare the journal entry to record Jorgen Company's payment to the bank when the note was dishonored.

Exercise 8-6 Accounting for a Note Payable

Campo Company borrowed $8,000 from its bank on March 1 and signed a six-month, 11% note payable for $8,000.

Required:

A. Prepare journal entries to record the issue of the note and its payment on its maturity date. Campo Company's fiscal year ends on December 31.

B. Assume that the note was issued on October 1, rather than March 1. Prepare journal entries to record the issue of the note, the accrual of interest on December 31, and the payment of the note.

Exercise 8-7 Borrowing by Discounting a Note Payable

On November 1, Dorsey Company borrowed money by issuing a $15,000, six-month note payable to a local bank. The bank deducted interest at 14% and gave Dorsey Company the proceeds.

Required:

A. Prepare all entries needed to record the issue of the note, the adjustment for interest expense at year-end, and the payment of the note on its maturity date. Dorsey Company's fiscal year ends on December 31.

B. Compute the effective interest rate that Dorsey Company paid for the use of the borrowed money.

PROBLEMS

Problem 8-1 Accounting for Bad Debts

On January 1, Dram Company had *Accounts Receivable* of $168,400 and an *Allowance For Uncollectible Accounts* with a credit balance of $8,700. During January of the current year, the following transactions occurred.

1. Sales on account	$493,000
2. Sales returns and allowances on credit sales	12,600
3. Accounts receivable collected	510,500
4. Accounts written off as uncollectible	2,600

Based on an aging of accounts receivable on January 31, the company determined that the *Allowance For Uncollectible Accounts* should have a credit balance of $11,450 on the January 31 balance sheet.

Required:

A. Prepare journal entries to record the summary data in the four items above and to adjust the *Allowance For Uncollectible Accounts*.

B. Show how *Accounts Receivable* and the *Allowance For Uncollectible Accounts* would appear on the January 31 balance sheet.

C. On March 23, Brad Company, whose $1,360 account had been written off as uncollectible in January, paid its account in full. Prepare the journal entries to record the collection.

D. Assume that Dram Company bases its estimate of uncollectible accounts on net credit sales and that 1% of net credit sales is expected to become uncollectible. Prepare the entry to recognize bad debts expense and determine the balance in the *Allowance for Uncollectible Accounts*.

Problem 8-2 Accounting for Bad Debts

All transactions related to a company's uncollectible accounts for the fiscal year ended December 31 are presented in the following list.

Jan.	19	Wrote off the $340 account of Rocky Company as uncollectible.
Apr.	9	Reestablished the account of James Fulbright and recorded the collection of $950 in full payment of his account, which had been written off earlier.
July	31	Received 40% of the $600 balance owed by Carl Wilson and wrote off the remainder as uncollectible.
Aug.	15	Wrote off as uncollectible the accounts of Welch Company, $1,600, and D. Fleetman, $2,100.
Sept.	26	Received 25% of the $1,040 owed by Western Company and wrote off the remainder as uncollectible.
Oct.	16	Received $641 from D. Jackson in full payment of his account, which had been written off earlier as uncollectible.
Nov.	20	Recorded an account receivable for a $4,000, 11%, 90-day note of N. Vassar that was dishonored at maturity date.
Dec.	31	Estimated bad debts expense for the year to be 1½% of net credit sales of $421,000.

The *Accounts Receivable* account had a balance at December 31 of $114,630, and the beginning (January 1) balance in the *Allowance For Uncollectible Accounts* was $6,200.

Required:

A. Prepare journal entries for each of the transactions.

B. Determine (1) the balance in the *Allowance* account after the December 31 adjustment; and (2) the expected realizable value of the accounts receivable as of December 31.

C. Assume that instead of basing the allowance for uncollectibles on net credit sales, the estimate of uncollectible accounts is based on an aging of accounts receivable and that $7,050 of the accounts receivable as of December 31 were estimated to be uncollectible. Determine

  1. The adjustment necessary to bring the *Allowance* account to the desired balance.

  2. The expected realizable value of the accounts receivable as of December 31.

Problem 8-3 Comparison of Direct Write-off and Allowance Methods

Ventura Company has used the direct write-off method of recording uncollectible accounts since it began operations four years ago. Recently, the company has liberalized its credit policy, which has resulted in a significant increase in credit sales and, therefore, the amount of uncollectible accounts. In light of these facts, the company is considering a change to the allowance method of accounting for uncollectible accounts.

The following information was extracted from the accounting records.

Year	Net Credit Sales	Total of Accounts Written Off	Year of Origin of Accounts Receivable Written off as Uncollectible			
			1	2	3	4
1	$ 30,000	$ 300	$300			
2	50,000	550	120	$430		
3	75,000	750	30	220	$500	
4	240,000	2,300		150	350	$1,800
			$450	$800	$850	$1,800

Management intends to estimate uncollectible accounts based on net credit sales, and they are curious as to the effect that an annual provision of 1½% of net credit sales would have had on the amount of bad debts expense reported during each of the last four years.

Required:

A. Determine for each year

  1. The amount of bad debts expense based on 1½% of net credit sales.
  2. The increase over the expense actually reported that such an estimate would cause.
  3. The balance in the *Allowance For Uncollectible Accounts* at year-end.

B. Do you think the 1½% figure is a good estimate, or would some other figure be more appropriate? Base your determination on the amount of uncollectible accounts originating during the first two years. (AICPA Adapted)

Problem 8-4 Comprehensive Problem on Receivables and Payables

Selected transactions of Landers Company for the year 1987 are presented here.

Feb.	13	Wrote off the $317 account receivable from Snider Company as uncollectible.
	28	Accepted a 60-day, 12% note in exchange for a $1,500 past-due account receivable of Morton Company.
Mar.	20	Sold merchandise to Silone Company and accepted a 90-day, 10% note in the amount of $8,000.
	30	Issued to Andrews Wholesale a $10,000, 11%, 90-day note for merchandise purchased.
	30	Discounted at First Bancorp the note received from Morton Company on February 28. The bank discount rate was 14%.
May	31	Borrowed $5,000 from Eastern Bank, issuing a $5,000, 12%, 9-month note.
June	2	Received from Betty Jolsen a 30-day, 12% note for $700 in settlement of her account receivable.
	18	Received from Silone Company the amount due on the note dated March 20.
	28	Paid the Andrews Wholesale note issued on March 30.
July	2	Betty Jolsen dishonored her note of June 2.
Dec.	31	Recorded accrued interest on the note payable to Eastern Bank.

Required:

A. Prepare journal entries to record the above transactions, assuming that Landers Company uses the allowance method of accounting for uncollectible accounts.

B. Prepare a journal entry to record the payment of the note payable to Eastern Bank on February 28, 1988.

Problem 8-5 Accounting for Notes Receivable, Including Discounting

During the last three months of the fiscal year, a company received the following notes.

Date of Note	Face Value	Term of Note	Interest Rate	Date of Discount	Discount Rate
1. Oct. 1	$ 5,000	60 days	12%	Oct. 31	13%
2. Nov. 2	8,000	90 days	9%	Dec. 10	10%
3. Nov. 15	10,000	60 days	11%		
4. Dec. 1	4,000	90 days	13%		
5. Dec. 8	12,000	90 days	10%	Dec. 23	12%
6. Dec. 16	10,000	60 days	10%		

Required:

A. Determine the due date and the maturity value for each note, and for notes 1, 2, and 5, determine the discount period, the amount of discount, and the proceeds.

B. Prepare journal entries to record the discounting of notes 1, 2, and 5 at the bank.

C. Prepare a journal entry to accrue interest on notes 3, 4, and 6 on December 31.

D. Prepare journal entries to record the collection of notes 3, 4, and 6 in the next fiscal period.

Problem 8-6 Comprehensive Problem on Accounts and Notes Receivable

The following transactions occurred during fiscal year 1987 (July 1, 1986, through June 30, 1987) at Chiles Company.

July	9	The company accepted a 10%, 90-day, $2,000 note in exchange for the past-due account receivable of Joe Lane.
Aug.	1	Wrote off the $340 account receivable of H. Roberts as uncollectible.
Sept.	7	The note receivable from Joe Lane was discounted at the bank at a discount rate of 11%.
Oct.	7	Joe Lane defaulted on his note and the bank assessed a protest fee of $23. Chiles Company paid the maturity value of the note, plus the $23 protest fee.
Nov.	6	Joe Lane unexpectedly paid the maturity value of his dishonored note, plus the protest fee and interest at 10% on both for 30 days beyond the note's maturity date.
Dec.	2	Chiles Company received $1,000 cash and a $5,000, 60-day, 10% note from P. Putnam in granting an extension on his past-due account receivable.
Jan.	31	Received payment from P. Putnam on his note of Dec. 2.
May	1	The company accepted a $4,000, 90-day, 11% note from C. Carr in settlement of an account receivable.
	1	The company discounted a 6-month, 10%, $15,000 note payable at a local bank.
June	30	Interest was accrued on the note receivable from C. Carr and on the note payable to the bank.
	30	Bad debts expense is to be recorded at 1½% times net credit sales of $416,000.

Required:

A. Prepare journal entries to record the transactions on Chiles Company's books, assuming the use of the allowance method of accounting for uncollectible accounts.

B. Prepare journal entries to record the collection of the C. Carr note and the payment of the note payable to the bank during fiscal year 1988.

ALTERNATE PROBLEMS

Problem 8-1A Accounting for Accounts Receivable

On March 1, Shriver Company had *Accounts Receivable* and an *Allowance For Uncollectible Accounts,* as follows.

Accounts Receivable

Mar. 1 Balance	641,300

Allowance for Uncollectible Accounts

Mar. 1 Balance	9,330

During March, the following transactions occurred.

1. Sales on account	$ 996,300
2. Sales returns and allowances on credit sales	20,100
3. Accounts receivable collected	1,060,100
4. Accounts written off as uncollectible	12,200

Based on an aging of accounts receivable on March 31, the company determined that the *Allowance For Uncollectible Accounts* should have a credit balance of $10,100 on the March 31 balance sheet.

Required:

A. Prepare journal entries to record the summary data for the four items above and to adjust the *Allowance For Uncollectible Accounts.*

B. Show how *Accounts Receivable* and the *Allowance For Uncollectible Accounts* would appear on the March 31 balance sheet.

C. On April 29, Travis Company, whose $1,350 account had been written off as uncollectible in March, paid its account in full. Prepare journal entries to record the collection.

Problem 8-2A Accounts and Notes Receivable

Transactions affecting Bradford Company's accounts receivable for the fiscal year ended December 31 are presented below.

Feb.	3	Wrote off the $497 account of Elm Company as uncollectible.
March	6	Received 50% of the $840 balance owed by Jack Wiley and wrote off the remainder as uncollectible.
Apr.	16	Recorded the collection of $300 from Glenn Rhodes in full payment of his account, which had been written off earlier.
July	15	Wrote off as uncollectible the accounts of Pauley Company, $700, and Bob Donley, $420.
Sept.	9	Received $350 from E. Dawkins in full payment of his account, which had been written off earlier as uncollectible.

Oct.   8 Received 30% of the $2,000 owed by North Company and wrote
            off the remainder as uncollectible.

Dec.   4 Recorded an account receivable for a $4,000, 12%, 90-day note of   12
            D. Martin that was dishonored at its maturity date.

        31 Estimated bad debts expense for the year to be 1¼% of net credit
            sales of $460,000.

Required:

A. Prepare journal entries for each of the transactions.

B. Determine the balance in *Allowance for Uncollectible Accounts* after the December
31 adjustment. Assume that the allowance account had a $4,700 credit balance on   7663
January 1.

C. Assume that instead of basing the allowance for uncollectibles on net credit sales,
the estimate of uncollectible accounts is based on an aging of accounts receivable
and that $6,210 of the accounts receivable at December 31 were estimated to be
uncollectible. Determine the adjustment necessary to bring the allowance account
to the desired balance. Assume that the allowance account had a $4,700 credit
balance on January 1.

Problem 8-3A Default on a Note Receivable

Boston Company sells much of its merchandise on credit with terms of n/30. Customers sometimes ask for an extension of credit beyond 30 days, in which case Boston
Company requires that the customer give an interest-bearing note. A sequence of
transactions with a customer, Nance Company, follows.

Mar.   10 Sold merchandise to Nance Company for $6,300; received $1,500
            cash and the balance was debited to *Accounts Receivable.*

Apr.   9 Received a 12%, 90-day note from Nance Company in settlement
            of its account receivable. The note was dated April 9.

July   8 On the due date of the note, Nance Company defaulted.

Sept.   6 Nance Company paid the defaulted note, plus interest at 12% on
            the defaulted amount from July 8 to September 6.

Required:

Prepare journal entries for the above events. Show interest computations and round
to the nearest dollar. Boston Company's fiscal year ends on December 31.

Problem 8-4A Discounting and Default of a Note Receivable

Jason's Imports entered into the following transactions during 1987.

Jan.   6 Accepted a 10%, 90-day, $2,000 note in exchange for the past-due
            account receivable of Jim Davies.

March   7 The note received from Jim Davies was discounted at the bank at
            a discount rate of 12%.

Apr.   6 Jim Davies defaulted on his note and the bank assessed a protest
            fee of $28. Jason's Imports paid the maturity value of the note, plus
            the protest fee.

May   6 Jim Davies paid the maturity value of his dishonored note, plus the
            protest fee and interest at 10% on both for 30 days beyond the
            note's maturity date.

Nov.   16 Accepted an $8,400, 90-day, 12% note from Tim Williams in settle-
            ment of his account receivable.

        30 Discounted a 6-month, 11%, $10,000 note payable at Central Bank.   45 dAys.

Dec.   31 Interest was accrued on the note receivable from Tim Williams. 126

        31 Interest expense was accrued on the note payable to Central Bank.

Required:

A. Prepare journal entries to record the transactions on Jason's Imports' books.

B. Prepare journal entries to record the collection of the Tim Williams note and the payment of the note payable to Central Bank during 1988.

Problem 8-5A Accounting for Notes Payable

On February 1, Prince Company purchased office equipment at a cost of $68,000. A cash down payment of $18,000 was made and a 13%, six-month note payable was given for the balance. The note requires two payments of $25,000 each plus interest on the amount of the payment. Payments are due on May 1 and August 1.

Required:

A. Prepare journal entries on February 1, May 1, and June 30, which is the end of the fiscal year for Prince Company.

B. Prepare the journal entry for the final payment on August 1.

CASE

CASE 8-1 Financial Report Analysis Case   Receivables and Payables

Refer to the financial statements of Holiday Inns, Inc., for the years ended December 28, 1984, and December 30, 1983, in Appendix A, and answer the following questions:

1. What types and classes of receivables did Holiday Inns hold on December 28, 1984?
2. Does Holiday Inns use the allowance method or direct-write-off method of accounting for uncollectible accounts?
3. What types of current liabilities did Holiday Inns owe on December 28, 1984?
4. What were the components of Holiday Inns' accrued expenses on December 28, 1984?
5. What was the balance in the *Allowance For Doubtful Accounts* at the end of 1983? At the end of 1984?
6. Holiday Inns had a significant increase in total receivables during 1984. Explain what caused most of the increase.

9

INVENTORY COSTING METHODS

CHAPTER OVERVIEW AND OBJECTIVES

This chapter describes various methods used to assign cost to ending inventory and to cost of goods sold. When you have completed the chapter, you should understand:

1. How to take a physical inventory.
2. How to determine when the title to inventory transfers.
3. How to allocate the cost of goods available for sale between ending inventory and cost of goods sold, using four different costing methods when the periodic inventory system is used.
4. How to determine inventory values by applying the *lower of cost or market rule*.
5. The effects of inventory errors on the balance sheet and income statement.
6. How to estimate a value for the ending inventory using the retail inventory and gross profit methods.
7. How to allocate the cost of goods available for sale between ending inventory and cost of goods sold, using four different costing methods when the perpetual inventory system is used (Appendix).

In Chapter 5, the term *merchandise inventory* was used to designate all goods owned by a merchandising firm and held for future sale to the firm's customers in the normal course of business. Illustrations in Chapter 5 were based on the assumption that the unit cost was the same for all units acquired by the firm. However, in today's markets the prices of most goods change frequently during an accounting period. When prices change, the firm is confronted with the problem of determining what portion of the total cost of goods available for sale should be assigned to ending inventory and what portion should be assigned to cost of goods sold to be matched against sales of the current period.

This chapter begins with a discussion of how to identify the units to be included in inventory. Next, four alternative methods used to allocate the cost of goods available for sale, between ending inventory and cost of goods sold, when prices are changing are discussed and illustrated. It is assumed that the company uses a periodic inventory system to account for inventory costs. The allocation of cost when using the perpetual inventory system is covered in the Appendix to this chapter.

Although cost is the primary basis for measuring inventory values, there are circumstances under which it is appropriate to value inventory at less than its historical cost. Several of these situations are discussed in this chapter. In addition, the effect of inventory errors on the company's financial statements are discussed. The chapter concludes with a discussion of two methods that are used to estimate ending inventory values.

DETERMINING THE INVENTORY ON HAND

Objective 1: Taking a physical inventory

When a periodic inventory system is maintained, the cost of inventory purchased during the period is recorded in the *Purchases* account, as discussed in Chapter 5. The balance in the *Merchandise Inventory* account is the cost of the inventory on hand at the beginning of the period. To determine the cost of the ending inventory, the units on hand must be counted and priced. The ending inventory is then reported as a current asset in the balance sheet, and is also deducted from the cost of goods available for sale in the income statement to determine the cost of goods sold. Although the inventory on hand and the cost of goods sold balances are available in the accounts when a perpetual inventory system is used, a physical inventory is also taken at least once a year to verify the balances reported.

Before conducting the actual physical count of units on hand (commonly referred to as *taking an inventory*) and pricing the units, the entire process must be carefully planned. The procedures established for the counting process must be carefully supervised to ensure that all units owned by the firm are properly counted. Although the specific details of procedures vary from firm to firm, this is a typical approach employed.

1. A prenumbered inventory ticket is issued for each type of item in stock and distributed to each department. The ticket provides a space to record
    a. A description or code number of the item.
    b. The number of units counted.
    c. The initials of the person making the count.
    d. The initials of the person verifying the count.
2. An employee counts the units, enters the number of units on hand on the inventory ticket, and initials it to identify the person performing the count. The inventory ticket is then attached to the units counted.
3. A supervisor recounts a sufficient number of items to ensure the accuracy of the recorded count and initials the inventory ticket.

4. A supervisor examines the inventory in each department to be sure that an inventory ticket has been attached to all items. Any group of like items without a ticket attached has not been counted.

5. The inventory tickets are collected and forwarded to the accounting department, where the prenumbered tickets are all accounted for. The information on the inventory tickets is summarized on an inventory summary sheet.

6. The unit cost of each individual item in stock is determined from purchase invoices or other supplementary records.

7. The number of units of the various individual items are multiplied by their unit cost and added together to compute the total ending inventory value.

The physical inventory is often conducted when the store is closed because of the difficulty of controlling the flow of goods.

TRANSFER OF OWNERSHIP

During an inventory count, care must be exercised to assure that all goods legally owned by the firm on the inventory date are included in the ending inventory, regardless of where the inventory is located. Transfer of ownership normally depends on the terms of the shipment. Recall from Chapter 5 that when goods are sold *FOB (free on board) shipping point,* freight is paid by the buyer and title ordinarily transfers when the goods are delivered to the transportation company by the seller. If the terms are *FOB destination,* the seller is responsible for paying the freight, and title usually does not transfer until delivery is made to the buyer.

Objective 2: Transfer of title

From an accounting point of view, at the time when title to the goods transfers, the seller should record a sales transaction and the buyer should record a purchase of inventory. In practice, however, sales are normally recorded when shipment is made, and purchases are recorded when the inventory is received, irrespective of the shipping terms.

To increase the accuracy of the financial statements at year-end, purchases and sales invoices for both the last week or two of the current accounting period and the first week or two of the next period should be reviewed to determine whether there were units in transit on the date of the inventory that should be included with the units counted. For example, goods purchased with the terms FOB shipping point and in transit at year-end should be recorded as a purchase and included in the physical count, even though they were not physically on hand when the actual count was made. Although exclusion of this inventory will have no effect on net income (purchases, goods available for sale, and ending inventory will each be understated by an equal amount), total assets and total liabilities are understated if the purchase is not recorded. Similarly, goods sold with the terms FOB destination should be included in the seller's ending inventory if in transit at year end, since title to the goods has not been transferred. The sale and related cost of goods sold are transactions to be recorded in the succeeding period.

In some cases, the seller may have received orders for goods that are part of the normal inventory but shipment may not have been made. In such situations, a sale is *not* recorded, because the revenue has not been earned. However, an exception is made when: (1) an order for goods has been received; (2) the goods are ready for shipment; and (3) the buyer has requested that the goods be held for later delivery. Such items should be excluded from the seller's inventory and included in the buyer's inventory. In still other cases, it may not be clear whether or not title has transferred. The accountant must then use his or her judgment and attempt to assess when the parties to the transactions intended the title to transfer.

GOODS ON CONSIGNMENT

Another problem sometimes encountered in taking an inventory is the treatment of goods held on consignment. A **consignment** is a marketing arrangement whereby a business (the **consignor**) ships goods to a dealer (the **consignee**) who agrees to sell the goods for a commission. Although a physical transfer of goods has taken place, title to the goods does not transfer. It remains with the consignor. Since title to the goods has not transferred, the shipment of consigned goods is not considered a sale/purchase transaction. Therefore, goods out on consignment are part of the consignor's inventory, even though physical possession of the goods is with the consignee. The goods are excluded from the consignee's inventory, since they remain the consignor's property.

DETERMINING THE COST OF INVENTORY

As with accounting for other assets, cost is the primary basis of accounting for inventory. Applied to inventory, cost means the sum of all direct and indirect costs incurred to bring the merchandise to a salable condition and to its existing location. Conceptually, the invoice price, freight charges, insurance on the goods while in transit, special handling costs, adjustments and assembly costs incurred in preparing the goods for sale, costs incurred to operate a purchasing department, costs associated with receiving and inspecting the goods, and storage costs incurred before the goods are sold are all among the costs that may be properly identified and allocated to inventory. However, when several types of inventory are acquired in one shipment, it may be difficult to allocate the incidental costs, such as freight and insurance, to individual items, so that a unit cost can be computed. In addition, the allocation of storage costs and costs related to operating a purchasing and receiving department requires an arbitrary allocation method and does not produce enough benefit to justify the additional cost of making the allocation. Therefore, many inventory costs are expensed in the period incurred, rather than added to the cost of inventory. As a result, often only the invoice price is used in computing the unit cost of goods purchased.

ALLOCATION OF INVENTORY COST BETWEEN ENDING INVENTORY AND COST OF GOODS SOLD—PERIODIC INVENTORY SYSTEM

Objective 3: Allocation of inventory costs

In Chapter 5, it was assumed that the unit cost was the same for all units acquired. However, since prices change, units purchased on different dates often have different unit costs. When this happens, management is confronted with the problem of selecting the unit cost to be matched against sales. To adhere to the matching principle, the allocation of total inventory cost between ending merchandise inventory and cost of goods sold is based on some cost flow assumption.

Four methods are commonly used to allocate cost: (1) specific identificaton; (2) first-in, first-out (FIFO), (3) last-in, first-out (LIFO); and (4) **average cost,** called the weighted average method when a periodic inventory system is used. All four methods are considered acceptable for accounting purposes, but, when prices are changing, each will produce different ending inventory and cost of goods sold amounts. FIFO, LIFO, and average cost are the most commonly used methods, as shown by a survey of 600 companies, reported in Figure 9–1, as shown on page 372.

The cost flow assumption does not have to conform to the actual physical movement of goods. A firm may rotate its stock so that the oldest units are sold first. However, in determining the cost of units sold, the cost of the most recent purchases may be assigned to cost of goods sold. All generally accepted accounting principles require is that the method selected be used consistently and that the cost allocation be systematic and rational.

ILLUSTRATION OF COST ALLOCATION METHODS

To illustrate the effects of the four inventory costing methods on the allocation of the total cost of goods available for sale ($412) to ending inventory and cost of goods sold, the following inventory record of a computer game will be assumed for the fiscal period.

Date	Number of Units	Unit Cost	Total Cost
Jan. 1 Beginning merchandise inventory	10	$10	$100.00
Purchases made during the current period:			
April 15 Purchase	12	11	$132.00
July 7 Purchase	15	12	180.00
Total purchases	27		312.00
Goods available for sale	37		$412.00
Sales made during the current period:			
April 20 Sales	8	?	?
August 12 Sales	10	?	?
Total cost of sales	18		?
Dec. 31 Ending merchandise inventory	19		?

Figure 9–1
Inventory Cost
Methods Used by
600 Companies

Costing Method	No.
FIFO	366
LIFO	408
Average cost	235
Other	52
Totals	1,061

(The total exceeds 600 companies because a company may adopt a different method for different types of inventory held.)
Source: Accounting Trends and Techniques, 1984 edition (New York: AICPA, 1985), p. 123.

In a periodic inventory system, the 19 units on hand on December 31 would have been determined by taking a physical inventory.

With a periodic inventory system, the number of units on hand at the end of the period must be counted and priced before the cost of goods available for sale ($412) can be allocated between the ending inventory and cost of goods sold. That portion of the total inventory cost allocated to the ending inventory depends on the cost flow assumption that the firm adopts. Once the cost of the ending inventory is determined, the cost of goods sold is computed by deducting the ending inventory cost from the cost of goods available for sale.

Specific Identification Method

The **specific identification** method requires that the cost of each unit sold and each unit on hand be identified with a specific purchase invoice. To do this, the firm must use some form of identification such as serial numbers. For purposes of illustration, assume that the 19 units in the ending inventory can be separately identified as 10 units from the July 7 purchase and 9 units from the beginning inventory. Costs are then assigned as follows.

Cost of goods available for sale—37 units				$412.00
Less: Cost of 19 units in the ending merchandise inventory				
Date	Units	Unit Cost	Total Cost	
1/1	9	$10	$ 90.00	
7/7	10	12	120.00	
Cost of ending merchandise inventory—19 units				210.00
Cost of goods sold—18 units				$202.00

As can be seen, the cost of goods sold is a residual amount, but the $202 can be verified as follows.

Cost of goods sold—18 units
1 unit from the beginning inventory at $10 per unit $ 10.00
12 units from the April 15 purchase at $11 per unit   132.00
5 units from the July 7 purchase at $12 per unit   60.00
Total cost of goods sold $202.00

Using the amounts computed for the specific identification method, the cost allocation procedure is diagrammed as follows.

	Cost of beginning		Cost of goods		Cost of ending	
$100	inventory		available		inventory	$210
	+	=	for sale	=	Cost of goods	
312	Cost of purchases				sold	202
$412		=	$412*	=		$412

*Allocation of the cost of goods available for sale to cost of ending inventory and cost of goods sold will vary, depending on the cost-flow method used.

Under a periodic inventory system, the ending inventory ($210) is reported as a current asset in the balance sheet and as a deduction from cost of goods available for sale in the income statement. As shown in Chapter 5, these amounts may be entered in the ledger accounts as part of the closing process. In one closing entry, *Merchandise Inventory* is credited for $100 to remove the beginning inventory balance from the account and transfer it to the *Income Summary* account. In a second closing entry, *Merchandise Inventory* is debited for $210 to record the ending inventory. These procedures are the same for the three other costing methods, but the amounts will vary with the costing method used.

First-in, First-out (FIFO) Method

The **First-in, First-out (FIFO)** method of determining the cost of goods sold is based on the assumption that the first units acquired are the first units sold. Therefore, the cost of the units on hand is that of the most recent purchases. Once again, this is a cost-flow assumption and need not represent the actual physical movement of goods. It should be emphasized that the name of the inventory method, FIFO, for example, refers to the flow of cost and the determination of cost of goods sold, and not to the ending inventory. That is, under FIFO, the cost of goods sold is made up of the first units purchased, while the ending inventory is made up of the last units purchased.

In the periodic inventory system, the ending inventory is computed first and is subtracted from the cost of goods available for sale to compute the cost of goods sold, as follows.

Cost of goods available for sale—37 units				$412.00
Less: Cost of 19 units in ending inventory				
Date	Units	Unit Cost	Total Cost	
7/7	15	$12	$180.00	
4/15	4	11	44.00	
Cost of ending merchandise inventory—19 units				224.00
Cost of goods sold—18 units				$188.00

Note that the 19 units in the ending inventory are associated with the last two purchases. In a periodic inventory system, the cost of goods sold is a residual amount, but in this example it can be verified as follows.

Cost of goods sold—18 units	
10 units from the beginning inventory at $10 per unit	$100.00
8 units from the April 15 purchase at $11 per unit	88.00
Total cost of goods sold	$188.00

The cost of the 18 units sold in this period consists of the beginning inventory and a portion of the cost of the first purchase made on April 15. The other four units from the April 15 purchase were assumed to be on hand as of December 31.

Last-in, First-out (LIFO) Method

Under the **last-in, first-out (LIFO)** method, the last units purchased are assumed to be the first units sold. Consequently, the costs of the most recent purchases are matched with sales revenue in the income statement. The cost of the ending inventory consists of the costs of the beginning inventory and the earliest purchases. The cost allocation is:

Cost of goods available for sale—37 units				$412.00
Less: Cost of 19 units in the ending inventory				
Date	Units	Unit Cost	Total Cost	
1/1	10	$10	$100.00	
4/15	9	11	99.00	
Cost of ending merchandise inventory—19 units				199.00
Cost of goods sold—18 units				$213.00

The cost of goods sold can be verified as follows.

Cost of goods sold—18 units

15 units from the July 7 purchase at $12 per unit	$180.00
3 units from the April 15 purchase at $11 per unit	33.00
Total cost of goods sold	$213.00

Note that when the LIFO method is used with a periodic inventory system, no attempt is made to compare the dates of sales with those of purchases. Units sold during the period are identified with the most recent purchases. In other words, it is possible to expense the cost of units sold, even though they were not on hand at the time of sale. For example, if a purchase had been made after August 12, the date of the last sale, those units would be considered sold first, in applying the LIFO method.

Weighted Average Method

Under the **weighted average** method, an average cost per unit is computed by dividing the total cost of goods available for sale including the cost of the beginning inventory and all purchases made during the accounting period, by the total number of units available for sale. This weighted average is then multiplied by the number of units on hand to determine the cost of the ending inventory, as follows.

$$\frac{\text{Cost of goods available for sale}}{\text{Number of units available for sale}} = \frac{\$412.00}{37 \text{ units}} = \$11.14 \text{ per unit*}$$

*Rounded to the nearest cent.

Ending inventory = 19 units × $11.14 per unit = $211.66

The cost of goods sold is:

Cost of goods available for sale—37 units	$412.00
Less: Cost of ending merchandise inventory—19 units	211.66
Cost of goods sold—18 units	$200.34

The cost assigned to cost of goods sold is confirmed as follows. (The difference is due to rounding the unit cost.)

18 units × $11.14 per unit = $200.52

The use of this method results in all units sold and on hand being priced at the average cost of $11.14 per unit.

COMPARISON OF COSTING METHODS

The preceding sections explained the procedural aspects of each costing method. This section will discuss justifications, features, and disadvantages of each method. In doing so, the effects of each of the four methods on the firm's financial statements are compared, and the results are illustrated in Figure 9–2. It is assumed that the 18 units were sold for a total of $360, that operating expenses totaled $120, and that the average income tax rate was 30%. The sales and operating expenses are the same in all cases because the inventory method used does not affect these income statement items. The beginning inventory in each case was assumed to be 10 units costing a total of $100. In the next period, the beginning inventory value will vary, depending on the costing method selected, and will be equal to the ending inventory computed in the current period.

Note that the computations in Figure 9–2 are based on the assumption that the unit cost increased steadily from $10 to $12 during the period. If the unit cost had not changed during the period, cost of goods sold, net income, and ending inventory values would be the same for all four methods. When costs change during a period, the costing method selected can have a significant effect on the firm's reported assets and net income figures. Even in this simple

Figure 9–2
Comparison of Four
Costing Methods

	Periodic Inventory System			
	Specific Identification	FIFO	LIFO	Weighted Average
Sales—18 units	$360	$360	$360	$360
Beginning inventory	$100	$100	$100	$100
Add: Purchases	312	312	312	312
Goods available for sale	412	412	412	412
Less: Ending inventory	210	224	199	212
Cost of goods sold	202	188	213	200
Gross profit on sales	158	172	147	160
Less: Operating expenses	120	120	120	120
Net income before taxes	38	52	27	40
Less: income taxes— 30%*	11	16	8	12
Net income	$ 27	$ 36	$ 19	$ 28
Ending inventory also reported in the balance sheet.	$210	$224	$199	$212

*Income taxes are rounded to the nearest dollar.

example, with increasing prices and only one inventory item held for sale, the FIFO net income was almost twice as much as the LIFO net income. The absolute difference between the methods could be even greater if the volume of purchases and sales and the variety of individual items held for sale were increased. However, keep in mind that all four methods are based on the cost concept. Although cost of goods sold and net income may vary between accounting periods, the total cost of goods sold and total net income reported over the life of the firm will be the same using all four methods, because only the actual cost incurred for inventory can be expensed.

SPECIFIC IDENTIFICATION METHOD

Under the specific identification method, when a sale is made, the item sold is identified and the cost of that item is matched against revenue. Thus, the method is based on the actual physical flow of goods.

Use of this method is primarily limited to businesses that sell easily identified items with a high unit cost (automobile dealerships and jewelry stores, for example). Most other firms will find this method impractical because it is both costly and time consuming. Another disadvantage of the method is that if the inventory units are identical and have different costs, it is possible for management to manipulate income by choosing to sell a unit with a low or a high cost.

FIRST-IN, FIRST-OUT METHOD

The FIFO method is widely used because it is easy to apply. When stock is rotated so that the oldest units are sold first, the method's cost flow assumption will approximate the actual physical flow of goods. The method does not permit manipulation of income, since management is not free to pick the cost of a certain item to be matched with revenue. Instead, management must expense the oldest unit cost available for sale.

As can be seen in Figure 9–2, during periods of rising unit cost, this method results in reporting a lower cost of goods sold and higher net income than either the LIFO or weighted average method. On the balance sheet, the ending inventory will reflect the higher cost of the most recent purchases—a more realistic measure of the inventory's current value than is provided by the other methods. On the other hand, during a period of declining unit cost, FIFO will produce the highest cost of goods sold, the lowest net income, and the lowest ending inventory values.

Many accountants argue that using FIFO during periods of rising prices results in an overstatement in real net income. To illustrate this point, consider the data used in our previous illustration.

January 1	Beginning inventory	10 units @ $10
April 15	Purchases	12 units @ $11
April 20	Sales	8 units @ $20
July 7	Purchases	15 units @ $12
August 12	Sales	10 units @ $20

On April 20, the firm sold 8 units for $20 per unit. Under FIFO, the company charged $10 per unit to cost of goods sold, which resulted in a gross profit of $10 per unit. However, these units were replaced on July 7 with units costing $12 each. Therefore, $2 of the gross profit per unit was used to replace the units sold, and only $8 per unit represents the real gross profit to the firm. Inclusion of the $2 in gross profit is considered misleading, because it cannot be distributed to the owners or reinvested in other aspects of the business without reducing the firm's ability to replace units sold. For this reason, it is sometimes called ''phantom profit'' or ''illusory profit.'' The same line of reasoning applies to the units sold on August 12, which, if prices continue to rise, must be replaced with higher-cost units.

LAST-IN, FIRST-OUT METHOD

The basic assumption of the LIFO method is that the firm must maintain a certain level of inventory to operate. When inventory is sold, it must be replaced at its current replacement cost. Income is not considered earned unless the sales price exceeds the cost to replace the units sold.

Although the cost of goods sold will not always equal the cost of replacing the unit sold because of price changes, it is frequently argued that LIFO provides the best measure of net income because it matches the more recent costs with current revenue. Since prices generally move upward, the effect of this method is to produce: (1) a higher cost of goods sold; and (2) a lower net income than the other methods (see Figure 9–2).

However, balance sheet values soon become outdated under LIFO because the oldest unit costs remain in the inventory. This creates some problems in evaluating the working capital position of a firm. In addition, if the level of inventory falls below normal, there is a matching of old costs with current revenue, which distorts income in the year of the inventory decrease. Another disadvantage of LIFO is that the possibility exists for management to manipulate net income by buying or not buying goods at the end of the year.

Note in Figure 9–2 that the income tax expense under LIFO is $8, the lowest of the four methods. Thus, although all four methods are acceptable for computing taxable income, using the LIFO method during periods of rising prices produces a tax benefit. This reduction in income taxes, coupled with high inflation, is one of the major reasons for the trend toward use of the LIFO method.

The reduced cash outflow for taxes makes more cash available for use in the firm's operations. However, as noted earlier, only the actual cost incurred is deductible as an expense. Thus, if the beginning inventory is eventually sold, or if prices decline, the total cost of goods sold will be lower and taxable income will be greater under LIFO. Of course, over the life of the firm these items will be the same for all four methods. Why then, has there been a switch to LIFO in recent years? The reason is that a tax reduction in the current period is preferred to one in a later period.

Despite the tax benefit, some firms have been reluctant to switch to LIFO because current tax laws require that if LIFO is used for tax purposes, it must also be used for financial reporting purposes. As a result, the firms will report lower earnings using LIFO, which may have an unfavorable effect on investors.

WEIGHTED AVERAGE METHOD

The average cost method is usually justified because the method is simple to apply and is not subject to income manipulation, as are some of the other methods. In applying this method, the average unit cost is affected: (1) by the number of units and the cost of the units in the beginning inventory; and (2) by all purchases made during the year. As a result, the cost of goods sold, net income, and ending inventory amounts reported under the average cost method will be between the extremes produced by FIFO and LIFO when prices are rising or falling. Thus, the use of the average cost method tends to smooth out net income and inventory values with neither the cost of goods sold nor the ending inventory reported at current values.

Although the average cost method is not used as frequently as FIFO and LIFO, it is sometimes used when the inventory units involved are homogeneous in nature and when it is difficult to establish a physical flow assumption. Examples of such inventory are grain in a grain elevator or gasoline in a storage tank.

WHICH METHOD TO SELECT?

The selection of the cost method to use for a particular type of inventory depends on many factors, including the effect that each method will have upon the firm's financial statements, income tax considerations, the information needs of management and statement users, and the clerical cost of applying the method. In practice, more than one of the methods may be considered appropriate in accounting for the same type of inventory. That is, generally accepted accounting standards do not prescribe the use of a specific costing method as being ''best'' for a particular set of inventory conditions. It is up to management and to the firm's accountant to decide which method both provides the most useful information to its statement users and satisfies other needs as well.

CONSISTENCY IN USING A COSTING METHOD

Clearly, the inventory costing method selected can have a significant impact on the firm's reported net income and asset figures. For this reason, the method used to assign cost to inventory and cost of goods sold should be disclosed in the financial statements.

Once a costing method has been selected, management cannot indiscriminately switch to another. When alternative accounting methods or procedures are considered acceptable in a given situation, the principle of **consistency** requires that a firm apply the same method from one accounting period to the next. If switching accounting methods between periods were permitted, the accounting data produced in different accounting periods would not be comparable.

The consistency principle does not completely rule out changing to an acceptable alternative method if the new method results in improved financial reporting. However, for tax purposes, a change in inventory costing methods can be made if the consent of the Internal Revenue Service is obtained. Generally, the approval to switch is automatic. A firm can switch to LIFO by merely using this method on the tax return and including a required form. Once a change is made, the nature of the change, the effect of the change on the financial statements, and the reasons the newly adopted method is preferred must be fully disclosed in notes accompanying the financial statements. Such disclosure is illustrated in Figure 9–3 for Arden Group, Inc. Without such disclosure, the statement reader may assume that no material changes in accounting methods were made during the period.

THE LOWER OF COST OR MARKET RULE

Objective 4: Lower of cost or market rule

Cost is the primary basis for recording and reporting most assets. The four inventory costing methods previously discussed are alternatives for arriving at the cost of inventory when the unit cost fluctuates during the accounting period. However, when there has been a decrease in the value of inventory or in the cost to replace the units in inventory, it is sometimes considered appropriate to report inventory at an amount below the cost. The decline in value could result from obsolescence, damage, deterioration, or a decline in the unit cost caused by supply and demand factors. If at the end of the period, the cost of replacing the inventory is less than its historical cost, the inventory is

Figure 9–3
Illustration of Reporting Change in Inventory Costing Methods

ARDEN GROUP, INC.
Notes to Consolidated Financial Statements
3 (in part): Inventories

In 1983, the Company adopted the last-in, first-out (LIFO) method of determining the cost of its non-perishable grocery merchandise ($26,943,000). Perishable merchandise and all other inventory is valued at the lower of first-in, first-out (FIFO) cost or market. The Company believes that the use of the LIFO method for nonperishable grocery merchandise results in a better matching of costs and revenues. At December 31, 1983, inventories valued by the LIFO method would have been $637,445 higher if they had been stated at the lower of FIFO cost or market. The effect of net income and income per share for the fifty-two weeks ended December 31, 1983 was a decrease of approximately $562,000 ($.20 per share). The 1982 results of operations do not reflect this accounting change. Pro-forma effects of retroactive application of LIFO to prior years are not determinable, and thus there is no cumulative effect on retained earnings at the beginning of the year.

Source: Accounting Trends and Techniques, 1984 Edition (New York: AICPA, 1984) p. 411.

written down to the lower replacement cost and a loss is reported. This valuation approach is referred to as the **lower of cost or market (LCM)** rule. Market, as the term is used here, is *the cost to replace* the inventory in the quantities typically purchased through the usual source of supply.

Using a valuation figure that is lower than cost is justified by the convention of **conservatism.** Under this convention, a decrease in value is recorded in the accounts in the period in which the decrease occurs. Thus, application of the LCM rule results in a loss in inventory value being recorded (matched against revenue) in the period in which the decline in value occurs, rather than in a subsequent period when the inventory is sold. Increases in the cost to replace inventory are not recorded, because they have not yet been realized by a sale (revenue principle).

To illustrate the application of the LCM rule, assume that 10 units of an item costing $180 per unit were priced to sell for $300 per unit and 5 units were sold during the period. The expected gross profit is $120 per unit or 40% ($120/$300) of the sales price. At the end of the period, the cost of replacing the units declined to $135, a 25% decrease in cost. Assume also that the decline in cost and competition resulted in the firm reducing the sales price per unit to $225 on the remaining inventory. Gross profit on sales based on cost and LCM is computed in the year of the price decline.

| | Ending inventory valued at | | |
	Cost	LCM	Difference
Sales (5 units × $300)	$1,500	$1,500	-0-
Cost of goods available for sale	$1,800	$1,800	-0-
Less: Ending inventory			
5 units × $180*	900		
5 units × $135		675	− $225
Cost of goods sold	900	1,125	+ 225
Gross profit on sales	$ 600	$ 375	− $225

*When the unit cost fluctuates, cost would be determined by using any of the four cost-flow assumptions.

Applying the LCM rule in this example results in the ending inventory being $225 [5 units × ($180 − $135)] less than the historical cost ending inventory figure. The reduction in the ending inventory value becomes a part of the cost of goods sold, reducing the gross profit by $225. In the next period, when the goods are sold, gross profit on sales based on cost and LCM is $225 and $450 respectively.

	Cost	LCM	Difference
Sales (5 units × $225)	$1,125	$1,125	-0-
Less: Beginning inventory	900	675	− $225
Gross profit on units sold	$ 225	$ 450	+ $225

As shown in the cost column, if the write-down was not made in the preceding period, gross profit is $225 in the year the units are sold. When the write-down of the inventory to LCM in the preceding period was made, the gross profit was expected to be $450, which is 40% of the sales price. Thus, applying the LCM rule resulted in the $225 decline in the replacement cost being recognized in the period in which it occurred, rather than in the period in which the goods were sold. As a result, a normal profit rate of 40% ($450/ $1,125) was reported in the year of the sale.

In the above example, it was assumed that a 25% decrease in the replacement cost resulted in the sales price being decreased 25% [($300 − $225) ÷ $300]. In practice, however, the cost of an item and its selling price do not always change proportionately. In some cases, the sales price may not be reduced. As a result, the asset has not lost its revenue-producing power. If so, then a write-down to replacement cost is not justified. In addition, if the anticipated sales price is decreased—but not in the same proportion as the decrease in replacement cost—the write down of the inventory to replacement cost may result in a misstatement in the asset and the reported income amounts. Because of this potential for misstatement, several modifications to the LCM rule as just illustrated are used in practice to determine the market value to be compared to historical cost. These modifications and other issues related to applying the LCM rule are discussed in Intermediate Accounting.

NET REALIZABLE VALUE

The inventory of a retail or wholesale business often contains units that have been used or that are obsolete, shopworn, or damaged. Such inventory items are generally reported at **net realizable value**—the anticipated sales price in the normal course of the business, less the estimated cost of selling and disposal. To illustrate, assume that a company is holding a tape deck that cost $380 and normally sells for $460. Because the unit was used as a demonstrator, however, it is estimated that it could be sold for $345 after the unit is reconditioned for a cost of $50. A sales commission on the unit is expected to be $20. The value of the unit is computed for inventory purposes as follows.

Estimated sales value	$345
Estimated selling and disposal cost	70
Estimated net realizable value	$275

Since the estimated net realizable value is below the historical cost of $380, the unit should be carried in the ending inventory at $275. This will result in a loss of $105 ($380 − $275) being reported in the period in which it occurs, rather than in the period in which the unit is sold. Under a periodic inventory system, the loss becomes a part of the cost of goods sold.

If the net realizable value is greater than the historical cost, the inventory is not written up to reflect the higher value. Again, the historical cost of the unit is the upper value to be used in valuation. In addition, if inventory is written down to its net realizable value or replacement cost, the new value substitutes for the original cost figure for computations in future periods.

INVENTORY ERRORS

The cost of goods sold is the largest expense for many firms. The inventory balance of unsold goods is often the largest current asset reported in the balance sheet. Therefore, the determination of correct dollar amounts to be reported for these two financial statement items is very important. Because of the large volume of inventory transactions and the necessity of making numerous computations, errors can occur at various stages in accounting for inventory.

Objective 5: Inventory errors

A common error is the failure to record goods in transit owned by the firm at the end of the period. As discussed earlier, such errors have no effect on net income, but inventory and accounts payable are both understated by the same amount. Another common error is the failure to observe a proper cut-off for recording sales and the related cost of goods sold. For example, a sale made after the year-end may have been recorded before the year-end. If this error occurs, sales, cost of goods sold, gross profit, and net income are overstated. In the balance sheet, accounts receivable are overstated and inventory is understated—resulting in a net overstatement in total assets and owner's equity equal to the amount of the gross profit on the sale.

Under a periodic inventory system, errors may occur in counting and pricing the inventory and in the failure to use the proper cut-off dates for recording purchases and sales. To illustrate the effects of errors in a periodic inventory system, it is helpful to reconsider the calculation of cost of goods sold.

In Figure 9–4, it is assumed that a $10,000 understatement in the ending

Figure 9–4

Comparative Income Statements Showing Effects of Inventory Errors in Two Opening Periods (all amounts are assets)

	1987 With a Correct Ending Inventory	1987 With an Understated Ending Inventory		1988 With an Understated Beginning Inventory	1988 With a Correct Beginning Inventory
Sales revenue	$300,000	$300,000		$300,000	$300,000
Cost of goods sold:					
Beginning inventory	50,000	50,000		50,000	60,000
Purchases	190,000	190,000		200,000	200,000
Goods available for sale	240,000	240,000		250,000	260,000
Less: Ending inventory	60,000	50,000		80,000	80,000
Cost of goods sold	180,000	190,000	(Ending inventory for one period becomes beginning inventory for next period.)	170,000	180,000
Gross profit on sales	120,000	110,000		130,000	120,000
Operating expenses	70,000	70,000		75,000	75,000
Net income	$ 50,000	$ 40,000		$ 55,000	$ 45,000

Total net income for two periods	Correct	Incorrect	Difference
1987	$50,000	$40,000	$(10,000)
1988	45,000	55,000	10,000
Total	$95,000	$95,000	–0–

inventory occurred while taking the physical inventory at the end of 1987. Comparison with the "correct" column shows that this error resulted in an overstatement in the cost of goods sold and an understatement in both gross profit and net income. Since the ending inventory is also reported as a current asset, this error will cause current assets, total assets, and owner's equity all to be understated by $10,000. The opposite occurs if the ending inventory is overstated, rather than understated.

Failure to discover the error in the ending inventory will also cause the income statement for the next period to be incorrect, since the ending inventory for one period becomes the beginning inventory for the next period. In the next year, cost of goods sold is understated by $10,000, and both gross profit and net income are overstated by $10,000. Again, the opposite is true if the beginning inventory had been overstated.

In the absence of any other errors, the balance sheet amounts are correct at the end of 1988. This results because inventory errors offset one another over two consecutive periods. That is, the net income in 1987 is understated by $10,000, but the net income in 1988 is overstated by $10,000. Thus, although each year is in error, the total net income for the two periods of $95,000 is correct and the owner's equity accounts at the end of 1988 will also be correct.

If the errors are discovered after 1988 and comparative financial statements are prepared, the appropriate amounts reported in the financial statements should be corrected, even though the errors are offsetting. Failure to do so will distort the trend of the firm's earnings. For example, in Figure 9–4 the correct inventory amounts yielded a declining earnings trend, whereas the incorrect amounts show increasing net income amounts. Finally, if the error is discovered before the close of the 1988 year end, a correcting entry should be made to increase the inventory account. The offsetting credit is made to owner's equity because the net income closed to owner's equity was understated by $10,000 at the end of 1987.

The effects of inventory errors in various financial statement items can be summarized as follows.

	Income Statement			Balance Sheet	
	Cost of Goods Sold	Gross Profit	Net Income	Inventory Balance	Owner's Equity
Year 1—Ending inventory is understated	+	−	−	−	−
Year 2—Beginning inventory is understated	−	+	+	0	0
Year 1—Ending inventory is overstated	−	+	+	+	+
Year 2—Beginning inventory is overstated	+	−	−	0	0

+ Overstated   − Understated   0 Correct Balance

ESTIMATING INVENTORIES

A periodic system requires that a physical inventory must be taken to determine the ending inventory balance. Taking a physical inventory is so time-consuming and expensive that it is usually performed only at the end of the fiscal period. However, management and other statement users often want interim financial statements at regular intervals during the accounting period so that they can assess the firm's performance. If a periodic inventory system is used, the preparation of the income statement requires that the inventory on hand be determined for the computation of the cost of goods sold.

Objective 6: Methods used to estimate ending inventory values

The *retail inventory method* and the *gross profit method* are two approaches commonly used to estimate the dollar amount of unsold goods without taking a physical count. The two methods are also useful to test the reasonableness of a physical inventory taken by the firm's employees, to provide some insights into the dollar amount of inventory shortages from such causes as theft and damage, and to compute an estimate of the goods on hand when a physical inventory cannot be taken (such as when the inventory has been destroyed by a fire or a flood). The retail method is also used by a retail business to convert a physical inventory taken at retail prices to an estimated cost amount.

RETAIL INVENTORY METHOD

To use the **retail inventory method,** the firm must maintain records of the beginning inventory and purchases made during the period both at cost and retail (selling price). The goods available for sale at cost are divided by the goods available for sale at retail to calculate a relationship between cost and selling price. This amount is called the ratio of cost to retail or simply the cost ratio. An estimate of the inventory at retail is then determined by subtracting the sales recorded during the period from the goods available for sale at retail. The ending inventory at retail is multiplied by the cost ratio to arrive at an estimate of the ending inventory at cost.

The accuracy of the ending inventory, determined by the retail inventory method, depends on the mix or composition of goods in the ending inventory in relation to the mix of goods used to compute the cost ratio. The method assumes that the ending inventory consists of the same mix of goods at various cost percentages as was contained in the goods available for sale.

To illustrate, assume that the following information was accumulated in the accounts and supplementary records.

	Cost	Retail
Beginning inventory	$24,500	$40,000
Purchases to date	35,500	60,000
Net sales	—	80,000

The ending inventory at cost is estimated as follows.

	Cost	Retail
Beginning inventory	$24,500	$ 40,000
Purchases	35,500	60,000
Goods available for sale	$60,000	$100,000

Ratio of cost to retail:

$$\frac{\$\ 60,000}{\$100,000} = 60\%$$

Less: Net sales		80,000
Estimate of ending inventory at retail		20,000
Cost ratio		× 60%
Estimate of ending inventory at cost		$ 12,000

The cost of goods sold can now be determined as $48,000 ($60,000 cost of goods available for sale minus $12,000 ending inventory at cost). The ending inventory, as computed above, is an estimate acceptable for interim statements. The firm should still conduct a physical inventory at least once a year for control purposes and to assure a proper measurement of the cost of goods sold.

The retail inventory method is also a convenient means to convert a physical inventory taken at retail to a cost amount. In other words, in a retail store each item for sale is generally marked to indicate the sales price. Consequently, during a physical inventory the units are listed at current retail prices as they are counted. This procedure eliminates the need to look up purchase invoices to determine the unit cost of each item. The retail dollar value of the ending inventory is converted to cost by applying the cost ratio, calculated as previously shown. Remember that the cost ratio is applied to the inventory value determined by a physical count. An estimate of the ending inventory at retail is still calculated as a control measure, because significant differences between the actual retail value and the estimate may indicate problems in the accounting system or excessive losses from theft or other causes.

Changes in the Initial Selling Price

In practice, the originally established sales price of many items does not remain constant during the period; instead, it changes frequently during the year as prices are reduced for special sales or increased as the market value of the item increases. For example, in the illustration just discussed, an item that cost $6 was initially priced to sell for $10. The $4 difference between the cost of the item and its selling price is called the **original markup** or **normal markup.** If the sales price is increased above the $10 to $12, the $2 increase in sales price is called an **additional markup.** Sometimes an increase above the original sales price is referred to as a **markup.** For clarity, we will use the term additional markup to refer to a markup above the initial selling price. A reduction in the initial selling price of $10 to $7 is called a **markdown** of $3. A store using the retail inventory method must also keep a record of the additional markups and markdowns. Changes in the original selling price actually make the calculation of a cost ratio more complicated than shown in the illustration. To illustrate the effects of additional markups and markdowns on the computation of the ending inventory, assume the following data.

	Cost	Retail
Beginning inventory	$20,000	$25,000
Purchases	70,000	92,000
Additional markups		3,000
Markdowns		4,000
Net sales		94,000

An estimate of the ending inventory is computed as follows.

	Cost	Retail
Beginning inventory	$20,000	$ 25,000
Purchases	70,000	92,000
Additional markups		3,000
Goods available for sale	$90,000	$120,000

Ratio of cost to retail:

$$\frac{\$ 90,000}{\$120,000} = 75\%$$

Less: Net sales	$94,000	
Markdowns	4,000	98,000
Estimate of ending inventory at retail		22,000
Cost ratio		× 75%
Estimate of ending inventory at lower of cost or market		$ 16,500

Inclusion of the additional markups, but not the markdowns, in the computation of the cost ratio is the traditional way that accountants apply the retail method. This approach is used because it results in a more conservative ending inventory estimate than if the markdowns were included in the computation. This approach is also used because it produces an ending inventory value that is an approximation of the lower of cost or market. A more detailed discussion of the modifications needed to adjust the retail inventory method for price changes is covered in Intermediate Accounting.

GROSS PROFIT METHOD

Some businesses do not maintain a record of the retail price of beginning inventory and purchases. If this information is not available, the retail inventory method cannot be used. However, the goods on hand may be estimated without taking a physical count by applying the **gross profit method.** This method is based on the assumption that the gross profit percent (gross profit / net sales) remains approximately the same from period to period.

To illustrate, assume that the inventory of a business was totally destroyed by fire. A review of the last two years' operations revealed that the gross profit percent was 40%. On the date of the fire, the ledger had been posted up to date and, as part of the company's internal control system, was locked in a fireproof safe. Selected account balances were:

	Dr. (Cr.) Balance
Sales	$(140,000)
Sales returns and allowances	8,000
Inventory—Beginning balance	16,300
Purchases	83,100
Purchases returns and allowances	(2,500)
Freight-in	700

Based on this data, an estimate of the cost of the ending inventory is computed as follows.

1. **Cost of goods available for sale**
   = Beginning inventory + Cost of goods purchased
   = $16,300 + $81,300
   = $97,600

2. **Estimated cost percent**
   = 100.0% − Gross profit percent
   = 100.0% − 40.0%
   = 60.0%

3. **Estimated cost of goods sold**
   = Net sales × Estimated cost percentage
   = $132,000 × 60%
   = $79,200

4. **Estimated cost of inventory**
   = Cost of goods available for sale − Estimated cost of goods sold
   = $97,600 − $79,200
   = $18,400

These computations are shown here in a partial income statement format.

Sales		$140,000	
Less: Sales returns and allowances		8,000	
Net sales		132,000	100%
Cost of goods sold:			
Beginning inventory		$16,300	
Purchases	$83,100		
Less: Purchases returns & allowances	(2,500)		
Add: Freight-in	700		
Net purchases		81,300	
Cost of goods available for sale		97,600	
Less: Estimated cost of ending inventory		?	
Estimated cost of goods sold ($132,000 × .60)		79,200	60%
Estimated gross profit on sales ($132,000 × .40)		$ 52,800	40%

The goods that were available for sale but had not been sold must have been on hand; their cost is the difference between the estimated cost of goods sold ($79,200) and the cost of goods available for sale ($97,600), which is $18,400.

The reliability of the ending inventory estimate depends on the estimate of the gross profit percent and the accuracy of the current accounting records. Since the gross profit percent is based on past relationships between gross profit and sales, adjustments to the percent should be made for known changes in the relationship.

PRESENTATION IN FINANCIAL STATEMENTS

The method used to account for inventory can significantly affect a firm's financial position and results of operations. Because of the importance of inventory, additional information is provided in footnotes to the financial statements. The disclosure commonly contains:

1. The cost-flow method that is used.
2. Whether that method is applied to all of the inventory.
3. The method of valuing the inventory (cost or lower of cost or market).
4. Whether the cost flow method was used consistently from one period to another.

Figure 9–5 on page 390 shows an example of disclosure information provided. Other examples are contained in Appendix A at the end of this book.

APPENDIX: ALLOCATION OF INVENTORY COST WHEN THE PERPETUAL INVENTORY SYSTEM IS USED

Recall that in Chapter 5 two inventory systems—periodic and perpetual—were discussed and illustrated. In this chapter, the specific identification, FIFO, LIFO, and weighted average cost flow assumptions were discussed and illustrated, assuming that the firm had adopted a periodic inventory system. One or more of these same four methods may also be adopted if the firm uses a perpetual inventory system. (The average cost flow method is called the moving average method when using a perpetual inventory system.) However, since the perpetual system determines the cost of goods sold at the time of sale, rather than at the end of the period, the two systems produce different net income and ending inventory amounts in some cases.

This Appendix illustrates the application of the four cost flow methods with a perpetual inventory system, using the same data used in the periodic illustrations. The inventory record of a computer game was:

Objective 7: Allocation of inventory costs—perpetual inventory system

Figure 9–5
Illustration of Inventory Disclosures in Financial Statement

FEDERATED DEPARTMENT STORES, INC.
Consolidated Balance Sheet

(in thousands)	January 28, 1984	January 29, 1983
Assets		
Current Assets:		
Cash	$ 64,505	$ 54,634
Accounts receivable	1,427,220	1,266,194
Merchandise inventories	1,128,476	943,932
Supplies and prepaid expenses	35,729	35,095
Total Current Assets	2,655,930	2,299,855

Notes to Financial Statements

1. Summary of Significant Accounting Policies
Merchandise inventories are substantially all valued by the retail method and stated on the LIFO (last-in, first-out) basis, which is lower than market. The LIFO basis is applied to give recognition to the effects of inflation in the cost of sales by matching current costs with current revenues.

4. Inventories
Merchandise inventories at the 1983 year-end were $1,128.5 million, compared with $943.9 million at the end of the preceding year. At year-end 1983, 1982, and 1981 inventories were $271.9 million, $261.2 million and $241.9 million lower than they would have been had the retail method been used without the application of the LIFO basis. This application resulted in charges of 13 cents per share in 1983, 18 cents per share in 1982 and 27 cents per share in 1981. Management believes that the LIFO method, which charges the most recent merchandise costs to the results of current operations, provides a better matching of current costs with current revenues in the determination of net income.

	Units	Unit Cost	Total Cost
Jan. 1 Beginning merchandise inventory	10	$10	$100
Purchases:			
April 15	12	11	132
July 7	15	12	180
Goods available for sale	37		$412
Sales:			
April 20	8		
August 12	10		
Total sales	18		
Dec. 31 Ending merchandise inventory	19		

The availability of more versatile and less costly computers has allowed more companies to adopt the perpetual inventory system, and thus achieve better inventory control.

PERPETUAL INVENTORY SYSTEM ILLUSTRATED

In a perpetual inventory system, an inventory card is maintained for each item in stock and an inventory control account is kept in the general ledger. To provide a continuous and current record of inventory transactions, the appropriate inventory card and the *Merchandise Inventory* account are adjusted as purchases and sales transactions occur. Inventory purchases are recorded at cost in the *Merchandise Inventory* account and in the individual inventory cards. Chapter 5 showed that the following two entries are made at the time of sale.

Mar.	15	Accounts Receivable (or Cash)	20	
		Sales		20
		Sold one unit of inventory for $20.		
	15	Cost of Goods Sold	10	
		Merchandise Inventory		10
		Transferred cost of unit sold to cost of		
		goods sold.		

The dollar amount of the first entry is based on the sales price. If the per-unit cost varies, the dollar amount recorded in the second entry depends on the cost flow method used.

SPECIFIC IDENTIFICATION METHOD

The computations for the specific identification method would be the same as those described for a periodic inventory system. They will not be repeated here. The only difference between the two methods is that under a perpetual system an entry is made at the time of sale to record the transfer of cost from the *Merchandise Inventory* account to the *Cost of Goods Sold* account.

FIRST-IN, FIRST-OUT METHOD

A perpetual inventory card using the same data presented earlier for the periodic inventory system is shown in Figure 9–6, which assumes a FIFO cost flow assumption. Note that the perpetual inventory record shows the unit and dollar amounts on a continuous basis for goods on hand, goods purchased, and goods sold.

Under the FIFO method, the cost of units removed from inventory is assumed to be from the first units available for sale at the time of each sale. The cost of the units on hand is composed of the most recent purchases. Thus, in Figure 9–6, the cost of the 8 units sold ($80) on April 20 is computed from the unit cost of the earliest units available, which are those in the beginning inventory. The 14 remaining unsold units are identified as: (1) two units from the beginning inventory; and (2) twelve units from the April 15 purchase.

The identification of units from separate purchases results in what are frequently called *inventory cost layers*. For the next sale, the cost of 2 units from

Item: Zonk III							Minimum Stock: 10		
Code: 1800		Location: Store Display					Maximum Stock: 30		

		Purchases			Cost of Goods Sold			Balance		
Date	Explanation	Units	Unit Cost	Total Cost	Units	Unit Cost	Total Cost	Units	Unit Cost	Total Cost
1/1	Beginning balance							10	10.00	100.00
4/15	Purchases	12	11.00	132.00				10	10.00	100.00
								12	11.00	132.00
4/20	Sales				8	10.00	80.00	2	10.00	20.00
								12	11.00	132.00
7/7	Purchases	15	12.00	180.00				2	10.00	20.00
								12	11.00	132.00
								15	12.00	180.00
8/12	Sales				2	10.00	20.00	4	11.00	44.00
					8	11.00	88.00	15	12.00	180.00

Figure 9–6
Inventory Card for Perpetual Inventory System—FIFO Cost-Flow Method

the beginning inventory ($20) and 8 units from the first purchase ($88) are transferred to cost of goods sold. This leaves an ending inventory of 19 units, valued at $224. Thus, at the end of the period, the *Cost of Goods Sold* account will show a balance of $188 ($80 + $108).

LAST-IN, FIRST-OUT METHOD

When the LIFO method (see Figure 9–7) is used in conjunction with a perpetual inventory system, the cost of goods sold is determined at the point of each sale, based on the assumption that the last units acquired are the first ones sold. Thus, the cost of the 8 units sold on April 20 consists of the cost of the most recent units purchased on April 15. The inventory balance of 14 units consists of two inventory cost layers—10 units from the beginning inventory and 4 units from the April 15 purchase. Similarly, the 10 units sold on August 12 are identified with the most recent units acquired on July 7. The cost of goods sold for the period is $208 ($88 + $120). The ending inventory is $204 ($100 + $44 + $60).

MOVING AVERAGE METHOD

Under the **moving average** method (see Figure 9–8), a new average cost per unit is computed after each purchase, rather than simply computing a weighted average at year-end. The moving average cost is used to compute the cost of goods sold and inventory on hand until additional units are acquired at a different unit price. It is computed as follows.

$$\frac{\text{Cost of goods available for sale currently}}{\text{Total number of units available for sale currently}} = \text{moving average cost}$$

Item: Zonk III   Minimum Stock: 10
Code: 1800   Location: Store Display   Maximum Stock: 30

		Purchases			Cost of Goods Sold			Balance		
Date	Explanation	Units	Unit Cost	Total Cost	Units	Unit Cost	Total Cost	Units	Unit Cost	Total Cost
1/1	Beginning balance							10	10.00	100.00
4/15	Purchases	12	11.00	132.00				{ 10	10.00	100.00
								{ 12	11.00	132.00
4/20	Sales				8	11.00	88.00	{ 10	10.00	100.00
								{ 4	11.00	44.00
7/7	Purchases	15	12.00	180.00				{ 10	10.00	100.00
								{ 4	11.00	44.00
								{ 15	12.00	180.00
8/12	Sales				10	12.00	120.00	{ 10	10.00	100.00
								{ 4	11.00	44.00
								{ 5	12.00	60.00

Figure 9–7
Inventory Card for Perpetual Inventory System—LIFO Cost-Flow Method

In our illustration, the average cost per unit after the April 15 purchase is:

$$(\$100 + \$132)/(10 \text{ units} + 12 \text{ units}) = \$10.55 \text{ per unit}$$

Since there were no additional purchases made before the sale of 8 units on April 20, the cost of the units sold is $84.40 (8 units $\times$ $10.55 per unit). The 14 units on hand are valued at $147.60 ($232.00 − $84.40). As a result of rounding, the cost of the units on hand is approximately equal to the 14 units times the $10.55 per unit. This average cost of $10.55 would be used

Item: Zonk III   Minimum Stock: 10
Code: 1800   Location: Store Display   Maximum Stock: 30

		Purchases			Cost of Goods Sold			Balance		
Date	Explanation	Units	Unit Cost	Total Cost	Units	Unit Cost	Total Cost	Units	Unit Cost	Total Cost
1/1	Beginning balance							10	10.00	100.00
4/15	Purchases	12	11.00	132.00				22	10.55	232.00
4/20	Sales				8	10.55	84.40	14	10.55	147.60
7/7	Purchases	15	12.00	180.00				29	11.30	327.60
8/12	Sales				10	11.30	113.00	19	11.30	214.60

Computations

4/15 ($100.00 + $132.00)/(10 units + 12 units) = $10.55 per unit*
7/7 ($147.60 + $180.00)/(14 units + 15 units) = $11.30 per unit*

*Rounded to the nearest cent.

Figure 9–8
Inventory Card for Perpetual Inventory System—Moving Average Cost-Flow Method

to cost additional units sold until another purchase is made, at which time a new moving average cost is computed, as shown in Figure 9–8.

COMPARISON OF THE COSTING METHODS—PERPETUAL INVENTORY SYSTEM

Justifications and disadvantages of using each method are the same as those discussed earlier for the periodic inventory system and will not be repeated here. Furthermore, the relative dollar amounts of cost of goods sold, net income, and ending inventory produced by the four methods would also be the same. That is, in periods of rising prices, LIFO will produce a higher cost of goods sold, a lower net income, and a lower ending inventory than the FIFO or average cost methods.

GLOSSARY

ADDITIONAL MARKUP. An increase in the sales price of an item above the initial selling price (p. 386).

AVERAGE COST. An inventory costing method in which an average unit cost is computed by dividing the total cost of goods available for sale by the total number of units available for sale. Moving average and weighted average are variations of the average cost method (p. 371).

CONSERVATISM. An accounting convention that specifies that when equally acceptable accounting procedures or estimates are available, an accountant should select the one that produces the lowest asset or net income amount. An example is the lower of cost or market approach to inventory valuation (p. 381).

CONSIGNEE. A firm or individual holding goods on consignment. The consignee does not own the goods held on consignment (p. 370).

CONSIGNMENT. A marketing arrangement whereby physical control of merchandise, but not title, is transferred from one business (the consignor) to another (the consignee) (p. 370).

CONSIGNOR. A firm or individual that ships goods on consignment. Title to the goods is retained by the consignor until the goods are sold by the consignee (p. 370).

CONSISTENCY. An accounting principle that calls for the use of the same acceptable accounting procedure from period to period (p. 379).

FIRST-IN, FIRST-OUT (FIFO). An inventory costing method that assumes that the first units purchased were the first units sold. The ending inventory consists of the cost of the most recently purchased units (p. 373).

GROSS PROFIT METHOD. A method used to estimate ending inventory value based on the assumption that the gross profit percentage is approximately the same from period to period (p. 387).

LAST-IN, FIRST-OUT (LIFO). An inventory costing method that assumes that the most recent units purchased were the first units sold. Ending inventory consists of the cost of the earliest units purchased (p. 374).

LOWER OF COST OR MARKET. An inventory valuation method by which inventory is valued at lower of original cost or market on the financial statement date (p. 381).

MARKUP. See additional markup and original markup (p. 386).

MARKDOWN. A decrease in the sales price of an item below the initial selling price (p. 386).

MOVING AVERAGE. An inventory costing method by which an average unit cost is computed after each purchase (p. 392).

NET REALIZABLE VALUE. The anticipated sales price of an item less the estimated cost of selling and disposal (p. 382).

ORIGINAL MARKUP (NORMAL MARKUP). The difference between the cost of an item and its initial selling price (p. 386).

RETAIL INVENTORY METHOD. A method used to estimate the ending inventory value based on the relationship of cost to retail prices (p. 385).

SPECIFIC IDENTIFICATION. An inventory costing method by which the cost of a specific item sold can be separately identified from the cost of other units held in the inventory (p. 372).

WEIGHTED AVERAGE. An inventory costing method by which an average cost per unit is computed by dividing the total cost of the units available for sale by the total number of units available for sale (p. 375).

DISCUSSION QUESTIONS

1. Explain the terms "FOB shipping point" and "FOB destination." If goods are shipped FOB shipping point at a cost of $600, which party to the transaction must pay the freight bill?
2. There are two parties to a consignment transaction. Which party should include goods being held on a consignment in his or her inventory?
3. What costs should be included in the cost of an inventory item?
4. Why are inventory costing methods needed?
5. Must a company use the inventory costing method that best conforms to the actual physical movement of the goods? Explain.
6. Explain the assumptions behind the FIFO method and the LIFO method.
7. Compare the effects of LIFO and FIFO on net income and ending inventory values during a period of increasing prices.
8. Explain the income tax benefits from using LIFO during periods of inflation.
9. What effect does the principle of consistency have on the selection of an inventory costing method? Why is it important that an accounting method be applied consistently from period to period?
10. Define the term "market," as used in the phrase "lower of cost or market."
11. What accounting convention justifies the use of the lower of cost or market valuation approach? Explain the convention.
12. Define net realizable value.
13. Why do inventory errors affect two periods?
14. If the ending inventory is mistakenly understated, what is the effect on net income in that period and the next period? What is the effect on the year-end balance sheet values reported for each year?
15. What uses can be made of the retail inventory method and the gross profit method of estimating the cost of inventory?
16. What records must be maintained to use the retail inventory method?
17. Explain the gross profit method as it is used to estimate the ending inventory.
18A. Differentiate between the weighted average cost method and the moving average cost method.

EXERCISES

Exercise 9-1 Inventory Cost-Flow Methods—Periodic Inventory System

The beginning inventory and the purchases of a product during June are shown here.

June	1	Inventory	500 units @ $4.00
	8	Purchase	200 units @ 4.15
	19	Purchase	100 units @ 4.17
	23	Purchase	300 units @ 4.26
	29	Purchase	400 units @ 4.25

On June 30, 300 units remain in inventory. The company uses a periodic inventory system. Determine the cost of the ending inventory and the cost of goods sold using three methods.

1. Weighted average.
2. FIFO.
3. LIFO.

Exercise 9-2 Lower of Cost or Market

The inventory of the O'Connor Company contains the following items as of December 31.

Item	Quantity	Unit Price Cost	Unit Price Market
#33	60	$ 4	$ 4.20
#24	25	8	7.00
#6	10	20	17.00
#45	70	6	6.00
#27	55	9	8.40

Required:
A. Determine the ending inventory value as of December 31, applying the lower of cost or market rule to the individual items.
B. What effect did application of the LCM rule have on the financial statements of the firm?

Exercise 9-3 Net Realizable Value

Premier Auto is an automobile dealership. One of its models was used as a demonstrator during the year. Presented here is the information related to the demonstrator as of December 31, the end of the current fiscal year.

Normal sales price	$10,530
Original cost	9,300
Estimated sales value in existing condition	8,500
Estimated selling and disposal cost	600

Required:
From the information provided, determine the value at which the demonstrator should be reported in the December 31 financial statements. Is there an effect on net income reported for the current period?

Exercise 9-4 Effects of Inventory Errors

The Grande Company's income statements for the past three years are as shown here.

	1986	1987	1988
Net Sales	$40,000	$50,000	$52,000
Beginning inventory	10,000	9,000	5,000
Purchases	20,000	20,000	26,000
Goods available for sale	30,000	29,000	31,000
Ending inventory	9,000	5,000	6,000
Cost of goods sold	21,000	24,000	25,000
Gross profit on sales	19,000	26,000	27,000
Operating expenses	6,000	8,000	10,000
Net income	$13,000	$18,000	$17,000

Because of errors, the 1986 ending inventory is understated by $3,000, and the 1987 ending inventory is overstated by $2,000. The 1988 ending inventory is correct.

Required:
A. Determine the correct amount of net income for each of the three years.
B. Determine the total income for the three-year period, as shown and as corrected.

Exercise 9-5 Effects of Inventory Errors
The SP Corporation was formed in 1987. Partial income statements for its first two years of operations are shown here.

	1987		1988	
Sales		$70,000		$80,000
Cost of goods sold:				
Beginning inventory	$25,000		$20,000	
Purchases	45,000		53,000	
Cost of goods available				
for sale	70,000		73,000	
Less: Ending inventory	20,000		26,000	
Cost of goods sold		50,000		47,000
Gross profit on sales		$20,000		$33,000

After the 1988 income statement was prepared, the firm's accountant noted that the gross profit percentage varied significantly between the two years, and that the 1988 gross profit increased $13,000 with only a $10,000 increase in sales. After an extensive review of the records, she found that inventory in the amount of $5,000 was correctly recorded as a purchase in 1987, but was not included in the physical count taken on December 31, 1987. The 1988 ending inventory was determined to be correct.

Required:
A. Prepare corrected partial income statements for the two years.
B. What effect did this error have on the gross profit of each year? What effect did the error have on the combined gross profit for the two years? Explain your answer.
C. What effect did this error have on the balance sheet accounts for each year?

Exercise 9-6 Retail Inventory Method
Using the following information, determine the cost of the April 30 inventory by the retail inventory method.

	Cost	Retail
Beginning inventory, April	$28,000	$43,000
Purchases during April	17,500	27,000
Sales during April		60,000

Exercise 9-7 Gross Profit Method

The following information relates to the inventory of the C. B. Owens Company during September.

Inventory, September 1	$30,000
Purchases	40,000
Purchases returns	3,000
Sales	80,000
Average gross profit on sales	35%

Use the gross profit method to estimate the cost of the inventory as of September 30.

Exercise 9A-8 Inventory Cost Methods—Perpetual Inventory System

The following information relates to the inventory of the Sheffield Company during March.

March	1	Beginning inventory	125 units @ $10
	3	Purchased	60 units @ $11
	10	Sold	50 units
	12	Purchased	50 units @ $12
	17	Sold	70 units
	25	Sold	20 units

Assume that the ending inventory on March 31 consisted of 12 units from the beginning inventory, 50 units from the March 3 purchase, and 33 units from the March 12 purchase. The Sheffield Company uses a perpetual system. Determine the cost of the ending inventory and the cost of goods sold, using four methods.

1. The moving average.
2. Specific identification.
3. LIFO.
4. FIFO.

Exercise 9A-9 LIFO and FIFO Cost-Flow Methods—Periodic and Perpetual Inventory Systems

The following transactions relate to the inventory of item C-7.

Jan.	1	Beginning Inventory	6 @ $50 = $300
Feb.	14	Purchased	7 @ $52 = $364
Mar.	25	Sold	9
July	8	Purchased	5 @ $55 = $275
Sept.	3	Purchased	8 @ $56 = $448
Oct.	13	Sold	9
Dec.	10	Sold	3

Required:

A. Using a periodic system and the LIFO method, determine the cost of the five items in inventory on December 31 and the cost of goods sold for the year.
B. Using a perpetual system and the LIFO method, determine the cost of the year-end inventory and the cost of goods sold.

C. Using a periodic system and the FIFO method, determine the cost of the five items in inventory on December 31 and the cost of goods sold for the year.

D. Using a perpetual system and the FIFO method, determine the cost of the year-end inventory and the cost of goods sold.

PROBLEMS

Problem 9-1 Inventory Cost-Flow Methods—Periodic Inventory System

During the year, the Irving Company sold 11,100 units of its product at $8 each. Operating expenses of $12,000 were incurred. Purchases of the product are shown below.

Jan.	1	Inventory	1,500 @ $4.00
Feb.	4	Purchases	2,000 @ $4.10
April	29	Purchases	2,800 @ $4.25
July	23	Purchases	3,000 @ $4.30
Sept.	6	Purchases	2,000 @ $4.35
Dec.	11	Purchases	1,500 @ $4.50

Irving Company uses a periodic inventory system.

Required:

A. Prepare a schedule to compute the number of units and cost of goods available for sale during the year.

B. Determine the cost of the ending inventory as of December 31, using the following inventory costing methods.
1. FIFO.
2. LIFO.
3. Weighted average.

C. Prepare three income statements in adjacent columns, using each of these inventory costing methods.

Problem 9-2 Lower of Cost or Market

The following information relates to barrels of oil held in the inventory of Starr Oil Company during 1987.

		Barrels	Unit Cost
January 1	Beginning inventory	50,000	$40
April 15	Purchases	20,000	40
May 13	Sales ($50 per barrel)	(50,000)	
August 9	Purchases	30,000	40
October 28	Sales ($50 per barrel)	(35,000)	

Due to an oil glut, the replacement cost for a barrel of the same grade of oil was $32 per barrel on December 31, 1987. In 1988, the company disposed of the 15,000 barrels of oil in the ending inventory for $615,000. No additional purchases were made in 1988. Starr Company uses a periodic inventory system and the average cost flow method.

Required:

Complete the following partial income statements for 1987 and 1988, using the average cost flow method and the lower of cost or market rule.

	Average Cost		LCM	
	1987	1988	1987	1988
Sales	___	___	___	___
Cost of goods sold				
Beginning inventory	___	___	___	___
Purchases	___	___	___	___
Cost of goods available for sale	___	___	___	___
Less: Ending inventory	___	___	___	___
Cost of goods sold	___	___	___	___
Gross profit on sales	___	___	___	___

Problem 9-3 Inventory Cost-Flow Methods—Periodic Inventory System

The following information relates to the inventory of the Millburn Company during the month of December.

	Units	Unit Cost	Total Cost
12/1 Beginning inventory	300	$6.00	$1,800
12/10 Purchases	500	6.25	3,125
12/23 Purchases	500	6.35	3,175
Totals	1,300		$8,100

Millburn uses the periodic inventory system. During the month, 700 units were sold for $7,600. A physical count on December 31 verified that 600 units were on hand.

Required:

A. Prepare an income statement through gross profit on sales for December, using each of the following costing methods.
  1. Specific identification, assuming that 300 units were sold from the beginning inventory and 400 units were sold from the first purchase.
  2. FIFO.
  3. LIFO.
  4. Weighted average.
B. Which cost-flow methods resulted in the highest gross profit on sales? The highest ending inventory? Explain why your results differ.
C. Prepare an income statement through gross profit on sales for December, using the FIFO and LIFO costing methods and assuming that the December 23 purchase had not been made.
D. Management of Millburn Company is expecting the unit cost to increase to $6.75 early in the next period. In anticipation of the price increase, assume that a purchase of 600 additional units was made on December 29 at a unit cost of $6.50. Prepare an income statement through gross profit on sales for December, using the FIFO and LIFO costing methods.
E. Compare your results obtained in requirements A, C, and D. Explain why your results are or are not the same.

Problem 9-4 Effects of Inventory Errors

The income statements for Babbitt Company for two years are shown here.

	1987	1988
Sales	$475,000	$500,000
Cost of goods sold		
Beginning inventory	85,000	50,000
Purchases	200,000	220,000
Goods available for sale	285,000	270,000
Ending inventory	50,000	70,000
Cost of goods sold	235,000	200,000
Gross profit on sales	240,000	300,000
Operating expenses	100,000	120,000
Net income	$140,000	$180,000

The following information has been discovered concerning 1987.

1. On December 23, Babbitt Company recorded goods purchased at a cost of $500. The terms were FOB shipping point. The goods were delivered by the seller to the transportation company on December 27. The goods were not included in the ending inventory, since they had not arrived.
2. Babbitt sells goods that it does not own, on a consignment basis. Consigned goods on hand at year-end were included in inventory at a cost of $1,500.
3. A purchase of goods worth $1,200 was made in December, but not recorded until January. The goods were received on December 28 and included in the physical inventory.
4. A sale of goods costing $800 was made and recorded in December. Since the buyer requested that the goods be held for later delivery, the items were on hand and included in inventory at year-end.
5. Babbitt sold goods costing $600 for $1,000 on December 26. The terms were FOB destination. The goods arrived at the destination in January. The sale was recorded in 1987, and the goods were excluded from the ending inventory.

Required:
A. Determine the correct ending inventory figure for 1987.
B. Prepare revised income statements for 1987 and 1988.
C. Determine the total net income for the two-year period, both before and after the revisions. Why are these figures similar or different?

Problem 9-5 Retail Inventory Method

Jenna's Boutique uses the retail inventory method to estimate the ending inventory for the purpose of preparing interim financial statements. The following information is available for the three months ended on March 31, 1987.

	Cost	Retail
Jan. 1 Beginning inventory	$45,000	$80,000
Net purchases	85,000	120,000
Net sales		175,000
Operating expenses	24,000	

Required:
A. Determine the cost of the March 31 inventory.
B. Prepare an income statement for the first quarter of the year.

Problem 9-6 Retail Inventory Method—Additional Markup and Markdown

Willie's Western Store takes the year-end physical inventory at retail and converts it to cost by the retail inventory method. Since Willie suspects that one of his employees has been stealing merchandise, he also wants to use the retail inventory method to estimate the cost of the ending inventory. The following information is available as of December 31.

	Cost	Retail
January 1 Beginning inventory	$24,000	$42,000
Purchases	93,000	149,000
Purchases returns	1,800	3,000
Additional markups		4,000
Markdowns		2,000
Net Sales		163,000
December 31 Physical inventory		22,000

Required:

A. Estimate the cost of the December 31 inventory.

B. Calculate the estimated loss due to theft at cost and at retail.

Problem 9-7 Gross Profit Method

The inventory of the Granny's Country Store was totally destroyed by fire on March 15. The accounting records were not destroyed, and they contained the following information for the period of January 1 through March 15.

Inventory balance, January 1	$25,600
Sales	75,200
Sales returns and allowances	2,700
Purchases	32,800
Purchases returns and allowances	800
Freight-in	1,200

The gross profit on sales over the last four years has averaged 45%. Estimate the inventory on hand at the date of the fire.

Problem 9A-8 Inventory Cost-Flow Methods—Perpetual Inventory System

The Fiesta Company buys and sells copy machines. The inventory on October 1 consisted of seven units at a cost of $1,800 each. Transactions during October are shown here.

Oct.	1	Purchased	3 units at $1,900 per unit
	11	Sold	4 units
	20	Purchased	6 units at $2,000 per unit
	23	Sold	3 units
	28	Sold	5 units

Fiesta Company uses a perpetual inventory system.

Required:

A. Record the information on perpetual inventory cards using each of the following methods.

1. LIFO.
2. FIFO.
3. Moving average.

B. Fiesta Company sold its product for $3,200 each, throughout October. Operating expenses for the month totaled $2,800. Prepare an income statement based on each of the following inventory costing methods.
   1. LIFO.
   2. FIFO.
   3. Moving average.
   4. Specific identification.

(For specific identification, assume the first sale was out of the beginning inventory, the second sale was out of the October 1 purchase, and the third sale was out of the October 20 purchase.)

Problem 9A-9 FIFO and LIFO Cost-Flow Methods—Perpetual Inventory System

Merlin's Games adopted a perpetual inventory system to account for its inventory in video games. The inventory on June 1 contained three units of Star Peace, a model that cost $180 per unit. The following data related to this model was accumulated during the month of June. All transactions were for cash.

	Purchases		Sales	
Date	Number of Units	Cost per Unit	Number of Units	Unit Sales Price
6/6	2	$200		
6/10			1	$375
6/16	3	250		
6/23			2	400
6/28			2	410

Operating expenses were $500 for the month.

Required:
A. Compute the cost of goods sold and the cost of the ending inventory for this model for the month of June assuming first the FIFO and then the LIFO cost-flow methods.
B. Record the sale of two units on June 23 for both the FIFO and the LIFO cost-flow methods.
C. Prepare income statements for both cost-flow methods, assuming a 30% income tax rate.
D. Which cost-flow method resulted in the highest gross profit from sales? Under what conditions would you expect the other method to result in the highest gross profit?
E. What amount is reported for the inventory in the June 30 balance sheet under each cost-flow method? Explain why there is a difference in inventory values when the number of units in the ending inventory is the same for both methods.
F. How much did income taxes differ between the two methods?
G. Assume that there were no additional units purchased and all of the units in the ending inventory were sold in the next period for $410 per unit. Which method will show the highest net income in the next period? The income tax rate for the next year is expected to be 30%.

ALTERNATE PROBLEMS

Problem 9-1A Inventory Cost Flow Methods—Periodic Inventory System

The A. D. Fisk Company sells only one product, which had a selling price of $15 per unit throughout the past year. Total sales for the year amounted to $65,625. Selling and administrative expenses of $14,800 were incurred. The product was purchased as follows.

January 1 inventory	750 @ $7.50
Purchases:	
Mar. 3	800 @ 7.70
May 14	825 @ 7.80
Aug. 2	1,000 @ 8.00
Sept. 23	1,100 @ 8.25
Nov. 5	800 @ 8.30

The company uses a periodic inventory system.   65625

Required:

A. Prepare a schedule to compute the number of units and cost of goods available for sale during the year.

B. Determine the cost of the year-end inventory, using each of the following methods.
   1. FIFO.
   2. LIFO.
   3. Weighted average.

C. Prepare three income statements in adjacent columns using each of these methods to determine the cost of goods sold.

Problem 9-2A Lower of Cost or Market

The following information applies to the inventory of the Campbell Camera Shop as of December 31.

Camera Model	Quantity	Unit Price	
		Actual Cost	Replacement Cost
A-4	15	$ 40	$ 35
C-7	23	100	100
G-1	12	65	62
Z-8	5	20	25

Required:

A. Compute the ending inventory value as of December 31, applying the lower of cost or market rule to each item in stock.

B. What effect did application of the LCM rule have on the financial statements of the firm?

C. Assume that at the end of the next fiscal period, 12 units of model A-4 are still on hand and the replacement cost is $38 per unit. How would this increase in replacement cost affect the inventory value of the 12 units?

Problem 9-3A Effects of Inventory Errors

Two consecutive annual income statements for the Omega Company are shown here.

	1987	1988
Sales Revenue	$150,000	$175,000
Cost of goods sold		
Beginning inventory	35,000	30,000
Purchases	90,000	100,000
Goods available for sale	125,000	130,000
Ending inventory	30,000	32,000
Cost of goods sold	95,000	98,000
Gross profit on sales	55,000	77,000
Operating expenses	26,000	31,000
Net income	$ 29,000	$ 46,000

The following information has been discovered concerning 1987.

1. Omega Company sells goods of the Alpha Corporation on consignment. Consigned goods on hand as of December 31 were included in the inventory, at a cost of $1,300.
2. On December 27, Omega sold goods costing $600 for $1,200. The terms were FOB destination, and the goods reached the buyer on January 6. Omega recorded the sale in 1987 and the goods were excluded from the ending inventory.
3. On December 19, Omega made and recorded a purchase of goods worth $1,800. The terms were FOB shipping point, and Omega received notice that the goods were delivered to the transportation company on December 23. Since the goods had not arrived by the end of the year, they were not included in inventory.
4. On December 31, a customer had goods costing $300 out on trial. These goods were excluded from ending inventory.
5. On December 26, Omega purchased goods for $750. The terms were FOB destination. Since the goods arrived in January, they were excluded from the ending inventory. The purchase was recorded in December.

Required:
A. Determine the correct ending inventory figure for 1987.
B. Prepare revised income statements for 1987 and 1988.
C. Determine the total net income for the two-year period, both before and after the revisions. Explain why the figures are similar or different.

Problem 9-4A Retail Inventory Method

Starry Day Paint Shop takes the year-end inventory at retail and converts it to cost by the retail inventory method. For control purposes, the paint shop also estimates the cost of the ending inventory, using the retail inventory method. The accounting records contain the following information on December 31.

	Cost	Retail
Inventory, January 1	$ 82,300	$120,000
Purchases	182,100	260,000
Purchases returns	4,000	8,000
Net sales		295,000
Physical inventory, December 31		68,800

Required:

A. Convert the retail dollar value of the December 31 physical inventory to cost.

B. Estimate the cost of the December 31 inventory.

C. Calculate the amount of the inventory shortage, at cost and at retail.

Problem 9-5A Retail Inventory Method—Additional Markups and Markdowns

Fighting Tigers Athletic Clothing uses the retail inventory method to estimate its ending inventory at lower of cost or market for the purpose of preparing interim statements. The following information is available on September 30, 1987.

	Cost	Retail
Beginning inventory	$ 42,300	$ 82,200
Net purchases	115,800	222,150
Additional markups		5,650
Markdowns		8,500
Net sales		228,300
Operating expenses		54,810

Required:

A. Estimate the cost of the inventory at the end of the first nine months of operations.

B. Prepare an income statement for the first nine months of operations.

Problem 9-6A Gross Profit Method

An explosion occurred at The Magic Shop on the night of April 11 and destroyed the entire inventory. The accounting records, which survived the explosion, contained the following information about the period of January 1 through April 11.

Sales	$37,200
Sales returns and allowances	2,100
Purchases	18,900
Purchases returns and allowances	1,200
Freight-in	500
Inventory balance, January 1	9,500

The gross profit on sales has averaged 37% over the last three years. Estimate the cost of the inventory that was destroyed.

Problem 9A-7A Inventory Cost-Flow Methods—Perpetual Inventory System

The Good Buy Company sells one type of phone answering machine. The November 1 inventory consisted of 15 units at a cost of $80 each. During November, the selling price was $150 and total operating expenses were $750. Transactions for the month were as follows.

Nov.	3	Purchased	8 units @ $85 per unit
	10	Sold	9 units
	16	Purchased	10 units @ $90 per unit
	21	Sold	6 units
	25	Sold	8 units

Required:

A. Record the information on perpetual inventory cards using each of the following methods.

  1. Moving average.

2. LIFO.
3. FIFO.
B. Prepare an income statement based on the perpetual inventory system for each of the following methods.
1. Moving average.
2. LIFO.
3. FIFO.
4. Specific identification. (For specific identification, assume that the first sale was out of the beginning inventory, the second sale was from the November 16 purchase, and the third sale was from the November 3 purchase.)

Problem 9A-8A FIFO and LIFO Cost-Flow Methods— Perpetual Inventory System

The beginning inventory of article LW4 and information about purchases and sales made during February are shown here.

Feb.	1	Inventory	1,000 units @ $6.00
	4	Purchase	2,500 units @ 6.25
	9	Sale	2,000 units
	12	Purchase	3,000 units @ 6.30
	21	Sale	1,000 units
	24	Sale	1,500 units
	26	Purchase	2,000 units @ 6.35
	27	Sale	1,000 units

The company uses the perpetual inventory system.

Required:
A. For both the LIFO and FIFO methods, compute the cost of goods sold and the cost of the ending inventory.
B. All the units sold on February 21 were sold for cash at $10 each. For both the LIFO and FIFO methods, prepare the general journal entry to record the sale, and the entry to record the cost of goods sold.

CASE

CASE 9-1 Financial Report Analysis Case   Analysis of Inventories
For this case, refer to the Chrysler Corporation's 1984 annual report presented in Appendix A. Complete the requirements in millions of dollars, as shown in the annual report.

Required:
Answer the following questions and perform the necessary computations.

A. What were the inventory balances reported in the 1984 and 1983 comparative balance sheets? Compute inventory as a percentage of current assets for both years. Discuss the primary reason for the change in the percentage.
B. What were the company's policies, with respect to accounting, for domestic productive inventories? Discuss the major advantages of using the LIFO method. With respect to balance sheet valuation, what is a major disadvantage of the LIFO method?

C. Did Chrysler Corporation change its methods of accounting for inventory? What reason did Chrysler give for making the change? Was there a material effect on net income (earnings) of the current year and on prior years? What would the inventory balances have been on December 31, 1984 if the FIFO method had been used? Ignoring income taxes, what effect did the change from LIFO and FIFO have on stockholders' equity? How did it affect operating income? Assuming an effective income tax rate of 40%, compute how much income taxes were reduced or increased in 1984 by using the LIFO method.

10

PLANT ASSETS: ACQUISITION AND ALLOCATION

CHAPTER OVERVIEW AND OBJECTIVES

This chapter discusses the nature of plant assets, the components of their cost, and the methods used to allocate their cost to expense. When you have completed the chapter, you should understand:

1. How the cost of different plant assets is determined.
2. How to apportion the cost of a lump-sum purchase of assets.
3. The nature of depreciation.
4. The factors that should be considered in determining a plant asset's useful life.
5. How to calculate depreciation expense under each of the commonly used depreciation methods.
6. The difference between capital expenditures and revenue expenditures.

The terms *plant assets, plant and equipment,* and *property, plant, and equipment,* are commonly used in accounting to describe those long-lived assets acquired by a business for use in operations, rather than for resale to customers. Examples of such assets include land, buildings, equipment, machinery, storage facilities, and vehicles. The term fixed assets, although seldom used today in the formal financial statements of large companies, often has been used in the past to describe this general category of assets and is still used frequently in conversation and in some of the general accounting literature.

It is management's intention to use plant assets for the future production of goods or services over several accounting periods that distinguishes them from other assets. Since they have value in use, they contain future service benefits for the business. For example, buildings contain future housing services for the company's operations; automobiles contain future transportation services; and computers contain future data processing services. Plant assets are expected to be used in the future to produce goods or services for sale to customers.

Assets that have physical characteristics similar to plant assets, but that are not intended for future use to produce goods or services, should not be included in the plant assets category. For example, construction equipment held by an equipment dealer is inventory, but the same type of equipment held by a construction company represents plant and equipment. Similarly, land held for future expansion or as an investment should be excluded from plant and equipment and classified as a long-term investment.

Because the service benefits contained in plant assets will be used over two or more accounting periods, the cost of the assets is allocated in a systematic manner to the accounting periods that benefit from their use. As the assets are used to produce goods or services, their cost is transferred to depreciation expense to match it with the revenue produced by the sale of the goods or services, which is an application of the ***matching principle***.

DETERMINING THE COST OF PLANT ASSETS

**Objective 1:
The cost of
plant assets**

The cost of a plant asset includes all of the expenditures necessary to obtain the asset and to get it ready for the use intended by the purchaser. An **expenditure** is either a cash payment or liability incurred to acquire a good or service. For example, the cost of acquiring a machine includes its invoice price (minus any cash discounts), sales taxes, freight, insurance in transit, installation expenditures (such as power hookup), and any initial adjustments needed to make the machine function properly. Assume, for example, the purchase of a machine at a list price of $25,000 with terms of 3/20, n/60. In addition, a sales tax of 4% must be paid, freight charges amount to $820, and installation expenditures amount to $675. The cost of the machine to be debited to the *Machinery* account is computed as follows.

List price of the machine	$25,000
Less: cash discount (3% × $25,000)	750
Net cash price	24,250
Sales tax (4% × $24,250)	970
Freight	820
Installation	675
Total	$26,715

The cost of an asset should not exceed the amount for which it could be acquired in a cash transaction, plus the other expenditures necessary to get the asset ready for use. Therefore, if payment is not made in time to take the cash discount, the $750 should be charged to interest expense, rather than to the asset account. In effect, an extra $750 was paid for the privilege of waiting an extra 40 days to make payment. The cost of a used or second-hand asset should include its purchase price plus initial expenditures made for repairs, new parts, paint, and any other conditioning necessary to get the asset ready for use.

Care should be taken that only *reasonable* and *necessary* expenditures are included. Expenditures that could be avoided or that do not increase the usefulness of the asset should be excluded from its cost. For example, expenditures required to repair damage to an asset caused by carelessness during installation should be charged to an expense account, rather than to the asset account.

When a company constructs an asset, for example a building, for its own use, the cost includes:

1. All expenditures made directly for construction (e.g., labor, materials, and insurance premiums paid during construction).
2. Architectural fees.
3. Engineering fees.
4. Building permits.
5. A reasonable amount of general overhead for things such as power, management supervision during construction, and depreciation on machinery used for construction.
6. Interest incurred on borrowed money during the construction period.[1]

The cost of *land* includes the price paid to the seller, the broker's commission, and other necessary expenditures, such as title search and survey fees. If the buyer pays delinquent taxes on the property, such taxes should also be included in the cost of the land. If the land contains a building that is to be demolished in order to construct a new building, the total purchase price plus the cost of removing the old building (less amounts received from the sale of salvaged materials) is included in the cost of the land. The cost of removing the old building is considered part of the land cost because it is incurred to get the land into condition for its intended use—the construction of a new building.

Although land cost is not depreciable because it has an unlimited life, some expenditures related to its acquisition and use, such as landscaping, driveways, fences, and parking lots, do have limited lives and are properly depreciated. Consequently, these items are normally charged to a separate *Land Improvements* account, and depreciated over their estimated useful lives.

APPORTIONING THE COST OF A LUMP-SUM ACQUISITION

Several plant assets may be acquired for a **lump-sum payment,** without the cost of each asset being identified separately. In these cases, the total cost must be systematically allocated to the assets purchased, because they may have different depreciable lives, or they may not be depreciable at all.

The most common method of apportionment is to allocate total cost on the basis of the relative fair values of the assets acquired. Fair values are estimates of current selling prices, which are often determined by appraisals. For ex-

Objective 2: Lump-sum purchase

---

[1]*Statement of Financial Accounting Standards No. 34,* "Capitalization of Interest Cost" (Stamford, Conn.: Financial Accounting Standards Board, 1979), par. 6.

ample, assume that a building, land, and office equipment were purchased as a lump-sum acquisition for a payment of $800,000. Fair values of the assets were determined by an independent appraisal, as follows.

	Fair Value
Building	$595,000
Land	170,000
Office equipment	85,000
Total fair value	$850,000

The total cost of $800,000 is allocated to each asset on the basis of these fair values by use of the following formula.

$$\frac{\text{Fair value of specific asset}}{\text{Total fair value of all assets}} \times \frac{\text{Acquisition}}{\text{Cost}} = \frac{\text{Cost allocated to}}{\text{the specific asset}}$$

Thus, the allocation would be as follows.

Building $\dfrac{595,000}{850,000} \times \$800,000 = \$560,000$

Land $\dfrac{170,000}{850,000} \times \$800,000 = 160,000$

Equipment $\dfrac{85,000}{850,000} \times \$800,000 = \underline{80,000}$

Total $\underline{\$800,000}$

The acquisition would be recorded with the following entry.

Jan.	2	Building	560,000	
		Land	160,000	
		Office Equipment	80,000	
		Cash		800,000
		To record the purchase of plant assets.		

EXCHANGING A NOTE FOR PLANT ASSETS

When a plant asset is purchased on credit, a note is often given in exchange. The note may contain a specified current interest rate, in which case the face value of the note will be equal to the cash price of the asset. For example, if a $20,000, 10%, 18-month note is exchanged for a machine, the transaction is recorded as follows.

Jan.	1	Machinery	20,000	
		Notes Payable		20,000
		Exchanged a $20,000, 10%, 18-month note for machinery.		

Notice that the *Machinery* account is debited only for the cash price of the asset. Interest on the note is not a part of the asset's cost and, therefore, is debited to *Interest Expense* when accrued or paid. Interest expense on the note will be accrued at the end of the year with the following entry.

Dec.	31	Interest Expense	2,000	
		Interest Payable		2,000
		To accrue interest on a note payable for		
		one year ($20,000 × 10%).		

When the note is paid on its maturity date, the entry is:

July	1	Notes Payable	20,000	
		Interest Payable	2,000	
		Interest Expense	1,000	
		Cash		23,000
		Paid a note payable plus interest.		

If no interest rate is specified on the note, or if the specified rate is unreasonable, a portion of the face value must be assumed to represent interest. The asset acquired with the note is recorded at its cash purchase price or the market value of the note, whichever is more clearly determinable. This process is called **imputing interest** on a note.[2] To illustrate, assume that an 18-month, $23,000 noninterest-bearing note was exchanged for a machine with a cash purchase price of $20,000.

The transaction would be recorded as follows.

Jan.	1	Machinery	20,000	
		Discount on Notes Payable	3,000	
		Notes Payable		23,000
		Exchanged a noninterest-bearing note for		
		machinery.		

Note that the machine is recorded at its cash value of $20,000, rather than at the face value of the note. This is the machine's cost and is the amount that is depreciated over the machine's useful life. The remaining $3,000 represents discount or interest on the note, which will be recognized as interest expense over the term of the note.

An adjusting entry is made on December 31 to recognize interest expense for the first year, as follows.

Dec.	31	Interest Expense	2,000	
		Discount on Notes Payable		2,000
		To record interest expense on a note		
		payable.		

[2]Accounting Principles Board, "Interest on Receivables and Payables," *APB Opinion No. 21* (New York: AICPA, August 1971), par. 12.

When the note is paid on its maturity date, the entry is:

July	1	Notes Payable	23,000	
		Interest Expense	1,000	
		Discount on Notes Payable		1,000
		Cash		23,000
		To record payment of a note payable.		

THE NATURE OF DEPRECIATION

Objective 3: What depreciation is

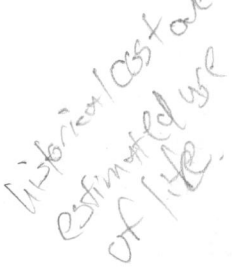

As described earlier, plant assets contain service benefits that a business intends to use over the life of the assets in the production of goods or services. All plant assets, except land, have limited useful lives, and their service benefits will be consumed by the end of their useful lives. Therefore, the cost of the service benefits is assigned to depreciation expense as the benefits are used.

Depreciation is the allocation of the cost of an asset to the accounting periods benefiting from its use. The meaning of depreciation is often misunderstood, because the term is generally used by nonaccountants to refer to the decline in the market value of assets. Although plant assets are subject to changes in market values, accountants are not concerned with recognizing these changes because plant assets are acquired for use, not for sale. Therefore, depreciation is an allocation process, not a valuation process.

DETERMINING THE AMOUNT OF DEPRECIATION

Factors needed to determine the amount of periodic depreciation for a plant asset are its cost, its estimated useful life, and its residual value. Determination of the initial cost of plant assets was discussed earlier. A discussion of estimated useful life and estimated residual value follows.

Estimated Useful Life

Objective 4: Determining a plant asset's useful life

A plant asset's **useful life** is the time period during which it is expected to be used by the purchaser in the production of goods or services. This period is generally much shorter than the asset's physical life. For example, the physical life of an automobile may be 8 to 10 years. Its useful life, however, may be only three years, because it will require more maintenance and will operate less efficiently after that time. The purchaser may decide that it is economical to trade in the automobile for a new one after three years of use. If that is the case, the cost of the automobile, less the estimated residual value, should be charged to depreciation expense over the three-year period.

Three major factors are considered in estimating the useful life of a plant asset.

The first factor is *physical wear and tear,* which is affected by such things as frequency of use, climatic conditions under which the asset is used, and the frequency of expected maintenance. For some assets, like construction equipment, these physical factors are the most important ones affecting useful life.

The second factor is **obsolescence,** which results when technological advances produce new assets that can provide the same service more efficiently than the existing assets, thereby causing them to become outdated. Obsolescence is the most important factor affecting the useful life of assets such as computers. The rapid improvements made in the design and performance of computers generally make them obsolete long before they wear out physically.

The third factor is **inadequacy,** which refers to the inability of an asset to meet the increasing needs of the user, caused by growth of the firm. When a company acquires plant assets, it generally attempts to acquire those that will provide adequate capacity to meet foreseeable operating needs. When demand for the company's products increases more rapidly than anticipated, the plant assets may not have the capacity to meet that demand and the assets are then said to have become inadequate.

Since the economic factors of obsolescence and inadequacy cannot be easily predicted, business managers are often conservative in estimating the useful lives of those plant assets that are most affected by these factors. Estimates of useful life are made on the basis of past experience. If the company has no past experience, the estimated useful lives of various assets can be obtained from industry publications.

Residual Value

The **residual value** of a plant asset is the amount expected to be received from the sale or other disposition of the asset at the end of its useful life. Assets such as automobiles and trucks may have significant resale values. Other assets, such as specifically designed machinery and equipment, may have value only as scrap metal at the end of their useful lives. Residual value is sometimes also called *salvage value* or *trade-in value.*

Depreciable Cost

The cost of an asset less its residual value is called its **depreciable cost.** It is the amount that should be charged to depreciation expense over the asset's useful life. When residual value is expected to be an insignificant amount in relation to the asset's cost, it is often ignored in computing depreciation.

Depreciation Methods

Several methods can be used to allocate the cost of an asset over its useful life. The four most frequently used methods are the straight-line, units-of-production, sum-of-years'-digits, and double declining-balance methods. Each of these methods is generally accepted in accounting, because each results in a systematic and rational allocation of the cost of a plant asset to the periods that benefit from that asset's use. Both the sum-of-years'-digits method and the double declining-balance method are often referred to as accelerated depreciation methods, because they charge relatively greater amounts of depreciation to the first year(s) of an asset's life.

A company does not have to use a single depreciation method for all of its depreciable assets. However, once a depreciation method is selected for a specific asset, it should be used consistently, year after year. The methods chosen will vary with management's expectations about the way the service benefits incorporated in the assets are to be used. In addition, the methods adopted by management for use in the accounts and financial statements may differ from those used in the preparation of income tax returns. For example, management may want to use the accelerated cost recovery system (which is discussed later in this chapter) for tax purposes. This is permitted even though the benefits from use of the asset are received evenly over time, thereby justifying the straight-line method for accounting and reporting purposes.

Objective 5: Calculating depreciation expense

Straight-line Method. The **straight-line depreciation method** allocates an equal amount of depreciation to each full accounting period in the asset's useful life. The amount of depreciation for each period is determined by dividing the cost of the asset, minus its residual value, by the number of periods in the asset's useful life. For example, assume that a machine has a cost of $33,000, a residual value of $3,000, and a useful life of five years. Depreciation for each full year is computed as follows.

$$\frac{\text{Cost} - \text{Residual value}}{\text{Useful life in years}} = \frac{\$33,000 - \$3,000}{5 \text{ years}} = \$6,000 \text{ annual depreciation}$$

The entry to record the depreciation is:

Dec.	31	Depreciation Expense	6,000	
		Accumulated Depreciation—Machinery		6,000
		To record depreciation for the year.		

Annual depreciation expense is $6,000. If the asset is acquired during a fiscal period, the annual depreciation amount should be prorated for the first and last partial years of its use. For example, if the machine were purchased on April 1, depreciation for the first year would be 9/12 × $6,000, or $4,500. Although depreciation could be computed to the exact day when an asset is acquired during a month, computation to the nearest month is generally sufficient. A full month's depreciation is taken on an asset acquired during the first half of a month, and no depreciation is taken for the month if the asset is acquired during the last half of the month. In fact, because depreciation is an estimate, many companies compute depreciation only to the nearest full year.

The straight-line method produces uniform charges to depreciation expense over the life of the asset. Under the straight-line method, depreciation is considered a function of time. Thus, this method is appropriate where the service benefits in the asset are received evenly throughout the asset's useful life.

Units-of-Production Method. The **units-of-production depreciation method** relates depreciation to use, rather than to time. Therefore, this method is particularly appropriate when the use of assets varies significantly from one period to another, because it results in a better matching of expenses with revenues. Accounting periods with greater production from the asset will be charged with a greater amount of depreciation expense.

A disadvantage of the units-of-production method is that it requires additional recordkeeping to determine the units produced during each period by each asset. It also requires an estimate of the total expected production of each asset over its useful life.

Under the units-of-production method, the depreciable cost of the asset (cost minus residual value) is divided by the estimated number of production units expected from the asset during its estimated life. Production units might be expressed in several ways—miles, operating hours, or units of product. The result of the division is a depreciation rate per production unit. The amount of depreciation for a period is then determined by multiplying the depreciation rate per production unit times the number of production units used or produced during the period.

To illustrate, assume that a machine with a cost of $33,000 and an estimated residual value of $3,000 is estimated to have a useful life of 15,000 operating hours. The depreciation rate per operating hour is:

$$\frac{\text{Cost} - \text{Residual value}}{\text{Operating hours}} = \text{Depreciation per operating hour}$$

or

$$\frac{\$33,000 - \$3,000}{15,000 \text{ hours}} = \$2.00 \text{ per operating hour}$$

If the machine was operated for 2,500 hours during an accounting period, that period would be charged with depreciation of $5,000 (2,500 hours × $2.00), and the following depreciation entry would be made.

Dec.	31	Depreciation Expense	5,000	
		Accumulated Depreciation—Machinery		5,000
		To record depreciation expense for the		
		year.		

No particular problem exists when the asset is acquired during a fiscal year. Since depreciation is a fixed amount per hour (or other production unit), depreciation expense is simply the hourly rate times the number of hours used during the partial year.

Sum-of-years'-digits Method. The **sum-of-years'-digits depreciation method** results in a decreasing depreciation charge over the useful life of the asset. Since more depreciation is charged to the early years of the asset's life and lesser amounts are charged to later years, the method is often called an **accelerated depreciation method.** Depreciation for each period is determined by multiplying the depreciable cost by successively smaller fractions. The fraction's denominator, which is constant, is determined by adding the years in the asset's useful life. The fraction's numerators, which change each year, are the years remaining in the asset's life at the beginning of the period. For example, if depreciation is computed for the sixth year of an asset's 10-year life, the numerator is five.

To illustrate, assume that the sum-of-years'-digits method is used to allocate depreciation on a machine with a cost of $33,000, a residual value of $3,000, and an estimated useful life of five years. The sum of the years' digits (the denominator) is computed as: $5 + 4 + 3 + 2 + 1 = 15$.

The depreciation charge for each year is then calculated as shown in the following table.

Year	Cost Less Residual Value	Fraction	Annual Depreciation Expense	Total Accumulated Depreciation	Book Value
1	$30,000 ×	5/15 =	$10,000	$10,000	$23,000
2	30,000 ×	4/15 =	8,000	18,000	15,000
3	30,000 ×	3/15 =	6,000	24,000	9,000
4	30,000 ×	2/15 =	4,000	28,000	5,000
5	30,000 ×	1/15 =	2,000	30,000	3,000

Note that the method results in a book value equal to the asset's residual value at the end of its useful life. The charge to depreciation expense decreases each year, and the addition to accumulated depreciation decreases each year by a constant amount ($2,000 in our example).

When the asset has a long life, the sum of the years' digits can be calculated by using the formula: $S = n\left(\dfrac{n + 1}{2}\right)$; where S equals the sum of the year's digits and n equals the number of years in the asset's life. Therefore, the sum of the years' digits for an asset with a 10-year life is $10\left(\dfrac{10 + 1}{2}\right) = 55$.

When an asset is acquired during a fiscal year, it is necessary to allocate each full year's amount to the fiscal years benefiting from the asset's use. Consequently, if the asset was acquired on April 1, the depreciation recorded in the first year would be $9/12 \times \$10,000$, or $7,500. Depreciation for the second year would be:

3/12 × $10,000 (from year 1 above)	$2,500
9/12 × $ 8,000 (from year 2 above)	6,000
Depreciation for second year	$8,500

Depreciation for each of the remaining years would be computed in a similar manner.

Declining-balance Method.
Like the sum-of-years'-digits method, the declining-balance depreciation method results in a decreasing depreciation

charge over the useful life of the asset. Consequently, it too is often called an accelerated depreciation method. Depreciation expense for each period is determined by multiplying a fixed depreciation rate times the declining **undepreciated cost** (i.e., the book value) of the asset at the beginning of the year. The depreciation rate is some multiple of the straight-line rate. Although this multiple can be several different numbers as computed by a formula, such as 1.25 or 1.50, it is often 2, and the method is called the **double declining-balance method.** Hereafter we will use a multiple of 2 and use the term double declining-balance method.

To illustrate, assume that an asset has a cost of $33,000, an estimated residual value of $3,000, and a useful life of five years. The straight-line rate is determined by dividing 100% by the useful life (5 years) of the asset. This rate (20%) is then doubled to determine the declining-balance rate (40%). The declining-balance rate is then applied to the book value of the asset at the beginning of the year to compute depreciation expense for each period, as indicated in the following table.

Year	Book Value at Beginning of Year		Rate		Annual Depreciation Expense	Book Value at End of Year
1	$33,000	×	.40	=	$13,200	$19,800
2	19,800	×	.40	=	7,920	11,880
3	11,880	×	.40	=	4,752	7,128
4	7,128	×	.40	=	2,851	4,277
5	4,277		.40		1,277	3,000

Three things should be specifically noted from this table.

1. The 40% depreciation rate is applied to the beginning of the year *book value* of the asset. Estimated residual value is *not* used to determine annual depreciation under the double declining-balance method (except that the asset may not be depreciated below its residual value).
2. The amount of depreciation declined each year.
3. Depreciation for the last year was *not* determined by multiplying $4,277 by 40%, because that would have resulted in a book value lower than the asset's residual value. Depreciation expense of $1,277 was computed for the last year by simply subtracting the residual value of $3,000 from the book value at the beginning of the year ($4,277), after it was determined that depreciation computed under the double declining-balance method would reduce the book value of the asset to less than its residual value.

It was assumed in this illustration that the asset was acquired at the beginning of the fiscal period, which is seldom actually the case. When an asset is acquired during a fiscal period, the amount of depreciation for the first year should be prorated. For example, if the asset was purchased on April 1, the first year's depreciation would be 9/12 × $13,200, or $9,900. The method of computing depreciation for subsequent years is unaffected, although the amounts will differ as shown in the table on page 420.

Year	Book Value at Beginning of Year	Rate		Annual Depreciation Expense	Book Value at End of Year
1	$33,000	× .40	= $13,200 × 9/12 =	$9,900	$23,100
2	23,100	× .40	=	9,240	13,860
3	13,860	× .40	=	5,544	8,316
4	8,316	× .40	=	3,326	4,990
5	4,990		(4,990 − 3,000) =	1,990	3,000

COMPARISON OF DEPRECIATION METHODS

The straight-line depreciaton method is most widely used, as shown in the following table from an annual survey of 600 companies conducted by the American Institute of Certified Public Accountants.

Depreciation Method	No. of Companies*
Straight-line	564
Declining-balance	57
Sum-of-years'-digits	17
Accelerated method (method not specified)	74
Units-of-production	65

*The number of companies exceeds 600 because some companies use more than one method.
Source: Accounting Trends & Techniques (AICPA, New York: 1984) p. 277.

The different methods allocate different amounts each year to depreciation expense over the life of an asset, even though the cost, residual value, and useful life are the same. The straight-line method produces uniform charges to depreciation over the life of the asset. Under the straight-line method, depreciation is considered a function of time. The benefits received from the use of the asset are assumed to be received evenly throughout the asset's life. The units-of-production method produces depreciation charges that may vary significantly from one accounting period to another as the use of the asset varies. Thus, under the units-of-production-method, depreciation is considered a function of asset use.

As mentioned earlier, both the sum-of-years'-digits and the double declin-ing-balance methods charge greater amounts of depreciation to the first year of an asset's life and gradually decrease charges thereafter. Although depre-ciation is considered a function of time, the benefits received from the use of the asset are assumed to be greater in the early years of use. As the asset ages, it becomes less efficient and requires increasing expenditures for repairs and maintenance. The combination of decreasing depreciation expense and increasing repair and maintenance expense tends to equalize the total periodic expense of the asset (as illustrated in Figure 10–1), thereby achieving a better matching of expense with revenue.

A comparison of the periodic depreciation charges under the different de-preciation methods for the machine used in previous illustrations is presented

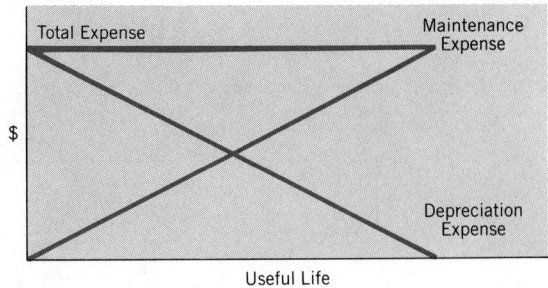

Figure 10–1
Depreciation and
Maintenance Expense

in the following table, based on a machine cost of $33,000, a residual value
of $3,000, and a useful life of five years.

Year	Straight-line	Units of Production (Amounts assumed)	Sum-of-years'-digits	Double Declining-balance
1	$ 6,000	$ 5,000	$10,000	$13,000
2	6,000	7,500	8,000	7,920
3	6,000	6,500	6,000	4,752
4	6,000	4,000	4,000	2,851
5	6,000	7,000	2,000	1,277
Total	$30,000	$30,000	$30,000	$30,000

Depreciation patterns under the four depreciation methods are shown graphically in Figure 10–2.

DEPRECIATION FOR INCOME TAX PURPOSES

Accelerated depreciation methods (for example, double declining-balance and
sum-of-years' digits) were widely used for income tax purposes for property
acquired prior to 1981. The Economic Recovery Act of 1981 established new
depreciation rules for income tax purposes under the *accelerated cost recovery
system (ACRS).* The ACRS provides that the cost of depreciable plant assets
acquired after 1980 are to be recovered over predetermined periods, which are

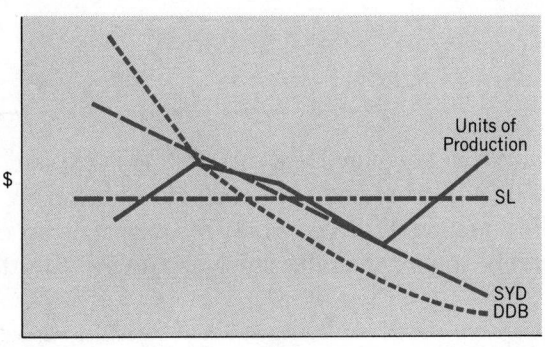

Figure 10–2
Comparison of De-
preciation Patterns

Figure 10–3
Rates for ACRS
Personal Property

PERCENTAGE BY PROPERTY CLASS

Recovery Year	3-year	5-year	10-year
1	25	15	8
2	38	22	14
3	37	21	12
4		21	10
5		21	10
6			10
7			9
8			9
9			9
10			9
	100	100	100

generally shorter than the useful lives of the assets (the cost is not reduced by residual value in computing the tax deduction).[3]

In general, the ACRS procedure classifies property into the two broad categories of personal property and real property. Most depreciable personal property is grouped into either a 3-, 5-, or 10-year category, and most depreciable real property is classified in an 18-year category. These categories represent the fixed recovery periods for ACRS property; the useful lives of the assets are irrelevant. Rates for ACRS personal property recovery are given in Figure 10–3.

The ACRS deduction for personal property is computed by applying the percentages in Figure 10–3 to the asset's cost. The percentages are based on the 150% declining-balance method. One-half year's depreciation is allowed in the year of purchase on all personal property acquired, regardless of when during the year the property was actually purchased.

Application of the ACRS percentages to the asset used in previous illustrations (cost, $33,000; residual value, $3,000; useful life, 5 years), assuming that the asset matched the description of 3-year category property, produces the following tax deductions.

Year	Computation	Amount
1	$33,000 × 25%	$ 8,250
2	33,000 × 38%	12,540
3	33,000 × 37%	12,210
Total		$33,000

Note that residual value is ignored and that the total cost is recovered for tax purposes over a three-year period, even though the asset's estimated useful life is 5 years. Because the ACRS generally recovers the cost of property over periods considerably shorter than the property's useful life, the ACRS does

---

[3]The ACRS does not apply to assets depreciated using the units-of-production method. In lieu of the ACRS percentages, taxpayers may elect to use the straight-line method over specified longer recovery periods.

not properly match expenses and revenues. Consequently, the ACRS is not an accepted method of determining depreciation expense for financial accounting purposes.

As indicated earlier, the new ACRS rules apply to property placed in service after 1980. For property placed in service prior to 1981, depreciation continues to be computed under the old methods.

The use of straight-line depreciation for financial accounting purposes and accelerated depreciation for tax purposes results in a larger tax depreciation expense, lower taxable income, and lower income tax payments during the early years of the asset's life. Tax payments are thereby deferred until later years, when the lower depreciation charges will result in higher taxable income and higher income taxes. Even though larger tax payments must be made in later years, the company has the interest-free use of the deferred tax dollars until the later years of the asset's life. Accounting for the differences between depreciation expense taken for financial reporting purposes and depreciation expense taken for income tax purposes is discussed in Chapter 17.

REVISION OF DEPRECIATION RATES

Two of the factors used to determine periodic depreciation, residual value and useful life, are based on estimates, which are rarely precise. Small misestimates occur frequently and are generally ignored because their effect is not material. Large misestimates, however, should be corrected when discovered. When it becomes known that an estimate should be revised, the generally accepted accounting procedure is to spread the remaining undepreciated cost of the asset over its remaining useful life.[4] Annual depreciation is increased or decreased enough in the current and future periods to offset the effect of the misestimate in prior periods. For example, assume the following case.

Equipment cost	$38,000
Estimated useful life	6 years
Estimated residual value	$ 8,000
Accumulated depreciation at the end of four years	
(assuming straight-line depreciation)	$20,000

Early in the fifth year, it is decided that the equipment will last for four more years. At the end of that time its residual value is estimated to be $4,000. The amount of depreciation to be recognized in the fifth year and each of the remaining years is $3,500, computed as follows.

Undepreciated cost at the end of the 4th year	
($38,000 − $20,000)	$18,000
Less: New estimated residual value	4,000
Remaining cost to be depreciated	$14,000
New estimated useful life remaining	4 years
Revised annual depreciation ($14,000 ÷ 4 years)	$ 3,500

At the end of eight years, the equipment will be depreciated to its residual

---

[4]Accounting Principles Board, "Accounting Changes," *APB Opinion No. 20* (AICPA; New York, July 1971), par. 31.

value and the *Equipment* and related *Accumulated Depreciation* accounts will appear as follows.

Equipment

Acquisition date	38,000

Accumulated Depreciation—Equipment

Year 1	5,000
Year 2	5,000
Year 3	5,000
Year 4	5,000
Year 5	3,500
Year 6	3,500
Year 7	3,500
Year 8	3,500
	34,000

Sometimes a company changes depreciation methods during a plant asset's useful life. A change in depreciation method—from straight-line to double declining-balance, for example—is called a *change in accounting principle*. The treatment of a change in accounting principle is presented in Chapter 16.

REPORTING DEPRECIATION IN THE FINANCIAL STATEMENTS

For financial reporting purposes, the Accounting Principles Board has ruled that depreciation expense must be disclosed, that both the cost of plant assets and their accumulated depreciation must be shown in the balance sheet, and that a general description of the depreciation method or methods used must be presented in the financial statements or in statement footnotes.[5] To comply with these requirements, companies generally report depreciation expense as a separate item in the income statement or in a footnote. Plant assets may be reported on the face of the balance sheet or in an accompanying schedule, as follows.

Property, Plant, and Equipment:			
Land			$164,000
Buildings		$849,000	
Less: Accumulated depreciation		231,500	617,500
Machinery and equipment		236,400	
Less: Accumulated depreciation		172,600	63,800
Total Property, Plant, and Equipment			$845,300

[5]Accounting Principles Board, "Omnibus Opinion—1967," *APB Opinion No. 12* (AICPA, New York: December 1967), par. 5.

With information presented in this manner and with knowledge of the depreciation methods used, the reader of the balance sheet can determine the approximate age of the plant assets. If the plant assets are old, they are likely to be less efficient in producing future goods and services. In addition, knowledge of the age of the assets is useful in judging the approximate time at which expenditures will be needed to replace them. For example, assuming the use of straight-line depreciation, the machinery and equipment just presented have been used for about 75% of their useful lives. Financing the replacement of these assets will probably be required in the relatively near future.

ACCUMULATED DEPRECIATION DOES NOT REPRESENT CASH

A common misunderstanding of those who are not well informed about accounting is that accumulated depreciation represents cash that can be used to replace the assets when they wear out. The informed person knows that accumulated depreciation represents nothing more than the portion of an asset's cost that has been transferred to depreciation expense since the asset was acquired. The cash account is not affected by the periodic entries made to transfer the asset's cost to depreciation expense. The accumulated depreciation account is a contra asset account with a credit balance and, as we have learned, cash is an asset having a debit balance.

This misunderstanding probably occurs because depreciation expense, unlike most other expenses, does not require a cash outlay in the same period in which the expense is deducted from revenue. As a result, most companies have a net cash inflow from operations (cash receipts from revenues less cash payments for expenses) in excess of reported net income.

To illustrate, assume that Beta Company sells services only in exchange for cash and pays cash for all expenses, with the exception of depreciation, in the same period in which the expense is incurred. During 1987, Beta Company made cash sales of $230,000, paid cash expenses of $170,000, and recognized depreciation expense of $10,000 on equipment purchased with cash in 1985. A comparison of cash flow from operations with net income reported for 1987 is:

	1987 Cash Flow		1987 Net Income	
Cash receipts from sales		$230,000		$230,000
Cash expenses	$170,000		$170,000	
Depreciation expense	-0-	170,000	10,000	180,000
Net cash flow		$ 60,000		
Net income				$ 50,000

Beta Company had a net cash flow from operations that was $10,000 greater than the amount of net income reported. This results because the depreciation expense deducted in arriving at net income did not require a cash payment in 1987.

But isn't the $10,000 cash in the bank account? Couldn't it be used to replace the equipment when it wears out? The answer is that the $10,000 may or may not be in the bank. It may have been used already, or it may be used before the equipment needs replacement, for any of the purposes for which a company normally uses cash. For example, it may be used to pay cash expenses or to pay off long-term debt, or it may be withdrawn by the owners for their personal use.

CAPITAL AND REVENUE EXPENDITURES

Objective 6: Capital expenditures vs. revenue expenditures

Expenditures made to acquire, improve, and maintain plant assets are either capital expenditures or revenue expenditures. **Capital expenditures** are those that add to the utility or usefulness of a plant asset for more than one accounting period, either by lengthening the asset's useful life or by increasing its capacity. Examples of capital expenditures are building additions, extraordinary repairs, asset replacement, or the installation of escalators to replace stairwells. Capital expenditures are debited to asset accounts and allocated to both the current and future periods through depreciation.

Revenue expenditures are those that benefit only the current accounting period, and they are debited to expense accounts when incurred. They are called revenue expenditures because they are matched against revenues in the period in which they are made. Ordinary recurring repairs and maintenance expenditures are examples of revenue expenditures.

It is important to distinguish carefully between capital expenditures and revenue expenditures, because improper treatment affects both the determination of periodic income and balance sheet values. For example, if the cost of equipment (a capital expenditure) is charged to expense when purchased, the net income of the current period will be understated and the net income of future periods will be overstated because of the absence of depreciation expense on the asset. In addition, plant assets, as well as owners' equity, will be understated on the balance sheet until the asset is either disposed of or until it reaches the end of its useful life.

ORDINARY REPAIRS AND MAINTENANCE

Ordinary repairs and maintenance are those relatively small recurring expenses necessary to keep a plant asset in good operating condition. Buildings need painting and minor repairs to their electrical and plumbing systems. Machines must be lubricated, cleaned, and reconditioned on a regular schedule. Engines require tune-ups and the replacement of small parts.

Expenditures for these purposes do not significantly add to the economic value or useful life of the asset. Rather, they are made to assure the obtaining of benefits from the asset over its original estimated useful life. Therefore, ordinary repairs and maintenance expenditures are matched against revenue of the current period. For example, if a company spent $675 for new tires, a new battery, and an engine tune-up for its delivery truck, the entry would be:

June	6	Repairs and Maintenance Expense	675	
		Cash		675
		To record ordinary repairs on delivery truck.		

EXTRAORDINARY REPAIRS

Extraordinary repairs are major reconditioning and overhaul expenditures made to extend a plant asset's useful life beyond the original estimate. For example, assume that a delivery truck was purchased for $14,000 and was estimated to have a useful life of five years, with a residual value of $2,000. At the end of the truck's fourth year, its book value is $4,400 (assuming straight-line depreciation), as shown here.

Cost	$14,000
Accumulated depreciation $\frac{(\$14,000 - \$2,000)}{5} \times 4$	9,600
Book value	$ 4,400

At the beginning of the fifth year, it is decided to replace the truck's engine at a cost of $4,200, after which the truck will last for three more years and have a residual value of $2,000. The entry to record this capital expenditure is:

Jan.	4	Accumulated Depreciation—Delivery Truck	4,200	
		Cash		4,200
		To record the installation of a new engine.		

The cost of the new engine is debited to the *Accumulated Depreciation* account, rather than to the asset account, with the reasoning that the expenditure cancels out some of the depreciation recorded in past periods. The effect of the debit to accumulated depreciation is to increase the book value of the asset, and the depreciation expense for each of the remaining years is computed as follows.

Cost of delivery truck	$14,000
Less: Accumulated depreciation ($9,600 − $4,200)	5,400
Book value after installing new engine	8,600
Less: New estimated residual value	2,000
New depreciable amount	$ 6,600
New annual depreciation expense ($6,600/3)	$ 2,200

BETTERMENTS

A **betterment** is the substitution of a better asset for one that is currently in use, or the substitution of a portion of an asset with an improved portion. The substitution of a tile roof for an asphalt one, or the substitution of computerized controls on machinery for manual ones are examples. Betterments generally result in more efficient or more productive assets, but often do not extend the asset's useful life.

The cost of betterments should be debited to the appropriate asset account and depreciated over the asset's remaining useful life. If possible, the cost and the related accumulated depreciation of the asset or asset portion substituted for should be removed from the accounts.

PLANT AND EQUIPMENT RECORDS

Plant assets are normally divided into functional groups with a separate general ledger account and accumulated depreciation account provided for each group. For example, a retail furniture company would have separate asset and accumulated depreciation accounts for delivery equipment, office equipment, and store equipment.

The company might have several delivery trucks, and numerous items of office equipment and store equipment. For example, the *Office Equipment* account may contain the cost of calculators, chairs, desks, typewriters, and filing cabinets. These items may have been acquired on different dates and will have different useful lives and residual values. In addition, the composition of the group of assets will change over time as individual assets are disposed of and new ones are acquired.

It is not practical to keep all of the detailed information needed for each asset in the general ledger accounts. Consequently, each plant asset account and its related accumulated depreciation account are control accounts, with the details about each item maintained in a subsidiary ledger.

Although there are many variations in the format of subsidiary ledgers, one commonly used method consists of a card file with a separate card for each item included in the control account. Each card contains a number, which is also placed on the asset, itself, as a means of identification and to aid in control over the item. To illustrate, assume a simplified case of a company that has two delivery trucks, both purchased on April 1, 1985. The general ledger *Delivery Equipment* and *Accumulated Depreciation* control accounts and subsidiary records for these assets are presented in Figure 10–4.

Note that the account number on the subsidiary ledger cards is the same as the general ledger account number for *Delivery Equipment*. Note, also, that the balance in the general ledger account, *Delivery Equipment,* is equal to the total of the balances of the asset section of the subsidiary ledger cards. Likewise, the balance in the general ledger account, *Accumulated Depreciation— Delivery Equipment,* is equal to the sum of the balances of the depreciation section of the subsidiary ledger cards. An inventory of plant assets is taken periodically to maintain control over the assets and to prove the equality of the general ledger accounts and their subsidiary records.

The subsidiary ledger cards provide information for the preparation of income tax returns and for supporting insurance claims in the event of loss from theft and casualty. The cards also contain information for preparing year-end adjustments for depreciation and space for entries to record the disposal of the asset. When the asset is disposed of, the asset section of the subsidiary card

General Ledger

Figure 10–4
Plant Asset Records

Delivery Equipment   Account No. **216**

Date	Explanation	P/R	Debit	Credit	Balance
4/1/85		CD 18	18,400		18,400

Accumulated Depreciation—Delivery Equipment   Account No. **217**

Date	Explanation	P/R	Debit	Credit	Balance
12/31/85		GJ 12		2,025	2,025
12/31/86		GJ 29		2,700	4,725
12/31/87		GJ 41		2,700	7,425

PLANT ASSET RECORD
Subsidiary Ledger

Account No. _____ 216 _____

Item __3/4 Ton Truck__   General Ledger Account __Delivery Equipment__
Serial No. __3AG64243321__
Purchased from   Bextell Motors
Useful Life ___5 years___   Estimated Residual Value ___$1,600___
Depreciation per Year ___$1,200___   Depreciation Method __straight-line__

Date	Explanation	P/R	Asset Dr.	Asset Cr.	Asset Bal.	Depreciation Dr.	Depreciation Cr.	Depreciation Bal.
4/1/85		CD 18	7,600		7,600			
12/31/85		GJ 12					900	900
12/31/86		GJ 29					1,200	2,100
12/31/87		GJ 41					1,200	3,300

PLANT ASSET RECORD

Account No. _____ 216 _____

Item _One-ton Truck_   General Ledger Account _Delivery Equipment_
Serial No. __4SG7215B4312__
Purchased from   Bextell Motors
Useful Life _6 years_   Estimated Residual Value ___$1,800___
Depreciation per Year $1,500   Depreciation Method _straight-line_

Date	Explanation	P/R	Asset Dr.	Asset Cr.	Asset Bal.	Accumulated Depreciation Dr.	Accumulated Depreciation Cr.	Accumulated Depreciation Bal.
4/1/85		CD 18	10,800		10,800			
12/31/85		GJ 12					1,125	1,125
12/31/86		GJ 29					1,500	2,625
12/31/87		GJ 41					1,500	4,125

is credited and the depreciation section is debited, thereby reducing both sections to zero. The card is then removed from the subsidiary ledger and filed in a permanent file for possible future reference.

GLOSSARY

ACCELERATED DEPRECIATION METHOD. Any depreciation method that results in greater depreciation expense in the early years of a plant asset's life than in the later years (p. 417).

BETTERMENT. The substitution of a better asset for the one that is currently in use, or the substitution of a portion of an asset with an improved portion (p. 427).

CAPITAL EXPENDITURE. An expenditure that adds to the utility or usefulness of a plant asset for more than one accounting period (p. 426).

DECLINING-BALANCE DEPRECIATION METHOD. A depreciation method under which some multiple of the straight-line rate is applied to the book value of a plant asset to arrive at an annual depreciation expense (p. 418).

DEPRECIABLE COST. The cost of a depreciable asset, minus its residual value (p. 415).

DEPRECIATION. The allocation of a plant asset's cost to the accounting periods benefiting from its use (p. 414).

EXPENDITURE. A cash outlay or the incurring of a liability to acquire a good or service (p. 410).

FIXED ASSETS. A term sometimes used to refer to plant assets (p. 409).

IMPUTING INTEREST. Assigning a portion of the face value of a note to interest when no interest rate is specified or when the interest rate specified is clearly unreasonable (p. 413).

INADEQUACY. The inability of a plant asset to meet the current demand for its product (p. 415).

LUMP-SUM ACQUISITION. The purchase of a group of plant assets for one total payment (p. 411).

OBSOLESCENCE. A condition under which a plant asset is out of date and can no longer produce on a competitive basis (p. 415).

RESIDUAL VALUE. The estimated value of a plant asset at the end of its useful life (p. 415).

REVENUE EXPENDITURE. An expenditure that benefits only the current accounting period (p. 426).

STRAIGHT-LINE DEPRECIATION METHOD. A depreciation method that allocates an equal amount of a plant asset's cost to each period in its useful life (p. 416).

SUM-OF-YEARS'-DIGITS DEPRECIATION METHOD. A depreciation method under which the cost of a plant asset is allocated to depreciation on a fractional basis. The denominator of the fraction is the sum of the digits in the asset's useful life. The numerators of the fractions are the years remaining in the asset's useful life at the beginning of the period (p. 417).

UNITS-OF-PRODUCTION DEPRECIATION METHOD. A depreciation method under which the cost of a plant asset is allocated to depreciation expense based on the number of production units produced during the period (p. 417).

USEFUL LIFE. The time period during which a plant asset is expected to be used to produce goods or services (p. 414).

DISCUSSION QUESTIONS

1. What are plant assets? What is the primary characteristic that distinguishes them from other assets?
2. Why is the cost of a plant asset allocated to accounting periods?
3. In a general sense, what should be included in the cost of a plant asset? Which of the following should be included in the cost of equipment.
   (a) Sales tax.
   (b) Installation charges.
   (c) Freight charges.
   (d) Cost of a permanent foundation.
   (e) New parts needed to replace those damaged while unloading.
4. Strum Company purchased a parcel of open land for speculation purposes. It is expected that the value of the land will increase so that it can be sold in the future at a gain. Where should this land be reported in the balance sheet?
5. Jones Company acquired land, a building, and office equipment for a lump-sum payment of $280,000. Fair values of each asset as determined by an independent appraiser are: land, $84,000; building, $186,000; and office equipment, $50,000. How much of the total payment of $280,000 should be allocated to each asset?
6. A $10,000, 12%, 12-month note was exchanged for a machine with a fair value of $10,000 on June 30. What entry should be made on December 31 to accrue interest expense on the note? How would this entry differ if a 12-month, non-interest-bearing note in the amount of $11,200 had been given?
7. Explain what is meant by the term "depreciation," as it is used in accounting.
8. Should depreciation be recorded on a building for a year in which the market value of the building has increased? Explain.
9. What is the difference between obsolescence and inadequacy, as it relates to plant assets?
10. What are accelerated depreciation methods? Why are they sometimes used?
11. Explain why accelerated depreciation methods are often used for income tax purposes.
12. What is the main advantage and the main disadvantage of using a units-of-production depreciation method?
13. An asset with a cost of $11,000, a residual value of $1,000, and an estimated life of four years was purchased at the beginning of year one. What is the amount of depreciation expense for years one and two if the sum-of-years'-digits method is used?
14. What would be the amount of depreciation for years one and two for the asset purchased in question 13 if the double declining-balance method were used?
15. What is the sum-of-the-years'-digits of a plant asset with an estimated useful life of 25 years?
16. Explain what the balance in the *Accumulated Depreciation—Machinery* account represents. How is the account treated in the financial statements?
17. What is meant by the term "book value"? Does a credit to *Accumulated Depreciation* increase or decrease book value?
18. If a company changes its estimate of the useful life of a plant asset, how should the change be accounted for?
19. What is the distinction between capital expenditures and revenue expenditures? Give an example of each and explain how the accounting treatment is different.

EXERCISES

Exercise 10-1 Lump-sum Purchase

Finger Lakes Manufacturing Company purchased a building, land, and equipment on March 7 for a cash payment of $1,300,000. Appraised values of the assets on the date of purchase were:

Building	$ 870,000
Land	435,000
Equipment	145,000
Total	$1,450,000

Required:

Compute the cost that should be assigned to each of the assets and prepare a journal entry to record the purchase.

✴Exercise 10-2 Determining Cost and Annual Depreciation

On January 2, 1987, Century Company purchased a machine with a list price of $37,500 and credit terms of 2/10, n/30. Payment was made within the discount period and included sales tax of 4% on the net price. Freight costs of $630 and installation costs of $450 were also paid. The machine has an estimated useful life of five years and a residual value at the end of its useful life of $4,300.

Required:

A. Determine the amount that should be debited to the *Machinery* account and prepare a journal entry to record the purchase.

B. Determine the amount of depreciation expense for each of the five years, assuming use of

    1. The straight-line depreciation method.

    2. The double declining-balance method of depreciation.

C. Prepare a journal entry to record depreciation expense for 1988 under the double declining-balance method.

Exercise 10-3 Acquisition by Issuing a Note Payable

On February 28, 1987, Alliance Garage purchased a machine on credit, giving a $16,800, 14%, 12-month note payable.

Required:

Prepare journal entries to:

A. Record the purchase of the machine.

B. Accrue interest on the note on December 31, 1987.

C. Record payment of the note in 1988.

✴Exercise 10-4 Depreciation Methods

Westfall Company purchased a new machine on January 2, 1987, for $73,500. The machine has an estimated useful life of four years and a residual value of $6,000.

Required:

A. Compute depreciation expense for each year (1987 through 1990) under the double declining-balance method and under the sum-of-years'-digits method.

B. Assume that Westfall Company decided to use the units-of-production depreciation method and that the useful life of the machine is estimated to be 50,000 operating hours. Prepare the journal entry to record depreciation expense on December 31, 1988, if the machine was operated for 10,000 hours during 1988.

Exercise 10-5 Depreciation Methods

Carlisle Company purchased office equipment on April 1, 1987, for $49,000. The equipment has an estimated useful life of five years and an estimated residual value of $7,000.

Required:

Determine the amount of depreciation expense to be recorded for each of the first two years under the straight-line, double declining-balance, and sum-of-years'-digits depreciation methods assuming that Carlisle Company records depreciation expense to the nearest month, and that the fiscal year ends on December 31.

Exercise 10-6 Revision of Depreciation Rates

Rochester Electric Company purchased a machine on January 2, 1987, for $39,000. The machine had an estimated useful life of four years and an estimated residual value of $7,000. Rochester Electric Company uses the straight-line depreciation method.

During 1989, following a review of the adequacy of depreciation rates, Rochester Electric Company's controller determined that the machine would have a useful life of four more years (including 1989) and an estimated residual value of $3,000.

Required:

A. Assuming that the fiscal year ends on December 31, compute the amount of depreciation expense that should be recognized for each of 1987 and 1988.

B. Compute the amount of revised depreciation expense to be recorded for 1989 and each year thereafter.

Exercise 10-7 Extraordinary Repairs and Revision of Depreciation

On January 2, 1986, Summit Company purchased for $13,500 a machine with an estimated useful life of six years and an estimated residual value of $1,500. In order to keep the machine running properly, the company has performed regular maintenance and repairs each year since its acquisition. In year four (1989), ordinary repairs amounted to $315.

At the beginning of 1990, Summit Company decided to completely overhaul the machine's major operating parts at a cost of $4,500, after which the machine is expected to have an estimated useful life and residual value of four more years and $1,600, respectively. Summit Company uses the straight-line depreciation method.

Required:

Prepare journal entries to record:

A. The purchase of the machine on January 2, 1986.
B. The ordinary repairs on the machine in 1989.
C. The major overhaul of the machine on January 3, 1990.
D. Depreciation expense on the machine as of December 31, 1990.

PROBLEMS

Problem 10-1 Depreciation Methods

Western Electronics Inc. recently paid $340,000 for manufacturing equipment, which is expected to have a useful life of five years and a residual value of $40,000. The manager of Western Electronics desired information about the effect that various depreciation methods will have on net income and asks you to prepare a schedule comparing the straight-line, double declining-balance, and sum-of-years'-digits methods of depreciation.

Required:
Prepare a schedule like the following and compute the annual depreciation charge and end-of-year book value for the expected life of the equipment.

	Straight-line		Declining-balance		Sum-of-years'-digits	
Year	Depreciation Expense	Book Value	Depreciation Expense	Book Value	Depreciation Expense	Book Value
Acquisition		$340,000		$340,000		$340,000
1						
2						
3						
4						
5						

Problem 10-2 Determining Cost of Various Assets

Plumbing Company began operations during 1987. The company had a building constructed and acquired manufacturing equipment during the first six months of the year. Manufacturing operations began early in July of 1987. The company's bookkeeper, who was unsure how to treat plant asset transactions, opened a *Plant Assets* account and debited (credited) that account for all of the expenditures and receipts involving plant assets as presented here:

1. Cost of real estate purchased: Land	$ 68,800
Old Building	32,800
2. Paid for the demolition of the old building to prepare the site for a new building	9,000
3. Paid for delinquent taxes on the property in (1)	5,400
4. Paid fee for title search on property in (1)	700
5. Received for sale of salvaged materials from old building	(4,000)
6. Paid architect for designing new building	30,000
7. Paid for a temporary fence around the construction site	2,700
8. Paid excavation costs for new building	13,300
9. Partial payment to building contractor	200,000
10. Paid for construction of parking lot and installation of parking lot lights	14,500
11. Paid interest on building loan during construction	17,600
12. Made final payment to building contractor	250,000
13. Paid for manufacturing equipment	96,000
14. Paid freight bill on manufacturing equipment	1,700
15. Paid installation costs of manufacturing equipment	2,000
16. Paid for removal of temporary fencing around construction site	1,400
17. Received for temporary fencing materials salvaged	(600)
18. Paid for repair of manufacturing equipment that was damaged during installation	750
Plant Assets account balance	$742,050

Required:

A. Prepare a schedule like the one following. Analyze each transaction, and enter the payment (receipt) in the appropriate column. Total the columns.

Item	Land	Land Improvements	Building	Manufacturing Equipment	Other

B. Prepare a journal entry to close the $742,050 balance in the *Plant Assets* account and allocate the transactions to their appropriate accounts.

C. Prepare an entry to record depreciation expense for one-half year on land improvements, building, and manufacturing equipment using straight-line depreciation. Useful lives and residual values are:

	Useful Life	Residual Value
Land improvements	10 years	$ -0-
Building	20 years	40,000
Manufacturing equipment	8 years	8,500

(AICPA adapted)

Problem 10-3 Comprehensive Problem

On January 1, 1987, Rainbow Industries purchased, by exchanging $400,000 cash and a $200,000, 15%, 18-month note payable, assets with the following independently determined appraised values:

	Appraised Value
Building	$390,000
Land	130,000
Machinery and equipment	130,000
Total	$650,000

The estimated useful life of the building is 25 years and its residual value is $80,000.

The $130,000 machinery and equipment amount consists of three machines independently appraised at $32,500 each, and some office equipment appraised at $32,500. The estimated useful lives and residual values for these assets are:

	Useful Life	Residual Value
Machine 1	5 years	$2,500
Machine 2	9 years	3,000
Machine 3	4 years	5,000
Office equipment	5 years	5,000

Rainbow Industries uses the straight-line depreciation method.

Required:

A. Prepare journal entries to record:
1. The purchase of the assets.
2. The accrual of interest expense on the note payable on December 31, 1987.
3. Depreciation expense for the year 1987.
4. The payment of the note on July 1, 1988.

B. Show how the plant assets would be reported on the December 31, 1987, balance sheet.

Problem 10-4 Comprehensive Problem

Over a five-year period, Castle Company completed the following transactions affecting plant assets. The company uses straight-line depreciation on all depreciable assets and records depreciation to the nearest month.

1985

Jan. 1 Purchased a new machine having a cash price of $32,000. A $38,000, 15-month, noninterest-bearing note payable was given in exchange. Freight charges of $450 and installation expenditures of $1,650 were paid in cash. The machine has an estimated useful life of five years and a residual value of $4,100.

June 20 Purchased a used delivery truck for $5,500 cash. The truck was repainted at a cost of $300, and a new battery (costing $55) and tires (costing $245) were installed. The truck has an estimated useful life of three years and an expected residual value of $700.

Dec. 31 Recorded depreciation expense on the assets.

31 Amortized discount on the note payable issued on January 1.

1986

Apr. 1 Paid the note payable issued on January 1, 1985.

July 30 Paid for ordinary repairs and maintenance on the machine and truck at a cost of $112.

Dec. 31 Recorded depreciation expense on the assets.

1987

Apr. 9 Installed a fence around the company property at a cost of $5,400. The fence has an estimated useful life of 12 years with no residual value. (Debit the cost to a *Land Improvements* account.)

Dec. 31 Recorded depreciation expense on the assets.

1988

June 30 Recorded the final depreciation on the delivery truck.

30 The company completed construction of a new warehouse. Construction costs incurred (all paid in cash) were: labor, $15,500; materials, $20,500; building permits, $900; architectural fees, $2,100; and overhead, $2,000. The warehouse is expected to have a residual value of $5,000 and a useful life of 30 years. (Debit the cost to a *Buildings* account.)

Dec. 31 Recorded depreciation expense on the assets.

1989

Jan. 2 Completely overhauled the machine purchased on January 1, 1985, at a cost of $6,000, after which the useful life was estimated to be four years. The new residual value was estimated to be $700.

Dec. 31 Recorded depreciation expense on the assets.

Required:

A. Prepare journal entries to record the transactions of Castle Company.

B. Prepare a schedule showing the cost and accumulated depreciation of each plant asset after recording depreciation on December 31, 1989.

Problem 10-5 Comprehensive Problem

Johnson Company completed the following transactions during 1987. The company uses sum-of-years'-digits depreciation and records depreciation to the nearest month.

1987

Jan. 6 Purchased a used machine (No. 1) for $8,600 cash. The machine was painted and reconditioned at a cost of $600. During installation, one of the major operating parts was dropped and had to be repaired at a cost of $400, paid in cash. The machine is expected to have a useful life of four years and a residual value of $600.

Mar. 7 Purchased land and a building with the intention of tearing down the building and constructing a new office complex. Johnson Company paid $120,000 for the property, plus a broker's commission of $9,000 and title search fees of $3,000.

20 Paid A to Z Demolition Company $8,000 to demolish the building acquired on March 7.

Apr. 10 The company's parking lot was paved at a cost of $22,000. The paving has an estimated useful life of 10 years with no residual value.

June 23 Purchased for cash a machine (No. 2) with a list price of $16,000. The seller granted a 3% cash discount. A sales tax of 5% on the net purchase price and freight charges of $204 were also paid. The machine's useful life is estimated to be five years and its residual value $1,500.

Nov. 1 Purchased for $29,000 cash a machine (No. 3) with an estimated useful life of six years and a residual value of $1,000.

Required:

A. Prepare journal entries to record the transactions of Johnson Company.

B. Prepare an entry to record depreciation expense on December 31, 1987.

Problem 10-6 Plant Asset Records

Selected transactions of Glendale Company are given here. The company uses straight-line depreciation and computes depreciation expense to the nearest month.

1987

Jan. 12 Purchased from Doubletree Sales Company a bottle washer (Serial No. BF1496) for $30,000 cash. The estimated life of the machine is seven years and its residual value is expected to be $2,000.

Apr. 10 Purchased from Goldenrod Distributors a dryer (Serial No. IZ17-6) for $9,000 cash. The machine has a useful life of four years and a residual value of $1,000.

Required:

A. Prepare journal entries to record the purchase of the assets and to record depreciation expense on December 31, 1987 and 1988.

B. Open a *Machinery* account (No. 140) and an *Accumulated Depreciation—Machinery* account (No. 141), and prepare subsidiary plant asset records for the two assets. Post the journal entries to the general ledger accounts and to the subsidiary plant asset records.

ALTERNATE PROBLEMS

Problem 10-1A Determining Cost of Various Assets

Budget Company was organized early in 1987. During the first nine months, the company acquired real estate for the construction of a building and other facilities. Operating equipment was purchased and installed and the company began operating activities in October, 1987. The company's accountant, who was not sure how to record some of the transactions, opened a *Plant Property* account and recorded debits and (credits) to the account as follows.

1. Cost of real estate purchased as a building site	$160,000
2. Paid architect's fee for the design of a new building	22,000
3. Paid for the demolition of an old building on the building site purchased in (1)	26,000
4. Paid delinquent property taxes on the real estate purchased as a plant site in (1)	1,500
5. Paid excavation costs for the new building	17,000
6. Made the first payment to the building contractor	200,000
7. Paid for equipment to be installed in the new building	156,000
8. Received from the sale of salvaged materials from the demolition of the old building	(7,700)
9. Made final payment to the building contractor	375,000
10. Paid interest on building loan during construction	24,200
11. Paid freight bill on equipment purchased	1,700
12. Paid installation cost of equipment	3,600
13. Paid for repair of equipment damaged during installation	3,100
Plant Property account balance	$982,400

Required:

A. Prepare a schedule like the one following. Analyze each transaction, and enter the payment (receipt) in the appropriate column. Total the columns.

Item	Land	Building	Equipment	Other

B. Prepare a journal entry to close the $982,400 balance in the *Plant Property* account and allocate the balances to their appropriate accounts.

C. Prepare an entry to record depreciation expense from October 1 to December 31, 1987. Useful lives and residual values are:

Building	25 years and $44,700
Equipment	5 years and $6,300

Budget Company uses the straight-line depreciation method.

Problem 10-2A Depreciation Methods

Oregon Industries purchased new equipment on July 1, 1987, at a cost of $360,000. The equipment has a useful life of four years and an estimated residual value of $40,000.

Required:

Assuming a fiscal year ended December 31, compute the amount of depreciation expense for each year (1987 through 1991) with each of the following methods.

A. Straight-line.

B. Sum-of-years'-digits.

C. Double declining-balance.

Problem 10-3A Extraordinary Repairs and Revision of Depreciation

Jaffe Company purchased machinery on January 2, 1986, at a cost of $196,400. The machinery is depreciated by the straight-line method over a useful life of four years with a residual value of $20,000.

On January 3, 1989, extraordinary repairs were made to the machinery at a cost of $24,400. Because of these extensive repairs, the useful life was reestimated at four years from January 3, 1989, and the residual value was reestimated at $4,500.

Required:
Prepare journal entries to record

A. The purchase of the machinery on January 2, 1986.
B. Depreciation expense for 1986, 1987, and 1988.
C. The expenditure for repairs on January 3, 1989.
D. Depreciation expense for 1989.

Problem 10-4A Comprehensive Problem

Over a four-year period, Cactus Enterprises completed the following transactions affecting plant assets. The company uses straight-line depreciaton and records depreciation to the nearest month.

1985
Jan.   1   Purchased a new machine having a cash price of $45,000. A $51,750, 18-month, noninterest-bearing note payable was given in exchange. Freight charges of $312 and installation expenditures of $1,688 were paid in cash. The machine has an estimated useful life of four years and a residual value of $3,000.

July   2   Purchased a used delivery truck for $5,000. Cash expenditures were made to repaint the truck at a cost of $600 and for new tires costing $250. The truck has an estimated useful life of four years and an expected residual value of $1,050.

Dec.   31   Recorded depreciation expense on plant assets.
         31   Amortized discount on the note payable issued on January 1.

1986
July   1   Paid the note payable issued on January 1, 1985.
         30   Paid for ordinary repairs and maintenance on the machine and truck at a cost of $190.

Dec.   31   Recorded depreciation expense on plant assets.

1987
June   26   Installed a fence around the company property at a cost of $6,600. The fence has an estimated useful life of ten years with no residual value. (Debit the cost to a *Land Improvements* account.)

Dec.   31   Recorded depreciation expense on plant assets.

1988
Jan.   5   Completely overhauled the machine purchased on January 1, 1985, at a cost of $10,000, after which the useful life was estimated to be three years. The new residual value was estimated to be $3,000.

Dec.   31   Recorded depreciation expense on plant assets.

Required:
A. Prepare journal entries to record the transactions of Cactus Enterprises.
B. Prepare a schedule showing the cost, accumulated depreciation, and book value of each plant asset after recording depreciation on December 31, 1988.

Problem 10-5A Correcting Errors

At the end of Apple Company's fiscal year, December 31, 1986, the following items must be resolved before financial statements can be prepared.

1. On January 1, 1986, Apple Company purchased a used machine for $53,000 cash. The cost was debited to the *Machinery* account. Prior to use, additional cash expenditures were made for painting and repairing the machine, $4,100, and installing and testing the machine, $3,900. These additional expenditures were debited to *Repairs and Maintenance Expense*. The repairs and installation were completed on April 1, 1986, and the machine was placed into use. The machine has an estimated useful life of five years with a residual value of $6,000. Apple Company uses straight-line depreciation and records depreciation to the nearest month.

2. A small building and land were purchased on January 2, 1986, for $90,000 cash, which was debited to the *Land* account. The appraised values of the building and land were $80,000 and $20,000, respectively. The building has an estimated useful life of 20 years with a residual value of $7,000. Apple Company uses straight-line depreciation for buildings.

3. A new truck was purchased on September 1, 1986, Apple Company giving cash of $2,500 and a 12-month noninterest-bearing note payable in the amount of $13,440. The *Trucks* account was debited for $15,940. The truck had a cash value of $14,500 on September 1. The truck has an estimated life of five years with a residual value of $3,250 and is depreciated by the double declining-balance method.

Required:

A. Prepare journal entries on December 31, 1986, to correct the accounts.
B. Prepare journal entries to record depreciation expense after the corrections in requirement (A) have been made.

Problem 10-6A Plant Asset Records

Selected transactions affecting the *Machinery* account of Dover Company are given here. The company uses double declining-balance depreciation and computes depreciation expense to the nearest month.

1987
Jan.   12 Purchased from Brighton Company a dye machine (Serial No. 6913A1) for $45,000 cash. The estimated life of the machine is five years and its residual value is expected to be $5,000.
June   30 Purchased from Park & Sons an automatic loom (Serial No. X12344) for $18,000 cash. The machine has a useful life of four years and a residual value of $7,000.

Required:

A. Prepare journal entries to record the purchase of the assets and to record depreciation expense on December 31, 1987 and 1988.
B. Open a *Machinery* account (No. 202) and an *Accumulated Depreciation—Machinery* account (No. 203), and prepare subsidiary plant asset records for the two assets. Post the journal entries to the general ledger accounts and to the subsidiary plant asset records.

CASE

CASE 10-1 Financial Report Analysis Case Plant Assets

Refer to the financial statements of Chrysler Corporation and Kmart Corporation in Appendix A and answer the following questions:

1. How much total depreciation expense was reported by Chrysler Corporation for 1984?

2. What depreciation method(s) is used by Chrysler Corporation? By Kmart Corporation?

3. What are the weighted average useful lives of Chrysler Corporation's buildings, machinery and equipment, and furniture, respectively?

4. What is the range of depreciation rates for Kmart Corporation's buildings, store fixtures, and other fixtures and equipment, respectively?

5. What was the book value of Owned Property and Property under Capital Leases, respectively, of Kmart Corporation on January 30, 1985?

6. What was the book value of Chrysler Corporation's investment in special tools on December 31, 1984? Does Chrysler use an accumulated amortization account for special tools?

7. Can you determine the book value of Kmart Corporation's buildings on January 30, 1985?

8. How much did Kmart invest in total capital expenditures during 1984?

11

PLANT ASSET DISPOSALS: NATURAL RESOURCES AND INTANGIBLES

CHAPTER OVERVIEW AND OBJECTIVES

This chapter covers the accounting procedures followed when disposing of plant assets, and those followed for the acquisition and allocation of natural resources and intangible assets. When you have completed the chapter, you should understand:

1. How to record the discard, sale, or exchange of plant assets.
2. The differences in accounting treatment for exchanges of similar and dissimilar assets.
3. How to account for the acquisition of natural resources.
4. How to account for depletion of natural resources.
5. How to account for the acquisition of various kinds of intangible assets.
6. How to account for the amortization of intangible assets.

PLANT ASSET DISPOSALS

Objective 1: Disposing of plant assets

When a plant asset is no longer useful, it is discarded, sold, or traded in on a new asset. The entry to record the disposal varies with the nature of the disposal. However, it is necessary in all cases to remove the book value of the asset from the accounts. This is accomplished by debiting the appropriate accumulated depreciation account for the amount of depreciation accumulated on the asset to the date of its disposal and crediting the asset account for its cost.

A plant asset should not be removed from the accounts merely because it has become fully depreciated. If the asset is still used, its cost and accumulated depreciation should remain on the books until it is sold, discarded, or traded in. If the asset is removed from the accounts, there will be no evidence of its continued use and the control provided by the subsidiary ledger will be eliminated. Of course, no additional depreciation can be recorded on the asset, because its cost has been fully allocated to expense.

DISCARDING PLANT ASSETS

When a plant asset is no longer useful to the business and has no sales value, it is discarded or scrapped. If the asset is fully depreciated, there is no loss on disposal. For example, if a machine with a fully depreciated cost of $7,000 is discarded because it is worthless, the entry is:

Jan.	2	Accumulated Depreciation—Machinery	7,000	
		Machinery		7,000
		Discarded a fully depreciated machine.		

Sometimes a plant asset is discarded as worthless before it is fully depreciated, in which case the undepreciated cost of the asset represents a loss on disposal. If the machine mentioned in the last paragraph was discarded when it had an accumulated depreciation balance of $6,500, a $500 loss would be recorded when the asset was removed from the accounts.

Jan.	2	Accumulated Depreciation—Machinery	6,500	
		Loss on Disposal of Plant Assets	500	
		Machinery		7,000
		Discarded a partially depreciated machine.		

If expenditures are incurred for the removal of the asset, they increase the loss on disposal. Assuming that the company had to pay $400 to have the machine dismantled and hauled away, the discarding entry would be:

Jan.	2	Accumulated Depreciation—Machinery	6,500	
		Loss on Disposal of Plant Assets	900	
		Machinery		7,000
		Cash		400
		Discarded a partially depreciated machine and paid disposal costs of $400.		

In this illustration, the asset was disposed of at the beginning of the year. When plant assets are disposed of during the year, an entry should be made to record depreciation expense for the fractional portion of the year prior to disposal, regardless of the method of disposal. If the monthly depreciation on the machine was $100, for example, and the machine was discarded on March

1, the entry to record depreciation for the two months prior to disposal would be:

Mar.	1	Depreciation Expense	200	
		Accumulated Depreciation—Machinery		200
		To record depreciation on discarded		
		machine.		

The entry to record the discarding of the machine would then be:

Mar.	1	Accumulated Depreciation—Machinery	6,700	
		Loss on Disposal of Plant Assets	300	
		Machinery		7,000
		Discarded a partially depreciated		
		machine.		

SALE OF PLANT ASSETS

Another means of disposing of a plant asset is to sell it. If the selling price exceeds the book value of the asset, there is a gain on disposal. Conversely, if the selling price is less than the book value, there is a loss on disposal. When material in amount, these gains and losses should be reported separately on the income statement in the other revenue and expense section. Immaterial gains and losses are generally offset against one another, and the net gain or loss is included on the income statement as other revenue or other expense.

To illustrate the various possibilities for reporting a gain or loss, assume that a machine with a cost of $22,000, an estimated residual value of $2,800, and a useful life of eight years was acquired on January 2, 1982. After the adjusting entry for depreciation was made on December 31, 1986, the accounts showed the following balances.

Machinery	$22,000
Accumulated Depreciation—Machinery	12,000*

*($22,000 − $2,800)/8 = $2,400
$2,400 × 5 years = $12,000

The machine was sold on August 1, 1987.

Before recording the sale, seven months' depreciation should be recorded for the period of January through July 1987.

Aug.	1	Depreciation Expense	1,400	
		Accumulated Depreciation—Machinery		1,400
		To record depreciation to the date of sale		
		($2,400 × 7/12 = $1,400).		

After recording depreciation to the date of sale, the book value of the machine is $8,600 ($22,000 − $13,400). Entries to record the sale of the machine under three different assumptions regarding selling price are presented here.

1. The machine is sold for $8,600.

Aug.	1	Cash	8,600	
		Accumulated Depreciation—Machinery	13,400	
		Machinery		22,000
		Sold a machine for its book value.		

Because the machine was sold for its book value, no gain or loss is recognized. The cash received is recorded and the cost of the machine and its related accumulated depreciation are removed from the accounts.

2. The machine is sold for $9,300.

Aug.	1	Cash	9,300	
		Accumulated Depreciation—Machinery	13,400	
		Machinery		22,000
		Gain on Disposal of Plant Assets		700
		Sold a machine for more than its book value.		

Since the machine was sold for more than its book value, a gain is recognized, equal to the difference between the selling price ($9,300) and the book value ($8,600) of the machine.

3. The machine is sold for $8,200.

Aug.	1	Cash	8,200	
		Accumulated Depreciation—Machinery	13,400	
		Loss on Disposal of Plant Assets	400	
		Machinery		22,000
		Sold a machine for less than its book value.		

Because the machine was sold for less than its book value, a loss is recognized, equal to the difference between the selling price ($8,200) and the book value ($8,600) of the machine.

EXCHANGING PLANT ASSETS

Another means of disposing of a plant asset is to trade it in for another asset. Such exchanges occur frequently with machinery, automobiles, and equipment. A trade-in allowance for the old asset is deducted from the price of the new asset, and the balance is paid in accordance with the credit terms. Accounting procedures used for the exchange of assets depend upon whether the assets exchanged are similar or dissimilar and whether a gain or loss results.

EXCHANGING SIMILAR ASSETS

Similar assets are those that are of the same general type and that perform the same function in a business. Some examples are the exchange of a truck for another truck or the exchange of a typewriter for another typewriter. The entry to record an exchange of similar assets will vary, according to whether there

Objective 2:
Exchanges of similar and dissimilar assets

is a gain or a loss on the exchange. When the trade-in allowance exceeds the book value of the asset traded in, a gain results. If the trade-in allowance is less than the book value of the asset traded in, a loss results. Losses on an exchange of similar assets are recognized immediately in accordance with the **conservatism convention.** Gains are not recognized, and the recorded value of the new asset is decreased by the amount of the unrecognized gain.[1]

Recognition of a Loss

To illustrate the recognition of a loss on an exchange, assume that a machine with a cost of $22,000 and accumulated depreciation to date of exchange of $15,000 is traded for a new machine with a cash price of $30,000. A trade-in allowance of $4,000 is received, and the remaining $26,000 is paid in cash. The excess of the book value of the old machine ($7,000) over the trade-in allowance received ($4,000) results in a loss of $3,000, and the exchange is recorded as follows.

Jan.	2	Machinery	30,000	
		Accumulated Depreciation—Machinery	15,000	
		Loss on Disposal of Plant Assets	3,000	
		Machinery		22,000
		Cash		26,000
		Exchanged an old machine plus cash for a new machine.		

This entry records the new machine at its cash price of $30,000, which is the amount that would have been paid in a straight cash transaction. Therefore, it is the maximum amount that should be debited to the asset account. The entry also removes the old machine and its related accumulated depreciation from the accounts and recognizes a loss on the exchange.

Nonrecognition of a Gain

When there is a gain on the exchange of similar assets, accounting rules require that the gain *not* be recognized at the time of the exchange. The amount of the gain serves to reduce the recorded value of the asset received, and the new asset is recorded at its cash price, less the unrecognized gain. Another way of viewing this is that the new asset is recorded at the book value of the old asset plus cash paid (generally called *boot*) in acquiring the new asset. To illustrate, assume that a trade-in allowance of $9,500, rather than $4,000, was received for the old machine in the preceding illustration, and the balance of $20,500 was paid in cash. Although the exchange results in a gain of $2,500 ($9,500 trade-in allowance minus $7,000 book value), the gain is not recognized and the exchange is recorded as follows.

[1]Accounting Principles Board, "Accounting for Nonmonetary Transactions," *APB Opinion No. 29* (New York: AICPA, May 1973), par. 22.

Jan.	3	Machinery	27,500	
		Accumulated Depreciation—Machinery	15,000	
		Machinery	~~42,500~~	22,000
		Cash		20,500
		Exchanged an old machine plus cash for		~~42,500~~
		a new machine.		

The recorded amount of the new machine is its cash price of $30,000, less the unrecognized gain of $2,500. Looked at another way, the recorded amount is equal to the book value of the old machine ($7,000) plus the amount of cash paid (boot) in the exchange ($20,500). The recorded amount of $27,500 is the machine's "cost." It is the amount that will be used in recording depreciation over its useful life.

The nonrecognition of the gain at the time of exchange is actually a *postponement* of the gain. Total depreciation expense over the life of the new machine will be $2,500 less, and net income will be $2,500 greater, than if depreciation were based on the $30,000 cash price of the machine. Thus, the gain is recognized gradually over the life of the new machine in the form of a lower annual depreciation expense.

The nonrecognition of gain is supported by the argument that revenue should not be recognized merely because one productive asset is substituted for a similar productive asset but, rather, should be considered to flow from the production and sale of the goods or services to which the substituted productive asset is committed. Thus, the exchange is considered a continuation of a past asset acquisition transaction, rather than the creation of a new one.

EXCHANGING DISSIMILAR ASSETS

When assets that perform different functions in a business are exchanged for each other, both gains and losses are recognized immediately. Examples of this would be the exchange of machinery for land or the exchange of a building for equipment. These exchanges are considered new asset acquisition transactions. The asset account and the related accumulated depreciation account for the old asset are removed from the books. The new asset received is recorded at its fair market value, and gain or loss is recognized for the difference between the book value of the old asset and the fair market value of the new asset.

To illustrate, assume that Dell Company exchanged a building with a cost of $125,000, accumulated depreciation of $60,000, and a fair market value of $90,000 for construction equipment with a fair market value of $90,000. The exchange would be recorded as follows.

Jan.	5	Construction Equipment	90,000	
		Accumulated Depreciation—Buildings	60,000	
		Buildings		125,000
		Gain on Disposal of Plant Assets		25,000
		Exchanged a building for construction		
		equipment.		

Note that the construction equipment received is recorded at its fair market value ($90,000); the cost of the building ($125,000) and its related accumulated depreciaton ($60,000) are removed from the accounts; and a gain is recognized in the amount of $25,000. The gain is the difference between the fair market value of the equipment received ($90,000) and the book value of the building given in exchange ($65,000).

If the fair market value of the construction equipment and building were $50,000, rather than $90,000, a $15,000 loss would be recognized and the entry would be:

Jan.	5	Construction Equipment	50,000	
		Accumulated Depreciation—Buildings	60,000	
		Loss on Disposal of Plant Assets	15,000	
		Buildings		125,000
		Exchanged a building for construction equipment.		

Notice in this case that a loss of $15,000 results, because the fair market value of the equipment received ($50,000) is less than the book value ($65,000) of the building given.

FEDERAL INCOME TAX RULES FOR EXCHANGES OF PLANT ASSETS

Federal income tax laws provide that neither gain nor loss is recognized for income tax purposes when an asset is traded for another similar asset. The cost basis of the new asset is the sum of the book value of the old asset, plus additional consideration given in the exchange. Thus, the tax treatment of a nonrecognized gain is consistent with the acceptable method for financial reporting purposes. Rules differ in the case of a trade-in involving a loss, however. Financial accounting rules require the immediate recognition of the loss, whereas income tax regulations do not permit a loss recognition.

To illustrate, assume that a machine with a cost of $22,000 and accumulated depreciation of $15,000 was traded for a new machine with a cash price of $30,000. A trade-in allowance of $4,000 was received and the remaining $26,000 was paid in cash. For income tax purposes, the new machine would be recorded as follows.

May	1	Machinery	33,000	
		Accumulated Depreciation—Machinery	15,000	
		Machinery		22,000
		Cash		26,000

For income tax purposes, the new machine has a depreciation basis of $33,000, which is equal to the book value of the old machine ($7,000) plus the $26,000 cash paid. The $3,000 difference between the book value of $7,000 and the trade-in allowance of $4,000 is not recognized immediately for tax purposes but is deferred and recognized over the useful life of the new machine. Depreciation expense for tax purposes will be based on $33,000, rather than on the cash price of $30,000. Thus the $3,000 loss will be recognized over the life of the new machine through higher depreciation charges.

NATURAL RESOURCES

Natural resources are assets, such as mineral deposits, oil and gas reserves, and standing timber, that are physically consumed as they are used. Thus, they are often called *wasting assets.* In their natural state, these assets represent inventories that will be consumed in the future by mining, pumping, or cutting, to convert them into various products. For example, a copper mine is a deposit of unmined copper ore, an oil field is a pool of unpumped oil, and standing timber is an inventory of uncut lumber. When mined, pumped, or cut they are converted into products for sale to customers. Until converted they are noncurrent assets, normally shown on the balance sheet under property, plant, and equipment, with such descriptive titles as "Mineral deposits," "Oil and gas reserves," and "Timberlands." For example, St. Regis Corporation reports its timberlands under the property, plant, and equipment caption in its 1983 annual report as follows.

Objective 3: Acquisition of natural resources

	(Thousands)	
	1983	**1982**
Timberlands	316,372	311,543
Less accumulated depletion	92,895	90,435
Timberlands, net	223,477	221,108

Natural resources are recorded in the accounts at their cost, which may include costs of exploration and development in addition to the purchase price. As the resource is converted by mining, pumping, or cutting, the asset account must be reduced proportionately. The carrying value of a copper mine, for example, is reduced for each ton of copper ore mined. As a result, the original cost is gradually transferred from the noncurrent asset account to inventory and from inventory to cost of goods sold, where it is matched against the revenue received from the copper produced and sold.

DEPLETION

The periodic allocation of the cost of natural resources to the units removed is called **depletion.** Depletion is computed in the same way that depreciation is under the units-of-production method. The cost of the natural resource (minus residual value) is divided by the estimated number of units available, such as tons of copper ore, to arrive at a depletion rate per unit. This depletion rate is then multiplied by the number of units removed during the period to determine the total depletion charge for the period. If a copper mine is purchased for $10,000,000, has an estimated residual value of $1,000,000, and contains an estimated 4,500,000 tons of copper ore, the depletion rate per ton is $2 ($10,000,000 − $1,000,000 = $9,000,000/4,500,000 tons). If 400,000 tons of ore are mined during the first year, the depletion charge for the year is $800,000, and is recorded as follows.

Objective 4: Depletion of natural resources

Dec.	31	Inventory of Copper Ore	800,000	
		Accumulated Depletion—Copper Mine		800,000
		To record depletion for the year.		

(Of course, the *Inventory of Copper Ore* account also would include labor costs and other extraction costs.)

On the balance sheet at the end of the first year, the copper mine would be reported as follows.

Copper mine	$10,000,000	
Less: Accumulated depletion	800,000	$9,200,000

Depletion represents a part of the cost of the resource extracted or product produced. It is possible that a natural resource extracted in one year may not be sold until a later year. In that case, the unsold portion represents inventory and should be reported as a current asset on the balance sheet. For example, if only 300,000 tons of the copper ore were actually processed and sold during the year, $600,000 would be reported on the income statement as depletion (included in cost of goods sold), and the remaining $200,000 would be shown as inventory of copper ore on the balance sheet. In other words, depletion is recorded in the year in which the copper ore is mined. It is then allocated to: (1) cost of goods sold and (2) inventory based on the number of units sold and the number of units retained in inventory. The following entry shows how this is done.

| Dec. | 31 | Cost of Goods Sold | 600,000 | |
| | | Inventory of Copper Ore | | 600,000 |

Of course, the amount of this entry actually would be larger than $600,000, because it also would include labor costs and other extraction costs related to the copper inventory sold.

DEPRECIATION OF RELATED PLANT ASSETS

The extraction of natural resources often requires the construction of on-site buildings and the installation of equipment that may be useful only at that particular location. These plant assets should be depreciated over their useful lives or over the life of the natural resource, whichever is shorter. Most often, depreciation is computed on the same basis as depletion by use of the units-of-production depreciation method.

To illustrate, assume that mining equipment with a cost of $450,000 and a normal useful life of 15 years is installed at the copper mine in the preceding illustration. The copper ore is being mined at a rate that will exhaust the mine in approximately 10 years. At the end of that time, the equipment will be abandoned. Thus, the useful life of the equipment is only 10 years. In this case, depreciation on the equipment should be based on the life of the mine and computed in the same way as depletion by use of the units-of-production method. The depreciation rate per ton would be $.10 ($450,000 ÷ 4,500,000 tons), and the depreciation charge for mining equipment in the first year would be $40,000 ($.10 × 400,000 tons). Like depletion, the depreciation of mining equipment is a part of the cost of the copper inventory produced. Thus, the depreciation entry would be:

Dec.	31	Inventory of Copper Ore	40,000	
		Accumulated Depreciation—Mining Equipment		40,000
		To record depreciation of mining equipment for the year.		

INTANGIBLE ASSETS

Long-lived assets that are useful to a business in the production of revenue but that have no physical substance are called **intangible assets.** Their value is derived from the long-term legal and economic rights or benefits obtained from ownership of them. Examples of intangible assets include patents, copyrights, leaseholds, and goodwill. Short-term assets that lack physical substance, such as accounts receivable and prepaid expense, are not classified as intangible assets.

The principles followed in accounting for intangible assets are similar to those used to account for plant assets. Accounting for intangibles is somewhat more difficult, however, because their lack of physical substance makes their identification, measurement, and useful life estimation more difficult.

Objective 5: Acquisition of intangible assets

Intangible assets are recorded initially at their acquisition cost. Some intangibles, like trademarks and trade names, may have been acquired without incurring any cost. Although they may be extremely valuable to the business— even essential to profitable operations—they should not be included in the balance sheet unless they have an acquisition cost. Intangible assets are normally shown in a separate section of the balance sheet immediately after the plant assets section and are reported at cost or at the portion of their cost that has not yet been amortized.

AMORTIZATION

The allocation of the cost of intangible assets to the periods benefiting from their use is called **amortization.** Amortization is similar to depreciation of plant assets. Unlike depreciation, however, an *Accumulated Amortization* account normally is not used. Instead, the amortization entry consists of a debit to *Amortization Expense* and a credit directly to the intangible asset account.

For many years, accountants supported the view that some intangible assets had unlimited lives and, therefore, should not be amortized. At the same time, many businesses elected to write their intangible assets down to the nominal figure of $1 on the basis of conservatism and because of an inability to determine a reasonable useful life. Accounting rules today require that all intangible assets be amortized over their legal or useful lives, with a maximum

Objective 6: Amortization of intangible assets

amortization period of 40 years.[2] The arbitrary write-down of intangible assets is not permitted. Significant changes in estimated useful life are accounted for by spreading the unamortized cost of the intangible assets over their remaining useful lives. The straight-line method of amortization is generally used to account for intangible assets.

PATENTS

A **patent** is an exclusive right, granted by the federal government, to produce and sell a particular product or to use a specific process for a period of 17 years. The reason for issuing patents is to encourage the invention of new machines, processes, and mechanical devices.

American businesses spend billions of dollars yearly on research and development of new products and new processes. These expenditures are a vital contribution to the nation's economic growth and increased productivity. Before 1975, some companies charged research and development expenditures to expense when incurred. Other companies capitalized such expenditures and amortized them over future periods. Because of this lack of uniformity, accounting rules were established requiring that all research and development expenditures that are not reimbursable by governmental agencies or other parties must be charged to expense in the period incurred.[3]

Since research and development expenditures are charged to expense as incurred, the only additional costs involved in an internally developed patent are the legal and filing fees paid to obtain it. Because these fees are usually relatively small, they are generally also charged to expense as incurred, which is justified under the *materiality convention.* When a patent is purchased from an inventor or patent holder, instead of being developed internally, the purchase price should be debited to the *Patents* account. In addition, any legal costs involved with the successful defense of the patent (which occurs quite frequently) should also be debited to the *Patents* account, because they represent costs incurred to establish legal rights to the patent.

For example, if a patent was purchased for $80,000 on January 4, the entry would be:

Jan.	4	Patents	80,000	
		Cash		80,000
		To record the purchase of a patent.		

Although a patent grants exclusive rights to the holder for 17 years, new inventions, such as the rapid changes in microcomputers, often make the patent obsolete before that period is up. Therefore, the cost of a patent should be amortized over its estimated economic life or 17 years, whichever is shorter. If the patent recorded in the previous example is expected to have a useful

[2]Accounting Principles Board, "Intangible Assets," *APB Opinion No. 17* (New York: AICPA, August 1970), par. 27, 29.

[3]Financial Accounting Standards Board, "Accounting for Research and Development Costs," *Statement of Financial Accounting Standards No. 2* (Stamford, Conn.: FASB, October 1974), par. 12.

life of eight years, the following adjusting entry is made each year to record amortization.

Dec.	31	Amortization Expense	10,000	
		Patents		10,000
		To record amortization of patents.		

Although most firms credit the asset account directly when amortization is recorded, some firms use an *Accumulated Amortization* account. Since intangible assets often are not directly replaceable, the relationship between cost and accumulated amortization does not have the same significance to statement readers that a similar relationship has for depreciable or depletable assets.

COPYRIGHTS

A **copyright** is an exclusive right, granted by the federal government, to reproduce and sell an artistic or published work. The exclusive right exists for the life of the creator, plus 50 years. If a copyright is purchased, the purchase price is debited to a *Copyrights* account and amortized over its economic life, or 40 years, whichever is shorter. As with a patent, the cost of a successful legal defense of a copyright should be debited to the *Copyrights* account. Since it is difficult to determine how long benefits will be received from a copyright, most copyrights are amortized over a relatively short period. Often the only additional cost to the creator of an artistic work is the fee paid for the copyright, because development costs have been expensed. Since the fee is nominal, it is often charged to expense immediately.

TRADEMARKS AND TRADE NAMES

The exclusive right to trademarks, such as the General Electric symbol, and to trade names, like Pepsi Cola, can be obtained by registering them with the federal government. The main cost of developing trademarks and trade names lies in advertising, which should be charged to expense in the period incurred. Other costs, such as registration fees and design costs, should be capitalized and amortized if their amount is material. Since these costs are often small, they are generally charged to expense when incurred. However, if a trademark or trade name is purchased, the purchase price may be material. If so, its cost should be debited to the appropriate intangible asset account and amortized over its useful life, not to exceed 40 years.

LEASEHOLDS

Many companies rent property under a contract called a **lease.** The owner of the property is the **lessor** and the person or company obtaining the rights of possession and use of the property is the **lessee.** The rights of possession and use granted to the lessee by the contract are called a **leasehold.**

Some leases provide for regular monthly rent payments and the lease generally can be canceled at any time by either the lessor or lessee. In these cases, a leasehold account is not used and the monthly rent payments are debited to rent expense. Sometimes a lease agreement provides that the rent for the entire period of the lease must be paid in advance, or a lump-sum payment is made in advance in addition to periodic rental payments. In these cases, it is necessary to allocate the payments to the accounting periods in which the asset is used.

If the lease covers a short period of time, the prepayments are debited to a current asset account, *Prepaid Rent,* and transferred to rent expense, as illustrated in earlier chapters. If the lease covers a long period of time, the prepayment is debited to a *Leasehold* account and is generally classified on the balance sheet as an intangible asset. The prepayment is allocated to rent expense as the lease benefits are received.

For example, assume that an agreement was made to lease a portion of a building from Baxter Realty for four years, beginning on January 1, 1987. The lease agreement requires a prepayment of $40,000, plus an annual payment of $20,000 on December 31 of each year. The prepayment would be recorded as follows.

Jan.	1	Leasehold	40,000	
		Cash		40,000
		To record a four-year building lease prepayment.		

On December 31 of each year the additional payment would be recorded and the leasehold (prepayment) would be amortized, as follows.

Dec.	31	Rent Expense	30,000	
		Leasehold		10,000
		Cash		20,000
		To record rent payment and the amortization of a leasehold.		

At times, the life of the lease covers most (75% or more) of the useful life of the leased property. In these cases, the lease is treated as the equivalent of an installment purchase of property, and the lessee records both the leased asset (such as leased machinery) and an equal long-term lease liability. Both the asset and the liability are recorded at the discounted present value of the future lease payments required under the lease contract. Accounting for this type of lease is discussed further in Chapter 17.

LEASEHOLD IMPROVEMENTS

Often, a lessee must make special improvements to leased property to make it suitable for its intended use. Examples of leasehold improvements are permanent partitions and permanent store fixtures installed in a leased building. These **leasehold improvements** become a permanent part of the property and title to them passes to the lessor at the end of the lease. Thus, these improvements cannot be removed by the lessee at the end of the lease. As a result, the cost of these improvements is debited to a *Leasehold Improvements* account, and amortized to expense over the life of the improvements or the life of the lease, whichever is shorter. The amortization entry consists of a debit to *Rent Expense* and a credit to *Leasehold Improvements*.

To illustrate, if $10,000 was paid to install partitions and permanent fixtures in a building leased for five years, the payment would be recorded as:

Jan.	2	Leasehold Improvements	10,000	
		Cash		10,000
		To record payment for improvements to leased building.		

The leasehold improvements would then be amortized each year, as follows.

Dec.	31	Rent Expense	2,000	
		Leasehold Improvements		2,000
		To record amortization of leasehold improvements.		

FRANCHISES

A **franchise** is a right granted by a company or a governmental body to an individual or firm to conduct business at a specified location or in a specific geographical area. Examples of franchises include the right to operate a fast-food operation, such as McDonald's or Kentucky Fried Chicken (a private franchise) and the right to operate a municipal bus line or private water company (a public franchise). The initial cost of a franchise may be substantial, and should be capitalized and amortized over the term of the franchise. If the franchise has no specific expiration date, it should be amortized over a period not to exceed 40 years. If initial franchise costs are small, they may be expensed when incurred. Periodic annual payments under a franchise agreement should be expensed.

GOODWILL

The term "goodwill" is used by accountants and the public to mean various things. In general terms, it is often thought of as the favorable reputation of a business among its customers. From an accounting standpoint, however, goodwill has a special meaning not limited to good customer relations. **Goodwill** is a business's potential to earn a rate of return on its net assets (assets minus liabilities) in excess of the normal rate of return in the industry in which the business operates. Goodwill arises from many factors, including customer confidence, superior management, favorable location, manufacturing efficiency, and good employee relations.

A successful business continually builds goodwill as it develops these factors, but the expenditures made in doing so generally cannot be specifically identified with the development of goodwill. Thus, goodwill is often called the unidentifiable intangible, represented by the overall ability of a business to earn above-normal returns on its identifiable net assets (net assets other than goodwill).

To illustrate the meaning of above-normal earnings, assume that two businesses in the same industry are offered for sale and that the normal return on the fair value of net assets in the industry is 15%. Data for the two companies follow.

	Able Company	Bay Company
Fair market value of net assets	$5,000,000	$5,000,000
Normal rate of return for the industry	× 15%	× 15%
Normal earnings	750,000	750,000
Actual average earnings for the past five years	900,000	750,000
Average earnings in excess of normal	$ 150,000	$ -0-

A potential buyer would be willing to pay $5,000,000 for Bay Company, because it is earning a normal return on the fair value of its net assets. Thus, assuming the same level of earnings in the future, the buyer would receive a 15% return on the purchase price of $5,000,000. Although Able Company has the same fair value of net assets, a potential buyer would be willing to pay more for Able Company than for Bay Company, because Able Company has been obtaining above-normal earnings, which are expected to continue for some time into the future.

Although a potential buyer would be willing to pay more for Able Company than for Bay Company, the data given do not tell us how much more the buyer would be willing to pay. The actual amount paid for goodwill will be the amount the buyer is willing to pay and the seller is willing to accept. Several approaches to estimating the amount of goodwill are available to the buyer and seller as a basis for negotiation.

1. The buyer and seller may agree on an arbitrary amount for goodwill. For example, if the buyer offers $5,400,000 for Able Company and the seller accepts the offer, the payment for goodwill is $400,000, the excess of the purchase price over the fair market value of the net assets. Thus, the buyer and the seller are placing an arbitrary value of $400,000 on the company's goodwill.

2. Goodwill may be computed arbitrarily at some multiple of excess earnings. For example, if excess earnings are expected to continue for about four years into the future, goodwill may be valued at four times the average above-normal earnings, or $600,000 (4 × $150,000) in our illustration. If agreed upon by the buyer and seller, the purchase price for Able Company would be $5,600,000, of which $600,000 represents payment for goodwill.

3. Goodwill may be computed by capitalizing the average above-normal earnings at the average rate of return for the industry. Capitalizing above-

normal earnings means dividing those earnings by the normal rate of return. For example, if Able Company is expected to continue to have $150,000 of excess earnings each year, these excess earnings may be capitalized at 15% and a $1,000,000 value may be placed on goodwill ($150,000/15% = $1,000,000). This approach values the goodwill at the amount that would have to be invested at the normal rate of return in order to earn the extra $150,000 each year ($1,000,000 × 15% = $150,000). This is the most theoretically correct approach if excess earnings are expected to continue indefinitely. However, because this will seldom be the case, the excess earnings are often capitalized at a higher capitalization rate to reflect the limited life of the goodwill. For example, if the excess earnings of Able Company are capitalized at 30%, goodwill is valued at $500,000 ($150,000/30%).

Regardless of the approach used to value goodwill, its recorded value will always be determined in the final analysis by the amount that the buyer is willing to pay and the seller is willing to accept. ***Goodwill is recorded in the accounts only when it has been purchased.*** Because goodwill generally cannot be purchased or sold separately, this usually occurs only when a business is purchased in its entirety. The purchase price of the business is assigned first to the fair market values of the identifiable assets and liabilities acquired, and any remainder of the purchase price is recorded as goodwill. Because goodwill is *not* amortizable for tax purposes, the purchaser will often try to attribute the full purchase price to identifiable assets.

Many businesses have goodwill that has been developed internally, by establishing good customer relations, acquiring or training superior management, and obtaining the other factors that contribute to above-normal earnings. This internally-developed goodwill is not recorded as an asset in the accounts, however, because the expenditures made to develop it have been charged to expense in the periods when they were incurred.

As with other intangible assets, goodwill is considered by accountants to have a limited life. Therefore, goodwill must be amortized to expense over its useful life, not to exceed a maximum period of 40 years.

GLOSSARY

AMORTIZATION. The systematic allocation of the cost of intangible assets to the periods benefiting from their use (p. 451).

COPYRIGHT. An exclusive right granted by the federal government to reproduce and sell an artistic or published work (p. 453).

DEPLETION. The systematic allocation of the cost of natural resources to the units removed (p. 449).

FRANCHISE. A right granted by a company or governmental body to conduct business at a specified location or in a specific geographical area (p. 455).

GOODWILL. The ability of a business to earn a rate of return in excess of the normal rate of return in the industry in which the business operates. It is recorded only when it is purchased and is measured by the excess of the purchase price over the fair value of the net assets acquired (p. 455).

INTANGIBLE ASSETS. Long-lived assets that are useful to a business in producing revenue but that have no physical substance (p. 451).

LEASE. A contract for the use (rental) of property (p. 453).

LEASEHOLD. The rights of possession and use of property granted under a lease contract (p. 453).

LEASEHOLD IMPROVEMENTS. Permanent improvements to leased property made by the lessee (p. 454).

LESSEE. The person or company obtaining the rights to possession and use of leased property (p. 453).

LESSOR. The owner of property that is leased to another person or company (p. 453).

PATENT. An exclusive right granted by the federal government to produce and sell a particular product or process for a period of 17 years (p. 452).

DISCUSSION QUESTIONS

1. Accounting for the disposal of a plant asset varies with the nature of the disposal. However, it is necessary to do one thing in all cases. What is this? How is it accomplished?

2. When a plant asset is sold for cash, how is the gain or loss measured? How is the gain or loss reported in the financial statements?

3. What entry should be made prior to the disposal of a plant asset in the middle of the year?

4. A factory machine and $8,000 cash are exchanged for a delivery truck. How should the cost of the delivery truck be determined for financial accounting purposes?

5. A duplicating machine with a cost of $12,000 and accumulated depreciation of $8,000 is traded for a new improved duplicating machine with a cash price of $17,000. Cash of $11,000 is also given. What is the cost of the new machine for financial accounting purposes? What is its cost for federal income tax purposes?

6. What logic supports the nonrecognition of gains on the exchange of similar assets?

7. At what amount are natural resources recorded in the accounts? What is the expense from the extraction of natural resources called? How is it computed?

8. Connor Coal Company recognizes $2 of depletion for each ton of coal mined. If 400,000 tons of coal are mined but only 300,000 tons are sold during the current year, how much should be charged to cost of goods sold for the year?

9. What are intangible assets? What are the most common types?

10. A building with an estimated life of 30 years is constructed on the site of a silver mine. The silver ore is expected to be entirely extracted over a period of 20 years. Assuming that the building will be abandoned after all the silver ore is extracted, over what time period should the building be depreciated? What depreciation method should probably be used?

11. What is amortization? In general, what should be the length of the amortization period? What amortization method is generally used?

12. Several years ago Baxter Company purchased, for $170,000, a patent for the manufacture of special "seal tight" plastic containers. After five years, the manufacture of these containers was discontinued because of the development of a new, improved container by a competitor. Baxter Company is continuing to deduct amortization expense of $10,000 per year based on a patent life of 17 years, which the president of Baxter Company says is required by generally accepted accounting standards. Do you agree?
13. What are leasehold improvements? Over what time period should they be amortized? Why?
14. What is goodwill, from an accounting standpoint? When and in what amounts is it recorded in the accounts? Is it necessary to amortize goodwill?

EXERCISES

Exercise 11-1 Discarding Plant Assets

Royal Company discarded the following machines as worthless.

Machine	Cost	Accumulated Depreciation Jan. 1, 1987	Removal Expense Paid	Date of Purchase	Date of Disposal
1	$ 9,300	$9,300	-0-	1/2/83	1/2/87
2	7,000	6,700	$100	6/30/82	1/2/87
3	10,000	8,400	-0-	6/30/83	4/1/87

Depreciation expense was recorded last on December 31, 1986.

Required:
Prepare separate entries to record the disposal of the machines.

Exercise 11-2 Sale of Plant Assets

On January 3, 1982, Worldwide Company paid $21,000 for a machine with an estimated useful life of ten years and a residual value of $3,000. On December 31, 1986, accumulated depreciation on the machine was $9,000. The machine was sold on May 31, 1987.

Required:
A. Prepare an entry to record depreciation expense on the machine for the five months in 1987. Use the straight-line depreciation method.
B. Prepare an entry to record the sale of the machine of May 31, 1987 assuming a selling price of
   1. $11,000.
   2. $12,000.

Exercise 11-3 Exchange of Similar Assets

On January 3, 1987, a company exchanged a machine with a cost of $23,000 and accumulated depreciation of $16,000 for a new similar machine with a cash price of $25,000.

Required:
A. Prepare an entry to record the exchange of the machines for financial accounting

purposes, assuming that a trade-in allowance of $6,000 was received for the old machine and the balance of $19,000 was paid in cash.

B. Prepare an entry to record the exchange of machines for financial accounting purposes, assuming that a trade-in allowance of $8,000 was received for the old machine and the balance of $17,000 was paid in cash.

Exercise 11-4 Exchange of Dissimilar Assets

A company exchanged machinery with a cost of $260,000 and accumulated depreciation of $180,000 for a parcel of land.

Required:

Prepare an entry to record the exchange assuming that

A. The fair value of the land was $95,000.
B. The fair value of the land was $70,000.

Exercise 11-5 Depletion of Natural Resources

Indian Copper Mine was purchased for $13,500,000, has an estimated residual value of $1,500,000, and contains an estimated 10,000,000 tons of copper ore. Mining equipment with an estimated useful life of 14 years was installed at a cost of $2,400,000. The ore is being extracted at a pace that will exhaust the mine in about 12 years, after which the equipment will be abandoned.

Required:

A. Prepare entries to record depletion of the mine and depreciation of the mining equipment for the first year, assuming that 780,000 tons of ore were mined and sold.
B. Prepare a partial balance sheet showing how the copper mine and the mining equipment would be reported at the end of the first year.

Exercise 11-6 Goodwill

Avon Company is considering the purchase of Seagreens Company, which produces a product that Avon uses in its manufacturing process. Relevant data for Seagreens Company is:

Fair market value of net assets	$1,800,000
Normal rate of return in the industry in which Seagreens Company operates	16%
Actual average annual earnings for the past five years	$ 318,000

Required:

Determine the total price Avon Company would pay for Seagreens Company under each of the following assumptions.

A. Avon will pay an amount equal to six years' above-normal earnings for Seagreens Company's goodwill.
B. Above-normal annual earnings are to be capitalized at 32% to determine the amount to be paid for goodwill.
C. Actual average annual earnings are to be capitalized at 16% to determine the total purchase price.

PROBLEMS

Problem 11-1 Exchanges and Disposals of Plant Assets

Phillips Company entered into the following transactions during 1987.

Jan.   4   Discarded a machine that cost $12,500 and had accumulated depreciation of $10,000. Disposal costs of $200 were incurred.

Mar.   29   Sold a machine for $6,000 that had cost $14,000 on January 2, 1983. The machine's estimated useful life and residual value were five years and $4,000, respectively. Accumulated depreciation on the machine through December 31, 1986 was $8,000.

Apr.   1   Exchanged a machine with a cost of $36,000 and accumulated depreciation to the date of exchange of $25,000 for a new similar machine with a cash price of $42,000. A trade-in allowance of $12,000 was received for the old machine and the remainder of the purchase price was paid in cash.

July   1   Exchanged a parcel of land that had cost $26,000 for machinery with a fair market value of $30,000.

Sept. 30   Exchanged a building with a cost of $250,000 and accumulated depreciation to the date of exchange of $200,000 for a machine with a fair market value of $40,000.

Oct.   31   Sold a machine for $17,000 cash that had cost $45,000 on November 1, 1982. The machine had an estimated useful life of six years and a residual value of $9,000 when purchased. On December 31, 1986, straight-line depreciation for $6,000 was recorded. No depreciation has yet been recorded for 1987.

Dec.   31   Recorded depletion of the company's mine. The mine was purchased on January 1, 1987, for $32,000,000. On the date of purchase, the mine was estimated to contain 8,000,000 tons of ore and to have a residual value of $2,800,000. One million tons of ore were mined during 1987.

Required:

Prepare journal entries to record the transactions.

Problem 11-2 Intangible Assets

The following transactions and events of Cochico Industries occurred during the current year.

1. The company's coal mine produced 900,000 tons of ore this year. The mine, which was purchased last year for $24,800,000, has an estimated residual value of $2,000,000 and is estimated to contain about 12,000,000 tons of coal. Production is expected to continue at about the same level as the current year.

2. A patent with an estimated useful life of eight years was purchased from its inventor for $160,000 in November of last year.

3. Mining equipment with a cost of $720,000 was installed at the coal mine [discussed in (1)] shortly after the mine was purchased. The equipment has a normal useful life of 15 years with no salvage value. The equipment cannot be salvaged when the mine is closed because the cost of removal would exceed the sales value of the equipment.

4. Timber rights were purchased for $750,000. The stand of timber is estimated to contain about 1,500,000 board feet. One hundred thousand board feet of timber were cut this year.

5. A five-year lease agreement was signed by the company at the end of last year, requiring that rent for the entire period in the amount of $150,000 be paid in advance.
6. In early July of this year, the company made some improvements to the property leased in (5) in the amount of $16,650. The improvements are estimated to have a useful life of seven years.
7. In late June of this year, the company purchased a franchise from a regional restaurant chain for $320,000. The franchise cost is to be amortized over 20 years.
8. On October 2 of the current year the company purchased a highly profitable local engineering firm for $2,000,000. The fair value of the net identifiable assets of the firm was $1,712,000. Goodwill is to be amortized over its expected life of six years.

Required:
Prepare separate journal entries to record amortization, depletion, and depreciation for the current year ended December 31.

Problem 11-3 Exchanges of Similar Assets
The beginning balance in the *Machinery* account and credits to the account for various machinery disposals during the year are presented here.

Machinery

1/1/87 Balance	452,500	1/5/87 Sold machine No. 102	11,000
1/11/87	?	1/8/87 Sold machine No. 94	8,000
1/14/87	?	1/11/87	12,000
4/2/87	?	1/14/87	32,000
8/30/87	?	2/26/87 Sold machine No. 98	19,000
		4/2/87	48,000
		6/30/87 Sold machine No. 104	9,500
		8/30/87	7,000

Four exchange transactions took place during 1987, as indicated here.

Jan. 11 Exchanged an old machine and $15,000 cash for a similar machine with a cash price of $20,000. The old machine had a cost of $12,000 and accumulated depreciation of $8,000.

14 A machine with a cost of $32,000 and accumulated depreciation of $27,000 was traded for a similar machine having a cash price of $39,000. A trade-in allowance of $4,000 was received, with the balance paid in cash.

Apr. 2 A machine with a cost of $48,000 and accumulated depreciation of $35,000 on December 31, 1986, was exchanged for a new similar machine with a cash price of $60,000. A trade-in allowance of $11,000 was received and the balance was paid in cash. Monthly depreciation on the old machine was $200.

Aug. 30 A machine with a cost of $7,000 and a book value at the date of exchange of $2,000 was traded in for a new similar machine with a cash price of $10,000. Received a trade-in allowance of $2,500 and paid the remaining $7,500 in cash.

Required:
A. Determine the amount that should be debited to the *Machinery* account for each of the exchanges and reproduce the *Machinery* account, showing its ending balance.

B. Determine the cost, for income tax purposes, of the four machines acquired during 1987.

Problem 11-4 Goodwill

Mary Michaels, who recently received an inheritance from her grandmother's estate, quit her high school music teaching position and began a search for a business that she would purchase and operate. She found what she believed was an ideal business for her background, Keyboard Music Store, which had been earning an average of $55,000 per year over the last four years.

Mary has a copy of Keyboard's current balance sheet as shown here.

Current Assets:			
Cash		$ 14,000	
Inventory		102,000	
Total Current Assets			$116,000
Plant Assets:			
Land		26,000	
Building	$113,000		
Less: Accumulated depreciation	20,000	93,000	
Equipment	26,000		
Less: Accumulated depreciation	4,000	22,000	
Total Plant Assets			141,000
Total Assets			$257,000
Liabilities:			
Accounts payable			$ 6,000
Mortgage payable			70,000
Total Liabilities			76,000
Bill Whitehurst, Capital			181,000
Total Liabilities and Owner's Equity			$257,000

Mary Michaels and Bill Whitehurst agree that the book values of assets and liabilities are equal to their fair market values with the exception of land, which has a fair market value of $60,000, and inventory, which has a fair market value of $110,000. Mary proposes to purchase the assets (except for cash) and assume the liabilities of Keyboard.

Required:
A. Determine the fair value of the net assets of Keyboard.
B. What is the average rate of return Keyboard has earned on its net assets as determined in (A)?
C. Determine the amount that Mary will pay for Keyboard assuming that she is willing to pay for goodwill.
   1. Four times average earnings in excess of an 18% return on the net assets acquired.
   2. Average earnings in excess of an 18% return on net assets acquired capitalized at 30%.

Problem 11-5 Correcting Errors

The following errors were made and discovered during the current year.

1. Depreciation of machinery, $4,600, was incorrectly credited to *Accumulated Depreciation—Buildings*.
2. A machine with a cost of $35,000 and accumulated depreciation to the date of

sale of $12,500 was sold for $25,000. The sale was recorded by a debit to *Cash* and a credit to *Machinery* for $25,000.

3. Property taxes of $5,280 were paid and debited to *Property Tax Expense*. Of this amount, $3,400 represented delinquent taxes from previous years on land purchased during the current year.

4. Delivery equipment, purchased on July 1 for $14,600, was debited to the *Purchases* account. The equipment has a useful life of five years and an estimated residual value of $2,600. The straight-line depreciation method is used for delivery equipment.

5. The cost of installing lighting in the company parking lot, which was $21,000, was charged to *Maintenance Expense* on January 4. The lights have a useful life of seven years and no residual value. Assume straight-line depreciation.

6. A machine with a cost of $57,000 and accumulated depreciation to the date of exchange of $40,000 was exchanged on December 23 for a new similar machine with a cash price of $49,000. A trade-in allowance of $19,000 was allowed on the old machine. The bookkeeper made the following entry.

Machinery	49,000	
Accumulated Depreciation—Machinery	40,000	
Machinery		57,000
Cash		30,000
Gain on Exchange		2,000

Required:

Prepare journal entries to correct the errors assuming that the books have not been closed for the current year ending December 31.

Problem 11-6 Comprehensive Review Problem

Westport Company completed the following transactions over a period of several years.

<u>1986</u>

Jan.   2   Purchased land and a building for $450,000 cash. The land and building had appraised values at that time of $150,000 and $350,000, respectively.

Mar. 20   Paid $15,000 to Re-Nu Company for renovation costs on the building acquired on January 2. Westport Company opened for business on March 25. The building has an estimated life of 20 years and an expected residual value of $30,000. Assume straight-line depreciation.

Dec. 31   Recorded depreciation expense on the building.

<u>1987</u>

May 21   Paid $4,600 to repair damage to the building caused by a windstorm.

Dec. 31   Recorded depreciation expense on the building.

<u>1988</u>

Jan.   6   Paid $56,250 for an addition to the building. The addition is expected to increase the useful life to 25 years from the date of the addition and to increase the building's residual value to $40,000.

Dec. 31   Recorded depreciation expense on the building.

<u>1989</u>

Oct.   4   The land and building were sold for $500,000 cash.

Required:

A. Prepare journal entries to record the transactions.

B. Open general ledger accounts for *Land, Buildings,* and *Accumulated Depreciation—Buildings,* and post the relevant portion of the entries to those accounts.

ALTERNATE PROBLEMS

Problem 11-1A Plant Asset Disposals

During 1987, Jax Company disposed of four different plant assets. On January 1, 1987, the accounts showed the following.

Asset	Cost	Residual Value	Estimated Life	Accumulated Depreciation
Truck No. 4	$21,000	$3,000	5 years	$10,800
Truck No. 6	18,000	2,000	4 years	12,000
Machine A	57,000	7,000	5 years	30,000
Machine B	32,000	2,000	15 years	21,000

Jax Company depreciates its trucks and machines by the straight-line method and records depreciation to the nearest month. Assets were disposed of as follows.

Truck No. 6, which was not insured, was completely destroyed by fire on January 6, 1987. A towing company was paid $560 to remove the truck and to clean up any debris.

Truck No. 4 was traded for a new truck on July 3, 1987. The new truck had a cash price of $31,000. The old truck, plus cash of $21,000, were given in exchange.

Machine A was sold for $22,000 cash on October 1, 1987.

Machine B was traded for a new similar machine with a cash price of $39,000 on December 22, 1987. The old machine, plus cash of $31,250, were given in exchange.

Required:

Prepare all journal entries needed to account for the transactions.

Problem 11-2A Various Methods of Disposing of a Plant Asset

On January 2, 1984, Mason Company purchased a truck for $38,000. The truck had an estimated life of five years and a residual value of $3,000. Straight-line depreciation is used.

Required:

Assuming that the truck is to be disposed of on July 1, 1987.

A. What entry should be made to record depreciation prior to the disposal?

B. Prepare journal entries to record the disposal of the truck under each of the following assumptions.

1. The truck is sold for $15,000 cash.
2. The truck is sold for $10,000 cash.
3. The truck and cash of $28,000 are exchanged for a new truck with a cash price of $42,000.

4. The truck was completely destroyed by fire and cash of $10,000 was received from the insurance company.
5. The truck and cash of $52,500 are exchanged for a new truck with a cash price of $65,000.

Problem 11-3A Intangibles

The following transactions and events affect the accounts of Dawn Company for the current year.

1. A patent with an estimated useful life of ten years was purchased for cash of $420,000 on January 3 of last year.
2. On January 8 of the current year, Dawn Company paid $22,000 in legal fees for the successful defense of a patent infringement suit against the patent purchased in (1).
3. On January 1 of the current year, Dawn Company signed a contract to lease a small warehouse from Ajax Company. The lease is for five years and required an advance payment of $105,000, plus a $45,000 cash payment at the end of each year.
4. On February 6 of the current year, Dawn Company purchased a coal mine for $5,750,000. Of the total purchase price, $4,950,000 was assigned to the coal mine and the remaining $800,000 was assigned to mining machinery. The mine has a residual value of $750,000 and contains an estimated 10,000,000 tons of coal. The mining machinery is expected to be useful for the entire life of the mine and will be abandoned when the coal deposits are depleted. During the current year, 1,500,000 tons of coal were mined.
5. Improvements were made to the leased warehouse in (3) on June 30 of the current year at a cost of $22,500. The estimated life of the improvements is eight years.

Required:
A. Prepare journal entries to record the expenditures made during the current year.
B. Prepare journal entries to record amortization, depletion, and depreciation for the current year. Record to the nearest month.

Problem 11-4A Intangibles

Morley Company has four different intangible assets at the end of 1987. Facts concerning each are as follows.

1. **Copyright.** On January 3, 1987, the company purchased a copyright for $55,200. The remaining legal life of the copyright was 26 years, and it is expected to have a useful life of 12 years to Morley Company with no residual value.
2. **Franchise.** On April 2, 1987, Morley Company purchased a franchise to distribute a new product for a ten-year period with no right of renewal. Cost of the franchise was $80,000.
3. **Patent.** Morley Company purchased a patent on July 1, 1987, from Bay Company for $77,700. The patent had been registered initially on January 1, 1981, and is expected to be useful to Morley Company until the end of its legal life.
4. **Goodwill.** Morley Company began operations on January 2, 1983, by purchasing another company for a total cash payment of $413,500. Included in the purchase price was a payment of $90,000 for goodwill. The president of Morley Company believes that "the goodwill is such an important long-term asset of the company that it should last for 100 years."

Required:
A. Prepare journal entries to record the acquisition of intangible assets during 1987.

B. Prepare the journal entries for each intangible asset that are necessary at the end of the annual accounting period on December 31, 1987.

Problem 11-5A Correcting Errors

During an audit of Lever Company at the end of 1987, the following errors, made in 1987, were discovered.

1. Store fixtures with a cost of $13,600 and accumulated depreciation to the date of sale of $9,400 were sold for $3,000 cash. The sale was recorded by a debit to *Cash* and a credit to *Store Fixtures* of $3,000.
2. The $12,200 cost of installing a fence around the office building was charged to *Maintenance Expense* on July 1. The fence has a useful life of ten years and no residual value. Assume straight-line depreciation.
3. The $14,250 cost of a truck purchased on January 4 was inadvertently debited to the *Purchases* account. The truck has a useful life of five years and is to be depreciated by the double declining-balance method with a residual value of $4,250.
4. On July 1, land with a cost of $31,000 was exchanged for a machine having a cash value of $57,000. The machine has a useful life of seven years and an estimated residual value of $1,000. The exchange was recorded by a debit to *Machinery* and a credit to *Land* for $31,000. Machinery is depreciated using the straight-line method.

Required:

A. Prepare the journal entries that should be made to correct the accounts at December 31, 1987, before the adjusting entries are made. Assume that closing entries have not yet been made.
B. Prepare adjusting entries on December 31, 1987, after the corrections in (A) have been made.

CASE

CASE 11-1 Discussion Case Goodwill

Fastgas Company, a retail fuel oil distributor, has increased its annual sales volume to a level four times greater than the annual sales of the dealer it purchased in 1979 in order to begin operations.

The board of directors of Fastgas Company recently received an offer from a large competitor for the purchase of Fastgas. As a result, the majority of the board wants to increase the stated value of goodwill on the balance sheet to reflect the larger sales volume developed through intensive promotion, and the current market price of sales gallonage. A few of the board members, however, would prefer to eliminate goodwill altogether from the balance sheet in order to prevent "possible misinterpretations." Goodwill was recorded properly in 1979.

1. Discuss the meaning of the term "goodwill."
2. What are the techniques often used to estimate the value of goodwill in negotiations to purchase a company?
3. Why are the book and market values of the goodwill of Fastgas Company different?
4. Discuss whether it is appropriate to
   (a) Increase the stated value of goodwill prior to the negotiations.
   (b) Eliminate goodwill completely from the balance sheet prior to negotiations.
   (AICPA adapted)

12

PAYROLL SYSTEMS

CHAPTER OVERVIEW AND OBJECTIVES

This chapter describes the essential features of a payroll system. When you have completed the chapter, you should understand:

1. The importance of accounting for labor costs and related payroll taxes.
2. How internal control is applied to payroll accounting.
3. The determination of an employee's gross earnings.
4. The different deductions from gross earnings.
5. The computation of an employee's net earnings.
6. Which payroll taxes are withheld from employees' earnings and which are paid by the employer.
7. The basic records and procedures used in a payroll system.
8. How to prepare journal entries for payroll accounting.

Objective 1: Importance of payroll accounting

The combined cost of labor and related payroll taxes represents a major expense of operating every business. Goodyear Tire and Rubber Company reported in 1983 that it employed 128,760 people with payroll expenses amounting to approximately $2.5 billion or 25.3 percent of sales. Ford Motor Company had 380,077 employees worldwide in 1983 with total labor costs of over $12 billion. The firm's average hourly labor cost (earnings and benefits) amounted to $22.67. Highly labor-intensive operations, such as a medical clinic, a hospital, or a university often have payroll expenses amounting to 75% to 80% of their total revenue. In addition to the large dollar amounts involved, accounting for payroll expenses is complicated by the impact of many federal and state laws. These laws require employers to maintain certain payroll records, collect and pay taxes on a timely basis, and comply with specific minimum standards for the amount of compensation paid and hours worked.

Another important consideration of payroll accounting is the increasing popularity of such fringe benefits as insurance premiums, education courses, child-care centers, physical fitness facilities, and retirement plans. In addition, employers must comply with their states' worker's compensation laws to provide employees benefits for job-related injuries or disease. The substantial dollar amounts involved with these benefits have added to the need for detailed payroll records. Large and small businesses alike must operate a sound payroll system that will ensure that each payroll is paid on time, that federal and state laws are complied with, and that sound internal control is maintained to prevent errors or fraudulent activities. A payroll system is an integral part of the accounting system discussed in Chapter 6. Like the accounting system itself, a good payroll system must be capable of receiving input data (such as employees' names, social security numbers, pay rates, and hours worked), processing the data, and generating output (such as payroll checks, payroll records, and reports to taxing authorities). This chapter describes the essential features of an effective payroll system.

IMPORTANCE OF INTERNAL CONTROL

Sound internal control, as discussed in Chapter 6, is a fundamental part of an effective payroll system. This is particularly important because payroll fraud has been experienced by many businesses in the past. Common payroll frauds, often substantial in amount, have been overpaid employee compensation, continuation of former employees on the payroll after termination, payments made to fictitious employees, overstatement of payroll deductions, and duplicate checks issued. In a small business with only a few employees, the owner may be able to handle all the payroll procedures personally. As a business grows, various payroll duties are delegated to several people, thereby introducing the possibility of fraud. The likelihood of error also increases with the separation of responsibilities for payroll functions.

Objective 2: Applying internal control to a payroll system

To achieve sound internal control over payroll procedures, a business should separate these duties: hiring employees, timekeeping, preparing checks and maintaining payroll records, and distributing checks to employees. In small businesses, two or more of these functions may have to be combined because of the lack of personnel. However, some separation of duties is essential, even in small businesses, in order to satisfy the basic characteristics of sound internal control. Internal control over payroll should begin when a new employee is hired and should continue until the employment is terminated. Written notice of employment, job description, amount of earnings, and deduction authorizations originate in the personnel department at the time of employment. Each new employee must complete an **Employee's Withholding Allowance Certificate, Form W-4,** such as the one shown on page 475, to indicate the appropriate number of withholding allowances. As discussed later, a withholding allowance is an amount of compensation that will not be taxed. Payroll deductions for such items as union dues, insurance, retirement plans, or uniforms must be authorized for each employee. Subsequent changes in pay rate, job assignment, or payroll deductions are recorded by the personnel department. The employee information maintained by the personnel department will be sent to the payroll department to place a new employee on the payroll and to assure that he or she is paid properly.

Some type of document must be utilized to record the amount of time for which the employee will be paid. Most businesses use a time clock to record the number of hours worked by each employee paid on an hourly basis. Employees clock-in when work begins and clock-out at the end of the work-day. The manager responsible for the related work activity is in charge of the time cards used for time-keeping purposes. A weekly or monthly time report is usually maintained for salaried personnel. At the end of each payroll period, the documents used to record employees' time are reviewed by the supervising managers in order to verify their accuracy, and are then sent to the payroll department.

Ideally, employees in the payroll department should have no payroll responsibilities other than checking the accuracy of the time-keeping documents, preparing payroll checks, and maintaining payroll records. Time-keeping forms are combined with information from the personnel department to process the payroll. In many cases, the payroll is processed with a computer, using the procedures discussed in Chapter 6. Payroll checks are prepared, and individual employee records of earnings and deductions are updated. The payroll checks are signed by the treasurer of the company or some other specified officer. In most cases, a separate bank account should be used to control payroll expenditures as will be discussed later. The final step in the payroll process is the distribution of paychecks. This should be accomplished by someone who is independent of the payroll function and is not responsible for supervising employees. In large businesses, this person is often called the paymaster. By separating the various duties involved in the payroll function for internal control purposes, collusion on the part of two or more people is necessary for fraudulent activity to be carried out.

EMPLOYER–EMPLOYEE RELATIONSHIP

Businesses obtain services from their own employees and from outsiders who are independent contractors. In the operation of a payroll system, a firm is concerned only with payments made as compensation to employees, and not with disbursements to independent contractors. Thus, we need to be able to recognize the essential features of an employer–employee relationship. In general, such a relationship exists when the business or person for whom the service is performed (the employer) has the right to direct and control not only the results to be achieved, but also *how* the results are to be achieved by another person (the employee). In contrast, an independent contractor chooses the specific means used to perform services and is at liberty to work for other businesses or persons at the same time.

A bookkeeper and the controller of a business are employees; a CPA performing an audit for the firm is an independent contractor. As such, the CPA is not an employee, because he or she will determine the scope of the audit work and will not be subject to the control of the client. The fees paid to independent contractors are kept separate from compensation to employees and, to reiterate, are not part of the payroll system.

GROSS EARNINGS

The first step in computing the amount paid to a particular employee during a given payroll period is determining his or her **gross earnings** (also called gross compensation) in the form of wages or salary. The term **wages** is used for compensation paid to an employee on the basis of an hourly rate or for piecework (this means that a worker is paid on the basis of some measure of productivity, such as the number of units produced). The term **salary** refers to compensation paid on a weekly, biweekly, or monthly basis. Usually salaries are paid to management, sales, and administrative personnel. Both wages and salaries may be supplemented by bonuses, profit sharing, commissions, and cost of living adjustments.

**Objective 3:
Calculating
gross earnings**

Gross earnings are also increased by overtime pay, which may be determined by agreement between an employer and employees (often in the form of a union contract), or by law. The **Federal Fair Labor Standards Act** (also called the Wages and Hours Law) regulates overtime pay for any employer who engages in interstate commerce. The act also establishes certain minimum-wage and equal-pay standards. For example, an employee covered by the act had to be paid a minimum wage of $3.35 in 1985. In most cases, the actual hourly wage agreed on by an employer and employee will be higher than the minimum.

The law also provides that a covered employee must be paid overtime at a rate that is at least 1½ times the regular rate for every hour worked in excess of 40 hours a week. Exemptions from the overtime requirements are provided in the law for executive, administrative, and certain supervisory personnel. Employees in certain industries, such as restaurants, motels, and farms are also exempt from overtime regulations. Many employment agreements provide an overtime pay rate in excess of 1½ times the regular rate for weekends or holidays. Some employment agreements recognize overtime rates for hours worked in excess of eight during any given day. The act also requires that females and males be paid equally for performing jobs involving equal skills, effort, responsibility, and working conditions.

To illustrate the calculation of gross earnings with overtime pay, assume that Leonard Smith, a construction worker for the Five Star Remodeling Company, earns a regular hourly wage of $8. In addition, he is paid an overtime rate of 1½ times the regular rate for all hours over eight in any weekday and twice the regular rate for work performed on a weekend or holiday. During the week ending February 9, 1985, Smith worked the following hours.

	Total Hours	Regular Hours	Overtime Hours
Monday	8	8	0
Tuesday	8	8	0
Wednesday	10	8	2
Thursday	9	8	1
Friday	10	8	2
Saturday	3	0	3
Total hours	48	40	8

Smith's gross earnings for the week are computed as follows.

Regular pay	40 hours × $8	= $320
Overtime pay, weekdays	5 hours × $8 × 1.5 =	60
Overtime pay, weekend	3 hours × $8 × 2 =	48
Gross earnings		$428

DEDUCTIONS FROM GROSS EARNINGS

Objective 4:
Difference between gross and net earnings

The **net earnings** paid an employee will be less than his or her gross earnings because of certain deductions that must be made. Many of these deductions are required because of federal, state, or local laws, while others are authorized by agreement between an employer and the employees. In the example above, Leonard Smith will not receive $428, because his employer will deduct certain amounts for such items as FICA taxes, federal income taxes, state income taxes, and union dues.

FICA Taxes

The Social Security System was created by the **Federal Insurance Contributions Act of 1935 (FICA).** The purpose of the system is to provide qualified workers with a continuing source of income during their retirement years. In addition, certain medical, disability, and survivorship benefits are provided by the system. The principal source of financing for the social security system is a tax on wages or salaries and on self-employment income. Most sources of compensation are subject to FICA taxes. Special rules apply to certain types of employment, such as agricultural labor, casual labor, domestic workers, and government employees.

FICA taxes are levied on both the employee and the employer, according to a schedule established by Congress. The schedule includes a tax rate on wages and salaries, up to a maximum or ceiling amount of earnings. While the amounts are subject to change, due to congressional action, the maximum compensation limit was $39,600 for 1985 and the tax rate for the employer and for the employee was 7.05%. Therefore, the combined rate for FICA taxes was 14.1%. We will assume throughout the discussion of FICA taxes and the homework at the end of the chapter that this maximum compensation limit is valid because the correct amount for a given year, beginning with 1986, will not be known until Congress determines it late in the preceding year, based on a cost of living adjustment. In addition to potential increases in the maximum compensation level, at the time of this writing the FICA rates for the employer and employee for years after 1985 are scheduled as follows.

Year	Tax on Employee	Tax on Employer
1986	7.15%	7.15%
1987	7.15	7.15
1988	7.51	7.51
1989	7.51	7.51
1990	7.65	7.65

We also will use the 7.05% rate throughout the discussion and illustration of FICA taxes. In 1985, the maximum amount of tax paid by both employer and employee was $2,791.80 ($39,600 × 7.05%). We should note that this amount has increased dramatically over the years; for example, in 1937 the maximum compensation level was $3,000 and the tax rate was 1%, for a maximum FICA tax of $30. As a result, FICA taxes today represent a significant cost of operating a business and reduction of spendable income for employees.

An employer must withhold from wages or salary the FICA taxes owed by each employee and must pay a payroll tax equal to the amount withheld. For example, assume that construction worker Leonard Smith earns $23,500 in 1985. His employer, Five Star Remodeling Company, would withhold FICA taxes amounting to $1,656.75 ($23,500 × 7.05%) during the year, and would owe a like amount as the employer's share of FICA taxes. Consequently, the total tax contributed to the social security system on Smith's behalf in 1985 is $3,313.50. If Smith's annual wages were $40,000, only $39,600 would be subject to FICA taxes and the total amount withheld would be $2,791.80. FICA taxes would not have to be paid on the $400 ($40,000 less $39,600) balance because it exceeds the maximum compensation taxable.

Federal Income Taxes

The federal income tax system of the United States is on a "pay-as-you-go" basis. This means that an employer must withhold certain amounts of federal income tax from each employee's wages or salary, based on the amount of gross earnings and the number of **withholding allowances** (amounts of income exempt from tax) claimed by the employee. Employers use **withholding tables,** such as the one illustrated in Figure 12–1, to determine the amount of federal income tax to be withheld, except in unusual cases. Each employee is required by law to complete a Form W–4, like the one in Figure 12–2, at the time that he or she is hired. At that time, the employee indicates the number of income tax withholding allowances (also called personal exemptions) claimed, and the marital status of the employee is recorded. In 1984, each allowance caused $1,000 of gross earnings to be exempted from federal income tax. Beginning in 1985, the $1,000 personal exemption is adjusted for inflation as measured by the Consumer Price Index for the preceding year. For example, the Consumer Price Index increased 4.08% in 1984, so the personal exemption for 1985 was $1,040 [$1,000 + (4.08% × $1,000)]. One allowance can be claimed for the employee, one for the employee's spouse, and one for each of the employee's dependents.

Additional allowances are taken if the employee or spouse is blind or at least 65 years old. Consequently, a married couple (neither of whom is blind nor 65 years old or older) with three dependent children would have claimed five allowances for a total dollar amount of $5,200 in 1985. Whenever the number of allowances or marital status changes, the employee must file a new Form W–4. The employer will match the gross earnings and the number of allowances with the proper withholding table to detemine the amount to be withheld from each paycheck. (It should be noted that an employee can, with

WEEKLY PAYROLL PERIOD — MARRIED PERSONS

the wages are— At least	But less than	And the number of withholding allowances claimed is—										
		0	1	2	3	4	5	6	7	8	9	10
		The amount of income tax to be withheld shall be—										
200	210	20	17	14	11	9	6	4	2			
210	220	21	18	16	13	10	8	5	3	1		
220	230	23	20	17	14	11	9	6	4	2		
230	240	24	21	18	16	13	10	8	5	3	1	
240	250	26	23	20	17	14	11	9	6	4	2	
250	260	28	24	21	18	16	13	10	8	5	3	1
260	270	29	26	23	20	17	14	11	9	6	4	2
270	280	31	28	24	21	18	16	13	10	8	5	3
280	290	32	29	26	23	20	17	14	11	9	6	4
290	300	34	31	28	24	21	18	16	13	10	8	5
300	310	36	32	29	26	23	20	17	14	11	9	6
310	320	38	34	31	28	24	21	18	16	13	10	8
320	330	39	36	32	29	26	23	20	17	14	11	9
330	340	41	38	34	31	28	24	21	18	16	13	10
340	350	43	39	36	32	29	26	23	20	17	14	11
350	360	45	41	38	34	31	28	24	21	18	16	13
360	370	47	43	39	36	32	29	26	23	20	17	14
370	380	48	45	41	38	34	31	28	24	21	18	16
380	390	50	47	43	39	36	32	29	26	23	20	17
390	400	52	48	45	41	38	34	31	28	24	21	18
400	410	55	50	47	43	39	36	32	29	26	23	20
410	420	57	52	48	45	41	38	34	31	28	24	21
420	430	59	55	50	47	43	39	36	32	29	26	23
430	440	61	57	52	48	45	41	38	34	31	28	24
440	450	63	59	55	50	47	43	39	36	32	29	26
450	460	66	61	57	52	48	45	41	38	34	31	28
460	470	68	63	59	55	50	47	43	39	36	32	29
470	480	70	66	61	57	52	48	45	41	38	34	31
480	490	73	68	63	59	55	50	47	43	39	36	32
490	500	75	70	66	61	57	52	48	45	41	38	34
500	510	78	73	68	63	59	55	50	47	43	39	36
510	520	80	75	70	66	61	57	52	48	45	41	38
520	530	83	78	73	68	63	59	55	50	47	43	39
530	540	85	80	75	70	66	61	57	52	48	45	41
540	550	88	83	78	73	68	63	59	55	50	47	43
550	560	90	85	80	75	70	66	61	57	52	48	45
560	570	93	88	83	78	73	68	63	59	55	50	47
570	580	95	90	85	80	75	70	66	61	57	52	48
580	590	98	93	88	83	78	73	68	63	59	55	50
590	600	101	95	90	85	80	75	70	66	61	57	52
600	610	103	98	93	88	83	78	73	68	63	59	55
610	620	106	101	95	90	85	80	75	70	66	61	57
620	630	109	103	98	93	88	83	78	73	68	63	59
630	640	112	106	101	95	90	85	80	75	70	66	61
640	650	115	109	103	98	93	88	83	78	73	68	63
650	660	117	112	106	101	95	90	85	80	75	70	66
660	670	120	115	109	103	98	93	88	83	78	73	68
670	680	123	117	112	106	101	95	90	85	80	75	70
680	690	126	120	115	109	103	98	93	88	83	78	73
690	700	129	123	117	112	106	101	95	90	85	80	75
700	710	132	126	120	115	109	103	98	93	88	83	78
710	720	136	129	123	117	112	106	101	95	90	85	80
720	730	139	132	126	120	115	109	103	98	93	88	83
730	740	142	136	129	123	117	112	106	101	95	90	85
740	750	146	139	132	126	120	115	109	103	98	93	88
750	760	149	142	136	129	123	117	112	106	101	95	90
760	770	152	146	139	132	126	120	115	109	103	98	93
770	780	155	149	142	136	129	123	117	112	106	101	95
780	790	159	152	146	139	132	126	120	115	109	103	98

Figure 12–1

Federal Income Tax Withholding Table

Form **W-4** (Rev. January 1982)

Department of the Treasury—Internal Revenue Service

Employee's Withholding Allowance Certificate

OMB No. 1545-0010
Expires 4-30-83

1 Type or print your full name: Leonard E. Smith

2 Your social security number: 306-39-6193

Home address (number and street or rural route): 1056 Rush Street

City or town, State, and ZIP code: Indianapolis, Indiana 46206

3 Marital Status: ☐ Single ☒ Married ☐ Married, but withhold at higher Single rate

Note: If married, but legally separated, or spouse is a nonresident alien, check the Single box.

4 Total number of allowances you are claiming (from line F of the worksheet on page 2) . . . 5

5 Additional amount, if any, you want deducted from each pay . . . $

6 I claim exemption from withholding because (see instructions and check boxes below that apply):

a ☐ Last year I did not owe any Federal income tax and had a right to a full refund of **ALL** income tax withheld, **AND**

b ☐ This year I do not expect to owe any Federal income tax and expect to have a right to a full refund of **ALL** income tax withheld. If both a and b apply, enter "EXEMPT" here . . . ▶

c If you entered "EXEMPT" on line 6b, are you a full-time student? . . . ☐ Yes ☐ No

Under the penalties of perjury, I certify that I am entitled to the number of withholding allowances claimed on this certificate, or if claiming exemption from withholding, that I am entitled to claim the exempt status.

Employee's signature ▶ Leonard E. Smith Date ▶ January 8 19 80

7 Employer's name and address (including ZIP code) (FOR EMPLOYER'S USE ONLY): Five Star Remodeling Company, Indianapolis, Indiana 46222

8 Office code

9 Employer identification number: 35-1299693

Figure 12–2
Employee's Withholding Allowance Certificate

certain limitations, claim a different number of allowances than he or she actually has because of the expected income tax liability for a given year.)

Other Income Taxes

Most states and some local authorities (city or county) levy income taxes that must be withheld by an employer. The procedures used for such taxes are similar to those already discussed for withholding federal income taxes.

Other Deductions

In addition to the mandatory deductions for taxes, several other deductions must be accounted for. Some examples are union dues, insurance premiums, retirement plan contributions, parking charges, savings bond purchases, uniform allowances, and charitable contributions. These deductions are taken out of the employee's paycheck by the employer and later remitted to the appropriate organizations.

COMPUTATION OF NET EARNINGS

Objective 5: Calculating net earnings

Gross earnings less the deductions already described equals the **net earnings** or take-home pay received by an employee. To illustrate how net earnings are computed, assume that construction worker Leonard Smith is paid weekly. Recall that his regular and overtime pay combined, for the period ending February 9, 1985, was $428. All of his earnings are subject to FICA taxes, and he has union dues of $4 per week. In addition, he has medical insurance premiums of $17.80 per week and contributes $5 per week to the United Way—a charitable organization. His federal and state income tax withholdings have been determined by his employer to be $39.00 and $12.84, respectively.

(The federal withholding is found in Figure 12–1 by looking at the intersection of the \$420–\$430 row and withholding allowances column 5, whereas we assume that the state withholding is taken from the appropriate state withholding table.) His net earnings are computed as follows:

Gross earnings		\$428.00
Deductions:		
FICA taxes (at 7.05%)	\$30.17	
Federal income taxes	39.00	
State income taxes	12.84	
Union dues	4.00	
Medical insurance	17.80	
United Way contribution	5.00	
Total deductions		108.81
Net Earnings		\$319.19

EMPLOYER'S LIABILITY FOR WITHHOLDING

The amounts withheld from an employee's paycheck are liabilities of the employer, who performs the duties of a collection agent. In the case of Leonard Smith, his employer owes a total of \$108.81 to the different parties involved with the withholdings. The various deductions must be paid when due to the federal government, state government, union, insurance company, and United Way. After the deductions are withheld, but before they are remitted to the appropriate organization, the amounts are *liabilities* of the employer. The employer, in turn, is responsible for maintaining adequate records which will provide the basis for filing any reports concerning the withholdings and for making payments on time. The withholdings are classified as current liabilities on the employer's balance sheet until they are paid.

EMPLOYER PAYROLL TAXES

Objective 6: Understanding who is responsible for payroll taxes

Payroll taxes are paid by both employers and employees. As indicated earlier, employers are required to match the amount of the employee's contribution to the social security system. In the case of Leonard Smith, his employer would pay FICA taxes amounting to \$30.17, based on his weekly earnings. Employers also must make payments for federal and state unemployment compensation tax. The **Federal Unemployment Tax Act (FUTA)** provides certain benefits for a limited period of time to employees who lose their jobs through no fault of their own. The Federal Unemployment Tax Act is a part of the social security system and is a joint federal and state unemployment program. The act establishes certain minimum standards that must be complied with by each state. The major portion of the tax is levied by the states, and a minor portion by the federal government. Actual unemployment benefits are paid by the state involved, while administrative expenses are paid from the amount of the tax remitted to the federal government.

The amount of the total FUTA tax can change, but in 1985, for most states, the federal and state portions combined amounted to 6.2 percent of the first \$7,000 earned by each employee. The federal portion of the unemployment tax itself is 6.2% by law, but a credit against that amount is granted for the state portion, up to a maximum of 5.4%. In turn, the actual amount paid to a state may be less than 5.4% if a particular employer has had a sufficiently low unemployment record in the past (according to a merit-rating plan). Nevertheless, the credit for federal purposes will still be 5.4%, so the federal liability is .8% (6.2% less 5.4%). A few states also require employees to pay state unemployment taxes. Indiana, the state in which Leonard Smith works, does not require a contribution from employees, but his employer has to pay the state the full 5.4% of the first $7,000 earned by each employee. The employer's share of the **state unemployment taxes** in a given year will be $378 ($7,000 × 5.4%) and the **federal unemployment taxes** $56 ($7,000 × .8%), a total of $434.

PAYROLL RECORDS AND PROCEDURES

The payroll system selected by a particular firm should depend on the number of employees and amount of automation, but several records and procedures are common to most payroll systems. Many small companies process their payrolls manually, although this has decreased significantly in recent years because of the increasingly detailed recordkeeping involved and the availability of in-house computers or timesharing services that process payrolls for a fee. One of the oldest and most popular computer applications in business is for preparing a payroll, because of its repetitive nature. A computer enables a business to process its payroll accurately, economically, and rapidly. This section describes the basic records and procedures common to most payroll systems.

Objective 7: Basic records and procedures with a payroll system

INPUT DATA

Two types of input data, *permanent* and *current,* are used to process a payroll. A permanent file, maintained at all times for each employee, includes such items as the employee's name, address, social security number, rate of pay, Form W–4 information, other deductions from gross earnings, and year-to-date payroll figures. A current file is developed each time a payroll is processed to record such items as regular hours worked, overtime hours worked, bonuses, commissions, vacation pay, tips, and sick pay. The permanent and current data are combined to determine net earnings, prepare a payroll check, and update year-to-date payroll figures, such as gross earnings, various types of deductions, and net earnings. Many businesses maintain payroll records on a departmentalized basis so that the source of the expenditure can be readily identified for control purposes. For example, a medical clinic can departmentalize its payroll for medical services performed, such as pediatrics, surgery, laboratory, radiology, and internal medicine.

PAYROLL REGISTER

A **payroll register** is a detailed listing of a firm's complete payroll for a particular pay period. Each employee's earnings and deductions for the period are reported in this register. The specific form chosen by a business for a payroll register will vary, depending on the number of employees, the payroll classifications required, and the use of automation. The Five Star Remodeling Company's payroll register, shown in Figure 12–3, is typical of one used by a business, and itemizes the gross-to-net earnings for each employee. The firm's payroll is divided into the categories *office salaries* and *construction wages*. Note that the beginning point of the accounting by employee is the gross earnings for a current payroll period. A column is presented for each type of deduction from gross earnings. Also, the net earnings (take-home pay) are reported, computed as gross earnings less the total deductions. The cumulative gross earnings column keeps the employer informed about the total compensation paid to date.

Objective 8: Journal entries required for a payroll

By totaling each of the columns, the business has the information required to record the payroll expense classified as office salaries and construction wages, as well as the related liabilities in the accounting system. This is accomplished with a general journal entry.

Feb.	9	Office Salaries Expense	420.00	
		Construction Wages Expense	2,086.00	
		FICA Taxes Payable		176.67
		Federal Income Taxes Payable		205.00
		State Income Taxes Payable		75.84
		Union Dues Payable		24.00
		Medical Insurance Payable		142.40
		United Way Contribution Payable		36.00
		Salaries and Wages Payable		1,846.09
		To record the payroll for the week ended February 9.		

Figure 12–3
Payroll Register

Employee	Hours	Regular	Over-time	Total	FICA Tax	Fed. Tax	State Tax	Union Dues	Insur-ance	United Way	Net Earnings	Cumulative Gross
Office Salaries												
M. Andrews	40	200.00		200.00	14.10	11.	6.00		17.80	2.00	149.10	1,200.00
J. Miller	40	220.00		220.00	15.51	17.	7.00		17.80	4.00	158.69	1,540.00
Subtotal		420.00		420.00	29.61	28.	13.00		35.60	6.00	307.79	2,740.00
Construction Wages												
A. Baker	40	240.00		240.00	16.92	17.	7.00	4.00	17.80	4.00	173.28	1,720.00
D. Cohn	40	240.00		240.00	16.92	11.	7.00	4.00	17.80	4.00	179.28	1,700.00
R. King	44	280.00	42.00	322.00	22.70	26.	10.00	4.00	17.80	6.00	235.50	2,260.00
B. Maier	50	320.00	136.00	456.00	32.15	52.	14.00	4.00	17.80	6.00	330.05	3,260.00
L. Smith	48	320.00	108.00	428.00	30.17	39.	12.84	4.00	17.80	5.00	319.19	2,100.00
C. Thomas	40	400.00		400.00	28.20	32.	12.00	4.00	17.80	5.00	301.00	2,700.00
Subtotal		1800.00	286.00	2086.00	147.06	177.	62.84	24.00	106.80	30.00	1538.30	13,740.00
Total		2220.00	286.00	2506.00	176.67	205.	75.84	24.00	142.40	36.00	1846.09	16,480.00

Payroll Register   2/9/85   Page 1

At the same time, the employer payroll taxes can be recorded, although some firms do so with an end-of-the-month adjusting entry. Remember that the employer is required to pay an amount equal to the employee's share of FICA taxes, as well as the unemployment taxes based on a maximum amount of compensation ($7,000 in 1985). Consequently, the employer would compute the federal and state unemployment tax liability, match the employees' FICA tax liability of $176.67, and make the following entry in the general journal.

Feb.	9	Payroll Taxes Expense	332.04	
		FICA Taxes Payable		176.67
		State Unemployment Taxes Payable		135.32
		($2,506 × 5.4% = $135.32)		
		Federal Unemployment Taxes Payable		20.05
		($2,506 × .8% = $20.05)		
		To record payroll taxes expense for the		
		week ended February 9.		

As a result, the total payroll expense for the week ended February 9 is $2,838.04 ($2,506.00 + $332.04). After the two payroll entries are recorded, the Five Star Remodeling Company also has liabilities amounting to $2,838.04, which must be paid on a timely basis to the employees, governmental agencies, and various other organizations. This will be done by debiting the liabilities and crediting *Cash* for the amounts accrued in the two entries, as will be discussed later.

EMPLOYEE EARNINGS RECORD

An **employee earnings record**, such as the one shown in Figure 12–4, provides a detailed description of an employee's hours worked, gross earnings, deductions, and net earnings for the year to date. This information is posted

Figure 12–4
Employee Earnings Statement

		Employee Earnings Record										1985

Name	Leonard E. Smith	Marital Status	M
Address	1056 Rush St. Indianapolis, IN 46206	Exemptions	5
Soc. Sec. No.	306-39-6193	Pay Rate	$8.00
Date of Birth	July 19, 1948	Position	Carpenter

Period Ending	Total Hours	Earnings			Deductions						Net Earnings	Cumulative Gross
		Reg.	O.T.	Gross	FICA	Fed.	State	Union	Insur.	United Way		
Jan. 5	42	320.00	24.00	344.00	24.25	26.	10.32	4.00	17.80	5.00	256.63	344.00
12	44	320.00	48.00	368.00	25.94	29.	11.04	4.00	17.80	5.00	275.22	712.00
19	40	320.00		320.00	22.56	23.	9.60	4.00	17.80	5.00	238.04	1,032.00
26	40	320.00		320.00	22.56	23.	9.60	4.00	17.80	5.00	238.04	1,352.00
Feb. 2	40	320.00		320.00	22.56	23.	9.60	4.00	17.80	5.00	238.04	1,672.00
9	48	320.00	108.00	428.00	30.17	39.	12.84	4.00	17.80	5.00	319.19	2,100.00

from the related line of the payroll register at the end of each pay period. The employee earnings record must be kept current, because it serves four important purposes: (1) It provides the information needed for certain payroll tax returns; (2) it indicates when an employee's gross earnings have reached the maximum limitations for FICA and unemployment taxes; (3) it furnishes the information required to prepare a Wage and Tax Statement, Form W–2 (discussed later), at the end of the year; and (4) it keeps the employer informed about the amount of earnings for each employee. Note in Figure 12–4 that the last column shows the cumulative gross earnings for the year to date.

PAYMENT OF EMPLOYEES

We noted earlier that for internal control reasons the preferred treatment is to pay employees with checks written on a separate **payroll bank account.** At the end of each pay period, a check is written for the total of the net earnings of all employees. It is drawn on the regular bank account and is deposited in the payroll bank account. Paychecks, such as the one illustrated in Figure 12–5, are later drawn on the payroll bank account, which should be reduced to zero after all the paychecks have cleared the bank. The use of one check drawn on the regular bank account for the payroll simplifies the reconciliation of that account at the end of the month, since only the one check has to be considered instead of all the individual payroll checks. Likewise, reconciling the payroll bank account is simplified because only payroll checks are involved. The separation of payroll checks drawn on a special cash account from nonpayroll checks drawn on the regular cash account facilitates the preparation, control, and reconciliation of what is often a large number of checks. In the case of the Five Star Remodeling Company, a check in the amount of $1,846.09 would be drawn on the regular bank account and deposited in the payroll bank account. *Salaries* and *Wages Payable* would then be debited, and *Cash* would be credited for $1,846.09 in the cash disbursements journal. The payroll register provides detailed information concerning specific amounts paid to individual employees.

A business with only a few employees may not need the control feature of a special payroll bank account. In such cases, paychecks are drawn from the regular bank account, and entries are made in the cash disbursements journal, debiting *Salaries and Wages Payable* and crediting *Cash.* Although it is not required by law, most employers provide each employee with an earnings statement for each pay period. As can be seen in Figure 12–5, the earnings statement is usually attached to the paycheck and shows hours worked, gross earnings, deductions, and net earnings for the current period and year to date.

WAGE AND TAX STATEMENT

By January 31 of every year, an employer must provide each employee several copies of a **Wage and Tax Statement, Form W–2,** for the preceding calendar year. The form shows the total earnings paid to the employee, the federal income taxes withheld, the state income taxes withheld, the earnings subject

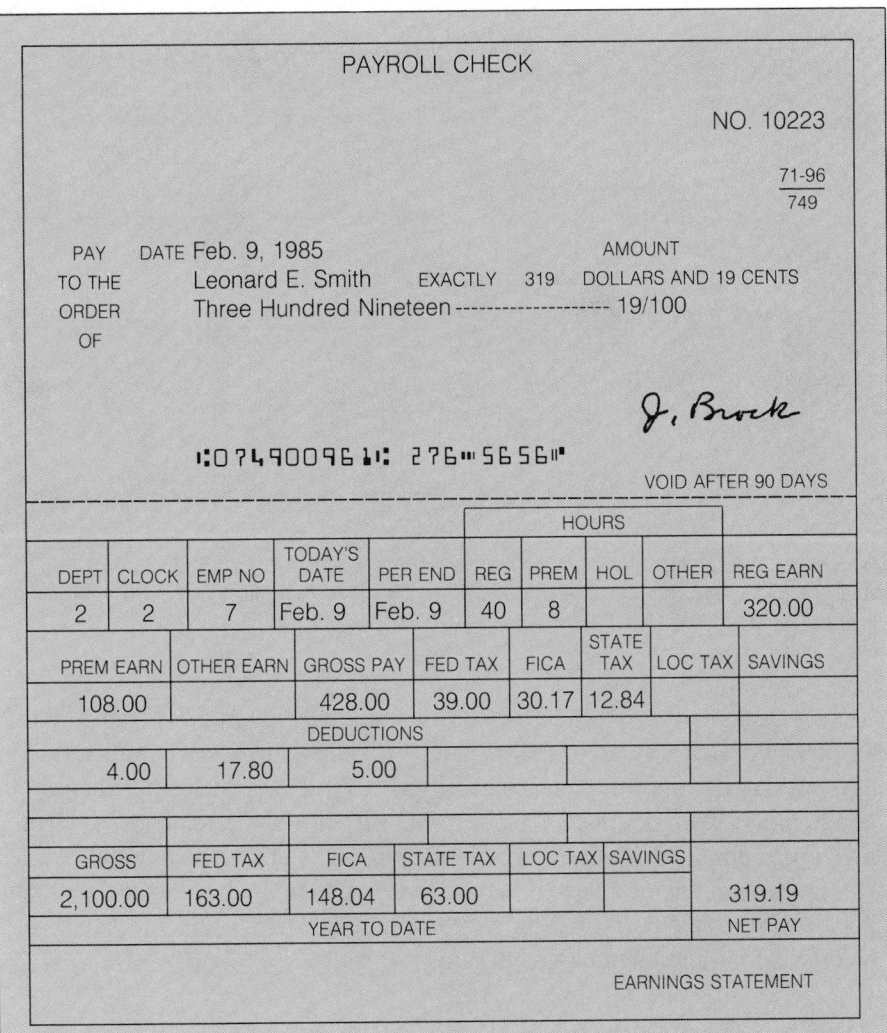

Figure 12–5
Paycheck/Earnings
Statement

to FICA taxes, the FICA taxes withheld, and certain other information. The employer also must send a copy of each employee's Form W–2 to the Social Security Administration, which processes the information and then sends the Internal Revenue Service the income tax information that it requires from the form. The Form W–2 furnishes information needed by the employee to file his or her income tax returns, and a copy of the form must be attached to each return filed. An example of a Form W–2, prepared for Leonard Smith, is shown in Figure 12–6.

PAYROLL TAX RETURNS

Employers are also required by law to file a number of payroll tax returns with governmental agencies. An example is the **Employer's Quarterly Federal Tax Return, Form 941,** shown in Figure 12–7. Every business must use a calendar year in accounting for payroll taxes, even if its fiscal year does not

		Copy B To be filed with employee's FEDERAL tax return	
Five Star Remodeling Company P.O. Box 682 Indianapolis, IN. 46222	3 Employer's identification number 35-1299693	4 Employer's State number	

5 Stat. employee ☐	De-ceased ☐	Pension plan ☐	Legal rep. ☐	942 emp. ☐	Cor-rection ☐

6	7 Advance EIC payment

2 Employer's name, address, and ZIP code

8 Employee's social security number	9 Federal income tax withheld	10 Wages, tips, other compensation	11 FICA tax withheld
306-39-6193	2348.00	23,500.00	1656.75

12 Employee's name, address, and ZIP code	13 FICA wages
Leonard E. Smith 1056 Rush Street Indianapolis, IN. 46206	23,500.00

14 FICA tips

16 Employer's use	

17 State income tax	18 State Wages, tips, etc.	19 Name of State
705.00		Indiana

20 Local income tax	21 Local wages, tips, etc.	22 Name of locality

Form **W-2 Wage and Tax Statement**   This information is being furnished to the Internal Revenue Service.   Department of the Treasury Internal Revenue Service   13-2678063 IRS APP

Figure 12–6
Wage and Tax Statement

end on December 31 for financial and income tax reporting. Form 941 must be prepared quarterly and filed no later than the end of the month following a given quarter. Information concerning FICA taxes and federal income tax withholdings are combined on Form 941. It shows the total gross earnings paid by an employer, the earnings subject to FICA taxes, the amount of FICA taxes, the amount of federal income taxes withheld, and the tax payments made. Similar payroll tax returns are required for state income taxes, local income taxes, and unemployment taxes.

PAYROLL TAX PAYMENTS

The employer acts as a collection agent and is liable to remit the amount of tax withheld to the appropriate governmental agency. Whenever the amounts withheld are large, they must be paid frequently by the employer. The exact timing of the payments depends on the nature of the tax and the amounts involved. For federal purposes, the FICA taxes (both employees' and employers' portions) and the federal taxes withheld must be combined, to determine when the total must be paid. Large amounts must be deposited on a timely basis prescribed by law at a **federal deposit bank** (a bank authorized by law to collect payroll tax deposits). Small amounts can be remitted directly to the Internal Revenue Service, along with the Form 941. The rules that define what are large amounts, small amounts, or something in between and how they are treated change frequently, so you should refer to the *Employer's Tax Guide,* published by the Internal Revenue Service, if you need more detailed information. Large businesses are required to make frequent deposits because of the size of their payrolls. The deposits are later reconciled with the tax liability, shown on Form 941 (see Figure 12–7). Similar procedures

Form **941** (Rev. January 1985) Department of the Treasury Internal Revenue Service	**Employer's Quarterly Federal Tax Return** ▶ For Paperwork Reduction Act Notice, see page 2. Please type or print

Your name, address, employer identification number, and calendar quarter of return. (If not correct, please change.)

Name (as distinguished from trade name) Five Star Remodeling Company	Date quarter ended March 31, 1985
Trade name, if any	Employer identification number 35-1299693
Address and ZIP code P.O. Box 682 Indianapolis, IN 46222	

4141

OMB No. 1545-0029
Expires: 12-31-85

T
FF
FD
FP
I
T

If address is ▶ different from prior return, check here ☐

If you are not liable for returns in the future, write "FINAL". . . . ▶ Date final wages paid . . . ▶

Complete for First Quarter Only

1 a Number of employees (except household) employed in the pay period that includes March 12th ▶	**1a**	8
b If you are a subsidiary corporation AND your parent corporation files a consolidated Form 1120, enter parent corporation employer identification number (EIN) . . ▶ **1b** −		
2 Total wages and tips subject to withholding, plus other compensation . . . . . ▶	**2**	32,820
3 Total income tax withheld from wages, tips, pensions, annuities, sick pay, gambling, etc . . . . ▶	**3**	2,685
4 Adjustment of withheld income tax for preceding quarters of calendar year (see instructions) . . ▶	**4**	
5 Adjusted total of income tax withheld	**5**	2,685
6 Taxable social security wages paid . . . . . $ 32,820 X 14.1% (.141) . .	**6**	4,628
7 a Taxable tips reported . . . . . . $ X 7.05% (.0705) . .	**7a**	
b Tips deemed to be wages (see instructions) . . $ X 7.05% (.0705) . .	**7b**	
8 Total social security taxes (add lines 6, 7a, and 7b)	**8**	4,628
9 Adjustment of social security taxes (see instructions) . . . . ▶	**9**	
10 Adjusted total of social security taxes	**10**	4,628
11 Backup withholding . . . . ▶	**11**	
12 Adjustment of backup withholding tax for preceding quarters of calendar year	**12**	
13 Adjusted total of backup withholding	**13**	
14 Total taxes (add lines 5, 10, and 13) . . . . ▶	**14**	7,313
15 Advance earned income credit (EIC) payments, if any (see instructions)	**15**	
16 Net taxes (subtract line 15 from line 14). **This must equal line IV below** (plus line IV of Schedule A (Form 941) if you have treated backup withholding as a separate liability.) . . . . ▶	**16**	7,313
17 Total deposits for quarter, including overpayment applied from a prior quarter, from your records ▶	**17**	7,313
18 Undeposited taxes due (subtract line 17 from line 16). Enter here and pay to IRS . . . . ▶	**18**	−0−
19 If line 17 is more than line 16, enter overpayment here ▶ $ and check if to be: ☐ Applied to next return or ☐ Refunded		

Record of Federal Tax Liability (Complete if line 16 is $500 or more)

See the instructions under rule 4 for details before checking these boxes.

Check only if you made eighth-monthly deposits using the 95% rule ▶ ☐ Check only if you are a first time 3-banking-day depositor ▶ ☐

Date wages paid	Tax liability (Do not show Federal tax deposits here.)					
		First month of quarter		Second month of quarter		Third month of quarter
1st through 3rd	A		I	555	Q	585
4th through 7th	B	550	J		R	
8th through 11th	C		K	558	S	565
12th through 15th	D	562	L		T	
16th through 19th	E	540	M	540	U	546
20th through 22nd	F		N		V	
23rd through 25th	G		O	537	W	554
26th through the last	H	588	P		X	633
Total liability for month	I	2,240	II	2,190	III	2,883
IV Total for quarter (add lines I, II, and III) . . . . ▶						7,313

Under penalties of perjury, I declare that I have examined this return, including accompanying schedules and statements, and to the best of my knowledge and belief it is true, correct, and complete.

Signature ▶ *William Jones*   Title ▶ Vice President   Date ▶ April 15, 1985.

Figure 12–7
Employer's Quarterly Federal Tax Return

must be followed with the federal portion of unemployment taxes. State and local governments also have specific schedules that must be complied with for timely payment of tax liabilities. When the amounts previously withheld are paid, an entry is made in the cash disbursements journal debiting the liability accounts and crediting *Cash*.

PAYMENT OF OTHER WITHHOLDINGS

The employer remits the amounts withheld for such items as union dues, insurance premiums, and charitable contributions at various times, according to agreements with the external organizations involved. Five Star Remodeling Company owes the union $24, an insurance company $142.40, and United Way $36. When the amounts accumulated in the three liability accounts are paid by the company, entries will be made in the cash disbursements journal debiting the liability accounts and crediting *Cash*.

SUMMARY OF JOURNAL ENTRIES FOR PAYROLL ACCOUNTING

The journal entries required to record the payroll of Five Star Remodeling Company, and the ultimate payment by the firm to the various parties are summarized in Figure 12–8. These entries are shown for illustration only; the actual entries may take different forms because of the timing of the cash payments involved.

GLOSSARY

EMPLOYEE EARNINGS RECORD. A record maintained for each employee showing hours worked, gross earnings, deductions, and net earnings for the year to date (p. 479).

EMPLOYEE'S WITHHOLDING ALLOWANCE CERTIFICATE (FORM W–4). A form completed by each employee, stating the number of withholding allowances claimed and the employee's marital status (p. 469).

EMPLOYER'S QUARTERLY FEDERAL TAX RETURN (FORM 941). A report prepared each quarter by the employer, to provide the federal government with information concerning gross earnings, FICA taxes, and income taxes withheld (p. 481).

FEDERAL FAIR LABOR STANDARDS ACT. A law that regulates overtime, minimum wages, and equal pay standards (p. 471).

FEDERAL INSURANCE CONTRIBUTIONS ACT (FICA). The law governing the social security system (p. 472).

FEDERAL UNEMPLOYMENT TAX ACT (FUTA). A law providing certain benefits, for a limited period, to employees who lose their jobs through no fault of their own (p. 476).

FEDERAL UNEMPLOYMENT TAXES. The federal portion of FUTA taxes paid by an employer (p. 477).

FICA TAXES. Taxes paid by both an employer and the employee to finance the social security system (p. 472).

Payroll Transaction	Journal Entry			Journal Used
Accrue Payroll	Office Salaries Expense	420.00		General
	Construction Wages Expense	2,086.00		
	FICA Taxes Payable		176.67	
	Federal Income Taxes Payable		205.00	
	State Income Taxes Payable		75.84	
	Union Dues Payable		24.00	
	Medical Insurance Payable		142.40	
	United Way Contribution Payable		36.00	
	Salaries and Wages Payable		1,846.09	
Accrue Payroll Taxes	Payroll Taxes Expense	332.04		General
	FICA Taxes Payable		176.67	
	State Unemployment Taxes Payable		135.32	
	Federal Unemployment Taxes Payable		20.05	
Pay Employees	Salaries and Wages Payable	1,846.09		Cash
	Cash		1,846.09	Disbursements
Pay Taxes	FICA Taxes Payable	353.34		Cash
	Federal Income Taxes Payable	205.00		Disbursements
	State Income Taxes Payable	75.84		
	State Unemployment Taxes Payable	135.32		
	Federal Unemployment Taxes Payable	20.05		
	Cash		789.55	
Pay Other Withholdings	Union Dues Payable	24.00		Cash
	Medical Insurance Payable	142.40		Disbursements
	United Way Contribution Payable	36.00		
	Cash		202.40	

Figure 12–8
Payroll Journal Entries Summarized

GROSS EARNINGS. The total amount of an employee's salary or wages before any payroll deductions (p. 471).

NET EARNINGS. Gross earnings of an employee, less the payroll deductions (p. 472).

PAYROLL BANK ACCOUNT. A special bank account used only for payroll purposes (p. 480).

PAYROLL REGISTER. A detailed listing of a firm's complete payroll for a given period (p. 477).

PAYROLL TAXES. Taxes withheld from an employee's gross earnings or paid by an employer on an employee's gross earnings (p. 476).

SALARY. Earnings paid to an employee on a weekly, biweekly, or monthly basis (p. 471).

STATE UNEMPLOYMENT TAXES. The state's portion of FUTA taxes paid by an employer or, in a small number of states, paid by an employee (p. 477).

WAGE AND TAX STATEMENT (FORM W–2). A form furnished by an employer to every employee, showing gross earnings and certain tax information for a particular year (p. 480).

WAGES. Earnings computed on an hourly rate or piecework basis and paid to an employee (p. 471).

WITHHOLDING ALLOWANCE. The amount of an employee's gross earnings not subject to income tax (p. 473).

WITHHOLDING TABLES. Tables showing the amounts of tax to be withheld for different levels of gross earnings (p. 473).

DISCUSSION QUESTIONS

1. Why is sound internal control essential for an effective payroll system? What duties should be separated to achieve good internal control in a payroll system?
2. What is the difference between an employee and an independent contractor? Why is this difference important for payroll accounting?
3. What are the two major types of gross earnings? Why is the Federal Fair Labor Standards Act important in the determination of gross earnings?
4. Identify the federal taxes that most employers are required to withhold from employees' gross earnings.
5. Explain which of the following taxes related to an employee's gross earnings are paid by the employee, by the employer, or by both.
   (a) FICA taxes.
   (b) Federal income taxes.
   (c) Federal unemployment taxes.
   (d) State unemployment taxes.
   (e) State income taxes.
6. Why are deductions from gross earnings liabilities of the employer?
7. Is the total compensation expense for a given period equal to gross earnings or net earnings? Why?
8. What is meant by the statement, ''an employer acts as a collection agent in the operation of a payroll system''?
9. What is the basic purpose of the Federal Insurance Contributions Act (FICA)?
10. What is the basic purpose of the Federal Unemployment Tax Act (FUTA)?
11. What is meant by the statement, ''the federal income tax system of the United States is on a pay-as-you-go basis''? Why is this important in the operation of an accounting system?
12. When is an Employee's Withholding Allowance Certificate (Form W–4) prepared? What is its purpose?
13. What are the two basic types of input data in a payroll system?
14. Why is a payroll register an essential part of a payroll system?
15. What is an employee earnings record? Distinguish between it and a payroll register.
16. Why is a separate bank account usually used, except with a small payroll?
17. What is the basic purpose of a Wage and Tax Statement (Form W–2)?
18. When is an Employer's Quarterly Federal Tax Return (Form 941) filed? Are all

payments for the employee's share of FICA taxes and the taxes withheld from gross earnings always paid when Form 941 is filed?

19. Robert Davis earns $400 per week. He is married and has two children. State income tax withholding is two percent of gross earnings. Insurance premiums amounting to $20 per week are deducted and all of his compensation is subject to FICA taxes (7.05%). Use the income tax withholding table on page 474 to compute his net earnings. Assuming that he is the only employee, what journal entry is required to accrue his compensation as an expense?

EXERCISES

Exercise 12-1 Determining Gross and Net Earnings

Bill Jones is a factory worker who is paid at the rate of $8 per hour. During the past week, he worked 46 hours. He is paid overtime at 1½ times his regular hourly rate. His gross earnings for the year prior to this past week were $4,000. Jones is married and claims 5 withholding allowances on his Form W–4. His union dues are $3 per week, and he has authorized a contribution to United Way of $2 each week. Assume a FICA tax rate of 7.05%. Use the withholding table on page 474 for federal taxes and assume that the state rate is 2%.

Required:

Compute the following for Jones' weekly wages.

1. Gross earnings.
2. Regular earnings.
3. Overtime earnings.
4. Deductions from gross earnings.
5. Net Earnings.

Exercise 12-2 Journal Entries for Payroll Accounting

On January 21, the weekly payroll register of the Darnell Company showed gross wages and salaries of $150,000. The entire payroll was subject to FICA and unemployment taxes. The company withheld $19,500 of federal income taxes, $3,000 of state income taxes, $2,300 of medical insurance premiums, and $970 of union dues from the employees' payroll checks. The applicable FICA rate is 7.05%, the state unemployment tax rate is 5.4%, and the federal unemployment tax rate is .8%.

Required:

A. Prepare a journal entry to record the payroll and payroll deductions.
B. Prepare a journal entry to record the employer's payroll tax expense.

Exercise 12-3 Computing Employer Payroll Tax Expenses

The Rostone Company is estimating its payroll taxes for the upcoming year. The company estimates that the amount of gross wages will be $790,000, of which $150,000 will be employee earnings not subject to FICA taxes. It also anticipates that $260,000 of the wages paid will not be subject to unemployment taxes. The FICA rate will be 7.05%, the state unemployment tax rate will be 5.4%, and the federal unemployment tax rate will be .8%.

Required:

Calculate the amounts the company estimates it will pay for payroll tax expenses for the year, showing the amount of each of the three taxes separately.

Exercise 12-4 Journal Entries for Payroll and Related Tax Expenses

The Underwood Company has four employees; the payroll data for the week ending October 29 are presented below.

Employee	Gross Earnings	Federal Income Tax	State Income Tax	Cumulative Earnings to End of Prior Week
A. Altone	$500	$ 61	$15	$ 5,700
C. David	450	50	14	6,500
E. Lymon	750	142	23	39,100
D. Mincher	700	136	23	40,200

The FICA tax rate is 7.05% on the first $39,600 paid each employee. The state unemployment tax rate is 5.4% and the federal unemployment tax rate is .8% on each employee's first $7,000 of wages.

Required:

Prepare journal entries to record the payroll and to record the employer's payroll tax expenses.

Exercise 12-5 Calculating and Recording a Payroll

The Donat Company is calculating the net pay of a married employee who claims four income tax withholding allowances. The employee worked 48 hours during the past week, and his hourly rate is $8.50. The company pays for all overtime hours at a rate of 1½ times the regular hourly rate, and the FICA rate is 7.05% on each employee's first $39,600 of wages. The employee's year-to-date pay to the end of the prior week was $39,200.

Required:

Prepare a journal entry to record the employee's payroll. Use the table on page 474 to calculate the federal income tax withholding. Assume a state income tax rate of 2% of gross wages.

Exercise 12-6 True/False Analysis of Payroll Accounting

Indicate whether each of the following statements is true or false.

1. A W–2 form must be completed by every person beginning employment.
2. FICA taxes are paid by both the employer and the employee.
3. To promote operating efficiency, the person who prepares a payroll should also distribute it to employees.
4. FICA taxes are paid to provide money for employees who are terminated through no fault of their own.
5. Payroll taxes withheld by employers are liabilities until paid because the employers are acting as collection agents.

PROBLEMS

Problem 12-1 Determining and Recording Gross and Net Earnings

Sheila Parker is a department supervisor at a local retail store who earns $8 per hour. She receives 1½ times her regular pay rate for any hours worked over eight hours on a weekday, twice her regular pay rate for any hours worked on the weekend, and three times her regular rate for hours worked on holidays. Sheila's hours for the past week were:

M	T	W	T	F	S	S
7	9	8	8	6	3	0

Monday was a legal holiday. The FICA rate is 7.05%, and the state income tax rate is 2% of gross pay. Sheila is married and claims one withholding allowance. She has authorized her employer to withhold $10 a week for health insurance premiums and $3 a week as a contribution to United Way. Her year-to-date gross earnings prior to this past week were $8,500.

Required:
A. Compute Sheila's gross and net earnings. Use the withholding table on page 474 for federal taxes.
B. Prepare a journal entry to accrue Sheila's compensation.

Problem 12-2 Calculations and Journal Entries for a Payroll

The following payroll data for the week ending September 20 were taken from the Preston Company's payroll records. The FICA tax rate is 7.05% on the first $39,600 paid to each employee. The state and federal unemployment tax rates are 5.4% and .8%, respectively, on each employee's first $7,000 of wages.

Employee	Gross Earnings	Federal Income Taxes	State Income Taxes	United Way Deductions	Health Insurance Deduction	Compensation to September 13
A. Foster	$300	$ 24	$ 9	$ 5	$ 8	$ 4,500
R. Garwell	600	90	18	5	10	8,100
H. Harris	750	142	23	15	12	38,900
D. Ralph	780	132	23	15	8	40,200

Required:
A. Calculate the FICA tax withheld and the net earnings for each employee.
B. Prepare a journal entry to accrue the payroll.
C. Prepare a journal entry to accrue the employer's payroll tax expense.

Problem 12-3 Preparing a Payroll Register and Recording a Payroll

The Kenney Company has provided the following information for the weekly payroll ending November 27.

Employee	M	T	W	T	F	S	Hourly Rate	Federal Income Taxes	State Income Taxes	Medical Insurance	Prior Earnings
R. Alt	8	8	9	9	8	0	$ 8	$26	$ 7	$15	$ 5,600
S. Bass	8	8	8	8	8	5	7	34	7	10	18,700
B. Jonn	12	8	10	8	8	2	10	63	16	15	39,300
L. Pall	8	8	10	8	8	0	6	21	6	15	5,100

The FICA tax rate is 7.05% of the first $39,600 paid each employee. All employees receive 1½ times their hourly rate for all hours over eight worked in any weekday and twice their regular rate for work performed on a weekend. The state unemployment tax rate is 5.4% and the federal unemployment tax rate is .8% of an employee's first $7,000 of wages.

Required:

A. Prepare a payroll register for the week ending November 27.

B. Prepare a journal entry to record the payroll and an entry to record the employer's payroll tax expense.

Problem 12-4 Preparing a Payroll Register and Recording a Payroll

The Stakem Company has provided the following information for the weekly payroll ending September 15.

Employee	M	T	W	T	F	S	Hourly Rate	Withholding Allowances	State Income Taxes	United Way	Prior Earnings
J. Carr	8	9	8	8	10	0	$10	1	$18	$ 5	$ 6,200
D. Doll	9	8	12	8	8	0	10	4	20	8	18,100
P. Popp	9	9	12	8	8	0	15	3	30	10	39,400
R. Ross	8	8	8	8	9	0	12	2	20	5	17,500

The FICA tax rate is 7.05% of the first $39,600 paid each employee. Each employee's first $7,000 of wages are subject to unemployment taxes; the state rate is 5.4%, and the federal rate is .8%. All employees are married and receive 1½ times their regular rate for all hours over eight worked in any day.

Required:

A. Prepare a payroll register for the week ending September 15. Refer to the schedule on page 474 to calculate the federal income tax withholdings.

B. Prepare journal entries to record the payroll and the employer's payroll tax expense.

Problem 12-5 Journalizing Payroll Transactions

The following accounts and balances appeared in the ledger of the Benning Company on August 30.

FICA taxes payable	$900
Federal income taxes payable	588
State income taxes payable	150
Medical insurance payable	228
United Way contributions payable	96

The following transactions occurred during September and October.

Sept. 1 Issued check payable to First National Bank (a federal depository bank) in payment of employees' federal income tax and FICA tax due.

 30 Prepared a journal entry to record the monthly payroll.

Gross wages	$4,200
Federal income taxes withheld	360
FICA taxes withheld	296
State income taxes withheld	84
Medical insurance premiums withheld	102
United Way deductions	48

30 Prepared a check on the regular bank account for the net amount of the monthly payroll and deposited it in the payroll bank account. Paid the employees.

30 Prepared a journal entry to record the employer's payroll tax expense. The federal unemployment tax rate is .8%, and the state unemployment tax rate is 5.4%. Gross wages earned by employees in excess of the unemployment tax limit amounted to $900.

Oct. 1 Issued a check payable to First National Bank in payment of the employees' federal income tax and FICA tax due.

15 Issued a check in payment of the company's federal unemployment taxes for the third quarter.

20 Issued a check payable to the United Way in payment of employee deductions to date.

25 Paid the ABC Insurance Co. the medical insurance premiums withheld from employees' paychecks during the quarter.

30 Remitted to the state department of revenue state income taxes payable for the quarter.

30 Issued a check to the state unemployment division for the quarter's state unemployment taxes.

Required:

Prepare journal entries to record the September and October transactions.

Problem 12-6 Payroll Accounting for Several Periods

The Folz Company's payroll is divided into categories for administrative salaries and production wages. Information from the company's permanent file on each employee is provided here.

Employee	Rate	Withholding Allowances	Withheld Uniform Allowance	Pension Plan	Cumulative Gross 4/7/87
Administrative:					
J. Hayes	$350.00 per wk.	2		$12.50 per wk.	$6,300
B. Roach	375.00 per wk.	4		12.50 per wk.	5,250
Production:					
N. Flood	8.00 per hr.	6	21 per wk.	8.00 per wk.	4,480
J. Folz	12.00 per hr.	8	21 per wk.	8.00 per wk.	6,448
M. Holly	9.00 per hr.	5	21 per wk.	8.00 per wk.	4,731
C. Riordan	10.50 per hr.	3	21 per wk.	8.00 per wk.	5,080

Folz Company's policy is to pay hourly workers 1½ times the regular pay rate for all hours over 40 in any week. Administrative employees receive their respective salaries regardless of how many hours are worked. All employees are married and the company's payroll is computed and distributed weekly.

The FICA tax rate is 7.05% of the first $39,600 paid each employee. The state unemployment tax rate is 5.4%, and the federal unemployment tax rate is .8% of an employee's first $7,000 of wages. The state income tax is a flat 2.25% of earnings, and federal income tax withholding is determined by consulting the withholding tables shown in the textbook.

Data from Folz's current file are given here.

	Hours Worked (pay period ending)			
Employee	**4/14/87**	**4/21/87**	**4/28/87**	**5/5/87**
J. Hayes	35	41	40	46
B. Roach	42	40	39	42
N. Flood	40	45	40	50
J. Folz	44	50	45	47
M. Holly	40	45	49	45
C. Riordan	40	40	45	50
Total	241	261	258	280

Required:

A. Prepare a payroll register for the pay periods ending 4/14, 4/21, 4/28, and 5/5.
B. For each pay period, prepare the required journal entries to record the payroll and the employer's payroll tax expense.
C. For the pay period ending 5/5/87, prepare the paycheck/earnings statement for N. Flood.

ALTERNATE PROBLEMS

Problem 12-1A Determining and Recording Gross and Net Earnings

Ronald Dare is a manager of a local store who earns $10 an hour. He receives overtime pay at a rate of 1½ times his regular pay rate for hours worked in excess of 40 from Monday through Friday, and twice his regular pay rate for any hours worked on the weekend. The FICA rate is 7.05%, and he lives in a state which imposes an income tax of 3% on gross wages. Ronald's employer withholds $15 from his weekly paycheck for health insurance and $5 for a United Way contribution. He is married and has year-to-date wages of $16,500, prior to this week. His hours for the week were as follows.

M	T	W	T	F	S	S
8	9	10	8	8	4	0

Required:

A. Calculate Ronald's gross and net earnings for the week. Use the withholding table on page 474 for federal taxes (2 exemptions).
B. Prepare a journal entry to record Ronald's paycheck.

Problem 12-2A Calculations and Journal Entries for a Payroll

The Scott Company is preparing the payroll for November 14 and has compiled the following data. The FICA rate is 7.05% on the first $39,600 paid each employee. The state unemployment rate is 5.4%, and the federal unemployment tax rate is .8% on each employee's first $7,000 of wages.

Employee	Gross Wages	Federal Income Taxes	State Income Taxes	Union Dues	Health Insurance Deduction	Compensation through November 7
S. Daly	$500	$ 59	$15	$10	$12	$ 5,700
K. May	450	57	13	10	12	6,000
S. Ness	700	103	21	15	18	39,200
C. Snow	600	98	18	15	20	39,600

Required:
A. Calculate the FICA taxes withheld for each employee.
B. Prepare a journal entry to record the payroll.
C. Prepare a journal entry to record the employer's payroll tax expense.

Problem 12-3A Preparing a Payroll Register and Recording a Payroll

The Springer Company has provided the following data for the week ending November 27.

Employee	M	T	W	T	F	S	Hourly Rate	Federal Income Tax	State Income Tax	United Way	Prior Earnings
M. Alt	8	8	8	8	8	2	$ 8	$32	$ 7	$ 5	$ 5,900
D. Kane	8	8	9	9	9	3	10	61	10	10	17,800
J. Mass	8	8	8	8	8	0	9	43	8	10	22,900
R. Stern	9	9	8	10	8	4	12	83	16	20	39,300

The state and federal unemployment tax rates are 5.4% and .8%, respectively, on the first $7,000 paid each employee. The FICA rate is 7.05% of each employee's first $39,600 of wages. The company pays each employee 1½ times the hourly rates for all hours over eight worked on a weekday and for all weekend hours worked.

Required:
A. Prepare a payroll register for the week ending November 27.
B. Prepare journal entries to record the payroll and to record the employer's payroll tax expense.

Problem 12-4A Preparing a Payroll Register and Recording a Payroll

The Roberts Company has asked you to record the payroll for the week ending October 12 and has provided the following data:

Employee	M	T	W	T	F	Personal Exemptions	Wage Rate	Earnings to End of Prior Week
A. Evans	8	8	8	8	10	0	$12	$ 5,800
B. Ford	8	9	9	9	9	1	10	21,500
C. Greg	8	8	8	9	9	2	11	12,100
D. Klein	8	9	8	8	10	1	14	39,400
F. Seit	8	8	8	8	10	3	10	6,500

Each employee receives 1½ times the regular pay rate for all hours over eight worked in any day. The FICA rate is 7.05% of each employee's $39,600 of wages.

Each employee's first $7,000 of wages are subject to federal and state unemployment taxes of .8% and 5.4%, respectively. The state income tax is 2% of gross wages.

Required:

A. Refer to the schedule on page 474 to calculate each employee's federal income tax withholding and prepare a payroll register for the week ending October 12.

B. Prepare a journal entry to record the payroll and an entry to record the employer's payroll tax expense.

Problem 12-5A Journalizing Payroll Transactions

The Evans Company has provided the following general ledger balances as of May 31.

Federal income taxes payable	$5,280
FICA taxes payable	3,523
Federal unemployment taxes payable	76
Medical insurance payable	564
State income taxes payable	912
State unemployment taxes payable	513
United Way contributions payable	240

The following transactions occurred in June and July.

June 1 Made a deposit at the Federal Trust Bank (a federal depository bank) for payment of employees' federal income taxes and FICA tax payable.

30 Prepared a journal entry to record the monthly payroll as follows.

Gross wages	$25,200
Federal income taxes withheld	4,680
FICA taxes withheld	1,777
State income taxes withheld	468
United Way deductions	120
Medical insurance premiums withheld	282

30 Issued a check from the regular bank account, payable to the payroll bank account for the net amount of the monthly payroll. Paid the employees.

30 Gross wages earned by employees in excess of the $7,000 unemployment limit were $18,000. The federal and state unemployment tax rate is .8% and 5.4%, respectively.

July 1 Issued a check for payment of the employees' federal income tax and FICA tax due from the June 30 payroll.

10 Paid the company's federal unemployment taxes for the second quarter.

18 Issued a check to the United Way for payment of unremitted employee deductions to date.

27 Issued a check to Safety Insurance Co. for medical insurance premiums withheld from employees' paychecks during the second quarter.

30 Issued a check to the state department of revenue for state income taxes payable in the quarter.

30 Remitted unemployment taxes to the state for the second quarter.

Required:
Prepare journal entries to record the June and July transactions.

CASE

CASE 12-1 Decision Case Evaluating Total Compensation Costs

The Pilgrim Moving and Storage Company is located in a midwestern university community. Last year's sales revenue totaled $600,000 and produced a net income of $48,000. Bill Shuman, president of the company, is concerned about profit margins that have been declining recently because of increasing labor costs and stable sales revenue. The moving and storage business in a campus town is seasonal, with 75% of sales typically occurring from May through September.

Mr. Shuman is looking for ways to reduce labor costs. During the busy season, 12 employees are needed to pack household goods for intrastate or interstate shipments. These people do not have chauffeur's licenses, so they cannot drive the trucks used to haul furniture and household goods. Each packer works approximately 860 hours from May through September. During the rest of the year, only six people are needed for a full 40 hours each week. However, the firm has found it necessary to guarantee the other six workers a minimum of 20 hours per week from October through April to retain their services during the busy season. Mr. Shuman estimates that the six people will be paid for a total of 3,600 hours during the period October through April, but only 1,800 of the hours will be spent productively. The rest will be idle time because the employees will have nothing to do.

Mary Dixie, a marketing representative of Temporary Help, Inc., has recently made a proposal to Mr. Shuman that is an alternative way for him to hire the extra six packers. Mrs. Dixie's firm provides temporary services with all types of skilled and unskilled workers. The workers supplied would be billed to Pilgrim on an hourly basis and would be on Temporary Help, Inc.'s payroll. Mrs. Dixie has offered to provide workers who are capable of packing household goods to replace the six employees for the entire year at a fixed hourly rate of $7.20 each. Pilgrim would pay only for the hours worked by the temporary help during the year. At first glance, Mr. Shuman is tempted to reject the offer because his company can hire packers at an hourly rate of $6. However, he realizes that the *true* cost of using his own employees must be greater than $6 per hour and has asked for your assistance in evaluating Mrs. Dixie's proposal. You have determined that in addition to the $6 per hour labor rate, the firm pays FICA taxes on all wages and unemployment taxes at full federal and state rates on the first $7,000 earned by each employee. The firm also pays $72 per month for each employee's health insurance.

Required:

A. Based strictly on the economics involved, should Pilgrim continue to hire the six additional packers or accept Mrs. Dixie's offer?

B. What other factors, if any, should Mr. Shuman consider in the decision-making process?

13

ACCOUNTING CONCEPTS: EFFECTS OF INFLATION

CHAPTER OVERVIEW AND OBJECTIVES

This chapter examines the nature of basic accounting concepts and principles as well as the effect of changing prices on financial reporting. When you have completed the chapter, you should understand:

1. Why accounting standards are needed.
2. The nature of generally accepted accounting principles.
3. The basic rules governing revenue recognition.
4. How to apply the percentage-of-completion method of recognizing revenue on long-term construction contracts.
5. How to apply the installment method of revenue recognition.
6. The matching principle and the basic rules governing the timing of expense recognition.
7. The nature of inflation.
8. The difference between general price-level changes and specific price changes.
9. The distinction between constant-dollar accounting and current value accounting.
10. Financial Accounting Standards Board (FASB) requirements for reporting the effects of inflation.

Chapter 1 contains a brief description of some basic accounting concepts, as well as the sources of accounting principles and practices. The theory underlying accounting concepts and standards has also been discussed throughout the preceding chapters as it related to the focus of those chapters. Thus, many important accounting concepts have been discussed in a relatively piecemeal fashion. In learning a new discipline, however, it is worthwhile to pause occasionally to consider what has been learned and to attempt to relate that learning to a general framework. That is one of the purposes of this chapter (Part I). An additional purpose is to study the effects of inflation on financial reporting (Part II).

PART I   ACCOUNTING CONCEPTS
THE NEED FOR ACCOUNTING STANDARDS

As explained earlier, the primary objective of financial reporting is providing financial information for use in making economic decisions. Business managers, investors, creditors, governmental agencies, and other outside parties use accounting information to make decisions concerning the allocation of scarce resources. These decisions have a significant effect on all of society, since they have impact on the form and direction of our economy. The effectiveness of decision makers is enhanced if they have information that is both reliable and understandable. In addition, decision making requires information about a business that is comparable with that of prior periods, as well as with that of other businesses. In other words, accountants need standards to guide them in preparing financial reports so that the reports contain information that is reliable, understandable, and comparable over time and between businesses.

**Objective 1:
Need for
Accounting
Standards**

GENERALLY ACCEPTED ACCOUNTING PRINCIPLES

The rules, conventions, and practices developed over time by the accounting profession are called **generally accepted accounting principles (GAAP).** Sometimes also called *standards,* these include the assumptions, principles, conventions, and practices that serve as general guidelines in the preparation of financial reports.

Principles or standards become ''generally accepted'' by obtaining the substantial authoritative support of the accounting profession. As noted in Chapter 1, the most active authoritative bodies are the American Institute of Certified Public Accountants, the Financial Accounting Standards Board, and the Securities and Exchange Commission. These groups, with the help of extensive research staffs, study reporting alternatives for various transactions and select the ones that result in the most useful presentation of financial information.

**Objective 2:
Nature of
GAAP**

Other groups, such as the American Accounting Association, the National Association of Accountants, and the Financial Executives Institute, also influence the development of accounting principles by conducting research and recommending reporting alternatives to those responsible for setting accounting standards, chiefly the FASB and the SEC. Selection of the best alternatives has come about gradually and in some areas has not yet been completed. Accounting standards are continually reviewed and revised to keep abreast with the increasing complexity of business operations. Accounting principles are not fundamental natural laws like those of the physical sciences; they are man-made guidelines, which attain their status when they are accepted by the accounting profession.

Since accounting principles evolve in accordance with changes in the business environment, it is not possible to present a complete list of generally accepted accounting principles. However, there are several broad assumptions, principles, and conventions that serve as basic guides in the selection of specific rules and practices. Knowledge of these will help to better understand the general framework within which accounting standards are developed.

BASIC ASSUMPTIONS

Accounting principles rest on four basic assumptions.

1. The entity assumption.
2. The going concern assumption.
3. The time period assumption.
4. The monetary unit assumption.

THE ENTITY ASSUMPTION

The **entity assumption** is a basic assumption that information is accumulated for a specific area or unit of accountability, called an entity. An **accounting entity** is an economic unit that controls resources and engages in economic activity. To accumulate financial information, the accountant must be able to clearly identify the boundaries of the unit being accounted for. Business activities of the entity are separated from both the personal activities of its owners and those of other entities. For accounting purposes, each entity is treated as though the entity owns its own assets, owes its own debts, and earns its own net income. However, this is not legally the case if the entity is a proprietorship or a partnership. Accountants sometimes overlook legal form, and instead report on the economic substance of business activities. For example, even though a proprietorship is not a legal entity, the business activities of the proprietorship are accounted for as though it were a legal entity.

An entity may be an individual, a governmental agency, a nonprofit organization, a business enterprise, or an organizational subunit. For example, accountants may want to prepare a report for a single division of a company, such as the Buick Division of General Motors Corporation, in which case the Buick Division is considered a separate unit of accountability.

Accounting attention is normally focused on the economic activities of individual businesses, but the boundaries of the accounting entity may not be the same as those of the legal entity. For example, a company that owns controlling interests in other companies, and the other companies it controls, are considered a single economic unit of accountability, for which consolidated financial statements are prepared, as discussed in Chapter 18. However, each of the individual companies is a legal entity and, therefore, is also an accounting entity. When financial reports are prepared, they must identify clearly the entity being reported on.

THE GOING CONCERN ASSUMPTION

Accounting reports are prepared under the assumption that the business will continue to operate in the future, unless there is evidence to the contrary. Because it is not possible to predict how long a business will exist, an assumption must be made. Past experience indicates that the continuation of operations in the future is highly probable for most companies. Thus, it is assumed that the business will continue to operate at least long enough to carry out its existing plans and commitments. This assumption is called the **going concern assumption** or sometimes called the **continuity assumption.**

   Adoption of the going concern assumption has important implications in accounting. For example, it provides justification for the use of historical costs in accounting for plant assets and for the systematic allocation of their costs to depreciation over their useful lives. Because it is assumed that the assets will not be sold in the near future, but will continue to be used in operating activities, current market values of the assets are of little importance. If the business continues to use the assets, fluctuations in their market values are not recorded as gains or losses because the fluctuations do not increase or decrease the usefulness of the assets. The going concern assumption also supports the inclusion of some assets, such as prepaid expenses and purchased goodwill, in the balance sheet, even though they may have little if any sales value.

   Although the going concern assumption is followed in most cases, it should not be applied when there is conclusive evidence that the business will not continue. If management intends to liquidate the business, the going concern and historical cost principles are set aside and financial statements are prepared on the basis of expected liquidation values. Thus, assets are reported at their expected sales values and liabilities are reported at the amount needed to settle them immediately.

THE TIME PERIOD ASSUMPTION

A completely accurate report of the degree of success achieved by a business cannot be obtained until the business is liquidated. Only then can net income be determined precisely. However, users of financial information need *timely* information for decision-making purposes. Thus, accountants must prepare periodic reports on the results of operations, financial position, and changes in financial position. To do so, accountants adopt the **time period assumption**—that is, they assume that economic activity can be associated realistically with relatively short time intervals.

   Because of the many estimates, professional judgments, and assumptions required, dividing the continuous economic activity of a business into time periods, such as months, quarters, and years, creates many problems for accountants. The shorter the time period, the more inaccurate are the cost allocations needed to determine net income. As a result, monthly net income is generally a less reliable figure than quarterly net income, which in turn is less reliable than net income determined on a yearly basis. Since cost allocations affect asset and liability amounts, the shorter the reporting period, the more inaccurate the balance-sheet amounts. Periodic measurements of net income and financial position are estimates and, therefore, are tentative. Users of financial statements should be fully aware of the tentative nature of the statement amounts when making decisions. There is a trade-off between the reliability of accounting information and its timely reporting—the more timely the information, the more subject it is to error.

THE MONETARY UNIT ASSUMPTION

Money is used in accounting as the common denominator by which economic activity is measured and reported. Under the **monetary unit assumption,** accountants assume that data expressed in terms of money are useful in making economic decisions and that the monetary unit (the dollar) represents a realistic unit of value that can be used to measure net income, financial position, and changes in financial position.

Inherent in the use of money as a unit of measure is the assumption that the value of money remains constant over time. As a result, 1986 dollars are combined with 1982 dollars and 1977 dollars as though they all represented the same purchasing power. For example, the amount paid for land purchased in 1977 ($50,000) is added to the amount paid for land purchased in 1986 ($100,000) and reported as a dollar investment of $150,000. Accountants recognize that when the general purchasing power of the dollar changes, the value of money also changes and that, therefore, money is not a stable unit of measure. These changes in the value of the measuring unit are ignored, however, because accountants disagree on the theoretical and practical means of adjusting for the changes. High inflation rates raise serious doubts about the wisdom of ignoring changes in the purchasing power of money. Current accounting standards require some supplementary disclosures of the effects of inflation. Methods of disclosure, as well as the problems and benefits involved, are discussed later in this chapter.

BASIC PRINCIPLES

Six basic principles constitute the basis for the development of accounting practices and procedures. They are:

1. The objectivity principle.
2. The cost principle.
3. The revenue principle.
4. The matching principle.
5. The consistency principle.
6. The full disclosure principle.

THE OBJECTIVITY PRINCIPLE

The **objectivity principle** holds that, if possible, accounting information should be reliable, that is, verifiable, and free from personal bias. Verifiable means that the validity of the data is supported by adequate evidence. If information is objective and verifiable, essentially similar measures and results should be produced if two or more qualified persons examine the same data. For example, the price agreed upon in an exchange transaction is objective, because it is based upon negotiation between independent parties. The price is also verifiable if it is supported by an invoice, contract, paid check, or other document. Accountants rely on various types of evidence to support the figures presented in accounting reports. Source documents, such as contracts, purchase orders, invoices, paid checks, and physical counts of inventory and other assets provide objective, verifiable evidence in accounting.

Although accountants seek the most objective evidence available, we must recognize that accounting data are not completely objective because there are many cases in which estimates must be made on the basis of personal judgments and observations. For example, the cost of a plant asset may be highly objective, but the amount of depreciation charged to each accounting period is affected by estimates of useful life and residual value, as well as by the selection of an appropriate depreciation method. However, as long as estimates are based on data and methods that can be verified by outside parties, the information is considered basically objective and verifiable.

THE COST PRINCIPLE

The need for objective, verifiable data is the basic reason for the use of historical costs in accounting. Under the **cost principle,** resources acquired are recorded at their cost, as measured by the amount of cash or cash equivalent given to acquire them. Changes in the market value of resources are generally ignored and the cost of the resources is allocated to the periods that benefit from their use. Thus, the income statement reports the cost of resources used as expenses, and the balance sheet reports the unallocated cost of the resources.

Some accountants believe that current market value (rather than cost) should be used as the basis for measuring resources and expenses. They argue that current values are more relevant to users of accounting data. However, some current values are less objective than historical costs, which raises the question of which factor is more important—reliability or relevancy. As discussed in a later section of this chapter, many accountants support the presentation of both historical cost data and current value data as at least a partial solution to the problem.

THE REVENUE PRINCIPLE

An important accounting function is the determination of periodic net income—the process of identifying and measuring revenues and expenses for a specified period of time. Revenue for a period is determined by applying the **revenue principle,** which provides guidance as to when revenue should be recognized. Essentially, the revenue principle provides that revenue should be recognized under accrual accounting when it is earned.

Some revenue, like interest revenue and rent revenue, is earned with the

Objective 3: Revenue Recognition

passage of time and is not difficult to associate with specific time periods. On the other hand, sales revenue is earned in a continuous process as the activities that give rise to revenue take place. For example, the earning process for a manufacturing firm involves the acquisition of goods and services, production of a product, sale of the finished product, and collection from customers. Although all of these activities contribute to the earning process, it is difficult to determine objectively how much revenue is earned at each step.

To provide a practical guide, accountants follow the revenue principle, which provides that revenue should be recognized (1) when the earning process is complete or essentially complete, and (2) when an exchange has taken place. Following this principle, most revenue is recognized when goods are sold (which normally means when they are delivered) or when services are rendered and become billable. At this point the earning process is essentially completed and the exchange price provides objective evidence of the amount of revenue to recognize. The only part of the earning process remaining is the collection of the sales price, which is considered relatively assured in our credit oriented society.

Although most revenue is recognized at the time of sale, two major exceptions are the percentage-of-completion method and the installment sales method.

PERCENTAGE-OF-COMPLETION METHOD

Objective 4: Applying the Percentage-of-completion Method

Construction companies often undertake projects that may take two or more years to complete. For example, assume that a company signed a contract to construct a major section of interstate highway, which is expected to take four years to complete. If the basic revenue principle were followed, net income on the project would not be recognized until the end of construction. Such accounting is called the *completed contract method.* Under that method, annual income statements would clearly be of little use to investors and other users who must make timely decisions. As a result, a departure from the revenue principle is recommended for long-term construction projects when estimates of costs to complete and the extent of progress toward completion are reasonably dependable.[1] Estimates are made of the percentage of the project completed each year and gross profit is recognized in proportion to the work completed. This approach is called the **percentage-of-completion method** of accounting for long-term contracts. The method works as follows.

1. An estimate is made of the total cost expected to be incurred on the project. The difference between the contract price and the total estimated cost is the construction company's estimated gross profit.
2. At the end of each year, the percentage of the project completed during the year is estimated. This may be done by comparing the actual project costs incurred during the year to the most recent estimate of the total cost of the project, or an estimate may be made by engineers or other qualified personnel.

---

[1]"Long-term Construction-type Contracts," *Accounting Research Bulletin No. 45* (AICPA, New York: 1955), par. 15.

3. The estimated gross profit on the project, as computed in step 1, is multiplied by the percentage determined in step 2 to determine the amount of gross profit for the year.
4. In the final year of the project, no estimate is needed, because total actual costs are known. The difference between the actual gross profit and the cumulative amount of gross profit recognized in prior years constitutes the gross profit for the final year.

   To illustrate, assume that Bates Construction Company signed a contract to construct a section of interstate highway at a price of $10,000,000. The project is expected to take three years to complete at an estimated cost of $7,000,000. Therefore, estimated gross profit on the project is $3,000,000. The actual costs incurred and the amount of gross profit recognized each year are:

Year	Actual Costs Incurred	÷	Estimated Total Costs	= Percent	×	Estimated Gross Profit	=	Gross Profit for the Year
1	$2,450,000	÷	$7,000,000	= 35%	×	$3,000,000	=	$1,050,000
2	2,800,000	÷	7,000,000	= 40%	×	3,000,000	=	1,200,000
3	1,850,000		Balance to complete the contract[a]					650,000
Total	$7,100,000							$2,900,000

[a]Balance to complete the contract:

Contract price	$10,000,000
Actual cost	7,100,000
Actual gross profit	2,900,000
Gross profit recognized in the first two years (1,050,000 + 1,200,000)	2,250,000
Remaining gross profit	$ 650,000

   In Year 1, the actual costs incurred represented 35% of the estimated total cost of the project. The percentage-of-completion method assumes that incurring costs represents a valid reflection of progress toward completion of the project. Thus, 35% of the estimated gross profit is recognized in Year 1. Similarly, 40% of the total estimated cost was incurred in Year 2 and thus, 40% of the estimated gross profit is recognized. In Year 3, gross profit is recognized in an amount equal to the actual total gross profit on the contract, minus the cumulative amount of gross profit recognized in Years 1 and 2.

   The percentage-of-completion method is based on estimates and, therefore, introduces an element of subjectivity into the determination of net income. In spite of this, the financial statements are considered more useful than they would be if none of the profit were recognized until the end of the project.

   Although the percentage-of-completion method is appropriate in accounting for long-term contracts expected to produce a profit, it is not an appropriate method if a loss is expected. When it becomes apparent that a loss is expected, the estimated loss must be recognized immediately under the *conservatism convention*.

THE INSTALLMENT METHOD

**Objective 5:
Applying the
Installment
Method**

It is common practice in some businesses to make sales on an installment basis. The purchaser normally makes a down payment and agrees to pay the remainder of the purchase price in equal installments at specified times. The seller often retains title to the property until final payment is received, or instead makes other arrangements to permit the repossession of the property in the event the purchaser defaults on payment. In spite of these provisions, installment sales ordinarily should be accounted for in the same manner as regular sales on account, and revenue should be recognized at the time of sale.[2] Of course, an appropriate provision should be made for estimated uncollectible accounts. In the relatively rare situations in which collection of the sales price is not reasonably assured, the installment method of accounting may be used.[3]

Under the **installment method,** each cash receipt is considered to consist of a partial recovery of the cost of the property sold and partially of gross profit. For example, if the gross profit rate on the installment sale is 40%, each cash receipt is considered to consist of 40% gross profit and 60% recovery of cost of goods sold. To illustrate, assume that on July 1, 1987, Croy Company sold land for $30,000 which had cost $18,000. The gross profit rate is 40% [($30,000 − $18,000)/$30,000]. The purchaser made a down payment of $6,000 and agreed to pay the remaining $24,000 at the rate of $1,000 per month for 24 months, beginning on August 1.[4] The amount of gross profit from installment sales recognized in each period, assuming all payments are received when due, is:

Year	Amount Collected	×	Gross Profit Rate	=	Gross Profit
1987	$11,000	×	40%	=	$ 4,400
1988	12,000	×	40%	=	4,800
1989	7,000	×	40%	=	2,800
Total	$30,000				$12,000

The $11,000 collected in 1987 consists of the down payment of $6,000 plus five monthly payments of $1,000 each. Under the installment method, gross profit is deferred and recognized when payment is received.

THE MATCHING PRINCIPLE

**Objective 6:
Expense Recog-
nition**

Revenue is an inflow of assets from the sale of goods or performance of services. Expenses are the assets used up in the process of producing revenue. In general terms, under accrual accounting, revenues are recognized when

---

[2]Accounting Principles Board, "Omnibus Opinion—1966," *APB Opinion No. 10* (AICPA, New York: 1966), par. 12.

[3]The Internal Revenue Code permits the use of the installment method. It is often used for income tax purposes because it permits the deferral of income tax payments until the cash is received.

[4]Installment sales contracts generally provide for interest on the unpaid balance. Although ignored in our illustration, the amount of each payment representing interest is recognized as interest revenue when received.

they are earned and expenses are recognized (matched against or related to revenue) as assets are used. Just as the revenue principle has been developed by accountants to serve as a guide in the timing of revenue, the **matching principle** has been developed to guide the timing of expense recognition. Three basic rules specify the bases for recognizing expenses. They are associating cause and effect, systematic and rational allocation, and immediate recognition.

Associating Cause and Effect

Some expenses are recognized on the basis of a relatively direct association with revenue earned and, therefore, are recorded in the same period that the revenue is recognized. Examples of this are the cost of goods sold during the period and sales commissions. The sale of goods produced the sales revenue; sales commissions relate directly to the revenue generated by the salespeople.

Systematic and Rational Allocation (Depreciation)

Many expenses cannot be associated directly with revenue-producing transactions but can be associated with specific accounting periods and thus are allocated to those accounting periods in a systematic and rational way. Examples of this are depreciation of plant assets, amortization of intangible assets, and allocation of rent and insurance. The depreciation, amortization, and allocation methods described in earlier chapters provide a systematic and rational allocation of asset costs to the periods that benefit from their use.

Immediate Recognition

Some expenses are associated with the current accounting period because (1) they cannot be associated directly with revenue transactions; (2) they have no discernible benefits for future accounting periods; or (3) their allocation among several accounting periods serves no useful purpose. Application of this rule results in a charge to expense in the period in which payment is made or a liability is incurred. Examples of this are officers' salaries, some selling expenses, such as advertising, and research and development expenditures. In addition, items carried as assets that are determined to have no discernible benefit for future periods are charged to expense. One example of this is equipment that has suddenly become obsolete before the end of its originally expected useful life.

In applying these expense-recognition rules, costs are first analyzed to see whether they can be associated with revenue on the basis of cause and effect. If not, an attempt is made to apply systematic and rational allocation procedures. If neither cause and effect nor systematic and rational allocation is appropriate, costs are recognized as expenses in the period incurred.

THE CONSISTENCY PRINCIPLE

Several generally accepted alternative accounting methods have been described in preceding chapters. For example, inventory methods include first-in, first-out (FIFO), last-in, first out (LIFO), and average, and depreciation methods include straight-line, sum-of-years'-digits, declining balance, and units-of-production. The methods adopted have a significant effect on the amount of net income reported for a period, as well as on the financial position at the end of the period. Although accounting statements for any given period may be useful in themselves, they are more useful if they can be compared with similar statements of prior periods. To improve the comparability of accounting data, accountants follow the **consistency principle.** The consistency principle requires that once a particular accounting method is adopted, it will not be changed from period to period. Without this principle, large changes in net income and financial position may result from an arbitrary change in the accounting methods used, rather than from changes in business conditions or general managerial effectiveness.

The consistency principle does not mean that a company can never change an accounting method. In fact, a change to a new method *should* be made if the new method provides more useful information than the old method. If a company changes an accounting method, however, the nature of and justification for the change, and its effect on net income, must be disclosed in the financial statements of the period in which the change is made.[5] The justification should explain clearly why the new method is preferable. For example, a change in method may be disclosed in a footnote such as this one.

During the year, the company changed from the first-in, first-out to the last-in, first-out method of accounting for inventory, because the last-in, first-out method more clearly reflects net income. The effect of the change was to decrease net income by $460,000 for the period.

The consistency principle does not require that a given accounting method be applied throughout the company. A company may use different inventory methods for different types of inventory and different depreciation methods for different kinds of plant assets.

THE FULL DISCLOSURE PRINCIPLE

The **full disclosure principle** requires that all relevant information affecting net income and financial position must be reported in the financial statements or in footnotes to the financial statements, although this does not mean that information must be reported in great detail. In fact, too much detailed information may impede, rather than improve, the usefulness of information. A list of the customers who owe money to a company and the amount owed by each would be of little use to statement users. On the other hand, if a single customer owes a large portion, say 60%, of the total accounts receivable, that fact may be significant and usually should be disclosed. In general, the goal is to disclose information in sufficient detail to permit the knowledgeable reader to make an informed decision.

Because many alternative accounting methods exist and because the meth-

[5]Accounting Principles Board, "Accounting Changes," *APB Opinion No. 20* (AICPA, New York: 1971), par. 17.

ods adopted can affect significantly the financial position and results of operations of a company, knowledge of the accounting methods used is essential for statement users. Therefore, a summary of the accounting methods used must be presented as an integral part of the financial statements.[6] This summary is generally included as the first footnote to the financial statements (for example, see the first note to the consolidated financial statements of Chrysler Corporation, on page A53). In addition to the disclosure of accounting methods, other items typically disclosed include:

1. The components of inventory, such as raw materials, work in process, and finished goods.
2. The components of the income tax provision.
3. The terms of major debt agreements.
4. The nature of any contingent liabilities, such as lawsuits.
5. Identification of assets pledged as security for loans.
6. The nature of contractual agreements for leases, pension plans, and stock option plans.
7. Major transactions affecting stockholders' equity.
8. The effect of changes in accounting methods and estimates.

Modifying Conventions

Because practical considerations sometimes require the modification of basic principles, two broad modifying conventions are followed in accounting.

1. Materiality.
2. Conservatism.

MATERIALITY

Materiality is used in accounting to refer to the relative size or importance of an item or event. Accounting is a practical art, rather than an exact science. Although accountants generally apply the most theoretically sound treatment to transactions and events, they sometimes deviate from that practice because the effect of a transaction or event is not significant enough to affect decisions—that is, the effect is not relevant. For example, small expenditures for plant assets are often expensed immediately, rather than depreciated over their useful lives. This is done both to save clerical costs of recording depreciation and because the effects on the income statements and balance sheets over the assets' lives are not large enough to affect decisions. Another example of the application of materiality is the common practice by large companies of rounding amounts to the nearest thousand dollars in their financial statements. In fact, very large companies like IBM and General Motors round amounts to the nearest million.

Materiality is a relative matter; what is material for one company may be immaterial for another. A $10,000 error in the financial statements of a multimillion-dollar company may not be important, but it may be critical to a

---

[6]Accounting Principles Board, "Disclosure of Accounting Policies," *APB Opinion No. 22* (AICPA, New York: 1972), par. 8.

small company. The materiality of an item may depend not only upon its relative size, but also on its nature. For example, the discovery of a $10,000 bribe is a material event, even for a large company.

Judgments as to the materiality of an item or event are often difficult to make. Accountants make them based on their knowledge of the company and on past experience, and users of financial statements must generally rely on the accountants' judgment. In summary, an item is material if there is a reasonable expectation that knowledge of it would influence the decisions of financial statement users.

CONSERVATISM

Accountants must make many difficult judgments and estimates when determining the proper treatment of business transactions. In reaching a decision, they must rely on the principles described earlier in an effort to make a fair presentation of the factual effects of the transactions. When this approach fails and doubt exists, accountants apply the convention of **conservatism,** which says in essence: *When in doubt, choose the solution that is least likely to overstate net assets and net income for the current period.*

Conservatism is apparent in the tendency to defer the recognition of gains until the earning process is essentially completed but to recognize losses as soon as they become known. For example, in the application of the lower of cost or market rule to inventory valuation, a loss is recognized if the market value of the inventory is less than its cost. However, if the market value exceeds cost, the gain is not recognized until the inventory is sold.

Conservatism is a useful approach in accounting but should be applied only when uncertainty prevents the reporting of factual results. Nothing in the convention of conservatism suggests that accountants should understate income or assets. An overapplication of conservatism produces incorrect results in both the current accounting period and in future periods.

PART II   EFFECTS OF INFLATION

Objective 7: Nature of Inflation

In our economy, money (the dollar) is used both as a medium of exchange and as a measure of "real" value, as determined by the amount of goods and services for which it can be exchanged. The amount of goods or services for which a dollar can be exchanged is called the **purchasing power** of the dollar. Although the prices of some goods (such as calculators, digital watches, and computers) have decreased in recent years, the economy of the United States and of most other countries has been characterized by significantly increasing prices of most goods and services. The general increase in prices results in **inflation,** which can be defined as a decrease in the purchasing power of the dollar or as an increase in the general price-level. The **general price-level** is the weighted average price of all goods and services in our economy.

Price changes are of two types: specific price changes and general price-level changes. It is important to distinguish between these two types because they reflect different things. **Specific price changes** are changes in the prices of specific goods or services, such as bread, computers, and medical services. Specific prices may increase or decrease from one period to another. As indicated earlier, the prices of calculators and digital watches, for example, have been decreasing, whereas the prices of real estate and medical services have increased steadily.

General price-level changes are changes in the weighted average price of all goods and services in the economy. Therefore, a general price-level change represents a change in the value of money in all its uses. Specific price changes affect the general price-level, because the prices of specific goods and services constitute the items used to determine the general price-level. Although the general price-level may decrease (deflation), this has occurred only once in the United States during the last 35 years—in 1949. Thus, the more common occurrence is an increase in the general price-level (inflation).

When the general price-level increases, it takes more dollars to acquire a given amount of goods or services. Stated another way, with an increased general price-level, a dollar will buy a smaller amount of goods or services. The general price-level is expressed in the form of an index number with a specific base year set equal to 100. Although agencies of the United States government publish several general price indexes, the most widely recognized is the *Consumer Price Index* (CPI), which is published monthly by the Bureau of Labor Statistics.

The CPI measures the average change in prices of a specific ''market basket'' of goods and services purchased by families living in cities. The Financial Accounting Standards Board recommends this index be used to restate financial data for general price-level changes because it is readily available, timely, and produces results that are comparable to other general price indexes. A partial listing of the CPI and the yearly inflation rate is shown in Figure 13–1.

As can be seen in Figure 13–1, the general price-level more than tripled from 1967 to 1984; that is, the 1984 dollar purchased less than one-third as much goods and services as the 1967 dollar. Stated another way, it would take $311.10 in 1984 to purchase the same goods and services that could have been purchased in 1967 for $100. The inflation rate is determined on the basis of the change in the average index for the year. Thus, for example, the inflation rate for 1984 was computed as $(311.1 - 298.4)/298.4 = 4.3\%$.

Objective 8:
General Price-level Changes vs. Specific Price Changes

REPORTING THE EFFECTS OF INFLATION

As discussed earlier, accountants prepare financial statements based on historical cost under the stable dollar assumption. These historical cost financial statements consist of aggregated amounts of dollars from different years, which represent different purchasing powers. The impact of inflation is difficult to assess by statement users. Because of the persistent nature of inflation and relatively high inflation rates, many accountants and users of financial information question the usefulness of the dollar measurements in the traditional

Inventory

Figure 13–1
Consumer Price
Index

Year	Average Index* (1967 = 100)	Year-end Index	Inflation Rate
1967	100.0	101.6	
1968	104.2	106.4	4.2%
1969	109.8	112.9	5.4
1970	116.3	119.1	5.9
1971	121.3	123.1	4.3
1972	125.3	127.3	3.3
1973	133.1	138.5	6.2
1974	147.7	155.4	11.0
1975	161.2	166.3	9.1
1976	170.5	174.3	5.8
1977	181.5	186.1	6.5
1978	195.4	202.9	7.7
1979	217.4	229.9	11.3
1980	246.8	258.4	13.5
1981	272.3	281.5	10.3
1982	289.1	292.4	6.2
1983	298.4	303.5	3.2
1984	311.1	315.5	4.3

*Source: U.S. Department of Labor, Bureau of Labor Statistics.

Objective 9: Distinction Between Constant-Dollar Accounting and Current Value Accounting

historical cost financial statements. They disagree, however, on what should be done to make the financial statements more useful.

Although several approaches have been suggested, two primary methods of reporting the effects of inflation have received relatively wide support. One is to restate the historical cost financial statements for changes in the general price level: **constant-dollar accounting.** The other is to prepare the financial statements on the basis of current prices: **current value accounting.**

CONSTANT-DOLLAR ACCOUNTING

Under constant-dollar accounting, historical cost figures in financial statements are converted to the number of current dollars representing an equivalent amount of purchasing power through the use of a general price level index, such as the CPI. This is accomplished by multiplying the historical cost amounts by a fraction. The numerator of the fraction is the current index number. The denominator is the index number at the date the historical cost figure originated. The objective is to state all amounts in dollars of current purchasing power. For example, assume that land was purchased on December 31, 1972 for $100,000. The land would be restated to an equivalent number of December 31, 1984 dollars as follows.

$$\frac{\text{Current price index}}{\text{Historical cost price index}} \times \text{Historical cost} = \text{Restated cost}$$

$$\frac{315.5}{127.3} \times \$100,000 = \$247,840$$

If additional land was purchased on December 31, 1975, for $50,000, it would be converted to 1984 purchasing power dollars as:

$$\frac{315.5}{166.3} \times \$50,000 = \$94,859$$

Land would be reported on the 1984 constant dollar balance sheet at $342,699 ($247,840 + $94,859).

Restatement for general price-level changes is not considered a departure from historical costs because historical costs are merely restated to a constant 1984 measuring unit. Thus, the restated amount for land of $342,699 does not represent the current market value of the land. The restatement does, however, represent a departure from the stable dollar assumption.

Monetary and Nonmonetary Items

When preparing constant-dollar financial statements, one must distinguish monetary items from nonmonetary items, because their treatment is different. **Monetary items** are money and those assets and liabilities that represent claims to receive or obligations to pay a fixed number of dollars. The number of dollars to be received or paid is fixed in amount, regardless of changes that may occur in the purchasing power of the dollar. Thus, cash, accounts receivable, and notes receivable are monetary assets. Most liabilities are monetary because they represent obligations to pay fixed amounts of dollars. Since monetary items represent claims to fixed amounts of dollars, they are already stated in terms of current purchasing power and do not need to be restated.

Purchasing power gains and losses result from holding monetary items over time. Holding monetary assets during a period of rising prices results in a loss in purchasing power, since the value of money is falling. On the other hand, owing money (holding monetary liabilities) during a period of rising prices results in a purchasing power gain, since the debts can be paid in the future with dollars of smaller purchasing power.

To illustrate a purchasing power loss, assume that Bray Company held $20,000 in cash throughout 1984. The loss in purchasing power would be:

Number of year-end dollars needed to maintain purchasing power

$20,000 \times \dfrac{315.5}{303.5}$	$20,791
Actual number of dollars held at year end	20,000
Purchasing power loss	$ 791

If Bray Company also held a $30,000 note payable throughout 1984, the gain in purchasing power would be:

Number of year-end dollars representing the same purchasing power as the amount owed at the beginning of the year

$30,000 \times \dfrac{315.5}{303.5}$	$31,186
Number of dollars actually owed	30,000
Purchasing power gain	$ 1,186

Nonmonetary items are those items that are not monetary in nature. Examples are inventory, plant assets, intangibles, and stockholders' equity. Since these items do not represent claims to fixed amounts of dollars, no purchasing power gain or loss results from them, and the nonmonetary items must be restated in terms of constant dollars. By restating them, recognition is given to the effect of changes in the general price-level from the time when the items were originally acquired.

Constant-dollar Balance Sheet

To illustrate the preparation of a constant-dollar balance sheet, the historical cost balance sheet, restatement computations, and constant-dollar balance sheet for Troy Company, adjusted to year-end dollars, are shown in Figure 13–2. Assumptions are that:

1. Restatement is based on the CPI (Figure 13–1).
2. Troy Company was formed on December 31, 1974. Common stock was issued and all plant assets and land were acquired at that time.
3. The 12/31 inventory was acquired evenly throughout 1984. The average CPI for 1984 was 311.1 (Figure 13–1).

Note that the monetary assets and liabilities are not restated. Nonmonetary assets and common stock are restated on the basis of the current year-end (1984) index over the index at the time the nonmonetary assets were acquired

Figure 13–2
Constant-dollar Balance Sheet

TROY COMPANY Constant-dollar Balance Sheet December 31, 1984			
	Historical Cost	Restatement Computations	Constant Dollar
Assets			
Cash	$ 48,000	Monetary—not restated	$ 48,000
Accounts receivable	76,000	Monetary—not restated	76,000
Inventory	80,000	(315.5/311.1) × $ 80,000	81,131
Plant and equipment	148,000	(315.5/155.4) × $148,000	300,476
Accumulated depreciation	(42,000)	(315.5/155.4) × $ 42,000	(85,270)
Land	60,000	(315.5/155.4) × $ 60,000	121,815
Total	$370,000		$542,152
Liabilities			
Accounts payable	$53,000	Monetary—not restated	$ 53,000
Notes payable, 1988	40,000	Monetary—not restated	40,000
Stockholders' Equity			
Common stock	180,000	(315.5/155.4) × $180,000	365,444
Retained earnings	97,000	Balancing amount	83,708
Total	$370,000		$542,152

and the common stock was issued. The restated retained earnings figure is an amount that is entered to bring the constant-dollar balance sheet into balance.

Constant-dollar Income Statement

A historical cost and constant-dollar income statement for Troy Company is shown in Figure 13–3. Assumptions are that:

1. Sales were made and expenses (other than depreciation) incurred evenly throughout the year.
2. The purchasing power loss of $1,032, which resulted because Troy Company carried an excess of monetary assets over monetary liabilities through the year, is an assumed amount. The computation of the purchasing power gain or loss in an actual situation is quite complex and, therefore, is covered in detail in more advanced accounting courses.

Note that sales, cost of goods sold, and other expenses were converted on the basis of the current CPI over the average CPI for the year. Depreciation expense is converted on the basis of the CPI that existed when the related depreciable assets were acquired in 1974.

The need for constant-dollar financial statements is an unsettled issue. Those who support their preparation argue that the stable dollar assumption does not reflect reality, particularly when inflation rates are high. They believe that the aggregation of dollars with different purchasing power may mislead users of financial information and thereby cause poor decisions. In addition, they argue that the financial data in constant-dollar statements are just as reliable and verifiable as historical cost data. Critics of constant-dollar accounting argue that both historical cost and constant-dollar financial statements are inadequate because they ignore real value changes. Most critics consequently support the preparation of current value financial statements.

Figure 13–3
Constant-dollar Income Statement

TROY COMPANY
Constant-dollar Income Statement
For Year Ended December 31, 1984

	Historical Cost	Restatement Computations	Constant Dollar
Sales	$394,000	(315.5/311.1) × $394,000	$399,572
Expenses:			
Cost of goods sold	241,000	(315.5/311.1) × $241,000	244,408
Depreciation	20,000	(315.5/155.4) × $ 20,000	40,605
Other expenses	73,000	(315.5/311.1) × $ 73,000	74,032
Total expenses	334,000		359,045
Net income	$ 60,000		
Net income before purchasing power loss			40,527
Purchasing power loss (assumed amount)			(1,032)
Constant-dollar net income			$ 39,495

CURRENT VALUE ACCOUNTING

As explained earlier, constant-dollar accounting does not depart from the historical cost concept. Rather, it merely restates historical costs in terms of the current purchasing power of money—that is, historical costs are restated only for general price-level changes. Current value accounting, however, is a departure from historical cost because it takes specific price changes into consideration. Two basic concepts of current value exist: net realizable value and current replacement cost (current cost). **Net realizable value** is an exit value, an estimate of the amount an asset could be sold for in its present condition minus disposal costs. **Current replacement cost** is an entry value, an estimate of the amount that would have to be paid currently to acquire an asset in its present condition, and is generally referred to simply as **current cost.**

Proponents of current value accounting tend to support the use of current cost, rather than net realizable value, for two reasons. First, current costs are believed to be more objectively determinable by the use of current price lists of suppliers, prices in established markets for used assets, and specific price indexes. Second, most assets are held for use, rather than for direct sale. Consequently, current replacement cost is considered more relevant to users than the current selling price of the assets. In addition, the FASB requires the disclosure of selected current cost information, as discussed later in this chapter. The following discussion, although limited, will thus concentrate on current cost accounting.

To illustrate the preparation of current-cost financial statements, assume that the replacement cost of Troy Company's nonmonetary assets on December 31, 1984, and the replacement cost of goods sold at the time they were sold were as follows.

Inventory	$ 92,000
Plant and equipment	400,000
Accumulated depreciation	(100,000)
Land	110,000
Cost of goods sold	275,000

Plant and equipment items are depreciated by the straight-line method and have a 10-year remaining life.

A balance sheet comparing historical cost with current cost is shown in Figure 13–4. In the current cost balance sheet, monetary assets (cash and accounts receivable) and monetary liabilities (accounts and notes payable) are not changed from their historical amounts because they already reflect current values. Nonmonetary assets are reported at the current cost to replace them in their present physical condition. Paid-in capital accounts are normally restated for general price-level changes and retained earnings is computed as a balancing amount.

An income statement comparing historical cost with current cost is presented in Figure 13–5. In the current cost income statement, sales and those expenses resulting from current cash payments or current accruals are reported at their historical cost amounts. Historical costs are used because sales resulted in an

Figure 13–4
Historical Cost and Current Cost Balance Sheet

TROY COMPANY
Balance Sheet
December 31, 1984

	Historical Cost	Current Cost
Cash	$ 48,000	$ 48,000
Accounts receivable	76,000	76,000
Inventory	80,000	92,000
Plant and equipment	148,000	400,000
Accumulated depreciation	(42,000)	(100,000)
Land	60,000	110,000
Total Assets	$370,000	$626,000
Accounts payable	$ 53,000	$ 53,000
Notes payable	40,000	40,000
Common stock (315.5/155.4) × $180,000)	180,000	365,444
Retained earnings (balancing amount)	97,000	167,556
Total Equities	$370,000	$626,000

increase in monetary assets (cash or accounts receivable) and expenses resulted in a decrease in monetary assets (cash) or an increase in monetary liabilities (accrued expenses). Expenses that will differ from historical costs (primarily cost of goods sold and depreciation) are reported at their current cost. Cost of goods sold is computed by multiplying the number of units sold by the replacement cost of the units at the time of sale. Depreciation expense is determined by applying the depreciation methods used to the plant assets' replacement costs. By reporting current costs, each company recognizes the effect of the specific price changes that affect the resources used by that company.

Proponents of current cost accounting argue that current cost information is much more realistic than historical cost or constant-dollar information—and

Figure 13–5
Comparative Historical Cost and Current Cost Income Statement

TROY COMPANY
Income Statement
For Year Ended December 31, 1984

	Historical Cost	Current Cost
Sales	$394,000	$394,000
Expenses:		
Cost of goods sold	241,000	275,000
Depreciation	20,000	30,000
Other expenses	73,000	73,000
Total expenses	334,000	378,000
Net income	$ 60,000	$ 16,000

therefore more useful. They also believe that a company has net earnings only if it has recovered the replacement cost of resources used, thereby permitting it to maintain its productive capacity. Critics of current cost accounting maintain that replacement costs are too subjective and difficult to verify and may, therefore, mislead decision makers. In addition, critics argue that essentially the same results can be obtained without departing from the historical cost basis. They believe that the use of LIFO to determine cost of goods sold and the use of accelerated depreciation methods are objective and verifiable and will result in reported earnings that approach those that would be reported under current cost accounting.

**Objective 10:
FASB Requirements for Reporting Inflation Effects**

FASB REQUIREMENTS

The Financial Accounting Standards Board has been concerned with the reporting problems created by inflation but has had difficulty reaching an agreement as to the proper solution. Each reporting basis—historical cost, constant-dollar, and current cost—has its advantages and disadvantages. Because decision makers use financial information daily, a major change in the reporting basis has the potential of disrupting the decision-making process and, therefore, the allocation of resources within our economy. In order to obtain experience in the preparation and use of different reporting bases, the FASB required that some companies present selected data on both a constant-dollar and a current cost basis in supplementary schedules to the historical-cost-based financial statements. Specific reporting requirements are contained in *Statement of Financial Accounting Standards No. 33,* "Financial Reporting and Changing Prices." Following an extended period of experimentation with reporting both current cost and constant-dollar data, in 1984 the FASB eliminated some constant-dollar disclosure requirements as provided in SFAS No. 82, "Financial Reporting and Changing Prices: Elimination of Certain Disclosures."

Statement No. 33 applies only to large publicly held companies—those with inventories and property, plant, and equipment (before deducting accumulated depreciation) of more than $125 million, or with total assets of more than $1 billion (after deducting accumulated depreciation). The main disclosures required by the modified *Statement No. 33* for each of the five most recent years, are:

1. Income from continuing operations on a current cost basis.
2. Purchasing power gain or loss on net monetary items.
3. Increase or decrease in the current cost or lower recoverable amount of inventory and property, plant, and equipment, net of inflation.
4. Net assets at year-end on a current cost basis.
5. Income per common share from continuing operations on a current cost basis.
6. Cash dividends declared per common share.
7. Market price per common share at year-end.
8. The average level of the Consumer Price Index.

GLOSSARY

ACCOUNTING ENTITY. An economic unit that controls resources and engages in economic activity (p. 498).

CONSERVATISM. An accounting convention which provides that, when in doubt, choose the solution least likely to overstate assets and income for the current period (p. 508).

CONSISTENCY PRINCIPLE. The concept that once a particular accounting method is adopted it should not be changed from period to period unless a different method provides more useful information (p. 506).

CONSTANT-DOLLAR ACCOUNTING. The restatement of historical cost financial statements for changes in the general price-level (p. 510).

COST PRINCIPLE. A basis on which resources and the allocation of resources are accounted for at their cost. Changes in the market value of resources are not recognized (p. 501).

CURRENT VALUE ACCOUNTING (CURRENT COST ACCOUNTING). The preparation of financial statements on the basis of current costs (p. 510).

CURRENT REPLACEMENT COST (CURRENT COST). The amount that would have to be paid currently to acquire an asset in its present condition (p. 514).

ENTITY ASSUMPTION. The assumption that information is accumulated for a specific unit of accountability, called an entity (p. 498).

FULL DISCLOSURE PRINCIPLE. The accounting principle that financial statements should disclose all relevant information affecting net income and financial position of a company (p. 506).

GENERAL PRICE-LEVEL. The weighted average of the prices of all goods and services in an economy (p. 508).

GENERAL PRICE-LEVEL CHANGE. A change in the weighted average of the prices of all goods and services in an economy (p. 509).

GENERALLY ACCEPTED ACCOUNTING PRINCIPLES (GAAP). The body of rules, conventions, and practices followed by accountants (p. 497).

GOING CONCERN ASSUMPTION (CONTINUITY ASSUMPTION). The assumption that a business will continue to operate in the future unless there is evidence to the contrary (p. 499).

INFLATION. A decrease in the purchasing power of money; also defined as an increase in the general price-level (p. 508).

INSTALLMENT METHOD. A method of accounting for installment sales under which gross profit is recognized in proportion to the amount of cash collected. Its use is permitted for financial reporting purposes only when collection of the sales price is not reasonably assured (p. 504).

MATCHING PRINCIPLE. The guide followed in accounting to determine the time period in which expenses will be deducted from revenues (p. 505).

MATERIALITY. The relative size or importance of an item or event. An item or event is considered material if knowledge of it would affect a user's decision (p. 507).

MONETARY ITEMS. Assets and liabilities that represent claims to fixed amounts of dollars (p. 511).

MONETARY UNIT ASSUMPTION. The use of money in accounting as the common denominator by which economic activity is measured and reported (p. 500).

NET REALIZABLE VALUE. The amount an asset could be sold for, less disposal costs (p. 514).

NONMONETARY ITEMS. All financial statement amounts that are not monetary in nature—that is, that do not represent claims to fixed amounts of cash (p. 512).

OBJECTIVITY PRINCIPLE. The concept that accounting data should be verifiable and free from personal bias (p. 500).

PERCENTAGE-OF-COMPLETION METHOD. A method of accounting for long-term projects under which gross profit is recognized in proportion to the work completed during the period (p. 502).

PURCHASING POWER. The amount of goods or services for which a dollar can be exchanged (p. 508).

PURCHASING POWER GAIN (LOSS). The gain (or loss) that results from holding monetary liabilities (assets) during a period of rising prices (p. 511)

REVENUE PRINCIPLE. The rule in accounting that revenue should be recognized when the earning process is substantially completed and an exchange has taken place (p. 501).

SPECIFIC PRICE CHANGE. A change in the price of a specific good or service (p. 509).

TIME PERIOD ASSUMPTION. Accountants' assumption that economic activity can be associated realistically with relatively short time intervals (p. 499).

DISCUSSION QUESTIONS

1. Why have accountants developed generally accepted accounting principles?
2. How do accounting principles become generally accepted?
3. Why is it so important that the business activities of an accounting entity be separated from the personal activities of its owners and the activities of other entities?
4. What is meant by the going concern assumption? What accounting practices receive their justification from this assumption?
5. How is the time period assumption related to the trade-off between the reliability of accounting information and its timely reporting?
6. What is the basic problem created by the monetary unit assumption when inflation rates are high?
7. What is the objectivity principle?
8. Explain what is meant by the cost principle. Why is it used instead of current market values?
9. Explain what is meant by the revenue principle.
10. What is the matching principle? Briefly explain each of the three bases for recognizing expenses, and give an example of each.
11. What is required by the consistency principle? Why?
12. What is meant by the full disclosure principle?
13. How is the materiality convention used in accounting?
14. Explain what is incorporated in the convention of conservatism and when it is applied. Give an example of its application.
15. Distinguish between general price-level changes and specific price changes.

16. What is constant-dollar accounting?
17. What is meant by the term *monetary items?* Give some examples.
18. What is current value accounting?

EXERCISES

Exercise 13-1 **Matching Accounting Concepts**
Match the items in Column I with the appropriate descriptions in Column II.

Column I	Column II
_8_ a. Conservatism	1. The measurement basis used to record and report economic activity.
_11_ b. Consistency	2. The normal basis used to account for assets.
_2_ c. Cost principle Historical	3. Business activity is separated from the owner's personal activity.
_3_ d. Entity assumption	4. Measurement of net income and financial position necessarily requires estimates.
_12_ e. Full disclosure	5. Data can be corroborated by reference to business documents, physical counts, and measurements by several qualified persons.
_9_ f. Going concern assumption	6. The basis for determining when expenses should be recognized.
_10_ g. Materiality	7. The earning process must be completed and an exchange must have taken place.
_6_ h. Matching principle	8. Used to discourage over-optimism in recording assets and net income.
_1_ i. Monetary unit assumption	9. An inappropriate assumption for a firm undergoing bankruptcy.
_7_ j. Revenue principle	10. Relates to the relative size or importance of an item or event.
_4_ k. Time period assumption	11. The same accounting methods should be used by a firm from one period to another.
_5_ l. Verifiability	12. Financial reports should include all relevant and significant information affecting net income and financial position.

Exercise 13-2 Violation of Accounting Principles

Several independent situations are described here.

1. The owner of a company included his personal medical expenses on the company's income statement.
2. No mention was made of a major lawsuit filed against the company, even though the company's attorney believes there is a high probability of losing the suit.
3. The LIFO inventory method was used in Year one, FIFO was used in Year two, and weighted-average was used in Year three.
4. Depreciation expense was not recorded, because to do so would result in a net loss for the period.
5. The cost of three small files (cost $8.27 each) was charged to expense when purchased, even though they had a useful life of several years.
6. Land was reported at its estimated selling price, which is substantially higher than its cost. The increase in value was included on the income statement.

Required:

For each situation, indicate the accounting principle(s) (if any) that is violated.

Exercise 13-3 Percentage-of-completion Method

Locke Construction Company signed a contract to construct a dam on the Verde River for $32,000,000. The project is expected to take four years to complete at an estimated cost of $24,000,000. Actual costs incurred each year were:

Year	Cost Incurred
1	$ 4,800,000
2	6,720,000
3	7,200,000
4	5,520,000
Total	$24,240,000

Assume that the estimated total cost of the project remained at $24,000,000 through the end of the third year.

Required:

Determine the amount of gross profit that should be recognized each year under the percentage-of-completion method.

Exercise 13-4 Installment Sale and Constant-dollar Accounting

On March 1, 1987, Hayes Company sold land held as an investment at a selling price of $400,000. The land had been acquired for $270,000 on January 1, 1980. The purchaser made a down payment of $200,000 and agreed to pay the remaining $200,000 at the rate of $5,000 per month for 40 months, beginning on April 1, 1987.

Required:

A. Assuming that all payments were received when due, determine the amount of gross profit that should be recognized each year under the installment method. Hayes' fiscal year-end is December 31.
B. Assume that the entire purchase price was received on the date of sale and that the price index was 226 on March 1, 1987, and 165 on January 1, 1980. Compute the gain or loss on the sale of land on a constant-dollar basis.
C. Assuming an income tax rate of 30%, and the situation described in (B), compute the after-tax gain or loss on a constant-dollar basis.

Exercise 13-5 Constant-dollar Accounting

Dibbs Company has landholdings that were purchased for a total of $315,000. The year of purchase and the purchase price for each of the three parcels owned are as follows.

Parcel	Year Purchased	Purchase Price
1	1978	$180,000
2	1980	52,500
3	1981	82,500

Required:

A. Determine the amount at which land should be reported on a 1983 constant-dollar balance sheet. Base your computation on the CPI presented in Figure 13–1 on page 510. All purchases were made at year-end, December 31.

B. Assuming the land was sold early in 1984 for $390,000, compute the gain or loss from the sale based on
   1. Historical cost measurement.
   2. Constant-dollar measurement.

Exercise 13-6 Purchasing Power Gain or Loss

Minor Company held $30,000 cash and a $20,000 note receivable throughout the year 1987. The company also held a note payable for $25,000 throughout the year. Assume that the price index was 196 on January 1, 1987, and 220 on December 31, 1987.

Required:

Determine the purchasing power gain or loss on the monetary items.

Exercise 13-7 Purchasing Power Gain or Loss

Mrs. Urbi had $30,000 cash in a safety deposit box at her bank during the entire year of 1987. On July 1, 1987, Mrs. Urbi borrowed $10,000 from a friend and promised to repay the loan one year later. No interest was charged. Assume that the price index was 160 on January 1, 1987; 165 on July 1, 1987; and 170 on December 31, 1987.

Required:

What purchasing power gain or loss did Mrs. Urbi have for 1987? (Round computations to the nearest dollar.)

Exercise 13-8 Comparing Historical Cost, Constant-dollar, and Current Cost

Blake Company purchased equipment for $100,000 on January 1, 1981, when the price index was 120. The equipment has a 10-year life and a residual vaue of $3,000. Replacement cost of the equipment on December 31, 1987, was $175,000 and its residual value was still estimated to be $3,000. The average price index for 1987 was 180.

Required:

Compute the amount of straight-line depreciation expense that would be deducted in the 1987 income statement, assuming that the income statement is prepared on the basis of

A. Historical cost.
B. Constant-dollar.
C. Current cost.

PROBLEMS

Problem 13-1 Violation of Accounting Principles

During an audit of Lilly Company, you discover that the following transactions and events were recorded during the current year.

1. A patent with a cost of $120,000 was being amortized over its useful life of 6 years. The amortization entry made at the end of the current year was:

Retained Earnings	20,000	
Patents		20,000

2. Ending inventory for the current year was overstated by ignoring the fact that the replacement cost of the inventory was $18,000 lower than its cost.
3. The company borrowed $500,000 from a bank, at an interest rate of 10%, to construct a new warehouse. At the completion of construction, the loan was repaid and the following entry was made.

Note Payable	500,000	
Warehouse	30,000	
Cash		530,000

4. An accelerator control device was installed on each of the company's 10 delivery trucks at a cost of $12.40 each. The transaction was recorded as follows.

Maintenance Expense	124	
Cash		124

5. Inventory was acquired at $29 per unit, throughout the current year, until the last purchase was made in November. At that time the company was able to negotiate a special price and acquired 10,000 units at $25 per unit. The purchase was recorded as follows.

Inventory	290,000	
Cash		250,000
Revenue		40,000

6. On January 2 of the current year, a new truck was purchased for $18,000. The truck had an estimated useful life of four years and a residual value of $2,000. Depreciation expense for the year was recorded as follows, in order to avoid reporting a net operating loss.

Depreciation Expense	1,000	
Accumulated Depreciation—Trucks		1,000

Required:

For each item, determine which generally accepted accounting principle(s) (if any) is violated, and explain why. For each violation, indicate the correct treatment.

Problem 13-2 Revenue Principle
This problem focuses on the revenue principle and consists of three parts.

Part 1. Required:
Critique each of the following statements.

A. Revenue should be recognized when the cash is received.
B. Revenue is earned when goods are shipped or delivered to the buyer.

Part II. Required:
Indicate the amount of revenue that should be recognized in 1986 in each of the following cases, and explain why.

A. Cash of $50,000 is received from a customer during 1986 in payment for special purpose machinery, which is to be manufactured and shipped to the customer early in 1987.
B. Net credit sales for 1986 amounted to $200,000, three-fourths of which were collected in 1986. Past experience indicates that about 96% of all credit sales are eventually collected.

Part III. Required:
Determine the amount of gross profit that should be recognized in 1986, 1987, and 1988 for each of the following cases.

A. Construction equipment with a cost of $169,000 was sold for $200,000. A $40,000 down payment was received in 1986 and the purchaser agreed to pay the balance in eight equal quarterly installments during 1987 and 1988. Collection of the full sales price is not reasonably assured.
B. Topful Construction Company signed a contract to construct an office complex at a contract price of $6,000,000. The project is expected to take three years to complete, at an estimated total cost of $4,200,000. Actual costs incurred on the project were: 1986, $1,260,000; 1987, $1,890,000; 1988, $1,125,000. Estimates of cost to complete and the extent of progress toward completion are reasonably dependable. Estimated total costs remained $4,200,000 until early in 1988.

Problem 13-3 Constant-dollar Accounting
CNC Inc. purchased land and machinery early in 1978 for $500,000, $150,000 of which was allocated to land. The machinery had an estimated useful life of eight years and a salvage value of $30,000. Machinery is depreciated on the straight-line basis. Additional land was purchased by CNC Inc. on January 1, 1980, for $50,000 and on December 31, 1982, for $70,000. The machinery purchased in 1978 was sold on January 1, 1984, for $187,500.

Required:
Using the CPI data in Figure 13–1 on page 510,

A. Determine the net amount at which machinery should be reported on a constant-dollar balance sheet on December 31, 1983.
B. Determine the amount at which land should be reported on a constant-dollar balance sheet on December 31, 1983.
C. Determine the amount of depreciation expense on machinery that should be reported on a constant-dollar income statement for 1982 and 1983.
D. How much gain would be reported on the sale of machinery in the historical cost income statement for the year ended December 31, 1984?

E. In terms of constant dollars, how much gain (loss) was realized on the sale of the machinery?

Problem 13-4 Constant-dollar Financial Statements

The December 31, 1983, balance sheet and 1983 income statement for Adnan Company are presented here.

ADNAN COMPANY
Balance Sheet
December 31, 1983

Assets

Cash	$ 40,000
Accounts receivable	57,000
Inventory	69,000
Plant and equipment	120,000
Accumulated depreciation	(25,000)
Land	35,000
Investment in bonds of Dan Company	10,000
Total Assets	$306,000

Liabilities

Accounts payable	$ 70,000
Notes payable due in 1988	65,000
Total Liabilities	135,000

Stockholders' Equity

Common stock	$85,000	
Retained earnings	86,000	171,000
Total Liabilities and Stockholders' Equity		$306,000

Income Statement
Year Ended December 31, 1983

Sales		$400,000
Cost of goods sold		230,000
Gross profit on sales		170,000
Expenses:		
Depreciation	$ 8,000	
Other expenses	115,000	123,000
Net Income		$ 47,000

Other Information:

1. Inventory was acquired evenly throughout 1983.
2. The company was formed on January 1, 1977, at which time the common stock was issued and the plant and equiment were acquired.
3. The investment in bonds of Dan Company was made on December 31, 1981.
4. Sales were made and expenses (except for depreciation) were incurred evenly throughout the year.

5. A purchasing power gain of $3,600 was computed for the year.

6. The land was acquired in two purchases. The first parcel was purchased with the plant and equipment in 1977 for $20,000; the second portion was acquired on January 1, 1980 for $15,000.

Required:
Using the CPI data in Figure 13–1 on page 510,

A. Prepare a constant-dollar balance sheet at December 31, 1983.

B. Prepare a constant-dollar income statement for the year ended December 31, 1983.

Problem 13-5 Constant-dollar and Current Cost Financial Statements

An income statement for the year ended December 31, 1986, and a balance sheet on December 31, 1986, for Darcy Company are presented here.

Income Statement

Net sales		$1,650,000
Cost of goods sold		1,205,000
Gross profit		445,000
Expenses:		
Depreciation	$ 38,000	
Other expenses	349,000	387,000
Net Income		$ 58,000

Balance Sheet

Assets		Liabilities and Owners' Equity	
Cash	$125,000	Accounts payable	$151,000
Accounts receivable	175,000	Notes payable	200,000
Inventory	240,000	Common stock	300,000
Plant and equipment (net)	416,000	Retained earnings	305,000
Total	$956,000	Total	$956,000

Darcy Company was formed in 1976, at which time the common stock was issued and the plant and equipment were purchased. Inventory was purchased evenly throughout 1986, and sales were made and cost of goods sold and expenses (other than depreciation) were incurred evenly throughout the year.

Other information:
1. Depreciation expense computed on the basis of plant asset replacement costs is $75,000.

2. The replacement cost of goods sold during 1986 was $1,205,000.

3. A purchasing power gain of $15,500 was computed for 1986.

4. The replacement cost of the December 31, 1986, inventory was $276,000.

5. The replacement cost of plant and equipment on December 31, 1986, was $701,500.

6. Assumed Price Indexes:

When the company was formed	145
December 31, 1986	200
Average for 1986	195

Required:

A. Prepare a constant-dollar and a current cost income statement for Darcy Company for the year ended December 31, 1986.

B. Prepare a constant-dollar and a current cost balance sheet at December 31, 1986.

ALTERNATE PROBLEMS

Problem 13-1A **Violation of Accounting Principles**

While reviewing the business activities of Santee Company, you discover that the following transactions and events were recorded.

1. A new machine was purchased at a warehouse auction sale for cash of $16,000. Since the cash price of the machine would have been $19,000 if purchased from Santee Company's normal supplier, the machinery account was debited for $19,000 and the following entry was made.

Machinery	19,000	
Cash		16,000
Gain from Bargain Purchase		3,000

2. Leasehold improvements with an estimated useful life of eight years were completed early in the current year at a cost of $90,000. Santee Company had a five-year nonrenewable lease on the property to which the improvements were made. To record amortization for the current year, the accountant made the following entry.

Amortization Expense	11,250	
Leasehold Improvements		11,250

3. On December 28 of the current year, Santee Company signed a contract with a customer under which Santee Company agreed to manufacture equipment for the customer during January of the following year at a price of $24,000. Santee Company received a check for $5,000 from the customer on December 28 and made the following entry.

Accounts Receivable	19,000	
Cash	5,000	
Sales		24,000

4. Steering wheel covers were installed in each of Santee Company's five delivery trucks at a cost of $20 each. The trucks had an average remaining useful life of four years. The transaction was recorded as:

Repairs Expense	100	
Cash		100

5. Ending inventory for the current year had a cost of $89,000 and a replacement cost of $85,000. The inventory was not reduced to its replacement cost because the company's accountant believed that the purchase price of similar inventory items would probably increase again during the next year.

6. Santee Company borrowed $200,000 from a bank at an interest rate of 15% to finance the construction of a new building. At the completion of construction the loan was repaid and the following entry was made.

Note Payable	200,000	
Buildings	22,000	
Cash		222,000

Required:
For each item, determine which generally accepted accounting principle(s), if any, is violated, and explain why. For each violation, indicate the correct treatment.

Problem 13-2A Constant-dollar Accounting

Wellbro Company purchased a building and land on January 4, 1981, for $300,000, of which $60,000 was assigned to land. The building had an estimated useful life of 15 years and a residual value of $40,000. Buildings are depreciated by the straight-line method. Additional land was purchased for $70,000 on January 2, 1983, and for $90,000 on July 1, 1984. The land purchased in 1983 was sold on January 2, 1987, for $110,000. The assumed price indexes at relevant dates were:

January 1, 1981	130
January 1, 1983	160
July 1, 1984	175
January 1, 1987	180
December 31, 1987	190

Required:
A. Determine the net amount at which the building should be reported on a constant-dollar balance sheet on December 31, 1987.
B. Determine the amount at which land should be reported on a constant-dollar balance sheet on December 31, 1987.
C. Determine the amount of depreciation expense on the building that should be reported on a constant-dollar income statement for 1986 and 1987.
D. How much gain or loss would be reported on the sale of land in the historical cost income statement for the year ended December 31, 1987?
E. In terms of constant dollars, how much gain or loss was realized on the sale of the land?

Problem 13-3A Revenue Principle

This problem concerns the correct application of the revenue principle and consists of three parts.

Part I. Required:
Critique each of the following statements.

A. Revenue is earned with the passage of time.
B. The revenue principle provides that revenue should be recognized under accrual accounting at the time of sale.

Part II. Required:
Indicate the amount of revenue that should be recognized in 1987 in each of the following cases and explain why.

A. Net credit sales for 1987 amounted to $150,000, three-fourths of which were collected in 1987. Past experience indicates that about 97% of all credit sales are eventually collected.

B. Cash of $35,000 is received from a customer during 1987 in payment for equipment that is to be manufactured and shipped to the customer during 1988.

Part III. Required:

Determine the amount of gross profit that should be recognized in 1986, 1987, and 1988, for each of the following cases.

A. Lenny Construction Company signed a contract to construct a dam on the Halo River at a contract price of $5,000,000. The project is expected to take three years to complete, at an estimated cost of $4,000,000. Actual costs incurred on the project were: 1986, $1,040,000; 1987, $1,620,000; 1988, $985,000. Estimates of costs to complete and the extent of progress toward completion are reasonably dependable. Estimated total costs remained $4,000,000 until early in 1988.

B. Office equipment with a cost of $75,000 was sold for $125,000. A $25,000 down payment was received in 1986 and the purchaser agreed to pay the balance in eight equal quarterly installments during 1987 and 1988. Collection of the full sales price is not reasonably assured.

Problem 13-4A Constant-dollar Financial Statements

An income statement for the year ended December 31, 1986, and a December 31, 1986, balance sheet for MAC Company follow.

MAC COMPANY
Income Statement
For the Year Ended December 31, 1986

Sales		$142,500
Expenses:		
Cost of goods sold	$71,300	
Depreciation expense	6,600	
Other expenses	22,200	100,100
Net Income		$ 42,400

MAC COMPANY
Balance Sheet
December 31, 1986

Assets		Liabilities	
Cash	$ 18,500	Accounts payable	$ 21,100
Accounts receivable	36,000	Notes payable	17,200
Inventory	32,500	Total Liabilities	38,300
Plant and equipment	58,600	Owners' Equity	
Accumulated depreciation	(18,300)	Common stock	79,000
Land	26,900	Retained earnings	36,900
Total	$154,200	Total	$154,200

MAC Company began operations in January, 1979, at which time the common stock was issued and plant, equipment, and land were purchased. Sales were made and expenses (except for depreciation) were incurred evenly throughout 1986. Inventory was acquired evenly throughout 1986. In addition, a purchasing power loss of $1,140 was computed for 1986.

Assume that the price index was:

144 on January 1, 1979.
206 on December 31, 1986.
202 average for 1986.

Required:
A. Prepare a constant-dollar income statement for 1986.
B. Prepare a constant-dollar balance sheet as of December 31, 1986. (Round to the nearest dollar.)

Problem 13-5A Constant-dollar Financial Statements

An income statement for 1987 and a balance sheet on December 31, 1987, for Petron Company are presented here.

PETRON COMPANY
Income Statement
For Year Ended December 31, 1987

Sales		$620,000
Cost of goods sold		350,000
Gross profit		270,000
Expenses:		
Depreciation	$ 21,560	
Other expenses	178,000	199,560
Net Income		$ 70,440

PETRON COMPANY
Balance Sheet
December 31, 1987

Cash		$ 56,000
Accounts receivable		79,800
Inventory		83,000
Plant and equipment		178,000
Accumulated depreciation		(35,000)
Land		49,000
Investment in bonds of S & S Company		15,000
Total Assets		$425,800
Accounts payable		$ 93,000
Notes payable, due in 1990		96,000
Total Liabilities		189,000
Common stock	$115,000	
Retained earnings	121,800	236,800
Total Liabilities and Stockholders' Equity		$425,800

Additional information:

1. Inventory was acquired evenly throughout 1987.
2. The company was formed in 1980, at which time the common stock was issued and the plant and equipment purchased.
3. The investment in bonds of S & S Company was made in 1983.
4. Sales were made and expenses (except for depreciation) were incurred evenly throughout the year.
5. A purchasing power gain of $4,650 was computed for the year.
6. The land was acquired in two purchases. The first parcel was purchased with the plant and equipment in 1980 for $30,000. The second portion was purchased in 1983 for $19,000.
7. The assumed price index on various dates was as follows.

In 1980, when the company was formed	155
In 1983, when the bond investment and land were purchased	185
On December 31, 1987	225
Average for the year 1987	215

Required:

A. Prepare a constant-dollar income statement for the year ended December 31, 1987.
B. Prepare a constant-dollar balance sheet as of December 31, 1987.

Problem 13-6A Constant-dollar and Current Cost Financial Statements

An income statement for the year ended December 31, 1987, and a balance sheet on December 31, 1987, for Rodin Company are presented here.

RODIN COMPANY
Income Statement
For the Year Ended December 31, 1987

Net sales		$1,355,200
Cost of goods sold		951,200
Gross profit		404,000
Expenses:		
Depreciation	$ 30,000	
Other expenses	282,900	312,900
Net Income		$ 91,100

RODIN COMPANY
Balance Sheet
December 31, 1987

Assets		Liabilities and Owners' Equity	
Cash	$100,000	Accounts payable	$130,000
Accounts receivable	151,000	Notes payable	120,000
Inventory	192,000	Common stock	280,000
Plant and equipment (net)	332,800	Retained earnings	245,800
Total	$775,800	Total	$775,800

Rodin Company was formed in 1982, at which time the common stock was issued and the plant and equipment acquired. Inventory was purchased evenly throughout 1987 and sales were made and cost of sales and expenses (other than depreciation) were incurred evenly throughout the year.

Additional information:
1. Depreciation expense computed on the basis of plant asset replacement costs is $49,900 for 1987.
2. The replacement cost of goods sold during 1987 was $955,000.
3. A purchasing power loss of $2,400 was incurred during 1987.
4. The replacement cost of the December 31, 1987, inventory was $203,500.
5. The replacement cost of plant and equipment on December 31, 1987 was $586,000.
6. Assumed price indexes were as follows.

When the company was formed in 1982	140
December 31, 1987	200
Average for 1987	195

Required:
A. Prepare a constant-dollar and a current cost income statement for Rodin Company for the year ended December 31, 1987.
B. Prepare a constant-dollar and a current cost balance sheet as of December 31, 1987.

CASE

CASE 13-1   Financial Report Analysis Case   **Effects of Changing Prices**
Refer to the financial statements and the supplementary financial data on the effects of changing prices for Chrysler Corporation in Appendix A and answer the following questions:

1. What was the net income (loss) from continuing operations for the year ended December 31, 1984, on an historical cost basis?
2. How much net income (loss) from continuing operations would have been reported for the year ended December 31, 1984, if the company had used current cost accounting?
3. What was the total amount of monetary assets held by Chrysler Corporation on December 31, 1984?
4. How much purchasing power gain or loss would have been reported on a constant-dollar income statement for the year ended December 31, 1984? Explain, in general terms, why the amount was a gain or loss.
5. What was the amount of Chrysler Corporation's net assets on December 31, 1984,
   (a) On an historical cost basis?
   (b) On a current cost basis?
6. What was the amount of Chrysler Corporation's inventory on December 31, 1984,
   (a) On an historical cost basis?
   (b) On a current cost basis?

PART 4

PARTNERSHIPS AND CORPORATIONS

14

ACCOUNTING FOR PARTNERSHIPS

CHAPTER OVERVIEW AND OBJECTIVES

This chapter discusses the partnership form of business organization and the accounting procedures used for it. When you have completed the chapter, you should understand:

1. The advantages of the partnership form of business organization.
2. The major characteristics of partnerships.
3. How to account for the formation of a partnership.
4. Methods of sharing profits and losses.
5. How to record the admission of a new partner.
6. How to record the withdrawal of a partner.
7. How to record the liquidation of a partnership.

Many of the accounting principles and practices discussed so far are also appropriate when accounting for a partnership. Nevertheless, some aspects of partnership accounting are different. These unique aspects mainly involve accounting for owners' equity transactions, allocation of net income or loss, the admission or withdrawal of a partner from the partnership, and partnership liquidation. We will briefly examine some of the characteristics of a partnership before these areas are discussed. Partnership law also has a significant influence on accounting practice. Most states have adopted the **Uniform Partnership Act (UPA)** or some modification of it to govern the formation, operation, and liquidation of partnerships. Provisions of the UPA will be discussed briefly throughout this chapter when appropriate. More extensive study of the legal aspects of a partnership is part of most business law courses.

PARTNERSHIP DEFINED

A **partnership,** as defined by the UPA, is ''an association of two or more persons to carry on as co-owners a business for profit.'' Because a written agreement is not necessary to form a partnership, it is sometimes difficult to determine if a partnership does, in fact, exist. Three attributes are necessary for a business partnership: (1) There must be an agreement between two or more legally competent persons; (2) the business must be operated for the purpose of earning a profit; and (3) members of the firm must be co-owners of the business. Co-ownership (often the most difficult attribute to determine) involves the right of each partner to share in the profits of the firm, to participate with the other partners in the management of the firm, and to own jointly with the other partners the property of the partnership. The right to participate in management may be limited by an express agreement among the partners.

REASONS FOR FORMING A PARTNERSHIP

We have already noted that a business can be a proprietorship, a partnership, or a corporation. Each of these forms has certain advantages and disadvantages. One of the major advantages of a partnership over a proprietorship is that it permits the pooling of both capital resources and the multiple skills of the individual partners. A partnership is easier and less costly to establish than a corporation and is generally not subject to as much governmental regulation. Furthermore, the partners may be able to operate with more flexibility because they are not subject to the control of a board of directors. There also may be certain tax advantages to a partnership, primarily because a partnership is not taxed as a separate entity.[1] Instead, the partnership's net income or net loss is allocated to the individual partners to be reported on their individual tax returns, whether or not the income is distributed to the partners. Except for an S Corporation, described in Chapter 28, a corporation is considered a separate taxable entity, and, therefore, its income is taxed to the corporation and again to the stockholders when distributed by the corporation.

Objective 1: Advantages of forming a partnership

CHARACTERISTICS OF A PARTNERSHIP

A prospective owner of a business should consider the tax and legal aspects of the various forms of business organizations carefully before selecting the one that meets his or her organizational objectives and personal goals. The partnership form may turn out to be unattractive because of one or more of the following characteristics.

Objective 2: Characteristics of partnerships

UNLIMITED LIABILITY

In a **general partnership,** each partner is personally liable for the obligations of the partnership. This means that if the creditors of the partnership are not paid from assets of the partnership, they can look to an individual partner's personal assets for recovery of any unpaid claims. In contrast, a **limited partnership** exists when one or more of the partners have limited their liability for partnership debts to the amount of assets they have invested in the partnership. However, a limited partner may not participate in the management

---

[1] The tax advantages of the various forms of business organizations are covered in Chapter 28.

of the business. In a limited partnership, one or more of the partners must be a general partner.

LIMITED LIFE

A partnership is dissolved for a number of reasons, including the death of a partner, the bankruptcy of the partnership or an individual partner, the withdrawal of a partner from the partnership, the expiration of the period specified in a contract, or a judgment by a court that a partner is not of sound mind and is thus incapable of performing his or her partnership duties. In some of these cases, the partnership activities are terminated and the partnership ceases to exist. In other cases, the continuing partners may form a new partnership and continue to operate without any visible interruption of business activities.

MUTUAL AGENCY

Normally, every partner acts as an agent for the partnership and for every other partner. Thus, a partner can represent the other partners and bind them to a contract if he or she is acting within the apparent scope of the business. For example, in the case of a merchandising firm, a partner can enter into contracts to buy and sell merchandise, hire employees, and acquire office equipment. Activities outside the normal course of the business, such as selling land owned by the partnership, must be authorized by all partners.

TRANSFER OF PARTNERSHIP INTEREST

The capital interest in a partnership is a personal asset of each individual partner; it can be sold or disposed of in any legal way. However, partnership law recognizes the highly personal relationship of partners and provides that the purchaser of a partner's interest does not have the right to participate in management of the firm unless he or she is accepted by all the other partners. The new partner is entitled to the selling partner's profit share and, in the event of liquidation, to receive whatever assets the selling partner would have received had he or she continued in the partnership. The necessity of obtaining approval to participate in management from the other partners may make it difficult to transfer a partnership interest.

The discussion thus far underlines the importance of care in selection of the individuals to be associated with in a partnership. In particular, the mutual agency and unlimited liability characteristics could result in extensive personal liability resulting from the acts of other partners.

Because of these characteristics, it may be more difficult for a partnership to raise capital than it is for a corporation to do so. Partnerships are thus most common in comparatively small businesses, professional organizations, such as a medical clinic or an accounting practice, and some limited projects undertaken to accomplish a single goal, such as an oil and gas exploration project or a real estate development project.

PARTNERSHIP AGREEMENT

A partnership is a voluntary association based on the contractual agreement between or among legally competent persons. The contract between the parties is called the **partnership agreement, partnership contract,** or **articles of partnership.** Although the partnership agreement may be oral, sound business practice dictates that the agreement be in writing for the protection of the individual partners. In the partnership agreement, the partners should clearly express their intentions, and the document should cover all aspects of operating the partnership. If there are subsequent disputes and the partners are unable to reach a satisfactory agreement, it may be necessary to resort to litigation. During litigation, the court will attempt to interpret the partnership agreement and the intentions of the partners. For example, in the absence of a specific agreement, courts have held that the intent of the individual partners must have been to share equally in profits of the firm. To avoid as many conflicts as possible, the partners should seek professional guidance from an attorney in drafting the partnership agreement.

Objective 3: Forming a partnership

The partnership agreement should be as explicit as possible and should include these important points.

1. Partnership name and identity of the partners.
2. Nature, purpose, and scope of the business.
3. Location of the place of business.
4. Provision for the allocation of profit and loss.
5. Provision for the withdrawal of assets by a partner.
6. Fiscal period of the partnership.
7. Whether or not an audit is to be performed.
8. Authority of each partner in contract situations.
9. Identification and valuation of initial asset investments and specification of capital interest each respective partner is to receive.
10. Accounting practices to be followed, such as depreciation methods to be used.
11. Procedures to be followed in the event of disputes among the partners.
12. Provisions covering how operations are to be conducted and how the various partners' interests are to be settled upon the death or withdrawal of a partner.

Some of these items will be discussed in more detail in subsequent sections of this chapter.

ACCOUNTING FOR A PARTNERSHIP

For accounting purposes, a partnership is a separate business entity. The transactions and events that affect the assets, liabilities, and capital accounts of the partnership are accounted for separately from the personal activities of the individual partners. For reporting purposes, however, a creditor may require information concerning the personal assets and debts of individual partners, as well as financial statements of the firm, because a general partner has unlimited liability for partnership debts.

Accounting for a partnership involves essentially the same procedures and generally accepted accounting principles examined in preceding chapters. A major difference, however, involves accounting for owners' equity. In a partnership, ownership interests are generally not equal, because the capital investments and withdrawals of each partner vary. Furthermore, as we shall see, the profit or loss reported for each fiscal period is allocated to the partners in accordance with the partnership agreement. Because the capital interest of each partner may vary, a separate capital account and separate withdrawal account are maintained for each partner.

The capital account of each partner is credited when assets are invested in the partnership by that person. Each partner's withdrawal account is debited to record the withdrawal of assets or the payment of personal expenses by an individual partner from partnership assets. At the end of the period, the withdrawal account of each partner is typically closed to his or her capital account and the balance in the *Income Summary* account is allocated to the partners and closed to their respective capital accounts. Except for the additional accounts and the need to divide the profit or loss, these are the same procedures followed in accounting for the capital transactions of a proprietorship.

RECORDING THE FORMATION OF A PARTNERSHIP

Assets invested in a partnership, liabilities assumed by a partnership, monetary amounts to be assigned to specific assets and liabilities, and the capital interest each partner is to receive should be agreed upon and specified in the partnership agreement. Once the agreement is made, the entry to record the initial investment can be made.

To illustrate, assume that Art Becker and Robin Cook, operators of competing businesses, agree to form the BC Partnership. The book values and fair values of the assets being invested and the liabilities assumed by the partnership were agreed upon, as shown in Figure 14–1. Assuming that Becker and Cook agree that each partner is to receive a capital credit equal to the amount of net assets invested, journal entries to record the initial investment are:

Jan.	1	Cash	60,000	
		Accounts Receivable	25,000	
		Inventory	19,000	
		Equipment	51,000	
		Allowance for Uncollectible Accounts		5,000
		Becker, Capital		150,000
	1	Cash	20,000	
		Inventory	10,000	
		Equipment	20,000	
		Land	40,000	
		Building	50,000	
		Mortgage Payable		40,000
		Cook, Capital		100,000

Figure 14–1
Assets Invested and
Liabilities Assumed
by Partnership

	Book Value		Fair Value	
	Becker	Cook	Becker	Cook
Cash	$ 60,000	$ 20,000	$ 60,000	$ 20,000
Accounts Receivable	25,000	-0-	25,000	-0-
Allowance for Uncollectible				
Accounts	(4,000)	-0-	(5,000)	-0-
Inventory	22,000	9,000	19,000	10,000
Equipment	80,000	42,000	51,000	20,000
Accumulated Depreciation	(35,000)	(18,000)	-0-	-0-
Land	-0-	15,000	-0-	40,000
Building	-0-	110,000	-0-	50,000
Accumulated Depreciation	-0-	(70,000)	-0-	-0-
Total Assets Invested	148,000	108,000	150,000	140,000
Mortgage Assumed	-0-	40,000	-0-	40,000
Net Assets Invested	$148,000	$ 68,000	$150,000	$100,000

The noncash assets and liabilities are recorded at their fair values and each partner receives a capital credit equal to the fair value of the net assets invested as agreed to by the two partners. Note that the receivables transferred to the partnership are recorded at their face amount and that an allowance is established based on an estimate of the uncollectible accounts at the time the partnership is formed. The amounts recorded in the books of the partnership may differ from the book value amounts reported in the books of the separate businesses. For example, the equipment recorded at $51,000 in the entry just shown had a book value of $45,000 ($80,000 − $35,000). The use of fair value provides a more equitable measure of the amount invested by each partner and is a better measure of the acquisition cost to the partnership. Entries to record additional investments after the partnership is formed are based on the same concepts.

ALLOCATION OF PARTNERSHIP NET INCOME OR NET LOSS

Partners may agree to any allocation of profit or loss that they consider appropriate, and the allocation method should be included in the partnership agreement. In the absence of an agreement or if the partners are unable to reach an agreement, the law provides that profits are to be divided equally, regardless of the amount invested by the individual partners. Also, if a profit agreement is made but a loss agreement is not, a loss is allocated in the same way as a profit.

In establishing an equitable way to allocate partnership profit and loss, the partners should consider the three distinct elements that make up partnership income: (1) a return for personal services performed by the partners; (2) a return on the capital provided by the partners; and (3) a return for the business risks assumed by the partners. If profits are to be allocated equitably, the allocation method should take into consideration any difference in the amount of resources and services provided. For example, if one partner is more ac-

**Objective 4:
Allocation of
net income or
net loss**

tively involved in the management of the firm or if his or her services are more valuable to the firm, this fact should be recognized in the profit and loss agreement. Likewise, if the partners' capital investments are not equal, a provision to recognize these differences should be included in the agreement.

As noted, the objective of the profit and loss agreement is to reward each partner for resources and services provided to the firm. Some of the more common agreements are:

1. A fixed ratio.
2. A ratio based on capital balances.
3. Interest on capital investments, salaries to partners for services rendered for the partnership, and the remainder in a fixed ratio established by the partners.

In the following illustrations, it is assumed that Art Becker and Robin Cook formed the BC Partnership with capital investments of $150,000 and $100,000, respectively. At the end of the first year of operations, the *Income Summary* account had a credit balance of $60,000 (net income). To complete the closing process, the *Income Summary* account is closed to the individual partner's capital accounts. The amount credited to each capital account is dependent on the income allocation method agreed to by the partners.

FIXED RATIO

One of the simplest profit and loss agreements is for each partner to be allocated profits or losses based on some specified ratio. This method may be appropriate if the partners' contribution can be stated in terms of a fixed percentage. For example, assume that Becker and Cook agree to a 70:30 sharing of profits and losses, respectively. The allocation to each partner would then be computed as follows.

```
Becker: $60,000 × 70% = $42,000
Cook:   $60,000 × 30% =  18,000
Net income             $60,000
```

The entry to close the *Income Summary* account is:

Dec.	31	Income Summary	60,000	
		Becker, Capital		42,000
		Cook, Capital		18,000

Losses would be allocated using the same 70:30 ratio, unless a separate loss agreement is stated in the partnership contract.

RATIO BASED ON CAPITAL BALANCES

The allocation of profits based on the ratio of capital balances may result in an equitable allocation when invested capital is considered the most important factor and/or when the partnership operations require little of the partners' time. Since the capital balances normally change during the period, the agreement should specify whether the ratio is to be computed from the original investment, the beginning-of-year balances, end-of-year balances, or from an average of the balances.

The $60,000 net income is allocated as follows, assuming that the ratio is to be computed from the beginning-of-year balances.

	Capital Investment	Net Income Allocation	
Becker:	$150,000	($150,000/$250,000) × $60,000 =	$36,000
Cook:	100,000	($100,000/$250,000) × $60,000 =	24,000
Total capital	$250,000	Net income	$60,000

The entry to close the *Income Summary* account is:

Dec.	31	Income Summary	60,000	
		Becker, Capital		36,000
		Cook, Capital		24,000

INTEREST, SALARIES, AND THE REMAINDER IN A FIXED RATIO

Frequently, the individual partners make unequal capital investments, and the amount of time as well as the nature of services performed in the management function are not the same for each partner. Unless provided for in the partnership agreement, however, a partner is not legally entitled to receive either compensation for services performed for the partnership or interest on capital investments. Thus, if an equitable allocation of net income is to be made to compensate the partners for unequal contributions, a profit allocation method that contains a provision for interest and/or salaries must be included in the partnership agreement. To illustrate, assume that the partnership agreement of BC Partnership contains this profit agreement.

1. Each partner is to receive annual interest of 10% on their initial capital investment.
2. Art Becker and Robin Cook are to receive salaries per year of $18,000 and $10,000, respectively.
3. Any remaining net income or loss is to be shared equally. (Equal percentages are used here under the assumption that business risk is assumed equally by each partner.)

The allocation of $60,000 net income would be as follows.

	Becker	Cook	Total
Net income to be allocated			$60,000
Interest on capital investment			
$150,000 × 10%	$15,000		
$100,000 × 10%		$10,000	(25,000)
Remaining income			35,000
Salaries to partners	18,000	10,000	(28,000)
Remaining income			7,000
Remainder to be divided equally	3,500	3,500	(7,000)
Remaining net income			-0-
Net income allocated to partners	$36,500	$23,500	$60,000

The entry to transfer the balance in the *Income Summary* account to the partners' capital accounts is:

Dec.	31	Income Summary		60,000	
		Becker, Capital			36,500
		Cook, Capital			23,500

Note that the salary and interest provisions are not accounted for as expenses of the partnership. Rather, they are factors used in the allocation of net income.

A salary agreement is sometimes confused with an agreement that permits withdrawals of assets. Since the term "salary" is commonly understood to mean a cash payment for services rendered, it is important that the partners specify clearly their intentions as to whether the salary is part of the profit agreement or an agreement to permit withdrawals during the period. That is, the partners may agree that each is permitted to withdraw living expenses. The partners may further agree that the withdrawals are salaries taken in anticipation of profitable operations and are to be considered part of the profit allocation to be made at the end of the period. Or the partners may provide for a profit agreement that is independent of the withdrawal agreement. In the remainder of this chapter and in the end-of-chapter materials, a salary agreement is considered an allocation of profit or loss only.

In the preceding example, the net income of $60,000 was greater than the interest and salary allocations of $53,000. The same procedures are used to allocate net income that is less than the interest and salary allocation or to allocate a net loss if the partners fail to provide alternative allocations for these two possibilities in the partnership agreement. For example, assume that the net income for the period was $41,000 rather than $60,000. The allocation would then be as shown on page 543.

	Becker	Cook	Total
Net income to be allocated			$41,000
Interest on capital investment	$15,000	$10,000	(25,000)
Remaining income			16,000
Salaries to partners	18,000	10,000	(28,000)
Excess allocated			(12,000)
Excess allocated equally	(6,000)	(6,000)	12,000
Remaining net income			-0-
Net income allocated to partners	$27,000	$14,000	$41,000

If there had been a loss of $12,000, the allocation of $53,000 for interest and salaries still follows the procedures shown, and the deficiency allocation of $65,000 ($53,000 + $12,000) would be allocated equally to the partners. Thus, the capital account of Becker would be credited for $500 and Cook's capital account would be debited for $12,500 as shown below.

	Becker	Cook	Total
Net loss to be allocated			($12,000)
Interest on capital investment	$15,000	$10,000	(25,000)
Excess allocated			(37,000)
Salaries to partners	18,000	10,000	(28,000)
Excess allocated			(65,000)
Excess allocated equally	(32,500)	(32,500)	65,000
Remaining excess			-0-
Net loss allocated to partners	$ 500	($12,500)	($12,000)

To avoid the above allocations when the net income is insufficient to cover the interest and salary allocations, the partnership agreement may contain an alternative allocation.

FINANCIAL STATEMENTS FOR A PARTNERSHIP

The income statement, balance sheet, and statement of changes in financial position for a partnership are prepared in much the same manner as they are for other forms of business organizations. The following items, which are specifically related to partnership reporting should be noted.

1. Each individual partner's equity in the business is reported separately on the balance sheet or in a separate schedule.
2. Salaries authorized for each partner and interest on capital investments are not reported as expenses but are recognized as allocations of net income.
3. There is no income tax expense, since a partnership is required to file only an information return.
4. The profit or loss allocation for the period is normally disclosed in the

Figure 14–2
Statement of
Changes in Partners'
Capital

BC PARTNERSHIP
Statement of Changes in Partners' Capital
For the Year Ended December 31, 1987

	Becker	Cook	Total
Capital balances, January 1, 1987	$150,000	$100,000	$250,000
Add: Additional investment*	10,000	-0-	10,000
Net income allocation	36,000	24,000	60,000
	196,000	124,000	320,000
Less: Withdrawals*	14,000	14,000	28,000
Capital balances, December 31, 1987	$182,000	$110,000	$292,000

*Additional investments and withdrawals amounts are assumed.

financial statements, either on the face of the income statement or in a supplementary schedule.

5. A statement, called a **statement of changes in partners' capital,** is prepared to report the changes in partners' capital that occurred during the period.

The statement of changes in partners' capital may appear as shown in Figure 14–2 for the BC Partnership.

CHANGES IN THE MEMBERS OF A PARTNERSHIP

It was noted earlier that one of the characteristics of the partnership form of business organization is its limited life. **Dissolution** of a partnership occurs when there is a change in the membership of the partners. There are many causes for dissolution of a partnership. They include the admission of a new partner, the withdrawal of a partner, the death of a partner, or the bankruptcy of a partner or the partnership.

In some cases, dissolution may lead to the operations of the partnership being terminated, such as when the partnership is bankrupt. In other cases, the old partnership may be dissolved, but the existing partners may continue the normal operations without any visible interruption of the firm's operations. For example, partners of an existing partnership may agree to admit an additional partner, or the surviving partners may continue to operate the firm after the death of one of the partners. Because the old partnership is dissolved, however, a new partnership agreement should be drafted.

RECORDING THE ADMISSION OF A NEW PARTNER

**Objective 5:
Admitting a
new partner**

A new partner may be admitted to an existing partnership by purchasing all or part of an interest directly from one or more existing partners or by making an investment in the partnership itself. In the first instance, a current member of the firm is selling all or part of an interest in the partnership. The net assets of the firm are not changed, since this is a personal transaction between individuals. If an investment is made in the partnership, however, the net assets and total capital of the firm are increased by the amount of the investment.

A partner cannot be prevented from selling his or her interest in a partnership, but the remaining partners must agree to the transfer of interest before the buyer can participate in management of the partnership. The UPA provides that the buyer of a partnership interest acquires the same right to share in profits and assets upon liquidation that the selling partner would otherwise be entitled to.

Admission of a New Partner by Purchasing an Existing Interest

When an individual buys an interest in a partnership by making payment directly to a current partner or partners, the only entry required in the partnership books is one to transfer the capital interest acquired from the selling partner to the buying partner. To illustrate, assume that Art Becker and Robin Cook are partners with current capital balances of $30,000 and $50,000, respectively. Their profit and loss sharing ratio is 60:40. Becker agreed to sell one-half of his capital interest to Mary Dart for $25,000. Cook approved of the sale and transfer of the interest to Dart. The credit to Dart's capital account is computed as follows.

Capital interest of Becker	$30,000
Percentage interest acquired by Dart	50%
Capital transfer to Dart	$15,000

The entry to record the transfer of the capital interest is:

May	6	Becker, Capital	15,000	
		Dart, Capital		15,000

Note that the capital transferred to Dart is one-half of Becker's current capital balance. The entry is the same, regardless of the amount paid by Dart. Note also that the net assets and total capital of the partnership are the same ($80,000) after the transfer as before the transfer because the cash transfer is between the partners as individuals and is not recorded in the partnership books.

Admission of a New Partner by Investing Assets in the Partnership

An individual may also gain admission to an existing partnership by investing assets in the business. A new partner may be admitted because the partnership is in need of additional cash (for example, the cash may be needed to finance expansion of the firm's operations or to take care of current operating needs). Or the new partner may be bringing some particularly needed talent, such as managerial skill, to the partnership. When cash or other assets are invested in the partnership, total assets and owners' equity of the partnership are increased by the amount invested.

To illustrate, assume again that Becker and Cook are partners with current capital account balances of $30,000 and $50,000, respectively. Their profit and loss sharing ratio is 60:40. Dart agrees to invest $20,000 for a one-fifth interest in the firm. Dart's capital interest is computed as follows.

Becker, Capital	$ 30,000
Cook, Capital	50,000
Investment by Dart	20,000
Total capital interest in the new partnership	100,000
Percentage capital interest acquired by Dart	20%
Capital interest of Dart	$ 20,000

The entry to record Dart's investment is:

May	6	Cash		20,000	
			Dart, Capital		20,000

After the entry is posted, the total capital is $100,000, of which Dart has a one-fifth interest of $20,000. If Dart had invested noncash assets, both the assets and the capital interest should be recorded at the fair value of the assets invested.

Although Dart has a one-fifth interest in the net assets of the firm, her right to share in profits of the new partnership may be be less than, equal to, or greater than one-fifth. As already pointed out, the profit-sharing ratio is a separate agreement and is not necessarily related to the capital interest. Thus, for the protection of the partners, a new profit and loss agreement should be determined and included in the partnership agreement.

A Bonus to the Old Partners. In the preceding illustration, Dart invested $20,000 in assets and received a $20,000 capital interest in the partnership. In some situations, an incoming partner may invest assets that have a fair value greater than the capital interest received. The difference between the two is called a bonus to the old partners and is credited to their capital accounts in the profit sharing ratio that existed prior to the admittance of the new partner. The incoming partner may be willing to give such a bonus to the old partners because the partnership has been earning above-normal profits and he or she wants to acquire the right to share in them; or the new partner may perceive other advantages in the partnership operations.[2]

Assume that Becker and Cook share profits in the ratio of 60:40 and currently report capital balances of $30,000 and $50,000, respectively. Dart agrees to invest $40,000 cash in the partnership for a one-fourth interest in capital. Dart's capital interest may then be computed as:

Capital interest of old partners ($30,000 + $50,000)	$ 80,000
Investment by Dart	40,000
Total capital interest in the new partnership	120,000
Percentage capital interest acquired by Dart	25%
Capital interest of Dart	30,000
Investment by Dart	40,000
Bonus to old partners	$ 10,000

---

[2]Another method, called the goodwill method, is sometimes used to record the admission of a new partner or the withdrawal of an existing partner. This method is covered in more advanced accounting courses.

Allocation of bonus to the old partners:

Becker:	$10,000 × 60% =	$ 6,000
Cook:	$10,000 × 40% =	4,000
Bonus to old partner		$10,000

Note that the $10,000 bonus is allocated to Becker and Cook in their profit and loss sharing ratio.

The entry to record the investment by Dart is:

May	6	Cash	40,000	
		Becker, Capital		6,000
		Cook, Capital		4,000
		Dart, Capital		30,000

After the investment, Dart has a capital interest equal to one-fourth of the net assets of $120,000 and the old partners have the remaining three-fourths interest of $90,000 (Becker, $36,000; Cook, $54,000).

A Bonus to the New Partner.

Sometimes a partnership needs additional working capital, or the new partner possesses some skills or business contacts needed by the firm. In such cases, the old partners may be willing to grant the incoming partner a capital interest greater than the fair value of the assets invested, that is, they may grant a bonus to the new partner.

To illustrate, assume the same facts as previously stated, except that Dart is to invest $40,000 for a one-half capital interest in the firm. The bonus is computed as:

Capital interest of old partners	$ 80,000
Investment by Dart	40,000
Total capital interest in the new partnership	120,000
Percentage capital interest acquired by Dart	50%
Capital interest of Dart	60,000
Investment by Dart	40,000
Bonus to the new partner	$ 20,000

Allocation of the bonus granted to the new partner:

Becker:	$20,000 × 60% =	$12,000
Cook:	$20,000 × 40% =	8,000
Bonus to new partner		$20,000

The entry to record the admission of the new partner is:

May	6	Cash	40,000	
		Becker, Capital	12,000	
		Cook, Capital	8,000	
		Dart, Capital		60,000

Note once again that the bonus of $20,000 to the new partner is debited to the old partners capital accounts according to their old profit and loss ratio.

The capital account balances are as follows, after the entry is posted to the accounts.

	Becker, Capital				Cook, Capital		
5/6	12,000		30,000	5/6	8,000		50,000
		Bal.	18,000			Bal.	42,000

	Dart, Capital	
	5/6	60,000

The old partners' total equity in the new partnership is $60,000, or one-half of $120,000. Dart has the remaining one-half interest of $60,000.

WITHDRAWAL OF A PARTNER

A partner wishing to withdraw from a partnership may sell his or her interest to an outside party or to one or more of the existing partners. In such cases, payment is made from the personal funds of the buying party or parties and goes directly to the withdrawing partner. The only entry required in the partnership books is to transfer the amount in the capital account of the withdrawing partner to the capital accounts of the buying party or parties. The transaction does not affect the assets of the partnership. In other cases, the equity interest of the withdrawing partner may be settled by withdrawing partnership assets.

The legal issues related to the withdrawal of a partner are rather complex and should be reviewed carefully by the parties involved. For example, the retiring partner may still have some responsibility for the liabilities existing at the time of withdrawal. Furthermore, to avoid as much conflict as possible, the partnership agreement should set out the procedures to be followed and the method for determining settlement. For example, the agreement may require an audit of the accounting records and a revaluation of assets and liabilities before a partner withdraws.

WITHDRAWAL OF ASSETS FROM THE PARTNERSHIP

In most cases, capital account balances do not reflect each partner's interest in the fair value of the net assets. To provide an equitable payment to a withdrawing partner, the partnership assets and liabilities should be revalued. Normally, any increase or decrease in values is allocated to the partners in their profit and loss ratio. The withdrawing partner is often permitted to withdraw assets or accept a note payable from the new partnership equal to his or her revalued capital interest.

Assume that Art Becker, Robin Cook, and Mary Dart are partners in the BCD Partnership, sharing profits 40:30:30, respectively. The partners agree that Cook is to retire from the partnership. The partnership agreement requires the revaluation of assets and liabilities on retirement of a partner and provides for the retiring partner to withdraw cash from the firm equal to his or her revalued capital account balance. Furthermore, if the cash balance is insufficient to settle the capital interest and leave enough cash to operate the business, the withdrawing partner is to receive promissory notes for the balance with a stated rate of interest equal to the current prime interest rate. A balance sheet for the BCD Partnership before the accounts are revalued is:

Cash	$ 25,000	Accounts payable	$ 35,000
Accounts receivable	20,000	Becker, Capital	30,000
Inventories	40,000	Cook, Capital	40,000
Plant assets (net)	70,000	Dart, Capital	50,000
Total	$155,000	Total	$155,000

Appraisals indicate that the inventories are understated by $3,000, due to the use of the LIFO inventory method, and plant assets are understated by $20,000. In addition, there is $8,000 of unrecorded accounts payable. The revaluation of the accounts and the changes in the capital accounts are computed as follows.

Gain on revaluation of assets ($3,000 + $20,000)	$23,000
Loss on revaluation of liabilities	8,000
Net increase in net assets and capital	$15,000

Allocation to partners:

Becker:	$15,000 × 40% =	$ 6,000
Cook:	$15,000 × 30% =	4,500
Dart:	$15,000 × 30% =	4,500
Increase in capital		$15,000

Note that the net gain resulting from the revaluation of the firm's assets and liabilities is allocated in the profit and loss sharing ratio.

Book Value of Assets Withdrawn is Equal to Capital Balance

The entries to record the revaluations and the withdrawal, assuming that Cook agrees to take cash of $12,000 ($13,000 is needed to operate the business) and the balance in a promissory note, are:

Nov.	5	Inventories	3,000	
		Plant Assets	20,000	
		Accounts Payable		8,000
		Becker, Capital		6,000
		Cook, Capital		4,500
		Dart, Capital		4,500
		To record the revaluation of assets and liabilities prior to withdrawal of a partner.		

5	Cook, Capital ($40,000 + $4,500)		44,500	
	Cash			12,000
	Notes Payable			32,500
	To record the withdrawal of Cook from the partnership.			

A balance sheet after these entries are posted would show:

Cash	$ 13,000	Notes payable	$ 32,500
Accounts receivable	20,000	Accounts payable	43,000
Inventories	43,000	Becker, Capital	36,000
Plant assets (net)	90,000	Dart, Capital	54,500
Total	$166,000	Total	$166,000

Since a new partnership is now formed, Becker and Dart should draft a new partnership agreement.

In this example, the book value of the assets and note received by Cook were equal to the book value of her revalued capital interest. Sometimes, however, a withdrawing partner may receive assets that have a value greater than the book value of his or her capital interest. This could happen because a profitable firm may be worth more than the fair value of its recorded net assets, or the continuing partners may be anxious to rid themselves of a specific partner. On the other hand, a partner may be anxious to withdraw from a partnership and may, therefore, be willing to receive assets that have a value less than the book value of his or her interest. When the book value of the net assets withdrawn does not equal the book value of the capital interest, the difference may be accounted for as a bonus to the remaining or withdrawing partner that is assigned to the remaining partners in their relative profit and loss ratio.

Book Value of Assets Withdrawn Is Greater than Capital Balance

To illustrate the withdrawal of assets with greater value than the book value interest, assume the same facts as in the previous example, but that Cook is to receive $12,000 in cash and a promissory note for $39,500 for her $44,500 capital interest. A bonus to Cook of $7,000 is computed as follows.

Cash	$12,000
Notes payable	39,500
Total consideration received	51,500
Book value of capital interest ($40,000 + $4,500)	44,500
Bonus to withdrawing partner	$ 7,000

The bonus is charged against the capital accounts of Becker and Dart in their profit and loss sharing ratio of 4:3. Thus Becker's capital account will be debited for $4,000 ($7,000 × 4/7), and Dart's capital account will be debited for $3,000 ($7,000 × 3/7).

The entries to record the revaluations and withdrawal are:

Nov.	5	Inventories	3,000	
		Plant Assets	20,000	
		Accounts Payable		8,000
		Becker, Capital		6,000
		Cook, Capital		4,500
		Dart, Capital		4,500
		To record the revaluation of assets and		
		liabilities prior to withdrawal of a		
		partner.		
	5	Cook, Capital	44,500	
		Becker, Capital	4,000	
		Dart, Capital	3,000	
		Cash		12,000
		Notes Payable		39,500
		To record the withdrawal of Cook from the		
		partnership.		

Book Value of Assets Withdrawn Is Less than Capital Interest

Assume now that Cook is anxious to withdraw and agrees to take a payment of $12,000 in cash and a $25,500 promissory note in settlement of her $44,500 capital interest. In this case, Cook grants a bonus of $7,000 to Becker and Dart. The entry to record the withdrawal is:

Nov.	5	Cook, Capital	44,500	
		Becker, Capital		4,000
		Dart, Capital		3,000
		Cash		12,000
		Notes Payable		25,500
		To record the withdrawal of Cook from the		
		partnership.		

In this case, Cook is receiving a settlement less than the book value of her equity interest. The bonus is credited to the capital accounts of the remaining partners in their profit and loss sharing ratio of 4:3.

DEATH OF A PARTNER

A partnership is dissolved upon the death of a partner and the deceased partner's estate is entitled to receive his or her current equity interest in the partnership assets. Determining a partner's equity interest in the firm can result in a number of controversies. To avoid litigation, the partnership agreement should contain procedures for determining a deceased partner's equity interest and the method of settlement. In the absence of specific provisions, the surviving partners and the executor of the estate must negotiate a settlement.

To determine a partner's equity interest at the time of death, the assets and liabilities are normally adjusted to their fair values and the accounts are closed to determine the net income or loss earned since the end of the last fiscal period. Although the old partnership is dissolved, the agreement usually provides that operations do not terminate but are continued by the surviving partners. If so, the method of settlement should be specified in the partnership agreement. Entries to record the settlement, either by the distribution of partnership assets to the estate or by the direct payment to the estate by those who purchase the interest, are similar to those of earlier illustrations.

PARTNERSHIP LIQUIDATION

Objective 7: Liquidation of a partnership

When a partnership is liquidated, the operations of the firm are discontinued and the business ceases to exist. The partnership agreement should contain procedures to be followed in completing the liquidation of the partnership. Before the firm begins the liquidation process, the partnership generally discontinues its normal operations and the accounts are adjusted and closed. The net income or loss (the balance in the *Income Summary* account) is allocated to the partners' capital accounts in accordance with their profit and loss ratio. As a result, the asset, liability, and capital accounts only will contain a balance.

The **liquidation** process involves the following steps.

1. Noncash assets are sold. This process of converting noncash assets into cash is called **realization.** If the sales price of an asset is greater than its book value, there is a gain from the realization; if the sales price is less than book value there is a loss from realization. A gain or loss on the sale of partnership assets is allocated to the partners in their profit and loss ratio.
2. As cash becomes available, it must be applied first to the payment of partnership liabilities.
3. Remaining assets are distributed to the partners according to their *capital balances*.

The partnership is terminated as a business when the liquidation process is completed.

To illustrate the accounting for a partnership liquidation, assume that BCD Partnership reported the trial balance in Figure 14–3 immediately after the closing process had been completed. Becker, Cook, and Dart share profits and losses in the ratio 50:30:20, respectively. Although the liquidation may result in a variety of financial outcomes, accounting for the liquidation will be described based on two examples: (1) all noncash assets are sold for $190,000; and (2) all noncash assets are sold for $80,000.

CAPITAL BALANCES SUFFICIENT TO ABSORB SHARE OF LOSSES

A schedule summarizing the transactions related to the partnership liquidation is shown in Figure 14–4, assuming that the noncash assets were sold for $190,000. In the liquidation schedule, a column is established for cash, non-

Figure 14–3
Partnership Trial
Balance

BCD PARTNERSHIP
Trial Balance
January 2, 1987

Account Title	Debit	Credit
Cash	$ 30,000	
Accounts Receivable	60,000	
Inventory	80,000	
Plant Assets (net)	130,000	
Accounts Payable		$ 50,000
Notes Payable		30,000
Becker, Capital		120,000
Cook, Capital		70,000
Dart, Capital		30,000
Totals	$300,000	$300,000

cash assets, liabilities, each partner's capital account, and loss or gain from
realization. The transactions entered in Figure 14–4 must be recorded in the
journal and posted to the ledger.

The sequence of events entered in Figure 14–4 is as follows.

1. The noncash assets are sold for $190,000 and the resulting loss from
realization is recorded. The loss is computed as follows.

Figure 14–4
Schedule of Partnership Liquidation

BCD PARTNERSHIP
Schedule of Partnership Liquidation
January 2, 1987

Explanation	Cash	Noncash Assets	= Liabilities	Becker	Cook	Dart	Loss or (Gain) From Realization of Assets
Balances before realization	$ 30,000	$270,000	($80,000)	($120,000)	($70,000)	($30,000)	
(1) Sale of noncash assets	190,000	(270,000)					$80,000
Balances	220,000	-0-	(80,000)	(120,000)	(70,000)	(30,000)	80,000
(2) Allocation of loss from realization				40,000	24,000	16,000	(80,000)
Balances	220,000	-0-	(80,000)	(80,000)	(46,000)	(14,000)	-0-
(3) Payment of liabilities	(80,000)		80,000				
Balances	140,000	-0-	-0-	(80,000)	(46,000)	(14,000)	-0-
(4) Distribution of cash to partners	(140,000)			80,000	46,000	14,000	
Balances	-0-	-0-	-0-	-0-	-0-	-0-	-0-

*Figures enclosed in parentheses indicate that an account has a credit balance or a credit is posted to the account.

Book value of noncash assets sold:	
Accounts Receivable	$ 60,000
Inventory	80,000
Plant Assets	130,000
Total book value of noncash assets	270,000
Sales price	190,000
Loss from realization	$ 80,000

2. The loss from realization is allocated to the partners according to their loss sharing ratio of 50:30:20, as follows.

	Allocation of Loss	**Amount allocated**
Becker	$80,000 × 50%	$40,000
Cook	$80,000 × 30%	24,000
Dart	$80,000 × 20%	16,000
Loss from realization		$80,000

3. Partnership liabilities are paid before assets are distributed to partners.
4. Cash is distributed to partners to satisfy their capital claims against the partnership assets.

The following entries are made to record the liquidation of the BCD Partnership. For reference purposes, the entries are numbered to correspond to the transactions numbered in the schedule of partnership liquidation.

1.	Jan.	2	Cash	190,000	
			Loss or Gain From Realization	80,000	
			Accounts Receivable		60,000
			Inventory		80,000
			Plant Assets		130,000
			To record the sale of all noncash assets.		
2.		2	Becker, Capital	40,000	
			Cook, Capital	24,000	
			Dart, Capital	16,000	
			Loss or Gain From Realization		80,000
			To allocate the loss on the sale of		
			noncash assets.		

If the assets had been sold at a gain, the *Loss or Gain From Realization* account would be credited in the first entry. The *Loss or Gain From Realization* account is a nominal account used after the partnership ceases its normal operations. The account is closed directly to the partners' capital accounts, rather than to the *Income Summary* account.

3.		2	Accounts Payable	50,000	
			Notes Payable	30,000	
			Cash		80,000
			To pay creditors in full.		

4.	2	Becker, Capital	80,000	
		Cook, Capital	46,000	
		Dart, Capital	14,000	
		Cash		140,000
		To record the distribution of cash to		
		partners.		

Note that the *amount of cash distributed to the partners is equal to the balances remaining in their respective capital accounts,* rather than in the profit and loss ratio. The distribution is a final settlement with the partners for their capital interest, as shown by the balance in their capital accounts, rather than an allocation of profit or loss. After the entries shown above are posted, all accounts in the partnership books will have a zero balance.

A PARTNER WITH A DEBIT CAPITAL BALANCE

In the preceding illustration, each partner's capital balance was sufficient to absorb his or her share of the $80,000 loss. In some cases, however, the allocation of the loss may result in a debit balance in one or more capital accounts. A debit capital balance is referred to as a **deficit** or **deficiency.** If a partner has a debit capital balance, the partnership has a claim against the partner for the amount of the debit balance. A partner must invest cash in the partnership to cover the deficit to the extent that he or she has personal assets to do so. The amount of cash invested is then credited to the partner's capital account. Any remaining deficit is written off to the other partners' capital accounts in their relative profit and loss sharing ratio. Available cash is then distributed to the partners, based on their capital account balances.

To illustrate, assume: (1) that the noncash assets of BCD Partnership were sold for $80,000; and (2) that all of the partners have sufficient personal assets to cover any deficit resulting from the liquidation. The liquidation is summarized in the schedule of partnership liquidation shown in Figure 14–5. The sequence of events is:

1. The noncash assets are sold for $80,000 and the resulting loss from realization of $190,000 ($270,000 book value − $80,000 sales price) is recorded.
2. The loss from realization is allocated to the partners as follows.

Becker:	$190,000 × 50% =	$ 95,000
Cook:	$190,000 × 30% =	57,000
Dart:	$190,000 × 20% =	38,000
Loss from realization		$190,000

3. Partnership liabilities are paid before assets are distributed to the partners.
4. Allocation of the loss from realization results in an $8,000 debit balance in Dart's capital account. Dart covers the deficit by investing $8,000 in the partnership.
5. Cash is distributed to the other two partners to settle their capital claims against the partnership assets.

BCD PARTNERSHIP
Schedule of Partnership Liquidation
January 2, 1987

Explanation	Cash	Noncash Assets	= Liabilities	Capital Balances*			Loss or (Gain) From Realization of Assets
				Becker	Cook	Dart	
Balances before realization	$ 30,000	$270,000	($80,000)	($120,000)	($70,000)	($30,000)	
(1) Sale of noncash assets	80,000	(270,000)					$190,000
Balances	110,000	-0-	(80,000)	(120,000)	(70,000)	(30,000)	190,000
(2) Allocation of loss from realization				95,000	57,000	38,000	(190,000)
Balances	110,000	-0-	(80,000)	(25,000)	(13,000)	8,000	-0-
(3) Payment of liabilities	(80,000)		80,000				
Balances	30,000	-0-	-0-	(25,000)	(13,000)	8,000	-0-
(4) Cash investment by Dart	8,000					(8,000)	
Balances	38,000	-0-	-0-	(25,000)	(13,000)	-0-	-0-
(5) Distribution of cash to partners	(38,000)			25,000	13,000		
Balances	-0-	-0-	-0-	-0-	-0-	-0-	-0-

*Figures enclosed in parentheses indicate that an account has a credit balance or a credit is posted to the account.

Figure 14–5
Schedule of Partnership Liquidation

Journal entries to record the liquidation are as follows.

1.	Jan.	2	Cash	80,000	
			Loss or Gain From Realization	190,000	
			Accounts Receivable		60,000
			Inventory		80,000
			Plant Assets		130,000
			To record the sale of all noncash assets.		
2.		2	Becker, Capital	95,000	
			Cook, Capital	57,000	
			Dart, Capital	38,000	
			Loss or Gain From Realization		190,000
			To allocate the loss on the sale of		
			noncash assets.		
3.		2	Accounts Payable	50,000	
			Notes Payable	30,000	
			Cash		80,000
			To pay creditors in full.		
4.		2	Cash	8,000	
			Dart, Capital		8,000
			To record additional investment by Dart.		

5.	2	Becker, Capital	25,000	
		Cook, Capital	13,000	
		Cash		38,000
		To record the distribution of the		
		remaining cash to partners.		

If Dart is unable to invest the $8,000 in the firm, the deficit is written off to the other partners' capital accounts in their respective profit and loss sharing ratio, 5:3 in this case. The allocation of Dart's deficit would be:

	Loss Ratio	Allocation of Deficit
Becker	5	5/8 × $8,000 = $5,000
Cook	3	3/8 × $8,000 = 3,000
	8	$8,000

The liquidation would then proceed as shown below.

			Capital Balances		
Explanation	Cash	=	Becker	Cook	Dart
Balances after payment of cash to creditors— (See Figure 14–5)	$30,000		($25,000)	($13,000)	$8,000
(4) Allocation of Dart's deficit			5,000	3,000	(8,000)
Balances	30,000		(20,000)	(10,000)	-0-
(5) Distribution of cash to partners	(30,000)		20,000	10,000	
Balances	-0-		-0-	-0-	-0-

The entries to record the allocation of the deficit balance and the final cash distribution to the partners are:

Jan.	2	Becker, Capital	5,000	
		Cook, Capital	3,000	
		Dart, Capital		8,000
		To allocate deficit in Dart's capital		
		account.		
	2	Becker, Capital	20,000	
		Cook, Capital	10,000	
		Cash		30,000
		To distribute cash to partners.		

Note again that the amount distributed to each partner is determined by the balances in their respective capital accounts.

GLOSSARY

DEFICIT (DEFICIENCY). A debit balance in the partner's capital account (p. 555).

DISSOLUTION. A change in the members making up the ownership of a partnership resulting from such causes as admission of a new partner, withdrawal of a partner, and death of a partner (p. 544).

GENERAL PARTNERSHIP. A partnership in which each partner is individually liable for the partnership liabilities (p. 535).

LIMITED PARTNERSHIP. A partnership in which one or more of the partners have limited their liability for partnership liabilities to the amount of their investment (p. 535).

LIQUIDATION. The termination of a business by the sale of noncash assets, payment of creditors, and distribution of the remaining cash to the owners (p. 552).

MUTUAL AGENCY. A characteristic of a partnership whereby each partner is an agent for the partnership and can bind the partnership to a contract if acting within the normal scope of the business (p. 536).

PARTNERSHIP. An association of two or more persons to carry on as co-owners a business for profit (p. 534).

PARTNERSHIP AGREEMENT (PARTNERSHIP CONTRACT, ARTICLES OF PARTNERSHIP). The contract or agreement made among the partners to form and operate a partnership (p. 537).

REALIZATION. The conversion of noncash assets into cash (p. 552).

STATEMENT OF CHANGES IN PARTNERS' CAPITAL. A financial statement that shows the changes in each partner's capital interest during the period (p. 544).

UNIFORM PARTNERSHIP ACT (UPA). A statute adopted by most states to govern the formation, operation, and liquidation of a partnership (p. 534).

UNLIMITED LIABILITY. A characteristic of a partnership whereby each general partner is responsible for all debts of the partnership (p. 535).

DISCUSSION QUESTIONS

1. Define a partnership and list some of the advantages of the partnership form of business organization.
2. A partner withdrew $20,000 from the partnership during the year. His share of partnership net income is $17,000. How much income from the partnership must he report on his individual income tax return?
3. Define the terms "unlimited liability" and "mutual agency," as they apply to a partnership.
4. Ray sells his partnership interest to Henry, even though the other partners do not agree to admit Henry as a partner. Does Henry have the right to take over Ray's position as manager of the business? Is Henry entitled to a share of the profits, and if so, how large a share?
5. Mark invests land with a book value of $75,000 and a fair value of $95,000 in a new partnership being formed. The partnership assumes a $35,000 mortgage on the land. What is Mark's capital interest in the partnership, assuming that he is to receive a capital credit equal to his net investment?

6. Their partnership agreement provides that Tom and Sue are to share profits in a 60:40 ratio, but does not mention losses. How would a $20,000 net loss be allocated?

7. Jan and Don receive salaries of $15,000 and $12,000, respectively. They allocate the remainder of the partnership income in a 40:60 ratio. How would they share a net income of $22,000?

8. Keith has a $20,000 capital balance when he sells his partnership interest to Scott for $25,000. What is Scott's capital balance?

9. Mary and Kay have partnership capital balances of $50,000 and $70,000, respectively, when they agree to give Larry a one-fourth capital interest in the partnership upon his investment of $35,000. How much is the bonus, and is it credited to Larry's account or to the accounts of Mary and Kay?

10. What is the purpose of revaluing assets and liabilities before a partner withdraws from the partnership?

11. In the liquidation process, how is a gain or loss on the sale of the assets shared by the partners?

60/40

12. Jerry and Ken share profits and losses in the ratio of 30:70. They have capital balances of $24,000 and $50,000, respectively, when they decide to liquidate. After they sell all noncash assets and pay the creditors, there is a cash balance of $100,000. How should the cash be distributed between the partners?

13. Explain how liquidation procedures can cause a partner to have a debit capital balance. What obligations does a partner with a debit balance have to the partnership?

EXERCISES

Exercise 14-1 Partnership Formation

Martha Layman and Jane Brawley agree to combine their businesses and form a partnership. The fair value and the book value of the assets invested by each partner and the liabilities assumed by the partnership are shown here.

	Martha Layman		Jane Brawley	
	Book Value	Fair Value	Book Value	Fair Value
Cash	$ 7,500	$ 7,500	$ 4,200	$ 4,200
Accounts Receivable	6,000	5,800	5,200	5,100
Inventory	16,800	15,500	10,700	13,000
Equipment	50,000	41,000	45,000	40,000
Accumulated Depreciation—Equipment	(20,000)	—	(25,000)	—
Accounts Payable	6,800	6,800	9,300	9,300

Required:

Prepare separate journal entries to record the initial investment of each partner, assuming that assets are accepted by the firm at fair value and that each partner is to receive a capital credit equal to the amount of the net assets invested by that partner.

Exercise 14-2 Allocation of Net Income

Walters and Harris form a partnership by investing $70,000 and $50,000, respectively. The partnership has a net income of $30,000 for the first year.   18000

Required:

A. Prepare the journal entry to record the allocation of net income under each of the following assumptions.

18000

12000

1. Walters and Harris agree to a 60:40 sharing of profits.
2. The partners agree to share profits in the ratio of their original capital investments.
3. The partners agree to a $12,000 per year salary allowance to Walters and a $6,000 per year salary allowance to Harris. Each partner is entitled to 8% interest on his original investment, and any remaining income is to be shared equally.

B. Repeat requirement (3), assuming that the partnership has a net income of $19,000 for the first year.

Exercise 14-3 Admission of a New Partner

Randall and Hopkins are partners having capital balances of $100,000 and $60,000, respectively. They share profits in the ratio of 70:30. They agree to admit White to the partnership for an investment of machinery worth $40,000.

Required:

Prepare the journal entry to record White's investment under each of the following conditions.

A. White receives a one-fourth capital interest.
B. White receives a one-fifth capital interest.
C. White receives a one-sixth capital interest.

Exercise 14-4 Admission of a New Partner

Randy Bryan and Laura Myers are partners. Their respective capital balances are $150,000 and $187,500, and they share profits and losses equally.

Required:

Prepare the journal entry to record the admission of Sharon Grand into the partnership under each of the following conditions.

A. Sharon acquires one-fourth of Randy's capital interest by paying $45,000 directly to him.
B. Sharon acquires one-fifth of both Randy's and Laura's capital interests. Randy receives $30,000 and Laura receives $35,000 directly from Sharon.
C. Sharon acquires a one-third interest for a $150,000 cash investment in the partnership.

Exercise 14-5 Withdrawal of a Partner

Greg Fall, Ed Mall, and Frank Stall are partners who share profits and losses in a 5:3:2 ratio. They have respective capital balances of $100,000, $80,000, and $70,000 at the time of Fall's withdrawal from the partnership.

Required:

Prepare the journal entry to record the withdrawal of Fall under each of the following assumptions.

A. Fall receives $100,000 in cash.
B. Fall receives $120,000 in cash.
C. Fall receives $80,000 in cash.

Exercise 14-6   **Partnership Liquidation**

Bart, Collins, and Masters are partners with capital accounts of $30,000, $22,000, and $43,000, respectively. They share profits and losses in the ratio of 30:30:40. When the partners decide to liquidate, the business has $25,000 in cash, noncash assets totaling $110,000, and $40,000 in liabilities. The noncash assets are sold for $140,000, and the creditors are paid.

Required:
A. Prepare a schedule of partnership liquidation.
B. Prepare journal entries to record each of the following transactions.
   1. The sale of the noncash assets.
   2. The allocation of the gain or loss from the sale of the assets.
   3. The payment to the creditors.
   4. The distribution of cash to the partners.

Exercise 14-7   **Partnership Liquidation—Partner with a Deficit Balance**

The partnership of Cherry, Drew, and Hardy is being liquidated. After the noncash assets are sold and the creditors are paid, the business has $85,000 cash. Cherry has a $50,000 credit capital balance, Drew's account has a $55,000 credit balance, and Hardy's capital account has a debit balance of $20,000. The partners share profits and losses in the ratio of 40:40:20.

Required:
A. Assuming that Hardy pays the money he owes to the partnership, prepare the journal entries to record Hardy's payment and the distribution of the cash to the partners.
B. Assuming that Hardy does not pay any of the money he owes, prepare the journal entries to record the allocation of Hardy's debit balance and the distribution of the cash.

Exercise 14-8   **Recording Partnership Transactions**

Warren and Fisher had capital balances of $50,000 and $30,000, respectively, on January 1, 1987. They completed the following transactions during the year.

March	8	Warren withdrew $15,000 in cash from the partnership. Fisher withdrew $3,000 of inventory.
July	27	Warren invested equipment valued at $10,000. Fisher invested $5,000 cash.
Dec.	31	The net income of $25,000 was allocated in the ratio of 60% to Warren and 40% to Fisher.
	31	The partners' withdrawal accounts were closed.

Required:
A. Prepare journal entries to record each of these transactions.
B. Prepare a statement of changes in partners' capital for the year ended December 31, 1987.

PROBLEMS

Problem 14-1   **Partnership Formation**

Debra Brown and Bill Thomas formed a partnership on September 1, 1986. They agreed to share profits and losses in the ratio of 80:20. Brown invested $60,000 in cash and land worth $140,000. Assets invested in the partnership and liabilities assumed by the partnership from Thomas's business are shown here at both book and fair value.

	Book Value	Fair Value
Cash	$ 5,000	$ 5,000
Accounts Receivable	4,000	3,700
Inventory	9,000	12,000
Equipment	34,000	36,000
Accounts Payable	8,000	8,000
Note Payable (Due Feb. 1, 1987)	3,000	3,000

During the first year, Brown invested an additional $5,000 in cash. The partnership's net income was $20,000. Brown withdrew $3,000, and Thomas withdrew $6,000.

Required:
A. Prepare the journal entries to record each partner's initial investment.
B. Prepare the partnership's balance sheet as of September 1, 1986.
C. Prepare a statement of changes in partners' capital for the year ended August 31, 1987.

Problem 14-2 Allocation of Net Income and Net Loss

Jill Wood and Henry Allen have agreed to form a partnership. Jill is to invest $120,000, and Henry is to invest $80,000. They are considering each of the following methods of allocating profits and losses.

1. Allocate in the ratio of 55:45.
2. Allocate in the ratio of their original investments.
3. Allocate interest of 10% on their original investments, a $15,000 salary to Jill, a $18,000 salary to Henry, and the remainder in the ratio of 60:40.
4. Allocate a $6,000 salary to Henry, interest of 6% on their original investments, and the remainder equally.

Required:
For each allocation method, prepare a schedule to determine each partner's share of the net income or loss assuming:

A. A net income of $80,000.
B. A net income of $20,000.
C. A net loss of $15,000.

Problem 14-3 Allocation of Net Income

Terry Rayburn, Sue Stewart, and Edwin Chandler are forming a partnership. Terry is investing $30,000, Sue is investing $50,000, and Edwin is investing $40,000. Terry will work full-time, Sue will work half-time, and Edwin will work one-fourth of the time. Profits and losses will be allocated according to one of the following plans.

1. Allocate interest of 10% on their original investments and the remainder in proportion to the time devoted to the business.
2. Allocate a $40,000 salary to Terry, a $25,000 salary to Sue, an $8,000 salary to Edwin, and the remainder in the ratio of their original investments.
3. Allocate a $9,000 salary to Terry and the remainder in the ratio of 25:45:30.
4. Allocate in the ratio of 20:40:40.

Required:
Prepare a schedule to determine each partner's share of the profits under each plan for a net income of

A. $100,000.
B. $30,000.

Problem 14-4 Admission of a New Partner

Diane, Sandra, and Carol are partners. They share profits and losses in the ratio of 50:30:20. On May 15, 1987, when they have capital balances of $80,000, $40,000, and $60,000, respectively, they agree to admit Glen to the partnership.

Required:
Prepare the journal entry to record Glen's admission to the partnership, given each of the following situations.

A. Glen invests $120,000 cash in the partnership for a 40% interest in the partnership.
B. Glen invests $40,000 cash in the partnership for a 20% interest.
C. Glen invests $40,000 cash in the partnership for a 10% interest.
D. Glen pays Sandra $25,000 for 50% of her interest.
E. Glen pays Diane $30,000 and Carol $20,000 for 25% of each of their partnership interests.

Problem 14-5 Withdrawal of a Partner

The November 16, 1987, balance sheet of the Main Partnership is shown here.

MAIN PARTNERSHIP
Balance Sheet
November 16, 1987

Assets	
Cash	$ 60,000
Accounts receivable	35,000
Inventory	75,000
Equipment	250,000
Total Assets	$420,000
Liabilities and Partners' Equity	
Accounts payable	$ 50,000
Keith, capital	170,000
Lawrence, capital	75,000
Daniels, capital	125,000
Total Liabilities and Partners' Equity	$420,000

Keith, Lawrence, and Daniels share profits and losses in the ratio of 45:20:35. Lawrence withdraws from the partnership on November 16, 1987.

Required:
Prepare the journal entry or entries to record the withdrawal of Lawrence, given each of the following situations.

A. Lawrence receives $50,000 cash and a $25,000 note from the partnership for his interest.

B. Daniels purchases Lawrence's interest for $85,000.

C. The partnership gives Lawrence $30,000 cash and equipment with a book value and a fair value of $55,000 for his interest.

D. The partnership gives Lawrence $55,000 cash for his interest.

E. Lawrence sells one-fourth of his interest to Keith for $25,000 and three-fourths to Daniels for $55,000.

F. Appraisals reveal that accounts receivable are overstated by $6,000, inventory is understated by $3,000, and equipment is understated by $8,000. These assets are revalued, and Lawrence is given a promissory note equal to his revalued capital account.

Problem 14-6 Partnership Liquidation

Amy, Lana, and Hank are partners who share profits and losses in the ratio of 30:20:50. On July 18, 1987, they decide to liquidate the business. The balance sheet on that date is presented here.

AMY, LANA, AND HANK
Balance Sheet
July 18, 1987

Assets		
Cash		$ 30,000
Accounts receivable	$ 25,000	
Less: Allowance for uncollectible accounts	5,000	20,000
Inventory		70,000
Equipment	180,000	
Less: Accumulated depreciation	30,000	150,000
Building	750,000	
Less: Accumulated depreciation	250,000	500,000
Land		300,000
Total Assets		$1,070,000
Liabilities and Partners' Equity		
Accounts payable		$ 60,000
Mortgage payable		400,000
Amy, capital		200,000
Lana, capital		70,000
Hank, capital		340,000
Total Liabilities and Partners' Equity		$1,070,000

Required:

A. Prepare a schedule of partnership liquidation based on the following information.

1. Collected $10,000 of accounts receivable and wrote off the remaining accounts.
2. Sold the inventory for $20,000.
3. Sold the equipment for $100,000.
4. Sold the building and the land for $500,000. The buyer assumed the mortgage and paid the balance in cash.

5. Allocate the loss to the partners' capital accounts.
6. Remaining liabilities are paid in full.
7. Cash in the amount of the deficit is received from the partner with a deficit balance.
8. Remaining cash is distributed to the partners.

B. Prepare one journal entry to summarize transactions 1 through 4.
C. Prepare journal entries to record transactions 5 through 8. *Hank Db. 205,000*

Problem 14-7 Partnership Liquidation

James, Mahon, and Gilbert are partners who share profits and losses in the ratio of 60:30:10. They have decided to liquidate the business. Their latest balance sheet appears here.

JAMES, MAHON, AND GILBERT
Balance Sheet
October 10, 1987

Assets	
Cash	$ 20,000
Other assets	90,000
Total Assets	$110,000
Liabilities and Partners' Equity	
Accounts payable	$ 40,000
James, capital	47,000
Mahon, capital	15,000
Gilbert, capital	8,000
Total Liabilities and Partners' Equity	$110,000

Required:
For each of the following four independent cases prepare

A. A schedule of partnership liquidation.
B. All necessary journal entries.
  1. The noncash assets are sold for $60,000.
  2. The noncash assets are sold for $25,000, and any partner with a deficit is unable to make additional investment in the partnership.
  3. The noncash assets are sold for $32,000, and any partner with a deficit is able to invest cash equal to the amount of the deficit.
  4. The noncash assets are sold for $125,000.

ALTERNATE PROBLEMS

Problem 14-1A Partnership Formation

On October 1, 1986, Pat King and Jack Queen formed a partnership. King invested some business assets and the liabilities assumed by the partnership, which are listed in the following table, at both book value and fair value.

	Book Value	Fair Value
Cash	$ 20,000	$ 20,000
Marketable Securities	10,000	16,000
Accounts Receivable	30,000	26,000
Inventory	70,000	75,000
Machinery and Equipment	175,000	180,000
Accounts Payable	50,000	50,000

Queen invested a building worth $200,000, land worth $80,000, and a $100,000 mortgage was assumed by the partnership. They agreed to share profits and losses in the ratio of 70:30. During the first year of the partnership, King invested $40,000 in the business and withdrew $30,000. Queen invested $80,000 and withdrew $25,000. The partnership had a net income of $100,000.

Required:

A. Prepare the journal entries to record the initial investments of each partner.

B. Prepare a balance sheet as of October 1, 1986.

C. Prepare a statement of changes in partners' capital for the year ended September 30, 1987.

Problem 14-2A   Allocation of Net Income and Net Loss

Alison Moore and John Graham have decided to form a partnership by investing $50,000 and $25,000, respectively. The following plans for dividing profits and losses are under consideration.

1. In the ratio of 50:50.

2. A $15,000 salary to Alison, a $25,000 salary to John, and the remainder in the ratio of 70:30.

3. A $20,000 salary to John, 10% interest on their original investments, and the remainder equally.

4. In the ratio of their original investments.

Required:

For each plan, prepare a schedule to determine the division of the net income or loss assuming

A. A net income of $90,000.

B. A net loss of $2,000.

C. A net income of $25,000.

Problem 14-3A   Allocation of Net Income

Harry, Gary, and Mary form a partnership by investing $100,000, $75,000, and $25,000, respectively. Harry will work 15 hours per week for the business. Gary will work 25 hours per week, and Mary will work 40 hours per week. The partners are considering the following plans for the division of profits and losses.

1. Divide according to the amount of time worked in the business.

2. Allocate a $10,000 salary to Harry, a $15,000 salary to Gary, a $24,000 salary to Mary, interest of 8% on their original investments, and the remainder in the ratio of 50:40:10.

3. Divide in the ratio of their original investments.

4. Allocate a $5,000 salary to Gary, a $7,500 salary to Mary, 12% interest on their original investments, and the remainder in the ratio of 40:40:20.

Required:
For each plan, prepare a schedule to determine each partner's share of the profits assuming a net income of

A. $80,000.
B. $36,000.

Problem 14-4A Admission of a New Partner

Able, Baker, and Charles are partners in the ABC Partnership. They share profits and losses in the ratio of 70:20:10. Their current capital balances are $300,000, $100,000, and $50,000, respectively. The partners have agreed to admit Dickens to the partnership.

Required:
Prepare the journal entry to record Dickens's admission to the partnership under each of the following conditions.

A. Dickens pays $185,000 directly to Able for 50% of his partnership interest.
B. Dickens invests $120,000 in the partnership for a 25% interest.
C. Dickens invests $50,000 in the partnership for a 10% interest.
D. Dickens invests $300,000 in the partnership for a 30% interest.
E. Dickens pays Able $150,000, Baker $60,000, and Charles $20,000 for 50% of each of their interests.

Problem 14-5A Withdrawal of a Partner

The balance sheet of the CHE partnership as of March 10, 1987, is shown here.

```
                    CHE PARTNERSHIP
                     Balance Sheet
                     March 10, 1987


    Assets
    Cash                                       $ 50,000
    Accounts receivable                          25,000
    Inventory                                     30,000
    Plant and equipment                          100,000
       Total Assets                            $205,000


    Liabilities and Partners' Equity
    Accounts payable                           $ 65,000
    Cleaver, capital                             20,000
    Harriet, capital                             80,000
    Evans, capital                               40,000
       Total Liabilities and Partners' Equity  $205,000
```

Cleaver, Harriet, and Evans divide profits and losses in a 20:50:30 ratio. On March 10, 1987, Cleaver retires from the partnership.

Required:
Prepare journal entries to record Cleaver's retirement from the partnership under each of the following assumptions.

A. Evans pays $18,000 directly to Cleaver for his partnership interest.

B. Cleaver receives $30,000 of partnership cash for his interest.

C. Cleaver receives inventory from the partnership with a book value of $17,000 and a $20,000 fair market value. The inventory is not revalued on the partnership books.

D. An analysis of the assets reveals that inventory is overstated by $5,000 and plant and equipment are understated by $20,000. The assets are to be revalued, and Cleaver is given $29,000 of partnership cash for his interest.

E. Cleaver sells one-half of his interest to his friend Kirk for $8,000. Harriet buys the other half for $13,000.

F. The partners agree that accounts receivable are overstated by $3,000. The account balance is adjusted, and Cleaver is given partnership cash equal to his adjusted capital balance for his interest.

Problem 14-6A Partnership Liquidation

On May 4, 1987, Janet, George, and Steve decide to liquidate their partnership. The balance sheet on that date appears here.

JANET, GEORGE, AND STEVE
Balance Sheet
May 4, 1987

Assets		
Cash		$ 15,000
Marketable securities		20,000
Accounts receivable	$ 24,000	
Less: Allowance for uncollectible accounts	2,000	22,000
Inventory		48,000
Plant and equipment	190,000	
Less: Accumulated depreciation	30,000	160,000
Total Assets		$265,000
Liabilities and Partners' Equity		
Accounts payable		$ 50,000
Notes payable		15,000
Janet, capital		97,000
George, capital		78,000
Steve, capital		25,000
Total Liabilities and Partners' Equity		$265,000

Janet, George, and Steve share profits and losses in a 40:40:20 ratio.

Required:

A. Prepare a schedule of partnership liquidation based on the following information.

1. The inventory is sold for $20,000.

2. Collections of accounts receivable total $8,000. The remaining accounts receivable are written off.

3. The plant and equipment are sold for $70,000. The buyer assumed the $15,000 notes payable and paid the balance in cash.

4. The marketable securities are sold for $22,000.
5. Allocate the gain or loss from realization to the partners' capital accounts.
6. Paid the creditors in full.
7. Received cash in the amount of the deficit from the partner(s) with deficit balances.
8. Distributed remaining cash to partners.

B. Prepare one journal entry to summarize transactions 1 through 4.
C. Prepare journal entries to record transactions 5 through 8.

Problem 14-7A **Partnership Liquidation**

The Apollo Partnership is being liquidated. The current balance sheet is shown here.

APOLLO PARTNERSHIP
Balance Sheet
January 14, 1987

Assets
Cash	$ 8,000
Other assets	45,000
Total Assets	$53,000

Liabilities and Partners' Equity
Accounts payable	$17,000
Ferris, capital	20,000
Jacobs, capital	13,000
Martin, capital	3,000
Total Liabilities and Partners' Equity	$53,000

Ferris, Jacobs, and Martin share profits and losses in a 40:30:30 ratio.

Required:
For each of the following four independent cases, prepare

A. A schedule of partnership liquidation.
B. All necessary journal entries.
1. The other assets are sold for $25,000, and any partner with a deficit is unable to eliminate any of the deficit.
2. The other assets are sold for $60,000.
3. The other assets are sold for $30,000, and any partner with a deficit is able to invest up to $10,000 of additional cash in the partnership.
4. The other assets are sold for $42,000.

CASE

CASE 14-1 Discussion Case **Valuation of Assets before Admission of a Partner.**

The AB Partnership was formed by Ann Allen and Bob Bauer in 1984. The partners agreed to share profits and losses equally. Allen manages the business, and spends

45 to 60 hours per week on it. Bauer is a salesperson with extensive experience in marketing. The balance sheet for AB Partnership as of December 31, 1987, is as follows.

Assets		Liabilities and Capital	
Cash	$ 10,000	Accounts payable	$100,000
Accounts receivable	70,000	Other current liabilities	85,000
Inventory (LIFO cost)	100,000	Long-term note (22%, due in 1991)	50,000
Land	60,000	Allen, Capital	60,000
Building (net)	75,000	Bauer, Capital	45,000
Equipment (net)	25,000		
Total	$340,000	Total	$340,000

Since its formation, the partnership has not produced a profit and has had cash flow problems. Unable to meet their short-term obligations, the partners borrowed $50,000 from Chris Cooper, giving a long-term note. Allen and Bauer feel that the major problems confronting the partnership have been eliminated and that the firm is an attractive investment. They recognize that management of their liquid assets will be required and they are also concerned about the high level of interest costs. Together they have approached Cooper and convinced him to become a partner in a new partnership to be called the ABC Partnership. The long-term note is to be converted to a partnership interest of the same amount, and Cooper is to invest cash in the firm so that he will have a 1/3 capital interest. Cooper has insisted, however, that the accounts be adjusted to reflect any errors and omissions. Allen and Bauer agree to this and counter by insisting that assets and liabilities should be adjusted to reflect current values. They argue that Cooper should not be permitted to benefit from price appreciations that have already occurred. After a review of the assets and the liabilities of the firm, the partners and Cooper agree that the following adjustments are needed.

1. The business has not followed a strict accrual basis of accounting. As a result, the following items were omitted from the December 31 balance sheet.

Accrued expenses	$1,800
Prepaid expenses	900
Unearned revenues	500

2. No provisions had been made for uncollectible accounts. It is estimated that 10% of the accounts receivable are uncollectible.
3. Current cost to replace the inventory is $115,000.
4. The fair value of the land is $78,400. The book value of the other fixed assets is equal to their current fair value.

Required:
A. Prepare the necessary journal entries on the books of the old partnership to adjust the accounts. Assume that the adjustments are made to an account called the *Valuation Adjustment* account. This account is then closed to the partners' capital accounts in accordance with their profit- and loss-sharing ratio.
B. Record the admission of Cooper by recognizing the conversion of the long-term debt to capital and the additional cash investment.
C. Prepare a balance sheet on December 31, 1987, as it would appear after the adjustments and the admission of Cooper.
D. Discuss why it is equitable to restate the accounts of the old partnership before the admission of Cooper.

15

CORPORATIONS: ORGANIZATION AND OPERATION

CHAPTER OVERVIEW AND OBJECTIVES

This chapter discusses how corporations are organized, the types of stock they issue, and accounting procedures for stockholders' equity. When you have completed the chapter, you should understand:

1. The advantages and disadvantages of the corporate form of business organization.
2. How a corporation is formed.
3. The management structure of a corporation.
4. The rights attached to stock ownership.
5. Why a distinction is made between paid-in capital and retained earnings.
6. The difference between authorized, issued, and outstanding stock.
7. How to record the issue of corporate stock.
8. The effect of dividends on assets and stockholders' equity.
9. The differences between common and preferred stock.
10. How to record stock subscriptions.
11. The meaning of book value per common share and how to compute it.

Although there are fewer corporations than proprietorships and partnerships in the United States, corporations transact about six times more dollar volume of business than the other two types of businesses combined. Corporations control vast amounts of resources. Most large businesses, as well as many small ones, are organized as corporations. It is important to have an understanding of corporations and their accounting practices, both because of their dominant economic role in society and because many people will at some time either work for or own shares in a corporation.

The domination of our economy by corporations has led to increasing demands for information about them. Almost everyone is affected by the activities of corporations. We all buy goods produced and services performed by them. Many people work for corporations, receive interest and dividends from them, or sell goods and services to them. All segments of society—including investors and prospective investors, creditors, labor unions, governmental agencies, and consumers—are necessarily interested in the financial strength and profitability of corporations as a means of assessing the efficiency with which they have used their resources.

THE CORPORATION

Probably the most widely quoted definition of a corporation is that given by Chief Justice John Marshall in the Dartmouth College Case in 1819, in which he described a corporation as "an artificial being, invisible, intangible, and existing only in contemplation of the law." A corporation is an artificial legal entity separate and distinct from its owners. As a separate entity, it has many of the rights and responsibilities of a person. As a legal entity, it can, through its agents, buy, own, and sell property in its own name, and engage in business activity by entering into contracts with others. It has an independent legal status in a court and, thus, can sue and be sued. It is legally responsible for its liabilities, and must pay income taxes just as a person does.

Corporations may be classified in several ways. They may be organized for profit or for nonprofit purposes. A **profit corporation** is one that engages in business activity with the goal of earning a profit for its owners. Its continued existence is dependent upon profitable operations. **Nonprofit corporations** are organized to engage in educational, charitable, health, and other activities benefiting society. Nonprofit corporations generally depend upon public contributions for their continued existence.

Corporations are also often classified as public corporations and nonpublic corporations. **Public corporations** are those whose shares of stock are widely held and traded through national stock exchanges. Corporations whose shares of stock are held by a small group, often by the members of a single family, and are not publicly traded are called **closely held** (or **nonpublic**) **corporations.**

ADVANTAGES OF THE CORPORATE FORM

Objective 1:
Advantages and
Disadvantages
of the Corpo-
rate Form of
Business

The corporate form of business has several advantages over the proprietorship and partnership forms. The main ones are discussed here.

Limited Liability

As a separate legal entity, a corporation is responsible for its actions and liabilities. Creditors have claims only against the assets of the corporation, not against the personal assets of the stockholders. Because the owners of a corporation are not personally liable for corporate debts, the maximum amount they can lose is the amount they invest. To investors, this is one of the most important advantages of the corporate form, since under the alternative forms of business organization, owners may be personally liable for business debts.

Broad Source of Capital

Ownership rights in corporations are represented by transferable shares of stock. By dividing ownership of the business into many shares with a relatively small value per share, both large and small investors are able to participate in the ownership of the business. Therefore, most large corporations can draw upon the savings of many investors to obtain needed capital.

Ready Transferability of Shares

Corporate shares may be transferred easily without disrupting the activities of the corporation. Shares in public corporations can be bought and sold on practically every weekday through one of the national or regional stock exchanges. Consequently, a stockholder can readily convert his or her investment into cash if the need arises.

Continuity of Existence

A corporation has an indefinite life and continues in existence even if its ownership changes. The transfer of shares from one owner to another has no effect on a corporation. In contrast, the death, incapacity, or withdrawal of an owner terminates a proprietorship or a partnership.

Use of Professional Management

Although the stockholders own the corporation, they normally do not manage its daily activities. Stockholders elect a board of directors, which has overall responsibility for administrative decisions. The board then hires a president and other officers to manage the business. In contrast to a partnership, no mutual agency exists in a corporation. An individual stockholder does not have the right to bind the corporation to a contract unless he or she has been hired as a corporate officer. This separation of management and ownership permits the corporation to hire the best managerial talent available.

DISADVANTAGES OF THE CORPORATE FORM

The corporate form also has some disadvantages when compared to the proprietorship and partnership forms. The main disadvantages are described here.

Heavier Tax Burden

Proprietorships and partnerships are not subject to income tax as separate business units. Instead, the income they earn is taxed only as personal income to the owners. In contrast, a corporation's income is taxed twice. Because the corporation is a separate legal entity, its income is subject to federal and state income taxes, the total of which may exceed 40% of corporate income. When the corporation's after-tax income is distributed to its stockholders as dividends, the income is taxed again as personal income to the stockholders receiving the dividends. This double taxation is the primary disadvantage of the corporate form of business.[1]

Greater Governmental Regulation

Corporations come into existence under specific state laws. Consequently, they are said to be creatures of the state and are subject to a much greater degree of control and supervision by the state than are proprietorships or partnerships. In addition, public corporations must file periodic reports with the Securities and Exchange Commission and the stock exchanges on which their shares are traded. Meeting these additional reporting requirements can be very costly in terms of management time, as well as in clerical expenses.

Separation of Ownership and Management

The use of professional managers was cited earlier as an advantage of the corporate form. In some cases, however, this separation of ownership from management may prove to be a disadvantage, because managers have sometimes operated corporations for their own benefit, rather than for the benefit of the stockholders. Considerable harm can be done before stockholders become aware of such conditions and take action to change management.

A summary comparison of the corporate form of business with the proprietorship or partnership form is shown in Figure 15–1.

FORMING A CORPORATION

Objective 2: How corporations are formed.

Some corporations, such as national banks and savings and loan associations, are formed under federal laws. The majority of corporations, however, are created by obtaining a charter from one of the 50 states. To form a corporation, states require that individuals called **incorporators** must sign an application

Figure 15–1
Summary Comparison of Forms of Business Organization

	Form of Business Organization	
Characteristic	Proprietorship/ Partnership	Corporation
Limited liability of owners	Disadvantage	Advantage
Ease of raising capital	Disadvantage	Advantage
Continuity of existence	Disadvantage	Advantage
Ease with which ownership may be transferred	Disadvantage	Advantage
Tax burden	Advantage	Disadvantage
Extent of government regulation	Advantage	Disadvantage

[1] When specific conditions of the Internal Revenue Code are met, the stockholders of some corporations may avoid the double taxation of income by electing to be taxed like partnerships.

for a corporate charter and file it with the appropriate state official. Although state laws vary, the application generally must include:

1. The name and address of the proposed corporation.
2. The purpose of the proposed corporation.
3. A description of the different classes of stock offered.
4. The number of shares of each class of stock authorized for sale.
5. A description of the rights, preferences, and restrictions of each class of stock.
6. The names and addresses of the incorporators and the number of shares of stock subscribed to by each.

Incorporation applications are generally approved if the application is completed correctly and the proposed corporation has a legal purpose. When the application is approved, a legal contract between the state and the incorporators, called a **corporate charter,** is entered into and the corporation is then authorized to conduct business.

The incorporators hold an initial meeting to: (1) adopt the corporation's bylaws, which are the rules and procedures followed in conducting corporate affairs; and (2) to elect a board of directors. The board of directors then meets to appoint the president and other officers who will manage the company. After capital is raised through the issue of shares of stock, the corporation is ready to begin operating activities.

Organization Costs

The costs incurred in forming a corporation are called **organization costs.** They include the incorporation fees paid to the state, attorneys' fees, promoters' fees, the cost of printing stock certificates and corporate records, and various other expenditures needed to form the corporation. These costs represent an intangible asset which will benefit the corporation throughout its life, and, therefore, are debited to an asset account called *Organization Costs.* Since the life of a corporation is indeterminate, the number of years that the corporation will benefit from organization costs is also indeterminate. Current accounting practice requires that organization costs, like other intangible assets, be amortized over their estimated useful life with a maximum of 40 years.

For example, an amortization entry would be made each year as follows.

Dec.	31	Amortization Expense	2,200	
		Organization Costs		2,200
		To record amortization of organization		
		costs (assumed amount).		

Current income tax rules permit a corporation to amortize organization costs over a period of not less than five years. Therefore, many companies amortize their organization costs over five years, for both income tax and accounting purposes. Although not conceptually correct, the practice is accepted by accountants because organization costs are generally not material in amount (materiality convention).

MANAGING THE CORPORATION

Objective 3:
Management
Structure of
Corporations

Although control of a corporation ultimately rests with its stockholders, that control is exercised only indirectly. Stockholders elect a board of directors, which sets overall corporate policies. The board, in turn, appoints a president and other officers to manage the corporation's day-to-day affairs and carry out the policies established by the board.

The Stockholders

An individual stockholder is not directly involved in the daily management of the company unless he or she has been elected to serve on the board of directors or has been appointed an officer or manager. Stockholders generally are involved only in electing the board of directors and voting on certain important corporate actions specified in the corporate bylaws. For example, many corporate bylaws provide that stockholders must approve such actions as the merger with or acquisition of another company, and changes in the corporation's capital structure.

Stockholders receive a stock certificate. A **stock certificate** is a legal document that provides evidence of ownership and identifies the number of corporate shares owned. It also contains the basic provisions of the stock ownership agreement, such as voting rights and dividend rights. An example of a stock certificate is shown in Figure 15–2.

Objective 4:
Stock Owner-
ship Rights

Ownership of stock usually carries certain rights and privileges, including:

1. The right to vote for directors and to vote on other matters described in the corporate bylaws. (This right is generally eliminated for preferred stockholders.)
2. The right to share in profits by receiving dividends declared by the board of directors.
3. The right to share in the distribution of the corporation's assets if it is liquidated. When a corporation is liquidated, creditors must be paid in full, and any remaining assets are distributed to the stockholders in proportion to the number of shares held.
4. The right to purchase a portion of any additional stock issued by the corporation. This right, called the **preemptive right,** permits stockholders to maintain their percentage interests in a corporation by purchasing new shares in proportion to their current holdings. For example, if Maria Martinez owns 4,000 of the 40,000 outstanding shares of a corporation, she has a 10% interest. If the corporation issues 10,000 additional shares, Maria has the right to purchase 10% of them, or 1,000 shares, so that she will maintain her 10% interest in the corporation after the issue of the additional shares. This right may unduly restrict the actions of management

Figure 15–2
Stock Certificate

of widely held corporations by hindering the timely issue of new shares. Consequently, the preemptive right is frequently waived by stockholders.

These rights and privileges can be modified only by specific contract between the corporation and the stockholders. For example, as indicated above, preferred stockholders generally give up the right to vote in exchange for dividend preferences, and stockholders often waive their preemptive right.

Stockholders generally meet once a year to elect directors and to conduct other business as provided by the corporate bylaws. Each share of stock is entitled to one vote. A stockholder who owns more than 50% of a corporation's stock can thus elect the board of directors and control the corporation. Because many of the stockholders of a widely held company do not exercise the voting right, however, a corporation can often be controlled through the ownership of a much smaller percentage of stock. Stockholders who do not attend the annual meeting may delegate their voting right to an agent by signing a legal document called a **proxy statement.** Often the voting right is delegated to the current management in order to permit them to continue to control the corporation.

The Board of Directors

Although the board of directors has final responsibility for managing the corporation, it normally restricts its role to formulating the major business policies of the company and to appointing the officers who will have responsibility for carrying out these policies. Duties of the board are normally identified in the corporate bylaws. They generally include such things as:

1. Taking responsibility for protecting the rights of stockholders and creditors.
2. Setting officers' salaries.
3. Declaring dividends.
4. Authorizing long-term borrowing, additional stock issues, and major expansion projects.
5. Reviewing the system of internal control.

The board of directors is normally composed of corporate executives and holders of large blocks of corporate stock. In addition, the board normally includes several outside directors to ensure a more objective evaluation of management performance.

Official actions of the board are recorded in the minutes of their meetings. The *minutes book* is important to the accountant because it contains board decisions that serve as the basis for the authorization of certain transactions, such as the payment of dividends, and the preparation of many accounting entries.

The Corporate Officers

A corporation's administrative officers usually include a president, several vice-presidents of specific functional areas, the controller, the treasurer, and the secretary. The president is the chief executive officer with responsibility to the board of directors for managing and controlling business activities. Often, the president is also the chief operating officer.

The president is normally supported by one or more vice-presidents, depending upon the size of the corporation. For example, a corporation may have a vice-president of finance, a vice-president of production, and a vice-president of marketing.

The *controller* is the chief accounting officer. As such, the controller's responsibilities generally include maintaining the corporation's accounting records, maintaining an adequate internal control system, preparing financial statements, tax returns and other reports, and developing the budget. The controller also often advises the board of directors about the accounting and tax consequences of proposed corporate actions.

The *treasurer* is primarily responsible for managing cash. He or she normally has custody of the company's funds, is responsible for establishing and maintaining cash security controls, and is responsible for planning and controlling the company's cash position.

The *secretary* maintains the minutes of meetings of the directors and stockholders. Often an attorney, the secretary represents the corporation in many legal and contractual matters. In a small corporation, the secretary also normally maintains the list of stockholders and the amount of their stock interests. Large corporations use outside registrars and transfer agents to perform this stockholder-record function. Some corporations, particularly smaller ones, combine the positions of secretary and treasurer.

The following diagram illustrates a typical corporate organization chart. Lines of authority extend from the stockholders to the board of directors to the president to other officers.

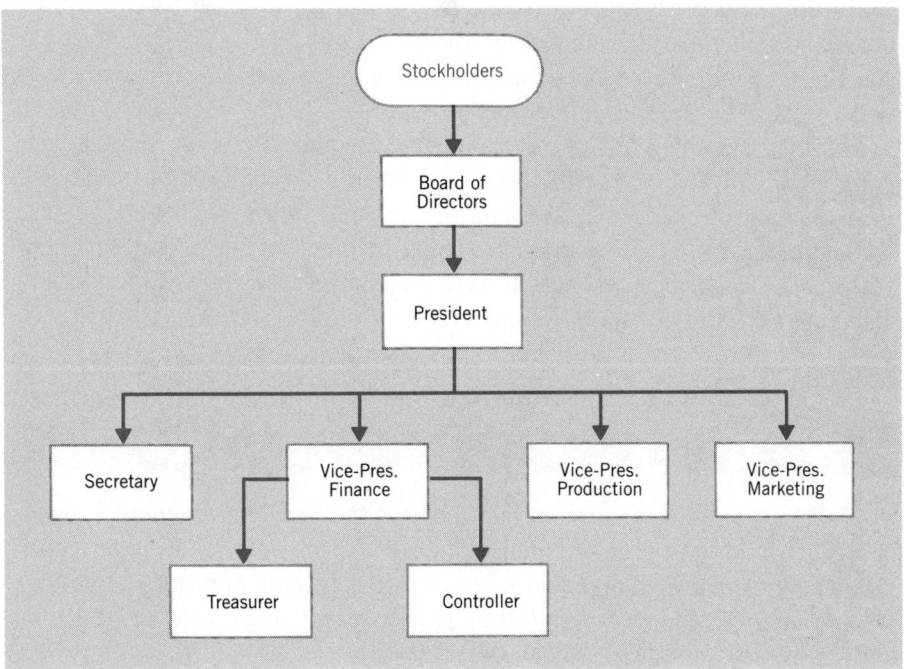

CORPORATE CAPITAL

Accounting for a corporation is similar in most respects to accounting for a proprietorship or a partnership. The income statement and the asset and liability sections of the balance sheet are essentially the same for all forms of business organization. There is a major difference, however, in accounting for corporate owners' equity. In a corporation, the term *stockholders' equity*— sometimes called *shareholders' equity* or simply *capital*—is used instead of *owners' equity.* The stockholders' equity section of a typical corporate balance sheet might appear as follows.

Stockholders' Equity	
Paid-in Capital:	
Preferred stock, $100 par value, 10,000 shares authorized, 5,000 shares issued and outstanding	$ 500,000
Common stock, $10 par value, 500,000 shares authorized, 200,000 shares issued and outstanding	2,000,000
Paid-in capital in excess of par value—preferred	50,000
Paid-in capital in excess of par value—common	1,450,000
Total paid-in capital	4,000,000
Retained Earnings	870,000
Total Stockholders' Equity	$4,870,000

110 issue price per share preferred

Legal capital = par of stock

Objective 5:
The Difference
Between Paid-in
Capital and Re-
tained Earnings

State incorporation laws generally require that stockholders' equity be separated into two broad categories: paid-in capital and retained earnings. **Paid-in capital** represents the amounts of assets invested in the corporation by its stockholders. When stockholders invest cash or other assets in a corporation, they are given shares of the corporation's stock as evidence of their investment. The paid-in capital category includes information about the types of stock, their par value, and the number of shares authorized and outstanding. Outstanding shares are those that have been issued to stockholders. These concepts will be discussed later in this chapter.

Retained earnings reflect the cumulative amount of income earned by the corporation and retained in the business. When a corporation's income statement accounts are closed at year-end, the *Income Summary* account is closed to *Retained Earnings*. For example, if net income for the year is $120,000, the *Income Summary* account will have a credit balance and will be closed to *Retained Earnings* by the following entry.

Dec.	31	Income Summary	120,000	
		Retained Earnings		120,000
		To close the income summary account.		

If the corporation incurred a net loss for the year, the *Income Summary* account would have a debit balance and the closing entry would consist of a debit to *Retained Earnings* and a credit to the *Income Summary* account. A debit balance in the *Retained Earnings* account is called a ***deficit*** and is deducted in arriving at total stockholders' equity.

AUTHORIZED CAPITAL STOCK

Objective 6:
Difference Be-
tween Author-
ized, Issued,
and Outstand-
ing Stock

When a corporation is formed, its charter indicates the maximum number of shares of stock it is permitted to issue and the par or stated value per share, if any. This maximum number of shares is called **authorized stock.** A corporation may be authorized to issue only one type of stock, called **common stock** or it may be authorized to issue both common stock and preferred stock. (Preferred stock is discussed later in this chapter.)

A corporation normally obtains permission, through its corporate charter, to issue more stock than it plans to sell immediately. This permits the corporation to raise additional capital in the future without asking the state to authorize more stock each time the corporation wishes to issue additional shares. For example, a corporation may be authorized to issue 500,000 shares of common stock, even though it intends to issue initially only 200,000 shares to raise the capital needed to begin operations. The remaining 300,000 shares may then be issued in the future if additional capital is needed.

OUTSTANDING STOCK

The outstanding stock of a corporation consists of the shares held by stockholders at any given time. As authorized stock is issued, it becomes outstanding stock. If 500,000 shares are authorized and 200,000 shares have been issued, the remaining 300,000 shares are called unissued stock and contain no rights until they are issued. The holders of the 200,000 outstanding shares own 100% of the corporation.

At times, a corporation's issued stock may exceed the number of shares outstanding because some of the shares may have been repurchased by the corporation. These repurchased shares are called ***treasury stock***. Accounting for treasury stock is discussed in Chapter 16.

Par Value

The par value of stock is an arbitrary amount per share placed on the stock by the incorporators at the time they apply for the corporate charter. They may select any value they wish, and par values of $1, $5, and $10 are common. For example, Alpha Portland Company's common stock has a par value of $10, Idaho Power Company's is $5, and J. C. Penney, Inc.'s is $.50. The incorporators generally set a par value substantially below the price at which they initially purchase the stock because most states prohibit the issue of stock for less than its par value. The initial purchase price establishes an approximate market price for the stock. If the market price of the stock later drops below its par value, the corporation is unable to issue additional stock. Establishing a relatively large spread between the initial issue price of the stock and its par value minimizes the possibility of its market price dropping below par value.

If a corporation issues par value stock, the par value is printed on each stock certificate and is the amount recorded in the capital stock accounts. For example, John Wiley & Sons' Class A common stock has a par value of $1 per share as shown in Figure 15–2. The only significance of par value (as well as stated value, which is discussed later) is that it establishes a minimum amount of capital, called ***legal capital***, which provides an element of protection for creditors. Legal capital cannot be reduced except by operating losses or legal action initiated by a majority vote of the stockholders. Because a corporation's creditors have claims only against the assets of the corporation, additional protection is provided to them by maintaining a minimum amount of assets equal to the legal capital. This minimum amount of assets cannot be returned to the stockholders until all creditors' claims have been paid. The total legal capital of a corporation issuing par value stock is equal to the number of shares outstanding multiplied by the par value per share.

The par value of stock has no relationship to its worth or market value. Par value is a fixed amount per share; market value generally fluctuates daily. For example, the market value of Holiday Inns, Inc.'s common stock ranged from $35.25 to $51.75 per share during 1984; its par value remained at $1.50 per share.

COMMON STOCK

Common stock is the residual equity in a corporation, which means that common stockholders are the last to receive asset distributions if the corporation is liquidated. Common stockholders take the greatest risk of loss if the corporation is unsuccessful, but they also have the greatest potential for gain if the company is profitable. As a result, the market value of common stock is closely related to profitability and will increase or decrease as actual profits increase and decrease and as stockholders' expectations about future profits rise and fall.

Common stock is issued to obtain resources for the corporation. Corporations normally issue common stock for cash, which then is used to acquire needed goods and services. In some cases, however, common stock is issued directly for noncash assets.

Issuing Common Stock for Cash

**Objective 7:
Recording the
Issuance of
Corporate
Stock**

When common stock is issued for cash, the *Cash* account is debited, the *Common Stock* account is credited for the par value of the shares issued (legal capital), and a separate account, called *Paid-in Capital in Excess of Par Value* is credited for the excess of the selling price over par value. For example, if 10,000 shares of $1 par value common stock are issued at $20 per share, the entry is:

Jan.	5	Cash	200,000	
		Common Stock		10,000
		Paid-in Capital in Excess of Par Value		190,000
		Issued 10,000 shares of common stock at $20 per share.		

It is important to recognize that the issue of capital stock does *not* constitute income to the corporation. Rather, it represents an investment in the corporation by owners. It is also important to remember that once the stock is issued and is being traded on security markets, the corporation itself is not involved in these transactions. Subsequent increases and decreases in the market value of the stock do not represent gains or losses to the corporation.

The total amount of the investment is reported as stockholders' equity, as follows.

Stockholders' Equity:	
Common stock, $1 par value, 60,000 shares authorized,	
10,000 shares issued and outstanding	$ 10,000
Paid-in capital in excess of par value	190,000
Total paid-in capital	200,000
Retained earnings (assumed amount)	50,000
Total Stockholders' Equity	$250,000

A few states permit the issue of stock for less than its par value, in which case a *Discount on Common Stock* account is debited for the difference between the issue price and the par value of the stock. If stock is issued at a discount, the initial purchasers of the stock are contingently liable to the corporation's creditors for the amount of the discount. Consequently, the issue of stock at a discount is rare.

Issuing Stock for Assets Other than Cash

At times, common stock is issued directly for assets such as land, buildings, or equipment. When this occurs, the assets received are recorded at the fair value of the stock issued or the fair value of the assets received, whichever is more objectively determinable. If the stock is publicly traded, the market value of the shares given is often a better measure of value than is the appraised value of the assets received.

For example, if 3,000 shares of common stock, with a market value of $15 per share, are exchanged for a piece of land, it is reasonable to record the cost of the land at $45,000 (3,000 × $15), since the stock could have been sold for $45,000 and the cash used to acquire the land.

For a new corporation, or a closely held one, the market value of the stock is unknown and the fair value of the assets received must be determined. For example, assume that a new corporation issued 10,000 shares of $10 par value common stock to one of the incorporators in exchange for land with an appraised value of $60,000 and a building appraised at $350,000. The issue of the stock would be recorded as follows.

Jan.	5	Land	60,000	
		Buildings	350,000	
		Common Stock		100,000
		Paid-in Capital in Excess of Par Value		310,000
		Exchanged 10,000 shares of common stock for land and a building.		

Because the fair value of the stock is unknown, the land and buildings are recorded at their appraised values. *Common Stock* is credited for the par value of the shares issued and the difference between the fair value of the assets and the par value of the stock is credited to *Paid-in Capital in Excess of Par Value*.

Sometimes a new corporation issues stock to its promoters in exchange for their services in organizing and promoting the corporation. If the fair value of the services received is $20,000, and 500 shares of $10 par value common stock is given, the entry is:

Jan.	5	Organization Costs	20,000	
		Common Stock		5,000
		Paid-in Capital in Excess of Par Value		15,000
		Exchanged 500 shares of stock for organizational services.		

DONATED CAPITAL

Sometimes a corporation may receive a donation of assets from a stockholder or other party. For example, in order to increase their tax base and provide employment to residents, cities often donate land to a corporation to encourage construction of facilities in their localities. When this occurs, the asset received is recorded at its fair value and a separate *Donated Capital* account is credited. For example, if a corporation received a donation of land with a fair value of $140,000, the entry would be:

Jan.	4	Land	140,000	
		Donated Capital		140,000
		To record the fair value of land donated		
		by Tuba City.		

If major restrictions are placed on the use of donated assets, a footnote explaining the restrictions should be included with the financial statements. Donated capital is normally reported as part of paid-in capital.

NO-PAR STOCK

In the early history of American corporations, all stock was required to have a par value. Today, however, all states permit the issue of **no-par value stock.** Some states require that the entire proceeds from the sale of no-par stock must be credited to the capital stock account as legal capital. This type of stock is referred to as *straight no-par stock.* In other states, the board of directors may assign a stated value per share to the no-par stock. *From an accounting standpoint, stated value and par value are the same thing, in that they both identify the amount that must be recorded as legal capital in the capital stock account. The entire proceeds from the issue of straight no-par stock constitutes legal capital.*

To illustrate the accounting for no-par stock, assume that a corporation issues 10,000 shares of no-par common stock at $25 per share. If the stock does not have a stated value, the entire proceeds are recorded in the no-par common stock account, as follows.

Jan.	5	Cash	250,000	
		Common Stock—No-par Value		250,000
		Issued 10,000 shares of no-par value		
		stock at $25 per share.		

If the board of directors has assigned a stated value of $5 to the no-par stock, the difference between the issue price and the stated value is credited to *Paid-in Capital in Excess of Stated Value,* as follows.

Jan.	5	Cash	250,000	
		Common Stock—No-par Value		50,000
		Paid-in Capital in Excess of Stated		
		Value		200,000
		Issued 10,000 shares of no-par value		
		stock with a stated value of $5 per		
		share for $25 per share.		

CASH DIVIDENDS

A **dividend** is a distribution of cash, other assets, or a corporation's own stock to its stockholders. Cash dividends are the most common and will be discussed in this chapter. Distributions of other assets and corporate stock are discussed and illustrated in Chapter 16.

Many corporations periodically distribute part of their earnings to their stockholders by declaring a cash dividend. The authority to declare dividends rests solely with the board of directors, which is responsible for determining both the legality of the dividend and the corporation's ability to pay it.

State laws vary with regard to dividends. Most states prohibit the payment of dividends in excess of retained earnings; however, some states permit the payment of dividends from any capital other than legal capital.

The corporation must have sufficient cash or other assets—in addition to retained earnings—to distribute dividends to stockholders without putting an undue strain on the ability of the corporation to continue to operate efficiently. Therefore, the board of directors must determine whether assets should be distributed to stockholders, or retained for operating activities or for financing growth. Once the board has declared a dividend, the obligation to pay it becomes a current liability and cannot be rescinded.

When a dividend is declared from capital other than retained earnings, the corporation is returning to its stockholders a portion of their paid-in capital. These dividends are called **liquidating dividends,** because they represent a return *of* stockholders' investments, rather than a return *on* their investments. They do not represent income to the stockholders.

Cash dividends are stated in terms of so many dollars or cents per share of stock. For example, if a corporation declares a dividend of $2 per share on outstanding stock, a stockholder owning 100 shares will receive a dividend check for $200.

A corporation's stockholders change as shares are traded in the market. To assure that dividends are paid to the rightful owner of the shares, dividends are declared on one date (the *declaration date*), and payable on some future date (the *payment date*) to the stockholders of record on some date in between (the *date of record*). The time period between the declaration date and the date of record allows new investors to record their shares before payment of the dividend.

To illustrate, assume that on May 25 the board of directors declared a $2-per-share dividend on 40,000 outstanding shares of common stock to be paid on June 20 to stockholders of record on June 10. Because a dividend liability is created on the declaration date that will not be settled until the payment date, two journal entries are required. The entry on the declaration date is.

✓ Close for retained earning at end of year

May	25	Dividends Declared	80,000	
		Dividends Payable		80,000
		Declared a cash dividend of $2 per share		
		on the 40,000 common shares		
		outstanding.		

Objective 8:
Effect of Cash Dividends on Assets and Stockholders' Equity

This entry recognizes the reduction of stockholders' equity and a dividend liability, which is reported as a current liability on the May 31 balance sheet.

The entry to record payment of the dividend is:

June	20	Dividends Payable	80,000	
		Cash		80,000
		To record payment of the dividend declared on May 25.		

No entry is required on the date of record, since that date is used only to determine the owners of the stock who are to receive the dividends.

The *Dividends Declared* account is a temporary retained earnings account that is closed to retained earnings at the end of the year. If a company declares dividends on both common and preferred stock, it may use a separate *Dividends Declared* and *Dividends Payable* account for each type of stock. Regardless of the procedures followed, the net effect of a cash dividend is to reduce both retained earnings and cash by the amount of the dividend.

PREFERRED STOCK

Objective 9: Differences Between Common Stock and Preferred Stock

In addition to common stock, many corporations issue one or more types of **preferred stock.** Preferred stock receives its name from the fact that preferred stockholders receive preferential treatment over common stockholders in one or more respects.

The most common preferences concern dividend distributions and asset distributions if the corporation is liquidated. In exchange for these preferences, preferred stockholders normally relinquish the right to vote. Preferences and other special features of preferred stock vary widely. For example, preferred stock can generally be recalled and retired at the option of the corporation and sometimes is convertible into common stock at the option of the preferred stockholders. Consequently, the preferred stock contract must be read carefully to determine its specific provisions.

DIVIDEND PREFERENCE

If stock is preferred as to dividends, its holders are entitled to a fixed dividend before any dividend is paid to common stockholders. The annual dividend is usually stated as a dollar amount per share or as a percentage of the stock's par value. For example, Armstrong Cork Company's balance sheet includes no-par value preferred stock with a $3.75 annual dividend per share, and Tenneco Inc.'s balance sheet shows 8.52%, $100 par value preferred stock. This means that $3.75 and $8.52, respectively, must be paid yearly on each share of preferred stock before a dividend can be paid to common stockholders.

Because the obligation to pay a dividend arises only if the board of directors declares one, preferred stockholders are not assured of receiving a dividend each year. Thus, if the board of directors decides not to declare a dividend on either preferred or common stock, either because of a lack of retained earnings, a shortage of cash, or both, then neither preferred stockholders nor common stockholders will receive a dividend.

Cumulative and Noncumulative Preferred Stock

The dividend preference on most preferred stock is **cumulative,** which means that undeclared dividends accumulate and the accumulated amount plus the current year's preferred dividend must be paid before any dividend can be paid to common stockholders. Dividends that are not declared in the year they are due are called **dividends in arrears.** Current accounting standards require that dividends in arrears must be disclosed. Disclosure is generally made in a footnote to the financial statements.

To illustrate cumulative dividends, assume that a corporation has 50,000 shares of $5 cumulative preferred stock outstanding and that no dividends were declared in the preceding year. In addition, there are 150,000 shares of common stock outstanding. If the board of directors declares a $700,000 dividend, it will be distributed to preferred and common stockholders, as follows.

	Preferred	Common	Cumulative Total
Dividends in arrears (50,000 × $5)	$250,000	-0-	$250,000
Current year's dividend	250,000		$500,000
Residual to common		$200,000	$700,000
Totals	$500,000	$200,000	

If the board declared a $400,000 dividend, it would all be distributed to preferred stockholders; common stockholders would receive no dividends, and dividends in arrears on preferred stock would still exist in the amount of $100,000.

If preferred stock is **noncumulative,** any undeclared dividends at the end of the year are lost. Because investors would be hesitant to purchase such stock, very little noncumulative preferred stock is issued.

Participating Preferred Stock

Sometimes preferred stockholders are not limited to a fixed amount of dividends for the current year, but are permitted to participate with common stockholders in dividends above a specified amount. This type of preferred stock is called participating preferred stock. The stock may be *fully participating* or *partially participating.* Fully participating means that preferred stockholders will share in all dividends paid in excess of: (1) dividends in arrears; (2) the current fixed dividend on preferred stock; and (3) a specified amount of dividends to common stockholders.

To illustrate the accounting for fully participating preferred stock, assume the par value of the preferred and common stock in the previous example was $50 per share. Assume also that the preferred stock is cumulative and participates fully with common stock in the ratio of their total par values after common stockholders have received dividends for the current year at the same fixed preference rate as preferred stockholders. Since the fixed preference rate on preferred stock is 10% ($5 current fixed dividend divided by $50 par value per share), a $1,650,000 dividend would be distributed, as follows.

	Preferred	Common	Cumulative Total
Dividends in arrears (50,000 × $5)	$250,000		$ 250,000
Current year's preferred dividend (50,000 × $5)	250,000		$ 500,000
Current year's common dividend (10% × $7,500,000)		$ 750,000	$1,250,000
Participation in ratio of total par values ($2,500,000 to $7,500,000) or 25% to 75%*	100,000	300,000	$1,650,000
Totals	$600,000	$1,050,000	

*Total par value of:
Preferred = 50,000 shares × $50 par value	$ 2,500,000
Common = 150,000 shares × $50 par value	7,500,000
Total par value of both preferred and common stock	$10,000,000

When participating preferred stock is limited as to the total amount of dividends it can receive for the current year, it is called *partially participating preferred stock*. For example, if the preferred stock in this example is limited to a 12% current dividend, the $1,650,000 total dividend would be distributed as follows.

	Preferred	Common	Cumulative Total
Dividends in arrears (50,000 × $5)	$250,000		$ 250,000
Current year's preferred dividend (50,000 × $5)	250,000		$ 500,000
Current year's common dividend (10% × $7,500,000 par value)		$ 750,000	$1,250,000
Participation feature (2% × $2,500,000 par value)	50,000		$1,300,000
Remainder of dividend to common		350,000	$1,650,000
Totals	$550,000	$1,100,000	

ASSET PREFERENCE

In addition to a dividend preference, most preferred stocks include a preference as to assets if the corporation is liquidated. If the corporation is liquidated, the preferred stockholders are entitled to receive payment (after creditors have been paid) equal to the par value of their stock—or a higher call price (explained in the next section) if one is included in the preferred stock contract—before common stockholders receive any of the corporation's assets. Normally, this preference also includes any dividends in arrears on cumulative preferred stock.

CALLABLE PREFERRED STOCK

Preferred stock contracts generally include a **call provision,** which gives the corporation the right to repurchase the stock from the stockholders at a predetermined call price. The call price—sometimes called *redemption price* or *liquidation price*—is usually slightly higher than par value. For example, Johns–Manville's $65 stated value preferred stock has a call price of $67.70 per share.

Preferred Shares Outstan X
cAll price

When preferred stock is called, the stockholder is paid the call price, plus any dividends in arrears, plus a pro rata portion of the current year's dividend. A call provision gives the corporation some flexibility in structuring its equity. A preferred stock may be called and retired, for example, in order to distribute greater dividends to common stockholders. Or a preferred stock may be retired and replaced with another preferred stock with a lower dividend rate.

Always more than pAr.

CONVERTIBLE PREFERRED STOCK

Some preferred stock is convertible. Convertibility permits the preferred stockholder to convert the stock into common stock at a predetermined exchange ratio. For example, each share of Borg–Warner Corporation's preferred stock is convertible into 2.5 shares of common stock at the option of the holder. The conversion privilege is an attractive feature to investors. If the corporation is successful and the market price of its common stock increases, the market price of the preferred stock will also increase proportionately, since it is convertible into common stock. If the market price of the common stock does not increase, the preferred stock still has its preference as to regular fixed dividends.

To illustrate, assume that a corporation issued 20,000 shares of 7%, $100 par value convertible preferred stock on January 2, 1984, at a price of $105 per share. Each preferred share is convertible into three shares of the corporation's $5 par value common stock at any time. The market price of the common stock was $30 per share on January 2, 1984, and an annual dividend of $1.50 per share was being paid. During the next several years, earnings increased significantly, and by January 1, 1987, the market price of the common stock had risen to $50 per share and annual dividends were increased to $3.50 per share. The preferred stock would have a market price of approximately $150 per share, since it could be converted into three shares of common stock with a total market price of $150.

When the market price and annual dividends on common stock increase, some preferred stockholders may convert their preferred stock into common stock. For example, if the holders of 5,000 of the preferred shares converted their stock, the entry would be.

Jan.	2	Preferred stock	500,000	
		Paid-in Capital in Excess of Par Value—		
		Preferred	25,000	
		Common Stock		75,000
		Paid-in Capital in Excess of Par		
		Value—Common		450,000
		Converted 5,000 shares of $100 par value		
		preferred stock into 15,000 shares of $5		
		par value common stock.		

This entry transfers the stockholders' equity associated with the preferred shares converted to appropriate common stockholders' equity accounts. The *Preferred Stock* account is reduced by $500,000 (5,000 shares × $100 par value per share), *Paid-in Capital in Excess of Par Value* on the preferred stock is reduced by $25,000 (5,000 shares × $5 per share), and the *Common Stock* account is credited for the par value of the common stock issued (15,000 shares × $5 = $75,000). The difference between the recorded value of the preferred stock retired and the par value of the common stock issued is credited to *Paid-in Capital in Excess of Par Value—Common*. Note that the market price of the common stock issued has no effect on the transaction.

CAPITAL STOCK SUBSCRIPTIONS

Objective 10: Recording Stock Subscriptions

Corporations sometimes issue stock on a subscription basis. This means that the purchaser (subscriber) agrees to pay for the shares at a future time or in a series of installments. In these cases, a receivable from the subscriber is recorded for the total purchase price. Legal capital is credited to a separate account called *Common* (or *Preferred*) *Stock Subscribed*. A separate *Stock Subscribed* account is used to show that the stock has not been fully paid for and that, therefore, the stock certificate has not yet been issued. The difference between legal capital and the issue price is credited to *Paid-in Capital in Excess of Par Value*.

To illustrate, assume that on January 2 a corporation sold 5,000 shares of $5 par value common stock on a subscription basis for $30 per share. Payment terms provide for a down payment of one-third of the purchase price, with the remainder due in two equal installments on March 1 and June 1. The entries to record the sale and collection of the down payment are.

Jan.	2	Subscriptions Receivable—Common	150,000	
		Common Stock Subscribed		25,000
		Paid-in Capital in Excess of Par		
		Value—Common		125,000
		To record subscriptions for 5,000 shares		
		of $5 par value common stock at $30		
		per share.		
Jan.	2	Cash	50,000	
		Subscriptions Receivable—Common		50,000
		To record collection of stock subscriptions		
		receivable.		

When installment payments are received on March 1 and June 1, *Cash* is debited and *Subscriptions Receivable—Common* is credited, as follows.

| March and June | 1 1 | Cash   Subscriptions Receivable—Common   To record collections of stock   subscriptions receivable. | 50,000 | 50,000 |

After full payment is received, the stock certificate is issued to the investor and the following entry is prepared.

| June | 1 | Common Stock Subscribed   Common Stock   To record the issue of a stock certificate   for 5,000 shares of $5 par value   common stock. | 25,000 | 25,000 |

Subscriptions receivable are reported as current assets on the balance sheet if they are expected to be collected within one year or during the normal operating cycle. The *Common Stock Subscribed* account is reported as an item of stockholders' equity (see Figure 15–3).

BOOK VALUE PER SHARE OF COMMON STOCK

Common stockholders' equity is often reported in statistical summaries in annual reports and in the financial press as an amount per share, generally called **book value per share of common stock.** It is computed by dividing total common stockholders' equity by the number of common shares outstanding. If a corporation has only one type of stock, book value per share is determined by dividing total stockholders' equity by the number of shares outstanding. For example, assume that a corporation has the following stockholders' equity.

Objective 11: Book Value Per Common Share

Common stock, $5 par, 100,000 shares authorized, 50,000 shares issued and outstanding	$ 250,000
Paid-in capital in excess of par value	600,000
Retained earnings	430,000
Total Stockholders' Equity	$1,280,000

Book value per share is $1,280,000 ÷ 50,000 shares = $25.60.

When a corporation has both preferred and common stock outstanding, total stockholders' equity must be allocated to the two classes of stock. Because book value per share is generally reported for common stock only, the approach is to subtract from total stockholders' equity the amount that would be distributed to preferred stockholders if the corporation were terminated. If a corporation is terminated, the corporation must pay the preferred stock call price to the preferred stockholders, plus any dividends in arrears. To illustrate, assume that a corporation has the following stockholders' equity.

7% Cumulative preferred stock, $100 par, 5,000 shares issued and outstanding, callable at $105	$ 500,000
Common stock, $5 par, 100,000 shares authorized, 50,000 shares issued and outstanding	250,000
Paid-in capital in excess of par value—common	600,000
Retained earnings	430,000
Total Stockholders' Equity	$1,780,000

Assume further that there is one year's dividends in arrears and that the current year's preferred dividend has not yet been declared. Book value per common share is computed as follows.

Total Stockholders' Equity		$1,780,000
Allocated to preferred stock:		
Call price (5,000 × $105)	$525,000	
Preferred dividends in arrears	35,000	
Current year's preferred dividends	35,000	595,000
Common stockholders' equity		1,185,000
Divided by common shares outstanding		÷50,000
Book Value per Common Share		$ 23.70

The main purpose of including the book value per share of common stock in statistical summaries is to give some indication to readers of financial statements of the effect of the retention of earnings on the growth of the corporation. For example, the book value per common share of Marathon Oil increased from $16.85 to $27.88 during a recent five-year period. Since the number of common shares outstanding remained relatively constant during this period, the effect of retaining earnings, rather than distributing them as dividends, was to increase book value per share by $11.03.

Book value should not be confused with liquidation value. If the corporation were liquidated, its assets would probably be sold at prices quite different from their book values. In addition, book value normally has little relationship to a stock's market value. The level of current earnings, earning capacity, and dividend policy are more important factors affecting the market value of common stock.

REPORTING STOCKHOLDERS' EQUITY

Several types of stockholders' equity accounts have been introduced in this chapter. An example of the stockholders' equity section of a balance sheet that includes these accounts is shown in Figure 15–3.

GLOSSARY

AUTHORIZED STOCK. The maximum amount of stock a corporation is permitted to issue under the terms of its charter (p. 580).

BOOK VALUE PER COMMON SHARE. The amount of common stockholders' equity related to each share of common stock (p. 591).

Figure 15–3
Stockholders' Equity Accounts

Paid-in Capital:	
Cumulative, 10%, preferred stock, $100 par value, 100,000 shares authorized, 20,000 shares issued and outstanding	$2,000,000
Common stock, $10 par value, 1,000,000 shares authorized, 300,000 shares issued and outstanding	3,000,000
Common stock subscribed, 10,000 shares	100,000
Paid-in capital in excess of par value—preferred	160,000
Paid-in capital in excess of par value—common	2,400,000
Donated capital	300,000
Total paid-in capital	7,960,000
Retained earnings	310,000
Total Stockholders' Equity	$8,270,000

Treasurer-issued & repurchased by Corporation

CALL PROVISION. The right of a corporation to repurchase preferred stock from its stockholders at a predetermined price (p. 589).

COMMON STOCK. Stock of a corporation having only one class of stock; or if there is more than one class, the class that has no preferences relative to the other classes of stock (p. 580).

CORPORATE CHARTER. The legal contract between the state and the incorporators (p. 575).

CUMULATIVE PREFERRED STOCK. Preferred stock on which undeclared dividends accumulate and must be paid before any dividend can be paid to common stockholders (p. 587).

DIVIDEND. A distribution of cash, other assets, or a corporation's own stock to its stockholders (p. 585).

DIVIDENDS IN ARREARS. Dividends on cumulative preferred stock that are not declared in the year in which they are due (p. 587).

INCORPORATORS. Individuals who form a corporation and sign the application for a corporate charter (p. 574).

LIQUIDATING DIVIDEND. A dividend declared from capital other than retained earnings. It is a return *of* capital, rather than a return *on* capital (p. 585).

NONCUMULATIVE PREFERRED STOCK. Preferred stock on which the right to receive dividends is lost in any year in which dividends are not declared (p. 587).

NONPROFIT CORPORATION. A corporation organized for nonprofit purposes; it generally depends upon public contributions for its continued existence (p. 572).

NONPUBLIC (CLOSELY HELD) CORPORATION. A corporation whose shares are not publicly traded (p. 572).

NO-PAR VALUE STOCK. A type of capital stock that is not assigned a par value (p. 584).

ORGANIZATION COSTS. The expenditures made to form a corporation. They include incorporation fees, attorneys' fees, and promoters' fees (p. 575).

PAID-IN CAPITAL. The capital invested in the corporation by its stockholders (p. 580).

PREEMPTIVE RIGHT. The right that permits stockholders to maintain their percentage interests in a corporation by purchasing new shares in proportion to their current holdings (p. 576).

PREFERRED STOCK. A type of stock that has certain preferences, such as a preference in dividend distribution, or a preference in asset distributions if the corporation is liquidated (p. 586).

PROFIT CORPORATION. A corporation organized with the goal of earning a profit for its shareholders (p. 572).

PROXY STATEMENT. A legal document by which a stockholder assigns his or her vote to an agent (p. 577).

PUBLIC CORPORATION. A corporation whose shares are widely held and traded through national stock exchanges (p. 572).

RETAINED EARNINGS. Earnings of a corporation that have been retained in the business, rather than distributed to stockholders (p. 580).

STOCK CERTIFICATE. A legal document that provides evidence of stock ownership (p. 576).

DISCUSSION QUESTIONS

1. What is the difference between public corporations and nonpublic corporations?
2. What are the main advantages of the corporate form of business organization? What are the main disadvantages?
3. What are organization costs? How should they be accounted for?
4. What is a proxy statement?
5. List the general rights of common stockholders.
6. Explain what is meant by the preemptive right.
7. Distinguish between paid-in capital and retained earnings.
8. When stock is issued for assets other than cash, accountants must determine the amount at which to record the transaction. What is the rule generally followed?
9. X Corporation has retained earnings at the beginning of the year of $200,000. The only entry affecting this account during the year was the entry to close the $220,000 debit balance in the *Income Summary* account. What is the balance in the *Retained Earnings* account at year-end? What is this balance called?
10. Why is an investment in noncumulative preferred stock generally not a desirable investment?
11. What is legal capital? What does it consist of?
12. What entry would be made to record the issuance of 10,000 shares of $2 par value common stock for $20 per share? How much (if any) of the amount received represents income to the corporation?
13. What accounts are involved when recording the declaration of a cash dividend? What accounts are involved when recording the payment of the cash dividend?
14. Define each of the following terms in the context of their application to preferred stock.
    (a) Cumulative.
    (b) Dividends in arrears.
    (c) Call provision.
    (d) Convertible.
15. Classify (as an asset, liability, stockholders' equity, revenue, expense) each of the following accounts.
    (a) Common Stock Subscribed.
    (b) Organization Costs.
    (c) Subscriptions Receivable.

(d) Dividends Payable.
(e) Paid-in Capital in Excess of Par Value.
(f) Retained Earnings.
16. How is book value per share of common stock determined when a corporation has both common stock and preferred stock outstanding?
17. What relationship is there between book value per share of common stock and the market price of the common stock?

EXERCISES

Exercise 15-1 Recording the Issue of Stock
Martel Company's charter contains authorization to issue 200,000 shares of common stock.

Required:
Prepare a journal entry to record the issue of 30,000 shares of stock at $35 per share assuming

A. The stock has a par value of $10 per share.
B. The stock is no-par stock.
C. The stock is no-par stock with a stated value of $15 per share.

Exercise 15-2 Preparing Stockholders' Equity Section of Balance Sheet
Crayola Corporation was organized on January 2, 1987, and was authorized to issue 100,000 shares of $100 par value, 11%, cumulative preferred stock and 300,000 shares of $5 par value common stock. One-half of the preferred stock was issued at par value and 50,000 shares of common stock were issued at $25 per share.

Required:
Prepare the stockholders' equity section of the balance sheet immediately after the issue of the shares.

Exercise 15-3 Dividend Distributions
Bar Corporation has 20,000 shares of $50 par value, 10%, cumulative preferred stock outstanding in addition to its common stock. The company began operations and issued both classes of stock on January 2, 1985. Dividends declared in each of the first four years were:

1985	$150,000	
1986	50,000	
1987	120,000	
1988	180,000	

Required:
Determine how the dividends will be distributed to each class of stock and the amount of dividends in arrears (if any) at the end of each year.

Exercise 15-4 Exchange of Stock for Noncash Assets
Sawyer Corporation completed the following transactions during its first year of operations.

1. Accepted land with a fair value of $130,000 as a donation from the city of Dover.
2. Exchanged 1,000 shares of $5 par value common stock for organizational services having a fair value of $15,000.

3. Issued 18,000 shares of $5 par value common stock in exchange for a building appraised at $270,000 and machinery with a fair value of $30,000.

Required:
Record the transactions in general journal form.

Exercise 15-5 Effects of Transactions on Retained Earnings

Kings Corporation completed the following transactions over a six-month period.

Dec.	31	Closed the $84,520 credit balance in the *Income Summary* account to *Retained Earnings*.
June	30	Declared a cash dividend of $1.50 per share on the 50,000 common shares outstanding.
July	30	Paid the dividends declared on June 30.

Required:
Prepared journal entries to record the transactions.

Exercise 15-6 Stock Subscriptions

On April 30, a corporation sold 10,000 shares of $1 par value common stock on a subscription basis for $30 per share. Payment terms required a down payment of 25% of the purchase price, with the remainder due in two equal installments on June 30 and August 30.

Required:
Prepare journal entries to record the stock subscription, cash collection, and the issue of the stock certificates.

Exercise 15-7 Conversion of Preferred Stock to Common Stock

Tatum Corporation has 10,000 shares of 9%, $50 par value convertible preferred stock outstanding, in addition to its 150,000 shares of $2 par value common stock. The preferred stock was originally issued at par value. Each preferred share is convertible into three shares of common stock. On June 1 of the current year, 5,000 of the preferred shares were converted into common stock.

Required:
A. Prepare the journal entry to record the conversion.
B. Assume that the common stock is no par, with a stated value of $10 per share. Prepare the journal entry to record the conversion.

Exercise 15-8 Book Value per Share of Common Stock

Lox Corporation has the following stockholders' equity.

Preferred stock, $100 par value, 10%, cumulative, 20,000 shares authorized, issued, and outstanding	$ 2,000,000
Common stock, $5 par value, 500,000 shares authorized, 200,000 shares issued and outstanding	1,000,000
Paid-in capital in excess of par value	4,500,000
Retained earnings	5,250,000
Total Stockholders' Equity	$12,750,000

There are no dividends in arrears on the preferred stock, but the current year's dividend has not yet been declared. The preferred stock is callable at $104 per share.

Required:
A. Determine the book value per share of common stock.
B. Assume that the preferred stock is callable at $106 and that no dividends have been declared in the current or prior year. Determine the book value per share of common stock.

PROBLEMS

Problem 15-1 Issuing Stock and Preparing Stockholders' Equity Section

Haven Corporation was organized early in 1986. The corporate charter authorizes the issue of 50,000 shares of $100 par value, 11%, cumulative preferred stock and 200,000 shares of $5 par value common stock. The following transactions affecting stockholders' equity were completed during the first year.

1. Issued 50 shares of preferred stock at par value for organizational services.
2. Issued, for cash, 4,000 shares of common stock at $25 per share and 1,000 shares of preferred stock at par.
3. Exchanged 8,000 shares of common stock for land with an appraised value of $60,000 and a building with an appraised value of $150,000.
4. Declared the required preferred stock dividend and a $2 per share dividend on common stock.
5. Closed the $126,000 credit balance in the *Income Summary* account.

Required:
A. Prepare journal entries to record these transactions.
B. Prepare the stockholders' equity section of the balance sheet.

Problem 15-2 Comprehensive Problem

Wayland Corporation received its charter authorizing the issue of 50,000 shares of $50 par value, 10%, cumulative preferred stock and 200,000 shares of no-par common stock. The board of directors elected to assign a stated value of $10 per share to the common stock. The preferred stock is callable at $55 per share. The following transactions affecting stockholders' equity were completed during the first year.

Jan.	8	Issued 25,000 shares of common stock at $20 per share and 2,000 shares of preferred stock at $55 per share.
	15	Received subscriptions to 10,000 shares of common stock at $21 per share along with one-third of the subscription price. The remainder of the subscription price is payable in two equal installments due on June 30 and September 30.
Apr.	26	Issued 3,000 shares of preferred stock in exchange for land with a fair value of $170,000.
June	30	Collected the first installment on the subscribed stock of Jan. 15.
Sept.	30	Collected the last installment on the subscribed stock of Jan. 15, and issued the stock certificates.
Dec.	9	Declared the required dividend on preferred stock and a $2 per share dividend on common stock.

18 Received subscriptions to 4,000 shares of common stock at $20 per share. The subscription price is payable in two equal installments on January 31 and May 31 of the following year.

31 Closed the $141,000 credit balance in the *Income Summary* account.

Required:

A. Prepare journal entries for these transactions.

B. Prepare the stockholders' equity section of the balance sheet as of December 31.

C. Compute book value per share of common stock. (The common shares subscribed should be included with common stock outstanding.)

Problem 15-3 Determining Number of Shares Outstanding

Stockholders' equity data for several corporations on December 31, 1986, are presented here.

1. Preferred stock, 10%, $100 par value, __?__ shares issued and outstanding, callable at 104% of par value — $ 800,000

Common stock, $5 par value, 100,000 shares authorized, __?__ shares issued and outstanding — 50,000

Paid-in capital in excess of par value — 1,450,000

Retained earnings — 425,000

Total Stockholders' Equity — $ 2,725,000

2. Cumulative preferred stock, 11%, $75 par, __?__ shares issued and outstanding, callable at $80 — $ 600,000

Common stock, $1 par value, 200,000 shares authorized, __?__ shares issued and outstanding — 20,000

Paid-in capital in excess of par value — 1,600,000

Retained earnings — 75,000

Total Stockholders' Equity — $ 2,295,000

Preferred dividends are in arrears for 1984 and 1985.

3. Cumulative preferred stock, 10%, $100 par, __?__ shares issued and outstanding, callable at $106 — $ 2,000,000

Paid-in capital in excess of par value—preferred — 40,000

Common stock, $5 par value, 500,000 shares authorized, __?__ shares issued and outstanding — 2,500,000

Paid-in capital in excess of par value—common — 10,000,000

Retained earnings — 2,500,000

Total Stockholders' Equity — $17,040,000

Dividends are in arrears on preferred stock for 1985.

4. Cumulative preferred stock, $6 preferred dividend, $70 par value, __?__ shares issued and outstanding, callable at $75 — $ 280,000

Common stock, no par value, 250,000 shares authorized, 150,000 shares issued and outstanding — 2,800,000

Retained earnings (deficit) — (70,000)

Total Stockholders' Equity — $ 3,010,000

Dividends are in arrears on preferred stock for 1984 and 1985.

Required:

A. Determine the number of preferred and common shares outstanding for each corporation.

B. Assuming that none of the corporations has yet declared dividends for 1986, determine book value per share of common stock.

Problem 15-4 Comprehensive Problem

The stockholders' equity section of Boxwood Corporation's balance sheet on December 31 of last year is presented here.

Stockholders' Equity		
Paid-in Capital:		
Convertible preferred stock, $100 par value, 10%, cumulative, 100,000 shares authorized, 20,000 shares issued and outstanding	$2,000,000	
Paid-in capital in excess of par value—preferred	220,000	$2,220,000
Common stock, $5 par value, 500,000 shares authorized, 200,000 shares issued and outstanding	1,000,000	
Paid-in capital in excess of par value—common	1,480,000	2,480,000
Retained earnings		650,000
Total Stockholders' Equity		$5,350,000

Each share of preferred stock is convertible into four shares of common stock. There are no preferred dividends in arrears.

Required:

A. Assume that each class of stock was issued in a single transaction. Prepare the entries that were made for the issue of each class of stock.

B. Assume that Boxwood Corporation paid total cash dividends last year in the amount of $250,000 on November 20 to stockholders of record on November 1. The dividends were declared on September 28. Prepare separate entries for each class of stock for each date if required. A single *Dividends Declared* account is used.

C. Prepare the entry that was made to close last year's net income of $520,000 from the *Income Summary* account to *Retained Earnings*.

D. Prepare an entry to record the conversion of 5,000 preferred shares into common shares.

Problem 15-5 Correcting Errors

Mulligan, Inc. completed its first year of operations as of December 31, 1987. The stockholders' equity section of the corporation's balance sheet, as prepared by Mulligan's bookkeeper, is presented here.

Stockholders' Equity

Preferred stock	$ 50,000
Common stock, no par	300,000
Retained earnings	80,000
Total Stockholders' Equity	$430,000

You have been asked to review the accounts and make any corrections necessary. During your review, you learn the following.

1. Preferred stock: $100 par value, $8 cumulative, 10,000 shares authorized, 500 shares issued and outstanding. The issue price was $103 per share and the difference between par value and the issue price was credited to *Retained Earnings*.
2. Common stock: No-par, stated value of $5 per share, 50,000 shares authorized, 25,000 shares issued and outstanding, 11,875 of which were issued for cash at $10 per share and credited in full to the *Common Stock* account. The other 13,125 shares were issued in exchange for a building with a fair value of $131,250. The *Common Stock* account was credited for the full $131,250.
3. Land with a fair value of $50,000 was donated to the corporation by the city of Yorktown. The bookkeeper debited *Land* and credited *Retained Earnings* for $50,000.
4. Common stock subscriptions were received for 5,000 shares of stock at $10 per share. The *Common Stock* account was credited for the full subscription price of $50,000. One-half of the subscription price was received as a down payment; the remainder is due early in 1988 and is included on the balance sheet as an account receivable. The stock certificates will not be issued until full payment is received.

Required:
A. Prepare individual entries to correct any errors in recording the transactions.
B. Prepare a corrected stockholders' equity section for Mulligan as of December 31, 1987.

Problem 15-6 Comprehensive Problem

Latana Corporation began operations five years ago by issuing 2,000 shares of $9 cumulative, $100 par value preferred stock at $102 and 30,000 shares of $5 par value common stock at $50 per share. The amount of stock outstanding has remained unchanged since the first day of operations (with the exception of the conversion of preferred stock into common stock). Dividends distributed each year are listed here. (Dividends in Year 5 were distributed before the preferred stock was converted.)

Year 1	$ -0-
Year 2	45,000
Year 3	15,000
Year 4	70,000
Year 5	135,000

Each share of preferred stock is convertible into three shares of common stock and is callable at $105. At the end of the fifth year, the corporation had a retained earnings credit balance of $260,000.

Required:

A. Determine, for each year, the total and per-share dividends on each class of stock, and the amount of dividends in arrears on preferred stock, if any.

B. Assume that in Year 5 dividends were declared on August 10 to be paid on September 30 to stockholders of record on September 18. Prepare entries for each class of stock for each date, if required. A *Dividends Declared* account is used, one for each class of stock.

C. Assume that 1,000 shares of preferred stock were converted into common stock on December 30 of Year 5. Prepare the journal entry to record the conversion.

D. Assume that 10,000 shares of preferred stock and 100,000 shares of common stock are authorized. Prepare the stockholders' equity section of the balance sheet at the end of Year 5. (Remember that preferred stock was converted into common stock prior to year-end.)

E. Determine the book value per share of common stock at the end of Year 5.

ALTERNATE PROBLEMS

Problem 15-1A Recording Stock Issues

Flamingo Corporation received a corporate charter authorizing it to issue 50,000 shares of $100 par value, 10%, cumulative preferred stock and 200,000 shares of no-par common stock with a stated value of $5 per share. The following transactions affecting stockholders' equity were completed during the first year.

1. Issued 100 shares of preferred stock at par value for organizational services.

2. Issued, for cash, 20,000 shares of common stock at $30 per share, and 1,000 shares of preferred stock at par.

3. Exchanged 13,000 shares of common stock for land with an appraised value of $250,000 and machinery with an appraised value of $140,000.

4. Declared the required preferred stock dividend and a $2 per share dividend on common stock.

5. Closed the *Income Summary* account. A $113,000 net income was earned.

Required:

A. Prepare journal entries to record the transactions.

B. Prepare the stockholders' equity section of the balance sheet.

Problem 15-2A Comprehensive Problem

Quill Corporation received a corporate charter in 1987, authorizing it to issue 200,000 shares of $2 par value common stock. It then completed the following transactions.

1987
March 8 Issued 4,000 shares of common stock for cash at $22 per share.
       10 Issued 400 shares of common stock to the corporation's attorney for services performed in organizing the corporation. The board of directors placed a value of $8,000 on the services.
June 16 Issued 16,000 shares of common stock in exchange for the following assets at their fair values: building, $180,000; land, $70,000; equipment, $80,000.
Dec. 5 Received subscriptions to 10,000 shares of common stock at $21

4 PARTNERSHIPS AND CORPORATIONS

per share. Twenty-five percent down payments were received with the subscriptions.

| | 31 | Closed the $3,600 debit balance in the *Income Summary* account. |

1988

| Mar. | 18 | Received the balance due on the stock subscriptions of December 5 and issued the stock. |
| Dec. | 31 | Closed the $48,000 credit balance in the *Income Summary* account. |

1989

| Feb. | 6 | The board of directors declared a $1 per share dividend on the common stock. The dividend was payable on March 1 to stockholders of record on February 22. |
| Mar. | 1 | Paid the dividends declared on February 6. |

Required:

A. Prepare journal entries for the transactions.

B. Prepare the stockholders' equity section of the balance sheet on December 31, 1987.

Problem 15-3A Issuing Stock for Assets and Preparing a Balance Sheet

Alex Winfield has operated a successful business for several years as a proprietorship. In June of 1987, Alex decided to incorporate the business in order to raise additional capital for expansion. On June 15, a corporate charter was received for Winfield Corporation, authorizing the corporation to issue 5,000 shares of $100 par, 10% cumulative preferred stock, and 100,000 shares of $2 par value common stock.

During June, Winfield Corporation completed the following transactions.

| June | 16 | Alex Winfield transferred assets with the following fair values from the proprietorship to the corporation in exchange for 20,000 shares of common stock. |

Inventory	$ 36,000
Equipment	80,000
Building	200,000
Land	50,000

| | 18 | Issued 200 shares of preferred stock for cash at $105 per share. |
| | 29 | Subscriptions to 1,000 shares of preferred stock were received at $105 per share. A down payment of 20% of the subscription price accompanied the subscription. |

Required:

A. Prepare journal entries to record the transactions.

B. Prepare a balance sheet for Winfield Corporation as of June 30, 1987.

Problem 15-4A Comprehensive Problem

The stockholders' equity section of the balance sheet of Morrow Corporation on December 31, 1987, is presented here.

MORROW CORPORATION
Stockholders' Equity
December 31, 1987

Cumulative preferred stock, 10%, $50 par value, 50,000 shares authorized:		
Issued	$500,000	
Subscribed	150,000	$ 650,000
Common stock, $5 par value, 500,000 shares authorized:		
Issued	200,000	
Subscribed	30,000	230,000
Paid-in capital in excess of par value:		
Preferred stock	26,000	
Common stock	920,000	946,000
Retained earnings (deficit)		(75,000)
Total Stockholders' Equity		$1,751,000

Listed as part of the assets on the balance sheet are: *Preferred Stock Subscriptions Receivable*, $145,750; *Common Stock Subscriptions Receivable*, $90,000.

Required:
Answer the following questions and show your computations.

A. How many shares of preferred and common stock have been issued?
B. How many shares of preferred and common stock have been subscribed to?
C. What is the total paid-in capital of Morrow Corporation?
D. What is the total legal capital of Morrow Corporation?
E. What was the average issue price of the preferred stock, including preferred stock subscribed?
F. What was the average issue price of the common stock, including common stock subscribed?
G. What is the average amount per share still owed by subscribers of common stock?
H. What is the book value per share of common stock, assuming that preferred stock dividends have all been paid and that preferred stock is callable at $54 per share?

Problem 15-5A Preparing a Classified Balance Sheet
The following data were taken from the general ledger of Harmon Company on December 31, 1987.

Cash	$ 13,600
Accounts Receivable	25,000
Common Stock	50,000
Accounts Payable	12,600
Preferred Stock	25,000
Inventory	52,100
Preferred Stock Subscriptions Receivable	28,000
Retained Earnings	88,800
Plant Assets	412,000

Accumulated Depreciation—Plant Assets	120,000
Mortgage Note Payable	80,000
Allowance for Uncollectible Accounts	1,400
Organization Costs	4,600
Preferred Stock Subscribed	50,000
Employee Wages Payable	4,500
Paid-in Capital in Excess of Par Value—Common	100,000
Paid-in Capital in Excess of Par Value—Preferred	3,000

The company is authorized to issue 10,000 shares of $50 par value, 10%, cumulative preferred stock and 50,000 shares of $5 par value common stock.

Required:
Prepare a classified balance sheet for Harmon Company.

CASE

CASE 15-1 Financial Report Analysis Case Stockholders' Equity
Refer to the annual reports in Appendix A and answer the following questions:

A. What is the par value or stated value per share of:
  1. Holiday Inns, Inc. common stock?
  2. Holiday Inns, Inc. special stock?
  3. Chrysler Corporation common stock?
  4. Kmart Corporation common stock?
B. With reference to Holiday Inns, Inc., how many shares of common stock on December 28, 1984 were:
  1. Authorized?
  2. Issued?
  3. Outstanding?
C. With reference to Chrysler Corporation:
  1. What was the annual dividend per share on preferred stock?
  2. How many shares of preferred stock on December 31, 1983 were
    (a) Authorized?
    (b) Issued?
    (c) Outstanding?
  3. What was the market price per share of common stock on December 31, 1983? On December 31, 1984?
D. With reference to Kmart Corporation, for the year ended January 30, 1985:
  1. What was the per share amount and total amount of dividends declared during the year?
  2. What was the total amount of dividends paid during the year?
  3. How many shares of common stock were issued during the year?

16

CORPORATIONS: OTHER TRANSACTIONS, INCOME, AND RETAINED EARNINGS

CHAPTER OVERVIEW AND OBJECTIVES

This chapter continues the discussion of transactions that affect stockholders' equity. When you have completed the chapter, you should understand:

1. The meaning of treasury stock and how to account for it.
2. How to record the retirement of stock.
3. The nature of stock dividends and stock splits and how to account for them.
4. The meaning of retained earnings restrictions.
5. How to report the effect of discontinued operations, extraordinary items, and changes in accounting principles.
6. How to compute and report earnings per share.
7. The nature of prior period adjustments and how to report them.

Chapter 15 included a discussion of how corporations are organized, the types of stock issued by corporations, accounting procedures for the issue of corporate stock, and the nature and accounting treatment of cash dividends. Chapter 16 treats several somewhat loosely related topics dealing with stockholders' equity and special items reported on the income statement. Because these topics are loosely related, the outline below may help in the transition from one topic to another.

Part I. Other Transactions Affecting Stockholders' Equity
A. Treasury stock.
B. Retirement of stock.
C. Stock dividends.
D. Stock splits.
E. Retained earnings restrictions.

Part II. Special Income Statement and Retained Earnings Items
A. Discontinued operations—Disposal of a business segment.
B. Extraordinary items (gains and losses).
C. Reporting the effects of a change in accounting principle.
D. Earnings per share.
E. Prior period adjustments.
F. The retained earnings statement.

PART I OTHER TRANSACTIONS AFFECTING STOCKHOLDERS' EQUITY

TREASURY STOCK

Objective 1: Accounting for Treasury Stock

Treasury stock is a corporation's own stock that:

1. Has been issued and fully paid for.
2. Has subsequently been reacquired by the corporation.
3. Has not been retired or reissued.

Treasury stock may be either preferred stock or common stock. When preferred stock is reacquired, however, it normally is retired. Therefore, most treasury stock is common stock. Among the most common reasons a corporation reacquires its own common stock are:

1. To support the current market price of the stock, since stockholders often judge management performance on the basis of the market value of the stock.
2. To have stock available for issue to employees and officers under bonus plans and employee stock purchase plans.
3. To have stock available for use in acquiring other companies.

For these reasons, many large corporations reacquire and reissue their own shares on a fairly regular basis.

Most treasury stock is acquired by cash purchase on the open market, which results in an equal amount of decrease in both the corporation's assets and in stockholders' equity. Treasury shares may be held for an indefinite period, reissued at any time, or retired.

While held by the corporation, treasury stock is similar to unissued stock, in that it contains none of the stockholder rights. Treasury stock is different from unissued stock, however, in one important respect. If stock was originally issued at an amount in excess of its par value and later purchased as treasury stock, it can be reissued for less than its par value without incurring a discount liability. When par value stock is originally issued at a price below its par value, the purchasers of the stock are contingently liable to the corporation's creditors for the amount of the discount.

PURCHASE OF TREASURY STOCK

Purchases of treasury stock are normally recorded at cost by debiting a *Treasury Stock* account and crediting *Cash*.[1] For example, assume that Brett Corporation purchased 2,000 shares of its own $10 par value common stock at $35 per share. The entry to record the purchase is:

[handwritten margin note: issued stock does not have to be outstanding.]

July	6	Treasury Stock	70,000	
		Cash		70,000
		Purchased 2,000 shares of treasury stock		
		at $35 per share. *Reacquired*		

The *Treasury Stock* account is debited for the total cost of the shares acquired. The par or stated value and the original issue price of the stock have no effect on the entry.

When treasury stock is purchased, the corporation essentially pays off some of its stockholders, thereby reducing both stockholders' equity and corporate assets. Because the stock may be reissued later, rather than formally retired, it is recorded in a *Treasury Stock* account. The *Treasury Stock* account is a contra stockholders' equity account that is subtracted from the total of paid-in capital and retained earnings in the stockholders' equity section of the balance sheet, as shown here.

Stockholders' Equity	
Paid-in capital:	
Common stock, $10 par value, 50,000 shares	
authorized, 30,000 shares issued, 28,000 shares	
outstanding	$300,000
Paid-in capital in excess of par value	185,000
Total paid-in capital	485,000
Retained earnings	162,000
Total paid-in capital and retained earnings	647,000
Less: Treasury stock, 2,000 shares, at cost	70,000
Total stockholders' equity	$577,000

The stockholders' equity section of the balance sheet shows that 30,000 shares of common stock have been issued, of which 2,000 are held as treasury stock. Therefore, the number of shares outstanding is 28,000, which constitutes the total ownership of the corporation.

---

[1]There are two acceptable methods of accounting for treasury stock, the cost method and the par value method. The cost method is more widely used in practice and is the method illustrated here.

Restriction of Retained Earnings for Treasury Stock Purchased

As mentioned earlier, when a corporation purchases treasury stock, some corporate assets are distributed to the stockholders from whom the shares were purchased. If assets are distributed to stockholders, the amount of assets left to pay creditors, of course, is reduced. To protect creditors, most states limit the distribution of assets to stockholders to the amount of retained earnings.

As discussed in Chapter 15, dividend distributions reduce both retained earnings and corporate assets. If a corporation were to declare dividends in the amount of its total retained earnings and also acquire treasury stock, it would obviously distribute assets in excess of retained earnings. Therefore, to limit total distributions of assets to the amount of retained earnings, most states restrict the payment of dividends to the extent of the cost of the treasury stock purchased. For the corporation whose stockholders' equity was just presented, dividend declarations would be limited to $92,000 ($162,000 − $70,000) until the corporation either obtains additional earnings or reissues part or all of the treasury stock.

REISSUE OF TREASURY STOCK

When treasury stock is reissued, *Cash* (or other assets received) is debited, the *Treasury Stock* account is credited for the cost of the shares reissued, and any difference between cost and the reissue price is credited or debited to *Paid-in Capital from Treasury Stock Transactions*.

To illustrate, assume that Brett Corporation reissues 1,000 of the 2,000 treasury shares acquired on July 6 for $35 per share at a reissue price of $38 per share. The reissue entry would be:

Oct.	9	Cash	38,000	
		Treasury Stock		35,000
		Paid-in Capital from Treasury Stock Transactions		3,000
		Reissued at $38 per share, 1,000 shares of treasury stock with a cost of $35 per share.		

If treasury stock is reissued at a price below its cost, *Paid-in Capital from Treasury Stock Transactions* is debited. For example, if Brett Corporation reissued 500 of its remaining 1,000 treasury shares at $30 per share, the entry would be:

Dec.	4	Cash	15,000	
		Paid-in Capital from Treasury Stock Transactions	2,500	
		Treasury Stock		17,500
		Reissued at $30 per share, 500 shares of treasury stock with a cost of $35 per share.		

If there is no paid-in capital from previous treasury stock transactions, or if the balance in that account is insufficient to cover the excess of cost over the reissue price, the debit is made to *Retained Earnings*. For example, if the 500 shares were reissued at $27 per share, the entry would be:

Dec.	4	Cash	13,500	
		Paid-in Capital from Treasury Stock		
		Transactions	3,000	
		Retained Earnings	1,000	
		Treasury Stock		17,500
		Reissued at $27 per share, 500 shares of treasury stock with a cost of $35 per share.		

The difference between the reissue price and cost of the treasury stock is credited or debited to *Paid-in Capital* (or possibly debited to *Retained Earnings*), rather than to a gain or loss account. Corporations earn profits or incur losses from the sale of goods or services to customers, not from the retirement or reissue of capital stock. Although not exactly the same, the purchase of treasury stock is similar to a withdrawal, and the reissue of the treasury stock is similar to a new investment by a proprietor or a partner. That is, these transactions are disinvestment and investment transactions that do not affect gain or loss.

RETIREMENT OF STOCK

A corporation may reacquire shares of its own stock with the intention of formally retiring them. When shares are retired, the stockholders' equity amounts related to the retired shares are removed from the capital accounts. If the shares are reacquired at a price less than their average issue price, the excess of the average issue price over cost is credited to *Paid-in Capital—Stock Retirement*. For example, assume that a corporation issued 100,000 shares of its $5 par value common stock at an average of $15 per share. The entry to issue the stock was:

Objective 2: Recording the Retirement of Capital Stock

Jan.	18	Cash	1,500,000	
		Common Stock		500,000
		Paid-in Capital in Excess of Par Value—Common		1,000,000

If 10,000 shares are later reacquired at $13 per share and formally retired, the entry is:

May	6	Common Stock (10,000 × $5)	50,000	
		Paid-in Capital in Excess of Par Value—		
		Common*	100,000	
		Cash		130,000
		Paid-in Capital—Stock Retirement		20,000
		Purchased and retired 10,000 shares of		
		common stock at $13 per share.		
		*(10,000 × $10)		

If the shares are reacquired at a price in excess of their average issue price, the excess of cost over average issue price is debited to *Retained Earnings*. For example, if the 10,000 shares were acquired at $18 per share, the entry would be:

May	6	Common Stock	50,000	
		Paid-in Capital in Excess of Par Value—		
		Common	100,000	
		Retained Earnings	30,000	
		Cash		180,000
		Purchased and retired 10,000 shares of		
		stock at $18 per share.		

Note that the retirement does not result in a gain or a loss to the corporation. Like treasury stock transactions, stock retirement transactions are disinvestments affecting only balance sheet stockholders' equity accounts. Revenues and expenses are unaffected.

If the stock being retired is held as treasury stock, the entries are similar to those just presented, except that the *Treasury Stock* account (rather than *Cash*) is credited. For example, if the stock had been purchased at $13 per share and held as treasury stock, the acquisition entry would have been:

Apr.	4	Treasury Stock	130,000	
		Cash		130,000
		Purchased 10,000 shares of treasury		
		stock at $13 per share.		

If the stock is later formally retired, the entry is:

May	6	Common Stock	50,000	
		Paid-in Capital in Excess of Par Value—		
		Common	100,000	
		Treasury Stock		130,000
		Paid-in Capital—Stock Retirement		20,000
		Formally retired 10,000 shares of stock		
		held as treasury stock.		

STOCK DIVIDENDS

A **stock dividend** is a pro rata distribution of additional shares of a corporation's stock to its stockholders. A stock dividend normally consists of the distribution of additional shares of common stock to common stockholders.

Stock dividends are not the same as cash dividends. Unlike cash dividends, which reduce both corporate assets and stockholders' equity, stock dividends have no effect on either corporate assets or on total stockholders' equity. The only balance sheet effect of a stock dividend is a transfer of retained earnings to paid-in capital.

Stock dividends sometimes are declared by successful companies that have used their earnings to expand operations, rather than using the earnings to declare dividends. A stock dividend gives stockholders tangible evidence of the increase in their equity in the corporation, without distributing cash or other assets to them.

Another reason for stock dividends is to reduce the market price of the common stock by increasing the number of shares outstanding. When a corporation grows, the market price of its common stock tends to increase. By reducing the market price of its shares, the corporation can encourage a broader ownership by both small and large investors. A stock dividend must be relatively large to accomplish this objective. As an alternative to declaring a large stock dividend, the corporation may undertake a stock split, which is described later in this chapter.

Objective 3:
Accounting for
Stock Dividends
and Stock Splits

ACCOUNTING FOR STOCK DIVIDENDS

When stock dividends are declared, retained earnings are transferred to paid-in capital. As discussed in Chapter 15, state incorporation laws generally require the maintenance of legal capital at an amount equal to the number of shares outstanding, times the par or stated value per share. Consequently, a minimum amount equal to the par or stated value of the additional shares issued must be transferred from *Retained Earnings* to the *Common Stock* account.

Accounting rules, however, distinguish between small and large stock dividends. *Small stock dividends* (defined as about 20% or less of outstanding shares) tend to have little immediate effect on the market price of the stock; some investors, therefore, consider them to be distributions of earnings. Accounting rules for small stock dividends provide that retained earnings should be transferred to paid-in capital in an amount equal to the number of additional shares issued, times the market price per share.

Small Stock Dividends

To illustrate a small stock dividend, assume that Brett Corporation has the following stockholders' equity.

Stockholders' Equity	
Paid-in capital:	
Common stock, $5 par value, 100,000 shares	
authorized, 50,000 shares issued and outstanding	$250,000
Paid-in capital in excess of par value	300,000
Total paid-in capital	550,000
Retained earnings	400,000
Total stockholders' equity	$950,000

Assume, further, that the board of directors declares a 5% stock dividend on December 20, distributable on January 10 to stockholders of record as of December 31. The market price of the stock was $22 per share on December 20. The entry to record the declaration of the stock dividend is:

Dec.	20	Stock Dividend Declared	55,000	
		Stock Dividend Distributable*		12,500
		Paid-in Capital in Excess of Par Value**		42,500
		To record the declaration of a 5% stock dividend on 50,000 shares of outstanding common stock.		
		*(2,500 × $5)		
		**[2,500 × ($22 − $5)]		

Like cash dividends, stock dividends are declared on outstanding shares only. Because this is a small stock dividend, the *Stock Dividend Declared* account is debited for the market value of the shares to be distributed, computed as follows.

$$50,000 \text{ shares} \times 5\% = 2,500 \text{ shares} \times \$22 = \$55,000$$

The *Stock Dividend Declared* account is a temporary retained earnings account that is closed to *Retained Earnings* at the end of the year.

The *Stock Dividend Distributable* account is credited for the par value of the shares to be issued, and the excess of the total market value over par value is credited to *Paid-in Capital in Excess of Par Value*. The *Stock Dividend Distributable* account would be reported as a separate item of paid-in capital on the December 31 balance sheet, as illustrated in Figure 16–1 on page 616. Note that it is not a liability because there is no obligation to distribute corporate assets.

When the shares are distributed on January 10, the entry is:

Jan.	10	Stock Dividend Distributable	12,500	
		Common Stock		12,500
		To record the distribution of a 2,500 share stock dividend.		

The net effect of the entries on December 20 and January 10 is to decrease retained earnings by $55,000 and to increase paid-in capital by the same amount, of which $12,500 is an increase in legal capital and $42,500 increases *Paid-in Capital in Excess of Par Value*. Thus, total stockholders' equity remains unchanged by the stock dividend, as demonstrated here.

	Before Stock Dividend	After Stock Dividend
Common stock	$250,000	$262,500
Paid-in capital in excess of par value	300,000	342,500
Retained earnings	400,000	345,000
Total stockholders' equity	$950,000	$950,000

Because total stockholders' equity remains unchanged, each stockholder's interest in total stockholders' equity also would remain unchanged. For example, assume that Paula Dean owns 5,000 shares (10%) of Brett Corporation before the distribution of the stock dividend. Her share of the stockholders' equity before and after the dividend is:

$$\text{Before: } \frac{5{,}000 \text{ shares}}{50{,}000 \text{ shares}} = 10\% \times \$950{,}000 = \$95{,}000$$

$$\text{After: } \frac{5{,}250 \text{ shares}}{52{,}500 \text{ shares}} = 10\% \times \$950{,}000 = \$95{,}000$$

Large Stock Dividends

Large stock dividends (those in excess of about 20% of shares outstanding) generally have the effect of an immediate and proportionate reduction in the market price of the stock. For example, if the market price of the stock was $50 before a stock dividend, the declaration of a 100% stock dividend reduces the market price immediately to about $25 per share, since there are twice as many shares outstanding. Because stockholders observe that the total market value of their shares remains unchanged after a large stock dividend, they do not tend to view it as a distribution of earnings. As a result, accounting rules for large stock dividends require the transfer of retained earnings in an amount sufficient only to comply with state laws, which is the par or stated value of the additional shares issued.

To illustrate the accounting for a large stock dividend, assume that Brett Corporation declared a 100% stock dividend. Brett Corporation's stockholders' equity before the stock dividend was as shown on page 612. The entry would be:

Dec.	20	Stock Dividend Declared	250,000	
		Stock Dividend Distributable		250,000
		To record the declaration of a 100% stock		
		dividend on 50,000 shares of common		
		stock (50,000 × $5 par value).		

[handwritten margin notes: "transfer par of stock from retained earnings to capital"; "2-1 double shares outstanding ½ par value"]

STOCK SPLITS

Stock is normally traded in 100-share lots. The purchase of 100 shares of stock selling at $100 per share requires an investment of $10,000. This is a rather large sum for most small investors, especially those who prefer to spread their investment risk by purchasing stock in several corporations. Consequently, a company that wants to attract small investors may want to reduce the market price of its stock to make it more attractive to them. One method of accomplishing this objective is to declare a large stock dividend. An alternative is a **stock split,** which decreases the par or stated value of the stock and increases the number of shares proportionately.

To illustrate, assume that Brett Corporation's stockholders' equity is as follows.

Stockholders' Equity	
Paid-in capital:	
Common stock, $5 par value, 100,000 shares authorized, 50,000 shares issued and outstanding	$250,000
Paid-in capital in excess of par value	300,000
Total paid-in capital	550,000
Retained earnings	400,000
Total stockholders' equity	$950,000

Assume, further, that the common stock has a current market price of $100 per share. In order to reduce the market price, the board of directors votes to split the stock four for one, which should reduce the market price per share to about $25. When the stock is split, the par value per share is decreased to $1.25 ($5 ÷ 4) and the number of authorized shares is increased to 400,000. Outstanding stock is recalled and new stock certificates are issued; four new shares given for each share recalled.

A stock split does not change the balance of any of the stockholders' equity accounts. Legal capital remains the same—at $250,000—since 200,000 shares are outstanding with a par value of $1.25 each. Thus, all that is necessary is a memo entry in the journal and the *Common Stock* account, indicating that the par value has been reduced and that the number of shares has been increased.

COMPARISON OF LARGE STOCK DIVIDENDS AND STOCK SPLITS

Large stock dividends are sometimes mistakenly called stock splits. Although both have the same effect on the market price of the stock (so that a two-for-one stock split and a 100% stock dividend both result in a doubling of the number of shares outstanding and a market price of about one-half of the previous market price), legally, they are different. All stock dividends result in an increase in the amount of legal capital and a decrease in retained earnings; stock splits do not.

RETAINED EARNINGS RESTRICTIONS

There are often restrictions on retained earnings that prevent the total amount of retained earnings reported in the balance sheet from being declared as dividends. Some of these are legal restrictions, some are contractual, and some are voluntary. As discussed earlier, an example of a legal restriction is the limitation on the availability of retained earnings for dividends to the extent of the cost of treasury stock purchased.

Objective 4: Retained Earnings Restrictions

Contractual restrictions are exemplified by bond indentures and other borrowing agreements that include restrictions on the amount of dividends that can be paid until the debt is repaid. The purpose of such restrictions is to provide additional protection to the lenders, since corporate assets that are not distributed as dividends are more likely to be available for interest payments and debt retirement.

Other retained earnings restrictions are made voluntarily by the board of directors to disclose limitations on dividend distributions. For example, many corporations have contingent liabilities, such as lawsuits in process. Without the restriction, there could be a double decrease in assets: (1) to pay dividends; and (2) to settle the lawsuits if their defense is unsuccessful. Regardless of the nature of the retained earnings restriction—legal, contractual, or voluntary—its purpose is to retain assets in the business, rather than distribute them as dividends.

Restrictions on the payment of dividends are normally disclosed in footnotes to the financial statements. For example, recent financial statements of St. Regis Corporation included the following footnote.

Agreements covering the long-term debt of St. Regis contain certain restrictions on the payment of cash dividends. The most restrictive of such agreements relates to the 8⅞% promissory notes. At December 31, 1983, the retained earnings that were free of such restrictions amounted to approximately $498,900,000.

The December 31, 1983, balance sheet reported total retained earnings of $1,059,893,000. Thus, less than one-half of St. Regis Corporation's retained earnings were available for dividends at that time.

COMPREHENSIVE ILLUSTRATION OF STOCKHOLDERS' EQUITY

In this and the preceding chapter, several illustrations of the treatment of stockholders' equity items were presented. Terminology used and the amount of detail provided vary considerably in practice. Figure 16–1 shows one possible presentation of stockholders' equity, in this case for Pratt Communications, Inc. at December 31, 1987.

The items listed under additional paid-in capital are normally combined and reported as one amount. The items making up the total additional paid-in capital are then presented in a footnote to the financial statements.

Figure 16–1
Stockholders' Equity

PRATT COMMUNICATIONS, INC.
Stockholders' Equity

Paid-in capital:	
8% Cumulative preferred stock, $100 par value, 50,000 shares authorized, 25,000 shares issued and outstanding	$2,500,000
Common stock, stated value $5 per share, 500,000 shares authorized, 200,000 shares issued, 195,000 shares outstanding	1,000,000
Common stock subscribed, 30,000 shares	150,000
Common stock dividend distributable, 20,000 shares	100,000
Additional paid-in capital:	
In excess of par value—preferred stock	200,000
In excess of stated value—common stock	1,870,000
From the retirement of preferred stock	75,000
From treasury stock transactions	160,000
Total paid-in capital	6,055,000
Retained earnings (of which $580,000 is restricted under debt agreements and for treasury stock purchased)	1,690,000
Total paid-in capital and retained earnings	7,745,000
Less: Treasury stock, 5,000 common shares at cost	125,000
Total stockholders' equity	$7,620,000

PART II SPECIAL INCOME STATEMENT AND RETAINED EARNINGS ITEMS

Objective 5: Reporting Discontinued Operations, Extraordinary Items, and Changes in Accounting Principles

Determining periodic net income is one of the primary functions of accounting. The amount of net income earned, as well as the trend of earnings over time, are important to users of accounting information because they serve as measures of management efficiency, as measures of creditworthiness, and as factors in the prediction of future earnings. Both stock market prices and dividends are affected by net income earned. Earnings from normal, recurring operating activities are presumed to be more useful in predicting future earnings. Consequently, earnings from normal operations are separated on the income statement from those earnings resulting from unusual transactions that are not expected to recur on a regular basis. Three categories of unusual transactions are identified by current accounting practice: discontinued operations, extraordinary gains and losses, and changes in accounting principle. Prior period adjustments (another category, discussed later in this chapter), are reported as direct adjustments to retained earnings in the retained earnings statement.

DISCONTINUED OPERATIONS— DISPOSAL OF A BUSINESS SEGMENT

Most large corporations have many segments. For the purpose of reporting discontinued operations, a **segment of a business** is defined as ''a component of an entity whose activities represent a separate major line of business or class of customer.''[2] For example, assume that Pratt Communications, Inc. has four segments—newspaper publishing, magazine publishing, radio, and television. If one of these segments is sold, the income statement for the year will not be comparable with those of other years. Current accounting standards require that for the segment sold, the gain or loss on sale and the operating net income or loss of the current year to the date of sale must be presented in a separate section of the income statement after income from continuing operations.

To illustrate, assume that Pratt Communications, Inc. sold its radio stations on August 1, 1987, at an after-tax gain of $800,000. Prior to August 1, the radio stations had earned $60,000 net income after taxes. The sale would be reported in a separate discontinued operations section of the income statement, as shown in Figure 16–2.

Revenues and expenses reported separately in the income statement include those of the newspaper, magazine, and television segments only. In determining the operating income of the discontinued segment, the revenues and expenses of the radio segment, between January 1 and August 1, are reported at their net amount, which is added to the gain on the sale of the radio division in the discontinued operations section. By reporting in this way, income from continuing operations can be used to estimate the earning power of those segments that will continue to operate in the future.

Figure 16–2
Income Statement—
Special Items

PRATT COMMUNICATIONS, INC.
Income Statement
For the Year Ended December 31, 1987

Revenues:		
Advertising revenue		$4,600,000
Subscription revenue		3,280,000
Total revenues		7,880,000
Expenses:		
Selling expenses	$4,800,000	
General and administrative expenses	1,640,000	
Interest expense	390,000	6,830,000
Income from continuing operations before tax		1,050,000
Income tax expense		420,000
Income from continuing operations		630,000
Discontinued operations:		
Operating income of discontinued segment (Net of $39,000 income tax)	$ 60,000	
Gain on sale of discontinued segment (Net of $267,000 income tax)	800,000	860,000
Net income		$1,490,000

[2]"Reporting the Results of Operations," *APB Opinion No. 30* (AICPA: New York, June 1973), par. 13.

INCOME TAX ALLOCATION

When a segment of the business is disposed of, the total income tax expense for the year of $726,000 ($420,000 + $39,000 + $267,000) must be allocated to show both the amount that relates to income from continuing operations ($420,000) and the amount identified with discontinued operations ($39,000 + $267,000). The income tax effects on discontinued operations are generally shown parenthetically, as illustrated in Figure 16–2. We will see later that this approach is also used in reporting extraordinary items and changes in accounting principle.

If a loss is incurred on operations of the discontinued segment to the date of sale, or if a loss is incurred on the sale of the segment, income tax savings result, which serve to reduce the amount of the loss incurred. For example, if Pratt Communication, Inc. incurred an operating loss of $99,000 before tax on the radio segment to the date of sale, the income statement presentation is:

Income from continuing operations before tax		$1,050,000
Income tax expense		420,000
Income from continuing operations		630,000
Discontinued operations:		
Operating loss of discontinued segment		
(Net of $39,000 tax savings)	$(60,000)	
Gain on sale of discontinued segment		
(Net of $267,000 income tax)	800,000	740,000
Net income		$1,370,000

Note that income from continuing operations remains the same; $630,000. The results of discontinued operations have no effect on the amount of income from continuing operations.

EXTRAORDINARY ITEMS

Some gains and losses result from events so unusual that they are reported separately on the income statement in order to distinguish them from the results of normal operating activities. These events, called **extraordinary items,** are relatively rare, because they must be both unusual in nature and occur infrequently. Unusual and infrequent events are described in *APB Opinion No. 30* as:

> *Unusual nature—the underlying events or transaction should possess a high degree of abnormality and be of a type clearly unrelated to, or only incidentally related to, the ordinary and typical activities of the entity, taking into account the environment in which the entity operates.*

> *Infrequency of Occurrence—the underlying event or transaction should be of a type that would not reasonably be expected to recur in the foreseeable future, taking into account the environment in which the entity operates.*[3]

[3]*Ibid.*, par. 20.

The environment includes such factors as the characteristics of the industry in which the firm operates, the geographical location of its operations, and the nature and extent of governmental regulations.

A given event may be unusual in nature for one firm but not for another because of differences in their environments. For example, an earthquake loss in Minnesota (where earthquakes rarely occur) would be unusual, whereas one in California may not be. The past experience of a company may be used to determine the probability of recurrence of an event, but is not sufficient, by itself, to satisfy the criterion of infrequency of occurrence. If the event is a type that occurs frequently in the environment in which the firm operates, it is not extraordinary.

Because the criteria for extraordinary items are somewhat subjective, judgment is required in order to distinguish extraordinary events from normal operating activities. *Accounting Principle Board (APB) Opinion No. 30* offers some guidance by including examples of events that might be considered extraordinary, as well as examples of events that generally are not extraordinary, as follows.

Extraordinary	Not Extraordinary
1. Major casualties such as an earthquake, if infrequent in the area. 2. Expropriation of assets by a foreign government. 3. Loss from a prohibition under a newly enacted law or regulation.	1. Write-down or write-off of receivables, inventories, equipment leased to others, deferred research and development costs, or other intangible assets. 2. Gains or losses from exchange or translation of foreign currencies, including those relating to major devaluations and revaluations. 3. Gains or losses on disposal of a segment of a business. 4. Other gains or losses from sale or abandonment of property, plant, or equipment used in the business. 5. Effects of a strike, including those against competitors and major suppliers. 6. Adjustments of accruals on long-term contracts.[4]

In addition, any material gain or loss on the early extinguishment of debt must be reported as an extraordinary item net of related income tax effect.[5]

When an event qualifies as an extraordinary item, it is reported on the income statement after discontinued operations (if any) under the caption of ''Extraordinary Items.'' To illustrate, assume that Pratt Communications, Inc. has a television station damaged by an earthquake in an area where no quake has ever occurred before. The loss is reported on the income statement, as shown in Figure 16-3 on page 624. Note that, as with the disposal of a segment

---

[4]*Ibid.*, par. 23.

[5]*Statement of Financial Accounting Standards No. 4.* ''Reporting Gains and Losses from Extinguishment of Debt'' (FASB: Stamford, Conn., March 1975), par. 8.

of a business, the extraordinary loss is reported net of its related tax effect. That is, we have assumed an $800,000 pretax earthquake loss, of which $200,000 reduces income tax expense, thereby producing a tax savings.

Sometimes events occur that meet only one of the criteria for extraordinary items. In those cases, any gain or loss resulting should be reported as a separate item in the determination of income from continuing operations. For example, assume that Pratt Communications, Inc. had a gain of $400,000 on the sale of securities held as an investment. The gain is not extraordinary because the sale of investments is not unusual. The gain is so large that it should be brought to the attention of users of the financial statements. Thus, it is reported separately in determining income from continuing operations, as illustrated in Figure 16–3 on page 624.

CHANGE IN ACCOUNTING PRINCIPLE

As discussed in earlier chapters, alternative methods may be used to account for some types of transactions. For example, several methods are acceptable in accounting for depreciation and for inventory. Different methods may result in material differences in income statement and balance sheet amounts.

The *consistency principle* in accounting generally requires that once an accounting method is adopted, it must be used consistently in order to provide comparable data from one accounting period to another. However, an exception to the consistency principle is permitted and an accounting method may be changed if a new method is preferable to the old one. A company may change from the straight-line method to an accelerated depreciation method for depreciating equipment, for example, because the service benefits incorporated in the equipment are actually being used on an accelerated basis.

When an accounting principle is changed, a description of the change, the reason for the change, and its effect on net income for the period must be disclosed in a footnote to the financial statements. In addition, the change in principle is assumed to have been made at the beginning of the year of change, and the cumulative effect of the change to the beginning of the year generally must be reported on the income statement immediately after extraordinary items, if any. The *cumulative effect* is the total effect the new method would have had on retained earnings if it had been applied in past periods instead of the old method.[6]

To illustrate, assume that Pratt Communications, Inc. adopted the sum-of-years'-digits depreciation method for printing equipment purchased at the beginning of 1985. The equipment cost $630,000 and had an estimated useful life of six years with a zero residual value. In 1987, management decides to change to the straight-line method, because it more closely reflects the true pattern of asset use. The cumulative effect of the change to the beginning of 1987 is computed as follows.

[6]Some changes in accounting principle are disclosed by restating the financial statements of prior years, rather than by recognition of the cumulative effect of the change in the current year. For a complete discussion of accounting changes, see *APB Opinion No. 20,* ''Accounting Changes.'' (AICPA: New York: 1972).

Depreciation taken under SYD method for 1985
and 1986:

$$\frac{6}{21} + \frac{5}{21} = \frac{11}{21} \times \$630,000 = \qquad \$330,000$$

Depreciation that would have been taken under the
straight-line method for 1985 and 1986:
$630,000 ÷ 6 years = $105,000 × 2 years = <u>210,000</u>
Cumulative effect of the change <u>$120,000</u>

A journal entry is prepared to adjust the *Accumulated Depreciation* account and to recognize the cumulative effect of the change, as follows.

Dec.	31	Accumulated Depreciation—Equipment	120,000	
		Cumulative Effect of Accounting Change		120,000
		To record the cumulative effect of a change from SYD to straight-line depreciation.		

The cumulative effect of the change, assuming an income tax rate of 40%, is reported on the income statement as shown in Figure 16–3 on page 624. Again, note that the cumulative effect of the accounting change is reported net of its related income tax effect. Because it is an income statement account, the *Cumulative Effect of Accounting Change* account is closed to the *Income Summary* account at year-end.

EARNINGS PER SHARE

One of the most widely publicized accounting statistics is **earnings per share** of common stock (EPS). Earnings per share data are used to evaluate the past performance of a business, to form an opinion as to its potential future performance, and to compare the operating performance of different companies. If a company has only common stock outstanding, earnings per share is computed by dividing net income by the average number of shares outstanding.

**Objective 6:
Computing and
Reporting
Earnings Per
Share**

The average number of shares is computed on a weighted average basis. For example, if Merk Company had 100,000 shares of common stock outstanding at the beginning of the year and issued 20,000 additional shares on April 1, the weighted average is based on the number of months that the shares were outstanding during the year ended December 31, and the computation is:

100,000 shares × 3/12 =	25,000
120,000 shares × 9/12 =	90,000
Weighted Average Shares Outstanding	115,000

or

100,000 shares × 12/12 =	100,000
20,000 shares × 9/12 =	15,000
Weighted Average Shares Outstanding	115,000

Basing the computation of EPS on the weighted average number of shares recognizes the fact that the assets received from the issue of shares on April 1 were available for earning revenue during three-fourths of the year only.

If Merk Company reports net income of $287,500 for the year, earnings per share is:

$$\frac{\text{Net income}}{\text{Average shares outstanding}} = \frac{\$287,500}{115,000} = \$2.50$$

Note that earnings per share pertain to common stock only. If a company has both cumulative preferred stock and common stock outstanding, the preferred dividend requirement for the year must be subtracted from net income. The remaining net income, which accrues to the benefit of the common stockholders, is divided by the average number of common shares outstanding. For example, assume that Merk Company has $400,000 of $100 par value, 6% cumulative preferred stock outstanding. The computation of earnings per share of common stock is:

$$\frac{\text{Net income} - \text{preferred dividends}}{\text{Average common shares outstanding}} = \frac{\$287,500 - \$24,000}{115,000} = \$2.29$$

PRIMARY AND FULLY DILUTED EARNINGS PER SHARE

When a company has a simple capital structure, like the one just illustrated, the computation of earnings per share is relatively straightforward. Many companies, however, have a **complex capital structure** that includes convertible securities, the conversion of which have the potential of decreasing (*diluting*) earnings per share of common stock. In other words, the conversion of preferred stock or the exercise of stock purchase rights will increase the number of common shares outstanding and, therefore, might reduce earnings per share.

To indicate the potential dilution, two earnings per share figures are generally presented, primary earnings per share and fully diluted earnings per share. **Primary earnings per share** is computed as illustrated above.[7] **Fully diluted earnings per share** is computed under the assumption that all potentially dilutive securities were converted or exercised at the beginning of the year. Thus, users are notified as to the potential dilution that might occur.

To illustrate, assume that each of the 4,000 shares of Merk Company's $100 par, 6%, cumulative preferred stock is convertible into 4 shares of common stock. The computation of primary and fully diluted earnings per share, assuming that the convertible preferred stock affects only the computation of fully diluted earnings per share, is:

$$\text{Primary} = \frac{\$287,500 - \$24,000}{115,000} = \$2.29$$

[7]Convertible securities and stock purchase rights that have a high probability of being converted or exercised are called common stock equivalents and are sometimes included in the computation of primary earnings per share. The rules for determining when and how to include them are beyond the scope of this book. They are described and illustrated in *APB Opinion No. 15*, ''Earnings Per Share'' (AICPA: New York, 1969).

$$\text{Fully diluted} = \frac{\$287{,}500}{115{,}000 + 16{,}000} = \$2.19$$

In the numerator of the fully diluted computation, the preferred stock is assumed to have been converted at the beginning of the year. Consequently, there would have been no dividends on the preferred stock. However, there would have been 16,000 additional shares of common stock outstanding during the year, which are added to the outstanding common shares in the denominator.

EARNINGS PER SHARE ON THE INCOME STATEMENT

Because of the significance attached by investors and others to earnings per share data, publicly held corporations are required to present earnings-per-share data on the face of the income statement. If a company has discontinued operations, extraordinary items, or the cumulative effect of a change in accounting principle reported on the income statement, earnings per share data must be presented for each of these components, as well as for final net income. The presentation of earnings per share is illustrated in Figure 16–3.

COMPREHENSIVE INCOME STATEMENT ILLUSTRATED

A comprehensive income statement for Pratt Communications, Inc., is shown in Figure 16–3. Although a company seldom has all of these transactions and events occur in a single year, they are included here to illustrate their treatment.

PRIOR PERIOD ADJUSTMENTS

Generally, all items of profit and loss recognized during a period must be included in the determination of net income of that period. A major exception to this general policy is the correction of a material error in the financial statements of a prior period.[8]

**Objective 7:
Reporting Prior
Period Adjust-
ments**

Errors result from mathematical mistakes, mistakes in the application of accounting principles, or oversight or misuse of facts that existed at the time that the financial statements were prepared. Errors discovered in the same period in which they occurred are corrected in the current period's financial statements. Errors in net income not discovered until a later accounting period are excluded from the current year's income statement to avoid distorting net income of the current period. Because net income is closed to retained earnings, the correction of an error in a prior year's net income is adjusted to the beginning balance of retained earnings in the year in which the error is discovered. These adjustments, which are made net of income tax effects, are called **prior period adjustments.**

---

[8]"Prior Period Adjustments," *Statement of Financial Accounting Standards No. 16* (FASB: Stamford, Conn., 1977), par. 11.

Figure 16–3
Comprehensive Income Statement

PRATT COMMUNICATIONS, INC.
Income Statement
For the Year Ended December 31, 1987

Revenues:		
Advertising revenue		$4,600,000
Subscription revenue		3,280,000
Total revenues		7,880,000
Expenses:		
Selling expenses	$4,800,000	
General and administrative expenses	1,640,000	
Interest expense	390,000	6,830,000
Income from operations		1,050,000
Gain on sale of securities		400,000
Income from continuing operations before tax		1,450,000
Income tax expense		580,000
Income from continuing operations		870,000
Discontinued operations:		
Operating income of discontinued segment (Net of $39,000 income tax)	60,000	
Gain on sale of discontinued segment (Net of $267,000 income tax)	800,000	860,000
Income before extraordinary item		1,730,000
Extraordinary item: Loss from earthquake (Net of $200,000 tax savings)		600,000
Income before effect of an accounting change		1,130,000
Cumulative effect on prior years' income of a change in depreciation method (Net of $48,000 income tax)		72,000
Net income		$1,202,000

Earnings (loss) per common share for:		Computations
Continuing operations	$3.44	(1)
Discontinued operations	4.41	(2)
Extraordinary loss	(3.08)	(3)
Cumulative effect of accounting change	.37	(4)
Net Income	$5.14	(5)

The earnings per share data are based on the data in Figure 16–1, with $200,000 preferred dividends ($2,500,000 × 8%), and 195,000 shares of common stock outstanding. Since there are no potentially dilutive securities, it is not necessary to report fully diluted earnings per share.

Computation of the various earnings per share figures are:
1. $870,000 − $200,000 preferred dividends = $670,000/195,000 shares.
2. $860,000/195,000 shares.
3. $600,000/195,000 shares.
4. $72,000/195,000 shares.
5. $1,202,000 − $200,000 preferred dividends = $1,002,000/195,000 shares.

Earnings per share for everything from Net Income down

Earnings ÷ Shares outstanding.

To illustrate, assume that in the process of preparing adjusting entries at the end of 1987, the accountant discovered that the company had failed to record depreciation of $65,000 on machinery acquired at the beginning of 1986. Assuming no income tax effect, the entry to correct the error would be made as follows.

Dec.	31	Retained Earnings	65,000	
		Accumulated Depreciation—Machinery		65,000
		To correct the failure to record		
		depreciation for 1986.		

The net income credited to retained earnings in closing the books at the end of 1986 was overstated by $65,000. In addition, accumulated depreciation on machinery was understated on the 1986 balance sheet. The debit to retained earnings in the entry shown corrects the balance in the *Retained Earnings* account, and the credit to *Accumulated Depreciation—Machinery* corrects the balance in that account. The correction of the beginning balance of retained earnings for 1987 is reported as shown on the retained earnings statement presented in Figure 16–4.

RETAINED EARNINGS STATEMENT

In addition to a balance sheet, an income statement, and a statement of changes in financial position, a retained earnings statement is prepared, either as a separate statement or as part of a combined statement of income and retained earnings. The retained earnings statement summarizes the changes that have taken place in the *Retained Earnings* account during the year. It also serves as a connecting link between the retained earnings balances reported on the balance sheets of successive accounting periods.

The retained earnings statement of Pratt Communications, Inc. shows that the company started the year with a retained earnings balance of $977,250. During 1987, retained earnings were reduced for the correction of an error in prior years' depreciation expense ($65,000) and for dividends declared

Figure 16–4
Retained Earnings
Statement

PRATT COMMUNICATIONS, INC.
Retained Earnings Statement
For the Year Ended December 31, 1987

Retained earnings balance, January 1		$ 977,250
Correction of error in prior years' depreciation		(65,000)
Retained earnings balance, January 1, as adjusted		912,250
Net income		1,202,000
Total		2,114,250
Less: Cash Dividends		
On preferred stock	$200,000	
On common stock—$1.15 per share	224,250	424,250
Retained earnings balance, December 31		$1,690,000

($424,250). Retained earnings were increased by income earned of $1,202,000 (Figure 16–3); thus, the retained earnings balance on December 31, 1987 is $1,690,000, which is also the amount shown in Figure 16–1.

GLOSSARY

COMPLEX CAPITAL STRUCTURE. A capital structure that contains potentially dilutive securities (p. 622).

EARNINGS PER SHARE. The amount of net income identified with each share of common stock (p. 621).

EXTRAORDINARY ITEM. An event that is unusual in nature and occurs infrequently, considering the environment in which a firm operates (p. 618).

FULLY DILUTED EARNINGS PER SHARE. An earnings per share figure computed under the assumption that all potentially dilutive securities were converted or exercised at the beginning of the year (p. 622).

PRIMARY EARNINGS PER SHARE. Net income identified with common stock divided by the weighted average number of common shares outstanding during the year (p. 622).

PRIOR PERIOD ADJUSTMENT. A direct adjustment to retained earnings to correct an error in the net income of a prior period (p. 623).

SEGMENT OF A BUSINESS. A component of an entity the activities of which represent a separate major line of business or class of customer (p. 616).

STOCK DIVIDEND. A pro rata distribution of additional shares of a corporation's own stock to its stockholders (p. 611).

STOCK SPLIT. A decrease in the par or stated value of stock with a proportionate increase in the number of shares (p. 614).

TREASURY STOCK. A corporation's own stock that has been issued and reacquired but not retired or reissued (p. 606).

DISCUSSION QUESTIONS

1. What is treasury stock? For what purposes might a corporation reacquire its own shares?
2. How is treasury stock similar to unissued stock? How is it different?
3. A corporation purchased 1,000 shares of its own $1 par value common stock at a price of $20 per share. What is the entry to record the purchase? What kind of account is the *Treasury Stock* account? How is this account reported on the balance sheet?
4. XYZ Corporation has retained earnings of $480,000 and holds treasury stock purchased at a cost of $180,000. In most states, what is the maximum amount of retained earnings that could be declared as a dividend? Why? Where is information regarding restrictions on retained earnings disclosed?
5. What accounts are involved when recording the purchase for cash of a corporation's own par value stock at a price less than its average issue price, if the shares are to be formally retired? How is this entry different if the shares are purchased at a price in excess of their average issue price?

6. What is a stock dividend? What effect do stock dividends have on corporate assets and on total stockholders' equity? How does a stock dividend affect book value per share of stock?

7. ABC Corporation has 50,000 shares of $1 par value common stock issued and outstanding. What entry would be made to record the declaration of a 5% stock dividend at a time when the market price of the shares is $25?

8. What is a stock split? What effect does a stock split have on total stockholders' equity?

9. A corporation with 20,000 shares of common stock outstanding splits its stock three for one. How many shares are outstanding after the split?

10. Indicate where each of the following items should be reported in the income statement.
    (a) Gain on sale of all refining operations by an oil company.
    (b) Loss on the disposal of obsolete manufacturing equipment.
    (c) An uninsured loss from the total destruction of a company's office building caused by a tornado. (Tornados are rare in the area in which the company operates.)
    (d) A change from the straight-line method of depreciation to the double declining-balance method.
    (e) Gain on the sale of one of several investments in the common stock of other companies.
    (f) Correction of an error in recording depreciation expense in a prior period.

11. Which of the following items would generally be considered extraordinary?
    (a) Bonus payments to management personnel.
    (b) Uninsured flood loss.
    (c) Bad debts expense.
    (d) Loss on the sale of a plant asset.
    (e) Loss from the passing of a new federal law prohibiting the sale of a certain product.
    (f) Loss from the expropriation of corporate assets by a Latin American government.

12. What is the general accounting practice followed when reporting the income tax effects of "special" income statement items?

13. A corporation decides in 1986 to change its method of depreciating plant machinery from the straight-line method to the double declining-balance method. The machinery was purchased for $100,000 at the beginning of 1984 and had an estimated useful life of four years with no residual value. What journal entry is necessary to adjust the accumulated depreciation account and to recognize the cumulative effect of the change?

14. Prepare a partial income statement showing how the effect of the accounting change in Question 13 would be reported. Assume an income tax rate of 40%. Income before the effect of the accounting change amounted to $964,000.

15. Lockhart Company had 60,000 shares of common stock outstanding at the beginning of the year and issued 30,000 additional shares on May 1. What is the weighted average number of shares outstanding during the year? How much is earnings per share, assuming a net income for the year of $680,000?

16. Assume that the company in Question 15 has $800,000 of $100 par value, 8%, cumulative preferred stock outstanding. What is earnings per share now? Assume, further, that each of the 8,000 preferred shares is convertible into three shares of common stock. What is fully diluted earnings per share under this assumption?

17. Is it necessary to present earnings per share data for such "special" income statement items as gains (or losses) from discontinued operations?
18. During 1986 an accountant discovered that her company failed to record a 1985 depreciation expense of $25,000 on equipment. What entry would be made to correct the error? What is this entry called? (Ignore income taxes.)
19. What is the purpose of the retained earnings statement?

EXERCISES

Exercise 16-1 Preparing Journal Entries and Stockholders' Equity Section
Farmington Corporation had the following stockholders' equity on January 1.

Common stock, $10 par, 100,000 shares authorized, 50,000 shares issued and outstanding	$ 500,000
Paid-in capital in excess of par value	480,000
Retained earnings	275,000
Total Stockholders' Equity	$1,255,000

During the year, the company entered into the following treasury stock transactions.

May 1 Purchased 6,000 of its own shares at $15 per share.
Aug. 6 Sold 2,400 of the treasury shares purchased on May 1 for $20 per share.
Dec. 3 Sold 1,600 of the treasury shares purchased on May 1 for $14 per share.

Required:
A. Prepare journal entries to record the transactions.
B. Prepare the stockholders' equity section of the balance sheet on December 31.

Exercise 16-2 Retirement of Stock
A corporation reacquired at $40 per share, 75,000 shares of its own $10 par value common stock that were issued at an average price of $46 per share. All 75,000 shares were then retired.

Required:
A. Prepare the journal entry to record the stock retirement.
B. Assume that the shares were reacquired at $50 per share, rather than $40 per share. Prepare the entry to record the stock retirement.
C. Assume that the shares purchased at $50 per share were initially intended to be held as treasury stock. Prepare the entries to record the purchase of the shares and the retirement of the shares at a later date.

Exercise 16-3 Retained Earnings Statement
In the process of preparing adjusting entries at the end of 1987, the accountant for Colony Corporation discovered that depreciation on one of the machines, in the amount of $8,000, had not been recorded at the end of 1986. The January 1, 1987, balance

in retained earnings was $810,000. Net income for 1987 is $81,000 and a cash dividend of $1.80 per share was declared on the 45,000 common shares outstanding. The company has no preferred stock.

Required:
A. Prepare the journal entry needed to correct for the failure to record depreciation. Assume there is no income tax effect.
B. Prepare a statement of retained earnings for the year ended December 31, 1987.

Exercise 16-4 Stock Dividends and Stock Splits

A Corporation with 100,000 shares of $5 par value common stock issued and outstanding declared a 10% stock dividend on July 18, distributable on August 15 to stockholders of record on July 31. The market price of the stock on July 18 was $32 per share. The corporation has paid-in capital in excess of par value of $425,000 and retained earnings of $720,000.

Required:
A. Prepare the journal entries to record the declaration and distribution of the stock dividend.
B. Assume that the corporation declared a 100% stock dividend instead of a 10% one. Prepare the entries to record the declaration and distribution of the stock dividend and prepare a schedule detailing the components of stockholders' equity before and after the stock dividend.
C. Assume that the board of directors choose to split the stock two for one, instead of declaring a stock dividend. Prepare the memo entry to record the stock split.
D. Prepare the stockholders' equity section of the balance sheet as it would appear assuming
  1. B had occurred.
  2. C had occurred.

Exercise 16-5 Preparation of Income Statements

Mozzer Company had sales revenue of $2,225,000 and service revenue of $402,500 for the year ended December 31, 1987. Cost of goods sold amounted to $1,362,500, selling and administrative expenses were $750,000 and income tax expense on continuing operations was $67,500.

During 1987, the company sold one of its operating divisions at a gain of $140,000 net of income tax of $40,000. Operating income of the division to the date of sale (which is excluded from the data just given) was $70,000 net of income tax of $30,500.

Required:
Prepare an income statement for Mozzer Company for the year ended December 31, 1987.

Exercise 16-6 Income Statement Classification

Selected transactions and events of Prokyone Corporation are given here.

1. An earthquake in Temville, where the company's largest plant is located, resulted in an uninsured loss of $1.8 million. Earthquakes have never occurred before in the Temville area.
2. Long-term investments were sold at a loss of $350,000.
3. A strike at the Darrey plant by the machinist's union resulted in a loss to the corporation of $2.3 million.

4. Excess machinery was sold at a gain of $240,000.
5. The company disposed of its unprofitable meat packing operation, incurring a loss of $1.1 million.
6. The meat packing operation had incurred a loss of $105,000 up to the date of sale.
7. The company sold one of its shoe manufacturing factories at a gain of $589,000.

Required:
Indicate in which section of the income statement each of the transactions or events should be reported. Your choices are

1. Income from continuing operations.
2. Disposal of a segment of the business.
3. Extraordinary item.

Exercise 16-7 Cumulative Effect of Accounting Change
Beebe Company had revenues and operating expenses for the year 1987, as follows.

Sales	$1,700,000
Cost of goods sold	780,000
Administrative expenses	190,000
Selling expenses	220,000
Depreciation expense	29,261

During 1987, the depreciation method used on two machines was changed from the straight-line method to the double declining-balance method. (The $29,261 depreciation expense shown above was computed under the new method.) Relevant data for the two machines is presented below.

	Cost	Date of Purchase	Estimated Useful Life	Estimated Salvage Value
Machine A	$180,000	1/1/85	10 years	$12,000
Machine B	72,000	1/1/84	5 years	5,000

Assume an income tax rate of 40%.

Required:
A. Prepare the journal entry needed to record the effect of the change in depreciation method.
B. Prepare an income statement for 1987 for Beebe Company.

Exercise 16-8 Earnings per Share
A partial income statement for Ventner, Inc., is given here.

Income from Continuing Operations		$650,000
Discontinued Operations:		
Operating Income of Discontinued Segment (Net of $28,000 Income Tax)	$ 70,000	
Gain on Sale of Segment (Net of $100,000 Income Tax)	250,000	320,000
Net Income		$970,000

The corporation had 200,000 common shares outstanding throughout the year, along with 10,000 shares of $100 par, 8% preferred stock. Each preferred share is convertible into three shares of common stock, which affects the computation of fully diluted earnings per share.

Required:
Determine primary and fully diluted earnings per common share for continuing operations, discontinued operations, and net income.

PROBLEMS

Problem 16-1   Journal Entries for Stockholders' Equity Items

Selected transactions and events affecting the stockholders' equity of Pepye Company during 1987 are given here.

1. Purchased 4,800 shares of treasury stock at $28 per share.
2. Reissued at $36 per share 1,800 of the treasury shares purchased in 1.
3. Reissued at $22 per share the 3,000 remaining treasury shares purchased in 1.
4. Declared a 10% common stock dividend on the 200,000 shares of outstanding $10 par value common stock. The market price of the common stock on the declaration date was $35 per share.
5. Distributed the stock dividend declared in 4.
6. Changed from the straight-line to the sum-of-years'-digits depreciation method for machinery purchased at the beginning of 1985. The machinery cost $190,000 and had an estimated useful life of five years with a salvage value of $10,000. Pepye's fiscal year ends on December 31.
7. The $10 par value common stock was split on a two for one basis.
8. Discovered that the bookkeeper failed to record depreciation expense of $27,000 on machinery for the prior year.

Required:
Prepare journal entries to record items 1 through 8.

Problem 16-2   Income Statement with Special Items

Gard Inc. had revenues and expenses for the year ended December 31, 1987 as follows.

Sales revenues	$10,580,000
Cost of goods sold	7,370,000
Administrative expenses	820,000
Selling expenses	760,000
Interest expense	320,000

Other events affecting 1987 net income were:

1. Gard sold its food processing division on May 31, 1987, at a pretax gain of $508,000. Operating income before tax for the division to the date of sale was $47,000, which is not included in the data given above.
2. A mining venture in Central America, partially owned by Gard in a joint venture with other firms, was expropriated by the foreign government. Gard's share of the loss amounted to $700,000 before tax effects.

Required:
Prepare an income statement for Gard Inc. for the year ended December 31, 1987. Assume a uniform income tax rate of 40%. Include earnings per share data under the assumption that Gard had 250,000 shares of common stock outstanding throughout the year.

dividends
cash ⎤ *outstanding*
stock ⎦

Problem 16-3 Preparing Journal Entries and Stockholders' Equity Section

Johnny Corporation had stockholders' equity at the beginning of 1987 as follows.

Common stock, $10 par value, 400,000 shares authorized, 150,000 shares issued and outstanding	$1,500,000
Paid-in capital in excess of par value	975,000
Retained earnings	1,096,000
Total Stockholders' Equity	$3,571,000

During 1987, the corporation completed the following transactions.

dividend rate

Jan. 6 Issued at par value 6,000 shares of $100 par, 9%, cumulative preferred stock.
15 Purchased 10,000 shares of common stock at $26 per share to be held as treasury stock.
Mar. 30 Reissued at $34 per share 2,000 of the treasury shares.
Dec. 15 Declared a 5% stock dividend on common stock, distributable on January 20, to stockholders of record on December 29. The market price of the stock was $25 per share.

Required:

A. Prepare journal entries to record the transactions.

B. Prepare the stockholders' equity section of the balance sheet on December 31, assuming that net income for 1987 was $356,000.

Problem 16-4 Dividends and Preparation of Stockholders' Equity Section

Curtis company had the following stockholders' equity at the beginning of 1987.

Common stock, $2 par value, 1,000,000 shares authorized, 500,000 shares issued and outstanding	$1,000,000
Paid-in capital in excess of par value	1,025,000
Retained earnings	2,384,000
Total Stockholders' Equity	$4,409,000

During 1987, the following transactions and events occurred.

1. On September 2 the company declared a $.45 per share cash dividend and a 5% stock dividend on its outstanding common stock. The dividends were payable or distributable on October 10 to stockholders of record on September 20. The market price of the stock on September 2 was $21 per share.

2. Net income for 1987 was $671,000.

3. While preparing adjusting entries at the end of 1987, the accountant discovered that the following two errors were made in recording depreciation for 1986.

(a) Depreciation of $30,000 on machinery was overlooked and, therefore, not recorded.

(b) Depreciation on office equipment was recorded in the amount of $110,000. The correct amount should have been $101,000.

Required:

A. Prepare journal entries for the declaration and payment (distribution) of dividends and to correct the accounts for the depreciation errors.

B. Prepare the stockholders' equity section of the balance sheet on December 31, 1987.

C. Prepare a retained earnings statement for the year ended December 31, 1987.

Problem 16-5 Earnings per Share

Marble Company had 142,000 shares of common stock and 50,000 shares of $50 par value, 8%, cumulative preferred stock outstanding on January 1. During the year, the company entered into the following transactions.

Feb.	1	Issued 20,000 shares of common stock.
June	1	Purchased 4,000 common shares as treasury stock.
Aug.	1	Reissued 2,000 shares of treasury stock.
Oct.	1	Issued 10,000 shares of common stock

Required:

A. Compute the weighted average number of common shares outstanding during the year.

B. Net income for the year was $632,500. Compute earnings per share assuming that:

1. The preferred stock is nonconvertible.

2. Each share of preferred stock is convertible into four shares of common stock, which affects the computation of fully diluted earnings per share.

ALTERNATE PROBLEMS

Problem 16-1A Comprehensive Problem

Beto Corporation has been in existence for several years. On January 1, 1987, its stockholders' equity consisted of the following.

Common stock, $5 par value, 500,000 shares authorized, 300,000 shares issued and outstanding	$1,500,000
Paid-in capital in excess of par value	600,000
Retained earnings	450,000
Total Stockholders' Equity	$2,550,000

During 1987 Beto Corporation completed the following transactions.

Jan.	9	Purchased 20,000 shares of treasury stock at $12 per share.
Feb.	16	Reissued at $17 per share 8,000 of the treasury shares purchased on January 9.

Mar. 10 Declared a 5% common stock dividend on the outstanding common stock. The market value of the common stock was $18 per share. (Reminder: Don't forget that some of the shares are held as treasury stock and, therefore, are not outstanding.)

Apr. 2 Reissued at $15 per share 5,000 of the treasury shares purchased on January 9.

5 Distributed the stock dividend declared on March 10.

June 12 Changed from the straight-line to the double declining-balance depreciation method for equipment purchased on January 2, 1985. The equipment cost $140,000 and had an estimated useful life of five years with a residual value of $10,000.

Sept. 8 Discovered that the accounting department failed to record depreciation expense of $12,500 on machinery for 1986.

Dec. 31 Closed the $86,400 credit balance in the *Income Summary* account.

Required:

A. Prepare journal entries to record the transactions.

B. What is the balance in the *Treasury Stock* account on December 31? How should the balance be reported in the December 31, 1987, financial statements?

C. How is the effect of changing from the straight-line to the double declining-balance method of depreciation reported in the financial statements.

D. What type of entry is the September 8 entry?

E. Determine the amount of total stockholders' equity on December 31, 1987.

F. Prepare a retained earnings statement for 1987.

Problem 16-2A Effects of Transactions and Earnings per Share

At the beginning of 1987, Robin Company had 70,000 shares of common stock outstanding and total stockholders' equity was $1,505,000. During 1987, Robin Company completed the following transactions.

Jan. 31 Purchased 8,000 shares of its outstanding stock as treasury stock at a price of $30 per share.

Apr. 1 Declared and distributed a 10% stock dividend on its outstanding common stock. The market price of the stock was $32 per share.

July 1 Reissued for $37 per share 4,000 of the treasury shares purchased on January 31.

Dec. 10 Declared a cash dividend of $1 per share payable on January 8, 1988.

31 Closed the $76,300 credit balance in the *Income Summary* account.

Required:

A. Set up a schedule with headings for (1) Total Stockholders' Equity, (2) Number of Shares Outstanding, and (3) Book Value per Share, and enter the amount of each of these three items on January 1, 1987, and after each of the transactions given.

B. Compute earnings per share for 1987.

Problem 16-3A Income Statement and Special Items

Girard Company earned revenues and incurred expenses for all operations except its fast-food division for the year ended December 31, 1986, as follows.

Sales revenues	$2,380,000
Cost of goods sold	1,588,000

Administrative expenses	212,000
Selling expenses	371,000
Interest expense	72,000

Other events affecting 1986 income were

1. An extraordinary loss of $145,000 before tax was incurred when a tornado severely damaged one of Girard Company's warehouses.
2. Girard sold its fast-food division on July 31, 1986, at a pretax gain of $168,000. An operating loss of $72,000 before tax was incurred by the division to the date of sale.
3. Girard changed from the double declining-balance method to the straight-line method of depreciation. The cumulative effect of the change to the beginning of 1986 was $52,000 (credit) before tax.

Required:
Prepare an income statement for Girard Company for the year ended December 31, 1986. Assume a uniform income tax rate of 30%. Include earnings per share data under the assumption that Girard had 102,000 shares of common stock outstanding throughout the year.

Problem 16-4A Earnings per Share
Doro-Spra Company had 210,000 shares of common stock and 30,000 shares of $100 par value, 8%, cumulative preferred stock outstanding on January 1. During the year, the company entered into the following transactions.

March	30	Issued 60,000 additional shares of common stock.
June	30	Purchased 20,000 common shares as treasury stock.
Nov.	1	Reissued 10,000 shares of treasury stock.

Required:
A. Compute the weighted average number of common shares outstanding during the year.
B. Net income for the year was $890,000. Compute earnings per share assuming that
  1. The preferred stock is nonconvertible.
  2. Each share of preferred stock is convertible into four shares of common stock, which affects the computation of fully diluted earnings per share.

Problem 16-5A Correction of Errors
Early in 1987, Amanda Ward, the head bookkeeper for Louis Company, became seriously ill and had to be hospitalized. During her absence, her relatively inexperienced assistant made the following journal entries to record the transactions described in the explanations.

1.	Cost of Goods Sold		20,000	
	Inventory			20,000
	To correct for the overstatement of inventory at the end of 1986.			
2.	Retained Earnings		120,000	
	Dividends Payable			120,000
	To record the declaration of a $1.25 per share dividend on 96,000 shares of outstanding common stock.			

3. Treasury Stock	15,000	
Cash		15,000
To record the purchase of 1,000 shares of $5 par value common stock for $15 per share to be held as treasury stock.		
4. Land	125,000	
Common Stock		125,000
To record the issue of 25,000 shares of $5 par value common stock in exchange for land with a fair value of $202,000.		
5. Dividend Payable	120,000	
Cash		120,000
To record payment of the dividend declared in 2.		
6. Cash	12,600	
Treasury Stock		12,600
To record the reissue of 700 shares of treasury stock at $18 per share.		
7. Paid-in Capital in Excess of Par Value	42,000	
Common Stock Dividend Distributable		10,000
Paid-in Capital in Excess of Par Value		32,000
To record a small stock dividend of 2,000 shares of $5 par value common stock with a market value of $21 per share.		
8. Common Stock Dividend Distributable	10,000	
Common Stock		10,000
To record the distribution of the stock dividend declared in 7.		
9. Accumulated Depreciation—Equipment	8,000	
Depreciation Expense		8,000
To correct for the overstatement of depreciation expense on equipment at the end of 1986.		

Required:

Analyze each transaction and state whether the entry made was correct or incorrect. If the entry is incorrect, make the entry that should have been made to record the transaction.

CASE

CASE 16-1   Financial Report Analysis Case   Treasury Stock and Earnings Per Share

Refer to the annual reports in Appendix A, and answer the following questions:

1. With reference to Kmart Corporation,
   (a) How many shares of common stock were held as treasury stock on January 30, 1985?
   (b) What was the total cost of the treasury shares on January 30, 1985?
2. With reference to Holiday Inns, Inc.,
   (a) What was the amount of retained earnings on December 28, 1984?
   (b) How did the purchase of treasury stock affect retained earnings during 1984?

    (c) Holiday Inns reported a $.56 loss per share from discontinued operations for the fiscal year ended December 31, 1982. What was the event that produced this loss per share?

3. With reference to Chrysler Corporation,

    (a) How much was primary earnings (loss) per share from continuing operations in 1984? in 1983? in 1982?

    (b) How much was fully diluted earnings per share for 1984?

    (c) How much of Chrysler's 1984 net earnings resulted from an extraordinary gain?

PART 5

ADDITIONAL FINANCIAL REPORTING ISSUES

17

ACCOUNTING FOR LONG-TERM LIABILITIES

CHAPTER OVERVIEW AND OBJECTIVES

This chapter describes accounting for bonds payable and other long-term liabilities. When you have completed the chapter, you should understand:

1. Why a firm obtains funds by long-term borrowing.
2. The features commonly included in a bond issue.
3. How to record the issuance of bonds at par value, at a discount, and at a premium.
4. How bond prices are determined.
5. How to amortize a bond discount or premium by the straight-line method of amortization.
6. How to account for bonds issued between interest payment dates.
7. Why an adjusting entry is needed to accrue bond interest expense and how to prepare the entry.
8. How to record the retirement of bonds before maturity.
9. How to record the conversion of bonds into common stock.
10. The purpose of a bond sinking fund and how to account for one.
11. How to amortize a bond discount or premium by the effective interest method of amortization.
12. How to account for a long-term note payable.
13. The difference between an operating lease and a capital lease.
14. The nature of a pension plan and when a pension liability results.
15. How to record income tax expense when there is a timing difference between taxable income and accounting income.

Firms obtain some of the funds needed to operate a business from a variety of lending sources. In securing financing for the acquisition of assets, it is sound financial practice to match the maturity of the debt with the cash flow produced by the assets acquired with the borrowed funds. Inventories that will be sold in the near future, for example, are usually financed through short-term credit. Cash needed to finance seasonal activities is generally borrowed on short-term notes because current operations are expected to produce sufficient cash to repay the loan. When a firm finds it necessary to obtain funds for long-term purposes, such as for the acquisition of plant assets, the funds are often obtained by long-term borrowing. Deferring the payment for an extended period allows time for the acquired assets to generate sufficient cash to cover interest payments and accumulate the funds needed to repay the loan. Also, because the interest rate is often fixed, the lender is able to lock in this rate and avoid fluctuations in the interest rate.

The repayment of long-term debt is often deferred for a period of 20 years or more. The agreement between the lender and the borrower usually provides for periodic interest payments on specified dates, as well as for repayment of the amount borrowed. The borrower receives current dollars in exchange for a promise to make payments to the lender at specified times in the future. Dollars received and paid at different times are made comparable by considering the time value of money. To fully understand the accounting for long-term liabilities, one should be familiar with the concept of present value. Appendix B to the text contains concepts and computations pertinent to that topic.

In order to focus on the fundamentals of accounting for bonds and to provide flexibility in assigning topics, this chapter is divided into three parts as follows:

Part I. Characteristics and Fundamentals of Accounting for and Reporting Bonds Payable.
Part II. Additional Problems Related to Accounting for Bonds Payable.
Part III. Accounting for and Reporting Other Long-term Liabilities.

PART I CHARACTERISTICS AND FUNDAMENTALS OF ACCOUNTING FOR BONDS PAYABLE

THE NATURE OF LONG-TERM LIABILITIES

A liability is considered long-term if it is due beyond one year from the balance sheet date or the operating cycle, whichever is longer. In other words, when the operating cycle is less than one year, a one-year period is used to classify liabilities as current or long-term. When the operating cycle is longer than one year, the length of the operating cycle is used to classify the obligations of the firm. The portion of long-term debt that will mature within one year or the operating cycle, whichever is longer, and which is to be retired with current assets is reported as a current liability.

BONDS PAYABLE

When a large amount of long-term financing is needed, one or a few lenders may not be able or willing to lend the total amount of money needed. In such situations, long-term funds may be obtained by issuing bonds to many investors. A **bond** is a written promise to pay a sum of money on a specified date and to pay interest each period as specified in the debt instrument. Thus, a bond is essentially a form of promissory note.

Bonds are generally issued in denominations of $1,000, which is called the **par value, face value, principal,** or **maturity value.** On the **maturity date** the borrower must pay the par value to the bondholders. Maturity dates vary, but terms of 20 to 30 years are common for corporate bonds. A total bond issue of $2 million generally consists of 2,000 individual bonds of $1,000 par value each. The division of the total issue into relatively small units permits more investors to participate in the issue.

A specified annual rate of interest is paid on the par value throughout the life of the bonds. The rate, called the **coupon rate, nominal rate, contract rate,** or **stated rate,** is expressed as a percentage of par value. Interest payments are normally made semiannually, although the stated rate of interest is expressed as an annual rate.

Bonds are issued by corporations and other entities, such as federal and state governments, school districts, cities, and universities. Bonds may be sold by the issuing company directly to investors, but normally the issuer sells them to an investment firm, called an **underwriter.** The underwriter expects to sell the bonds to investors at a higher price, thereby earning a profit.

A bond certificate is given to the buyer as evidence of the firm's indebtedness. The terms of the agreement constitute a contract called the bond **indenture.** The bond indenture indicates the interest rate to be paid, the dates on which interest is to be paid, the maturity date, the principal amount, and any other features, such as the bondholder's right to convert the bonds into common stock. An example of a bond certificate is shown in Figure 17–1.

Because the bonds may be held by numerous individual investors, a third party, called a **trustee,** is appointed by the issuing company to represent the bondholders. In most cases the trustee is a large bank or trust company with the primary duty of ensuring that the issuing company fulfills the terms of the bond indenture. The issuing company pays the trustee's expenses.

After the bonds are initially issued, they are listed on one of the securities exchanges. Thus, they may be bought or sold through brokers, who charge a commission for their services. Bond prices are quoted as a percentage of par value. For example, the price of a $1,000 par value bond quoted at 104 is $1,040 ($1,000 × 104%). The minimum variation in a bond price is ⅛ of a dollar. Thus a $1,000 bond quoted at 83⅝ would sell for $836.25 ($1,000 × 83.625%).

Bonds may be sold at par, which means that the bond price was 100. If the bond price is below 100, the bonds sell at a **discount;** if the bond price is above 100, the bonds sell at a **premium.** The amount of the discount or premium is the difference between the issue price and the par value of the bond. For example, a bond quoted at 104 is selling at a $40 ($1,040 − $1,000) premium. Alternatively, if the firm received $920 for a bond, there is an $80 discount.

Figure 17–1
Example of a Bond Certificate

ADVANTAGES AND DISADVANTAGES OF ISSUING DEBT

Firms primarily obtain additional long-term resources by either issuing long-term notes or bonds or by selling additional shares of preferred or common stock. One management function is selecting the types of financing that are most advantageous to the firm. There are a number of reasons why management will elect to issue bonds instead of stock.

Objective 1:
Why long-term debt is issued

1. As a creditor, the bondholder does not hold an ownership interest in the firm and, accordingly, does not have a voting right. As a result, the issuance of bonds does not dilute the control of the existing owners.
2. Net income available to the common stockholders can be increased through the use of financial leverage. **Financial leverage** is the borrowing of funds at a fixed rate. The firm then expects to invest the funds in such a way as to earn a return greater than the fixed rate. For example, if funds borrowed at a fixed interest rate of 12% are used to earn an 18% return, the additional 6% earnings accrue to the stockholders. If the rate earned on the funds borrowed is less than the interest rate—unfavorable financial leverage—the earnings per share is reduced.
3. Interest charges are an expense that are deductible from revenue in computing taxable income, whereas dividends on preferred and common stock are not.

The major disadvantages and limits on issuing debt are as follows:

1. Default (failure to make payment when due) on the amount borrowed or on the interest commitment could result in the bondholders taking legal action against the firm to enforce their claims. Such action could force the borrower into declaring bankruptcy. In bankruptcy, creditors must be paid in full before any asset distribution is made to the stockholders.

2. There is a limit to the amount of new funds that a firm can obtain by borrowing. Because the bondholders are creditors, the interest payments must be made, regardless of the firm's income level. The use of increasing amounts of debt increases the firm's fixed interest costs. At lower levels of net income, the firm may be unable to generate sufficient cash from operations to satisfy the periodic interest payments and could be forced into bankruptcy. Because the risk of default increases as the amount borrowed increases, the interest rate required by investors increases to reflect this added risk. At first, the rate increases slowly for moderate amounts of debt, but at some level investors consider any new debt excessive and the market rate increases rapidly. At some point, the interest rate will exceed the rate that management is willing to incur. Determination of a favorable balance between debt and equity financing is discussed in more detail in finance courses.

3. Bondholders may place restrictions on the firm, such as requiring that a minimum level of working capital be maintained or limiting the amount of dividends a firm can pay.

CLASSIFICATION OF BONDS

**Objective 2:
Features in a
bond issue**

A bond indenture is written to satisfy the financial needs of the borrower, but the agreement must also be attractive to a sufficient number of investors. Consequently, individual bond issues with a variety of features have been created. Some of the more common features are presented here.

Bond Features Related to the Underlying Security

Secured or Mortgage Bonds. A secured bond is backed by specific physical assets of the firm which serve as collateral for the bond. **Collateral** is something of value, acceptable to the lender, that can be converted into cash to satisfy the debt if the borrower defaults. If the firm fails to make payments as specified in the bond indenture, the specific assets may be sold and the proceeds used to pay the bondholders.

Debenture Bonds or Unsecured Bonds. Holders of debenture bonds rely on the general credit standing of the issuing firm for their security. As a result, debenture bonds are generally issued by financially strong companies. Debenture bonds may be *subordinated* or *junior* to other types of debt. This means that in the event of bankruptcy, the claims of subordinated debenture holders to the firm's earnings and assets are met only after higher priority claims, called senior debt, have been satisfied.

Bond Features Related to Evidence of Ownership and Payment of Interest

Registered Bonds. The names and addresses of all holders of a registered bond are recorded in a record, called the bond register, with either the issuing company or the trustee. Interest payments are made by check to the currently registered owners. If ownership of the bond is transferred, the issuing company must be notified so that the new owner can be entered in the bond register.

Coupon (Bearer) Bonds. These bonds have a printed coupon attached to the bond for each interest payment. The amount of interest due and interest payment date is specified on each coupon. When interest is due, the bondholder detaches the proper coupon from the bond, endorses it, indicates his or her address, and then presents it to a bank for collection. When coupon bonds are issued, neither the issuing company nor the trustee maintains a record of the coupon bondholders. The title to the bond is assumed to be with the holder or bearer.

Bond Features Related to the Maturity Date

Term Bonds. The principal of term bonds is paid in full on a single specified date. That is, the entire issue matures on the same date.

Serial Bonds. The principal of serial bonds matures in installments on a series of specified dates. For example, $100,000 of a $1 million bond issue may mature at the end of each year for a period of 10 years.

Bond Features Related to Potential Early Retirement

Callable Bonds. Some bonds can be called in by the issuing company before they mature. The price that the issuer must pay, called the *call price,* is stipulated in the indenture and is usually slightly higher than the par value of the bonds. Most bonds issued today are callable bonds.

Convertible Bonds. These are bonds that can be exchanged for common stock at the bondholder's option.

A bond issue may contain other special features. For example, the agreement may prohibit a corporation from paying dividends to stockholders unless a stipulated level of working capital is maintained, or it may also require that the issuing company make periodic deposits to a bond retirement fund (called a *bond sinking fund*) to accumulate the cash needed to retire the bonds when they mature.

Since most bonds are issued with a fixed coupon rate for the life of the bond issue, accounting and reporting for fixed interest rate bonds are illustrated in this chapter. However, during periods of high, unstable interest rates, and during periods of high inflation, other forms of debt instruments are often used. An example is the issue of variable interest rate debt, for which the interest rate is tied to the prevailing market rate. As an example, the interest rate paid by U.S. Steel on one of its bond issues is tied to the interest rate of United States Treasury bills. Variable interest rate mortgages on real estate offered by lending institutions is another example of variable rate lending. Another type of financing is zero coupon bonds. With zero coupon bonds, the semiannual interest on the bonds is added to the principal and both the interest and principal are paid at maturity. Because periodic interest is not paid, zero coupon bonds sell for much less than their par value.

FINANCIAL STATEMENT DISCLOSURE

Although bond issues may contain different features, accounting for the various issues is similar. Because the features of long-term debt are important to potential investors, they are disclosed in a footnote to the financial statements. The disclosure usually contains the interest rate, maturity date, restrictions on the payment of dividends, and any assets pledged as security. An example of such disclosure is presented in Figure 17–2 for Zenith Radio Corporation.

ACCOUNTING FOR BONDS ISSUED AT PAR VALUE

Objective 3: Recording the issue of bonds

A formal journal entry is not required when bonds are authorized for sale, but a memorandum entry describing the issue may be entered in the *Bonds Payable* account. To illustrate, assume that on May 15, 1987, Jordon Corporation's board of directors authorized the issue of $100,000 of 11%, five-year bonds

Figure 17–2
Illustration of Long-term Debt Disclosure Footnote Accompanying Financial Statement

NOTE 6—LONG-TERM DEBT
The components of long-term debt were:

In millions	December 31 1983	December 31 1982
9.95% promissory note due 1999	$110.0	$110.0
8⅜% convertible subordinated debentures due 2005	—	50.0
Capitalized lease obligations	1.5	2.0
	111.5	162.0
Less—current portion	6.9	—
Total long-term debt	$104.6	$162.0

The terms of the 9.95% note include annual sinking fund requirements of $6.9 million, beginning December 1984. The principal restrictive covenants in the note agreement require a minimum level of working capital and place restrictions concerning additional borrowing and retained earnings available for stock repurchases and payment of dividends. At December 31, 1983, $56.3 million of retained earnings were free of limitations set forth in the agreement.

During the third quarter of 1983, the Company called for redemption all of its outstanding 8⅜% convertible subordinated debentures due 2005. Substantially all of the debenture holders chose to convert, which resulted in 2.5 million shares of common stock being issued in August 1983.

dated June 30, 1987. (For illustrative purposes, the bonds are issued for an unusually small amount and are assumed to be outstanding for a relatively short period of time.) Interest is payable semiannually on June 30 and December 31. There are no other special features contained in the bond indenture. The memorandum may take the following form.

Bonds Payable

1987		
May 15	Received authorization to issue $100,000 of 11%, 5-year debenture bonds dated June	30, 1987. Interest is payable semiannually on June 30 and December 31.

Assuming that the entire bond issue is sold at par value on June 30, the entry to record the issue is:

June	30	Cash	100,000	
		Bonds Payable		100,000
		Issued 11%, 5-year bonds at par value.		

The bonds are reported as a long-term liability until the maturity date is within one year or the next operating cycle, whichever is longer. They are then switched to the current liability classification. An exception to reporting the liability as current is made when the bondholders are to be paid from resources classified as noncurrent assets, such as when a bond sinking fund is established. If noncurrent assets are specifically identified as available to retire the debt, then the debt is reported as a long-term liability.

In this case, interest of $5,500 is due each June 30 and December 31 until the bonds mature. The cash interest payment is computed as follows.

$$\text{Interest} = \text{Par Value} \times \text{Rate} \times \text{Time}$$
$$= \$100,000 \times 11\% \times 6/12$$
$$= \$5,500$$

The entry to record the first semiannual interest payment is:

Dec.	31	Bond Interest Expense	5,500	
		Cash		5,500
		Paid semiannual interest on 11% bonds.		

Once the bonds are issued, they may be traded on the open market. Depending on a number of factors, such as current interest rates and the financial position of the borrower, the market price of the bonds will fluctuate. Changes in the market price are not entered in the firm's books because such changes do not alter the firm's commitment to make the stated semiannual interest payments and to pay the par value when the bonds mature.

THE EFFECT OF MARKET INTEREST RATES ON BOND PRICES

In the previous example, Jordan Corporation agreed to pay $100,000 when the bonds mature on June 30, 1992, and 11% of the par value annually in two semiannual payments of $5,500 each on June 30 and December 31. Thus, the

**Objective 4:
Determining a
bond price**

stated rate of interest, interest payment dates, the maturity value, and the maturity date are specified in the bond indenture and usually remain fixed during the life of the bond. Although the stated rate of interest of 11% establishes the amount of interest to be paid annually, the actual interest rate incurred by the firm will be equal to the market rate of interest at the time that the bonds are issued.

The **market rate** of interest on a bond, sometimes called the **effective rate** or **yield rate,** is the actual rate of interest an investor will earn if bonds purchased at a certain price are held to maturity. The market rate tends to fluctuate daily as investors' perceived risk of an investment changes. The greater the risk associated with an investment, the greater will be the rate of return required by investors. Because securities vary in risk, there is no single market rate of interest. Instead, there is *a schedule of rates corresponding to the risk associated with a particular security*. For example, in February 1985, the interest rate on U.S. Treasury bonds due in one year was 9.2%, while bonds of Eastern Airlines due in 1998 were selling to yield 18%. Obviously, the treasury bonds were considered less risky than the airline bonds.

In the case of Jordan Corporation, the firm will receive the $100,000 par value for the bonds only if the market rate of interest for comparable alternative investments is equal to the stated rate of 11% on the bonds. If the market rate of interest is higher on other investments of similar risk, investors will offer less than the par value so that they can earn the prevailing market rate of interest. That is, investors will not pay $1,000 for a Jordan Corporation bond and get $110 interest per year if another comparable investment would yield 12%, or $120 annually. In contrast, if other investments of similar risk are selling to yield 10%, or $100 per year, investors will bid up the price of Jordan Corporation's $1,000 bond paying $110 per year, until a price is reached that will yield the market rate of 10%.

Thus, the market price of a bond is determined by the prevailing market rate of interest for comparable alternative investments. Because the stated rate is fixed by contract, an adjustment to the price of the bond is necessary to bring the yield on the bonds in line with the prevailing market rate of interest.

The issuer generally establishes a stated rate of interest approximately equal to the market rate on the date that the bonds are to be issued. However, to allow sufficient time for printing the certificates, drafting a bond indenture, and obtaining the necessary approvals from state and federal securities agencies (such as the Securities and Exchange Commission), the stated rate must be determined in advance of the issue date. Thus, the daily fluctuations in the market rate and the sometimes wide variations in the rates mean that the issue price is often not equal to par value. The bond prices will reflect these variations by being issued at a discount or at a premium.

HOW THE ISSUE PRICE OF A BOND IS DETERMINED

This section relies heavily on the reader's understanding of the present value concepts presented in Appendix B at the end of the text.

BONDS SOLD AT A DISCOUNT

To illustrate how the issue price of a bond is determined, assume that the Jordan Corporation's 11%, five-year bonds were issued when the market rate of interest was 12% (6% per semiannual period). Jordan Corporation will pay $1,000 per bond, five years later when the bonds mature, and an interest payment of $55 every six months for the next five years. To determine an issue price that will yield a return of 12% to an investor, the two separate cash flows—principal, which is a single amount, and the interest payments, which are an annuity—are discounted using the market rate of interest as shown here.

Present value of $1,000 due after 10 semiannual periods at 6%: $1,000
  × .5584 (Table B–3, page B–9)   = $558.40
Present value of $55 payable semiannually for 10 periods at 6%: $55 ×
  7.3601 (Table B–4, page B–10)   = 404.80
Present value of future cash flows discounted at 6% per discount period $963.20

Because the market rate of interest is higher than the fixed stated rate, the bond issue will sell at a discount. An investor paying $963.20 for a bond and holding it until maturity will earn a return of 12% on the bonds.

Once the bonds are issued, their market price will fluctuate with changes in the market rate of interest. The market price of the bonds necessary to yield a given market rate can be determined by using essentially the same procedures just shown after the market rate is established.

BONDS SOLD AT A PREMIUM

To illustrate the computation of the bond price when the bonds are issued at a premium, assume that the market rate of interest was 10% (5% per semiannual period) when the bonds were issued. The issue price per bond is computed as follows.

Present value of $1,000 due after 10 semiannual periods at 5%: $1,000
  × .6139 (Table B–3, page B–9)   = $613.90
Present value of $55 payable semiannually for 10 periods at 5%: $55
  × 7.7217 (Table B–4, page B–10)   =   424.70
Present value of future cash flows discounted at 5% per discount period $1,038.60

The bonds will be issued for a premium because the market rate of interest is lower than the stated rate.

Note that bond prices move in an opposite direction to the market rate of interest. If the market rate of interest increases, the price of a bond will decline. Conversely, if the market rate of interest decreases, the price of a bond will increase. These relationships are summarized in Figure 17–3.

Figure 17–3
Relationship of Market Rate to Issue Price of Bonds

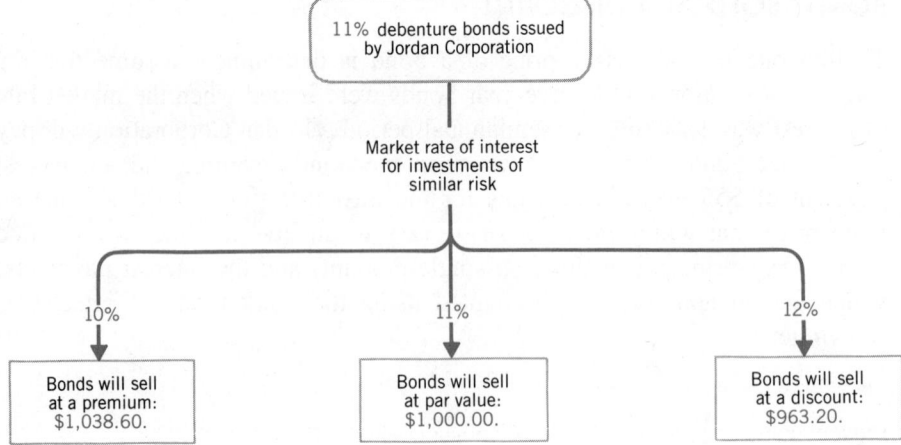

ACCOUNTING FOR BONDS ISSUED AT A DISCOUNT

Objective 5: Amortizing a bond discount or premium

To illustrate accounting for bonds issued at a discount, assume that Jordan Corporation issued its $100,000, 11%, five-year bonds on June 30 for $96,320 to yield the prevailing market rate of interest of 12%. The issuance of the bonds is recorded as follows.

June	30	Cash	96,320	
		Discount on Bonds Payable	3,680	
		Bonds Payable		100,000
		Issued 11%, 5-year bonds at a discount.		

In recording the issue of bonds, *Cash* is debited for the amount received, *Bonds Payable* is credited for the par value of the bonds, and *Discount on Bonds Payable* is debited for the difference between the two.

In a balance sheet prepared immediately after the bonds were issued, the bonds would be reported in this manner.

Long-term Liabilities:
11% Bonds payable, due 6/30/1992 $100,000
    Less: Unamortized discount on bonds payable   3,680 $96,320

The discount is deducted from the par value of the bonds to show the **carrying value** of the bonds. On the date of issuance, the carrying value is equal to the amount borrowed, which was determined by computing the present value of the future cash flows. In subsequent periods, the debit balance in the discount account is amortized (allocated to interest expense) over the life of the bonds, which results in a gradual increase in the carrying value from period to period. When the bonds mature, the discount will be fully amortized and the carrying value of the bonds will equal their par value.

AMORTIZING THE BOND DISCOUNT

Because the par value, rather than the amount received, must be paid to the bondholders at the maturity date, the discount is an increased interest cost to the firm. The total cost for using the borrowed funds is computed as follows.

Cash to be paid to the bondholders:	
Principal at maturity	$100,000
Interest payments ($100,000 × 11% × 5 years)	55,000
Total cash paid to bondholders	155,000
Cash received when the bonds are issued	96,320
Total interest cost	$ 58,680

As can be seen, the total interest cost is the difference between the amount borrowed ($96,320) from the bondholders and the amount paid back to them ($155,000). The total interest cost consists of the discount of $3,680 paid when the bonds mature plus the $55,000 total cash interest payments. In other words, the amount of cash received when the bonds were issued ($96,320) is less than the cash to be paid back at maturity ($100,000) by the amount of the discount ($3,680). Therefore, the company must pay back $3,680 more than was borrowed, in addition to the 10 semiannual interest payments that total $55,000.

Although the discount is not paid until the bonds mature, it is allocated (called **amortization**) over the life of the bonds because each period benefits from the use of the money. Thus, the amount of the discount increases the cost of borrowing, and, as shown later, amortization of the discount results in an interest expense each period, which is greater than the semiannual cash payment. The effect of the discount is to increase the stated rate of interest of 11% to the effective rate of 12% required by the investors.

Two methods may be used to amortize a discount or premium, the *straight-line method* and the *effective-interest method.* The straight-line method of amortization is easier to apply because it allocates the interest cost evenly over the life of the bonds. The method is often used in practice. However, the method is conceptually deficient because it does not report the effective rate of interest. The effective-interest method (described in a later section of this chapter) is theoretically preferred. However, a discount or premium may be amortized using the straight-line method if the results obtained from using the method are not materially different from those that would be obtained if the effective-interest method were used.

Straight-line Method of Amortization

The straight-line method allocates an equal amount of the discount to bond interest expense in each interest period. In our illustration, the bonds were issued for $96,320. The amount of the $3,680 discount amortized each period is computed as follows.

$$\frac{\text{Discount amortization}}{\text{per interest period}} = \frac{\text{Total discount}}{\text{Number of interest periods bonds}}$$
are outstanding

$$= \frac{\$3,680}{10 \text{ six-month periods}}$$

$$= \$368 \text{ per six month period}$$

The cash interest payment is:

$$\text{Interest} = \text{Par value} \times \text{Rate} \times \text{Time}$$
$$= \$100,000 \times 11\% \times 6/12$$
$$= \$5,500$$

The entry to record the first semiannual interest payment is:[1]

Dec.	31	Bond Interest Expense	5,868[2]	
		Discount on Bonds Payable		368
		Cash		5,500
		Paid semiannual interest and amortized discount on 11%, 5-year bonds.		

Note that interest expense of $5,868 is reported although cash of only $5,500 is paid. The added expense of $368 does not involve cash until the par value is paid when the bonds mature. The *Bonds Payable* and *Discount on Bonds Payable* accounts will appear as follows after the December 31 entry is posted.

Bonds Payable		**Discount on Bonds Payable**	
6/30	100,000	6/30 3,680 12/31	368
		12/31 Bal. 3,312	

The credit of $368 to the contra liability account, *Discount on Bonds Payable*, results in an increase of $368 in the carrying value of the bonds. The bonds would be reported as follows in the December 31 balance sheet.

Long-term Liabilities:
11% Bonds payable, due 6/30/1992 $100,000
Less: Unamortized discount on bonds payable   3,312 $96,688

In each subsequent six-month period, the carrying value will increase $368 as the discount is amortized. The amortization of the discount will increase the

[1]In this chapter, one compound journal entry is made to amortize any discount or premium on bonds payable. However, it is sometimes easier to see the effects of amortization on the accounts if two entries are made: (1) to record the payment of interest; and (2) to record the amortization of the discount or premium. For this illustration, these entries are as follows.

Dec.	31	Bond Interest Expense	5,500	
		Cash		5,500
		To record the payment of semiannual interest.		
	31	Bond Interest Expense	368	
		Discount on Bonds Payable		368
		To record the amortization of discount.		

Both the compound journal entry and the two entries above are considered acceptable alternatives.

[2]When the straight-line method of amortization is used, the bond interest expense can be verified by dividing the total interest cost of $58,680 by the 10 semiannual interest periods.

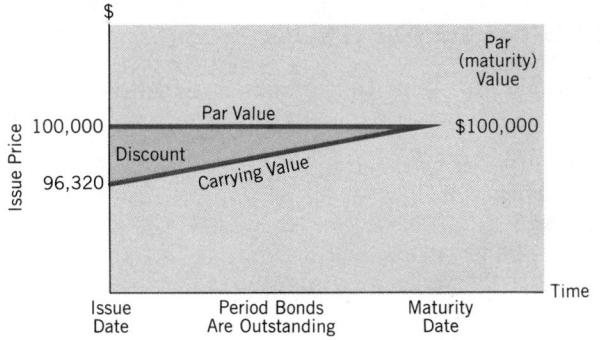

Figure 17–4

Effect of Discount on Carrying Value of Bonds Payable

carrying value of the bonds payable to its par value of $100,000 on its maturity date, as shown in Figure 17–4.

ACCOUNTING FOR BONDS ISSUED AT A PREMIUM

Bonds will sell at a premium if the stated rate of interest on the bonds is greater than the prevailing market rate of interest at the time of sale. For example, as shown on page 649, the 11%, five-year bonds of the Jordan Corporation will sell for $103,860 if the market rate of interest is 10% at the time of issue. The entry to record the sale on June 30 is:

June	30	Cash	103,860	
		Premium on Bonds Payable		3,860
		Bonds Payable		100,000
		Issued 11%, 5-year bonds at a premium.		

In this entry, *Cash* is debited for the amount received, *Bonds Payable* is credited for the par value of the bonds, and a premium is recorded for the difference between the two.

The bonds would be shown in a balance sheet prepared immediately after their issue as:

Long-term Liabilities:
11% Bonds payable, due 6/30/1992 $100,000
Add: Unamortized premium on bonds payable   3,860 $103,860

Both the unamortized bond premium and bonds payable accounts have a credit balance, so they are added together to derive the carrying value of the debt. The $103,860 was computed by discounting the future cash flows at the market rate of interest on the date of issue. In subsequent periods, the premium is allocated over the life of the bonds as a reduction in interest expense to reflect the fact that the actual rate of borrowing is less than the stated rate. By the time the bonds mature, the premium account will be reduced to a zero balance, leaving a carrying value of $100,000, which is the amount due the bondholders at that time.

AMORTIZING THE BOND PREMIUM

Because the bonds were issued at a premium, the cost of borrowing is $51,140, as computed here.

Cash to be paid to the bondholders:	
Principal at maturity	$100,000
Interest payments ($100,000 × 11% × 5 years)	55,000
Total cash paid to bondholders	155,000
Cash received when the bonds were issued	103,860
Total interest cost	$ 51,140

The total interest cost is equal to the sum of the periodic interest payments, less the amount of the premium. That is, the amount of cash received when the bonds were issued ($103,860) is greater, by the amount of the premium ($3,860), than the amount to be paid back at maturity ($100,000). The premium received over the cash to be paid back reduces the total cost of borrowing and is amortized over the life of the bonds because each period benefits from the lower interest cost. Amortization of the premium results in an interest expense each period that is less than the semiannual cash payment.

The bond premium may be amortized using the straight-line method of amortization or the effective-interest method of amortization, although the latter is preferred on conceptual grounds.

Straight-line Method of Amortization

If the straight-line method is used to amortize a premium, an equal amount is amortized as a reduction in interest expense each period. Thus, amortization per period is $386 as computed here.

$$\frac{\text{Premium amortization}}{\text{per interest period}} = \frac{\text{Total premium}}{\text{Number of interest periods bonds}}$$
$$\text{are outstanding}$$

$$= \frac{\$3,860}{10 \text{ six-month periods}}$$

$$= \$386 \text{ per six month period}$$

The entry to record the first interest payment on December 31 is:[3]

Dec.	31	Bond Interest Expense		5,114	
		Premium on Bonds Payable		386	
		Cash			5,500
		Paid semiannual interest and amortized			
		the premium on 11%, 5-year bonds.			

[3]The payment and amortization may be recorded by making two entries, as follows.

Dec.	31	Bond Interest Expense		5,500	
		Cash			5,500
		To record the payment of semiannual interest.			
	31	Premium on Bonds Payable		386	
		Bond Interest Expense			386
		To record the amortization of premium.			

This entry is the same in each interest period. Note that the interest expense is less than the cash payment by the amount of the premium amortization. The interest expense is lower because the actual cost of borrowing (10%) is less than the 11% stated rate. However, interest expense reported each period, as a percentage of the bond carrying value, does not portray the actual effective rate of interest incurred by the firm.

After the December 31 entry is posted, the *Bonds Payable* and *Premium on Bonds Payable* accounts will appear as follows.

Bonds Payable				Premium on Bonds Payable			
		6/30	100,000	12/31	386	6/30	3,860
						12/31 Bal.	3,474

These accounts will be reported in the December 31 balance sheet, as shown here:

Long-term Liabilities:
11% Bonds payable, due 6/30/1992 $100,000
Add: Unamortized premium on bonds payable   3,474 $103,474

Note that the carrying value of $103,474 is $386 less than the carrying value of $103,860 on June 30, the date of issue. In each subsequent interest period, the carrying value will decrease $386 until the bonds mature, at which time the carrying value will be equal to the par value of the bonds, as shown in Figure 17–5.

When the straight-line method is used, total interest cost is allocated equally to each period over the life of the bonds. When bond discount is amortized, the carrying value increases each period, and interest expense, as a percentage of the carrying value of the debt, will decrease over time. Conversely, the straight-line amortization of a bond premium will result in a decreasing carrying value for the bonds, and interest, as a percentage of carrying value, will increase. Since the effective rate of interest is a fixed rate, use of the straight-line method distorts the actual cost of borrowing. For this reason, the APB and its successor, the FASB, have supported the use of the effective-interest method of amortization. Although the effective-interest method is required, the straight-line method of amortization is permitted ''if the results obtained

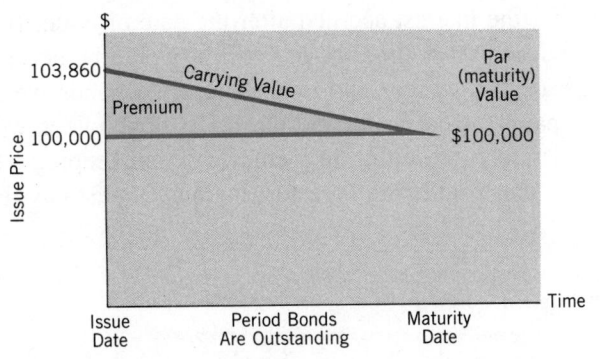

Figure 17–5

Effect of Premium on Carrying Value of Bonds Payable

are not materially different from those which would result from the 'interest method.' ''[4]

PART II ADDITIONAL PROBLEMS RELATED TO ACCOUNTING FOR BONDS PAYABLE

Accounting for bonds is a complex topic. In order to focus on the basic issues of accounting for bonds payable, the previous section of this chapter assumed that:

1. The bonds were sold on their issue date.
2. The bonds had one interest payment date, which coincided with the fiscal year-end.
3. The straight-line method of amortization was used.
4. The bonds were outstanding to maturity.

Accounting for a bond issue when these assumptions do not hold is discussed and illustrated in this section of the chapter, along with several other related topics. These topics are:

1. Accounting for bonds issued between interest payment dates.
2. Year-end adjusting entry for bond interest expense.
3. Retirement of bonds before maturity.
4. Conversion of bonds into common stock.
5. Accounting for a bond sinking fund.
6. The effective-interest method of amortization.

BONDS ISSUED BETWEEN INTEREST PAYMENT DATES

Objective 6: Issue of bonds between interest payment dates

The Jordan Corporation example used in the previous section assumed that the bonds were issued on an interest payment date and were outstanding a full six-months before the first semiannual interest payment was made. However, bonds are frequently issued between interest payment dates. In such cases, the buyer must pay the issuing company the interest accrued from the interest payment date to the date of issue, plus the issue price of the bonds. On the first interest payment date, a full six-months' interest is paid on the bonds outstanding, regardless of when the bonds were issued. Thus, in the first payment, the accrued interest collected from the buyer is returned along with the payment for the interest accrued after the date of issue. If the firm did not collect accrued interest at the time of issue, it would be necessary to maintain a record of each bondholder and of the dates the bonds were issued. At the first interest payment date, interest due each bondholder would have to be computed separately—resulting in increased recordkeeping costs.

If a bond is later sold by an investor, the buyer must pay the seller accrued

[4]"Interest on Receivables and Payables," *Opinion of the Accounting Principles Board No. 21* (AICPA: New York, 1971), par. 15.

interest from the last payment date to the sales date. The holder of the bond then receives a full six months' interest on the next interest payment date.

To illustrate, assume that the Jordan Corporation bonds dated June 30 were issued on September 30 at par value plus three months' accrued interest. The entry to record the issue is:

Sept.	30	Cash	102,750	
		Bonds Payable		100,000
		Bond Interest Expense		2,750
		Issued 11%, 5-year bonds at par value		
		plus accrued interest for 3 months		
		($100,000 × 11% × 3/12 = $2,750).		

Note that the credit of $2,750 for the accrued interest is made to the *Bond Interest Expense* account. Although the credit balance represents a liability at this time, a credit to an expense account avoids the need to split the first interest payment between a liability and the expense portion that accrues after the date of issue.

On December 31, the first semiannual interest payment date, a full six months' interest is paid to the bondholders, even though the bonds were not issued until September 30. The entry is:

Dec.	31	Bond Interest Expense	5,500	
		Cash		5,500
		Paid semiannual interest on 11% bonds.		

After these two entries are posted, the *Bond Interest Expense* account would appear in T account format, as follows

Bond Interest Expense

12/31 (Interest Payment)	5,500	9/30 (Accrued Interest)	2,750
Balance	2,750		

The balance in the account is the proper amount of interest expense for the three-month period that the bonds were outstanding ($100,000 × 11% × 3/12 = $2,750).

YEAR-END ADJUSTING ENTRY FOR BOND INTEREST EXPENSE

A company's fiscal year-end often does not correspond with an interest payment date. In such cases, an adjusting entry must be made at year-end to record the interest accrued on the bonds and to amortize any discount or premium from the last interest payment date to the fiscal year-end. For example, assume that Jordan Corporation's 11%, five-year bonds were issued for $103,860 on June 30, 1987, as in a previous illustration. Interest is paid on June 30 and December 31. The entry to record the first interest payment on December 31, 1987, is:

Objective 7:
Accruing bond
interest expense

Dec.	31	Bond Interest Expense	5,114	
		Premium on Bonds Payable	386	
		Cash		5,500
		Paid semiannual interest and amortized the premium on 11%, 5-year bonds.		

If Jordan has a January 31 fiscal year-end, the following adjusting entry must be made on January 31, 1988, to accrue one month's interest and to amortize one month's bond premium.

1988 Jan.	31	Bond Interest Expense	853	
		Premium on Bonds Payable	64	
		Accrued Bond Interest Payable		917
		To accrue interest and amortize premium for one month on 11% bonds. ($100,000 × 11% × 1/12 = $917; premium amortization for 6 months of $386 ÷ 6 = $64).		

On January 31, 1988, the *Bond Interest Expense* account would appear as follows.

Bond Interest Expense

1987		
12/31	5,114	
1988		
1/31	853	
1/31 Bal.	5,967	

The $5,967 balance in the account is closed to the *Income Summary* account as part of the closing process.

When interest is paid on June 30, the following entry is made.

1988 June	30	Bond Interest Expense	4,261	
		Premium on Bonds Payable	322	
		Accrued Bond Interest Payable	917	
		Cash		5,500
		Paid semiannual interest, a portion of which was accrued at fiscal year-end, and amortized premium for 5 months on 11% bonds. ($386 − $64 = $322)		

In this entry, the interest expense and premium amortization for the remaining five months is recorded and the accrued liability recorded at January 31 is paid. If bonds are issued at a discount, the accrual of interest and amortization of the discount is recorded in a similar manner.

RETIREMENT OF BONDS BEFORE MATURITY

As mentioned earlier, most bond issues are callable by the issuing company if it pays a price specified in the bond indenture to the bondholders. Bonds are made callable to enable the company to retire the bonds and issue new ones at a lower effective interest rate. Bonds may also be retired if the issuer purchases them on the open market.

In accounting for the early retirement of bonds, a material difference between the price paid and the bond's carrying value is reported separately in the income statement as an extraordinary gain or loss.[5] An extraordinary gain results if the purchase price of the bonds is less than their carrying value, and an extraordinary loss is incurred if the purchase price is greater than their carrying value.

To illustrate, assume that the $100,000 Jordan Corporation bonds issued for $103,860 contained a provision that the bonds could be called at 104 on any interest date after June 30, 1989. The company exercised its call option on July 1, 1990, when the unamortized bond premium was $1,544. The entry is:

1990					
July	1	Bonds Payable	100,000	
		Premium on Bonds Payable	1,544	
		Extraordinary Loss on Retirement of Bonds	2,456	
		Cash		104,000
		Retired bonds by paying call price of $104,000 (100,000 × 104%).		

A gain would result if the company were able to purchase the bonds for a price less than the carrying value of $101,544.

Objective 8: Recording the retirement of bonds

CONVERSION OF BONDS INTO COMMON STOCK

A bond is convertible into common stock of the issuing company at the option of the bondholder if that option is provided for in the bond indenture. The terms of conversion, such as the conversion ratio (the number of shares received for each bond converted) and the conversion period or dates, must be specified in the bond agreement.

Convertible bonds are popular because they offer advantages to both issuer and investor. From the point of view of the investor, a convertible bond provides a fixed rate of return and the security of being a creditor of the firm, while at the same time allowing the option of converting the bonds into common stock should conversion become attractive. The conversion option also gives the investor the opportunity to benefit from the price appreciation of the common stock because the price of a convertible bond will increase with increases in the market price of the underlying common stock. To illustrate, assume that a firm issued a convertible bond, which can be exchanged for 50

Objective 9: Recording a bond conversion

[5]"Reporting Gains and Losses fron Extinguishment of Debt," *Statement of Financial Accounting Standards No. 4* (FASB: Stamford, Conn., 1975), par. 8.

shares of stock. If the market value of the firm's common stock is $15 per share, the conversion feature makes the bonds worth $750 (50 shares × $15). However, the bond value may be more than $750. As a straight bond (i.e., without the conversion feature) it has a value equal to the present value of the future cash flows. If the market price of the common stock increases to $25 per share, the bond would have a market price of approximately $1,250, since it could be converted into 50 shares of stock with a total market value of $1,250. An advantage to the issuing company is that the effective rate of interest is generally lower for convertible bonds than for nonconvertible bonds.

Up to the date of conversion, convertible bonds are accounted for in the same way as debenture bonds. If the bonds are converted, the carrying value of the debt is transferred to paid-in capital accounts. For example, assume that each of the $1,000 Jordan Corporation bonds is convertible into 30 shares of $10 par value common stock. One-half of the bondholders (50 bonds with a $50,000 par value) elect to convert their bonds after the interest payment has been made on June 30, 1990. The unamortized premium on the converted bonds is $772 ($1,544 × 50%). Fifteen hundred shares of common stock are issued as computed here.

$$\begin{aligned} \text{Shares issued} &= \text{Conversion ratio} \times \text{Number of bonds converted} \\ &= \text{30 shares per bond} \times \text{50 bonds} \\ &= \text{1,500 shares} \end{aligned}$$

The entry for the conversion is:

1990					
July	1	Bonds Payable		50,000	
		Premium on Bonds Payable		772	
		Common Stock			15,000
		Paid-in Capital in Excess of Par Value			35,772

Note that there is no gain or loss recognized on the transaction. The essence of this entry is to recognize the carrying value of the debt as the payment for the stock. Accordingly, the excess of the carrying value of the bonds ($50,772) over the par value of the common stock ($15,000) is credited to *Paid-in Capital in Excess of Par Value*.

BOND SINKING FUND

Objective 10: Accounting for a bond sinking fund

When bonds mature, the issuing company must have sufficient cash available to pay their maturity value. Bond indentures often provide that periodic deposits must be made to a **bond sinking fund** during the life of the bonds. In other cases, management may decide to make voluntary deposits to accumulate the cash needed at the maturity date. Sinking fund deposits are usually made to a trustee, who invests the cash in income-earning securities. The periodic deposits, plus the earnings on the investments, accumulate until the bonds mature, at which time the trustee sells the investments and uses the proceeds to retire the bonds. Any deficiency in the fund is made up by an additional deposit by the issuing company. If there is an excess of cash in the fund, it is returned to the issuing company.

The amount of each periodic deposit will depend on the rate of return earned from the investments. For example, assume that on January 1, 1987, Grant Corporation issued $1 million of five-year bonds and agreed to deposit with a trustee at the end of each year for the next five years $200,000, less the earnings made on the fund investments during the year. The initial deposit is recorded as follows.

1987					
Dec.	31	Bond Sinking Fund	200,000		
		Cash		200,000	
		Made annual deposit to sinking fund.			

Although the assets in the sinking fund are physically held by the trustee, they are still the property of Grant Corporation. The *Bond Sinking Fund* account is reported in Grant Corporation's balance sheet as a long-term investment, because the funds are not available for use in current operations.

The trustee will report the earnings on the investments each period to Grant Corporation. The entries at the end of 1988, assuming that earnings of $18,000 were reported by the trustee, are:

1988					
Dec.	31	Bond Sinking Fund	18,000		
		Sinking Fund Revenue		18,000	
		To record revenue earned from sinking fund investments.			
	31	Bond Sinking Fund	182,000		
		Cash		182,000	
		Made annual deposit to sinking fund.			

Revenue earned from sinking fund investments is reported in the income statement in the other revenue section.

Similar entries are made at the end of each year for the remainder of the accumulation period. As the maturity date approaches, the trustee will sell the investments and will inform the company of any final deposit required to bring the accumulated balance up to the $1,000,000 needed to retire the debt. The entry to record the bond retirement is:

1992					
Jan.	1	Bonds Payable	1,000,000		
		Bond Sinking Fund		1,000,000	
		To record the payment of bonds at maturity.			

EFFECTIVE-INTEREST METHOD OF AMORTIZATION

**Objective 11:
Effective-interest method of amortization**

As noted earlier, the effective-interest method is the preferred method for computing interest expense. In order to contrast the effective-interest method with the straight-line method, the same data used earlier to illustrate the straight-line method of amortizing a discount or premium will now be used to illustrate the effective-interest method.

AMORTIZATION OF A DISCOUNT—EFFECTIVE-INTEREST METHOD

The following facts are assumed for a bond issue.

Date of issue	June 30, 1987
Par value	$100,000
Stated rate of interest	11%
Interest payment dates	June 30, December 31
Term to maturity	5 years
Market rate of interest	12%
Issue price to yield 12%	$ 96,320

The journal entry to record the bond issue is:

1987					
June	30	Cash		96,320	
		Discount on Bonds Payable		3,680	
		Bonds Payable			100,000

A discount amortization table for the Jordan Corporation bonds is presented in Figure 17–6. Amounts have been rounded to the nearest dollar. Under the

Figure 17–6
Amortization Table for Bonds Issued at a Discount—Effective-interest Method

Semiannual Interest Periods	(A) Carrying Value Beginning of Period (Col. G for previous period)	(B) Effective Semiannual Interest Expense (Col. A × 6%)	(C) Semiannual Cash Payment ($100,000 × 5½%)	(D) Discount Amortization (Col. B – Col. C)	(E) Par Value	(F) Bond Discount Balance (Col. F for previous period – Col. D)	(G) Carrying Value—End of Period (Col. E – Col. F)
6/30/87					$100,000	$3,680	$ 96,320
12/31/87	$96,320	$ 5,779	$ 5,500	$ 279	100,000	3,401	96,599
6/30/88	96,599	5,796	5,500	296	100,000	3,105	96,895
12/31/88	96,895	5,814	5,500	314	100,000	2,791	97,209
6/30/89	97,209	5,832	5,500	332	100,000	2,459	97,541
12/31/89	97,541	5,852	5,500	352	100,000	2,107	97,893
6/30/90	97,893	5,874	5,500	374	100,000	1,733	98,267
12/31/90	98,267	5,896	5,500	396	100,000	1,337	98,663
6/30/91	98,663	5,920	5,500	420	100,000	917	99,083
12/31/91	99,083	5,945	5,500	445	100,000	472	99,528
6/30/92	99,528	5,972*	5,500	472	100,000	—	100,000
Totals		$58,680	$55,000	$3,680			

*In the last period, interest expense is equal to the semiannual interest paid plus the remaining balance in the bond discount column ($5,500 + $472 = $5,972). The carrying value at the beginning of the tenth interest period times 6% may not exactly equal this amount due to the accumulated effects of rounding errors.

effective-interest method, interest expense for each period (Column B) is computed by multiplying the carrying value of the bonds at the beginning of the period (Column A) by the effective interest rate per period. Since the bonds were sold to yield 12% annually, the semiannual effective interest rate is 6%. The amount of the discount amortized each period (Column D) is the difference between interest expense and the semiannual interest payment.

During the first period, interest expense was $5,779 ($96,320 × 6%), but only $5,500 was paid to the bondholders. The difference of $279 is the amount of the discount amortization for the period. The entry to record the payment and discount amortization is:

Dec.	31	Bond Interest Expense	5,779	
		Discount on Bonds Payable		279
		Cash		5,500
		Paid semiannual interest and amortized		
		discount on 11%, 5-year bonds		

In period two, interest expense is the net liability of $96,599 multiplied by 6%, or $5,796. Because the carrying value of the liability increased during the first period, the interest cost is greater in the second period. In subsequent periods, the interest expense increases as the carrying value increases.

Note that interest expense (Column B), as a percentage of the beginning carrying value (Column A), is a constant 6% each period. Although the bond indenture requires a semiannual interest payment of $5,500, the interest expense reported each period reflects the effective interest rate incurred by the firm.

AMORTIZATION OF A PREMIUM—EFFECTIVE-INTEREST METHOD

To illustrate the amortization of a bond premium, we assume that the Jordan Corporation bonds were issued for $103,860 to yield an effective annual interest rate of 10%, 5% per semiannual period. A premium amortization table for the Jordan Corporation bonds under the effective-interest method is presented in Figure 17–7. The computations are based on the same concepts discussed earlier for the amortization of a discount. Note, however, that the amount of premium amortized each period decreases interest expense. Interest expense reported each period is the effective semiannual rate of 5% times the carrying value of the bonds at the beginning of the period.

The first interest payment is recorded as follows:

Dec.	31	Bond Interest Expense	5,193	
		Premium on Bonds Payable	307	
		Cash		5,500
		Paid semiannual interest and amortized		
		premium on 11%, 5-year bonds.		

Over the life of the bonds, the interest expense debit decreases with a corresponding increase in the debit to the premium account. This results because the carrying value of the bonds is decreasing each period as the premium is reduced through amortization.

Semiannual Interest Period	(A) Carrying Value Beginning of Period (Col. G for previous period)	(B) Effective Semiannual Interest Expense (Col. A × 5%)	(C) Semiannual Cash Payment ($100,000 × 5½%)	(D) Premium Amortization (Col. B − Col. C)	(E) Par Value	(F) Bond Premium Balance (Col. F for previous period − Col. D)	(G) Carrying Value—End of period (Col. E + Col. F.)
6/30/87					$100,000	$3,860	$103,860
12/31/87	$103,860	$ 5,193	$ 5,500	$ 307	100,000	3,553	103,553
6/30/88	103,553	5,178	5,500	322	100,000	3,231	103,231
12/31/88	103,231	5,162	5,500	338	100,000	2,893	102,893
6/30/89	102,893	5,145	5,500	355	100,000	2,538	102,538
12/31/89	102,538	5,127	5,500	373	100,000	2,165	102,165
6/30/90	102,165	5,108	5,500	392	100,000	1,773	101,773
12/31/90	101,773	5,089	5,500	411	100,000	1,362	101,362
6/30/91	101,362	5,068	5,500	432	100,000	930	100,930
12/31/91	100,930	5,047	5,500	453	100,000	477	100,477
6/30/92	100,477	5,023*	5,500	477	100,000	—	100,000
Totals		$51,140	$55,000	$3,860			

*In the last period, interest expense is equal to the semiannual interest paid less the remaining balance in the bond premium account ($5,500 − $477). The carrying value at the beginning of the tenth period times 5% may not exactly equal this amount due to the accumulated effects of rounding errors.

Figure 17–7
Amortization Table for Bonds Issued at a Premium—Effective-interest Amortization

PART III OTHER LONG-TERM LIABILITIES

Balance sheets often contain a number of different kinds of long-term liabilities other than bonds payable. Examples are long-term notes payable, lease obligations, liabilities related to an employee pension plan, and deferred income tax credits, all discussed below.

ACCOUNTING FOR AND REPORTING LONG-TERM NOTES PAYABLE

Objective 12: Accounting for long-term notes

Companies often issue long-term notes payable to obtain resources to finance the acquisition of operating assets. As defined in Chapter 8, a note payable is an unconditional promise to pay a sum certain in money on demand or at a future determinable date. Long-term unsecured notes and mortgages are normally issued when money is borrowed from one or a few lending institutions, such as banks or insurance companies. Long-term notes are also frequently issued for a shorter period of time, and/or issued to borrow smaller amounts of money than bonds. Smaller companies generally use notes, rather than bonds, whereas a large company may issue both.

Long-term notes may take various forms. In one common form, the note requires periodic interest payments with the principal payable in full at maturity. Another common form provides that both the interest and principal must be paid in installments. This latter type of note is often used by consumers to finance the purchase of a home or an automobile. Both types of notes may be unsecured, but frequently, when a company borrows money to finance the purchase of plant assets, a promissory note secured by a legal document, called a mortgage, is given to the lender or seller. A **mortgage** is a lien on specific property of the borrower. The promissory note given is called a **mortgage note payable.** If the debt is not paid, the mortgage holder may have the specific property sold and the proceeds applied to the debt. An **unsecured note payable** is a promissory note that is backed by a legal claim against the borrower's general assets.

NOTES REQUIRING PERIODIC INTEREST PAYMENTS WITH THE PRINCIPAL PAID AT MATURITY

Long-term interest bearing notes that provide for periodic interest payments with the principal repaid at the maturity date have cash flows similar to those required in a bond agreement. Thus, the accounting for and reporting of such notes is, in essence, the same as those for bonds payable. That is, the note is measured by the present value of the future cash flows and any discount or premium is amortized over the life of the note.

In the balance sheet, a note is classified as long-term if it is to be settled beyond one year from the balance sheet date or beyond the operating cycle, whichever is longer. As with bonds, a discount is subtracted from and a premium is added to the face amount of the note.

INSTALLMENT NOTES PAYABLE

Installment contracts generally require the borrower to make equal periodic payments that include both accrued interest and a reduction in principal. Each payment is first applied to the accrued interest and the remainder of the payment reduces the principal. As the principal balance declines over time, the portion of each payment assigned to interest decreases and the portion assigned to a reduction of principal increases.

To illustrate, assume that Midwest Airlines purchased a passenger airplane for $2,500,000 on September 1, 1987. Midwest gave the seller a 12% mortgage note that provided for a $252,250 down payment and 60 monthly payments of $50,000 each, to begin on October 1, 1987.[6] Since the payments are made monthly, the annual interest rate of 12% must be converted to a monthly rate of 1%. The entry to record the purchase is:

Sept.	1	Aircraft	2,500,000	
		Mortgage Note Payable		2,247,750
		Cash		252,250

---

[6]Given a 1% effective interest rate per month, the monthly payment of $50,000 can be verified as follows.

$$\frac{\text{Present value factor of ordinary}}{\text{annuity for 60 periods at 1\%}} = 44.955$$

$$\text{Monthly payment} = \text{Amount borrowed} / \frac{\text{Present value of ordinary}}{\text{annuity for 60 periods at 1\%}}$$

$$= \$2,247,750 / 44.955$$

$$= \$50,000$$

Monthly Payment Number	Payment Date	(A) Unpaid Balance at Beginning of Month	(B) Cash Payment	(C) Interest for One Month (Col. B × 1%)	(D) Reduction in Principal (Col. C – Col. D)	(E) Principal Balance at End of Month (F)
	1987					
	Sept. 1	$2,500,000	$252,250	$ —	$252,250	$2,247,750
1	Oct. 1	2,247,750	50,000	22,478	27,522	2,220,228
2	Nov. 1	2,220,228	50,000	22,202	27,798	2,192,430
3	Dec. 1	2,192,430	50,000	21,924	28,076	2,164,354
	1988					
4	Jan. 1	2,164,354	50,000	21,644	28,356	2,135,998
5	Feb. 1	2,135,998	50,000	21,360	28,640	2,107,358
	1993					
59	Aug. 1	98,520	50,000	985	49,015	49,505
60	Sept. 1	49,505	50,000	495	49,505	–0–

Figure 17-8
Monthly Payment Schedule

The division of the first five and last two monthly payments between interest and principal is shown in Figure 17–8. The portion of each payment allocated to interest expense is computed as follows.

$$\frac{\text{Interest}}{\text{expense}} = \frac{\text{Unpaid principal at the}}{\text{beginning of each month}} \times \frac{\text{Effective monthly}}{\text{interest rate}}$$

The principal portion of each payment is:

$$\text{Principal reduction} = \text{Cash payment} - \text{Interest expense}$$

For the first payment on October 1, these computations are:

$$\text{Interest expense} = 2,247,750 \times .01$$
$$= 22,478$$

$$\text{Principal reduction} = 50,000 - 22,478$$
$$= 27,522$$

The entry to record the October 1 payment is:

Oct.	1	Interest Expense	22,478	
		Mortgage Note Payable	27,522	
		Cash		50,000
		Made the monthly mortgage payment.		

For reporting purposes, the part of the unpaid principal balance to be paid during the next year should be classified as a current liability, with the balance of the principal classified as a long-term liability.

LEASE OBLIGATIONS

A **lease** is a rental agreement in which the *lessor* (the owner) conveys to the *lessee* the right to use property for a specified period of time in return for periodic rental payments. Many companies lease much of their equipment, rather than purchasing it, for one or more of the following reasons.

**Objective 13:
Accounting for
lease obligations**

1. Leasing permits 100% financing, rather than making a substantial down payment, as required in most credit purchases.
2. The full lease payment, even for land, is deductible for tax purposes.
3. Lease contracts may be more flexible and contain fewer restrictions than most debt agreements.

Because of these advantages, the use of leasing has grown rapidly in recent years. As a result, the accounting profession has devoted a great deal of effort to the establishment of accounting standards for lease reporting.

For accounting purposes, leases are of two types: capital leases and operating leases. Leases that transfer substantially all the benefits and risks of ownership to the lessee are installment purchases in substance and are called **capital leases.** Because the provisions contained in lease contracts vary widely, the FASB established four criteria to be applied in assessing whether a particular lease contract is, in substance, an installment purchase of property. A lease is classified as a capital lease if it is noncancelable and meets one or more of these four criteria.

1. The lease transfers ownership of the property to the lessee by the end of the lease term.
2. The lease permits the lessee to acquire the property at the end of the lease for a bargain price.
3. The length of the lease (lease term) is equal to 75% or more of the estimated economic life of the leased property.
4. The present value of the lease payments at the beginning of the lease term equals or exceeds 90% of the fair value of the leased property.[7]

To illustrate, assume that a major airline entered into an equipment lease to acquire its airplanes. The lease has a fixed noncancelable term of eight years. The estimated economic life of the airplanes is 10 years. Because the lease satisfies criterion three (8/10 = 80%), the airline would account for the lease as a capital lease.

Capital leases are accounted for as if they were installment purchases. Accounting by the lessee is similar to that described earlier for a mortgage note payable. The lessee records the leased property as a plant asset and credits a long-term liability for the future lease payments. The asset and liability are recorded at an amount equal to the present value of the future lease payments. Part of each lease payment is recorded as interest expense, and the remainder

---

[7]"Accounting for Leases," *Statement of Financial Accounting Standards No. 13* (FASB: Stamford, Conn., 1976), par. 7.

is a reduction in the principal balance. In addition, the leased asset is depreciated over the period that it is expected to be used, in this case the life of the lease of eight years.

To illustrate, assume that the lease contract for the airplanes required a $1,000,000 payment at the end of each of the eight years and that the lease provided for 12% interest. The ownership of the airplanes does not transfer to the lessee. The present value of the lease payments is computed by multiplying $1,000,000 times the present value of an annuity factor, found in Appendix B. Thus the leased asset and lease obligation are recorded at $4,967,600 ($1,000,000 × 4.9676), as follows.

Jan.	1	Leased Airplanes	4,967,600	
		Lease Obligation		4,967,600
		To record acquisition of leased airplanes.		

The first lease payment, on December 31, is divided between interest and principal. The entry to record the payment is:

Dec.	31	Interest Expense	596,112	
		Lease Obligation	403,888	
		Cash		1,000,000
		To record first lease payment (Interest expense = $4,967,600 × 12%).		

The cost of the asset, as measured by the present value of the future cash payments, is allocated to the periods during which it is to be used (8 years). It is assumed that the straight-line method of depreciation is used.

Dec.	31	Depreciation Expense	620,950	
		Accumulated Depreciation— Leased Airplanes		620,950
		To record depreciation on leased airplanes ($4,967,600 / 8 years).		

Accounting in the remaining seven years would be similar to that just shown, except that the portion of the $1,000,000 lease payment pertaining to interest will decrease each year (since the lease obligation is decreasing), and the portion pertaining to the lease obligation will increase. Note that these procedures are the same as those illustrated in the previous section for an installment note payable.

Leases that do not meet at least one of the four criteria for a capital lease are classified as operating leases. **Operating leases** are generally short-term or cancelable, with the lessor retaining the usual risks and rewards of ownership. For example, a company that leases delivery trucks on a weekly basis during its peak demand periods would account for the truck lease as an operating lease. The periodic lease payments are accounted for by the lessee as rent expense. The leased property is not recorded as an asset, and the related obligation to make the lease payments is not recognized in the accounts. However, if the amounts involved are significant, the minimum future rental payments for each of the next five years and the total rental expense included in each income statement presented must be disclosed in a footnote.

PENSION PLANS

Most firms have **pension plans** to provide payments to eligible employees when they retire. The company normally appoints a trustee, such as an insurance company, to administer the plan, and satisfies its pension obligation by making regular payments to the trustee. The trustee then invests the funds and uses the fund earnings and contributions to pay benefits to retired employees. This type of plan is called a **funded plan.**

The amount to be paid into the fund is determined jointly by the policies of the company, the trustee, and the provisions of the Pension Reform Act of 1974. Measurement of the pension expense is complex and beyond the scope of this book. However, the amount reported as expense in the income statement is determined independently of the cash contribution. Payments to the pension funds are recorded by a debit to *Pension Expense* and a credit to *Cash*. If payments to the pension fund are equal to the pension expense computed each period, a liability will not appear in the balance sheet. A liability *will* arise, however, if payments to the fund are less than the pension expense recognized. Therefore, the liability that often appears in the balance sheet represents the accumulated excess of pension expense over the cash paid into the pension fund.

Objective 14: The nature of a company's pension plan

DEFERRED INCOME TAXES

There are differences in the recognition of revenue and expenses between the tax law and generally accepted accounting principles that result in differences between accounting income and taxable income. **Accounting income** is the amount reported for income, before income taxes, in the firm's income statement prepared for external reporting purposes. If a particular item of revenue or expense creates a **permanent difference,** it will enter into the computation of either taxable income or accounting income—but not both. For example, interest received on a bond issued by a state government is reported on the books as income, but is not taxable income. Consequently, accounting income in the year that the interest is accrued is greater than taxable income.

In other cases, the differences will cause taxable income to exceed accounting income. For example, legally imposed fines and penalties are not deductible in computing taxable income, but such payments *are* expensed for accounting purposes. When the difference between the amount of taxable income and accounting income is the result of a permanent difference, the income tax expense reported in the income statement will be equal to the income tax

Objective 15: Accounting for the difference between accounting income and taxable income

liability. In such cases, the effective tax rate, as a percentage of accounting income, will not equal the statutory tax rate.

In contrast with permanent differences, other differences between taxable income and accounting income, called **timing differences,** arise when an item of revenue or expense enters into the computation of both taxable income and accounting income, but in different periods. A timing difference may result because the timing of certain revenues and expenses, as required by the tax law, differs from the timing of revenues and expenses in accordance with generally accepted accounting principles. For example, the tax law specifies that an advance receipt of rent is fully taxable in the year received, but for financial reporting purposes it is recognized as revenue as it is earned. Although the rent is reported as revenue earlier for tax purposes, the total revenue for tax and financial reporting will be the same over the rental period. The only difference is the pattern of recognizing the annual income amounts.

In addition, for some items, the tax law permits a taxpayer to select accounting methods for tax purposes that are different from those used for financial reporting purposes. For example, many firms elect to use an accelerated depreciation method in computing taxable income and the straight-line method in computing accounting income. In this case, the total depreciation recognized over the useful life of the asset will be the same for both financial reporting and tax purposes, but the amounts computed for each purpose each year will not be equal.

When the use of alternative accounting methods results in a timing difference, a financial accounting problem arises as to the proper measurement of the income tax expense. To illustrate the nature of this problem, assume that Ewing Oil Company purchased an asset for $600,000 that had a four-year useful life and a zero expected residual value. The company reported accounting income of $500,000 before taxes and depreciation on the new asset in each of four years. The company elected to use the straight-line method of depreciation for book purposes and the accelerated cost recovery system (ACRS) for tax purposes. Recall from Chapter 10, that the ACRS provides that the cost of assets acquired after 1980 is to be recovered over predetermined periods, which are generally shorter than the useful life of the assets. The ACRS deduction is computed by applying prescribed percentages to the asset's cost. The asset falls into the three-year class under the ACRS. The ACRS percentage table provides for a deduction of 25% of the cost in the first year, 38% in the second year, and 37% in the third year. To simplify the tax computations, a fixed corporate tax rate of 40% is assumed. Depreciation expense under both methods, the income tax liability, and a condensed income statement for each of the four years are shown in Figure 17–9. Figure 17–9 is developed to illustrate the justification for the allocation of income taxes. As shown later, the income statement results are not in accordance with generally accepted accounting principles.

Note that the total depreciation computed over the life of the asset is the same for tax purposes and accounting purposes. However, more depreciation is deducted under the ACRS method in the early years of the asset's useful life, which results in a taxable income lower than the accounting income before

		Year			
	1	2	3	4	Total
Depreciation Expense					
Depreciation expense—book purposes ($600,000 ÷ 4 years)	$150,000	$150,000	$150,000	$150,000	$600,000
Tax purposes	$150,000	$228,000	$222,000	–0–	$600,000

Year 1 $600,000 × 25% = $150,000
  2 $600,000 × 38% = $228,000
  3 $600,000 × 37% = $222,000
  4 $600,000 × 0% = –0–
The useful life of 3 years and rates are derived from tables provided by the Internal Revenue Service.

Income Tax Liability					
Taxable income before depreciation	$500,000	$500,000	$500,000	$500,000	$2,000,000
Depreciation expense	150,000	228,000	222,000	–0–	600,000
Taxable income	$350,000	$272,000	$278,000	$500,000	$1,400,000
Income tax liability (40%)	$140,000	$108,800	$111,200	$200,000	$ 560,000

Income Statement
Income tax expense is not reported in accordance with generally accepted accounting principles.

	1	2	3	4	Total
Income before depreciation and taxes	$500,000	$500,000	$500,000	$500,000	$2,000,000
Depreciation expense	150,000	150,000	150,000	150,000	600,000
Income before taxes	350,000	350,000	350,000	350,000	1,400,000
Income tax expense (actual tax liability)	140,000	108,800	111,200	200,000	560,000
Net income	$210,000	$241,200	$238,800	$150,000	$ 840,000

Figure 17–9
Illustration of Reporting Income Tax Expense—Income Taxes Not Allocated

taxes. In later years this reverses, since less depreciation is deducted for tax purposes than for accounting purposes, and taxable income exceeds accounting income. In the income statement, the income tax expense reported each period is equal to the tax liability computed each period. This approach results in a fluctuating tax expense and, except for the second year, in a decreasing net income, even though the pretax accounting income was the same each year. Opponents of this method contend that such results are misleading and confusing to statement readers.

In order to avoid such distortion in the income statement, *the APB concluded that income tax allocation procedures should be followed* when the difference between accounting and taxable income is caused by timing differences.[8] Income tax allocation procedures result in the accrual of income tax expense based on accounting income, rather than on taxable income. Using tax allocation procedures, income statements for Ewing Oil Company would appear as follows.

[8]Accounting Principles Board, ''Accounting for Income Taxes,'' *APB Opinion No. 11* (AICPA: New York, 1967), par. 34.

Income Statement	Year 1	Year 2	Year 3	Year 4	Total
Income before depreciation and taxes	$500,000	$500,000	$500,000	$500,000	$2,000,000
Depreciation expense	150,000	150,000	150,000	150,000	600,000
Income before taxes	350,000	350,000	350,000	350,000	1,400,000
Income tax expense (40%)	140,000	140,000	140,000	140,000	560,000
Net income	$210,000	$210,000	$210,000	$210,000	$ 840,000

Using this tax allocation approach, the income tax expense for each period is computed by multiplying the pretax accounting income reported in the income statement by the tax rate. Since the tax expense does not equal the tax liability, an account called *Deferred Income Tax* is created to balance the two, as shown in these journal entries.

			Debit	Credit
Year	1	Income Tax Expense	140,000	
		Income Tax Payable		140,000
Year	2	Income Tax Expense	140,000	
		Income Tax Payable		108,800
		Deferred Income Tax		31,200
Year	3	Income Tax Expense	140,000	
		Income Tax Payable		111,200
		Deferred Income Tax		28,800
Year	4	Income Tax Expense	140,000	
		Deferred Income Tax	60,000	
		Income Tax Payable		200,000

The four-year history of the *Deferred Income Tax* account is:

Deferred Income Tax

Date		Explanation	Post. Ref.	Debit	Credit	Balance
Year	1				-0-	-0-
	2				31,200	31,200
	3				28,800	60,000
	4			60,000		—

The credit balance in the *Deferred Income Tax* account is generally reported as a liability, because the balance in the account represents an obligation for taxes that will be paid in future tax years when taxable income exceeds accounting income. The classification of the account as current or long-term depends on the classification of the asset or liability that gave rise to the timing difference.[9] In this illustration, the balance in the *Deferred Income Tax* account is reported as long term, since it results from a difference in depreciation expenses computed on an asset classified as long-term. If the difference were related to alternative methods used to account for a current asset, the deferred income tax liability account would be classified as a current liability.

In the preceding illustration, tax payments were postponed as a result of taking a deduction for tax purposes before it was recognized as an expense in the accounting records. Taxes may also be postponed if revenue is recognized for book purposes before it is subject to tax. In contrast, taxes may be prepaid when expenses are recognized in computing accounting income before they are deducted in computing taxable income, or when revenues are included in taxable income before they are recognized in the books. In these latter cases, taxable income is greater than accounting income, which creates a tax liability greater than tax expense. The excess of the tax liability over the tax expense, is a debit to *Deferred Income Tax,* which is reported as an asset in the balance sheet. The prepaid tax is then expensed when the income is later reported in the income statement.

Note in Figure 17–9 that the cumulative income tax of $560,000 is equal to the income tax liability for the four years and that the total net income is $840,000 whether income taxes were allocated or not. Why then does a company elect to use an alternative method for tax purposes? The attraction of the accelerated method for tax purposes can be shown by comparing the pattern of cash payments for taxes had the straight-line method been used for tax purposes rather than the ACRS.

Tax Payments	Straight-line	ACRS	Difference
Year 1	$140,000	$140,000	$ -0-
2	140,000	108,800	31,200
3	140,000	111,200	28,800
4	140,000	200,000	(60,000)
Total tax payments	$560,000	$560,000	$ -0-

Although the total tax payment is the same in both cases, the use of an accelerated depreciation method results in the postponement of a portion of the payment for income taxes in the first three years. Thus, at the end of Year 2, the company has $31,200, and has an additional $28,800 available in Year 3 for use in operations until it must be paid in Year 4.

The use of different methods for book and tax purposes requires keeping two sets of depreciation records. To avoid this duplication, some firms keep their accounting records on the same basis as their tax records. This practice is acceptable when the tax method does not result in a material difference from what would be reported in accordance with generally accepted accounting

---

[9]*Ibid.,* par. 57. Also, Financial Accounting Standards Board, "Balance Sheet Classification of Deferred Income Taxes," *Statement No. 37* (Stamford: 1980), par 4.

Figure 17–10
Liability Section of
Balance Sheet

Liabilities and Stockholders' Equity	
Current Liabilities:	
Notes payable to banks	$100,000
Accounts payable	62,000
Current maturities of long-term liabilities	10,000
Bank overdraft	4,500
Accrued liabilities:	
Salaries, wages, and employee benefits	10,200
Interest	5,400
Property and payroll taxes	4,800
Other	2,500
Federal and state income taxes	6,700
Cash dividends payable	4,300
Advance deposits received from customers	2,800
Total current liabilities	213,200
Long-term Liabilities:	
Notes and bonds payable, net of current maturities	140,000
7% convertible subordinated debentures	100,000
Obligations under capital leases	31,500
Deferred income taxes	18,400
Accrued pension costs, not to be funded currently	7,200
Total long-term liabilities	297,100
Total liabilities	510,300
Stockholders' Equity:	

principles. If the difference between the two methods is material, the proper accounting method should be used for external reporting purposes.

COMPREHENSIVE ILLUSTRATION OF REPORTING LIABILITIES

In this and the preceding chapters, various types of current and long-term liabilities were discussed. Although the terminology used and the amount of detail provided vary considerably in practice, Figure 17–10 shows one possible presentation of the liability section of the balance sheet. Additional information, such as interest rates, maturity dates, minimum cash payments, and restrictions, is presented in footnotes. The annual reports presented in Appendix A to the text contain illustrations of such footnote disclosures.

GLOSSARY

ACCOUNTING INCOME.   The income amount reported for external reporting purposes (p. 669).

BOND (BOND PAYABLE).   A certificate containing a written promise to pay the principal amount at a specified time, plus interest on the principal at a specified rate per period (p. 642).

BOND SINKING FUND. An investment fund established to provide for the retirement of bonds (p. 660).

CALLABLE BOND. A bond that may be purchased before the bond matures at the option of the issuing company for a specified price stated in the indenture (p. 645).

CAPITAL LEASE. A lease that is, in substance, an installment purchase of property (p. 667).

CARRYING VALUE OF BONDS. The par value of a bond issue, less any unamortized discount or plus any unamortized premium (p. 650).

COLLATERAL. Something of value that is acceptable to a lender as security for a loan (p. 644).

CONVERTIBLE BOND. A bond that may be converted into common stock of the issuing company (p. 645).

COUPON RATE (NOMINAL RATE, CONTRACT RATE, OR STATED RATE). The interest rate stated as a percentage of par value and used to determine the amount paid periodically to the bondholder (p. 642).

COUPON (BEARER) BOND. A bond that has a printed interest coupon attached for each interest payment date. Title is assumed to be with the holder of the bond (p. 645).

DEBENTURE BOND (UNSECURED BOND). A bond backed only by the general credit rating of the company (p. 644).

DISCOUNT. The excess of the par value of a bond over its sale price (p. 642).

FINANCIAL LEVERAGE. The use of borrowed funds that have a fixed cost to earn a higher rate of return for the purpose of increasing the earnings of the owners (p. 643).

FUNDED PLAN. A pension plan in which deposits are made to an outside agency appointed to manage the fund (p. 669).

INCOME TAX ALLOCATION. An accounting procedure under which the reported income tax expense is based on accounting income, rather than on taxable income (p. 671).

INDENTURE. The terms of a bond agreement contained in a contract between the borrowing firm and the bondholder (p. 642).

LEASE. A rental agreement in which the lessor conveys to the lessee the right to use property for a specified period of time in return for periodic rental payments (p. 667).

MARKET RATE (EFFECTIVE RATE, YIELD RATE). The actual rate of interest an investor will earn if bonds are purchased at a certain price and held to maturity (p. 648).

MATURITY DATE. The date on which the borrower must pay the par value of a note or bond (p. 642).

MORTGAGE. A legal document setting forth the specific assets serving as collateral for a loan (p. 665).

MORTGAGE NOTE PAYABLE. A form of a promissory note in which specific property of the borrower serves as collateral for a loan (p. 665).

OPERATING LEASE. A lease that is not a capital lease. In an operating lease, the lessor retains the risks and rewards of ownership (p. 668).

PAR VALUE (FACE VALUE, PRINCIPAL, MATURITY VALUE). The amount due to a lender when a debt matures (p. 642).

PENSION PLAN. A plan established to provide payments to eligible employees when they retire (p. 669).

PERMANENT DIFFERENCE. An item of revenue or expense that enters into the computation of accounting income or taxable income, but not both (p. 669).

PREMIUM.   The excess of the sale price of a bond over its par value (p. 642).

REGISTERED BOND.   A bond whose owner's name is on file with the issuing firm (p. 645).

SECURED (MORTGAGE) BOND.   A bond secured by a prior claim against specific property of the issuing company (p. 644).

SERIAL BONDS.   A bond issue that matures in installments (p. 645).

TERM BONDS.   A bond issue in which all of the bonds mature on one date (p. 645).

TIMING DIFFERENCE.   A revenue or expense item that enters into the determination of both accounting income and taxable income but in different time periods (p. 670).

TRUSTEE.   A third party appointed to represent the bondholders (p. 642).

UNDERWRITER.   An investment firm that markets a bond issue (p. 642).

UNSECURED NOTE PAYABLE.   A promissory note backed by a legal claim against the general assets of the borrower (p. 665).

DISCUSSION QUESTIONS

1. What are the advantages and disadvantages of debt financing, rather than equity financing?

2. Regis Company issued $1,000,000 of bonds on an interest payment date. What amount of cash was received from the sale, assuming that the bonds sold at: 100; 98; and 102¼?

3. Differentiate between the following bond terms:
   (a) Secured and debenture.
   (b) Registered and coupon.
   (c) Term and serial.

4. A corporation issued $1,000,000 of 7½% bonds at 96⅜ to yield 8%.
   (a) Were the bonds issued at a premium or at a discount?
   (b) What is the maturity value of the bonds?
   (c) What is the nominal (stated) rate of interest?
   (d) What is the effective rate of interest?

5. How do the market rate of interest and the stated rate of interest compare when a bond is sold at a discount?

6. The unamortized premium on a $1,000,000 bond issue is $68,100. What is the carrying value of the bonds?

7. Why must the buyer of a bond sold between interest payment dates pay the seller accrued interest?

8. A company calls $500,000 of bonds at 99 when the discount account has a $21,000 balance.
   (a) What is the amount of the company's gain or loss?
   (b) What type of gain or loss is it?

9. What is the advantage to the issuing company of issuing convertible bonds?

10. (a) Where is the *Bond Sinking Fund* account classified on the balance sheet?
    (b) Where is the *Bond Sinking Fund Revenue* listed on the income statement?

11. Why does interest expense change each period when the effective-interest method of amortization is used?

Ex 17-1

A1 1,124,632

1166 400

Cash 1124632

D.

9.8 181

589086

254545

214500

.2145

50000

payable would look like this (payment)

Interest+Expense
   Mortgage Notes Payable
      Cash

2. a 1,000,000
   b   980,000
   c 1,022,500

4. a discount
   b ~~1,600,015~~ 1,600,000
   c 9½% 7½%
   d 7½% 12.5% 8%

5 it goes up.

6 it goes up, market rate is higher than stated rate.

6. 1,068,100

7. The buyer pays the seller Accrued interest when
   he buys A bond.

8   500,000
    21,000 discount
    a loss
    b discount

(handwritten: 4632 / 3600 / 132)

12. What accounts are debited in an entry to record a payment on a mortgage note payable?
13. What criteria must be met before a leasee can properly account for a lease as a capital lease?
14. Differentiate between the journal entries to record a lease payment with a capital lease and with an operating lease.
15. When would a company have a credit balance in the *Pension Fund Liability* account?
16. Distinguish between a permanent difference and a timing difference between accounting income and taxable income.
17. When are income tax allocation procedures used? Why are they used?
18. Why is the balance in the *Deferred Income Tax* account sometimes classified as an asset and sometimes as a liability?

EXERCISES

(For the exercises and problems in this chapter, round all computations to the nearest dollar.)

Exercise 17-1 Computing Issue Price of Bonds and Recording the Issue

On June 11, the Barrett Corporation received authorization from its board of directors to issue $1,000,000 of 12%, 10-year bonds dated July 1. Interest is payable semi-annually, on December 31 and June 30. *60,000 cash*

Required:
A. Compute the issue price of the bonds on July 1 for each of the following three cases.
   1. The bonds are sold to yield 10%. *1123,600*
   2. The bonds are sold to yield 12%. *par*
   3. The bonds are sold to yield 16%.
B. Record the issuance of the bonds for each case.

(handwritten margin: yield-effective market 76.85)
(handwritten: Cash / Premium on Bonds Payable / Bonds Payable)

Exercise 17-2 Straight-line Method of Amortization

On July 1, 1987, Koret Corporation issued $400,000, 9%, 10-year bonds. The bonds were dated July 1, 1987, and interest is payable each June 30 and December 31. Koret Corporation's annual year-end is December 31, and because the difference between the two methods of amortization is not material, the company uses the straight-line method of amortization.

Required:
A. Prepare journal entries to record the issuance of the bonds and the payments of interest and the amortization of discount or premium on December 31, 1987, and June 30, 1988, assuming that
   1. The bonds were issued at par.
   2. The bonds were issued for $375,080.
   3. The bonds were issued for $424,920.
B. Complete the following schedule as of December 31, 1987, after the December 31 interest payment had been recorded.

Premium not written off yet (handwritten, left margin)

Face value (handwritten)

	Issue Price		
	$400,000	$375,080	$424,920
Bonds payable	400,000	400,000	400,000
Unamortized discount	0	-23,674	0
Unamortized premium	0	0	23,674
Carrying value of the bonds	400,000	376,326	423,674
Change in carrying value from July 1	0	+1,246	-1,246
Bond interest expense for 1987	19,000	19,246	16,754
Cash payment for interest during 1987	19,000	19,000	18,000
Discount or premium amortization during 1987	0	1,246	-1,244

Exercise 17-3 Bonds Issued Between Interest Payment Dates

The Royer Corporation issued $100,000 of 10-year, 8% bonds on May 1 at par value plus accrued interest. Interest is payable on February 1 and August 1. The corporation is a calendar year firm.

Required:

Prepare general journal entries to record the following transactions.

A. Issuance of the bonds on May 1. *Feb, March, April, .25* (handwritten)
B. First interest payment on August 1. *May June July,* (handwritten)
C. Accrued interest on December 31. *Aug Sep Oct Nov Dec* (handwritten)
D. The interest payment on February 1.

Exercise 17-4 Accrual of Bond Interest

On September 1, 1987, Heinz Company issued $1,000,000 of 8%, 20-year bonds for $960,000. Interest is payable on August 31 and February 28. The fiscal year of the company is the calendar year, and the company uses the straight-line method of amortization.

Required:

Prepare journal entries to record the following transactions.

A. Issue of the bonds on September 1, 1987.
B. Accrual of interest and amortization of the discount on December 31, 1987.
C. Payment of interest and amortization of discount on February 28, 1988.
D. Payment of interest and amortization of discount on August 31, 1988.

Exercise 17-5 Retirement of Bonds Before Maturity

The Harper Company issued $1,000,000 of 11%, 10-year callable bonds on January 1, 1983, at 102. Interest is payable on June 30 and December 31, and the company uses the straight-line method of amortization.

Required:

A. Prepare the journal entry to record the interest payment and the amortization of the premium on June 30, 1987.
B. Prepare the entry to record the retirement of the bonds on July 1, 1987, at 104.

Exercise 17-6 Bond Conversion

The Madison Corporation has $900,000 of 13% convertible bonds outstanding. Each

$1,000 bond is convertible into 25 shares of $20 par value common stock. On March 1, 1987, an interest-payment date, unamortized discount amounted to $9,000 after recording the current interest payment. On March 1, 1987, $400,000 of the bonds were converted.

Required:
Prepare the journal entry to record the conversion of the bonds.

Exercise 17-7   Bond Sinking Fund
On January 1, 1987, G & B Electronics Corporation issued $350,000 of 10-year bonds. The bond indenture requires that every January 1 for the next 10 years G & B deposit $35,000, less any earnings made on the fund investment during the year.

Required:
Prepare journal entries to record each of the following transactions.

A. The first deposit is made in the sinking fund on January 1, 1988.
B. On December 31, 1988, it is determined that the sinking fund investments earned $4,315 during the year.
C. The second deposit is made in the sinking fund on January 1, 1989.
D. The $350,000 accumulated in the sinking fund is used to retire the bonds on January 1, 1997.

Exercise 17-8   Effective-Interest Method of Amortization
The Hartford Corporation issued $1,000,000 of 10-year, 9% bonds on July 1, 1987, for $937,700. Interest is payable on June 30 and December 31. The market rate of interest is 10%.

Required:
A. Prepare the journal entry to record the issue of the bonds on July 1, 1987.
B. Using the effective-interest method of amortization, prepare the general journal entries to record the payments of interest and the amortization of the discount or premium on the following dates: December 31, 1987; June 30, 1988; and December 31, 1988.
C. Show how the bonds payable would be reported on the December 31, 1988, balance sheet.
D. How much bond interest expense is reported in the 1988 income statement?
E. How much cash was paid to the bondholders during 1988?
F. Explain why your answers to requirements (D) and (E) are different.
G. Prepare the journal entry to retire the bonds at the maturity date.

Exercise 17-9   Effective-Interest Method of Amortization
Use the same information as is given in Exercise 17-8, except that the bonds were issued for $1,067,965 to yield 8%.

Required:
Complete requirements (A) through (G), as given in Exercise 17-8.

Exercise 17-10   Mortgage Notes Payable
The Taylor Corporation purchased a warehouse on May 1, 1987, for $350,000. Taylor gave a down payment of $70,000 and signed a 9.75% mortgage note with monthly payments of $2,700. (Use effective interest method.)

Required:
A. Give the journal entry to record the first monthly payment on June 1, 1987.

B. Give the entry to record the payment on August 1, 1987.

Exercise 17-11 Accounting for a Lease Obligation

Newton Company operates the Landmark Motel. The motel is leased under the following lease agreement.

Inception of the Lease	January 1, 1986
Term	20 years, noncancelable
Ownership	The lease contains no bargain purchase option and ownership does not transfer to Newton Company
Lease payments	$100,000 per year (due on December 31)

The motel has an estimated economic life of 25 years and the lease provides for a 16% rate of interest. Newton Company uses the straight-line method of depreciation.

Required:

A. Is this a capital lease or an operating lease? Explain your answer.

B. Compute the present value of the lease payment.

C. Record the necessary journal entries to account for the lease in 1986.

Exercise 17-12 Income Tax Allocation

The records of the Lasser Corporation contain the following income tax information.

	1987	1988	1989
Actual Income Tax	$48,700	$51,900	$52,700
Income Tax Reported on the Income Statement	51,100	51,100	51,100

Required:

A. Prepare journal entries to record the income tax expense and liability for each of the years.

B. Post the entries to a T account entitled *Deferred Income Tax.*

PROBLEMS

Problem 17-1 Computing Issue Price and Straight-line Method of Amortization

On July 1, 1987, Wilbur Corporation issued $300,000 of 10-year bonds with a stated interest rate of 16%. The market rate of interest was 20% on that date. Semiannual interest is payable on June 30 and December 31. The company's fiscal year ends December 31.

Required:

A. Determine the issue price of the bonds.

B. Prepare a journal entry to record the issuance of the bonds.

C. Using the straight-line method, prepare journal entries to record bond interest expense and amortization on the first three interest payment dates.

D. Compute the carrying value of the bonds on December 31, 1988. Show how the bonds would be reported in the balance sheet.

E. Compute the total bond interest expense that would be reported in the 1988 income statement. How is the interest reported?

F. Prepare the journal entry to retire the bonds on their maturity date.

✳ Problem 17-2   Accrual of Interest and Bond Retirement Before Maturity

The following transactions of the Continental Corporation relate to its issuance of $2,000,000 of 12%, 20-year, callable bonds. Interest-payment dates are September 1 and March 1. The company's fiscal year is the calendar year, and it uses the straight-line method of amortization.

Sept. 1, 1987	The bonds are issued for $2,150,000.
Dec. 31, 1987	An adjusting entry is made to record accrued interest and to amortize a portion of the premium.
Mar. 1, 1988	Interest is paid and a portion of the premium is amortized.
Sept. 1, 1989	Interest is paid and a portion of the premium is amortized.
Sept. 1, 1989	The company retires one-fourth of the bonds by calling them at 105.

Handwritten margin note: 20 yr. × 12 months = 240 months. Credit Premium

Required:

Prepare general journal entries to record each of the transactions.

Problem 17-3   Bond Transactions and Sinking Fund

Birmingham Corporation decided to issue $500,000 of 13%, five-year bonds. Interest is payable on June 30 and December 31. The fiscal year of the corporation ends June 30. The bond indenture requires Birmingham Corporation to deposit $78,725 in a bond sinking fund at the end of every fiscal year during the life of the bonds. The sinking fund cash is invested in securities, which will yield a 12% annual return each period. Some of the transactions relating to the bond issue and the sinking fund are listed here.

July 1, 1987	Sold the bond issue at 92¼.
Dec. 31, 1987	Paid the semiannual interest and amortized the discount using the straight-line method.
June 30, 1988	Paid the interest on the bonds and amortized the discount.
June 30, 1988	Made the first sinking fund deposit.
June 30, 1989	Paid the interest on the bonds and amortized the discount.
June 30, 1990	Recorded the interest earned by the sinking fund investments during the fiscal year. The investments earned 12% as expected.
June 30, 1991	Made the fourth sinking fund deposit.
June 30, 1992	Retired the bonds and transferred the excess in the sinking fund to the cash account.

Required:

A. Complete the following table, showing the interest earned by the sinking fund during the fiscal year and the fund balance as of June 30 for each of the five years during the life of the bonds.

DATE	CASH DEPOSITS	INTEREST EARNED	ACCUMULATED BALANCE

B. Prepare journal entries to record the transactions.

Problem 17-4 Bonds Issued Between Interest Payment Dates, Accrual of Interest, Bond Conversion, and Bond Retirement Before Maturity

J. T. Robbins Company decided to issue $1,500,000 of 9%, 15-year, convertible bonds dated May 1, 1987. Each $1,000 bond is convertible into 50 shares of $10 par value common stock. Semiannual interest is due on April 30 and October 31. The fiscal year of the company is the calendar year and it uses the straight-line method to amortize bond discount and premium. J. T. Robbins Company completed the following transactions.

Aug. 31, 1987	Issued the entire bond issue at a price of 100, plus accrued interest.
Oct. 31, 1987	Paid the semiannual interest.
Dec. 31, 1987	Recorded the accrued interest.
April 30, 1988	Paid the semiannual interest.
May 1, 1988	Bondholders converted $500,000 of the bonds.
Oct. 31, 1988	Paid the semiannual interest on the bonds outstanding.

J. T. Robbins Company then decided to issue $450,000 of 11%, 20-year, callable bonds dated December 31, 1987. Interest is payable on June 30 and December 31. The following transactions were completed.

Dec. 31, 1987	Issued the entire issue at 98.
June 30, 1988	Paid the semiannual interest and amortized the discount.
Dec. 31, 1988	Paid the semiannual interest and amortized the discount.
July 1, 1991	Called the bonds at 99½.

Required:
Prepare journal entries to record each of the transactions.

Problem 17-5 Effective-Interest Method of Amortization

The Ross Corporation issued $600,000 of three-year bonds on February 1, 1987. Semiannual interest payments are due on January 31 and July 31. The fiscal year of the company ends July 31. The accountant prepared the following interest expense and amortization schedule.

Interest Payment Date	Cash Paid	Interest Expense	Amount Amortized
July 31, 1987	$36,000	$31,522	$4,478
January 31, 1988	36,000	31,298	4,702
July 31, 1988	36,000	31,063	4,937
January 31, 1989	36,000	30,816	5,184
July 31, 1989	36,000	30,557	5,443
January 31, 1990	36,000	30,299	5,701

Required:
A. Determine the stated rate of interest.
B. Were the bonds sold at a discount or at a premium?
C. What method of amortization was used?
D. Determine the effective rate of interest.
E. Prepare the entry to record the sale of the bonds.
F. Prepare journal entries to record the interest payment and amortization on July 31, 1987, and on January 31, 1989.

Problem 17-6 Effective-Interest Method of Amortization

 *nominal or stated*

On January 1, 1987, the TRW Corporation issued five-year, 10% bonds with a par value of $200,000. Interest is payable June 30 and December 31. The bonds were issued at a price to yield 8%.

Required:

A. Compute the issue price of the bonds.

B. Prepare the journal entries to record the following transactions.
   1. January 1, 1987. All of the bonds were issued for cash.
   2. June 30, 1987. Paid the semiannual interest and amortized the premium or discount. (Use the effective-interest method to amortize the discount or premium.)
   3. December 31, 1987 (end of annual period). Paid the semiannual interest and amortized the premium or discount.
   4. June 30, 1988. Paid the semiannual interest and amortized the premium or discount.
   5. January 1, 1992. Paid the bonds at maturity.

C. Show how the bonds payable will be reported in the December 31, 1987 balance sheet.

D. Answer the following questions.
   1. What amount of bond interest expense is reported in 1987?
   2. Will the bond interest expense reported in 1988 be the same as, greater than, or less than the amount reported in 1987?
   3. Assuming that the bonds are outstanding the full five-year period, what is the total bond interest expense to be recognized during the life of the bonds?
   4. Would the straight-line method of amortization result in the same amount, more than, or less than the bond interest expense reported in 1987 under the effective-interest method?
   5. If the straight-line method had been used, would the carrying value of the bonds be less than or greater than the carrying value computed in requirement (C)?
   6. Would the total bond interest expense recognized over the life of the bonds using the straight-line method be the same as, greater than, or less than the amount computed in question (3)? Explain.

Problem 17-7 Mortgage Notes Payable

Southwest, Incorporated, has decided to open another department store. It purchased a building and land for $2,475,000 on May 1, 1987, by giving a down payment of $232,932 and signing a 16% mortgage note. The note provides for 80 quarterly payments of $93,750. The first quarterly payment was made on August 1, 1987. The company's fiscal year-end is December 31.

Required:

A. Prepare a quarterly payment schedule for payments made in 1987 and 1988. Head the columns with the following titles: Payment Date; Unpaid Balance at Beginning of Quarter; Cash Payment; Interest for One Quarter; Reduction in Principal; and Principal Balance at end of Quarter.

B. Prepare journal entries to record the purchase of the land and building, the first three quarterly payments, and the adjusting entry at December 31 (80% of the purchase price is attributed to the building).

C. Show how the unpaid mortgage note principal would be classified on the balance sheet as of December 31, 1987.

Problem 17-8 Preparation of Amortization Table—Effective-Interest Method

On January 1, 1987, Porter Company issued $1,000,000, 11.5%, 5-year bonds to yield 10%. The bonds were dated January 1, 1987 and interest is payable on June 30 and December 31. The company's year-end is December 31. Porter Company uses the effective-interest method of amortization.

Required:
A. Determine the issue price of the bonds.
B. Prepare an amortization table.

Problem 17-9 Accounting for Lease Obligation

The Dole Corporation signed an agreement on January 1, 1987 to lease equipment for 5 years. Rental payments of $24,769 are due on December 31 of each year. The equipment has a fair value of $89,287. The lease is considered a capital lease. Dole made the first payment on December 31, 1987. The interest rate on the lease is 12%.

Required:
A. Prepare an amortization table using the following headings.

Date	Annual Lease Payment	Interest on Unpaid Obligation	Reduction of Lease Obligation	Balance of Lease Obligation

B. Record the leased asset and leased obligation.
C. Record the first lease payment on December 31, 1987.

Problem 17-10 Income Tax Allocation

The Crest Corporation purchased a machine on January 2 for $170,000. The machine has a four year useful life and a zero residual value. The corporation uses the ACRS method of depreciation (25% year 1; 38% year 2; 37% year 3) for tax purposes, and the straight-line method for financial statement purposes. The corporation's annual income before depreciation and income tax is $275,000. Assume a fixed corporate tax rate of 40% and a calendar year-end.

Required:
A. Determine the taxable income and income tax liability for each of the four years.
B. For each year, determine accounting net income in accordance with generally accepted accounting principles.
C. Prepare journal entries to record each year's income tax expense and liability.
D. Set up a T account entitled *Deferred Income Tax* and post the journal entries to this account.

Problem 17-11 Income Tax Allocation

On July 1, 1987, Villa Serena Development Corporation received $28,800 as advance payment for 24 months' rent. The rental period began on that date. Villa Serena has an annual taxable income, without considering the rent, of $220,000. Assume a fixed corporate tax rate of 40% and a calendar year-end. (Assume that the cash basis is used for income tax purposes and the accrual basis is used for financial statement purposes.)

Required:
A. Compute the income tax liability for 1987, 1988, and 1989.
B. Determine the accounting net income for 1987, 1988, and 1989, assuming that the actual tax liability is reported on the income statement.
C. Determine the accounting net income for each year, assuming that income tax allocation procedures are used.
D. Prepare journal entries to allocate the tax expense and record the tax liability.

ALTERNATE PROBLEMS

Problem 17-1A Computing Issue Price and Straight-line Method of Amortization

Campbell Company issued $3,000,000 of 13.5%, 15-year bonds on October 1, 1987, when the market rate was 12%. Interest payments are due on March 31 and September 30. The fiscal year of the company ends September 30.

Required:
A. Determine the issue price of the bonds.
B. Prepare a journal entry to record the issuance of the bonds.
C. Prepare journal entries to record bond interest expense and amortization for the first three interest payments. Use the straight-line method of amortization.
D. Compute the carrying value of the bonds on October 1, 1988. Show how the bonds would be reported in the balance sheet.
E. Compute the total bond interest expense that would be reported in the income statement for the year ended September 30, 1988.
F. Prepare the journal entry to retire the bonds on their maturity date.

Problem 17-2A Accrual of Interest and Bond Retirement Before Maturity

The Welch Company issued $1,800,000 of 11%, 15-year, callable bonds. Interest payment dates are May 31 and November 30. The company's fiscal year ends December 31 and it uses the straight-line method of amortization. The following transactions relate to the bond issue.

Dec. 1, 1987	The bonds are issued for $1,937,250.
Dec. 31, 1987	An entry is made to record interest accrued and to amortize a portion of the premium.
May 31, 1988	The first interest payment is made and a portion of the premium is amortized.
Nov. 30, 1989	The fourth interest payment is made and a portion of the premium is amortized.
Nov. 30, 1989	One-third of the bonds are called at 108 and retired.

Required:
Prepare general journal entries to record each of the transactions.

Problem 17-3A Bond Transactions and Sinking Fund

Bailey Corporation decided to issue $900,000 of 12%, four-year bonds. Semiannual interest payments are due on June 30 and December 31. The company has agreed to deposit $194,040 in a bond sinking fund at the end of each year during the life of the bond issue. The sinking fund investments will earn an annual return of 10%. Bailey Corporation uses the straight-line method of amortization. Some of the company's transactions are listed here.

Jan. 1, 1987	Sold the entire issue for 98⅜.
June 30, 1987	Paid the first interest payment and amortized a portion of the discount.
Dec. 31, 1987	Deposited cash into the sinking fund.
June 30, 1988	Paid the third interest payment and amortized a portion of the discount.
Dec. 31, 1988	Recorded the income earned during the year by the sinking fund investments.
Dec. 31, 1989	Deposited cash into the sinking fund.
Dec. 31, 1990	Recorded the sinking fund earnings for the year.
Dec. 31, 1990	Paid the bondholders with proceeds from the sinking fund and received cash for the excess amount in the fund.

Required:

A. Prepare a table showing the interest earned by the sinking fund during the year and the year-end fund balance for each year during the life of the bonds. The table should appear as follows.

Date	Cash Deposits	Interest Earned	Accumulated Balance

B. Prepare journal entries to record the transactions listed.

Problem 17-4A Bond Issued Between Interest Payment Dates, Accrual of Interest, Bond Conversion, and Bond Retirement Before Maturity

The Remington Corporation decided to issue $2,000,000 of 9%, 10-year convertible bonds. The bonds are dated October 1, 1987, and interest is payable on March 31 and September 30. Each $1,000 bond can be converted into 40 shares of $20 par value common stock. The company's fiscal year ends December 31. Because the difference between the two amortization methods is immaterial, the company uses the straight-line amortization method. The following transactions relating to the bond issue were completed.

Dec. 1, 1987	Issued the entire bond issue at par, plus accrued interest.
Dec. 31, 1987	Recorded the accrued interest.
Mar. 31, 1988	Paid the semiannual interest.
Sept. 30, 1988	Paid the semiannual interest.
Sept. 30, 1988	$1,000,000 of the bonds were converted.
Dec. 31, 1988	Recorded the accrued interest on the outstanding bonds.

Remington Corporation then decided to issue $1,300,000 of 10.5%, 20-year, callable bonds. The bonds are dated January 1, 1989, and interest-payment dates are June 30, and December 31. Remington completed these transactions.

Jan. 1, 1989	Issued all the bonds for $1,313,000.
June 30, 1989	Paid the semiannual interest and amortized the premium.

June 30, 1993   Paid the semiannual interest and amortized the premium.
June 30, 1993   The entire bond issue was called at 102.5 and retired.

Required:
Prepare the general journal entries to record each transaction.

Problem 17-5A Effective-Interest Method of Amortization
On July 1, 1987, Baltimore Corporation issued $500,000 of three-year bonds. Interest payment dates are June 30 and December 31. The corporation's fiscal year is the calendar year. The following amortization table was prepared.

Interest Payment Date	Cash Paid	Interest Expense	Amount Amortized
December 31, 1987	$28,750	$35,841	$ 7,091
June 30, 1988	28,750	36,408	7,658
December 31, 1988	28,750	37,021	8,271
June 30, 1989	28,750	37,682	8,932
December 31, 1989	28,750	38,397	9,647
June 30, 1990	28,750	39,143	10,393

Required:
A. What is the stated rate of interest on the bonds?
B. Were the bonds issued at a premium or at a discount?
C. Which method of amortization was used?
D. What was the market rate of interest when the bonds were sold?
E. Prepare the entry to record the sale of the bonds.
F. Prepare journal entries to record interest expense and amortization on June 30, 1988, and on June 30, 1989.

Problem 17-6A Effective-Interest Method of Amortization
On January 1, 1987, the FTD Corporation issued five-year, 10% bonds with a par value of $300,000. Interest is payable June 30 and December 31. The bonds were issued at a price to yield 12%.

Required:
A. Compute the issue price of the bonds.
B. Prepare journal entries to record the following transactions:
  1. January 1, 1987. All of the bonds were issued for cash.
  2. June 30, 1987. Paid the semiannual interest and amortized the premium or discount. (Use the effective-interest method to amortize the discount or premium.)
  3. December 31, 1987 (end of annual period). Paid the semiannual interest and amortized the premium or discount.
  4. June 30, 1988. Paid the semiannual interest and amortized the premium or discount.
  5. January 1, 1992. Paid the bonds at maturity.
C. Show how the bonds payable will be reported on the December 31, 1987 balance sheet.
D. Answer the following questions.
  1. What amount of bond interest expense is reported in 1987?
  2. Will the bond interest expense reported in 1988 be the same as, greater than, or less than the amount reported in 1987?

PART 5 ADDITIONAL FINANCIAL REPORTING ISSUES

3. Assuming that the bonds are outstanding the full five-year period, what is the total bond interest expense to be recognized during the life of the bonds?
4. Would the straight-line method of amortization result in the same amount, more than, or less than the bond interest expense reported in 1987 under the effective-interest method?
5. If the straight-line method had been used, would the carrying value of the bonds be less than or greater than the carrying value computed in requirement (C)?
6. Would the total bond interest expense recognized over the life of the bonds using the straight-line method be the same as, greater than, or less than the amount computed in question (3)? Explain.

Problem 17-7A Mortgage Notes Payable

Wesley Corporation purchased a building and the land it is on for $1,000,000. It gave the seller a down payment of $203,520 and a 14% mortgage note requiring 100 quarterly payments of $28,800 due the fifteenth of March, June, September, and December. Wesley Corporation purchased the building and land and made the down payment on June 16, 1987. It made the first quarterly payment on September 15, 1987. The company's fiscal year-end is December 31.

Required:
A. Prepare a quarterly payment schedule for 1987 and 1988. Use the following headings: Payment Date; Unpaid Balance at Beginning of Quarter; Cash Payment; Interest for One Quarter; Reduction in Principal; and Principal Balance at End of Quarter.
B. Prepare journal entries to record the purchase and the first three quarterly payments, and the adjusting entry as of December 31 (85% of the purchase price is attributed to the building).
C. Show how the mortgage note payable would be classified in the balance sheet as of December 31, 1987.

Problem 17-8A Preparation of Amortization Table—Effective-Interest Method

On February 1, 1987, Beckman Corporation issued $500,000, 9%, four-year bonds to yield 10%. The bonds were dated February 1, 1987 and interest is payable on July 31 and January 31. The company's year-end is December 31. Beckman uses the effective-interest method of amortization.

Required:
A. Determine the issue price of the bonds.
B. Prepare an amortization table.

Problem 17-9A Income Tax Allocation

The Standard Corporation received $27,000 on October 1, 1987, as an advance payment of rent for the 18 month period beginning that day. Standard has taxable income from other sources of $140,000 per year. Assume a fixed corporate tax rate of 40% and a calendar year-end. Rent is reported as taxable income in the year received.

Required:
A. Determine Standard's income tax liability for 1987, 1988, and 1989.
B. Determine Standard's accounting net income for each of the years, assuming that the actual tax liability appears on the income statement.
C. Determine Standard's accounting net income, assuming that income tax allocation procedures are used.

D. Prepare journal entries to record the allocated tax expense and the actual tax liability.

CASES

CASE 17-1   Financial Report Analysis Case   Analysis of Long-Term Debt

For this case you are to refer to the Kmart Corporation's annual report presented in Appendix A to the text. Complete the requirements in millions of dollars, as shown in the annual report.

Required:
A. Compute the net increase or decrease in the firm's "Long-term Debt" category during the fiscal year ended January 30, 1985. What type of financing primarily caused the change?
B. Determine the amount of "Long-term Debt" reported in the Janaury 30, 1985 balance sheet that matures within the next fiscal year.
C. Prepare a list of the firm's "Long-term Debt" that require a sinking fund payment, the amount of the payment required, and the date the first payment is to be made.
D. Are there restrictions on the payment of cash dividends to the common stockholders? How can the lender benefit from a restriction on dividends?
E. Determine the following with regard to the 6% convertible debentures.
  1. Maturity date.
  2. Coupon rate.
  3. How many shares of common stock will be issued if one $1,000 par value debenture is converted.
  4. The number of shares of authorized stock reserved for conversion.
  5. The approximate market price of a $1,000 par value bond related to the conversion feature, assuming that the common stock was selling for $41 per share.

CASE 17-2   Financial Report Analysis Case   Analysis of Lease Obligation

For this case you are to refer to the Holiday Inns, Inc. annual report presented in Appendix A. Complete the requirements in thousands of dollars, as shown in the annual report.

Required:
A. What is the amount of capital lease obligations included with the company's long-term debt?
B. The company shows total minimum lease payments for capital leases of $71,192. However, only $37,636, including current maturities, is reported as a liability in the balance sheet. What does the difference between these two amounts represent? Explain how this difference is accounted for.
C. The company discloses the minimum lease payments for both capital leases and operating leases. What criteria must the company use to classify its leases as capital or operating?
D. The company reports property and equipment, net of accumulated depreciation, in the amount of $1,673,430. What is the dollar amount of leased assets included in this category?

18

LONG-TERM INTERCORPORATE INVESTMENTS, CONSOLIDATED FINANCIAL STATEMENTS, AND INTERNATIONAL ACCOUNTING

Ex 1,2,3

Stocks

Cost *Equity*

Cost *Equity*
∧ *|*
temp. Lt. *L.T.*

Cost *Equity*
20% *over 20%*

Income of purchased comp. stocks
Dividends "
Reduction in market "

CHAPTER OVERVIEW AND OBJECTIVES

This chapter discusses accounting for long-term intercorporate investments, consolidated financial statements, and international accounting procedures. When you have completed the chapter, you should understand:

1. The nature of long-term investments.
2. The purpose of holding long-term investments in securities.
3. The difference between the cost and equity methods of accounting for long-term investments in voting stock.
4. How to account for long-term investments in bonds.
5. The purpose of consolidated financial statements.
6. The differences between the purchase and pooling of interests methods of preparing consolidated financial statements.

7. The conditions that must be met before a subsidiary is included in the consolidated financial statements.
8. Limitations in the use of information contained in consolidated financial statements.
9. The effect of changes in foreign exchange rates on receivables and payables to be settled in foreign currency.
10. How to translate a foreign subsidiary's financial statements into U.S. dollars.

This chapter includes three separate but related, topics: long-term investments in corporate securities, consolidated financial statements, and international accounting.

LONG-TERM INVESTMENTS IN CORPORATE SECURITIES

In the three preceding chapters, we discussed accounting for the issue of securities and the payment of dividends and interest from the viewpoint of the issuing corporation. We now turn our attention to the accounting procedures followed by the investors who purchase these securities. Investors may be individuals, mutual funds, pension funds, or other companies.

As discussed earlier, investments are classified as either temporary or long-term, depending upon the objective of the investment. Securities that management intends to hold for a short time, (i.e., those securities that management will convert to cash as needed for normal operating activities) are classified as temporary investments. Accounting for temporary investments was discussed in Chapter 7.

Long-term investments are those that are not intended to be converted into cash for normal operating activities; they may be defined simply as all investments that are not temporary. Just like temporary investments, they may consist of equity securities or debt securities.[1] Long-term investments are normally reported in a separate section of the balance sheet, immediately aftᵉʳ current assets, under the caption "Long-term investments" or simply "Investments."

Although there are several reasons why a company makes long-term investments in the securities of other companies, the primary objective is to increase net income. Net income is increased, of course, by the receipt of interest or dividends and through market appreciation of the securities, which is recognized when the securities are sold.

Another important means of increasing net income is through growth. A company may expand by enlarging existing facilities or by purchasing or building new factories or other facilities in various locations. This process requires large amounts of capital and produces results rather slowly.

Objective 1: Nature of long-term investments

Objective 2: Purpose for holding long-term investments in securities

---

[1]Long-term investments also include funds set aside for special purposes, such as a bond sinking fund, and land or other assets owned by the company but not used in normal operations.

ACCOUNTING FOR LONG-TERM INVESTMENTS IN COMMON STOCK

As an alternative to expanding by enlarging existing facilities or by purchasing new facilities, a company may expand its operations by acquiring sufficient voting stock of another company to influence or control its operations by electing members of its board of directors. The company acquiring the stock is called the **investor company** and the company whose stock is acquired is called the **investee company.** Many companies expand in this way for several reasons. One reason is that this type of expansion is accomplished rapidly, since the investee company already has operating facilities, customers, and suppliers, and may also own natural resources needed in the investor company's operations. Another reason is that expansion can be obtained with a smaller capital commitment than is otherwise possible. By acquiring more than 50% of the voting stock of another company, the investor can control the investee with a much smaller investment than would be required to build or buy equivalent facilities.

Objective 3: Cost method vs. equity method for common stock investments

Long-term investments in common stock are recorded initially at their total acquisition cost. However, the accounting method chosen for the investment subsequent to acquisition depends upon whether the investor owns enough stock to exercise significant influence over the investee's operating and financing policies. If the investor can exercise significant influence over the investee, the investment is accounted for by the **equity method;** otherwise it is accounted for by the **cost method,** applying the lower of cost or market procedures. In order to provide a reasonable degree of uniformity in practice, current accounting rules state that—unless there is evidence to the contrary—the ownership of 20% or more of the voting stock of a corporation provides presumptive evidence of the ability to exercise significant influence.[2] Thus, common stock investments of 20% or more are normally accounted for by the equity method, whereas those of less than 20% are accounted for by the cost method.

An investor corporation sometimes acquires all or a majority (over 50%) of the voting stock of an investee corporation in order to control the investee's activities. In these cases, consolidated financial statements are generally prepared. Consolidated financial statements are discussed later in this chapter.

The Cost Method

When less than 20% of a corporation's common stock is purchased and held as a long-term investment, the investment is recorded at its cost, including any broker's commission. For example, assume that Apex Company purchased 10,000 (10%) of Lux Corporation's 100,000 outstanding common shares as a long-term investment for 18¾, plus a broker's commission of $1,000. The investment is recorded as follows.

[2]"The Equity Method of Accounting for Investments in Common Stock," *Opinion of the Accounting Principles Board No. 18* (New York: AICPA, 1971), par. 17.

Jan.	8	Investment in Lux Corp. Stock	188,500	
		Cash		188,500
		To record the purchase of 10,000 shares of Lux Corporation common stock at $18.75 per share, plus $1,000 commission.		

Because less than 20% of Lux Corporation's outstanding stock was acquired, the investment is accounted for by the cost method. When the cost method is used, dividends declared by the investee may be recognized as dividend revenue by the investor through a debit to *Dividends Receivable* and a credit to *Dividend Revenue*. The *Dividends Receivable* account is then credited when the cash is received. As an alternative, because dividend revenue is often immaterial and is not taxable until received in cash, many companies defer recognition of the dividend until cash is received. For example, if Lux Corporation paid a $1 per share dividend, the entry by Apex Company would be:

Aug.	6	Cash	10,000	
		Dividend Revenue		10,000
		To record dividends received.		

A group of long-term common stock investments, each less than 20% of the outstanding stock of the respective investee company, constitutes the investor's long-term stock portfolio.[3] Lower of cost or market procedures are applied to a long-term stock investment portfolio accounted for by the cost method. Thus, the aggregate cost of the portfolio is compared with aggregate market value at the end of each accounting period. If aggregate market value is less than aggregate cost, an *Unrealized Loss on Long-term Investments* account is debited and an *Allowance to Reduce Long-term Investments to Market Value* account is credited.

Accounting procedures are similar to those used for the temporary stock portfolio described in Chapter 7 except that *the Unrealized Loss on Long-term Investments account is reported as a contra stockholders' equity item, rather than as a deduction in the income statement*. Thus, the *Unrealized Loss* account is not closed at the end of the period. In subsequent periods, both the *Unrealized Loss* account and the *Allowance* account are adjusted by an amount sufficient to report the long-term stock investment at the lower of its cost or market. Any balance in the *Unrealized Loss* account is deducted directly from stockholders' equity and the *Allowance* account is deducted as a contra to *Long-term Investments*.

For example, assume that on December 31, 1987, a long-term stock investment portfolio has an aggregate cost of $490,000 and an aggregate market

---

[3]The long-term stock portfolio also includes investments in other types of equity securities, such as preferred stock, and stock warrants (rights to purchase stock at a fixed price), regardless of the percentage owned.

value of $420,000. The entry made on December 31, 1987 to reduce the long-term stock portfolio to the lower of cost or market would be:

Dec.	31	Unrealized Loss on Long-term Investments	70,000	
		Allowance to Reduce Long-term		
		Investments to Market Value		70,000

The unrealized loss and allowance accounts would be reported on the December 31, 1987 balance sheet as follows.

Assets		
Current assets		$169,000
Long-term investments in stock	$490,000	
Less: Allowance to reduce long-term		
investments to market value	70,000	420,000
Plant and equipment (net of depreciation)		281,000
Total assets		$870,000
Liabilities		$100,000
Stockholders' Equity		
Common stock, $10 par	500,000	
Retained earnings	340,000	
Total	840,000	
Less: Unrealized loss on long-term investments	70,000	770,000
Total Liabilities and Stockholders' Equity		$870,000

The unrealized loss is subtracted directly from stockholders' equity, rather than being deducted in the income statement as is done with the unrealized loss on temporary stock investments. The loss in value of temporary investments is more likely to be realized because management intends to sell the investment in the near future. Because management intends to hold the long-term stock investments for several years, during which time the market value of the stock may rise again, the Financial Accounting Standards Board (FASB) decided that these fluctuations in stock values should not be reflected in net income.

If the market value of the long-term stock portfolio is greater than its cost, the unrealized gain is not recorded and the portfolio is reported at its aggregate cost. If the portfolio's aggregate market value at the end of a subsequent period is higher than its carrying value (cost minus allowance account), both the *Unrealized Loss* account and the *Allowance* account are decreased sufficiently to report the portfolio at the lower of its aggregate cost or aggregate market value. Thus, when the long-term stock portfolio has been written down to its market value, it may be written up only to its original cost. In other words, the *Allowance* account is adjusted upward and downward so that the *Allowance* account balance equals the excess of cost over market value of the portfolio on the balance sheet date. For example, if the market value of the portfolio was $460,000 on December 31, 1988, the following entry would be made.

Dec.	31	Allowance to Reduce Long-term Investments to Market Value	40,000	
		Unrealized Loss on Long-term Investments		40,000

When long-term stock portfolio securities that previously were written down to a lower market value are sold, the gain or loss recognized is the difference between the selling price and the original purchase cost, regardless of the balance in the allowance account. The balance in the allowance account is adjusted up or down to reflect the difference between aggregate portfolio cost and a lower aggregate portfolio market value at the end of the period.

The Equity Method

As mentioned earlier, when a company acquires 20% or more of the voting stock of a corporation, the investment is normally accounted for by the equity method. When the stock is acquired, the investment is recorded at its cost, just as it is with the cost method. However, two main features distinguish the equity method from the cost method. Under the equity method:

1. The investor company recognizes its proportional share of the investee's income as an increase in the investment account and as revenue for the period. If the investee reports a loss for the period, the investor decreases the investment account for its proportional share and recognizes a loss.
2. Dividends received from the investee are credited to the investment account, rather than to dividend revenue. The receipt of cash is treated as a recovery of a portion of the investment, because the investor's share of the investee's income has already been recognized as income and as an increase in the investment account.

To illustrate, assume that on January 2, 1987, Apex Company purchased 25,000 (25%) of the 100,000 outstanding common shares of Lux Corporation at 18¾, plus a broker's commission of $2,000. On September 1, Lux Corporation paid a dividend of $1 per share, and on December 31 it reported net income of $200,000. To record the effects of these events, Apex Company would make the following entries.

Jan.	2	Investment in Lux Corporation	470,750	
		Cash		470,750
		To record the purchase of 25,000 common shares of Lux Corporation at $18.75 per share, plus $2,000 commission.		
Sept.	1	Cash	25,000	
		Investment in Lux Corporation		25,000
		To record dividends received.		
Dec.	31	Investment in Lux Corporation	50,000	
		Investment Revenue		50,000
		To record 25% of Lux Corporation's reported net income of $200,000.		

The investment is recorded at its initial cost. The distribution of the dividend on September 1 reduced Lux Corporation's stockholders' equity by $100,000 and reduced Apex Company's share of Lux Corporation's stockholders' equity by $25,000 (25% × $100,000). Consequently, the receipt of the dividend is credited to the investment account to reflect the decrease in equity. Because Apex Company can significantly influence the operating policies of Lux Corporation, Apex Company recognized its share of Lux Corporation's net income for the period. Lux Corporation's stockholders' equity increased by the amount of income earned during the year ($200,000), and Apex Company's share of $50,000 (25% × $200,000) is added to the investment account. Thus, the investor's share of the increases and decreases in the investee's stockholders' equity are recorded as increases and decreases in the investment account. After recording these transactions, the investment account will appear as follows.

Investment in Lux Corporation

Jan. 2 Purchase	470,750	Sept. 1 Dividends	25,000
Dec. 31 Net income	50,000		
Dec. 31 Balance	495,750		

Recording the Sale of Stock Investments

When stock investments are sold, the appropriate investment account is credited for the carrying value of the shares sold, and the difference between the selling price (less broker's fees) and the carrying value is credited to *Gain on Sale of Investments* or debited to *Loss on Sale of Investments*. For example, assume that Apex Company sold 2,500 shares of Lux Corporation stock on January 2, 1988, for $22 per share and paid a broker's fee of $1,000. The entry to record the sale of 10% of the shares (2,500/25,000) would be:

Jan.	2	Cash (2,500 × $22) − $1,000	54,000	
		Investment in Lux Corp.*		49,575
		Gain on Sale of Investments		4,425
		To record the sale of 2,500 shares of Lux Corporation stock at $22 per share less $1,000 broker's fees.		
		*(10% × $495,750)		

A comparison of accounting for temporary and long-term stock investment portfolios under the lower of cost or market method is presented in Figure 18–1. A comparison of accounting for long-term stock investments under the cost method versus the equity method is shown in Figure 18–2.

ACCOUNTING FOR LONG-TERM INVESTMENTS IN BONDS

Objective 4: Accounting for long-term bond investments

The investor's accounting for long-term bonds is essentially the reverse of the accounting done for the issue of the bonds by the borrowing (issuing) company. The bond investment is recorded at its cost, including broker's fees. Since interest on bonds accrues over time, the purchaser must also pay interest accrued between the date of the last interest payment and the purchase date.

Figure 18–1
Accounting for
Temporary and
Long-term Stock In-
vestment Portfolios
Under the Lower of
Cost or Market
Methods

Item	Portfolio	
	Temporary	Long-term
Balance sheet location	Current assets.	Investments.
Allowance to reduce to lower of aggregate cost or market	Deducted from the cost of investment.	Same as temporary.
Unrealized loss	Unrealized loss in income statement (decrease net income).	Unrealized loss subtracted from stockholders' equity (no effect on net income).
Recovery of market value	Adjusted through recovery account in income statement (increases net income).	Adjusted through unrealized loss account in stockholders' equity (no effect on net income).
Sale of investment	Results in realized gain or loss in income statement.	Same as temporary.
Dividends declared	Reported as revenue in the income statement.	Depends on use of cost or equity method, as shown in Figure 18–2.

The amount paid for accrued interest is normally debited to *Interest Revenue*, so that it will be offset against the credit to *Interest Revenue* when the first interest payment is received.

The amount paid for bonds often will be more or less than par value; that is, the bonds are purchased at a premium or a discount. As explained in Chapter 17, if the market rate of interest is less than the stated rate on the bonds, the bonds will sell at a premium. If the market interest rate is more than the stated rate, the bonds will sell at a discount. Premium or discount represents an adjustment to interest revenue and, therefore, must be amortized over the remaining life of the bonds.

The premium or discount on a bond investment normally is not recorded in a separate account as is done for bonds payable. Rather, the bonds are recorded at their cost, and the difference between cost and the par value of the investment is amortized by direct entries to the *Investment in Bonds* account. Consequently, on each balance sheet date the *Investment in Bonds* account will contain the carrying value of the investment, which is equal to cost plus amortized discount, or cost minus amortized premium. The amortization of

Figure 18–2
Comparison of Cost
and Equity Methods

	Accounting Method	
Item	Cost	Equity
Acquisition of investment	Recorded at acquisition cost (remains unchanged).	Same as Cost but balance changes each year.
Revenue from investment	Recorded only when dividends are declared.	Investment account increased by investor's share of net income.
Dividends declared	Revenue recognized.	No revenue recognized. Credit investment account.
Use of lower of cost or market method	Compare total cost and total market value of all equity securities classified as long-term. Write down in a contra account if market is lower than cost.	Investment account not written down unless market decline is material and permanent.

discount will increase the carrying value of the bond investment to its maturity (par) value on its maturity date. Likewise, the amortization of premium will decrease the carrying value of the bond investment to its maturity value on its maturity date, as shown in Figure 18–3.

Bonds Purchased at a Premium

To illustrate bonds purchased at a premium, assume that on May 1, 1987, Bay Company purchased 300, $1,000 par value, 10% bonds of Croy Corporation on the open market at 105, plus accrued interest of $7,500 and broker's fees of $3,000. The bonds pay interest semiannually on July 31 and January

Figure 18–3
Effect of Premium
and Discount Amor-
tization on the Car-
rying Value of a
Bond

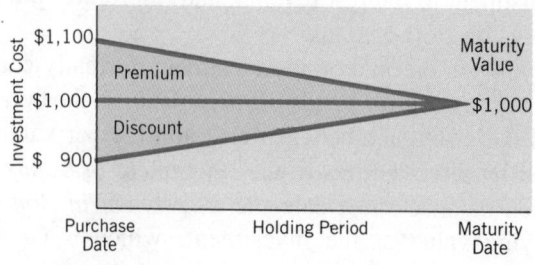

31. They mature on January 31, 1991, and thus have 45 months remaining to maturity date. The entry to record the purchase is:

May	1	Investment in Croy Corp. Bonds	318,000	
		Interest Revenue	7,500	
		Cash		325,500
		To record the purchase of Croy Corp.		
		bonds.		

The investment account is debited for the total cost of the bonds [(300 × $1,000 × 105%) + $3,000 broker's fee] and *Interest Revenue* is debited for the three months accrued interest of $7,500 ($300,000 × 10% × 3/12). As an alternative, the $7,500 accrued interest could be debited to *Interest Receivable*. If that is done, *Interest Receivable* is credited for $7,500 and *Interest Revenue* is credited for $6,300 when the interest payment is received on July 31. Note that, unlike the accounting for bonds by the issuing company, when accounting for bonds purchased, a separate premium account for the investment is not used.

The receipt of the first semiannual interest payment and amortization of premium for three months are recorded as follows.

July	31	Cash	15,000	
		Investment in Croy Corp. Bonds		1,200
		Interest Revenue		13,800
		To record the receipt of interest and the		
		amortization of premium.		

Because there were 45 months between the purchase of the bonds and their maturity date, amortization per month under the straight-line method is computed as follows.

Cost of the investment	$318,000
Par value of the bonds	300,000
Amount to be amortized	18,000
Amortization period (45 months)	÷ 45
Amortization per month	$ 400[4]

The debit to cash represents the amount received for the semiannual period ($300,000 × 10% × 6/12). The credit to the investment account reflects the amortization of premium for the months of May, June, and July (3 × $400).

When bonds are purchased at a premium, the amount of interest revenue is less than the cash received, by the amount of premium amortization. Thus, the amount of interest earned each month is equal to $2,500 ($300,000 × 10% × 1/12) less $400 per month amortization, or $2,100. The amount can be verified, as follows.

[4]As mentioned in Chapter 17, the interest method of amortization should be used if the difference between it and the straight-line method is material in amount. The straight-line method is generally used by companies that make only incidental investments in long-term bonds because interest revenue constitutes only a small part of their total income.

Amount to be received by the investor:	
Maturity value	$300,000
Interest for 45 months ($300,000 × 10% × 45/12)	112,500
Total cash to be received	412,500
Cost of investment	318,000
Total interest revenue	94,500
Number of months to maturity	÷ 45
Interest revenue per month	$ 2,100

After the interest receipt entry of July 31 is posted, the *Interest Revenue* account will appear thus.

Interest Revenue

May 1	7,500	July 31	13,800

The credit balance in the account ($6,300) reflects the correct amount of interest earned for the three months from May 1 to July 31 ($2,100 × 3 months).

On December 31, the end of the fiscal year, interest is accrued and amortization is recorded as follows.

Dec.	31	Interest Receivable (1)	12,500	
		Investment in Croy Corp. Bonds (2)		2,000
		Interest Revenue (3)		10,500
		To accrue interest for 5 months and		
		amortize premium.		
		(1) $300,000 × 10% × 5/12		
		(2) $400 × 5 months		
		(3) $2,100 × 5 months		

Notice that amortization is credited directly to the *Investment in Croy Corporation Bonds* account. This process will reduce the investment account to the par value of the bonds ($300,000) by their maturity date, at which time Bay Company will receive the maturity value and make the following entry.

1991				
Jan.	31	Cash	300,000	
		Investment in Croy Corp. Bonds		300,000
		To record receipt of maturity value.		

Bonds Purchased at a Discount

If the bonds are purchased at a discount, rather than at a premium, the amount of interest revenue is greater than the cash received, and the amount of periodic amortization is debited (rather than credited) to the investment account. In this way the investment account is gradually increased over time and will be equal to the maturity value of the bonds on their maturity date.

For example, assume that the Croy Corporation bonds in the previous illustration were purchased for $295,500 (including the broker's fee), plus accrued interest. Thus, the bonds were purchased at a $4,500 discount ($300,000

− $295,500). Therefore, the monthly amortization of the discount is $100 ($4,500/45 months). During the first year, the investment in bonds would be accounted for as follows.

May	1	Investment in Croy Corp. Bonds	295,500	
		Interest Revenue	7,500	
		Cash		303,000
		To record the purchase of Croy Corp. bonds.		
July	31	Cash	15,000	
		Investment in Croy Corp. Bonds	300	
		Interest Revenue		15,300
		To record the receipt of interest and amortization of discount. ($100 × 3 months.)		
Dec.	31	Interest Receivable	12,500	
		Investment in Croy Corp. Bonds	500	
		Interest Revenue		13,000
		To accrue interest for 5 months and amortize discount. ($100 × 5 months.)		

After the entries have been posted, the *Interest Revenue* account will show:

Interest Revenue

May 1	7,500	July 31	15,300
		Dec. 31	13,000
		Dec. 31 Balance	20,800

The $20,800 interest revenue earned during 1987 can be verified with the following computation.

Total amount to be received by the investor:	
Maturity value	$300,000
Interest for 45 months ($300,000 × 10% × 45/12)	112,500
Total cash to be received	412,500
Cost of investment	295,500
Total interest revenue	117,000
Number of months to maturity	÷ 45
Interest revenue per month	2,600
Number of months from May through December	× 8
Total interest revenue earned	$ 20,800

Recording the Sale of Bond Investments

When bond investments are sold, the accounting procedure is similar to that used for the sale of stock investments. However, in addition to the selling price of the bonds, the seller will receive interest accrued since the last interest payment date. Also, amortization of premium or discount on the investment to the date of sale should be recorded.

To illustrate, assume that Bay Company sold one-half of its Croy Corporation bonds on April 1, 1989, for $160,000 (net of broker's fees), plus accrued interest of $2,500. Assume, also, that the bonds were purchased at a premium, as illustrated previously. Before recording the sale, amortization should be recorded from the last interest payment date to the date of sale, as follows.

Apr.	1	Interest Revenue	800	
		Investment in Croy Corp. Bonds		800
		To record amortization for February and		
		March at $400 per month.		

After this entry is posted, the *Investment in Croy Corporation Bonds* account will appear as presented here.

Investment in Croy Corporation Bonds

5/1/87	318,000	7/31/87 Amortization	1,200
		12/31/87 Amortization	2,000
		1/31/88 Amortization	400
		7/31/88 Amortization	2,400
		12/31/88 Amortization	2,000
		1/31/89 Amortization	400
		4/1/89 Amortization	800
4/1/89 Balance	308,800		9,200

The sale of the bonds can now be recorded by the following entry.

Apr.	1	Cash	162,500	
		Interest Revenue		2,500
		Investment in Croy Corp. Bonds		154,400
		Gain on Sale of Investments		5,600
		To record the sale of one-half of the Croy		
		Corporation bonds.		

Cash is debited for the proceeds from the sale of $160,000, plus $2,500 accrued interest ($150,000 × 10% × 2/12), the investment account is credited for half of its carrying value (½ × $308,800), since only half the bonds were sold, and a gain on the sale of $5,600 is recorded. The gain can be verified as follows.

Selling price	$160,000
Carrying value of bonds sold (½ × $308,800)	154,400
Gain on sale of investment	$ 5,600

Since half the bonds were sold, interest received on each subsequent July 31 and January 31 will be $7,500 ($150,000 × 10% × 6/12), and amortization of premium will be $200 per month, rather than $400.

CONSOLIDATED FINANCIAL STATEMENTS

Corporations often own all or a majority (more than 50%) of the voting stock of other corporations. The company owning the stock is called the **parent company,** and the company whose stock is more than 50% owned is called a **subsidiary.** Thus, if Pratt Company owns more than 50% of the voting stock of Sweet Company, Pratt Company is the parent company and Sweet Company is a subsidiary. By owning more than 50% of the voting stock, Pratt Company can elect the board of directors of Sweet Company and thereby effectively control its activities and resources.

Each company is a separate legal entity, so each maintains its own accounting records and prepares separate financial statements. In the separate financial statements of Pratt Company, the investment in Sweet Company will appear in the balance sheet as an investment accounted for by the equity method, and the income statement will include Pratt Company's share of Sweet Company's net income or net loss. However, the equity method does not show the individual asset and liability amounts of Sweet Company represented by the investment account, or the individual revenues and expenses of Sweet Company that produced Pratt Company's share of Sweet Company's net income.

Because the parent company controls the activities and resources of the subsidiary, *the two companies effectively function as a single economic entity.* Investors in the parent company want financial information about all of the resources and operations under the control of the parent company. Consequently, the separate financial statements of the parent company and its subsidiary (or subsidiaries) are combined into a single set of statements, called **consolidated financial statements.**

The preparation of consolidated financial statements is quite difficult and is normally the subject of an advanced accounting course. However, because most publicly held corporations consist of a parent company owning one or more subsidiary companies, it is important to understand the basic principles followed in the preparation of consolidated financial statements.

Objective 5:
Purpose of consolidated financial statements

PRINCIPLES OF CONSOLIDATION

Consolidated financial statements are prepared by combining the individual account balances of the parent company with those of the subsidiaries in order to report them as single accounts. For example, the cash balance of the parent company is combined with the cash balance of the subsidiaries; the parent company's accounts payable are combined with the subsidiaries' accounts payable; and the parent company's sales are combined with those of the subsidiaries. Before combining account balances, however, certain duplicate items must be eliminated so that the combined amounts are not overstated from a single-entity standpoint. Three basic types of elimination must be made: *elimination of the investment account and subsidiary stockholders' equity; elimination of intercompany receivables and payables;* and *elimination of intercompany revenues and expenses.* The first two types of elimination are discussed in the following section on the preparation of the consolidated balance sheet.

Elimination of intercompany revenues and expenses will be discussed in the later section on the preparation of a consolidated income statement.

ACCOUNTING METHODS

Objective 6:
Purchase
method vs.
pooling-of-inter-
ests method

When a corporation and one or more other companies are brought together (become affiliated) into one economic unit, the transaction is called a **business combination.** Two methods of accounting for business combinations—the purchase method and the pooling of interests method—are acceptable under generally accepted accounting principles. However, the two methods may not be used as alternatives for the same business combination. That is, if certain specified conditions are met, the pooling of interests method must be used. If any of these conditions are not met, the purchase method is required.

Purchase Accounting

In some cases a parent company acquires its controlling interest in a subsidiary by purchasing the subsidiary's shares. Payment may be made by giving cash, other assets, debt securities, equity securities, or a combination of these. This type of acquisition is called a purchase, and the consolidated financial statements are prepared under the **purchase method** of accounting. Under the purchase method, the investment in subsidiary is recorded at its cost, which is assigned to the assets acquired and liabilities assumed in an amount equal to their fair values. Any excess of cost over the fair value of the net assets acquired is recorded as consolidated goodwill. Under the purchase method, it is assumed that the former stockholders of the subsidiary sell their shares to the parent company in exchange for the cash, other assets, or securities received.

Pooling of Interests Accounting

If the parent company exchanges its voting stock for essentially all (defined as 90% or more) of the voting stock of a subsidiary and if certain other specific conditions are met as well, the business combination must be accounted for as a **pooling of interests.**[5] Because the former stockholders of the subsidiary become stockholders in the combined or consolidated entity, and because no resources are distributed, the business combination is viewed as a transaction under which the stockholders of the combining companies pool their resources and stockholder interests to form a new company. In other words, no purchase and sale of the subsidiary's stock occurs. Based on this reasoning, the market price of the shares given and the fair values of the subsidiary's assets and liabilities are ignored. The assets and liabilities of the subsidiary are not revalued in the consolidated balance sheet. The *book values* of the subsidiary's assets and liabilities are combined with those of the parent company in the consolidated balance sheet, and no excess of cost over book value (or excess of book value over cost) exists. As a consequence, no consolidated goodwill exists in a pooling of interests.

[5]"Business Combinations," *Opinion of the Accounting Principles Board No. 16* (New York: AICPA, August 1970), pars. 45–48.

Under the pooling of interests method, the investment in a subsidiary is normally recorded at an amount equal to the par or stated value of the parent company shares issued. The investment account is then eliminated on the consolidated worksheet in a manner similar to that which occurs under the purchase method.

The pooling of interests method is used in practice less frequently than the purchase method, and will not be illustrated here. Examples of the preparation of consolidated financial statements follow, using the purchase method of accounting.

CONSOLIDATED BALANCE SHEET

The consolidated balance sheet shows the total assets under control of the parent company's board of directors, the total debts owed by the consolidated entity to outsiders, and the owners' equity in the assets. To illustrate the preparation of a consolidated balance sheet, assume that Pratt Company and Sweet Company had the following balance sheets on January 1, 1987.

	Pratt Company	Sweet Company
Assets		
Cash	$320,000	$ 49,000
Note receivable from Sweet Company	30,000	-0-
Accounts receivable (net)	80,000	52,000
Inventory	125,000	71,000
Plant and equipment (net)	396,000	76,000
Total Assets	$951,000	$248,000
Liabilities and Stockholders' Equity		
Accounts payable	$ 86,000	$ 48,000
Note payable to Pratt Company	-0-	30,000
Common stock, $10 par value	500,000	100,000
Retained earnings	365,000	70,000
Total Liabilities and Stockholders' Equity	$951,000	$248,000

On January 2, 1987, Pratt Company purchased all of the outstanding common stock of Sweet Company for $170,000 on the open market. Late in 1986 Pratt Company had loaned Sweet Company $30,000, obtaining a note receivable as evidence of the loan.

To record the purchase of Sweet Company's stock, Pratt Company made the following entry.

Jan.	2	Investment in Sweet Company	170,000	
		Cash		170,000
		To record the purchase of 100% of Sweet Company's outstanding stock.		

Notice that the purchase price of the stock was equal to the book value of Sweet Company's net assets (stockholders' equity). The total purchase price of the stock is often greater (or less) than the book value of the net assets purchased. Accounting for such situations is discussed later in this chapter.

Data for the preparation of consolidated statements are normally accumulated on a worksheet similar to that shown in Figure 18–4. Because no operating activity has yet taken place, the only consolidated financial statement prepared on the date of stock acquisition is a consolidated balance sheet.

Notice in Figure 18–4, that Pratt Company's balance sheet includes cash of $150,000 (since $170,000 was used to buy Sweet Company's stock) and also includes its investment in Sweet Company. The $170,000 cash was paid to Sweet Company's stockholders and, therefore, is not included in Sweet Company's balance sheet.

The theory of consolidated statements is that the parent company and its subsidiary are viewed as a single economic entity. Thus, before the accounts of Pratt Company and Sweet Company are combined, it is necessary to prepare the two types of eliminating entries mentioned earlier. *The eliminating entries are worksheet entries only—they are not made on either the parent company's or subsidiary company's books.*

Eliminating entry (1) (Figure 18–4) is made to eliminate the *Investment in*

Figure 18–4

Worksheet for a Consolidated Balance Sheet—100% Ownership

PRATT COMPANY AND SUBSIDIARY
Worksheet for a Consolidated Balance Sheet
January 2, 1987

	Pratt Company	Sweet Company	Eliminations Dr.	Eliminations Cr.	Consolidated Balances
Cash	150,000	49,000			199,000
Note receivable from Sweet Company	30,000			(2) 30,000	
Accounts receivable	80,000	52,000			132,000
Inventory	125,000	71,000			196,000
Investment in Sweet Company	170,000			(1) 170,000	
Plant and equipment	396,000	76,000			472,000
Total	951,000	248,000			999,000
Accounts payable	86,000	48,000			134,000
Note payable to Pratt Company		30,000	(2) 30,000		
Common stock:					
Pratt Company	500,000				500,000
Sweet Company		100,000	(1) 100,000		
Retained earnings:					
Pratt Company	365,000				365,000
Sweet Company		70,000	(1) 70,000		
Total	951,000	248,000	200,000	200,000	999,000

(1) To eliminate the investment in Sweet Company.
(2) To eliminate intercompany note receivable and note payable.

Sweet Company account and Sweet Company's stockholders' equity. When Pratt Company purchased the stock of Sweet Company, it effectively acquired Sweet Company's net assets, which were recorded in the *Investment in Sweet Company* account. Because Sweet Company's assets and liabilities will be combined with those of Pratt Company, failure to eliminate the interest in the net assets reported in the investment account would result in a double counting. In addition, since Sweet Company's stockholders' equity represents the source of the net assets, it too must be eliminated. In other words, one part of the consolidated entity (Pratt Company) owns the stock of another part of the consolidated entity (Sweet Company). An entity's ownership of its own stock does not constitute either an asset or stockholders' equity. Consequently, both the investment account and the subsidiary's stockholders' equity are eliminated to report the parent company and subsidiary company as a single economic entity.

Eliminating entry (2) is made to eliminate the intercompany *Note Receivable* and *Note Payable*. Failure to eliminate them would result in an overstatement of both assets and liabilities, since the receivable and payable result from the transfer of funds within the consolidated entity—that is, no outside party is involved. Since a company cannot owe money to itself, both the intercompany note receivable and note payable are eliminated.

After the eliminating entries have been made on the worksheet, the remaining balance sheet accounts are combined and carried into the consolidated balances column as assets, liabilities, and stockholders' equity of the consolidated entity. The consolidated balances column is then used to prepare the consolidated balance sheet, as shown in Figure 18–5. Notice that the stockholders' equity of the consolidated entity is the same as Pratt Company's, since Sweet Company's stockholders' equity has been eliminated.

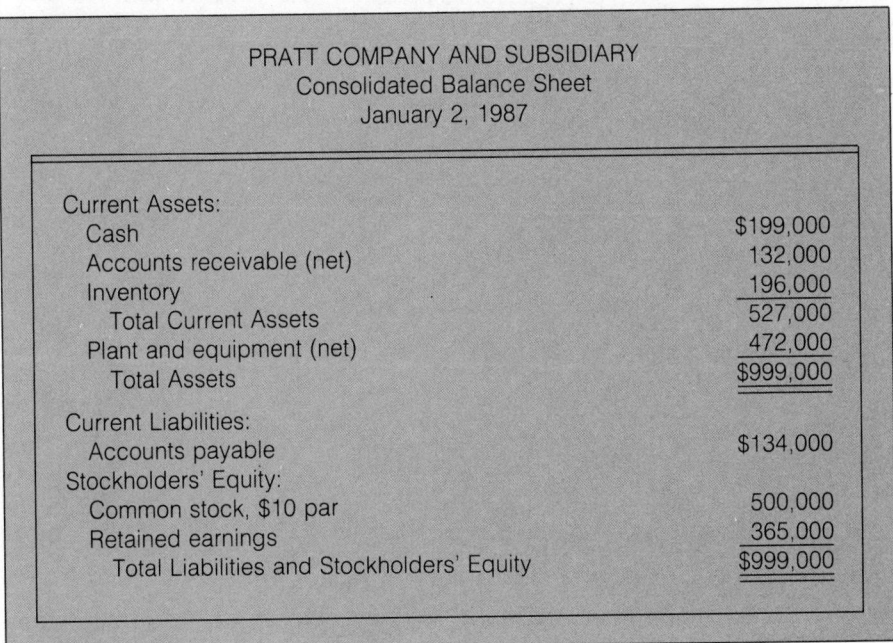

Figure 18–5
Consolidated Balance Sheet

PRATT COMPANY AND SUBSIDIARY
Consolidated Balance Sheet
January 2, 1987

Current Assets:	
Cash	$199,000
Accounts receivable (net)	132,000
Inventory	196,000
Total Current Assets	527,000
Plant and equipment (net)	472,000
Total Assets	$999,000
Current Liabilities:	
Accounts payable	$134,000
Stockholders' Equity:	
Common stock, $10 par	500,000
Retained earnings	365,000
Total Liabilities and Stockholders' Equity	$999,000

Purchase of Less than 100% of Subsidiary Stock

In the preceding case, we assumed that Pratt Company purchased all (100%) of Sweet Company's outstanding stock. As mentioned earlier, however, control can be achieved by acquiring only a majority (less than 100%) of the subsidiary's outstanding shares. When this occurs, the subsidiary has stockholders other than the parent company. These other stockholders are called minority stockholders and their interest in the net assets of the subsidiary is called a **minority interest.** All of the subsidiary's assets and liabilities are included in the consolidated balance sheet in order to show the total resources and obligations under control of the parent company's board of directors. The minority interest in the net assets of the subsidiary is set out on the worksheet when the investment account and subsidiary's stockholders' equity is eliminated, as shown in Figure 18–6.

For example, assume that Pratt Company purchased only 70% of Sweet Company's stock on January 2, 1987, at a cost of $119,000. A worksheet for a consolidated balance sheet on the date of acquisition is shown in Figure 18–6.

Figure 18–6
Worksheet for Consolidated Balance Sheet—Minority Interest

PRATT COMPANY AND SUBSIDIARY
Worksheet for a Consolidated Balance Sheet
January 2, 1987

	Pratt Company	Sweet Company	Eliminations Dr.	Eliminations Cr.	Consolidated Balances
Cash	201,000	49,000			250,000
Notes receivable from Sweet Company	30,000			(2) 30,000	
Accounts receivable	80,000	52,000			132,000
Inventory	125,000	71,000			196,000
Investment in Sweet Company	119,000			(1) 119,000	
Plant and equipment	396,000	76,000			472,000
Total	951,000	248,000			1,050,000
Accounts payable	86,000	48,000			134,000
Notes payable to Pratt Company		30,000	(2) 30,000		
Common stock:					
Pratt Company	500,000				500,000
Sweet Company		100,000	(1) 100,000		
Retained earnings:					
Pratt Company	365,000				365,000
Sweet Company		70,000	(1) 70,000		
Minority interest				(1) 51,000	51,000
Total	951,000	248,000	200,000	200,000	1,050,000

(1) To eliminate the investment in Sweet Company
(2) To eliminate intercompany note receivable and note payable.

Again, notice that the purchase price of the stock ($119,000) was equal to the book value of Sweet Company's net assets acquired (70% × $170,000 = $119,000). Also, since Pratt Company used only $119,000 in cash to acquire Sweet Company stock, the cash balance is $201,000 ($320,000 − $119,000). Eliminating entry (1) is made to eliminate the investment account and Sweet Company's stockholders' equity. However, since only 70% of Sweet Company's stock was purchased, a minority interest in its net assets exists in the amount of $51,000 (30% × $170,000). The minority interest is set up on the last line of the worksheet as part of eliminating entry (1) and is reported as a separate item on the consolidated balance sheet. Most companies report minority interest as a separate item between liabilities and stockholders' equity. An example of such treatment is shown here.

Liabilities and Stockholders' Equity	
Current liabilities:	
Accounts payable	$ 134,000
Minority interest	51,000
Stockholders' equity:	
Common stock, $10 par	500,000
Retained earnings	365,000
Total liabilities and stockholders' equity	$1,050,000

Eliminating entry (2) is made to eliminate intercompany notes receivable and notes payable, as explained in the preceding illustration.

Purchase of Stock for More (or Less) than Book Value

In the preceding examples we assumed that the parent company purchased its shares in the subsidiary company at a price equal to their book value. That assumption was made to simplify the example and concentrate attention on the fundamentals followed in the preparation of a consolidated balance sheet. Actually, when a corporation purchases stock in another corporation, it must pay the market price of the shares—which normally will be more or less than their book value. In the preparation of consolidated statements, this difference between the cost of the investment and the book value of the subsidiary's equity acquired must be reported properly.

If the parent company pays more than book value for the shares, an excess of cost over book value will remain when the investment account is eliminated against the subsidiary's stockholders' equity. Among the main reasons why a company may pay more than book value for shares are that:

1. The fair values of the subsidiary's assets may be greater than their book values. The application of conservative accounting procedures, such as the use of accelerated depreciation and of the LIFO inventory method, often produces book values for plant and equipment and for inventory that are less than their fair values. In addition, some subsidiary assets, such as land, may have appreciated in value.

2. Long-term subsidiary liabilities may be overvalued as a result of an increase in general market interest rates.

3. The subsidiary may have unrecorded goodwill, as evidenced by its above-normal earnings.

4. The parent company may be willing to pay a premium for the right to acquire a controlling interest in the subsidiary and the economic advantages it expects to obtain from integrated operations.

The Accounting Principles Board specified the standards to be followed in assigning the cost of shares in a subsidiary company as follows: First, all identifiable assets acquired and liabilities assumed, whether or not shown in the financial statements of the acquired company, should be assigned a portion of the cost of the acquired company, normally equal to their fair values at the date of acquisition. Second, the excess of cost over the sum of the amounts assigned to identifiable assets acquired less liabilities assumed should be recorded as goodwill.[6]

To illustrate, assume that Pratt Company and Sweet Company had balance sheets on January 1, 1987, as shown on page 705. On January 2, 1987, Pratt Company purchased all of Sweet Company's stock for $220,000. Since the book value of Sweet Company's net assets (stockholders' equity) is $170,000, there is an excess of cost over book value of $50,000 ($220,000 − $170,000). Assume, further, that $30,000 of this excess relates to an undervaluation of Sweet Company's plant and equipment and that the remaining $20,000 represents consolidated goodwill. A worksheet for the preparation of a consolidated balance sheet on the date of acquisition is shown in Figure 18–7.

Pratt Company's cash balance on January 2 is $100,000 because $220,000 was used to acquire Sweet Company's stock. Note that when the investment account is eliminated against Sweet Company's stockholders' equity, a $50,000 excess of cost over equity acquired remains, $30,000 of which is added to plant and equipment and $20,000 of which represents consolidated goodwill. The $30,000 must be charged to depreciation expense on future worksheets over the remaining life of the plant assets in determining consolidated net income. Likewise, consolidated goodwill is amortized to expense on the worksheet over its estimated life, not to exceed 40 years.

Sometimes the parent company pays less than book value for the subsidiary company's share because the fair values of the subsidiary's assets are less than their book values, because its liabilities are understated, or because it has incurred operating losses, which have decreased the market value of its shares. When the amount paid is less than book value, the accounting standards require that the excess of book value over cost should be allocated to reduce the values assigned to noncurrent assets in determining their fair values.[7]

CONSOLIDATED INCOME STATEMENT

The consolidated income statement is prepared by combining the individual revenue and expense accounts of the parent company and its subsidiaries.

[6]Ibid., par. 87.

[7]Ibid., par. 91.

PRATT COMPANY AND SUBSIDIARY
Worksheet for a Consolidated Balance Sheet
January 2, 1987

	Pratt Company	Sweet Company	Eliminations Dr.	Eliminations Cr.	Consolidated Balances
Cash	100,000	49,000			149,000
Note receivable from Sweet Company	30,000			(2) 30,000	
Accounts receivable	80,000	52,000			132,000
Inventory	125,000	71,000			196,000
Investment in Sweet Company	220,000			(1) 220,000	
Plant and equipment	396,000	76,000	(1) 30,000		502,000
Goodwill			(1) 20,000		20,000
Total	951,000	248,000			999,000
Accounts payable	86,000	48,000			134,000
Note payable to Pratt Company		30,000	(2) 30,000		
Common stock:					
Pratt Company	500,000				500,000
Sweet Company		100,000	(1) 100,000		
Retained earnings:					
Pratt Company	365,000				365,000
Sweet Company		70,000	(1) 70,000		
Total	951,000	248,000	250,000	250,000	999,000

(1) To eliminate the investment in Sweet Company.
(2) To eliminate intercompany note receivable and note payable.

Figure 18–7
Worksheet for Consolidated Balance Sheet—Excess Cost

Before combining the accounts, however, any intercompany revenues and expenses must be eliminated so that the consolidated income will reflect only the results of operations from transactions with parties outside the affiliated group. Examples of intercompany items that must be eliminated are intercompany sales and purchases, intercompany rent revenue and rent expense, and intercompany interest revenue and interest expense.

To illustrate, assume that Pratt Company and Sweet Company had revenues and expenses during 1987 as shown in Figure 18–8. Assume, also, that Pratt Company sold $80,000 worth of merchandise to Sweet Company during the year, and that Sweet Company paid $2,400 in interest to Pratt Company on the note payable to Pratt Company. Sweet Company sold all of the merchandise purchased from Pratt Company during the year. A worksheet for the preparation of a consolidated income statement is shown in Figure 18–8.

Eliminating entry (1) eliminates intercompany sales and purchases (included here in the cost of goods sold) so that the total sales and cost of goods sold reported on the consolidated income statement will include only those resulting from transactions with parties outside the affiliated group. Eliminating entry (2) eliminates intercompany interest revenue and interest expense, since the

PRATT COMPANY AND SUBSIDIARY
Worksheet for a Consolidated Income Statement
Year Ended December 31, 1987

	Pratt Company	Sweet Company	Eliminations Dr.		Eliminations Cr.		Consolidated Balances
Sales	642,000	374,000	(1)	80,000			936,000
Interest revenue	2,400		(2)	2,400			
Total revenue	644,400	374,000					936,000
Cost of goods sold	376,000	208,000			(1)	80,000	504,000
Operating expenses	169,000	122,000					291,000
Interest expense		2,400			(2)	2,400	
Total expenses	545,000	332,400					795,000
Net Income	99,400	41,600		82,400		82,400	141,000

(1) To eliminate intercompany sales and purchases.
(2) To eliminate intercompany interest revenue and interest expense.

Figure 18–8
Worksheet for Consolidated Income Statement

intercompany note receivable and note payable were eliminated on the consolidated balance sheet. In addition, the interest payment resulted in a cash transfer within the consolidated entity, since no outside party was involved.

The preparation of a consolidated income statement is normally much more complex than illustrated here. The consolidated financial statements would also include a consolidated retained earnings statement and a consolidated statement of changes in financial position. Because their preparation is complex, they are topics appropriate to an advanced accounting course.

CONDITIONS FOR THE PREPARATION OF CONSOLIDATED FINANCIAL STATEMENTS

**Objective 7:
Criteria for inclusion of subsidiary in consolidated financial statements**

Certain conditions must be met before a given subsidiary can be included in a corporation's consolidated financial statements. The most important condition is that the parent company must actually control the subsidiary by owning more than 50% of its voting stock. In addition, the management of the parent company should actively exercise control of the subsidiary and should expect to continue to do so in the future. A parent company should not consolidate a subsidiary that it expects to sell in the near future.

Even though control conditions are met, there may be some situations, such as the following, in which a subsidiary should be excluded from consolidated statements.

1. The activities of the subsidiary may be so unrelated to those of other subsidiaries or the parent company that it would be more informative to exclude the subsidiary from consolidation and disclose its activities sep-

arately. For example, General Motors Corporation does not consolidate its finance subsidiary, General Motors Acceptance Corporation.

2. The resources of the subsidiary, such as a bank or insurance company, may be so restricted by statute that they are not generally available for use throughout the affiliated group. For example, Sears, Roebuck and Company does not consolidate its insurance subsidiary, Allstate Insurance Company.

3. The subsidiary may be in a foreign country that has imposed currency restrictions such that the income and assets of the subsidiary cannot be withdrawn by the parent company.

When a subsidiary is excluded from consolidation, it is generally reported in the financial statements as an investment accounted for by the equity method.

LIMITATIONS OF CONSOLIDATED FINANCIAL STATEMENTS

Consolidated financial statements are prepared primarily for use by management, stockholders, and creditors of the parent company. Consolidated financial statements are of limited use to minority stockholders and creditors of the subsidiary companies, because they contain no detailed information about the individual subsidiaries. Creditors and minority stockholders of a subsidiary have legal claims only against the resources of that subsidiary, not against those of the parent company, and thus, must rely on the individual financial statements of the subsidiary to assess the safety and earning potential of their investments.

Objective 8:
Limitations of consolidated financial statements

Information in the consolidated financial statements of highly diversified companies that operate in several industries is often of limited use to investors and prospective investors in the parent company. Financial position and the results of operations of these companies cannot be compared with industry standards or with other companies, since the companies often operate in different industries. To partially counter this deficiency, accounting standards require that diversified companies must report certain information by segments of the business. Specific requirements of segment reporting are contained in *Financial Accounting Standards No. 14,* "Financial Reporting for Segments of a Business Enterprise," and are covered in more advanced accounting courses.

INTERNATIONAL ACCOUNTING

Growth is a major objective of many businesses. To increase revenues, business managers often search for ways to expand existing markets or to enter into new markets for their products and services. They also continually look for new, more economic sources of supply as a means of helping to control costs. In their search for these new markets and sources of supply, managers naturally consider expansion into other countries. Today, many large businesses, called **multinational corporations,** operate throughout the world. Foreign operations often make up a significant part of their total operations, as shown in Figure 18–9.

Figure 18–9
Amount of Foreign
Operations for Se-
lected Companies

| | Percentage of | |
| | Foreign Revenue to | Foreign Operating Profit to |
Company	Total Revenue	Total Operating Profit
Apple Computer, Inc.	22.2	35.8
Sperry Corporation	32.9	43.9
General Electric Company	19.6	17.7
Holiday Inns, Inc.	14.9	12.2
Borg-Warner Corporation	21.7	20.7
The H. J. Heinz Company	36.3	37.8
Hewlett–Packard Company	41.4	28.4

Source: Computed by authors from 1983 annual report data.

Multinational companies engage in two broad types of foreign activities: (1) import/export transactions; and (2) ownership activities, (that is, the complete or partial ownership of foreign companies). Accounting problems are encountered when transactions with a foreign company are to be settled in a foreign currency. In addition, the financial statements of foreign subsidiaries or investees must be translated into U.S. dollars before the subsidiary can be consolidated or the equity method applied to common stock investments.

EXCHANGE RATES—TRANSLATION

Objective 9: Effect of changes in exchange rates on foreign receivables and payables

Sale and purchase contracts (transactions) between firms in different countries specify the currencies to be used to settle the transactions. For example, a U.S. firm that purchases goods from a French firm may have to pay in francs and, therefore, have to exchange dollars for francs in order to pay for the goods. The number of dollars to be exchanged for the specified number of francs is determined by the exchange rate between dollars and francs. The **exchange rate** is the ratio between a unit of one currency and the amount of another currency for which that unit can be exchanged at a particular time. Exchange rates change continually to reflect changes in the demand for and supply of different currencies.

Companies normally record transactions in their books in the currency of the country in which they operate. Consequently, as mentioned earlier, the financial statements of foreign companies must be translated into U.S. dollars before they can be consolidated with U.S. companies or before the equity method can be applied to common stock investments.

Transactions that are to be settled in a foreign currency, and the financial statements of foreign subsidiaries or investees, are translated into U.S. dollars by multiplying the number of units of foreign currency by a direct exchange rate. Thus, *translation* is the process of expressing monetary amounts that are stated in terms of a foreign currency in the currency of the reporting company.

A *direct exchange quotation* is one in which the exchange rate is quoted in terms of how many units of the domestic currency can be converted into *one unit of foreign currency*. For example, a direct quotation of U.S. dollars for one British pound of 1.238 means that $1.238 can be exchanged for one British pound. To translate 100 pounds into dollars, the 100 pounds is multiplied by the direct exchange rate of $1.238.

Exchange rates may also be expressed in terms of converting *one unit of domestic currency* into units of a foreign currency, which is called an **indirect quotation.** In the example just given, one U.S. dollar could be converted into .8078 pounds (1.00/1.238). To translate pounds into dollars, the number of pounds could be divided by the indirect exchange rate. Direct exchange rates will be used in the illustrations that follow.

Figure 18–10 shows the direct rate of selected currencies in terms of U.S. dollars.

ACCOUNTING FOR IMPORT AND EXPORT TRANSACTIONS

A common activity for many companies engaged in international business is the purchase and sale of goods and services. For example, a U.S. manufacturer may attempt to reduce costs by purchasing some less expensive components from another country. Or, a U.S. company may attempt to increase revenues by selling goods in another country or by purchasing foreign goods for sale in this country. The accounting methods chosen for these transactions depends on whether the transactions are to be settled in U.S. dollars or in the currency of the other country.

Importing Transactions

When a U.S. company purchases goods and services from a foreign company, the contract may specify payment in either U.S. dollars or the currency of the foreign company. If payment is to be made in dollars, no accounting problem arises. For example, assume that a U.S. company purchases $80,000 worth of goods from a French company on December 1, 1986. Payment is to be made in U.S. dollars on February 28, 1987. The accounting entries are the same as those illustrated in earlier chapters.

Country	Prices in U.S. Dollars
Britain (Pound)	$1.0875
Canada (Dollar)	.7210
Denmark (Krone)	.08337
France (Franc)	.09775
Israel (Shekel)	.001317
Japan (Yen)	.003845
Mexico (Peso)	.004049
West Germany (Mark)	.2979

Source: The Wall Street Journal, March 14, 1985.

Figure 18–10
Selected Foreign Currency Exchange Rates

	1986				
	Dec.	1	Purchases	80,000	
			Accounts Payable, French Company		80,000
	1987				
	Feb.	28	Accounts Payable, French Company	80,000	
			Cash		80,000

If the transaction is to be settled in francs, however, the U.S. company must purchase francs for payment to the French company. Since exchange rates change daily, the U.S. company may incur an exchange gain or loss between the December 1, 1986 purchase date and the February 28, 1987 payment date.

Three dates are important in accounting for transactions to be settled in a foreign currency. These dates and the appropriate exchange rate to use for translation are the following.

1. **The transaction date.** Each element (asset, liability, etc.) is measured and recorded in dollars by multiplying the units of foreign currency by the current exchange rate.
2. **Each balance sheet date between the transaction date and the settlement date.** Balance sheet amounts that are to be settled in a foreign currency are adjusted to reflect the current exchange rate at the balance sheet date and an exchange gain or loss may be recognized at that time.
3. **The settlement date.** In the case of a foreign currency payable, the U.S. company must exchange U.S. dollars for foreign currency to settle the account. Foreign currency units received in settlement of a foreign currency receivable will be exchanged for dollars. An exchange gain or loss is recognized if the number of dollars paid or received does not equal the balance of the payable or receivable.

To illustrate the application of these rules, assume the previous example (the purchase by a U.S. company of $80,000 worth of goods from a French company), except that payment for the purchase is to be made by paying the French company 800,000 francs. Assume, further, that the direct exchange rate for the franc is as follows.

Date	Rate
December 1, 1986	$.100
December 31, 1986	.110
February 28, 1987	.105

Journal entries would be:

	1986				
	Dec.	1	Purchases	80,000	
			Accounts Payable, French Company		80,000
			(800,000 × $.100)		

On December 31, 1986, the balance sheet date, the payable due in foreign currency is adjusted, using the exchange rate in effect at that time. The entry is:

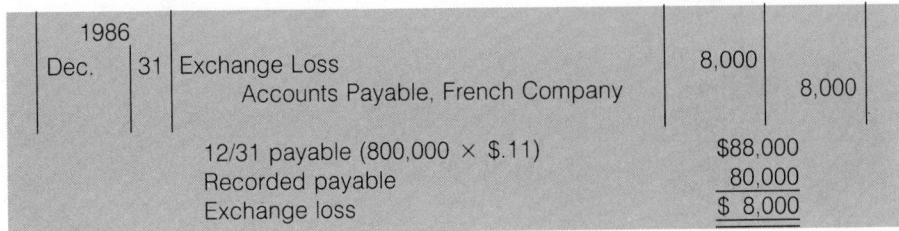

1986					
Dec.	31	Exchange Loss	8,000	
		Accounts Payable, French Company		8,000

12/31 payable (800,000 × $.11)	$88,000
Recorded payable	80,000
Exchange loss	$ 8,000

On February 28, 1987 the U.S. company must purchase 800,000 francs to settle the transaction. Since the exchange rate on this date is $.105, the company must pay $84,000 (800,000 × $.105) to acquire the necessary francs. The journal entry to record the settlement is:

1987					
Feb.	28	Accounts Payable, French company	88,000	
		Cash		84,000
		Exchange Gain		4,000

Over the course of the entire transaction, the U.S. company has incurred a $4,000 net exchange loss, because it agreed to pay a fixed number of French francs, and before payment was made the cost to acquire each franc increased from $.10 to $.105. This net loss is recorded in the records as an exchange loss of $8,000 in 1986 and an exchange gain of $4,000 in 1987.

Realized versus Unrealized Exchange Gains and Losses

Note in the example just used that an exchange loss on the account payable was recognized on the balance sheet date, December 31. The loss is unrealized, because the account has not yet been settled. When an account payable (or receivable) is settled, an exchange gain or loss on the settlement is considered realized. The Financial Accounting Standards Board believes that users of financial statements are served best by reporting the effects of exchange rate changes in the period in which they occur, even though they are unrealized and may reverse or partially reverse in a later period. This procedure is criticized, however, because under generally accepted accounting principles gains and losses are not normally reported until realized, and the recognition of unrealized gains and losses results in increased earnings volatility.

Exporting Transactions

Since sale transactions are the opposite of purchase transactions, the same general logic discussed in the previous section applies to them, except that the relationship of exchange gains and losses to changes in the exchange rate is reversed. For example, assume that the U.S. company in the previous example sold $80,000 of merchandise to the French company. As before, if the transaction is to be settled in U.S. dollars, no accounting problem exists and the journal entries are:

1986 Dec.	1	Accounts Receivable, French company	80,000	
		Sales		80,000
1987 Feb.	28	Cash	80,000	
		Accounts Receivable, French company		80,000

If the agreement is that the French company will pay for the goods in francs, however, the U.S. company will incur an exchange gain or loss if the exchange rate for the franc changes between the date of sale and the settlement date. The entries on the U.S. company's books in this case would be:

1986 Dec.	1	Accounts Receivable, French company	80,000	
		Sales		80,000
		(800,000 × $.10)		
1986 Dec.	31	Accounts Receivable, French company	8,000	
		Exchange Gain		8,000

Receivable value on 12/31 (800,000 × $.11)	$88,000
Recorded receivable	80,000
Exchange gain	$ 8,000

1987 Feb.	26	Cash*	84,000	
		Exchange Loss	4,000	
		Accounts Receivable, French company		88,000
		*(800,000 × $.105)		

A comparison of the entries to record an exporting transaction with those to record an importing transaction reveals that the same movement in the exchange rate has an opposite effect on the company's reported income. That is, the increase in the exchange rate from $.10 to $.105 results in a net $4,000 exchange loss in the case of a foreign currency payable, whereas a net exchange gain of $4,000 is reported in the case of a foreign currency receivable.

TRANSLATION OF FOREIGN FINANCIAL STATEMENTS

Objective 10: Translating a foreign subsidiary's financial statements into U.S. dollars

As mentioned earlier, multinational corporations often engage in international business activity by owning all or part of foreign companies. Financial statements expressed in foreign currencies must be translated into U.S. dollars before the equity method of accounting can be applied or a foreign subsidiary can be consolidated with its U.S. parent company. Because we are interested only in the general principles of translation here, discussion is limited to the translation of the financial statements of a foreign subsidiary. Although several different translation methods might be used, the **current rate method** is most widely used and, therefore, is discussed here.

Current Rate Translation Method

Under the current rate method, revenue and expense accounts (and gains and losses) are translated into U.S. dollars using the exchange rate in effect when those items were recognized during the period. Because individual translation of numerous revenue and expense transactions is impractical, an appropriate average rate for the period is normally used.

In the balance sheet, all assets and liabilities are translated into U.S. dollars, using the current exchange rate at the balance sheet date. Common stock and other paid-in capital accounts are translated using the historical exchange rate, that is, the exchange rate existing on the date that the subsidiary was acquired. The retained earnings amount is determined by setting the beginning retained earnings balance equal to the ending balance from the preceding year. Net income as reported on the translated income statement is then added to this. Dividends paid are translated at the exchange rate existing on the payment date and the translated amount is deducted to derive the ending retained earnings balance.

Translation Illustration.   As an illustration of the translation of a foreign subsidiary's financial statements, assume that Brock Company has a 100% owned subsidiary in West Germany, named Rolf Company. Before year-end financial statements can be prepared, Rolf Company's financial statements must be translated into U.S. dollars. Assume the following exchange rates for the West German mark.

1. When the subsidiary was acquired, $.24.
2. Average for 1987, $.33.
3. December 31, 1987, $.34
4. When dividends were paid, $.32.

The December 31, 1987 balance sheet and the 1987 income statement for Rolf Company are shown in Figure 18–11 in both West German marks and U.S. dollars.

The translation adjustment (sometimes called a translation gain or loss) is the amount needed to balance the total debits and credits in the balance sheet after the individual accounts have been translated. It results because some items are translated at current rates and other items are translated at historical rates.

A MOVE TOWARD UNIFORM INTERNATIONAL ACCOUNTING STANDARDS

The growth in international business and an increased interest in international companies by investors emphasize the need for developing international accounting standards. Currently, there are no accounting standards required

Figure 18–11
Translation of Foreign Subsidiary's Financial Statements

ROLF COMPANY
Balance Sheet
December 31, 1987

	Marks	Exchange Rate	Dollars
Cash	50,000	.34	$ 17,000
Accounts receivable (net)	130,000	.34	44,200
Inventory	110,000	.34	37,400
Plant and equipment (net)	470,000	.34	159,800
Total Assets	760,000		$258,400
Accounts payable	45,000	.34	$ 15,300
Notes payable	100,000	.34	34,000
Common stock	300,000	.24	72,000
Retained earnings	315,000	Assumed amount	122,800
Translation adjustment			14,300
Total Liabilities and Stockholders' Equity	760,000		$258,400

ROLF COMPANY
Income Statement
For the Year Ended December 31, 1987

	Marks	Exchange Rate	Dollars
Sales	800,000	.33	$264,000
Cost of goods sold	360,000	.33	118,800
Gross profit	440,000		145,200
Expenses	240,000	.33	79,200
Net income	200,000		66,000
Dividends declared and paid	50,000	.32	16,000
Increase in retained earnings	150,000		$ 50,000

worldwide. Progress toward development of international accounting standards is slow, primarily because different countries often have fundamentally different business practices, legal and regulatory constraints, and economic environments. However, several supranational organizations—such as the International Accounting Standards Committee, the European Economic Community, and the United Nations—are attempting to harmonize international accounting and reporting standards. The most active of these organizations is the International Accounting Standards Committee (IASC).

The IASC was established in 1973 to develop accounting standards to be followed in the preparation of financial statements, and to promote the worldwide acceptance and observance of those standards. The committee's objective is not to adopt any particular country's accounting principles as the only acceptable ones, but rather, to improve and harmonize accounting standards globally.

The International Accounting Standards (IAS) issued by the IASC have no formal authority. However, member organizations of the IASC, such as the AICPA in the United States, have agreed to use their "best efforts" to ensure that published financial statements in their countries comply with the IAS in all material respects. Some countries, such as Singapore, have adopted these standards as part of their generally accepted accounting principles. Others have encouraged their use. For example, the stock exchange regulatory body in Italy has recommended that listed companies follow these standards in areas where no local standards or laws apply.[8]

Since its inception, the IASC has issued 24 IAS, covering topics ranging from the general principles of revenue recognition to the standards to be followed in accounting for leases and the capitalization of interest charges. In order to obtain greater international comparability, an increasing acceptance of IAS by multinational companies is needed.

GLOSSARY

BUSINESS COMBINATION.   A transaction under which a corporation and one or more other companies are brought together into one economic unit (p. 704).

CONSOLIDATED FINANCIAL STATEMENTS.   The financial statements of a parent company and its subsidiaries in which the assets and liabilities of the affiliates are combined into a consolidated balance sheet and their revenues and expenses are combined into a consolidated income statement (p. 703).

COST METHOD OF ACCOUNTING FOR STOCK INVESTMENTS.   An accounting method under which the investment is recorded at its cost. With this method, revenue is recognized on the investment as dividends are received (p. 692).

EQUITY METHOD OF ACCOUNTING FOR STOCK INVESTMENTS.   An accounting method under which the investor company recognizes its share of the investee company's income or losses as they are reported by the investee. The investor increases or decreases the investment account for its share of the investee's income or losses, and decreases the investment account for dividends received (p. 692).

EXCHANGE RATE.   The ratio between a unit of one currency and the amount of another currency for which that unit can be exchanged at a particular time (p. 714).

INVESTEE COMPANY.   A corporation whose stock is owned by another company (p. 692).

INVESTOR COMPANY.   A company that owns stock in another company (p. 692).

LONG-TERM INVESTMENTS.   Investments that are not intended to be converted into cash for normal operating needs (p. 691).

MINORITY INTEREST.   The minority stockholders' interest in the net assets of a subsidiary company (p. 708).

MULTINATIONAL CORPORATIONS.   Corporations that operate in different countries throughout the world (p. 713).

PARENT COMPANY.   A company that owns more than 50% of the voting stock of a corporation (p. 703).

[8]*Financial Reporting & Accounting—1984 Update* (New York: Arthur Young, 1984), p. 21.

POOLING OF INTERESTS. A method of accounting for a business combination in which the parent company exchanges its voting stock for essentially all of the voting stock of a subsidiary and certain other specific conditions are met as well. The assets and liabilities of the separate companies are combined at their book values (p. 704).

PURCHASE METHOD. A method of accounting for a business combination in which the stockholders of the subsidiary company sell their shares to the parent company. Assets and liabilities of the subsidiary are reported at their fair values as measured by the total cost of the shares (p. 704).

SUBSIDIARY COMPANY. A corporation which has more than 50% of its shares owned by another company (p. 703).

DISCUSSION QUESTIONS

1. What is the distinction between temporary investments and long-term investments?
2. Long-term investments in voting stock are initially recorded at their cost. Subsequent to acquisition they are accounted for by one of two methods. Name each method and explain when the use of each is appropriate.
3. Gray Company purchased 10,000 of the 40,000 outstanding common shares of Busy Company on January 1, 1987, paying $20 per share. During 1987, Busy Company declared a dividend of $90,000 and reported income for the year of $200,000. The market value of the stock was $18 per share on December 31, 1987. What should be the balance in the *Investment in Busy Company Stock* account on December 31, 1987?
4. Assume that the stock in (3) was purchased on July 1, 1987, instead of January 1 and that the dividends were declared on April 1, 1987. Income of Busy Company for the year were $200,000. What would be the balance in the investment account to be reported on the December 31, 1987, balance sheet of Gray Company?
5. Under what circumstances will a company's bonds sell on the market at (a) par, (b) a premium, and (c) a discount?
6. Why is it necessary to amortize a discount or a premium that arises from the purchase of a long-term investment in bonds at an amount below or above par value? Over what period should the discount or the premium be amortized?
7. Spare Company purchased a $1,000 par value, 15% bond of Craye Company on July 1, 1987, for $1,132. The bond matures on December 31, 1992. How much interest revenue should be reported by Spare Company for the year ended December 31, 1987?
8. Describe how the sale of a stock investment is recorded.
9. What are consolidated financial statements? What is their purpose?
10. What are the three basic types of eliminations that must be made in the preparation of consolidated financial statements?
11. Why are the investment account and the subsidiary's stockholders' equity accounts eliminated on a worksheet for a consolidated balance sheet?
12. What is meant by the term *minority interest*? Where is this item generally reported on a consolidated balance sheet?
13. Briefly, explain when a business combination must be accounted for as a pooling

of interests. Why does no consolidated goodwill ever result in such a combination?

14. Why might consolidated net income be greater under the pooling of interests method than under the purchase method?
15. Explain why the problem of accounting for currency exchange rates exists.
16. Distinguish between a direct and an indirect exchange rate quotation.
17. Explain what causes an unrealized foreign exchange gain or loss and tell when such gains or losses are recognized. Why has the FASB been criticized for its requirements regarding this question?

EXERCISES

Exercise 18-1 Long-term Stock Investment—Cost and Equity Methods

On January 1, 1987, Onion Company purchased 10% of Mandy Company's 100,000 outstanding common shares as a long-term investment at 31¼, plus a broker's commission of $1,500. On July 6, Mandy Company paid a dividend of $1.50 per share on all outstanding common shares, and reported net income of $240,000 for the year.

Required:
A. Prepare the entries to record the purchase of the stock and the receipt of the cash dividend.
B. Assuming that the market value of the Mandy stock investment was $306,000 at the end of 1987, explain how the difference between cost and market value should be reported in the financial statements.
C. Assume that Onion Company purchased 25% of Mandy Company's outstanding common stock instead of 10%. Prepare the journal entries Onion Company would make to account for its investment during 1987.

Exercise 18-2 Long-term Stock Investment—Equity Method

On January 1, 1987, Marta Company purchased 9,000 of the 30,000 outstanding common shares of Revell Company, as a long-term investment, paying $40 per share. On August 6, 1987, Revell Company paid a dividend of $.50 per share, and on December 31, Revell Company reported income for the year of $75,000. The market value of Revell Company's stock on December 31, 1987, was $36 per share.

Required:
A. Prepare all journal entries on the books of Marta Company to account for its investment in Revell Company for 1987.
B. Compute the balance in the investment account after all entries for 1987 have been posted.
C. Assume Marta Company sold 1,350 of its shares in Revell Company on January 1, 1988, for $39 per share, less a broker's commission of $500. Prepare the journal entry to record the sale.

Exercise 18-3 Long-term Bond Investment

On May 1, 1987, Eastern Company purchased 100, $1,000 par value, 10% bonds of Zanor Company on the open market, as a long-term investment, at 102 plus accrued interest of $2,500 and broker's fees of $3,000. The bonds pay interest semiannually on July 31 and January 31 and mature on July 31, 1993. Eastern Company's fiscal year ends on December 31.

Required: (Round amounts to the nearest dollar.)

A. Prepare all journal entries that would be made by Eastern Company to account for the bond investment during 1987.

B. Assuming that Eastern Company held the bonds until their maturity date, prepare the journal entry on Eastern's books on July 31, 1993.

Exercise 18-4 Sale of Bond Investment

Refer to Exercise 18-3. Assume that Eastern Company sold one-half of its Zanor Company bonds on April 30, 1989, for $54,000 (net of broker's fees) plus accrued interest of $1,250.

Required:

Prepare the journal entries that Eastern Company should prepare on the date of sale.

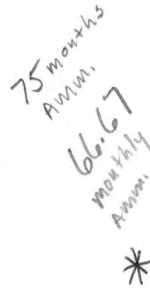

Exercise 18-5 Long-term Bond Investment

On March 1, 1987, Woody Company purchased 50, $1,000 par value, 12% bonds of Bex Company on the open market, as a long-term investment, for $47,000 (including broker's fee) plus accrued interest. The bonds pay interest semiannually on June 30 and December 31 and mature on December 31, 1991.

Required:

A. Prepare all journal entries that would be made by Woody Company to account for this investment during 1987, assuming its fiscal year ends on December 31.

B. How much interest revenue was earned during 1987?

C. Assume that Woody Company sold all of the bonds on July 1, 1989, for $48,800. Prepare the entry to record the sale.

Exercise 18-6 Consolidated Worksheet Entries—100% Ownership

Burke Company and Saver Company had balance sheets on January 2, 1987, as follows.

	Burke	Saver
Cash	$290,000	$ 50,000
Note receivable from Saver Company	50,000	-0-
Accounts receivable	90,000	24,000
Inventory	100,000	30,000
Plant and equipment (net)	305,000	104,000
Total Assets	$835,000	$208,000
Accounts payable	$ 92,000	$ 20,000
Note payable to Burke Company	-0-	50,000
Common stock, $2 par value	400,000	70,000
Retained earnings	343,000	68,000
Total Liabilities and Stockholders' Equity	$835,000	$208,000

On January 2, 1987, Burke Company purchased all of the outstanding common stock of Saver Company on the open market for $138,000.

Required:

A. Prepare the entry Burke Company would make to record the purchase of Saver Company's stock.

B. Prepare, in general journal form, the eliminating entries that would be needed to prepare a consolidated balance sheet worksheet on the date of acquisition, January 2, 1987.

Exercise 18-7 Consolidated Worksheet Entries—70% Ownership

Refer to the data in Exercise 18-6 and assume that Burke Company had purchased only 70% of Saver Company's common stock (instead of 100%), at a purchase price of $96,600.

Required:

A. In general journal form, prepare the eliminating entries that would be needed in the preparation of a consolidated balance sheet worksheet on January 2, 1987.

B. Assume that Burke Company purchased 100% of Saver Company's stock for $180,000 and that $25,000 of the excess of cost over book value acquired relates to the undervaluation of Saver Company's plant and equipment. The remainder of cost over book value acquired represents goodwill. In general journal form, prepare the eliminating entries that would be needed in the preparation of a consolidated balance sheet worksheet on January 2, 1987.

Exercise 18-8 Consolidated Income Statement

Poffer Company and Senco Company had revenues and expenses for the year 1987 as follows.

	Poffer	Senco
Sales	$800,000	$250,000
Interest revenue	5,000	-0-
Total revenue	805,000	250,000
Cost of goods sold	510,000	179,000
Operating expenses	215,000	60,000
Interest expense	-0-	5,000
Total expenses	725,000	244,000
Net Income	$ 80,000	$ 6,000

Senco Company is a wholly owned subsidiary of Poffer Company. During 1987, Poffer Company sold $40,000 worth of merchandise to Senco Company. The $5,000 interest expense of Senco Company was paid to Poffer Company on a note payable.

Required:

A. In general journal form, prepare the eliminating entries needed to prepare a consolidated income statement worksheet for 1987.

B. Prepare a consolidated income statement for the year ended December 31, 1987.

Exercise 18-9 Import and Export Transactions

The following transactions were entered into by Hardware International, a tool company.

Feb.   1   Purchased tools from a French manufacturer for 120,000 francs. The exchange rate was $.12.

      15   Sold merchandise to a British company for 59,000 pounds. The exchange rate was $1.20.

24 Purchased precision tools from a Japanese manufacturer for 2,400,000 yen. The exchange rate was $.004.

Mar. 2 Paid one-half of the amount owed to the French company when the exchange rate was $.13. (Payment was made in francs.)

7 Received 59,000 British pounds from the British company in settlement of the transaction of 2/15. The exchange rate was $1.25.

11 Paid 2,400,000 yen to settle the 2/24 purchase from the Japanese manufacturer. The exchange rate was $.0038.

Apr. 1 Paid the remainder of the amount owed the French company when the exchange rate was $.12. (Payment was made in francs.)

Required:

Prepare journal entries to record the transactions.

Exercise 18-10 Import and Export Transactions

Marianne Company, a toy dealer, entered into the following transactions. Marianne's fiscal year ends on December 31.

1987

Dec. 1 Purchased porcelain dolls from a manufacturer in Denmark. The invoice price was 110,000 kroner, and the exchange rate was $.0902. The contract calls for payment in kroner.

10 Sold an assortment of toys to a Canadian firm. The invoice price was 10,000 Canadian dollars, and the exchange rate was $.76. The contract calls for payment in Canadian dollars.

1988

Jan. 30 Paid the Denmark company 110,000 kroner when the exchange rate was $.0918.

Feb. 10 Received 10,000 Canadian dollars from the Canadian firm when the exchange rate was $.77.

Required:

A. Prepare journal entries to record the 1987 transactions.

B. Prepare journal entries to adjust the account payable and account receivable at December 31. The exchange rates on 12/31/87 were:

Kroner	$.0921
Canadian dollar	$.775

C. Prepare journal entries to record the settlement transactions in 1988.

PROBLEMS

※ Problem 18-1 Cost vs. Equity Method for Long-term Stock Investment

Blake Company purchased some of the 20,000 shares of the outstanding common stock of Ladd Company as a long-term investment. The annual accounting period for each company ends on December 31. The following transactions took place during 1987.

Jan. 1 Purchased shares of common stock of Ladd Company at $30 per share, as follows.

Case A 2,000 shares purchased 60,000

Case B 5,000 shares purchased 150,600

Dec. 31   Received financial statements of Ladd Company for the year ended December 31, 1987. Reported net income was $84,000.

     31   Received a cash dividend of $1 per share from Ladd Company.

     31   The market value of Ladd Company common stock was $27 per share.

Required:

A. For each case, what accounting method should be used by Blake Company? Explain why.

B. Prepare the journal entries that Blake Company should make for each case.

C. Give the amounts for each case that would be reported on the financial statements of Blake Company on December 31, 1987. Use the following format.

	Case A	Case B
Balance Sheet:		
Long-term investment		
Less: Allowance to reduce investment to		
market value		
Net investment		
Stockholders' equity:		
Unrealized loss on Long-term Investments		
Income Statement:		
Investment (dividend) revenue		

Problem 18-2   Long-term Stock Investment

On January 3, 1987, Bane Company purchased, as a long-term investment, 30,000 of the 100,000 outstanding common shares of Prince Company for $13 per share plus a broker's commission of $1,000. Prince Company declared and paid a cash dividend of $.75 per share on August 8, 1987, and reported net income for the year of $93,900 on December 31, 1987. The market value of Prince Company's stock on December 31, 1987, was $15 per share.

Required:

A. What method should Bane Company use to account for the investment in Prince Company? Why?

B. Prepare the entries Bane Company would make during 1987 to account for its investment in Prince Company.

C. Assume that Bane Company sold 3,000 of its shares of Prince Company on January 2, 1988, for $15 per share, less a broker's commission of $750. Prepare the entry to record the sale.

Problem 18-3   Long-term Bond Investment

On June 1, 1987, Lutler Company purchased 200, $1,000 par value, 9% bonds of Saley Company, as a long-term investment, at 103 plus accrued interest of $3,000 and a broker's commission of $2,360. The bonds pay interest semiannually on March 31 and September 30 and mature on September 30, 1993. On November 30, 1988, Lutler Company sold one-half of the bonds for $105,292 (net of broker fees), plus accrued interest of $1,500, in order to finance plant expansion.

Required:

A. Prepare all journals entries concerning the bond investment during the years of 1987 and 1988. (Lutler Company's fiscal year ends on December 31.)

B. What is the net amount of interest revenue earned during 1987?

C. Prepare the entry that would be made on September 30, 1993, when the remaining unsold bonds mature.

Problem 18-4 Long-term Bond Investment

Assume the same information given in Problem 18-3, except that the bonds were purchased at 96 instead of 101 and that the broker's commission was $2,452 instead of $2,360.

Required:

A. Prepare all journal entries concerning the bond investment during the years 1987 and 1988. (Lutler Company's fiscal year ends on December 31.)

B. What is the net amount of interest revenue earned during 1987?

C. Prepare the entry that would be made on September 30, 1993, when the remaining unsold bonds mature.

Problem 18-5 Worksheet for Consolidated Balance Sheet—80% Ownership

Balance sheets of Napier Company and Olson Company on January 4, 1987, are as follows.

	Napier Company	Olson Company
Cash	$ 520,000	$ 85,000
Note receivable from Olson Company	40,000	-0-
Accounts receivable (net)	102,000	59,000
Inventory	68,000	89,000
Plant and equipment (net)	510,000	170,000
Total Assets	$1,240,000	$403,000
Accounts payable	$ 190,000	$115,000
Note payable to Napier Company	-0-	40,000
Common stock, $10 par	700,000	175,000
Retained earnings	350,000	73,000
Total Liabilities and Stockholders' Equity	$1,240,000	$403,000

On January 4, 1987, Napier Company purchased 80% of the outstanding common stock of Olson Company on the open market for $198,400.

Required:

A. Prepare the entry to record the purchase of Olson's stock.

B. Prepare a worksheet for a consolidated balance sheet on January 4, 1987.

C. Prepare a consolidated balance sheet.

Problem 18-6 Worksheet for Consolidated Balance Sheet—100% Ownership

Refer to the data in Problem 18-5 and assume that Napier Company purchased all of the stock of Olson Company for $285,000. Assume, also, that $34,000 of the excess of cost over book value relates to an undervaluation of Olson Company's plant and equipment and that the remainder represents goodwill.

Required:
A. Prepare the entry to record the purchase of Olson Company's stock.
B. Prepare a worksheet for a consolidated balance sheet on the date of acquisition.

Problem 18-7 Import and Export Transactions

The S&S Company, a U.S. firm, engaged in the following transactions with foreign companies.

Date	Transaction	Billing Amount	Direct Rate of Exchange
1987			
11/10	Purchased inventory from a Japanese firm, Mitoi Company	2,500,000 Yen	$.0041
12/18	Sold merchandise to Phillips Company, a British firm	100,000 Pounds	1.32
12/29	Paid one-half of the amount due Mitoi Company		.004
12/31	Close of S&S Company's fiscal year		
1988			
1/7	Purchased goods from a West German company	32,000 Marks	$.3235
3/18	Paid the remainder of the amount due Mitoi Company		.0043
3/19	Received payment in full from Phillips Company		1.28
4/4	Paid the West German Company		.323

Required:
A. Prepare general journal entries for S&S Company for 1987.
B. Adjust the accounts at year-end, December 31, 1987. Year-end exchange rates were:

Japanese yen	$.0042
British pound	$1.31

C. Assuming S&S Company engaged in no other foreign transactions during 1988, prepare journal entries for 1988 and compute the net exchange gain or loss for the year.

Problem 18-8 Foreign Operations

On January 1, 1987, a U.S. parent company formed a wholly owned subsidiary, Parke Ltd., located in England. Parke Ltd.'s financial statements for 1987 in British pounds were as follows.

PARKE LTD.
Income Statement
For the Year Ended December 31, 1987
(In British pounds)

Sales revenue	160,000
Cost of goods sold	50,000
Gross profit	110,000
Operating expenses	70,000
Net income	40,000
Dividends declared and paid	20,000
Increase in retained earnings	20,000

PARKE LTD.
Comparative Balance Sheets
December 31, 1987
(In British pounds)

	Beginning of Year	End of Year
Cash	16,000	24,000
Accounts receivable (net)	30,000	41,000
Inventory	34,000	51,000
Plant and equipment (net)	80,000	72,000
Total assets	160,000	188,000
Accounts and notes payable	80,000	88,000
Common stock	80,000	80,000
Retained earnings	-0-	20,000
Total equities	160,000	188,000

Relevant exchange rates for the British pound are:

	U.S. dollars per pound
January 1, 1987	$1.26
December 31, 1987	1.32
Average for 1987	1.30
Dividend payment date	1.31

Required:
Translate the year-end balance sheet and the income statement of Parke Ltd. into U.S. dollars so that they can be included in the consolidated financial statements.

ALTERNATE PROBLEMS

Problem 18-1A Cost vs. Equity Method of Accounting

Darrow Company had 50,000 shares of $10 par value common stock outstanding. On January 1, 1987, Elis Company purchased, as a long-term investment, some of Darrow Company's common stock at $31 per share. On December 31, 1987, Darrow Company reported a net operating loss of $50,000 and declared and paid a cash dividend of $.50 per share. The market value of Darrow Company's stock on December 31, 1987, was $26 per share.

Required:

A. For each case given below, indicate the method of accounting that should be used by Elis Company. Explain why.

Case A   Elis Company purchased 5,000 shares of Darrow Company stock.
Case B   Elis Company purchased 20,000 shares of Darrow Company stock.

B. For each case, give the journal entries that Elis Company should make for each of the events below. (If no entry is required, explain why.)
  1. To record the purchase of the shares.
  2. To recognize the net loss reported by Darrow Company for 1987.
  3. To record the receipt of cash dividends.
  4. To recognize the effect of the market value on December 31, 1987.
C. Indicate the amounts that would be reported in the financial statements of Elis Company on December 31, 1987, relative to these cases. Follow the format presented here.

	Case A	Case B
Balance Sheet:		
Long-term investment in Darrow Stock	_____	_____
Less: Allowance to reduce to market	_____	_____
Net investment	_____	_____
Stockholders' equity:		
Unrealized loss on Long-term Investments	_____	_____
Income Statement:		
Investment or dividend revenue (loss)	_____	_____

Problem 18-2A Long-term Stock Investment

At the beginning of 1987, Umber Company purchased 30,000 of the 100,000 outstanding common shares of Witney Company as a long-term investment for $18 per share plus a broker's commission of $5,000. Witney Company declared and paid a cash dividend of $.40 per share on September 9, 1987, and reported a net loss of $86,000 for the year ended December 31, 1987.

Required:

A. What method should Umber Company use to account for the investment in Witney Company? Why?

B. Prepare the entries Umber Company would make during 1987 to account for its investment in Witney Company.

C. Assume that Umber Company sold 3,000 of its shares of Witney Company on January 1, 1988, for $13 per share, less a broker's commission of $800. Prepare the entry to record the sale.

Problem 18-3A Long-term Bond Investment

On October 1, 1987, Duff Company purchased 50, $1,000 par value, 12% bonds of HiTec Company as a long-term investment, for $47,984 (including broker fees) plus accrued interest of $2,000. The bonds pay interest semiannually on May 31 and November 30 and mature on May 31, 1992. On August 1, 1988, Duff Company sold one-half of the bonds for $24,372 (net of broker's fees) plus accrued interest of $500, in order to finance plant expansion.

Required:

A. Prepare all journal entries concerning the bond investment during the years 1987 and 1988. (Duff Company's fiscal year ends on December 31.)

B. What is the net amount of interest revenue earned during 1987?

C. Prepare the entry that would be made on May 31, 1992, when the remaining bonds mature.

Problem 18-4A Long-term Bond Investment

Assume the same information given in Problem 18-3A, except that the bonds were purchased for a total cost of $52,240, plus accrued interest of $2,000.

Required:

A. Prepare all journal entries concerning the bond investment during the years 1987 and 1988. (Duff Company's fiscal year ends on December 31.)

B. What is the net amount of interest revenue earned during 1987?

C. Prepare the entry that would be made on May 31, 1992, when the bonds mature.

Problem 18-5A Worksheet for Consolidated Balance Sheet—90% Ownership

Peabody Company and Shaw Company had balance sheets on January 1, 1987, as follows.

	Peabody Company	Shaw Company
Cash	$ 735,000	$105,000
Note receivable from Shaw Company	70,000	-0-
Accounts receivable (net)	177,500	103,000
Inventory	295,000	156,250
Plant and equipment (net)	892,800	297,800
Total Assets	$2,170,300	$662,050
Accounts payable	$ 485,200	$199,050
Note payable to Peabody Company	-0-	70,000
Common stock, $5 par value	1,225,000	260,000
Retained earnings	460,100	133,000
Total Liabilities and Stockholders' Equity	$2,170,300	$662,050

On January 1, 1987, Peabody Company purchased 90% of the outstanding common stock of Shaw Company on the open market for $353,700.

Required:

A. Prepare the entry to record the purchase of Shaw Company stock.
B. Prepare a worksheet for a consolidated balance sheet on January 1, 1987.
C. Prepare a consolidated balance sheet.

Problem 18-6A Worksheet for Consolidated Balance Sheet—100% Ownership

Using the data in Problem 18-5A, assume that Peabody Company purchased all of the stock of Shaw Company for $477,500. Any excess of cost over book value relates to an undervaluation of Shaw Company's land, which is included in the plant and equipment account.

Income statements for the two companies for the year ended December 31, 1987, are given here.

	Peabody	Shaw
Sales	$3,025,000	$1,254,000
Interest revenue	5,000	-0-
Total Revenue	3,030,000	1,254,000
Cost of goods sold	1,960,500	790,350
Operating expenses	827,300	353,500
Interest expense	-0-	9,800
Total Expenses	2,787,800	1,153,650
Net Income	$ 242,200	$ 100,350

During 1987, Shaw Company made sales to Peabody Company of $400,000. Shaw Company paid $5,000 in interest to Peabody Company on the note payable.

Required:

A. Prepare the entry to record the purchase of Shaw Company's stock.
B. Prepare a worksheet for a consolidated balance sheet on the date of acquisition.
C. Prepare a worksheet for a consolidated income statement for 1987.

Problem 18-7A Translating Foreign Financial Statements

Chicago Steel Company has a 100% owned West German subsidiary, Ubehorst Corporation, located in Buchholz, West Germany. The West German mark is the currency used by Ubehorst in its accounts and financial reports. Ubehorst's financial statements for 1987, in West German marks, are given here.

UBEHORST CORPORATION
Balance Sheet
December 31, 1987
(In West German marks)

Assets	
Cash	40,000
Accounts receivable (net)	90,000
Inventory	85,000
Property, plant, and equipment (net)	403,000
Total Assets	618,000

Liabilities and Stockholders' Equity

Accounts payable	136,000
Taxes payable	14,000
Common stock	301,000
Retained earnings	167,000
Total liabilities and stockholders' equity	618,000

UBEHORST CORPORATION
Income Statement
For the Year Ended December 31, 1987
(In West German marks)

Sales	1,100,000
Cost of goods sold	660,000
Gross profit	440,000
General and administrative expenses	110,000
Net income before income taxes	330,000
Income tax expense	175,000
Net income	155,000

On December 31, 1986, the translated retained earnings balance was $19,500. Assume the following exchange rates for the West German mark.

Historical	$.25
January 1, 1987	.30
Average for 1987	.32
December 31, 1987	.31

Required:

Translate Ubehorst Corporation's financial statements into U.S. dollars. (Hint: Translate the income statement first and use net income plus the December 31, 1986 translated retained earnings of $19,500, to find the correct ending retained earnings for the balance sheet.)

CASE

CASE 18-1   Financial Report Analysis Case   Consolidated Financial Statements

Refer to the annual report of Kmart Corporation in Appendix A and answer the following questions:

1. What method is used to account for nonconsolidated subsidiaries and affiliated companies?
2. How much income was earned from investments in nonconsolidated subsidiaries and affiliated companies during the year ended January 30, 1985?

3. What is the general principle followed by Kmart in determining which subsidiaries should be included in the consolidated financial statements?

4. Why isn't Kmart Insurance Services, Inc., consolidated with other subsidiaries in the consolidated financial statements?

5. What was Kmart's equity in Kmart Insurance Services, Inc., on December 31, 1984?

19

STATEMENT OF CHANGES IN FINANCIAL POSITION

CHAPTER OVERVIEW AND OBJECTIVES

This chapter discusses the preparation and uses of a statement of changes in financial position. When you have completed the chapter, you should understand:

1. The different concepts of funds.
2. The normal sources and uses of working capital.
3. The kinds of transactions that produce changes in working capital.
4. How to report the effects of exchanges of noncurrent items.
5. How to prepare a statement of changes in financial position worksheet.
6. How to prepare a formal statement of changes in financial position.
7. How to prepare a cash basis statement of changes in financial position.

As discussed in Chapter 1, a complete set of financial statements includes a balance sheet, an income statement, a retained earnings statement, and a statement of changes in financial position (SCFP). The first three statements were presented in preceding chapters. The SCFP is discussed in this chapter. However, the fact that the SCFP is discussed last does not imply that it is less important than the other financial statements. The SCFP is a very useful statement for both investors and creditors, because it identifies the sources and uses of resources, as well as the changes that have taken place in the financial position of a business from one period to another. This chapter will discuss the different concepts of funds and the preparation of the SCFP on both a working capital basis and cash basis.

THE STATEMENT OF CHANGES IN FINANCIAL POSITION

An analysis of comparative balance sheets for successive periods will identify the total changes that have taken place in asset, liability, and owners' equity accounts, but will not provide a ready explanation of what caused those changes. The income statement and retained earnings statement provide a partial explanation by indicating the sources and uses of funds from operating activities, the amount of earnings paid as dividends, and the amount of earnings retained for other uses. Neither statement, however, gives a full report of the sources of resources during the period and the uses to which they were committed.

The statement specifically designed to summarize all of the financing (sources of funds) and investing (uses of funds) activities of a business for a period— including those involving operating activities—is the statement of changes in financial position (SCFP). This statement aids users by providing answers to questions such as: How were the funds obtained to pay off long-term debt and to acquire new plant assets during the period? How was the firm able to pay regular dividends, even though it incurred a significant operating loss for the period? How were the funds from a new stock issue utilized? Why is the company in a worse working capital position when it had profitable operations for the period?

The SCFP provides answers to these and similar questions, because it shows the individual sources and uses of funds during the period. In fact, in the past many firms called it a statement of sources and applications of funds, or simply a funds statement, but today the great majority of firms use the title statement of changes in financial position.

CONCEPTS OF FUNDS

The term **funds** means different things to different people. Funds are thought of as:

Objective 1: Different concepts of funds

1. Cash.
2. Cash plus readily marketable securities.
3. **Working capital**—the excess of current assets over current liabilities.[1]

Any of these concepts may be used in the preparation of the SCFP. However, there has been a rather dramatic shift from the working capital basis to the cash basis over the past several years. This shift is shown by the results of two surveys of 600 companies.

	1983	1980
Number of Companies Reporting:		
Changes in working capital	286	541
Changes in cash and cash equivalents	314	59
Total Companies	600	600

Source: Accounting Trends & Techniques (New York: AICPA, 1984), p. 366.

[1]Terminology used in the accounting and finance literature varies somewhat. Some authors refer to current assets as working capital and call the excess of current assets over current liabilities net working capital.

Although the cash concept of funds is more prevalent in practice today, the preparation of the SCFP is easier to demonstrate with the working capital concept. Consequently, the preparation of a working capital basis statement of changes in financial position will be discussed and illustrated first. The cash basis is treated in a later section of this chapter.

WORKING CAPITAL BASIS SCFP

The working capital concept of funds is sometimes used because business and financial executives recognize that short-term credit is often used as a substitute for cash. Over the operating cycle, current liabilities are incurred to acquire inventory and services. The inventory is exchanged for an account receivable in a sales transaction, the account receivable is collected, and the cash is used in part to pay current liabilities. In other words, current liabilities are continually being incurred, current assets are constantly being converted into cash, and cash is continuously being used to pay current liabilities. At any given time, the excess of current assets over current liabilities (i.e., working capital) represents a fund of relatively liquid resources. For example, assume that Clark Corporation had the following current assets and current liabilities on January 1.

Cash	$ 60,000	Notes payable	$ 35,000
Accounts receivable	80,000	Accounts payable	90,000
Inventory	120,000	Accrued expenses	10,000
Total Current Assets	$260,000	Total Current Liabilities	$135,000

Clark Corporation's working capital is $125,000 ($260,000 − $135,000). As the inventory is sold and accounts receivable are collected, cash becomes available to pay off the current liabilities. In addition, there will be cash left over that management can use to replace inventory, pay current expenses, invest in plant assets, pay off long-term debt, or distribute as dividends. Thus, business executives generally think of working capital as a fund of net liquid assets that can be used for various operating and investing activities.

It is important to recognize that transactions involving only current assets and current liabilities do not normally change the amount of working capital. For example, if Clark Corporation collects $40,000 of accounts receivable, total current assets and current liabilities remain unchanged; thus, working capital also remains unchanged. Likewise, if $35,000 cash is used to pay off the notes payable, current assets will be reduced to $225,000, current liabilities will be reduced to $100,000, and working capital will remain unchanged at $125,000.

SOURCES AND USES OF WORKING CAPITAL

When the SCFP is prepared to report the sources and uses of working capital, any transaction that increases working capital is a **source of funds** and any transaction that decreases working capital is a **use of funds.** Therefore, it is important to recognize the effect of various transactions on working capital. As an aid in analyzing the effect of different transactions on working capital, it is helpful to view the balance sheet in account form, as shown below.

Objective 2: Sources and uses of working capital

a. Current Assets	b. Current Liabilities
c. Noncurrent Assets	d. Noncurrent Liabilities and Owners' Equity

To affect working capital, a transaction must involve both a current account and a noncurrent account. In other words, to affect working capital, a transaction must involve accounts on both sides of the solid line (which might be called the working capital line) in the balance sheet. Transactions that affect accounts within one of the four parts only, as well as transactions that affect accounts on both sides of the broken line only, have no effect on working capital. Applying these rules, we can identify 10 general types of transactions, six of which do not affect working capital and four that do affect it.

Transactions That Do Not Affect Working Capital

Type of Transaction	Parts of Balance Sheet Affected	Examples
1.	Current assets (Part a) only.	Purchased a temporary investment for cash; collected an account receivable.
2.	Current liabilities (Part b) only.	Exchanged a short-term note payable for an account payable.
3.	Noncurrent assets (Part c) only.	Exchanged land for equipment.
4.	Noncurrent liabilities and owners' equity (Part d) only.	Exchanged common stock for bonds payable.
5.	Current assets and current liabilities (Parts a and b).	Paid an account payable; purchased inventory on account.
6.	Noncurrent assets and noncurrent liabilities or owners' equity (Parts c and d).	Issued common stock for land; exchanged a long-term note payable for equipment.

Note that none of these six types of transactions involve accounts on both sides of the solid line. Types 1, 2, 3, and 4 affect accounts within each part only. An exchange of one current asset for another of equal value, or the exchange of one current liability for another of equal value, does not change total working capital. Likewise, an exchange of one noncurrent asset for another, or an exchange of a noncurrent liability for another noncurrent liability or for stock, has no effect on working capital. Type 5 transactions reduce or increase current assets and current liabilities by equal amounts and, therefore, do not affect total working capital. Type 6 transactions do not involve working capital because no current asset or current liability is affected.

Transactions That Affect Working Capital

Type of Transaction	Parts of Balance Sheet Affected	Examples
7.	Current assets and noncurrent assets (Parts a and c).	Purchased plant assets for cash; sold plant assets for a short-term receivable.
8.	Current liabilities and noncurrent assets (Parts b and c).	Purchased plant assets on short-term credit.
9.	Current assets and noncurrent liabilities or owners' equity (Parts a and d).	Issued common stock or bonds payable for cash; retired preferred stock for cash; purchased treasury stock for cash.
10.	Current liabilities and noncurrent liabilities or owners' equity (Parts b and d).	Exchanged a short-term note payable for a long-term note payable.

Each of these four types of transactions involves a current asset or current liability and a noncurrent asset, noncurrent liability, or element of owners' equity. Each type affects accounts on both sides of the solid line, thereby resulting in a source or use of working capital.

It may be useful to think of sources of working capital as producing a pool of funds, which can be used for various purposes, as depicted in Figure 19–1.

SOURCES OF WORKING CAPITAL

Firms obtain working capital primarily from four basic sources: current operating activities, the sale of noncurrent assets, the issue of long-term debt, and the issue of capital stock.

Current Operations

The main source of working capital for many companies is current operating activities. Sales result in an increase in both current assets (cash or receivables) and owners' equity (revenue). The increase in current assets increases working capital. Cost of goods sold and most expenses decrease current assets or increase current liabilities and decrease owners' equity. Therefore, most expenses reduce working capital. If the increase of funds from revenues exceeds the decrease of funds for cost of goods sold and operating expenses, there is

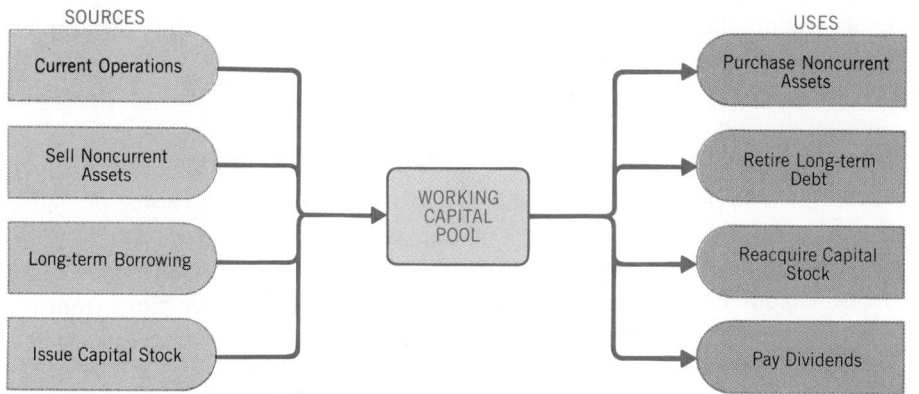

Figure 19–1
Sources and Uses
of Working Capital

a net increase of funds and, therefore, a net increase in working capital. Conversely, if the decrease of funds for cost of goods sold and operating expenses exceeds the increase of funds from revenues, a net decrease in working capital results.

If all revenues represented an increase in current assets or a decrease in current liabilities, and all expenses represented a decrease in current assets or an increase in current liabilities, net income would represent a net increase in working capital for the period. This is seldom the case, however. Some expenses deducted on the income statement (such as depreciation, depletion, and amortization) do not reduce current assets or increase current liabilities during the current period. Depreciation, for example, is recorded by a debit to depreciation expense and a credit to accumulated depreciation (a contra to a noncurrent asset account). Current assets and current liabilities are unaffected. The same is true for depletion of natural resources and amortization of intangible assets.

Some items increase net income but do not increase current assets or decrease current liabilities. One such item, gain on the sale of an asset, is discussed later in this chapter. Other items are covered in more advanced accounting courses.

In the preparation of the SCFP, total revenues and those expenses that decrease working capital could be reported separately. However, since this detail is already provided in the income statement, net income is generally shown as the first item on the SCFP. Expenses that did not decrease working capital during the period are then added, as illustrated here.

CLARK CORPORATION
Statement of Changes in Financial Position
For the Year Ended December 31, 1987

Sources of Working Capital:	
Net income as reported on the income statement	$421,600
Add: Expenses not requiring working capital:	
Depreciation expense	68,200
Total Working Capital Provided by Operations	489,800

Other sources and uses of working capital are then listed separately to complete the statement, as will be shown later.

Depreciation is Not a Source of Working Capital.

Unfortunately, the addition of depreciation expense to net income might lead some people to view depreciation as a source of working capital. It is important to avoid this misconception. The depreciation entry does not involve a current asset or current liability. Thus, no working capital flows into the company from the depreciation entry. The source of the $489,800 working capital from operations for Clark Corporation was the excess of sales revenues over those expenses that required the use of working capital. Depreciation and similar items, such as amortization and depletion, are expenses which are deducted from revenue in arriving at net income. However, they do not require the use of working capital. Thus, they are added back to net income merely as a convenient shortcut for determining working capital provided by operations.

It is possible for a company to report a net operating loss for the period and still show working capital provided by operations. This will result when the total of depreciation, depletion, and amortization added back is greater than the operating loss. For example, Stone Container Corporation reported a net operating loss of $2,922,000 for the year ended December 31, 1983. Working capital provided by operations, however, amounted to $26,508,000.

Nonoperating Gains and Losses.

Another type of adjustment to net income made in determining working capital provided by operations is that needed for nonoperating gains and losses. Current accounting standards require that these gains and losses must be reported on the income statement. For example, if land with a cost of $40,000 is sold for $100,000, the sale would be recorded as follows.

June	5	Cash	100,000	
		Land		40,000
		Gain on Sale of Land		60,000

The entire proceeds from the sale ($100,000) is reported on the statement of changes in financial position as working capital provided from the sale of land. Since the $60,000 gain is reported in the income statement and included in net income, it must be deducted from net income on the statement of changes in financial position in order to prevent the double counting of the $60,000 and to reflect properly the working capital provided by operations. If the gain is not deducted, working capital provided by the transaction would be incorrectly reported as $160,000. In a similar manner, if the land was sold for $30,000 and a $10,000 loss was reported, the loss must be added to net income in arriving at working capital provided by operations.

Sale of Noncurrent Assets

A company may obtain working capital by selling a plant asset, long-term investment, or other noncurrent asset in exchange for a current asset. Working capital will increase by the amount of current assets received, regardless of whether the noncurrent asset is sold at a gain or a loss. For example, if long-term investments with a cost of $50,000 are sold for $70,000 cash, working capital increases by the $70,000 increase in current assets. If the cost of the long-term investments had been $80,000, resulting in a loss of $10,000, the increase in working capital would still be $70,000—since that is the amount by which current assets increased. As discussed earlier, any gain is deducted from (and any loss is added to) net income in determining working capital provided by operations.

Issue of Long-term Debt

The issue of long-term debt, such as bonds payable, for cash, increases current assets and noncurrent liabilities and is a major source of working capital for many companies. Short-term borrowing, however, increases both current assets and current liabilities by an equal amount and, therefore, is not a source of working capital.

Issue of Capital Stock

An additional issue of capital stock or the reissue of treasury stock for cash or other current assets is another source of working capital because current assets increase with an offsetting increase in stockholders' equity. In a similar manner, an additional investment of current assets by an individual owner or partner is a source of working capital to a proprietorship or partnership. Capital stock issued in a stock dividend or stock split does not provide working capital, however, because these events do not produce an increase in the corporation's assets. Rather, only stockholders' equity accounts are affected without an increase in total stockholders' equity.

USES OF WORKING CAPITAL

Most uses of working capital come about from transactions that are the opposite of those that provide working capital. For example, a business may incur an operating loss in excess of depreciation and other items added back, thereby reducing working capital. Other uses of working capital are the purchase of noncurrent assets, the retirement of long-term debt, the retirement or reacquisition of capital stock, and the declaration of cash dividends.

Purchase of Noncurrent Assets

The purchase of plant assets, long-term investments, or other noncurrent assets in exchange for current assets or current liabilities is a major use of working capital for many companies. Noncurrent assets are increased, and the decrease in current assets or increase in current liabilities reduces working capital.

Retirement of Long-term Debt

If current assets are used to pay long-term liabilities, working capital is reduced. In addition, when a portion of long-term debt becomes due within the next accounting period, it must be reclassified as a current liability. Since current liabilities increase with an offsetting decrease in noncurrent liabilities, the reclassification results in a decrease in working capital. Subsequent payment of the portion classified as a current liability will not affect working capital, because both current assets and current liabilities will be reduced.

Retirement or Reacquisition of Capital Stock

When current assets are used to reacquire capital stock that is to be retired or held as treasury stock, working capital is decreased by the amount of the current assets given up. Likewise, the withdrawal of current assets by an individual owner or partner is a use of working capital in a proprietorship or partnership.

Declaration of Cash Dividends

The declaration of a cash dividend results in a debit to *Dividends Declared* and a credit to a current liability, *Dividends Payable*. Since current liabilities are increased, the declaration of the dividend is a use of working capital. The later payment of the dividend reduces a current asset and a current liability by equal amounts and, therefore, does not affect working capital. In other words, it is the declaration of cash dividends, rather than their payment, that represents a use of working capital.

THE SPECIAL CASE OF EXCHANGE TRANSACTIONS

Objective 4: Reporting effects of exchanges of noncurrent items

Companies sometimes give a long-term note payable or issue their capital stock in direct exchange for a noncurrent asset. For example, assume that common stock was issued in exchange for a building and the following entry was made.

June	4	Buildings	600,000	
		Common Stock		600,000
		Exchanged common stock for a building.		

Since the transaction does not involve current assets or current liabilities, it has no effect on working capital. However, because the transaction *does* represent a significant financing and investing event, accounting standards require that the effects of the transaction be disclosed by reporting it as both a source and a use of working capital.[2] Therefore, the issue of common stock is reported

[2]Accounting Principles Board, "Reporting Changes in Financial Position," *APB Opinion No. 19* (New York: AICPA, 1971), par. 8.

as a $600,000 source of working capital, and the acquisition of the building is reported as a $600,000 use of working capital. In this way, significant financing and investing transactions are disclosed, even though the net effect on working capital is zero. This approach to reporting exchange transactions is sometimes referred to as the **all financial resources approach.**

Other types of exchange transactions that are reported as both a source and a use of working capital include the conversion of bonds payable or preferred stock into common stock, and the exchange of long-term debt for plant assets. Most transactions that affect only noncurrent accounts are exchange transactions. A major exception is the issue of a stock dividend. Stock dividends are not exchange transactions and do not affect the company's resources, but merely result in a transfer of retained earnings to other stockholders' equity accounts. Thus, stock dividends are not reported in the statement of changes in financial position.

PREPARING A WORKING CAPITAL BASIS SCFP

The SCFP consists of two main sections, one for reporting the sources of working capital and the other for reporting the uses of working capital. The difference between the totals of the two sections represents the increase or decrease in working capital for the period. The SCFP is supported by a schedule showing the changes in individual current assets and current liabilities for the period.

Most of the information needed to prepare the SCFP is found in the comparative balance sheets, the income statement, and the retained earnings statement. Additional information is obtained by analyzing the changes that have taken place in the noncurrent general ledger accounts during the period. Since transactions that increase or decrease working capital must involve both current and noncurrent accounts, an examination of the changes in the noncurrent accounts identifies the individual sources and uses of working capital.

WORKING CAPITAL FLOW—A BASIC ILLUSTRATION

Ace Company is a small corporation engaged in the retail sale of men's clothing. The company rents its store building but owns its store equipment. A statement of income and retained earnings for 1987 and comparative balance sheets on December 31, 1986 and 1987, are shown in Figure 19–2.

In addition to normal operating activities, the following events occurred during 1987.

1. Land costing $55,000 was purchased for cash for the future construction of a store building.
2. Common stock was issued at par value for cash of $50,000.
3. Cash dividends of $20,000 were declared and paid.

The first step in the preparation of a statement of changes in financial position is the computation of the change in working capital for the year. This can be done by preparing a schedule of changes in the components of working capital (Figure 19–3).

Figure 19–2
Ace Company Financial Statements

ACE COMPANY
Statement of Income and Retained Earnings
For the Year Ended December 31, 1987

Sales		$380,000
Cost of goods sold		196,000
Gross profit		184,000
Operating expenses:		
Administration expense	$76,000	
Selling expense	56,000	
Depreciation expense	8,000	140,000
Net income		$ 44,000
Retained earnings, January 1, 1987		25,000
Total		69,000
Less: Cash dividends declared		20,000
Retained earnings, December 31, 1987		$ 49,000

ACE COMPANY
Comparative Balance Sheets

	December 31	
	1987	1986
Assets		
Cash	$ 47,000	$ 36,000
Accounts receivable	26,000	18,000
Inventory	54,000	49,000
Store equipment	88,000	88,000
Less: Accumulated depreciation	(43,000)	(35,000)
Land	55,000	-0-
Total Assets	$227,000	$156,000
Liabilities and Owners' Equity		
Short-term notes payable	$ 15,000	$ 10,000
Accounts payable	13,000	21,000
Common stock	150,000	100,000
Retained earnings	49,000	25,000
Total Liabilities and Owners' Equity	$227,000	$156,000

The statement of changes in financial position can then be prepared, as shown in Figure 19–4.

Working capital provided by operations can be determined by analyzing the income statement. Net income of $44,000 is adjusted for expenses not requiring the use of working capital during the period, in this case depreciation expense of $8,000. Note that the $8,000 also represents the increase in accumulated depreciation (a noncurrent account) on the comparative balance sheets.

Figure 19-3
Change in Components of Working Capital

Changes in Components of Working Capital

	December 31		Increase or (Decrease) in Working Capital
	1987	1986	
Current assets:			
Cash	$ 47,000	$ 36,000	$11,000
Accounts receivable	26,000	18,000	8,000
Inventory	54,000	49,000	5,000
Total current assets	127,000	103,000	
Current liabilities:			
Short-term notes payable	$ 15,000	$ 10,000	(5,000)
Accounts payable	13,000	21,000	8,000
Total current liabilities	28,000	31,000	
Working capital	$ 99,000	$ 72,000	
Increase in working capital			$27,000

Figure 19-4
Working Capital SCFP

ACE COMPANY
Statement of Changes in Financial Position
For the Year Ended December 31, 1987

Working capital was provided by:		
Operations:		
Net income as reported on the income statement		$ 44,000
Add: Expenses not requiring working capital:		
Depreciation expense		8,000
Total working capital provided by operations		52,000
Issue of common stock		50,000
Total working capital provided		102,000
Working capital was used for:		
Purchase of land	$55,000	
Payment of dividends	20,000	75,000
Increase in working capital		$ 27,000

Remember that sources and uses of working capital must involve both current and noncurrent accounts. Thus, the other sources and uses of working capital can be determined by analyzing the changes in noncurrent accounts on the comparative balance sheets. The land account increased by $55,000, reflecting the purchase of land, which is a use of working capital. The common stock account increased by $50,000, which represents a source of working capital from the issue of stock. In addition, the change in retained earnings for the year can be verified as follows.

Retained earnings balance, 1/1/87	$25,000
Add net income for 1987	44,000
Total	69,000
Less dividends declared in 1987	20,000
Retained earnings balance, 12/31/87	$49,000

A MORE COMPLEX ILLUSTRATION

The preparation of a more complex statement of changes in financial position involves four basic steps.

1. The change in working capital for the period is calculated by preparing a schedule of changes in the components of working capital, as illustrated in Figure 19–3 and 19–7 (p. 755).
2. A worksheet is prepared to analyze the changes in noncurrent accounts.
3. Changes in noncurrent accounts are analyzed to determine whether they have resulted in a source of or use of working capital.
4. The SCFP is prepared from the information gathered on the worksheet.

The comparative balance sheets and statement of income and retained earnings of Clark Corporation presented in Figure 19–5 are used to illustrate the preparation of the statement of changes in financial position.

During 1987, Clark Corporation entered into these transactions, which affected noncurrent accounts.

1. A new wing was added to the building at a cost of $400,000 cash.
2. New equipment was purchased at a cost of $158,000. Cash of $58,000 and a note payable for $100,000 due January 1, 1990, were given in exchange.
3. Long-term stock investments were sold for $160,000.
4. Bonds payable with a par value of $100,000 were issued for cash at par.
5. An additional 20,000 shares of $5 par value common stock were issued for $173,000.
6. Depreciation expense for the year was $33,000 on buildings and $35,000 on equipment.
7. Cash dividends of $116,000 were declared and paid.

Figure 19–5
Clark Corporation
Financial Statements

CLARK CORPORATION
Comparative Balance Sheets

Assets	December 31	
	1987	1986
Current assets:		
Cash	$ 188,000	$ 162,000
Accounts receivable (net)	231,000	176,000
Inventory	314,000	322,000
Prepaid expenses	36,000	14,000
Total current assets	769,000	674,000

Long-term stock investment (at cost which is less than market)	100,000	200,000
Property, plant, and equipment:		
Buildings	1,200,000	800,000
Accumulated depreciation—buildings	(348,000)	(315,000)
Equipment	674,000	516,000
Accumulated depreciation—equipment	(267,000)	(232,000)
Land	300,000	300,000
Total property, plant, and equipment	1,559,000	1,069,000
Total Assets	$2,428,000	$1,943,000

Liabilities and Stockholders' Equity

Current liabilities:		
Accounts payable	$ 238,000	$ 269,000
Accrued expenses	83,000	66,000
Total current liabilities	321,000	335,000
Long-term liabilities:		
Notes payable, due January 1, 1990	100,000	-0-
Bonds payable, due July 1, 1998	600,000	500,000
Total long-term liabilities	700,000	500,000
Stockholders' equity:		
Common stock, $5 par	650,000	550,000
Paid-in capital in excess of par value	299,000	226,000
Retained earnings	458,000	332,000
Total stockholders' equity	1,407,000	1,108,000
Total Liabilities and Stockholders' Equity	$2,428,000	$1,943,000

CLARK CORPORATION
Statement of Income and Retained Earnings
For the Year Ended December 31, 1987

Net sales		$4,620,000
Cost of goods sold		2,440,000
Gross profit on sales		2,180,000
Operating expenses other than depreciation	$1,770,000	
Depreciation expense	68,000	
Total operating expenses		1,838,000
Operating income		342,000
Gain on sale of investments		60,000
Net income before income tax		402,000
Income tax expense		160,000
Net income		242,000
Retained earnings, January 1		332,000
Total		574,000
Less: Cash dividends declared		116,000
Retained earnings, December 31		$ 458,000

COMPUTATION OF THE CHANGE IN WORKING CAPITAL FOR THE YEAR

The first step in the preparation of a statement of changes in financial position for Clark Corporation is to compute the increase or decrease in working capital during 1987. This is normally done by preparing a schedule of changes in the components of working capital, as follows.

	December 31		Working Capital Increase (Decrease)
	1987	1986	
Current assets:			
Cash	$188,000	$162,000	$ 26,000
Accounts receivable	231,000	176,000	55,000
Inventory	314,000	322,000	(8,000)
Prepaid expenses	36,000	14,000	22,000
Total current assets	769,000	674,000	95,000
Current liabilities:			
Accounts payable	238,000	269,000	31,000
Accrued expenses	83,000	66,000	(17,000)
Total current liabilities	321,000	335,000	14,000
Working capital	$448,000	$339,000	
Increase in working capital			$109,000

Current assets increased by $95,000 from the end of 1986 to the end of 1987, resulting in an increase in working capital. In addition, current liabilities decreased by $14,000, which also represents an increase in working capital. Since working capital increased by a total of $109,000 during the year, the sources of working capital reported in the statement of changes in financial position must exceed the uses of working capital by $109,000.

PREPARATION OF THE WORKSHEET

Objective 5: Preparing a working capital basis SCFP worksheet

After determining the net change in working capital, noncurrent accounts and source documents are analyzed to identify the individual sources and uses of working capital. To aid in this analysis and to gather the information needed to prepare the statement of changes in financial position, many accountants prepare a worksheet. Although the statement could be prepared directly from an analysis of the changes in noncurrent accounts, the worksheet is particularly helpful when there have been numerous transactions affecting noncurrent accounts during the period. The worksheet for Clark Corporation, presented in Figure 19–6, consists of two main sections. The top section is used to reconcile beginning-of-year with end-of-year noncurrent account balances and to identify the individual sources and uses of working capital, which are listed in the bottom section. The basic steps in the preparation of the worksheet are as follows.

CLARK CORPORATION
Worksheet for Statement of Changes in Financial Position
Year Ended December 31, 1987

	Account Balance 1/1/87	Analysis of Transactions for 1987 Debit	Analysis of Transactions for 1987 Credit	Account Balance 12/31/87
Debits				
Working capital	339,000	109,000		448,000
Buildings	800,000	(3) 400,000		1,200,000
Equipment	516,000	(4) 158,000		674,000
Land	300,000			300,000
Long-term investments	200,000		(5) 100,000	100,000
Total Debits	2,155,000			2,722,000
Credits				
Accumulated depreciation—buildings	315,000		(2) 33,000	348,000
Accumulated depreciation—equipment	232,000		(2) 35,000	267,000
Notes payable	0		(4) 100,000	100,000
Bonds payable	500,000		(6) 100,000	600,000
Common stock	550,000		(7) 100,000	650,000
Paid-in capital in excess of par value	226,000		(7) 73,000	299,000
Retained earnings	332,000	(8) 116,000	(1) 242,000	458,000
Total Credits	2,155,000	783,000	783,000	2,722,000
Sources of Working Capital		**Sources**	**Uses**	
Operations:				
Net income		(1) 242,000		
Add: Depreciation		(2) 68,000		
Less: Gain on sale of investment			(5) 60,000	
Issue of note payable for equipment		(4) 100,000		
Sale of long-term investments		(5) 160,000		
Issue of bonds payable		(6) 100,000		
Issue of common stock		(7) 173,000		
Uses of Working Capital				
Building addition			(3) 400,000	
Purchase of equipment			(4) 158,000	
Cash dividends declared			(8) 116,000	
		843,000	734,000	
Increase in working capital			109,000	
		843,000	843,000	

Figure 19–6
Worksheet for Statement of Changes in Financial Position

1. Columns are used in the top section to record noncurrent account balances at the beginning of the year, analyze transactions for the year, and record noncurrent account balances at the end of the year.
2. Noncurrent accounts with debit balances are separated from those with credit balances. Working capital balances at the beginning of the year and the end of the year are listed as the first debit item, and the increase (or

decrease) in working capital is entered as a debit (or credit) in the Analysis of Transactions column. The beginning-of-year and end-of-year debit balances are then listed, followed by the beginning-of-year and end-of-year credit balances.[3]

3. After beginning-of-year and end-of-year debit and credit balances are entered, the debits and credits are added to prove their equality.

4. After debits and credits are added, the heading Sources of Working Capital is entered in the bottom section of the worksheet. Several lines are skipped and then the heading Uses of Working Capital is entered.

5. Changes in each noncurrent account are analyzed and explained. Entries are then made in the Analysis of Transactions columns to reconcile the beginning-of-year and end-of-year balances and to list the individual sources and uses of working capital in the bottom section of the worksheet. (Because the analysis of transactions is critical in the preparation of the statement of changes in financial position, an analysis of each transaction is presented in the next section.)

6. Each debit and credit item is totaled horizontally (crossfooted) to prove the reconciliation of the beginning-of-year and end-of-year balances. Any item that does not reconcile is an indication that a transaction has been omitted.

7. The debits and credits in the Analysis of Transactions columns are added to prove their equality.

8. The Sources and Uses columns in the bottom section are totaled, and the increase (or decrease) in working capital is entered as a balancing use (or source) of working capital.

After the worksheet is completed, all of the information needed to complete the statement of changes in financial position is contained in the bottom section and is then used to prepare the formal statement.

ANALYSIS OF TRANSACTIONS

The most important step in the preparation of the statement of changes in financial position is the analysis of the transactions that affected noncurrent accounts during the year. An analysis of each transaction is presented here, and the explanations are keyed to the numbers in parentheses in Figure 19–6.

1. Clark Corporation reported net income of $242,000 for 1987. Net income represents an increase in retained earnings (a noncurrent account) and, as discussed earlier, is an increase in working capital. Therefore, on the worksheet, net income is debited to a source of working capital from operations and is credited to the beginning balance of *Retained Earnings* as one reconciling item between the beginning and ending *Retained Earnings* balances. Recall, however, that the net income figure must be adjusted for items that affected net income but that did not affect current assets or

---

[3]If the company has negative working capital at the beginning or end of the year (if current liabilities exceed current assets), this is entered as the first item in the credit part of the top section.

current liabilities during the period, in order to report the net working capital provided by operations.

2. As explained earlier, depreciation expense reduces net income but does not decrease a current asset or increase a current liability during the period. Therefore, depreciation has no effect on working capital. Depreciation expense was $33,000 on the building and $35,000 on equipment. Depreciation expense of $68,000 is shown on the worksheet as an addition to net income and as an addition to accumulated depreciation on buildings ($33,000) and equipment ($35,000). The worksheet entry adjusts working capital provided by operations, and reconciles the beginning and ending balances in the *Accumulated Depreciation* accounts.

3. Cash of $400,000 was paid for a building addition during the year. This decrease in current assets represents a use of working capital. The worksheet entry is a debit to buildings and a credit to uses of working capital of $400,000. The entry reconciles the beginning and ending balances in the *Buildings* account and reports the separate use of working capital.

4. Equipment was purchased during the year at a cost of $158,000, of which $58,000 was paid in cash and a $100,000 long-term note payable was given for the balance. The worksheet entry for this transaction is:

Source of Working Capital—Issue Note Payable	100,000	
Equipment	158,000	
Notes Payable		100,000
Use of Working Capital—Purchase Equipment		158,000

Notice that the purchase of equipment was financed in part by the use of working capital and in part by the issue of a long-term note payable. The net effect of the transaction is a $58,000 use of working capital. Under the all financial resources approach, however, the issue of the long-term note payable is shown as a source of working capital and the entire cost of the equipment ($158,000) is shown as a use of working capital. The debit to *Equipment* and credit to *Notes Payable* serve to reconcile the beginning and ending balances of the *Equipment* and *Notes Payable* accounts.

5. Long-term investments with a cost of $100,000 were sold during the year for $160,000. The book entry to record the sale was:

Cash	160,000	
Long-term Investments		100,000
Gain on Sale of Investments		60,000

The $160,000 cash received increased current assets and, therefore, increased working capital. The $60,000 gain on sale of investments was included in net income on the income statement. Notice that the worksheet entry for this transaction shows the $160,000 source of working capital and that the $100,000 credit to long-term investments reconciles the beginning and ending balances in the *Long-term Investments* account. In addition, the $60,000 gain is subtracted from net income to show working capital provided by operations. Since the full $160,000 cash received is shown as a source of working capital, failure to subtract the $60,000 gain would result in a double reporting of sources of working capital.

6. The issue of bonds payable provided $100,000 of working capital during the year. The worksheet entry shows the source of working capital and reconciles the beginning and ending balances in the *Bonds Payable* account.

7. The issue of common stock provided $173,000 of working capital. The worksheet entry shows the source of working capital and reconciles the beginning and ending balances in the *Common Stock* and *Paid-in Capital in Excess of Par Value* accounts.

8. Cash dividends declared decreased working capital by $116,000. The worksheet entry shows the use of working capital and completes the reconciliation of the beginning and ending balances in the *Retained Earnings* account.

PREPARATION OF THE SCFP

Objective 6: Preparing a working capital basis SCFP

When the worksheet is completed, all sources and uses of working capital have been identified. The formal statement is then prepared from the bottom section of the worksheet, as shown in Figure 19–7. Notice that the net working capital provided by operations is $250,000, that the other individual sources and uses of working capital are identified, and that the increase in working capital for the year of $109,000 is shown as the final item.

In addition to the statement of changes in financial position, the net changes in each component of working capital must be disclosed, either in the statement or in a separate schedule. (A schedule of changes in the components of working capital for Clark Corporation is included in Figure 19–7.)

CASH BASIS SCFP

Objective 7: Preparing a cash basis SCFP

As indicated earlier, the cash concept of funds is sometimes used as the basis for the preparation of the SCFP. In that case, the statement reports the sources and uses of cash, rather than the sources and uses of working capital. Even when the working capital basis is used for external reporting purposes, some type of **cash flow statement** is normally prepared for internal use in planning and controlling cash flows.

A cash flow statement may be prepared in any of various formats. If prepared for internal use only, it is often a simple listing of cash receipts (sources) and cash disbursements (uses) during the period. If prepared for external reporting purposes, it takes the same format as the SCFP prepared on a working capital basis. *Cash provided by operations* is reported first, followed by *other sources* and *uses* of cash. The difference between total sources and uses of cash represents the net increase or decrease in cash during the period. Following the all financial resources approach, exchange transactions are reported as both sources and uses of cash. An exchange of a long-term note payable for

Figure 19–7
Working Capital
SCFP

CLARK CORPORATION
Statement of Changes in Financial Position
For the Year Ended December 31, 1987

Sources of Working Capital		
Operations		
Net income	$242,000	
Add: Depreciation	68,000	
Less: Gain on sale of investments	(60,000)	
Net working capital provided by operations		250,000
Other Sources of Working Capital		
Issue of long-term notes payable		100,000
Sale of long-term investments		160,000
Issue of bonds payable		100,000
Issue of common stock		173,000
Total sources of working capital		783,000
Uses of Working Capital		
Building addition	$400,000	
Purchase of equipment	158,000	
Cash dividends	116,000	
Total uses of working capital		674,000
Increase in working capital		$109,000

Changes in Components of Working Capital

	December 31		Working Capital Increase (Decrease)
	1987	1986	
Current assets:			
Cash	$188,000	$162,000	$ 26,000
Accounts receivable	231,000	176,000	55,000
Inventory	314,000	322,000	(8,000)
Prepaid expenses	36,000	14,000	22,000
Total current assets	769,000	674,000	
Current liabilities:			
Accounts payable	238,000	269,000	31,000
Accrued expenses	83,000	66,000	(17,000)
Total current liabilities	321,000	335,000	
Working capital	$448,000	$339,000	
Increase in working capital			$109,000

[handwritten marginalia: Working Capital = CA – CL]

[handwritten marginalia: NI]

equipment, for example, is reported as though the note were issued for cash and the cash was then used to purchase equipment.

CASH PROVIDED BY OPERATIONS

The first step in the preparation of a cash basis SCFP is determining the amount of cash provided by operations. Cash inflow to the company from current operations results from cash sales and the collection of accounts receivable.

Cash outflow for operations results from the payment of current operating expenses and current liabilities that were incurred to obtain goods and services. The difference between the cash inflow and the cash outflow from operating activities represents the net increase or decrease in cash provided by operations.

Net cash flow from operations can be determined by listing separately the cash received from cash sales and collections of accounts receivable and the cash paid out for operating expenses and payment of current liabilities. Another approach is similar to that used to determine working capital provided by operations, where items that affected net income but that did not provide or use working capital were added to or subtracted from net income.

In determining cash flow, changes in current assets (other than cash) and current liabilities constitute sources and uses of cash. The normal approach in computing cash flow from operations is to convert the accrual basis income to a cash basis income. Each current asset (except cash) and each current liability is adjusted to reflect its effect on revenues and expenses, as if a cash basis, rather than an accrual basis, of determining income were used.

To convert the accrual basis income to cash basis income, the relationship between the effect of operating transactions on accrual income and cash movements within the company must be considered. Thus, accrual basis revenue is adjusted to show cash received from customers and accrual basis expenses are adjusted to show cash expenses. The difference between cash received from customers and cash paid for expenses represents the net cash flow from operating activities. The conversion process is presented in the following sections.

Cash Receipts from Customers

Under accrual accounting, sales on account are recognized by a debit to *Accounts Receivable* and a credit to *Sales* at the time each sale is made. Under the cash basis, revenue is not recognized until cash is received. The conversion of accrual basis sales revenue to cash basis sales revenue may be done as follows.

$$\text{Accrual basis}\atop\text{net sales} \left\{ {+\text{ Beginning accounts receivable} \atop -\text{ Ending accounts receivable}} \right\} = {\text{Cash received} \atop \text{from customers}}$$

Clark Corporation's comparative balance sheets (Figure 19–5, page 748–749) show that accounts receivable on 12/31/86 and 12/31/87 were $176,000 and $231,000, respectively. Thus, cash receipts from customers may be computed as:

Accrual basis net sales (Figure 19–5)	$4,620,000
Add: Beginning accounts receivable	176,000
Total cash collectible	4,796,000
Less: Ending accounts receivable	231,000
Cash received from customers	$4,565,000

The beginning balance of accounts receivable is added to accrual basis sales. The total shows the amount of cash that could have been collected during the current period, including collections of sales recognized in prior years. The ending accounts receivable balance is subtracted because it represents sales that have not yet been collected. The result is cash collected from customers during the current period.

Cash Payments for Purchases

Under accrual accounting, purchases of merchandise on account are recognized when made by a debit to *Purchases* (in a periodic system) and a credit to *Accounts Payable*. Under the cash basis, purchases are not recognized until cash is paid. Thus, to convert from accrual basis cost of goods sold to cash basis purchases, adjustments must be made for the changes during the year in inventory and in accounts payable, as follows.

$$\left.\begin{array}{l} \text{Accrual basis} \\ \text{cost of goods sold} \end{array}\right\} \left\{\begin{array}{l} - \text{ Beginning inventory} \\ + \text{ Ending inventory} \end{array}\right\} = \begin{array}{l} \text{Accrual basis} \\ \text{purchases} \end{array}$$

$$\left.\begin{array}{l} \text{Accrual basis} \\ \text{purchases} \end{array}\right\} \left\{\begin{array}{l} + \text{ Beginning accounts payable} \\ - \text{ Ending accounts payable} \end{array}\right\} = \begin{array}{l} \text{Cash paid} \\ \text{for purchases} \end{array}$$

Clark Corporation's comparative balance sheets (Figure 19–5) show that on 12/31/86 and 12/31/87: (1) inventory balances were $322,000 and $314,000, respectively; and (2) accounts payable balances were $269,000 and $238,000, respectively. Thus, cash paid for merchandise purchased during 1987 can be computed as follows.

Accrual basis cost of goods sold (Figure 19–5)	$2,440,000
Less: Beginning inventory	322,000
Total	2,118,000
Add: Ending inventory	314,000
Accrual basis purchases for the year	2,432,000
Add: Beginning accounts payable	269,000
Total possible cash payments for purchases	2,701,000
Less: Ending accounts payable	238,000
Cash paid for purchases during the year	$2,463,000

   The amount of purchases made during the year is computed first, by deducting the beginning inventory balance from accrual basis cost of goods sold and adding the ending inventory balance to accrual basis cost of goods sold. After the amount of purchases for the year is determined, the amount of cash paid for purchases can be computed. This is done by adding beginning accounts payable (goods purchased last year are paid for during the current year) and deducting ending accounts payable (goods purchased this year that have not yet been paid for).

Cash Payments for Expenses

Under accrual accounting, expenses are recognized when resources are used to earn revenues. Some expenses are prepaid, some are paid during the current period as incurred, and some are accrued at the end of the period. Under the cash basis, expenses are recognized when they are paid for. The relationship between expenses and cash payments depends upon the changes in prepaid expenses and accrued expenses. Thus, the conversion of accrual basis expenses to cash basis expenses may be made as follows.

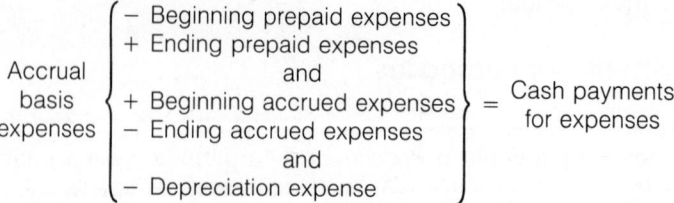

Clark Corporation's comparative balance sheets show that on 12/31/86 and 12/31/87: (1) prepaid expenses were $14,000 and $36,000, respectively; and (2) accrued expenses were $66,000 and $83,000, respectively. Consequently, cash paid for operating expenses, including income tax expense was:

Accrual basis expenses including income taxes	
($1,838,000 + $160,000) (Figure 19–5)	$1,998,000
Less: Beginning prepaid expenses	14,000
Balance	1,984,000
Add: Ending prepaid expenses	36,000
Total	2,020,000
Add: Beginning accrued expenses	66,000
Total	2,086,000
Less: Ending accrued expenses	83,000
Balance	2,003,000
Less: Depreciation expense	68,000
Cash paid for expenses	$1,935,000

Beginning prepaid expenses are deducted from accrual basis expenses to remove expenses that were paid for in prior years. Ending prepaid expenses are then added, to show expenses paid for this year that will not be charged to expenses until later years.

Beginning accrued expenses are added, since they were paid for this year, even though they were added to expenses last year. Ending accrued expenses are then deducted, because they were charged to expenses this year but will not be paid for until next year.

Depreciation (as well as amortization and depletion) does not use cash during the current period. Thus, depreciation expense also must be deducted in converting accrual basis expenses to cash basis expenses.

Using the cash basis information determined in the preceding paragraphs, we can compute the amount of cash provided by operations, as shown in Figure 19–8.

A summary of the computation of cash provided by operations is presented in Figure 19–9.

PREPARING THE CASH BASIS SCFP

The cash provided by operations, computed in Figure 19–8, does not explain the full story of cash flows during the year. Sources (uses) of cash from the nonoperating financing and investing activities of the company must be added

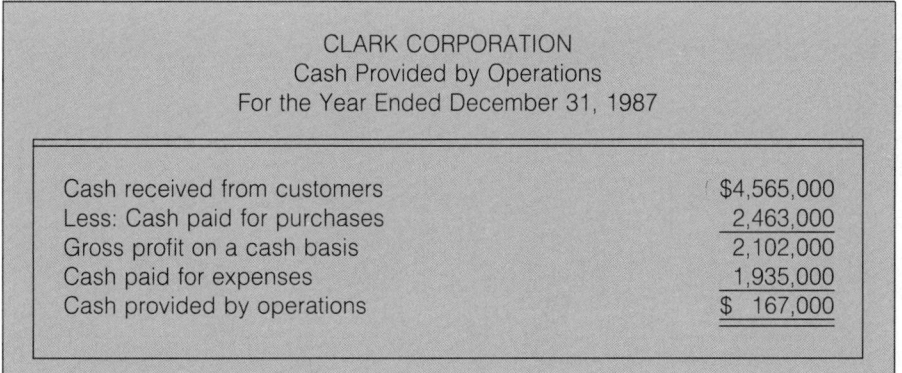

Figure 19–8
Cash Provided by
Operations

(or deducted) to explain fully the $26,000 increase in cash during the year, as shown in Figure 19–10.

Note that the other (nonoperating) sources and uses of cash are the same as those shown in the statement of changes in financial position prepared on a working capital basis in Figure 19–7. Note, also, that the gain on sale of investments reported in the income statement (Figure 19–5) is not reported separately. Rather, the full $160,000 cash received from the sale of long-term investments is included as a separate, other source of cash.

The sources and uses of cash, other than those provided by operations, are relatively self-explanatory. Cash was obtained from the issue of bonds payable and from the issue of common stock. Cash was used to acquire a building addition, to purchase equipment, and to pay dividends. In addition, as mentioned earlier, the exchange of the long-term note for equipment is reported

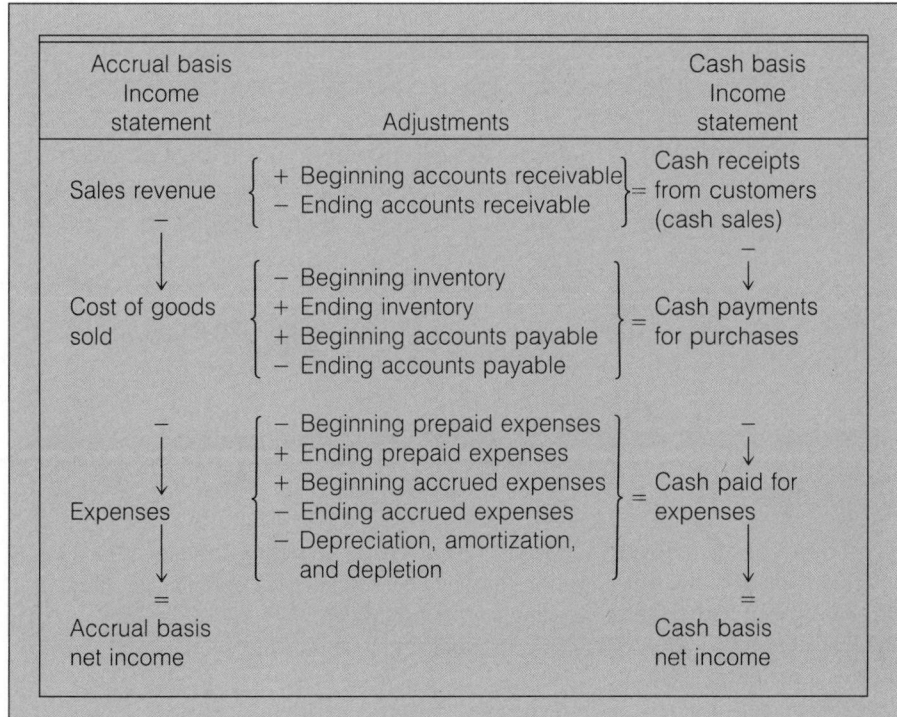

Figure 19–9
Summary Computation of Cash Provided by Operations

Figure 19–10
Cash Flow State-
ment

<table>
<tr><td colspan="3" align="center">CLARK CORPORATION
Cash Flow Statement
For the Year Ended December 31, 1987</td></tr>
<tr><td>Sources of Cash</td><td></td><td></td></tr>
<tr><td> Cash provided by operations (Figure 19-8)</td><td></td><td>$167,000</td></tr>
<tr><td> Other sources:</td><td></td><td></td></tr>
<tr><td>   Issue of long-term notes payable</td><td>$100,000</td><td></td></tr>
<tr><td>   Sale of long-term investment</td><td>160,000</td><td></td></tr>
<tr><td>   Issue of bonds payable</td><td>100,000</td><td></td></tr>
<tr><td>   Issue of common stock</td><td>173,000</td><td>533,000</td></tr>
<tr><td>   Total sources of cash</td><td></td><td>700,000</td></tr>
<tr><td>Uses of Cash</td><td></td><td></td></tr>
<tr><td> Building addition</td><td>400,000</td><td></td></tr>
<tr><td> Purchase of equipment</td><td>158,000</td><td></td></tr>
<tr><td> Cash dividends</td><td>116,000</td><td></td></tr>
<tr><td>   Total uses of cash</td><td></td><td>674,000</td></tr>
<tr><td>Increase in cash</td><td></td><td>26,000</td></tr>
<tr><td>Cash balance, January 1</td><td></td><td>162,000</td></tr>
<tr><td>Cash balance, December 31</td><td></td><td>$188,000</td></tr>
</table>

both as a source of cash from the issue of long-term notes payable and as a use of cash for the purchase of equipment.

Cash Basis SCFP—A Shortcut Approach

In practice, the cash basis statement of changes in financial position is often presented in a different format. Rather than computing separate cash amounts for receipts from customers, payments for purchases, and payments for expenses, the statement begins with reported (accrual basis) net income. To derive cash provided by operations, the net income figure is then adjusted for items that affected net income but that did not require or provide cash during the period. Other sources and uses of cash are then included in a manner similar to that used in preparing a statement of changes in financial position on a working capital basis.

To illustrate, the alternate form of cash basis statement of changes in financial position for Clark Corporation is shown in Figure 19–11.

GLOSSARY

ALL FINANCIAL RESOURCES APPROACH. A reporting format for the statement of changes in financial position that includes exchanges of noncurrent items as both a source of and a use of working capital or cash (p. 745).
CASH FLOW STATEMENT. A statement that reports the sources and uses of cash for a period (p. 754).
FUNDS. When used in the statement of changes in financial position, funds are

Figure 19–11
Cash Basis Statement of Changes in Financial Position

CLARK CORPORATION
Statement of Changes in Financial Position
For the Year Ended December 31, 1987

Sources of Cash:		
Cash provided by operations:		
Net income from the income statement		$242,000
Add: Decrease in inventory	$ 8,000	
Increase in accrued expenses	17,000	
Depreciation expense	68,000	93,000
Deduct: Increase in accounts receivable	55,000	
Increase in prepaid expenses	22,000	
Decrease in accounts payable	31,000	
Gain on sale of investments	60,000	(168,000)
Cash provided by operations		167,000
Other cash sources:		
Issue of long-term notes payable	100,000	
Sale of long-term investment	160,000	
Issue of bonds payable	100,000	
Issue of common stock	173,000	533,000
Total sources of cash		700,000
Uses of cash:		
Building addition	400,000	
Purchase of equipment	158,000	
Cash dividends	116,000	
Total uses of cash		674,000
Increase in cash		26,000
Cash balance, January 1		162,000
Cash balance, December 31		$188,000

defined as working capital, cash, or cash and readily marketable securities (p. 737).
SOURCE OF FUNDS. A transaction that increases working capital or cash (p. 739).
USE OF FUNDS. A transaction that decreases working capital or cash (p. 739).
WORKING CAPITAL. The excess of current assets over current liabilities (p. 737).

DISCUSSION QUESTIONS

1. What are the primary concepts of "funds" that may be used in the preparation of a SCFP?
2. What are the primary sources and uses of working capital?
3. Why are expenses such as depreciation and depletion added back to net income in determining working capital provided by operations? List some other items that would require adjustments to net income.

4. What is the effect on working capital of each of the following transactions? (Consider each item individually.)
   (a) The collection of a $6,000 account receivable.
   (b) The issue of a $1,000 par value bond payable at a premium of $20.
   (c) The purchase of equipment in exchange for a 90-day note payable amounting to $15,000.
   (d) The purchase of $5,000 of merchandise inventory on credit.
   (e) The exchange of a 120-day, $1,000, 10% note payable in settlement of an account payable.
   (f) The exchange of 2,000 shares of common stock with a market value of $20 per share for machinery.
   (g) The sale for $16,000 of temporary marketable securities with a cost of $12,000.

5. If long-term investments with a cost of $25,000 are sold for $35,000, what will be the effect on working capital? What will be the effect on cash?

6. Is depreciation a source of working capital? Why or why not?

7. What effect would the issue of a stock dividend have on working capital? How would the issue affect cash flow?

8. A company reported a net loss of $40,000 on its income statement and a $20,000 source of working capital from operations on its SCFP. Explain how this could happen.

9. What effect would the amortization of $500 of discount on bonds payable have on working capital? How should the $500 be treated on a SCFP?

10. During the year, the holders of $100,000 of convertible bonds payable converted their bonds into 30,000 shares of $5 par value common stock. What effect would the conversion have on working capital? Do you think the conversion should be reported on the SCFP? If so, how?

11. Explain how accrual basis net sales can be adjusted to show the amount of cash received from customers.

12. Total cost of goods sold for a company during the year under accrual accounting amounted to $80,000. If inventory decreased by $6,000 and accounts payable decreased by $12,000 during the year, how much cash was paid for purchases?

13. Accrual basis operating expenses for a company, other than depreciation, amounted to $62,000 for the year. If prepaid expenses increased by $8,000 and accrued expenses decreased by $6,000 during the year, how much cash was paid for operating expenses during the year?

14. Zee Company's fiscal year ends on June 30. The board of directors declared a cash dividend on June 20 of the current year, payable on July 15 to stockholders of record on June 30. What effect would this declaration have on a SCFP prepared on a working-capital basis for the current year? What would be the effect on a cash basis SCFP for the current year? What would be the effect on working capital and cash flow in the following year, when the dividend was paid?

EXERCISES

Exercise 19-1 Effects of Transactions on Working Capital

Given here is a list of transactions of Lore Company during 1987. For each transaction, indicate whether it resulted in a source or use of working capital and the amount, if any. Use the letter S for source, U for use, and N for neither a source nor a use.

Transaction	Effect on Working Capital	Amount
1. Collected $84,000 of accounts receivable.	N	$ ____
2. Sold a machine with a book value of $3,000 for $4,800 cash.	S	4800
3. Borrowed $20,000 from a bank, giving a note payable on July 5, 1990.	S	20,000
4. Paid $15,000 in settlement of accounts payable.	N	____
5. Issued 2,000 shares of $10 par value common stock at $20 per share.	S	40000
6. Purchased a machine for $8,000, giving $4,000 cash and promising to pay the balance in 60 days.	U	8000
7. Recorded depreciation expense on equipment, $8,000.	N	____
8. Issued a $20,000 long-term note payable in settlement of a $20,000 short-term note payable.	S	____
9. Issued 50 $1,000 par value bonds payable at 90%.	S	45000
10. Purchased treasury stock, $76,000.	U	76000
11. Purchased land, giving a $60,000 note, payable in 1990, in exchange.	N	____
12. Declared a cash dividend of $18,000.	U	____
13. Settled an account payable of $16,000 by giving the creditor 500 shares of unissued common stock.	S	____
14. Sold a temporary investment with a cost of $7,000 for $10,000 cash. *non-current*	S	3000
15. Declared and distributed a 10% stock dividend on 100,000 shares of outstanding common stock when the market price of the stock was $6 per share.	N	____
16. Issued 1,000 shares of $10 par value common stock with a market price of $25 per share in exchange for land.	SU	____
17. Wrote off a $500 uncollectible account receivable against the *Allowance for Uncollectible Accounts*.	N.	____
18. Reissued one-half of the treasury stock acquired in (10) for $50,000.	S	50000

All financial resources concept

Dividend Decl.
Dividend Pay

Payed-Cash Dividend
No effect

Exercise 19-2 **Effects of Transactions on Cash**

For each transaction in Exercise 19-1, indicate whether it resulted in a source or a use of cash and the amount, if any. Use the letter S for source, U for use, and N for neither a source nor a use.

Exercise 19-3 **Determining Working Capital Provided by Operations**

The following income statement was prepared for Stayman Company at the end of 1987.

STAYMAN COMPANY
Income Statement
For the Year Ended December 31, 1987

Sales		$3,465,000
Cost of goods sold		1,800,000
Gross profit		1,665,000
Operating expenses:		
Distribution expense	$450,000	
Salaries and wages expense	650,000	
Depreciation expense	145,000	
Rent expense	45,000	
Patent amortization expense	13,250	
Bad debts expense	5,100	1,308,350
Operating income		356,650
Gain on sale of investments		5,000
Net income before income tax		361,650
Income tax expense		137,500
Net Income		$ 224,150

Required:

Determine the amount of working capital provided by current operating activities for the year.

Exercise 19-4 Changes in Components of Working Capital

The current sections of Mayvell Company's balance sheets at December 31, 1986 and 1987, were as follows.

	1987	1986
Current Assets:		
Cash	$ 72,000	$ 46,500
Accounts receivable (net)	94,000	110,000
Inventory	241,000	200,000
Prepaid expenses	31,000	35,200
Total Current Assets	$438,000	$391,700
Current Liabilities:		
Notes payable	$ 70,000	$ 40,000
Accounts payable	52,000	83,000
Accrued expenses payable	64,000	50,000
Total Current Liabilities	$186,000	$173,000

Required:

Prepare a schedule showing the net change in each component of working capital during 1987.

Exercise 19-5 Working Capital and Cash Provided by Operations

The following information was taken from the comparative financial statements of Clyde Company, which were prepared on an accrual basis.

	1987	1986
Net sales	$392,000	$360,000
Cost of goods sold	164,000	142,000
Operating expenses (including depreciation expense of $28,000 each year)	148,000	140,000
Net income	80,000	78,000
Year-end accounts receivable (net)	74,000	68,000
Year-end inventory	52,000	60,000
Year-end accounts payable	34,000	32,000
Year-end wages payable	10,000	16,000

Required:
A. Prepare a schedule to show the amount of working capital provided by operations during 1987.
B. Prepare a schedule to show the amount of cash provided by operations during 1987.

Exercise 19-6 Conversion from Accrual Basis to Cash Basis
The following information was taken from the general ledger accounts of Bayton Company, which uses the accrual basis of accounting.

	Year-end	
	1987	1986
Accounts receivable	$ 46,700	$31,800
Inventory	39,000	42,100
Prepaid insurance	1,800	2,200
Accounts payable for merchandise purchased	28,600	30,400
Wages payable	2,600	3,800
Sales	105,600	
Cost of goods sold	58,900	
Operating expenses (including $19,000 depreciation expense)	35,400	

Required:
Compute

A. The amount of cash collected from customers during 1987.
B. The amount of cash paid for merchandise purchased during 1987.
C. The amount of cash paid for operating expenses during 1987.

Exercise 19-7 Preparing a SCFP Without a Worksheet
Comparative balance sheet information for 1987 and 1986 and income statement data for 1987 for Leeber Company are presented here.

	1987	1986
Cash	$ 18,600	$ 22,400
Accounts receivable	26,900	25,200
Inventory	32,700	34,800
Plant assets	68,000	50,000
Accumulated depreciation—plant assets	(30,000)	(27,000)
Total Assets	$116,200	$105,400
Accounts payable	$ 23,400	$ 22,100
Accrued expenses	12,900	13,900
Long-term note payable	10,000	-0-
Common stock	20,000	20,000
Retained earnings	49,900	49,400
Total Liabilities and Owners' Equity	$116,200	$105,400
Sales	$ 98,700	
Cost of goods sold	56,600	
Gross profit on sales	42,100	
Operating expenses including depreciation	36,600	
Net income	$ 5,500	

Plant assets were purchased during the year, but none were sold. Dividends were declared and paid during November of 1987.

Required:

A. Compute the increase or decrease in working capital during 1987.

B. Prepare a working capital basis statement of changes in financial position. (Because this is a relatively easy exercise, a worksheet should not be necessary.)

PROBLEMS

Problem 19-1 Preparing a SCFP Without a Worksheet

The following data were taken from the financial statements of Bauer Company.

	December 31	
	1987	1986
Current assets	$ 84,500	$167,000
Building	115,000	115,000
Less: Accumulated depreciation	(45,000)	(40,000)
Equipment (Fixed Assets)	44,000	38,000
Less: Accumulated depreciation	(14,000)	(11,000)
Long-term investments	10,000	20,000
Current liabilities	44,500	38,000
Common stock	87,500	75,000
Retained earnings	62,500	76,000

No equipment was sold during the year. Cash dividends declared and paid during the year amounted to $33,500. Net income for 1987 was $20,000. Long-term investments were sold at a gain of $2,000.

Required:
Prepare a statement of changes in financial position for 1987 on a working-capital basis. A worksheet should not be necessary.

Problem 19-2 Worksheet for Working Capital Basis SCFP

Snyder Company had balance sheet data at the end of December, 1986 and 1987, as follows.

Assets	1987	1986
Cash	$ 90,800	$ 40,320
Accounts receivable (net)	71,200	79,800
Inventory	312,000	268,000
Prepaid expenses	32,000	10,000
Equipment	356,000	232,000
Accumulated depreciation—equipment	(67,200)	(40,320)
Total Assets	$794,800	$589,800
Liabilities and Owners' Equity		
Notes payable	$ 21,200	$ 12,800
Accounts payable	117,120	110,000
Accrued expenses	10,400	12,800
Long-term notes payable	56,000	80,000
Common stock, $5 par value	280,000	220,000
Paid-in capital in excess of par value	140,000	20,000
Retained earnings	170,080	134,200
Total Liabilities and Owners' Equity	$794,800	$589,800

An inspection of the firm's 1987 income statement and general ledger accounts revealed the following.

1. Net income for the year was $91,880.
2. Depreciation expense was recorded in the amount of $30,880, and a fully depreciated machine with a cost of $4,000 was discarded and its cost and accumulated depreciation removed from the accounts.
3. New equipment was purchased during the year at a cost of $128,000.
4. A long-term note payable of $24,000 was paid off.
5. Twelve thousand shares of common stock were issued during the year at an issue price of $15 per share.
6. Cash dividends of $1 per share were declared and paid on outstanding shares, including those issued during the year.

Required:
A. Prepare a worksheet for a statement of changes in financial position on a working capital basis.
B. Prepare a formal statement of changes in financial position, including a schedule of changes in the components of working capital.

Problem 19-3 Cash Flow Statement

Using the data presented in Problem 19-2, plus the additional income statement detail given here, prepare a cash flow statement for Snyder Company for the year ended December 31, 1987.

Income Statement Detail	
Net sales	$836,800
Cost of goods sold	543,200
Operating expenses other than depreciation	170,840

Problem 19-4 Preparing a SCFP Without a Worksheet

Drill Company had the following condensed balance sheet at the end of 1986.

DRILL COMPANY
Balance Sheet
December 31, 1986

Current assets	$112,500	Current liabilities	$ 45,000
Long-term investments	60,000	Long-term notes	
Plant and equipment (net)	202,500	payable	76,500
Land	120,000	Bonds payable	75,000
		Common stock	225,000
		Retained earnings	73,500
	$495,000		$495,000

During 1987, the following events occurred.

1. Net income for 1987 was $63,000 after deducting depreciation of $27,000.
2. Bonds payable in the amount of $15,000 were retired at par.
3. Dividends totaling $22,500 were declared and paid.
4. Land was purchased at a cost of $18,000 cash.
5. Additional common stock of $30,000 was issued at par.
6. Land was purchased by exchanging $54,000 in bonds payable.
7. Long-term investments that cost $30,000 were sold for $30,900.

Required:

A. Prepare a working capital basis statement of changes in financial position for 1987.

B. Prepare a condensed balance sheet for Drill Company as it would appear on December 31, 1987. Assume that current liabilities remained at $45,000.

Problem 19-5 Worksheet for Working Capital Basis SCFP

Comparative balance sheet data for Dickerson Company on June 30, 1986 and 1987, follow.

	June 30	
	1987	1986
Current Assets:		
Cash	$ 210,000	$ 245,200
Accounts receivable (net)	130,700	111,300
Inventory	275,000	221,200
Prepaid expenses	22,800	23,000
Total current assets	638,500	600,700
Plant and Equipment:		
Buildings	639,000	339,000
Accumulated depreciation—buildings	(111,400)	(97,600)
Equipment	361,200	331,200
Accumulated depreciation—equipment	(89,900)	(67,000)
Land	168,000	39,000
Total plant and equipment	966,900	544,600
Long-term investments	70,000	160,000
Total Assets	$1,675,400	$1,305,300
Current Liabilities:		
Notes payable	$ 45,000	$ 50,000
Accounts payable	170,000	168,000
Accrued expenses	10,500	14,000
Total current liabilities	225,500	232,000
Long-term Liabilities:		
Notes payable, due 3/30/90	305,000	272,600
Bonds payable, due 9/1/96	300,000	200,000
Total long-term liabilities	605,000	472,600
Stockholders' Equity:		
Common stock, $10 par	230,000	200,000
Paid-in capital in excess of par value	272,100	188,100
Retained earnings	342,800	212,600
Total stockholders' equity	844,900	600,700
Total Liabilities and Stockholders' Equity	$1,675,400	$1,305,300

Examination of the company's income statement and general ledger accounts disclosed the following.

1. Net income for the year was $199,200.
2. Depreciation expense of $13,800 was recorded during the year on buildings, and depreciation of $22,900 on equipment.
3. A new wing was added to the building at a cost of $300,000 cash.
4. Long-term investments with a cost of $90,000 were sold for $125,000.
5. A vacant lot next to the company's plant was purchased for $129,000, with payment consisting of $96,600 cash and a note payable for $32,400, due on June 30, 1990.
6. Bonds payable of $100,000 were issued for cash at par.
7. Three thousand shares of common stock were issued at $38 per share.
8. Equipment was purchased for $30,000 cash.
9. Cash dividends of $69,000 were declared and paid.

Required:

A. Prepare a worksheet for a statement of changes in financial position (working-capital basis).

B. Prepare a formal statement of changes in financial position. A schedule of changes in the components of working capital is not necessary.

Problem 19-6 Cash Flow Statement

Using the data provided in Problem 19-5 and the income statement detail given here, prepare a cash flow statement for Dickerson Company for the year ended June 30, 1987.

Income Statement Detail	
Net sales	$875,600
Cost of goods sold	525,300
Operating expenses other than depreciation	149,400

ALTERNATE PROBLEMS

Problem 19-1A Effects of Transactions on Working Capital and Cash

A list of business transactions and adjustments is given here.

A. Declared a cash dividend.

B. Recorded depreciation expense for the period.

C. Paid an account payable.

D. Sold a plant asset at a loss.

E. Paid a cash dividend previously declared.

F. Paid the income tax liability that was accrued at the end of last year.

G. Purchased equipment, giving a 90-day note payable.

H. Sold a temporary investment at a gain.

I. Wrote off an account receivable against the *Allowance for Uncollectible Accounts*.

J. Issued common stock in exchange for convertible bonds, which were converted by the bondholders.

K. Recorded amortization expense on patents.

L. Exchanged 30,000 shares of authorized common stock for a building.

M. Paid in advance for a one-year insurance policy.

Required:

For each item in the list, indicate the effect (increase, decrease, or no effect on both working capital and cash. Use the following format.

Item	Working Capital	Cash
A.	Decrease	No effect

Problem 19-2A Preparing a SCFP Without a Worksheet

Maris Company's financial statements contained the following information.

	September 30	
	1987	1986
Current assets	$248,000	$167,000
Building	271,000	271,000
Less: Accumulated depreciation	(129,000)	(118,000)
Machinery	200,000	98,000
Less: Accumulated depreciation	(41,000)	(32,000)
Long-term investments	23,000	47,000
Current liabilities	115,000	102,000
Common stock	340,000	200,000
Retained earnings	117,000	131,000

No machinery was sold during the year. Cash dividends declared and paid during the year amounted to $12,000. A net operating loss of $2,000 was incurred during the year. Long-term investments were sold at a loss of $6,000.

Required:
Prepare a statement of changes in financial position for the year ended September 30, 1987, using a working capital basis. A worksheet is not necessary.

Problem 19-3A Worksheet for Working Capital Basis SCFP

Comparative balance sheet data for Flair Company as of June 30, 1987 and 1986 are as follows.

	1987	1986
Cash	$ 99,200	$112,600
Accounts receivable (net)	116,400	121,900
Inventory	93,300	58,400
Prepaid expenses	18,600	17,100
Long-term investments in stock	45,000	76,500
Plant assets	399,400	281,300
Less: Accumulated depreciation	(112,200)	(96,700)
Total Assets	$659,700	$571,100
Accounts payable	$ 98,400	$ 72,700
Accrued expenses	18,900	21,600
Long-term notes payable	40,000	60,000
Common stock, $10 par value	300,000	250,000
Paid-in capital in excess of par value	100,000	90,000
Retained earnings	102,400	76,800
Total Liabilities and Stockholders' Equity	$659,700	$571,100

Reference to Flair Company's income statement and general ledger accounts showed the following.

1. The income statement reported net income of $43,600.
2. Plant assets were purchased for cash during the year. No plant assets were sold.
3. Part of the long-term investment in stock was sold at a $7,500 loss.

4. Five thousand shares of common stock were issued during the year for $12 per share.

5. Cash dividends of $.60 per share were declared and paid on outstanding shares, including those issued during the year.

6. Long-term notes payable became due and were paid during the year.

Required:

A. Prepare a worksheet for a working capital basis statement of changes in financial position.

B. Prepare a formal statement of changes in financial position, including a schedule of changes in the components of working capital.

Problem 19-4A Cash Flow Statement

Using the data provided in Problem 19-3A, plus the additional income statement detail given here, prepare a cash flow statement for Flair Company for the year ended June 30, 1987.

Income Statement Detail

Net sales	$862,600
Cost of goods sold	529,400
Operating expenses, including depreciation expense	282,100

Problem 19-5A Preparing a SCFP Without a Worksheet

Borro Company had the following condensed balance sheet at the end of 1986.

BORRO COMPANY
Balance Sheet
December 31, 1986

Current assets	$119,400	Current liabilities	$ 64,350
Long-term investment	71,250	Long-term notes payable	75,000
Plant assets (net)	245,850	Bonds payable	150,000
Land	112,500	Common stock	225,000
Patents	66,900	Retained earnings	101,550
	$615,900		$615,900

The following events occurred during 1987.

1. Net income of $27,600 was reported in 1987 after deducting depreciation expense of $42,000 and amortization expense on patents of $6,000.

2. Bonds payable in the amount of $30,000 were issued at par.

3. Land valued at $37,500 was purchased by exchanging 1,500 shares of $25 par value common stock.

4. Dividends totaling $24,000 were declared and paid.

5. Long-term investments, which cost $39,000, were sold for $43,500.

6. Plant assets were purchased for cash, $54,000.

Required:

A. Prepare a working capital basis statement of changes in financial position for 1987.

B. Prepare a condensed balance sheet for Borro Company, as it would appear on December 31, 1987. Assume current liabilities remained at $64,350.

Problem 19-6A Worksheet for Working Capital Basis SCFP

Balance sheets for Zenno Company on December 31, 1987 and 1986, contained the following items.

	1987	1986
Assets		
Cash	$ 28,200	$ 44,600
Accounts receivable, net	37,400	31,200
Inventory	100,400	102,800
Prepaid expenses	2,600	2,200
Long-term investments	-0-	30,000
Equipment	60,800	57,000
Accumulated depreciation—equipment	(13,200)	(9,800)
Building	200,000	-0-
Accumulated depreciation—building	(2,400)	-0-
Land	40,000	-0-
Total Assets	$453,800	$258,000
Liabilities and Owners' Equity		
Accounts payable	$ 40,600	$ 43,400
Income taxes payable	2,800	2,200
Mortgage payable	130,000	-0-
Common stock, $5 par	200,000	160,000
Additional paid-in capital	10,000	2,000
Retained earnings	70,400	50,400
Total Liabilities and Stockholders' Equity	$453,800	$258,000

Zenno Company's 1987 income statement and general ledger accounts showed the following.

1. Net income earned during the year, $34,000.
2. Equipment was purchased during the year at a cost of $5,000.
3. Equipment with a cost of $1,000 and accumulated depreciation of $600 was traded for new equipment with a list price of $1,600. A trade-in allowance of $600 was received.
4. Fully depreciated equipment, which cost $1,600, was discarded during the year and written off in the accounts.
5. Long-term investments were sold during the year for an amount equal to their cost.
6. Zenno Company purchased the building and land it had been previously renting for a total of $240,000; $110,000 was paid in cash and a mortgage was given for the balance.
7. Depreciation expense for the year was $5,600 for equipment and $2,400 for the building.
8. Eight thousand shares of common stock were issued during the year for cash of $6 per share.
9. Cash dividends of $14,000 were declared and paid during the year.

Required:

A. Prepare a worksheet for a statement of changes in financial position on a working capital basis.

B. Prepare a formal statement of changes in financial position, including a schedule of changes in the components of working capital.

Problem 19-7A Cash Flow Statement

Using the data provided in Problem 19-6A, plus the additional income statement detail provided here, prepare a cash flow statement for Zenno Company for the year ended December 31, 1987.

Income Statement Detail	
Net sales	$537,600
Cost of goods sold	361,200
Operating expenses including depreciation expense	142,400

CASE

CASE 19-1 Financial Report Analysis Case Funds Analysis

Refer to the financial statements of Kmart Corporation for the year ended January 30, 1985 in Appendix A and answer the following questions:

A. What concept of funds is used in the Statement of Changes in Financial Position?
B. What was the amount of funds provided by (used for) operations during the year?
C. What was the increase (decrease) in funds for the year?
D. What was the amount of funds used for additions to owned and leased property during the year?
E. What was the amount of funds provided by the issue of common stock during the year?
F. How much working capital did Kmart have on January 30, 1985? on January 25, 1984?
G. What were the two primary sources of funds?

20

ANALYSIS OF FINANCIAL STATEMENTS

CHAPTER OVERVIEW AND OBJECTIVES

This chapter describes some of the techniques used to analyze a firm's financial statements. When the chapter is completed, you should understand:

1: The objectives of financial statement analysis.
2. How to perform horizontal analysis, trend analysis, and vertical analysis.
3. How to compute and use ratios to analyze a firm's profitability, liquidity, and solvency.
4. The limitations of financial statement analysis.

A firm's financial statements are used by various parties to evaluate the firm's financial performance. The preceding chapter demonstrated how the statement of changes in financial position could be used to supplement the balance sheet and income statement in analyzing a firm's financing and investing activities. This chapter focuses on the basic techniques commonly employed to analyze a firm's balance sheet and income statement. These statements are emphasized because they are the primary source of financial data for most outside parties.

SOURCES OF FINANCIAL INFORMATION

The firm's financial statements contained in the annual report are the end products of the accounting process. To report on the progress of a firm during the year, most publicly held firms also issue interim reports each quarter. (Recall that an interim report covers a period of less than 12 months.) Interim reports focus primarily on the income statement and contain summary data, rather than a full set of financial statements. Still, they provide additional information for evaluating the profitability and financial position of the firm's operations. Unlike the annual report, however, interim reports are unaudited reports. Annual and interim reports, with their accompanying schedules and explanatory notes, are one of the primary means by which management communicates information about the firm to interested outside parties.

A wealth of information is also available from other sources, however. Probably the most detailed information available on publicly held companies is contained in the reports that must be filed with the Securities and Exchange Commission (SEC). Financial advisory services, such as Moody's Investors Service and Standard and Poor's Corporation, also publish financial data for both publicly and privately owned companies. These are normally not as detailed as the SEC reports or the company reports. The advantage of advisory service reports is their accessibility, as they are available at most public and university libraries.

A comparison of the company under study with firms in a similar line of business and with industry norms is also useful. Industry data are available from a number of financial services. For example, Robert Morris Associates' *Annual Statement Studies* provides income statement and balance sheet data and 16 financial ratios for many industries. Dun & Bradstreet publishes an *Industry Norms and Key Business Ratios* book, which contains typical balance sheets and income statements, and 14 selected financial ratios for over 800 different lines of business. The 14 ratios for the most recent year, by industry groups, are also published in a *Key Business Ratios* book by Dun & Bradstreet. Individual company and industry analyses are also available from stock brokerage firms. An abundance of useful information is available in various economic and financial newspapers and magazines, such as the *Wall Street Journal, Forbes, Fortune, Business Week,* and *Barron's.*

In making comparisons with other companies, an analyst must recognize that the company under review may not be similar to other companies because of diversification into other product lines. Also, because of diversification, industry data may not clearly resemble the company under study. In such cases, the analyst attempts to identify the industry that the company best fits, and uses that industry's data and companies in that industry group for comparison.

THE NEED FOR ANALYTICAL TECHNIQUES

Information contained in the various sources of financial data is expressed primarily in monetary terms. When the absolute dollar amounts for most items reported in the financial statements are considered individually, they are generally of limited usefulness. Significant relationships may not be apparent from a review of absolute dollar amounts, because no indication is given of whether a particular item is good or bad for a firm. For example, merely knowing that a company reported earnings of $100,000 for the current year is of limited use unless the amount is compared to other information, such as last year's earnings, the current year's sales, the earnings of other companies in the same business, or some predetermined standard established by the statement user.

To simplify the identification of significant changes and relationships, the dollar amounts reported in the financial statements are frequently converted into percentages or ratios by the statement user. Some commonly recognized percentages are sometimes shown in supplementary schedules to the financial statements, as part of the firm's annual report. The analysis of relationships between the dollar amount of each item to some base amount is referred to as *horizontal analysis* and *vertical analysis*. *Ratio analysis* is the interpretation of the relationship between two items, such as current assets to current liabilities.

OBJECTIVES OF FINANCIAL STATEMENT ANALYSIS

Percentage analysis and ratio analysis have been developed to provide an efficient means by which a statement user can identify: (1) important relationships between items in the same statements; and (2) trends in financial data. Percentages and ratios simplify the evaluation of financial conditions and past operating performances.

Objective 1: Objectives of statement analysis

The information is used primarily to forecast a firm's ability to pay its debts when due and to operate at a satisfactory profit level. However, because the analytical techniques are almost limitless—and so are the users' special interests and objectives—the choice of proper ratios and percentages must fit their purpose. For example, some users of financial data are concerned with evaluating the firm's ability to produce enough cash to pay its short-term debts when they mature and still have sufficient cash left to carry out its other activities (i.e., the firm's *liquidity*). The focus of this type of investigation is generally on the firm's current assets and current liabilities.

Other users, such as long-term creditors and stockholders, are also concerned with the firm's liquidity but, in addition, are interested in a firm's ability to pay its long-term obligations. This aspect of the analysis is concerned with the **solvency** of the firm. In a solvency analysis, the statement user assesses the financial structure of the firm and its prospects for operating at an earnings level adequate to provide sufficient cash for the payment of interest, dividends, and debt principal.

To serve as a basis for the discussion of percentage and ratio analysis, balance sheets and income statements for the Gordon Corporation, during a two-year period (1988 and 1987), are presented in the first two columns of Figures 20–1 and 20–2. In order to show the computations of ratios for two periods, a December 31, 1986 balance sheet is also included in Figure 20–1. The statements in Figures 20–1 and 20–2 are not in a format as they would appear in an annual report. For example, the Change During the Year and the Common Size Statement columns are not part of the annual report presentation. These computations must be made by the analyst, as discussed later in this chapter.

It cannot be emphasized too strongly that, for the statement analysis of an individual company to be useful, the relationships must be compared to other data or standards. Comparisons of the company under study may be made to industry averages, to the past performance of the company, and to the per-

GORDON CORPORATION
Comparative Balance Sheets
December 31, 1988, 1987, and 1986
(000's omitted)

	Year Ended December 31			Change During the Year 1987–1988*		Common Size* Statements	
	1988	1987	1986	Dollar Amount	Percent	1988	1987
Assets							
Current assets:							
Cash	$ 390	$ 300	$ 290	$ 90	30.0	5.2	4.7
Marketable securities	380	440	460	(60)	(13.7)	5.1	7.0
Accounts receivable (net)	1,460	1,290	1,320	170	13.2	19.6	20.5
Inventory	2,010	1,770	1,860	240	13.6	27.1	28.1
Prepaid expenses	100	100	100	-0-	-0-	1.3	1.6
Total current assets	4,340	3,900	4,030	440	11.3	58.3	61.9
Long-term investments	400	500	500	(100)	(20.0)	5.4	7.9
Plant and equipment	2,600	1,800	1,770	800	44.4	35.0	28.6
Other assets	100	100	100	-0-	-0-	1.3	1.6
Total assets	$7,440	$6,300	$6,400	$1,140	18.1	100.0	100.0
Liabilities							
Current liabilities:							
Notes payable	$ 620	$ 600	$ 750	$ 20	3.3	8.4	9.5
Accounts payable	1,040	900	1,050	140	15.6	14.0	14.3
Accrued expenses	100	100	100	-0-	-0-	1.3	1.6
Total current liabilities	1,760	1,600	1,900	160	10.0	23.7	25.4
Long-term liabilities—11%	1,900	1,700	1,800	200	11.8	25.5	27.0
Total liabilities	3,660	3,300	3,700	360	10.9	49.2	52.4
Stockholders' Equity							
Preferred stock	300	300	300	-0-	-0-	4.0	4.8
Common stock ($10 par value)	1,500	1,200	1,200	300	25.0	20.2	19.0
Additional paid-in capital	502	400	400	102	25.5	6.7	6.3
Retained earnings	1,478	1,100	800	378	34.4	19.9	17.5
Total stockholders' equity	3,780	3,000	2,700	780	26.0	50.8	47.6
Total liabilities and stockholders' equity	$7,440	$6,300	$6,400	$1,140	18.1	100.0	100.0

*Computations are explained on pages 778–782.

Figure 20–1
Comparative Balance Sheets, Change During the Year, and Common Size Statements

formance of companies in the same industry. (In the following discussion, rather than stating the need for comparison every time a particular analysis is performed, it will be assumed that this additional step is taken by the statement user.)

PERCENTAGE ANALYSIS

HORIZONTAL ANALYSIS

Objective 2: Performing horizontal, trend, and vertical analysis

An analysis of the change from year to year in individual statement items is called **horizontal analysis**. Horizontal analysis of the preceding year's financial statements is generally performed as a starting point for forecasting future performance. Most firms' annual reports include financial statements for the two most recent years (**comparative statements**), and selected summary data

GORDON CORPORATION
Comparative Income Statements
For the Years Ended December 31, 1988 and 1987
(000 omitted)

	Year Ended December 31		Change During Year		Common Size Statements	
	1988	1987	Dollar Amount	Percent	1988	1987
Sales	$10,320	$9,582	$ 738	7.7	100.0	100.0
Less: Cost of goods sold	7,719	6,975	744	10.7	74.8	72.8
Gross profit on sales	2,601	2,607	(6)	(0.2)	25.2	27.2
Expenses:						
Selling expense	1,080	830	250	30.1	10.5	8.6
Administrative expense	567	620	(53)	(8.5)	5.5	6.5
Interest expense	252	230	22	9.6	2.4	2.4
Income tax expense	144	237	(93)	(39.2)	1.4	2.5
Total expenses	2,043	1,917	126	6.6	19.8	20.0
Net income	558	690	(132)	(19.1)	5.4	7.2
Preferred stock dividends	30	30	-0-		0.3	0.3
Net income available to common stockholders	$ 528	$ 660	$(132)	(20.0)	5.1	6.9

Figure 20–2
Comparative Income Statements, Change During the Year, and Common Size Statements

for five to ten years. For an example of comparative statements see the Holiday Inn, Inc. annual report in Appendix A.

In horizontal analysis, the individual items or groups of items on comparative financial statements are generally first placed side by side, as in the first columns of Figures 20–1 and 20–2. Because it is difficult to compare absolute dollar amounts, the differences between the figures of one year and the next are computed in both dollar amounts and percentage change. In computing the increase or decrease in dollar amounts, the earlier year is used as the base year. The percentage change is computed by dividing the increase or decrease from the base year in dollars by the base year amount. For example, from 1987 to 1988 the *Cash* account of Gordon Corporation increased by $90,000, from $300,000 to $390,000 (Figure 20–1). The percentage change is 30%, computed as follows.

$$\text{Percentage increase} = \frac{90,000}{300,000} = 30.0\%$$

A percentage change can only be computed when a positive amount is reported in the base year; the amount of change cannot be stated as a percentage if the item in the base year was reported as a negative or a zero amount.

A review of the percentage increases or decreases will reveal those items that showed the most significant change between the periods under study. Important and unusual changes, such as a significant percentage change in sales, should be investigated further by the analyst. The objectives of this investigation are:

1. To determine the cause of the change.
2. To determine whether the change was favorable or unfavorable.
3. To attempt to assess whether a trend is expected to continue.

The analyst must also consider changes in other related items. For example, when reviewing the percentage changes in the balance sheet accounts included in Figure 20–1, attention is directed to the change in the *Plant and Equipment* account, because of the size and direction of the change (44.4% increase). The cause of the change is an expansion in the firm's operations. In assessing whether the change is favorable or unfavorable, an analyst would seek further answers to such questions as: How is the added investment being financed? Is expansion going to cause severe cash flow problems? Are sales markets adequate to support the additional output? Answers to these questions, and announcements by management, will assist the analyst in determining whether further expansion is expected to continue. The analyst may look to the balance sheet, the income statement, the statement of changes in financial position, and supplementary disclosures for additional data in answering these questions.

Sales in Figure 20–2 increased 7.7%, by itself a favorable trend. However, the rate of increase in cost of goods sold was 10.7%, and selling expenses increased by 30.1%. Thus, during the period, the firm was unable to maintain its profit margin percentage [(sales − cost of goods sold)/sales]. It appears that the increase in sales is at least partially the result of an increased sales effort. These items warrant further investigation by an analyst who is concerned with the profitability and long-term future of the firm. In this case, the analyst should try to determine whether inventory costs are continuing to increase, the extent of competitive pressures on the revenues of the firm, and the effect of the increased selling costs on future sales.

TREND ANALYSIS

Trend analysis is commonly employed when financial data are presented for three or more years (see Holiday Inns, Inc. annual report in Appendix A). In this analysis, the earliest period is the base period. Each financial statement item of the base year is set equal to 100. In subsequent years, statement items are stated as a percentage of their value in the base year by dividing the dollar amount in the succeeding year by the dollar amount in the base year. For example, assume that sales and net income were reported for the last five years as follows.

			Year		
	(Base Year) 1984	1985	1986	1987	1988
Sales	1,000,000	1,050,000	1,120,000	1,150,000	1,220,000
Net income	200,000	206,000	218,000	222,000	232,000

It is clear that the dollar amounts of both sales and net income are increasing. However, the relationship between the change in sales and net income can be interpreted more easily if the changes are expressed in percentages by dividing the amount reported for each subsequent year by the base-year amount, thus producing:

	1984	1985	1986	1987	1988
Sales	100	105	112	115	122
Net income	100	103	109	111	116

Now it can be seen that net income is increasing more slowly than sales.

The relationship between sales and net income is only one trend that should be reviewed. The trend in other accounts should also be investigated, particularly since the level of net income is affected not only by sales, but also by the expenses of the firm. In this case, it is possible that the firm's inventory costs are increasing faster than selling prices. Or the increase in sales may be the result of granting liberal credit terms, which are resulting in larger bad debt expenses. The point is that other related operating data must also be reviewed before drawing conclusions about the significance of one particular item. The overall objective is to evaluate various related trends and attempt to assess whether the trend can be expected to continue.

VERTICAL ANALYSIS

Horizontal analysis compares the proportional changes in a specific item from one period to the next. **Vertical analysis** involves restating the dollar amount of each item reported on an individual financial statement as a percentage of a specific item on the same statement. This specific item is referred to as the base amount. For example, on the balance sheet, individual components are stated as a percentage of total assets or total liabilities and stockholders' equity. On the income statement, net sales or total revenue are usually set equal to a base of 100%, with each income statement item expressed as a percentage of the base amount. Such statements are often called **common size statements,** since all items are presented as a percentage of some common base amount.

Vertical analysis for Gordon Corporation is presented in the last two columns of Figures 20–1 and 20–2 (pages 778 and 779). Vertical analysis is useful for identifying the relative importance of items to the base used. For example, it can be readily observed that the cost of goods sold as a percentage of sales increased from 72.8% to 74.8%. Vertical analysis is also an important tool for comparing data to other standards, such as the past performance of the firm, the current performance of competing firms, and averages developed for the industry in which the firm operates.

RATIO ANALYSIS

Objective 3: Computing and using ratios

A financial statement **ratio** is computed by dividing the dollar amount of one item reported in the financial statements by the dollar amount of another item reported. The purpose is to express a relationship between two relevant items that is easy to interpret and compare with other information. For example, the relationship of current assets to current liabilities—called the current ratio—is of interest to most statement users. For a firm reporting current assets of $210,000 and current liabilities of $120,000, the current ratio is 1.75 (210,000/120,000). This means that the company has $1.75 in current assets for every $1.00 of its current liabilities.

The relationship could be converted to a percentage (175%) by multiplying the ratio by 100. In ratio form, or as a percentage, the relationship between the two items can be more easily compared to other standards, such as, for example, the current ratio of other companies, or industry-wide ratios.

Relevant relationships can exist between items in the same financial statement or between items reported in two different financial statements, so there are many ratios that can be computed. The analyst must give careful thought to which ratios best express the relationships relevant to the area of immediate concern. The user must keep in mind that a ratio shows a significant relationship that may have little significance when used alone. Consequently, to evaluate the adequacy of a certain relationship, the ratio should be compared to other standards, such as industry averages, and the historical record of the company under study.

Ratios are classified according to their evaluation of a firm's **profitability, liquidity,** and **solvency.** Unless otherwise noted, the computations in the remainder of this chapter are based on the financial statements presented for Gordon Corporation in Figures 20–1 and 20–2. A summary of the ratios discussed in this chapter is presented in Figure 20–3.

RATIOS TO ANALYZE PROFITABILITY

Profitability analysis consists of tests used to evaluate a firm's earning performance during the year. The results are combined with other data to forecast the firm's potential earning power. Potential earning power is important to long-term creditors and stockholders because, in the long run, the firm must operate at a satisfactory profit to survive. Potential earning power is also important to statement users, such as suppliers and labor unions, who are interested in maintaining a continuing relationship with a financially sound company. A firm's financial soundness depends on its future earning power.

Adequacy of earnings is measured in terms of the relationship between

Ratio	Method of Calculation	Significance of Each Ratio
Profitability Ratios		
Return on total assets	$$\frac{\text{Net income} + \text{Interest expense (net of tax)}}{\text{Average total assets}}$$	Measures rate of return earned on total assets provided by both creditors and owners.
Return on common stockholders' equity	$$\frac{\text{Net income} - \text{Preferred dividend requirements}}{\text{Average common stockholders' equity}}$$	Measures rate of return earned on assets provided by owners.
Return on sales	$$\frac{\text{Net income}}{\text{Net sales}}$$	Measures net profitability of each dollar of sales.
Earnings per share	$$\frac{\text{Net income} - \text{Preferred dividend requirements}}{\text{Weighted average number of common shares outstanding}}$$	Measures net income earned on each share of common stock.
Price-earnings ratio	$$\frac{\text{Market price per share of common stock}}{\text{Earnings per share}}$$	Measures the amount investors are paying for a dollar of earnings.
Dividend yield	$$\frac{\text{Annual dividend per share of common stock}}{\text{Market price per share of common stock}}$$	Measures rate of return to stockholders based on current market price.
Dividend payout	$$\frac{\text{Total dividends to common stockholders}}{\text{Net income} - \text{Preferred dividend requirements}}$$	Measures the percentage of income paid out to common stockholders.
Liquidity Ratios		
Current ratio	$$\frac{\text{Current assets}}{\text{Current liabilities}}$$	A measure of short-term liquidity. Indicates the ability of a firm to meet its short-term debts from its current assets.
Quick ratio	$$\frac{\text{Cash} + \text{Marketable securities} + \text{Net receivables}}{\text{Current liabilities}}$$	A more rigorous measure of short-term liquidity. Indicates the ability of the firm to meet unexpected demands from liquid current assets.
Receivable turnover	$$\frac{\text{Net sales}}{\text{Average receivable balance}}$$	Measures effectiveness of collections; used to evaluate whether receivable balance is excessive.
Inventory turnover	$$\frac{\text{Cost of goods sold}}{\text{Average inventory balance}}$$	Indicates the liquidity of inventory. Measures the number of times inventory was sold on the average during the period.
Solvency Ratios		
Debt to total assets	$$\frac{\text{Total liabilities}}{\text{Total assets}}$$	Measures percentage of assets provided by creditors and extent of using leverage.
Times interest earned	$$\frac{\text{Net income} + \text{Interest expense} + \text{Income tax expense}}{\text{Interest expense}}$$	Measures the ability of the firm to meet its interest payments out of current earnings.

Figure 20–3
Summary of Ratios

earnings and either total assets or common stockholders' equity, the relationship between earnings and sales, and the availability of earnings to common stockholders. If earnings appear to be inadequate, the next step is to determine whether the sales volume is too low. Are the cost of goods sold and/or other expenses too high? Is the investment in assets excessive in relation to the firm's sales?

Rate of Return on Total Assets

Rate of return on total assets is determined by dividing the sum of net income plus after-tax interest expense by average total assets for the year.

$$\text{Return on total assets} = \frac{\text{Net income} + \text{Interest expense (net of tax)}[1]}{\text{Average total assets}}$$

Interest expense (net of tax) is computed as:

$$\text{Interest expense} \times (1.0 - \text{income tax rate})$$

Interest is added back to net income in the numerator to derive the total return earned on all of the assets used, regardless of how they were acquired. In other words, interest is a return to the creditors for the use of their money to finance the acquisition of assets. The net of tax interest expense is used, because that is the net cost to the firm for using borrowed funds. Average total assets is used in the denominator, because the earnings were produced by employing resources throughout the period. The sum of the beginning and ending total assets is divided by two, to compute average total assets. If sufficient information were available, a monthly or quarterly average would be preferred, in order to minimize the effects of seasonal fluctuations.

The management of Gordon Corporation produced a return on average total assets of 11.0% in 1988 and 13.5% in 1987, as computed below assuming the tax rate was 21% and 26%, respectively.

1988	1987
$\frac{558 + 252(1.00 - .21)}{(6,300 + 7,440)/2} = 11.0\%$	$\frac{690 + 230(1.00 - .26)}{(6,400 + 6,300)/2} = 13.5\%$

During 1988, management produced approximately 11 cents in profit for every dollar of assets invested, compared with 13.5 cents for every dollar in 1987. The decrease in rates between the two years is significant, and results from decreased net income combined with an increased investment base. Such a decrease highlights the need for further investigation by the analyst.

Rate of Return on Common Stockholders' Equity

The return on total assets does not measure the return earned by management on the assets provided by the common stockholders. The return to the common stockholders may be greater or less than the return on total assets because of the firm's use of financial leverage. As discussed in Chapter 17, financial leverage is the use of debt securities or other fixed-return securities, such as preferred stock, to earn a return greater than the interest or dividends paid to the creditors or preferred stockholders. If a firm is able to earn more on the borrowed funds than the fixed amount that must be paid to the creditors or preferred stockholders, the return to the common stockholders will be greater than the return on total assets. If the amount earned on the borrowed funds is less than the fixed interest and preferred dividend, the return to the common

[1]There are variations in the way analysts compute the same ratios. For example, some analysts prefer to compute the return on total assets using one of the following alternatives as a substitute for the numerator.

a. Net income + Interest expense
b. Net income before interest expense and income taxes.
c. Net income

The various approaches to computing the same ratio point out the need for an analyst to exercise care when comparing ratios computed by different individuals.

stockholders will be less than the return on total assets. The return may be computed as:

$$\text{Return on common stockholders' equity} = \frac{\text{Net income} - \text{Preferred dividend requirement}}{\text{Average common stockholders' equity}}$$

The preferred dividend requirement is subtracted from net income to yield the portion of net income allocated to the common stockholders' equity. The denominator excludes the preferred stockholders' equity in the firm.

The computations for Gordon Corporation are shown here.

| | December 31 | | |
	1988	1987	1986
Common stock	$1,500	$1,200	$1,200
Additional paid-in capital	502	400	400
Retained earnings	1,478	1,100	800
Total common stockholders' equity	$3,480	$2,700	$2,400

$$\underline{\quad 1988 \quad}$$
$$\frac{558 - 30}{(2,700 + 3,480)/2} = 17.1\%$$

$$\underline{\quad 1987 \quad}$$
$$\frac{690 - 30}{(2,400 + 2,700)/2} = 25.9\%$$

Note that both of these rates are higher than the corresponding returns computed on total assets, because the company earned a return on the assets financed by the creditors and preferred stockholders greater than the interest or dividends paid to them. However, the percentage decreased from 25.9% to 17.1%, a decrease worthy of further investigation.

Return on Sales

Return on sales—also called profit margin—is calculated during a vertical analysis of the income statement. It reflects the portion of each dollar of sales that represents income. Return on sales is computed by dividing net income by net sales.

$$\text{Return on sales} = \frac{\text{Net Income}}{\text{Net sales}}$$

For Gordon Corporation the rates are:

$$\underline{\quad 1988 \quad}$$
$$\frac{558}{10,320} = 5.4\%$$

$$\underline{\quad 1987 \quad}$$
$$\frac{690}{9,582} = 7.2\%$$

For 1988, each dollar of sales produced 5.4 cents in income. Consistent with the other rates computed, this ratio indicates a declining profitability trend for the firm. The rates should, of course, be compared to other standards to be more useful. If the return on sales for competing firms is 5%, for example, the 5.4% appears favorable. Even so, other data, such as increases in major expenses, should be investigated further because other problem areas or poor management practices could be discovered to explain the decline between the two years. ·

Earnings Per Share

The earnings per share (EPS) of common stock is widely used in evaluating the performance of a firm. The ratio is commonly used to compile earnings data for the press and for statistical services. It is a widely publicized ratio, because it converts the absolute dollar amount of net income to a per share amount. That is, the EPS ratio is the amount of net income earned on one share of stock. It is computed as follows.

$$\text{EPS} = \frac{\text{Net income} - \text{Preferred dividend requirements}}{\text{Average number of common shares outstanding}}$$

In the Gordon Corporation illustration, the calculations are:

1988	1987
$\dfrac{558 - 30}{150} = \$3.52$	$\dfrac{690 - 30}{120} = \$5.50$

The average number of common shares outstanding is computed on a weighted-average basis. The weighted average is based on the number of months that the shares were outstanding. The average number of shares for 1987 and 1988 is computed on the assumption that there were 120,000 shares outstanding during 1987 and that 30,000 additional shares were issued at the beginning of 1988.

The EPS ratio means that for 1988 the firm earned $3.52 per share of common stock outstanding. Current generally accepted accounting standards require that the EPS must be disclosed on the face of the income statement.

The computation of EPS is much more complex than it appears as shown here. These complexities are discussed in detail in more advanced accounting courses.

Price–Earnings Ratio

The price–earnings ratio (P/E ratio) indicates how much investors are currently paying for each dollar of earnings. It enhances a statement user's ability to compare the market value of one common stock, relative to earnings, to that of other companies. It is computed by dividing the current market price of a share of common stock by the earnings per share.

$$\text{P/E ratios} = \frac{\text{Market price per share of common stock}}{\text{Earnings per share}}$$

Assuming a market price of $40 per share for Gordon Corporation common stock on December 31, 1988, the P/E ratio is:

$$\frac{40.00}{3.52} = 11.36 \text{ times}$$

The common stock of Gordon Corporation is said to be selling for 11.4 times its earnings.

Price–earnings ratios vary widely between industries, since they represent investors' expectations about the future earnings power of a company. Thus, high P/E stocks are associated with companies with prospects of high earnings growth, whereas more stable firms have low P/E stocks. For example, in the early part of 1985, companies associated with high-technology generally had a high P/E ratio. Apple Computer had a P/E of approximately 30. On the other hand, companies in the auto industry had low P/E ratios. Ford Motor Company and General Motors, for example, had P/E ratios of 3 and 6, respectively.

Dividend Yield

The dividend yield is normally computed by investors who are investing in common stock primarily for dividends, rather than for appreciation in the market price of the stock. The percentage indicates a rate of return on the dollars invested and permits easier comparison to returns from alternative investment opportunities. The dividend yield is computed as:

$$\text{Dividend yield} = \frac{\text{Annual dividend per share of common stock}}{\text{Market price per share of common stock}}$$

Cash dividends of $150,000 ($1 per share) were paid during 1988 to the common stockholders of Gordon Corporation.[2] Assuming a market price of $40 per share, the dividend yield is computed as follows.

$$\frac{1.00}{40.00} = 2.5\%$$

Dividend Payout

Investors interested in dividend yields may also compute the percentage of common stock earnings distributed as dividends to the common stockholders each period. This ratio is referred to as the dividend payout ratio.

---

[2]The $150,000 can be verified as follows.

Retained earnings, 1/1/88 (Figure 20–1)		$1,100,000
Add: Net income (Figure 20–2)		558,000
Less: Cash dividends		
Preferred stock	$ 30,000	
Common stock	150,000	180,000
Retained earnings, 12/31/88 (Figure 20–1)		$1,478,000

Dividends per share is computed as follows:

$$\text{Dividend per share} = \frac{\text{Dividends to common stockholders}}{\text{Number of common shares outstanding}}$$

$$= \frac{\$150,000}{150,000 \text{ shares}}$$

$$= \$1 \text{ per share}$$

$$\text{Dividend payout} = \frac{\text{Total dividends to common stockholders}}{\text{Net income} - \text{Preferred dividend requirements}}$$

For the Gordon Corporation the 1988 ratio is:

$$\frac{150}{558 - 30} = 28.4\%$$

This ratio provides an investor with some insights into management's policy of distributing dividends as a percentage of net income available to the common stockholders. A low payout ratio would indicate that management is reinvesting earnings internally. Such a company would be desirable for someone interested in investing for growth in the market price of the shares. A company with a consistently high payout ratio would be of interest to an investor who depends on dividends as a source of current income, for example, a retired individual.

Some recent dividend payout percentages for selected companies are given in Figure 20–4. Over the years, the aggregate dividend payout ratio for U.S. corporations generally has averaged about 40% to 60%.

RATIOS TO ANALYZE LIQUIDITY

Liquidity—that is, the firm's ability to meet its short term obligations—is an important factor in financial statement analysis. After all, a firm that cannot meet its short-term obligations may be forced into bankruptcy and, therefore, will not have the opportunity to operate in the long run. The focus of this aspect of analysis is on working capital or some component of working capital.

Current Ratio

Perhaps the most commonly used measure of a firm's liquidity is the current ratio, which is computed as:

$$\text{Current ratio} = \frac{\text{Current assets}}{\text{Current liabilities}}$$

Figure 20–4
Dividend Payment
Ratio for Selected
Companies

Company	Dividend Payout Ratio (percent)
Apple Computer, Inc.	-0-
Cincinnati Gas & Electric Company	73.9
Firestone Tire & Rubber Company	36.3
General Electric Company	42.1
General Motors Corporation	23.7
Holiday Inns, Inc.	25.2
Kmart Corporation	27.4
Levitz Furniture	17.3
McDonald's Corporation	16.9
Sperry	47.4

Source: Computed from annual reports by authors.

The current ratio, a measure of the firm's liquidity, measures the creditors' margin of safety. It indicates the relationship of current assets to current liabilities on a dollar-per-dollar basis. A low ratio may indicate that the firm would be unable to meet its short-term debt in an emergency. A high ratio is considered favorable to creditors, but may indicate excessive investment in working capital items, such as holding slow-selling inventory items, that may not be producing income for the firm.

Analysts often contend that the current ratio should be at least two to one. In other words, a firm should maintain $2 of current assets for every $1 of current liabilities. Although such a rule is one standard of comparison, it is arbitrary and subject to exceptions and numerous qualifications in the modern approach to statement analysis. Deviations from the 2:1 rule nevertheless indicate an area in which additional tests are needed to evaluate the firm's liquidity. For example, a firm with a ratio of 1:1 may have a difficult time meeting its short-term commitments. Therefore, to assess its liquidity, the quick ratio and turnover ratios discussed below and the cash flow should be carefully investigated.

The current ratios for Gordon Corporation for 1988 and 1987 are:

1988	1987
$\dfrac{4{,}340}{1{,}760} = 2.47$	$\dfrac{3{,}900}{1{,}600} = 2.44$

Gordon Corporation shows a slight improvement in the relationship between current assets and current liabilities and, in the absence of other information, would be considered liquid, at least in the short run. However, a ratio of 2.4 or higher may signify excessive investments in current assets. That is, a high ratio may indicate that the company is holding too many assets that are not producing revenue.

Quick Ratio

One of the limitations of the current ratio is that it includes inventory and prepaid expenses in the numerator. However, these items are not as liquid as cash, marketable securities, notes receivable, or accounts receivable. In the normal course of business, inventories must first be sold, and then the cash collected, before cash is available. Also, most prepaid expenses, such as prepaid insurance, are to be consumed and cannot be readily converted into cash. A ratio that is used to supplement the current ratio and that provides a more rigorous measure of liquidity is the quick ratio or acid test ratio, as it is sometimes called. The quick ratio is computed as follows.

$$\text{Quick ratio} = \frac{\text{Cash + Marketable securities + Net receivables}}{\text{Current liabilities}}$$

The higher the ratio, the more liquid the firm is considered. A lower ratio may indicate that, in an emergency, the company would be unable to meet its immediate obligations.

The quick ratio for Gordon Corporation is computed as follows.

	1988	**1987**
Cash	$ 390	$ 300
Marketable securities	380	440
Accounts receivable (net)	1,460	1,290
Total quick assets	$2,230	$2,030

$$\frac{2,230}{1,760} = 1.27 \qquad \frac{2,030}{1,600} = 1.27$$

A ratio of 1.27:1 in both years indicates that the firm is highly liquid. However, this observation is somewhat dependent on the collectibility of the receivables included in the numerator.

The current ratio and quick ratio are used to measure the adequacy of the firm's current assets to satisfy its current obligations as of the balance sheet date. However, these ratios ignore how long it takes for a firm to collect cash—an important aspect of the firm's liquidity. Since receivables and inventories normally make up a large percentage of a firm's current assets, the quick ratio and current ratio may be misleading if there is an extended interval between purchasing inventory, selling it, and collecting cash from the sale. Thus, the receivable turnover and inventory turnover ratios are two other measures of liquidity that are often used to yield additional information. These turnover ratios are sometimes called activity ratios.

Receivable Turnover

The receivable turnover ratio is a measure of how many times the average receivable balance was converted into cash during the year. It is also considered a measure of the efficiency of the firm's credit-granting and collection policies. It is computed as follows.

$$\text{Receivable turnover} = \frac{\text{Net sales}}{\text{Average receivable balance}}$$

The higher the receivable turnover ratio, the shorter the time period between recording a sale and collecting the cash. To be competitive, the firm's credit policies are influenced by industry practices. Comparison of this ratio to industry norms can reveal deviations from competitors' operating results.

In computing this ratio, credit sales should be used in the numerator whenever the amount is available. However, such information is normally not available in financial statements, so net sales is used as a substitute. An average of monthly receivable balances should be used in the denominator. In the absence of monthly information, the year-end balance, an average of the beginning of the year and end of the year balances, or averages of quarterly balances are used in the calculation. The average of the receivable balances is used, because net sales are earned over a period of time. Therefore, the denominator should approximate what the receivable balance was throughout the period.

The computations for Gordon Corporation are:

$$\underline{1988}$$

$$\frac{10{,}320}{(1{,}290 + 1{,}460)/2} = 7.51 \text{ times}$$

$$\underline{1987}$$

$$\frac{9{,}582}{(1{,}320 + 1{,}290)/2} = 7.34 \text{ times}$$

Frequently, the receivable turnover is divided into 365 days to derive the average number of days it takes to collect receivables from sales on account.

$$\underline{1988}$$

$$\frac{365 \text{ days}}{7.5} = 48.7 \text{ days}$$

$$\underline{1987}$$

$$\frac{365 \text{ days}}{7.3} = 50.0 \text{ days}$$

During 1988, the corporation collected the average account receivable balance 7.51 times. Expressed another way, it took an average of 48.7 days to collect sales on account, an improvement of one day over 1987. These measures are particularly useful if one knows the credit terms granted by the firm. Assuming credit terms of 60 days, the average 49-day collection period provides some indication that the firm's credit policy is effective and that the firm probably is not burdened by excessive amounts of uncollectible accounts that have not been written off. A collection period significantly in excess of 60 days indicates a problem with either the granting of credit, collection policies, or both.

Inventory Turnover

The control of the amount invested in inventory is an important aspect of managing a business. The size of the investment in inventory and inventory turnover are dependent upon such factors as type of business and time of year. A grocery store has a higher turnover than an automobile dealership; the inventory level of a seasonal business is higher at certain times in the operating cycle than at others. The inventory turnover ratio is a measure of the adequacy of inventory and how efficiently it is being managed. The ratio is an expression of the number of times the average inventory balance was sold and then replaced during the year. The ratio is computed as follows.

$$\text{Inventory turnover} = \frac{\text{Cost of goods sold}}{\text{Average inventory balance}}$$

Cost of goods sold, rather than sales, is used in the numerator because: (1) it is a measure of the cost of inventory sold during the year; and (2) the cost measure is consistent with the cost basis of the denominator. Ideally, an average of monthly inventory balances should be computed, but this information is generally not available to external parties in published reports. A quarterly average can be computed if quarterly interim reports are published by the firm.

The inventory turnover for Gordon Corporation is:

$$\underline{1988}$$

$$\frac{7{,}719}{(1{,}770 + 2{,}010)/2} = 4.08 \text{ times}$$

$$\underline{1987}$$

$$\frac{6{,}975}{(1{,}860 + 1{,}770)/2} = 3.84 \text{ times}$$

The average days per turnover can be computed by dividing 365 days by the turnover ratio.

$$\frac{365 \text{ days}}{4.1} = 89.0 \text{ days} \qquad \frac{365 \text{ days}}{3.8} = 96.1 \text{ days}$$

The 1988 turnover ratio indicates that the average inventory was sold 4.08 times during the year, as compared to 3.84 times in 1987. In terms of days, the firm held its inventory approximately 89 days in 1988 before it was sold, as compared to about 96 days in 1987.

The increased turnover in 1988 is generally considered a favorable trend. Inventory with a high turnover is less likely to become obsolete and decline in price before it is sold. A higher turnover also indicates greater liquidity, since the inventory will be converted into cash in a shorter period of time. However, given the nature of the firm's business, a very high turnover may indicate that the company is carrying insufficient inventory and is losing a significant amount of sales.

RATIOS TO ANALYZE SOLVENCY

A firm is using financial leverage whenever it finances a portion of its assets with a fixed charge security. Issuing bonds to finance the purchase of plant assets is an example of using financial leverage. Such debt securities commit the firm to making interest payments and repaying the principal on specified dates. If a firm fails to meet these commitments, the bondholders can force the firm into bankruptcy. Thus, borrowing increases the risk of default. The advantage to the common stockholders is that their return may be increased if the return earned on the funds borrowed is greater than the cost of the debt.

Several ratios are used to analyze the firm's ability to satisfy its long-term commitments and still have sufficient working capital left over to operate successfully. These ratios test the firm's solvency.

Debt to Total Assets

The percentage of total assets financed by creditors indicates the extent to which the firm uses debt financing. The ratio of debt to total assets, also called the debt ratio, is a measure of the relationship between total liabilities and total assets and is computed thus.

$$\text{Debt to total assets} = \frac{\text{Total liabilities[3]}}{\text{Total assets}}$$

A high debt to total assets ratio indicates a greater risk of default and less protection for the creditors. This percentage is important to long-term creditors and stockholders, since the creditors have a prior claim to assets in the event of liquidation—that is, the creditors must be paid in full before assets are distributed to stockholders. The greater the percentage of assets contributed

---

[3]Some analysts include preferred stock with the total debt, rather than with equity, on the basis that it has a preference to assets in liquidation and that it is often issued to obtain financial leverage for the common stockholders. Preferred stock is not included here because it does not have a maturity date and because dividends do not have to be paid.

by stockholders, the greater the protection to the creditors. For Gordon Corporation the ratio is:

1988	1987
$\dfrac{3,660}{7,440} = 49.2\%$	$\dfrac{3,300}{6,300} = 52.4\%$

Thus, for both years, approximately 50% of the assets were provided by the firm's creditors.

Because of the trade-off between increased risk for potentially greater returns to common stockholders, there is no percentage that is considered better than another. Other things being equal, firms with stable income can issue a greater percentage of debt than firms with volatile income. Stable income levels enables a statement user to better predict, from period to period, the level of debt costs that can be covered from cash generated by operations. Some selected examples of debt to equity ratios computed from recent balance sheets are shown in Figure 20–5.

Times Interest Earned

The times interest earned ratio is an indication of the firm's ability to satisfy periodic interest payments from current earnings. The rough rule of thumb is that the company should earn three to four times its interest requirement. Since current interest charges are normally paid from funds provided by current operations, analysts frequently compute the relationship between earnings and interest.

$$\text{Times interest earned} = \frac{\text{Net income + Interest expense + Income tax expense}}{\text{Interest expense}}$$

Interest expense and income taxes are added back to net income in the numerator, because the ratio is a measure of income available to pay the interest charges. For Gordon Corporation the ratio is:

Company	Debt to Total Assets Ratio (percent)
Apple Computer, Inc.	32.1
Circle K Corporation	60.8
Deere & Co.	61.3
Exxon	51.3
Ford Motor	67.8
General Electric	51.6
General Motors	54.6
RCA Corporation	66.8
Sperry	54.6
Standard Oil of Ohio	51.6

Source: Computed from annual reports by authors.

Figure 20–5
Debt to Total Assets Ratio for Selected Companies

	1988	**1987**
Net Income	$558	$ 690
Interest expense	252	230
Income tax expense	144	237
Totals	$954	$1,157

1988   1987

$$\frac{954}{252} = 3.79 \text{ times} \qquad \frac{1,157}{230} = 5.03 \text{ times}$$

In 1987, earnings before interest and income taxes were 5.03 times interest expense. This ratio declined to 3.79 in 1988. The 1988 result is marginal, but it is still an adequate coverage, according to the rule of thumb. However, the result should be considered in relation to other trends in the company's financial status, especially the trend in this ratio, and in comparison with other standards, such as industry averages.

LIMITATIONS OF FINANCIAL ANALYSIS

**Objective 4:
Limitations
of statement
analysis**

The analytical techniques introduced in this chapter are useful for providing insights into the financial position and results of operations of a particular firm. Statement users must be careful in interpreting trends and ratios computed from reported financial statements. Certain basic limitations and an explanation of each follow.

1. Financial analysis is performed on historical data, primarily for the purpose of forecasting future performance. The historical relationships may not continue because of changes in:
   a. The general state of the economy.
   b. The business environment in which the firm must operate.
   c. Management.
   d. The policies established by management.
2. The measurement base used in computing the analytical measures is historical cost. Failure to adjust for inflation or for changes in fair values may result in some computations providing misleading information on a trend basis and in any comparison between companies. For example, the return on total assets includes net income in the numerator, which is affected by the current year's sales and current operating expenses, measured in current dollars. However, fixed assets and other nonmonetary items are measured in historical dollars—which are not adjusted to reflect current price levels. Thus, the ratio divides items primarily measured in current dollar amounts by a total measured primarily in terms of historical dollars. This limitation is partially overcome by the requirement that firms must report inflation-adjusted data as supplementary information to the historical cost statements (see Chapter 13).
3. Year-end data may not be typical of the firm's position during the year. Knowing that certain ratios are computed at year-end, management may improve a ratio by entering into certain types of transactions near the end of the year. For example, the current ratio can be improved by using cash

to pay off short-term debt. To illustrate, assume that a firm reported current assets of $200,000 and current liabilities of $100,000 before paying $50,000 on accounts payable. The payment will increase the current ratio, as shown here.

	Before Payment	Payment	After Payment
Current assets	$200,000	$50,000	$150,000
Current liabilities	100,000	50,000	50,000

$$\text{Current ratio} = \frac{200{,}000}{100{,}000} = 2 \qquad \text{Current ratio} = \frac{150{,}000}{50{,}000} = 3$$

Also, a firm usually establishes a fiscal year-end that coincides with the low point of activity in its operating cycle. Therefore, account balances, such as receivables, accounts payable, and inventory, may not be representative of the balances carried in these accounts during the year.

4. Companies may not be comparable. Data among companies may not provide meaningful comparisons because of factors such as the use of different accounting methods, the size of the companies, and the diversification of product lines—despite the fact that this chapter has emphasized such comparisons.

GLOSSARY

COMMON SIZE STATEMENT. A financial statement in which the amount of each item reported in the statement is stated as a percentage of some specific base amount, also reported in the same statement (p. 781).

COMPARATIVE STATEMENTS. Financial statements for the current year and prior years presented together to facilitate the analysis of changes in account balances (p. 778).

HORIZONTAL ANALYSIS. That part of an analysis based on the comparison of amounts reported for the same item in two or more comparative statements with an emphasis on the change from year to year (p. 778).

RATIO. Division of the amount reported for one financial statement item by the amount reported for another. Ratio analysis is the evaluation of the relationship indicated by this division (p. 782).

SOLVENCY. A firm's ability to satisfy its long-term obligations (p. 777).

TREND ANALYSIS. That part of the analysis involved with comparing the changes in a particular item over a series of years. In trend analysis a base year is selected. Statement items in subsequent statements are expressed as a percentage of the base year value (p. 780).

VERTICAL ANALYSIS. That part of an analysis in which the focus of the study is on the proportion of individual items expressed as a percentage of some specific item reported in the same statement (p. 781). (See also *Common Size Statement.*)

DISCUSSION QUESTIONS

1. The dollar amounts of one year's financial statements have limited significance when presented alone. To what could the dollar amounts be compared to provide a more meaningful analysis?
2. Differentiate between horizontal analysis, trend analysis, and vertical analysis.
3. What is the purpose of computing ratios?
4. Name and define each of the three financial aspects of a firm that are commonly analyzed.
5. Identify the financial statement users who would have a primary interest in each of the three financial aspects of a firm.
6. Explain how the price-earnings ratios, dividend yield ratios, and dividend payout ratios of growth firms and more stable firms tend to differ.
7. What ratio will help to answer each of the following questions.
   (a) How effective are the credit policies of the firm?
   (b) How much confidence do investors have in the firm?
   (c) Are the assets being used efficiently?
   (d) How is the firm being financed?
8. How are the current ratio and the quick ratio similar? How do they differ?
9. Why is it preferable to use only credit sales as the numerator in computing the receivable turnover? Comment on a firm's credit policies if the receivable turnover is 8.1 and its credit terms are 30 days.
10. What risk does a company assume as the inventory turnover increases?
11. How could earnings per share decrease even though net income has increased from the previous year?
12. How can ratios be used to determine whether common stockholders benefit from the assets provided by creditors and preferred stockholders?
13. A firm has a current ratio of 2.0 and a quick ratio of 1.5. If the current liabilities total $100,000, what is the sum of the inventory and prepaid assets?
14. Explain why financial statement analysis should be merely the beginning of a thorough investigation of a firm.
15. Why is the usefulness of financial analysis particularly limited during periods of high inflation?

EXERCISES

Exercise 20-1 Common Size Statements

Comparative income statements of the Bradley Company are shown here.

	1987	1986
Sales	$500,000	$470,000
Cost of goods sold	320,000	289,050
Gross profit on sales	180,000	180,950
Operating expenses	155,000	150,400
Net income	$ 25,000	$ 30,550

Required:

Prepare common size statements for both years.

Exercise 20-2 Trend Analysis
A company reported the following financial data over a five-year period.

	1985	1986	1987	1988	1989
Sales	$620,000	$651,000	$669,600	$688,200	$700,600
Gross profit on sales	248,000	262,880	272,800	280,240	285,200
Operating expenses	185,000	190,550	196,100	197,950	203,500

Required:
A. Prepare a trend analysis of the data.
B. Do the trends signify a favorable or an unfavorable situation? Explain.

Exercise 20-3 Trend Analysis
The asset section of the balance sheet of the Durbin Company is shown here.

	1987	1986
Cash	$ 23,000	$ 21,500
Accounts receivable	41,000	43,000
Inventory	115,700	112,800
Prepaid insurance	1,200	1,350
Furniture and fixtures	62,100	58,500
Machinery and equipment	100,000	95,000

Required:
Compute the change in each account in both dollars and percentage.

Exercise 20-4 Liquidity Analysis
The following information is taken from the financial statements of the Miranda Company.

	1987	1986
Cash	$ 40,000	$ 44,000
Marketable securities	100,000	90,000
Accounts receivable	85,000	82,000
Inventory	210,000	208,000
Prepaid expenses	7,000	9,000
Plant and equipment	350,000	345,000
Current liabilities	230,000	227,000
Sales	980,000	965,000
Cost of goods sold	588,000	582,000

Required:
Compute the following items for 1987.

A. Current ratio.
B. Quick ratio.
C. Receivable turnover ratio.
D. Average collection period of accounts receivable.
E. Inventory turnover ratio.
F. Average period for inventory turnover.

Exercises 20-5 Profitability and Solvency Analysis

The following information is available for the Young Company.

	1987	1986
Sales	$800,000	$735,000
Interest expense	32,000	34,000
Income tax expense	62,000	68,000
Net income	73,000	72,000
Preferred stock cash dividends	4,000	4,000
Total assets	650,000	615,000
Total liabilities	370,000	405,000
Preferred stock	75,000	75,000
Common stock	130,000	120,000
Retained earnings	75,000	15,000

Required:

A. Compute the following ratios for 1987.
1. Return on total assets. (Assume a tax rate of 46%.)
2. Return on common stockholders' equity.

B. Compute the following ratios for 1986 and 1987.
1. Return on sales.
2. Debt to total assets.
3. Times interest earned.

Exercise 20-6 Profitability Analysis

The Wood Corporation had a net income of $525,000. The company distributed preferred stock cash dividends of $23,000, and dividends to common stockholders of $300,000. Throughout the year, 200,000 shares of common stock were outstanding. Common stock is currently selling for $25 per share.

Required:
Compute the following ratios.

A. Earnings per share.
B. Price-earnings ratio.
C. Dividend yield.
D. Dividend payout.

Exercise 20-7 Effect of Transactions on Current Ratio

Presented here is information related to Bidwell Company on December 29, 1987.

BIDWELL COMPANY
Partial Balance Sheet
December 29, 1987

Cash	$150,000	Short-term notes payable	$ 50,000
Accounts receivable	105,000	Accounts payable	150,000
Inventories	225,000	Accrued liabilities	45,000
Prepaid expenses	20,000		
Total	$500,000	Total	$245,000

Required:

A. Compute the current and quick ratio, based on the data as of December 29, 1987.

B. A long-term debt agreement entered into by the company two years ago requires the company to maintain a minimum working capital ratio of 2:1. Management is concerned that this requirement will not be met and is considering entering into one or more of the following transactions before the close of the fiscal year-end, December 31. Compute the current ratio after each of the following transactions and indicate whether the ratio would be increased, decreased, or unaffected by the transaction.

1. Borrow $50,000 on a long-term note.
2. Pay $50,000 on accounts payable.
3. Give existing creditors a $50,000 short-term note in settlement of accounts payable.
4. Give existing creditors a $50,000 long-term note in settlement of accounts payable.

Exercise 20-8 Limitations of Ratio Analysis

A Company and B Company began operations on January 1, 1987. For illustrative purposes, we will assume that at that date their financial positions were identical and that their operations during 1987 were also identical. The only difference between the two companies is that they elected to use different accounting methods, as shown here.

	A Company	**B Company**
Inventory	FIFO	LIFO
Plant and equipment	Straight-line depreciation	Accelerated depreciation

Financial statements for the two companies prepared at the end of 1987 are presented here.

Income Statement		
	A Company	B Company
Revenues	$200,000	$200,000
Cost of goods sold	120,000	132,300
Gross profit on sales	80,000	67,700
Expenses*	43,000	58,000
Net income	$ 37,000	$ 9,700

*Includes interest expense of $7,000. Depreciation expense was $15,000 for A Company and $30,000 for B Company.

Balance Sheet

	A Company	B Company
Assets		
Cash	$ 20,000	$ 20,000
Accounts receivable	45,000	45,000
Inventories	35,000	22,700
Property, plant, and equipment (net)	45,000	30,000
Total Assets	$145,000	$117,700
Liabilities and Stockholders' Equity		
Current liabilities	$ 25,000	$ 25,000
Long-term liabilities	40,000	40,000
Common stockholders' equity	80,000	52,700
Total Liabilities and Stockholders' Equity	$145,000	$117,700

Required:
Compute the following items for each company.

A. Return on total assets. (Assume a tax rate of 30%.)
B. Return on common stockholders' equity.
C. Return on sales.
D. Current ratio.
E. Receivable turnover.
F. Inventory turnover.
G. Debt to total assets.

Exercise 20-9 Ratio Significance
Match the ratio listed in the left-hand column to the definition of its significance listed in the right-hand column.

Ratio	**Significance**
1. Debt to total assets.	A. Measures rate of return earned on total assets provided by both creditors and owners.
2. Earnings per share.	
3. Receivable turnover.	
4. Current ratio.	B. Measures rates of return earned on assets provided by owners.
5. Times interest earned.	
6. Return on total assets.	C. Measures net profitability of each dollar of sales.
7. Price-earnings ratio.	
8. Return on common stockholders' equity.	D. Measures net income earned on each share of common stock.
9. Dividend payout.	E. Measures the amount investors are paying for a dollar of earnings.
10. Return on sales.	
11. Quick ratio.	F. Measures rate of return to stockholders based on current market price.
12. Dividend yield.	
13. Inventory turnover.	G. Measures the percentage of income paid out to common stockholders.

H. A measure of short-term liquidity. Indicates the ability of a firm to meet its short-term debts from its current assets.

I. A more rigorous measure of short-term liquidity. Indicates the ability of the firm to meet unexpected demands from the liquid current assets.

J. Measures effectiveness of collections; used to evaluate whether receivable balance is excessive.

K. Indicates the liquidity of inventory. Measures the number of times inventory was sold on the average during the period.

L. Measures the percentage of assets provided by creditors and the extent financial leverage is used.

M. Measures the ability of the firm to meet its interest payments out of current earnings.

PROBLEMS

Problem 20-1 Horizontal and Vertical Analysis

The comparative financial statements of Jasper Company are shown here.

JASPER COMPANY
Comparative Income Statements
For the Years Ended December 31, 1987 and 1986
(000 omitted)

	1987	1986
Sales	$8,000	$7,600
Less: Cost of goods sold	5,300	5,350
Gross profit on sales	2,700	2,250
Selling expenses	1,000	980
Administrative expenses	950	830
Income tax expense	220	170
Total Expenses	2,170	1,980
Net Income	$ 530	$ 270

JASPER COMPANY
Comparative Balance Sheets
December 31, 1987 and 1986
(000 omitted)

	1987	1986
Assets		
Cash	$ 100	$ 120
Accounts receivable	220	180
Inventory	460	420
Long-term investments	100	120
Plant and equipment	1,800	1,500
Total Assets	$2,680	$2,340
Liabilities and Stockholders' Equity		
Accounts payable	$ 260	$ 240
Note payable	50	70
Long-term liabilities	950	950
Common stock	1,000	850
Retained earnings	420	230
Total Liabilities and Stockholders' Equity	$2,680	$2,340

Required:

A. Compute the changes in the financial statements from 1986 to 1987 in both dollar amounts and percentages.

B. Prepare a common size income statement and balance sheet for 1987 and 1986.

C. Comment on the significant relationships revealed by the horizontal and vertical analyses.

Problem 20-2 Trend Analysis

The comparative income statements and balance sheets of the Jefferson Company are shown here.

JEFFERSON COMPANY
Comparative Income Statements
For the Years Ended December 31, 1985–1990
(000 omitted)

	1985	1986	1987	1988	1989	1990
Sales	$150	$155	$154	$160	$200	$215
Less: Cost of goods sold	92	93	89	95	118	141
Gross profit on sales	58	62	65	65	82	74
Expenses	40	41	42	48	48	52
Net Income	$ 18	$ 21	$ 23	$ 17	$ 34	$ 22

JEFFERSON COMPANY
Comparative Balance Sheets
December 31, 1985–1990
(000 omitted)

	1985	1986	1987	1988	1989	1990
Assets						
Cash	$ 8	$ 9	$ 9	$ 11	$ 9	$ 7
Accounts receivable	13	15	14	16	26	34
Inventory	37	39	43	60	80	78
Plant and equipment	90	93	95	175	173	172
Total Assets	$148	$156	$161	$262	$288	$291
Liabilities and Stockholders' Equity						
Accounts payable	$ 23	$ 22	$ 25	$ 24	$ 54	$ 56
Long-term liabilities	30	29	26	71	60	60
Common stock	75	75	75	125	125	125
Retained earnings	20	30	35	42	49	50
Total Liabilities and Stockholders' Equity	$148	$156	$161	$262	$288	$291

Required:

A. Prepare a trend analysis of the data.

B. Comment on any significant situations revealed by the trends.

Problem 20-3 **Ratio Analysis**

The comparative financial statements of the Parker Corporation are shown here.

PARKER CORPORATION
Comparative Income Statements
For the Years Ended December 31, 1987 and 1986

	1987	1986
Sales	$395,000	$386,500
Less: Cost of goods sold	247,000	228,000
Gross profit on sales	148,000	158,500
Operating expenses	110,000	120,500
Interest expense	7,500	7,000
Income tax expense (50%)	15,250	15,500
Total expenses	132,750	143,000
Net income	$ 15,250	$ 15,500

PARKER CORPORATION
Comparative Balance Sheets
December 31, 1987 and 1986

	1987	1986
Assets		
Current Assets:		
Cash	$ 10,000	$ 9,000
Marketable securities	10,500	12,500
Accounts receivable	39,500	37,000
Inventory	105,000	101,500
Prepaid expenses	2,000	2,500
Total Current Assets	167,000	162,500
Plant and Equipment	80,000	70,500
Total Assets	$247,000	$233,000
Liabilities		
Current Liabilities:		
Accounts payable	$ 38,500	$ 32,000
Notes payable	20,000	15,000
Total Current Liabilities	58,500	47,000
Bonds payable	70,000	70,000
Total Liabilities	128,500	117,000
Stockholders' Equity		
Preferred stock	20,000	20,000
Common stock ($2.50 par value)	25,000	25,000
Additional paid-in capital	57,500	57,500
Retained earnings	16,000	13,500
Total Stockholders' Equity	118,500	116,000
Total Liabilities and Stockholders' Equity	$247,000	$233,000

During 1987, Parker Corporation declared and paid cash dividends on preferred stock of $1,400 and common stock of $11,350. On December 31, 1987, the market price of the common stock was $14 a share.

Required:
Compute the following ratios for 1987.

A. Return on total assets.
B. Return on common stockholders' equity.
C. Return on sales.
D. Earnings per share.
E. Price-earnings ratio.
F. Dividend yield.
G. Dividend payout.
H. Current ratio.
I. Quick ratio.
J. Receivable turnover.

K. Inventory turnover.
L. Debt to total assets.
M. Times interest earned.

Problem 20-4   Effect of Transactions on Ratios

The Quality Corporation completed the transactions listed here in the left-hand column.

Transaction	Ratio
1. Retired bonds payable by issuing common stock.	Return on common stockholders' + equity
2. Purchased inventory on account.	Quick ratio —
3. Sold inventory for cash.	Current ratio +
4. Issued additional shares of common stock for cash.	Debt to total assets –
5. Declared a cash dividend on common stock.	Dividend payout +
6. Paid the cash dividend.	Dividend yield *unchanged*
7. Wrote off an uncollectible account receivable to *Allowance for Uncollectible Accounts*.	Current ratio *unchanged*
8. Collected on accounts receivable.	Receivable turnover +
9. Paid on accounts payable.	Return on total assets +
10. Sold obsolete inventory at cost.	Return on sales +
11. Issued a stock dividend on common stock.	Earnings per share +
12. Sold inventory on account.	Inventory turnover +

Required:
State whether each transaction would cause the ratio listed opposite it to increase, decrease, or remain unchanged.

Problem 20-5   Using Ratios to Compute Data Missing in Financial Statements

The incomplete financial statements of the Barrett Corporation are shown here.

BARRETT CORPORATION
Income Statement
For the Year Ended December 31, 1987

Sales	$?
Less: Cost of goods sold	?
Gross profit on sales	?
Operating expenses	20,000
Interest expense	?
Total expenses	?
Income before taxes	38 ?000
Less: Income tax (50%)	19,000
Net income	$ 19 ?000

```
                    BARRETT CORPORATION
                        Balance Sheet
                     December 31, 1987

   Assets
   Current Assets:
     Cash                                            $    ?
     Accounts receivable                                  ?
     Inventory                                            ?
       Total Current Assets                               ?
   Plant and equipment                                    ?
       Total Assets                                  $    ?95,000

   Liabilities and Stockholders' Equity
   Current liabilities                               $    ?
   Long-term liabilities, 10% interest                 20,000
   Common stock, $10 par value                            ?
   Retained earnings                                      ?
       Total Liabilities and Stockholders' Equity    $95,000
```

The following additional information is available.

1. The current ratio is 2.0.
2. The quick ratio is 1.0.
3. The receivable turnover is 10.0 and the balance in *Accounts Receivable* on January 1, 1987 was $10,000.
4. The inventory turnover is 2.0. The January 1, 1987 inventory was $22,000.
5. The debt to total assets ratio is 40.0%.
6. Earnings per share are $3.80. No additional common stock was issued during the year.
7. All the interest expense is attributable to the long-term liabilities.

Required:

Complete the income statement and the balance sheet. Show all computations. (Hint: The debt to total assets ratio is the key to this problem.)

Problem 20-6 Comparison of Two Companies

Hardy Company and Oliver Company are competing businesses in the community. The two companies are quite similar, except that Hardy uses the LIFO method for inventory accounting and Oliver uses the FIFO method. Financial statements for the two companies are shown on the next page.

Required:

A. Compute the following ratios for each company.
  1. Return on total assets (assume that both companies incurred an interest expense of $110 during 1987).
  2. Return on sales.
  3. Current ratio.
  4. Receivable turnover.

Income Statements
For the Year Ended December 31, 1987

	Hardy	Oliver
Sales	$5,000	$5,000
Less: Cost of goods sold	3,000	2,370
Gross profit	2,000	2,630
Operating and interest expenses	1,500	1,500
Income tax expense (30%)	150	340
Total expenses	1,650	1,840
Net Income	$ 350	$ 790

Balance Sheets
December 31, 1987 and 1986

	Hardy		Oliver	
	1987	1986	1987	1986
Assets				
Cash	$ 500	$ 400	$ 500	$ 400
Accounts receivable	420	415	420	415
Inventory	100	100	745	115
Equipment	1,500	1,500	1,500	1,500
Total Assets	$2,520	$2,415	$3,165	$2,430
Liabilities and Stockholders' Equity				
Current liabilities	$ 500	$ 450	$ 500	$ 450
Long-term liabilities	1,100	1,000	1,100	1,000
Stockholders' equity	920	965	1,565	980
Total Liabilities and Stockholders' Equity	$2,520	$2,415	$3,165	$2,430

5. Inventory turnover.
6. Debt to total assets.

B. Why do the two companies' ratios differ? Which, if either, company appears superior?

ALTERNATE PROBLEMS

Problem 20-1A **Horizontal and Vertical Analysis**

Comparative income statements and balance sheets of the Granada Corporation appear here.

GRANADA CORPORATION
Comparative Income Statements
For the Years Ended December 31, 1987 and 1986

	1987	1986
Sales	$430,000	$380,000
Less: Cost of goods sold	200,000	195,000
Gross profit on sales	230,000	185,000
Operating expenses	126,000	65,000
Interest expense	10,000	6,000
Income tax expense	28,200	32,000
Total expenses	164,200	103,000
Net Income	$ 65,800	$ 82,000

GRANADA CORPORATION
Comparative Balance Sheets
December 31, 1987 and 1986

	1987	1986
Assets		
Cash	$ 23,500	$ 30,000
Accounts receivable	46,000	43,000
Inventory	70,000	62,000
Plant and equipment	250,000	160,000
Total Assets	$389,500	$295,000
Liabilities and Stockholders' Equity		
Accounts payable	$ 65,000	$ 50,000
Bonds payable	100,000	40,000
Common stock	175,000	175,000
Retained earnings	49,500	30,000
Total Liabilities and Stockholders' Equity	$389,500	$295,000

Required:

A. Compute the changes in the income statements and balance sheets from 1986 to 1987 in dollar amounts and in percentages.

B. Prepare common size financial statements for both years.

C. Comment briefly on the relationships revealed by the horizontal and vertical analyses.

Problem 20-2A Trend Analysis

Comparative financial statements for the Highland Corporation appear here.

HIGHLAND CORPORATION
Comparative Income Statements
For the Years Ended December 31, 1985–1989
(000 omitted)

	1985	1986	1987	1988	1989
Sales	$900	$936	$1,062	$1,593	$1,809
Less: Cost of goods sold	530	551	604	890	1,023
Gross profit on sales	370	385	458	703	786
Selling expenses	100	109	113	125	175
Administrative expenses	75	72	82	90	94
Interest expense	15	15	15	23	24
Income tax expense	62	64	88	178	184
Total Expenses	252	260	298	416	477
Net Income	$118	$125	$ 160	$ 287	$ 309

HIGHLAND CORPORATION
Comparative Balance Sheets
December 31, 1985–1989
(000 omitted)

	1985	1986	1987	1988	1989
Assets					
Current assets	$280	$314	$311	$ 353	$ 358
Plant and equipment	535	556	589	754	824
Total Assets	$815	$870	$900	$1,107	$1,182
Liabilities and Stockholders' Equity					
Current liabilities	$150	$174	$212	$ 186	$ 204
Bonds payable	160	162	163	258	259
Common stock	450	450	450	450	450
Retained earnings	55	84	75	213	269
Total Liabilities and Stockholders' Equity	$815	$870	$900	$1,107	$1,182

Required:
A. Perform a trend analysis on the financial statements.
B. Comment on any significant relationships revealed by the trend analysis.

Problem 20-3A Ratio Analysis

The 1987 annual report of the Jordan Company contains the following information.

Preferred dividends declared and paid during 1987: $20,000.

Common dividends declared and paid during 1987: $830,000.

Market price per share of preferred stock on December 31, 1987: $20.00.

Market price per share of common stock on December 31, 1987: $60.00.

JORDAN COMPANY
Income Statement
For the Year Ended December 31, 1987
(000 omitted)

Sales	$18,000
Less: Cost of goods sold	11,500
Gross profit on sales	6,500
Selling expenses	2,400
Administrative expenses	1,800
Interest expense	500
Income tax expense (30%)	540
Total Expenses	5,240
Net Income	$ 1,260

JORDAN COMPANY
Comparative Balance Sheets
December 31, 1987 and 1986
(000 omitted)

	1987	1986
Assets		
Current Assets:		
Cash	$ 600	$ 550
Marketable securities	120	100
Accounts receivable	1,800	2,000
Inventory	2,000	2,240
Total Current Assets	4,520	4,890
Plant and equipment	8,400	7,800
Total Assets	$12,920	$12,690
Liabilities		
Current Liabilities:		
Accounts payable	$ 2,500	$ 2,640
Accrued expenses	50	100
Total Current Liabilities	2,550	2,740
Notes payable	100	90
Bonds payable	3,500	3,500
Total Liabilities	6,150	6,330
Stockholders' Equity		
Preferred stock (10%, $10 par value)	200	200
Common stock ($5 par value)	1,000	1,000
Paid-in capital in excess of par value	3,100	3,100
Retained earnings	2,470	2,060
Total Stockholders' Equity	6,770	6,360
Total Liabilities and Stockholders' Equity	$12,920	$12,690

Required:
Compute the following ratios as of December 31, 1987.

A. Return on total assets.
B. Return on common stockholders' equity.
C. Return on sales.
D. Earnings per share.
E. Price-earnings ratio.
F. Dividend yield.
G. Dividend payout.
H. Current ratio.
I. Quick ratio.
J. Receivable turnover.
K. Inventory turnover.
L. Debt to total assets.
M. Times interest earned.

Problem 20-4A   Effect of Transactions on Ratios

Selected transactions of the Palmer Company are listed here in the left-hand column.

Transaction	Ratio
1. Buy machinery on account.	Debt to total assets
2. Write off an uncollectible account receivable to *Allowance for Uncollectible Accounts*.	Quick ratio
3. Retire bonds payable with cash.	Return on total assets
4. Issue common stock in exchange for land.	Return on common stockholders' equity
5. Pay on accounts payable.	Debt to total assets
6. Declare a cash dividend on common stock.	Current ratio
7. Sell inventory on account.	Quick ratio
8. Collect on accounts receivable.	Current ratio
9. Sell inventory for cash.	Receivable turnover
10. Pay a cash dividend previously declared.	Dividend payout
11. Record accrued interest on notes payable.	Return on sales
12. Issue bonds payable.	Return on total assets

Required:
Indicate whether each transaction will increase, decrease, or have no effect on the ratio listed across from it.

Problem 20-5A   Using Ratios to Compute Data Missing in Financial Statements

The financial statements of the Kramer Corporation appear here with most of the dollar amounts missing.

KRAMER CORPORATION
Income Statement
For the Year Ended June 30, 1987

Sales	$800,000
Less: Cost of goods sold	?
Gross profit on sales	?
Operating expenses	?
Interest expense	?
Total Expenses	?
Income before taxes	?
Less: Income tax (50%)	?
Net income	$?

KRAMER CORPORATION
Balance Sheet
June 30, 1987

Assets	
Current Assets:	
Cash	$?
Accounts receivable	?
Inventory	?
Total Current Assets	?
Plant and equipment	?
Total Assets	$?
Liabilities and Stockholders' Equity	
Current liabilities	$ 65,000
Long-term liabilities, 10% interest	200,000
Common stock, $10 par value	?
Retained earnings	?
Total Liabilities and Stockholders' Equity	$?

The following additional information is available.

1. The current ratio is 2.0.
2. The quick ratio is 1.0.
3. The receivable turnover is 16.0, and the *Accounts Receivable* balance on July 1, 1986, was $60,000.
4. The inventory turnover is 7.15, and the balance in the *Inventory* account on July 1, 1986 was $46,888.
5. Return on sales is 11.25%.
6. Debt to total assets is 66.25%.
7. Earnings per share are $9.00. The number of shares of common stock outstanding remained constant during the year.
8. Times interest earned is 10.0.

Required:
Fill in all the missing dollar amounts. Show all computations. (Hint: The current ratio
is the key to solving this problem.)

Problem 20-6A Comparison of Two Companies

Hogan Corporation and Schultz Corporation are competing businesses. The two companies are quite similar, except that Hogan uses the LIFO method for inventory
accounting and Schultz uses the FIFO method.

Financial statements for the two companies are shown here.

Income Statements
For the Year Ended December 31, 1987

	Hogan	Schultz
Sales	$50,000	$50,000
Less: Cost of goods sold	35,000	30,000
Gross profit	15,000	20,000
Operating and financing expenses	8,000	8,000
Income tax expense (30%)	2,100	3,600
Total Expenses	10,100	11,600
Net Income	$ 4,900	$ 8,400

Balance Sheets
December 31, 1987 and 1986

	Hogan 1987	Hogan 1986	Schultz 1987	Schultz 1986
Assets				
Cash	$ 5,000	$ 4,000	$ 5,000	$ 4,000
Accounts receivable	4,300	4,100	4,300	4,100
Inventory	5,000	5,000	8,000	3,000
Equipment	10,000	8,000	10,000	8,000
Total Assets	$24,300	$21,100	$27,300	$19,100
Liabilities and Stockholders' Equity				
Current liabilities	$ 7,000	$ 6,500	$ 7,000	$ 6,500
Long-term liabilities	9,000	7,000	9,000	7,000
Stockholders' equity	8,300	7,600	11,300	5,600
Total Liabilities and Stockholders' Equity	$24,300	$21,100	$27,300	$19,100

Required:
A. Compute the following ratios for each company.
  1. Return on total assets (assume that each company incurred interest expense of
  $900 for 1987).
  2. Return on sales.
  3. Current ratio.

4. Receivable turnover.
5. Inventory turnover.
6. Debt to total assets.

B. Why do the two companies' ratios differ? Which, if either, company appears superior?

CASE

CASE 20-1 Financial Report Analysis Case Percentage and Ratio Analysis of Comparative Statements

For this case, you must use the 1984 and 1980 annual reports for Chrysler Corporation presented in Appendix A.

Required:

A. In each annual report after the notes to the financial statements, an "Accountant's Report," prepared by the company's auditors, Touche Ross & Co., is presented. In the opinion of Touche Ross, were both sets of financial statements fairly presented?

B. Compute the following ratios and percentages for both years.
  1. Current ratio.
  2. Debt to total assets.
  3. Return on sales.
  4. Dividend payout.
  5. Compute the following as a percentage of total liabilities and shareholders' equity.
    (a) Total current liabilities.
    (b) Long-term debt (excluding deferred liabilities, other liabilities, and accrued employees' benefits).
    (c) Preferred stock.
    (d) Common stock.
  6. Compute the following as a percentage of net sales.
    (a) Costs, other than the items below.
    (b) Depreciation of plant and equipment.
    (c) Selling and administrative expenses.
    (d) Pension plans.

C. Compute the percentage change from 1980 to 1984 in the following items.
  1. Net sales.
  2. Costs, other than the items below.
  3. Current assets.
  4. Net property, plant, and equipment.
  5. Current liabilities.
  6. Total assets.

D. Comment on significant changes that are evident from your computations.

PART 6

MANAGERIAL ACCOUNTING FUNDAMENTALS

21

MANAGERIAL ACCOUNTING AND BUSINESS SEGMENTS

CHAPTER OVERVIEW AND OBJECTIVES

This chapter presents a transition from *financial accounting* to *managerial accounting*. When you have completed the chapter, you should understand:

1. The way organizational structure affects the information needs of management.
2. The role of management in an organization.
3. The importance of efficiency and effectiveness in an organization.
4. The concept of different costs for different purposes.
5. The basic nature of business segmentation.
6. The importance of responsibility accounting in a business firm.
7. The use of departmental accounting.
8. The difference between departmental gross profit, departmental contribution to indirect expenses, and departmental net income as profitability measures.
9. The basic nature and limitations of indirect operating expense allocations.
10. The analysis required to identify an unprofitable department.
11. The basic procedures required for branch accounting.

As we mentioned at the outset, modern accounting serves a wide variety of users who have economic interests in business firms. In the preceding chapters, we have examined the fundamentals of financial accounting with our primary attention directed toward external parties, such as creditors and investors. We now turn to the subject of managerial accounting, which is concerned with internal reporting to managers, who use the information at all levels of an organization for planning, controlling, and decision making. The information needs of management are quite different from those of parties external to the firm. *Managerial accounting is not restricted to the generally accepted accounting principles required for financial accounting*, so management can establish its own guidelines for the type of accounting information it uses. However, both managerial and financial accounting information should be developed within the same general accounting system. The cost of maintaining two separate systems would be excessive, if not prohibitive, because of the duplication of such items as charts of accounts, journals, ledgers, bookkeeping costs, and computer time. Since it is management-oriented, our coverage of managerial accounting should be preceded by an understanding of what managers do and the organizational structure within which they operate.

ORGANIZATIONAL CONSIDERATIONS

The most basic form of economic enterprise is a one-person business. Its management and information needs are relatively simple because all decision-making responsibilities for functions such as purchasing, selling, producing, accounting, and financing rest with the owner. This simple situation seldom exists, and if it does, it will normally be found only during the initial stage of a business firm's life cycle. As soon as the first employee is hired, a division of labor occurs and an organization is born. An **organization** can be defined as a group of people who share common goals with a well defined division of labor. The managers of an organization need relevant information to integrate the activities of the various segments of the organization and to ensure that they are directed toward common goals. As an organization develops in size and complexity, authority and responsibility for performance are delegated to many people. Consequently, the role of management becomes increasingly important. This is true for a manufacturing corporation, a bank, an accounting firm, a medical clinic, or a retail store.

Objective 1:
How an organizational structure affects the information needs of managers

ROLE OF MANAGEMENT

A major goal of every firm is to achieve satisfactory financial results. The management of a business firm is accountable to its owners for adequate profits as indicators of a successful operation. Even not-for-profit entities, such as charitable organizations, must be certain that their expenses do not exceed revenues for an extended period. Every firm must accept the fact that its resources will be in limited supply and must be conserved if a satisfactory financial performance is to be achieved. Such factors as inflation, technological change, competition, government regulation, high interest rates, increased energy costs, and declining productivity have an adverse effect on most firms' financial performance.

Objective 2:
The role of management in an organization

If a business is to be financially successful, management must be both efficient and effective. **Efficiency** means maintaining a satisfactory relationship between a firm's resource inputs and its outputs of products or services (for example, the minimum number of labor hours as input required to produce a product as output). **Effectiveness** refers to how well a firm attains its goals

Objective 3:
Distinguishing between efficiency and effectiveness

Figure 21–1
Management Process

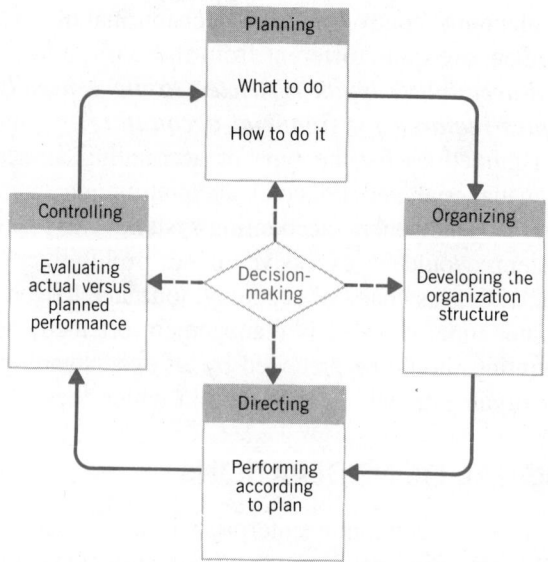

(for example, the number of products sold compared with the number planned). The efficiency and effectiveness of the management process, diagrammed in Figure 21–1, is essential to the overall success of any business. It is important to note that these **management functions** are not always as sequentially dependent as Figure 21–1 may suggest, since they are often performed concurrently and are constantly interacting with each other.

PLANNING

A successful business plans for the future by carefully setting goals. Management must decide what actions the firm should take in the future and how goals should be accomplished. Alternative courses of action are identified, their probable results are evaluated, and the courses of action that appear best for the achievement of the firm's goals are selected. Planning is required so that management can anticipate future events, rather than react to actual circumstances once they are known. Much of managerial planning will be concerned with the efficiency and effectiveness of future operations.

ORGANIZING

Plans are only words and numbers on paper until they are implemented. The organizing function provides the structure or capacity within which management will work to achieve its plans. The firm is divided into segments (such as departments, branches, divisions, plants, and offices) to take advantage of the specialization of skills and abilities. The right people are hired, trained, and assigned to specific jobs. Well defined lines of authority and responsibility are established. Sources of operating resources (such as materials, utilities, and advertising) are selected, physical facilities (land, buildings, machinery, and equipment) are obtained, and financing commitments are arranged to fund the operations.

DIRECTING

This function deals with the day-to-day management of the firm. Actions, decision making, communication, and leadership are combined to carry out the planned activities within the organizational structure. Problems are solved, questions are answered, disagreements are resolved, and coordination of the various operating segments is achieved.

CONTROLLING

Management must be sure that the actual performance of the firm and its segments compares favorably with the goals established during the planning function. If managers are to be held accountable for their performances, they should know where and why actual results differ from those planned. Control is based upon the concept of **management by exception**, which recognizes that since management time is a scarce resource, the primary concern should be detecting any performance that deviates significantly from the related plan. Performance reports are issued periodically to inform management of any significant variations from the expected results, so that corrective action can be taken to improve the efficiency or effectiveness of future operations whenever possible.

DECISION MAKING

Competent decision making is at the core of each of the functions performed by management. A wide range of decisions must be made. Top management will be concerned with strategic decisions relating primarily to the firm's environment (such as economic conditions, social problems, and market considerations). At lower levels of management, operating decisions are made regularly for such activities as product pricing, choice of inventory levels, production scheduling, and advertising media selection. All management decisions are concerned with the selection between alternatives and have one thing in common—*the need for reliable information*. Some of the information needed will be historical, while much of it will reflect management's expectations about the future. Most of the information needed will be objective, but some will be subjective. Much of the information needed will be available from internal sources, although some will be externally oriented. As we shall see, a significant amount of the information needed will come from managerial accounting.

DIFFERENT COST CLASSIFICATIONS

**Objective 4:
Why there are
different costs
for different
purposes**

Two of the most frequently used terms in the accountant's vocabulary are *cost* and *expense.* Both the distinction between the two terms and the many ways that costs are classified are of extreme importance in accounting. While the terms cost and expense are often used synonymously, there is a technical difference between the two. A *cost* is an economic sacrifice of resources made in exchange for a product or service, whereas an *expense* is an expired cost. In general, as long as a cost has a future benefit, it is reported on the balance sheet as an asset. The cost expires when it is consumed in the production of revenue or when it no longer has future benefit. Then the cost is presented on the income statement as an expense. For example, we may pay cash for an annual insurance policy for liability protection. The payment is initially a cost, which later is treated as a monthly expense as the future benefits of the insurance expire.

Managerial accountants identify specific types of costs that are suitable for specific purposes. Examples of different types of costs are direct cost, indirect cost, controllable cost, uncontrollable cost, variable cost, and fixed cost. Since most costs ultimately become expenses, the same categories or types can be associated with expenses. The important issue is that *different costs will be applicable for different purposes.* Once the purpose of the cost information is known, the managerial accountant will choose from the many cost classifications available to select the most pertinent meaning. We will explain each of the major cost classifications in our discussion of managerial accounting topics.

BUSINESS SEGMENTATION

**Objective 5:
The basics of
business seg-
mentation**

We noted earlier that a key aspect of the organizing function is the structuring of a business firm's segments. **Business segmentation**, the division of work into specialized units, enables a firm to accomplish more than it otherwise could. Segmented decision making is usually better, since managers of the segments are closest to the day-to-day activities and can control them more effectively. Departments, divisions, and branches are typical business segments within the same entity. Some corporations use subsidiaries organized as separate entities with common ownership of stock and top management. The choice of business segments depends upon such factors as the size of the organization, the nature of the products or services, the type of customers, management philosophy, and geographical factors. For example, a franchised automobile dealership might be segmented into six departments: new car sales, used car sales, leasing, repair shop, body shop, and parts, as shown in Figure 21–2. Even service firms divide their activities into well defined segments. An accounting firm is typically structured into departments for auditing, management services, and tax work.

Once the choice of specific business segments is made, a manager is assigned to each of them. He or she is given a certain amount of authority to make decisions and take whatever action is necessary to accomplish the goals

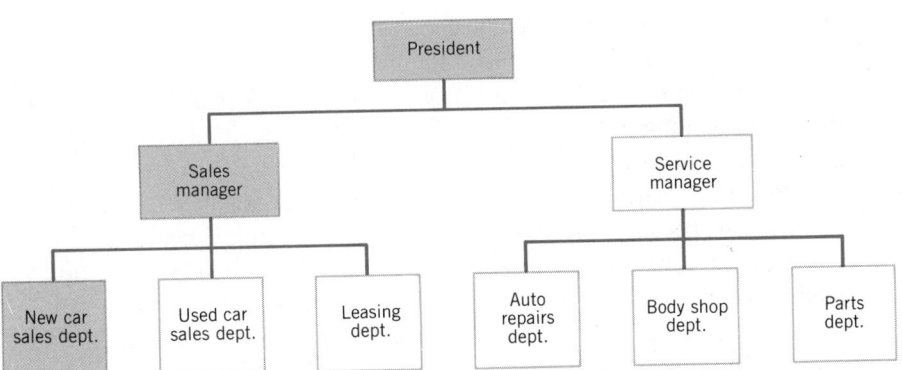

Figure 21–2
Automobile Dealer-
ship Organization
Chart

of the segment. In turn, the manager is held responsible for the segment's performance, which means the person is obligated to achieve desired operating results. Ideally, both efficiency and effectiveness measures will be used to evaluate the performance of the segments. This means that whenever possible, resource inputs, outputs in the form of products or services, and the goals of the segment will be considered in the evaluation process.

To evaluate the performance of a segment, the accounting system must be designed so that detailed financial information for each segment will be available. This detailed information is not usually made public, since it would be valuable to competitors. Instead, managers use it to plan activities for each segment, allocate scarce resources, evaluate actual performances, and take corrective action, whenever necessary, to improve the efficiency and effectiveness of future operations.

RESPONSIBILITY ACCOUNTING

Responsibility accounting is an important managerial accounting topic that provides much of the personalized information needed to manage the segments of a business. In essence, responsibility accounting requires each manager to participate in the development of financial plans for his or her segment and provides timely performance reports that compare actual results with those planned. When responsibility accounting is used along with budgeting (which we will discuss in Chapter 24), the combination provides management with an effective means of planning and controlling a firm's financial performance.

**Objective 6:
The importance
of responsibility
accounting**

FUNDAMENTALS OF RESPONSIBILITY ACCOUNTING

The most essential features of responsibility accounting can be summarized as follows.

Choice of Responsibility Centers. A **responsibility center** is a business segment, such as a department, that can be established as a cost center, a profit center, or an investment center. The choice among the three depends on the answer to the question, "What aspect of the financial performance is to be controlled?" If management is concerned only with the costs incurred in a particular department, it will be defined as a **cost center.** Cost centers are the most common form of responsibility center, since many departments do not produce revenue. For example, a retail firm's accounting department could be established as a cost center. A **profit center** exists when revenue, as well as costs, can be traced to a department. A sales department of a retail store can be organized as a profit center, because earnings from the segment's activity can be measured. However, the most complete form of responsibility center is an **investment center,** in which management is held responsible for the return on the resources used by the segment. As such, the manager of an investment center will be accountable for costs, revenue, and operating assets, with the goal of generating a satisfactory return on investment. A department store operated by a chain-store organization is an example of an investment center.

Matching Accounting System and Organization. Once the choice between the different types of responsibility centers has been made, the accounting system must be designed to collect financial data for each responsibility center. Consequently, the accounting system itself is segmented to provide information for individual managers, as well as for the firm as a whole, through the numbering system used to code the general ledger accounts.

Controllability Focus. In the evaluation of their responsibility centers' financial performances, managers should be accountable for only the financial items over which they have control. At their level of management, they must be able to regulate, or at least to influence, all costs, revenues, or invested resources classified as being controllable during a given accounting period. Thus, the two key dimensions of controllability in responsibility accounting are the *specific level of management* and the *given time period.* For example, a **controllable cost or expense** is one that can be authorized by a particular manager during a specified time period. The manager of a sales department in a retail store is usually able to control the labor costs of the department, but can *not* influence the real estate taxes paid on the building occupied by the store. He or she would be held accountable for the labor cost, but not for the property taxes.

Participative Management. The managers accountable for the performance of the responsibility centers should participate actively in the development of the planned financial performance, which is usually expressed in terms of a budget. When managers prepare their own estimates, goals become *self-imposed,* instead of being established by higher management. This approach should motivate managers to achieve the planned performance.

Performance Reporting. The manager of a responsibility center is evaluated with performance reports that show the financial items for which he or she is responsible. The reporting phase of responsibility accounting is based on the premise that the assignment of authority and responsibility flows from top to bottom in an organization, while accountability flows from bottom to top. In other words, top managers transfer the authority and responsibility for operating results to lower levels of management

	Budget	Actual	Variance
President's Report:			
President's office	$ 12,800	$ 13,900	$ 1,100 U
Sales departments	102,900	112,370	9,470 U
Service departments	92,500	98,600	6,100 U
Total	208,200	224,870	16,670 U
Sales Manager's Report:			
Sales manager's office	9,500	9,900	400 U
New car sales department	56,600	61,970	5,370 U
Used car sales department	28,200	32,100	3,900 U
Leasing department	8,600	8,400	200 F
Total	102,900	112,370	9,470 U
New Car Sales Manager's Report:			
Sales salaries	18,200	19,800	1,600 U
Advertising	20,000	23,200	3,200 U
Utilities	4,400	4,850	450 U
Insurance	3,200	3,200	—
Rent	10,000	10,000	—
Other	800	920	120 U
Total	$ 56,600	$ 61,970	$ 5,370 U

Figure 21–3
Automobile Dealership Partial Responsibility Reporting System, Month of January, 1987

and receive periodic reports accounting for the actual and planned performance in return. Consequently, the performance reports start at the lowest level of management and build upward. Each manager receives information concerning his or her own performance, as well as that of any other manager who reports to him/her. Figure 21–3 is a partial version of a responsibility reporting system used to control the operating expenses of the automobile dealership shown in Figure 21–2. Cost centers have been established at three levels of management—departmental, sales or service manager, and the president of the firm. For illustrative purposes, we have restricted our attention to the shaded area of Figure 21–2, although all segments would be included in a real-life situation.

As the performance information flows from bottom to top, it is cumulative and less detailed. At the top of the organization, the president is accountable for one large responsibility center representing the entire business. The expected operating expenses are shown in the budget column, and the actual operating expenses incurred are presented in the actual column. The **variances** shown in the right-hand column are the differences between the expected and the actual expenses. The ''U'' indicates an unfavorable variance whenever the actual results are greater than those expected. A favorable variance, ''F,'' occurs when the actual expenses are less than those planned.

Management by Exception. Significant variances between the planned and actual performance of each responsibility center should be emphasized in the performance reports so that their causes can be determined and corrective action taken whenever necessary. For example, in the automobile dealership illustration, the unfavorable variances would be investigated to explain why the actual expenses reported are $16,670 higher than expected. The president can request the detailed copies of the performance reports from all levels of responsibility and can trace the variances downward through the performance reports to identify their sources so that corrective action can be taken to improve future operations. In turn, each accountable manager can do the same thing within his or her span of authority.

DEPARTMENTAL ACCOUNTING

Objective 7: How departmental accounting is used

Many firms are divided into departments in order to take advantage of the benefits of business segmentation and to differentiate between the products or services offered. More detailed accounting procedures are required to evaluate the financial performance of each department within an organization than are needed for the firm as a whole. **Departmental accounting** is used most frequently by large businesses, which typically have control problems. Such companies want to continuously evaluate the profitability of their different activities. However, even small firms can utilize departmental accounting to determine where their resources can best be used. For example, a small accounting firm may account separately for its accounting and tax services, so that management can decide where the professional time of employees should be devoted to achieve desired financial results. Many of the procedures used for departmental accounting are actually extensions of responsibility accounting.

Typically, the income statement is the only accounting report used for departmental accounting, since the balance sheet is common to the entire firm. In developing departmental accounting information, the accountant must decide how complete the income statement should be for each of the departments. Some small firms segregate only revenue by departments. Many merchandising firms restrict their attention to the gross profit on sales, which is calculated by subtracting cost of goods sold from net sales. Other businesses consider certain direct operating expenses of the departments, and some prepare a complete income statement for each department by allocating indirect expenses among the departments. Each of these approaches has certain advantages, but keep in mind that the managers of the various departments should be held accountable for only those financial items that they can control.

DEPARTMENTAL GROSS PROFIT—MERCHANDISING FIRM

Objective 8: Different departmental profit measures and income statement formats

Departmental gross profit (also called gross margin) on sales is a key indicator of profitability, and is closely watched by the management of a merchandising firm. As we noted in Chapter 9, the gross profit percentage can even be used to estimate ending inventories. If a merchandising business is to achieve its profit goals, the gross profit must be sufficient to cover the operating expenses and produce the desired net income. The factors influencing department gross profit are the number of units sold, selling prices, mix of merchandise sold, and the cost of units sold. In most cases, all four factors are controllable by the department managers, so the gross profit receives a significant amount of attention. Faster inventory turnover, higher prices, a more profitable sales mix, and effective cost control are among the most important objectives of the department managers. This does not mean that management should ignore the operating expenses, because the ultimate measure of financial performance is net income. As we shall see, however, many of the operating expenses are beyond the control of the department managers.

A merchandising firm must select between two basic approaches for the development of departmental gross profit information. The most common approach is to establish a complete set of general ledger accounts for the items that contribute to the gross profit in each department. Such accounts as *Sales, Purchases, Inventory, Sales Returns and Allowances, Freight in,* and *Purchase Returns and Allowances* are used in each department to record transactions as they occur. An alternative that is less accurate, but which may save time and expense, is to use a single set of general ledger accounts for the firm as a whole and then distribute the total amounts recorded to the various departments at the end of the accounting period. Analysis sheets, which are not actually part of the general ledger, provide the detail required in the alternative treatment. A separate analysis sheet would be used for sales, purchases, sales returns, freight in, and purchase returns. Figure 21–4 illustrates an analysis sheet used to account for the monthly sales of a hardware store. By combining the data in the analysis sheets with the amount of actual or estimated ending inventory for each department at the end of an accounting period, the departmental gross profit can be computed.

Electronic Data Processing

More detailed and reliable departmental accounting information has been made available in recent years by electronic data processing applications. Data terminals located at customer checkout stations can capture sales and inventory information while they function as cash registers at the point of sale. In some cases, the data are collected through the terminal and transmitted directly or

Figure 21–4
Sales Analysis Sheet

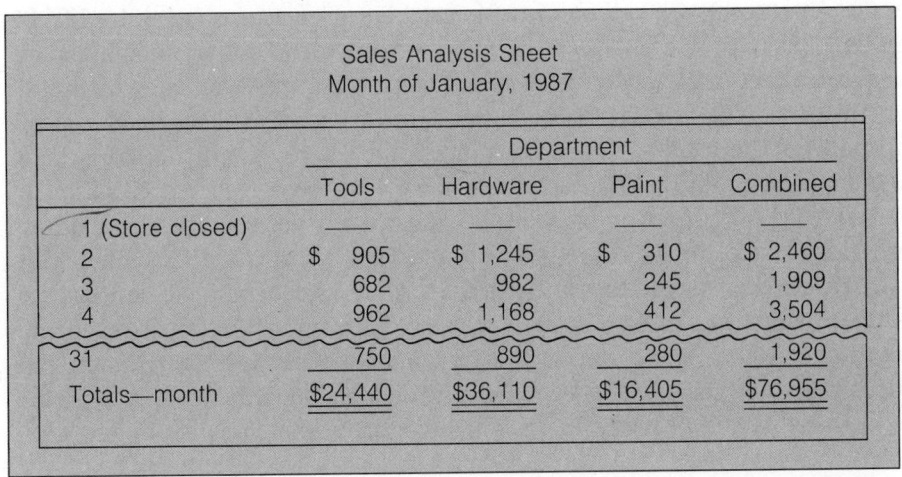

Sales Analysis Sheet
Month of January, 1987

	Tools	Hardware	Paint	Combined
		Department		
1 (Store closed)	——	——	——	——
2	$ 905	$ 1,245	$ 310	$ 2,460
3	682	982	245	1,909
4	962	1,168	412	3,504
31	750	890	280	1,920
Totals—month	$24,440	$36,110	$16,405	$76,955

indirectly to a computer. In more modern applications, the data terminals are freestanding devices, which in essence means they have their own electronic capability to collect, process, and report information.

Data terminals used at the point of sale have become popular in drugstores, supermarkets, hardware stores, discount stores, and department stores. Even small stores often find a data terminal to be the most effective and economical means of performing departmental accounting. Inventory tags or labels are coded with such information as department, type of merchandise, price, vendor, style, color, and original purchase cost. A coding system can be used to prevent customers from identifying anything except the price of the item. The checkout clerk punches the information into the terminal, where it is captured for subsequent processing into valuable management reports concerning the sales and inventory performance. For automatic data capture, an optical wand reader can be used at the point of sale to read the coded information and enter it into the terminal. Key entry of the inventory information by humans is eliminated, which saves time and can increase the accuracy of the data collection. The person operating the terminal simply passes the wand reader over the inventory tag and the information is automatically entered into the terminal. Alternatively, the reader may be contained in the checkout counter, in which case the inventory items pass over it. Newer data terminals even have a voice system that informs customers of the prices they are being charged.

The electronic data processing capability provides management with timely and reliable information concerning each department's performance. Inventory turnover, gross profit calculations, the percentage of total inventory invested in each item, sales results by salesperson, and pricing structure information are among the many statistics made available to management.

INCOME STATEMENT WITH DEPARTMENTAL GROSS PROFITS

Figure 21–5 shows an income statement prepared for the Andrews Hardware Store, which operates three departments. The statement reveals departmental gross profits and their combined total. The operating expenses are not assigned to the departments when this format is used but, instead, are subtracted from the total gross profit. The gross profit is presented as a dollar amount and as a percentage of sales. The income statement provides management with useful information with which departmental performance can be evaluated and sources of profit can be identified. The combination of the volume of inventory sold and the gross profit rate for each sales dollar must be considered because the same total gross profit can be achieved with a large volume of sales at a low gross profit rate, or with a smaller volume of sales at a higher gross profit rate. However, it should be noted that the analysis is not complete, since some of the operating expenses will be related to specific departments, and the ultimate objective is to earn a satisfactory amount of net income. Because the focus of the income statement in Figure 21–5 is on departmental gross profit, an itemized listing of the selling and administrative expenses is omitted.

ANDREWS HARDWARE STORE
Income Statement
(Departmental Gross Profit Format)
Year Ended December 31, 1987

	Tools Department		Hardware Department		Paint Department		Combined Departments
Sales	$352,000		$448,000		$224,000		$1,024,000
Less returns	8,000		4,800		3,200		16,000
Net sales	344,000		443,200		220,800		1,008,000
Cost of goods sold:							
Beginning inventory	68,800		88,640		36,800		194,240
Purchases	262,480		278,968		129,680		671,128
Freight in	4,800		5,600		3,200		13,600
Goods available for sale	336,080		373,208		169,680		878,968
Ending inventory	71,200		89,560		37,200		197,960
Cost of goods sold	264,880		283,648		132,480		681,008
Gross profit (%)	$ 79,120	(23.0)	$159,552	(36.0)	$ 88,320	(40.0)	326,992 (32.4)
Operating expenses:							
Selling expenses							146,400
Administrative expenses							132,800
Total operating expenses							279,200
Net income							$ 47,792

Figure 21–5
Departmental Income Statement

DEPARTMENTAL NET INCOME

Objective 9: How indirect expense allocation is used

Departmental profitability reporting can be extended beyond the gross profit calculation to show the net income of each department through the use of **operating expense allocation.** The reasoning behind such an extension is that a department is merely a part of the entire firm and could not function without the benefits provided by such operating expenses as advertising, rent, utilities, property taxes, insurance, and salaries. Since the firm's revenue is generated by the sales departments, a fair share of all expenses should be matched with it. Unfortunately, difficult expense allocation problems are inevitable in the determination of departmental net income and will usually have an adverse effect on the accuracy of the results. When **departmental net income** (net sales less all expenses) is computed, the reports must be interpreted and used carefully. They should not be utilized for responsibility accounting purposes if they contain expenses over which the departmental managers have no control. Instead, complete departmental income statements should be used by top management to assess the approximate profitability of the departments as separate businesses providing their own goods and services, given the methods used to allocate the operating expenses.

Direct and Indirect Operating Expenses

To determine departmental net income, a distinction must be made between direct and indirect operating expenses. Managerial accountants often use the terms *direct* and *indirect* in relation to some **cost objective,** which is defined as any activity for which separate cost measurement is performed. In general, a **direct cost or expense** can be traced to a specific cost objective, whereas an **indirect cost or expense,** also called a common cost (expense), is incurred for multiple cost objectives. In this chapter, the cost objective is a department in a merchandising firm. However, managerial accounting uses a wide range of other cost objectives, such as a product produced by a manufacturing firm, a service performed by a bank, or a branch office operated by an insurance company.

A direct operating expense can be traced to a particular department as a cost objective, since it is incurred solely for the benefit of that department. Examples of this are the sales salaries and commissions paid to salespeople who work exclusively in one department. The direct operating expenses can be charged to separate departmental expense accounts when they are incurred. Alternatively, some accountants prefer to assign the direct expenses to the departments using a worksheet at the end of an accounting period. This approach reduces the number of departmental accounts needed without any loss of accuracy.

In contrast, an indirect operating expense is incurred for the benefit of the firm as a whole, so it can *not* be traced to a particular department as a cost objective. An indirect operating expense is a common expense since it is incurred for the benefit of more than one cost objective. Rent, utilities, insurance, property taxes, and top management salaries are examples of indirect operating expenses. Another type of indirect operating expense would be one incurred by a service department. A **service department** supports the sales departments in some specific way that enables the sales departments to function. A personnel department, an advertising department, a general office department, an accounting department, and a maintenance department are service departments. Although certain expenses, such as salaries and supplies, are directly related to the service departments, they are indirect operating expenses for the selling departments.

Since none of the indirect operating expenses can be traced to the merchandising departments, they can be assigned to them only on some allocation basis. This means that the indirect expenses are apportioned among the various departments that jointly benefit from them. A number of bases have been developed by accountants as potentially equitable ways to allocate indirect expenses. Since the guiding principle for proper allocation should be to match the expenses with the revenue that they help produce, the merchandising departments will ideally be charged for indirect expenses on the basis of the benefits that they receive. However, these benefits are often difficult to measure, and sound judgment, rather than absolute rules, may be the only approach possible. Unfortunately, even equally competent accountants will often disagree on the choice of the best allocation basis for a specific indirect expense. As a result, extreme caution must be exercised in interpreting income statements in which indirect expenses have been allocated.

Bases for Allocating Expenses

To illustrate the allocation of indirect expenses to departments, we will continue to use the example of Andrews Hardware Store. We assume that the direct operating expenses are assigned to the departments at the end of the accounting period instead of being recorded regularly in departmental accounts. The indirect operating expenses are allocated at the end of the period on bases that the firm's accountant believes best represent the benefits received from the expenses. A departmental expense allocation worksheet is used to allocate the operating expenses to the three departments: tools, hardware, and paint. The methods used for the distribution of the operating expenses are discussed next, and the results are shown on the allocation worksheet in Figure 21–6.

Sales Salaries. Each salesperson employed by Andrews Hardware Store works exclusively in one department, so all sales salaries are *direct expenses.* The payroll register is departmentalized and shows that the sales salaries are $36,960, $34,240, and $21,200 for the Tools Department, Hardware Department, and Paint Department, respectively.

Advertising Expense. Andrews Hardware Store relies primarily on newspaper and radio media for its advertising. The department managers have the

Figure 21–6
Expense Allocation Worksheet

ANDREWS HARDWARE STORE
Departmental Expense Allocation Worksheet
Year Ended December 31, 1987

Operating Expenses	Amount	Allocation Base	Tools	Hardware	Paint
Selling expenses:					
Sales salaries	$ 92,400	Direct—payroll register	$36,960	$34,240	$21,200
Advertising	12,600	Direct—invoices	5,200	2,400	5,000
Advertising	17,640	Indirect—net sales	6,015	7,762	3,863
Inventory insurance	5,760	Direct—insurance policy	2,056	2,615	1,089
Bad debts	4,200	Direct—accounts written off	1,432	1,848	920
Sales supplies	3,800	Direct—requisitions	1,200	1,100	1,500
Depreciation—equipment	5,200	Direct—property records	1,900	1,500	1,800
Miscellaneous	4,800	Indirect—net sales	1,637	2,112	1,051
Total	146,400		56,400	53,577	36,423
Administrative expenses:					
Management salaries	48,000	Indirect—time	16,000	16,000	16,000
Building expenses	46,800	Indirect—space	11,700	23,400	11,700
Purchasing department	16,000	Indirect—purchases	6,240	6,656	3,104
General office department	16,200	Indirect—employees	6,480	5,670	4,050
Miscellaneous	5,800	Indirect—net sales	1,978	2,552	1,270
Total	$132,800		$42,398	$54,278	$36,124

authority to authorize a limited amount of advertising for their individual departments. Invoices indicate that the direct departmental advertising amounted to $5,200, $2,400, and $5,000 for the three departments, or a total of $12,600. The remaining $17,640 was spent on store advertising, which featured all three departments and which is allocated on the basis of sales as the most realistic distribution of the related benefits. The indirect advertising expense of Andrews Hardware Store would be allocated according to the following schedule.

Department	Tools	Hardware	Paint	Combined
1987 net sales	$344,000	$433,200	$220,800	$1,008,000
Percentage of combined sales	34.1	44.0	21.9	100.0
Allocation of $17,640	$ 6,015	$ 7,762	$ 3,863	$ 17,640

Alternative treatments would be to distribute the indirect advertising on the basis of the direct advertising expense or the relative number of departmental products presented in the indirect advertising.

Inventory Insurance.   The insurance premium paid to insure the store's merchandise inventory is treated as a direct expense since it is calculated on the basis of the average dollar amount of inventory maintained during the year. Consequently, the total insurance expense is divided among the departments proportionate to their average inventory balances. The computation of the average departmental inventories as percentages of the average inventory of the store is as follows.

Department	Tools	Hardware	Paint	Combined
Beginning inventory	$68,800	$88,640	$36,800	$194,240
Ending inventory	71,200	89,560	37,200	197,960
Average inventory	70,000	89,100	37,000	196,100
Percentage of combined average inventory	35.7	45.4	18.9	100.0
Allocation of $5,760	$ 2,056	$ 2,615	$ 1,089	$ 5,760

Bad Debts.   Bad debt expense is charged directly to the departments on the basis of the accounts receivable written off during the period. When this approach is not feasible, bad debts are usually apportioned on the basis of departmental credit sales. The bad debt expenses are $1,432, $1,848, and $920 for the three departments.

Sales Supplies.   The sales supplies are treated as direct expenses for each of the departments. The dollar amounts per department are determined from the requisition forms used to order the supplies. The amounts for the three departments are $1,200, $1,100, and $1,500.

Depreciation Expense. Depreciation on the equipment used in each department is calculated from the property records, which are maintained on a departmental basis. Consequently, the depreciation expense is directly related to each department. The amounts are $1,900, $1,500, and $1,800 for the three departments.

Miscellaneous Selling Expenses. Since the expenses listed in this category originated from a variety of sources, it is assumed that allocating them on the basis of sales provides the best overall measure of the benefits received by each department. Therefore, the same percentages used in the distribution of indirect advertising expense would be applied to the miscellaneous sales expenses, which total $4,800.

Management Salaries. These expenses are allocated on the basis of the approximate time devoted by the top management of the store to each department. Considerations such as sales volume, personnel requirements, promotional effort, and operating problems will affect the time spent by management on departmental activities. In the case of Andrews Hardware Store, management estimates that it devotes about the same amount of time to each department, so the total of $48,000 is divided equally among the departments.

Building Expenses. All of the building occupancy expenses including rent, cleaning, real estate taxes, utilities, maintenance, and insurance are charged to one account—*Building Expenses*—and allocated to the sales departments on the basis of square feet occupied. If the building were owned, its depreciation would be allocated on the same basis. The Tools, Hardware, and Paint departments occupy one-quarter, one-half, and one-quarter of the total space respectively, so their respective charges are $11,700, $23,400, and $11,700. All of the space is of approximately the same value. If significant differences in value exist because of a department's location in a store, they should be taken into consideration in the allocation of any building expenses affected. For example, if management believes that the space near the store entrance is worth twice as much as the same area on the second floor because of higher sales in the area, the building rent allocated should be twice as much for the more valuable space.

Purchasing Department Expenses. The Purchasing Department is one of two service departments used by Andrews Hardware Store. This department has the responsibility of finding the best suppliers for purchases required by the selling departments and for placing specific orders. A variety of service departments may provide support to the selling departments of merchandising firms. Commonly used bases for allocating service department expenses to the selling departments are shown in Figure 21–7. Andrews Hardware Store uses the purchases of a given year to allocate the Purchasing Department's expenses, since this is considered the best aproximation of the services rendered to the selling departments. The resulting distribution is as follows.

Figure 21–7
Service Department
Expense Allocation
Bases

Service Department	Expense Allocation Bases
Advertising	Sales or number of ads placed in each selling department.
General office	Number of employees or sales in each selling department.
Janitorial	Square feet of floor space in each selling department.
Maintenance	Service rendered to each selling department.
Personnel	Number of employees in each selling department.
Purchasing	Dollar amounts of purchases by each selling department.
Storeroom	Dollar amounts of purchases or merchandise handled for each selling department.

Department	Tools	Hardware	Paint	Combined
1987 purchases (including freight in)	$267,280	$284,568	$132,880	$684,728
Percentage of combined purchases	39.0	41.6	19.4	100.0
Allocation of $16,000	$ 6,240	$ 6,656	$ 3,104	$ 16,000

General Office Department Expenses. The other service department of Andrews Hardware Store provides personnel, accounting, and payroll services to the three selling departments. The number of employees per department is the basis used to allocate the General Office Department expenses to the selling departments, since this is considered the best approximation of the benefits provided. An evaluation of the personnel employed in each department indicates that the following schedule is appropriate.

Department	Tools	Hardware	Paint	Combined
Percentage of total employees	40	35	25	100
Allocation of $16,200	$6,480	$5,670	$4,050	$16,200

Miscellaneous Administrative Expenses. The miscellaneous administrative expenses are allocated to the departments on the basis of sales for the same reason discussed earlier for the miscellaneous selling expenses. Consequently, the distribution of the total amount of $5,800 is $1,978, $2,552, and $1,270 to the Tools Department, Hardware Department, and Paint Department respectively.

DEPARTMENTAL INCOME STATEMENT

Once the assignment of operating expenses is completed, an income statement showing the net income from operations by department can be prepared, such as the one presented in Figure 21–8. The results indicate that two of the

ANDREWS HARDWARE STORE
Income Statement
(Departmental Net Income Format)
Year Ended December 31, 1987

	Tools Department	Hardware Department	Paint Department	Combined Departments
Net sales	$344,000	$443,200	$220,800	$1,008,000
Cost of goods sold	264,880	283,648	132,480	681,008
Gross profit	79,120	159,552	88,320	326,992
Operating expenses				
Selling expenses:				
Sales salaries	36,960	34,240	21,200	92,400
Advertising	11,215	10,162	8,863	30,240
Insurance	2,056	2,615	1,089	5,760
Bad debts	1,432	1,848	920	4,200
Supplies	1,200	1,100	1,500	3,800
Depreciation	1,900	1,500	1,800	5,200
Miscellaneous	1,637	2,112	1,051	4,800
Total	56,400	53,577	36,423	146,400
Administrative expenses:				
Management salaries	16,000	16,000	16,000	48,000
Building expenses	11,700	23,400	11,700	46,800
Purchasing	6,240	6,656	3,104	16,000
General office	6,480	5,670	4,050	16,200
Miscellaneous	1,978	2,552	1,270	5,800
Total	42,398	54,278	36,124	132,800
Total operating expenses	98,798	107,855	72,547	279,200
Net income (loss)	$ (19,678)	$ 51,697	$ 15,773	$ 47,792

Figure 21–8
Departmental Income Statement

departments, Hardware and Paint, were profitable, with net incomes of $51,697 and $15,773, respectively, whereas the Tools Department incurred a loss of $19,678. Remember, however, that these results should be evaluated cautiously. They represent estimates of the bottom-line net income performances of the departments when they are assigned their share of the indirect operating expenses. In turn, they represent approximations of the operating results of the departments as independent businesses. As suggested earlier, however, "their share" is subject to a great deal of judgment and depends upon the choice of the bases used to allocate the indirect operating expenses.

Different accountants may choose different allocation bases and, obviously, will achieve different results. Also, the departmental income statements can be criticized on the basis that the departments are not really separate businesses but, instead, segments of the same firm. Therefore, their bottom-line evaluation should only be concerned with the expenses for which they are directly accountable and the indirect expenses should be a common pool that benefits the entire firm, rather than individual departments. Such a presentation would avoid arbitrary allocations and represent the contribution of each department to the united efforts of the firm as a whole. As we will see later in manufacturing accounting, certain cost allocations are necessary to comply with generally accepted accounting principles; they should be easier to understand once you have learned the basics of the allocation process introduced here.

DEPARTMENTAL CONTRIBUTION TO INDIRECT EXPENSES

Objective 10: Evaluating an unprofitable department

An analysis of the net income results shown in Figure 21–8 may lead to the conclusion that the Tools Department is so unprofitable that management should consider eliminating it. The net loss of $19,678 may suggest to management that profits would have been $67,470 instead of $47,792 without the Tools Department. *But is this an accurate conclusion?* While it is true that the Tools Department does not have a sufficient amount of gross profit to cover its direct operating expenses plus its allocated indirect expenses, it nevertheless is making a contribution to the firm's profit results. The **departmental contribution to indirect expenses** is considered by many accountants and managers to be a more realistic assessment of a department's profitability performance than net income, which involves the allocation process described earlier. The advantage of departmental contribution to indirect expenses is that it usually consists of the revenue and expenses that would disappear if the department did not exist. Its use avoids the somewhat arbitrary allocation of indirect expenses required when an attempt is made to measure departmental net income.

The departmental contribution to indirect expenses is found by subtracting the direct operating expenses of a department from the departmental gross profit. In most cases, the direct operating expenses will be controllable by the department managers, so the departmental contribution to indirect expenses can be used effectively in responsibility accounting. In Figure 21–9, the operating results of Andrews Hardware Store have been restated in the format of departmental contribution to indirect expenses. Since the indirect expenses are outside the control of the department managers, they are left as common expenses, which are deducted from the total departmental contribution to indirect expenses. The departmental contributions of $30,372, $115,849 and $56,811 identify the controllable profit performances of the three departmental managers.

In Figure 21–9, we see that the Tools Department has made a contribution of $30,372 to the indirect expenses. Consequently, rather than increasing the total net income by $19,678, the elimination of the Tools Department would actually cause a decrease in net income of $30,372. This decrease in profit would occur because the two remaining departments have a combined departmental contribution to indirect expenses of $172,660 and will have to absorb all of the indirect operating expenses, amounting to $155,240. Thus, the net income would be only $17,420 in contrast to the profit of $47,792 from a three-department operation. The difference is the $30,372 contributed by the Tools Department. An alternative way to evaluate the results of elimi-

Figure 21–9
Departmental In-
come Statement

ANDREWS HARDWARE STORE
Income Statement
(Departmental Contribution to Indirect Expenses Format)
Year Ended December 31, 1987

	Tools Department	Hardware Department	Paint Department	Combined Departments
Net sales	$344,000	$443,200	$220,800	$1,008,000
Cost of goods sold	264,880	283,648	132,480	681,008
Gross profit	79,120	159,552	88,320	326,992
Direct operating expenses				
Sales salaries	36,960	34,240	21,200	92,400
Advertising	5,200	2,400	5,000	12,600
Insurance	2,056	2,615	1,089	5,760
Bad debts	1,432	1,848	920	4,200
Supplies	1,200	1,100	1,500	3,800
Depreciation	1,900	1,500	1,800	5,200
Total	48,748	43,703	31,509	123,960
Departmental contribution to indirect operating expenses	$ 30,372	$115,849	$ 56,811	203,032
Indirect operating expenses				
Advertising				17,640
Miscellaneous selling				4,800
Management salaries				48,000
Building expenses				46,800
Purchasing				16,000
General office				16,200
Miscellaneous administration				5,800
Total				155,240
Net income				$ 47,792

nating the Tools Department is to consider the gross profit of $79,120 given up versus the decreased direct operating expenses of $48,748. Again, the difference is $30,372 in favor of keeping the department. The most significant point in this analysis is that profitability measurement involving allocated expenses can generate misleading information when it is applied incorrectly.

A complete analysis of the Tools Department would have to take into consideration alternative uses of the space currently occupied by it and any adverse effect on the sales of the Hardware and Paint Departments from its elimination. Customers may only want to shop at a store with a complete line of hardware products, so the elimination of tools might adversely affect the sales of the other two departments. Also, we have assumed that all of the direct operating expenses are avoidable expenses, while all of the indirect expenses are unavoidable. **Avoidable costs or expenses** are ones that can be eliminated by the termination of a department, but **unavoidable costs or expenses** are those that will continue even when a department is eliminated. Consequently, only the direct operating expenses can be eliminated by disposing of the Tools Department, whereas the indirect expenses will not change, since the store will require essentially the same amount of services to support the remaining departments. In some cases, certain indirect operating expenses may also be avoidable, because they can be eliminated by reducing the size of the operation. For example, the expenses of the purchasing department may be decreased with fewer sales departments to serve. Conversely, some direct operating expenses are *not* avoidable, since they will continue even if the department is eliminated. For example, the department manager may be a valuable employee who has years of experience with the firm and, because of this, management may not terminate the person. The key issue in considering the discontinuation of any department is a careful assessment of each operating expense to determine whether it also will be eliminated with the decision.

FUNDAMENTALS OF BRANCH ACCOUNTING

Objective 11: The basic procedures used in branch accounting

Our final concern with business segmentation is a brief coverage of **branch accounting** procedures, used to account for branch operations. As merchandising firms grow, they often open branch stores to serve new marketing territories. National and regional chain-store operations have become increasingly popular in recent years. The growth of suburban shopping centers has contributed significantly to the number of branch operations.

In chain-store operations, a branch manager is assigned to each store and usually given broad responsibilities for operating the store within the general guidelines established by top management. The branch maintains its own inventories, sells the merchandise, approves customer credit, and may even collect its own accounts receivable. A branch may obtain all of its merchandise from the home office or some of it may be purchased from outside suppliers. Regardless of how much independence a branch is given, an accounting system is needed to control the transactions between the home office and the branch store, as well as to provide management with the information required to evaluate the branch's operating results.

CENTRALIZED VERSUS DECENTRALIZED ACCOUNTING

Management must decide whether the accounting for its branch operation will be accomplished with a centralized or a decentralized system. Many small merchandising firms use a centralized accounting system in which most of the records are maintained by the home office. The preparation of basic source documents, such as sales invoices or summaries, payroll time cards, and purchase vouchers, is the only accounting work performed by the branch. Copies of the basic documents are sent periodically to the home office for processing through the accounting system. All the journals and ledgers are maintained by the home office, which usually operates a computerized accounting system. Separate branch accounts for sales, cost of goods sold, and operating expenses are maintained in the home office general ledger. Basically, the same procedures discussed earlier for departmental accounting are used to process the accounting data and prepare timely reports with which the operating performance can be evaluated, since each branch is, in essence, a department.

As a system of branch operations grows, the volume of transactions and the accounting problems associated with the geographical separation of the stores force many firms to use decentralized accounting. Each branch maintains a self-contained accounting system, including an on-site computer in many large operations. The accounting principles and procedures used by each branch are basically the same as those of an autonomous store. The one exception is that a **Home Office account** is used by a branch instead of capital accounts. The *Home Office* account will show the net investment in the branch on the part of the firm. The account will be credited for cash, inventory, and other resources provided by the home office for the branch. It will be debited for cash, inventory, and other resources sent by the branch to the home office or to other branches. The *Home Office* account also will replace retained earnings in closing the branch books and will be credited for branch net income or debited for a branch net loss.

In a decentralized accounting system, a **Branch Investment account** will be maintained on the home office books to record transactions affecting a firm's investment in the branch operation. The *Home Office* account and the *Branch Investment* account are defined as **reciprocal accounts,** since they basically measure the same thing and should always be equal when all the accounting is completed. The *Branch Investment* account is debited for cash, inventory, and other resources provided for the branch by the home office, as well as for the net income earned by the branch. It is credited for any cash, inventory, or other resources transferred from the branch, as well as any net loss incurred by the branch. When combined financial statements for the home office and branch operations are prepared, neither the *Home Office* account nor the *Branch Investment* account are included, because of their reciprocal nature. Instead, the equal but opposite balances in the two accounts are offset against each other before the balance sheet accounts are combined. As a result, the assets and liabilities of the branch are substituted for the *Branch Investment* account, since the purpose of the combined balance sheet is to show the financial position of the firm as a whole.

Branch Accounting Illustration

The Caine Company, with a home office in Chicago, operates a major department store chain. The firm recently opened its eighth branch store (Branch 8) in a suburban shopping center and will continue to use a decentralized accounting system because of the number of branches and the distance between the home office and the branch stores. During January, 1987, the following transactions took place.

1. The home office transferred $5,000 in cash, $75,000 in inventory, and $20,000 of display equipment to the new branch store.
2. Sales for January at Branch 8 amounted to $86,500.

3. The cost of the merchandise sold by Branch 8 during January was $61,200. In addition, the operating expenses incurred by the branch were $7,890, divided as follows.

Branch manager's salary	$1,800
Sales salaries	3,800
Advertising	600
Insurance	350
Utilities	280
Depreciation—equipment	810
Other expenses	250

4. Collections on customers' accounts totaled $32,100 at Branch 8.
5. A cash transfer of $3,000 was made to the home office by Branch 8.
6. The branch books were closed at the end of January and the monthly net income was reported to the home office.

The journal entries required to account for the January transactions of the home office and its branch are shown in Figure 21–10. You should note that the two reciprocal accounts, *Branch 8 Investment* and *Home Office,* are in agreement at the end of January as follows:

Home Office Books		Branch Books	
Branch 8 Investment		**Home Office**	
100,000	3,000	3,000	100,000
17,410			17,410
117,410	3,000	3,000	117,410
Balance 114,410			114,410 Balance

GLOSSARY

AVOIDABLE COSTS OR EXPENSES. Costs or expenses that can be eliminated if a department or a product is terminated (p. 837).

BRANCH ACCOUNTING. Procedures used to account for branch operations (p. 838).

BUSINESS SEGMENTATION. The division of a business into well defined components directed toward common goals (p. 822).

CONTROLLABLE COSTS OR EXPENSES. Costs or expenses that can be regulated or influenced at a particular level of management during a specified time period (p. 824).

COST CENTER. A responsibility center in which only controllable costs are considered, with no concern for revenue or invested assets (p. 824).

COST OBJECTIVE. Any activity for which separate cost measurement is performed. Examples are a department, a product, or a branch office (p. 830).

DEPARTMENTAL ACCOUNTING. Accounting procedures required to evaluate the financial performance of individual departments within an organization (p. 826).

book value = original cost − Acc. Depn (handwritten)

CAINE COMPANY
Journal Entries for Home Office and Branch 8
Month of January, 1987

Home Office Books			Branch 8 Books		
1. Branch 8 investment	100,000		Cash	5,000	
Cash		5,000	Merchandise inventory	75,000	
Merchandise inventory		75,000	Display equipment *at book value*	20,000	
Display equipment		20,000	Home Office		100,000
To record transfer of assets to Branch 8.			To record assets received from home office.		
2. No entry			Accounts receivable	86,500	
			Sales		86,500
			To record January branch sales		
3. No entry			Cost of goods sold	61,200	
			Management salaries expense	1,800	
			Sales salaries expense	3,800	
			Advertising expense	600	
			Insurance expense	350	
			Utilities expense	280	
			Depreciation expense	810	
			Other expenses	250	
			Merchandise inventory		61,200
			Accrued salaries payable		5,600
			Accumulated depreciation		810
			Cash		1,480
			To record January branch cost of goods sold and operating expenses		
4. No entry			Cash	32,100	
			Accounts receivable		32,100
			To record January branch cash collections.		
5. Cash	3,000		Home office	3,000	
Branch 8 investment		3,000	Cash		3,000
To record transfer of cash from branch.			To record transfer of cash to home office.		
6. No entry			Sales	86,500	
			Cost of goods sold		61,200
			Management salaries expense		1,800
			Sales salaries expense		3,800
			Advertising expense		600
			Insurance expense		350
			Utilities expense		280
			Depreciation expense		810
			Other expenses		250
			Income summary		17,410
			To close sales and expenses to income summary		
Branch 8 investment	17,410		Income summary	17,410	
Branch 8 net income		17,410	Home office		17,410
To record branch net income			To close income summary account.		

Figure 21–10
Branch Accounting Journal Entries

DEPARTMENTAL CONTRIBUTION TO INDIRECT EXPENSES. The revenue of a department, less its cost of goods sold and direct operating expenses (p. 836).

DEPARTMENTAL GROSS PROFIT. The revenue of a department, less its cost of goods sold (p. 826).

DEPARTMENTAL NET INCOME. The revenue of a department, less its cost of goods sold, its direct operating expenses, and an allocated portion of indirect expenses (p. 829).

DIRECT COSTS OR EXPENSES. Costs or expenses that can be traced to a specific cost objective (p. 830).

EFFECTIVENESS. A measure of how well a firm attains its goals (p. 819).

EFFICIENCY. Maintaining a satisfactory relationship between a firm's resource inputs and its outputs of products or services (p. 819).

INDIRECT COSTS OR EXPENSES. Costs or expenses incurred for the common benefit of multiple cost objectives (p. 830).

INVESTMENT CENTER. A responsibility center in which the controllable revenue, costs, and investments in operating assets are considered in evaluating its performance (p. 824).

MANAGERIAL ACCOUNTING. A branch of accounting that provides management information for planning, controlling, and decision making (p. 818).

MANAGEMENT BY EXCEPTION. The concentration on performance results that deviate significantly from those planned (p. 821).

MANAGEMENT FUNCTIONS. The planning, organizing, directing, and controlling required to manage an organization (p. 820).

OPERATING EXPENSE ALLOCATION. A systematic and rational process used to apportion indirect expenses to departments (p. 829).

ORGANIZATION. A group of people who share common goals, with a well defined division of labor (p. 819).

PROFIT CENTER. A responsibility center in which both controllable revenue and costs are considered in the evaluation of the center's performance (p. 824).

RESPONSIBILITY ACCOUNTING. The accounting procedures used to evaluate the financial performance of responsibility centers (p. 823).

RESPONSIBILITY CENTER. A business segment organized as a cost center, a profit center, or an investment center so that responsibility accounting can be performed (p. 823).

SERVICE DEPARTMENT. A department that provides supporting services such as personnel, advertising, accounting, maintenance, or purchasing (p. 830).

UNAVOIDABLE COSTS OR EXPENSES. Costs or expenses that will not be eliminated if a department or a product is terminated (p. 838).

VARIANCE. A measure of the difference between a planned financial performance and the actual results achieved. For example, a favorable cost variance arises when the actual cost is less than the amount planned. In contrast, an unfavorable cost variance exists when the actual cost exceeds the amount expected. (p. 825).

DISCUSSION QUESTIONS

1. What are the basic differences between financial accounting and managerial accounting? Identify an example of each of these two types of accounting.
2. Distinguish between efficiency and effectiveness measurements. Which of the two concepts is being measured in the following?
   (a) Departmental sales salaries required for July sales in a retail store.
   (b) Actual July sales compared with those planned by a retail store.
   (c) Labor costs required to perform laboratory tests during July in a medical clinic.
   (d) New car sales for an automobile dealership in July were 48 units. The sales manager had forecast 55 units for the month.

(e) The labor cost per tax return prepared by a CPA firm.

3. Identify the essential steps in the management process.

4. Explain why managerial accounting information is essential for good decision making in a business.

5. A university basketball team is an organization. How are such managerial considerations as goals, management functions, and the role of information important to the success of the team?

6. Differentiate between a cost and an expense. What is meant by the saying, "there are different costs for different purposes"?

7. Explain how the amount of an insurance premium can be both a cost and an expense.

8. Why is a business divided into segments, and how does segmentation relate to responsibility accounting?

9. Distinguish between a cost center, a profit center, and an investment center. Give an example of a business segment established as each type of responsibility center.

10. How is the term ***controllable*** used in responsibility accounting? Which of the following items would you expect to be controllable by the manager of the hardware department in a large discount store during a given month?
    (a) Depreciation on departmental equipment.
    (b) Rent on the building in which the store is located.
    (c) Cost of goods sold.
    (d) Departmental sales salaries.
    (e) Advertising expenses.

11. Explain the concept of management by exception.

12. What is a variance in a responsibility accounting application?

13. Why is departmental gross profit important in a merchandising firm?

14. How have electronic data terminals improved departmental accounting in recent years?

15. Distinguish between direct and indirect expenses. What must each be related to before the terms direct and indirect have meaning? Refer to question 10. Which of the five items are direct expenses for the hardware department? Are direct expenses always controllable expenses?

16. What is the role of a service department in a merchandising operation? Suggest the best ways to allocate the costs of the following service departments to the selling departments.
    (a) Personnel.
    (b) Purchasing.
    (c) Advertising.
    (d) Maintenance.
    (e) Janitorial.

17. Identify the advantages and disadvantages of departmental income statements prepared on the basis of
    (a) Departmental gross profit.
    (b) Departmental net income.
    (c) Departmental contribution to indirect expenses.

18. In considering the elimination of what appears to be an unprofitable department, identify the most important considerations. How do avoidable and unavoidable expenses affect the decision? Given the following facts, should the merchandise department of the Campus Bookstore be eliminated? Why or Why not?

	Merchandise Department	Book Department	Total
Sales	$600,000	$900,000	$1,500,000
Direct expenses	480,000	390,000	870,000
Indirect expenses	180,000	270,000	450,000
Operating income (loss)	$ (60,000)	$240,000	$ 180,000

19. Explain briefly what a branch operation is and why branch accounting is required.
20. Distinguish between a centralized and a decentralized branch accounting system. When are the reciprocal accounts, *Home Office* and *Branch Investment*, used and why are they necessary?

EXERCISES

Exercise 21-1 Distinguishing between Financial and Managerial Accounting Applications

Listed below are five accounting applications used by the Keller Company. Indicate whether each application would be classified primarily as financial accounting or managerial accounting.

1. A monthly income statement for a new branch store is prepared for the bank that financed the project.
2. A department manager in a large retail store receives a monthly report concerning advertising costs.
3. A federal tax return is prepared for a department store.
4. A detailed analysis of the costs involved with purchasing or leasing a new microcomputer system is developed.
5. A company's annual report is prepared and sent to interested parties.

Exercise 21-2 Identifying Managerial Accounting Information for Various Management Functions

Indicate whether each of the following types of managerial accounting information would be used primarily for planning, organizing, directing, or controlling.

1. A sales forecast of customer demand for a particular product.
2. A memo from a departmental manager to an employee explaining how a new compensation plan will affect that person.
3. A personnel report showing the number of new accountants needed by a CPA firm during the next year.
4. A projection of net incomes for several sales levels.
5. A report showing the difference between planned sales and those actually achieved.

Exercise 21-3 Distinguishing between Costs and Expenses

Indicate which of the following is a cost and which is an expense.

1. Cash payment of $14,000 for a new truck.
2. Purchase of a one-year liability insurance policy for $1,200.
3. Annual depreciation of $4,000 on a business automobile.
4. Cash payment of $188 for advertising in a local newspaper.
5. Lease payment for store equiment.

Exercise 21-4 Departmental Gross Profit

The Ritebuilt Store operates two departments, Farm Supplies and Hardware. An income statement is prepared on the basis of departmental gross profit. Operating data for the year 1987 are as follows.

	Farm Supplies	Hardware	Total Store
Sales	$1,008,000	$768,000	$1,776,000
Gross profit percentage	50%	37.5%	
Operating expenses			$ 648,000

Required:

A. What is the cost of goods sold for each of the departments?

B. Prepare an income statement that emphasizes departmental gross profit. (Disregard income taxes.)

Exercise 21-5 Departmental Contribution to Indirect Expenses

The Well-Read Bookstore operates two departments, Books and General Merchandise. During 1987, the store had the following operating results.

	Books	General Merchandise
Sales	$261,600	$504,000
Sales returns	9,600	14,400
Direct operating expenses	51,600	134,400
Gross profit percentage of net sales	30%	40%

In addition, indirect operating expenses that are not allocated to the departments amounted to $61,440.

Required:

Prepare a departmental income statement for 1987 based on the contribution to indirect expenses approach. Use three columns, headed Books Department, General Merchandise Department, and Total, respectively. (Disregard income taxes.)

✝Exercise 21-6 Evaluating the Effect of Unavoidable Costs

One of the Beck Clothing Store's four departments has reported a net loss of $11,000 after deducting $56,000 of operating expenses. Assume that only $26,000 of the operating expenses can be eliminated if the department is discontinued.

Required:

A. Should Beck keep operating the department based only on these facts?

B. Will the performance of the three other departments ever be considered in the decision? *Yes because you must take into the whole business. If you discontinue one department you might lose customers for the others as well.*

✓Exercise 21-7 Evaluating Avoidable versus Unavoidable Costs

The Sell-Low Variety Store operates three departments, including a hardware department that has consistently showed net losses when the firm's accountant prepares a departmentalized income statement for the store. For the year just ended, the hardware department showed the following performance.

Sales	$168,000
Cost of goods sold	115,200
Gross profit	52,800
Operating expenses	96,500
Net loss	$(43,700)

The operating expenses include allocated indirect expenses amounting to $62,500, which will be incurred whether the department is operated or not. The remainder of the operating expenses are direct for the hardware department, but include $14,000 that will have to be reassigned to another department because that amount is the salary of the owner's nephew who will be kept on the payroll regardless of the decision made about the hardware department. *Gross Profit -20000, reduction every year*

Required:

Should the hardware department be eliminated? Support your answer with calculations showing the effect on store profits of eliminating the department.

⁺Exercise 21-8 Indirect Operating Expense Allocation

The Star Clothing Store operates three selling departments. Certain indirect operating expenses are allocated to the selling departments, as follows.

Expense	Amount	Basis of Allocation
Personnel department	$28,800	Payroll
Building rent	43,200	Square feet of floor space
Advertising	72,000	Sales
Insurance on inventory	18,000	Amount of inventory

The following information is obtained from store records for 1987.

	Dept. A	Dept. B	Dept. C
Payroll	$100,800	$ 72,000	$115,200
Square feet of floor space	3,600	4,608	6,192
Sales	$270,000	$225,000	$405,000
Amount of inventory	63,000	48,600	68,400

Required:

Prepare a schedule allocating the indirect operating expenses to the three selling departments.

+Exercise 21-9 Indirect Operating Expense Allocation with Sales

The Harly Variety Store allocates indirect operating expenses to its three departments on the basis of sales. In 1986, the following allocations were made.

	Dept. A	Dept. B	Dept. C	Total
Sales	$600,000	$480,000	$120,000	$1,200,000
Indirect operating expenses	288,000	230,400	57,600	576,000

Assume that in 1987 Departments A and B have sales of $600,000 and $480,000, respectively, but Department C's sales increase to $360,000 because of the popularity of a new product line. Assume further that the total indirect operating expenses of $576,000 remain the same in 1987.

Required:

A. Determine the allocation of indirect operating expenses in 1987, using the same approach taken in 1986.

B. Are the results of requirement (A) logical for an equitable allocation of indirect operating expense?

Exercise 21-10 Elimination of a Department

The Kesel Company operates a discount store with three departments. John Kesel, the president of the company, wants to eliminate Department C because it continually shows a net operating loss. During the past year (1986), the departmental operating performances were as follows.

	Dept. A	Dept. B	Dept. C
Sales	$480,000	$288,000	$192,000
Cost of goods sold	288,000	187,200	144,000
Gross profit	192,000	100,800	48,000
Direct expenses	48,000	28,800	24,000
Indirect expenses	84,000	50,400	33,600
Net income (loss)	$ 60,000	$ 21,600	$ (9,600)

In analyzing these operating results, the company's accountant determines that advertising expenses amounting to $4,800 are the only indirect operating expenses that can be avoided if Department C is eliminated. All direct expenses are avoidable.

Required:

What would be the effect on the company's profits of eliminating Department C? (Disregard income taxes.)

Exercise 21-11 Branch Accounting Fundamentals

Home Office Records
Ft. Wayne Branch

Date	Explanation	Post. Ref.	Debit	Credit	Balance
12/1	Beginning balance				139,680
12/10	Merchandise shipped to branch		19,440		159,120
12/27	Cash received from branch			5,400	153,720
12/8	Fixtures sent to branch		4,320		158,040

Ft. Wayne Branch Records
Home Office

Date	Explanation	Post. Ref.	Debit	Credit	Balance
12/1	Beginning balance				139,680
12/10	Merchandise from home office			19,440	159,120
12/27	Cash sent to home office		5,400		153,720
12/31	December net income			11,520	165,240

At the end of 1987, the *Ft. Wayne Branch* and *Home Office* accounts of the Dillon Department Store were as shown on the previous page.

Required:

A. Explain why the two reciprocal accounts have different balances as of December 31. What is the correct balance?

B. Prepare the journal entries required in the home office records and branch records to reconcile the *Ft. Wayne Branch* and *Home Office* accounts, as of December 31, 1987.

PROBLEMS

Problem 21-1 Indirect Expense Allocation

The Arden Department Store operates four departments, A through D, at its Binghamton location. In order to prepare a departmental income statement, the store's accountant allocates indirect operating expenses with the following allocation bases.

Indirect Expense	Allocation Base	Total Amount
Rent	Relative value of square footage	$ 9,600
Personnel Department	Number of employees	14,400
Insurance	Value of inventory	6,720
Utilities	Square footage	3,840

The accountant has also been provided the following data relative to the four departments.

	Dept. A	Dept. B	Dept. C	Dept. D
Square footage	840	360	480	720
Number of employees	10	8	12	10
Value of inventory	$24,000	$30,000	$12,000	$14,000

Departments A and B are located on the first floor and Departments C and D are on the second floor. The company believes that the first floor is three times as valuable as the second floor for the allocation of the rent expense.

Required:

Prepare a schedule that correctly allocates the indirect operating expenses to the four departments.

Problem 21-2 Departmental Contribution to Indirect Expenses

The Alert Appliance Store operates two departments: Kitchen Appliances and Video Appliances. The store's income statement for the year ending October 31, 1987, has been prepared from the accounting records, as follows.

ALERT APPLIANCE STORE
Income Statement
Year Ended October 31, 1987

Sales		$1,002,000
Cost of goods sold:		
Beginning inventory	$102,000	
Purchases	366,000	
Goods available for sale	468,000	
Ending inventory	(70,800)	
Cost of goods sold		397,200
Gross profit		604,800
Expenses:		
Sales salaries	222,000	
Advertising	74,400	
Depreciation	43,200	
Managerial salaries	102,000	
Rent	63,600	
Property taxes	14,400	
Interest	45,600	
Total expenses		565,200
Net income		$ 39,600

The store's records indicate that the following percentages of each expense or revenue account are directly chargeable to the departments. (Any balance left in an expense account is an indirect expense.)

	Kitchen Appliances	Video Appliances
Purchases	60%	40%
Sales salaries	53%	47%
Advertising	45%	25%
Depreciation	21%	16%
Property taxes	29%	23%
Sales	55%	45%

Direct

The beginning inventory for the Kitchen Appliances department was $84,000 and the ending inventory was $62,400. The beginning inventory for the Video Appliances department was $18,000 and the ending inventory was $8,400.

Required:
Prepare a departmental income statement for the year ending October 31, 1987 that shows each department's contribution to indirect expenses.

Problem 21-3   Departmental Accounting
The Anniversary Limited Corporation has prepared an income statement using the departmental gross profit format for its two departments, the Jewelry department and the Fine China department, as follows.

ANNIVERSARY LIMITED CORPORATION
Income Statement
Year Ended April 30, 1987

	Jewelry	Fine China	Total
Sales	$756,000	$294,000	$1,050,000
Cost of goods sold	419,850	139,950	559,800
Gross profit	$336,150	$154,050	490,200
Operating Expenses:			
Salaries			198,000
Advertising			80,400
Depreciation			55,200
Rent			28,800
Utilities			20,400
Payroll taxes			11,400
Total operating expenses			394,200
Net income			$ 96,000

The store's accountant has been able to divide the ending balance in each expense account into three components: direct expenses chargeable to the Jewelry department, direct expenses chargeable to the Fine China department, and indirect expenses. The breakdown, presented as a percentage of the expense account balance, and the allocation bases for the indirect expenses are as follows.

	Direct Expenses by Department		Indirect	
Item	Jewelry (Percent)	Fine China (Percent)	Expenses (Percent)	Allocation Base for Indirect Expenses
Salaries	65	25	10	Sales
Advertising	40	20	40	Cost of ads placed
Depreciation	42	30	28	Fixed asset cost
Rent	52	26	22	Space occupied
Utilities	60	20	20	Space occupied
Payroll taxes	65	25	10	Sales

Assume that the floor space is of equal value. The following data are also available.

	Jewelry	Fine China
Cost of ads placed	$36,846	$12,282
Floor space in square feet	15,000	7,500
Fixed asset cost	$78,000	$19,500

Required:

A. Prepare a departmental income statement showing departmental contribution to indirect expenses.

B. Prepare a departmental income statement showing departmental net income.

Problem 21-4 Elimination of a Department

The Buy-More Furniture Store operates three departments at its Indianapolis location:

a Commercial Furniture Department, a Residential Furniture Department, and an Assemble-Yourself Furniture Department for the budget conscious. The store's accountant has prepared an income statement by department for the most recent year, and, for the third year in a row, the Assemble-Yourself Furniture department has shown a loss. If the company decides to eliminate the unprofitable department, 60% of the space occupied by the Assemble-Yourself Furniture Department will be used by the Residential Furniture Department and the remaining 40% will be used by the Commercial Furniture Department. The firm does not believe that eliminating the Assemble-Yourself Furniture Department, while at the same time enlarging the remaining two departments, will change the sales or gross profits of the Residential and Commercial departments.

The accountant has also provided the following information.

1. The president's salary of $90,000 per year has been allocated equally among the departments.
2. At present, there are three sales people and a manager in the Assemble-Yourself Furniture Department. If the department is eliminated, the manager would be transferred to the Commercial Furniture Department and the three sales people would be terminated. The manager's salary is $42,000 per year.
3. The utilities, rent, and insurance are allocated on the basis of square footage. The insurance would decrease $2,400 a year if the department is eliminated; the rent and utilities would not change.
4. Indirect advertising expenses in the amount of $96,000 were allocated to the departments on the basis of sales. The direct advertising expenditures incurred by the Assemble-Yourself Furniture Department would be eliminated.
5. The equipment in the Assemble-Yourself Furniture Department would be transferred to the other departments: 70% to the Commercial Furniture Department and 30% to the Residential Furniture Department.

BUY-MORE FURNITURE STORE
Income Statement
Year Ended December 31, 1987

	Commercial Furniture	Residential Furniture	Assemble-Yourself Furniture	Total
Sales	$1,020,000	$612,000	$408,000	$2,040,000
Cost of goods sold	408,000	275,400	142,800	826,200
Gross profit	612,000	336,600	265,200	1,213,800
Operating expenses:				
Salaries	192,900	99,000	107,700	399,600
Utilities	18,480	21,720	17,400	57,600
Advertising	168,000	104,400	115,200	387,600
Rent on building	33,600	44,400	30,000	108,000
Depreciation on equipment	42,000	31,200	26,400	99,600
Insurance	9,720	14,580	8,100	32,400
Total Operating Expenses	464,700	315,300	304,800	1,084,800
Net Income (Loss)	$ 147,300	$ 21,300	$ (39,600)	$ 129,000

Required:

A. Should the Assemble-Yourself Furniture Department be eliminated? What will the impact be on total net income if it is eliminated?

B. Prepare a departmental income statement that would result if the department is dropped.

Problem 21-5 Branch Accounting

The Sugar Plum Shop has branch retail outlets throughout the state of Florida. The home office is in Tampa. In June, 1987, the corporation opened a branch in Orlando, and the following transactions took place during the first month of operations.

June	1	Sugar Plum transferred $7,800 in cash to the Orlando branch, along with $10,080 of store equipment from the home office. The equipment is estimated to have a seven-year life with no residual value and should be depreciated using the straight-line method.
	2	The branch received $6,000 of merchandise, which it had ordered from an outside supplier on account.
	4	The branch received $26,400 of inventory from the home office.
	7	The branch paid rent for June in the amount of $1,200.
	15	Branch sales for the first two weeks of June were $44,400, sales on account and $3,600 in cash sales.
	16	The branch paid for the merchandise it had received June 2.
	18	Branch collections of accounts receivable, $34,800.
	20	The branch paid the following bills.

Utilities	$ 420
Telephone	210
Salaries	14,400

	25	The branch transferred $12,000 to the home office.
	26	The branch paid the following bills:

Payroll taxes	$ 990
Insurance	1,440
Advertising	738

	28	The branch received $21,600 of inventory from the home office.
	30	Branch sales for the last two weeks of the month were: sales on account, $30,000; cash sales, $3,120.
	30	The branch ending inventory was $9,384.
	30	The branch books were closed at the end of June, and the net income was reported to the home office.

Required:

A. Record the journal entries to be made by the home office and the Orlando branch for the month of June.

B. Calculate the balance in the *Home Office* account and the *Orlando Branch* account as of June 30.

ALTERNATE PROBLEMS

Problem 21-1A Indirect Expense Allocation

The Don Hall Department Store has four departments. The indirect operating expenses of the store are allocated to the departments with the following allocation bases.

Indirect Expense	Allocation Base	Total Amount
Office expense	Number of employees	$18,600
Advertising	Sales	3,840
Rent	Relative value of square footage	30,240
Utilities	Square footage	6,720

In order to prepare a departmental income statement, the firm's accountant has compiled the following data.

	Dept. A	Dept. B	Dept. C	Dept. D
Number of employees	12	8	6	14
Sales	$48,000	$30,000	$18,000	$24,000
Square footage	3,000	1,000	2,400	1,600

Departments A and B are located on the first floor and Departments C and D are on the second floor. The company believes that the space on the first floor is twice as valuable as the space on the second floor for the allocation of rent expense.

Required:
Prepare a schedule showing the allocation of indirect operating expenses to the four departments.

Problem 21-2A Departmental Contribution to Indirect Expenses

The Small World Store operates two departments: a Children's Clothing Department and a Toy Department. The store's accountant has prepared the following income statement for the year ending May 31, 1987.

SMALL WORLD STORE
Income Statement
Year Ended May 31, 1987

Sales		$752,000
Cost of goods sold		
Beginning inventory	$ 84,000	
Purchases	488,000	
Goods available for sale	572,000	
Ending inventory	73,600	
Cost of goods sold		498,400
Gross profit		253,600
Expenses:		
Salaries	100,000	
Insurance	34,400	
Advertising	36,000	
Depreciation	13,600	
Supplies	20,800	
Interest	28,800	
Total Expenses		233,600
Net Income		$ 20,000

The beginning inventory of the Children's Clothing Department was $34,400, and the ending inventory was $30,400. The beginning inventory for the Toy Department was $49,600, and the ending inventory was $43,200.

The store's records indicate that the following percentages of each expense or revenue are directly chargeable to the departments. (Any balance left in an expense account is an indirect expense.)

Item	Children's Clothing Department (%)	Toy Department (%)
Sales revenue	45	55
Salaries	21	34
Insurance	26	36
Advertising	32	43
Depreciation	23	19
Supplies	33	35
Purchases	47	53

Required:

Prepare a departmental income statement for the year ended May 31, 1987, showing each department's contribution to indirect expenses.

Problem 21-3A Departmental Accounting

The Rural Cleaning Materials Company has used the departmental gross profit format to prepare an income statement for its two departments, Commercial Linen and Household Items.

RURAL CLEANING MATERIALS COMPANY
Income Statement
Year Ended November 30, 1987

	Commercial Linen	Household Items	Total
Sales	$426,120	$209,880	$636,000
Cost of goods sold	192,720	71,280	264,000
Gross profit	$233,400	$138,600	372,000
Operating expenses:			
Salaries			144,000
Depreciation			27,000
Insurance			21,600
Advertising			27,600
Supplies			38,400
Utilities			23,400
Total Operating Expenses			282,000
Net Income			$ 90,000

The company has been able to determine the percentage of each expense category that is chargeable as direct expense to Commercial Linen, as direct expense to Household

Items, or as indirect expense. The breakdown, presented as a percentage of the expense account balance and the allocation bases for indirect expenses are as follows.

Expense Item	Direct Expenses by Department Commercial (%)	Household (%)	Indirect Expenses (%)	Allocation Base for Indirect Expenses
Salaries	55	30	15	Sales
Depreciation	46	20	34	Fixed asset cost
Insurance	52	35	13	Fixed asset cost
Advertising	32	21	47	Cost of ads placed
Supplies	42	33	25	Cost of goods sold
Utilities	61	29	10	Space occupied

The following data are also available.

	Commercial	Household
Fixed asset cost	$113,400	$48,600
Cost of ads placed	25,632	17,088
Floor space in square feet	9,120	2,280

Required:

A. Prepare a departmental income statement showing departmental contribution to indirect expenses.

B. Prepare a departmental income statement showing departmental net income.

Problem 21-4A   Elimination of a Department

Mr. King operates a hardware store with three departments: Hardware, Plumbing, and Paint. For the past three years, the Paint Department has shown a net loss, and the owner of the store has asked you to determine whether the Paint Department should be eliminated. If Mr. King decides to eliminate the Paint Department, 75% of the space occupied by the Paint Department will be used by the Hardware Department and the remaining 25% will be used by the Plumbing Department. Neither sales nor gross profits of the Hardware or Plumbing departments will change if the Paint Department is eliminated.

The following additional information describes the expenses currently related to the Paint Department.

1. The owner's salary of $36,000 has been allocated equally among the three departments.
2. At present, there is one salesperson and a manager in the Paint Department. If the Paint Department is eliminated, the manager would be transferred to the Hardware Department and the salesperson would be terminated. The salesperson's salary is $14,400.
3. The office expense, telephone, and supplies are allocated on the basis of sales. The supplies expense would decrease by $1,200 if the paint department is eliminated, but the office expense and telephone expense would not change.
4. The rent expense is allocated on the basis of square footage, and the rent expense would not change if the paint department is eliminated.

The most recent income statement for the store is shown next.

KING HARDWARE
Income Statement
Year Ended July 31, 1987

	Hardware	Plumbing	Paint	Total
Sales	$205,920	$110,880	$54,600	$371,400
Cost of goods sold	95,820	51,780	16,380	163,980
Gross profit	110,100	59,100	38,220	207,420
Operating expenses:				
Salaries	61,200	34,800	42,000	138,000
Office expenses	7,200	5,184	2,016	14,400
Telephone	3,300	2,376	912	6,588
Supplies	13,200	9,504	3,696	26,400
Rent	9,600	5,400	4,200	19,200
Total expenses	94,500	57,264	52,824	204,588
Net Income (Loss)	$ 15,600	$ 1,836	$(14,604)	$ 2,832

Required:

A. Should the paint department be eliminated?

B. Prepare a departmental income statement showing the results if the department is dropped.

Problem 21-5A Branch Accounting

The General Auto Store, Inc., opened a branch retail outlet in Dallas, Texas on April 1. The following transactions took place during the first month of operations.

April   1   The home office transferred $9,000 in cash to the Dallas branch, along with $4,320 of store fixtures and equiment. The store fixtures and equipment are estimated to have a five-year life with no residual value and should be depreciated using the straight-line method.

        3   The branch received $18,000 of inventory from the home office.

        5   The branch received $19,200 of inventory it had ordered from an outside supplier on account.

        6   The branch paid the rent for April in the amount of $960.

        9   Branch sales for the first two weeks in April were $21,600 of sales on account and $6,000 in cash sales.

      10   The branch paid the following bills.

Utilities	$ 180
Supplies	1,080
Telephone	240
Salaries	4,800

      12   The branch paid for the inventory it received on April 5.

      15   Branch collections on accounts receivable amounted to $15,600.

      27   The branch received $12,000 of inventory from the home office.

      29   Branch sales for the last two weeks of the month were sales on account of $14,400 and cash sales of $7,200.

      29   The branch paid the following expenses:

Salaries	$6,000
Insurance	360

      30   The branch ending inventory was $19,680.

      30   The branch books were closed at the end of April, and the net income was reported to the home office.

Required:

A. Record the journal entries to be made by the home office and the branch office for the month of April.

B. Calculate the balance in the *Home Office* account and the *Branch* account, as of April 30.

CASE

CASE 21-1 Decision Case **Responsibility Accounting**

Andrews Automobiles, Inc. is a franchised dealership operating in the midwest. In recent years, the firm has experienced unsatisfactory profit results because of slumping sales in the area. At the suggestion of the firm's CPA, responsibility accounting was implemented at the beginning of 1987. The following departments were organized as profit centers.

1. New Car Sales
2. Used Car Sales
3. Service—Mechanical
4. Service—Body Shop
5. Parts and Accessories

Monthly reports are prepared showing the profit results of each of the five departments. On April 20, 1987, the Parts and Accessories manager and the Used Car manager have demanded a meeting with the firm's president, Bill Andrews, to discuss the way responsibility accounting is being applied. In particular, they are protesting two policies that currently are in effect.

1. The Parts and Accessories Department must transfer all parts and accessories to other departments internally at their original invoice cost.
2. The Used Car Sales Department is charged the full dollar amount allowed by the New Car Sales Department on a used car traded in for a new car. In many cases, this amount exceeds the ultimate selling price of the used car. The used car sales manager tells the president about a recent case that is typical. A 1981 model automobile with a wholesale market value of $4,800 was traded in on a new car with a list price of $12,240 and a dealer cost of $9,792. An allowance of $6,528 was given on the used car to promote the deal, and the customer paid cash of $5,712. Consequently, a profit of $2,448 ($6,528 + $5,712 − $9,792) was recognized by the New Car Sales Department. The retail market value of the used car was $5,520, and it was sold at that price two weeks later. Since the used car sales department was charged $6,528 when the used car was added to inventory, it incurred a loss of $1,008 on the ultimate sale.

Both managers (Parts and Accessories as well as Used Car Sales) are upset by what they consider unfair practices and a violation of the basic premise of responsibility accounting as it was originally explained to them.

Required:

A. Do you agree or disagree with the two managers?

B. What would you do to improve the situation, if anything?

C. Why is your answer to part B important to Mr. Andrews, as well as to the other two managers?

22

ACCOUNTING FOR A MANUFACTURING FIRM

CHAPTER OVERVIEW AND OBJECTIVES

This chapter presents the accounting fundamentals required for a manufacturing operation. When you have completed the chapter, you should understand:

1. The basic nature of a manufacturing operation.
2. The difference between the inventories of a manufacturing firm and those of a merchandising business.
3. The distinction between product costs and period costs.
4. The three manufacturing cost elements—direct materials, direct labor, and manufacturing overhead—used in a production operation.
5. The basic nature of absorption costing and a cost classification based upon cost behavior.
6. The preparation of an income statement for a manufacturing firm and the supporting information reported in a cost of goods manufactured statement.
7. The additional accounts and accounting procedures required for a manufacturing firm.
8. The use and limitations of a periodic inventory system in a manufacturing operation.
9. The role of a worksheet in a manufacturing firm and how to prepare financial statements from it.
10. The problems associated with the valuation of inventories when a periodic inventory system is used by a manufacturing firm.

Objective 1: The basic nature of a manufacturing operation

In earlier chapters, we have been concerned with the development of accounting fundamentals for service and merchandising firms. We have purposefully avoided manufacturing operations so far, because of certain complexities associated with them. A **manufacturing firm** is the most complete type of business enterprise because it involves production, selling, and administrative functions. Manufacturers convert raw materials that they purchase into salable finished products. An automobile manufacturing firm purchases steel, aluminum, glass, and other basic materials and converts them through a production process into automobiles, which are sold to the firm's franchised dealers. In contrast, the dealers are merchandisers, who sell the automobiles to the public. A manufacturing firm will use most of the accounting fundamentals discussed earlier in this book, but will require additional accounting procedures for the collection, reporting, and control of production costs.

To help you visualize what manufacturing is all about, consider the simplified production flow of Designer Jeans, Inc., a maker of high-quality jeans, shown below. The firm has two production departments, Cutting and Sewing. Skilled labor and a highly automated production process are combined to make a pair of jeans that is sold to a retail store. Raw materials (primarily denim) are purchased from an outside supplier, kept in the Stores Department, and issued as needed to the Cutting Department. In the Cutting Department, each pair of jeans is cut to an appropriate size and then transferred to the Sewing Department, where the product is finished through an elaborate sewing process.

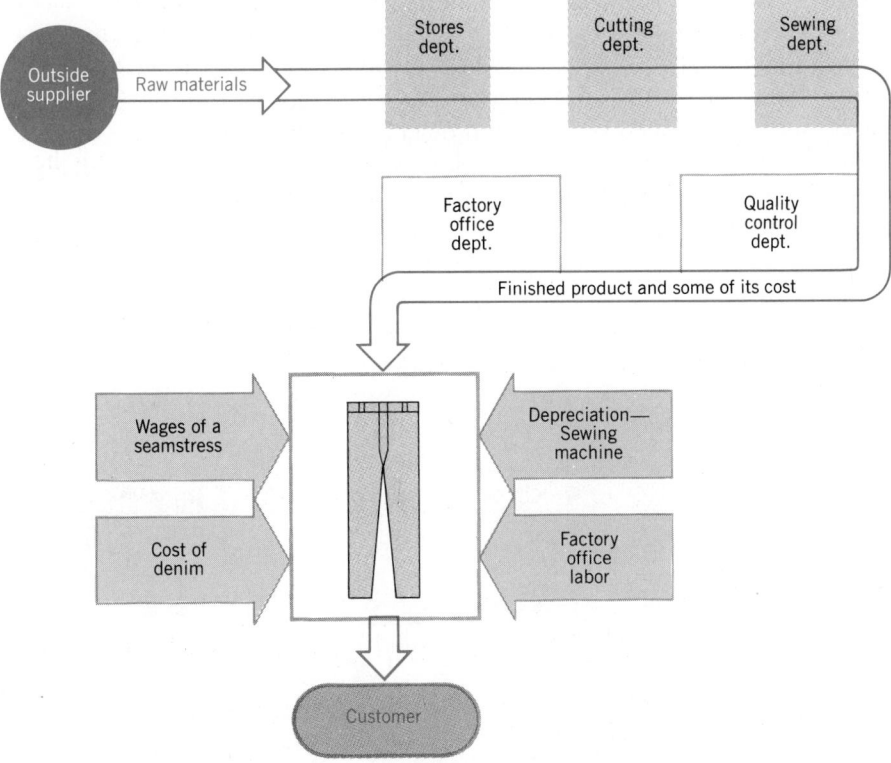

Management must be able to account for the costs incurred for the production of jeans to make decisions such as pricing the finished product and evaluating the profitability of the operation. Note that production occurs in only the two production departments, Cutting and Sewing, even though the company operates five departments in the manufacturing process. The other three departments—Stores, Factory Office, and Quality Control—are called service departments because they support the two production departments. For example, the Factory Office Department provides such services as accounting, payroll, personnel, and purchasing. Remember that we identified service departments used for merchandising in the previous chapter and the only difference here is that they support production departments instead of sales departments. Note also that selling and administrative functions are not part of the manufacturing process. This is an important point that will have an impact on how we determine the costs that should be charged to inventory in a manufacturing firm. We now turn to the accounting fundamentals required for a manufacturing operation.

MANUFACTURING VERSUS NONMANUFACTURING FIRMS

Objective 2: Comparing inventories in manufacturing and merchandising firms

Manufacturing and nonmanufacturing firms are alike, in that they depend upon revenue from the products or services that they sell. They also engage in many of the same selling and administrative activities, such as advertising, calling on customers, issuing credit, doing clerical work, and performing general management functions. The valuation of a manufacturing firm's inventories, however, introduces some important accounting differences between it and a service entity that does not have an inventory, or a merchandising enterprise that buys goods that are ready for resale. The cost flow associated with the manufacturing process used to convert raw materials into finished products causes more complicated accounting problems than those experienced by nonmanufacturing businesses. For example, consider the comparison of the inventory cost flows of a merchandising business and a manufacturing firm, as shown in Figure 22–1.

Figure 22–1

Merchandising and Manufacturing Firms Inventory Cost Flow

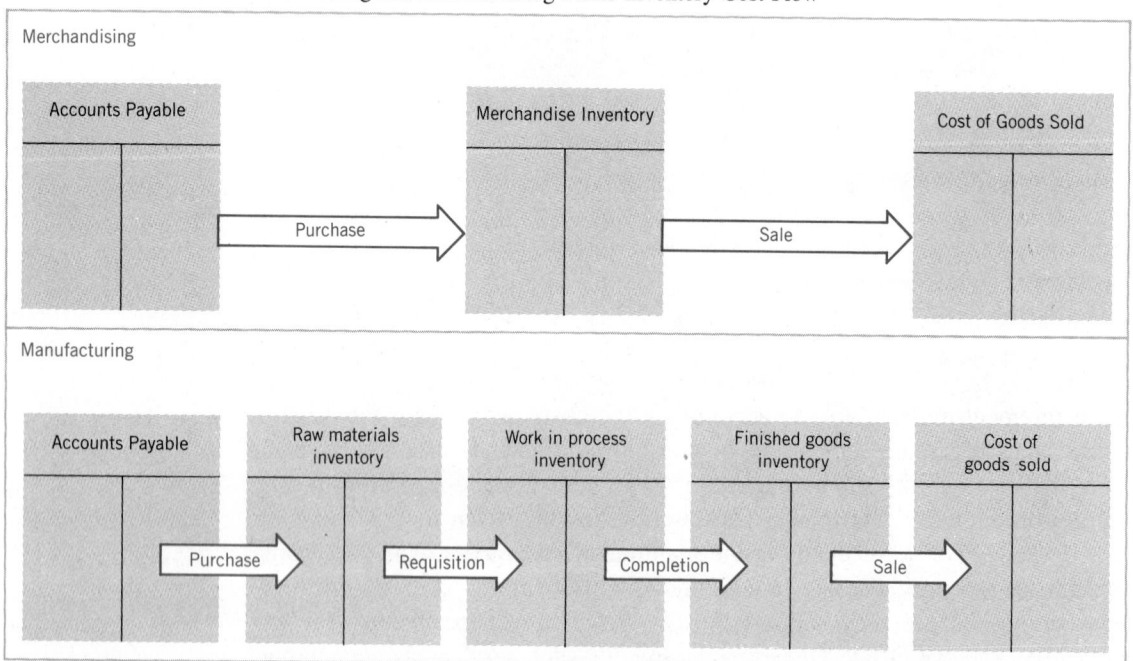

Three different inventory accounts must be maintained by a manufacturing firm: raw materials, work in process, and finished goods. At the end of any accounting period, the balance in each of these three inventory accounts will be reported as a current asset on the balance sheet. In contrast, a merchandising firm uses a single inventory account. A proper matching of revenues and expenses will be dependent upon the accuracy with which the costs of the three inventories are accumulated throughout the production process. Costs are transferred from raw materials to work in process to finished goods and, ultimately, to cost of goods sold. The *three types of inventory* for manufacturing are the following.

Raw Materials. The cost of the basic materials and parts that have been purchased and are available for future conversion into salable products are classified as **raw materials** inventory. Examples are the steel, aluminum, glass, zinc, rubber, plastics, paint, and other basic ingredients used to manufacture automobiles.

Work in Process. Inventory that is partially finished but requires further processing before it can be sold is classified as **work in process** inventory. For example, all the automobiles placed into production on an assembly line but unfinished at the end of an accounting period will be treated as work in process inventory.

Finished Goods. The total cost recorded during the production process for all products fully manufactured and ready for sale is classified as **finished goods** inventory. For example, all the costs incurred to produce automobiles that have been completed but are awaiting delivery to the manufacturer's dealers will be shown as finished goods inventory. These costs would have been recorded during the work in process stage as the automobiles were being worked on and transferred to the finished goods inventory account when they were completed.

PRODUCT AND PERIOD COSTS

We learned in Chapter 21 that managerial accountants classify costs in many ways. We also noted that a cost is an asset as long as it has future benefit. Expired costs are charged to the income statement as expenses, since they no longer have future benefit.

The terms *product cost* and *period cost* are particularly important in the development of a manufacturing firm's income statement. A proper matching of revenues and expenses must be based upon a well defined distinction between the product and period costs. The reason for this is that the period in which the benefit of any cost is received is the period in which the cost should be deducted as an expense. **Product costs** are necessary for the physical existence of a salable product. They are inventoried as assets until the products are sold because this is the period of time during which the costs have value to the business. At the point of sale, the product costs have been consumed in the production of revenue, so they can no longer benefit the business and are expensed on the income statement of the period. **Period costs** are identified

Objective 3: Distinguishing between product and period costs

with a specific time interval since they are not required to have a salable product. Consequently, they are not inventoried and are charged as expenses to a period according to the matching principle discussed in Chapters 3 and 13. In most cases, this means they are expensed as they are incurred. Certain exceptions to this general rule, such as prepaid rent and depreciation, are required in order to comply with accrual accounting. The flows of product costs and period costs through the financial statements can be illustrated as follows.

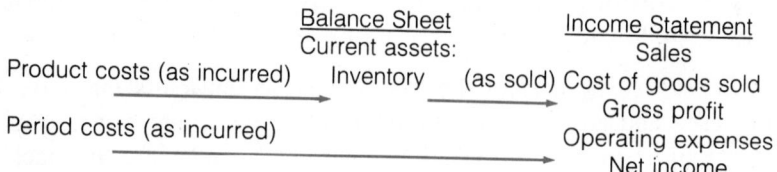

A merchandise firm's product costs will consist only of its *purchase costs,* as we have seen earlier, since the merchandise purchased is ready for resale. The purchase costs are kept in an inventory account until they are matched against revenue as cost of goods sold. All other costs, including labor, are charged to a specific period as selling or administrative expenses. A service firm, such as an accounting practice or a real estate business, *will not have product costs,* since it does not maintain an inventory for resale. As a result, all costs are period costs because they are expensed in specific periods.

In a manufacturing firm, all the manufacturing cost elements that are needed to produce products in the manufacturing process are treated as product costs. They are kept in inventory as assets as long as the related products are held, since their benefits to the business have not ended. When the products are sold, the related product costs are transferred as expenses to the cost of goods sold section of the income statement. At that point, the product costs are no longer beneficial because the firm does not hold the inventory. Note that the result of this treatment of product costs is that they may occur in one account-ing period, but be treated as an expense in a following period. The nonproduct or period costs are not inventoried in a manufacturing firm because they are charged to specific time intervals, instead of to the inventory being produced. Selling and administrative costs are always treated as period costs and, gen-erally, are deducted on the income statement when the revenue that they help the firm earn is recognized. For example, advertising expense and the presi-dent's salary would be treated by a manufacturing firm as period costs. The next consideration is the identification of the manufacturing cost elements that are inventoried as product costs.

MANUFACTURING COST ELEMENTS

Objective 4: The three man-ufacturing cost elements

The inventory cost flow of a manufacturing firm, illustrated in Figure 22–1, can be expanded to the more complete manufacturing cost flow shown in Figure 22–2. A flow of **manufacturing cost elements** is associated with the *physical flow of products* through the production process. Managerial account-ants must record the manufacturing cost elements as they are incurred so that

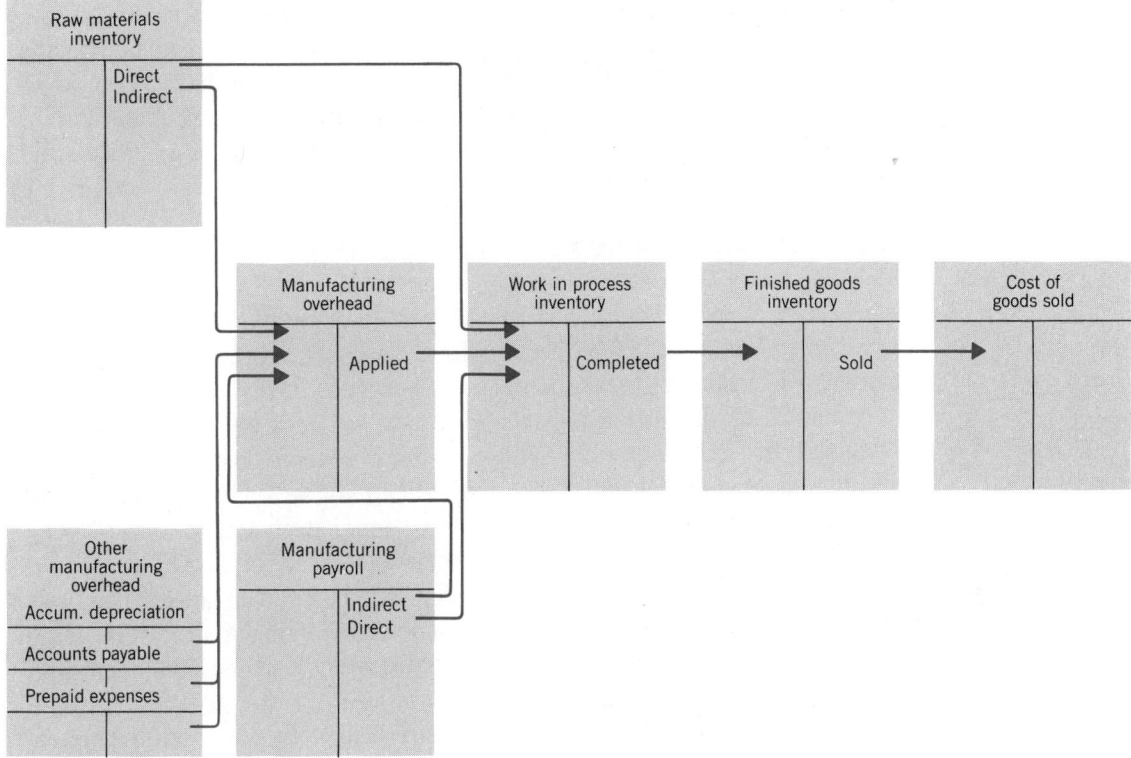

Figure 22–2
Manufacturing Cost Flow

they can be accumulated as assets and properly matched with revenue once the related products are sold. The cost of a finished product consists of three manufacturing cost elements: *direct materials, direct labor,* and *manufacturing overhead.*

Direct Materials. The raw materials directly traceable as an integral part of a finished product are called **direct materials.** The aluminum used for an automobile, the plastic used for a calculator, the crude oil used for gasoline, and the steel used for a golf club are examples of direct materials. Since direct materials physically become part of a finished product, they can be traced to the product or, in some situations, batches of products. Direct materials do not include such miscellaneous items as lubricants, glue, screws, or nails, which are treated as indirect materials and included in manufacturing overhead. It may not be possible to trace such items to the products or it may not be economically feasible to do so.

Direct Labor. The wages paid to employees whose time and effort can be traced to products are classified as **direct labor.** As long as the employees perform tasks that can be identified specifically with the conversion of direct materials into finished goods, the labor is a direct cost. Examples of this are the wages paid to welders on an automobile manufacturing assembly line. The direct labor becomes a part of the finished product, so it can be traced to a product or to batches of products. Other labor will be required to support the production process but will not be traceable to finished products. The wages or salaries paid to janitors, maintenance personnel, production supervisors, cafeteria workers, and material handlers will be classified as indirect labor and included in manufacturing overhead.

Manufacturing Overhead. All manufacturing costs except direct materials and direct labor are included in **manufacturing overhead.** Other terms used instead of manufacturing overhead are indirect manufacturing cost, factory overhead, and factory burden. Indirect materials, indirect labor, utilities, maintenance, insurance, rent, depreciation, property taxes, and payroll taxes are examples of manufacturing overhead. Three issues must be resolved in accounting for manufacturing overhead. First, several costs, such as rent, depreciation, insurance, and real estate taxes *may be applicable in part* to manufacturing and *in part* to selling and administrative functions. Consequently, these are common costs, since they are incurred for all three activities. In Chapter 21, we discussed methods that can be used to allocate indirect operating expenses to the departments of a merchandising firm. The same procedures can be utilized to distribute common costs to the manufacturing, selling, and administrative functions.

Second, manufacturing overhead is incurred in both **production departments** and **service departments**, although products are worked on only in the production departments. The service departments provide support to the production departments, with such activities as maintenance, production control, inspection, storage, and engineering. The service department overhead costs must be assigned in some way to the production departments so that, ultimately, they can be included in the product cost. Again, the allocation procedures discussed in Chapter 21 are applicable to the assignment of service department costs to the production departments.

Finally, the indirect nature of manufacturing overhead (for example, property taxes) prevents it from being traced to the products in the same manner as direct materials and direct labor. Nevertheless, such items as indirect labor, rent, property taxes, insurance, and utilities are indispensable for the production process, because without them manufacturing could not take place. A manufacturing firm must develop a reliable method with which the overhead costs can be assigned as product costs. Instead of tracing manufacturing overhead to the production process, the costs are applied on some basis that closely relates the costs incurred with the work performed. Commonly used bases for the application of manufacturing overhead are direct labor cost, direct labor hours, or units produced. An **overhead application rate** (also called a burden rate) is developed by dividing the total manufacturing overhead cost by the basis used to measure production activity.

For example, if manufacturing overhead costs are $200,000 and direct labor hours are 50,000, an overhead application rate of $4 per hour can be computed by dividing manufacturing overhead costs by direct labor hours ($200,000 divided by 50,000). Manufacturing overhead will be assigned as product costs by applying the $4 rate to each direct labor hour worked during the production process. It is important to note that an overhead application rate is usually based on estimates of both manufacturing overhead cost and production activity, rather than on actual results. This subject is discussed in more detail in Chapter 23.

INVENTORY VALUATION CONSIDERATIONS

Two inventory valuation methods, absorption costing and variable costing, are available to a manufacturing firm. With **absorption costing**, all manufacturing costs are treated as product costs, regardless of whether or not they may change in relation to production levels. Consequently, all direct materials, direct labor, and manufacturing overhead are treated as product costs. In contrast, **variable costing**, sometimes called direct costing, recognizes *only* those manufacturing costs that change in relation to production levels as product costs. We will limit our coverage of product costing to the procedures used with absorption costing until Chapter 26, where we will discuss variable costing. Generally accepted accounting principles require the application of absorption costing for external financial reporting with the justification that all of the manufacturing cost elements needed to produce a salable product must be inventoried.

Objective 5: Differentiating between absorption costing and variable costing

Management also uses absorption costing for many of its internal accounting applications. However, management must often evaluate the effect of changes in sales or production volume on the profits of the firm. One of the most widely used ways to classify costs in managerial accounting is by their **cost behavior,** which is the measure of how a cost will react to changes in the level of business activity. Our primary concern at this point is with the cost behavior of manufacturing costs, although the same basic concepts can also be applied to selling and administrative expenses.

VARIABLE COST

A **variable cost** will vary in total amount *proportionately* with some measure of business activity, such as sales dollars, units produced, or direct labor hours worked. Direct materials, direct labor, and certain manufacturing overhead items, such as the cost of electricity for machinery operation, will be variable costs. For example, if a direct labor cost of $40 is required to produce one unit of a product, the total direct labor cost will increase and decrease proportionately with the number of units produced, as illustrated in the following schedule.

Number of Units Produced	Direct Labor Cost per Unit	Total Direct Labor Cost
1	$40	$ 40
25	40	1,000
50	40	2,000
100	40	4,000

While the direct labor rate per unit is constant, the total direct labor cost varies with the level of production.

FIXED COST

A **fixed cost** will remain constant in total amount over a wide range of business activity. In a manufacturing operation, a fixed cost *will be the same* regardless of the amount produced. Many of the manufacturing overhead items will be fixed costs. Some examples are depreciation, rent, property taxes, and supervisory salaries. While a fixed cost remains constant in total, regardless of the level of activity, it will have a unit cost that varies inversely with volume. For example, a $500 monthly depreciation charge for production equipment will be constant regardless of the production level, but would change as a unit cost as follows.

Number of Units Produced	Monthly Depreciation	Depreciation per Unit
1	$500	$500
25	500	20
50	500	10
100	500	5

Since variable and fixed costs are not segregated in the product costing process with absorption costing, cost behavior information is not readily available from the accounting system. In contrast, the distinction between variable and fixed costs is actually incorporated into the formal accounting procedures with variable costing, as we will see in Chapter 26.

COST OF GOODS SOLD

The major difference between accounting for a merchandising firm and a manufacturing operation is the *calculation of cost of goods sold*. As we saw in Chapter 5, a merchandising firm calculates cost of goods sold as follows.

Beginning merchandise inventory + Purchases of merchandise − Ending merchandise inventory = Cost of goods sold

In contrast, a manufacturing operation determines cost of goods sold in the following way.

Beginning finished goods inventory + Cost of goods manufactured − Ending finished goods inventory = Cost of goods sold

At first glance, the two cost of goods sold calculations may appear to be the same, but actually they are somewhat different because of the production flow associated with manufacturing. In effect, the cost of goods manufactured in a manufacturing firm results from the conversion of raw materials to finished goods through work in process and replaces the purchases of merchandise in a merchandising enterprise. This difference carries forward into the development of an income statement.

COMPARISON OF INCOME STATEMENTS

In Figure 22–3, the cost of goods sold calculation process is shown as the difference between income statements prepared for merchandising and manufacturing firms. Sales revenue, selling expenses, administrative expenses, and income taxes are treated the same. Again, we see that the cost of goods manufactured in the manufacturing firm's income statement replaces the purchases of the merchandising business. The next step is to identify what constitutes the cost of goods manufactured.

**Objective 6:
Preparing an income statement for a manufacturing firm**

COST OF GOODS MANUFACTURED STATEMENT

The cost of goods manufactured can be computed as:

$$\begin{array}{l}\text{Cost} \\ \text{of goods} \\ \text{manufactured}\end{array} = \begin{array}{l}\text{Direct} \\ \text{materials} \\ \text{cost}\end{array} + \begin{array}{l}\text{Direct} \\ \text{labor} \\ \text{cost}\end{array} + \begin{array}{l}\text{Manufacturing} \\ \text{overhead} \\ \text{cost}\end{array} + \begin{array}{l}\text{Beginning} \\ \text{work in} \\ \text{process} \\ \text{inventory}\end{array} - \begin{array}{l}\text{Ending} \\ \text{work in} \\ \text{process} \\ \text{inventory}\end{array}$$

A **cost of goods manufactured statement** is prepared to show the supporting calculations for the cost of goods manufactured reported on the income statement. In Figure 22–3, the cost of goods manufactured amounts to $710,000, and the purpose of the supporting statement shown in Figure 22–4 is to provide a detailed explanation of the total. The total of the direct materials cost, the direct labor cost, and the manufacturing overhead cost represents the manufacturing costs of the period. The direct materials used, totaling $142,000, are determined by adding the purchases of the period ($141,000) to the beginning materials ($48,000) and subtracting the ending materials ($47,000). You should

Figure 22–3
Comparison of Income Statements

A MERCHANDISING FIRM Income Statement Year Ended December 31, 1987			A MANUFACTURING FIRM Income Statement Year Ended December 31, 1987		
Sales		$1,000,000	Sales		$1,000,000
Cost of goods sold:			Cost of goods sold:		
Beginning merchandise inventory	$150,000		Beginning finished goods inventory	$150,000	
Purchases of merchandise	710,000		Cost of goods manufactured (Figure 22-4)	710,000	
Goods available for sale	860,000		Goods available for sale	860,000	
Ending merchandise inventory	160,000		Ending finished goods inventory	160,000	
Cost of goods sold		700,000	Cost of goods sold		700,000
Gross profit		300,000	Gross profit		300,000
Operating expenses:			Operating expenses:		
Selling expenses	110,000		Selling expenses	110,000	
Administrative expenses	120,000		Administrative expenses	120,000	
Total operating expenses		230,000	Total operating expenses		230,000
Net income before taxes		70,000	Net income before taxes		70,000
Income taxes		16,000	Income taxes		16,000
Net income		$ 54,000	Net income		$ 54,000

Figure 22–4
Cost of Goods Manufactured Statement

A MANUFACTURING FIRM Cost of Goods Manufactured Statement Year Ended December 31, 1987		
Direct materials:		
Beginning raw materials	$ 48,000	
Purchases (net)	141,000	
Raw materials available for production	189,000	
Ending raw materials	47,000	
Direct materials used		$142,000
Direct labor		355,000
Manufacturing overhead:		
Indirect labor	56,000	
Supplies	5,000	
Utilities	42,000	
Rent	22,600	
Insurance	18,000	
Payroll taxes	28,400	
Depreciation	32,000	
Miscellaneous	4,000	
Total manufacturing overhead		208,000
Manufacturing costs for the period		705,000
Beginning work in process		35,000
Total work in process		740,000
Ending work in process		30,000
Cost of goods manufactured		$710,000

note that the presentation of the direct materials used is basically the same as the cost of the goods sold shown on the income statement of a merchandising business. The direct labor cost amounting to $355,000 and the manufacturing overhead of $208,000 would be recorded during the period. Consequently, the total manufacturing costs for the period are $705,000.

The individual manufacturing overhead items are listed and totaled on the statement as long as they are not too numerous. If a large number of accounts are involved, they may be shown on a separate schedule to keep the cost of goods manufactured statement from being too lengthy. The beginning work in process inventory of $35,000 represents costs that have been incurred in the previous period, and they are added to the manufacturing costs of the current period. Since the ending work in process of $30,000 consists of costs associated with products that will be finished later, it must be subtracted to compute the cost of goods manufactured for the period. The cost of goods manufactured of $710,000 represents the production cost of the products that have been completed and transferred to finished goods inventory during the period. This figure is also inserted on the income statement in Figure 22–3.

ACCOUNTING SYSTEM CONSIDERATIONS

A manufacturing firm's accounting system will be *more complex* than one utilized by a nonmanufacturing business because of the manufacturing cost flow illustrated in Figure 22–2. The basic accounts used for assets, liabilities, owners' equity, revenue, selling expenses, and administrative expenses in nonmanufacturing businesses are also needed in a manufacturing firm. Additional asset and income statement accounts will be required in manufacturing to accurately determine the cost of goods sold and to provide management with reliable product cost information.

A manufacturing firm must decide between a periodic and a perpetual inventory system in accounting for the manufacturing costs. We introduced the essential features of periodic and perpetual inventories in Chapter 5. In this chapter, we will illustrate the use of a periodic inventory approach in manufacturing and then extend these procedures to a perpetual inventory system in the next chapter.

**Objective 7:
The accounts
and accounting
procedures
needed for a
manufacturing
firm**

PERIODIC INVENTORY SYSTEM FOR MANUFACTURING

Small manufacturing firms may be able to use a periodic inventory system if a single product or a few similar products are produced. As such, the manufacturing accounting is performed within the general accounting system by extending the basic procedures used for merchandising accounting. The additional accounts required with a periodic inventory system in a manufacturing operation are

**Objective 8:
How a periodic
inventory sys-
tem works in a
manufacturing
operation**

1. *Raw Materials Inventory.*
2. *Raw Materials Purchases.*
3. *Work in Process Inventory.*
4. *Finished Goods Inventory.*
5. *Manufacturing Plant and Equipment.*
6. *Manufacturing Payroll.*
7. *Manufacturing Overhead.*
8. *Manufacturing Summary.*

Many of these accounts will be set up as control accounts supported by the detailed information of a subsidiary ledger. For example, the balance in the *Manufacturing Overhead* account will be the sum of the amounts recorded in subsidiary ledger accounts for such items as indirect labor, supplies, utilities, and rent.

The *Manufacturing Summary* account is used at the end of an accounting period to summarize the costs incurred and to determine the cost of goods manufactured. It should be kept in mind that beginning balances are carried in the three inventory accounts (*Raw Materials, Work in Process,* and *Finished Goods*) during an accounting period when a periodic inventory system is used. At the end of each accounting period, a physical count of raw materials, work in process, and finished goods must be made and costs must be assigned to inventory units before financial statements can be prepared. Consequently, the manufacturing cost flow shown in Figure 22–2 is not accounted for as it takes place, and the inventory cost information is made available through the closing of the accounts at the end of the period. For example, the *Manufacturing Summary* account would be used by a manufacturing firm with the information in Figures 22–3 and 22–4 as follows.

Manufacturing Summary

1987			1987		
Dec. 31	Beginning raw materials	48,000	Dec. 31	Ending raw materials	47,000
31	Purchases of raw materials	141,000	31	Ending work in process	30,000
31	Manufacturing payroll	355,000	31	Close cost of goods manufactured	710,000
31	Manufacturing overhead	208,000			
31	Beginning work in process	35,000			
		787,000			787,000

Income Summary

1987					
Dec. 31	Beginning finished goods	150,000	Dec. 31	Ending finished goods	160,000
31	Cost of goods manufactured	710,000			
	Balance	700,000			

The $700,000 balance shown in the *Income Summary* account before the revenue, selling expenses, administrative expenses, and income taxes are closed represents the cost of goods sold and coincides with the amount shown in Figure 22–3. After the revenue and other expenses are closed to the *Income Summary* account, a credit balance of $54,000 will remain as the net income for the period.

The net income of $54,000 will be closed to *Retained Earnings* as a final step in the closing process. The cost of goods manufactured under a periodic inventory system will usually be calculated on a manufacturing worksheet, similar to the one introduced in Chapter 5 for a merchandising business. A description of a manufacturing worksheet and a more complete illustration of manufacturing accounting with a periodic inventory system follow.

WORKSHEET FOR A MANUFACTURING FIRM

Objective 9: Using a worksheet in a manufacturing firm

The worksheet of a merchandising firm can easily be adapted for use by a manufacturing firm. Two additional columns are required to record the financial data reported in the cost of goods manufactured statement. The **manufacturing worksheet** of Boyles Precision Manufacturing Company, a midwestern producer of small metal parts, is presented in Figure 22–5. The balances of the general ledger accounts are listed as a trial balance in the first two

BOYLES PRECISION MANUFACTURING COMPANY
Manufacturing Worksheet
Year Ended December 31, 1987

Account	Unadjusted Trial Balance Dr.	Cr.	Adjustments Dr.	Cr.	Manufacturing Dr.	Cr.	Income Statement Dr.	Cr.	Balance Sheet Dr.	Cr.
Cash	24,500								24,500	
Accounts receivable	102,000								102,000	
Allowance for uncollectible accounts		2,100		(1) 7,000						9,100
Inventories:										
Finished goods	210,000						210,000	201,500	201,500	
Work in process	49,000				49,000	50,700			50,700	
Raw materials	67,200				67,200	71,500			71,500	
Prepaid expenses	2,600			(2) 1,700					900	
Manufacturing machinery	86,000								86,000	
Accumulated depreciation—machinery		26,000		(5) 10,750						36,750
Manufacturing equipment	32,000								32,000	
Accumulated depreciation—equipment		11,000		(6) 6,400						17,400
Small tools	14,100			(9) 3,300					10,800	
Patents	9,600			(7) 1,100					8,500	
Accounts payable		18,000								18,000
Accrued payroll taxes		1,400		(3) 574						1,974
Notes payable (long term)		28,000								28,000
Common stock ($10 par value)		50,000								50,000
Retained earnings		316,336								316,336
Sales		1,400,000						1,400,000		
Raw materials purchases	194,600				194,600					
Freight in	2,800				2,800					
Direct labor	490,000		(3) 7,000		497,000					
Indirect labor	77,200		(3) 1,200		78,400					
Supplies	8,726				8,726					
Utilities	58,800				58,800					
Rent	31,640				31,640					
Insurance	22,120		(2) 1,700		23,820					
Payroll taxes	39,270		(3) 574		39,844					
Other expenses	5,600				5,600					
Advertising	20,800						20,800			
Sales salaries	121,520						121,520			
Other selling expenses	11,680						11,680			
Administrative salaries	156,800						156,800			
Other administrative expenses	11,200						11,200			
Interest expense	3,080		(4) 280				3,360			
Totals	1,852,836	1,852,836								
Bad debt expense			(1) 7,000				7,000			
Accrued wages payable				(3) 8,200						8,200
Accrued interest expense				(4) 280						280
Depreciation expense—machinery			(5) 10,750		10,750					
Depreciation expense—equipment			(6) 6,400		6,400					
Amortization expense—patent			(7) 1,100		1,100					
Income tax expense			(8) 35,040				35,040			
Accrued income taxes				(8) 35,040						35,040
Depreciation expense—tools			(9) 3,300		3,300					
Cost of goods manufactured						956,780	956,780			
Totals			74,344	74,344	1,078,980	1,078,980				
Net income							67,320			67,320
Totals							1,601,500	1,601,500	588,400	588,400

Figure 22–5

Manufacturing Worksheet

columns. The end-of-period adjustments are made in the adjustments columns, and the cost of goods manufactured information is recorded in the manufacturing columns. Income statement columns and balance sheet columns are used for the data needed to prepare the two basic financial statements. As we saw in Chapter 4, a worksheet is used by a business firm to *organize* financial information in a systematic manner and to *prepare* the financial statements. This is especially important for a manufacturing operation because of the complexities associated with the production process and the additional financial data that are involved.

Once the trial balance data are entered on the worksheet, the end-of-period adjustments must be made. The Boyles Precision Manufacturing Company has identified the following adjustments that are required as of December 31.

1. Bad debt expense is estimated at one-half of one percent (.005) of credit sales of $1,400,000.
2. Expired insurance on manufacturing equipment, currently recorded as a prepaid expense, is $1,700.
3. Accrued wages amount to $8,200—distributed as $7,000 for direct labor and $1,200 for indirect labor. The associated employer payroll taxes are $574.
4. Accrued interest expense on a long-term note payable is $280.
5. Depreciation on the machinery used in manufacturing is $10,750.
6. Depreciation on the manufacturing equipment is $6,400.
7. Amortization of patents is $1,100.
8. Federal and state income tax expense amounts to $35,040.
9. An inventory of the small tools used in manufacturing was taken on December 31. Small tools amounting to $10,800 were on hand as compared with the $14,100 shown in the small tools account. Consequently, $3,300 is written off in 1987.

The debits and credits associated with the adjustments are in balance at $74,344. The amounts in the adjustments columns are combined with the amounts in the trial balance columns, and the results are transferred according to their ultimate presentation in the financial statements to the manufacturing columns, income statement columns, or balance sheet columns. Those items that will appear on the cost of goods manufactured statement are shown in the manufacturing columns. All items except the ending work in process and raw materials inventories will have debit balances, since they will be expenses on the statement. The beginning work in process and raw materials inventories of $49,000 and $67,200, respectively, are entered as debit balances in the manufacturing section.

The ending work in process and raw materials inventories amounting to $50,700 and $71,500, respectively, are entered in the manufacturing credit column, since they will be deducted on the cost of goods manufactured statement. They are then extended to the balance sheet debit column to be reported as assets on the balance sheet. The $956,780 figure required to balance the debits and credits in the manufacturing columns is the cost of goods manufactured for the period, which is transferred to the income statement debit column.

The beginning finished goods inventory of $210,000 is entered in the income statement debit column, since it represents an addition in the determination of cost of goods sold. The ending finished goods inventory of $201,500 is entered into the income statement credit column because it will be subtracted from goods available in the determination of cost of goods sold. The same figure is also entered in the balance sheet debit column to be reported as an asset on the balance sheet. The sales of $1,400,000 are recorded in the income statement credit column. The operating expenses totaling $329,000, the interest expense of $3,360, and the income tax expense amounting to $35,040 are recorded in the income statement debit column. The debit of $67,320 needed to balance the income statement columns is the annual net income, which will ultimately be closed to retained earnings. All asset, liability, and stockholders' equity items are carried forward to the balance sheet columns. Formal statements prepared by the Boyles Precision Manufacturing Company from the worksheet are presented in Figures 22–6, 22–7, and 22–8.

Figure 22–6
Income Statement

BOYLES PRECISION MANUFACTURING COMPANY
Income Statement
Year Ended December 31, 1987

Sales			$1,400,000
Cost of goods sold			
Beginning finished goods inventory		$ 210,000	
Cost of goods manufactured (Figure 22-7)		956,780	
Goods available for sale		1,166,780	
Ending finished goods inventory		201,500	
Cost of goods sold			965,280
Gross profit			434,720
Operating expenses			
Selling expenses:			
Advertising	$ 20,800		
Sales salaries	121,520		
Other selling expenses	11,680		
Total selling expenses		154,000	
Administrative expenses:			
Administrative salaries	156,800		
Bad debt expense	7,000		
Other administrative expenses	11,200		
Total administrative expenses		175,000	
Total operating expenses			329,000
Operating income			105,720
Interest expense			3,360
Net income before tax			102,360
Income taxes			35,040
Net income			$ 67,320

Figure 22–7
Cost of Goods Man-
ufactured Statement

BOYLES PRECISION MANUFACTURING COMPANY
Cost of Goods Manufactured Statement
Year Ended December 31, 1987

Direct materials		
Beginning raw materials	$ 67,200	
Purchases	194,600	
Freight in	2,800	
Raw materials available for production	264,600	
Ending raw materials	71,500	
Direct materials used		$ 193,100
Direct labor		497,000
Manufacturing overhead		
Indirect labor	78,400	
Supplies	8,726	
Utilities	58,800	
Rent	31,640	
Insurance	23,820	
Payroll taxes	39,844	
Other expenses	5,600	
Depreciation expense	20,450	
Patent amortization expense	1,100	
Total manufacturing overhead		268,380
Total manufacturing costs for the period		958,480
Beginning work in process		49,000
Total work in process		1,007,480
Ending work in process		50,700
Cost of goods manufactured		$ 956,780

CLOSING ENTRIES FOR A MANUFACTURING FIRM

The account balances that are used to determine the cost of goods manufactured are closed through the *Manufacturing Summary* account, which is then
closed to the *Income Summary* account. The Boyles Precision Manufacturing
Company would require the following entries to close the account balances
shown on the worksheet in Figure 22–5 (the numbers 1–5 identify specific
closing entries for the discussion that follows).

1.					
Dec.	31	Manufacturing Summary		1,078,980	
			Raw Materials Inventory		67,200
			Work in Process Inventory		49,000
			Raw Material Purchases		194,600
			Freight In		2,800
			Direct Labor		497,000
			Indirect Labor		78,400
			Supplies Expense		8,726

		Utilities Expense		58,800
		Rent Expense		31,640
		Insurance Expense		23,820
		Payroll Taxes Expense		39,844
		Other Expenses		5,600
		Depreciation Expense—Machinery		10,750
		Depreciation Expense—Equipment		6,400
		Patent Amortization Expense		1,100
		Small Tools Depreciation		3,300
		To close manufacturing accounts with debit balances		
2.	31	Raw Materials Inventory	71,500	
		Work in Process Inventory	50,700	
		Manufacturing Summary		122,200
		To establish ending raw materials and work in process inventories		
3.	31	Income Summary	1,534,180	
		Finished Goods Inventory		210,000
		Advertising Expense		20,800
		Sales Salaries Expense		121,520
		Other Selling Expenses		11,680
		Administrative Salaries Expense		156,800
		Other Administrative Expenses		11,200
		Interest Expense		3,360
		Bad Debt Expense		7,000
		Income Tax Expense		35,040
		Manufacturing Summary		956,780
		To close the income statement accounts with debit balances.		
4.	31	Finished Goods Inventory	201,500	
		Sales	1,400,000	
		Income Summary		1,601,500
		To establish the ending finished goods inventory and close the sales account		
5.	31	Income Summary	67,320	
		Retained Earnings		67,320
		To close net income to retained earnings.		

You should note that all of the account balances used in the closing process are taken directly from the worksheet. The first entry credits all debit balances in the manufacturing section of the worksheet, resulting in the elimination of the beginning raw materials inventory, beginning work in process inventory, raw material purchases, freight in, and manufacturing expense account balances. The second entry sets up the ending raw materials and work in process

Figure 22–8
Balance Sheet

BOYLES PRECISION MANUFACTURING COMPANY
Balance Sheet
December 31, 1987

Assets			Liabilities	
Current assets:			Current liabilities:	
Cash		$ 24,500	Accounts payable	$ 18,000
Accounts receivable	$102,000		Accrued payroll	
Allowance for uncol-			taxes	1,974
lectible accounts	(9,100)	92,900	Accrued wages	
Inventories:			payable	8,200
Finished goods	201,500		Accrued interest	
Work in process	50,700		expense	280
Raw Materials	71,500		Accrued income	
Total inventories		323,700	taxes	35,040
Prepaid expenses		900	Total current	
Total current assets		442,000	liabilities	63,494
Plant assets:			Long term liabilities:	
Machinery	86,000		Notes payable	28,000
Accumulated			Total liabilities	91,494
depreciation	(36,750)	49,250		
Equipment	32,000		Stockholders' Equity	
Accumulated			Common stock	
depreciation	(17,400)	14,600	($10 par value)	50,000
Small tools		10,800	Retained earnings	383,656
Total plant assets		74,650	Total stockholders'	
Patents		8,500	equity	433,656
			Total liabilities and	
			stockholders'	
Total assets		$525,150	equity	$525,150

inventories, which are shown as credits in the manufacturing section of the worksheet. The balance left in the *Manufacturing Summary* account after the second closing entry is $956,780, which is the cost of goods manufactured for the period. The $956,780 balance is closed along with the other debit balances of the income statement section of the worksheet in the third closing entry. Included is the elimination of the beginning finished goods inventory. In the fourth entry, the ending finished goods inventory is established and the sales for the year are closed to *Income Summary*. The credit balance left in the *Income Summary* account is $67,320, which is the annual net income. The final closing entry transfers the net income to the *Retained Earnings* account.

ESTIMATING COSTS TO BE INCLUDED IN INVENTORIES

When a periodic inventory system is used in a manufacturing firm, such as the Boyles Precision Manufacturing Company, the three types of inventory must be valued at the end of an accounting period before the financial statements can be prepared. The worksheet shown in Figure 22–5 indicates that the ending balances of raw materials, work in process, and finished goods are $71,500, $50,700, and $201,500, respectively. We must next consider the procedures needed to determine these ending inventory values. Remember that a periodic inventory system requires that the inventory items be counted and costed to determine the value of the ending inventories. The valuation of the raw materials inventory is relatively straightforward, because it is very similar to the procedures used for merchandise inventory. Since the inventory is in the same form in which it was purchased, a count is made and the cost is determined from original purchase invoices. A choice between the various flow assumptions (for example, FIFO or LIFO) must also be made.

The valuation of work in process and finished goods with a periodic inventory approach is more complex. As Figure 22–2 illustrates, the production flow used to convert raw materials to finished goods is a constant process. Yet, we must stop the process at the end of a period for accounting purposes to count and place a value on the ending inventories, without the benefit of detailed records concerning the costs incurred during production. Because of the addition of direct labor and manufacturing overhead during the period, the ending work in process and finished goods inventories are in different forms than they were at the beginning of the manufacturing process. But the question is "How much of the total manufacturing costs incurred should be assigned to the ending inventories and how much should be charged to the cost of goods manufactured?" Most manufacturing firms produce more than one product, so a unit cost for each product cannot be computed by simply dividing the total cost of goods manufactured by the number of units produced. Also, the units in work in process will be unfinished and are usually at different stages of production.

A manufacturing firm using a periodic inventory system must rely on the sound judgment of the managerial accountant and the production manager to approximate the value of the ending work in process and the finished goods inventories. The amount of direct materials assignable to the ending inventory can normally be found by referring to the product specifications for the units in work in process and finished goods. Each finished product will require a certain amount of direct materials compatible with its quality level and selling price. The same product specifications will indicate how much labor cost should be required to complete a product. Based on the percentage of completion for the various products in the ending inventories, management can assign an approximate amount of labor that should have been used. Since the direct materials and direct labor are directly related to the production of products, these estimates are usually reasonably accurate in the valuation of ending inventories.

Objective 10: Problems associated with a periodic inventory system used by a manufacturing firm

We discovered earlier that manufacturing overhead is not directly traceable to the products manufactured since it is, by definition, an indirect cost. Instead, an overhead application rate is used to assign manufacturing overhead costs to inventories. When a periodic inventory system is used, the most common practice is to express manufacturing overhead as a percentage of direct labor costs. The use of this overhead application rate is based on the assumption that the ratio of manufacturing overhead costs to direct labor costs is the same for all products produced during the period. The overhead rate is multiplied times the direct labor cost estimated for the ending work in process and finished goods inventories so that manufacturing overhead cost can be charged to each of the inventories. In the case of Boyles Precision Manufacturing Company, the firm incurred manufacturing overhead costs of $268,380 and direct labor amounted to $497,000 (see Figure 22–7). Therefore, the overhead application rate is $268,380 divided by $497,000, or 54% of direct labor cost. Consequently, 54 cents of manufacturing overhead will be assigned as product costs for every dollar of direct labor cost. We assume that the procedures discussed in this section have been used to value the Boyles Precision Manufacturing Company's ending inventories. The amounts of direct materials, direct labor, and manufacturing overhead assigned to work in process and finished goods are the following—based on management's estimates of the direct costs incurred and the use of the 54% overhead application rate.

	Direct Materials	Direct Labor	Manufacturing Overhead	Total
Work in process	$24,674	$ 16,900	$ 9,126	$ 50,700
Finished goods	46,345	100,750	54,405	201,500

LIMITATIONS OF A PERIODIC INVENTORY SYSTEM

We must emphasize that only a small manufacturing firm can utilize a periodic inventory system. Even then, the results may not be adequate to satisfy the cost information needs of management. Product costs are calculated in manufacturing for three basic purposes: *inventory valuation, income determination, and management decision-making applications* such as product pricing, cost control, product profitability analysis, and resource allocations. As we can see in the example of the Boyles Precision Manufacturing Company, the cost information will be available only at the end of an accounting period after physical inventories have been taken for raw materials, work in process, and finished goods. The cost information from a periodic inventory system will not be sufficiently timely, accurate, and detailed to serve the day-to-day needs of management, except in extremely simple situations.

As we have previously demonstrated, counting and pricing an ending inventory is very time consuming—particularly for work in process and finished goods inventories. Consequently, a complete inventory is usually taken only at the end of the year, despite the fact that management needs the information for decisions that must be made regularly throughout the period. We noted in the Boyles Precision Manufacturing Company example that rough approximations may be the only measures possible for the ending work in process and finished goods inventories. Any errors made with the estimates will have an adverse effect on the income reported for the period and the management decision-making process. In addition, management may have trouble controlling costs over time because the cost results are not adequately detailed. Since unit costs for each product are not computed, it will be difficult to evaluate the effect of changes in costs between periods. Management needs to relate the cost information to responsibility centers and to products. The use of responsibility accounting requires the determination of what costs should be, as well as what they actually are. Timely reports that pinpoint the responsibility for variances between the planned and actual cost performance must be based upon a detailed description of the costs incurred.

The deficiencies of a periodic inventory system increase with the number of products and producing departments. A cost accumulation system is used by many manufacturing firms to correct the deficiencies of a periodic inventory system. Cost accumulation procedures provide management with the cost information necessary to plan, control, and evaluate the performance of the production function. Perpetual inventories are maintained so that the cost information is timely, accurate, and detailed. The emphasis of cost accumulation is on unit cost determination for each type of product, instead of on the total cost of goods manufactured during the period. The two types of cost accumulation systems, job order costing and process costing, are discussed in the next chapter.

GLOSSARY

ABSORPTION COSTING. The inventory valuation method used by a manufacturing firm in which all manufacturing costs are charged as product costs, regardless of whether or not they may change in relation to production levels (p. 865).

COST OF GOODS MANUFACTURED STATEMENT. A detailed accounting of the manufacturing cost performance reported on the income statement of a manufacturing firm (p. 867).

COST BEHAVIOR. The measure of how a cost will react to changes in the level of business activity (p. 865).

DIRECT LABOR. Represents the wages paid to employees whose time and effort can be traced to specific products (p. 863).

DIRECT MATERIALS. Consist of the raw materials that can be traced as an integral part of a finished product (p. 863).

FINISHED GOODS. The cost of the products that have been manufactured completely and are ready for sale (p. 861).

FIXED COST. A cost that will remain constant in total amount over a wide range of business activity (p. 866).

MANUFACTURING COST ELEMENTS. The direct materials, direct labor, and manufacturing overhead required to produce a salable product (p. 862).

MANUFACTURING FIRM. A business that converts raw materials into salable products (p. 858).

MANUFACTURING OVERHEAD. All manufacturing costs except direct materials and direct labor required in the production process (p. 864).

MANUFACTURING WORKSHEET. Working papers used by a manufacturing firm to organize financial data (including the manufacturing costs) and to prepare financial statements (p. 870).

OVERHEAD APPLICATION RATE. A rate used to assign manufacturing overhead costs as product costs (p. 864).

PERIOD COSTS. Costs charged to the income statement of the period in which they are incurred, rather than being inventoried as product costs (p. 862).

PRODUCT COSTS. Costs inventoried as assets during the production process and charged to the income statement when the related finished goods are sold (p. 861).

PRODUCTION DEPARTMENTS. Departments directly engaged in the manufacturing operation required to convert raw materials into finished goods (p. 864).

RAW MATERIALS. Represent the cost of the basic materials and parts that have been purchased by a manufacturing firm and are available for conversion into salable products (p. 861).

SERVICE DEPARTMENTS. Departments that support the production departments with such activities as maintenance, production control, and storage (p. 864).

VARIABLE COST. A cost that will vary in total amount proportionately with some measure of business activity (p. 865).

VARIABLE COSTING. The inventory valuation method used for internal reporting purposes by a manufacturing firm. Only variable manufacturing costs are charged as product costs with this method (p. 865).

WORK IN PROCESS. Inventory that has been partially converted into finished products (p. 861).

DISCUSSION QUESTIONS

1. Explain the basic differences between the inventories of a manufacturing firm and those of a merchandising enterprise. What is the effect of these differences on the income statements of the two types of businesses?
2. Distinguish between product and period costs. Identify which of the following is a product cost and which is a period cost.
   (a) Indirect materials.
   (b) Depreciation—manufacturing equipment.
   (c) Gas heat—sales office.
   (d) President's salary.
   (e) Direct labor.
   (f) Insurance—factory.
   (g) Sales manager's salary.
   (h) Production supervisor's salary.
   (i) Depreciation—president's car.
3. What are the three manufacturing cost elements? Which of the nine items in Question 2 would be classified as a manufacturing cost and how would each be classified (direct materials, direct labor, or manufacturing overhead)?
4. Explain the basic difference between a fixed cost and a variable cost. On the basis of their most likely cost behavior, how would each of the items in Question 2 be categorized (fixed or variable)?

5. Explain the basic difference between manufacturing costs for the period, cost of goods manufactured, and cost of goods sold.
6. The Merrill Company incurred the following manufacturing costs during the year.

Direct materials	$140,000
Direct labor	350,000
Manufacturing overhead	210,000

   (a) Assume that the company had no work in process inventory at the beginning or end of the year. How much was the firm's cost of goods manufactured?
   (b) Assume, instead, that the company had a work in process inventory of $20,000 at the beginning of the year but none at the end of the year. How much was the firm's cost of goods manufactured?
   (c) Assume instead that the company had a work in process inventory of $20,000 at the beginning of the year and $40,000 at the end of the year. How much was the firm's cost of goods manufactured?
7. During the previous year, the cost of raw materials used by a manufacturing firm was $80,000. The raw materials inventory decreased by $9,000 during the period. What was the cost of raw materials purchased?
8. Explain what the balance of the *Manufacturing Summary* account represents before the account is closed.
9. What is the purpose of a worksheet in the accounting cycle of a manufacturing firm?
10. Why is the cost of goods manufactured entered as a credit in the manufacturing columns of a worksheet and a debit in the income statement columns?
11. Why is the beginning finished goods inventory entered as a debit in the income statement columns of a worksheet instead of in the balance sheet columns?
12. If a given cost is incurred for the common benefit of manufacturing, selling, and administrative activities, how should the amount be divided among the three?
13. The Do-Rite Company evaluates the performance of its manufacturing operation by considering controllable costs only. All direct costs are classified as being controllable and all indirect costs are considered uncontrollable. Do you agree with this approach?
14. What are the basic procedures involved when valuing inventories in a manufacturing operation with a periodic inventory system?
15. What are the limitations of a periodic inventory system used by a manufacturing firm? How would a perpetual inventory system eliminate these deficiencies?
16. What is an overhead application rate and why is it used by manufacturing firms?
17. The Kemper Company uses an overhead application rate of 60% of direct labor cost to charge overhead to work in process inventory. If manufacturing overhead amounting to $32,520 is applied to work in process at the end of the year, what is the proper amount of direct labor charged to the inventory?

EXERCISES

Exercise 22-1 Identifying Product or Period Costs
Classify the following items as being either product costs or period costs.

A. Salaries of workers handling inventory during production.
B. Depreciation on an airplane used by the firm's president.

C. Lease payments on automobiles used by sales representatives.
D. Plant manager's salary.
E. Social security payments for production workers.
F. Containers used to package finished goods.

Exercise 22-2 Evaluating Basic Cost Behavior

The Fast Speedboat Company produces ski boats. Each boat contains a dual battery system, which is purchased from an outside supplier for $110 each. The firm's production process is highly automated with an annual depreciation charge of $800,000.

Required:
A. What are per boat and total costs of the battery systems for 10 boats, 100 boats, 1,000 boats, and 10,000 boats?
B. What is the depreciation charge per boat if 1,000 boats are produced each year? What would it be for 10,000 boats?
C. What kind of cost behavior is involved in A and B?
D. If absorption costing were used, would the depreciation expense be inventoried? What if variable costing were used?

Exercise 22-3 Basic Format of a Manufacturing Income Statement

Listed below are selected financial data from the 1987 accounting records of the Hall Company.

Cost of goods manufactured	$244,000
Ending finished goods	44,000
Sales	408,000
Beginning finished goods	36,000
Selling and administrative expenses	84,000

Required:
Prepare an income statement for 1987.

Exercise 22-4 Preparing a Cost of Goods Manufactured Statement

Listed below are selected financial data from the 1987 accounting records of the Miller Manufacturing Company.

Beginning raw materials	$ 55,000
Ending raw materials	53,000
Beginning work in process	40,320
Direct labor	408,960
Manufacturing overhead	239,616
Ending work in process	34,560
Purchases of raw materials	162,432

Required:
Prepare a cost of goods manufactured statement for 1987.

Exercise 22-5 Determining Beginning Work in Process

The information given here is taken from the financial records of the Jackson Company for the year ended December 31, 1987.

Manufacturing overhead, 62.5% of direct labor cost	$ 72,000
Raw materials inventory, January 1, 1987	12,000

Cost of goods manufactured	327,200
Raw materials inventory, December 31, 1987	18,000
Work in process inventory, December 31, 1987	36,000
Raw materials purchased in 1987	158,400

Required:
Compute the cost of work in process inventory on January 1, 1987.

Exercise 22-6 Valuing Manufacturing Inventories

During 1987 the Hagstrom Corporation incurred the following costs in its manufacturing activities.

Direct labor	$116,000
Direct materials	157,600
Manufacturing overhead	174,000

The company charges manufacturing overhead to work in process inventory and finished goods inventory, using an overhead application rate based on direct labor costs.

Required:
A. Determine the company's overhead application rate.
B. If the company's ending finished goods inventory of $18,400 included $3,200 of direct material costs, determine the inventory's labor and overhead costs.
C. The company's ending work in process inventory amounted to $20,000. If the direct labor costs included in the ending inventory figure amounted to $5,600, calculate the inventory's raw materials and manufacturing overhead costs.

Exercise 22-7 Manufacturing Accounting with Missing Data

For each company fill in the missing data. Each company is independent of the others.

Income Statements			
	Company X	Company Y	Company Z
Sales	$42,400	?	$48,800
Beginning finished goods	5,600	?	12,000
Cost of goods manufactured	15,200	$32,000	?
Ending finished goods	?	12,000	16,800
Cost of goods sold	16,000	29,600	?
Gross profit	?	35,200	?
Operating expenses	12,000	?	18,400
Net income	?	20,000	?
Beginning work in process	?	8,400	9,600
Direct labor	5,600	12,000	16,800
Raw materials used	5,200	7,200	13,600
Manufacturing overhead	6,400	9,600	12,000
Ending work in process	7,200	?	24,000

Exercise 22-8 Manufacturing Accounting with Missing Data

Income statement data for the Lawsom Corporation are presented below for four years.

Income Statements				
	1985	1986	1987	1988
Sales	?	?	$368,000	$360,000
Beginning finished goods	$ 52,000	?	?	?
Beginning work in process	18,000	?	?	12,000
Raw materials used	71,200	$ 76,000	48,000	68,000
Direct labor	?	84,000	64,000	44,000
Manufacturing overhead	76,000	?	60,000	48,000
Ending work in process	24,000	?	?	?
Cost of goods manufactured	?	?	180,000	152,000
Ending finished goods	68,000	?	?	18,400
Cost of goods sold	232,800	231,200	193,600	?
Gross profit	220,000	?	?	168,000
Operating expenses	68,000	60,000	?	40,000
Net income	?	144,000	96,000	?

Required:

Fill in the missing data. (*Hint:* 1988 data provide information required to find 1987 unknowns).

Exercise 22-9 Evaluating Cost Classifications

Identify the most likely correct answer for each of the following costs as a product or period cost and as a variable or fixed cost, with respect to level of activity.

	Product	Period	Variable	Fixed
1. Manufacturing utilities				
2. Manufacturing supplies				
3. Direct materials				
4. President's salary				
5. Depreciation on manufacturing equipment				
6. Manufacturing rent				
7. Sales office utilities				
8. Depreciation on sales office equipment				
9. Nails used in production				
10. Maintenance contract on manufacturing equipment				

Exercise 22-10 Evaluating the Use of Raw Materials

The Poland Tool Company produces and sells high-quality woodworking tool sets. Each set of tools is contained in a wooden carrying case, which is purchased from an outside supplier. The wooden carrying cases are held as raw materials inventory until they are placed into production and combined with the related tool sets. The production and purchasing departments have provided the following information for the month of January.

1. Beginning raw materials inventory included 760 wooden cases at a cost of $17,480.
2. The company purchased 1,600 additional cases at $23 each.
3. A total of 1,800 cases were transferred into production.
4. An additional 120 cases were given to managers of prospective retail outlets for promotional purposes.

Of the cases placed into production, 65% were combined with tool sets, which were completed and transferred to finished goods. Of the cases transferred to finished goods during January, 70% had been sold by month's-end. There was no beginning inventory of wooden cases in finished goods or in work in process.

Required:
Determine the cost of the wooden cases that would be included in the following accounts as of January 31.

A. Raw materials.
B. Work in process.
C. Finished goods.
D. Selling expense.
E. Cost of goods sold.

PROBLEMS

Problem 22-1 **Fundamentals of Manufacturing Accounting**
During 1987, the Organ Manufacturing Company incurred the following expenses in connection with its production activities.

Manufacturing utilities	$ 24,400
Indirect labor	34,400
Raw material purchases	140,000
Direct labor	104,000
Depreciation on manufacturing equipment	19,200
Plant rent expense	20,000
Supplies used in production	10,400
Repairs to manufacturing equipment	21,600

The beginning and ending inventory values were:

	Beginning Inventory	Ending Inventory
Raw materials	$17,600	$15,200
Work in process	29,600	33,600
Finished goods	34,400	28,000

Required:
A. Calculate the relationship between direct labor cost and manufacturing overhead costs.
B. Prepare a cost of goods manufactured statement for the year ended December 31, 1987.
C. Prepare closing entries for the manufacturing accounts using the *Manufacturing Summary* account.
D. Prepare the entry to close the *Manufacturing Summary* account.

Problem 22-2 **Determining Cost of Goods Sold**

The accountant for the Overly Company has compiled information concerning the company's 1987 manufacturing costs. The beginning inventories included raw materials—$76,800; work in process—$51,200; and finished goods—$94,400. The company incurred direct labor costs of $541,440, and its total costs of goods manufactured for 1987 amounted to $1,928,000. Manufacturing overhead costs are assigned to work in process and finished goods, using the relationship between direct labor costs and manufacturing overhead incurred. The ending inventories are comprised of the following costs.

	Raw Materials	Work in Process	Finished Goods
Raw materials	$70,400	$17,600	$24,000
Direct labor	—	17,920	21,120
Manufacturing overhead costs	—	?	31,680
Total ending inventory	$70,400	?	$76,800

Required:

Prepare a schedule showing the cost of goods sold for 1987.

Problem 22-3 **Manufacturing Income Statement**

The following accounts and amounts were taken from the records of the Spore Manufacturing Company.

Advertising	$ 33,600
Sales travel	8,800
Depreciation—production machinery	12,000
Depreciation—office equipment	4,800
Direct labor	202,400
Manufacturing utilities	8,560
Manufacturing rent	62,400
Manufacturing supplies	40,000
Finished goods, 1/1/87	73,600
Finished goods, 12/31/87	68,000
Freight-in	6,400
Indirect labor	43,200
Machinery repairs	11,200
Administrative office rent	16,800
Officers' salaries	123,200
Property taxes—manufacturing equipment	4,800
Property taxes—office equipment	10,400
Purchase discounts on raw materials	9,600
Raw materials inventory, 1/1/87	35,200
Raw materials inventory, 12/31/87	42,400
Raw material purchases	360,000
Sales	1,000,800
Sales returns	17,600
Sales commission expense	32,000
Work in process, 1/1/87	13,600
Work in process, 12/31/87	16,800

Required:

Prepare an income statement and a cost of goods manufactured statement for the year ending December 31, 1987.

Problem 22-4 Correcting a Manufacturing Income Statement

The president of the Spade Manufacturing Company hired his daughter, who had just completed her first accounting course in college, as summer help in the accounting department. Her first assignment was to prepare an income statement for the month of May. Applying the knowledge she had acquired in her financial accounting course, she prepared the following statement.

SPADE MANUFACTURING COMPANY Income Statement Month Ended May 31, 1987	
Sales	$394,400
Operating expenses:	
Raw material purchases	77,600
Rent	49,600
Depreciation	12,000
Utilities	24,000
Direct labor	100,000
Indirect labor	18,400
Office salaries	24,800
Administrative and selling expenses	37,600
Total operating expenses	344,000
Net income	$ 50,400

The president questions these results and has decided that a correct income statement should be based on the following data.

1. The beginning and ending inventories of raw materials were $16,800 and $19,200, respectively.

2. Three of the expenses listed on his daughter's income statement were applicable to both manufacturing operations and the selling and administrative functions. The percentages applicable to each are as follows.

	Manufacturing	Selling and Administrative
Rent	65%	35%
Depreciation	75%	25%
Utilities	60%	40%

3. The work in process and finished goods inventories were:

	May 1	May 31
Work in process	$29,600	$28,000
Finished goods	23,200	24,800

Required:

Prepare a corrected income statement for the month of May

Problem 22-5 Use of a Manufacturing Worksheet

The unadjusted trial balance of the Stevens Manufacturing Company on December 31, 1987 is presented here.

STEVENS MANUFACTURING COMPANY
Unadjusted Trial Balance
December 31, 1987

Account Title	Debits	Credits
Cash	$ 8,000	
Accounts receivable	16,800	
Allowance for uncollectible accounts		$ 800
Finished goods inventory, 1/1/87	28,000	
Work in process inventory, 1/1/87	13,600	
Raw materials inventory, 1/1/87	7,200	
Prepaid insurance	2,400	
Machinery and equipment	72,800	
Accumulated depreciation		26,000
Accounts payable		15,200
Notes payable		24,000
Common stock		1,000
Retained earnings		34,680
Sales		864,000
Raw material purchases	324,000	
Direct labor	195,200	
Indirect labor	50,400	
Manufacturing supplies	27,200	
Utilities—manufacturing	19,600	
Rent—manufacturing	33,600	
Insurance—manufacturing	15,200	
Property taxes—manufacturing	7,200	
Selling expenses	84,480	
Administrative expenses	43,200	
Interest expense	16,800	
Totals	$965,680	$965,680

Additional information:

1. On September 1, 1987, the company paid $2,400 for a 12-month insurance premium. *Prepaid Insurance* was debited at the time of the purchase.
2. The *Machinery and Equipment* account includes $25,200 of administrative office equipment and $47,600 of manufacturing equipment. All machinery and equipment is depreciated using the straight line method, with a seven year life and no residual value. No additions or deletions were made to the *Machinery and Equipment* account during 1987.
3. The inventories as of December 31, 1987 were:

Raw materials	$ 6,000
Work in process	15,200
Finished goods	32,000

4. Expenses incurred at year end but not yet recorded: direct labor—$5,000; indirect labor—$1,200; and selling expenses—$3,760.
5. An additional bad debt expense of $208 must be recognized.
6. Ignore income taxes.

Required:

A. Prepare a manufacturing worksheet, including pairs of columns for unadjusted trial balance, adjustments, manufacturing, income statement, and balance sheet. Complete the worksheet properly.

B. Prepare a cost of goods manufactured statement for the year ended December 31, 1987.

C. Prepare the closing entries using a *Manufacturing Summary* account.

D. Calculate the relationship between manufacturing overhead and direct labor costs as an overhead application rate. Using that rate, calculate the direct labor and manufacturing overhead included in the ending inventories, if the ending work in process contains $5,064 of raw materials, and if $7,384 of raw materials is included in the finished goods inventory.

ALTERNATE PROBLEMS

Problem 22-1A Fundamentals of Manufacturing Accounting

The following costs were incurred by the Tansey Company in its manufacturing operation in 1987.

Manufacturing insurance	$ 16,000
Direct labor	96,000
Raw material purchases	122,400
Manufacturing utilities	34,400
Repairs to manufacturing equipment	13,600
Indirect labor	43,200
Manufacturing supplies	27,200

The beginning and ending inventory values were:

	Beginning	Ending
Raw materials	$21,600	$19,200
Work in process	32,800	36,000
Finished goods	26,400	24,800

Required:

A. Calculate the relationship between direct labor costs and manufacturing overhead costs.

B. Prepare a cost of goods manufactured statement for the year ending December 31, 1987.

C. Prepare closing entries for the manufacturing accounts using the *Manufacturing Summary* account.

D. Prepare the entry to close the *Manufacturing Summary* account.

Problem 22-2A Determining Cost of Goods Sold

The Terrell Manufacturing Corporation incurred direct labor costs of $302,400 and its total cost of goods manufactured during 1987 was $920,000. The company assigns manufacturing overhead costs to work in process and finished goods, using the relationship between direct labor costs and manufacturing overhead incurred. The beginning inventories included raw materials—$60,000; work in process—$67,200; and finished goods—$100,000.

The ending inventories were comprised of the following costs.

	Raw Materials	Work-in Process	Finished Goods
Raw materials	$64,000	$22,680	$33,240
Direct labor	—	20,400	33,200
Manufacturing overhead	—	26,520	?
Totals	$64,000	$69,600	?

Required:

Prepare a schedule showing the cost of goods sold for 1987.

Problem 22-3A Manufacturing Income Statement

The Swedran Manufacturing Company, Inc. has compiled the following accounts and amounts for the preparation of the annual financial statements.

Work in process, 1/1/87	$ 21,600
Raw materials, 1/1/87	28,000
Finished goods, 1/1/87	60,000
Indirect labor	53,600
Sales commission expense	110,112
Sales	917,600
Raw material purchases	288,000
Freight-in	12,000
Purchase discounts on raw materials	5,600
Manufacturing rent	13,760
Advertising	20,000
Finished goods, 12/31/87	54,400
Sales returns	12,800
Manufacturing supplies	27,600
Depreciation—administrative equipment	39,600
Raw materials, 12/31/87	31,200
Direct labor	157,600
Manufacturing utilities	10,960
Administrative salaries	125,760
Work in process, 12/31/87	25,280
Plant insurance	7,280
Depreciation—manufacturing equipment	12,880

Required:

Prepare an income statement and a cost of goods manufactured statement for the year ending December 31, 1987.

Problem 22-4A Correcting a Manufacturing Income Statement

Mr. Swango has offered to perform accounting services for the manufacturing company his nephew has organized. Using his financial accounting textbook, he has prepared the following income statement.

VICKER MANUFACTURING, INC.
Income Statement
Month Ended August 31, 1987

Sales	$36,000
Operating expenses:	
Raw material purchases	17,600
Rent	1,600
Depreciation	1,200
Insurance	720
Direct labor	9,600
Indirect labor	1,440
Administrative and selling expenses	2,480
Total operating expenses	34,640
Net income	$ 1,360

Mr. Swango's nephew has compiled the following data in order to prepare a corrected income statement.

	Beginning	Ending
Raw materials	$1,600	$2,000
Work in process	3,440	3,760
Finished goods	1,440	1,680

Three of the expenses listed on the income statement were required for both manufacturing operations and the selling and administrative functions. The percentages applicable to each are:

	Manufacturing	Selling and Administrative
Rent	70%	30%
Depreciation	80%	20%
Insurance	62%	38%

Required:
Prepare a corrected income statement for August 31, 1987.

Problem 22-5A Use of a Manufacturing Worksheet

The unadjusted trial balance of the Sperry Manufacturing Company on December 31, 1987 is presented here.

SPERRY MANUFACTURING CO.
Unadjusted Trial Balance
December 31, 1987

Account Title	Debits	Credits
Cash	$ 11,760	
Accounts receivable	26,400	
Allowance for uncollectible accounts		$ 2,160
Finished goods inventory, 1/1/87	18,400	
Work in process, 1/1/87	6,000	
Raw materials inventory, 1/1/87	2,960	
Prepaid rent	43,200	
Machinery and equipment	156,800	
Accumulated depreciation		28,000
Accounts payable		14,400
Notes payable		60,000
Common stock		32,000
Retained earnings		29,600
Sales		688,000
Direct labor	172,800	
Raw materials purchases	164,000	
Indirect labor	56,800	
Manufacturing supplies	14,400	
Utilities	44,800	
Insurance	13,040	
Selling expenses	25,600	
Administrative expenses	53,600	
Interest expense	18,400	
Rent expense	25,200	
Totals	$854,160	$854,160

Additional information:

1. The *Machinery and Equipment* account is made up of $117,600 of manufacturing machinery and $39,200 of office equipment. All machinery and equipment is depreciated using a seven-year life, no residual value, and the straight-line method.
2. On July 1, 1987, the company paid $43,200 for the next 12 months' rent. Prepaid rent was debited at the time of the transaction.
3. The inventories as of December 31, 1987 were:

Raw materials	$ 2,480
Work in process	6,960
Finished goods	20,000

4. The utilities, rent, and insurance expenses are related to manufacturing operations.
5. Expenses incurred as of year-end, but not yet recorded are: direct labor—$3,200; indirect labor—$960; and administrative expenses—$560.
6. Ignore income taxes.

Required:

A. Prepare a worksheet, including a pair of columns for unadjusted trial balance, adjustments, manufacturing, income statement, and balance sheet. Complete the worksheet properly.

B. Prepare a cost of goods manufactured statement.
C. Prepare the closing entries, using a *Manufacturing Summary* account.
D. Calculate the relationship between manufacturing overhead and direct labor costs as an overhead application rate. Using that rate, calculate the direct labor cost and manufacturing overhead included in the ending inventories, if ending work in process contains $1,920 of raw materials, and if $3,200 worth of raw materials is included in the ending finished goods.

CASE

CASE 22-1   Decision Case   Manufacturing Accounting with Missing Records

The Combustible Company produces a highly flammable chemical product. The company experienced a fire on April 1, 1987, which destroyed its entire work in process inventory but did not affect the raw materials or finished goods inventories because they were located elsewhere. You have been asked to assist the firm's insurance company in determining the amount of work in process inventory at the time of the fire. Combustible Company uses a periodic inventory system, so perpetual records are not available.

A periodic inventory taken after the fire indicated that raw materials were valued at $48,000 and finished goods at $62,400. The company's accounting records show that the inventories as of January 1, 1987 were:

Raw materials	$16,000
Work in process	48,000
Finished goods	73,600

In addition, the accounting records indicate that the costs recorded during the first quarter of 1987 amounted to:

Purchase of raw materials	$86,400
Direct labor	48,000

In the past, manufacturing overhead costs have amounted to 150% of direct labor costs.

Sales for the first quarter of 1987 amounted to $320,000. The firm's gross profit margin has been 40% of sales for a long time.

Required:
Prepare a report that shows the best estimates for:
A. The firm's cost of goods sold for the first quarter of 1987.
B. The firm's cost of goods manufactured for the first quarter of 1987.
C. The firm's work in process inventory as of March 31, 1987, broken down as direct materials, direct labor, and manufacturing overhead.

23

COST ACCUMULATION SYSTEMS

CHAPTER OVERVIEW AND OBJECTIVES

This chapter presents the essential features of cost accumulation systems. When you have completed the chapter, you should understand:

1. The basic nature of a cost accumulation system.
2. The basis for choosing between job order costing and process costing.
3. The role of a job order cost sheet in product costing.
4. The accounting procedures used in job order costing.
5. The difference between actual and applied manufacturing overhead.
6. Why product costs with process costing are average costs.
7. How equivalent units are used in process costing.
8. Why the weighted-average method or FIFO method is used when a beginning work in process inventory exists with process costing.
9. The basic difference between equivalent units with the weighted-average method and the FIFO method.
10. How inventories are costed with the weighted-average and FIFO methods.
11. The accounting procedures applied in process costing.
12. The role of a cost of production report.

Objective 1: The basic nature of a cost accumulation system

We demonstrated in Chapter 22 the difficulties caused by the production process and its associated cost elements in determining the cost of manufacturing specific units of output. Nevertheless, every manufacturing firm must know what it costs to produce each product so that a selling price adequate to earn a satisfactory gross profit can be established. **Cost accumulation** is a specialized type of accounting used by a manufacturing firm to record product costs as production takes place. In contrast to the periodic inventory procedures discussed in the preceding chapter, a perpetual inventory system is maintained as a *continuous record* of the costs, and the emphasis is on the *unit cost* of the products, rather than on the total manufacturing costs of a period. Production cost data are collected in separate ledger accounts included in the general accounting system. The cost information, developed through cost accumulation procedures and used for both external and internal reporting, serves two basic purposes: product costing and managerial decision making.

Product costs are used to value a manufacturing firm's work in process and finished goods inventories, as well as to periodically determine its net income. Product costing on a perpetual basis eliminates the need for the rough estimates of ending inventory values used in a periodic inventory system. In addition, management requires reliable cost information on a regular basis for such decision-making functions as projecting a firm's financial performance, product pricing, product profitability analysis, production cost control, and resource allocations.

Although the emphasis of this chapter is on the use of cost accumulation in a manufacturing operation, it is also applicable in many nonmanufacturing businesses such as hospitals, banks, retail stores, insurance companies, accounting firms, and construction companies. Nonmanufacturing firms use cost accumulation procedures to determine the costs of performing services or activities, instead of producing products. Some examples of this are a bank costing its credit card service, an insurance company costing the policies written by its agents, a hospital costing a medical procedure, and an accounting firm costing the preparation of a corporate tax return.

The two basic types of cost accumulation systems available are *job order costing* and *process costing.* The choice between the two will depend upon the nature of the manufacturing operation. When products are produced as separately identifiable units or groups of units, job order costing is appropriate. An example of a job order costing application is a publishing firm producing a textbook, such as the one you are reading. The costs associated with distinctly separate activities such as writing, editing, class testing, and printing are accumulated for a specific publishing project and later assigned to the number of books printed. If the products are manufactured on a continuous or homogeneous basis, they cannot be separated realistically, and process costing should be used. An example of a process costing application is a firm producing paint that is sold to retail stores. It would be impossible to determine the cost of any particular gallon of paint because of the continuous flow of liquid and associated production costs involved. Product costing with both methods is an averaging procedure, although a job order unit cost is usually more accurate than a unit cost computed with process costing.

Objective 2:
The difference between job order costing and process costing applications

JOB ORDER COSTING

Job order costing is most appropriate when products are manufactured according to customers' orders or specifications and when the identity of each **job** must be kept separate. A major characteristic of a manufacturing operation in which a job order costing system is appropriate is that it must have a well defined beginning and completion time. The technique can be used to accumulate the costs of a single product (for example, a large airplane being produced) or a group of identical or similar products (for example, several dining-room tables being manufactured). Such industries as commercial printing, aerospace, shipbuilding, heavy machinery, and furniture rely on job order costing for the determination of product costs. It is also utilized by construction businesses, hospitals, repair shops, accounting firms, and motion picture companies.

CONTROL DOCUMENT—JOB ORDER COST SHEET

Objective 3: The role of a job order cost sheet for product costing

A control document is required with a job order cost system in order to accumulate the production costs and report the results to management. In job order costing, the job itself is the focal point for recording the product costs. The control document used in job order costing, a **job order cost sheet,** has two basic purposes. It provides an *itemized listing* of all direct materials, direct labor, and manufacturing overhead charged to a job, and it serves as a *subsidiary ledger* during and after the manufacturing operation. (Remember from Chapter 6 that a subsidiary ledger is the detailed accounting of a balance of a control account maintained in the general ledger.) A job order cost sheet is illustrated in Figure 23–1. The information recorded on the cost sheet will be explained subsequently.

A control number is assigned to each job entered into production and is recorded on a job order cost sheet. Information concerning the customer and product description is also entered before the cost sheet is filed in the work in process subsidiary ledger file. The cost sheet in Figure 23–1 indicates that the Village Manufacturing Company, which produces furniture, started Job 691 on January 12 and finished it on January 19.

One hundred dining-room tables were produced for the customer, Carr, Inc. The subsidiary ledger of cost sheets is controlled by the *Work in Process Inventory* account (a control account) while production takes place. The reference columns show the original sources of data recorded in the job order cost sheet (for example, a specific labor time ticket). When direct materials are requisitioned from the storeroom for a specific job, their cost is charged to the job in the material column of the job's cost sheet. The direct labor cost required to convert raw materials to finished goods is charged to the job in the labor column of the job's cost sheet, and an appropriate amount of manufacturing overhead is also recorded on the cost sheet. When the job is completed, its total cost can be determined by adding the cost recorded in the three columns.

The manufacturing costs recorded on the job order cost sheets must also be debited periodically to the *Work in Process Inventory* account. At the end of a month, the sum of the costs shown on the cost sheets assigned to unfinished jobs should equal the balance in the *Work in Process Inventory* account after the monthly accounting is finished. When a job is completed, the costs recorded on its cost sheet are totaled and the amount is debited to *Finished Goods Inventory,* with the same amount credited to the *Work in Process Inventory* account. The cost sheet is then removed from the work in process subsidiary

Job No. 691			JOB ORDER COST SHEET					
			VILLAGE MANUFACTURING COMPANY					
Customer		Carr, Inc.						
Product		L-100			Quantity		100	
Date Started			1/12	Date Finished			1/19	

Labor			Material			Overhead	
Date	Reference	Amount	Date	Reference	Amount	Direct Labor Hours	1,350
1/12	12-30	$ 1,920	1/12	1126	$6,000	Overhead rate	$ 4.50
1/13	13-30	1,920	1/19	1198	1,500	Overhead applied	$6,075
1/14	14-30	1,920	Total		$7,500		
1/15	15-30	1,920				Summary	
1/16	16-30	1,920				Direct labor	$10,800
1/19	19-17	1,200				Direct material	7,500
Total		$10,800				Manufacturing Overhead	6,075
						Total cost	24,375
						Unit cost	$243.75

Figure 23–1
Job Order Cost Sheet

ledger file and transferred to the finished goods subsidiary ledger file, which is controlled by the *Finished Goods Inventory* account in the general ledger. When a job is sold, the total cost of the job is charged to the *Cost of Goods Sold* account and credited to *Finished Goods Inventory*. The job order cost sheet is transferred to the cost of goods sold subsidiary ledger file (maintained on an annual basis) as a final step in the job order costing flow, illustrated in Figure 23–2. All aspects of the manufacturing cost flow illustrated in Figure 23–2 are perpetually accounted for as a job progresses from the raw materials stage to the point of sale.

We now turn our attention to the specific procedures required to perform job order costing with perpetual inventories. The Village Manufacturing Company's January, 1987 performance will be used to illustrate the job order costing procedures.

ACCOUNTING FOR MATERIALS

The purchasing cycle discussed in the Appendix to Chapter 7 can be used to control the raw materials acquired. All raw materials are kept in a storeroom under the supervision of a stores manager and are issued to work in process upon receipt of a properly prepared and authorized **material requisition form,** such as the one shown in Figure 23–3. The material requisition form is prepared and signed by the manager responsible for the work being performed.

**Objective 4:
The accounting procedures used in job order costing**

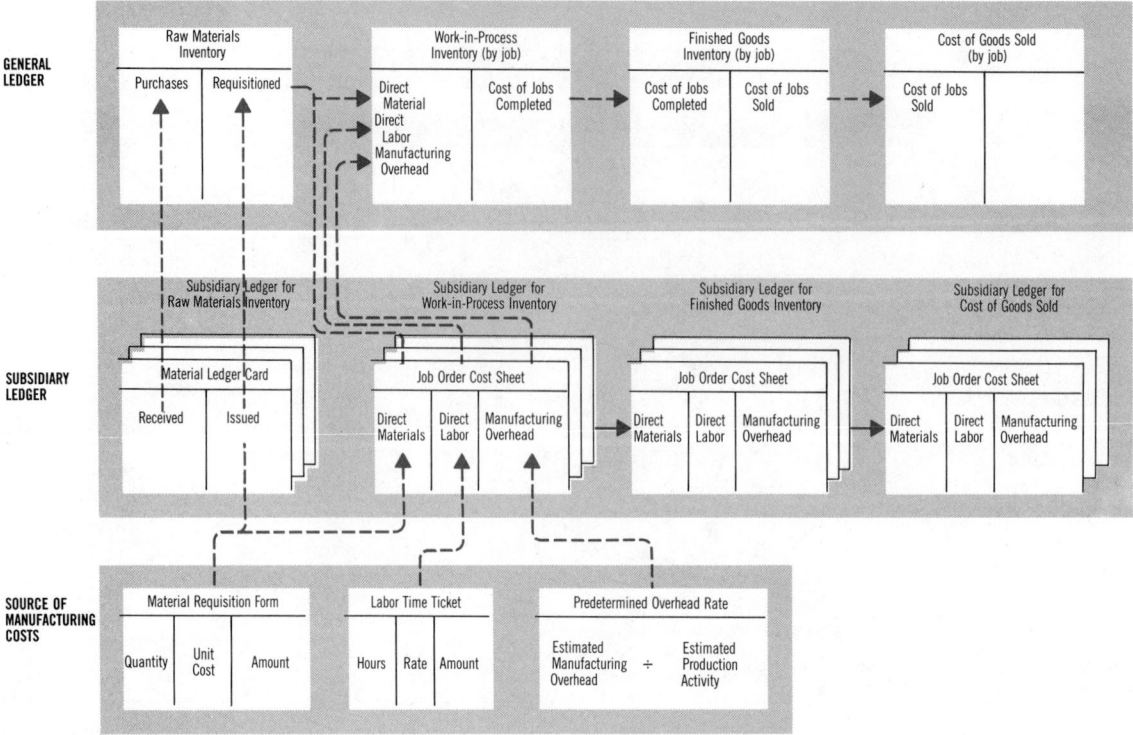

Figure 23–2
Job Order Costing Flow

It identifies the specific material required and shows the job or manufacturing overhead account to which it is to be charged as direct or indirect material. The material requisition forms are sent to the accounting department at the end of each day for further processing. Figure 23–3 indicates that 250 units of raw material were charged to Job 691 at a total cost of $6,000 on January 12.

Figure 23–3
Material Requisition
Form

MATERIAL REQUISITION FORM		Number	1126
Job Number	691	Date	1/12
Overhead Account	—		
Authorized By	JGH		

Description	Quantity	Unit Cost	Amount
AZ 100	250	$24	$6,000

MATERIAL LEDGER CARD
Item   AZ 100

Date	Reference	Received			Issued			Balance		
		Quantity	Unit Cost	Total Cost	Quantity	Unit Cost	Total Cost	Quantity	Unit Cost	Total Cost
1/6	18/20	300	24	$7,200				300	24	$7,200
1/12	1126				250	24	$6,000	50	24	$1,200

Figure 23–4
Material Ledger Card

Material ledger cards, such as the one presented in Figure 23–4, are maintained for each type of material used and serve as the subsidiary ledger for the *Raw Materials Inventory* account. The ledger cards provide perpetual inventory control with columns for receipts, issues, and a current balance. The raw materials requisitioned during an accounting period are recorded as direct materials on the job order cost sheets or as indirect materials charged to manufacturing overhead by someone in the accounting department. The $6,000 of materials requisitioned to Job 691 have been deducted in Figure 23–4 in order to maintain a current balance of goods on hand. The costs must also be charged to the control accounts established for *Work in Process Inventory* and *Manufacturing Overhead*. We assume that the Village Manufacturing Company makes all entries to the general ledger accounts at the end of the month, although they may be recorded throughout the month in other situations. The entries in the ledger cards should be made perpetually during the period. The company purchased raw materials in January with a total cost of $42,500, including $7,200 for the material in Figure 23–4, so the following entry would be required (the journal entries used for the job order costing are numbered to summarize the procedures later).

		(1)		
Jan.	31	Raw Materials Inventory	42,500	
		Accounts Payable		42,500
		To record raw materials purchased during January.		

Five jobs, including Job 691, were worked on during the month and each would have a separate job order cost sheet, although we will consider only the one for Job 691. As we saw in Figure 23–1, raw materials with a total cost of $7,500 were requisitioned for Job 691 during January. The total raw materials requisitioned for the five jobs amounted to $36,550, and those charged to *Manufacturing Overhead* were $1,680. Thus, the following journal entry would be made.

		(2)		
Jan.	31	Work in Process Inventory	36,550	
		Manufacturing Overhead	1,680	
		Raw Materials Inventory		38,230
		To record raw materials requisitioned during January.		

ACCOUNTING FOR LABOR

A time reporting system consisting of *labor time tickets, time cards,* and a *payroll register* is used to accumulate labor costs with job order costing. A labor time ticket, such as the one illustrated in Figure 23–5, is used to record the time spent by each employee on a specific job or an overhead assignment. A time card is utilized to control the total daily labor hours; each employee is required to clock in when work begins and clock out at the end of the day. A payroll register, similar to the one discussed in Chapter 12, is also maintained as a detailed description of the manufacturing payroll, usually classified on a departmental basis.

The labor time tickets are prepared daily under the supervision of the manager responsible for the work activity. Each labor hour recorded on the time tickets is multiplied times the appropriate wage rate, and the total cost is charged either to jobs as direct labor, or to manufacturing overhead as indirect labor. In large organizations, a timekeeper may perform the clerical work associated with the tickets, which are usually in a form appropriate for computerized processing. During each day, a time ticket is prepared each time an employee changes from one job or overhead assignment to another. For example, the employee accounted for in Figure 23–5 spent eight hours on Job 691. At the end of the day, all of the time tickets are sent to the accounting department for classification as direct or indirect labor. Since labor cannot be inventoried like raw materials, the entire manufacturing payroll must be distributed each period as direct or indirect labor. Based on the payroll accounting, we assume that the Village Manufacturing Company incurred a manufacturing payroll of $48,200 during January. In addition, the labor time tickets

Figure 23–5
Labor Time Ticket

LABOR TIME TICKET					
Employee Name	J. Ford		Number		12-18
Employee Number	18		Date		1/12
Work Performed	Assembly		Job		691
Approved By	JGH		Overhead Account		—
Time Started	Time Stopped		Hours	Rate	Amount
7:00	11:00		4	$8	$32
12:00	4:00		4	8	32
Total Cost					$64

indicate that the firm's direct labor was $42,000 (including $10,800 for Job 691, or 1,350 hours times $8 per hour according to Figure 23–1), and the indirect labor amounted to $6,200. The following entry would be recorded. (Payroll withholdings are ignored.)

			(3)		
Jan.	31	Work in Process Inventory		42,000	
		Manufacturing Overhead		6,200	
		Wages Payable			48,200
		To record the direct and indirect labor for			
		January.			

ACCOUNTING FOR MANUFACTURING OVERHEAD

The accumulation of the direct manufacturing costs for the Village Manufacturing Company was basically straightforward, since they could be traced to production with a materials requisition or labor time reporting system. Accounting for manufacturing overhead is more complicated because of its indirect nature and the need to accumulate costs currently in a perpetual inventory system. Accounting for the total manufacturing overhead of a given period is relatively simple. The difficult accounting problem is to relate the manufacturing overhead cost to production output on some reliable basis. We learned in Chapter 22 that manufacturing overhead is an indirect cost incurred for the benefit of all products and, therefore, it cannot be traced to specific jobs, as the direct costs can be. Instead, it must be charged to the jobs on some production activity basis that closely relates the *cost* to the work performed. The choice of a production activity basis depends on which one will provide the best causal relationship between it and manufacturing overhead; that is, the amount of production activity required for a job will determine the amount of manufacturing overhead needed. Examples of some production activity bases used are direct labor hours, direct labor cost, machine hours, and units produced. The best choice of a production activity basis will depend on the nature of the manufacturing operation. If the production process is labor intensive, direct labor hours or direct labor costs will typically be used. In contrast, machine hours would be more appropriate for a highly automated operation.

    With a perpetual inventory system, a firm *cannot* wait until the end of an accounting period to charge the manufacturing overhead actually incurred to the jobs, since management needs the product cost information for decision-making purposes during the period. Also, fluctuations in either the amount of manufacturing overhead or the level of production activity between short time periods, such as months, may produce inconsistent results if actual costs and actual production activity are used. For example, assume that a toy manufacturing firm has a monthly depreciation charge for its machinery of $50,000, which must be included in the product cost. Assume further that production activity is seasonal and that 25,000 units are produced in January while 100,000 units are manufactured in September. If actual manufacturing overhead and

Objective 5:
The difference between actual and applied manufacturing overhead

actual production activity are used, the unit cost for depreciation would be $2 for January and $.50 for September. In months of high production, the unit cost would be low, while in months of low production the unit cost would be high, despite the fact that the products and the manufacturing process are identical from month to month. In order to avoid these accounting problems, a predetermined overhead rate is used to apply the cost to the jobs as they are worked on. A **predetermined overhead rate** can be computed for an upcoming year based on the following fraction.

$$\frac{\text{Estimated annual manufacturing overhead cost}}{\text{Estimated annual level of production activity}} = \frac{\text{Predetermined}}{\text{overhead rate}}$$

For example, assume that the Village Manufacturing Company forecasted manufacturing overhead of $270,000 for 1987 and expected to work 60,000 direct labor hours. Its predetermined overhead rate would be:

$$\frac{\$270,000}{60,000} = \$4.50 \text{ per direct labor hour}$$

Once the predetermined overhead rate is known, we simply multiply it by the direct labor hours recorded for a job, in order to apply the manufacturing overhead. Since 1,350 direct labor hours were incurred for Job 691 (see Figure 23–1), the manufacturing overhead applied would be $6,075; or 1,350 hours times $4.50 (also shown in Figure 23–1). The amounts charged to the various job order cost sheets would be totaled and recorded in the *Work in Process Inventory* account with an entry as follows (we assume that the payroll records show that a total of 5,280 direct labor hours were worked in January).

			(4)		
Jan.	31		Work in Process Inventory	23,760	
			Manufacturing Overhead		23,760
			To record manufacturing overhead applied during January (5,280 hours at $4.50 per hour).		

The applied manufacturing overhead is credited to the *Manufacturing Overhead* account, which is a control account supported by a subsidiary ledger that contains a detailed listing of the individual overhead items incurred. The actual manufacturing overhead incurred is debited to the same control account and to subsidiary ledger accounts established for the individual manufacturing overhead items, such as depreciation, rent, insurance, real estate taxes, utilities, indirect material, and indirect labor. The Village Manufacturing Company has already recorded $1,680 for indirect material and $6,200 for indirect labor. Additional manufacturing overhead charges for January were:

Depreciation	$ 8,200
Rent	2,200
Insurance	850
Real estate taxes	600
Utilities	3,470
Total	$15,320

The total actual manufacturing overhead for January, 1987 was $23,200 ($1,680 + $6,200 + $15,320), and the following entry would be required to record the additional charges.

		(5)		
Jan.	31	Manufacturing Overhead	15,320	
		Accounts Payable		5,670
		Accumulated Depreciation		8,200
		Accrued Taxes Payable		600
		Prepaid Insurance		850
		To record the balance of actual		
		manufacturing overhead for January.		

Overapplied and Underapplied Manufacturing Overhead

Note that with the journal entries presented above for manufacturing overhead, we have debited the manufacturing overhead control account for the actual amount of overhead incurred and credited the same account for the amount applied to work in process with the predetermined overhead rate. As a result, we can show the manufacturing overhead control account in T account form, as follows.

Manufacturing Overhead

Jan. 31 Indirect materials	1,680	Jan. 31 Applied overhead	23,760
31 Indirect labor	6,200		
31 Other overhead	15,320		
		Jan. 31 Balance	560

The use of the single manufacturing overhead account makes it easy to compare the amount of overhead actually incurred with the amount applied to work in process. Remember that we used a predetermined overhead rate because we could not wait to determine the actual manufacturing overhead and production results and we wanted to spread cost or production differences from month to month over a longer period of time. Since the predetermined overhead rate is based on estimated manufacturing overhead and estimated production activity, instead of on actual amounts, we would expect differences in the debit and credit sides of the manufacturing overhead account as the actual cost and production results vary from those planned. As such, the actual manufacturing overhead and the applied manufacturing overhead *are seldom equal* at the end of any given month. If the applied amount exceeds the actual costs, the *Manufacturing Overhead* account will have a credit balance, so the overhead will be **overapplied.** This means that more overhead is charged to work in process than is actually incurred. When the amount applied is less than the actual costs, a debit balance will exist and manufacturing overhead will be **underapplied.** In the example of the Village Manufacturing Company, manufacturing overhead is overapplied by $560, since $23,760 was applied to the jobs but only $23,200 was actually incurred. Ideally, the estimates used for the predetermined overhead rate will be accurate, and any balance in the

Manufacturing Overhead account will be small, particularly at the end of the annual period.

At the end of the year, any over- or underapplied manufacturing overhead can be subtracted from or added to the annual cost of goods sold to reconcile the actual and applied amounts. Alternatively, the difference may be disposed of by prorating it among the ending work in process inventory, ending finished goods inventory, and annual cost of goods sold. In most cases, this proration is not practical, unless the difference is significantly large, because of the accounting time required and the adjustment is made only to the cost of goods sold. When the amount of over- or underapplied manufacturing overhead is significant (large compared with the amount of overhead involved), generally accepted accounting principles require that the proration approach for financial reporting be used. To illustrate the basic principles involved with proration, assume that a firm ended an accounting period with the following account balances.

Account	Ending Balance	Percent of Total
Work in Process Inventory	$ 30,000	6
Finished Goods Inventory	70,000	14
Cost of Goods Sold	400,000	80
Total	$500,000	100

Assume that manufacturing overhead is underapplied by $20,000; we would prorate this difference and increase the three accounts as follows.

Work in Process Inventory — $30,000 + (.06) $20,000 = $31,200
Finished Goods Inventory — $70,000 + (.14) $20,000 = $72,800
Cost of Goods Sold — $400,000 + (.80) $20,000 = $416,000

If the manufacturing overhead had been overapplied by $20,000, these same prorated amounts would have been subtracted from the three account balances.

On an interim basis, the balance in the *Manufacturing Overhead* account is usually *carried forward on the balance sheet* from month to month as a current asset (underapplied) or a current liability (overapplied) until the end of the year. An underapplied balance is an asset, because more overhead has been incurred than the amount charged to work in process. In contrast, an overapplied balance is shown as a liability because that amount has not actually been incurred. As such, the credit balance of $560 for the Village Manufacturing Company would be shown as a current liability on a balance sheet prepared as of January 31, 1987. If the same condition existed at the end of the year, the overapplied balance, which is not material in amount, could be closed to cost of goods sold, as follows.

Dec.	31	Manufacturing Overhead	560	
		Cost of Goods Sold		560
		To eliminate overapplied manufacturing overhead for the year.		

ACCOUNTING FOR THE COMPLETION OF A JOB

When a job is completed, its costs are totaled on the job order cost sheet and transferred from *Work in Process Inventory* to *Finished Goods Inventory*. In addition, the job order cost sheet is removed from the work in process subsidiary ledger, marked *completed,* and refiled in the finished goods subsidiary ledger. In order to record the completion of Job 691, the Village Manufacturing Company would make the following entry.

		(6)		
Jan.	31	Finished Goods Inventory	24,375	
		Work in Process Inventory		24,375
		To record the completion of Job 691 and		
		transfer it to finished goods inventory.		

ACCOUNTING FOR THE SALE OF A JOB

Since perpetual inventories are maintained with job order costing, the total costs accumulated for each job are known at the point of completion. As we see in Figure 23–1, Job 691 consisted of 100 tables produced at a unit cost of $243.75. This information is important to management for decision-making functions, such as **product pricing, production performance evaluation, profitability analysis, forecasts of future operations,** and **cost control.** Job ordering costing also permits the recording of the cost of goods sold at the time of sale. For example, if Job 691 is sold on credit for $39,000, the transaction would be recorded as follows.

		(7)		
Jan.	31	Accounts Receivable	39,000	
		Sales		39,000
		Cost of Goods Sold	24,375	
		Finished Goods Inventory		24,375
		To record the sale of Job 691.		

The job order cost sheet for Job 691 would be removed from the finished goods subsidiary ledger, marked *sold,* and transferred to the cost of goods sold subsidiary ledger as the final step in the job order costing flow. Note that the difference between the selling price of Job 691 ($39,000) and the cost of goods sold ($24,375) is the job's gross profit ($14,625).

SUMMARY OF JOB ORDER COSTING FLOW

Let's summarize what we have learned about the job order costing flow of the Village Manufacturing Company by tracing the various transactions involved through the appropriate T accounts to see their interrelationships. The numbers (1) through (7) refer to the journal entries recorded earlier in the chapter starting with the purchase of raw materials and ending with a job at the point of sale.

Accounts Receivable		Raw Materials Inventory		Work in Process Inventory	
(7) 39,000		(1) 42,500	(2) 38,230	(2) 36,550	(6) 24,375
				(3) 42,000	
				(4) 23,760	

Finished Goods Inventory		Prepaid Insurance		Accumulated Depreciation	
(6) 24,375	(7) 24,375	1/1 Bal. 10,200	(5) 850		(5) 8,200

Accounts Payable		Wages Payable		Accrued Taxes Payable	
	(1) 42,500		(3) 48,200		(5) 600
	(5) 5,670				

Manufacturing Overhead		Sales		Cost of Goods Sold	
(2) 1,680	(4) 23,760		(7) 39,000	(7) 24,375	
(3) 6,200					
(5) 15,320					

PROCESS COSTING

Objective 6: Why product costs with process costing are average costs

Process costing is used by manufacturing firms with the ***continuous production flows*** usually found in mass-production industries. The homogeneity of the production output prevents the separation of units, or groups of units, required in job order costing. Firms producing chemicals, rubber, plastics, petroleum, and pharmaceuticals rely on process costing. The technique can also be applied to accumulate costs for a number of nonmanufacturing activities, such as the services performed by a utility company, mail sorting in a post office, similar condominium units built by a contractor, and check clearing in a bank. The focal point of process costing is the **processing center**, in which the work is performed during a specified period of time. A processing center can be a department, a work station, an assembly line, or a division. Output is usually measured in such units as gallons, pounds, liters, tons, barrels, or square feet. Unit costs are computed for raw material costs and conversion costs in each processing center. **Conversion costs** are defined as the combined total of the direct labor and manufacturing overhead costs incurred by a processing center. In its most basic form, process costing produces an average unit cost computed as:

$$\frac{\text{Total processing center costs for a period}}{\text{Total processing center output for a period}} = \text{Average unit cost}$$

This deceptively simple computation becomes more complicated in most cases for the following reasons.

1. When a processing center has work in process at the beginning or at the end of a period, its output cannot be measured solely in terms of the units actually completed. Costs will have been incurred for any partially completed units that are part of the center's output, despite the fact they are not in a finished form.

2. The various manufacturing cost elements will not usually be uniformly incurred during the production process. For example, the conversion costs that consist of direct labor and manufacturing overhead are typically consumed continuously during the production process, whereas raw materials are normally added at specific points in time. Consequently, a work in process inventory may be at different stages of completion for different cost elements.

CONCEPT OF EQUIVALENT UNITS

Since any unfinished work must be costed along with the finished units, production output in a process costing system cannot usually be expressed entirely in terms of physical or whole units. Unfinished work in process inventory on hand at the end of a period will require additional work and costs in the next period. Any beginning work in process inventory will include work and costs incurred in a previous period. The partial units cannot be equated with whole units, since their form is obviously not the same. **Equivalent units** are used to overcome this problem and represent the number of units that would have been produced if all the work and costs had been applied to complete units. In other words, any partially processed inventories must be *restated* to the equivalent number of finished units they would represent before they are combined with the completed units. For example, 500 units that are 50% completed are the equivalent of 250 units that are 100% finished. Since no additional work is required for the completed units, they automatically become equivalent units. Consequently, the equivalent units for a particular period will be a measure of how many whole units of production are represented by the units finished, plus the units partially finished.

The stage of completion for each manufacturing cost element must be evaluated separately in the calculation of equivalent units, except in the rare case where all of the manufacturing costs are incurred in the same manner. To illustrate the most basic form of equivalent units, assume that there is no beginning inventory and that 108,000 units are entered into production. During the period, 90,000 units are finished and 18,000 are left in the ending work in process inventory, 20% finished as far as conversion costs are concerned. The equivalent units for the conversion costs would be 93,600, as shown below (90,000 units completed plus 20% of the 18,000 unfinished). If the conversion costs for the period are $280,800, the unit conversion cost would be $3. Assume further that raw materials are added at the beginning of the production process at a cost of $216,000. Since the stage of completion for raw materials is 100% (the materials are added at the beginning and all the units, finished and partially finished, are beyond that point), their equivalent units are 108,000 and the unit cost for raw materials is $2.

Objective 7:
Why equivalent units are necessary

	Raw Material Costs	Conversion Costs
Production units started	108,000	108,000
Production units finished	90,000	90,000
Plus equivalent units in ending inventory		
18,000 physical units × 100%	18,000	
18,000 physical units × 20%		3,600
Total equivalent units (a)	108,000	93,600
Total cost (b)	$216,000	$280,800
Unit cost (b ÷ a)	$2	$3

Equivalent Units With a Beginning Inventory

Objective 8: Why the weighted-average method or FIFO method is used

A beginning work in process inventory complicates the equivalent unit computations, since some of the work will have been performed in an earlier period and part of it will occur in the current period. A flow assumption must be made for costing purposes in order to determine which costs are transferred out of a processing center and which are left in ending inventory. The flow assumption concept is essentially the same one discussed in Chapter 9 and usually consists of two possibilities in a process costing situation: (1) the weighted-average method or (2) the FIFO method. When the **weighted-average method** is used, the units and costs in the beginning work in process inventory are *combined* with those of the current period. In contrast, the **First-in, First-out (FIFO) method** requires that a *distinction* be made between the units and costs of different periods by assigning them to separate layers of inventory. The choice between the two methods depends on how important it is to keep track of cost differences between short periods, such as months. If production costs per unit of product fluctuate significantly from period to period, management may want to evaluate the differences for control purposes with the FIFO method. Otherwise, the weighted-average method will be used, because it is simpler and the product costing results will be essentially the same as those with the FIFO method.

Objective 9: Why equivalent units are different with the weighted-average method and the FIFO method

Equivalent units with the two methods will be different, since we are combining production costs and units in the beginning inventory and those of the current period with the weighted-average method, but keeping them separate when the FIFO method is used. To illustrate these equivalent unit differences, assume that a firm's beginning work in process inventory consists of 10,000 units that are 40% completed as to conversion costs. Raw materials are added at the beginning of the process, so the 10,000 units are completed as to the raw materials. 108,000 units are entered into production during the current month, and 18,000 units are 20% finished for conversion costs at the end of the month. As a result, 100,000 units were finished during the month (10,000 + 108,000 − 18,000). The FIFO assumption tells us that the beginning inventory of 10,000 units would be finished first; so only 90,000 of the units entered into production during the month were completed (100,000 − 10,000). The remaining 18,000 units started during the month would be left in work in process at the end of the period. Since we want to separate the accounting for the 10,000 units from that of the current month's production with the FIFO method, equivalent units are computed as follows.

| | Equivalent Units | |
	Raw Material Costs	Conversion Costs
Equivalent units needed to complete beginning inventory of 10,000 units during the month		
10,000 × 0%	-0-	
10,000 × 60%		6,000
Plus 90,000 units started and finished during the month	90,000	90,000
Plus equivalent units in ending inventory of 18,000 units		
18,000 × 100%	18,000	
18,000 × 20%		3,600
Equals total equivalent units for FIFO costing	108,000	99,600

These equivalent unit figures would be used to determine the cost of completing the beginning inventory (the additional 60% conversion costs needed) and accounting for the current production costs. In contrast, the computation of equivalent units with the weighted-average method is much simpler because we do not have to keep the beginning inventory and the current production separate. We simply pool both and average the results between the two periods. The calculation of equivalent units with the weighted-average method is as follows.

| | Equivalent Units | |
	Raw Material Costs	Conversion Costs
100,000 units completed	100,000	100,000
Plus equivalent units in ending inventory of 18,000 units		
18,000 × 100 %	18,000	
18,000 × 20%		3,600
Equals total equivalent units for weighted-average costing	118,000	103,600

Since we do not distinguish between the units or costs in the beginning inventory and those of the current period with the weighted-average method, we will have 103,600 equivalent units for the conversion costs (100,000 + 20% of 18,000). The percentage of completion for the beginning inventory can be ignored, since the units and costs of the different periods are combined. The equivalent units for raw materials are the same as the total units involved, or 118,000 because the raw materials are added at the beginning of the process and no additional raw materials are required. With the weighted-average method, we assume, in essence, that the units in the beginning inventory were started and completed during the current period.

COSTING FIFO INVENTORY

Objective 10: Compute unit costs with the two flow assumptions

To illustrate how the equivalent units computed for the FIFO and weighted-average methods can be used to determine inventory costs, assume that the following cost data pertain to the beginning inventory of 10,000 units and the current month's production performance (108,000 units started and 18,000 units left in ending inventory).

Costs from previous month in the beginning inventory	
Raw material costs	$20,000
Conversion costs	12,000
Total	$32,000

Costs incurred during the current month	
Raw material costs	$216,000
Conversion costs	298,800
Total	$514,800

Total costs incurred − $32,000 + $514,800 = $546,800

Remember that the only additional costs required to complete the beginning inventory are the conversion costs because no additional raw materials are needed. Consequently, all of the $216,000 of raw materials will be assigned to units started during the current month. However, part of the conversion costs incurred during the current month ($298,800) must be charged to the beginning inventory to account for the 60% additional work needed to finish the beginning inventory according to the FIFO flow assumption. To do so, we must first determine unit costs for the current month, as follows.

Current month's production

Cost item	(a) Amount	(b) Equivalent units	(a)/(b) Unit cost
Raw material costs	$216,000	108,000	$2
Conversion costs	298,800	99,600	3
Total cost per unit			$5

Note that we are using the current month's costs and equivalent units only in determining the unit costs, because of the FIFO requirement that we keep the beginning inventory separate from the current month's production results. The only effect of these unit costs on the beginning inventory is that we will use the conversion cost per unit to account for the completion of the beginning inventory during the current month. To complete the FIFO inventory costing, we can use the unit costs to account for the beginning and current month's inventories in the following manner.

Costs assigned to beginning inventory:		
Costs from previous month in beginning inventory		$ 32,000
Costs from current month (conversion costs only):		
10,000 units × 60% × $3		18,000
Total costs of beginning inventory finished		
during the current month		50,000
Costs assigned to 90,000 units started and		
finished during the current month:		
90,000 units × $5 (total cost per unit)		450,000
Costs assigned to 18,000 units started but not		
finished during the current month:		
Raw material costs		
18,000 units × $2	$36,000	
Conversion costs		
18,000 units × 20% × $3	10,800	
Total ending inventory costs		46,800
Total costs assigned to beginning and current		
month's inventories		$546,800

Note that we have total costs of $546,800 to be accounted for and that we have done so by assigning $50,000 to the beginning inventory that was completed during the current month, $450,000 to the units started and completed, and $46,800 to the units started but unfinished at the end of the current month (the beginning inventory for the next month). The total costs to be accounted for are the costs from the beginning inventory ($32,000) and those of the current month ($514,800). Since the raw materials are added at the start of the process, we do not have to assign any current month's raw material costs to the units in the beginning inventory. Additional conversion costs are needed to advance the beginning inventory from the 40% finished stage to a finished state, an increase of 60%. Thus, we assign the $3 unit conversion cost to 6,000 equivalent units (10,000 × 60%). As a result, we have valued the beginning inventory at a total cost of $50,000 (the $32,000 we started with, plus the additional conversion costs of $18,000). These 10,000 units are assumed to be finished first during the current month, according to the FIFO flow assumption.

The 90,000 units started and finished during the month are costed at a unit cost of $5 for a total cost of $450,000 because they are the result of the current month's production only. These units are assumed to be finished after the beginning inventory is completed. In assigning costs to the ending inventory, we must differentiate between the equivalent units for raw materials and conversion costs when we use the unit costs for raw materials and conversion costs of $2 and $3. The $2 unit cost for raw materials pertains to all 18,000 units left in ending inventory, which is complete as to the raw materials. Thus, the total raw material costs in the ending inventory are $36,000 (18,000 × $2). However, the 18,000 units in the ending inventory must be converted to

3,600 equivalent units (18,000 × 20%) for the conversion costs before the $3 unit cost for conversion costs can be used. This adjustment is consistent with the one we made earlier when we determined the equivalent units in ending inventory with the FIFO method. As a result, the total conversion costs in the ending inventory are $10,800 (3,600 × $3), giving us a total ending inventory cost of $46,800 (raw materials of $36,000 plus conversion costs of $10,800). When we finish costing the inventories with the FIFO method, we can see that we have accounted for the total costs of $546,800 that were included in the beginning inventory or recorded during the current period, as follows.

Beginning inventory finished during the month	$ 50,000
Units started and finished during the month	450,000
Units left in ending inventory	46,800
Total costs accounted for	$546,800

COSTING WEIGHTED-AVERAGE INVENTORY

We will use the same cost and production data introduced for the FIFO method to illustrate the weighted-average method. Since we do not have to differentiate between the costs and units in the beginning inventory and those of the current month with the weighted-average method, the costing calculations involved are much simpler. We just combine the beginning and current costs for each cost element and use the equivalent units computed earlier for the weighted-average method, as follows.

Cost Element	(a) Beginning Inventory	(b) Current Month	(a) + (b) = (c) Total Costs	(d) Equivalent Units	(c)/(d) Unit Cost
Raw material costs	$20,000	$216,000	$236,000	118,000	$2
Conversion costs	12,000	298,800	310,800	103,600	3
Total cost per unit					$5

Note that the total unit cost of $5 with the weighted-average method is the same as it was with the FIFO method. The reason is that, in this example, the unit costs for raw materials and conversion costs in the beginning inventory are the same as those in the current month. In other words, the unit costs of $2 for raw materials and $3 for conversion costs remained constant between the two months [e.g., the unit conversion cost for the beginning inventory is $12,000 divided by the 4,000 equivalent units we started with (since 10,000 units were 40% finished) or $3—the same unit cost for the current month]. This will not always be the case, and unit cost differences will occur with the two methods when costs change from month to month. These differences are the result of averaging the changing costs with the weighted-average method over beginning and current units, but separating them with the FIFO method.

Once we have the unit costs with the weighted-average method, we can assign costs to the units finished and to those in the ending inventory, as follows.

Costs assigned to the units finished during the month:		
100,000 units × $5		$500,000
Costs assigned to ending inventory:		
Raw material costs (18,000 units × $2)	$36,000	
Conversion costs (18,000 units × 20% × $3)	10,800	
Total ending inventory costs		46,800
Total costs assigned to finished and ending inventories		$546,800

With the weighted-average method, we do not care whether the units finished during the current month came from the beginning inventory or those started during the month. Thus, we cost the 100,000 finished units at the same average cost (in this case, $5). The ending inventory in this illustration is the same as it was with the FIFO method ($46,800) since the unit costs did not change between months. Note that the total costs to be accounted for ($546,800) have been assigned to the units finished ($500,000) and those left in ending inventory ($46,800).

Remember that we have assumed that the unit costs did not change between months and, therefore, the costing results are the same with the FIFO method and the weighted-average method in this illustration. Since the differences between the two methods over relatively short periods, such as months, are often minor, and since the weighted-average method is easier to use and understand than the FIFO method, we will limit further coverage of process costing to the weighted-average method, deferring a more complete consideration of the FIFO method to a cost accounting textbook.

PROCESS COSTING PROCEDURES

The flow of costs for a firm operating two departments, Blending and Finishing, with process costing is summarized in Figure 23–6. Raw materials, direct labor, and manufacturing overhead are accumulated within each processing center with procedures similar to those discussed earlier for job order costing. However, the absence of jobs simplifies the accounting significantly, since costs are accumulated by processing centers instead of by separate jobs. Therefore, detailed job order cost sheets are not required. In many cases, costs are accounted for over a longer period, such as a month, rather than over the life of each job, which is usually shorter. Many of the employees work in only one department, so the labor time reporting requirements are minimal. For example, a departmentalized payroll register may provide all the information required to distribute labor costs without the detailed job assignments recorded on labor time tickets. Also, the distinction between direct and indirect costs (raw materials and labor) required in job order costing is not necessary, since the costing objective changes to a processing center. All of the raw materials and labor costs are direct for the processing center. In some situations where

Objective 11:
The accounting
procedures used
with process
costing

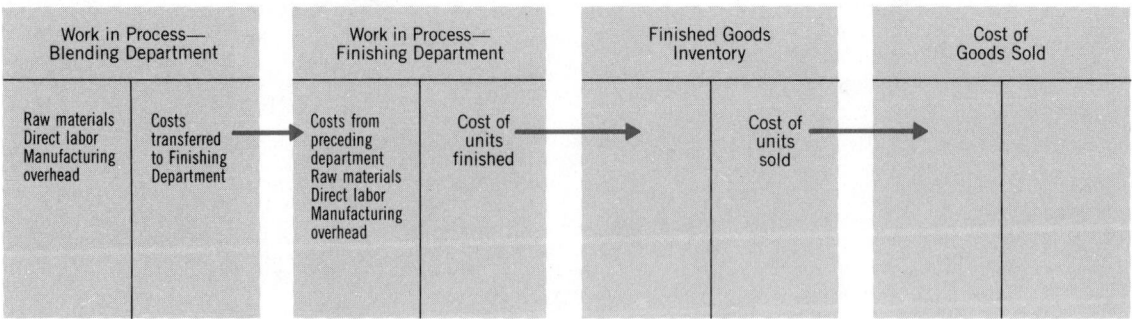

Figure 23–6
Process Costing Flow

the amount of manufacturing overhead and the production level are relatively constant from month to month, actual manufacturing overhead may be used for costing purposes instead of utilizing a predetermined overhead rate.

A *Work in Process Inventory* account is established for each processing center and is debited for the manufacturing costs incurred during a given period. Once the amount of each manufacturing cost is known, a total unit cost can be calculated. The total unit cost of the production output of each processing center is computed by dividing the costs accumulated for each cost element by its respective number of equivalent units and adding the resulting quotients together (as we have illustrated earlier). When multiple processing centers are involved, the *output of a given center becomes the input of a succeeding center,* costed with the total unit cost accumulated up to the point of transfer. The receiving center's *Work in Process Inventory* account is debited for the total cost transferred, and the transferring center's account is credited for the same amount. When the production process is completed, a *Finished Goods Inventory* account is debited and the final processing center's *Work in Process Inventory* account is credited. Cost of production reports (defined in the next section) are prepared for each processing center's periodic performance, in order to monitor the physical flow of production, the costs to be accounted for, and the costs accounted for.

CONTROL DOCUMENT—COST OF PRODUCTION REPORT

Objective 12: Preparing a cost of production report

A **cost of production report** serves as the control document in process costing, since it is used to account for the costs charged to a processing center during a specified period of time. The report is usually prepared on a monthly basis, although a shorter or longer period may be chosen if the benefits of doing so exceed the costs. A cost of production report, such as the one shown in Figure 23–7, has three sections.

1. A *physical flow schedule* section shows the physical flow of production through a processing center. Included are the number of production units for which a processing center is responsible, their stage of completion, where they are at the end of the period, and the number of equivalent

Figure 23–7
Cost of Production
Report

MARCO CHEMICAL COMPANY
Blending Department
Cost of Production Report
Month Ended January 31, 1987

	Total Units	Equivalent Units Raw Material Costs	Equivalent Units Conversion Costs
Physical Flow Schedule			
Beginning work in process	8,000		
Units started	106,000		
Units to be accounted for	114,000		
Units finished	108,000	108,000	108,000
Ending work in process	6,000	6,000	2,000*
Units accounted for	114,000	114,000	110,000

Cost Element	Beginning Costs	Current Costs	Total Costs	Equivalent Units	Unit Cost
Costs to be Accounted For					
Raw material costs	$12,000	$159,000	$171,000	114,000	$1.50
Conversion costs	16,000	424,000	440,000	110,000	4.00
Costs to be accounted for	$28,000	$583,000	$611,000		$5.50

Costs Accounted For

Units transferred to
Finishing Department (108,000 gallons × $5.50) $594,000
Ending work in process
Raw material costs (6,000 gallons × $1.50) $9,000
Conversion costs (6,000 gallons × 1/3 × $4) 8,000 17,000
Costs accounted for $611,000

*6,000 gallons × 1/3 completion

units involved with the physical flow. This section provides a check to make sure that the number of units worked on during a period (the units to be accounted for) are actually accounted for (e.g., the number of units finished and those in process at the end of the period).

2. A *costs to be accounted for* section identifies the amounts accumulated for each cost element (e.g., raw materials) within the processing center during the period, the equivalent units for each cost element, and the unit costs computed for the various cost elements. By adding together the unit costs for the various cost elements, we can determine the total cost of producing one unit in the processing center.

3. A *costs accounted for* section indicates what happened to the costs for which the processing center is responsible in terms of the amounts assigned to finished units and those left in process at the end of the period.

ILLUSTRATION OF PROCESS COSTING

The Marco Chemical Company produces a single product, *Stayclean,* used for swimming-pool maintenance. Two departments, Blending and Finishing, are operated as processing centers with the output of the Blending Department becoming the input of the Finishing Department. Raw materials, in the form of chemical powders, are issued at the start of production in the Blending Department and at the end of the processing in the Finishing Department. Conversion costs (direct labor and manufacturing overhead) are incurred uniformly throughout the processing in each of the departments. The following data summarize the January, 1987 operating performance of the two departments.

Beginning Work in Process Data		
	Blending Department	**Finishing Department**
Units in beginning inventory	8,000 gallons	13,000 gallons
Raw material costs	$12,000	-0-
Conversion costs	$16,000	$18,850
Cost from preceding department (Blending)		$71,500

January Processing Data		
	Blending Department	**Finishing Department**
Units started	106,000 gallons	108,000 gallons
Units finished	108,000 gallons	100,000 gallons
Units in ending inventory	6,000 gallons	21,000 gallons
Raw material costs	$159,000	$160,000
Conversion costs	$424,000	$291,450
Costs from preceding department (Blending)		$594,000

The beginning and ending work in process inventories of the Blending Department are respectively one-half and one-third complete, in terms of the conversion costs of that department. The same stages of completion prevail for the beginning and ending work in process inventories of the Finishing Department. The January cost of production reports for the two departments are shown in Figures 23–7 and 23–8, respectively. Essentially the same procedures and concepts are required to prepare either report. Therefore, we will concentrate on the basic features of the cost of production report for the Finishing Department.

The physical flow schedule shows the units (gallons) for which the Finishing Department is accountable, as well as their disposition. A total of 121,000 units are involved, with 100,000 completed and 21,000 remaining in the ending inventory—one-third complete. Also shown are the equivalent units for each cost element. The costs to be accounted for section identifies the *costs incurred for the various cost elements, their equivalent units, and the average*

Figure 23–8
Cost of Production
Report

MARCO CHEMICAL COMPANY
Finishing Department
Cost of Production Report
Month Ended January 31, 1987

		Equivalent Units		
	Total Units	Preceding Department Costs	Raw Material Costs	Conversion Costs
Physical Flow Schedule				
Beginning work in process	13,000			
Units started	108,000			
Units to be accounted for	121,000			
Units finished	100,000	100,000	100,000	100,000
Ending work in process	21,000	21,000	-0-	7,000*
Units accounted for	121,000	121,000	100,000	107,000

Costs to be Accounted For

Cost Element	Beginning Costs	Current Costs	Total Costs	Equiv- alent Units	Unit Cost
Preceding department costs	$71,500	$ 594,000	$ 665,500	121,000	$ 5.50
Raw material costs	0	160,000	160,000	100,000	1.60
Conversion costs	18,850	291,450	310,300	107,000	2.90
Costs to be accounted for	$90,350	$1,045,450	$1,135,800		$10.00

Costs Accounted For

Units transferred to finished goods	(100,000 gallons × $10)	$1,000,000
Ending work in process		
Preceding department costs	(21,000 gallons × $5.50)	$115,500
Raw material costs	(21,000 gallons × 0 × $1.60)	0
Conversion costs	(21,000 gallons × 1/3 × $2.90)	20,300 135,800
Costs accounted for		$1,135,800

*21,000 gallons × 1/3 completion

unit cost calculations. The weighted-average method is used for inventory costing. All units are finished as far as the preceding department's (Blending) costs are concerned, so their equivalent units amount to 121,000. These preceding department costs can be thought of as being like raw materials purchased from an outside supplier and added at the beginning of the Finishing Department's process. We have a total of 121,000 equivalent units for the preceding department's costs because we started the month with 13,000 units and had 108,000 units transferred from the Blending Department to the Finishing Department during the month. Since the raw materials used by the Finishing Department are added at the end of the process, none are in the ending inventory (it is not at that point yet) and the equivalent units are equal to those physically finished, or 100,000. The equivalent units for the conversion costs are the total of the finished units plus one-third of the 21,000 units in process at the end of January, or 107,000. Again, the percentage of completion for the beginning inventory is irrelevant, because the weighted-average method is used. Unit costs are computed by dividing the total costs accumulated for each cost element by the respective number of equivalent units. The unit cost computations involved in the Finishing Department's cost of production report can be detailed as follows.

	Equivalent Units		
	Preceding Department Costs	Raw Material Costs	Conversion Costs
Units completed	100,000	100,000	100,000
Plus equivalent units in ending inventory			
21,000 × 100%	21,000		
21,000 × 0%		-0-	
21,000 × 33⅓%			7,000
Equals equivalent units (a)	121,000	100,000	107,000
Production costs			
Beginning inventory	$ 71,500	0	$ 18,850
January costs	594,000	$160,000	291,450
Total costs to be accounted for (b)	$665,500	$160,000	$310,300
Unit costs (b)/(a)	$5.50	$1.60	$2.90
Total unit costs ($5.50 + $1.60 + $2.90)			$10.00

The total unit cost after both departments are finished with production is $10. Note that the unit cost of $5.50 incurred in the Blending Department is applied to each of the units transferred to the Finishing Department, as shown on both cost of production reports.

The final section of the report shows the accountability for the department cost performance. The Finishing Department has costs of $1,135,800 for which it is accountable. The units transferred to finished goods are costed at $1,000,000, and $135,800 is left in the ending inventory that will be completed in February. Note that separate computations must be made for the various cost elements in the ending inventory because of the different equivalent units and unit costs. The ending work in process inventory of $135,800 will be shown as a current asset on the balance sheet as of January 31, 1987, along with that amounting to $17,000 in the Blending Department.

We assume that 80,000 gallons of *Stayclean* are sold by the Marco Chemical Company on credit at a price of $18 per gallon. The remaining 20,000 gallons produced during January will be left in finished goods inventory at a cost of $200,000. Essentially the same journal entries shown earlier for job order costing are made to record the work in process costs of each department. The journal entries required to transfer units from the Blending Department to the Finishing Department, record the finished goods, and record the sales for January are:

Jan.	31	Work in Process Inventory—Finishing	594,000	
		Work-in-Process Inventory—		
		Blending		594,000
		To record the transfer of inventory		
		from the Blending Department to		
		the Finishing Department.		
	31	Finished Goods Inventory	1,000,000	
		Work in Process Inventory—		
		Finishing		1,000,000
		To record the finished goods		
		inventory.		
	31	Accounts Receivable	1,440,000*	
		Sales		1,440,000
		Cost of Goods Sold	800,000**	
		Finished Goods Inventory		800,000
		To record the sale of 80,000 gallons		
		of product.		
		* 80,000 gallons × $18		
		**80,000 gallons × $10		

GLOSSARY

CONVERSION COSTS. The combined total of direct labor and manufacturing overhead costs incurred by a processing center (p. 906).

COST ACCUMULATION. The use of a job order costing system or a process costing system to record product costs with a perpetual inventory flow (p. 894).

COST OF PRODUCTION REPORT. The control document used in process costing to account for the manufacturing costs of a processing center during a specified time period (p. 914).

EQUIVALENT UNITS. A measure of how many whole units of production are represented by the units finished plus the units partially finished in a process costing operation (p. 907).

FIFO METHOD. The flow assumption used with process costing in which beginning units and costs are kept separate from those of the current period (p. 908).

JOB. A product or group of products being produced when job order costing is used (p. 895).

JOB ORDER COSTING. A cost accumulation system with which costs are accumulated for a job (p. 895).

JOB ORDER COST SHEET. The control document used with job order costing to provide a detailed listing of the manufacturing costs related to the production of a job (p. 896).

LABOR TIME TICKET. A record of how much time an employee spends on a job or on an overhead assignment (p. 900).

MATERIAL REQUISITION FORM. A record of the amount of raw material requisitioned from the storeroom for a job or as indirect material (p. 897).

OVERAPPLIED MANUFACTURING OVERHEAD. The excess of the manufacturing overhead applied to work in process with a predetermined rate during a given period over the actual manufacturing overhead incurred (p. 903).

PREDETERMINED OVERHEAD RATE. The rate determined by dividing estimated manufacturing overhead for a period by some measure of the estimated production activity, and used to apply overhead to work in process (p. 902).

PROCESS COSTING. A cost accumulation system with which costs are accumulated for a processing center during a specified period of time (p. 906).

PROCESSING CENTER. A segment of the manufacturing operation in which costs are accumulated with process costing (p. 906).

UNDERAPPLIED MANUFACTURING OVERHEAD. The excess of the actual manufacturing overhead incurred during a particular period over the manufacturing overhead applied to work in process (p. 903).

WEIGHTED-AVERAGE METHOD. The flow assumption used with process costing in which the beginning units and costs are combined with those of the current period (p. 908).

DISCUSSION QUESTIONS

1. What is a cost accumulation system and what are its benefits?
2. How are perpetual inventories maintained with a cost accumulation system?
3. Distinguish between job order costing and process costing.
4. What is a job order cost sheet?
5. Identify the basic business forms required for job order costing.
6. What is a predetermined overhead rate and why is it used by most manufacturing firms?
7. Johnson Manufacturing Company applies overhead to jobs on the basis of 60% of direct labor cost. Job 691 has been charged with $8,400 of direct labor cost and $6,200 of direct materials. If 100 units were produced in Job 691, what is the cost per unit?
8. What is underapplied manufacturing overhead? What is overapplied manufacturing overhead? How would each be disposed of at the end of a period?
9. What is meant by the proration of over- or underapplied manufacturing overhead? What problems are associated with this proration?
10. When a job order costing system is used, does indirect labor become a part of work in process inventory? Explain.
11. What type of industry is likely to use job order costing? Give some examples.
12. What type of industry is likely to use process costing? Give some examples.
13. What is meant by the average unit cost in process costing?
14. What are equivalent units and why are they necessary with process costing?
15. Decker Company began the period with no work in process inventory, started producing 75,000 units, and had 10,000 units in ending work in process inventory

that were one-fourth finished in terms of conversion costs. How many equivalent units were involved for the conversion costs that are incurred uniformly throughout the process?

16. Why is a choice between the weighted-average method and the FIFO method often necessary with process costing?

17. The Cook Manufacturing Company uses a process costing system. At the beginning of June, the firm had 5,000 units in the beginning work in process inventory that were fully finished in terms of raw materials and 40% finished for conversion costs. During June, 52,000 units were entered into production and 15,000 units were left in work in process inventory at the end of the month that were fully completed in terms of raw materials and 20% completed for conversion costs. What are the equivalent units with the weighted-average method and with the FIFO method?

18. What is the role of a cost of production report? What are the three major sections of such a report?

19. Distinguish between the costs to be accounted for and the costs accounted for in a process costing application.

20. How is the cost of the ending work in process inventory computed in a cost of production report?

21. Are the accounting procedures required for process costing usually more or less detailed than those used for job order costing? Explain.

EXERCISES

Exercise 23-1 Determining Job Costs

The Stewart Company uses a job order costing system. On July 1, the firm had no beginning work in process inventory. During July, the following costs were recorded.

Direct materials	$32,000
Direct labor (3,780 hours)	34,020
Actual manufacturing overhead	26,100

Manufacturing overhead is applied using a predetermined overhead rate of $6.80 per direct labor hour. None of the jobs were finished in July.

Required:
Determine the July 31 work in process inventory.

Exercise 23-2 Use of Predetermined Overhead Rates

The estimated cost and operating data for two manufacturing companies are presented here.

	Company	
	A	B
Units produced	31,200	20,400
Manufacturing overhead costs	$146,640	$215,424
Direct labor hours	50,400	67,320
Direct labor cost	$228,000	$252,400

Company A applies overhead on the basis of units of production, while Company B uses direct labor hours. During the past year, Company A actually produced 28,800 units and incurred manufacturing overhead costs of $138,240. Company B's actual manufacturing overhead costs were $232,560, and 68,400 direct labor hours were used.

Required:
A. Calculate the predetermined overhead rate of each company.
B. Determine whether the overhead was overapplied or underapplied for each company.

Exercise 23-3 Job Order Costing Procedures

Job order cost data for jobs 1 through 10 are shown here. The costs were incurred by the Heffner Company during April and May, the firm's first two months of operations.

Job Order No.	Costs as of May 1	May Production Costs
1	$5,040	
2	4,440	
3	3,120	
4	2,280	$ 960
5	2,640	2,520
6		4,440
7		5,532
8		1,848
9		1,548
10		948

Jobs 1 through 3 were completed in April. Jobs 4 through 7 were completed in May. Jobs 8 through 10 were incomplete as of May 31. Jobs 1, 3, 5, 7 were sold during May.

Required:
Calculate the following.

A. Work in process inventory, May 1.
B. Work in process inventory, May 31.
C. Finished goods inventory, May 1.
D. Finished goods inventory, May 31.
E. Cost of goods sold for May.

Exercise 23-4 Job Order Costing Procedures

The Landmark Furniture Company uses a job order costing system. The October cost and operating data were as follows.

Raw materials purchased	$171,600
Direct labor costs	177,600
Raw materials issued to production	159,600
Actual manufacturing overhead costs (including depreciation of $13,200)	133,200
Cost of goods manufactured	457,200
Machine hours	32,400
Sales (all credit)	$504,000

The company applies manufacturing overhead to production at a rate of $4.80 per machine hour. The beginning raw materials inventory was $19,200. The beginning work in process inventory was $32,400. The beginning and ending finished goods inventories were $48,000 and $62,400, respectively.

Required:
A. Prepare journal entries to record the October transactions.
B. Was overhead overapplied or underapplied for the month of October?
C. Calculate the ending balances of raw materials and work in process. (*Hint:* Prepare T accounts for the inventories.)

Exercise 23-5 Determining Equivalent Units
The Denice Company operates a process costing system in the production of perfume. Conversion costs are incurred uniformly throughout the production process. Three different raw material costs are incurred during the production process, as follows.

1. Raw material A—added at the beginning of the process
2. Raw material B—added when the production process is 1/2 finished
3. Raw material C—added at the end of the production process

The firm had no beginning work in process inventory as of November 1, completed 60,000 units during November, and had 10,000 units in work in process inventory on November 30.

Required:
A. Assume that the ending work in process inventory is 40% completed as to conversion costs. How many equivalent units are there for each of the four cost elements?
B. Assume that the ending work in process inventory is 75% completed as to conversion costs. How many equivalent units are there for each of the four cost elements?

Exercise 23-6 Equivalent Units—Weighted-average and FIFO Methods
The Cleanit Company produces shampoo. At the beginning of February, 28,200 liters of shampoo were in process, 100% complete as to raw materials and 40% complete as to conversion costs. During the month, 152,000 liters of raw materials were placed into production. At the end of the month, 8,500 liters of shampoo were in work in process inventory, 100% completed as to raw materials and 70% completed in terms of conversion costs.

Required:
A. Prepare a schedule of equivalent units for February, using the weighted-average method.
B. Prepare a schedule of equivalent units for February, using the FIFO method.
C. Why are the equivalent units different for the conversion costs in parts A and B?

Exercise 23-7 Computing Unit Costs with Beginning Inventory
Refer to Exercise 23-6. Assume that the following costs were recorded by the Cleanit Company for the beginning work in process and the production performance for February.

Beginning inventory:	
Raw material costs	$11,280
Conversion costs	6,768

February production costs:

Raw material costs	$60,800
Conversion costs	99,822

Required:

A. Compute the unit cost for each liter of shampoo if the weighted-average method is used.

B. Determine the total costs of the liters of shampoo finished during February, using the weighted-average method. What is the balance of the ending work in process inventory?

C. Compute the unit cost for each liter of shampoo if the FIFO method is used.

D. Determine the total costs of the liters of shampoo finished during February, using the FIFO method. What is the balance of ending work in process inventory?

Exercise 23-8   Process Costing without Beginning Inventory

The Allman Company produces a single product, using two production departments. The November cost and operating data for the first department is:

Beginning work in process inventory	-0-
Units started in Department 1	40,800
Units transferred to Department 2	33,600
Raw material costs	$368,640
Conversion costs	198,240

The work in process inventory in Department 1 at November 30 is 25% complete as to conversion costs and two-thirds complete as to materials.

Required:

Prepare a cost of production report for the November performance of Department 1.

Exercise 23-9   Process Costing without a Beginning Inventory

The Independent Pipe Company manufactures plastic pipe in a continuous flow production system. Below are production data for the month of July in the Molding Department.

Beginning work in process	-0-
Units started	67,200
Cost of raw materials added at the beginning	$252,000
Direct labor costs	196,560
Manufacturing overhead costs	287,280
Ending work in process units (all raw materials included and 1/2 finished for conversion costs)	13,440

Finished units are transferred to the Coating Department.

Required:

Prepare a cost of production report for the July operating performance of the Molding Department.

Exercise 23-10   Process Costing Flows

The Poulos Company produces a single product, which passes through two processing centers, Baking and Shaping. The following T accounts show the flow of costs through the two processing centers during March.

Work in Process—Baking

Bal. 3/1	19,200	Transferred to	
Raw materials	69,120	Shaping Dept.	288,000
Direct labor	76,800		
Manuf. overhead	153,600		

Work in Process—Shaping

Bal. 3/1	11,520	Transferred to	
Transferred in	288,000	finished goods	470,400
Direct labor	61,440		
Manuf. overhead	122,880		

Required:
Prepare journal entries to record the flow of costs through the two processing centers during March.

Exercise 23-11 Process Costing with Beginning Inventory

The Bowers Company produces plastic novelty gifts in a single Molding Process Department. Materials are added at the beginning of the molding process, and conversion costs are incurred continuously throughout the process. As of June 1, there were 7,200 units in beginning inventory, at a cost of $57,600. This cost was comprised of $36,000 for materials and $21,600 for conversion costs. The beginning inventory was 40% complete as to conversion costs.

During June, raw material costs amounted to $72,000 and conversion costs were $100,800. During the month, 14,400 units were started in the molding process and 16,800 units were transferred to finished goods. The ending inventory in the molding process was 75% complete as to conversion costs.

Required:
Prepare a cost of production report for the month of June. The Bowers Company uses the weighted-average method in its process costing system.

PROBLEMS

Problem 23-1 Job Order Costing and Manufacturing Overhead

The Sanborn Company uses a job order cost system to control production costs in its two departments. The accounting records for Job 333 show the following data.

	Department 1	Department 2
Direct labor hours	800	1,140
Direct labor cost	$9,600	$9,690
Raw materials	3,600	5,160
Machine hours	60	84

The company applies manufacturing overhead to production on the basis of direct labor cost in Department 1 and on the basis of machine hours in Department 2. At the beginning of the year, the firm estimated the following production performance.

	Department 1	Department 2
Direct labor hours	52,000	116,400
Direct labor cost	$624,000	$989,400
Machine hours	7,800	8,140
Manufacturing overhead	$748,800	$244,200

Required:

A. Calculate the overhead rate for each department.

B. Calculate the total cost of Job 333.

C. If actual machine hours used in Department 2 were 8,320 and actual overhead was $253,760, was overhead overapplied or underapplied?

Problem 23-2 Job Order Costing Procedures

The Vanwinkle Products Company uses a job order cost system. Cost and operating data for 1987 are as follows.

1. Total payroll incurred—$97,200, of which $25,200 was indirect labor and the remainder was direct labor.
2. Raw materials purchased—$102,000.
3. Raw materials issued to production—$106,800; $10,800 of these materials were indirect.
4. Manufacturing overhead is applied at 140% of direct labor cost.
5. Manufacturing costs paid:

Utilities	$14,400
Rent	28,800
Supplies	13,200
Insurance	8,400
Miscellaneous	12,000

6. Manufacturing equipment depreciation—$9,600.
7. Jobs completed and transferred to finished goods—$174,000.
8. Jobs with a cost of $168,000 were sold for $261,603 on credit.
9. The beginning inventories for 1987 were: raw materials—$10,800, work in process—$24,000, and finished goods—$6,000.

Required:

A. Prepare all necessary journal entries to record the transactions.

B. Calculate the ending balances in *Raw Materials Inventory, Work in Process Inventory,* and *Finished Goods Inventory.*

C. Was manufacturing overhead underapplied or overapplied in 1987?

Problem 23-3 Journal Entries for Job Order Costing

The Lyan Company uses a job order cost system. On January 1, 1987, job order numbers 33 and 34 were in process, with costs of $420 and $455, respectively. Part of the production data for January is as follows.

1. Manufacturing payroll of $5,200 was paid. Each worker earns $8 per hour. Ignore income taxes and other payroll deductions.
2. The payroll was distributed as follows.

Job 33	$1,300
Job 34	1,700
Job 35	1,295

Job 36	360
Indirect labor	545

3. Raw materials requisitioned were charged as follows.

Job 33	$ 995
Job 34	1,600
Job 35	2,221
Job 36	1,050
Indirect use	665

4. Additional manufacturing overhead costs incurred and paid during the month to-taled $5,100.
5. Manufacturing overhead is applied at $9 per direct labor hour.
6. Jobs 33, 34, and 35 were completed and transferred to finished goods.
7. Jobs 33 and 35 were sold at cost plus a 40% markup on cost.

Required:
A. Prepare the journal entries to record the January transactions. Use a *Work in Process Inventory* control account.
B. Prepare a job order cost sheet for each of the jobs worked on in January.
C. What is the balance in the *Work in Process Inventory* account on January 31? What is the balance in the *Finished Goods Inventory* account?

Problem 23-4 Weighted-average and FIFO Costing

The Bonita Company manufactures suntan lotion and utilizes a process cost accounting system. The lotion is produced in the Blending Department and is then transferred to the Bottling Department. The Blending Department's production performance for April can be summarized as follows.

Beginning work in process inventory:	
Gallons (100% finished as to raw materials, 40% finished as to conversion costs)	21,000
Raw material costs	$16,800
Conversion costs	13,440
Production during April:	
Gallons started	210,000
Gallons left in ending work in process inventory (100% finished as to raw materials, 20% finished as to conversion costs)	16,000
Raw material costs	$168,000
Conversion costs	335,680

Required:
A. Compute the equivalent units for the Blending Department, assuming that the weighted-average method is used.
B. Compute the unit cost of producing one gallon of lotion with the weighted-average method.
C. Compute the equivalent units for the Blending Department, assuming that the FIFO method is used.
D. Compute the unit cost of producing one gallon of lotion, using the FIFO method.

E. Compare the unit costs in parts B and D. Explain the comparison of the unit costs with the two methods.

F. Prepare a cost of production report for the Blending Department, using the weighted-average method.

Problem 23-5 Cost of Production Report with a Beginning Inventory

The Stayon Company produces paint in a single Mixing Department. Production costs are accumulated with a process costing system, and the weighted-average method is used to compute unit costs. The following information is available on the work performance of the Mixing Department during May.

	Gallons	Percent Completed Raw Materials	Percent Completed Conversion Costs
Beginning work in process	56,000	100	40
Started in production	540,000		
Ending work in process	36,000	100	25

Costs in the beginning work in process inventory and those accumulated during the May production performance were as follows.

	Raw Material Costs	Conversion Costs
Beginning work in process	$ 123,200	$ 98,560
May production	1,188,000	2,405,040

Required:

Prepare a cost of production report for the Mixing Department's performance during May.

Problem 23-6 Cost of Production Reports with Beginning Inventories and Two Departments

The Taste-Rite Company prepares a special blend of salad dressing using two departments, a Blending Department and a Finishing Department. The finished product is sold in large quantities to several companies which bottle it and sell it with their own labels. The weighted-average method is applied to calculate unit costs in the Taste-Rite Company's process costing system. Raw materials are added at the beginning of each department's process, and conversion costs are incurred uniformly throughout the two processes. The salad dressing flows from the Blending Department to the Finishing Department, and then to finished goods inventory when all the work is completed.

Production data in gallons for the month of June with completed percentages for the conversion costs were as follows.

	Beginning Inventory	Percent Complete	Units Started	Ending Inventory	Percent Complete
Blending Department	30,000	30	110,000	40,000	25
Finishing Department	15,000	40	?	35,000	20

Beginning work in process inventory costs on June 1 were:

	Blending Department	Finishing Department
Previous department costs	-0-	$105,000
Raw materials	$120,000	22,500
Conversion costs	27,000	15,000

Production costs incurred during June were:

	Blending Department	Finishing Department
Raw material costs	$440,000	$150,000
Conversion costs	303,000	202,500

Required:
Prepare cost of production reports for the June production performances of the two departments. Remember that the production output of the Blending Department is the input of the Finishing Department.

ALTERNATE PROBLEMS

Problem 23-1A   Job Order Costing and Manufacturing Overhead

The Stern Company utilizes a job order cost system to control production costs in its two departments. Manufacturing overhead is applied on the basis of machine hours in Department A and on the basis of direct labor cost in Department B. The firm prepared the following estimates for its 1987 production performance.

	Department A	Department B
Machine hours	12,600	16,400
Direct labor cost	$212,500	$348,480
Direct labor hours	25,000	39,600
Manufacturing overhead	$340,200	$906,048

The accounting records for job 998 shows the following data.

	Department A	Department B
Machine hours	86	98
Direct labor cost	$1,496	$1,690
Direct labor hours	176	192
Raw materials	$1,042	$1,202

Required:
A. Calculate the predetermined overhead rate for each department.
B. Calculate the total cost of job 998.
C. If the actual direct labor cost in Department B was $352,200 and the actual manufacturing overhead was $914,400, was the overhead overapplied or underapplied?

Problem 23-2A   Job Order Costing Procedures

The head accountant of the Hare Company has asked you to journalize the following transactions, which took place during May, 1987. The company uses a job order cost system.

1. Raw materials purchased—$30,000.
2. Total manufacturing payroll included $36,000 of direct labor and $8,000 of indirect labor.
3. Manufacturing overhead is applied at 125% of direct labor cost.
4. Raw materials issued to production—$28,000 direct materials and $4,000 indirect materials.
5. Other manufacturing expenses incurred:

Rent	$5,400
Supplies	6,000
Insurance	5,000
Utilities	8,400

6. Manufacturing equipment depreciation—$7,000.
7. Jobs completed and transferred to finished goods—$106,200.
8. Jobs with a cost of $104,000 were sold for $130,000 cash.
9. The beginning inventories were:

Raw materials	$ 7,000
Work in process	11,200
Finished goods	9,600

Required:

A. Prepare the journal entries to record the transactions.
B. Calculate the ending balances in work in process, raw materials, and finished goods. (*Hint:* Prepare T accounts.)
C. Was overhead underapplied or overapplied in May?

Problem 23-3A Journal Entries for Job Order Costing

The Riggs Company accounts for its manufacturing costs using a job order cost system and has provided the following production data for its performance during the month of June.

1. Job 103 was in process as of June 1 with a cost of $8,500.
2. The purchases of raw materials on credit during the month amounted to $27,500. Raw materials requisitioned were charged to the following.

Job 103	$7,000
Job 104	6,500
Job 105	9,500
Indirect materials	3,500

3. Manufacturing payroll of $24,375 was incurred. Each worker earns $7.50 per hour. Ignore income taxes and other payroll deductions.
4. The manufacturing payroll was distributed as follows.

Job 103	$6,900
Job 104	8,100
Job 105	7,350
Indirect labor	2,025

5. Additional manufacturing overhead costs incurred during the month were $4,300 (assume that *Accounts Payable* was credited for $3,200 and the rest went to accumulated depreciation).
6. Manufacturing overhead is applied at $3.35 per direct labor hour.
7. Jobs 103 and 104 were completed and transferred to finished goods.
8. Job 103 was sold at a markup of 40% above cost.

9. The beginning raw materials were $8,500.

Required:
A. Prepare the journal entries to record the June transactions.
B. Determine the balances of the *Raw Materials Inventory* and *Work in Process Inventory* accounts at the end of June.

Problem 23-4A Weighted-average and FIFO Costing

The Kulsrud Company produces a cleaning solvent in a single processing center, the Blending Department, and uses process costing to accumulate the production costs. You are provided with the following information about the firm's August production performance.

Beginning work in process inventory:	
Gallons (100% finished as to raw materials, 60% finished as to conversion costs)	28,000
Raw material costs	$140,000
Conversion costs	50,400
Production during August:	
Gallons started	160,000
Gallons left in ending work in process inventory (100% finished as to raw materials, 30% finished as to conversion costs)	18,000
Raw material costs	$800,000
Conversion costs	475,800

Required:
A. Compute the equivalent units with the weighted-average method.
B. Compute the unit cost of producing one gallon with the weighted-average method.
C. Compute the equivalent units with the FIFO method.
D. Compute the unit cost of producing one gallon with the FIFO method.
E. Prepare a cost of production report for the firm's August production performance with the weighted-average method.

Problem 23-5A Cost of Production Report with a Beginning Inventory

The Presto Company produces antifreeze in a single Mixing Department. Process costing is used to accumulate production costs, and the weighted-average method is applied to calculate unit costs. The following data concerning the Mixing Department's September performance were obtained from the firm's accounting records.

		Percent Completed	
	Gallons	**Raw Materials**	**Conversion Costs**
Beginning work in process	12,000	100	25
Started in production	108,000		
Ending work in process	20,000	100	40
		Raw Material Costs	**Conversion Costs**
Beginning work in process		$ 6,000	$ 2,400
September production		54,000	84,000

Required:

Prepare a cost of production report for the September production performance of the Mixing Department. Remember that the weighted-average method is used to compute unit costs.

Problem 23-6A Process Costing with Beginning Inventory

The Big-C Company produces a special blend of fruit juice in two departments, Blending and Canning. Raw materials are added at the beginning of the blending process and at the end of the canning process. All conversion costs are incurred continuously in each department. The weighted-average method is used to compute unit costs, and the fruit juice flows from the blending process to the canning process and then to finished goods.

Production data in gallons for the month of December with completed percentages for the conversion costs were as follows.

	Beginning Inventory	Percent Complete	Units Started	Ending Inventory	Percent Complete
Blending department	22,000	10	420,000	15,000	20
Canning department	8,000	75	?	12,000	80

Beginning work in process inventory costs on December 1 were:

	Blending Department	Canning Department
Previous department costs	$ -0-	$5,600
Raw material costs	8,800	0
Conversion costs	660	3,000

The production costs incurred during December were:

	Blending Department	Canning Department
Raw material costs	$168,000	$ 42,300
Conversion costs	128,340	213,300

Required:

Prepare cost of production reports for the Blending and Canning Departments' December performances.

CASE

CASE 23-1 Decision Case Evaluating Problems with Fluctuating Unit Costs

The Fine Toy Company produces a single product, which is sold to retail stores throughout the Southeast. The demand for the toy is very seasonal, with peak retail sales in the summer months and at Christmas. Joe Spillery, the president of the company, is very concerned because of the variation in unit costs from quarter to quarter and wants to know whether there is a better way to determine unit product costs than the method currently being used. Unit costs are computed quarterly by dividing the total manufacturing costs for a quarter by the units produced during the quarter. The company's estimated costs and production, by quarter, for the next year are:

	First Quarter	Second Quarter	Third Quarter	Fourth Quarter
Direct material costs	$ 24,000	$ 48,000	$ 24,000	$ 96,000
Direct labor costs	48,000	96,000	48,000	192,000
Variable manufacturing overhead	14,400	28,800	14,400	57,600
Fixed manufacturing overhead	192,000	192,000	192,000	192,000
Totals	278,400	364,800	278,400	537,600
Units produced	10,000	20,000	10,000	40,000
Unit cost	$ 27.84	$ 18.24	$ 27.84	$ 13.44

Required:

What suggestions would you make to Mr. Spillery to improve the way the firm computes unit costs?

PART 7

FINANCIAL PLANNING AND CONTROLLING OPERATIONS

24

FINANCIAL PLANNING AND CONTROL WITH BUDGETING

CHAPTER OVERVIEW AND OBJECTIVES

This chapter presents the basic concepts of budgeting for a business. When you have completed the chapter, you should understand:

1. The basic nature of financial planning and control.
2. The importance of goal congruence for an organization.
3. The benefits of budgeting.
4. The steps involved in preparing a master budget.
5. The significance of an accurate sales forecast.
6. The difference between an operating budget and a financial budget.
7. The preparation and use of each of the individual budgets included in the master budget.
8. The use of budgets for performance reporting and financial control.

Objective 1: Financial planning and control concepts

A **budget** is a detailed plan that shows how resources are expected to be acquired and used during a specified time period. Virtually every person and every organization use some form of budget to identify the resources that must be available to support the expenditures of a period. Sometimes we do this in our personal lives without even recognizing it as a formal application of budgeting. For example, assume that we are considering the purchase of a new automobile. We must determine if we have enough cash available, given our other financial commitments, or whether we can afford monthly payments if we decide to finance the transaction with an auto loan. This situation requires the preparation of a relatively simple budget to make sure that we can pay for the new automobile without straining ourselves financially. A budget prepared by a business is typically much more detailed and formalized than one used by an individual, although all budgets serve the same basic purpose. The process of preparing a budget, called **budgeting**, is an essential phase of managing a business in an efficient and effective manner. Budget information is utilized throughout the management process discussed in Chapter 21, although its primary application is in the planning and controlling functions.

A budget, as a management tool, can be compared to the architectural drawings used by a contractor to build a house. If the contractor is to build the house efficiently (with the proper amount of resources in the form of labor and materials) and effectively (so that the results are compatible with the predetermined specifications), he or she must follow the blueprint drawings carefully in order to guide the building process from beginning to end. A budget serves management in much the same manner, by providing a formal plan for the firm's future course of action according to well defined organizational goals. Initially, budgeting identifies certain financial and operating targets, which become management's goals for the future. These targets provide the direction for the firm's activities and transactions, which are expected to lead to satisfactory profit results. Then, as the actual performance occurs, it is monitored and checked against the related targets for control purposes. When significant variances are found between the actual and the planned performances, they are investigated and corrected whenever possible, through the responsibility accounting procedures introduced in Chapter 21. Budgeting and responsibility accounting are closely related, since the budget provides many of the performance targets used in responsibility accounting. While the primary emphasis of this chapter is on budgeting for a business, many of the concepts and procedures are useful in nonbusiness activities as well.

IMPORTANCE OF GOAL CONGRUENCE

Every organization must be certain that all of its segments work toward common goals. Since the performances of the various segments will be interrelated in many ways, each segment manager must know not only his or her own role, but also how it interacts with the rest of the organization. For example, the accounting, finance, marketing, personnel, production, and purchasing functions of a manufacturing firm must be coordinated. The same is true for the agencies of a government, the services of a bank, or the departments of a hospital. Otherwise, inefficiency and ineffectiveness will develop in the allocation and utilization of resources.

This coordination will not occur automatically, because individuals within an organization and the organization as a whole may have different goals. For example, consider the potential conflict that could develop in a manufacturing firm from differing inventory policies of the managers responsible for production and marketing. The production manager is concerned primarily with using the manufacturing facilities efficiently and maintaining stable inventory levels. In contrast, the marketing manager is concerned primarily with having enough inventory available at all times to meet customers' demands—even if

Objective 2: Goal congruence in an organization

large variations in sales volume occur between periods. The stable inventory levels and fluctuating sales demand are not compatible, and thus, a compromise becomes necessary. Without a formal coordination system, individual managers would tend to operate in different directions and, in many cases, against the best interests of the organization. This problem becomes increasingly difficult as an organization grows and management responsibility is delegated to more people. **Goal congruence** occurs when the managers of a firm accept the organizational goals as their own. The various activities of a business must be planned and controlled with the full participation and support of the managers responsible for them.

BENEFITS OF BUDGETING

Objective 3:
The benefits of budgeting

Achieving satisfactory profits in today's competitive and uncertain business world is no easy matter. For example, the average profit margin for large corporations in the United States is only about 5%, which means that the typical company has approximately *five cents out of every sales dollar* with which to pay dividends, retire debt, and reinvest in the business. The biannual profit performances of eight large corporations from 1978 to 1984 are shown in Figure 24–1, to illustrate how small corporate profits really are.

The profit margin measure is calculated by dividing net income by net sales. Little room exists for error with these tight profit results, and management must do everything possible to operate efficiently and effectively. A firm's financial performance must be planned and controlled as thoroughly as possible with sound budgeting procedures if acceptable profit results are to be achieved. The major benefits of budgeting, which can ultimately lead to a profitable operation are as follows.

1. It *forces* management to *plan ahead* and anticipate the future on a systematic basis. Most managers are very busy with their day-to-day activities and may resist formalized planning unless budgeting is part of their job. Nevertheless, every successful manager knows what he or she wants to

Figure 24–1
Profitability Performance for Eight Large Corporations

Company	Profit Margin Percent			
	1978	1980	1982	1984
American Airlines	4.5	def.*	def.	4.8
Ford Motor Company	4.1	def.	def.	4.2
General Foods	3.5	3.7	3.4	3.7
Holiday Inns	5.6	7.6	5.2	7.8
IBM Corporation	14.7	13.2	11.8	13.7
Pabst Brewing	1.6	1.3	0.1	0.5
Sears, Roebuck and Co.	4.7	2.2	2.4	3.6
Texas Instruments	5.6	5.3	3.2	def.

*def. indicates a net loss for the period.
Source: "Annual Report on American Industry," *Forbes* (January 1979, 1981, 1983, 1985).

accomplish and when it should be done. The regularity of the budgeting process forces managers to formalize their thinking and participate in the goal-setting activities of the firm.

2. It provides management with *realistic performance targets,* against which actual results can be compared with responsibility accounting. Management by exception is performed by identifying significant variances, which require corrective action if the firm is to achieve its goals. Consequently, the budget plays an important role in controlling the acquisition and use of resources.

3. It *coordinates* the various segments of the organization and makes each manager aware of how the different activities fit together. Goal congruence can be achieved by the unifying effect budgeting has on an organization—particularly when it is combined with responsibility accounting.

4. It serves as a *communication device* with which the various managers can exchange information concerning goals, ideas, and achievements. Since direct contact will decrease as an organization increases in size, a formal communication network is required. Budgeting enables the managers to interact and develop an awareness of how each of their activities contributes to the firm's overall operation.

5. It furnishes management with *motivation,* in the form of the goals to be achieved. Few people work for the sheer joy of it; most of us need some form of stimulus to work hard and maintain an enthusiastic attitude toward our job. A properly used budget is a motivating device that provides performance targets against which actual results can be evaluated. Unfortunately, an improperly prepared budget may have an adverse effect on the motivation of managers, who may then criticize the process as being unfair. Two key aspects of a correct application of budgeting are that the budgeted level of performance should be attainable with a reasonably efficient amount of effort, and that the managers who will be evaluated with the budget data should participate actively in the budget's development. Managers will be more highly motivated with *self-imposed* budget estimates, than with ones established by someone at a higher level in the organization.

FINANCIAL PLANNING WITH BUDGETING

The primary objective of the financial planning phase of budgeting is to identify how management intends to acquire and use the firm's resources during a budget period in order to achieve organizational goals. A **master budget,** consisting of several interrelated budgets, provides the basis for financial planning. The major steps in developing a master budget are the following.

Objective 4:
The basic steps used for a master budget

1. Management identifies the organizational goals for the budget period, including those that are financially oriented, such as desired net income, profit margins, return on investment, liquidity, share of the market, and financial position.

2. The managers of the various responsibility centers participate in the development of the parts of the master budget for which they are accountable.

3. Sales for the budget period are forecasted.
4. Cost of goods sold and operating expenses for the budget period are estimated.
5. Capital expenditures for the budget period are identified.
6. Accrual accounting is converted to a cash basis to determine cash receipts and disbursements. Any nonoperating sources or uses of cash (such as the sale of stock, issue of debt, payment of dividends, or retirement of debt) are considered.
7. A set of estimated financial statements is prepared, based on the initial version of the financial performance projections.
8. The estimated financial performance results are compared with the organizational goals, and revisions are made wherever necessary to make the final version of the budget compatible with the overall goals.

IMPORTANCE OF THE SALES FORECAST

Objective 5: Why an accurate sales forecast is so important

An accurate sales forecast is the cornerstone of successful budgeting, since virtually everything else is dependent on it. The sales information provides the basis for preparing a sales budget, for predicting cash receipts, and for constructing a variety of expense budgets. At the same time, the sales forecast is usually subject to more uncertainty than any other aspect of budgeting. Unless a business firm has a large number of unfilled orders that guarantee future sales, or unless it has a highly consistent demand for its products or services, sales forecasting will be complicated by the uncertainties of the future. The general economy, industry conditions, effect of proposed advertising, actions of competitors, consumer buying habits, population changes, and technological developments are factors that influence the reliability of a sales forecast.

A combination of several methods can be used to forecast sales. The most common methods are *predictions by members of the sales staff, group estimates prepared by top management,* and *the use of statistical or mathematical techniques.* The sales staff is generally aware of current market conditions and should participate actively in the preparation of the sales forecast. Field surveys can be conducted to predict revenue by products or services, geographical areas, customers, and sales representatives. In large businesses, a market research staff may be available to conduct the field studies of consumer demand and to develop sales revenue estimates.

All members of the top management team—including marketing, production, finance, purchasing, and corporate officers—should collectively develop their own estimate of expected revenue based on their knowledge of the total business and the environment in which the firm will operate. In addition, a number of statistical and mathematical techniques beyond the scope of this text are available. The basic reason for using alternative forecasting methods is that they provide a check on each other and produce a compromise representing management's best estimate of sales revenue.

STRUCTURE OF THE MASTER BUDGET

The master budget includes several interrelated budgets that collectively represent a comprehensive plan of action for a specified time period. A budget committee is normally appointed and given responsibility for coordinating the development of the master budget. It is typically prepared for a one-year period that coincides with a firm's fiscal year, although more and more businesses are preparing long-term budgets for periods of 3 to 5 years. The budget for a year should be subdivided into shorter periods, such as months or quarters, so that timely comparisons of actual and budgeted results can be made. Alternatively, the budget may be developed for a continuous period of 12 months or more by adding a month or a quarter in the future as the month or quarter just ended is eliminated. In any case, the budgeted targets often *must be revised,* as time progresses and new information concerning the business and its environment becomes available.

The master budget consists of two major parts, the operating budget and the financial budget. The **operating budget** is a detailed description of the revenue and costs required to achieve satisfactory profit results. The **financial budget** shows the funding and financial position needed for the planned operations. Each of these two components has several separate but interrelated budgets, such as those shown schematically in Figure 24–2 for a typical manufacturing firm. The page numbers shown in Figure 24–2 refer to the presentation of the related budgets in an illustration later in the chapter. Essentially,

Objective 6: Differentiating between an operating budget and a financial budget

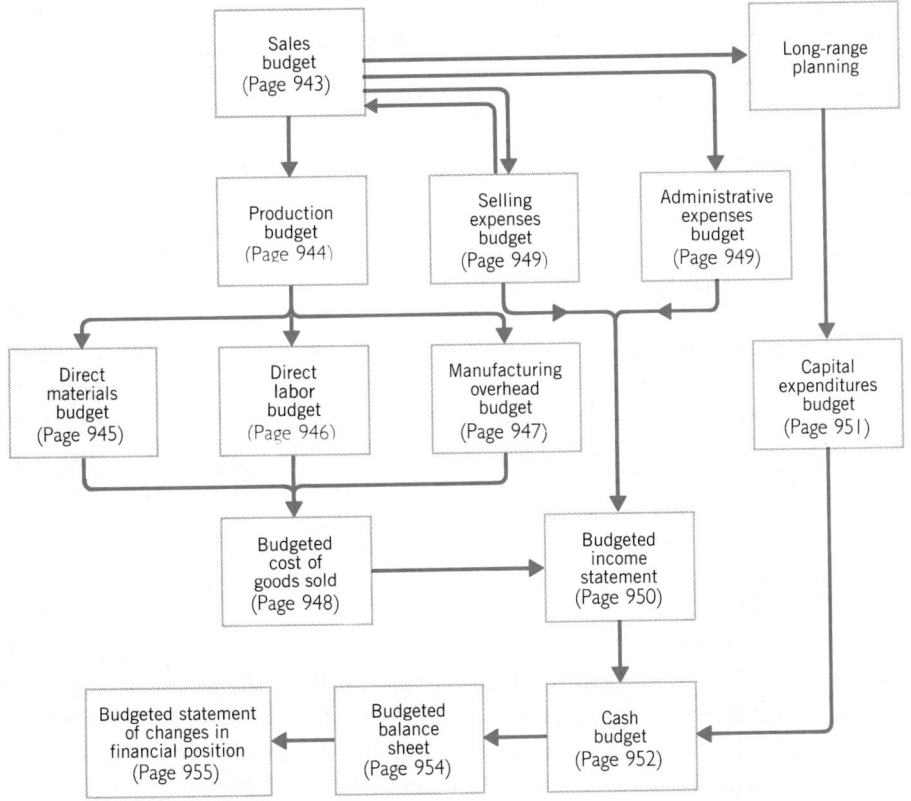

Figure 24–2
Master Budget Inter-relationships

the same budgeting cycle as the one illustrated in Figure 24–2 is applicable in a nonmanufacturing business, although some of the individual budgets may differ (for example, a merchandising firm would not need a production budget). In the preparation of a master budget, a manufacturing firm will prepare the following budgets.

Master Budget	
Operating Budget	**Financial Budget**
Sales budget	Capital expenditures budget
Production budget	Cash budget
Direct materials budget	Budgeted balance sheet
Direct labor budget	Budgeted statement of changes
Manufacturing overhead budget	in financial position
Cost of goods sold budget	
Selling expenses budget	
Administrative expenses budget	
Budgeted income statement	

MASTER BUDGET PREPARATION ILLUSTRATION

Objective 7: Preparing and using the budgets included in the master budget

To illustrate the preparation of a master budget, we will refer to the Kort Company, which produces two types of medallions that are sold to campus bookstores. A deluxe medallion is larger and requires more direct labor than a standard medallion. Ounces of a special metal alloy are purchased by Kort Company and converted into medallions with skilled labor and specialized manufacturing equipment. The following data represent the direct costs estimated for the production of each medallion.

	Deluxe	Standard
Direct materials	2.4 ounces @ $2.50 per ounce	2.0 ounces @ $2.50 per ounce
Direct labor	2 hours @ $8.00 per hour	1 hour @ $8.00 per hour

The master budget is prepared for a calendar year and is subdivided into quarters. In the following illustration, we are concerned with a summary of the steps taken by Kort Company in the preparation of the master budget. Work in process inventories are negligible for Kort Company, so they are ignored here in order to concentrate on the basic principles of budgeting.

SALES BUDGET

As noted earlier, virtually every phase of the master budget is dependent on the sales forecast. The **sales budget** is prepared from the sales forecast. Detailed information concerning sales volume, selling prices, and sales mix is presented in the sales budget. Kort Company has used the forecasting methods discussed earlier to develop the sales budget shown in Figure 24–3. In addi-

KORT COMPANY
Sales Budget
Year Ending December 31, 1987

| | Quarter | | | | Annual |
	1	2	3	4	Total
Deluxe Medallion					
Budgeted sales units	4,000	6,000	6,500	5,000	21,500
Budgeted price per unit	48	48	48	48	48
Budgeted sales dollars	$192,000	$288,000	$312,000	$240,000	$1,032,000
Standard Medallion					
Budgeted sales units	6,000	8,000	8,500	7,000	29,500
Budgeted price per unit	25	25	25	25	25
Budgeted sales dollars	$150,000	$200,000	$212,500	$175,000	$ 737,500
Total					
Budgeted sales dollars	$342,000	$488,000	$524,500	$415,000	$1,769,500

Figure 24–3
Sales Budget

tion, management has considered the influence of selling expenses, such as advertising, on the projected demand for the two products. The sales budget also furnishes the information required to prepare the cash receipts part of the cash budget, shown later in Figure 24–13.

PRODUCTION BUDGET

Once the sales budget has been prepared, the production requirements for the period are determined as:

$$\text{Production units required} = \text{Forecast sales units} + \text{Desired ending finished goods} - \text{Beginning finished goods}$$

Note that we must make an inventory level decision before the production requirements can be established. Kort Company plans its inventory level for each finished product, so as to have an adequate number of units available to satisfy the expected sales demand for a current quarter and have enough ending inventory for future sales. The right amount of inventory is an important factor for the firm's profitability. An excessive inventory will result in unnecessary costs, such as insurance, handling, and funds invested. In contrast, inventory shortages will cause lost sales, dissatisfied customers, and production scheduling problems.

We assume that the company has decided that the desired ending finished goods inventory for a particular quarter should be equal to the expected sales for the *first month of the succeeding quarter*. This policy has enabled the company to maintain an adequate, but not excessive, ending inventory in the past. For example, the desired ending inventory for deluxe medallions at the end of the first quarter is set to be equal to the sales expected for April. Since the **production budget** is developed before the budget year 1987 starts, the beginning inventory has to be estimated. The production budget for 1987 is shown in Figure 24–4.

DIRECT MATERIALS BUDGET

After the production requirements have been determined, the **direct materials budget** can be developed. Inventory level decisions must again be made by management in the preparation of the direct materials budget. Essentially the same approach used for the production budget is taken with budgeted direct materials purchases, calculated as:

$$
\begin{array}{llll}
\text{Budgeted} & \text{Budgeted} & \text{Desired} & \text{Beginning} \\
\text{purchases} = & \text{direct} & + \text{ending} & - \text{direct} \\
\text{in units} & \text{materials} & \text{direct} & \text{materials} \\
& \text{usage} & \text{materials} &
\end{array}
$$

The direct materials required are initially determined in ounces and then converted to dollars by multiplying the ounces needed by the cost of an ounce of metal alloy. Kort Company requires 2.4 ounces of direct materials to produce one deluxe medallion and 2 ounces of direct materials for a standard medallion. Each ounce costs $2.50. In Chapter 25, we will see how the prices and quantities of the resources required for production can be predetermined as standard costs. The firm also uses a one-month supply for the estimate of

Figure 24–4
Production Budget

KORT COMPANY
Production Budget
Year Ending December 31, 1987

	Quarter				Annual
	1	2	3	4	Total
Deluxe Medallion					
Forecast sales units (Figure 24-3)	4,000	6,000	6,500	5,000	21,500
Desired ending finished goods	3,000	2,150	1,650	1,950	1,950
Total units needed	7,000	8,150	8,150	6,950	23,450
Beginning finished goods	1,350	3,000	2,150	1,650	1,350
Production required—units	5,650	5,150	6,000	5,300	22,100
Standard Medallion					
Forecast sales units (Figure 24-3)	6,000	8,000	8,500	7,000	29,500
Desired ending finished goods	2,500	3,000	2,500	2,400	2,400
Total units needed	8,500	11,000	11,000	9,400	31,900
Beginning finished goods	2,000	2,500	3,000	2,500	2,000
Production required—units	6,500	8,500	8,000	6,900	29,900

KORT COMPANY
Direct Materials Budget
Year Ending December 31, 1987

	Quarter				Annual Total
	1	2	3	4	
Deluxe Medallion					
Production units required (Figure 24-4)	5,650	5,150	6,000	5,300	22,100
Ounces of materials per unit	2.4	2.4	2.4	2.4	2.4
Ounces of materials required	13,560	12,360	14,400	12,720	53,040
Desired ending materials	4,104	4,800	4,248	4,776	4,776
Ounces needed	17,664	17,160	18,648	17,496	57,816
Beginning materials	4,560	4,104	4,800	4,248	4,560
Purchases required—ounces	13,104	13,056	13,848	13,248	53,256
Cost per ounce	$2.50	$2.50	$2.50	$2.50	$2.50
Cost of purchases	$32,760	$32,640	$34,620	$33,120	$133,140
Standard Medallion					
Production units required (Figure 24-4)	6,500	8,500	8,000	6,900	29,900
Ounces of materials per unit	2	2	2	2	2
Ounces of materials required	13,000	17,000	16,000	13,800	59,800
Desired ending materials	5,650	5,500	4,600	4,200	4,200
Ounces needed	18,650	22,500	20,600	18,000	64,000
Beginning materials	4,150	5,650	5,500	4,600	4,150
Purchases required—ounces	14,500	16,850	15,100	13,400	59,850
Cost per ounce	$2.50	$2.50	$2.50	$2.50	$2.50
Cost of purchases	$36,250	$42,125	$37,750	$33,500	$149,625
Total purchases	$69,010	$74,765	$72,370	$66,620	$282,765

Figure 24–5
Direct Materials Budget

desired ending direct materials inventory. The total budgeted purchases of direct materials are $282,765, as shown in Figure 24–5.

DIRECT LABOR BUDGET

The **direct labor budget** is also developed from the production budget and provides important information concerning the size of the labor force that is necessary during each quarter. The primary objective is to maintain a labor force large enough to satisfy the production requirements but *not so large that it results in costly idle time*. At the same time, it must be large enough to avoid an excessive amount of overtime charges, which also would be costly. The first step in the development of the direct labor budget is to estimate the time needed to produce each type of medallion. Two hours are required for one deluxe medallion and one hour is needed for a standard medallion. The total labor hours required are computed by multiplying these hourly measures by the respective number of medallions to be produced. For the year, 74,100 direct labor hours are projected. Multiplication of the total direct labor hours

KORT COMPANY
Direct Labor Budget
Year Ending December 31, 1987

| | Quarter | | | | Annual |
	1	2	3	4	Total
Deluxe Medallion					
Production units required (Figure 24-4)	5,650	5,150	6,000	5,300	22,100
Direct labor hours per unit	2	2	2	2	2
Total hours required	11,300	10,300	12,000	10,600	44,200
Labor rate per hour	$8.00	$8.00	$8.00	$8.00	$8.00
Direct labor cost	$ 90,400	$ 82,400	$ 96,000	$ 84,800	$353,600
Standard Medallion					
Production units required (Figure 24-4)	6,500	8,500	8,000	6,900	29,900
Direct labor hours per unit	1	1	1	1	1
Total hours required	6,500	8,500	8,000	6,900	29,900
Labor rate per hour	$8.00	$8.00	$8.00	$8.00	$8.00
Direct labor cost	$ 52,000	$ 68,000	$ 64,000	$ 55,200	$239,200
Total direct labor cost	$142,400	$150,400	$160,000	$140,000	$592,800
Total direct labor hours	17,800	18,800	20,000	17,500	74,100

Figure 24–6
Direct Labor Budget

by the hourly labor rate of $8 gives the budgeted total direct labor cost, which amounts to $592,800 for the year, as shown in Figure 24–6.

MANUFACTURING OVERHEAD BUDGET

Kort Company applies manufacturing overhead to inventory on the basis of the 74,100 budgeted direct labor hours found in the direct labor budget. Total budgeted manufacturing overhead is $518,700, so the predetermined overhead rate used for product costing purposes is $7 per direct labor hour ($518,700 divided by 74,100). The company distinguishes between variable and fixed manufacturing overhead. As we see in Figure 24–7, the estimated variable manufacturing overhead costs total $177,840 for the year, or $2.40 per budgeted direct labor hour ($177,840 divided by 74,100). The total fixed manufacturing overhead costs are $340,860 or $4.60 per budgeted direct labor hour ($340,860 divided by 74,100). For every hour of direct labor recorded during the actual production performance, $7 will be applied for manufacturing overhead.

The fixed portion of the **manufacturing overhead budget** is determined by spreading the annual fixed costs equally over the four quarters, since we assume that the Kort Company does not have any seasonal differences in its fixed costs. As a result, the fixed manufacturing costs are $85,215 per quarter. Cost behavior analysis has shown that the variable costs fluctuate with the production level per quarter, based on the following rates.

KORT COMPANY
Manufacturing Overhead Budget
Year Ending December 31, 1987

| | Quarter | | | | Annual |
	1	2	3	4	Total
Variable Costs					
Indirect labor	$ 5,340	$ 5,640	$ 6,000	$ 5,250	$ 22,230
Indirect materials	1,780	1,880	2,000	1,750	7,410
Employee benefits	28,480	30,080	32,000	28,000	118,560
Utilities	7,120	7,520	8,000	7,000	29,640
Total	42,720	45,120	48,000	42,000	177,840
Fixed Costs					
Supervision	36,715	36,715	36,715	36,715	146,860
Property taxes	5,400	5,400	5,400	5,400	21,600
Insurance	4,200	4,200	4,200	4,200	16,800
Maintenance	9,500	9,500	9,500	9,500	38,000
Utilities	8,600	8,600	8,600	8,600	34,400
Depreciation	16,000	16,000	16,000	16,000	64,000
Other	4,800	4,800	4,800	4,800	19,200
Total	85,215	85,215	85,215	85,215	340,860
Total manufacturing overhead	$127,935	$130,335	$133,215	$127,215	$518,700
Direct labor hours	17,800	18,800	20,000	17,500	74,100
Manufacturing overhead rate per direct labor hour					$7.00

Figure 24–7
Manufacturing Overhead Budget

Manufacturing Overhead Item	Estimated Variable Rate per Direct Labor Hour
Indirect labor	$ .30
Indirect materials	.10
Employee benefits	1.60
Utilities	.40
Total	$2.40

The direct labor hours of 17,800, 18,800, 20,000, and 17,500 for the four quarters, respectively, are multiplied by the variable cost rates to determine the budgeted variable overhead costs per quarter, as shown in Figure 24–7.

COST OF GOODS SOLD BUDGET

The **cost of goods sold budget** is shown in Figure 24–8. The unit costs of $36 and $20 for deluxe and standard medallions, respectively, can be multiplied by the number of units sold, in order to determine the cost of goods sold

KORT COMPANY
Cost of Goods Sold Budget
Year Ending December 31, 1987

	Deluxe Medallion		Standard Medallion		Total	
Beginning finished goods		$ 48,600		$ 40,000	$	88,600
Direct materials used						
Beginning materials	$ 11,400		$ 10,375		$ 21,775	
Budgeted purchases						
(Figure 24-5)	133,140		149,625		282,765	
Ending materials	11,940		10,500		22,440	
Direct materials used	132,600		149,500		282,100	
Direct labor (Figure 24-6)	353,600		239,200		592,800	
Manufacturing overhead						
(direct labor hours × $7)	309,400		209,300		518,700	
Total manufacturing cost		795,600		598,000		1,393,600
Ending finished goods		70,200		48,000		118,200
Cost of goods sold		$774,000		$590,000		$1,364,000
Unit costs per product						
Direct materials	2.4 lbs. @ $2.50 =	$ 6.00		2 lbs. @ $2.50 =	$ 5.00	
Direct labor	2 hrs. @ $8.00 =	$16.00		1 hr. @ $8.00 =	$ 8.00	
Manufacturing overhead ˙	2 hrs. @ $7.00 =	$14.00		1 hr. @ $7.00 =	$ 7.00	
Unit Cost		$36.00			$20.00	

Figure 24–8
Cost of Goods Sold Budget

for each product. The budgeted sales units of deluxe medallions are 21,500 (Figure 24–3), so the cost of goods sold is $774,000, while 29,500 standard medallions (Figure 24–3) are planned at a cost of $590,000. The total budgeted cost of goods sold is $1,364,000 ($774,000 + $590,000). The same result is obtained for each product by working through the traditional form of the cost of goods sold computational schedule, as shown in Figure 24–8.

SELLING EXPENSES BUDGET

We noted earlier that the influence of selling expenses on the sales budget must be evaluated carefully. The management of the Kort Company does this by preparing the **selling expenses budget** along with the sales budget, and the expected effect on sales from the selling effort is considered when the sales volume is forecasted. We assume for illustrative purposes that all the selling expenses are fixed and amount to $128,600, spread evenly over the four quarters. In reality, several selling expenses, such as sales commissions, advertising, and travel may be variable expenses in many businesses because their total amounts change with different sales levels. The selling expenses budget is presented in Figure 24–9.

KORT COMPANY
Selling Expenses Budget
Year Ending December 31, 1987

Selling Expenses	Quarter 1	Quarter 2	Quarter 3	Quarter 4	Annual Total
Advertising	$ 4,500	$ 4,500	$ 4,500	$ 4,500	$ 18,000
Sales salaries	23,450	23,450	23,450	23,450	93,800
Travel	1,200	1,200	1,200	1,200	4,800
Entertainment	800	800	800	800	3,200
Insurance	320	320	320	320	1,280
Property taxes	380	380	380	380	1,520
Utilities	200	200	200	200	800
Depreciation	1,200	1,200	1,200	1,200	4,800
Other	100	100	100	100	400
Total	$32,150	$32,150	$32,150	$32,150	$128,600

Figure 24–9
Selling Expenses Budget

ADMINISTRATIVE EXPENSES BUDGET

The **administrative expenses budget** provides a listing of the estimated administrative expenses for the period. All the administrative expenses of the Kort Company are fixed; their total is $100,004. Administrative expenses are typically fixed because their total amount does not change with different sales levels. An exception would be a bonus paid to certain managers based on a percentage of sales. Again, we assume that the total administrative expenses are spread evenly among the quarters, as shown in Figure 24–10.

KORT COMPANY
Administrative Expenses Budget
Year Ending December 31, 1987

Administrative Expenses	Quarter 1	Quarter 2	Quarter 3	Quarter 4	Annual Total
Management salaries	$21,441	$21,441	$21,441	$21,441	$ 85,764
Clerical salaries	2,500	2,500	2,500	2,500	10,000
Insurance	130	130	130	130	520
Property taxes	160	160	160	160	640
Supplies	150	150	150	150	600
Depreciation	500	500	500	500	2,000
Other	120	120	120	120	480
Total	$25,001	$25,001	$25,001	$25,001	$100,004

Figure 24–10
Administrative Expenses Budget

Figure 24–11
Budgeted Income
Statement

KORT COMPANY
Budgeted Income Statement
Year Ending December 31, 1987

	Deluxe Medallion	Standard Medallion	Total
Sales—units (Figure 24-3)	21,500	29,500	51,000
Sales—dollars (Figure 24-3)	$1,032,000	$737,500	$1,769,500
Cost of goods sold (Figure 24-8)	774,000	590,000	1,364,000
Gross profit	258,000	147,500	405,500
Operating expenses:			
Selling (Figure 24-9)			128,600
Administrative (Figure 24-10)			100,004
Total operating expenses			228,604
Net income before tax			176,896
Income tax (from tax schedule)			65,686
Net income			$ 111,210

BUDGETED INCOME STATEMENT

The budgeted income statement shown in Figure 24–11 is developed from the individual budgets previously discussed. At first glance, the statement may appear to be the result of simply combining the end products of the other budgets once they are available. However, remember that the basic premise of budgeting is a planned financial performance that is acceptable to management. The control feature of the budgeted statement is exercised when management compares the actual operating results with the plan. Top management starts the budgeting process by establishing certain guidelines within which the business will plan its financial performance. These guidelines may pertain to such goals as profit margin, return on investment, share of the market, growth rate, cash flow, research and development, cost control, financial position, and productivity. We assume that the management of Kort Company included among its guidelines the goals of achieving a before-tax profit margin of 10% of sales and a before-tax return on average stockholders' equity in the range of 23% to 25%. The before-tax net income is budgeted at $176,896, which is about 10% of sales and approximately a 23.3% before-tax return on average stockholders' equity. The average stockholders' equity is calculated from the balance sheets presented later by adding the beginning and ending balances of stockholders' equity for the year and dividing the result by two.

CAPITAL EXPENDITURES BUDGET

The **capital expenditures budget** included in the master budget shows the acquisition of facilities and equipment planned for the period. Capital expenditures represent investments that are expected to yield benefits over a relatively long period of time. Most firms, including Kort Company, prepare

Figure 24–12
Capital Expenditures
Budget

KORT COMPANY
Capital Expenditures Budget
Year Ending December 31, 1987

	Quarter				Annual
	1	2	3	4	Total
Manufacturing equipment—machines		$25,000		$25,000	$50,000
Office equipment—typewriter			$ 1,000		1,000
Sales equipment—automobiles			14,000		14,000
Total	–0–	$25,000	$15,000	$25,000	$65,000

long-term capital expenditures budgets for periods of five years or more. Therefore, the amounts shown in Figure 24–12 would represent the current portion planned for the upcoming year. (Capital budgeting is discussed in Chapter 27). Kort Company will finance capital expenditures of $65,000 out of operating income during 1987.

CASH BUDGET

The revenue and expenses of the operating budget must be translated into *cash receipts* and *cash disbursements* for financial planning purposes. The goal of this is to make sure that the business has sufficient liquidity to pay its bills as they come due. The **cash budget** (Figure 24–13) and the supporting schedule of the projected cash receipts from sales and cash disbursements for direct material purchases (Figure 24–14) are used to plan an adequate but not excessive cash balance for each quarter. Excess cash can be used more productively by investing it in earning assets. A satisfactory income statement does not guarantee sufficient liquidity because of the time lag between accrual and cash accounting. An estimate of the time lag between revenue recognized and cash collections, as well as that associated with expenses charged and cash payments, must be carefully considered. In addition, any noncash expenses (such as depreciation) must be eliminated in the preparation of the cash budget. Note also that many businesses have to prepare cash budgets for periods within a quarter, in order to protect against cash shortages on a daily, weekly, or monthly basis, even though the projected ending quarterly balance may be adequate.

We assume that the Kort Company has analyzed its previous experience with cash receipts from sales and has decided that 70% of each quarter's sales should be collected currently and 30% collected the following quarter. Bad debts are negligible, so they are ignored. In addition, the company projects that 80% of its direct material purchases will be paid for in the quarter in which they are acquired and 20% will be paid for in the following quarter.

KORT COMPANY
Cash Budget
Year Ending December 31, 1987

| | Quarter | | | | Annual |
	1	2	3	4	Total
Beginning cash balance	$ 62,000	$ 31,206	$ 16,606	$ 94,641	$ 62,000
Cash collections from sales of:					
Current quarter (.7)	239,400	341,600	367,150	290,500	1,238,650
Previous quarter (.3)	123,000	102,600	146,400	157,350	529,350
Total cash from sales	362,400	444,200	513,550	447,850	1,768,000
Total cash available	424,400	475,406	530,156	542,491	1,830,000
Cash disbursements:					
Direct materials purchased in:					
Current quarter (.8)	55,208	59,812	57,896	53,296	226,212
Previous quarter (.2)	13,200	13,802	14,953	14,474	56,429
Total cash for purchases	68,408	73,614	72,849	67,770	282,641
Direct labor	142,400	150,400	160,000	140,000	592,800
Manufacturing overhead	111,935	114,335	117,215	111,215	454,700
Selling expenses	30,950	30,950	30,950	30,950	123,800
Administrative expenses	24,501	24,501	24,501	24,501	98,004
Total cash for operations	378,194	393,800	405,515	374,436	1,551,945
Net cash available from operations	46,206	81,606	124,641	168,055	278,055
Capital expenditures	–0–	25,000	15,000	25,000	65,000
Cash dividends	–0–	25,000	–0–	50,000	75,000
Estimated quarterly income tax	15,000	15,000	15,000	15,000	60,000
Ending cash balance	$ 31,206	$ 16,606	$ 94,614	$ 78,055	$ 78,055

Figure 24–13
Cash Budget

The receipts and disbursements of cash for accounts receivable and accounts payable are detailed in Figure 24–14. All expenses other than those related to the purchases of direct materials are assumed to be paid for in the quarter in which they occur. Depreciation amounting to $70,800 has been eliminated from the various budgets ($64,000 from the manufacturing overhead budget in Figure 24–7, $4,800 from the selling expenses budget in Figure 24–9, and $2,000 from the administrative expenses budget in Figure 24–10), since it is a noncash expense. Kort Company expects to begin the year with $62,000 and end it with $78,055 after all cash receipts from sales ($1,768,000) are added to the beginning balance and the total disbursements of $1,751,945 are subtracted. The total disbursements shown in Figure 24–13 are for operating cash outlays ($1,551,945), capital expenditures ($65,000), cash dividends ($75,000), and estimated taxes ($60,000), for a total of $1,751,945. We assume that an estimated tax payment of $15,000 will be paid each quarter. The remaining balance of the total tax liability shown on the income statement ($5,686) will be paid when the tax returns are filed. The cash available each

KORT COMPANY
Schedule of Cash Receipts and Disbursements
Year Ending December 31, 1987

	Quarter				
	1	2	3	4	Total
Cash receipts:					
From beginning accounts receivable balance of $123,000 (Fig. 24–15)	$123,000				$ 123,000
From 1st quarter sales of $342,000 (Fig. 24–3)	(.7) 239,400	(.3) $102,600			342,000
From 2nd quarter sales of $488,000 (Fig. 24–3)		(.7) 341,600	(.3) $146,400		488,000
From 3rd quarter sales of $524,500 (Fig. 24–3)			(.7) 367,150	(.3) $157,350	524,500
From 4th quarter sales of $415,000 (Fig. 24–3)				(.7) 290,500	290,500
Total cash receipts	$362,400	$444,200	$513,550	$447,850	$1,768,000
Cash disbursements:					
For beginning accounts payable balance of $13,200 (Fig. 24–15)	$ 13,200				$ 13,200
For 1st quarter purchases of $69,010 (Fig. 24–5)	(.8) 55,208	(.2) $ 13,802			69,010
For 2nd quarter purchases of $74,765 (Fig. 24–5)		(.8) 59,812	(.2) $ 14,953		74,765
For 3rd quarter purchases of $72,370 (Fig. 24–5)			(.8) 57,896	(.2) $ 14,474	72,370
For 4th quarter purchases of $66,620 (Fig. 24–5)				(.8) 53,296	53,296
Total cash disbursements	$ 68,408	$ 73,614	$ 72,849	$ 67,770	$ 282,641

Figure 24–14
Schedule of Cash Receipts and Disbursements

quarter is within the guidelines established by management for the budget period.

BUDGETED BALANCE SHEET

Since the budget for 1987 is prepared by the Kort Company before the end of 1986, the balance sheet as of December 31, 1986 must be estimated. It is shown in Figure 24–15 and provides the beginning balances for the 1987 budgeting process. Once the actual results are known, the beginning balance sheet may be revised if significant differences occur. The budgeted balance

Figure 24–15
Budgeted Balance
Sheet

KORT COMPANY
Budgeted Balance Sheet
December 31, 1987
(With Comparative Estimates as of December 31, 1986)

	1986		1987	
Assets				
Cash	$ 62,000		$ 78,055	
Accounts receivable	123,000		124,500	
Finished goods inventory	88,600		118,200	
Raw materials inventory	21,775		22,440	
Total current assets		$295,375		$343,195
Land		110,000		110,000
Building and equipment	629,585		694,585	
Accumulated depreciation	(280,000)	349,585	(350,800)	343,785
Total assets		$754,960		$796,980
Liabilities				
Accounts payable		$ 13,200		$ 13,324
Accrued income taxes		–0–		5,686
Total current liabilities		13,200		19,010
Stockholders' Equity				
Common stock (100 shares outstanding, no par)		100,000		100,000
Retained earnings		641,760		677,970
Total stockholders' equity		741,760		777,970
Total liabilities and stockholders' equity		$754,960		$796,980

sheet for December 31, 1987, also presented in Figure 24–15, is the result of translating the beginning balances through the budgeting process into ending balances. For example, cash increases from $62,000 to $78,055 as a result of the cash receipts and disbursements shown in the cash budget. Accounts receivable increase from $123,000 to $124,500 because of the sales recorded but not collected (total sales of $1,769,500 from Figure 24–3 and cash receipts of $1,768,000 from Figure 24–13, or a difference of $1,500). The other beginning and ending balances in Figure 24–15 can be reconciled by referring to their respective budgets. Management must evaluate the budgeted balance sheet carefully to make sure that it reflects a sufficiently strong financial position. If the projected balance sheet is not acceptable, revisions to the budget should be made.

BUDGETED STATEMENT OF CHANGES IN FINANCIAL POSITION

The budgeted statement of changes in financial position is the final step in the preparation of the financial budget and is presented in Figure 24–16. The statement of changes in financial position provides management with valuable

Figure 24–16
Budgeted Statement
of Changes in Fi-
nancial Position

KORT COMPANY
Budgeted Statement of Changes in Financial Position
Year Ending December 31, 1987

Sources of working capital		
Net income (Figure 24-11)	$111,210	
Add expenses not requiring working capital:		
Depreciation (Figures 24-7, 24-9, 24-10)	70,800	
Working capital from operations		$182,010
Uses of working capital		
Purchases of equipment (Figure 24-12)	65,000	
Payment of dividends (Figure 24-13)	75,000	
Total uses of working capital		140,000
Increase in working capital		$ 42,010

Budgeted Schedule of Working Capital Changes
Year Ending December 31, 1987

	Beginning	Ending	Increase/(Decrease) in Working Capital
Cash	$ 62,000	$ 78,055	$16,055
Accounts receivable	123,000	124,500	1,500
Finished goods inventory	88,600	118,200	29,600
Raw material inventory	21,775	22,440	665
Total current assets	295,375	343,195	47,820
Accounts payable	13,200	13,324	(124)
Accrued income taxes	–0–	5,686	(5,686)
Total current liabilities	13,200	19,010	(5,810)
Change in working capital			$42,010

information concerning the proposed financing and investing activities of the firm. It shows the sources of working capital, the uses of working capital, and the changes in working capital expected during the year. The increase in working capital of $42,010 can be reconciled with the changes in working capital items shown in Figure 24–16. The content and benefits of the statement were explained more fully in Chapter 19.

FINANCIAL CONTROL WITH BUDGETING

The control phase of budgeting consists of three major steps.

1. Comparing the actual financial performance with the budget estimates.
2. Identifying any significant variances.
3. Deciding what management action should be taken.

The emphasis of budgetary control is on both efficiency and effectiveness measures. **Budget performance reports** that show significant variances be-

**Objective 8:
Using a budget
for per-
formance re-
porting and fi-
nancial control**

Figure 24–17
Budget Performance
Report

KORT COMPANY
Sales Department
Budget Performance Report
Quarter Ending March 31, 1987

Controllable Expenses	Budgeted	Actual	Variance
Advertising	$ 4,500	$ 5,200	$ 700 U
Sales salaries	23,450	24,550	1,100 U
Travel	1,200	1,750	550 U
Entertainment	800	980	180 U
Utilities	200	210	10 U
Other	100	95	5 F
Total	$30,250	$32,785	$2,535 U

tween the actual and planned performance provide the feedback necessary to evaluate the financial results on the basis of management by exception. Unfavorable variances will be investigated to determine whether corrective action can be taken to improve future performance. Even significantly large favorable variances should be evaluated to be sure that the related estimates were correct. If they were too easy to attain, the estimates should be changed for the future. The performance reports are prepared for the business as a whole and for its various segments on a responsibility accounting basis. Only controllable revenues and costs should be included in the performance reports; it would be unfair to hold managers accountable for uncontrollable items.

To illustrate the basic format of a performance report, one prepared for the sales manager of the Kort Company is shown in Figure 24–17. The report includes the controllable expenses of the sales department during the first quarter. The "actual" column shows the actual costs incurred by the department, and the "budgeted" column contains the budget estimates for each category. The "U" indicates an unfavorable variance, while the "F" refers to a favorable variance. The sales department incurred expenses that exceeded its budget by $2,535. Unless sales are substantially higher because of the increased spending, these results will have an adverse effect on the firm's profits and will require corrective action if the financial goals of future quarters are to be achieved.

GLOSSARY

ADMINISTRATIVE EXPENSES BUDGET. Estimates of the administrative expenses for the budget period (p. 949).

BUDGET. A quantitative plan showing how resources are expected to be acquired and used during a specified time period (p. 936).

BUDGETING. The process of preparing a budget for financial planning and control (p. 937).

BUDGET PERFORMANCE REPORT.   A report showing a comparison of the actual and budgeted performance with an emphasis on any variances (p. 955).

CAPITAL EXPENDITURES BUDGET.   The acquisition of long-term assets planned during a future period (p. 950).

CASH BUDGET.   The cash receipts and disbursements expected during the budget period (p. 951).

COST OF GOODS SOLD BUDGET.   An estimate of the cost of goods sold required for the budget period (p. 947).

DIRECT LABOR BUDGET.   A projection of the direct labor needs of a budget period based on the expected production level (p. 945).

DIRECT MATERIALS BUDGET.   A projection of the direct materials that must be purchased to satisfy the production requirements of a budget period (p. 944).

FINANCIAL BUDGET.   The part of the master budget that shows the funding and financial position needed for the planned operations (p. 941).

GOAL CONGRUENCE.   The reconciliation of the goals of individual managers with those of the organization (p. 938).

MANUFACTURING OVERHEAD BUDGET.   A projection of the manufacturing overhead items required to support the expected production level (p. 946).

MASTER BUDGET.   A set of interrelated budgets representing a comprehensive plan of action for a specified time period (p. 939).

OPERATING BUDGET.   The component of the master budget that describes the revenue and costs required to achieve a satisfactory financial performance (p. 941).

PRODUCTION BUDGET.   An estimate of the number of units that will be manufactured during the budget period (p. 944).

SALES BUDGET.   A translation of the sales forecast for a budget period into detailed information concerning the products or services that are expected to be sold (p. 942).

SELLING EXPENSES BUDGET.   Estimates of the selling expenses needed to generate the expected sales volume for the budget period (p. 948).

DISCUSSION QUESTIONS

1. What is a budget? Think about your personal life and indicate how a budget can be used for your personal financial planning.
2. Why can it be said that the budgeting process in the typical business actually consists of multiple budgets?
3. How is a budget used for (a) planning and (b) control?
4. What is goal congruence and why is it important for a business?
5. What are the major benefits of budgeting?
6. What are the two major components of a master budget?
7. Why is an accurate sales forecast essential for effective budgeting? Why is it difficult to forecast sales accurately?
8. What are the most popular methods used to forecast sales?
9. Distinguish between a sales budget and a production budget.
10. What are the major purposes of an operating budget and a financial budget?
11. Why are inventory level decisions important in the budgeting process?
12. How are responsibility accounting and budgeting related?
13. The McDonald Company expects to sell 60,000 units during the upcoming year. It has 9,000 units available at the beginning of the year and wants to have 12,000

units on hand at the end of the year. How many units should the firm produce during the year?

14. Why is a reliable cash budget required even with an accurate prediction of a business's income statement performance?
15. You recently overheard a local businesswoman say, "My business involves too many uncertainties for budgeting to be practical." Do you agree? Explain.
16. Why is it important to distinguish between fixed costs and variable costs in preparing a manufacturing overhead budget?
17. How does budgeting assist management in developing its employment policies?
18. Is the budgeted income statement simply the product of combining a number of revenue and expense budgets?
19. What are the major steps in the control phase of budgeting?
20. How should management decide what costs to include in budget performance reports?

EXERCISES

Exercise 24-1 Preparing a Sales Budget
The Lettuce-Patch Company produces three dolls, which are sold to retail stores throughout the East. The company expects the following sales performance for the next year.

Doll	Selling Price	Annual Sales (Units)
Baby	$ 8	72,000
Mother	12	48,000
Father	10	96,000

The budgeted annual sales are distributed by month in the following percentages.

Month	Portion of Annual Sales
January	.03
February	.06
March	.04
April	.04
May	.02
June	.05
July	.06
August	.02
September	.14
October	.20
November	.22
December	.12

Required:
Prepare a monthly sales budget in units and dollars for the three dolls combined.

Exercise 24-2 Preparing a Sales Budget
The Russell Company is preparing a sales budget for 1987. In reviewing the actual sales data for the previous year, the managers involved agree that the number of units

of product A sold in 1987 should represent a 15% increase over 1986 sales; product B unit sales should increase 5%; product C sales should decrease 4%. The managers' projections took into consideration the general economic conditions and the anticipated changes in selling prices. The selling price of products A and B will increase 10% while the selling price of product C will drop 5%. The percentage of each product's sales occurring in a given quarter are:

	First Quarter	Second Quarter	Third Quarter	Fourth Quarter
Product A	25%	30%	15%	30%
Product B	20%	25%	35%	20%
Product C	30%	20%	25%	25%

The actual 1986 product sales data were:

	Unit Selling Price	Total Sales
Product A	$16.80	$394,800
Product B	10.80	194,400
Product C	14.40 × .05	302,400

Required:
Prepare a sales budget for 1987 showing projected dollar sales by quarter. Round all calculations to the nearest dollar.

Exercise 24-3 Basic Production Budget Preparation
The Accuracy Company produces two models of calculators, Basic and Memory. The projected operating performance data for the month of June are as follows.

	Basic	Memory
Estimated beginning inventory (units)	3,000	2,520
Estimated June sales (units)	7,920	7,380
Desired ending inventory (units)	3,300	2,340

Required:
Prepare a production budget for June.

Exercise 24-4 Analysis of the Budgeting Process
Choose the best answer to each of the following questions.

A. The normal starting point for the preparation of a master budget is the
  1. Direct labor budget.
  2. Budgeted income statement.
  3. Production budget.
  4. Sales forecast.
B. Which of the following would not normally be part of a firm's operating budget?
  1. Sales budget.
  2. Production budget.
  3. Budgeted balance sheet.
  4. Direct labor budget.
C. Which of the following would not normally be part of a firm's financial budget?
  1. Capital expenditures budget.
  2. Selling expenses budget.
  3. Cash budget.
  4. Budgeted balance sheet.

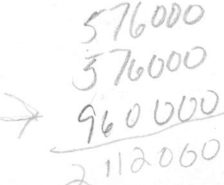

D. The concept of management by exception refers to management
1. Considering only unusual items.
2. Developing an assessment of all large items.
3. Considering only unfavorable items.
4. Considering only those items that deviate significantly from plan.

E. Which of the following is not a benefit of budgeting?
1. Performance evaluation.
2. Increased coordination.
3. Effective communication.
4. Required planning.
5. None of the above.

F. Whenever a firm prepares a sales forecast
1. It does not represent a firm commitment that cannot be altered if necessary.
2. It should be based only on sound quantitative analysis.
3. It should always be an extension of past performance.
4. It should be more detailed than the sales budget later developed.

Exercise 24-5 Determining Budgeted Purchases and Cash Disbursements

The Tyler Department Store has prepared a budget for the fiscal year ending April 30, 1988, based on the following data

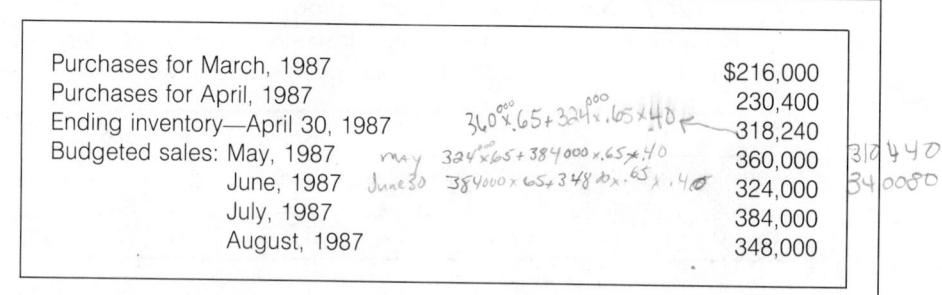

Purchases for March, 1987	$216,000
Purchases for April, 1987	230,400
Ending inventory—April 30, 1987	318,240
Budgeted sales: May, 1987	360,000
June, 1987	324,000
July, 1987	384,000
August, 1987	348,000

The cost of goods sold is 65% of sales, and the company's policy is to maintain a month-end inventory balance sufficient to meet the projected sales requirement for the following month and 40% of the sales requirements for the second following month. The company pays for 50% of its purchases in the month of purchase, pays 35% in the following month, and pays 15% in the second month following.

Required:
A. Calculate the amount of purchases for May and June of 1987.
B. Calculate the cash disbursements in May and June for merchandise purchased.

Exercise 24-6 Preparing a Direct Labor Budget

The Western Manufacturing Company maintains a finished goods inventory balance at the end of a month equal to 60% of the sales requirements of the following month. The ending inventory balance on October 31 was comprised of 648 units, and the projected unit sales for November, December, and January were 1,080, 1,152, and 840 units, respectively.

The labor requirements per unit produced are as follows.

	Time Required (Hours)	Rate Per Hour
Welder	3.5	$14.40
Assembly labor	2.7	12.00
Painter	5.0	8.40

Required:
Prepare a direct labor budget for November and December.

Exercise 24-7 Calculating Cash Receipts

The Roundout Department Store's budgeted monthly gross sales for July through December are presented below. The company's experience is that 70% of the monthly sales are on credit. All payments received during the month of sale are subject to a 2% cash discount. This policy applies to both cash and credit sales. Approximately 45% of the credit sales are collected in the month of sale, 30% are collected in the month following the sale, and 20% are collected in the second month following the sale; 5% are never collected.

The budgeted gross sales by month are:

July	$48,000
August	72,000
September	60,000
October	66,000
November	54,000
December	78,000

Required:
Calculate the forecast cash receipts for October, November, and December.

Exercise 24-8 Evaluating Future Cash Flow

The Barry Company is preparing a cash budget for May, 1987 and has provided the following information.

1. Seventy percent of each month's sales are on account, with 79% of the accounts being collected in the month of sale. The remaining accounts are collected the following month.
2. The cost of goods sold equals 65% of sales. Sixty percent of all purchases are paid for in the month of sale and 40% are paid for the following month.
3. The company policy is to maintain an inventory level equal to 50% of the next month's sales requirement. The requirement was met on May 1, 1987.
4. Selling and administrative expenses are budgeted at $12,000 for May. This includes $3,600 of depreciation. All selling and administrative expenses, except depreciation, are paid in the month incurred.
5. Cash balance, May 1 $12,600

April sales	42,000
May sales	62,400
June sales	54,000
April purchases	33,930

Required:
A. Prepare a budgeted income statement for May.
B. Prepare a cash budget for May.

Exercise 24-9 Evaluating Future Cash Flows

The Donovan Company has prepared a budgeted income statement for the month of June. The company pays for 60% of its merchandise in the month of purchase and pays 40% in the following month. Seventy percent of all sales are collected in the month of sale and 30% are collected in the following month. The annual insurance premium was prepaid in February, and the annual property taxes are due in November. All other cash expenses are paid currently. The company maintains a minimum cash balance of $600, and the cash balance as of June 1 was $1,020. A new piece of equipment costing $360 will be paid for in June.

Additional information:

May sales	$1,920
May purchases	1,080
June purchases	1,440

DONOVAN COMPANY
Budgeted Income Statement
For the Month of June

Sales		$2,400
Cost of goods sold		1,080
Gross profit		1,320
Operating expenses:		
Insurance	$ 90	
Property taxes	108	
Rent	180	
Wages	660	
Depreciation	60	
Total expenses		1,098
Net income		$ 222

Required:

A. Prepare a cash budget for the month of June.

B. How much cash can the owners of the Donovan Company withdraw during June and still maintain the minimum cash balance required?

Exercise 24-10 Preparing a Budget Performance Report

Southern Indiana University has used the following budget amounts for its management department's controllable costs during 1987.

Cost items	Fixed Amount	Variable cost per student enrolled
Employee salaries	$62,400	$ .60
Utilities	20,400	.18
Maintenance	21,600	.20
Supplies	16,800	.80
Duplicating	6,400	5.00
Travel	21,000	-0-

The actual enrollment for the management department for the year was 4,000 students. The actual costs incurred for the year were as follows.

Employee salaries	$67,100
Utilities	23,120
Maintenance	22,100
Supplies	21,750
Duplicating	28,400
Travel	25,600

Required:
Prepare a budget performance report for 1987.

PROBLEMS

Problem 24-1 **Preparing a Sales Forecast**
The Bailey Company manufactures a line of water heaters designed for apartment use. The company markets this line in two cities—Bay City and Cove City. Approximately 60% of all new apartment complexes in the two areas will have a water heater installed in each apartment. They have also projected that 5% of the existing apartments will install new water heaters to improve existing systems or replace old heaters that cannot be repaired. Based on past experience, the Baily Company anticipates it can obtain 30% of the new apartment construction market and 10% of the replacement market.

The company sells two models of water heaters—the standard and the deluxe, a more energy-efficient unit. Builders will use the standard model in 70% of the apartments they construct and the deluxe model in 30%. When an existing complex installs new water heaters, it will use the standard model in 25% of the apartment units and the deluxe in 75%.

The other information available is:

	Bay City	Cove City
Number of units to be constructed	50,400	61,200
Number of existing units	600,000	480,000
Selling price—standard	$190	$190
Selling price—deluxe	250	245

Required:
Prepare a sales forecast in units and dollars for the Bailey Company by market area.

Problem 24-2 **Preparing a Production Budget and Related Budgets**
The McCabe Company manufactures redwood patio and lawn furniture. The manager in charge of the production of picnic tables has been asked to prepare a production budget, a direct materials budget, and a direct labor budget for part of 1987 based on the firm's sales forecast.

The materials and labor requirements per table are:

	Quantity	Cost
Lumber	20 feet	$6 per foot
Stain	1 quart	3 per quart
Cutting labor	3 hours	9.60 per hour
Finishing labor	8 hours	13.20 per hour

The company requires an ending finished goods inventory for each quarter that equals 40% of expected sales for the next quarter. Also, the ending inventory balance of direct materials should equal 30% of the next quarter's production requirements. The inventory balances on January 1, 1987, are forecast as:

Lumber	30,240 feet
Stain	1,512 quarts
Picnic tables	1,440 units

The forecast quarterly sales in units are:

First quarter, 1987	3,600
Second quarter, 1987	7,200
Third quarter, 1987	4,800
Fourth quarter, 1987	2,400

Required:

A. Prepare a quarterly production budget for the first three quarters of 1987.

B. Prepare a direct materials budget for the first two quarters of 1987.

C. Prepare a direct labor budget for the first two quarters of 1987.

Problem 24-3 Preparing a Cash Budget

The Ely Company is in the process of preparing a cash budget for the coming year. The company collects 70% of its sales in the same quarter that the sale was made, 25% in the quarter following the sale, and the remainder in the subsequent quarter. Seventy-five percent of all materials are paid for in the quarter in which they are purchased, with the remaining 25% paid for in the following quarter.

The selling expenses are $12,000 each quarter, plus 10% of sales. Administrative expenses are $72,000 per quarter, including $24,000 of depreciation expense. The company is planning to buy equipment during the second quarter at a cost of $14,400 and to pay an $8,400 dividend in the first quarter. The cash balance on January 1, 1987, is $13,800.

The following sales and purchases data have been compiled for the preparation of the budget:

	Sales	Purchases
Third quarter, 1986	$120,000	$48,000
Fourth quarter, 1986	108,000	43,200
First quarter, 1987	126,000	50,400
Second quarter, 1987	132,000	44,400

Required:

Prepare a cash budget by quarter and in total for the first two quarters of 1987.

Problem 24-4 Preparing Budgeted Financial Statements

The King Company is preparing a quarterly budget for the three months ending March 31, 1987. The information available for the budget is as follows.

1. Cash sales represent 30% of all monthly sales. Seventy percent of all credit sales are collected in the month of sale and the remainder are collected in the month following the sale.

2. Merchandise purchases that are made on account equal 60% of the sales forecast for that month. Sixty percent of the purchases are paid for in the month of purchase, and 40% are paid for the following month.

3. Ending inventory on March 31, 1987, is projected to be $27,600.
4. Equipment purchases for the first quarter are budgeted at $2,400.
5. Other quarterly expenses are budgeted as follows: utilities—$5,520; rent—$15,600; salaries—$30,000. These expenses are paid when incurred.
6. Depreciation for the first quarter will be $4,800.
7. The balance sheet as of January 1, 1987, is projected to have the following account balances.

Cash	$ 8,520	Accumulated depreciation	$28,800
Accounts receivable	5,880	Accounts payable	2,880
Inventory	12,000	Common stock	24,600
Equipment	67,200	Retained earnings	37,320

8. Budgeted sales are: January—$62,400; February—$60,000; March—$57,600.
9. Ignore income taxes.

Required:
Prepare a budgeted income statement and a budgeted balance sheet for the quarter ending March 31, 1987.

Problem 24-5 Comprehensive Budgeting Problem

The Kiki Company is preparing a master budget for the first quarter of 1987 and has compiled the following data.

1. The company sells a single product at a price of $13 per unit. The sales forecast (in units) for the last quarter of 1986 and the first seven months of 1987 is:

	Number of Units
October	12,000
November	13,200
December	12,840
January	11,040
February	14,400
March	13,800
April	12,600
May	13,080
June	12,120
July	11,400

(handwritten: units 65,280 × 13 = 848640)

2. Sixty percent of the sales are collected in the month of sale, 25% are collected in the following month, and 15% are collected in the second month following the sale.
3. There will be no beginning inventories on January 1, 1987. The ending finished goods inventory should equal 15% of the sales requirements for the next three months, and the raw materials ending inventory should equal 40% of the next month's production requirement.
4. Ignore income taxes.
5. Eighty percent of the material purchases are paid in the quarter of purchase and 20% are paid the following quarter. Unpaid purchases from 1986 are $66,000 as of January 1, 1987. *(handwritten: .03 × 13 × 39240)*
6. Variable selling expenses are 3% of sales. Administrative expenses are $43,200 per quarter, of which $4,800 represents depreciation expense. Fixed selling expenses are $16,800 each quarter. All selling and administrative expenses are paid in the quarter in which they are incurred.

7. The product requirements are:

	Direct Material	Direct Labor
Per unit	1 lb.	.3 hours

The direct materials are purchased for $3.60 a pound. The direct labor wage rate is $12 an hour. The manufacturing overhead is $107,784 for the first quarter of 1987 (including $17,964 for depreciation) and is paid in the month incurred.

8. The January 1, 1987 cash balance is expected to be $7,200.

Required:

A. Prepare a sales budget for the period of November 1986 through March 1987.
B. Determine cash collections for the first quarter of 1987.
C. Calculate the number of units to be produced in the first quarter of 1987.
D. Prepare a direct materials budget for the first quarter of 1987.
E. Prepare a cash budget for the first quarter of 1987.
F. Prepare a budgeted income statement for the first quarter of 1987.

ALTERNATE PROBLEMS

Problem 24-1A Preparing a Sales Forecast

The Last-Long Corporation manufactures a line of dishwashers designed for residential use in the cities of Holbrook and Perry. Dishwashers will be installed in approximately 80% of all new residential units, and the company projects that 5% of all existing residential units will be replacing older dishwashers during the next year. Based on past experience, the company anticipates that it can obtain 25% of the new residential construction market and 10% of the replacement market.

The company markets two types of dishwashers—the standard and the deluxe. The standard model will be placed in 75% of new units constructed, and 25% of the builders will choose the deluxe model. Thirty percent of existing homeowners who buy will choose the standard model to replace their older dishwashers, while 70% will choose the deluxe model.

The Last-Long Corporatin has compiled the following data in the preparation of a sales forecast.

	Holbrook	Perry
Number of existing residential units	900,000	624,000
Number of units to be constructed	12,000	9,600
Selling price—standard	$350	$355
Selling price—deluxe	415	425

Required:
Prepare a sales forecast for the Last-Long Corporation by city.

Problem 24-2A Preparing a Production Budget and Related Budgets

The Pinacle Company manufactures upholstered furniture and is in the process of preparing a production budget, direct materials budget, and direct labor budget.

The labor and materials requirements per finished unit are:

Cutting labor	1 hour at $9 per hour
Finishing labor	2 hours at $10.80 per hour

| Fabric | 7 yards at $6.00 per yard |
| Lumber | 15 feet at $7.20 per foot |

The forecasted quarterly sales in units are:

First quarter, 1987	4,800
Second quarter, 1987	3,000
Third quarter, 1987	3,600
Fourth quarter, 1987	2,400

The company requires an ending inventory balance of raw materials that is equal to 10% of the next quarter's production requirements. Also, the ending inventory balance of finished goods should be equal to 20% of the next quarter's expected sales. The projected inventory balances as of January 1, 1987, are:

Fabric	3,108 yards
Lumber	6,660 feet
Finished goods	960 units

Required:
A. Prepare quarterly production budgets for the first three quarters of 1987.
B. Prepare direct materials budgets for the first two quarters of 1987.
C. Prepare direct labor budgets for the first two quarters of 1987.

Problem 24-3A Preparing a Cash Budget

The Howarth Company wants to prepare a cash budget for the first two quarters of 1987. The company's experience has been that 60% of sales will be collected during the quarter in which the sale is made, 25% will be collected in the quarter following the sale, 10% will be collected in the second quarter following the sale, and 5% will be collected in the third quarter following the sale. The company pays for 70% of its materials in the quarter of the purchase, and the balance is paid in the following quarter.

Selling expenses amount to $18,000 per quarter plus 15% of sales. Administrative expenses are estimated to be $48,000 per quarter, which includes $14,400 of depreciation expense. All selling and administrative expenses, except depreciation, are paid when incurred.

The company is planning to purchase equipment during the first quarter at a cost of $24,000. The company will pay off a $36,000 note, which will mature during the second quarter. The interest due at maturity will be $4,200. The company's anticipated cash balance as of January 1, 1987, is $18,000.

The company's estimated sales and purchases data are as follows.

	Sales	Purchases
Second quarter, 1986	$144,000	$84,000
Third quarter, 1986	132,000	72,000
Fourth quarter, 1986	168,000	96,000
First quarter, 1987	228,000	60,000
Second quarter, 1987	156,000	72,000

Required:
Prepare a cash budget for the first two quarters of 1987, by quarter and in total.

Problem 24-4A Preparing Budgeted Financial Statements

The McBride Company has compiled the following data in order to prepare a quarterly budget for the three months ending June 30, 1987.

1. Merchandise purchases are made on account and monthly purchases amount to 55% of the forecasted sales for that month. Seventy percent of the purchases are paid for in the current month and 30% are paid for in the following month.
2. Sales on account represent 80% of all monthly sales. Sixty percent of all credit sales are collected in the month of sale, and the remainder are collected in the month following the sale.
3. Principal payments on the company's note payable to be made during the quarter are budgeted at $6,000. Interest payments during the quarter will be $1,440.
4. Other quarterly expenses are budgeted as follows: salaries—$120,000; rent—$12,000; insurance—$3,600. These expenses will be paid when incurred.
5. The depreciation expense per quarter is $7,200.
6. The ending inventory as of June 30, 1987, is projected to be $14,400.
7. The projected balance sheet as of April 1, 1987 included the following accounts.

Cash	$10,800
Accounts receivable	41,400
Inventory	12,000
Equipment	62,400
Accumulated depreciation	9,360
Accounts payable	21,600
Note payable	30,000
Common stock	12,000
Retained earnings	53,640

8. Budgeted sales are as follows: April—$122,400; May—$132,000; June—$138,000.

Required:
Prepare a budgeted income statement and a budgeted balance sheet for the quarter ending June 30, 1987.

Problem 24-5A Comprehensive Budgeting Problem
The Dorr Company is in the process of preparing a master budget for the last quarter of 1987.

1. The company's single product sells for $37 a unit. The sales manager has prepared the following sales forecast (in units).

July, 1987	24,600
August, 1987	21,600
September, 1987	23,160
October, 1987	26,040
November, 1987	24,480
December, 1987	23,520
January, 1988	22,020
February, 1988	24,900
March, 1988	22,920

2. Sixty-five percent of all sales are collected in the month of sale, 20% are collected in the following month, and 15% are collected in the second month following the sale.
3. The beginning inventory of finished goods on October 1, 1987, is expected to be 10,104 units. There will be no beginning raw materials inventory. The ending finished goods inventory should equal 20% of the next two months' sales requirements. The ending raw materials inventory should equal 30% of the production requirements for the next month.

4. Eighty percent of the purchases are paid for in the quarter of purchases and 20% are paid for in the following quarter. Unpaid purchases from the third quarter of 1987 total $342,000 as of October 1, 1987.

5. The product requirements per unit are 2.5 pounds of material A and 1.5 hours of direct labor. Material A can be purchased for $7.20 per pound, and the direct labor rate is $9.60 per hour.

6. The budgeted manufacturing overhead amounts to $4.80 per unit based on expected production (including $.80 for depreciation), and all manufacturing overhead is paid in the month incurred.

7. Fixed selling expenses are $90,000 per quarter. Fixed administrative expenses are $111,600 per quarter. Fixed quarterly administrative expenses include $18,000 of depreciation expense. Variable selling expenses are 2% of sales. All selling and administrative expenses, except depreciation, are paid in the quarter in which they are incurred.

8. The beginning cash balance as of October 1 is expected to be $12,000.

9. Ignore income taxes.

Required:

A. Prepare a sales budget for the period of August through December, 1987.

B. Prepare a cash collections schedule for the fourth quarter of 1987.

C. Calculate the number of units to be produced during the fourth quarter of 1987.

D. Prepare a direct materials budget for the last quarter of 1987.

E. Prepare a cash budget for the last quarter of 1987.

F. Prepare a budgeted income statement for the last quarter of 1987.

CASE

CASE 24-1   Decision Case   Budgeted Income Statement and Cash Budget

The Bayside Medical Center is located in southern Florida. During the months of December through April, the center operates an outpatient clinic for the treatment of minor illnesses and injuries. Because of the seasonal nature of tourism in the area, the clinic is closed for the remainder of the year and regular patients are treated by other departments of the center. The clinic is organized as a separate profit center with its own budget and accounting records. You have just been assigned the responsibility of preparing a budget for the clinic's next five months of operations (December–April).

You have determined from past clinic performance and discussions with the medical center's management that the following are realistic projections for the next five months of operations.

Salaries. Six people will be employed in the clinic with a total monthly salary expense of $27,840.

Operating expenses. Monthly operating expenses for the clinic are expected to be $7,200. Depreciation charges of $1,200 are included.

Collections. Past experience has shown that 40% of the bills are paid in cash when the services are performed. Twenty percent of the bills are on credit without insurance and are paid in the month following the service. Thirty-eight percent of the bills are on credit and are covered by insurance. They are paid two months after services are performed, and the other 2% of the bills are never collected. The average bill per patient appointment is $30.

Payments. All salaries are paid in the month in which the services are performed. Eighty percent of the monthly cash operating expenses are paid in the same month, while 20% are paid in the next month.

Patient activity. The number of patient appointments expected for the period are:

December	1,320
January	2,640
February	3,120
March	3,720
April	1,800

Cash balance. The clinic will have a cash balance of $24,000 on December 1. A minimum cash balance of $2,400 is required for the clinic by the management of Bayside Medical Center at the end of each month. Whenever the cash balance at the end of a month is below $2,400, the clinic has to borrow the required cash from the center for the next month or as long as it is required, whichever is longer, at 15% interest. Whenever the cash balance exceeds $24,000 at the end of a month, the excess is transferred to the general bank account of the center.

Required:

A. Prepare a budgeted income statement for each month during the December through April period.

B. Prepare a cash budget for each month during the December through April period.

FLEXIBLE BUDGETS AND STANDARD COSTS

CHAPTER OVERVIEW AND OBJECTIVES

This chapter discusses flexible budgets and standard costs. When you have completed the chapter, you should understand:

1. The basic difference between a flexible budget and a fixed budget.
2. How a flexible budget is constructed.
3. The use of a flexible budget for performance evaluation.
4. The basic nature of standard costs and their role in financial planning and control.
5. The benefits of standard costs.
6. The various methods used to establish standard costs and the types of standards possible.
7. The use of standard cost variances.
8. The procedures required to calculate standard cost variances and charge standard costs to the *Work in Process Inventory*.
9. How a specific capacity level is chosen in the development of a predetermined overhead rate with a flexible budget.
10. How standard cost variances are disposed of at the end of an accounting period.

Flexible budgets and standard costs are two important managerial accounting tools. The master budgeting procedures discussed in the preceding chapter have a potential deficiency in many applications: all budgeted costs are estimated on the basis of a *single* level of activity for sales or production. A budget of this type is called a **fixed** or **static budget** since *only one* level of activity is considered. As long as the level of activity actually achieved is

Objective 1: Difference between a flexible budget and a fixed budget

approximately the same as the one planned, the fixed budget serves as a useful managerial tool. When significant differences between the actual and the budgeted levels of activity take place, however, the budgets should be revised to reflect these changes. This can be done with the use of a **flexible budget**, which is a series of budgets for different levels of activity. As we will see later in this chapter, a flexible budget is particularly important for planning and controlling manufacturing overhead costs.

Standard costs are predetermined costs used as performance targets for an efficient manufacturing operation. They are analogous to other performance targets used as the basis for measuring the level of achievement in many aspects of our lives, such as a B+ rating for recognition of academic performance, a par round of golf for a serious golfer, a recipe used by a restaurant to prepare a pizza, and the engineering specifications followed in the production of a calculator. Many of the performance targets required for financial planning and control will be in the form of standard costs.

PERFORMANCE EVALUATION WITH A FIXED BUDGET

As we learned in Chapter 24, the starting point in the development of a master budget is the sales forecast for the budget period. The planning phase of the management cycle is served effectively by this approach since all of the firm's activities are directed toward a common level of achievement. The production level and all budgets for manufacturing, selling, and administrative activities are based on the single estimate of sales. This is an example of a fixed budgeting approach, since cost and revenue estimates are developed for only one level of activity. A potential problem with using a fixed budget for control purposes is that it does not take into consideration the possibility that the sales or production goals of the firm may not be achieved. If the actual level of activity for sales or production differs *significantly* from that planned, performance evaluation is difficult to make with a fixed budget. For example, consider the comparison of the budgeted performance and the actual cost results achieved by the production department of the Naville Manufacturing Company shown in Figure 25–1.

Can we really say that the production department's actual cost performance was $64,550 less than its budget? This might be the conclusion based upon a fixed budgeting approach, although it would be erroneous. We also note that the department did not produce the 25,000 units budgeted, so all of the variable costs should automatically be lower with the 20,000 units actually produced. Remember that a variable cost changes in total amount over different levels of production.

The budget estimates in Figure 25–1 simply do not reflect what costs should be for the actual units produced. We cannot compare the manufacturing costs of one production level with those of another production level and expect the results to be of any value to management. Since the Naville Manufacturing Company's fixed budget is based on 25,000 units and only 20,000 were produced, a comparison of the actual variable costs for 20,000 units with budgeted

Figure 25–1
Fixed Budget Performance Report

NAVILLE MANUFACTURING COMPANY
Fixed Budget Performance Report
Year Ended December 31, 1987

	Budget	Actual	Variance
Production units	25,000	20,000	5,000 U
Variable costs			
Direct materials	$125,000	$110,000	$15,000 F
Direct labor	300,000	260,000	40,000 F
Indirect materials	12,500	11,400	1,100 F
Indirect labor	18,750	16,200	2,550 F
Utilities	31,250	24,600	6,650 F
Total variable costs	487,500	422,200	65,300 F
Fixed costs			
Supervision	60,500	61,400	900 U
Property taxes	8,700	8,700	0
Insurance	5,200	5,300	100 U
Maintenance	4,700	4,450	250 F
Depreciation	15,300	15,300	0
Total fixed costs	94,400	95,150	750 U
Total manufacturing costs	$581,900	$517,350	$64,550 F

U indicates an unfavorable variance.
F indicates a favorable variance.

amounts for 25,000 units will lead to incorrect conclusions. Instead, a flexible budget should be used to provide a **comparable basis** for evaluating financial performance when the actual level of activity is different from the one budgeted.

PREPARATION OF A FLEXIBLE BUDGET

A flexible budget is developed for a *range of activity,* rather than for a single activity level. As such, a flexible budget is said to be dynamic, since it enables management to *adjust the budget* to the actual level achieved. The adjusted budget will consist of the costs that should have been incurred for the actual activity level. The initial step in the preparation of a flexible budget is to distinguish between the fixed and variable costs. The cost behavior of each cost item over past periods can be studied to see whether it changes as the activity level changes. In Chapter 22, we illustrated how a **variable cost** varies in total amount proportionally with changes in volume, whereas the variable cost rate is constant on a per-unit basis. We also showed that a **fixed cost** will remain constant in total amount over a wide range of activity but will vary inversely on a per-unit basis. We will consider procedures for analyzing the cost behavior of specific costs in Chapter 26.

In the case of Naville Manufacturing Company, three of the manufacturing overhead items—indirect materials, indirect labor, and utilities—have been classified as variable costs along with the direct materials and direct labor.

Objective 2:
How a flexible budget is developed

The firm has established the following variable cost rates for the manufacturing cost performance.

Cost Item	Variable Cost Rate per Unit
Direct materials	$ 5.00
Direct labor	12.00
Indirect materials	.50
Indirect labor	.75
Utilities	1.25
Total	$19.50

The variable cost portion of the flexible budget will change for different levels of production, as we see in Figure 25–2. The range of production activity is from 20,000 units to 30,000 units. The variable cost rates are multiplied by a specific number of units to determine the expected variable costs for that level of production. For example, the indirect materials budgeted for 30,000 units amount to $15,000 (30,000 × $.50). The five fixed cost items remain constant over the entire range of activity (Figure 25–2). Consequently, the variable costs are the costs that "flex" over different levels of activity.

Figure 25–2
Flexible Budget

NAVILLE MANUFACTURING COMPANY
Flexible Budget
Year Ended December 31, 1987

	Per Unit	Levels of Activity 20,000	25,000	30,000
Production units				
Variable costs				
Direct materials	$ 5.00	$100,000	$125,000	$150,000
Direct labor	12.00	240,000	300,000	360,000
Indirect materials	.50	10,000	12,500	15,000
Indirect labor	.75	15,000	18,750	22,500
Utilities	1.25	25,000	31,250	37,500
Total variable costs	19.50	390,000	487,500	585,000
Fixed costs				
Supervision		60,500	60,500	60,500
Property taxes		8,700	8,700	8,700
Insurance		5,200	5,200	5,200
Maintenance		4,700	4,700	4,700
Depreciation		15,300	15,300	15,300
Total fixed costs		94,400	94,400	94,400
Total manufacturing costs		$484,400	$581,900	$679,400

PERFORMANCE EVALUATION WITH A FLEXIBLE BUDGET

The use of a flexible budget for cost performance reporting makes the budget estimates and actual results comparable, since they are both based on the same level of activity. Figure 25–3 presents a *flexible budget performance report* for the production department of the Naville Manufacturing Company. Instead of achieving favorable financial results that might be reported with the fixed budget shown earlier, the department *actually incurred an unfavorable variance of $32,950.* Both the "budget" column and the "actual" column in the report are based on the production level of 20,000 units. The flexible budget performance report represents a much more realistic evaluation of the departmental cost performance than the fixed budget performance report.

The variances shown in Figure 25–3 have meaning, since they relate to the cost performance only. Production differences have been eliminated by adjusting the flexible budget to the level of 20,000 units. The performance report provides management with a realistic indication of the areas that should be further investigated in order to control the production costs. For example, direct materials cost and direct labor cost exceeded the budget estimates by $10,000 (10%) and $20,000 (8.3%), respectively. Corrective action will be required if future profitability goals are to be achieved.

The dynamic nature of a flexible budget permits management to adjust it to any level as long as the same cost behavior patterns prevail. In the Naville

Objective 3: Using a flexible budget for performance evaluation

NAVILLE MANUFACTURING COMPANY
Flexible Budget Performance Report
Year Ended December 31, 1987

	Budget	Actual	Variance
Production units	20,000	20,000	
Variable costs			
Direct materials	$100,000	$110,000	$10,000 U
Direct labor	240,000	260,000	20,000 U
Indirect materials	10,000	11,400	1,400 U
Indirect labor	15,000	16,200	1,200 U
Utilities	25,000	24,600	400 F
Total variable costs	390,000	422,200	32,200 U
Fixed costs			
Supervision	60,500	61,400	900 U
Property taxes	8,700	8,700	0
Insurance	5,200	5,300	100 U
Maintenance	4,700	4,450	250 F
Depreciation	15,300	15,300	0
Total fixed costs	94,400	95,150	750 U
Total manufacturing cost	$484,400	$517,350	$32,950 U

U indicates an unfavorable variance.
F indicates a favorable variance.

Figure 25–3
Flexible Budget Performance Report

Manufacturing Company case, the actual level of activity was the same as one of the levels in the original flexible budget (20,000 units). Even if the actual activity level is not found in the flexible budget, management can easily adjust the budget to that level. For example, if the Naville Manufacturing Company had produced 22,400 units, the budget would be adjusted to that level and the results would be compared with the associated actual costs. The variable cost rates (totaling $19.50 per unit) would be multiplied by 22,400 to determine the total variable costs of $436,800, and the fixed costs would be the same as they were for the production of 25,000 units ($94,400). The total budgeted manufacturing costs for 22,400 units would be $531,200 ($436,800 + $94,400).

USE OF STANDARD COSTS

**Objective 4:
How standard
costs are used**

Chapter 23 demonstrated how a cost accumulation system can be used to determine the actual costs of producing a product. This information furnishes management with a *detailed record* of the manufacturing costs that are incurred in the production of a job or the operation of a processing center. The cost data are also used in the inventory valuation and income determination aspects of financial reporting. However, the results have serious limitations concerning the measurement of the efficiency of the manufacturing operation. Management planning must be founded on reliable projections of an efficient utilization of resources. Management control is concerned with a comparison of actual results with those planned, as we saw in the discussion of budgeting.

The limitation of historical or actual cost data is that they represent what happened, which is not necessarily what should have happened. Consequently, it is difficult to determine a reliable performance measurement base with historical cost data. Are the costs too high? If so, who is responsible? How can they be reduced? Are the costs representative of the future? These typical questions are difficult to answer with historical cost data. Efficiency evaluations are limited to historical comparisons, such as unit costs from month to month, and to management's judgment about what costs should be. The problem with trend analysis is that there is no guarantee that the operation was efficient to begin with, so it may be meaningless to compare the costs of one period with those of another period. In addition, difficulties will be encountered in assessing the impact of changes in such factors as the volume of production, wage rates, product quality levels, productivity, raw materials prices, and the cost of overhead items. Management judgment about what costs should be is hindered by the same limitations.

If a manufacturing firm is to operate efficiently, it must be certain that economical amounts of resource inputs are utilized in the production of its products. This is true for both job order and process costing operations. Standard costs are carefully predetermined measures of what costs should be to produce a product or perform an operation in accordance with management's planned performance. They serve as benchmarks against which the actual performance can be realistically evaluated. While our primary concern in this chapter is the application of standard costs in manufacturing firms, standard costs are also used in a wide range of other businesses, such as hospitals, restaurants, accounting firms, banks, and automobile service centers. In practice, standard costing is potentially applicable whenever the activities of a business are repetitive.

In a manufacturing operation, standards are used to plan and control direct materials, direct labor, and manufacturing overhead. The objective is to establish a standard cost for each unit of product by predetermining the cost per unit of the direct materials, direct labor, and manufacturing overhead required to produce it. Both the per-unit dollar amounts that should be incurred for the three manufacturing cost elements and the quantity of each that should be used are identified. The standard direct materials cost consists of a standard price per unit of material multiplied by the standard number of units to be used. Likewise, the standard direct labor cost is composed of a standard labor rate per hour, multiplied by the standard number of hours required. The standard amount of manufacturing overhead for a product is found by multiplying a predetermined overhead rate by some measure of standard production activity, such as standard direct labor hours. The predetermined overhead rate is the same as the one introduced in Chapter 23 when actual costs were accumulated.

BENEFITS OF STANDARD COSTS

The most important *benefits* of standard costs are the following.

Objective 5: The benefits of standard costs

1. Standard costs provide *reliable estimates* for the planning phase of budgeting. We noted in Chapter 24 that accurate projections for direct materials, direct labor, and manufacturing overhead are necessary to perform effective budgeting. Since standard costs are carefully predetermined costs, they provide the best basis for estimating future cost performance. Consequently, standard costs contribute significantly to the planning function of management.
2. Standard costs serve as **targets** in the application of responsibility accounting to evaluate performance and to control manufacturing costs. The standard costs represent measures of what costs should be, so any variances between them and the actual costs incurred can be investigated for potential corrective action. Cost control does not necessarily mean minimizing costs, but it does mean keeping them within acceptable limits. Responsible managers receive periodic reports that reveal any significant variances through the application of management by exception.
3. Standard costs can be used for inventory valuation with cost savings in the recordkeeping function. The inventories are maintained on the basis of standard costs without the detailed accounting of the actual costs needed in an actual costing system. Since the standard costs are predetermined costs, they are used to record the materials, labor, and manufacturing overhead as production takes place. A reconciliation of the actual costs is made at the end of an accounting period with variance analysis, eliminating much of the detailed accounting work and clerical cost incurred during the period.
4. Standard cost information is available on a timely basis for managerial decision making. Management must regularly make decisions concerning

such activities as product pricing, product profitability analysis, departmental performance evaluation, and utilization of resources. Standard costs can be used in many cases without waiting for the results of the actual performance.

5. Standard costs make employees *more aware of costs* and of their impact on the operation. Most employees will not be trained accountants and will be more concerned with operating procedures than with the costs associated with them. Since the standard costs represent what costs should be, they make the employees more cost conscious and time conscious, thereby promoting an efficient use of resources. An incentive wage system, tied in with standard costs, can be implemented to further increase the benefits from cost awareness. For example, a bonus may be offered to employees who perform their work within the standard amount of time allotted.

ESTABLISHING STANDARD COSTS

**Objective 6:
How standard costs are established and the types of standards possible**

A standard cost is made up of an input quantity and a unit price. For example, the production of one finished product may require five pounds of direct materials at a cost of $2 per pound. The standard direct materials cost would be $10 per finished unit. Product specifications must be considered carefully in the establishment of standard costs to ensure that desired quality levels are maintained. Standard costs are usually established with one or some combination of the following three methods: an engineering approach, analysis of historical performance data, and management's judgment concerning future operating conditions. Time studies, work sampling, and synthesizing procedures are examples of engineering techniques that can be used to develop standards. Their major purpose is to determine economical quantities of material and labor on a scientific basis. For example, a time study may be performed to determine the best combination of labor steps needed for a particular job. Historical cost data should not be ignored in the development of standard costs, even though they may have the deficiencies mentioned earlier. The most recent past, in particular, can provide valuable insight into what can be expected in the future. Finally, management's judgment concerning future performance must be weighed heavily. The managers responsible for the various activities are the persons closest to the day-to-day operations, so their opinions and knowledge must be considered. This is particularly important whenever external influences, such as union negotiations for wage rates and market conditions for material prices, are involved. In many businesses, a standards committee is formed and given the responsibility of coordinating the development and revision of standard costs.

Management must also decide what types of standards the firm will use. The choice between ideal standards and attainable standards depends upon *how demanding* management wants the planned performance to be. **Ideal standards** require the highest possible level of effort if they are to be achieved. They represent maximum efficiency and do not consider allowances for factors such as waste, spoilage, fatigue, work interruptions, and human error. Few businesses use ideal standards because they produce significant variances from all but the very best performances and may discourage average or above-average workers.

Attainable standards are preferred, because they represent targets that can be achieved with a reasonably efficient effort. As such, they are difficult but possible to attain and include allowances for departures from maximum efficiency. Once the standards are established, they should be reviewed regularly and revised whenever necessary to coincide with internal and external changes. For example, in inflationary times, material price standards will be changed frequently to keep pace with market conditions.

STANDARD COST VARIANCES

Standard cost variances arise when actual costs are different from standard costs. The cost variances enable management to evaluate the efficiency of the manufacturing operation and to improve the cost performance whenever necessary. *Standard cost variance analysis* is used to determine the amount of any difference between actual and standard costs, as well as to discover what caused the deviation. When the actual costs exceed the standard costs, a variance is **unfavorable**. A *favorable* variance occurs when the actual costs are less than the standard costs.

Standard costs can be used for analytical purposes only or can be incorporated into the formal accounting system. When they are used only for analytical purposes, standard cost variances are shown on management performance reports used to control manufacturing costs. As such, they are not recorded in the general ledger. The more complete treatment is to establish cost variance accounts that are used to accumulate any differences between the actual and standard cost performance in the general ledger. When the cost variances are recognized in the general ledger, the costs charged to inventories and, ultimately, to cost of goods sold are standard costs, instead of the actual costs incurred. The differences between the actual costs incurred and the standard costs included in the inventories or cost of goods sold are recorded in separate accounts. One account is established for each type of variance (e.g., the material price variance). An unfavorable variance will have a debit account balance, since, in essence, it is an *added cost* (the actual cost is more than the standard cost used). A favorable variance will have a credit account balance because it represents a *reduced cost* (the actual cost is less than the standard cost used).

In the following discussion of specific standard cost variances, we assume that standard costs and the related variances are recorded within the accounting system. To illustrate standard cost variances, we will refer to the Jackson Manufacturing Company's cost performance for January, 1987. The company has predetermined the following standard costs for the production of one drum of *Cleanup,* an industrial cleaning compound that is the only product produced by the firm.

Objective 7:
Use of standard cost variances

Direct materials—4 pounds @ $8.00 per pound	$32
Direct labor—2 hours @ $8.50 per hour	17
Manufacturing overhead—2 hours @ $7.00 per direct labor hour	14
Standard cost per drum	$63

The firm plans to produce one unit of product at a total cost of $63. During the month of January, the actual manufacturing costs incurred in the production of 4,100 drums were:

Direct materials—purchased and used 17,200 pounds @ $8.50 per pound		$146,200
Direct labor—8,100 hours @ $8.70 per hour		70,470
Manufacturing overhead:		
Variable overhead cost—	$18,200	
Fixed overhead cost—	45,100	
Total overhead cost		63,300
Total actual manufacturing costs for January		$279,970

Objective 8: Calculating standard cost variances and accounting for them

The first step in variance analysis is to compare the actual costs incurred to produce 4,100 units of product with the standard costs that should have been incurred. Any difference will be a total cost variance, which can be explained by a combination of material variances, labor variances, and manufacturing overhead variances. The total cost variance is computed as follows.

Total actual costs for January (shown previously)	$279,970
Total standard costs for January (4,100 units × $63)	258,300
Total unfavorable cost variance	$ 21,670

The next step is to identify the sources of the unfavorable cost variance of $21,670 incurred during January.

MATERIAL VARIANCE ANALYSIS

Any difference between the actual material cost and the standard material cost can be explained by a combination of a material price variance and a material quantity variance. The **material price variance** is the result of recording an actual quantity of direct materials at an actual price that is different from the standard price. It is used to *evaluate the performance* of the purchasing department and to *measure the effect* of price increases or decreases on the firm's profit results. In many cases, an unfavorable material price variance is not controllable by management because of unavoidable changes in market prices. Other causes of unfavorable material price variances are rush orders with large transportation charges, choosing the wrong supplier, an incorrect choice of quality for the materials involved, and lost purchase discounts because of late payments.

The **material quantity variance** arises when the actual amount of direct materials used is different from the standard amount of materials allowed for the units produced. The standard amount of materials allowed will be the number of units actually produced as finished products, multiplied by the standard materials required for each unit completed. The material quantity variance will provide a measure of a production department's efficiency in utilizing direct materials and will be the responsibility of the manager in charge of the related manufacturing activity. Common causes of unfavorable material quantity variances are materials of inferior quality, inexperienced labor, inadequate supervision, and faulty equipment.

Material variances can be computed and journalized as follows.

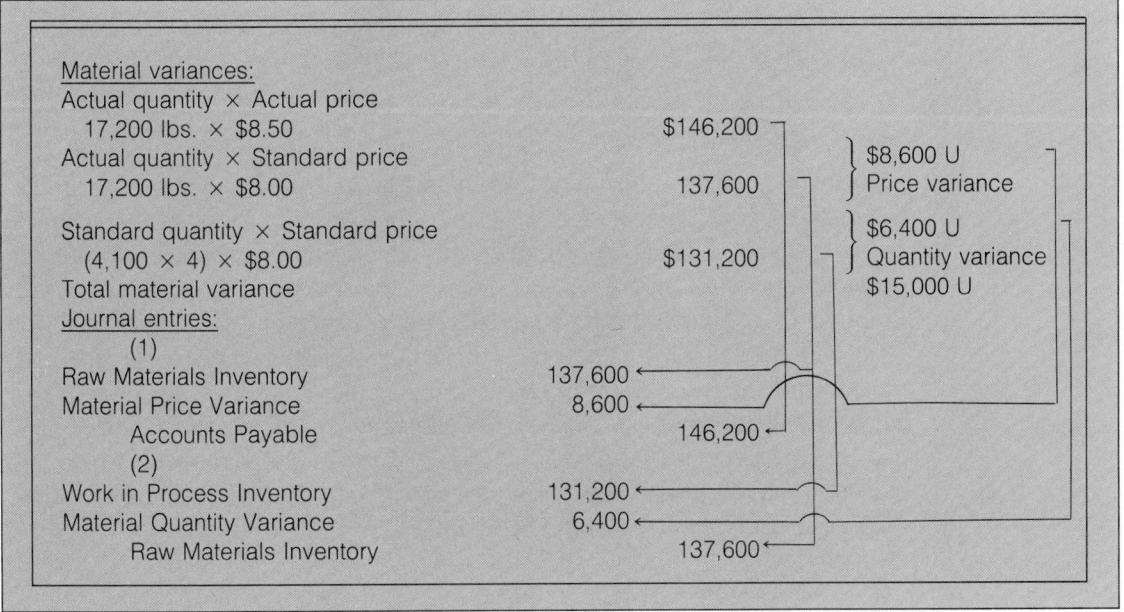

The "U" indicates an unfavorable variance. Since the actual cost of the material used ($146,200) exceeded the standard amount allowed ($131,200) by $15,000, an unfavorable total material variance was incurred. The material price variance was the result of a $.50 per-pound deviation from standard, multiplied by 17,200 pounds, or $8,600. The production of 4,100 units of product called for only 16,400 standard pounds of material (4,100 × 4) in contrast with the 17,200 pounds used. The difference of 800 pounds multiplied by the standard price of $8 indicates an unfavorable quantity variance of $6,400. Note that after the two journal entries are recorded, the work in process inventory has been charged for standard material price and quantity with the two variances isolated for performance evaluation. In journal entry (1), we record the purchase of the raw materials and isolate the material price variance at the point of purchase. This enables management to recognize the material price variance as early as possible and respond quickly to unfavorable situations. If we waited until the materials were used to record the material price variance, too much time might have passed for effective corrective action and cost control. Frequently, the purchase and usage of materials occur several months apart. Therefore, the safest approach is to determine the materials price variance at the time of purchase to allow for timely reporting. In journal entry (2), we record the materials issued to production and the related material quantity variance. Both unfavorable variances will require further investigation and corrective action if future profit goals are to be achieved. Some managers prefer a more simplified calculation of the two material variances, as follows.

Material price
variance = Actual quantity × (Actual price − Standard price)
= 17,200 pounds ×   ($8.50   − $8.00)
= $8,600 U

Material quantity
variance = Standard price × (Actual quantity − Standard quantity)
= $8.00   ×   (17,200   −   16,400)
= $6,400 U

Note also, that we have assumed that the actual quantity purchased and used are equal in this illustration. When they are not equal, we should compute the material price variance for the quantity purchased, instead of the quantity used, because we want to recognize the material price variance as soon as possible for control purposes. In such cases, the actual quantity purchased will be utilized in computing the material price variance and the actual quantity used will be utilized for the material quantity variance. Otherwise, the calculations of the two variances are the same as those shown in the case of the Jackson Manufacturing Company. To illustrate, assume that the firm purchased 18,200 pounds of material, instead of the 17,200 assumed earlier, but still used the 17,200 pounds during the production process. The computation of the material variances would be as follows.

Material price
variance = Actual quantity × (Actual price − Standard price)
=   18,200   ×   ($8.50   − $8.00)
= $9,100 U

Materials quantity
variance = Standard price × (Actual quantity − Standard quantity)
= $8.00   ×   (17,200   −   16,400)
= $6,400 U

As we see, the material price variance is based on the actual quantity *purchased*, whereas the material quantity variance is based on the actual quantity *used* during the production process. As a result, we have a material price variance of $9,100, which is $500 higher than the $8,600 variance computed earlier because of the 1,000 pounds of material that were purchased but left in inventory at the end of the period (18,200 pounds purchased and 17,200 pounds issued to production). Each of the 1,000 pounds cost an extra $.50 when compared with the standard price ($8.50 versus $8.00), for a total variance of $500. The journal entries required to record the purchase and usage transactions in this case are as follows.

Raw Materials Inventory (18,200 pounds × $8)	145,600	
Material Price Variance (18,200 pounds × $.50)	9,100	
Accounts Payable (18,200 pounds × $8.50)		154,700
To record the purchase of materials and the material		
price variance.		
Work in Process Inventory (16,400 pounds × $8)	131,200	
Material Quantity Variance (800 pounds × $8)	6,400	
Raw Materials Inventory (17,200 pounds × $8)		137,600
To record the direct materials requisitioned and the		
material quantity variance.		

LABOR VARIANCE ANALYSIS

A deviation between the actual direct labor cost and the standard direct labor cost can be divided into a labor rate variance and a labor efficiency variance. A **labor rate variance** occurs for the actual labor hours when the actual labor rate is different than the standard rate planned. In many cases, standard labor rates are determined through a collective bargaining agreement according to employees' *experience, skills,* and *seniority.* In other situations, the rates are established by the personnel department in conjunction with higher management. Consequently, the responsibility for a labor rate variance must be carefully assigned. The manager in charge of the production performance will be accountable for assigning workers with the correct wage rates to specific jobs. If an employee earning a wage rate different from the standard rate specified is assigned to a job, a labor rate variance—controllable by the related manager—will arise. For example, a highly-skilled worker may be assigned to a job requiring less skill and a lower labor rate. The result will be an unfavorable labor rate variance, which may be offset somewhat by a favorable labor efficiency variance (discussed next) if the work is performed faster than the standard hours allowed because of the employee's superior ability. This trade-off is particularly beneficial when an excess of highly skilled labor is available and would otherwise be idle if it were not assigned to the lower skilled work.

The **labor efficiency variance** is the result of using more or less direct labor hours as production input than the standard hours allowed for the units of output produced. The labor efficiency variance, used to measure the productivity of the labor force in achieving production results, will be the responsibility of the manager in charge of the manufacturing operation. Labor productivity is the output of products produced divided by the number of hours required to achieve that output. If a firm's labor productivity is rising, the business is producing more units of output with a given number of labor hours, which, in turn, has a positive effect on unit product costs and profits. The standard direct labor hours allowed are determined by multiplying the units produced by the standard direct labor hours per unit. We then compare the actual direct labor hours recorded in the accounting system with the standard hours allowed, in order to determine how efficiently the labor has been used. Unlike direct materials, direct labor hours are ''purchased'' and used at the same time, so we do not have a difference between the actual hours included in the variance calculations, as we did earlier with direct materials. Typical causes of unfavorable labor efficiency variances are faulty equipment, inexperienced workers, poor-quality materials, and inadequate supervision.

The two labor variances can be calculated and journalized in the following ways.

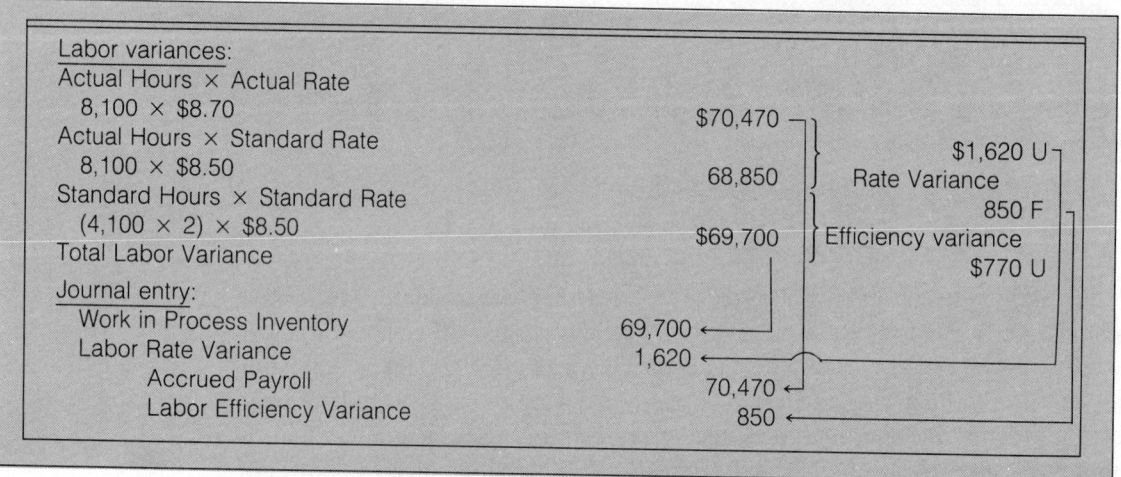

Again, the "U" indicates an unfavorable variance while the "F" identifies a favorable variance. The labor rate variance is unfavorable by $1,620, because the actual rate exceeded the standard rate by $.20 per hour ($8.70 − $8.50) multiplied by 8,100 hours. In contrast, the labor efficiency variance is favorable, since 8,100 actual hours of labor were required for the production output when the standard hours allowed were 8,200 (4,100 units produced × 2 hours per unit). Each of the 100 hours below standard saved the firm $8.50, for a total of $850. The journal entry for labor also charges the standard rate and hours to the *Work in Process Inventory*, so that it can be maintained purely on the basis of standard costs. Management will have to look at both labor variances to determine what corrective action is required. In doing so, any interrelationship between the two variances must be considered carefully. For example, the favorable efficiency variance may have occurred because, as we discussed earlier, highly skilled workers were used who could complete the job faster. This, in turn, may have caused the unfavorable rate variance, because highly skilled labor costs more than the standard rate paid for an unskilled job.

The two labor variances can be determined with a more simplified calculation, as follows.

Labor rate
variance = Actual hours × (Actual rate − Standard rate)
= 8,100 × ($8.70 − $8.50)
= $1,620 U

Labor efficiency
variance = Standard rate × (Actual hours − Standard hours)
= $8.50 × (8,100 − 8,200)
= $850 F

STANDARD APPLICATION OF MANUFACTURING OVERHEAD

In effect, the predetermined overhead rate discussed in Chapter 23 is a standard cost. When the rate is applied to the actual direct labor hours worked, the charge to *Work in Process Inventory* is a **partial standard cost.** The standard amount of manufacturing overhead in a standard cost system is determined by multiplying the predetermined overhead rate by some measure of standard production activity, such as standard direct labor hours, standard direct labor cost, or standard machine hours. For example, the standard cost information presented earlier for the Jackson Manufacturing Company indicates that the predetermined rate is $7 and that two standard direct labor hours are required per drum of *Cleanup.* Therefore, the standard amount of manufacturing overhead is $14 for each finished unit. In a standard cost system, the actual hours worked are not considered in the application of manufacturing overhead, since the applied overhead should not vary from the standard amount just because the actual and standard labor hours are different.

FLEXIBLE BUDGET FOR MANUFACTURING OVERHEAD

When we introduced the concept of a predetermined overhead rate in Chapter 23, we assumed for illustrative purposes that the consideration of one level of production activity was sufficient. As a result, we used a fixed budgeting approach, which we now know to be of limited value because of the fact that actual cost results can be compared only with budget estimates for the single level of activity. A flexible budget can be prepared for manufacturing overhead to avoid the limitations of a fixed budget. A distinction between variable and fixed costs is made and the budget is prepared for a range of production levels so that management can evaluate the impact of attaining an activity level different from the one planned. The production activity levels are based on the same measure of standard production used to apply the overhead. Whenever the standard production performance is different from that planned, management can easily adjust to the change by revising the original budget. The budgeted fixed manufacturing overhead for the standard production level attained will be the same as the amount in the original budget, but the budgeted variable manufacturing overhead will change because of its cost behavior.

Objective 9:
How capacity affects a predetermined overhead rate

A manufacturing overhead flexible budget for the Jackson Manufacturing Company is shown in Figure 25–4. The budget represents the January portion of the annual flexible budget used by the firm to calculate a predetermined overhead rate and to provide the basis for cost performance evaluation with variance analysis. Standard direct labor hours are used to measure the level of production activity, and they range from 7,000 to 10,000 for the budget period. Four production levels are budgeted as percentages of maximum capacity at 70%, 80%, 90%, and 100%. *Maximum capacity* is the measure of the highest production level a firm can achieve with its existing physical facilities and organizational structure. The variable overhead costs change at a rate of $2 per standard direct labor hour within the budgeted range of activity.

The fixed costs remain constant at $45,000. As a result, the total manufacturing overhead at any level of activity can be calculated with the following formula.

Manufacturing overhead = $45,000 + $2 (Standard direct labor hours)

Since a range of production activity is considered in the flexible budget, a single level of production must be selected for the calculation of the predetermined overhead rate. The choice of a specific production level is important because different overhead rates will be computed for different levels of production. These differences are caused by the fact that the fixed manufacturing costs per standard direct labor hour decrease as the number of hours increases. The following schedule illustrates the effect of cost behavior on the calculation of a predetermined overhead rate from the flexible budget of the Jackson Manufacturing Company.

		70%	80%	90%	100%
Standard direct labor hours	(A)	7,000	8,000	9,000	10,000
Variable overhead cost	(B)	$14,000	$16,000	$18,000	$20,000
Fixed overhead cost	(C)	45,000	45,000	45,000	45,000
Total overhead cost	(D)	$59,000	$61,000	$63,000	$65,000
Variable overhead rate per hour	(B ÷ A)	2.00	2.00	2.00	2.00
Fixed overhead rate per hour	(C ÷ A)	6.43	5.63	5.00	4.50
Total overhead rate per hour	(D ÷ A)	$ 8.43	$ 7.63	$ 7.00	$ 6.50

As a result, the total overhead rate decreases from $8.43 per hour to $6.50 per hour as the capacity increases from 70% to 100%. If the correct production level is not selected at the beginning of the period, the *wrong amount of overhead* will be applied to *Work in Process Inventory*, even if the actual cost performance is the same as the related budget estimates. For example, if the Jackson Manufacturing Company selects its predetermined overhead rate from the maximum capacity level, the fixed portion of the rate will be $4.50. If the firm only works 8,000 standard direct labor hours, the fixed overhead applied will be $36,000 (8,000 × $4.50), despite the fact that the budgeted fixed costs are $45,000. The variable costs do not cause the same problem, since they automatically adjust to the level of 8,000 standard direct labor hours, with the applied amount and budgeted amount being equal at $16,000 (8,000 × $2). The following four concepts of capacity can be considered for the choice of a production level within a flexible budget.

1. **Maximum capacity.** Highest level of production activity possible if optimal operating conditions exist with no delays, material shortages, or maintenance problems.
2. **Practical capacity.** Maximum capacity less reasonable allowances for departures from an optimal performance.
3. **Expected capacity.** Level of production activity expected for a specific year, given the firm's operating conditions and market demand for its products.

Figure 25–4
Manufacturing Over-
head Flexible
Budget

JACKSON MANUFACTURING COMPANY
Manufacturing Overhead Flexible Budget
Month of January, 1987

	Per hour	70	80	Normal Capacity 90	100
Percentage of capacity		70	80	90	100
Units of production		3,500	4,000	4,500	5,000
Standard direct labor hours		7,000	8,000	9,000	10,000
Budgeted manufacturing overhead					
Variable costs					
Indirect materials	$ .20	$ 1,400	$ 1,600	$ 1,800	$ 2,000
Maintenance	1.10	7,700	8,800	9,900	11,000
Utilities	.70	4,900	5,600	6,300	7,000
Total variable costs	2.00	14,000	16,000	18,000	20,000
Fixed costs					
Supervision		9,500	9,500	9,500	9,500
Insurance		3,000	3,000	3,000	3,000
Property taxes		9,300	9,300	9,300	9,300
Supplies		2,200	2,200	2,200	2,200
Rent		6,000	6,000	6,000	6,000
Depreciation		15,000	15,000	15,000	15,000
Total fixed costs		45,000	45,000	45,000	45,000
Total manufacturing overhead		$59,000	$61,000	$63,000	$65,000

Predetermined overhead rate per standard direct labor hour
   ($63,000 ÷ 9,000 hours) $7.00

4. **Normal capacity.** The average annual production activity that will satisfy
the market demand over a relatively long time, such as a three to five year
period.

Since sales demand is ignored with both maximum and practical capacities,
they are not popular methods for predetermining a manufacturing overhead
rate. If the sales volume does not fluctuate significantly from year to year,
expected capacity and normal capacity will be approximately equal. Many
accountants believe that normal capacity produces the *most accurate* manufacturing overhead rate when significant fluctuations in sales volume occur
between years. The longer period will *normalize* the fluctuations between
years and provide more consistent overhead application rates. We assume that
the Jackson Manufacturing Company uses normal capacity for the calculation
of the predetermined overhead rate and that it amounts to 9,000 standard direct
labor hours for the month of January. Consequently, the predetermined overhead rate is $7, as shown in Figure 25–4 and in the standard cost information
presented earlier. The rate consists of $2 for the variable costs and $5 for the

fixed costs. Each time that a standard direct labor hour is recorded, $7 will be applied to the *Work in Process Inventory* for manufacturing overhead.

UNDERAPPLIED AND OVERAPPLIED OVERHEAD

The difference between the actual manufacturing overhead and the standard amount applied to production is an overapplied or underapplied variance. If the actual overhead exceeds the amount applied, the result is an underapplied variance. In contrast, an overapplied variance exists when the standard amount of overhead applied to the work in process inventory during the period exceeds the actual overhead incurred. An underapplied condition is *unfavorable* because the cost of the inventory is understated while the reverse is true (it is *favorable*) for an overapplied situation. In order to control manufacturing overhead costs, management needs to be able to identify the sources underlying any difference between the actual and the applied overhead, just as it did with materials and labor.

OVERHEAD VARIANCE ANALYSIS

The division of the total manufacturing overhead variance for analytical purposes is analogous to the variance analysis discussed earlier for materials and labor, when a total variance was separated into *price* and *quantity components*. While manufacturing overhead variances can be computed in several ways, we will restrict our attention in this text to a *two-variance approach* consisting of a controllable overhead variance and a capacity variance. A **controllable overhead variance** is the difference between the actual manufacturing overhead and the manufacturing overhead budgeted for the standard production activity level attained (in this case the standard direct labor hours allowed). The actual manufacturing overhead will be recorded in the general ledger during an accounting period and the budgeted overhead will be determined by adjusting the flexible budget to the standard production level of the period. The controllable overhead variance is a measure of management's efficiency in utilizing the manufacturing overhead costs and will be the responsibility of the manager in charge of the related manufacturing operation. Common causes of controllable overhead variances are changing prices or rates for such overhead cost items as utilities, excessive use of indirect materials or indirect labor, and equipment breakdowns.

A **capacity variance** is the difference between the manufacturing overhead budgeted for the standard production activity level attained and the standard amount of overhead applied to the *Work in Process Inventory* during the period. The capacity variance is also called a volume variance or denominator variance because it results from having used the estimated level of production activity, rather than the actual level as the denominator when calculating the predetermined overhead rate. As pointed out earlier, the fixed overhead costs applied will not equal those budgeted when the standard production activity level attained differs from the original capacity level budgeted. Therefore, a capacity variance is the result of absorbing the budgeted fixed manufacturing overhead over a different production level. It is an important measure of the cost of capacity available but not utilized. For example, in the case of the Jackson Manufacturing Company, management's goal was to operate at a normal capacity of 9,000 standard direct labor hours, but only 8,200 standard direct labor hours were recorded. Consequently, the fixed cost portion of the predetermined overhead rate ($5) was not adequate to absorb all of the fixed overhead costs budgeted ($45,000). The reasons for the idle capacity may range from manufacturing problems to a lack of sales orders. As a result, either the production department or the sales department may be responsible for a capacity variance, depending on the circumstances.

The controllable overhead variance and the capacity variance for the Jackson Manufacturing Company can be computed and journalized as follows.

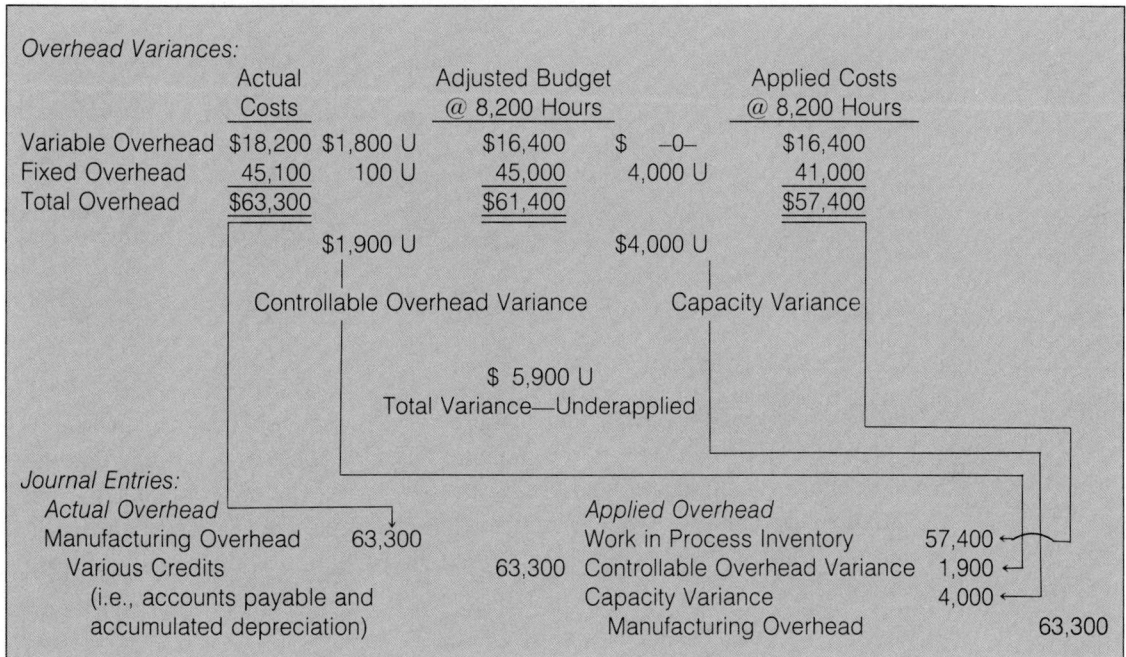

An unfavorable controllable overhead variance of $1,900 was incurred because the actual variable manufacturing overhead and the actual fixed manufacturing overhead exceeded the budget by $1,800 and $100, respectively. The unfavorable controllable overhead variance of $1,900 can be analyzed in more detail for each of the cost items involved, by developing the report shown in Figure 25–5. The unfavorable capacity variance of $4,000 was the result of working 8,200 standard direct labor hours instead of the 9,000 hours representing normal capacity. The 800 hour difference multiplied times the fixed cost rate of $5 per hour is equal to the capacity variance. The sum of the two overhead variances is equal to the amount of underapplied manufacturing overhead or $5,900. Again, notice that the *Work in Process Inventory* is charged only with the standard manufacturing overhead costs, which are calculated by multiplying the predetermined rate of $7 times the standard direct labor hours of 8,200, or a total of $57,400.

Figure 25–5
Controllable Variance Report

			Controllable Overhead
	Budget*	Actual	Variance
JACKSON MANUFACTURING COMPANY Controllable Overhead Variance Report Month Ended January 31, 1987			
Variable overhead costs			
Indirect materials	$ 1,640	$ 1,690	$ 50 U
Maintenance	9,020	10,150	1,130 U
Utilities	5,740	6,360	620 U
Total	16,400	18,200	1,800 U
Fixed costs			
Supervision	9,500	9,500	—
Insurance	3,000	3,000	—
Property taxes	9,300	9,300	—
Supplies	2,200	2,300	100 U
Rent	6,000	6,000	—
Depreciation	15,000	15,000	—
Total	45,000	45,100	100 U
Total manufacturing overhead	$61,400	$63,300	$1,900 U

*Adjusted budget for 8,200 standard direct labor hours.
U Indicates an unfavorable variance.

Recap of Variances

Earlier we noted that the actual manufacturing costs for the Jackson Manufacturing Company exceeded the standard costs by $21,670 (assuming that the direct materials purchased and used were the same). Having computed the six variances attributable to the manufacturing cost performance, we can divide the total variance, as follows, for further investigation with management by exception.

Unfavorable material price variance	$ 8,600
Unfavorable material quantity variance	6,400
Unfavorable labor rate variance	1,620
Favorable labor efficiency variance	(850)
Unfavorable controllable overhead variance	1,900
Unfavorable capacity variance	4,000
Total unfavorable manufacturing cost variances	$21,670

DISPOSITION OF COST VARIANCES

Objective 10: How standard cost variances are treated at the end of an accounting period

When cost variances are recorded in general ledger accounts, as they were in the illustration of the Jackson Manufacturing Company, their balances at the end of an accounting period must be disposed of in the preparation of financial statements. Cost variances are normally allowed to accumulate for external reporting from month to month, since unfavorable variances in one month are often offset by the favorable variances of another month. For interim reporting purposes, they are shown on the balance sheet with an unfavorable variance as an asset, and a favorable variance as a liability. At the end of the year, relatively small balances in the variance accounts are adjusted to cost of goods sold in the income statement. When the variances are significant, they should be prorated to the *Work in Process Inventory, Finished Goods Inventory,* and *Cost of Goods Sold,* because only actual costs can be used with generally accepted accounting principles.

The treatment of standard cost variances for internal reporting purposes is somewhat different. Since the standard costs represent management's goals for a specific period, it is customary to report the variances to management as they occur. This is accomplished by adjusting each period's cost of goods sold in the income statement prepared for management. For example, assume that the Jackson Manufacturing Company sold all 4,100 drums of *Cleanup* that it produced in January. The cost of goods sold section of a monthly income statement prepared for management would show the following.

Standard cost of goods sold (4,100 units @ $63)		$258,300
Plus unfavorable cost variances:		
Material price variance	$8,600	
Material quantity variance	6,400	
Labor rate variance	1,620	
Controllable overhead variance	1,900	
Capacity variance	4,000	
Less favorable cost variances:		
Labor efficiency variance	850	21,670
Adjusted cost of goods sold		$279,970

GLOSSARY

ATTAINABLE STANDARDS. Performance targets that can be achieved with a reasonably efficient effort (p. 979).

CAPACITY VARIANCE. The difference between the budgeted manufacturing overhead for the standard production activity level attained and the standard amount of overhead applied to the work in process inventory (p. 988).

CONTROLLABLE OVERHEAD VARIANCE. The difference between the budgeted manufacturing overhead for the standard production activity level attained and the actual manufacturing overhead for the period (p. 988).

EXPECTED CAPACITY. The level of production activity expected for a specific year, given the firm's operating conditions and market demand for its products (p. 986).

FIXED (STATIC) BUDGET. A budget prepared for only one level of business activity (p. 971).

FLEXIBLE BUDGET. A series of budgets prepared for a range of business activity (p. 972).

IDEAL STANDARDS. Performance targets that can be achieved only with an optimal performance (p. 978).

LABOR EFFICIENCY VARIANCE. A measure of the effect of a difference in the actual direct labor hours used and the standard direct labor hours that should have been used (p. 983).

LABOR RATE VARIANCE. A measure of the effect of a difference in the actual labor rate paid workers and the standard labor rate that should have been paid (p. 983).

MATERIAL PRICE VARIANCE. A measure of the effect of a difference between the actual price paid for material and the standard price that should have been paid (p. 980).

MATERIAL QUANTITY VARIANCE. A measure of the effect of a difference between the actual amount of direct materials used and the amount of direct materials that should have been used (p. 981).

MAXIMUM CAPACITY. The highest level of production activity possible if optimal conditions exist (p. 986).

NORMAL CAPACITY. The average annual production activity that will satisfy the market demand over a relatively long time, such as a three to five year period (p. 987).

PRACTICAL CAPACITY. The maximum production capacity of a firm, less reasonable allowances for departures from an optimal performance (p. 986).

STANDARD COSTS. Carefully predetermined costs that should be incurred to produce a product or perform an operation (p. 972).

STANDARD COST VARIANCES. The difference between standard costs and actual costs, which can be used in the application of management by exception (p. 979).

DISCUSSION QUESTIONS

1. Differentiate between a fixed budget and a flexible budget.
2. What is the deficiency of a fixed budget for performance evaluation purposes?
3. What are the major steps involved in the preparation of a flexible budget?
4. "The flexible aspect of a flexible budget consists of variable costs." Do you agree? Explain.
5. "Fixed costs are not important in the use of a flexible budget." Do you agree? Explain.
6. What is a standard cost?
7. What is wrong with comparing actual performance with past performance, in order to evaluate a firm's efficiency?
8. What are the benefits of standard costs?
9. How are standard costs established?
10. Distinguish between ideal and attainable standards.
11. Who is usually responsible for a material price variance? Who is responsible for a material quantity variance?
12. Who is usually responsible for a labor rate variance? Who is responsible for a labor efficiency variance?
13. The Balton Company has a standard labor rate of $8.60 per hour. Each of its finished products requires 5 hours of labor. During the month of July, 5,200 units are produced with 26,800 labor hours and an actual labor cost of $236,920.

What is the total labor cost variance? How much of it is attributable to labor rate? Labor efficiency?

14. What is a controllable overhead variance? What is a capacity variance?
15. Why is the determination of a specific capacity level important in the application of manufacturing overhead with a flexible budget?
16. Explain the following terms.
    (a) Maximum capacity.
    (b) Practical capacity.
    (c) Expected capacity.
    (d) Normal capacity.
17. The Colt Company uses normal capacity, measured in standard direct labor hours, to apply manufacturing overhead. During 1987, normal capacity was 12,000 standard direct labor hours, while the standard direct labor hours allowed for the production level achieved amounted to 11,520. Actual hours worked amounted to 12,240. The predetermined overhead rate was $6.00, of which $2.00 was variable. How much overhead was applied to *Work in Process Inventory*? What was the capacity variance?
18. Explain the basic difference in disposing of standard cost variances in internal reports, as compared with the treatment of them for external reporting.

EXERCISES

Exercise 25-1 Basic Concepts of a Flexible Budget

The Kelsey Company wants to prepare flexible budget cost estimates for the following items within a range of 10,000 to 12,000 direct labor hours.

	Fixed Cost	Variable Cost per Direct Labor Hour
Maintenance	$3,600	$.25
Depreciation	6,000	—
Supplies	840	.45
Utilities	1,800	.15
Rent	2,400	—
Insurance	3,600	—
Indirect labor	7,200	.75

Required:

A. Prepare a flexible overhead budget for 10,000, 11,000 and 12,000 direct labor hours.
B. Calculate the fixed, variable, and total overhead rates if 10,000 direct labor hours are chosen as the normal capacity.
C. Calculate the fixed, variable, and total overhead rates if 12,000 direct labor hours are chosen as the normal capacity.

Exercise 25-2 Developing a Flexible Budget and a Performance Report

The Robinson Company uses an annual flexible budget based on standard direct labor hours for the following manufacturing overhead items.

	Variable Cost per Standard Direct Labor Hour	Fixed Cost
Indirect labor	$.50	$3,600
Supplies	.15	4,500
Utilities	.25	8,100

During the year, the firm recorded 8,700 standard direct labor hours while working 9,100 actual direct labor hours and incurring the following actual costs.

Indirect labor — $ 8,000
Supplies — 5,790
Utilities — 10,315

Required:

A. Prepare a flexible budget for the three cost items using 8,000, 9,000, and 10,000 standard direct labor hours.

B. Prepare a flexible budget performance report for the three cost items, based on the firm's operating results for the year.

Exercise 25-3 Computing Material Price and Quantity Variances

The Lomax Company uses a standard cost system with which 30 board-feet of lumber at $4.20 per board-foot should be used to manufacture one office desk. The company purchased and used 9,900 board-feet of lumber to produce 300 desks. The total actual cost of the materials used in production was $42,570.

Required:

A. Calculate the material price and quantity variances.

B. How would your answer to part A change if the company had purchased 10,500 board-feet at a cost of $45,150 and used only 9,900 board-feet?

Exercise 25-4 Computing Materials Variances

The Darnell Company produces a laundry detergent labeled *Clean-all*. The firm uses a standard cost system, and the standard direct materials required for one box of *Clean-all* are as follows.

Chemical compound—3 pounds @ $1.32 per pound
Container —1 box @ $.06 per box

During March, the company purchased and used 76,000 pounds of chemical compound at $1.50 each and 25,600 containers at $.05 each. The actual production of *Clean-all* amounted to 25,440 boxes.

Required:

A. Compute the material price variances and the material quantity variances.

B. If the firm had purchased 80,000 pounds of chemical compound and used 76,000 pounds, what would the materials price variance amount to?

C. Who would be responsible for the variances in A and B?

D. What are some likely causes of these variances?

Exercise 25-5 Computing Labor Variances

The Destin Company has determined that 3.6 standard direct labor hours are needed for each unit produced and that the standard direct labor rate should be $8.50. During the month just ended, 12,000 units were produced, actual direct labor cost was $383,195, and actual direct labor hours were 44,300.

Required:

A. What was the total direct labor cost variance for the year?

B. Divide the total direct labor cost variance into the labor rate variance and the labor efficiency variance.

C. Who would be responsible for each of the variances in part B?

Exercise 25-6 Computing Labor Rate and Efficiency Variances

The Mitchell Company has decided that the labor standards for each unit produced are 3 hours of assembly labor at $8.50 per hour and 2.5 hours of finishing labor at $9.50 per hour. During May, the company produced 840 units using 2,820 hours of assembly labor and 2,200 hours of finishing labor. The company's direct labor payroll was $24,534 for assembly labor and $20,680 for finishing labor.

Required:

Calculate the labor rate and efficiency variances for the assembly labor and the finishing labor.

Exercise 25-7 Computing Controllable Overhead and Capacity Variances

The Watkins Company manufactures washing machines and applies manufacturing overhead using standard direct labor hours. The company estimated that it would take 36,000 standard direct labor hours to produce 7,200 washing machines during 1987. At this level of production, the company budgeted variable manufacturing overhead of $54,000 and fixed overhead of $162,000. Actual production for 1987 was 7,100 units, and the actual manufacturing overhead incurred was $222,100, of which $59,100 was variable manufacturing overhead.

Required:

Calculate the controllable overhead variance and capacity variance.

Exercise 25-8 Evaluating Labor Efficiency and Overhead Capacity Variances

The following six companies apply fixed manufacturing overhead on the basis of standard direct labor hours. For each company, the budgeted standard direct labor hours used to calculate the predetermined overhead rate, the actual direct labor hours worked, and the standard direct labor hours allowed for the actual production are presented.

Company	Budgeted Direct Labor Hours	Actual Direct Labor Hours	Standard Direct Labor Hours
Company A	14,400	12,600	13,200
Company B	19,200	18,360	19,200
Company C	15,600	16,800	17,400
Company D	12,000	13,200	12,240
Company E	13,200	12,000	12,000
Company F	18,000	18,600	18,600

Required:

For each company, indicate whether there would be a favorable or unfavorable overhead capacity variance. Also specify whether each company incurred a favorable or unfavorable labor efficiency variance.

Exercise 25-9 Direct Labor and Manufacturing Overhead Cost Variances

The Clifton Company uses a standard cost system. Direct labor information for the month of November is as follows.

Standard labor rate	$7.20 per hour
Actual labor rate	7.40 per hour
Actual direct labor hours	1,650 hours
Unfavorable labor efficiency variance	$1,080

The company had planned to produce 800 units of finished product during the month. Each unit requires two standard direct labor hours. Budgeted manufacturing overhead for the month was: variable costs—$3 per standard direct labor hour and fixed costs of $9 per standard direct labor hour, based on the estimated production of 800 units. The actual manufacturing overhead for the month was: variable costs—$4,650 and fixed costs—$14,900.

Required:

A. How many units must have been produced during the month?

B. Calculate the labor rate variance for the month.

C. Calculate the controllable overhead and capacity variances for the month.

Exercise 25-10 Evaluation of Standard Costing Basics

Select the best answer to the following questions.

A. When standard costs are used, the material price variance is computed by multiplying the

1. Actual price by the difference between the actual quantity purchased and the standard quantity used.
2. Standard price by the difference between the standard quantity purchased and the standard quantity used.
3. Standard quantity purchased by the difference between the actual price and the standard price.
4. Actual quantity purchased by the difference between the actual price and the standard price.

B. Which of the following would be least likely to cause an unfavorable materials quantity variance?

1. Machinery that has not been working right.
2. Workers with superior abilities.
3. Scheduling a great deal of overtime.
4. Direct materials of lower quality than is required by the standards.

C. Assume that

AH = Actual hours.

SH = Standard hours allowed for production.

AR = Actual labor rate.

SR = Standard labor rate.

Which of the following formulas should be used to calculate the labor efficiency variance?

1. $AR (AH - SH)$.
2. $SH (AR - SR)$.
3. $SR (AH - SH)$.
4. $AH (AR - SR)$.

D. An unfavorable labor efficiency variance indicates that
   1. The actual labor rate was higher than the standard rate.
   2. The total labor cost variance must be unfavorable.
   3. Overtime labor was used during the period.
   4. Actual labor hours exceeded the standard hours allowed.
F. A debit balance in the labor efficiency variance account indicates that
   1. Actual hours exceeded standard hours.
   2. Standard hours exceeded actual hours.
   3. Standard rate and standard hours exceeded actual rate and actual hours.
   4. Actual rate and actual hours exceeded standard rate and standard hours.
G. Information on the Harris Company's direct materials cost is as follows.
   Standard price per unit $7.20
   Actual quantity purchased   1,600
   Favorable materials price variance $480
   The actual purchase price per unit is
   1. $6.12.
   2. $6.90.
   3. $6.22.
   4. $7.50.

PROBLEMS

Problem 25-1   Use of a Flexible Budget Performance Report
The Frey Company has prepared a fixed budget performance report for the year ending December 31, 1987, as follows.

	Budget	Actual	Variance
Units of production	42,000	44,400	2,400 U
Manufacturing costs			
Direct materials	$273,000	$296,148	$23,148 U
Direct labor	346,500	364,524	18,024 U
Manufacturing overhead			
Variable costs			
Indirect labor	68,040	75,036	6,996 U
Supplies	23,940	22,200	1,740 F
Repairs	13,860	15,984	2,124 U
Total variable overhead	105,840	113,220	7,380 U
Fixed costs			
Insurance	4,800	5,040	240 U
Rent	14,400	14,400	0
Depreciation	12,000	12,000	0
Supervisory salaries	25,200	25,800	600 U
Total fixed overhead	56,400	57,240	840 U
Total manufacturing overhead	162,240	170,460	8,220 U
Total manufacturing costs	$781,740	$831,132	$49,392 U

Required:

Convert the fixed budget performance report to a flexible budget performance report.

Problem 25-2 Evaluating Variances from Standard Costs

The JGH Company had a total favorable direct labor variance of $264 for the month of May. The standard labor rate was $7.20, but due to a recent pay increase the labor rate variance for May was $312, unfavorable. The actual hours of direct labor used in production were 624. The company's total direct material variance for May was $96, unfavorable, and the material quantity variance was $360, unfavorable. The actual cost of the materials used in production was $3,696; the standard quantity of direct materials for May's production was 1,200 pounds.

Required:

Calculate the actual labor wage rate per unit and the standard direct labor hours allowed for the units produced. Also determine the standard price, the actual price, and the actual number of pounds for the materials used in production.

Problem 25-3 Determining Standard Cost Variances

The Arnold Company uses a standard cost system and has prepared the following flexible budget.

	75%	90%
Capacity		
Production in units	3,600	4,320
Manufacturing overhead		
Variable costs		
Indirect labor	$11,700	$14,040
Supplies	2,700	3,240
Repairs	720	864
Utilities	1,260	1,512
Total variable costs	16,380	19,656
Fixed costs		
Rent	10,800	10,800
Insurance	6,000	6,000
Property taxes	3,600	3,600
Depreciation	2,064	2,064
Total fixed costs	22,464	22,464
Total manufacturing overhead	$38,844	$42,120

The standard cost data for the company's single product are:

> Direct labor —5 hours at $8 per hour
> Direct materials—20 pounds at $2 per pound

Manufacturing overhead is five standard direct labor hours at an unknown cost per hour. The company uses normal capacity of 90% for the calculation of the predetermined overhead rate applied to standard direct labor hours. The company actually operated at 75% of capacity and produced 3,600 units. The actual costs were:

Direct labor: 18,640 hours at $7.80 per hour	$145,392
Direct materials: 71,640 pounds at $2.10 per pound	150,444
Rent	10,800
Insurance	6,000
Property taxes	3,600
Depreciation	2,064
Indirect labor	11,772
Supplies	2,556
Repairs	648
Utilities	1,440

Required:

A. Calculate the predetermined overhead rate.

B. Calculate the price (rate) and quantity (efficiency) variances for material (labor).

C. Compute the controllable overhead and capacity variances for manufacturing overhead.

Problem 25-4 Calculating Standard Cost Variances

The Ester Company has provided the following information about the company's only product.

Standard direct materials price	$1.60 per pound
Standard direct labor rate	8.20 per hour
Standard direct labor hours per unit	3 hours
Standard materials per unit	5 pounds
Variable manufacturing overhead	$3 per standard direct labor hour
Fixed manufacturing overhead	7.50 per standard direct labor hour
Normal capacity for the month	7,200 units

During the preceding month, the actual production was 7,560 units. The company purchased and used 39,000 pounds of material at a cost of $1.75 per pound. The average rate paid for the 22,800 hours of direct labor was $8.40 per hour. The actual variable manufacturing overhead was $67,080, and the actual fixed manufacturing overhead was $163,000.

Required:

A. Compute the material price and quantity variances and the labor rate and efficiency variances.

B. Calculate the controllable overhead and capacity variances.

C. Calculate the material price variance if the company purchased 41,000 pounds of materials instead of 39,000 pounds.

Problem 25-5 Accounting for Variances from Standard Performance

The Bond Company has predetermined the following standard costs needed to produce one unit of product. Also shown are the actual costs incurred during the previous month. The actual production was 2,880 units; budgeted production was a normal capacity of 3,000 units. The firm uses the normal capacity to calculate its predetermined overhead rate.

	Standard Cost	Actual Cost
Materials	7 feet @ $6.50 per yard	6.8 feet @ $6.65 per yard
Labor	3.2 hours @ $9.20 per hour	3.4 hours @ $9.60 per hour
Variable manufacturing overhead	3.2 hours @ $1.10 per hour	3.4 hours @ $1.25 per hour
Fixed manufacturing overhead	3.2 hours @ $5.20 per hour	$17.65 per unit produced

Required:
A. Calculate the labor rate and efficiency variances.
B. Calculate the material price and quantity variances.
C. Calculate the controllable overhead and capacity variances.
D. Prepare journal entries to record the costs incurred in work in process and related variances for materials, labor, and manufacturing overhead.

ALTERNATE PROBLEMS

Problem 25-1A Use of a Flexible Budget Performance Report

Kevin's Supply Company has prepared the following fixed budget performance report for the year ending July 31, 1987.

	Budget	Actual	Variance
Units of production	18,000	15,600	2,400 U
Manufacturing costs			
Direct materials	$162,000	$144,300	$17,700 F
Direct labor	126,000	107,640	18,360 F
Manufacturing overhead			
Variable costs			
Indirect labor	18,000	16,380	1,620 F
Supplies	27,000	27,300	300 U
Repairs	13,500	14,040	540 U
Total variable overhead	58,500	57,720	780 F
Fixed costs			
Depreciation	63,600	63,720	120 U
Insurance	1,200	960	240 F
Rent	6,000	6,000	—
Salaries	8,400	8,640	240 U
Total fixed overhead	79,200	79,320	120 U
Total manufacturing overhead	137,700	137,040	660 F
Total manufacturing costs	$425,700	$388,980	$36,720 F

Required:
Prepare a flexible budget performance report that corrects the deficiencies of the report just shown.

Problem 25-2A Evaluating Variances from Standard Costs

The Burton Company had a total unfavorable material cost variance of $360. The material price variance was $240, unfavorable. The standard cost of material was $2 per pound, and the total standard cost of the materials for May's production was $4,680. The company's total direct labor variance was $120, unfavorable. The actual cost of labor was $10,350, and the actual labor rate was $11.50. The labor efficiency variance was $330, favorable.

Required:
A. Calculate the standard direct labor hours for the units produced.
B. Determine the actual number of direct labor hours incurred, and the standard labor rate.
C. Calculate the actual quantity of materials used in production, the actual unit price of the materials, and the standard quantity of materials allowed for the production level achieved.

Problem 25-3A Determining Standard Cost Variances

The Arias Company has prepared the following summarized manufacturing overhead budget used in a standard cost system.

	90%	95%
Capacity	90%	95%
Production in units	21,600	22,800
Manufacturing overhead		
Variable costs	$ 64,800	$ 68,400
Fixed costs	171,000	171,000
Total	$235,800	$239,400

The standard cost data for the company's only product are:

Direct materials	18 pounds at $4 per pound
Direct labor	6 hours at $12 per hour
Manufacturing overhead	6 hours at $1.75 per hour

The company uses normal capacity of 95% for the calculation of the predetermined overhead rate, which is based on standard direct labor hours. The company actually operated at 90% of capacity, producing 21,600 units and incurring the following costs.

Direct materials—391,500 pounds at $3.90 per pound	$1,526,850
Direct labor—131,400 hours at $12.10 per hour	1,589,940
Variable manufacturing overhead	67,392
Fixed manufacturing overhead	172,300

Required:
A. Calculate the price (rate) and quantity (efficiency) variances for direct materials (and labor).
B. Calculate the controllable overhead and capacity variances for manufacturing overhead.

Problem 25-4A Calculating Standard Cost Variances

The Milton Company produced 4,560 units during the previous month. The company had purchased and used 37,680 pounds of material at a cost of $3.60 per pound. The actual variable manufacturing overhead was $58,700, and the actual fixed manufacturing overhead was $115,800. The company used 18,820 actual hours of direct labor, and the actual wage rate was $7.30 per hour.

The company's standard costs for the product are.

Standard quantity of direct materials per unit	8 pounds
Standard hours of direct labor per unit	4 hours
Standard direct material cost per pound	$3.70
Standard direct labor rate per hour	7.10
Variable overhead rate per standard direct labor hour	$3.00
Fixed overhead rate per standard direct labor hour	6.00
Predetermined overhead rate	$9.00
Normal capacity in units	4,800

Required:

A. Calculate the material price and quantity variances.
B. Calculate the labor rate and efficiency variances.
C. Calculate the controllable overhead and capacity variances.
D. Assume that the company purchased 42,680 pounds of materials instead of 37,680 pounds. What is the materials price variance as a result of this change?

Problem 25-5A Accounting for Variances from Standard Performance

The Tuttle Company has compiled the following data for the standard costs planned and actual costs incurred for each unit produced during the previous month.

	Standard Costs	Actual Costs
Labor	6 hours @ $8.00 per hour	6.2 hours @ $8.20 per hour
Material	4.5 pounds @ $5.10 per pound	4.7 pounds @ $4.90 per pound
Variable manufacturing overhead	6 hours @ $3.50 per hour	6.2 hours @ $3.65 per hour
Fixed manufacturing overhead	6 hours @ $7.60 per hour	$45 per unit produced

The actual production was 6,120 units; budgeted production was for a normal capacity of 6,000 units. The firm uses normal capacity to calculate the predetermined overhead rate.

Required:

A. Calculate the material price and quantity variances.
B. Calculate the labor rate and efficiency variances.
C. Calculate the controllable overhead and capacity variances.
D. Prepare journal entries to record the costs incurred in work in process and the related variances for materials, labor, and manufacturing overhead.

CASE

CASE 25-1 Decision Case Establishing the Basis for Standard Labor Hours

The Botwil Company produces several models of robots that are used to manufacture automobiles. The firm has been in existence for only five years and has experienced significantly higher production costs during the past three years than previously. A job order cost system using actual cost data has been used to accumulate product costs. The president of the firm, Bill Botwil, has an engineering background. He has analyzed the cost data from the performance of the past three years and is alarmed because labor costs have increased 60% during that period. In turn, the company's profits have declined by 80%.

Mr. Botwil hired an engineering consulting firm to evaluate the labor cost performance and establish labor standards for the future. In analyzing the report prepared by the engineering consulting firm, the president notes the following amounts of time required by several workers to perform a certain operation in the production of a particular robot.

Worker	Time Required (Hours)
J. Jackson	5.5
H. Hegerty	5.5
J. Metzger	5.5
R. Hart	5.8
D. Madden	6.2
B. Burns	6.2
V. Rogers	6.2
D. Douglas	6.6
B. Liebman	7.2
S. Starr	7.3
Average	6.2

In addition, the president is further confused because the engineering consulting firm has informed him that the operation in question should be performed in five hours if ideal operating conditions and labor efficiency exist. The firm's head accountant advises the president that the standard labor quantity should be 5.5 hours for the operation because that time has been achieved by three workers. However, the production manager involved says that the average amount of labor (6.2 hours) should be used as the standard. The president believes that the choice of an appropriate labor standard for this operation is an important decision because the same reasoning will be used for all production operations in order to control future labor costs.

Required:

A. What is the difference between an ideal standard cost and an attainable standard cost?

B. What should be established as the standard hours of labor in this case? Why?

PART 8

BUSINESS DECISION MAKING

26

COST-VOLUME-PROFIT RELATIONSHIPS

CHAPTER OVERVIEW AND OBJECTIVES

This chapter covers the subject of cost–volume–profit relationships. When you have completed the chapter, you should understand:

1. The importance of cost behavior analysis for managerial accounting applications.
2. The basic techniques used to determine linear cost functions.
3. The significance of the relevant range.
4. The benefits of a contribution margin-oriented income statement.
5. The basic differences between absorption costing income statements and variable costing income statements.
6. The benefits and limitations of variable costing.
7. How profits can be planned with cost–volume–profit analysis.
8. The calculation and application of break-even sales.
9. The use of a cost–volume–profit chart to evaluate the profitability of different levels of business activity.
10. The evaluation of changes in such factors as selling price, sales volume, sales mix, and costs with cost–volume–profit analysis.
11. How to use contribution margin variance analysis.

In Chapter 24, we emphasized the importance of a planned profit performance. Managers are constantly faced with decisions concerning *selling prices, sales volume, sales mix,* and *costs* in their search for the combination of these factors that will produce acceptable profits. To find the right combination, management must be able to evaluate the effect on net income of interrelationships among the four factors. **Cost–volume–profit (CVP) analysis** is an important managerial accounting technique used to determine how costs and profits are affected by changes in the level of business activity. It can assist in answering such questions as:

1. What is the firm's break-even point—the sales level at which the business will neither earn a profit nor incur a loss?
2. What will be the impact on sales volume and profit of increasing advertising expenses?
3. What level of sales must be achieved to earn a desired amount of net income?
4. If selling prices are increased or decreased, what will be the effect on sales volume?
5. If a variable cost, such as direct labor, is replaced with a fixed cost, such as equipment depreciation, what will be the impact on profits?
6. How much additional sales volume is required to offset a pending increase in direct materials cost by a vendor?
7. If additional plant capacity is acquired at a higher level of fixed manufacturing overhead cost, what will happen to net income?
8. What is the most profitable sales mix?

When the cost behavior concepts introduced in Chapter 22 are combined with information concerning selling prices, sales volume, and sales mix, the effect of a change in the level of business activity can be evaluated effectively with CVP analysis. Thus, knowledge about cost behavior patterns is an integral part of CVP analysis. Many manufacturing firms develop the cost data required for CVP analysis within the accounting system by using the variable costing method of inventory valuation (also introduced in Chapter 22) instead of the absorption costing method we have been concerned with so far in our discussion of manufacturing accounting.

COST BEHAVIOR ANALYSIS REVISITED

Chapter 22 introduced the concept of **cost behavior**, which is the measure of how a cost will respond to changes in the level of business activity. Several types of cost behavior are possible, but the three most important ones for CVP analysis are variable costs, fixed costs, and mixed costs. Recall that a variable cost will *vary in total amount proportionately with some measure of activity or volume,* such as sales dollars, products produced, or direct labor hours. In contrast, a fixed cost will *remain constant in total amount* over a wide range of activity. A third type of cost behavior is a **mixed cost** (sometimes called a semivariable cost), which contains both fixed cost and variable cost components.

The managerial accountant must be able to evaluate each cost item incurred by the firm, in order to determine the cost function that best describes the item's cost behavior. In its most basic form, a **cost function** is a relationship between cost as a dependent variable and some measure of activity or volume as an independent variable. For example, total manufacturing cost depends on

Objective 1:
Why cost behavior is important

the number of units produced, so that cost would be the dependent variable and the units produced would be the independent variable. In more advanced cases (which are beyond the scope of this text), more than one independent variable can be considered.

Objective 2: How a linear cost function is determined

An important aspect of CVP analysis is that all cost functions are assumed to be **linear** (in the form of a straight line) so that the rate of change is constant and easy to predict. As such, the cost function used in CVP analysis can be expressed as a linear equation, as follows.

$$y = a + bx$$

{ You should recall from your algebra course that this is called the slope-intercept form of the equation for any straight line

where:

- y = the total cost as a dependent variable.
- a = the fixed cost portion of the total cost (also called the y intercept because it is the point where a linear cost function that is graphed touches the vertical axis as we will see later).
- b = the variable cost rate that is the slope (rate of change) of the linear cost function.
- x = the measure of activity or volume as an independent variable. Examples are sales dollars, units produced, and direct labor hours.

Remember that we developed a flexible manufacturing overhead budget in Chapter 25 based on the following formula.

Manufacturing overhead = $45,000 + $2 (Standard direct labor hours)

This is an example of a linear cost function in which manufacturing overhead (y) is equal to the sum of the fixed cost portion (a) plus the variable cost rate of $2 ($b$) multiplied by the standard direct labor hours as a measure of activity (x). In this case, manufacturing overhead is a mixed cost, because it contains both fixed and variable costs.

The three basic cost functions—fixed, variable, and mixed—can be graphed as shown in Figure 26–1. Unfortunately, many firms experience some costs that are not exactly variable and others that are not exactly fixed, over the

Figure 26–1
Three Basic Cost Functions

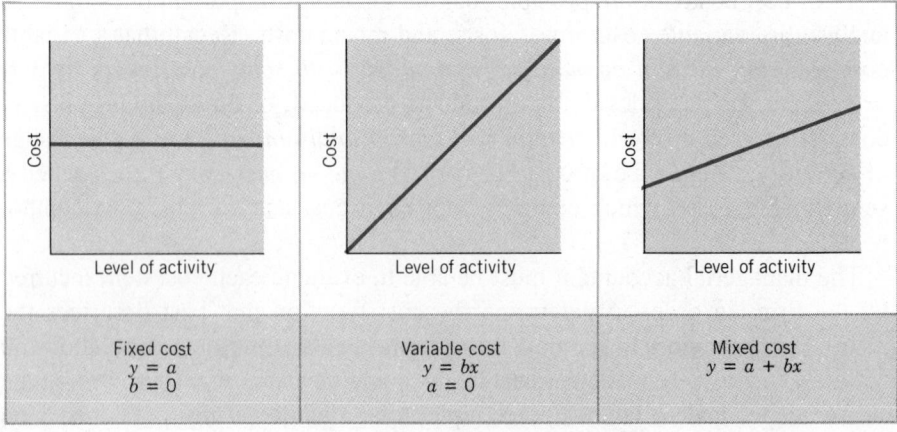

Fixed cost	Variable cost	Mixed cost
$y = a$	$y = bx$	$y = a + bx$
$b = 0$	$a = 0$	

entire range of business activity possible. In order to understand and justify how managerial accountants treat the more complex cost behavior patterns in the application of CVP analysis, we must first consider some of the complications associated with variable and fixed cost behavior.

VARIABLE COST BEHAVIOR

Few variable costs behave exactly as linear functions with constant slopes over all levels of activity. Two notable exceptions, a *curvilinear function* and a *step function,* are found in many businesses. A graphic version of each of these cost functions is shown in Figure 26–2. The curvilinear variable cost shown in graph (a) is the result of what economists describe as economies and diseconomies of scale. At extremely low levels of activity, a firm does not have sufficient volume to take advantage of such factors as automation and the specialization of labor. Consequently, the variable cost function increases at an increasing rate. When unusually high levels of activity are achieved, inefficiencies and bottlenecks occur, so a variable cost again increases at an increasing rate. Within the shaded area of graph (a), the cost function is approximately linear, because the rate of increase is relatively constant. The shaded area of the graph is called the **relevant range**, which is the range of activity within which a firm expects to operate. Since the business does not intend to operate outside the relevant range, the curvilinear cost behavior at very low or very high levels of activity is ignored. The relevant range concept is important for CVP analysis because it provides the justification for the linearity assumption without any significant loss of accuracy as long as the firm's activity stays within the relatively narrow limits.

A step cost function, such as the one exhibited in graph (b), will be incurred for some variable cost items because they cannot be purchased in divisible units. For example, labor services are generally acquired on the basis of 40 hours per week. The associated costs cannot be inventoried for future use, since they must be utilized or lost as each workday passes. Consequently, each worker's wages represent a step in the cost function shown in graph (b). The cost function increases abruptly as an additional worker is hired to satisfy the needs of a higher level of activity. Again, the managerial accountant converts the step function into a linear function, as shown in graph (b), by connecting the points representing the highest level of activity for each step.

Objective 3:
The significance of the relevant range

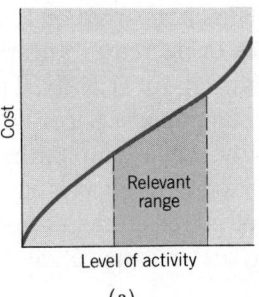

(a)

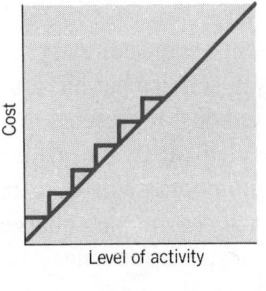

(b)

Figure 26–2
Curvilinear and Step Cost Functions

Figure 26–3
Fixed Cost Function

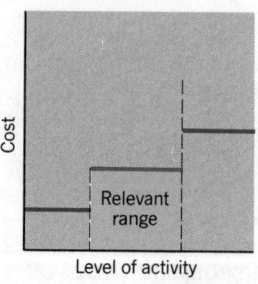

The justification for the conversion is that the business will want to fully utilize the labor cost for any given step by attaining the highest level of activity.

FIXED COST BEHAVIOR

The relevant range concept also permits management to assume that the total fixed costs will remain constant over a range of activity. In reality, the total fixed costs may change over a complete range of activity in wide steps, as shown in Figure 26–3. Many fixed costs are defined as **discretionary fixed costs** because they can be reduced or discontinued by management if adequate time is available. At low levels of activity, management may decide to reduce or eliminate such activities as advertising, research and development, and employee training programs. At an extremely low level of activity such as one caused by a prolonged strike, drastic measures may be necessary to eliminate all but the committed fixed costs through layoffs and curtailments. The **committed fixed costs** are required even if the operation is shut down temporarily. They consist of such items as depreciation, property taxes, insurance, and top management salaries.

At an extremely high level of activity, added capacity will be necessary to satisfy the market demand for the firm's products or services, so fixed costs, such as depreciation and managerial salaries, will increase. Again, the relevant range concept permits management to ignore the low and high levels by concentrating on the normal range of operation. Within the relevant range, the fixed costs will remain constant in total amount.

MIXED COST BEHAVIOR

As we can see in Figure 26–1, a mixed cost contains *both* fixed and variable components. Consequently, a mixed cost increases or decreases linearly with changes in activity but has a positive amount at zero activity. The fixed portion of a mixed cost represents the minimum cost of obtaining a service, while the variable element is the result of a change in activity. For example, the rental of an automobile will be a mixed cost when a fixed amount per day and a certain rate per mile are charged. Other examples of mixed costs in some cases are utilities, maintenance, sales salaries, employees' insurance, and office machine rental.

COST BEHAVIOR ANALYSIS OF MIXED COSTS

For mixed costs to be planned and controlled, they must be divided into their fixed and variable components. A number of techniques based on the equation $y = a + bx$ can be used for the separation of mixed costs. The three most popular techniques are ***visual fit of a scatter diagram, the high-low method,*** and ***linear regression analysis.*** All three techniques are based on the collection of historical data that represent the mixed costs incurred at different levels of activity. The objective is to develop a cost function that best reflects the cost behavior pattern of the mixed costs. As a simplified example, assume that a manufacturing firm has experienced the following maintenance costs and machine hours during the past 12 months.

Month	Maintenance Costs	Machine Hours
January	$27,550	2,920
February	28,600	3,625
March	31,680	4,380
April	33,350	4,752
May	36,000	5,986
June	37,700	7,250
July	41,760	8,640
August	38,610	7,150
September	36,250	6,525
October	34,560	5,720
November	30,030	5,005
December	29,930	4,350

The monthly maintenance costs can be plotted as a function of machine hours, as shown in Figure 26–4. The visual fit of a scatter diagram method is applied by drawing a straight line through the relationships of the dependent

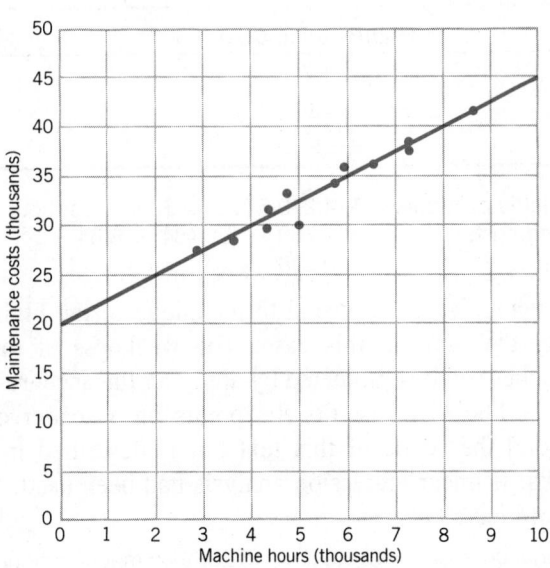

Figure 26–4
Scatter Diagram—
Maintenance Costs

and independent variables. The straight line through the points representing the various relationships of maintenance costs and machine hours is chosen as the best visual fit by the person performing the analysis. This means that the differences between the scatter points and the straight line are minimal, compared with other lines that might be drawn through the scatter diagram. The fixed portion of maintenance costs is determined by extending the line to the vertical axis, and amounts to approximately $20,000.

The variable costs can be found for any given number of machine hours by subtracting the fixed costs of $20,000 from the total costs related to that level of activity. For example, total maintenance costs of $35,000 are estimated for 6,000 machine hours; therefore, the variable costs would be $15,000 ($35,000 less $20,000). In turn, the variable cost rate is approximately $2.50 ($15,000/ 6,000). Consequently, the maintenance cost function is equal to $20,000 plus $2.50 per machine hour. While the visual fit method often provides a useful estimation technique, it is dependent on the judgment of the person performing the analysis and, therefore, is subject to significant error. In other words, a given person may not visualize the best fit of a line to the scatter points.

The high-low method is a quantitative technique that can be used to estimate a mixed cost function. As long as the costs at the highest level of activity and those at the lowest level are representative of the straight line that best describes a cost function, they provide useful information for cost estimation. The high-low method is based on the procedure used to determine the slope of any linear function, because it compares the cost at the highest level of activity with the cost at the lowest level of activity. The difference in cost caused by variable costs is divided by the difference in activity to find the variable cost rate. Once the variable costs for a given level of activity are known, they can be subtracted from the total costs to determine the fixed costs. This method must be used carefully, however, since the high and low points in many cases will not represent the true cost function. The high-low method can be applied to the maintenance cost data, as follows.

	Maintenance Cost	Machine Hours
High	$41,760	8,640
Low	27,550	2,920
Difference	$14,210	5,720

Variable cost rate = $14,210/5,720 = $2.484 per hour
Fixed costs = $41,760 − ($2.484 × 8,640)
= $20,298

The results of using either the visual fit technique or the high-low method are approximately the same in this case. The weakness of these two cost estimation approaches can be eliminated by applying linear regression analysis to find the straight line that best fits the points on a scatter diagram. The technique is beyond the scope of this text but is described in introductory statistics textbooks. If linear regression analysis had been used, the estimated cost function would have been

Maintenance costs = $19,645 + ($2.568 × machine hours)

In this example, the two less accurate estimation techniques produced approximately the same cost function as the more sophisticated one, but this will not always be the case.

COST BEHAVIOR AND THE INCOME STATEMENT

The primary concern in CVP analysis and many other managerial accounting applications is an income statement expected in the future. To project a future earnings performance, management must be able to evaluate how *costs and profits will fluctuate with changes in sales volume.* Unfortunately, the conventional income statement discussed in earlier chapters will be of limited value in predicting cost–volume–profit relationships. In a conventional income statement, costs are classified by business function (manufacturing, selling, and administrative) without any consideration of the cost behavior involved. While such a statement may be very factual concerning the historical earnings performance of a specific period, it will not indicate what should happen to costs and profits with a different sales volume in the future. For example, consider the conventional income statement of the Butler Manufacturing Company, shown in Figure 26–5.

Objective 4:
The benefits of
an income
statement with
a contribution
margin format

The firm earned net income of $120,000, which was 12% of sales. Suppose management expects sales to increase by $200,000 to $1,200,000, or 20%, in 1987, because more units will be sold, and thus, wants to predict the related net income. Can management simply multiply the projected sales revenue of $1,200,000 by the profit margin of 12% to predict a 1987 net income of $144,000 (which would also be a 20% increase)? The answer is *no*; many of the costs involved will be fixed and will not change with the increase in sales volume as long as the firm remains within the relevant range. We know from our discussion of absorption costing in Chapter 22 that fixed manufacturing overhead costs will be included in the cost of goods sold section of the income statement because they are assigned to the products during the production

Figure 26–5
Income Statement—
Conventional Format

BUTLER MANUFACTURING COMPANY
Income Statement
Year Ended December 31, 1987

	Amount	Percentage
Sales	$1,000,000	100
Cost of goods sold	520,000	52
Gross profit	480,000	48
Operating expenses		
Selling expenses	200,000	20
Administrative expenses	160,000	16
Total operating expenses	360,000	36
Net income	$ 120,000	12

operation. We also know that the selling and administrative expenses will typically be both fixed and variable. Even if the Butler Manufacturing Company were a retailing business, its operating expenses would most likely be partially fixed and partially variable.

To eliminate the deficiency of a conventional income statement, many businesses construct the statement on the basis of cost behavior. Here, the emphasis is on the **contribution margin**—sales revenue less all variable costs. The **contribution margin rate** is found by dividing the contribution margin by sales. The contribution margin represents the amount of sales revenue available, first to absorb the fixed costs and then to contribute toward profit. Since only the variable costs are deducted to calculate the contribution margin, it will vary directly as a fixed percentage with sales volume. Before an income statement emphasizing the contribution margin can be prepared, each cost item must be analyzed carefully with the procedures discussed earlier in this chapter in order to determine its cost behavior. We assume that the cost behavior classifications shown in Figure 26–6 have been developed for the Butler Manufacturing Company.

The information contained in the revised income statement in Figure 26–6 will enable management to evaluate the effect on net income of a change in sales volume. If sales of $1,200,000 are expected, the resulting net income can be computed as follows.

Projected contribution margin ($1,200,000 × .4)	$480,000
Fixed costs	280,000
Net income	$200,000
Net income as a percentage of sales	16.7

The net income projected for 1987 is $200,000 and is a higher percentage of sales than that of 1986 because the fixed costs remain at $280,000. Only the variable costs have increased on the basis of 60% of sales. Thus, the

Figure 26–6
Income Statement—
Contribution Margin
Format

BUTLER MANUFACTURING COMPANY
Income Statement
Year Ended December 31, 1987

	Amount	Percentage
Sales	$1,000,000	100
Variable cost of goods sold	400,000	40
Variable operating expenses	200,000	20
Contribution margin	400,000	40
Fixed costs		
Manufacturing	120,000	12
Operating	160,000	16
Total fixed costs	280,000	28
Net income	$ 120,000	12

contribution margin in dollars increases from $400,000 to $480,000, but as a percentage of sales remains constant at 40%. Alternatively, the increase in net income of $80,000 can be computed by multiplying the sales increase of $200,000 by the contribution margin rate of .40. An income statement that emphasizes the contribution margin will be used for internal purposes only and will provide the basis for CVP analysis. Since a manufacturing firm can develop an income statement of this type with variable costing instead of the absorption costing method with which we have been concerned in previous chapters, let us turn to a brief coverage of variable costing before proceeding with the subject of CVP analysis.

VARIABLE COSTING

We learned in Chapter 22 that absorption costing must be used for external reporting purposes because generally accepted accounting principles require both fixed and variable manufacturing overhead to be absorbed as product costs. However, we have demonstrated that management often needs income statement information that is useful in predicting the impact of changes in sales volume on the costs and profits of a firm. This information is difficult, if not impossible, to obtain with absorption costing since there is no clear-cut distinction between fixed and variable costs.

Objective 5: Difference between absorption costing and variable costing

Variable costing is an alternative product costing method that can be used for internal reporting purposes to overcome the deficiencies of absorption costing. With variable costing, only the variable manufacturing costs (direct materials, direct labor, and variable manufacturing overhead) are treated as product costs. This approach eliminates the problems associated with unit fixed costs that vary inversely with production volume, since the fixed manufacturing costs are treated as period costs, rather than product costs. Three major steps are involved in the application of variable costing.

1. All costs—manufacturing, selling, and administrative—are analyzed carefully to determine which are fixed and which are variable. A mixed cost is separated into its fixed and variable parts.
2. Variable manufacturing costs—direct materials, direct labor, and variable manufacturing overhead—are assigned as product costs. Therefore, work in process, finished goods, and cost of goods sold will be valued on the basis of the costs that vary proportionately with volume.
3. All fixed manufacturing costs, as well as the selling and administrative expenses, are treated as period costs and charged to the income statement of the period in which they are incurred. However, the variable selling and administrative expenses are separated from the fixed selling and administrative expenses for presentation on the income statement. The variable selling and administrative expenses are deducted from sales, along with the variable cost of goods sold, in order to determine the contribution margin of a period. In contrast, the fixed selling and administrative expenses are subtracted (along with the fixed manufacturing overhead costs) from the contribution margin to determine the net income of a period.

An income statement developed with variable costing has the same basic format as the one shown in Figure 26–6. The only difference may be the presentation of a **manufacturing margin**, which is optional and is the difference between sales revenue and the variable cost of goods sold. The **manufacturing margin rate** is the manufacturing margin expressed as a percentage of sales. Proponents of variable costing support its format on the premise that it distinguishes between the *costs of doing business* (the variable costs deducted to determine the contribution margin) and the *costs of being in business* (the fixed costs subtracted from the contribution margin). The costs of doing business will rise and fall as the level of business activity increases and decreases. In contrast, the costs of being in business represent capacity costs that will occur regardless of the volume of business achieved.

RECONCILING VARIABLE COSTING AND ABSORPTION COSTING NET INCOME

The major difference between variable costing and absorption costing is the timing of the fixed manufacturing costs as deductions on the income statement. The variable costing method charges the fixed manufacturing costs to the income statement as they are incurred. Absorption costing applies the fixed manufacturing costs to the products produced during a period, so they are deducted from the income statement when the products are sold. The amount of fixed manufacturing costs left on the balance sheet at the end of a given period will be in proportion to the number of units left in the ending inventory.

When sales and production volumes are equal, inventories do not increase or decrease so the same amount of fixed manufacturing costs will be charged to the income statement with both methods. Consequently, the net income with variable costing will be equal to the net income with absorption costing. If sales and production volumes are different, variable costing net income and absorption costing net income also will be different. When production exceeds sales (resulting in an increase in inventory), part of the fixed manufacturing costs inventoried with absorption costing will be deferred in inventory to a future period. As a result, absorption costing net income will be greater than variable costing net income. In contrast, variable costing net income will be higher than that of absorption costing when sales exceed production (resulting in a decrease in inventory). This is caused by the fact that, as inventory is depleted, fixed manufacturing costs of a previous period will be combined with those of the current period with absorption costing. We can reconcile the difference between net incomes with absorption costing and variable costing with the following formula.

$$\text{Difference in net incomes} = \begin{array}{c}\text{Fixed costs in the}\\\text{ending inventory with}\\\text{absorption costing}\end{array} - \begin{array}{c}\text{Fixed costs in the}\\\text{beginning inventory with}\\\text{absorption costing}\end{array}$$

When the fixed costs in the ending inventory with absorption costing are greater than those in the beginning inventory, net income with absorption costing will exceed net income with variable costing by the same amount.

This difference in fixed costs will be deferred to the future with absorption costing but expensed in the current period with variable costing. In contrast, fixed costs in the ending inventory with absorption costing that are less than those in the beginning inventory will cause net income with absorption costing to be lower than that of variable costing by the same amount. When this happens, fixed costs that have previously been expensed with variable costing will be charged to the income statement of the current period with absorption costing, resulting in less net income. If there is no change in the fixed costs included in the ending and beginning inventories with absorption costing, the net income will be the same with the two methods, because an equal amount of fixed costs will have been charged to the income statement of the current period with both methods.

ILLUSTRATION OF VARIABLE COSTING

The basic difference between variable costing and absorption costing can be illustrated by preparing income statements using each method. To do so, the January and February operating performance of the Component Company, a west coast electronics manufacturer, is utilized.

Sales in units	40,000 in January
	50,000 in February
Production in Units	50,000 in January
	40,000 in February
Inventory as of January 1	none
Selling price per unit	$20
Variable manufacturing costs per unit	$5
Variable selling and administrative expenses per unit	$2
Fixed manufacturing overhead per month	$400,000
Fixed selling and administrative expenses per month	$80,000

A comparison of income statements prepared with absorption costing and variable costing is presented in Figure 26–7. In January, production exceeded sales by the 10,000 units transferred to ending inventory at a cost of $130,000 with absorption costing. The variable costs in the ending inventory are $50,000 (10,000 units × $5), and the balance of $80,000 represents fixed manufacturing costs (1/5 of $400,000). Net income with absorption costing is greater than with variable costing by the same $80,000, since one-fifth of the fixed manufacturing costs are deferred from the January income statement. In other words, the fixed costs in the ending inventory are $80,000 more than those of the beginning inventory. In contrast, the total fixed manufacturing costs of $400,000 are charged to the January income statement with variable costing. The situation is reversed in February, when sales exceed production by 10,000 units. The fixed manufacturing costs charged to the income statement under absorption costing are $400,000 for February, plus the $80,000 balance carried forward from January. The result is a decrease of $80,000 in the fixed costs

Figure 26–7
Absorption Costing
and Variable Costing

COMPONENT COMPANY
Comparison of Income Statements
Absorption Costing and Variable Costing

	January	February	Total
Absorption Costing			
Sales	$800,000	$1,000,000	$1,800,000
Cost of goods sold (1)	520,000	730,000	1,250,000
Gross profit	280,000	270,000	550,000
Selling and administrative expenses (2)	160,000	180,000	340,000
Net income	$120,000	$ 90,000	$ 210,000

(1) Cost of goods sold

	January	February	Total
Beginning inventory	–0–	130,000	–0–
Production costs			
(50,000 × $5) + $400,000 =	650,000		
(40,000 × $5) + $400,000 =		600,000	
Total			1,250,000
Ending inventory (1/5)	130,000	–0–	–0–
Cost of goods sold	520,000	730,000	1,250,000

(2) Selling and administrative expenses

	January	February
(40,000 × $2) + 80,000	160,000	
(50,000 × $2) + 80,000		180,000

	January	February	Total
Variable Costing			
Sales	$800,000	$1,000,000	$1,800,000
Cost of goods sold (3)	200,000	250,000	450,000
Manufacturing margin	600,000	750,000	1,350,000
Variable selling and administrative expenses (4)	80,000	100,000	180,000
Contribution margin	520,000	650,000	1,170,000
Fixed costs			
Manufacturing	400,000	400,000	800,000
Selling and administrative	80,000	80,000	160,000
Net income	$ 40,000	$ 170,000	$ 210,000

(3) Cost of goods sold

	January	February
Beginning inventory	–0–	50,000
Production costs		
(50,000 × $5)	250,000	
(40,000 × $5)		200,000
Ending inventory (1/5)	50,000	–0–
Cost of goods sold	200,000	250,000

(4) Variable selling and administrative expenses

	January	February
(40,000 × $2)	80,000	
(50,000 × $2)		100,000

in the ending inventory from the amount in the beginning inventory. Again, the fixed manufacturing costs shown on the variable costing income statement are $400,000, so its net income is $80,000 higher than the net income with absorption costing. During the two-month period, sales and production both equal 90,000 units, so the total net income is $210,000 with either method.

In Figure 26–7, the variable costing net income moves in the same direction as sales. The manufacturing margin (sales less the variable cost of goods sold) is a constant percentage of sales (75% in this case). The contribution margin is also a *constant* 65% of sales. Consequently, management can easily predict the impact of a change in sales volume on net income, because of the linear relationships involved. When sales increased by $200,000 from January to February, the increase in net income of $130,000 is logical because of the following computation.

$$\begin{array}{ccccc} \text{Increase in} & \times & \text{Contribution} & = & \text{Increase in} \\ \text{sales volume} & & \text{margin rate} & & \text{net income} \\ \$200,000 & \times & .65 & = & \$130,000 \end{array}$$

However, the absorption costing results are much more difficult to interpret and explain. Despite the fact that sales increased by $200,000 in February, the net income was actually $30,000 lower than that of January. The basic reason for these inconsistent results is the fact that the net income with absorption costing is *affected by changes in inventory* (sales not equal to production) because of the absorption of fixed manufacturing costs as product costs. As such, absorption costing net income is a function of both sales and production, as compared to variable costing net income, which is a function only of sales.

BENEFITS AND LIMITATIONS OF VARIABLE COSTING

Many manufacturing firms use variable costing for internal reporting purposes during an accounting period and convert to absorption costing at the end of the period by adding fixed manufacturing costs to inventories and to cost of goods sold. The primary benefits and limitations of variable costing must be evaluated carefully so that it can be properly used.

Objective 6:
Benefits and
limitations of
variable costing

Benefits of Variable Costing

1. Variable costing forces management to evaluate the cost behavior pattern of each cost item.
2. The information needed for CVP analysis can be obtained directly from the income statement, rather than from special analysis independent of the income statement.
3. The effect of fixed costs on profits is emphasized because the total fixed costs are treated as period costs and are reported in one place on the income statement, rather than being scattered throughout the statement.
4. Variable costing provides the basis for the preparation of a flexible budget in which variable costs and fixed costs are separated.
5. Since variable costs and fixed costs are divided, variable costing assists

management in such decision-making activities as profit planning, cost control, pricing, and resource allocations.

Limitations of Variable Costing

1. The separation of many cost behavior patterns into variable and fixed elements is very difficult, and the results are only approximations, at best.
2. Variable costing is not acceptable for financial reporting or income tax reporting.
3. Variable costing may give the misleading impression that only the variable costs must be considered in pricing decisions. In the long run, both variable costs and fixed costs must be recovered before net income can be earned. As we shall see in Chapter 27, short-run pricing may be based on variable costing.
4. Balance sheet inventories valued with variable costing will be understated so working capital will be lower than it would be with absorption costing.

ASSUMPTIONS OF COST–VOLUME–PROFIT ANALYSIS

Now that we have considered the basic aspects of a contribution margin-oriented income statement, we can turn to the following assumptions underlying CVP analysis.

1. The unit sales price remains constant.
2. All costs can be identified as variable or fixed costs with a reasonable amount of accuracy.
3. Variable costs will change proportionately with volume.
4. The fixed costs will remain constant.
5. Efficiency will remain unchanged.
6. Whenever more than one product is sold, total sales will be in some predictable proportion or sales mix.
7. Variable costing will be used or, if absorption costing is used, the number of units sold will be equal to the number of units produced.

PROFIT PLANNING WITH CVP ANALYSIS

Objective 7: Using CVP analysis to plan profits

As indicated earlier, CVP analysis is used by management to evaluate the interrelationships of selling price, sales volume, sales mix, and costs so that acceptable profits can be earned. Profit goals are established during the budgeting process and are reevaluated continuously during the budget period. In order to plan profits, management must estimate the selling price of each product, the variable costs required to produce and sell it, and the fixed costs expected for a given period. This information is combined with estimates concerning the expected sales volume and sales mix. The variable costing concepts previously discussed provide the foundation for profit planning with CVP analysis. The coverage of CVP analysis that follows refers to the operating performance of the Stabilizer Company, which began manufacturing a single model of cross-country skis on January 1, 1986, in a Midwestern plant. A condensed income statement for the firm's first year of operation is shown below.

STABILIZER COMPANY Income Statement Year Ended December 31, 1986	Amount	Percentage
Sales (8,000 units @ $50)	$400,000	100.0
Variable cost of goods sold	240,000	60.0
Manufacturing margin	160,000	40.0
Variable selling and administrative expenses	40,000	10.0
Contribution margin	120,000	30.0
Fixed costs		
Manufacturing	110,000	27.5
Selling and administrative	40,000	10.0
Net income (loss)	$(30,000)	(7.5)

BREAK-EVEN ANALYSIS

Break-even analysis is the typical starting point for CVP analysis. The **break-even point** is the sales volume at which revenue and total costs are equal, with no net income or loss. Net income is earned above the break-even point; a net loss is incurred below it. Both the variable and fixed costs are covered by sales revenue at the break-even point. While a break-even point is not a desired performance target because of the lack of profit, it does indicate the level of activity necessary to avoid a loss. As such, the break-even point represents a target of the minimum sales volume that must be achieved by a business. In addition, break-even analysis provides valuable information concerning the impact of cost behavior patterns at different sales levels. We will see later that the basic procedures of break-even analysis can be extended to plan for a *desired amount of profit* and to evaluate the *margin of safety* associated with the expected sales volume.

Objective 8: Calculating break-even sales

Break-Even Equation

The break-even point can be determined mathematically or graphically and can be expressed in either sales units or sales dollars. Mathematically, the basic variable costing income statement format can be stated as:

$$\text{Sales} - \text{Variable costs} - \text{Fixed costs} = \text{Net income}$$

or:

$$\text{Sales} = \text{Variable costs} + \text{Fixed costs} + \text{Net income}$$

which can be expanded to:

$$\begin{array}{c} \text{No. of units sold} \\ \times \\ \text{Selling price} \end{array} = \begin{array}{c} \text{No. of units sold} \\ \times \\ \text{Variable cost rate} \end{array} + \text{Fixed costs} + \text{Net income}$$

At the break-even point, the net income is obviously zero. Note that the left side of the last equation consists of: 1) the number of units that must be sold; 2) the selling price that must be achieved; and 3) the total sales dollars found by multiplying 1) times 2). Consequently, we can apply break-even analysis by determining the required amount for one or more of these three items, depending on our objective. If we know the selling price, we can find the number of units that must be sold. If we know the number of units expected to be sold, we can use the equation to determine the selling price needed to break even. Finally, we can let the total sales dollars required to break even be the unknown, without breaking the left side of the equation into the number of units and the selling price.

To illustrate the use of the break-even equation, consider the financial data presented earlier for the Stabilizer Company. The firm operated below its break-even point in 1986 because it incurred a net loss of $30,000. Note that fixed costs were $150,000 and variable costs were 70% of sales: $280,000 ($240,000 + $40,000) divided by $400,000, or $35 per unit ($280,000 divided by 8,000). The number of units required for break-even sales can be established as an unknown (S) and determined as:

(1)
$$\begin{aligned} \$50S &= \$35S + \$150,000 \\ \$15S &= \$150,000 \\ S &= 10,000 \text{ units} \end{aligned}$$

The break-even sales in units can be converted to sales dollars of $500,000 by multiplying the 10,000 units by the selling price of $50. If we had expected to sell 10,000 units and wanted to determine the selling price needed to break even (without knowing the $50 price given), we could do so by letting the selling price be the unknown (S) as follows.

(2)
$$\begin{aligned} 10,000S &= 10,000 \ (\$35) + \$150,000 \\ 10,000S &= \$350,000 + \$150,000 \\ 10,000S &= \$500,000 \\ S &= \$50 \end{aligned}$$

Finally, we can use the cost–volume–profit relationships to find the total sales dollars required to break even as the unknown (S).

(3)
$$\begin{aligned} S &= .7S + \$150,000 \\ .3S &= \$150,000 \\ S &= \$500,000 \end{aligned}$$

The break-even sales dollars can be converted to sales units of 10,000 by dividing $500,000 by $50, the selling price. We can prove that sales of $500,000 will produce break-even results by preparing the following income statement.

Sales (10,000 units × $50)	$500,000
Variable costs (10,000 units × $35 or 70% of sales)	350,000
Contribution margin	150,000
Fixed costs	150,000
Net income	$ -0-

Contribution Margin Approach

Remember that the contribution margin is found by subtracting all variable costs from sales. The contribution margin rate or percentage is determined by dividing the contribution margin by sales. The contribution margin is shown on the left side of equations (1) and (3) in the previous section. In the first equation, 15S$ represents the contribution margin as a dollar amount, whereas, in the third equation, $.3S$ is the contribution margin as a percentage (30%) of sales. If we multiply $15 by the number of units sold, we will have the total contribution margin. Or, if we multiply the total sales dollars by .3, we will also have the total contribution margin. When the contribution margin was stated as a dollar figure, the break-even point was calculated in sales units. However, the use of the contribution margin measured as a percentage resulted in a break-even point in sales dollars. An alternative way to calculate a break-even point using the contribution margin directly is as follows.

$$\text{Break-even sales} = \frac{\text{Fixed costs}}{\text{Unit contribution margin}} = \frac{\$150,000}{\$15} = 10,000 \text{ units}$$

or:

$$\text{Break-even sales} = \frac{\text{Fixed costs}}{\text{Contribution margin \%}} = \frac{\$150,000}{.3} = \$500,000$$

Graphic Approach

For visual purposes, the break-even point can be plotted on a **cost–volume–profit chart**, such as the one shown in Figure 26–8 for the Stabilizer Company. In addition to the break-even point, the profitability of various revenue and cost relationships over a range of volume can be evaluated using such a chart. The vertical scale of the chart represents dollars of revenues and costs in thousands, while the volume of units in thousands is measured along the horizontal axis. The steps used to prepare this cost–profit–volume chart are:

Objective 9:
Developing a
CVP chart

1. Plot the revenue line, which begins at the origin and increases at the rate of $50 per unit.
2. Plot the variable cost function, which begins at the origin and increases at the rate of $35 per unit.
3. Plot the fixed cost line, which begins at $150,000 and runs parallel to the variable cost function.

The chart indicates that the Stabilizer Company's break-even point is $500,000 in sales or 10,000 units—the same results obtained with the mathematical approaches earlier. The profit or loss anticipated for any sales volume can be

Figure 26–8
Stabilizer Company
Cost–Volume–Profit
Chart

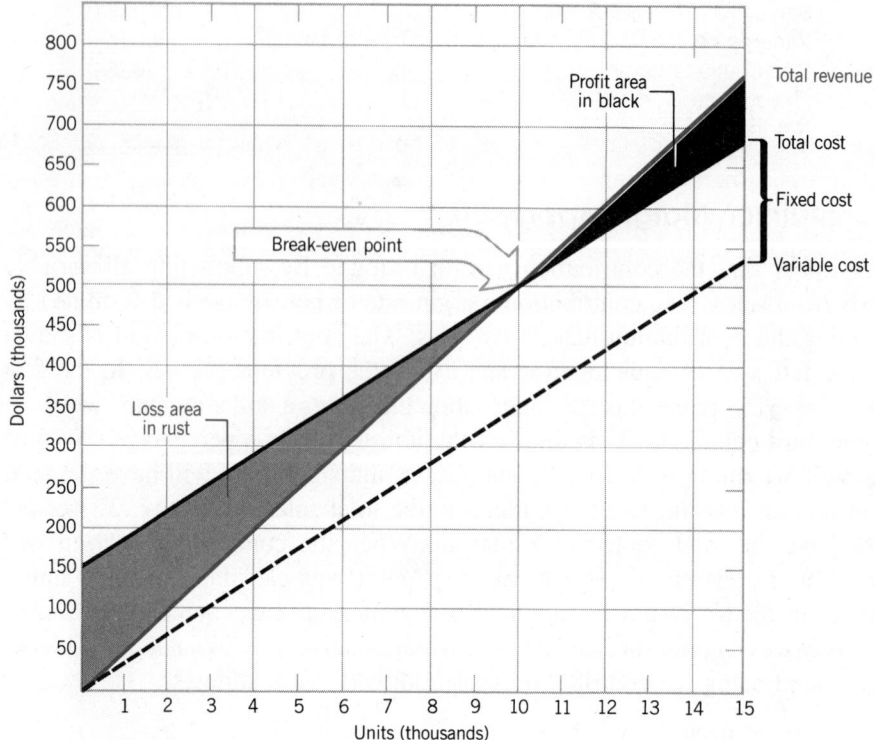

found on the chart. If the company does not achieve sales of $500,000, it will incur an operating loss (the rust colored area). A profit will be earned when sales exceed $500,000 (the black colored area). By comparing the variable costs with revenue, the contribution margin in dollars can also be determined at any sales volume from the cost–volume–profit chart. For example, the contribution margin at the break-even point is the $150,000 needed to cover the fixed costs.

MARGIN OF SAFETY CONCEPT

An important extension of the break-even point is its use to determine a firm's **margin of safety**—the amount by which sales can decrease before a loss occurs. The margin of safety is the excess of actual or expected sales over the break-even sales. A large margin of safety is an indication that a business can absorb a significant decline in sales volume without incurring a loss. As such, the margin of safety is an important measure of the risk involved with operating a business when such factors as a weak economy, changes in consumer buying, and competition are considered. We can determine the margin of safety as a dollar amount or as a percentage of sales. For example, assume that the manager of the Stabilizer Company expects sales of $600,000 in 1987, without any change in its break-even point of $500,000. Its margin of safety for 1987 would be $100,000 ($600,000 − $500,000) or 16.7% ($100,000/$600,000).

TARGET NET INCOME

The basic procedures of break-even analysis also can be used to determine the sales volume needed to *earn a desired net income*. A profit goal can be expressed as a fixed amount of net income or as a percentage of sales. In either case, the basic income statement equation presented earlier is used, in order to find the sales volume required for the desired profit. We simply drop the assumption used earlier that net income is equal to zero. Assume that the management of the Stabilizer Company wants to earn a net income, before tax, of $60,000 in 1987 and expects the same selling price and costs as those experienced in 1986. The necessary sales target can be computed as:

S = Sales dollar target
S = Variable costs + Fixed costs + Target net income before tax
S = .7S + $150,000 + $60,000
.3S = $210,000
S = $700,000 [or 14,000 units ($700,000/$50)]

With the sales of $700,000, the following income statement shows that net income before tax will be $60,000.

Sales (14,000 units @ $50)	$700,000
Variable costs (14,000 units @ $35)	490,000
Contribution margin	210,000
Fixed costs	150,000
Net income before tax	$ 60,000

Alternatively, assume that management's goal is to achieve before-tax profits that are 10% of sales. The equation required to determine the sales target is:

S = Sales dollar target
S = .7S + $150,000 + .1$S$
.2S = $150,000
S = $750,000 [or 15,000 units ($750,000/$50)]

Again, an income statement can be prepared to prove that a sales level of $750,000 will produce a before-tax profit equaling 10% of sales.

Sales (15,000 units @ $50)	$750,000	
Variable costs (15,000 units @ $35)	525,000	
Contribution margin	225,000	10%
Fixed costs	150,000	
Net income before tax	$ 75,000	

Many firms choose to define their profit target as net income after tax, in which case an additional computation is required to determine the net income before tax. To do so, the after-tax net income is divided by the factor (1 − tax rate). For example, assume that the Stabilizer Company's profit goal for 1987 is to earn after-tax net income of $42,000 with a tax rate of 30%. The required sales volume can be calculated as follows.

S = Variable costs + Fixed costs + Target net income before taxes
S = .7S + $150,000 + [$42,000/(1 − .3)]

$$.3S = \$150{,}000 + \$60{,}000$$
$$.3S = \$210{,}000$$
$$S = \$700{,}000 \text{ [or 14,000 units (\$700,000/\$50)]}$$

Alternatively, the income before tax can be calculated as follows.

$$X = \text{Income before tax}$$
$$.3X = \text{Tax}$$
$$X - .3X = \text{Income after tax}$$
$$X - .3X = \$42{,}000$$
$$.7X = \$42{,}000$$
$$X = \$60{,}000$$

Then, the $60,000 can be inserted into the equation to solve for S, the sales volume required to earn an after-tax profit of $42,000.

It should be noted that the sales level necessary to achieve the after-tax net income goal is the same as that found earlier for a before-tax net income target of $60,000, since $42,000 divided by $.7 = \$60{,}000$.

EVALUATING THE IMPACT OF CHANGE

**Objective 10:
The impact of
change with
CVP analysis**

Once the cost–volume–profit relationships are known, management can use the information to find the combination of revenue and costs that will produce acceptable profits. Cost–volume–profit analysis is particularly important to management during the budgeting process, when various alternative strategies regarding the future financial performance must be evaluated. Effective profit planning must be concerned with the impact on profits of:

1. changes in selling prices.
2. changes in sales volume.
3. changes in sales mix.
4. changes in variable costs.
5. changes in fixed costs.

To illustrate the CVP analysis used to evaluate potential changes, we will continue to use the 1986 financial data of the Stabilizer Company. Management would undoubtedly be dissatisfied with its first-year financial results, since a net loss of $30,000 occurred. Assume that the initial version of the 1987 budget has been prepared with the 1986 selling prices and costs, but that sales volume is expected to increase by 2,000 units. As a result the following income statement is projected without any additional changes.

Sales (10,000 units @ $50)	$500,000
Variable costs (10,000 units @ $35)	350,000
Contribution margin	150,000
Fixed costs	150,000
Net income	$ -0-

While the projected performance is better than the results of 1986, it is not acceptable to management because the firm will only operate at a break-even sales level. Consequently, the firm is considering a number of changes and will apply CVP analysis to evaluate their impact on profits. We will consider each of these changes independently, although they would be evaluated concurrently in a real-life situation.

Change in Selling Price

The sales manager of the Stabilizer Company estimates that a price reduction of 10% will increase the number of units sold by 20%, from 10,000 units to 12,000 units. If this happens, the impact on break-even sales and net income is:

$$S = \text{Break-even sales units}$$
$$\$45S = \$35S + \$150,000$$
$$\$10S = \$150,000$$
$$S = 15,000 \text{ units [or } \$675,000 \text{ (15,000 units} \times \$45)]$$

Sales (12,000 units × $45)	$540,000
Variable costs (12,000 units × $35)	420,000
Contribution margin	120,000
Fixed costs	150,000
Net income (loss)	$(30,000)

Despite the fact that sales revenue would increase by $40,000 with this proposal, the firm would incur a net loss of $30,000 instead of operating at break-even. The reason is the $5 loss of contribution margin per unit, which is not offset by selling 2,000 additional units. The break-even point also increases from $500,000 to $675,000, so this change would not produce favorable results for the firm.

Change in Variable Costs

The firm's production manager believes that changes in the manufacturing process will make labor utilization more efficient and reduce the variable costs by $5 per unit. The impact on the break-even sales and net income would be:

$$S = \text{Break-even sales units}$$
$$\$50S = \$30S + \$150,000$$
$$\$20S = \$150,000$$
$$S = 7,500 \text{ units [or } \$375,000 \text{ (7,500 units} \times \$50)]$$

Sales (10,000 units @ $50)	$500,000
Variable costs (10,000 units @ $30)	300,000
Contribution margin	200,000
Fixed costs	150,000
Net income	$ 50,000

The improved efficiency will increase the firm's profits by $50,000 because the contribution margin per unit will be $20 instead of $15. The $5 increase in contribution margin multiplied by the 10,000 units in sales equals the $50,000 net income. In addition, the break-even point is reduced from 10,000 to 7,500 units.

Change in Fixed and Variable Costs

The management of the firm is considering changing the method of compensating its sales manager, whose 1986 salary was based on a commission of 10% of sales. Instead of the commission, management is proposing to pay the person a fixed sum of $40,000 per year. Without the commission, the variable costs will be 60% (70% less 10%) and the contribution margin 40%. The effect on the firm's break-even point and net income would be:

$$S = \text{Break-even sales dollars}$$
$$S = .6S + \$190,000$$
$$.4S = \$190,000$$
$$S = \$475,000 \ [\text{or } 9,500 \text{ units } (\$475,000/\$50)]$$

Sales (10,000 units @ $50)	$500,000
Variable costs (10,000 units @ $30)	300,000
Contribution margin	200,000
Fixed costs	190,000
Net income	$ 10,000

The net income is increased by $10,000 with this proposed change because the total contribution margin increases by $50,000 (10,000 units times $5 per unit) while the fixed costs increase by only $40,000.

Change of Fixed Costs and Sales Volume

Another proposal being considered by the management of the Stabilizer Company is an advertising campaign that would cost the firm $30,000 per year. Management estimates that sales will increase by 30%, from 10,000 units to 13,000 units, as a result of the additional advertising. The new break-even point and net income would be:

$$S = \text{Break-even sales units}$$
$$\$50S = \$35S + \$180,000$$
$$\$15S = \$180,000$$
$$S = 12,000 \text{ units } [\text{or } \$600,000 \ (12,000 \text{ units} \times \$50)]$$

Sales (13,000 units @ $50)	$650,000
Variable costs (13,000 units @ $35)	455,000
Contribution margin	195,000
Fixed costs	180,000
Net income	$ 15,000

The break-even point would increase by 2,000 units because an additional contribution margin of $30,000 (2,000 units @ $15 per unit) is necessary to cover the proposed advertising expenditures. Since the sales are expected to increase by 3,000 units, the projected net income will be $15,000—the result of earning a contribution margin of $15 for each of the 1,000 units above the break-even point.

EXTENSION TO MULTIPLE PRODUCTS

In the Stabilizer Company illustration, we considered cost–volume–profit analysis with only one product. Earlier we stated a basic assumption of CVP analysis that total sales must be in *some predictable proportion or sales mix whenever more than one product is sold*. Cost–volume–profit analysis is performed by a multiproduct firm with a weighted average contribution margin for a given sales mix. For example, assume that the Stabilizer Company can produce and sell two models of cross-country skis with the following data.

	Standard Model	Deluxe Model
Selling price	$50	$80
Variable costs	35	48
Contribution margin	$15	$32
Contribution margin percent	30	40

The fixed costs are $184,000, and the firm's product mix is four standard models for each deluxe model. The weighted average contribution margin per unit would be $18.40, computed as follows.

Total contribution margin for 5 units of product ($15 × 4) + $32 × 1)	=	$92.00
Divided by number of units	÷	5
Average contribution margin per unit	=	$18.40

Thus, the break-even sales with the two products would be:

S = Break-even sales units

$$S = \frac{\text{Fixed costs}}{\text{Weighted average contribution margin per unit}}$$

$$S = \frac{\$184,000}{\$18.40}$$

$S = 10,000$ units

Since the sales mix is four standard models for one deluxe model, the 10,000 units will be divided into 8,000 standard models and 2,000 deluxe models ($\frac{4}{5}$ × 10,000 = 8,000 standard models and $\frac{1}{5}$ × 10,000 = 2,000 deluxe models). The break-even income statement will be:

	Standard Model	Deluxe Model	Total
Sales—units	8,000	2,000	10,000
Sales—dollars	$400,000	$160,000	$560,000
Variable costs	280,000	96,000	376,000
Contribution margin	$120,000	$ 64,000	$184,000
Fixed costs			184,000
Net income			$ -0-

This same weighted average contribution margin approach can be used to determine break-even sales or plan profits in any multiproduct firm, as long as the sales mix can be predicted.

CONTRIBUTION MARGIN VARIANCE ANALYSIS

Objective 11:
Contribution margin variance analysis

Another important use of the contribution margin in managerial accounting is to evaluate why that part of a planned profit performance was not achieved during a particular period. In the previous sections of this chapter, we have been concerned with the use of the contribution margin to project a future profit performance, which involves the planning phase of management. We now turn our attention to the application of **contribution margin variance analysis** to assist management in controlling actual profit results compared with those planned. When carefully planned profits are not achieved, management needs information concerning the causes so that it can decide who and what are to blame, as we saw with standard cost variance analysis. Contribution margin variance analysis enables management to evaluate why the contribution margin of a given period is different from that planned in the budget, or different from that of a previous period. Essentially the same analysis can be applied to differences in gross profit instead of contribution margin. Since the contribution margin is the difference between sales and the variable costs, any change in it will be due to one or a combination of the following.

1. A variation of selling price per unit sold.
2. A variation of the number of units sold.
3. A variation of the mix or combination of units sold.
4. A variation of the variable costs of producing and selling each unit.

To illustrate the fundamentals of contribution margin variance analysis, we will consider a firm that sells only one product. This means that the firm cannot incur a sales mix variance, a subject we defer to more advanced accounting textbooks. Assume that the management of the Stabilizer Company decided that sales of 15,000 units, a selling price of $50, and variable costs of $35 should be budgeted for 1987. As a result, the budgeted contribution margin is $225,000 (15,000 units × $15). Assume that after the year 1987 is over, the company reported the following income statement performance showing the actual contribution margin earned compared with the one budgeted.

	Budget	Actual	Variance
Sales—units	15,000	16,000	1,000 F
Sales—dollars	$750,000	$752,000	$ 2,000 F
Variable costs	525,000	592,000	67,000 U
Contribution margin	$225,000	$160,000	$65,000 U

Management wants an explanation of why the actual contribution margin was $65,000 less than the budgeted contribution margin, despite the facts that the actual number of units sold exceeded those budgeted by 1,000 and actual sales dollars were $2,000 more than the amount budgeted. Three separate variances—selling price, sales volume, and variable costs—must be computed, in order to determine the causes of the unfavorable contribution margin variance of $65,000. We must consider only one factor (selling price, sales volume, or variable costs) at a time, while holding the other two factors constant, as follows.

Selling Price Variance

The budgeted selling price was $50 per unit ($750,000/15,000 units), but the actual selling price was only $47 per unit ($752,000/16,000 units). The selling price variance is unfavorable and is computed by multiplying the difference of $3 per unit by the 16,000 units actually sold. The 16,000 units actually sold are used to eliminate the effect of sales volume, and the result is an unfavorable selling price variance of $48,000 (16,000 units × $3).

Sales Volume Variance

A favorable sales volume variance was incurred because the actual units sold (16,000) were 1,000 units more than those budgeted (15,000). The additional units will cause both sales revenue and the variable costs to increase, so the net result is a higher contribution margin. To eliminate the effect of changes in selling price or variable costs from the amounts planned, we use the budgeted contribution margin of $15 (budgeted selling price of $50 less budgeted variable costs of $35, or $225,000/15,000 units) to compute the sales volume variance for the 1,000 additional units. As a result, the favorable sales volume variance was 1,000 units times $15, or $15,000.

Variable Cost Variance

The budgeted variable costs for each unit sold were $35 ($525,000/15,000 units), whereas the actual unit variable costs were $37 ($592,000/16,000). As a result, the actual variable costs per unit were $2 higher than expected. The $2 per-unit deviation is multiplied by the 16,000 units sold (again holding sales volume constant at the actual units sold) to compute an unfavorable variable cost variance of $32,000.

The algebraic summation of the three variances should equal the unfavorable contribution margin variance of $65,000. The unfavorable variances for selling price ($48,000) and variable costs ($32,000), less the favorable sales volume variance ($15,000), equals $65,000. These variances will be reported to the managers responsible for the related financial performances so that corrective action can be taken wherever possible to improve the future profitability of the firm. This variance analysis is another example of the application of the management by exception principle.

GLOSSARY

BREAK-EVEN POINT. The sales volume at which revenue and total costs are equal with no net income or loss (p. 1021).
COMMITTED FIXED COSTS. Fixed costs that are required even if the operation is shut down temporarily (p. 1010).
CONTRIBUTION MARGIN. The sales revenue less all variable costs (p. 1014).
CONTRIBUTION MARGIN RATE. The contribution margin expressed as a percentage of sales (p. 1014).

CONTRIBUTION MARGIN VARIANCE ANALYSIS. A technique used to evaluate the difference between the actual contribution margin for a given period and the contribution margin budgeted for the same period or one for a previous period (p. 1030).

COST BEHAVIOR. How a cost responds to changes in the level of business activity (p. 1007).

COST FUNCTION. The relationship between a cost as a dependent variable and some measure of the level of business activity as an independent variable (p. 1007).

COST–VOLUME–PROFIT (CVP) ANALYSIS. A managerial accounting technique used to evaluate how costs and profits are affected by changes in the level of business activity (p. 1006).

COST–VOLUME–PROFIT CHART. A graphic display of the break-even point, as well as the net income or loss for a range of activity (p. 1023).

DISCRETIONARY FIXED COSTS. Fixed costs that can be reduced or discontinued by management if adequate time is available (p. 1010).

LINEARITY ASSUMPTION. A key assumption of CVP analysis that all revenue and costs will behave as straight-line functions (p. 1008).

MANUFACTURING MARGIN. The sales revenue less the variable cost of goods sold (p. 1016).

MANUFACTURING MARGIN RATE. The manufacturing margin expressed as a percentage of sales (p. 1016).

MARGIN OF SAFETY. The amount by which sales can decrease before a loss results (p. 1024).

MIXED COST. A cost that has both a variable component and a fixed component (p. 1007).

RELEVANT RANGE. The range of activity within which a business expects to operate and incur variable costs with constant slopes, as well as fixed costs that are constant in total amount (p. 1009).

VARIABLE COSTING. The inventory valuation technique used for internal reporting in which only the variable manufacturing costs are inventoried (p. 1015).

DISCUSSION QUESTIONS

1. Why is cost–volume–profit analysis such an important managerial accounting subject?
2. Identify the major characteristics of a
   (a) Variable cost.
   (b) Fixed cost.
   (c) Mixed cost.
3. Explain what is meant by the relevant range concept. How does this concept contribute to the linearity of cost functions?
4. What is a cost function and how does a linear cost function respond to changes in activity?
5. Differentiate between a variable cost that actually is a curvilinear function and

one that is a step function. How is the treatment of each one as a linear function justified?

6. Distinguish between a discretionary fixed cost and a committed fixed cost. Give an example of each.

7. The Hi-Lo Company wants to estimate the cost behavior of its manufacturing supplies. Selected data are as follows.

Manufacturing Supplies	Production Level
$27,936	5,184 hours
$25,056	3,744 hours

Using these data, estimate the cost behavior of manufacturing supplies.

8. What is the basic limitation of the income statement format used for external reporting in projecting a firm's future profitability?

9. What is the contribution margin? Why is it an important managerial accounting measure?

10. What are the major characteristics of variable costing? How does it differ from absorption costing?

11. How can variable costing net income and absorption costing net income be reconciled for a given accounting period?

12. What are the benefits and limitations of variable costing?

13. The Rock Company uses variable costing for internal reporting, and absorption costing for external reporting. During the previous year, the firm produced 72,000 units and sold 90,000 units. The variable costs required to manufacture one unit were $2.20 and the fixed costs were $6.00 per unit. Which of the two methods, variable costing or absorption costing, would report the highest net income? By how much, based on the facts given?

14. What are the basic assumptions underlying cost–volume–profit analysis?

15. Define the following terms.
    (a) Break-even point.
    (b) Break-even equation.
    (c) Cost–volume–profit chart.
    (d) Margin of safety.

16. How can break-even analysis be extended to determine the sales volume required to earn a desired net income?

17. The Alt Corporation sells a product for $40. Variable costs are $24 per unit and fixed costs are $48,000 per month.
    (a) What is the firm's break-even point?
    (b) If the firm wants to earn a before-tax profit of $12,000 per month, how many units must be sold?
    (c) If the firm wants to earn a before-tax profit of 16% of sales, what sales volume is necessary?

18. In recent years, the airlines have received a great deal of publicity with their ''no frills'' air fares. Since these fares are discounted significantly, how can they be justified on the basis of cost–volume–profit relationships?

19. What are the major changes that must be evaluated in order to find the combination of revenue and costs that will produce acceptable profits?

20. What is meant by the weighted average contribution margin when CVP analysis is applied to multiple products?

21. Why is contribution margin variance analysis an important managerial accounting tool?

22. The budget of the Byars Company for the year just ended indicated that 40,000 units of product should have been sold at a price of $15 each, with unit variable costs of $10. Actual sales were 44,000 units at a price of $12 each, with unit variable costs of $10. Identify the dollar amounts of the three variances that may have caused a different actual contribution margin than the one planned.

EXERCISES

Exercise 26-1 High-low Method and Cost Behavior

The Meeks Company rents a copy machine for which it pays a per-copy charge and a fixed annual rental fee. The company has estimated that the total costs of the machine are $22,600 if 800,000 copies are made during a year. If the company makes 1,250,000 copies per year, the total copy cost is $32,500.

Required:
A. Calculate the variable rate per copy and the fixed annual rental fee.
B. What total cost would the company incur if the company makes 1,100,000 copies during a year?

Exercise 26-2 Evaluating Mixed Costs with the High-low Method

The Williams Company wants to develop a reliable cost function for its manufacturing overhead. Its high and low levels of production activity are 180,000 direct labor hours and 120,000 direct labor hours, respectively. At 180,000 hours, the firm expects to incur costs of $616,000, and at 120,000 hours the costs will be $544,000.

Required:
A. Compute the fixed costs and the variable cost rate for the manufacturing overhead.
B. What should the total manufacturing overhead be for 150,000 direct labor hours?

Exercise 26-3 Absorption Costing Versus Variable Costing

During 1987, the Herman Company manufactured 4,000 units and recorded the following results.

Direct materials per unit	$ 15
Direct labor per unit	10
Variable manufacturing overhead per unit	3
Selling price per unit	50
Fixed selling and administrative expenses	15,000
Fixed manufacturing overhead	48,000

There was no beginning inventory in 1987 and 3,800 units were sold during the year.

Required:
A. Calculate the unit cost with absorption costing.
B. Calculate the unit cost with variable costing.
C. Calculate the net income for 1987 under absorption costing.
D. Calculate the net income for 1987 under variable costing.
E. Reconcile the net income under absorption costing and variable costing.

Exercise 26-4 Basic Contribution Margin Income Statement

The Glide Company produces a high quality model of downhill skis. During the past year, the firm prepared the following income statement for its president.

```
                          GLIDE COMPANY
                          Income Statement
                     Year Ended December 31, 1986

Sales                                                        $800,000
Less cost of goods sold                                       480,000
Gross profit                                                  320,000
Less operating expenses:
  Selling expenses                          $160,000
  Administrative expenses                     80,000          240,000
Net income                                                  $ 80,000
```

The president wants to use this income statement to project the profits for 1987. He wants to know what the projected net income will be if the unit sales of skis increase by 20% and has asked you to assist him. The following information is available from the firm's accounting records.

Selling price of a pair of skis	$ 200
Variable manufacturing costs per pair	80
Annual fixed manufacturing costs	160,000
Percent of selling expenses that are variable	25
Annual fixed administrative expenses	$ 80,000

Required:
A. Convert the 1986 income statement to one with a contribution margin format.
B. What is the contribution margin for each pair of skis?
C. Assuming that the selling price and all costs remain unchanged, what will the net income be for 1987?

Exercise 26-5 Basics of CVP Analysis

The Sell-Low Company is the distributor of a new product. The product sells for $80 per unit with a contribution margin rate of 40 percent. The company's annual fixed costs are $800,000.

Required:
A. What are the variable costs per unit?
B. How many units must the firm sell to break even?
C. What is the break-even point in sales dollars?
D. If the firm wants to earn a net income before tax of $96,000, how many units must be sold? What sales dollar level is required?
E. If the firm wants to earn a before-tax net income of 15% of sales, how many units must be sold? What are the sales dollars?
F. Prepare a CVP chart for the firm.

.15 s(80x)=

.12x

Exercise 26-6 Evaluating Changes with CVP Analysis

The Roller Company sells its only product at a price of $240 per unit. Variable expenses are $180 per unit and total fixed expenses are $270,000. Current annual sales are 6,000 units.

Required:

A. What is the firm's break-even point in sales units? What is the break-even point in sales dollars?

B. Calculate the company's net income under each of the following independent situations.

    1. Variable expenses increase 20%.

    2. Sales volume decreases 20%.

    3. Fixed costs increase 20%.

    4. Sales price increases 20%.

    5. Sales price increases 20%, variable expenses increase 20%, sales volume decreases 20%, and fixed costs decrease 20%.

Exercise 26-7 Evaluating CVP Relationships

Information for four independent companies is presented below.

1. Company A has a product that sells for $48 and is produced at a variable cost of $36 per unit. The variable costs can be reduced 20% by installing a new piece of equipment. Installation of the new equipment will increase fixed costs from the present level of $62,400 to $92,160. Calculate the present break-even point and the new break-even point if the equipment is installed.

2. Company B wishes to attain a before-tax net income equal to 35% of sales revenue. Variable expenses are 47.5% of sales and fixed expenses are $315,000. Calculate the dollar amount of sales necessary to achieve the profit goal.

3. Company C incurs variable costs of $18 per unit for a product that has a selling price of $30. If the break-even point is $96,000 of annual sales, what are the company's annual fixed costs?

4. Company D has annual fixed costs of $144,000. The variable costs are $3 per unit and the break-even point is 18,000 units. Determine the selling price per unit.

Exercise 26-8 Cost–Volume–Profit Analysis with Two Products

The Harper Company sells two products, A and B. During 1986, fixed costs were $166,464 and sales were in the ratio of six units of product A to each four units of product B. Product A sells for $62 each, and the variable costs are $44 per unit. Product B sells for $80 each and the variable costs are $56 per unit.

Required:

A. Compute the break-even point in total units and the number of units of each product that must be sold at the break-even point.

B. How many units of product A and product B must the company sell to achieve a before-tax net income of $20,808?

Exercise 26-9 Contribution Margin Variance Analysis

The Cavanaugh Company has prepared the following income statement information showing the actual contribution margin earned from the sales of the company's only product as compared with the budgeted performance.

	Budget	Actual
Sales—units	5,200	5,100
Sales—dollars	$468,000	$453,900
Variable costs	260,000	244,800
Contribution margin	$208,000	$209,100

Required:
Calculate the selling price variance, sales volume variance, and variable cost variance.

PROBLEMS

Problem 26-1 Cost Behavior Analysis with the High-low Method

The Gregory Company's manufacturing overhead has changed significantly from year to year in relation to the direct labor hours worked. The costs at the high and low levels of activity during the past 5 years are as follows.

	Level of Activity	
	High	**Low**
Manufacturing overhead	$464,000	$344,000
Direct labor hours	120,000	80,000

The manufacturing overhead consists of four items: indirect materials, maintenance, property taxes, and utilities. The firm has analyzed these costs at the low level of activity and determined that the costs are incurred as follows, at that level.

Indirect materials (variable)	$120,000
Maintenance (mixed)	110,000
Property taxes (fixed)	38,000
Utilities (variable)	76,000
Total	$344,000

Required:
A. Determine the cost function for the total manufacturing overhead using the format of $y = a + bx$.
B. If direct labor hours of 110,000 are expected for the next year, what is the estimate of total manufacturing overhead?
C. Calculate how much of the total manufacturing overhead is maintenance cost, at the high activity level of 120,000 direct labor hours. Note that this is the only mixed cost involved, since the other three costs are either fixed or variable.

Problem 26-2 Absorption Costing Versus Variable Costing

The Des Company has prepared income statements for the past three years with absorption costing that is used for external reporting purposes. The company applies fixed manufacturing costs to the units of production on the basis of the actual production for that year. The annual fixed manufacturing costs are $45,000, and the contribution margin is 25%. The company's selling and administrative expense is a mixed cost. The company's unit sales and production data for the past three years are:

	1986	**1987**	**1988**
Sales	12,000	16,000	15,000
Production	15,000	15,000	15,000

The income statements under absorption costing are:

	1986	1987	1988
Sales	$480,000	$640,000	$600,000
Beginning inventory	-0-	96,000	64,000
Cost of goods manufactured	480,000	480,000	480,000
Less: ending inventory	96,000	64,000	64,000
Cost of goods sold	384,000	512,000	480,000
Gross profit	96,000	128,000	120,000
Selling and administrative expense	22,000	26,000	25,000
Net income	$ 74,000	$102,000	$ 95,000

Required:

A. Calculate the fixed manufacturing overhead rate that was used to apply overhead in each year.

B. Calculate the variable selling and administrative expense per unit sold.

C. Prepare income statements for the three years, using variable costing.

D. Reconcile the difference between the net income with absorption costing and variable costing for each of the three years.

Problem 26-3 Performing CVP Analysis

The Mailey Company has provided the following production and sales information for each unit of product.

Direct materials	$ 7
Direct labor	12
Variable manufacturing overhead	6
Sales commissions	10% of the selling price
Selling price	$50

The fixed costs for the period are $286,000.

14,300

Required:

A. Calculate the company's break-even point.

B. Calculate the number of units that must be sold to achieve a before-tax profit of $18,000.

C. Would it be better if the company sold 15,000 units at a selling price of $50 each or 18,000 units at a selling price of $46? 14000

D. If the company spends an additional $14,400 on fixed advertising costs, what level of dollar sales must be attained to earn a before-tax net income of $18,000? Assume that there has been no change in the sales price.

E. Assume that the income tax rate is 40%. How much additional advertising can be incurred at a sales level of 16,000 units if the company is still to earn an after-tax net income of $18,000?

Problem 26-4 Evaluating Alternatives with CVP Analysis

The Merkel Company has prepared an income statement for the past year as follows.

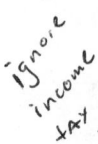
ignore income tax

Sales (30,000 units)		$1,200,000
Cost of sales:		
Direct materials	$285,000	
Direct labor	420,000	

Variable manufacturing overhead	45,000	
Fixed manufacturing overhead	150,000	900,000
Gross profit		300,000
Variable selling expenses	90,000	
Fixed selling and administrative expenses	30,000	120,000
Net income before taxes		180,000
Income taxes (40%)		72,000
Net income		$ 108,000

Required:
Consider each of the following independent situations.

A. Determine the company's break-even point in units and sales dollars.
B. If the company desires to attain an after-tax net income of $144,000, what is the dollar level of sales necessary to reach its goal?
C. If the company's sales volume increases by 10% as a result of increasing fixed selling expenses by $18,000 and variable selling expenses by $.60 per unit, what is the company's after-tax net income?
D. If direct material costs increase 10%, direct labor costs increase 15%, variable overhead costs increase 8%, and fixed overhead increases by $6,000, how many units must be sold to earn an after-tax net income of $90,000? Round your calculations to the nearest unit.
E. If the sales volume is 30,000 units, what is the selling price needed to achieve an after-tax profit of $144,000?

Problem 26-5 Evaluating the Impact of Change with CVP
The REN Company has prepared its 1987 income statement, which is presented below. The company is evaluating three independent situations and has asked for your assistance.

Sales (24,000 units)	$96,000
Variable expenses	55,200
Contribution margin	40,800
Less fixed expenses	33,600
Net income	$ 7,200

Required:
A. If a new marketing method would increase variable expenses by an unknown amount (that you should compute), increase sales units 10%, decrease fixed costs 5%, and increase net income by 25%, what would be the company's break-even point in terms of dollar sales if it adopts this new method? Assume that the sales price per unit would not be changed. Round your answer to the nearest number.
B. If sales units increase 30% in the next year and net income increases 150%, did the manager perform better or worse than expected in terms of net income? Assume that there was adequate capacity to meet the increased volume without increasing fixed costs.
C. If the company hires a new salesperson at a salary of $19,125, how much must sales increase in terms of dollars to maintain the company's current net income?

Problem 26-6 Performing CVP Analysis with Multiple Products

The Munson Company has provided the following per-unit cost and sales data for 1987.

	Product A	Product B	Product C	Product D
Selling price	$60	$70	$40	$30
Direct labor	16	20	16	10
Direct materials	24	20	10	6
Variable manufacturing overhead	6	8	4	2
Variable selling expenses	2	4	2	2
Units sold in 1987	10,000	12,500	7,500	20,000
Budgeted 1988 unit sales	17,500	21,000	7,000	24,500

The company's fixed manufacturing overhead costs are $382,200 per year, and the annual fixed selling and administrative costs are $126,000.

Required:

A. Calculate the break-even point for 1987 and 1988 in total units and the number of units of each product that will be sold at the break-even point.

B. Calculate the number of units of each product that would have to be sold in 1987 in order to achieve an after-tax net income of $152,460. The company's tax rate is 40%.

C. Calculate the number of units of each product that would have to be sold in 1988 to achieve an after-tax net income of $167,520.

Problem 26-7 Contribution Margin Variance Analysis

The president of the Carter Company has just finished reviewing her firm's income statement for the quarter just ended and is disturbed by the profit results involved. Her main concern is the significant difference between the budgeted contribution margin and the one actually incurred. The company sells one product. A summary of the profit results follows here.

	Budget	Actual
Sales—units	14,400	15,000
Sales—dollars	$146,880	$144,000
Variable costs	86,400	93,000
Contribution margin	$ 60,480	$ 51,000

Required:

Compute the three variances that are the sources of the contribution margin variance for the quarter.

ALTERNATE PROBLEMS

Problem 26-1A Cost Behavior Analysis with the High-low Method

The Caty Company has experienced different levels of manufacturing overhead in relation to machine hours during recent years. The costs at the high and low activity levels during the past four years are as follows.

	Levels of Activity	
	High	**Low**
Manufacturing overhead	$644,000	$564,000
Machine hours	110,000	70,000

The manufacturing overhead consists of four items: indirect materials, maintenance, depreciation, and utilities. The firm has analyzed these costs at the high level of activity and determined that the costs are incurred at that level as follows.

Indirect materials (variable)	$ 55,000
Maintenance (mixed)	164,000
Depreciation (fixed)	304,000
Utilities (variable)	121,000
Total	$644,000

Required:
A. Use the format of $y = a + bx$ to establish the cost function for total manufacturing overhead.
B. If machine hours of 102,000 are expected for the next year, what is the estimate for total overhead?
C. Calculate how much of the total manufacturing overhead at the low activity level of 70,000 machine hours is maintenance cost. Note that this is the only mixed cost involved, because the other three costs are either fixed or variable.

Problem 26-2A Absorption Costing Versus Variable Costing

The Pallet Company prepares income statements under absorption costing for external reporting purposes, but uses variable costing for managerial decision making. The company applies the annual fixed manufacturing overhead cost of $84,000 to the units of production on the basis of actual production for that year. The company's only product has a contribution margin of 30%, and the selling and administrative expense is a mixed cost. The income statements, under absorption costing, for the past three years are:

	1985	**1986**	**1987**
Sales	$720,000	$720,000	$540,000
Beginning inventory	0	72,000	74,000
Cost of goods manufactured	504,000	444,000	324,000
Less: ending inventory	72,000	74,000	40,500
Cost of goods sold	432,000	442,000	357,500
Gross profit	288,000	278,000	182,500
Selling and administrative expense	184,000	184,000	148,000
Net income	$104,000	$ 94,000	$ 34,500

The company's unit sales and production data for the past three years are:

	1985	**1986**	**1987**
Sales	24,000	24,000	18,000
Production	28,000	24,000	16,000

Required:
A. Calculate the variable selling and administrative expense per unit sold.
B. Prepare income statements for the three years, using variable costing.
C. Reconcile the difference between the net incomes with absorption costing and variable costing for each of the three years.

Problem 26-3A Performing CVP Analysis

The Brenner Company has provided the following production and sales information for each unit of product.

Direct materials	5 pounds at $3 per pound
Direct labor	3 hours at $7 per hour
Variable manufacturing overhead	3 hours at $3 per hour
Sales commissions	$3
Selling price	60

The firm's annual fixed costs are $480,000.

Required:

A. Calculate the company's break-even point.
B. If the company desires to attain a before-tax profit of $48,000, calculate the number of units the company must sell to reach its goal.
C. In order to maximize the company's before-tax profit, should the company sell 42,000 units with a retail price of $60 each, or 40,000 units at $62 each?
D. If the company increases fixed costs by $60,000, what level of dollar sales must be attained to earn a before-tax income of $48,000? The sales price and variable costs per unit will not change.
E. If the company's income tax rate is 20%, how much additional fixed costs can the company incur at a sales level of 46,000 units and still maintain an after-tax net income of $48,000?

Problem 26-4A Evaluating Alternatives with CVP Analysis

The Cogen Company has prepared the following income statement for the previous year.

Sales (36,000 units)		$2,160,000
Cost of sales:		
Direct materials	$612,000	
Direct labor	648,000	
Variable manufacturing overhead	252,000	
Fixed manufacturing overhead	108,000	1,620,000
Gross profit		540,000
Variable selling expenses	144,000	
Fixed selling and administrative expenses	172,000	316,000
Net income before taxes		224,000
Income taxes (40%)		89,600
Net income		$ 134,400

Required:

Consider each of the following independent situations.

A. What is the dollar level of sales necessary to attain an after-tax net income of $252,000?
B. If the company increases fixed selling expenses by $10,000 and variable selling expenses by $4 per unit, unit sales are expected to increase by 20%. Calculate the company's after-tax net income with these changes.

C. If direct labor costs increase 10%, direct materials costs increase 5%, variable manufacturing overhead increases 20%, and fixed manufacturing overhead increases $20,000, how many units must be sold to maintain an after-tax income of $134,400? Round your calculations to the nearest unit.

Problem 26-5A Evaluating the Impact of Change with CVP

The Ray Company has prepared the following income statement for the previous fiscal year.

Sales (13,000 units)	$260,000
Variable expenses	149,500
Contribution margin	110,500
Less fixed expenses	96,200
Net income	$ 14,300

Required:

Answer the following questions for each of the four independent situations.

A. If the company's president is considering increasing his salary by $20,400, how much must dollar sales increase to maintain the company's current net income?

B. If the company decreases sales commissions, variable expenses would decrease by 10%. The company believes that unit sales would decrease 5%, due to the loss of sales representatives, even though the company plans to increase its advertising budget by $10,000. Should the company decrease the sales commissions?

C. If the company changes its production and marketing techniques, it is projected that variable expenses will increase 10%, fixed expenses will decrease 15%, and sales will increase 20%. Calculate the company's break-even point in terms of sales dollars if the new strategy is adopted. Assume that the sales price per unit would not be changed. Round your answer to the nearest dollar.

D. If the company's net income increases 250% next year due to a 28% increase in sales units, did the company perform better or worse than expected? Assume that the company has adequate capacity to meet the increased volume without increasing fixed costs.

Problem 26-6A Performing CVP Analysis with Multiple Products

The Lanark Company has compiled the following sales and per-unit cost data.

	Product A	Product B	Product C	Product D
Selling price	$25	$30	$40	$20
Direct labor	9	10	12	6
Direct materials	5	5	8	4
Variable manufacturing overhead	2	3	4	2
Variable selling expense	1	2	2	2
Units sold in 1986	16,000	28,000	24,000	12,000
Budgeted 1987 unit sales	25,000	30,000	35,000	10,000

The company's fixed manufacturing and administrative costs are $428,400. The company's tax rate is 40%.

Required:

A. Calculate the number of units of each product that will be sold at the break-even point for 1986 and 1987.

B. Calculate the number of units of each product that would have had to be sold in 1986 to achieve an after-tax net income of $122,400.

C. Calculate the number of units of each product needed to earn an after-tax net income of $189,000 in 1987.

Problem 26-7A Contribution Margin Variance Analysis

The sales manager of the Philip Company cannot understand the contribution margin results of the firm's most recent quarterly income statement. He had been monitoring sales volume carefully during the quarter and knew that it was substantially above the amount budgeted. However, the actual contribution margin earned was less than the amount budgeted. The sales manager has asked for your assistance in interpreting the results. The company only sells one product, and a summary of the income statement results is as follows.

	Budget	Actual
Sales—units	21,000	23,200
Sales—dollars	$420,000	$440,800
Variable costs	252,000	348,000
Contribution margin	$168,000	$ 92,800

Required:
Determine why the actual contribution margin was so much less than the amount budgeted by computing the variances that caused the deviation.

CASE

CASE 26-1 Decision Case   CVP Analysis and Variable Costing

The Juliono Company, located in the northern part of California, produces and sells a selection of medium-priced bottled wines. The firm has been in operation for 10 years but has not been able to achieve profit results that are acceptable to its president and majority stockholder, William Juliono. These results have occurred despite the facts that sales demand for the product in recent years has been increasing and production last year was very near the limit of the firm's capacity of 2,000,000 bottles per year. The firm's most recent income statement, prepared with absorption costing, shows the following operating results.

Sales (1,960,000 bottles @ $4)		$7,840,000
Cost of goods sold		
Beginning inventory (20,000 bottles @ $3,60)	$ 72,000	
Production cost (1,970,000 bottles @ $3.60)	7,092,000	
Total	7,164,000	
Ending inventory (30,000 bottles @ $3.60)	108,000	
Cost of goods sold		7,056,000
Gross profit		784,000
Selling and administrative expenses		680,000
Net income before taxes		$ 104,000

The president has hired you to find ways to improve the firm's profitability. Your first step is to evaluate the cost behavior patterns involved, as follows.

Production costs:
Variable — $2.00 per bottle
Fixed — $3,152,000 for 1,970,000 bottles, or $1.60 per bottle
Selling and administrative expenses:
Variable — $.10 per bottle sold
Fixed — $484,000

Required:

A. Prepare an income statement for the firm using variable costing.
B. Why is the net income in requirement (A) different from that shown earlier with absorption costing?
C. What is the firm's break-even point in bottles? What is it in dollars?
D. The company's marketing manager believes that a $40,000 increase in advertising expenses will result in sales of 2,000,000 bottles. Should this decision be made?
E. In addition to the $40,000 in advertising expenses, the firm can increase its capacity to 2,400,000 bottles per year by increasing the fixed manufacturing costs by $720,000. There will not be any change in the variable manufacturing costs or selling and administrative expenses. What would be the effect on the firm's break-even point? Assuming all 2,400,000 bottles can be sold, what would be the effect on the firm's net income?

27

DECISION MAKING AND CAPITAL BUDGETING

CHAPTER OVERVIEW AND OBJECTIVES

This chapter describes the role of managerial accounting in decision making and capital budgeting. When you have completed the chapter, you should understand:

1. The nature of decision making.
2. The major steps in the decision-making process.
3. The application of differential analysis to choices between alternative courses of action.
4. How to evaluate special orders, make or buy decisions, and joint product costs.
5. The essential features of product mix decisions.
6. How to use return on investment and residual income analysis.
7. The basic nature and importance of capital budgeting.
8. The use of cash flows in capital budgeting decisions.
9. The concept of discounted cash flows based on the time value of money.
10. How to evaluate an investment with the net present value method and the internal rate of return method.
11. The basic features of the cost of capital.
12. The use of a profitability index with the net present value method.
13. The role of depreciation as a tax shield in capital budgeting.
14. The use and limitations of capital budgeting methods that do not involve the time value of money.

**Objective 1:
Nature of decision making**

We saw in Chapter 21 that managers make decisions continuously as they *plan activities, organize resources, direct operations,* and *control performance*. The managerial accounting topics covered in previous chapters assist management in making decisions, either directly or indirectly. This chapter deals specifically with the subject of decision making and the kind of accounting information required for the decision-making process. **Decision making** involves a choice between alternative courses of action, and the alternative chosen is usually selected on the basis of some measure of profitability or cost savings. What products to produce, how to produce them, how to sell them, what price to charge, how to allocate resources, what equipment to buy, and whether or not to expand operating capacity are examples of business decisions.

While all business decisions are future oriented, some will have longer-term implications than others. Initially, we are primarily concerned in this chapter with operating decisions (introduced in Chapter 21) that are short-run oriented. Managers must make good operating decisions if their firm is to utilize the existing capacity of the business in a profitable way. Many of the topics covered with operating decisions are also useful to top management in strategic decision making. Later, we shift to the subject of capital budgeting, which is an important long-term decision-making tool, used by management to establish a firm's operating capacity.

In general, the quality of decision making is highly dependent on the quality of the information available to the decision maker. Good information leads to good decisions, while bad information leads in the opposite direction. A discussion of the role of accounting information in decision making must be preceded by a basic understanding of the decision-making process used by managers.

BASICS OF MANAGERIAL DECISION MAKING

Business decisions range from the routine and repetitive to the complex and nonrecurring. Except for the simplest cases, managerial decision making is both an art and a science because a combination of qualitative (subjective) and quantitative (objective) factors enter the picture. Such qualitative factors as public image, social responsibility, competitive reaction, management intuition, and employee attitudes often have an important bearing on a decision. At the same time, management will attempt to structure a decision-making situation in quantitative terms whenever possible, so that a choice can be made on a systematic basis. Managerial accounting provides most of the quantitative information (revenues, costs, invested capital, and operating statistics) required to evaluate alternative courses of action.

While there is no universal way in which managers make decisions, the **decision-making process**, in general, consists of these four steps.

Objective 2: Major steps in the decision-making process

1. Definition of the problem.
2. Selection of alternative courses of action.
3. Obtaining relevant information.
4. Making a decision.

In the problem-definition phase of decision making, a manager should develop a complete understanding of the problem that must be solved and the objective that he or she wants to accomplish. The problem should be identified precisely, and all pertinent facts associated with it should be carefully interpreted. This first step is essential because the other phases of the decision-making process depend upon it. If the problem is incorrectly defined, time and resources will be wasted by ineffective decision making.

The second step is the selection of the possible alternative courses of action. In some cases, only two alternatives are considered. For example, a firm may decide whether to produce a certain part needed in a production process or to purchase it. More complex decisions involve more than two alternatives. The major consideration when numerous alternatives are possible is to limit the analysis to a manageable number of alternatives, but still find a satisfactory solution. For example, a medical clinic may be trying to decide what kind of computer to install for data processing. Rather than consider every computer manufacturer, the clinic will consider only those companies known for their expertise in the health-care field.

The third step in the decision-making process is the collection of information by means of which the various alternatives can be evaluated. Only *relevant* information should be considered—information that will be useful in influencing the decision. All irrelevant information should be discarded, but both qualitative and quantitative information should be gathered. Some of the information will be internal to the business; some will be external. Whenever the information is the result of past performance, it should be recast as a projection of what is expected or desired in the future.

Once the pertinent facts have been thoroughly analyzed, a decision is made. The final choice among alternative courses of action is the one that the decision maker believes will lead to the desired objective, which was identified in the problem-definition step. In many cases, a **decision model** (a formalized method for evaluating alternatives) is used as an aid in the selection process. The cost–volume–profit analysis methods, discussed in Chapter 26, are examples of decision models that can be used to evaluate the profitability of various alternatives. Other decision models, based on mathematical or statistical procedures, are also available for decision making in well structured situations.

DIFFERENTIAL ANALYSIS

**Objective 3:
Understanding
differential
analysis**

Differential analysis, also called **incremental analysis**, is a decision model that can be used to evaluate the differences in revenues and costs for alternative courses of action. The costs considered are not necessarily those used in conventional financial reporting. As noted earlier, there are different costs for different purposes. For decision-making purposes, relevant costs, differential costs, unavoidable costs, sunk costs, and opportunity costs are important classifications. **Relevant costs** are expected future costs, which will differ among alternatives. The difference between the relevant costs of two or more alternatives is called the **differential cost**. For example, if a production manager is deciding which of two machines to buy, direct labor cost may or may not be relevant. If the same skilled labor, with an hourly rate of $12, is required to operate either machine, the cost is not relevant. However, if one machine requires less skill, with a $10-per-hour operator, the labor cost is relevant and the differential cost is $2 per hour.

All costs are relevant in decision making, except the unavoidable costs; these will be the same, regardless of the alternative selected. **Unavoidable costs** are either future costs that will not differ between alternatives (the $12 direct labor costs needed for both machines is an unavoidable cost) or sunk costs. **Sunk costs** are not relevant in decision making because they have already been incurred and cannot be changed. An example is the book value of an item of equipment that a business is trying to decide whether or not to replace. Assume that the equipment does not have any residual value. If the item is replaced, the book value will be written off in the period of disposal. If it is kept, the same amount will be depreciated over the remaining life of the asset. Consequently, the book value will be expensed in either case, so it is a sunk cost.

An **opportunity cost** is the potential benefit forgone by rejecting one alternative while accepting another. Opportunity costs are not found in the general ledger but are considered, either formally or informally, as part of virtually every decision. For example, if a student decides to attend summer school instead of accepting a job that will pay $2,200, the true cost of attending school is more than books, tuition, and housing. The opportunity cost of attending summer school is $2,200. As a business example, if a firm is considering the investment of working capital in land to be held for future expansion, the income that will be lost from an alternative investment, such as a bank certificate of deposit, will be an opportunity cost associated with the land acquisition.

The concepts of relevancy and differential can also be applied to revenues. **Relevant revenues** are those that will differ between alternatives; **differential revenue** is the difference between the relevant revenues of two or more alternatives. Whenever there are no relevant revenues (meaning that the differential revenue is zero) for a given decision, the selection between alternatives is usually made on the basis of the lowest cost. For an example of relevant revenues, assume that a firm is considering the addition of a new product to utilize available production capacity. Two choices are being evaluated: cross-country skis or downhill skis. The projected revenue with cross-country skis is $286,000, while that of downhill skis is $326,000, or a differential revenue of $40,000. The related costs would also be considered if they are relevant.

Differential analysis can assist management in making several types of business decisions. We used differential analysis, without identifying it as such, in Chapter 21, when we considered a department's contribution to indirect expenses in evaluating whether or not to discontinue the Tools Department. Other examples of decisions made using differential analysis are:

Should a special order be accepted? Should a product or product line be discontinued? Is it better to produce or to purchase a part needed in manufacturing? Does a product need further processing or is it ready to sell? Should a fixed asset be replaced?

In the following sections, we will consider the application of differential analysis to some of these decisions.

EVALUATION OF A SPECIAL ORDER

Objective 4: Evaluating decisions with differential analysis

Business firms must often decide whether or not to accept a special order, usually at a price lower than the regular selling price. The long-term pricing policy of any business must be based on a consideration of all costs incurred, if the firm is to be profitable. When idle capacity exists, however, a special order may be attractive, even though a lower than normal selling price is involved. Differential analysis can be applied to evaluate the differential revenue and costs associated with a special order. (Remember that a pricing decision based on differential analysis is valid for a one-time order, but normally is not valid for a firm's regular line of business.)

To illustrate a decision concerning a special order, let's refer to the Western Hardball Company, a manufacturer of baseballs sold with a Western label to discount stores. The company has the capacity to produce 100,000 baseballs per month, although the sales forecast for January is only 60,000 units because of seasonal demand for the product. An exporter located in Miami has offered to purchase 10,000 baseballs, at a price of $1.90 each, for distribution in a South American country. The regular selling price per baseball is $2.50. The variable costs required to produce a baseball are $.80, and the monthly fixed production costs are $84,000. No additional selling and administrative expenses will be required with the order, but there will be a setup cost of $5,000 for a special label that must be imprinted on each baseball. Should the offer be accepted? If the decision is made on the basis of the average production cost per baseball with the order, the offer will be rejected because the $1.90 price is less than the average cost of $2.07 [$.80 + ($89,000/70,000)]. However, the average cost of production is irrelevant, as shown by differential analysis.

	Without Order	With Order	Differential Analysis	
Sales 60,000 @ $2.50	$150,000	$150,000		
10,000 @ $1.90		19,000	$19,000	(Differential Revenue)
Variable costs				
60,000 @ $.80	48,000	48,000		
10,000 @ $.80		8,000	(8,000)	(Differential Costs)
Fixed costs—regular	84,000	84,000		
—setup		5,000	(5,000)	(Differential Costs)
Gross profit	$ 18,000	$ 24,000	$ 6,000	

The firm's profit will be $6,000 higher with the offer, even though the price is lower than normal. As long as the company does not have a better alternative use of the production capacity (an opportunity cost for the special order) and is certain that the special offer will not have an adverse effect on its regular business, the offer should be accepted.

EVALUATION OF A MAKE OR BUY DECISION

Most manufacturing firms use many component parts in the assembly of their finished products. The parts can be produced by the manufacturer or purchased from an outside source. An automobile manufacturer may produce its own engines but purchase its tires. In turn, certain parts of the engine (such as nuts and bolts) may be acquired from other manufacturers. Whenever a manufacturing firm has the production capacity and expertise to produce a given part, the decision to make it or buy it should be based on the relevant costs of each alternative. Differential analysis can be used to evaluate the relevant costs of making or buying a part. For example, assume that the Beech Company has been operating at 75% of capacity and has been paying $8 each to purchase a small gear used in its production process. A forecast of the future indicates that regular production will remain at approximately 75% of capacity. As a means of utilizing some of the unused capacity, the firm is considering the possibility of producing 20,000 gears, instead of purchasing them. Based on the firm's normal product costing approach with absorption costing, the following costs are estimated for 20,000 gears.

Direct materials	$ 42,000
Direct labor	73,000
Variable manufacturing overhead	20,000
Fixed manufacturing overhead	55,000
Total costs	$190,000
Cost of each gear (20,000 gears)	$9.50

At first glance, it may appear that the cost of producing a gear exceeds the purchase price by $1.50 ($9.50 less $8.00). However, differential analysis requires a review of the manufacturing costs to determine which costs are actually avoidable if the gears are purchased. Assume that this has been done and that all direct materials, all direct labor, all variable manufacturing overhead, and fixed manufacturing overhead amounting to $5,000 can be eliminated by purchasing the gears. Fixed manufacturing overhead of $50,000 will be incurred whether the gears are produced or purchased, so it is not a relevant cost. Differential analysis shows:

	Make the Gears	Buy the Gears	Differential Analysis
Direct materials	$ 42,000		$ 42,000
Direct labor	73,000		73,000
Variable manufacturing overhead	20,000		20,000
Fixed manufacturing overhead	55,000	$ 50,000	5,000
Purchase costs (20,000 @ $8)		160,000	(160,000)
Total costs	$190,000	$210,000	$(20,000)

The relevant costs of producing the gears are $140,000 ($42,000 + $73,000 + $20,000 + $5,000), or $7 per unit ($140,000/20,000 units). Therefore, a cost savings of $1 per unit ($8 less $7) will result if the firm produces the gears—for a total cost savings of $20,000. The firm should also consider any alternative uses of the unused capacity with a contribution margin (opportunity cost) in excess of $20,000, since they would generate even higher profits than the production of gears. Also, the desire to control the quality of the gears internally may be an important factor in the analysis. In addition, any potentially adverse effect on the business relationship with the outside supplier of the gear, who may provide other components used in the production process, must be carefully evaluated.

TREATMENT OF JOINT PRODUCT COSTS

Many manufacturing firms produce several products from common raw materials or from the same production process. For example, an oil refinery may produce gasoline, fuel oil, kerosene, lubricating oils, naphtha, and paraffin from crude oil. Chemical, lumber, mining, and meatpacking are other industries in which it is not possible to produce a single product without producing other products. These multiple products are called **joint products**; the common costs required to produce them before they are identifiable as separate units of output are termed **joint product costs**. The point in the production process at which the joint products become separately identifiable products is called the **split-off point**. Some products may be in salable form at the split-off point, while others may require further processing before they can be sold. Graphically, the production flow of a manufacturing firm with two products (A and B) that are salable at the split-off point and one product (C) that must be processed further is:

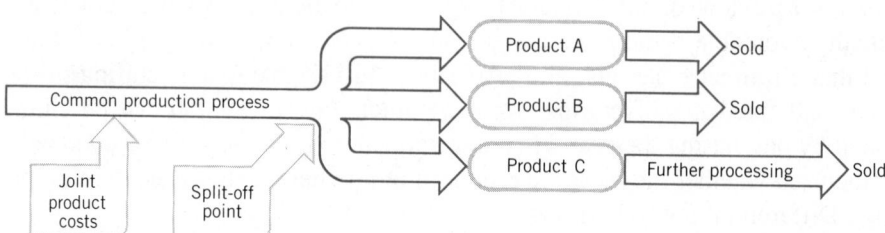

In the treatment of joint product costs, a distinction must be made between the valuation of inventories and decision making concerning the point at which the products should be sold. Joint product costs are common costs that must be allocated to the individual products involved to value inventories for financial reporting purposes. The most popular practice is to allocate joint product costs on the basis of the products' relative sales value. Assume that a chemical company produces 12,000 gallons of Alodane and 6,000 gallons of Balodane, while incurring joint product costs of $108,000. Alodane sells for $8 per gallon and Balodane sells for $9 per gallon. Therefore, the sales of Alodane are $96,000 and the sales of Balodane are $54,000, for total sales of $150,000. Using the relative sales value method, the joint product costs of $108,000 would be assigned to the two products as follows.

$$\text{Alodane} - \frac{\$96,000}{\$150,000} \times \$108,000 = \$ \ 69,120$$

$$\text{Balodane} - \frac{\$54,000}{\$150,000} \times \$108,000 = \underline{\$ \ 38,880}$$

Total joint costs $\underline{\underline{\$108,000}}$

The allocation of joint product costs must be performed so that the production costs can be divided between inventories and the cost of goods sold. However, like any cost allocation procedure, the results must be interpreted carefully since they are only approximations of the true costs of producing individual products.

Managers must often decide whether to sell a joint product at the split-off point or to process it further. Joint product costs are irrelevant in such decisions since they are *sunk costs* and should not be allocated to the joint products involved for decision-making purposes. Instead, differential analysis should be used to evaluate the relevant costs and revenues. For example, assume that the two products, Alodane and Balodane, can either be sold at the split-off point for $8 and $9 per gallon, respectively, or can be processed further and subsequently sold. The following data are relevant.

Product	Selling Price per Gallon at Split-off Point	Further Processing Costs per Gallon	Selling Price per Gallon after Further Processing
Alodane	$8.00	$4.00	$14.00
Balodane	9.00	7.00	15.50

The joint product costs of $108,000 are ignored because they are sunk costs. Alodane would be processed further and sold for $14 per gallon and Balodane would be sold at the split-off point for $9 because of this differential analysis.

Product	Differential Revenue with Further Processing	Differential Cost of Further Processing	Profit (or Loss) of Further Processing
Alodane	$6.00 ($14.00 less $8.00)	$4.00	$ 2.00
Balodane	6.50 (15.50 less 9.00)	7.00	(.50)

The gross profit earned by selling Alodane after further processing and Balodane at the split-off point would be $66,000 [(12,000 × $14) + (6,000 × $9) − (12,000 × $4) − $108,000]. This is $24,000 higher than the gross profit of $42,000 ($150,000 − $108,000) that would be earned by selling both products at the split-off point. The reason for this is the additional income of $24,000 (12,000 × $2) earned by the further processing of Alodane.

PRODUCT MIX DECISIONS

**Objective 5:
Key features of
product mix de-
cisions**

Any business that sells more than one product must continuously evaluate the profitability of its various products to determine the most profitable product mix. In many cases, this cannot be done by simply selecting the products with the highest individual contribution margins because *scarce resources and other limiting factors* are characteristic of virtually every business. For example, a manufacturing firm will have a limited amount of production capacity, as measured by direct labor hours or machine hours. In a department store, the limitation is the amount of floor space available. These limitations are called **constraints,** and management's job is to maximize the use of resources, given their constraints. The most profitable product mix should be determined in these situations by relating the contribution margin of each product to the constraints of the firm. For example, consider a company that produces and sells two types of furniture—tables and chairs—with these selling prices and variable costs.

	Table	**Chair**
Selling price	$30	$24
Variable costs	15	18
Contribution margin	$15	$ 6
Contribution margin percent	50	25

At first glance, a table appears to be the more profitable product, and management might be tempted to produce as many tables as can be sold. Assume, however, that the same machines are used to produce both products and that only 60,000 machine hours are available each month. Six machine hours are required to produce a table, two machine hours are required for each chair. If an unlimited number of either product can be sold, only chairs should be produced because they are more profitable on the basis of contribution margin per machine hour.

	Table	Chair
Contribution margin per machine hour	$\dfrac{\$15}{6} = \$2.50$	$\dfrac{\$6}{2} = \$3.00$

By producing a maximum of 30,000 chairs (60,000/2), the total contribution margin earned will be $180,000 (30,000 chairs × $6 or 60,000 hours × $3). It is unlikely, however, that an unlimited number of chairs can be sold, since the market usually imposes constraints that must be recognized in product mix decisions. For example, a minimum number of tables may have to be produced to satisfy the needs of customers who want to buy both tables and chairs. In addition, the maximum number of chairs that can be sold may be less than

30,000. Other constraints, such as limited raw materials and direct labor hours, may also require consideration in the analysis. In most cases, more than two products must be evaluated, so the determination of the most profitable product mix is a complex decision. Linear programming is a mathematical tool that can be used to overcome the complexities of multiple constraints and multiple products. The subject of linear programming, which is a series of algebraic manipulations, is beyond the scope of this text but is described in most decision-science textbooks.

RETURN ON INVESTMENT ANALYSIS

In Chapter 20, we showed how the rate of return on certain measures of investment can be used as important evaluations of a business firm's profitability. When **return on investment (ROI) analysis** is combined with the business segmentation topics discussed in Chapter 21, management has an effective means of deciding which segments of the business are most profitably using their resources. Recall from Chapter 21 that a responsibility center can be established as an ***investment center*** if the manager of that center has control of the revenue, costs, and resources invested. Return on investment analysis can be applied to such investment centers as divisions, product lines, plants, and retail stores with this formula.

Objective 6: Understanding ROI and residual income analysis

$$\text{ROI} = \text{Margin earned} \times \text{Turnover of assets}$$

$$= \frac{\text{Net operating income}}{\text{Sales}} \times \frac{\text{Sales}}{\text{Operating assets}}$$

Since sales are obviously canceled out in the ROI computation, the same result can be found by dividing net operating income by operating assets. The expanded version of ROI just shown is preferred by most managers because it emphasizes the fact that ROI is actually a function of two variables, ***margin earned*** and ***turnover of assets***. To achieve a desired ROI, management must control both of these variables. Improvements in ROI can be achieved by *increasing sales, reducing costs, or reducing assets*. Net operating income is typically income before interest expense and taxes in ROI analysis. The interest expense is eliminated because it is considered a return to creditors for the assets they have provided. Operating assets are usually defined as the average of the annual beginning and ending asset balances. All productive assets—cash, accounts receivable, inventories, and fixed assets—are included. To illustrate the application of ROI analysis, let's look at the G & P Company, which operates two divisions as investment centers. Top management wants to know which of the two earned the highest ROI during the past year, so that it can decide which segment of the business to expand in the future. The following data indicate that the Personal Products Division has a higher ROI than the Cleaning Products Division, even though it is much smaller.

		Personal Products Division	Cleaning Products Division
Net income before taxes	(a)	$ 420,000	$ 880,000
Interest expense	(b)	30,000	44,000
Net operating income	(c = a + b)	450,000	924,000
Sales	(d)	3,600,000	8,400,000
Average operating assets	(e)	2,400,000	6,000,000
Margin earned	(c/d)	12.5%	11.0%
Turnover of assets	(d/e)	1.5	1.4
ROI	(c/e)	18.75%	15.4%

The Cleaning Products Division has a lower margin earned and a lower turnover of assets than the Personal Products Division. As a result, the Cleaning Products Division's ROI is only 15.4%, compared with 18.75% for the Personal Products Division. Future expansion should take place in the Personal Products Division and resources might be moved to it from the Cleaning Products Division. If a higher ROI is to be achieved, the divisions will have to increase sales, reduce costs, or reduce operating assets.

RESIDUAL INCOME ANALYSIS

An alternative way to evaluate the performance of an investment center is by applying residual income analysis. **Residual income** is the net operating income earned in excess of a certain minimum rate of return on operating assets. When residual income is used to evaluate performance, the objective is to maximize the amount of residual income rather than the return on investment. The advantage of residual income analysis is that it prevents the possibility of a segment manager rejecting an opportunity to earn a return on investment that is acceptable to the firm as a whole but below the ROI of his or her investment center. For example, assume that the G & P Company has decided that a minimum ROI of 12% is acceptable. Since the Personal Products Division has an ROI of 18.75%, its manager may reject an opportunity to earn 15% with a new product, even though it is acceptable to the firm because the division's ROI will decrease. The residual income approach would charge the division manager only 12%, so all projects with a return in excess of 12% will be accepted. The major limitation of the residual income approach is that it is difficult to compare the performance of business segments of different sizes with it, since the larger segments will have more residual income than the smaller ones. Nevertheless, it is useful for evaluating the profitability of a specific segment's operating results. The following analysis illustrates the application of the residual income approach to the G & P Company's performance.

		Personal Products Division
Average operating assets	(a)	$2,400,000
Minimum return at 12%	(b = .12a)	288,000
Net operating income	(c)	450,000
Residual income	(c − b)	$ 162,000

TRANSFER PRICING DECISIONS

One of the most important considerations in performance evaluation with either ROI or residual income analysis is the firm's transfer pricing policy. **Transfer pricing** refers to the prices charged by one segment of a decentralized firm for products or services transferred to another segment. For example, the Delco Electronics Division of General Motors Corporation provides radios for the Oldsmobile Division. The key question is, what prices should be charged for such interdivisional transfers? Since both the buyer and the seller are segments of the same organization, the transactions will not be independent, as they are with external sources. The most basic form of transfer price is the transferring segment's *cost,* which we used in the process costing illustration in Chapter 23. There, the Finishing Department was charged for the full cost of the products transferred from the Blending Department. However, one of the main objectives in a decentralized organization is to achieve a certain amount of autonomy for each of the segments. The use of a cost-based transfer price does not provide any profit incentive for the transferring segment. Consequently, performance evaluation of the various segments based on ROI or residual income will be impossible.

Some form of *market price* is typically used to provide the profit incentive needed for segment performance measurement. If the product or service being transferred has a market price determinable from external sources, it can be used. Otherwise a *negotiated price* may be determined by bargaining between the buying division and the selling division to obtain an amount equitable to both parties. Some firms use a *cost-plus basis* for transfer pricing, in which the price is set at the transferring segment's cost, plus a fixed amount or a certain percentage of cost. Several other transfer pricing methods are available and are discussed in most cost accounting textbooks.

CAPITAL BUDGETING

The types of managerial decisions considered so far in this chapter have been primarily short-term oriented. **Capital budgeting**, which involves the planning and financing of capital investments such as the replacement of equipment, expansion of production facilities, and introduction of a new product line, is

Objective 7: Fundamentals of capital budgeting

another important area of managerial decision making. Capital budgeting decisions are concerned with a current expenditure, which will pay for itself and yield an acceptable rate of return over a relatively long period of time. As such, capital budgeting decisions are critical to the long term profitability of a firm since they will determine its capacity to do business. Capital budgeting decisions must be carefully considered by top management for several reasons.

1. They involve large sums of money.
2. The resources invested are committed for a long period of time.
3. They cannot be easily reversed, since the investment becomes a sunk cost, which can be recovered only through the productive use of the related assets or their ultimate sale, if possible, for their residual value.
4. Since they are long term oriented, substantial risk is involved because of such uncertainties as economic conditions, technological developments, consumer preferences, and social responsibilities.
5. In many cases, the success or failure of a firm may be dependent on a single decision.

To give you an appreciation of the magnitude and nature of capital budgeting decisions, consider the following excerpt from Procter and Gamble's 1984 annual report.

Capital expenditures amounted to $906 million, which was considerably higher than the $604 million of the previous year. Investments in manufacturing capacity for new products contributed importantly to the increased spending. Other major areas of spending included cost savings and productivity improvement projects, and projects designed to improve the quality of our existing products. In the coming year, we anticipate that capital spending will be somewhat higher than this past year with continuing emphasis in the areas mentioned above.

USE OF CASH FLOWS IN CAPITAL BUDGETING

Objective 8:
Why cash flows
are used in cap-
ital budgeting

Most capital budgeting methods require the use of *cash flows* to evaluate the return on an investment. The analysis involves a cash outlay made currently, or in the future, to obtain net cash flows (defined as the cash receipts in excess of cash disbursements or, instead, as the cost savings) from the investment in future years. An exception to the use of cash flows is the return on average investment method, which we will discuss later. The basic reason for using cash flows instead of accounting net income to measure the return from an investment is the time value of money, a concept discussed in Appendix B at the end of the book. The cash received today from an investment is worth more than the same amount of cash received next month or next year.

Since net income is based on accrual accounting, it typically does not reflect the flow of cash in and out of a business. The cash flows involved with an accrual income statement may precede or follow the net income reported.

Sales usually do not produce immediate cash receipts because of the time needed to collect accounts receivable. Expenses may require cash payments before they appear on the income statement (e.g., the depreciation on equipment and the inventory included in cost of goods sold) or after the income statement period (e.g., accrued salaries and taxes). Consequently, accrual accounting must be converted to cash accounting before the time value of money can be evaluated accurately in capital budgeting. A more complete discussion of the conversion of accrual accounting to cash accounting is presented in Chapter 19.

The most common cash inflows considered in a capital budgeting decision are:

1. Revenue from increased sales resulting from an investment.
2. Cost reductions from an investment that improves efficiency.
3. Any residual value at the end of the useful life of the investment.

Typical cash outflows associated with capital budgeting decisions are the initial cost of the investment and the operating expenses incurred for the investment (including income taxes on the profit involved). In many cases, an additional cash outflow is the increase in working capital (e.g., accounts receivable and inventory) required to support the investment. In such cases, incremental working capital is part of the initial investment. When the life of the investment is finished, the added working capital can be eliminated, so the decrease would be treated as a cash inflow. The same dollar increase and decrease in working capital will not simply cancel out because of the time value of money. We should also point out that depreciation does not require a cash outlay when it is recorded each period, so it should not be included as an operating cost for capital budgeting purposes. The related cash outflow is recognized when the initial investment is made. As we will see later, however, the impact of depreciation on income taxes (cash outflows) must be considered in capital budgeting.

TIME VALUE OF MONEY: AN OVERVIEW

If you need a complete review of the time value of money, you should read Appendix B at the end of the book because we will only be concerned with a brief coverage here. The basic issue with the time value of money is that a dollar held today is worth more than a dollar held at any time in the future. If we have the money today, it can be invested to earn interest and, thus, will grow in amount as future periods pass. Consequently, one year from now we will have the original investment plus one year's interest. If we invest $1,000 today at 12% compounded annually (the interest is calculated once a year), we will have $1,120 one year later [$1,000 + (.12) $1,000]. As a result, we can say that the $1,120 one year from now is worth only $1,000 to us today.

The time value of money can be expressed in terms of its future value or its present value. The $1,120 is the future value of the $1,000 because of the

Objective 9:
Using the time value of money to discount cash flows

interest earned for one year. In contrast, the $1,000 is the present value of the $1,120 if we discount the future value back to today's dollars. The process of converting a future value into what has to be a smaller present value is called discounting, and we use the term ***discount rate*** to indicate that a present value is being calculated, instead of a future value involving an interest rate. However, the interest rate and the discount rate are both the same amount in a given future value–present value relationship, or 12% in the case just given. In capital budgeting, we are concerned with discounted cash flows so that we can compare the cost of an investment with the present value of the net cash flows expected from it in the future. The expected future net cash flows from an investment can be compared with the investment only when both are measured in equivalent dollars. This can be accomplished by discounting the future dollars to their present value, which is the equivalent dollar value today of a known future amount (given a certain discount rate and time period of receipt or payment).

The same basic concepts of the time value of money can be applied to an annuity, which is a series of equal payments over a specified number of periods. The future value of an annuity is the sum of all payments made plus the interest accumulated on each payment. In contrast, the present value of an annuity is the amount that would have to be invested today at a certain interest rate in order to receive a series of future payments over a specified period of time. This means that the future payments are discounted to their present value by removing the amount of interest involved. If we think of a capital budgeting decision as consisting of making an investment today to receive a series of equal annual payments over the life of the investment that will recover the original investment and yield a desired rate of return, we have an example of the present value of an annuity.

The tables presented in Appendix B are used to evaluate the time value of money to avoid the tedious mathematics that otherwise would be required. Since capital budgeting decisions consist of present value applications, we will use Tables B–3 and B–4 in the illustrations of discounted cash flows. Table B–3 provides factors for various combinations of discount rates and number of periods related to the present value of a single amount, whereas Table B–4 contains the factors for the present value of an annuity. When equal net cash flows per year are involved, we can use Table B–4 for the discounting process. Otherwise, we consider the net cash flow of each year separately, using Table B–3. The net present value method and the internal rate of return method are two important discounted cash flow techniques used for capital budgeting decisions in the business world. To illustrate the basics of each method, assume that the Carson Company is evaluating the possibility of producing a new product, which will require the acquisition of a new machine that will be paid for in cash. The machine will cost $163,715, and we initially assume that it is expected to have no residual value at the end of its useful life of five years. The company estimates that the new product will increase its annual net cash flows by $50,000, summarized as follows.

Estimated cash inflows from sales of new product	$160,000
Estimated cash outflows for operating expenses (including income taxes)	110,000
Estimated annual net cash flows	$ 50,000

USE OF THE NET PRESENT VALUE METHOD

BASIC OBJECTIVE WITH THE NET PRESENT VALUE METHOD

The Carson Company is considering an investment of $163,715 in current dollars, which will yield expected net cash flows of $50,000 for each of five years. In making any investment, the expected future cash flows must be compared with the amount of the investment required to obtain them. The objective is to return the amount invested, as well as to earn a satisfactory return on the investment. By discounting the expected future cash flows into present value terms, they can be directly compared with the investment cost. The **net present value method** is a discounted cash flow technique, which can be used for this comparison. The discount rate chosen for the discounting process is the firm's required rate of return, often called the cost of capital or the hurdle rate.

Objective 10:
Net present value and internal rate of return methods

ROLE OF COST OF CAPITAL

The **cost of capital** is the firm's cost of obtaining funds in the form of debt and owners' equity. As such, the cost of capital is not the same as the interest rate at which money can be borrowed because the cost of *all* means of financing used by a firm must be considered. For example, a given firm may use three types of financing—debt, preferred stock, and common equity (common stock and retained earnings). The concepts and calculations underlying a complete coverage of the cost of capital are complex and beyond the scope of this book, so they are deferred to a finance textbook. However, the basic principles involved can be illustrated with a simple example. Assume that the after-tax costs of a firm's debt, preferred stock, and common equity are 6%, 12%, and 15.6%, respectively. Further, the capital structure of the firm consists of the following.

Objective 11:
Basics of cost of capital

Type of Financing	Percent of Total Capital
Debt	30
Preferred stock	20
Common equity	50

The cost of capital is a weighted average, computed as the sum of the products of each financing source's cost multiplied by its percentage of the total capital, or in this case:

$$\begin{aligned} \text{Cost of capital} &= (.06).3 + (.12).2 + (.156).5 \\ &= .018 + .024 + .078 \\ &= .12 \text{ or } 12\% \end{aligned}$$

As long as an investment offers a rate of return higher than the cost of capital, it should be accepted because the return will exceed the cost of the funds used to finance it. This will occur when the net present value (which is the difference between the discounted expected future net cash flows and the cost of the investment) is positive (discounted expected future net cash flows exceed the cost of the investment). In contrast, a negative net present value should be rejected since the cost of the investment will exceed its return to the firm. If the net present value of an investment is zero, management will be indifferent about accepting or rejecting it because no net gain in assets will result (the cost of the investment will be equal to the amount returned).

ILLUSTRATION OF NET PRESENT VALUE METHOD

To illustrate the net present value method, assume that the management of the Carson Company requires a return in excess of 12% because its cost of capital is the same as the one calculated above. The expected future cash flows can be discounted by one of two approaches. They can be discounted year by year, using the present value of $1 table (12% and five periods), as shown in Figure 27–1. The factors shown in the third column are from the present value of $1 table (Table B–3 in Appendix B at the end of the book). Since the amount received each year is the same, the expected future net cash flows of $50,000 per year can be discounted more easily by using the present value of an annuity of $1 table (12% and five periods). The present value of an annuity of $1 is presented in Appendix B as Table B–4. The alternative treatment would be determined as follows.

Present value of expected annual net cash flows ($50,000 × 3.6048)	$180,240
Cost of initial investment	163,715
Net present value	$ 16,525

Whenever the expected future net cash flows are not constant each year, they must be discounted on a year-by-year basis with the present value of $1 table. Carson Company should buy the machine because the investment has a net present value of $16,525. The total present value of $180,240 represents the maximum amount the firm could pay and still earn the required 12%. However, it can make the investment for only $163,715. As a result, the actual rate of return must be higher than the minimum of 12% required. Note, in Figure 27–1, that the $50,000 expected annual net cash flow is worth less and less in present value terms as time passes. If a discount rate higher than 12% had been used, the total present value of the net cash flows would have

Figure 27–1
Present Value Analysis of Investment in Machine

Year	(a) Expected Net Cash Flow	(b) Present Value of $1 @ 12%	(a) × (b) Present Value of Net Cash Flow
1	$50,000	.8929	$ 44,645
2	50,000	.7972	39,860
3	50,000	.7118	35,590
4	50,000	.6355	31,775
5	50,000	.5674	28,370
Total present value of net cash flows			180,240
Cost of initial investment			163,715
Net present value			$ 16,525

been lower than $180,240. In contrast, a lower discount rate would have produced a total present value of the net cash flows in excess of $180,240. An inverse relationship will exist between the discount rate chosen and the present value of the net cash flows, which means that a business will be willing to pay more for an investment when it requires a lower return on the investment.

EVALUATING INVESTMENTS WITH A PROFITABILITY INDEX

An extension of the net present value method, called a profitability index, can be used to compare investments that involve different amounts of money. The net present value of one investment cannot be compared directly with the net present value of another investment, unless both are of equal size. For example, a net present value of $10,000 from an investment of $50,000 is more attractive than a net present value of $10,000 from an investment of $500,000. We can use a profitability index to provide the relative measurement needed to compare two or more competing investments. Competing investments are mutually exclusive, which means that the acceptance of one investment results in the rejection of the other. A **profitability index** is computed by dividing the present value of the net cash flows by the cost of the investment required. In the case of the Carson Company, the profitability index is determined as:

Objective 12:
Computing and using a profitability index

$$\text{Profitability index} = \frac{\text{Present value of net cash flows}}{\text{Cost of investment}}$$

$$= \frac{\$180,240}{\$163,715}$$

$$= 1.1009$$

The simple decision rule used with the profitability index is that the investment with the largest index is preferred over others with lower indexes. The profitability index can be used to rank investments in their descending order, so that the firm's resources will be channeled into the most potentially profitable investments.

USE OF INTERNAL RATE OF RETURN METHOD

In the Carson Company case, we observed that the actual rate of return from the machine must be higher than 12% because the net present value is positive at that discount rate. Suppose we discounted the net cash flows at 20%, using Table B–4 (present value of an annuity of $1 for 20% and 5 periods) from the Appendix.

Present value of expected annual net cash flows	
($50,000 × 2.9906)	$149,530
Cost of initial investment	163,715
Net present value	$(14,185)

Note that we have a negative net present value of $14,185 at 20%. This means that the investment in the machine will not yield a 20% return, so the actual rate of return must be less than 20%. Since we had a positive net present value at 12% (meaning that the actual rate must be higher than 12%) and a negative net present value at 20% (meaning that the actual rate must be lower than 20%), the actual rate of return from the investment must be somewhere in between the two discount rates. The **internal rate of return**, also called the time adjusted rate of return or the actual rate of return, is defined as the discount rate that will produce a net present value of zero for an investment. In other words, the discounted net cash flows will be equal to the cost of the investment. An investment with an internal rate of return that exceeds the firm's cost of capital will be attractive to a business.

Since the net cash flows for the Carson Company are equal each year and the machine is paid for initially, the calculation of the internal rate of return is relatively easy. We simply treat the net cash flows as an annuity and find the factor from Table B–4 in the Appendix that will make the discounted cash flows equal to the cost of the investment. The appropriate factor is found as follows.

$$\text{Internal rate of return factor} = \frac{\text{Cost of the investment}}{\text{Annual net cash flows}}$$

$$= \frac{\$163,715}{\$50,000}$$

$$= 3.2743$$

Remember that a specific factor, such as 3.2743, from a time value of money table represents a particular combination of discount (interest) rate and number of time periods. Referring to the row for five periods in Table B–4 of the Appendix, we see that the factor 3.2743 gives us a 16% rate, which is the internal rate of return. If we multiply the internal rate of return factor times the $50,000 annual net cash flows, the result is $163,715 − the cost of the initial investment. Whenever we have a factor that is not shown in the table, we can estimate the internal rate of return based on the factor's approximate position in the table, or use mathematical interpolation to determine the exact rate. If the net cash flows are not equal each year, we must use a trial and error approach to find the correct internal rate of return. This consists of choosing an arbitrary discount rate and calculating the net present value of the cash flows involved. If the net present value is positive, we know that the discount rate being tried is lower than the internal rate of return, so we repeat the process with a higher rate until we find a net present value that is negative. Once the internal rate of return is bracketed, we continue to choose discount rates until we find the one with a net present value of zero. Fortunately, computer programs are readily available to eliminate the tedious manual calculations involved with the trial and error process.

IMPACT OF UNEVEN CASH FLOWS—INCLUDING RESIDUAL VALUE

Cash flows from an investment can differ from year to year for several reasons. For example, the annual net cash flows from operations may be different, a major overhaul of the asset may be required at a future date, or the asset may have an estimated residual value at the end of its useful life. To illustrate, let's change the facts with the Carson Company case and assume that the $163,715 investment is expected to produce the following net cash flows over its five-year life.

Year	Amount
1	$30,000
2	40,000
3	50,000
4	60,000
5	70,000

Note that the total net cash flows over the five-year period are $250,000, the same as they were in the original case. However, the timing of the net cash flows is different. Assume, further, that the firm will have to spend $10,000 on a major overhaul of the equipment at the end of the third year to keep it operational, and that the equipment is expected to have a residual value, less income taxes, of $20,000 at the end of its five-year life. Note that the residual value estimated at the end of the equipment's useful life must be reduced by any income taxes expected with the disposition because we are concerned with cash flows. In general, the excess of the selling price of such an asset over its book value at the time of sale is taxed. Thus, to estimate the cash inflow from the ultimate disposition of the equipment, we must consider any income taxes involved. The discounted cash flows involved with this case are shown in Figure 27–2.

The net present value in this case is $12,628, indicating that the actual rate of return is higher than 12%, so the investment is attractive to the firm. The original investment cost is not discounted because it already is in current dollars. The unequal annual net cash flows from operations ranging from $30,000 to $70,000 are discounted at 12% on a year-to-year basis using factors from the present value of $1 table (Table B–3 from the Appendix). Since the major overhaul is required at the end of the third year, its estimated cost (a cash outflow) of $10,000 is converted to current dollars with a factor of .7118.

Year	Item	(a) Cash Flow	(b) Present Value of $1 @ 12%	(a) × (b) Present Value of Cash Flows
Current	Original investment	$(163,715)	1.0000	$(163,715)
1	Annual net cash flow	30,000	.8929	26,787
2	Annual net cash flow	40,000	.7972	31,888
3	Annual net cash flow	50,000	.7118	35,590
3	Major overhaul	(10,000)	.7118	(7,118)
4	Annual net cash flow	60,000	.6355	38,130
5	Annual net cash flow	70,000	.5674	39,718
5	Residual value (after income taxes)	20,000	.5674	11,348
Net present value				$ 12,628

Figure 27–2
Present Value Analysis of Investment in Machine

The residual value, after income taxes, is a single sum, which will be recovered in five years as a cash inflow, so it is discounted using the present value of $1 table with a factor of .5674. We should note that if the firm had required additional working capital to support the investment, that dollar amount would have been added to the initial cost of the investment. At the end of the five year period, the reduction in working capital would have been discounted like the residual value was (but without any income-tax effect), as a release of funds for the business.

DEPRECIATION AS A TAX SHIELD

Objective 13: Depreciation as a tax shield

We emphasized earlier that depreciation should not be included as a cash outflow in capital budgeting because it does not require a cash payment when it is recorded. Instead, the cost of the asset is considered as a cash outflow when it is paid for. However, depreciation *does* affect the amount of income taxes paid because it is deductible for tax purposes, and income taxes require cash outflows. Consequently, the choice of depreciation method will have an impact on the cash flows evaluated in a capital budgeting decision. We are concerned with the depreciation method used for the tax return, not the one used for financial reporting, in capital budgeting. The specific depreciation methods available in a given year depend on the tax law, which changes over time. For example, the Economic Recovery Act of 1981 introduced the concept of an accelerated cost recovery system (ACRS) that allows the most rapid depreciation for tax purposes according to predetermined schedules. The ACRS ignores both the useful lives of assets and any residual values that they are expected to have. The cost of many types of business equipment (e.g., office equipment that has a useful life of ten years) is expensed over a five-year period with ACRS according to the following schedule.

Year of Ownership	Cost Recovery Percent
1	15
2	22
3	21
4	21
5	21

The schedule shows the percentage of a five-year asset's original cost that can be depreciated in each of the years. For example, a $10,000 asset would produce $1,500 of depreciation (.15 × $10,000) during the first year it is used, regardless of when it is purchased during the year. Since depreciation is deductible for tax purposes, it shields revenue from tax, even though it does not require any cash payment when it is recorded. Thus, depreciation is called a **tax shield.** The amount of tax savings from a tax shield depends on the tax rate involved. If a company has a 35% tax rate, the tax savings from a depreciation deduction of $1,000 is $350 ($1,000 × .35), based on the following general formula.

$$\text{Tax savings from depreciation tax shield} = \text{Depreciation deduction} \times \text{Tax rate}$$

The net cash flow of the firm will be $350 higher with the depreciation than it would have been without it. We can see the tax shield effect in the following comparison of the tax liability of Company A, which has such a deduction, with Company B, which does not have the $1,000 depreciation deduction. To illustrate only the impact of the depreciation on net cash flow, we assume that the sales for each firm are equal to cash receipts and that all operating expenses other than depreciation are paid in cash.

	Company A	Company B	Difference
Sales (equal to cash receipts)	$25,000	$25,000	$ -0-
Less expenses:			
Cash operating expenses	15,000	15,000	-0-
Depreciation (1)	1,000	-0-	1,000
Net income before taxes	9,000	10,000	(1,000)
Income taxes @ 35%	3,150	3,500	(350)
Net income after taxes (2)	5,850	6,500	(650)
Net cash flows (2) + (1)	$ 6,850	$ 6,500	$ 350

Note that Company A has $350 less income taxes and higher net cash flows of the same amount because it has the $1,000 depreciation tax shield. The net cash flows for the two companies are determined by adding depreciation, which does not affect cash flow, back to the net income after taxes. Alternatively, the net cash flows can be computed by subtracting all cash outlays from the sales (for Company A, this would be $25,000 − $15,000 − $3,150 = $6,850; and for Company B, it would be $25,000 − $15,000 − $3,500 = $6,500). Even though Company B has $650 more net income than Company A, the depreciation tax shield has resulted in the larger net cash flows of $350 for Company A.

The true impact of depreciation as a tax shield is also affected by the time value of money. That is, the tax deductions will be worth more to a business in early years than in later years because of the time value of money. As a result, the present value of the net cash flows involved with timing differences in depreciation deductions must be carefully considered. To illustrate, assume that an asset with a 12-year useful life and no expected residual value is purchased for $240,000 by a firm with a tax rate of 35%. The firm's cost of capital is 16%. We can compare the discounted tax savings with the rapid ACRS schedule shown earlier and the discounted tax savings with the straight-line method used over a 12-year period, as shown here.

Discounted Tax Savings of Rapid Depreciation Schedule – Five Years

Year	(a) Annual* Depreciation	(b) Tax Rate	(a × b = c) Tax Savings	(d) Present Value of $1 @ 16%	(c × d) Discounted Tax Savings
1	$36,000	.35	$12,600	.8621	$10,862
2	52,800	.35	18,480	.7432	13,734
3	50,400	.35	17,640	.6407	11,302
4	50,400	.35	17,640	.5523	9,743
5	50,400	.35	17,640	.4761	8,398
Totals	$240,000		$84,000		$54,039

*Annual depreciation

Year		Amount
1	($240,000 × .15) =	$36,000
2	($240,000 × .22) =	52,800
3–5	($240,000 × .21) =	50,400

Discounted Tax Savings of 12-Year Depreciation Schedule (Straight-line method)

Total tax savings from depreciation – $240,000 × .35 =	$84,000
Annual depreciation – ($240,000/12)	$20,000
Tax rate	× .35
Annual tax savings	7,000
Present value of an annuity factor of $1 at 16% for 12 years (Table B–4 from the Appendix)	× 5.1971
Discounted tax savings	$36,380

Since the annual tax savings change with the rapid five-year depreciation schedule, we discount the tax savings on a year-to-year basis. In contrast, the annual depreciation with the 12-year schedule is $20,000, because the straight-line method is used. As a result, the tax savings of $7,000 ($20,000 × .35) are the same each year, and we can discount them using the annuity approach. Note that in both cases the tax savings from the depreciation are $84,000 ($240,000 × .35) over the total time period considered. However, the five-year schedule will result in much higher discounted tax savings because they will occur early in the asset's life when the time value of money is high. The discounted tax savings from the five-year schedule are $54,039 compared with $36,380 from the twelve-year schedule, or an added savings of $17,659 in current dollars. Consequently, the concept of depreciation as a tax shield is important to a business, both in terms of the amount of tax savings involved and in terms of the timing of the tax savings (reduced cash outflows).

OTHER CAPITAL BUDGETING METHODS

PAYBACK PERIOD METHOD

Capital budgeting techniques that are not based on the time value of money are sometimes used to approximate the profitability of an investment. The **payback period method** is a measure of the length of time required to recover the cost of an investment from the net cash flows it generates. This is the period of time needed for an investment to pay for itself. The payback period is simple to compute and easy to understand. Often, use of the shortest payback period possible is desirable for two reasons.

Objective 14: Payback period and return on average investment

1. The sooner the cash is recovered, the sooner it can be reinvested in other productive assets, something particularly important in times of high inflation.
2. A quick payback period may reduce the risk of the investment, since uncertainty usually increases with the passage of time.

The primary disadvantages of the method are that it ignores the total life of the investment and the time value of money. An investment selected because of its short payback period may, therefore, be less profitable over its entire life than an alternative investment with a longer payback period and total life. Managers may use this method to maximize short-term profits and make themselves look good, even though the long-term results are detrimental to the business. In addition, cash flows in later years are assumed to be equivalent to those in early years—a serious violation of the time value of money concept. Nevertheless, many firms use the payback period method to make a final choice among alternatives when other methods of evaluation indicate they are equally attractive. The payback period in the Carson Company's decision (in the original case) is computed as:

$$\text{Payback period} = \frac{\text{Initial cost of investment}}{\text{Annual net cash flows}}$$

$$= \frac{\$163,715}{\$50,000} = 3.2743 \text{ years}$$

Note that the payback formula is the same as the one we used earlier to determine the annuity factor for the internal rate of return. The payback period concept is an easy way to remember this important step in computing the internal rate of return.

RETURN ON AVERAGE INVESTMENT METHOD

The **return on average investment method** is a rough approximation of an investment's profitability in terms of net income from the income statement. It is calculated by dividing the average annual net income after tax from an investment by the average investment. When straight-line depreciation is used, the book value of an asset decreases uniformly over its life. As a result, the average investment is computed as:

$$\text{Average investment} = \frac{\text{Initial cost} + \text{Residual value}}{2}$$

When the residual value is zero, the average investment is simply the initial cost divided by two. Remember that we have been using cash flows in the Carson Company case, so we would have to convert back to an income statement based on accrual accounting to use the return on average investment method. Assume that we have made the conversion and the average net income is found to be $20,536 (after all accrual adjustments including the deduction for depreciation). Also, assume that the firm expects the machine to have a $19,645 residual value at the end of 5 years. The average investment and return from it would be computed as follows.

$$\text{Average investment} = \frac{\$163,715 + \$19,645}{2}$$

$$= \frac{\$183,360}{2}$$

$$= \$91,680$$

$$\text{Return on average investment} = \frac{\text{Average net income}}{\text{Average investment}}$$

$$= \frac{\$20,536}{\$91,680}$$

$$= 22.4\%$$

The 22.4% return would be compared with the returns of alternative investments and with the minimum return required by management to determine whether it should be accepted. The proponents of this method support it on the premise that it follows the income statement in measuring the return on an investment. The $20,536 used in the example is the estimate of annual net income, rather than the estimated net cash flows. Unlike the payback period method, the return on average investment method *does* consider the profitability of an investment over its useful life. However, it has a serious weakness: *it does not consider the time value of money*. The use of the average annual net income ignores the timing of cash receipts and disbursements. Consequently, the net cash flows from an investment's last year of life are valued the same as those of its first year. In addition, the method does not distinguish between an investment requiring an immediate payment of cash and one that will be paid for in the future. Since cash available in the current year is clearly worth more than cash available in the distant future, the time value of money should be taken into consideration for effective capital budgeting.

GLOSSARY

CAPITAL BUDGETING. The planning and financing of capital investments (p. 1057).

COST OF CAPITAL. A firm's cost of obtaining funds in the form of debt and owners' equity (p. 1061).

DECISION MAKING. Making a choice among alternative courses of action (p. 1047).

DECISION-MAKING PROCESS. Defining the problem, selecting alternative courses of action, obtaining relevant information, and arriving at a decision (p. 1047).

DECISION MODEL. A formalized method for evaluating alternative courses of action (p. 1048).

DIFFERENTIAL ANALYSIS (INCREMENTAL ANALYSIS). A decision model used to evaluate the differences in relevant revenues and costs between alternative courses of action (p. 1048).

DIFFERENTIAL COST. The difference between the relevant costs of two alternatives (p. 1048).

DIFFERENTIAL REVENUE. The difference between the relevant revenues of two alternatives (p. 1049).

INTERNAL RATE OF RETURN. The discount rate that will discount the cash flows associated with an investment, so that the net present value is equal to zero (p. 1064).

JOINT PRODUCTS. More than one product produced from common raw materials or the same production process (p. 1052).

JOINT PRODUCT COSTS. Common costs required to produce joint products before they are identifiable as separate units (p. 1052).

NET PRESENT VALUE METHOD. A capital budgeting method used to discount future cash flows into present value terms with the firm's cost of capital or hurdle rate (p. 1061).

OPPORTUNITY COST. The potential benefit forgone by rejecting one alternative while accepting another (p. 1049).

PAYBACK PERIOD METHOD. A measure of the length of time required to recover the cost of an investment from the net cash flows it generates (p. 1069).

PROFITABILITY INDEX. The present value of the net cash flows from an investment divided by the cost of the investment (p. 1063).

RELEVANT COSTS. Expected future costs that will differ between alternatives (p. 1048).

RELEVANT REVENUES. Expected future revenues that will differ between alternatives (p. 1049).

RESIDUAL INCOME. The net operating income earned in excess of a certain minimum rate of return on operating assets (p. 1056).

RETURN ON AVERAGE INVESTMENT METHOD. A capital budgeting method that provides a rough approximation of an investment's profitability in terms of net income from the income statement (p. 1070).

RETURN ON INVESTMENT (ROI) ANALYSIS. A technique used to evaluate the profitability of segments of a business (p. 1055).

SPLIT-OFF POINT. The point in the production process at which joint products become separate products (p. 1052).

SUNK COSTS. Costs that are not relevant in decision making because they have already been incurred and cannot be changed (p. 1049).

TAX SHIELD. The total amount of a tax-deductible expense, such as depreciation, that shields that amount of revenue from being taxed (p. 1067).
TRANSFER PRICING. The prices charged by one segment of a decentralized firm for products or services transferred to another segment (p. 1057).
UNAVOIDABLE COSTS. Either future costs that will not differ between alternatives or sunk costs (p. 1049).

DISCUSSION QUESTIONS

1. What is decision making? What are the basic steps followed in the decision-making process?
2. You recently heard a business manager make the following comment. "Quantitative analysis may be all right for some businesses, but I'd rather make decisions based on my intuition and years of experience." Do you agree? Explain.
3. What is differential analysis?
4. Define each of the following terms.
   (a) Relevant costs.
   (b) Differential costs.
   (c) Unavoidable costs.
   (d) Sunk costs.
   (e) Opportunity costs.
5. The All-Sports Company produces golf balls, which are sold for $8 per dozen. Under what circumstances might the firm consider an order at a price lower than $8?
6. The Back Camper Company uses a number of parts to produce several models of campers. The company has been purchasing a certain part from another firm at a price of $110, even though it has the expertise to produce the part internally. The chief accountant has estimated that the following costs would be incurred in the production of each of the parts.

Direct costs	$ 90
Variable manufacturing overhead	10
Fixed manufacturing overhead	22
Total	$122

Do you agree that the firm should buy the part based on this analysis? Explain your reasoning.
7. Define the following terms.
   (a) Joint products.
   (b) Joint product costs.
   (c) Split-off point for joint products.
8. Why can't a firm simply select the products with the highest contribution margins to find the most profitable product mix?
9. Differentiate between return on investment analysis and residual income analysis.
10. Why are transfer pricing decisions important in evaluating the profit performance of the segments of a business?
11. What is capital budgeting? Why are capital budgeting decisions critical to the overall success of a firm?
12. Differentiate between cash flows and net income, as the terms are used in capital budgeting. Why are cash flows used in most capital budgeting models?

13. Why are discounted cash flows the best basis upon which capital budgeting decisions can be made?
14. What is a firm's cost of capital? How does it relate to capital budgeting decisions?
15. What does the term *net present value* mean?
16. Discounting future cash flows at 16% provides a lower present value than discounting them at 12%. Why?
17. What is a profitability index? How is it used with the net present value method?
18. Define the internal rate of return. How is it different from the net present value?
19. Explain the concept of a depreciation deduction tax shield. If a business has a depreciation deduction of $4,000 and a tax rate of 30%, how much tax savings does the deduction provide? What is the impact on the firm's cash flows?
20. What is the payback period method? What are the primary limitations of the use of the payback period method in capital budgeting?
21. What is the main advantage of using the return on average investment method? What is the major disadvantage?

EXERCISES

Exercise 27-1 **Evaluating a Special Order**
The Zare Company manufactures portable cassette players at a per unit cost of:

Direct labor	$18
Direct materials	24
Variable manufacturing overhead	14
Fixed manufacturing overhead	22
Total unit cost	$78

The company sells each cassette player for $95 and is presently operating at 75% of its capacity of 50,000 units per year. The company has received a special order at a price of $63 per unit from a mail-order firm for 1,000 units per month for one year only. The units sold to the mail-order firm would be identical to the firm's regular players, except for a special name plate. The Zare Company would have to purchase a new machine for $35,000 in order to produce the special name plate. The machine will have no alternative use or residual value at the end of the year. The sales by the mail-order firm would not affect the company's regular sales because of the different label and markets involved.

Required:
Should the company accept the special order? What would be the impact on profits?

Exercise 27-2 **Evaluating a Make or Buy Decision**
The Stevens Company manufactures calculators and has always produced all necessary parts for the calculators, including the subassembly. The cost per unit of the subassembly at a production level of 50,000 units is:

Direct materials	$ 9
Direct labor	10
Variable manufacturing overhead	6
Fixed manufacturing overhead	8
Total unit cost	$33

One-fourth of the fixed manufacturing overhead is a common cost that is allocated to the subassembly production. The remaining fixed manufacturing overhead cost is direct, and one-half of direct fixed overhead cost could be eliminated if the subassemblies are purchased, rather than produced. An outside supplier has offered to produce and sell the Stevens Company 50,000 subassemblies at a price of $29 per unit.

Required:
A. Should the offer be accepted if there are no alternative uses for the manufacturing space currently being used to produce the subassembly?
B. Should the offer be accepted if the manufacturing space currently being used could be rented for $80,000 per year?

Exercise 27-3 Differential Analysis and Joint Products
The Levine Company produces four joint products—A, B, C, and D—at a total cost of $40,000. The company can sell the products immediately after the split-off point for $12,000, $9,600, $10,800, and $14,400, respectively. The products also can be processed further and sold as follows.

Product	Additional Processing Costs	Sales
A	$14,400	$24,000
B	16,800	28,800
C	26,400	42,000
D	7,200	16,800

All costs after the split-off point can be eliminated for any product that is not processed beyond the split-off point.

Required:
Which products should be processed further and which should be sold at the split-off point?

Exercise 27-4 Combining Contribution Margin and a Scarce Resource
The Morgan Company produces and sells four products—A, B, C, and D. The selling prices, variable costs, and number of machine hours required to produce each product are:

Product	Selling Price	Variable Costs	Machine Hours Per Unit
A	$32	$20	2
B	40	16	3
C	30	20	1
D	60	28	8

The company can produce each of the four products with a single machine, which has a maximum operating capacity of 6,600 hours per year.

Required:
A. How many units of each of the four products can be produced in a year if the company produces only that product?
B. Assuming that the company can sell all the units it produces, which product or mix of products should be produced?
C. Assuming the firm must produce 400 units of Product A, what additional products should be produced?

Exercise 27-5 Evaluating Profitability Performance

The Bunnell Company operates four departments. The company has gathered the following departmental data.

Department	Sales	Cost of Goods Sold	Operating Expenses	Operating Assets Beginning Balance	Ending Balance
1	$ 80,000	$ 60,000	$ 6,000	$ 60,000	$ 80,000
2	36,000	14,000	9,400	88,000	80,000
3	600,000	500,000	78,000	360,000	520,000
4	500,000	300,000	110,400	500,000	620,000

Required:
1. Rank the four departments on the basis of return on investment.
2. Assume that the company requires a minimum return on the average investment in operating assets of 10%. What is the residual income of each department?

Exercise 27-6 Basic Capital Budgeting Methods

The Blazer Company is evaluating the purchase of a new machine that will cost $33,540 and have no residual value. Annual net cash flows (including tax payments) for each of the next 10 years are expected to be $8,000. The related annual net income is expected to be $4,696, and depreciation is computed for financial reporting purposes on a straight-line basis. The company has a cost of capital of 12%.

Required:
A. Compute the payback period.
B. Compute the net present value.
C. Compute the internal rate of return.
D. Compute the return on average investment.

Exercise 27-7 Determining Cost of Capital

The Howard Company wants to determine its cost of capital to use in capital budgeting decisions. The firm's capital structure is as follows.

Source of Capital	Amount
Debt financing	$ 40,000
Preferred stock	20,000
Common equity	140,000

The firm's president has determined that the after-tax costs of the three financing sources are 8%, 12%, and 18%, respectively.

Required:
Compute the firm's cost of capital.

Exercise 27-8 Evaluating Depreciation as a Tax Shield

The head accountant of the Rogers Company, a new company just beginning operations, is trying to evaluate the after-tax effect of depreciation on the firm's cash flows. The company has recently purchased depreciable assets costing $200,000, with no residual value at the end of a 10-year life. Assume that the firm has two options for the annual rates of depreciation, shown as follows.

Year	Option 1	Option 2
1	.15	.10
2	.22	.10
3	.21	.10
4	.21	.10
5	.21	.10
6	—	.10
7	—	.10
8	—	.10
9	—	.10
10	—	.10

The firm expects to have to pay income taxes each year with either option at a tax rate of 35%. It has a cost of capital of 12%.

Required:
Compute the discounted tax savings with each option.

Exercise 27-9 Use of Discounted Cash Flows and Payback Period

The Luth Company is considering the purchase of a new machine, which will cost $70,000 and which will be paid for in cash. The machine has a useful life of seven years with no residual value. Annual before-tax cash savings from better productivity are expected to be $18,000. The company has a cost of capital of 12% and an income tax rate of 35%. Straight-line depreciation is used.

Required:
A. Determine the annual after-tax cash savings from the machine.
B. What is the payback period for the investment?
C. What is the net present value of the investment?

Exercise 27-10 Capital Budgeting Evaluations

The Gatlob Company is evaluating three investment alternatives and has compiled the following information.

	Investment		
	A	**B**	**C**
Initial investment:	$91,276	$151,632	$83,946
Net cash inflows:			
Year 1	20,000	40,000	30,000
2	20,000	40,000	30,000
3	20,000	40,000	30,000
4	20,000	40,000	30,000
5	20,000	40,000	—
6	20,000	—	—
7	20,000	—	—

The company requires a 12% minimum return on new investments.

Required:
A. Calculate the payback period for each investment.
B. Calculate the net present value for each investment.
C. Determine the profitability index for each investment.
D. Calculate the internal rate of return for each investment.

Exercise 27-11 Evaluating Relationships Between Net Present Value and Internal Rate of Return

Given here are four independent cases in which the life of each investment is 10 years, with no residual value.

Case	Initial Investment Cost	Annual Net Cash Flows	Cost of Capital	Internal Rate of Return	Net Present Value
1	—	$ 70,000	12%	16%	—
2	$193,328	—	—	16%	$ 32,680
3	282,510	—	10%	—	24,720
4	—	100,000	—	16%	(64,070)

Required:
Fill in the blanks based on the relationships between the initial cost of the investment, the annual net cash flows, the cost of capital, the internal rate of return, and the net present value.

PROBLEMS

Problem 27-1 Evaluating a Special Order with Opportunity Costs

The White Company produces flower vases. The operating results of the preceding year were.

Sales (77,000 units @ $16)	$1,232,000
Cost of goods sold	
Direct materials	231,000
Direct labor	308,000
Manufacturing overhead	184,800
Total	723,800
Gross Profit	508,200
Selling expenses	77,000
Administrative expenses	46,200
Total operating expenses	123,200
Net income	$ 385,000

The company has received a special order to sell 10,000 vases at a unit cost of $13.80. Material costs per unit would not change, but the labor costs for the special order would be 25% greater than normal, since some overtime wages would be incurred. Fixed manufacturing overhead is 50% of the variable manufacturing overhead at the present level of production. Fixed manufacturing overhead would not change, and there would be no additional variable or fixed selling expenses. The administrative expenses, which are all fixed, would increase by $4,000 if the special order is accepted. Current variable selling expenses are $.40 per unit. The company has a maximum capacity of 85,000 vases, so the company would have to reduce its regular sales by 2,000 units if it accepts the special order.

Required:

Should the company accept the special order? What would be the effect on the firm's profits?

Problem 27-2 Evaluating a Make or Buy Decision

The Radar Company has realized a significant increase in demand for its products and is presently producing at a full capacity level of 100,000 units. The company is considering expanding output to 125,000 units by the adoption of one of the following alternatives.

1. The additional 25,000 units could be purchased from an outside source at a price of $12 per unit.
2. The company could expand its production capacity, which would result in added direct fixed expenses of $100,000 per year. The company's sales and cost data at the 100,000 unit level of output are:

Sales	$1,500,000
Direct materials	200,000
Direct labor	300,000
Variable manufacturing overhead	100,000
Direct fixed manufacturing overhead	500,000
Allocated fixed manufacturing overhead	150,000
Net income	$ 250,000

Common fixed costs allocated to production would increase from $150,000 to $187,500, since the common fixed overhead is allocated on the basis of sales volume, although the firm's total common fixed costs would not increase under either alternative.

Required:

Which of the two alternatives should the company adopt? What would be the effect of each alternative on profits?

Problem 27-3 Differential Analysis and Joint Products

The Straight-Shoot Company produces two joint products, X and Y. The annual production is 20,000 units of X and 12,000 units of Y at a joint cost of $208,000. Product X can be sold for $10 per unit at the split-off point, and product Y can be sold for $16 per unit. Product Y can be further processed at a cost of $20,000 into products A and B. The additional processing will produce 8,000 units of A and 4,000 units of B. The selling price of product A is $12 per unit, and product B sells for $20 per unit. Product X can be processed further at an annual cost of $40,000 and sold for $20 per unit.

Required:

Which products should be sold at the split-off point and which should be processed further?

Problem 27-4 Profitability Analysis

The Darnell Company has compiled the following budgeted data for next year's operations.

	Account Balance on 1/1	Account Balance on 12/31
Cash	$ 20,000	$ 50,000
Accounts receivable	50,000	70,000
Inventory	90,000	100,000
Plant and equipment	160,000	140,000
Accounts payable	40,000	60,000
Total fixed costs	$100,000	
Variable costs per unit	10	
Estimated volume	20,000 units	

Required:

A. If the company wants to earn net income at the estimated volume that is a 15% before-tax return on its average investment in operating assets, what should the selling price per unit be? (*Hint:* Use CVP analysis)

B. If the company actually produces and sells 18,000 units at the price computed in requirement (A), what is the firm's actual rate of return on its average investment in operating assets?

C. If the company actually sells 24,000 units at a selling price of $17 per unit, what is the company's residual income, assuming a minimum acceptable return on assets of 12%?

Problem 27-5 Capital Budgeting Evaluations

The Beasley Company is considering a project that would require the purchase of a new machine at a cost of $59,812. The new machine would have a five-year life and no residual value at the end of its life. The new project would produce a net cash flow of $20,000 each year. The company has a cost of capital of 12%.

Required:

A. What is the payback period for the machine?

B. Calculate the net present value of the machine.

C. Determine the internal rate of return for the machine.

Problem 27-6 Using Alternative Capital Budgeting Methods

The president of Star Enterprises is evaluating three investment projects. The net cash flows for each project are estimated as follows.

	Investment Project		
Year	1	2	3
1	$ 90,000	$ 60,000	$ 50,000
2	90,000	60,000	50,000
3	90,000	60,000	50,000
4	—	60,000	50,000
5	—	60,000	50,000
6	—	—	50,000
7	—	—	50,000
8	—	—	50,000
Initial cost	$216,162	$227,448	$217,180

The firm's cost of capital is 12%.

Required:

A. Compute the payback period for each investment.
B. What is the net present value for each investment?
C. What is the profitability index for each investment?
D. Calculate the internal rate of return for each investment.

Problem 27-7 Using Cash Flows in a Capital Budgeting Decision

The Larsen Company is considering a new robotics system, which will significantly decrease its manufacturing costs. The annual after-tax cost savings are expected to be $110,000, and the system will cost $470,000. Its useful life will be eight years and its residual value is estimated at $10,000, net of tax. However, a major overhaul costing $37,500 will be required at the end of the fifth year. The firm's cost of capital is 16%, and straight-line depreciation is used.

Required:

Using the net present value method, determine whether the robotics system should be purchased.

Problem 27-8 Evaluating a Capital Expenditure Decision

The Hoosier Company operates a computer service bureau that provides data-processing services to the business community. The firm is currently considering the purchase of a new specialized computer that will cost $110,000 and have no residual value at the end of its five-year life. Straight-line depreciation is used for all equipment. The firm's accountant expects the revenue and expenses associated with operating the computer to be about equal to cash receipts and cash disbursements, except for depreciation. The projected operating performance is summarized as:

Year	Revenue	Expenses (including depreciation)
1	$ 86,450	$58,000
2	96,000	61,500
3	102,250	61,500
4	108,500	61,500
5	114,750	61,500

The company's expected tax rate is 20%, and its cost of capital is 12%. Income taxes are not included in the expenses shown.

Required:

A. Compute the return on average investment for the computer.
B. Determine the annual net cash flows (after tax) expected from the operation of the computer.
C. Calculate the net present value for the investment.
D. Determine the profitability index for the investment.

ALTERNATE PROBLEMS

Problem 27-1A Evaluating a Special Order with Opportunity Costs

The Burn-Rite Company manufactures gas grills and is considering expanding production. A distributor has asked the company to produce a special order of 10,000 grills to be sold in another country. The grills would be sold under a different brand name and would not influence Burn-Rite Company's current sales. The plant is currently producing 92,000 units per year. The company's maximum capacity is 100,000 units per year, so the company would have to reduce the production of units sold under its own brand name by 2,000 units if the special order is accepted.

The company's income statement for the previous year is presented below.

Sales (92,000 units)		$6,900,000
Cost of goods sold		
Direct materials	$2,300,000	
Direct labor	1,840,000	
Manufacturing overhead	1,380,000	5,520,000
Gross profit		1,380,000
Selling expenses	575,000	
Administrative expenses	$ 237,500	812,500
Net income		$ 567,500

The company's variable manufacturing overhead is $10 per unit, and the variable selling expense is $5 per unit. The administrative expense is completely fixed and would increase by $5,000 if the special order is accepted. There would be no variable selling expense associated with the special order, and variable manufacturing overhead per unit would remain constant.

The company's direct labor cost per unit for the special order would increase 5%, while direct material cost per unit for the special order would increase 10%. Fixed manufacturing overhead and fixed selling expense would not change.

Required:
If the distributor has offered to pay $67 per unit for the special order, should the company accept the offer?

Problem 27-2A Evaluating a Make or Buy Decision

The Blow-Hard Company produces air compressors. The motors for the compressors are purchased directly from an outside supplier at a cost of $55 each. The company has some factory space, which it currently rents to another firm as warehouse space. The annual rental income is $55,000. If the company decides to manufacture the motors, it would have to purchase a new machine at a cost of $75,000. The new equipment would enable the firm to produce its annual requirement of 5,000 motors, and would have no residual value at the end of a five-year useful life. In addition, the company has compiled the following costs per unit, which do not reflect the cost of the new machine.

Direct labor	$12
Direct materials	15
Variable manufacturing overhead	8
Fixed manufacturing overhead—direct	2
Fixed manufacturing overhead—allocated	5
Total	$42

Required:
Should the firm make or buy the motors for the air compressors?

Problem 27-3A Differential Analysis and Joint Products

The Raye Chemical Company produces two products, A and B, at a joint cost of $48,000. The company can sell 8,000 units of product A for $4 per unit, or the units can be processed further at a cost of $20,000, to produce 3,000 units of product X, 4,000 units of product Y, and 1,000 units of a third product, Z. The unit selling prices for products X, Y, and Z are $6, $4, and $8, respectively. The company can sell 5,000 units of product B, or they can be processed further to produce 2,000 units of product C and 3,000 units of product D. The additional processing to produce products C and D will cost $6,000. The per unit selling prices are: product B—$6; product C—$10; and product D—$6.

Required:

Which of the products should be sold at the split-off point and which should be processed further?

Problem 27-4A Profitability Analysis

The Fly-Right Company, an overnight package delivery service, wants to maintain a 20% before-tax return on the average investment in operating assets. The operating assets totaled $900,000 on January 1 and are estimated to be $940,000 on December 31. The company anticipates that it will deliver 60,000 packages during the next calendar year. The variable costs per package average $5, and total fixed costs are budgeted to be $200,000.

Required:

A. What should the company charge to deliver a package in order to achieve its goal? (*Hint:* Use CVP analysis)

B. If the company actually delivers 56,000 packages at the price determined in requirement (A), what is the firm's actual rate of return on its average investment in operating assets?

C. If the company actually delivers 58,000 packages at a delivery fee of $11.20 per package, what is the company's residual income, assuming a minimum acceptable return on assets of 15%?

Problem 27-5A Capital Budgeting Evaluations

The Porter Company is considering the purchase of a new machine. The machine would cost $124,000 and have a useful life of five years. At the end of five years, the machine is expected to have no residual value. The new machine would provide a net cash flow and operating income before depreciation and taxes of $44,000 each year. Straight-line depreciation is to be used. The company's income tax rate is 40%, and it requires a rate of return of at least 12% on investments of this type.

Required:

A. What is the payback period for the machine?

B. Calculate the net present value of the investment.

Problem 27-6A Evaluating Investments with Capital Budgeting Methods

The Tanto Company is considering three investments for the upcoming year. The firm has a cost of capital of 16%. Summary information concerning the net cash flow of the investments and their initial costs is shown here.

	Investment		
Year	A	B	C
1	$ 70,000	$ 50,000	$ 30,000
2	70,000	50,000	30,000
3	70,000	50,000	30,000
4	70,000	50,000	30,000
5	—	50,000	30,000
6	—	50,000	30,000
7	—	—	30,000
8	—	—	30,000
9	—	—	30,000
10	—	—	30,000
11	—	—	30,000
12	—	—	30,000
Initial cost	181,209	205,570	155,913

Required:
A. Calculate the payback period for each investment.
B. What is the net present value for each investment?
C. What is the profitability index for each investment?
D. Compute the internal rate of return for each investment.

Problem 27-7A Using Cash Flows in a Capital Budgeting Decision

The McCormick Company is evaluating a new computer that would be used for data processing. The increased capacity of the equipment is expected to save the firm $40,000 (after tax) for each of the five years of its useful life. A residual value of $10,000 after taxes is expected for the computer at the end of the five years. The cost of the equipment is $150,000, and it will be paid for in cash. The equipment's manufacturer estimates that an overhaul, costing $15,000, will be required at the end of the third year. The firm's cost of capital is 16%, and straight-line depreciation is used.

Required:
Use the net present value method to determine whether the computer should be purchased.

Problem 27-8A Evaluating a Capital Expenditure Decision

Graham Electronics is an engineering consulting firm specializing in the installation of highly sophisticated electronic communications systems. The company is considering the purchase of testing equipment that would be used on jobs. The equipment would cost $132,000 and would have no residual value at the end of its five-year life. Straight-line depreciation would be used if the equipment is purchased. The firm's accountant projects revenue and expenses with the operation of the equipment that are equal to the cash receipts and cash disbursements associated with it, except for depreciation. A summary of the cash flows expected from the equipment (without considering taxes) is as follows.

Year	Revenue	Expenses (including depreciation)
1	$103,740	$69,600
2	115,200	73,800
3	122,700	73,800
4	130,200	73,800
5	137,700	73,800

The firm's expected tax rate is 20%, and its cost of capital is 12%.

Required:

A. Compute the return on average investment for the equipment.

B. Determine the annual net cash flows (after tax) expected from the operation of the equipment.

C. Calculate the net present value for the investment.

D. Determine the profitability index for the investment.

CASE

CASE 27-1 Decision Case Make or Buy Decision

You are an accountant with the Roll-On Company, a producer of golf carts. At a recent management meeting, the vice president, Ed Rogers, reported that the equipment used to manufacture a particular component of the golf cart is worn out and will have to be replaced. It has no residual value. Alternatively, he informed the other managers at the meeting, the company could consider purchasing the component from an outside supplier and not replacing the equipment that is used only for that component.

The president of the company listened to Mr. Rogers's report and asked you to develop an analysis of the costs associated with the two alternatives, making or buying the component. You have accumulated the following facts.

Making the Component. The new equipment required to manufacture the component has a cost of $432,000 and a five-year useful life. Straight-line depreciation is used by the company and the equipment will not have a residual value. Each year, 48,000 components are required, and the firm's costs incurred to produce one unit last year were:

Direct materials		$ 3.96
Direct labor		5.76
Manufacturing overhead:		
Variable portion	$ .86	
Fixed portion	5.26	
Total		6.12
Total cost per unit		$15.84

Included in the fixed manufacturing costs is depreciation on the old equipment, amounting to $2.16 per unit. Ed Rogers believes that the new equipment will be more efficient and will reduce direct labor cost and variable overhead cost by 25%. The direct materials cost and fixed manufacturing overhead cost, other than depreciation, will not change if the new equipment is acquired. The firm can produce a maximum of 72,000 components each year with the new equipment and has no other use for the space involved.

Purchasing the component. The components can be purchased from a reliable outside supplier at a price of $10.30 each. The supplier is willing to sign a contract guaranteeing that the price will be the same for five years.

Required:

A. Assuming that the company will continue to use 48,000 components each year, should the components be produced or purchased?

B. Assuming that the company will require 72,000 components each year, would your decision be different?

C. Suppose that the space involved with the production of the components can be leased for five years at an annual rent of $19,200. Would this affect your decision if the company will require 72,000 components each year?

D. Can you think of any nonfinancial considerations that should be analyzed in the decision to make or buy the component?

28

INCOME TAXES: AN OVERVIEW

CHAPTER OVERVIEW AND OBJECTIVES

This chapter contains two parts. Part I is an overview of federal income tax laws as they pertain to individual taxpayers. Part II discusses the computation of a corporation's income tax liability and the impact of income taxes on business decisions. When you have completed this chapter, you should understand:

1. Some basic features of the federal income tax system.
2. The importance of tax planning.
3. The major components of an individual tax return, such as gross income, deductions from gross income, itemized deductions, personal exemptions, and tax credits.
4. How to compute the tax liability for an individual using both tax tables and tax-rate schedules.
5. The computation of taxable income and income tax liability for a corporation.

In preceding chapters, the impact of taxes on business decisions has not been emphasized, but tax payments to various governmental bodies are a significant part of the cost of doing business. Corporations often report an income tax expense of 40% or more of their pretax income. For example, in its 1984 annual report, Apple Computer, Inc. reported income before taxes of $109.2 million and an income tax expense of $45.1 million—41.3% of its pretax income. Because of the magnitude of taxes, few business decisions are made without first considering their effect.

The various taxes levied by federal, state, and local governments also have a significant effect on individuals. Federal income tax rates vary according to income. The rates for individuals range between an 11% minimum and a 50%

maximum of taxable income. Therefore, planning to minimize the legal tax liability is as vitally important for individual taxpayers as it is for businesses.

Because of the complexity of tax rules and regulations, tax specialists are often engaged to determine the tax consequences of various alternatives. To benefit fully from the advice of specialists, decision makers must understand the basic structure of the tax system, so that they will be aware of the tax consequences of their decisions.

The basic provisions of the federal income tax laws that affect individuals are discussed in Part I. Part II discusses the income tax laws that affect corporations. The aspects of the federal tax laws covered include the provisions of the Economic Recovery Tax Act of 1981 (ERTA), the Tax Equity and Fiscal Responsibility Act of 1982 (TEFRA), and the Tax Reform Act of 1984 (TRA). Federal income tax laws are emphasized because they have the greatest impact on both personal and business income. However, while state and local tax laws are not covered in this chapter, they should not be ignored in tax planning. They do increase the total tax burden—even though their tax rates are lower than the federal rates.

PART I. INTRODUCTION TO THE FEDERAL TAX SYSTEM AND TAX CONSIDERATIONS FOR INDIVIDUALS

A BRIEF HISTORY OF FEDERAL INCOME TAXATION

Federal income taxes were first collected in this country to help finance the American Civil War. However, in the late 1800s the Supreme Court ruled the income tax unconstitutional, because it was levied in proportion to the income of individuals, rather than in proportion to a census, as permitted by the Constitution. In 1913, Congress enacted the first permanent income tax law after the Sixteenth Amendment to the Constitution was ratified. The Sixteenth Amendment gave Congress the power to levy and collect taxes on individual incomes without regard to a census. Since then, Congress has enacted numerous other tax laws, all of which are compiled in the **Internal Revenue Code**.

The U.S. Treasury Department, operating through an agency called the Internal Revenue Service (IRS), is responsible for administering and enforcing the income tax laws. The IRS periodically issues regulations that reflect its interpretations of income tax laws. The ultimate interpretation of the tax laws, however, lies with the federal court system, which handles disputes between the IRS and taxpayers.

The original purpose of the income tax was to raise revenue. Although that is still its primary purpose, Congress has also used its taxing authority to accomplish other economic and social goals, such as attaining full employment, providing an incentive to small businesses, providing economic stimulation to certain industries or to the national economy, redistributing national income, and controlling inflation.

SOURCES AND USES OF FEDERAL GOVERNMENT FUNDS

For 1985, the federal government budgeted receipts of $745.1 billion, excluding borrowing, and outlays of $925.5 billion. Individual income tax is the primary source of funds for the U.S. government. It is expected to account for 36 cents of every dollar of receipts for the 1985 fiscal year (See Figure 28–1). Another eight cents comes from corporate income taxes. The major budget outlays are direct benefit payments for individuals, national defense, and interest payments, in that order.

SOME FEATURES OF THE FEDERAL INCOME TAX SYSTEM

Objective 1: Features of the federal tax system

Before discussing some of the specific tax provisions related to computing taxable income for individuals and businesses, it is helpful to discuss some of the basic features of the federal income tax system.

CLASSIFICATIONS OF TAXABLE ENTITIES

For purposes of federal income tax, there are four classifications of taxable entity: individuals, corporations, estates, and trusts. Each must file a tax return and pay taxes on taxable income. Discussion is limited here to individual and corporate taxes. Taxation of estates and trusts is covered in more advanced courses.

Proprietorships and partnerships are recognized as separate business entities

Figure 28–1
The Budget Dollar—
Fiscal Year 1985
Estimate

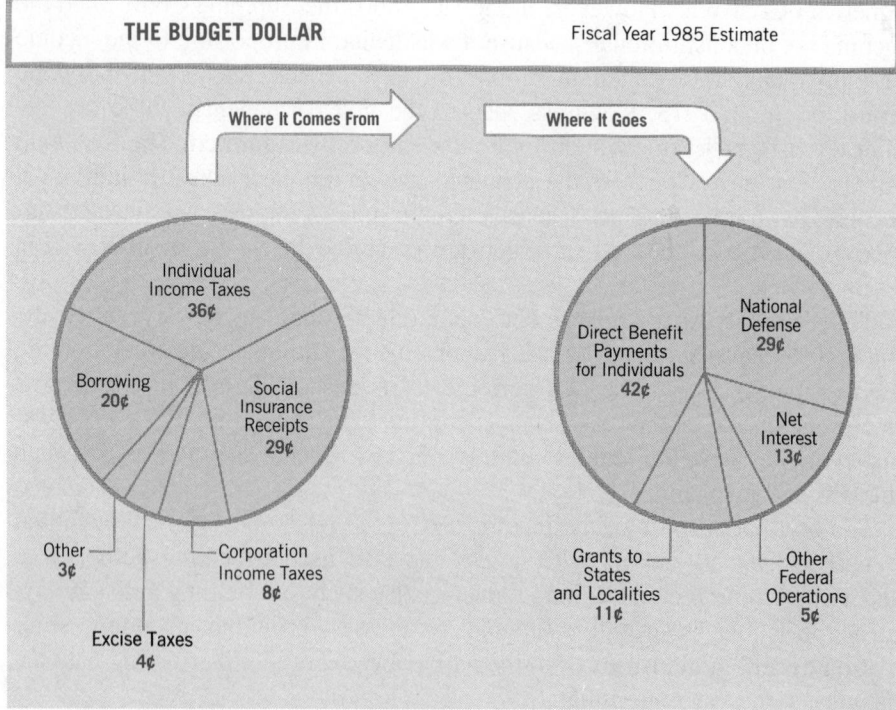

Source: The United States Budget in Brief, 1985

for accounting purposes, but they are not subject to tax as separate taxable entities. Instead, a proprietor must include the income or loss from a business in his or her individual tax return. A partnership must file an information return showing the results of operations and a computation of how the income or loss is allocated to each partner. In turn, the partners must include their share of the income or loss in their respective individual tax returns. Remember that the income of a proprietorship or the allocable share of partnership income is taxed directly to the individual owners, whether or not it is actually withdrawn from the business.

A corporation, on the other hand, is a separate taxable entity, which must file a tax return and pay a tax on its taxable income. When after-tax income is distributed to stockholders, dividends in excess of an excluded amount must be included as income in the stockholders' individual tax returns. This taxing of income when it is earned by the corporation and again when it is distributed to the stockholders has led to the assertion that corporate income is subject to double taxation.

Corporations that satisfy certain criteria can avoid the direct tax on corporate income by electing to be considered an **S Corporation** (previously called a Subchapter S Corporation). An S Corporation is treated similarly to a partnership for tax purposes. An S Corporation may have one stockholder, but one of the basic conditions for S Corporation treatment is that the number of stockholders cannot exceed a specified maximum (currently 35). Thus, the option generally is available only to relatively small businesses.

RELATIONSHIP OF TAX LAW TO GENERALLY ACCEPTED ACCOUNTING PRINCIPLES

To accomplish the purposes of raising revenues and implementing certain economic and social policies, Congress has enacted an increasingly complex and ever-changing set of tax laws. Under these laws, taxable income is based on objectives and rules that are sometimes different from the generally accepted accounting principles applied in determining accounting income. Furthermore, a taxpayer often is permitted or required to use one accounting method for tax purposes and another for accounting purposes. Consequently, taxable income often does not equal accounting income.

THE ROLE OF TAX PLANNING

The potential effect of income taxes is usually a significant factor in evaluating alternative courses of action. **Tax planning** or **tax avoidance** involves evaluating the impact of alternative courses of action on taxable income. The objective of tax planning is to legally structure business and personal transactions in such a way that the tax liability resulting from them is legally minimized. In contrast, **tax evasion** is the deliberate misstatement of a tax liability by failing to report income received or by claiming fraudulent deductions. For example, taxes are evaded when interest, tips, and gains on the sale of investments are not reported, when excessive depreciation is deducted, and

Objective 2:
The importance of tax planning

when a contribution to a charitable organization is deducted but not made. Tax evasion is illegal and the penalties for it can be severe.

In most business decisions, however, the tax factor is only one variable and should be considered in the light of other objectives. For example, the tax consequences of incorporating will be different from the tax consequences of forming a partnership, since each alternative will have a different effect on the amount of taxable income allocable to the owners. In addition, the cost of incorporating, the fact that partners have unlimited liability, and the amount of funds needed should also be considered—and may ultimately be more important than the tax implications of the decision. Nevertheless, regardless of other considerations, the goal of tax planning is to choose and implement the alternative that produces the lowest legal tax liability.

THE CHOICE OF ACCOUNTING METHODS

The taxable year in which an item is reported as income or is reported as an expense depends on the accounting method adopted—accrual basis or cash basis. Most individual taxpayers use the cash basis of accounting. A taxpayer who engages in a business and who also has other sources of income, such as salaries, rental income, and interest, may elect to report the business income on the accrual basis, but report other income and deductions on a cash basis.

Accrual Basis of Accounting

The *accrual basis* of accounting described throughout the preceding chapters is used by many businesses. Under this method, revenues are recognized when a sale is made or when services are rendered, and expenses are recognized when used in the production of revenue, regardless of when cash is received or paid. Any taxpayer (other than an individual whose only income is salary) who maintains a set of accounting records can elect to use the accrual basis for tax purposes. When inventories are a significant factor in the calculation of net income, the accrual basis is required for purchase and sales figures.

Cash Basis of Accounting

The *cash basis* of accounting—that is, revenue recognized when cash is received and expenses or deductions claimed when cash is paid—is used by most individuals not engaged in a business and by businesses that do not have significant inventories. Therefore, this method is widely used by service businesses.

For income tax purposes, the cash basis is modified in two major ways.

1. Revenue is reported as income when it is available to the taxpayer. In tax terms, this is called **constructive receipt**. For example, interest credited to a savings account is taxable even though it was not withdrawn by the taxpayer.
2. The cost of depreciable assets cannot be deducted in full in the year of purchase, but must be depreciated in accordance with tax laws.

The cash basis of accounting is simple to use and requires a minimum of recordkeeping. However, a major advantage often is that it permits a taxpayer greater flexibility in tax planning. When this method is used, a taxpayer may legally control the timing of receipts for services performed and payments for deductible items. For example, a doctor may purposely delay billing patients until after year-end, or reasonable amounts of office supplies may be purchased in advance and deducted in the current tax year. Thus, taxable income is reduced in the current year as a result of both actions.

Most transactions for a service firm are in cash. However, receipt of noncash items for services rendered must be included at their fair value for income tax purposes. For example, if an accountant agrees to maintain the accounting records and prepare the tax returns for a dentist in exchange for dental care for his family, both the accountant and the dentist have taxable income resulting from this arrangement. This income is measured by the fair value of the services received by each party. The dentist also has a deduction for the accounting services received. If either the dentist or the accountant fails to report the value of the services received, he or she could be charged with income tax evasion and be subject to possible penalties.

TAX CONSIDERATIONS FOR INDIVIDUAL TAXPAYERS

Tax returns are filed on forms provided by the federal government. Although the listing of specific data on a tax form varies from time to time, the general approach to computing taxable income for an individual taxpayer is shown in Figure 28–2. Conceptually, the Internal Revenue Code defines gross revenue and deductions as diagrammed in Figure 28–2. That is, revenues are defined

**Objective 3:
Components of
a tax return**

Income from all sources		$81,420
Less: Exclusions from income		1,180
Gross income for tax purposes		80,240
Less: Deductions from gross income		7,000
Adjusted gross income		73,240
Less: Deductions from adjusted gross income		
Itemized deductions	$16,760	
Less: Zero bracket amount	3,400	$13,360
Exemptions		4,000
		17,360
Taxable income		$55,880
Gross tax liability from tax tables or tax rate schedules		$13,602
Less: Tax credits	$ 100	
Tax prepayments	13,180	13,280
Net tax liability (or refund)		$ 322

Figure 28–2
Approach to Determining Taxable Income for an Individual Taxpayer

as gross income and expenses incurred to produce the gross income are subtracted to arrive at adjusted gross income. On the tax forms, however, some revenue and related expenses are reported on separate schedules and the net income or loss is carried forward in the computation of adjusted gross income. For example, expenses related to operating a trade or business are subtracted from revenues earned from operating a trade or business in Schedule C, rent and royalty income and related expenses are reported in Schedule E, and capital gains and losses are computed in Schedule D.

Ordinarily, tax returns for individuals must be filed within 3½ months after the close of the tax year. Most individuals are on a calendar year and, therefore, must file their individual returns by April 15. However, any taxpayer who keeps adequate records may elect to be on a fiscal year.

Note that Figure 28-2 shows three types of subtractions in deriving the net tax liability: exclusions, deductions, and credits. **Exclusions** are items that are omitted by law from the tax computation. In most cases, exclusions are not listed in the tax return because they are not part of the tax concept of income. **Deductions** are items that reduce the amount of income subject to tax. **Tax credits** are direct reductions in the amount of tax liability.

TOTAL INCOME, EXCLUSIONS, AND GROSS INCOME

The starting point for computing an individual's tax liability is the identification of all income, from any source, that is associated with the current tax year. Not all income is included in the tax concept of gross income. For tax purposes, **gross income** is defined as all income not specifically excluded by statutory law, IRS regulations, or court decisions. An item of income that is not included in gross income is called an exclusion. Figure 28-3 lists examples of items to be included in gross income and items excluded from gross income.

Note in Figure 28-3 that certain types of income are exempt from taxation. In addition, there are other specific exclusions and deductions provided for by law. For example, corporate dividends received totaling $100 during the year ($200 if a married couple files a joint return) or less are excluded from taxable income. In addition, certain income items receive favorable tax treatment by qualifying for special deductions. For example, as discussed in a later section, a $100 gain on the sale of a capital asset held longer than a specified period (currently six months) qualifies for a $60 deduction that is not subject to tax. This means that taxable income will be increased by only $40 by the sale of the item. Thus, the nature of the income item can have a significant impact on the tax liability.

DEDUCTIONS FROM GROSS INCOME

There are two types of deduction in Figure 28-2: (1) deductions from gross income to arrive at **adjusted gross income**; and (2) deductions from adjusted gross income to arrive at **taxable income** (i.e., the amount taxes are paid on). This distinction is important, because the amount of certain deductions made from adjusted gross income is limited to a percentage of adjusted gross income.

Figure 28–3
Examples of Items
Included in the Sec-
tions of an Individ-
ual's Tax Return

These items represent general rules and are subject to certain exceptions.

Items Excluded from Gross Income	Items Included in Gross Income
Interest on state and municipal bonds	Wages and salaries
Certain life insurance proceeds	Bonuses
Social security benefits	Interest on savings account
Scholarship not requiring a service from the recipient	Severance pay
Group health and accident insurance premiums paid by an employer	Gambling gains
Corporate dividends up to $100* per person	Corporate dividends in excess of $100*
Gifts	Tips for services rendered
Inheritance	Rents
Accident and disability benefits	Royalties
Return of capital, as opposed to income	Vacation payments
	Business income from sole proprietorship
	Allocable share of partnership income
	Prizes
	Proceeds from lotteries
	Gains from sale or exchange of real estate, investments, and other property

*200 for a married couple filing a joint return.

Figure 28–3

Examples of Items Included in the Sections of an Individual's Tax Return

Such deductions are deductible only if the total of all allowable deductions exceed a certain specified amount, as discussed later in this chapter.

An item can be deducted from gross income only if it is specifically authorized by the Internal Revenue Code. In addition, a taxpayer must maintain adequate records to support any deduction claimed. Tax rules require the maintenance of adequate written records to support business related deductions. Failure to keep them will result in the disallowance of the deduction by the IRS. The major authorized deductions from gross income to arrive at adjusted gross income are:

1. Expenses of a trade or business. All ordinary and necessary expenses paid or incurred during the taxable year in carrying on a trade or business are deductible. In general, the expenses included in this category are those that appear on the income statement of a business prepared in accordance with generally accepted accounting principles.

2. Expenses for the production of rental and royalty income. A taxpayer may deduct ordinary and necessary expenses associated with producing rental and royalty income. For example, although the expenses incurred in the management and maintenance of a single rental property are not deductible from gross income as a business expense—because such limited activity does not constitute a trade or business—they are deductible if related to producing rental income.

3. Employee business expenses. The following specific expenses incurred by an employee are deductible in determining adjusted gross income.
   a. Automobile expenses, excluding commuting expenses between home and the place of employment, associated with performing service as an employee.
   b. Expenses for travel, meals, and lodging while away from home on business related travel.
   c. Expenses of a salesperson soliciting business away from the employer's place of business (called an outside salesperson).
   d. Costs incurred in moving to a new residence because of a new job location that is at least 35 miles further from the old residence than the old job site was.

   Amounts received from an employer as reimbursement for employee job related expenses are subtracted from the total expense in determining the amount of the deduction.

   For an employee, the only expenses incurred in connection with employment that are deductible in determining adjusted gross income are those just specified. In general, these relate to travel, transportation, meals, and lodging. Other employee expenses, such as union and professional dues, tools, and uniforms, may be deducted as part of the itemized deductions, as discussed later.

4. Contributions to retirement accounts. An individual can accumulate funds for retirement in several types of retirement plans. The two most common plans are Individual Retirement Accounts (IRA's) and Keogh plans.
   a. A salaried individual can contribute the lesser of $2,000 or 100% of compensation to an IRA. The maximum is $2,250 if an IRA account is also set up for a nonworking spouse.
   b. A self-employed individual can contribute a limited amount of his or her income to a Keogh plan. The deduction is 25% of self-employment income after deducting the Keogh contribution, up to a maximum contribution of $30,000. This deduction is available to the self-employed, as well as to an employee who receives outside income from moonlighting, such as providing consulting, computer programming, and freelance writing services.

5. Long-term capital gains deduction. As discussed later in this chapter, 60% of net long-term capital gains are deductible.

6. Reduction for a two-earner married couple. A married couple filing a joint return is permitted to deduct 10% of income earned by the spouse with the lower income, up to $30,000 of income reduced by employee business expenses, and payments to IRA and Keogh plans.

7. Other deductions. Deductions are permitted for losses from the sale or exchange of property used in a trade or business or the production of income, alimony payments, and disability income. Generally, each item must satisfy some criterion before it is deductible, and limits are usually placed on the amount of each item that can be deducted.

DEDUCTIONS FROM ADJUSTED GROSS INCOME

The two categories of allowable deductions from adjusted gross income are deductions for: (1) specified expenses; and (2) personal and dependent exemptions. In the case of specified expenses, taxpayers have the option of reducing their adjusted gross income by either: (1) itemizing their deductions; or (2) subtracting an amount called the zero bracket amount. The taxpayer should elect whichever alternative produces the greater deduction.

Zero Bracket Amount

Deductions for personal, living, or family expenses are disallowed except those expressly provided for in the Internal Revenue Code. Taxpayers are permitted to deduct a specific standard deduction for personal expenses. This deduction is referred to as the **zero bracket amount**—that is, the amount of income on which no tax will be paid. The zero bracket amounts currently are:

Married persons filing a joint return	$3,400
Married person filing a separate return	1,700
Single individual	2,300

The zero bracket amount is incorporated into the tax tables and schedules provided by the IRS.

Itemized Deductions

Certain categories of personal expenses, called **itemized deductions**, are allowable by law. If the total of a taxpayer's itemized deductions is in excess of the zero bracket amount, the taxpayer should itemize. If a taxpayer elects to itemize deductions, only the excess over the zero bracket amount may be deducted. If deductions are itemized, adequate records must be maintained to support the deduction.

The tax laws specify the circumstances under which an item qualifies as an itemized deduction and any limitations of the amount that may be deducted. The categories of itemized deductions are presented here.

1. **Medical and dental expenses.** Medical and dental expenses of the taxpayer and his or her family that exceed 5% of adjusted gross income are deductible.
2. **Taxes.** Federal taxes do not qualify as an itemized deduction, but many state and local taxes do. For example, state and local income taxes, sales taxes, real estate taxes, and personal property taxes are deductible. However, state and local taxes on gasoline, liquor, tobacco, and most types of license fees (such as marriage, driver's, and pet licenses) are not deductible.
3. **Interest.** Interest paid on almost any form of personal indebtedness is deductible.

4. **Charitable contributions.** Cash contributions to public charities, such as religious, educational, scientific, or literary organizations are deductible with a maximum deduction of 50% of adjusted gross income. Noncash gifts are subject to other limitations.

5. **Casualty or theft losses.** Uninsured casualty and theft losses in excess of $100 per loss are deductible to the extent they exceed 10% of adjusted gross income. A casualty is a sudden, unexpected, or unusual event such as a hurricane, flood, fire, lightning, or earthquake. Automobile accidents also qualify. However, gradual damage to property caused by termites, moths, or other insects or events does not qualify as a casualty loss.

6. **Miscellaneous deductions.** This category is a catchall for all allowable expenses related primarily to a taxpayer's employment or to the management of income-producing assets that are not deductible in arriving at adjusted gross income. These include:

    Union dues.

    Safety equipment and protective clothing, such as hard hats.

    Small tools and supplies needed on the job.

    Uniforms required by an employer and which cannot usually be worn away from work.

    Physical examinations required by an employer.

    Educational expenses required by an employer or by law.

    Rental charges on a safety deposit box to keep records of income-producing properties.

    Fees paid to have a tax return prepared and for income tax advice.

    Subscriptions to professional journals.

    Dues to professional organizations.

    Investment counsel fees.

Exemptions

A taxpayer is entitled to deduct a certain amount ($1,000 in 1984) from adjusted gross income for each personal exemption claimed. A separate **exemption** is allowed for the taxpayer, for his or her spouse if a joint return is filed, and for each dependent. Additional exemptions are allowed if the taxpayer or spouse is 65 or over, or if either is blind.

To qualify as a dependent, a person must satisfy all of the following tests.

1. Has received over half of his or her support from the taxpayer.
2. Is closely related to the taxpayer or has been a member of the taxpayer's household for the entire year.
3. Has received less than $1,000 in income. (This test does not have to be satisfied if a taxpayer's child was under 19 at the end of the year or was a full-time student for at least five months of the year.)
4. Is a citizen of the United States or a resident of the United States, Canada, or Mexico.
5. If the dependent is married, he or she has not filed a joint return with his or her spouse.

COMPUTING THE TAX LIABILITY

Once the taxpayer's taxable income is computed, the next step is to compute the gross tax liability from the appropriate tax table or tax rate schedule. Tax tables and rate schedules are provided for a single taxpayer, married taxpayers filing joint returns, married taxpayers filing separate returns, a qualifying widow and widower with dependent children, and a head of household.[1]

**Objective 4:
Computing the
tax liability for
an individual**

Tax Tables

The appropriate tax table or tax rate schedule used to determine the gross tax liability depends on the taxpayer's filing status and the amount of taxable income. Tax tables are normally used if the amount of taxable income is less than $50,000. Figure 28–4 shows part of a tax table. Note that the table incorporates the zero bracket income amount. Thus, for a married couple filing jointly, the table does not show a tax liability below a taxable income of $3,400.

Tax tables may be used whether or not the taxpayer elects to itemize deductions. For example, assume that Jim and Carol Newhart filed a joint return and reported adjusted gross income of $8,090 during 1987. The Newharts claimed exemptions for two children, and their itemized deductions totaled $2,980. Because their deductions were less than the $3,400 zero bracket amount for a joint return, they would not itemize deductions. Their taxable income was $4,090 ($8,090 − $4,000 for exemptions) and their gross tax liability of $74 was determined directly from the tax table. (See Figure 28–4, income bracket $4,050 to $4,100.)

Now, assume that the Newharts earned $53,600 and had itemized deductions of $9,620. Their tax table income would be computed as follows.

Adjusted gross income			$53,600
Less: Itemized deductions	$9,620		
Less: Zero bracket amount	3,400	$6,220	
Personal exemptions (4 × $1,000)		4,000	10,220
Taxable income			$43,380

The excess itemized deductions are subtracted to compute the tax table income, because the $3,400 zero tax bracket amount is already incorporated in the tax table. The gross tax liability, taken from the tax table in Figure 28–4, is $8,972.

Tax Rate Schedules

Taxpayers must use tax rate schedules if their taxable income equals or exceeds $50,000, or they qualify for using an alternative method to figure their tax. Tax rate schedules are shown in Figure 28–5.

To illustrate the use of the tax rate schedules, assume that Jim and Carol Newhart, who have two children, filed a joint return. Their taxable income was computed as shown on page 1100.

[1]In general, a head of household is an unmarried taxpayer who provides more than half the cost of maintaining a home (which could be a separate home) for certain qualified persons, such as an unmarried child or a parent of the taxpayer.

Top section

If line 37 (taxable income) is— At least	But less than	Single	Married filing jointly *	Married filing separately	Head of a house-hold	At least	But less than	Single	Married filing jointly *	Married filing separately	Head of a house-hold	At least	But less than	Single	Married filing jointly *	Married filing separately	Head of a house-hold
		Your tax is—						Your tax is—						Your tax is—			
$0	$1,700	$0	$0	$0	$0	2,400	2,425	12	0	78	12	3,400	3,450	124	3	197	124
						2,425	2,450	15	0	81	15	3,450	3,500	130	8	203	129
1,700	1,725	0	0	a1	0	2,450	2,475	18	0	84	18	3,500	3,550	136	14	209	135
1,725	1,750	0	0	4	0	2,475	2,500	21	0	87	21	3,550	3,600	142	19	215	140
1,750	1,775	0	0	7	0												
1,775	1,800	0	0	10	0	2,500	2,525	23	0	89	23	3,600	3,650	148	25	221	146
						2,525	2,550	26	0	92	26	3,650	3,700	154	30	227	151
1,800	1,825	0	0	12	0	2,550	2,575	29	0	95	29	3,700	3,750	160	36	233	157
1,825	1,850	0	0	15	0	2,575	2,600	32	0	98	32	3,750	3,800	166	41	239	162
1,850	1,875	0	0	18	0	2,600	2,625	34	0	100	34	3,800	3,850	172	47	245	168
1,875	1,900	0	0	21	0	2,625	2,650	37	0	103	37	3,850	3,900	178	52	252	173
						2,650	2,675	40	0	106	40	3,900	3,950	184	58	259	179
1,900	1,925	0	0	23	0	2,675	2,700	43	0	109	43	3,950	4,000	190	63	266	184
1,925	1,950	0	0	26	0							**4,000**					
1,950	1,975	0	0	29	0	2,700	2,725	45	0	111	45						
1,975	2,000	0	0	32	0	2,725	2,750	48	0	114	48	4,000	4,050	196	69	273	190
2,000						2,750	2,775	51	0	117	51	4,050	4,100	202	74	280	195
						2,775	2,800	54	0	120	54	4,100	4,150	208	80	287	201
2,000	2,025	0	0	34	0	2,800	2,825	56	0	123	56	4,150	4,200	214	85	294	206

Bottom section

At least	But less than	Single	Married filing jointly *	Married filing separately	Head of a house-hold	At least	But less than	Single	Married filing jointly *	Married filing separately	Head of a house-hold	At least	But less than	Single	Married filing jointly *	Married filing separately	Head of a house-hold
42,000						**45,000**						**48,000**					
42,000	42,050	10,540	8,526	12,635	9,760	45,000	45,050	11,800	9,516	13,961	10,833	48,000	48,050	13,060	10,618	15,311	12,093
42,050	42,100	10,561	8,543	12,656	9,777	45,050	45,100	11,821	9,533	13,984	10,854	48,050	48,100	13,081	10,637	15,334	12,114
42,100	42,150	10,582	8,559	12,677	9,795	45,100	45,150	11,842	9,549	14,006	10,875	48,100	48,150	13,102	10,656	15,356	12,135
42,150	42,200	10,603	8,576	12,698	9,812	45,150	45,200	11,863	9,566	14,029	10,896	48,150	48,200	13,123	10,675	15,379	12,156
42,200	42,250	10,624	8,592	12,719	9,830	45,200	45,250	11,884	9,582	14,051	10,917	48,200	48,250	13,144	10,694	15,401	12,177
42,250	42,300	10,645	8,609	12,740	9,847	45,250	45,300	11,905	9,599	14,074	10,938	48,250	48,300	13,165	10,713	15,424	12,198
42,300	42,350	10,666	8,625	12,761	9,865	45,300	45,350	11,926	9,615	14,096	10,959	48,300	48,350	13,186	10,732	15,446	12,219
42,350	42,400	10,687	8,642	12,782	9,882	45,350	45,400	11,947	9,632	14,119	10,980	48,350	48,400	13,207	10,751	15,469	12,240
42,400	42,450	10,708	8,658	12,803	9,900	45,400	45,450	11,968	9,648	14,141	11,001	48,400	48,450	13,228	10,770	15,491	12,261
42,450	42,500	10,729	8,675	12,824	9,917	45,450	45,500	11,989	9,665	14,164	11,022	48,450	48,500	13,249	10,789	15,514	12,282
42,500	42,550	10,750	8,691	12,845	9,935	45,500	45,550	12,010	9,681	14,186	11,043	48,500	48,550	13,270	10,808	15,536	12,303
42,550	42,600	10,771	8,708	12,866	9,952	45,550	45,600	12,031	9,698	14,209	11,064	48,550	48,600	13,291	10,827	15,559	12,324
42,600	42,650	10,792	8,724	12,887	9,970	45,600	45,650	12,052	9,714	14,231	11,085	48,600	48,650	13,312	10,846	15,581	12,345
42,650	42,700	10,813	8,741	12,908	9,987	45,650	45,700	12,073	9,731	14,254	11,106	48,650	48,700	13,333	10,865	15,604	12,366
42,700	42,750	10,834	8,757	12,929	10,005	45,700	45,750	12,094	9,747	14,276	11,127	48,700	48,750	13,354	10,884	15,626	12,387
42,750	42,800	10,855	8,774	12,950	10,022	45,750	45,800	12,115	9,764	14,299	11,148	48,750	48,800	13,375	10,903	15,649	12,408
42,800	42,850	10,876	8,790	12,971	10,040	45,800	45,850	12,136	9,782	14,321	11,169	48,800	48,850	13,396	10,922	15,671	12,429
42,850	42,900	10,897	8,807	12,994	10,057	45,850	45,900	12,157	9,801	14,344	11,190	48,850	48,900	13,417	10,941	15,694	12,440
42,900	42,950	10,918	8,823	13,016	10,075	45,900	45,950	12,178	9,820	14,366	11,211	48,900	48,950	13,438	10,960	15,716	12,471
42,950	43,000	10,939	8,840	13,039	10,092	45,950	46,000	12,199	9,839	14,389	11,232	48,950	49,000	13,459	10,979	15,739	12,492
43,000						**46,000**						**49,000**					
43,000	43,050	10,960	8,856	13,061	10,110	46,000	46,050	12,220	9,858	14,411	11,253	49,000	49,050	13,480	10,998	15,761	12,513
43,050	43,100	10,981	8,873	13,084	10,127	46,050	46,100	12,241	9,877	14,434	11,274	49,050	49,100	13,501	11,017	15,784	12,534
43,100	43,150	11,002	8,889	13,106	10,145	46,100	46,150	12,262	9,896	14,456	11,295	49,100	49,150	13,522	11,036	15,806	12,555
43,150	43,200	11,023	8,906	13,129	10,162	46,150	46,200	12,283	9,915	14,479	11,316	49,150	49,200	13,543	11,055	15,829	12,576
43,200	43,250	11,044	8,922	13,151	10,180	46,200	46,250	12,304	9,934	14,501	11,337	49,200	49,250	13,564	11,074	15,851	12,597
43,250	43,300	11,065	8,939	13,174	10,197	46,250	46,300	12,325	9,953	14,524	11,358	49,250	49,300	13,585	11,093	15,874	12,618
43,300	43,350	11,086	8,955	13,196	10,215	46,300	46,350	12,346	9,972	14,546	11,379	49,300	49,350	13,606	11,112	15,896	12,639
43,350	43,400	11,107	8,972	13,219	10,232	46,350	46,400	12,367	9,991	14,569	11,400	49,350	49,400	13,627	11,131	15,919	12,660
43,400	43,450	11,128	8,988	13,241	10,250	46,400	46,450	12,388	10,010	14,591	11,421	49,400	49,450	13,648	11,150	15,941	12,681
43,450	43,500	11,149	9,005	13,264	10,267	46,450	46,500	12,409	10,029	14,614	11,442	49,450	49,500	13,669	11,169	15,964	12,702
43,500	43,550	11,170	9,021	13,286	10,285	46,500	46,550	12,430	10,048	14,636	11,463	49,500	49,550	13,690	11,188	15,986	12,723
43,550	43,600	11,191	9,038	13,309	10,302	46,550	46,600	12,451	10,067	14,659	11,484	49,550	49,600	13,711	11,207	16,009	12,744
43,600	43,650	11,212	9,054	13,331	10,320	46,600	46,650	12,472	10,086	14,681	11,505	49,600	49,650	13,732	11,226	16,031	12,765
43,650	43,700	11,233	9,071	13,354	10,337	46,650	46,700	12,493	10,105	14,704	11,526	49,650	49,700	13,753	11,245	16,054	12,786
43,700	43,750	11,254	9,087	13,376	10,355	46,700	46,750	12,514	10,124	14,726	11,547	49,700	49,750	13,774	11,264	16,076	12,807
43,750	43,800	11,275	9,104	13,399	10,372	46,750	46,800	12,535	10,143	14,749	11,568	49,750	49,800	13,795	11,283	16,099	12,828
43,800	43,850	11,296	9,120	13,421	10,390	46,800	46,850	12,556	10,162	14,771	11,589	49,800	49,850	13,816	11,302	16,121	12,849
43,850	43,900	11,317	9,137	13,444	10,407	46,850	46,900	12,577	10,181	14,794	11,610	49,850	49,900	13,837	11,321	16,144	12,870
43,900	43,950	11,338	9,153	13,466	10,425	46,900	46,950	12,598	10,200	14,816	11,631	49,900	49,950	13,858	11,340	16,166	12,891
43,950	44,000	11,359	9,170	13,489	10,442	46,950	47,000	12,619	10,219	14,839	11,652	49,950	50,000	13,879	11,359	16,189	12,912

*This column must also be used by a qualifying widow(er).

50,000 or over—use tax rate schedules

Figure 28–4
Tax Tables

Figure 28–5
Tax Rate Schedules

Schedule X
Single Taxpayers

Taxable Income		Tax Liability		
Over	But Not Over	Amount	Plus Percent	Of the Amount Over
-0-	$ 2,300	-0-	-0-	-0-
$ 2,300	3,400	-0-	11	$ 2,300
3,400	4,400	$ 121	12	3,400
4,400	6,500	241	14	4,400
6,500	8,500	535	15	6,500
8,500	10,800	835	16	8,500
10,800	12,900	1,203	18	10,800
12,900	15,000	1,581	20	12,900
15,000	18,200	2,001	23	15,000
18,200	23,500	2,737	26	18,200
23,500	28,800	4,115	30	23,500
28,800	34,100	5,705	34	28,800
34,100	41,500	7,507	38	34,100
41,500	55,300	10,319	42	41,500
55,300	81,800	16,115	48	55,300
81,800	———	28,835	50	81,800

Schedule Y
Married Taxpayers Filing Joint Returns

Taxable Income		Tax Liability		
Over	But Not Over	Amount	Plus Percent	Of the Amount Over
-0-	$ 3,400	-0-	-0-	-0-
$ 3,400	5,500	-0-	11	$ 3,400
5,500	7,600	$ 23	12	5,500
7,600	11,900	483	14	7,600
11,900	16,000	1,085	16	11,900
16,000	20,200	1,741	18	16,000
20,200	24,600	2,497	22	20,200
24,600	29,900	3,465	25	24,600
29,900	35,200	4,790	28	29,900
35,200	45,800	6,274	33	35,200
45,800	60,000	9,772	38	45,800
60,000	85,600	15,168	42	60,000
85,600	109,400	25,920	45	85,600
109,400	162,400	36,630	49	109,400
162,400	———	62,600	50	162,400

Adjusted gross income			$66,380
Itemized deductions	$13,280		
Less: Zero bracket amount	3,400	$9,880	
Personal exemptions (4 × $1,000)		4,000	13,880
Taxable income			$52,500

From Schedule Y in Figure 28–5, the Newharts' gross tax liability would be computed as follows.

Tax on first $45,800	$ 9,772
Tax on the remaining income ($52,500 − $45,800 = $6,700 × 38%)	2,546
Gross tax liability	$12,318

The percentage indicated in the tax table—38% in this case—is referred to as the **marginal tax rate**, because it is the rate applied on the next dollar of income. The marginal tax rate is often used by taxpayers to identify their income-tax bracket. However, because lower income levels are taxed at lower rates, the effective or average tax rate for the Newharts is 23.5% ($12,318 ÷ $52,500).

One can see the highly progressive nature of the income tax rates from the tax rate schedules. A **progressive tax** is one in which the tax rate becomes higher as the amount of taxable income increases.

TAX CREDITS

A tax credit is a reduction in the amount of tax liability computed on taxable income. A tax credit is more beneficial to a taxpayer than a deduction, because it is a direct dollar-per-dollar reduction in the tax liability. In contrast, a deduction reduces the amount of income subject to tax. For example, one-half of the amounts contributed to political candidates up to a maximum of $50 ($100 on a joint return) may be taken as a credit against the tax liability. Thus, a contribution of $100 will reduce the tax liability by $50. If the $100 had been considered a deduction and a tax rate of 40% is assumed, taxes would have been reduced by only $40.

Other income tax credits are available to the elderly, for child care while the taxpayer or spouse is at work, for payments of income taxes to foreign countries, for homeowners who have installed energy-saving items, and for taxpayers who have income below $10,000. Generally, there are specific limitations to each of these income tax credits.

TAX PREPAYMENTS

During the tax year, income tax payments are withheld by employers from the salaries paid to employees, as noted in Chapter 12. The amount withheld is based on the employee's earnings for the year, his or her marital status, and the number of exemptions claimed by the employee. The amount withheld must be reported to each employee on a Form W-2 by January 31 for the preceding calendar year.

Taxpayers who receive income not subject to withholding generally must estimate their tax for the year and make quarterly installment payments to the IRS. The sum of the amounts withheld, any quarterly estimated payments, and any tax credits are subtracted from the gross tax liability to determine the amount of unpaid taxes due or the refund claimed at the time a tax return is filed.

THE IMPORTANCE OF THE MARGINAL TAX RATE

When considering the various alternatives affecting taxable income, it is important for individual taxpayers and other taxable entities to use the marginal tax rate in assessing the impact of taxes on their decisions. Assume, for example, that a married couple with taxable income of $58,000 is considering whether to invest $10,000 in a municipal bond paying 9% nontaxable interest or a corporate bond paying 14% interest. The after-tax cash flow from each investment can be computed as follows.

	Invest in Municipal Bonds	Invest in Corporate Bonds
Cash flow from interest	$900	$1,400
Less: Increase in cash outflow for taxes*	-0-	532
Net after-tax cash flow	$900	$ 868

$$\begin{array}{cccc} \text{*Marginal} & \text{Increase in} & \text{Increase in cash} \\ \text{tax} \times & \text{taxable} = & \text{outflow for} \\ \text{rate} & \text{income} & \text{taxes} \end{array}$$

Investment in municipal bonds.
Interest of $900 is
nontaxable income
(38% × -0-) = -0-

Investment in corporate bonds.
Interest of $1,400 is
taxable income
(38% × $1,400) = $532

(The marginal tax rate for taxable income between $45,800 and $60,000 is 38% from Figure 28–5).

Although the interest rate is higher on the corporate bonds, the after-tax cash flow is greater when the $10,000 is invested in municipal bonds.

The increase in taxes of $532 is verified here.

	No Additional Investment	Invest in Corporate Bonds	Difference
Taxable income before interest	$58,000	$58,000	$ -0-
Taxable interest	-0-	1,400	+ 1,400
Taxable income	$58,000	$59,400	+$1,400
Income tax			
Income tax on $45,800 (from Figure 28–5)	$ 9,772	$9,772	$ -0-
Income tax on amount over $45,800			
($58,000 − $45,800) × 38%	4,636		
($59,400 − $45,800) × 38%		5,168	+ 532
Total income taxes	$14,408	$14,940	+$ 532

A similar analysis can be performed in assessing the net cost of a tax deduction that results in a decrease in taxable income. For example, the net cost of a $10,000 contribution is $5,000 for a married couple with taxable income over $162,400, because the marginal tax rate is 50%, as shown in Figure 28–5.

CHANGES IN 1985 TAX YEAR

Beginning January 1, 1985, tax tables and schedules for individuals, personal and dependency exemptions, and zero bracket amounts are to be adjusted annually for increases in the Consumer Price Index (CPI). The adjustments are called indexing. The indexing provision of the law was enacted as part of the Economic Recovery Tax Act of 1981, (but did not become effective until 1985) for the purpose of reducing the impact of inflation on the tax system. That is, in the past, a taxpayer receiving a cost-of-living pay raise equal to the rate of inflation was pushed into a higher tax bracket and paid more tax, even though he or she did not have an increase in real income.

Here is how indexing works. The CPI for the 12 months ending September 30, 1983 will serve as the base year. In subsequent years, the increase in the CPI will be computed on September 30 of the current year over the index on September 30, 1983. For example, the government announced that the CPI increased 4.1% for the 12-month period ending September 30, 1984. Thus, tax brackets, exemptions, and zero bracket amounts for 1985 will be increased approximately 4.1%. For the 1985 taxable year, personal and dependency exemptions will increase to $1,040 from $1,000; the zero bracket amount for an individual will rise to $2,390 from $2,300 and, for joint returns, the amount will increase to $3,540 from $3,400; and the individual tax brackets will be widened by 4.1% to allow more income to be taxed at the same rate. (Since these amounts will change each year, the illustrations in this chapter are based on—and the end-of-chapter problem material should be worked using—the unadjusted amounts for 1984 given in this chapter.)

The tax reductions resulting from indexing will be substantial. The Treasury Department estimates that taxpayers will save more than $9 billion in taxes in 1985.

CAPITAL GAINS AND LOSSES

Capital gains or losses are realized gains or losses on the sale of capital assets. **Capital assets** are defined in the Internal Revenue Code as any item of property *except*

1. Inventories.
2. Trade accounts and notes receivable.
3. Land, buildings, and equipment used in a trade or business.
4. Certain intangible assets, such as copyrights and literary works or artistic compositions.

Thus, most property held for personal use or investment is a capital asset.

Stock and bond investments, a personal residence, an automobile, and a coin collection are examples of capital assets that may be held by an individual. Although depreciable and real property used in a trade or business (item 3) are not capital assets, such assets may be treated as capital assets under certain conditions.

When a capital asset is sold, the capital gain or loss reported is the difference between the selling price and the basis of the asset. Determining the basis of the asset for tax purposes may be complex, but, in general, it is the asset's cost adjusted for any depreciation taken on the asset in computing taxable income.

A gain or loss on each sale of a capital asset is classified as short-term or long-term. The classification depends on the date that the asset was acquired and the length of the time it was held. Before 1976, if a capital asset was held for longer than six months, the gain or loss was classified as a **long-term capital gain** or a **long-term capital loss**. A gain or loss from the sale of a capital asset held less than six months was classified as a **short-term capital gain** or a **short-term capital loss**. In 1976, the holding period for long-term capital gains treatment was extended from six months to twelve months. As part of the 1984 Tax Reform Act, the holding period was reduced to six months for assets acquired after June 22, 1984 and before January 1, 1988. The reduction in the holding period is intended to create investment incentives. The holding period is scheduled to revert to twelve months in 1988, but Congress intends to evaluate the effects of the six months holding period before 1988.

A detailed discussion of the different tax treatments that may be given the sale of a capital asset is beyond the scope of this book. However, in tax planning, an individual taxpayer should recognize that the tax consequences are significantly affected by the classification of a gain or loss as short-term or long-term. Short-term capital gains are fully taxable as ordinary income while short-term capital losses are offset against capital gains or ordinary income dollar-for-dollar. In the case of a long-term capital loss, it takes two dollars of long-term losses to offset one dollar of income. In addition, a maximum of $3,000 of capital losses can be offset against income in any one year. Any remaining losses may be carried forward to offset income. On the other hand, 60% of the excess of long-term capital gains over short-term losses, if any, is deducted from the gain in determining the taxable portion of the gain. To illustrate the tax benefit of the long-term capital gain treatment, assume that an individual taxpayer in the 50% tax bracket sold one capital asset during the year for a gain of $6,000. The asset had been held for 14 months and, therefore, qualifies as a long-term capital gain. The taxable gain and income tax associated with the sale are computed here.

Short-term capital loss	$ -0-
Long-term capital gain	6,000
Excess of long-term capital gain over short-term capital loss	6,000
Less: 60% capital gain exclusion ($6,000 × 60%)	3,600
Reported as part of taxable income	$2,400
Income tax associated with gain ($2,400 × 50%)	$1,200

The effective tax rate on this transaction is 20% ($1,200 tax/$6,000 gain on the sale). Had the gain been classified as short-term, the income tax associated with the sale would have been $3,000 ($6,000 × 50%).

Although timing the sale of a capital asset is an important tool in tax planning, the decision to sell or retain a capital asset is an investment decision. Other economic considerations and investment strategy can be equally or more important than the tax consequences.

COMPUTATION OF INCOME TAX FOR A JOINT RETURN

To illustrate the computation of the federal income tax, assume that Julie and Tom George, ages 34 and 32, respectively, file a joint tax return. They have two children who qualify as dependents. Julie George, a real estate agent, earned commissions of $22,000 and made quarterly estimated federal income tax payments totaling $3,900 during the year. Julie's employer does not have a retirement plan established for his employees. She, however, contributed $2,000 to a qualified individual retirement account. Tom George earned $50,000 during the year working as an accountant, and had $9,280 withheld from his salary for federal income taxes. During the year the Georges sold a coin collection for an $8,000 gain, which they had held for five years, and also disposed of a common stock investment at a $3,000 loss, which they had held for five months. Dividends in the amount of $2,800 were received on a jointly owned stock investment. Interest of $980 on municipal bonds was received during the year and $640 was credited to their savings account and was available for withdrawal. The itemized deductions and computation of tax shown in Figure 28–6 are determined on the basis of our previous discussion. In Figure 28–6, the information is presented in condensed form. In practice, some of the information would have been shown in more detail and in separate schedules.

Figure 28–6
Computation of Federal Income Tax—Julie and Tom George, Joint Return

Gross Income:		
Salary		$50,000
Real estate commissions		22,000
Dividends income	$2,800	
Less: Exclusion	200	2,600
Capital gains:		
Net long-term capital gains	8,000	
Net short-term capital losses	3,000	5,000
Interest received or credited to account:		
Savings accounts		640
(Interest on municipal bonds of $980 is excluded.)		
Gross income for tax purposes		$80,240

Deductions from gross income:
  Long-term capital gains deductions
    (60% × $5,000 excess of net long-
    term capital gain over net short-term
    capital losses) 3,000
  Contribution to individual retirement
    account* 2,000
  10% of lower earning spouse's income
    reduced by IRA contribution
    ($22,000 − $2,000) × 10% 2,000   7,000
Adjusted gross income 73,240
Deductions from adjusted gross income:
Itemized deductions:
  Medical and dental expenses (doctors'
    fees, dentists' fees, nursing
    services, hospital care, X-rays,
    medical insurance premiums,
    prescription drugs, eyeglasses,
    ambulance service, lab fees,
    crutches, and physical therapist) 4,222
  Less: 5% of adjusted gross income 3,662   560
  Taxes: Real estate 2,460
    General sales tax 480
    State and local income taxes 1,050
    Personal property 460
  Interest on home mortgage 6,280
  Other interest payments 2,300
  Charitable contributions 2,490
  Miscellaneous (dues to professional
    organizations and safety deposit
    box rental) 680
  Total Itemized deductions 16,760
  Less: Zero bracket amount 3,400
  Excess itemized deductions 13,360
Personal exemptions (4 × $1,000) 4,000
Total deductions from adjusted gross
  income 17,360
Taxable income $55,880

Computation of federal income tax (See
  Figure 28–5 for tax rate schedules)
  $9,772 + 38% ($10,080) $13,602
Less: Tax credits—Political contribution,
  $400 ($400 × 50% = $200: limited to
  $100) .... $ 100
Prepayments—Federal income tax
            withheld 9,280
            Estimated quarterly tax
            payments 3,900   13,280
Net tax liability due with tax return .... $ 322

*Tom George also qualifies for a $2,000 contribution to an IRA account, but the
contribution was not made this year.

PART II. TAX CONSIDERATIONS FOR CORPORATIONS

Objective 5: Computing the tax liability for a corporation

A corporation is a separate taxable entity that must file tax returns and pay taxes on its taxable income. Corporate returns are due within 2½ months after the close of the corporation's fiscal year. Some corporations, such as S Corporations and charitable organizations organized as corporations, are exempt by law from taxation. Other corporations, such as banks and insurance companies, are subject to special tax regulations. For corporations without special regulations, the computation of taxable income centers around an income statement similar to the one prepared for external reporting. However, the computation of taxable income can still be very complex. For this reason, only some of the major distinguishing features of the corporate tax system will be discussed here.

There are fewer steps in determining the taxable income of a corporation than in determining that of an individual, because there is no distinction between gross income and adjusted gross income for a corporation. Furthermore, a corporation does not itemize personal deductions or deduct personal exemptions, and there is no deduction for corporations comparable to the zero bracket amount. The steps for determining the corporate tax liability are shown in Figure 28–7.

TOTAL REVENUES AND EXCLUSIONS

The first step in the computation of taxable income for a corporation is the determination of the corporation's total revenue and gains recognized during the year. Examples are revenues from the sale of goods or the performance of services, interest and dividends on investments, gains from the sale of assets, rental receipts, and royalties. In most cases, revenues recognized for accounting purposes are also considered revenues for tax purposes. There are, however, some exceptions. For example, interest on obligations of state and local governments and life insurance proceeds received by the corporation on the death of an insured employee or officer are reported in the income statement but are excluded from gross income for tax purposes.

Figure 28–7
Steps in Computing Corporate Tax Liability

Total Revenues	$780,000
Less: Exclusions from revenue	32,000
Gross income	748,000
Less: Deductions from gross income	612,000
Taxable income	$136,000
Compute tax liability from rate schedule	$42,310
Less: Tax credits	4,200
Net tax liability	$38,110

DEDUCTIONS FROM GROSS INCOME

Most of the deductions from gross income are the usual expenses incurred in operating the corporation and producing revenue. These include cost of goods sold, selling expenses, and administrative expenses. There are certain other deductions and limitations on some expenses that are specified by law and that result in a difference between accounting income and taxable income. Some of the more common differences are:

1. **Capital gains and losses.** A corporation's capital losses cannot be offset against ordinary income; capital losses can be used to offset capital gains only. The unused portion of the loss can be carried back to the three years preceding the year of the loss and carried forward five years following the loss year. However, the loss carryback and carryforward can be offset against capital gains only. If carried back, the tax liability for that year is recomputed and a refund claim is filed with the IRS for the difference between the original tax and the recomputed tax.

   Short-term capital gains are included in taxable income and subject to taxation at the regular tax rates. Long-term capital gains are taxed at the regular corporate rate or 28%, whichever is lower. If the marginal regular corporate tax rate is greater than 28%, the excess of net long-term capital gains over net short-term capital losses is taxed at a maximum rate of 28%. Corporations are not permitted the long-term capital gain deduction of 60% that is available to individuals.

2. **Dividends received deduction.** A corporation is permitted a deduction of 85% of dividends received from shares of stock in other U.S. corporations. The intent of this deduction is to reduce the effects of taxing three entities for the same income. That is, if the deduction was not permitted, the distributing corporation would have already paid a tax on its net income, the dividend would be taxed to the receiving corporation, and when distributed to the stockholders of the receiving corporation, another layer of tax would be imposed.

3. **Net operating loss.** A corporation is permitted to offset losses of a particular year against income of other years. Losses may be carried back to the three preceding years. The tax is recomputed and the difference between this amount and the original tax is refunded to the corporation. Any unused loss may be carried forward successively to the next 15 years following the loss year and deducted from income. A corporation may elect to forgo the carryback and only carry the loss forward.

4. **Charitable contributions.** A corporation may deduct charitable contributions but the amount that can be deducted is limited to 10% of taxable income before deducting any contributions and the 85% dividend-received deduction. Contributions in excess of the 10% limitation may be carried forward to the five succeeding years, subject to the 10% limitation in each year.

5. **Expenses not deductible.** Premiums paid for employees' life insurance policies under which the corporation is the named beneficiary and the amortization of goodwill are not deductible for tax purposes.

Figure 28–8
Tax Rate Schedule
for Corporations

Taxable Income		Tax Liability		
Over	But Not Over	Amount Plus	Percent	Of the Amount Over
$ -0-	$ 25,000	$ -0-	15	$ -0-
25,000	50,000	3,750	18	25,000
50,000	75,000	8,250	30	50,000
75,000	100,000	15,750	40	75,000
100,000	———	25,750	46	100,000

Corporation income tax rates for tax years beginning in 1983.

COMPUTING THE TAX LIABILITY

The tax liability is computed by applying the appropriate tax rate to the taxable income. The current corporation income tax rate structure is shown in Figure 28–8. The corporate tax is also a progressive tax. To illustrate the use of this schedule, a corporation with reported taxable income of $80,000 would compute its tax liability as:

Tax on first $75,000	$15,750
Tax on excess ($80,000 − $75,000 = $5,000 × 40%)	2,000
Total tax liability	$17,750

Like individuals, a corporation may qualify for certain tax credits to be deducted from the gross tax liability and must pay estimated taxes in quarterly installments.

TAX PLANNING AND BUSINESS DECISIONS

As noted before, income taxes have a significant effect on most business decisions and are often the most important factor influencing a business decision. Because of the complexity of the tax laws, most firms hire a tax specialist to review the tax implications of alternative courses of action and to provide guidance in arranging business transactions so that taxes are minimized legally. The following are some examples of the tax impact on alternative approaches to various business problems.

TAX IMPLICATIONS OF THE CHOICE OF BUSINESS ORGANIZATION

One of the first decisions an owner or owners of a business must make at the time of organization is whether to operate as a corporation, a proprietorship, or a partnership. Because of the difference between individual and corporate tax rates, and because other tax provisions vary greatly with the legal form of business, the tax consequences should be carefully considered in making this decision. The major tax factors are these.

1. A corporation is a separate taxable entity and must report and pay taxes on its income at rates ranging from 15% to 46%. Dividends paid are not a tax-deductible business expense. Furthermore, dividends in excess of the dividend exclusion ($200 for a married couple) are taxed again to the individual stockholders when received.

2. Partners or proprietors must report business income on their individual returns when it is earned, whether it is withdrawn for personal use or left in the business. Business income and dividends are taxed to individuals at rates that range from 11% to 50%.

3. Corporations may deduct reasonable salaries paid to stockholders who also work for the corporation as a business expense from gross income.

4. In the case of a partnership or a proprietorship, salaries to the owner(s) are considered an allocation of income.

As previously noted, a business may obtain the legal benefits of a corporation and also receive the tax benefits of a partnership by electing S Corporation status if certain criteria are satisfied.

To illustrate the impact of taxes on the form of business organization, assume that Jack Jones is going to form a business, which he expects will produce an annual income of about $100,000 before deducting his own salary of $60,000. That salary is considered reasonable for the services he performs. There will be no other withdrawals from the business. The corporate tax and the individual tax for Jones are compared under a corporation and proprietorship in Figure 28–9 on page 1110.

Under these assumed conditions, his combined tax burden is $9,872 lower ($26,550 − $16,678) if he incorporates than if he operates as a proprietor. This is a result of the fact that the $40,000 earnings retained in the business are taxed as ordinary income when operating as a proprietorship. His individual marginal tax rate on this income was higher than the marginal tax rate used to compute the corporate tax on the $40,000. If a part or all of the $33,550 corporate net income is distributed in subsequent periods, the dividends are taxable to Jones as ordinary income. Should the dividends not be withdrawn and he is later able to sell his shares of capital stock at an increased price that reflects the retained earnings, the gain will be treated as a long-term capital gain. In either case, he is able to postpone the tax on the portion of earnings retained by the corporation. A corporation, however, may be subject to a penalty tax on accumulated earnings deemed excessive and retained for the purpose of avoiding the tax on dividends.

Unfortunately, determining the tax advantage of one form of organization over another is not as straightforward as it appears from this illustration. The apparent tax advantage one form of organization may have over another can vanish with a change in such variables as the individual's and the corporation's marginal tax rates, the level of income, what constitutes a reasonable salary, and the amount of earnings retained in the business. To illustrate, the combined corporate and individual income tax is computed here, assuming that all of the corporate net income was distributed to Jones.

Taxable Income:	
Salary	$60,000
Dividends of $33,550 (see Figure 28–9)	
less $200 exclusion	33,350
	$93,350
Less: deductions	13,000
Taxable income	$80,350
Income tax liability:	
Individual tax:	
Tax on first $60,000	$15,168
Excess $20,350 × 42%	8,547
	$23,715
Plus the corporate tax	6,450
Combined tax liability:	$30,165

The combined tax liability is $30,165 when all of the corporate net income is distributed. The change in assumption does not affect the combined tax liability when a proprietorship is operated; it remains the same at $26,550, as computed in Figure 28–9. Thus, when all of the corporate net income is distributed, the lowest combined tax liability is incurred when the proprietorship form of organization is adopted ($26,550 compared to $30,165).

Figure 28–9
Comparison of Tax Impact on Forms of Business Organizations

	Legal Form of Business Organization	
	Corporation	Proprietorship
Business income excluding		
salary to owner	$100,000	$100,000
Less: Salary to owner	60,000	-0-
Taxable income	40,000	-0-
Corporate tax expense:		
First $25,000 $3,750		
Tax on excess $15,000 × 18% 2,700	6,450	-0-
Net income	$ 33,550	$100,000
Individual tax*	$ 10,228	$ 26,550
Tax paid by business	6,450	-0-
Combined tax	$ 16,678	$ 26,550
Individual income	$ 60,000	$100,000
Less: Itemized deductions and		
personal exemptions	(13,000)	(13,000)
Taxable income	$ 47,000	$ 87,000
Income tax liability		
First $45,800	$ 9,772	First $85,600 $ 25,920
Excess $1,200 × 38%	456	Excess $1,400
		× 45% 630
Total	$ 10,228	$ 26,550

*From tax rate schedule in Figure 28–5, assuming a joint return and total deductions and exemptions of $13,000. Figure 28–4 would normally be used for some of these computations if a complete table was available.

CHOICE OF FINANCING METHODS

When a corporation seeks additional funds for long-term purposes, it may obtain them by retaining earnings generated from operations, by issuing additional shares of capital stock, or by issuing long-term debt. As discussed in Chapter 17, there are a number of factors to consider in making financial decisions. In any case, a significant factor in the decision is the overall tax effect on the business and the stockholders. The tax impact of the various forms of financing varies, because interest on debt is a tax-deductible expense, whereas a dividend paid on capital stock is not. To illustrate this point, assume that a firm needs to raise $500,000 for plant expansion, on which a return of 18% is expected.

Management is considering whether to issue shares of 12% preferred stock or borrow at a 14% rate of interest. The firm is in the 46% marginal tax bracket. The after-tax results for the two alternatives are shown here.

	Issue Stock	Issue Bonds
Increase in earnings ($500,000 × 18%)	$90,000	$90,000
Interest expense ($500,000 × 14%)	-0-	70,000
Taxable income	90,000	20,000
Income tax expense:		
$90,000 × 46%	41,400	
$20,000 × 46%		9,200
Net income before dividends	48,600	10,800
Preferred dividends ($500,000 × 12%)	60,000	
Net income available to common stockholders	($11,400)	$10,800

Clearly, in certain situations, the tax advantage of debt encourages its use to finance a business.

OPERATING THE BUSINESS

Once the business is organized, management should use the marginal tax rate to assess the impact of taxes on alternative decisions, as illustrated earlier for an individual. There are also many ways that transactions can be arranged so that a favorable tax treatment is obtained legally. Primarily, these relate to the timing of transactions and to the choice of accounting methods. The latter was discussed in Chapter 17.

The *timing of business transactions* is one of the simplest tax-planning techniques available. A company seeking to reduce taxable income can move discretionary expenses (such as routine plant and equipment maintenance) planned for the next year into the current year. Charitable contributions are another example of a discretionary expense. In addition, sales transactions near the end of the current year may be deferred until the next year. Capital assets that are to be disposed of at a gain should be held for a sufficient period, if at all possible, in order to qualify for long-term capital gains treatment. The preferential treatment given capital gains is so significant that it may be beneficial to defer the sale, even if it means that a smaller gain will be realized.

GLOSSARY

ADJUSTED GROSS INCOME. Gross income less ordinary and necessary business expenses and other deductions permitted by law (p. 1092).

CAPITAL ASSET. Any item of property except (1) inventories; (2) trade accounts and notes receivable; (3) land, building, and equipment used in a trade or business; and (4) certain intangible assets (p. 1102).

CONSTRUCTIVE RECEIPT. The point in time when a cash receipt is taxable because it is controlled by a taxpayer, even though it is not actually received (p. 1090).

DEDUCTION. An item that reduces an amount subject to tax (p. 1092).

EXCLUSION. An item omitted from gross income, as provided by the tax laws (p. 1092).

EXEMPTIONS. A deduction from adjusted gross income for each exemption claimed by a taxpayer. A separate exemption is allowed for the taxpayer, the taxpayer's spouse, and each qualified dependent (p. 1096).

GROSS INCOME. All income not specifically excluded by statutory law, IRS regulation, or court decision (p. 1092).

INTERNAL REVENUE CODE. A compilation of all current federal income tax laws (p. 1087).

ITEMIZED DEDUCTIONS. Expenses that are permitted by law to be deducted from adjusted gross income in computing taxable income (p. 1095).

LONG-TERM CAPITAL GAIN. A gain from the sale of a capital asset held longer than a specified period; six months as of 1985 (p. 1103).

LONG-TERM CAPITAL LOSS. A loss from the sale of a capital asset held longer than a specified period; six months as of 1985 (p. 1103).

MARGINAL TAX RATE. The tax rate applied to the next dollar of taxable income (p. 1100).

PROGRESSIVE TAX. A tax in which the tax rate increases as the level of taxable income increases (p. 1100).

S CORPORATION. A corporation that elects to be taxed similarly to a partnership, which can be done when certain criteria are satisfied (p. 1089).

SHORT-TERM CAPITAL GAIN. A gain from the sale of a capital asset held less than a specified period; six months as of 1985 (p. 1103).

SHORT-TERM CAPITAL LOSS. A loss from the sale of a capital asset held less than a specified period; six months as of 1985 (p. 1103).

TAXABLE INCOME. The amount of income on which the gross tax liability is computed (p. 1092).

TAX CREDIT. An item that is a direct reduction in the amount of tax liability (p. 1092).

TAX EVASION. The deliberate misstatement of taxable income, tax credits, prepayments, and/or other taxes (p. 1089).

TAX PLANNING (TAX AVOIDANCE). A legal means of reducing or deferring an income tax liability (p. 1089).

ZERO BRACKET AMOUNT. A standard deduction permitted in lieu of itemized deductions. The zero bracket amount is incorporated in the tax tables and rate schedules (p. 1095).

DISCUSSION QUESTIONS

1. What are the four classifications of taxpayers for federal income tax purposes?
2. The taxable income of a proprietorship is $63,000, and the owner withdrew $35,000 during the year. How much business income must the owner report on his income tax return?
3. Explain the meaning of the expression "double taxation of corporate income."
4. Define tax planning and tax evasion.
5. How is the cash basis of accounting modified for income tax purposes?
6. What are the advantages of using the cash basis of accounting for income tax purposes?
7. An individual taxpayer has a net short-term capital loss of $1,000 and a net long-term capital loss of $2,000. What amount can be offset against the current year's ordinary income?
8. An individual taxpayer has a net short-term capital loss of $4,500 and a net long-term capital gain of $7,000.
   (a) What is the net capital gain?
   (b) What is the amount of the net increase in adjusted gross income resulting from the net capital gain?
9. Define the following terms.
   (a) Exclusion.
   (b) Deduction.
   (c) Zero bracket amount.
   (d) Tax credit.
10. Arrange the following items in the correct order to arrive at the net tax liability or refund due for an individual taxpayer.
   (a) Tax credits.
   (b) Exclusions from income.
   (c) Deductions from gross income.
   (d) Exemptions.
   (e) Adjusted gross income.
   (f) Taxable income.
   (g) Total income.
   (h) Excess itemized deductions.
   (i) Tax prepayments.
   (j) Gross income.
   (k) Gross tax liability.
11. Does it make any difference if an item is deducted to arrive at adjusted gross income or from adjusted gross income? Why?
12. A married couple filing a joint return has taxable income of $52,000.
   (a) What is their gross tax liability?
   (b) What is the marginal tax rate?
   (c) What is their effective or average tax rate?
13. List, in order, the steps used to compute corporate net tax liability.
14. What are some ways in which the treatment of corporate capital gains and losses differs from the treatment of the capital transactions of individual taxpayers?

15. Differentiate between the tax treatment of the owners' salaries for a corporation and for a partnership.
16. What is the tax advantage of financing with debt, rather than with stock?

EXERCISES

(For the exercises and problems in this chapter, round all computations to the nearest dollar.)

Exercise 28-1 Identifying Items of Income and Expense

Possible sources of income for an individual taxpayer are listed here.

1. Lottery winnings.
2. Tips.
3. Royalties.
4. Scholarship received for academic achievement.
5. Profit from a proprietorship.

Possible expenses incurred by an individual taxpayer appear here.

6. Alimony payments.
7. Contribution to the Salvation Army.
8. Fee paid to a CPA to have tax return prepared.
9. Cost of a marriage license.
10. Payments to an individual retirement account.
11. Interest paid on credit cards used for personal use.

Required:

A. Determine whether each source of income should be included in gross income or excluded from gross income for tax purposes.
B. Determine whether each expense is deductible to arrive at adjusted gross income, deductible from adjusted gross income, or not deductible.

Exercise 28-2 Capital Gains and Losses

The Alcotts have decided to sell a capital asset within the next month. If they sell it within the next week they expect to have a short-term capital gain of $6,000. If they wait until later in the month, they expect to have a long-term capital gain of $5,000. In addition, they have a short-term capital loss of $1,500 for the year. The Alcotts are in the 50% tax bracket.

Required:

Determine whether the Alcotts should make the sale next week or whether they should wait until later in the month.

Exercise 28-3 Computation of Tax Liability for an Individual

Beth Williams is single and has no dependents. She compiled the following tax-related information.

Total income	$56,850
Income tax withheld from salary	14,780
Itemized deductions	5,155
Exclusions from income	2,800
Deductions from gross income	1,000

Required:
Determine the following.

A. Taxable income.
B. Gross tax liability. (Use the tax table in Figure 28–4.)
C. Net tax liability or refund.
D. Average tax rate.

Exercise 28-4 Computation of Tax Liability for a Corporation
The records of the Allstar Corporation contain the following information.

Operating revenue	$415,000
Dividends from U.S. corporations	10,000
Net long-term capital gain	11,000
Net short-term capital loss	12,000
Operating expenses	275,000

Required:
Compute the tax liability of the Allstar Corporation.

Exercise 28-5 Computation of Tax Liability for a Corporation
The records of the Valley Corporation contain the following information.

Sales revenue	$350,000
Dividends from U.S. corporations	20,000
Losses carried forward	75,000
Interest revenue	12,500
Operating expenses	202,500

Required:
Compute the tax liability of the Valley Corporation.

Exercise 28-6 Tax Effects on Financing Decisions
Hallmark Company needs to raise $100,000 for plant expansion on which a return of 20% is expected. Management is considering whether to issue shares of 10% preferred stock or borrow at a 12% rate of interest. The corporation is in the 30% tax bracket.

Required:
Calculate the effect of each proposal on the firm's net income available to stockholders.

PROBLEMS

Problem 28-1 Computation of Tax Liability for a Married Couple
Bill and Karen Johnson are married and have one dependent child. They are both in their thirties. Bill is a psychologist with his own private practice. Karen heads the public relations department of a large firm. They plan to file a joint return, and they compiled the following information to give to their accountant.

Gross revenue from Bill's practice	$76,700
Expenses of Bill's practice	55,000
Estimated tax paid by Bill	8,500
Karen's salary	39,800
Income tax withheld from Karen's salary	10,950

Interest earned on savings in the bank	400
Sales tax	710
Property tax	590
Inheritance received	4,500
Medical and dental expenses	4,825
Net long-term capital gains	3,500
Net short-term capital losses	2,700
Interest on home mortgage	9,270
Theft loss	485
Dividends	1,100

Required:

Compute the Johnson's adjusted gross income, taxable income, and net income tax liability or refund due (use the tax table in Figure 28–4).

Problem 28-2 **Computation of Tax Liability for a Married Couple**

Robert and Ginger Carlson file a joint tax return. Robert is 65 and Ginger is 60. They support their 21-year-old daughter who is a full-time student and who earned $1,500 during the summer. Robert is a photographer and Ginger works part-time as a sales-clerk. Their records contain the following information.

Robert's salary	$55,595
Ginger's salary	6,590
Received a gift of cash	3,000
Interest on savings account	200
Interest on City of Phoenix bonds	150
Sold stock purchased three years ago for $6,700	4,000
Sold gold coins purchased three months ago for $3,200	3,000
Political contributions	200
Charitable contributions	4,500
Interest expense on loans	2,850
Medicine and drugs	450
Doctor and hospital payments	2,870
Uninsured loss from flood damage	7,630
Safe deposit box rental	45
Sales tax	590
State gas tax	110
Income tax withheld from Robert's salary	13,290
Income tax withheld from Ginger's salary	400

Required:

Compute the Carlson's taxable income, gross tax liability (use the tax table in Figure 28–4 if taxable income is covered in the table), and amount of unpaid taxes due or refund to be received.

Problem 28-3 **Type of Business Organization**

Rick Webber and Steve Tyler plan on starting a business by investing equal amounts of money. They would like to organize the business as either a partnership or a corporation. They anticipate an annual net income of $90,000 before deducting their salaries of $22,000 each for services performed. Both Rick and Steve are single and have no dependents. Neither of them itemizes deductions. The business would be Rick's only source of income. Steve has yearly income from other sources of $15,000. For this problem, use the tax rate schedules in Figure 28–5 to compute their individual income tax liability, even though taxable income may be less than $50,000.

Required:
A. Assuming that the business is organized as a partnership, determine the income tax liability of both Rick and Steve. Profits of the partnership are shared equally.
B. Assume that the business is organized as a corporation and that no dividends are distributed. Allocate one-half of the corporate income tax to each owner, and determine the tax liability of both Rick and Steve.
C. Assume that a corporation is formed and that all the net income is distributed as dividends. Allocate one-half of the corporate income tax to each owner, and determine the tax liability of both Rick and Steve.

Problem 28-4 Computation of Tax Liability for a Corporation
The records of the National Corporation contain the following information.

Sales revenue	$325,000
Interest on investments	15,000
Dividends from U.S. corporations	20,000
Cost of goods sold	190,000
Selling expenses	39,000
Administrative expenses	26,000
Net short-term capital loss	8,000
Net long-term capital gain	7,000
Goodwill amortization	7,500
Charitable contributions	9,000
Losses carried forward	8,000
Premium for employees' life insurance policies (National is the beneficiary)	6,500

Required:
Compute the tax liability of the National Corporation.

Problem 28-5 Computation of Tax Liability for a Corporation
The records of the Pepper Corporation contain the following information.

Sales revenues	$650,000
Royalty revenue	75,000
Interest received on state obligation	12,000
Interest on other investments	18,000
Dividends from U.S. corporations	15,000
Cost of goods sold	400,000
Selling expenses	75,000
Administrative expenses	45,000
Net long-term capital gain	30,000
Tax credits	5,000
Goodwill amortization	15,000
Charitable contributions	22,000
Premiums for employees' life insurance (part of employees' benefit package)	50,000

Required:
Compute the net tax liability of the Pepper Corporation.

Problem 28-6 Tax Effects on Financing Decisions
The Nova Corporation needs $700,000 to introduce a new product line. The investment is expected to yield a return of 18% before taxes. The following methods of raising the capital are being considered.

1. Issue $700,000 of 10-year, 13% bonds at par.
2. Issue 7,000 shares of 9.5%, cumulative, nonparticipating preferred stock for $100 a share.
3. Issue 28,000 shares of common stock for $25 a share.

Nova Corporation currently has 50,000 shares of common stock outstanding. The firm has a 46% marginal tax rate.

Required:
Determine the effect of each of the three financing methods on the income tax expense, net income, net income available to common stockholders, and earnings per share on common stock.

ALTERNATE PROBLEMS

Problem 28-1A Computation of Tax Liability for a Married Couple
Mark and Brooke Dalton, a married couple in their forties, have four dependent children. They compiled the following information for use in preparing their joint return.

Mark's salary	$31,950
Income tax withheld from Mark's salary	6,090
Brooke's salary	28,600
Income tax withheld from Brooke's salary	5,450
Sales tax	520
Charitable contributions	170
Net long-term capital gains	4,000
Net short-term capital gains	1,000
Interest on home mortgage	4,800
Interest on credit cards	210
Medical and dental expenses	2,410
Interest on corporate bonds	970
Interest on municipal bonds	170
Dividends	790
Lottery winnings	2,250
State income tax	3,720

Required:
Compute the Dalton's adjusted gross income, taxable income, and net tax liability. (Use the tax table in Figure 28–4 if taxable income is covered in the table.)

Problem 28-2A Computation of Tax Liability for a Married Couple
Ross and Ellen Spencer are a married couple in their twenties. They have three children and support Ross's 17-year-old sister, who lives with them. Ross is an engineer. Ellen, who is blind, is a lawyer. Their records contain the following information, which may be used in preparing their joint return.

Ellen's salary	$22,800
Ross's salary	49,360
Interest on savings account	170
Dividends	210
Gambling gains	3,120
Sold a painting purchased eight years ago for $3,000	6,800
Sold stock purchased four months ago for $2,600	1,950

Political contributions	180
Sales tax	550
Medical and dental expenses	5,140
Uninsured loss from automobile accident	780
Alimony payments to Ross's first wife	4,350
Subscriptions to professional journals	80
Property tax	660
Interest on home mortgage	11,900
Income tax withheld from Ellen's salary	4,095
Income tax withheld from Ross's salary	10,605

Required:

Compute the Spencer's taxable income, gross tax liability, and amount of unpaid taxes due or refund to be received.

Problem 28-3A Type of Business Organization

Mike Reese and Peter Matheson have decided to start a small business. They will invest equal amounts of capital and share profits equally. They anticipate an annual net income of $120,000 before deducting their salaries of $35,000 each, which is reasonable compensation. Mike is single with no dependents. The business will be his only source of income. Peter is married and has one young child. The business and his wife's salary of $13,500 (after deducting 10% from her lower earnings) are the only sources of income to be reported on his joint return. Neither Mike nor Peter itemizes deductions. Use the tax rate schedule shown in Figure 28–5 to compute their income tax liability, even though taxable income may be less than $50,000.

Required:

A. Assume that the business is organized as a partnership. Compute the tax liability of both Mike and Peter.
B. Assume that a corporation is organized and that no dividends are distributed. Allocate one-half of the corporate income tax liability to each owner, and then compute the total tax liability of both Mike and Peter.
C. Assume that the business is organized as a corporation and that all the net income is distributed as dividends. After allocating one-half of the corporate tax liability to each owner, compute the total tax liability of both Mike and Peter.

Problem 28-4A Computation of Tax Liability for a Corporation

The records of T-Top Corporation contain the following information.

Interest received on state obligations	$ 12,500
Sales	675,000
Dividends from U.S. corporations	17,500
Dividends from foreign corporations	7,500
Net long-term capital gain	15,000
Life insurance proceeds (death of an insured officer)	75,000
Interest on investments	9,500
Cost of goods sold	350,000
Selling expenses	85,000
Administrative expenses	75,300
Net short-term capital loss	13,500
Tax credits	10,000
Goodwill amortization	15,000
Charitable contributions	20,000

Required:

Compute the tax liability of the T-Top Corporation.

Problem 28-5A Tax Effects on Financing Decisions

ADR Corporation would like to purchase several pieces of machinery and equipment for $500,000. Three proposals have been suggested to raise the capital.

1. Sell 50,000 shares of common stock for a total price of $500,000.
2. Sell 10,000 shares of 10.5% preferred stock for $50 a share.
3. Sell $500,000 of 13% bonds at par value.

   ADR Corporation expects a pretax yield on the investment of 19%. There are 100,000 shares of common stock currently outstanding. The firm has a 40% marginal tax rate.

Required:

Calculate the expected effect of each proposal on the firm's income tax expense, net income, net income available to common stockholders, and earnings per share on common stock.

APPENDIX A
CONSOLIDATED
FINANCIAL
STATEMENTS

K MART CORPORATION
1984 ANNUAL REPORT

REPORTS BY MANAGEMENT AND INDEPENDENT ACCOUNTANTS

K mart Responsibility for Financial Statements

K mart Corporation management is responsible for the integrity of the information and representations contained in this annual report. This responsibility includes making informed estimates and judgments in selecting the appropriate accounting principles in the circumstances. Management believes the financial statements conform with generally accepted accounting principles and have been prepared on a consistent basis except for the change in the method of accounting for foreign currency translation, effective January 27, 1983 as described in Note (A) to the consolidated financial statements.

To assist management in fulfilling these obligations, the company utilizes several tools, which include the following:

♦ The company maintains a system of internal accounting controls to provide for the integrity of information for purposes of preparing financial statements and to assure assets are properly accounted for and safeguarded. This concept of reasonable assurance is based on the recognition that the cost of the system must be related to the benefits to be derived. Management believes its system provides this appropriate balance.

♦ An Internal Audit Department is maintained to evaluate, test and report on the application of internal accounting controls in conformity with standards of the practice of internal auditing.

♦ The Board of Directors appoints the independent accountants to perform an examination of the company's financial statements. This examination includes, among other things, a review of the system of internal controls as required by generally accepted auditing standards.

♦ The Audit Committee of the Board of Directors, consisting solely of outside directors, meets regularly with management, internal auditors and the independent accountants to assure that each is carrying out its responsibilities. The internal auditors and independent accountants both have full and free access to the Audit Committee, with and without the presence of management.

B. M. FAUBER
Chairman of the Board
and Chief Executive Officer

R. E. BREWER
Senior Vice President
Finance

Report of Independent Accountants

To the Shareholders and Board of Directors of K mart Corporation

In our opinion, the accompanying consolidated balance sheets and the related consolidated statements of income, shareholders' equity and changes in financial position present fairly the financial position of K mart Corporation and its subsidiaries at January 30, 1985 and January 25, 1984, and the results of their operations and the changes in their financial position for each of the three fiscal years in the period ended January 30, 1985, in conformity with generally accepted accounting principles consistently applied during the period except for the change effective January 27, 1983, with which we concur, in the method of accounting for foreign currency translation as described in Note (A) to the consolidated financial statements. Our examinations of these statements were made in accordance with generally accepted auditing standards and accordingly included such tests of the accounting records and such other auditing procedures as we considered necessary in the circumstances.

200 Renaissance Center
Detroit, Michigan
March 13, 1985

Price Waterhouse

CONSOLIDATED STATEMENTS OF INCOME

(Millions, except per-share data)	Fiscal Year Ended		
	January 30, 1985	January 25, 1984	January 26, 1983
Sales	$21,095.9	$18,597.9	$16,772.2
Licensee fees and rental income	207.5	191.3	169.5
Equity in income of affiliated retail companies	58.8	51.7	44.5
Interest income	39.7	38.0	54.6
	21,401.9	18,878.9	17,040.8
Cost of merchandise sold (including buying and occupancy costs)	15,259.8	13,447.4	12,298.6
Selling, general and administrative expenses	4,427.7	3,880.1	3,602.9
Advertising	554.4	424.6	401.7
Provision for store closings			44.5
Interest expense:			
Debt	146.5	84.1	97.7
Capital lease obligations	193.5	189.0	176.5
	20,581.9	18,025.2	16,621.9
Income before income taxes	820.0	853.7	418.9
Income taxes	327.1	366.5	162.0
Income from retail operations	492.9	487.2	256.9
Equity in income of insurance operations	6.2	5.1	4.9
Net income for the year	$ 499.1	$ 492.3	$ 261.8
Earnings per common and common equivalent share	$3.84	$3.80	$2.06

See accompanying Notes to Consolidated Financial Statements.

CONSOLIDATED BALANCE SHEETS

(Millions)	January 30, 1985	January 25, 1984
Assets		
Current Assets:		
Cash (includes temporary investments of $294.3 and $762.9, respectively)	$ 492.0	$1,027.7
Accounts receivable	179.0	134.8
Merchandise inventories	4,587.8	3,581.6
Operating supplies and prepaid expenses	52.0	44.4
Total current assets	5,310.8	4,788.5
Investments in and Advances to:		
Affiliated retail companies	219.2	211.8
Insurance operations	173.1	128.6
Property and Equipment–net	3,338.8	2,973.7
Cost in Excess of Fair Value of Net Assets Acquired–net	140.6	14.4
Other Assets	79.3	66.1
	$9,261.8	$8,183.1
Liabilities and Shareholders' Equity		
Current Liabilities:		
Long-term debt due within one year	$ 1.9	$ 3.2
Capital lease obligations due within one year	74.1	70.6
Notes payable	234.9	
Accounts payable–trade	1,916.9	1,717.2
Accrued payrolls and other liabilities	362.5	328.0
Taxes other than income taxes	200.0	172.9
Income taxes	98.8	228.9
Total current liabilities	2,889.1	2,520.8
Capital Lease Obligations	1,780.1	1,822.3
Long-Term Debt	1,106.9	711.2
Other Long-Term Liabilities	163.4	127.8
Deferred Income Taxes	88.5	60.9
Shareholders' Equity	3,233.8	2,940.1
	$9,261.8	$8,183.1

See accompanying Notes to Consolidated Financial Statements.

CONSOLIDATED STATEMENTS OF CHANGES IN FINANCIAL POSITION

	Fiscal Year Ended		
(Millions)	January 30, 1985	January 25, 1984	January 26, 1983
Cash Provided by (Used for):			
Operations			
Net income for the year	**$ 499.1**	$ 492.3	$ 261.8
Noncash charges (credits) to earnings:			
Depreciation and amortization	302.9	264.5	251.1
Provision for store closings			44.5
Deferred income taxes	15.6	21.5	7.6
Undistributed equity income	(15.7)	(16.8)	(15.9)
Increase in other long-term liabilities	35.6	33.8	21.2
Other–net	9.3	.8	6.4
Total from net income	846.8	796.1	576.7
Cash provided by (used for) current assets and current liabilities:			
Increase in inventories	(792.5)	(285.4)	(159.8)
Inventories of acquired companies	(213.7)	(1.3)	
Increase in accounts payable	199.7	203.8	260.4
Other–net	(121.4)	106.6	130.2
Net cash provided by (used for) operations	(81.1)	819.8	807.5
Financing			
Increase in long-term debt and notes payable	645.7	123.4	197.2
Reduction in long-term debt and notes payable	(16.7)	(10.4)	(181.4)
Obligations incurred under capital leases	43.8	78.9	141.8
Reduction in capital lease obligations	(77.5)	(75.5)	(63.0)
Common stock issued	21.1	22.9	8.2
Purchase of treasury shares	(50.8)		
Net cash provided by financing	565.6	139.3	102.8
Dividends Paid	(150.7)	(132.2)	(123.0)
Investments			
Additions to owned and leased property	(646.0)	(405.7)	(391.4)
Owned property of acquired companies	(94.0)	(10.0)	
Cost in excess of fair value of net assets acquired	(128.0)		
Proceeds from the sale of property	62.0	91.4	49.7
Increased investment in affiliated retail companies and insurance operations	(46.2)	(24.5)	(3.8)
Other–net	(17.3)	(4.2)	(3.2)
Net cash used for investments	(869.5)	(353.0)	(348.7)
Net Increase (Decrease) in Cash	**$(535.7)**	$ 473.9	$ 438.6

See accompanying Notes to Consolidated Financial Statements.

CONSOLIDATED STATEMENTS OF SHAREHOLDERS' EQUITY

($ Millions)	Number of Shares Issued	Common Stock	Capital in Excess of Par Value	Retained Earnings	Treasury Shares	Foreign Currency Translation Adjustment	Total Shareholders' Equity
Balance at January 27, 1982	**123,976,386**	**$124.0**	**$264.2**	**$2,067.4**	**$**	**$**	**$2,455.6**
Net income for the year				261.8			261.8
Cash dividends declared, $1.00 per share				(124.3)			(124.3)
Common stock sold under stock option and purchase plans and conversion of debentures	517,960	.5	7.7				8.2
Balance at January 26, 1983	**124,494,346**	**124.5**	**271.9**	**2,204.9**			**2,601.3**
Net income for the year				492.3			492.3
Cash dividends declared, $1.08 per share				(135.1)			(135.1)
Common stock sold under stock option and employees' savings plans and conversion of debentures	654,619	.6	16.9				17.5
Common stock issued for acquisition of Bishop Buffets, Inc.	761,840	.8	4.6	7.0			12.4
Cumulative foreign currency translation adjustment (includes $8.7 for current year)						(48.3)	(48.3)
Balance at January 25, 1984	**125,910,805**	**125.9**	**293.4**	**2,569.1**		**(48.3)**	**2,940.1**
Net income for the year				499.1			499.1
Cash dividends declared, $1.24 per share				(155.4)			(155.4)
Common stock sold under stock option and employees' savings plans and conversion of debentures	785,488	.8	20.3				21.1
Purchase of 1,678,500 treasury shares, at cost					(50.8)		(50.8)
Foreign currency translation adjustment net of applicable income taxes of $.1						(20.3)	(20.3)
Balance at January 30, 1985	**126,696,293**	**$126.7**	**$313.7**	**$2,912.8**	**$(50.8)**	**$(68.6)**	**$3,233.8**

Common stock, authorized 250,000,000 shares, $1.00 par value.

Ten million shares of no par value preferred stock with voting and cumulative dividend rights are authorized but unissued. Currently there are no plans for its issuance.

See accompanying Notes to Consolidated Financial Statements.

NOTES TO CONSOLIDATED FINANCIAL STATEMENTS

(A) Summary of Significant Accounting Policies

Fiscal Year: The company's fiscal year ends on the last Wednesday in January. Fiscal year 1984 consisted of 53 weeks and ended on January 30, 1985. Fiscal years 1983 and 1982 consisted of 52 weeks and ended on January 25, 1984 and January 26, 1983, respectively.

Basis of Consolidation: The company includes all majority-owned retail subsidiaries in the consolidated financial statements. The accounts of Furr's Cafeterias, Inc. and Bishop Buffets, Inc. are included in the consolidated financial statements on the basis of fiscal years generally ending on December 31. Investments in affiliated retail companies owned 20% or more and the wholly owned insurance operations are accounted for by the equity method using their December financial statements. All significant intercompany transactions and accounts have been eliminated in consolidation.

Foreign Operations: Effective in fiscal 1983, K mart Corporation changed its method of accounting for foreign currency translation to comply with the requirements of Financial Accounting Standard No. 52, "Foreign Currency Translation." Foreign currency assets and liabilities are translated into U.S. dollars at the exchange rates in effect at the balance sheet date except for operations in countries with high inflation. Results of operations are translated at average exchange rates during the period for revenue and expenses. Translation gains and losses resulting from fluctuations in the exchange rates are accumulated as a separate component of shareholders' equity. Translation gains and losses of operations in highly inflationary countries continue to be included in consolidated results of operations. Prior to 1983 all translation gains and losses were included in net income.

Inventories: Merchandise inventories are valued at the lower of cost or market, using the retail method, on the last-in, first-out basis for substantially all domestic inventories and the first-in, first-out basis for the remainder.

Property Owned: Land, buildings, leasehold improvements and equipment are recorded at cost. Major replacements and refurbishings are charged to the property accounts while replacements, maintenance and repairs that do not improve or extend the life of the respective assets are expensed currently. The company capitalizes interest cost as part of the cost of constructing capital assets.

The cost of all properties retired and the accumulated depreciation thereon are eliminated from the accounts and the resulting gain or loss is taken into income.

Depreciation: The company computes depreciation on owned property principally on the straight-line method for financial statement purposes and on accelerated methods for income tax purposes. Most store properties are leased, and improvements are amortized over the term of the lease but not more than 25 years. Other annual rates used in computing depreciation for financial statement purposes are 2% to 10% for buildings, 10% to 14% for store fixtures and 5% to 33% for other fixtures and equipment.

(A) Summary of Significant Accounting Policies continued

Leased Property under Capital Leases: The company accounts for capital leases, which transfer substantially all of the benefits and risks incident to the ownership of property, as the acquisition of an asset and the incurrence of an obligation. Under this method of accounting for leases, the asset is amortized using the straight-line method and the obligation, including interest thereon, is liquidated over the life of the lease. All other leases (operating leases) are accounted for by recording periodic rental expense over the life of the lease.

Licensee Sales: The company's policy is to exclude sales of licensed departments from total sales.

Preopening and Closing Costs: The company follows the practice of treating store operating costs incurred prior to opening a new retail unit as current period expenses. When the decision to close a retail unit is made, the company provides for future net lease obligations, nonrecoverable investments in fixed assets, other expenses directly related to discontinuance of operations and estimated operating losses through expected closing dates.

Income Taxes: Deferred income taxes are provided on nonpermanent differences between financial statement and taxable income.

The company accrues appropriate U.S. and foreign taxes payable on all of the earnings of subsidiaries and affiliates, except with respect to earnings that are intended to be permanently reinvested. Any additional taxes or credits related to subsequent distributions of such earnings are determined and taken into account at the time of distribution.

Investment Credit: The company uses the "flow through" method of accounting for investment credit whereby income tax expense is reduced for the period in which expenditures create the tax benefit.

(B) Store Closings

During 1982, the company made a thorough review of operations, which resulted in a determination that a number of stores and auto service departments were operating at unacceptable levels of profitability. Following this review process, the company closed eight K mart stores, a total of 66 Kresge and Jupiter stores and 361 automotive service departments and planned a phaseout of 17 additional K mart stores in 1983, resulting in a pretax provision of $44.5 million ($.19 per share after tax) in 1982.

(C) Acquisitions

On August 9, 1984, K mart Corporation completed the acquisition of Walden Book Company, Inc. (Waldenbooks) for $300.0 million. Headquartered in Stamford, Connecticut, Waldenbooks is the nation's largest retail bookstore chain. As of January 30, 1985, Waldenbooks operated 898 stores in all 50 United States.

On September 27, 1984, the company completed the acquisition of Builders Square, Inc. (formerly Home Centers of America, Inc.) through a merger with a wholly owned subsidiary. The company purchased 100% of the shares of Builders Square for $11.00 per share, aggregating $88.2 million. Based in San Antonio, Texas, Builders Square operated 15 home improvement stores in the states of Texas, Illinois and Oklahoma as of January 30, 1985.

The acquisitions of Waldenbooks and Builders Square have been accounted for as purchases, and accordingly the results of operations have been consolidated with those of the company from the respective dates of acquisition. The excess of cost over the fair value of net assets acquired approximating $93.9 million related to Waldenbooks and $34.1 million related to Builders Square are being amortized on a straight-line basis over 40 years. Assuming the Waldenbooks and Builders Square acquisitions had occurred at the beginning of fiscal 1984 rather than during the third quarter of 1984 at the same purchase price, unaudited pro forma consolidated sales, net income and earnings per share for 1984 would approximate $21.4 billion, $483.5 million and $3.72, respectively. The pro forma financial information assumes adjustments to combined historical results of operations for imputed interest on the purchase price, amortization of goodwill and the effects of revaluation of assets and liabilities under purchase accounting. Combined pro forma amounts for 1983 would not have been materially different from the reported amounts because the financing costs of the acquisitions and the amortizations resulting from the purchase accounting method largely offset the additional earnings.

On December 20, 1983, K mart Corporation issued 761,840 shares of common stock, through a wholly owned subsidiary, for all the common shares of Bishop Buffets, Inc. (Bishop). Bishop operates a chain of cafeterias in eight midwestern and western states. The acquisition was accounted for as a pooling of interests; however, the financial statements were not restated for periods prior to the acquisition due to immateriality.

(D) Subsequent Event

On January 13, 1985, K mart Corporation and Pay Less Drug Stores Northwest, Inc. (Pay Less) executed a definitive merger agreement providing for the acquisition of Pay Less through a wholly owned subsidiary of the company. Pursuant to the agreement, Pay Less shareholders will receive $27.00 in cash for each of their shares. The total value of the transaction will be approximately $500.0 million and will be accounted for under the purchase method. Pursuant to a tender offer in February 1985, approximately 92% of the outstanding shares of common stock of Pay Less was acquired. It is expected that the acquisition will be completed on March 29, 1985. K mart Corporation will include the results of Pay Less operations in fiscal 1985. Pay Less is headquartered in Wilsonville, Oregon and operates a chain of 164 super drug stores in Oregon, Washington, California, Idaho and Nevada.

If the acquisitions of Waldenbooks, Builders Square and Pay Less had all taken place at the beginning of fiscal 1984 at the same purchase price, unaudited pro forma consolidated sales, net income and earnings per share for 1984 would approximate $22.3 billion, $470.0 million and $3.62, respectively. The pro forma financial information assumes adjustments to combined historical results of operations for imputed interest on the purchase price, amortization of goodwill and the effects of revaluation of assets and liabilities under purchase accounting. The pro forma effect on 1984 earnings per common and common equivalent share by quarter is illustrated in Note (R).

(E) Merchandise Inventories

A summary of inventories by method of pricing and the excess of current cost over stated LIFO value follows:

(Millions)	January 30, 1985	January 25, 1984
Last-in, first-out (cost not in excess of market)	$4,072.3	$3,108.0
Lower of cost (first-in, first-out) or market	515.5	473.6
Total	$4,587.8	$3,581.6
Excess of current cost over stated LIFO value	$ 507.0	$ 526.6

(F) Property and Equipment

The components of property and equipment are:

(Millions)	January 30, 1985	January 25, 1984
Property owned:		
Land	$ 54.4	$ 57.6
Buildings	228.0	174.4
Leasehold improvements	395.3	303.9
Furniture and fixtures	2,170.4	1,738.0
Construction in progress	24.5	57.5
Property under capital leases	2,409.3	2,386.1
	5,281.9	4,717.5
Less—accumulated depreciation and amortization:		
Property owned	1,100.0	976.6
Property under capital leases	843.1	767.2
Total	$3,338.8	$2,973.7

The components of depreciation and amortization expense and capital expenditures are:

(Millions)	Property Owned	Capital Leases	Total
Depreciation and amortization expense:			
1984	$202.6	$100.3	$302.9
1983	$ 167.8	$ 96.7	$ 264.5
1982	$ 157.4	$ 93.7	$ 251.1
Capital expenditures:			
1984—Additions	$621.7	$ 24.3	$646.0
—From acquired companies	94.0		94.0
Total	$715.7	$ 24.3	$740.0
1983—Additions	$ 367.9	$ 37.8	$ 405.7
—From acquired companies	10.0		10.0
Total	$ 377.9	$ 37.8	$415.7
1982—Additions	$ 306.4	$ 85.0	$ 391.4

The owned property of acquired companies includes Waldenbooks and Builders Square for 1984 and Bishop Buffets for 1983.

(G) Equity Company Information

Meldisco Subsidiaries of Melville Corporation

All U.S. K mart footwear departments are operated under license agreements with the Meldisco subsidiaries of Melville Corporation, substantially all of which are 49% owned by the company and 51% owned by Melville. Fees and income earned under the license agreements in 1984, 1983 and 1982 of $150.1 million, $137.4 million and $117.3 million, respectively, are included in licensee fees and rental income. The company's equity in the income of these operations and dividends received in 1984, 1983 and 1982 were as follows:

(Millions)	1984	1983	1982
Equity in income of Meldisco operations	$ 44.8	$ 40.2	$ 31.9
Dividends	$ 40.9	$ 33.3	$ 26.6

Meldisco subsidiaries' summarized financial information follows:

(Millions)	Year Ended December 31,		
	1984	1983	1982
Net sales	$932.6	$848.4	$759.3
Gross profit	$399.6	$364.9	$312.1
Net income	$ 92.5	$ 83.1	$ 66.2

(Millions)	December 31,		
	1984	1983	1982
Inventory	$104.9	$ 94.9	$ 90.6
Other current assets	101.1	102.5	75.6
Noncurrent assets	2.1	2.8	3.4
Total assets	208.1	200.2	169.6
Current liabilities	42.5	42.3	27.1
Net assets	$165.6	$157.9	$142.5
Equity of K mart Corporation	$ 80.1	$ 76.3	$ 68.7

G. J. Coles & Coy. Limited

The company has a 20% equity interest in G. J. Coles & Coy. Limited (Coles), the major food and general-merchandise retailer in Australia. Income earned under the K mart license agreement in 1984, 1983 and 1982 of $2.5 million, $2.4 million and $2.5 million, respectively, is included in licensee fees and rental income. The company's equity in the income of Coles' operations, dividends, year-end investment in Coles and the market value of Coles common stock owned by the company follows. The cumulative effect of translating the company's equity in the investment of Coles as of January 30, 1985 and January 25, 1984 according to FAS 52 was a reduction of $41.4 million and $31.4 million, respectively.

(G) Equity Company Information continued

(Millions U.S. $)	1984	1983	1982
Equity in income	$ 19.6	$ 17.2	$ 21.6
Dividends	$ 8.4	$ 6.7	$ 7.0
Equity of K mart Corporation	$107.5	$102.8	$109.2
Market value of Coles common stock	$173.6	$176.9	$103.4

Summarized financial information adjusted for conformity with U.S. generally accepted accounting principles for Coles' most recent fiscal years follows. Information presented for 1984 and 1983 was translated into U.S. dollars under the principles of FAS 52. The 1982 financial statements were translated according to FAS 8. [See Note (A).]

(Millions U.S. $)	Fiscal Year Ended		
	July 29, 1984	July 31, 1983	July 25, 1982
Net sales	$4,901.3	$4,404.7	$4,423.6
Net income	$ 88.8	$ 73.0	$ 70.2

(Millions U.S. $)	July 29, 1984	July 31, 1983	July 25, 1982
Current assets	$ 526.6	$ 471.6	$ 449.5
Noncurrent assets	949.3	922.6	974.8
Total assets	$1,475.9	$1,394.2	$1,424.3
Current liabilities	$ 616.6	$ 533.1	$ 535.9
Noncurrent liabilities	325.9	340.5	313.4
Equity	533.4	520.6	575.0
Total liabilities and equity	$1,475.9	$1,394.2	$1,424.3

K mart Insurance Services, Inc.

K mart Insurance Services, Inc. summarized financial information follows:

(Millions)	Year Ended December 31,		
	1984	1983	1982
Premium and other income	$141.1	$112.9	$ 95.7
Costs and expenses	134.9	107.8	90.8
Net income	$ 6.2	$ 5.1	$ 4.9

(Millions)	December 31,		
	1984	1983	1982
Cash and receivables	$ 22.5	$ 18.4	$ 9.2
Investments	214.8	173.9	160.0
Policy acquisition costs and other assets	108.6	99.6	80.1
Total assets	345.9	291.9	249.3
Policy and claim reserves	146.4	· 136.2	119.0
Other liabilities	26.4	27.1	16.0
Equity of K mart Corporation	$173.1	$128.6	$114.3

Unremitted earnings of unconsolidated subsidiaries included in consolidated retained earnings were $128.7 million at January 30, 1985.

(H) Income Taxes

Components of income before income taxes follow:

(Millions)	1984	1983	1982
U.S.	$791.0	$828.3	$397.8
Foreign	29.0	25.4	21.1
Total	$820.0	$853.7	$418.9

The provision for income taxes consists of:

(Millions)	1984	1983	1982
Current:			
Federal	$257.7	$304.7	$131.7
State and local	49.0	35.5	19.6
Foreign	4.8	4.8	3.1
Deferred:			
Excess of tax over book depreciation	47.6	19.3	24.8
Lease capitalization	(13.6)	(14.2)	(14.9)
Store closings provision			(18.7)
Other	(18.4)	16.4	16.4
Total income taxes	$327.1	$366.5	$162.0

A reconciliation of the company's effective tax rate to the federal statutory rate follows:

(Millions)	1984	1983	1982	% of Pretax Income 1984	1983	1982
Federal statutory rate	$377.2	$392.7	$192.7	46.0%	46.0%	46.0%
State and local taxes, net of federal tax benefit	26.5	19.6	11.1	3.2	2.2	2.6
Tax credits	(48.7)	(25.6)	(19.6)	(5.9)	(3.0)	(4.7)
Equity in income of affiliated retail companies subject to lower tax rates	(23.6)	(23.3)	(21.8)	(2.9)	(2.7)	(5.2)
Other	(4.3)	3.1	(.4)	(.5)	.4	
Total income taxes	$327.1	$366.5	$162.0	39.9%	42.9%	38.7%

The amounts shown on the balance sheets for deferred income taxes result principally from the difference between financial statement and income tax depreciation, reduced by the effect of accounting for certain leases as capital leases of $138.2 million at January 30, 1985 and $125.6 million at January 25, 1984. At January 30, 1985, the net amount of current deferred taxes included in operating supplies and prepaid expenses was $3.4 million, which related primarily to the current portion of property taxes and uninsured claims offset by timing differences arising from LIFO and layaways. At January 25, 1984, the net amount of current deferred taxes of $8.6 million, included in income taxes payable, relates principally to LIFO, layaways and the timing difference in certain taxes.

Undistributed earnings of consolidated subsidiaries, which are intended to be permanently reinvested, totaled $192.3 million at January 30, 1985.

(I) Long-Term Debt

(Millions)	January 30, 1985	January 25, 1984
6% convertible subordinated debentures due 1999	$ 188.3	$ 199.3
9⅞% notes due 1985 (net of unamortized discount of $.1 million and $.4 million, respectively)	199.9	199.6
Commercial paper and notes payable to banks	700.0	300.0
Other	20.6	15.5
	1,108.8	714.4
Portion due within one year	1.9	3.2
Long-term debt	$1,106.9	$ 711.2

The debentures due 1999 are convertible into common stock at $35.50 per share. The indenture relating to the debentures provides that the company shall pay $11.0 million into a sinking fund on July 15 each year from 1985 to 1998, inclusive. The debentures are subject to redemption through the sinking fund at 100% of the principal amount, or at any time at the option of the company at prices declining from 106% to 100% of the principal amount after July 15, 1994. During fiscal 1984, the company purchased $11.0 million principal amount of debentures in order to satisfy the July 1985 sinking fund requirements. At January 30, 1985, a total of 5,304,629 shares of authorized common stock are reserved for conversion.

The 9⅞% notes are unsecured obligations of the company due July 15, 1985 and may be redeemed at a redemption price equal to 100% of the principal amount plus accrued interest.

The company has entered into revolving credit agreements with various banks in the aggregate amount of $950.0 million as of the year ended January 30, 1985, of which $300.0 million had been in effect as of the year ended January 25, 1984. The agreements, which are for terms of either three or five years, provide for borrowings at an interest rate based on the prime rate, "CD-based rate" or "LIBOR-based rate" at the company's election. The revolving credit agreements contain certain restrictive provisions regarding the maintenance of net worth, working capital, coverage ratios and payment of cash dividends. At January 30, 1985, $1,111.7 million of consolidated retained earnings were free of such restrictions.

During March 1985, K mart Corporation completed three debt offerings. The company issued $250.0 million of 12¾% sinking fund debentures due March 1, 2015. The debentures will be redeemable at 100% of the principal amount through annual sinking fund payments on March 1, 1996 through 2014 of not less than $12.5 million nor more than $37.5 million. Prior to March 1, 1995, the company may not redeem any debentures from or in anticipation of borrowed funds having an interest cost to the company of less than 12.78% per year. The debentures are otherwise redeemable in whole or in part, at any time at the option of the company at prices declining from 112.5% to 100% of the principal amount. The company issued $150.0 million of 12⅛% notes due March 1, 1995. The notes are not redeemable prior to maturity. The company issued $100.0 million of 12½% debentures due March 1, 2005. The debentures are not redeemable prior to maturity. Interest is payable semi-annually beginning September 1, 1985 with respect to each of these issues.

At January 30, 1985, the revolving credit agreements and portions of the subsequent debt offerings, which have been or will be used to refinance current amounts outstanding, support $700.0 million of commercial paper and the $200.0 million 9⅞% notes due July 15, 1985. These amounts have been classified as long-term debt based on the company's intention to maintain at least that amount of similar debt outstanding during fiscal 1985. At January 25, 1984, the revolving credit agreements support $300.0 million of commercial paper and notes payable to banks classified as long-term debt.

Principal payments on long-term debt (excluding $900.0 million in commercial paper and notes payable classified as long-term debt for 1984) for the five years subsequent to 1984, in millions, are: 1985–$1.9; 1986–$15.4; 1987–$11.9; 1988–$11.4; 1989–$11.4.

(J) Compensating Balances and Current Notes Payable

At January 30, 1985, the company had bank lines of credit aggregating $764.1 million with interest rates approximating the "prime" lending rate. In support of certain lines of credit, it is expected that compensating balances will be maintained on deposit with the banks, which will average 10% of the line to the extent that it is not in use and an additional 10% on the portion in use, whereas other lines require fees in lieu of compensating balances. The company is free to withdraw the entire balance from its accounts at any time.

At January 30, 1985, notes payable included $213.1 million of the company's commercial paper (weighted average interest rate 8.1%) and $21.8 million of notes payable to banks (weighted average interest rate 7.7%).

(K) Leases

Description of Leasing Arrangements: The company conducts operations primarily in leased facilities. K mart store leases are generally for terms of 25 years with multiple five-year renewal options which allow the company the option to extend the life of the lease up to 50 years beyond the initial noncancellable term. Certain leases provide for additional rental payments based on a percent of sales in excess of a specified base. Also, certain leases provide for the payment by the lessee of executory costs (taxes, maintenance and insurance), and some selling space has been sublet to other retailers in certain of the company's leased facilities.

(K) Leases continued

Lease Commitments: Future minimum lease payments with respect to capital and operating leases are:

(Millions)	Minimum Lease Payments	
	Capital	Operating
Fiscal Year:		
1985	$ 342.2	$ 266.8
1986	336.4	263.4
1987	330.2	258.2
1988	325.4	249.2
1989	319.1	239.9
Later years	3,910.9	2,508.5
Total minimum lease payments	5,564.2	3,786.0
Less—minimum sublease rental income		(177.2)
Net minimum lease payments	5,564.2	$ 3,608.8
Less:		
Estimated executory costs	(1,527.0)	
Amount representing interest	(2,183.0)	
Obligations under capital leases, of which $74.1 is due within one year	$ 1,854.2	

The company has guaranteed indebtedness related to certain leased properties financed by industrial revenue bonds. As of January 30, 1985, the total amount of such guaranteed indebtedness is $274.0 million, of which $117.7 million is included in capital lease obligations.

Rental Expense: A summary of operating lease rental expense and short-term rentals follows:

(Millions)	1984	1983	1982
Minimum rentals	$260.3	$227.5	$202.2
Percentage rentals	49.5	38.4	32.2
Less—sublease rentals	(36.5)	(35.5)	(33.5)
Total	$273.3	$230.4	$200.9

Reconciliation of Capital Lease Information: The impact of recording amortization and interest expense versus rent expense on capital leases is as follows:

(Millions)	1984	1983	1982
Amortization of capital lease property	$100.3	$ 96.7	$ 93.7
Interest expense related to obligations under capital leases	193.5	189.0	176.5
Amounts charged to earnings	293.8	285.7	270.2
Related minimum lease payments net of executory costs	(264.3)	(255.1)	(239.4)
Excess of amounts charged over related minimum lease payments	$ 29.5	$ 30.6	$ 30.8

Related minimum lease payments above exclude executory costs for 1984, 1983 and 1982 in the amounts of $80.0 million, $76.7 million and $73.6 million, respectively.

In 1984 and 1983, there were no currency gains or losses recognized from the inclusion of capital leases for foreign operations due to the adoption of FAS 52. The inclusion of capital leases of foreign operations increased currency fluctuation gains by $3.0 million in 1982. [See Note (A).]

(L) Segment and Geographic Information

The dominant portion of the company's operations is in a single industry, retailing general merchandise through the operation of a chain of discount department stores.

The company has both domestic and foreign operations, which are summarized as follows:

(Millions U.S. $)	1984	1983	1982
Sales:			
U.S.	$20,329.0	$17,785.7	$16,007.1
Canada	766.9	812.2	765.1
Total	$21,095.9	$18,597.9	$16,772.2
Licensee fees and other income:			
U.S.	$ 279.4	$ 258.1	$ 240.9
Canada	4.5	3.3	3.7
Australia	22.1	19.6	24.0
Total	$ 306.0	$ 281.0	$ 268.6
Income from retail operations:			
U.S.	$ 462.4	$ 459.7	$ 229.2
Canada	9.8	9.4	4.5
Australia	20.7	18.1	23.2
	492.9	487.2	256.9
Equity in income of insurance operations	6.2	5.1	4.9
Net income for the year	$ 499.1	$ 492.3	$ 261.8
Identifiable assets:			
U.S.	$ 8,499.1	$ 7,497.6	$ 6,642.0
Canada	370.4	345.1	371.1
	8,869.5	7,842.7	7,013.1
Investments in and advances to:			
Affiliated retail companies–			
U.S.	80.3	76.3	68.7
Australia	107.5	102.8	109.2
Mexico	31.4	32.7	38.4
Insurance operations	173.1	128.6	114.3
Total assets	$ 9,261.8	$ 8,183.1	$ 7,343.7

Operating results of certain foreign operations, which are not significant, are included in U.S. amounts.

(L) Segment and Geographic Information continued

The company's equity in income of G. J. Coles & Coy. Limited (Coles) of Australia and license fees from Coles are included under the caption "Licensee fees and other income." [See Note (G).]

In 1984 and 1983, due primarily to the adoption of FAS 52, currency gains or losses included in income from retail operations were insignificant. [See Note (A).] Currency fluctuations, which are included in income from retail operations for 1982, reflect the effect of exchange rate changes recognized when financial statements of foreign operations are translated into U.S. dollars. Currency fluctuations, including net amounts reported in Australian and Mexican equity income, consisted of a $3.7 million gain in 1982.

Identifiable assets are those assets of the company that are identified with operations in a specific geographic area. Corporate assets (assets used by two or more geographic operations) and transfers between geographic areas are insignificant.

(M) Earnings Per Common and Common Equivalent Share

Earnings per common and common equivalent share were computed by dividing net income by the weighted average number of shares of common stock and dilutive common stock equivalents outstanding during each year. Common shares at the beginning of each year were increased by the number of shares issuable on conversion of the 6% convertible debentures (issued in 1974), and net income was adjusted for interest expense net of the related tax effect. The number of common shares was increased by the number of shares issuable under the Stock Purchase Incentive Plan (1982 only) and the Stock Option Plans, less the number of shares that were assumed to have been purchased at average market prices with the proceeds of sales under the plans. The shares issued in 1983 for the pooling of interests with Bishop Buffets, Inc. were not assumed to be outstanding prior to the date of acquisition because net income prior to date of acquisition was not restated due to immateriality. [See Note (C).]

(N) Pension Plans

The company and its subsidiaries have noncontributory pension plans covering most employees. Total pension expense was $49.4 million for 1984, $42.2 million for 1983 and $42.7 million for 1982. The increase in pension expense for 1984 compared with 1983 resulted from a benefit improvement and elimination of a prior credit balance in the funding standard account, partially offset by favorable investment performance. In 1983 the effect of a change in the assumed rate of employee turnover, based on the company's actual experience, decreased total pension expense for 1983 by $6.0 million. The effect of the change was offset by a general increase in total pension costs in 1983. The company's policies are to fund pension costs accrued and to amortize prior service costs principally over 30 years.

A comparison of accumulated benefits and net assets for the company's principal pension plan as of the two most recent valuation dates follows:

(Millions)	January 25, 1984	January 26, 1983
Actuarial present value of accumulated plan benefits:		
Vested	$318.3	$269.8
Nonvested	87.6	82.2
Total	$405.9	$352.0
Net assets available for benefits	$574.0	$475.4

The weighted average assumed rate of return used in determining the actuarial value of accumulated plan benefits was 7.0% for both years.

(O) Employees' Savings Plan

The Employees' Savings Plan (the Savings Plan), which commenced July 1, 1982, provides that employees of the company and certain subsidiaries who have completed two "Years of Service" can invest from 2% to 12% of their earnings in the employee's choice of a diversified common stock fund, an insured guaranteed investment fund or a K mart common stock fund. For each dollar the employee invests up to 6% of his or her earnings, the company will contribute an additional 50 cents which is invested in the K mart common stock fund.

Contributions for the K mart common stock fund may be remitted to the Trustee in cash or in the form of company common stock. Contributions remitted to the Trustee in cash may be used to acquire K mart common stock pursuant to market purchases or directly from the company by subscription or purchase.

As of September 1, 1983, 2,000,000 shares of K mart common stock were made available for issuance or sale to the Trustee, and as of January 30, 1985, 1,223,391 shares remained available. The company's expense related to the Savings Plan was $29.7 million for 1984, $25.5 million for 1983 and $13.2 million for a partial year in 1982.

Effective October 1, 1983, the company added a Payroll-Based Stock Ownership Plan (PAYSOP). Under the PAYSOP provisions, the company makes an additional annual contribution for all eligible employees to be invested in the K mart common stock fund, equal to ½% of each participant's compensation paid in fiscal 1984 and 1983. The company receives a direct income tax credit for the full amount of the PAYSOP contribution.

(P) Stock Option Plans

Under the company's 1973 Stock Option Plan (the 1973 Plan), as most recently amended in 1982, options to acquire up to 4,000,000 shares of common stock may be granted to officers and key employees at no less than 100% of the fair market value on the date of grant.

Options under the 1973 Plan may have a maximum term of ten years and are exercisable two years after the date of grant, except that the two-year limitation does not apply if employment terminates due to total and permanent disability or death. Payment upon exercise of an option may be made in cash, already-owned shares or a combination of both. Such shares will be valued at their fair market value as of the date of exercise.

The 1973 Plan provides for stock appreciation rights (SARs) in tandem with nonqualified stock options for officers and eligible directors who are limited under the Securities Exchange Act of 1934 in dealing with shares of the company's stock. Such an optionee may request that the Compensation and Incentives Committee permit the optionee to surrender all or part of an exercisable option in return for stock, cash or a combination of both equal to any appreciation in the value of the surrendered shares over the option price. Compensation expense of $4.0 million in 1984, $2.2 million in 1983 and $.8 million in 1982 was recorded for the excess of the market price of the option over the grant price.

Under the terms of the 1981 Incentive Stock Option Plan (the 1981 Plan), options to acquire up to 5,000,000 shares of common stock may be granted to officers and other key employees of the company at no less than 100% of the fair market value on the date of grant. Options under the 1981 Plan are intended to be incentive stock options (ISOs) pursuant to Section 422A of the Internal Revenue Code. Such options may have a maximum term of ten years and are exercisable two years after the date of grant, except that an ISO may not be exercised by an optionee who has a prior ISO outstanding. Payment upon exercise of an option may be made in cash, already-owned shares or a combination of both. Such shares will be valued at their fair market value as of the date of exercise. SARs do not apply to ISOs under the 1981 Plan.

Pertinent information covering the plans follows:

	1984		1983	
	Number of Shares	Option Price Per Share	Number of Shares	Option Price Per Share
Outstanding at beginning of year	3,159,390	$19.31-$35.75	2,854,400	$19.31-$37.63
Granted	1,599,500	29.69- 34.63	1,235,300	32.81- 35.75
Exercised	(281,967)	19.31- 34.94	(472,925)	19.31- 34.94
Cancelled	(152,166)	19.31- 34.94	(457,385)	19.31- 37.63
Outstanding at end of year	4,324,757	19.31- 35.75	3,159,390	19.31- 35.75
Exercisable at end of year	1,556,957	$19.31-$34.94	1,948,490	$19.31-$34.94
Available for grant at end of year	3,904,823		5,353,070	

(Q) Contingent Obligations

On January 29, 1982, Astra, S.A. (Astra), the company's Mexican retail affiliate, made a public offering of long-term debt in the principal amount of $100.0 million to finance the acquisition of land and the construction and fixturing of new Astra discount department and food stores in Mexico. The 16¾% notes due 1992 are unconditionally guaranteed by K mart Corporation. The company has additionally guaranteed a bank loan of $12.0 million.

The company and G. J. Coles & Coy. Limited (Coles) have guaranteed indebtedness related to certain properties in Australia on a joint and several basis. Coles subsequently indemnified K mart Corporation from any liability incurred pursuant to its guarantees. As of January 30, 1985, the amount guaranteed was $30.0 million.

(R) Quarterly Financial Information (Unaudited)

Each of the quarters includes 13 weeks, except for the fourth quarter of 1984, which includes 14 weeks.

(Millions, except per-share data)

		Quarter		
1984	**First**	**Second**	**Third**	**Fourth**
Gross revenue	$4,223.5	$5,114.3	$5,052.1	$6,972.3
Cost of merchandise sold	2,972.3	3,595.6	3,592.4	5,099.5
Net income	58.0	144.4	92.4	204.3
Earnings per common and common equivalent share	.45	1.11	.71	1.57
Pro forma earnings per common and common equivalent share*	.35	1.02	.67	1.58

		Quarter		
1983	**First**	**Second**	**Third**	**Fourth**
Gross revenue	$3,977.8	$4,736.6	$4,385.9	$5,740.7
Cost of merchandise sold	2,851.8	3,391.9	3,120.8	4,082.9
Net income	44.6	117.7	81.4	248.6
Earnings per common and common equivalent share	.35	.91	.63	1.91

*Pro forma earnings per share includes the acquisitions of Waldenbooks, Builders Square and Pay Less as if they had been effective at the beginning of fiscal 1984. [See Notes (C) and (D).]

Cost of merchandise sold was calculated during each interim period utilizing estimated gross profit rates, including an estimate of inflation in the prices of merchandise purchased during the year. If the results of the physical inventory and the annual rate of inflation determined by using the Bureau of Labor Statistics Department Store Index had been known on a quarterly basis, income before estimated income taxes would have been increased (decreased) as shown:

(Millions)

Quarter	1984	1983
First	$10.6	$ 2.9
Second	8.3	2.4
Third	(1.1)	2.4
Fourth	(17.8)	(7.7)

Impact of Inflation (Unaudited)

Under generally accepted accounting principles, the financial statements of K mart Corporation have been prepared on a historical cost basis. Under Financial Accounting Standards No. 33 (FAS 33), "Financial Reporting and Changing Prices" as amended by FAS 70, adjustments have been made for inflation under the current cost method, which attempts to provide reasonable approximations of changes in specific prices of goods and services. Under the guidelines of FAS 33, only cost of merchandise sold and depreciation and amortization expense are required to be adjusted, since these items are thought to be most affected by inflation.

K mart Corporation, like most nonfood retailers, uses the last-in, first-out (LIFO) method of inventory valuation in its historical financial statements. Thus, cost of merchandise sold valued on the LIFO method approximated current cost. For purposes of FAS 33 disclosure, LIFO cost of merchandise sold was estimated for the small portion of inventory not valued under the LIFO method.

Depreciation and amortization expense for owned and leased properties in 1984 was $423.1 million on a current cost basis, compared with $302.9 million in the historical financial statements. Current cost depreciation is calculated using a combination of average costs and building indexes for owned and leased assets. As a result of the company's experience with the application of FAS 33, the methodology for computing current cost amortization of leased properties was changed in 1984 and prior years have been restated for conformity.

In accordance with FAS 33, income tax expense remains the same for current cost accounting as that reported in the historical financial statements. This is because present tax laws do not allow deductions for additional cost of merchandise sold and depreciation expense resulting from the effects of inflation. As a result, the effective tax rate for 1984 rises from 39.9% on a historical cost basis to 47.1% on a current cost basis.

A "purchasing power gain" is created where monetary liabilities (such as capital lease obligations and long-term debt) exceed monetary assets (cash, receivables, etc.). This net monetary liability position results in a gain in purchasing power since the obligation will presumably be settled in dollars of lower value. Such a gain does not represent earnings or funds available for dividends.

The current cost method involves the use of assumptions, approximations and estimates. Thus, this method should be viewed in this context and not as a precise indicator of the effects of inflation on K mart Corporation.

Statements of Income Adjusted for Changing Prices

(Millions)	As Reported in the Primary Financial Statements	Adjusted for Changes in Specific Prices (Current Cost)
	Fiscal Year Ended January 30, 1985	
Sales and other income	$21,362.2	$21,362.2
Cost of merchandise sold	15,125.3	15,130.6
Depreciation and amortization	302.9	423.1
Other costs and expenses	5,114.0	5,114.0
Income before income taxes	820.0	694.5
Income taxes	327.1	327.1
Net income (includes $6.2 equity income of insurance operations)	$ 499.1	$ 373.6
Effective tax rate	39.9%	47.1%
Unrealized gain from decline in purchasing power of net amounts owed		$ 160.3
Increase in general price level (constant dollar)		$ 317.5
Increase in specific prices (current cost) of merchandise inventories, property owned and leased		54.1
Excess of increase in general price level over increase in specific prices		$ 263.4

Five-Year Comparison of Selected Supplementary Financial Data Adjusted for Effects of Changing Prices
(Millions, except per-share amounts, of average fiscal 1984 dollars)

	1984	1983	1982	1981	1980
Net sales and other operating revenue (in constant dollars)	$21,362.2	$19,633.9	$18,274.7	$19,028.3	$18,011.1
Current Cost:					
Net income	$ 373.6	$ 368.2	$ 152.9	$ 101.7	$ 213.6
Earnings per share	$ 2.89	$ 2.81	$ 1.18	$ .79	$ 1.66
Net assets	$ 5,207.3	$ 5,181.3	$ 4,818.5	$ 4,826.3	$ 4,977.5
Excess of increase (decrease) in general price level over increase in specific prices	$ 263.4	$ (136.2)	$ 55.1	$ (228.9)	$ 272.9
Gain from decline in purchasing power of net amounts owed	$ 160.3	$ 171.8	$ 160.6	$ 341.2	$ 452.6
Other data (in constant dollars):					
Cash dividends declared per share	$ 1.24	$ 1.13	$ 1.07	$ 1.09	$ 1.15
Market price per share at year end	$ 39	$ 32	$ 28	$ 17	$ 21
Average Consumer Price Index	312.0	299.4	290.0	274.2	249.1

Amounts presented in the above table were converted to average fiscal 1984 dollars as measured by the CPI-U.

At January 30, 1985, current cost of merchandise inventories was $5,094.8, current cost of property owned (net of accumulated depreciation) was $2,129.4 and current cost of leased property under capital leases (net of accumulated amortization) was $2,606.5.

Holiday Inns, Inc. 1984 Annual Report

**Summary of Selected Financial
and Stock Data**

	1984	1983	1982	1981	1980	1979
Operating Results (millions)						
Continuing Operations						
Revenues	1,759.8	1,585.1	1,425.3	1,351.8	1,156.6	834.6
Operating Income	336.5	291.6	234.8	244.6	190.3	152.7
Tax Rate	43.0%	45.0%	39.0%	36.4%	43.8%	46.3%
Income	131.0	124.4	97.2	98.7	69.9	61.7
Discontinued Operations—Income (Loss)	—	—	(21.2)	38.7	38.4	(5.8)
Net Income	131.0	124.4	76.0	137.4	108.3	55.9
Cash Flow from Continuing Operations	372.6	317.5	264.6	233.8	182.7	146.3
Common Stock Data						
Income per Share—Continuing	3.59	3.28	2.50	2.68	1.94	1.94
Income (Loss) per Share—Discontinued	—	—	(.56)	.98	.98	(.18)
Income per Share	3.59	3.28	1.94	3.66	2.92	1.76
Cash Dividends Declared per Share	.90	.84	.80	.74	.70	.66
Book Value per Share	28.99	27.35	24.94	24.73	21.51	18.93
Price Range of Common Stock	51¾-35¼	59-34¼	38¾-23¾	33¼-21⅛	32½-13¾	22⅞-15¼
Average Number of Common and Common Equivalent Shares Outstanding (thousands)	36,487	37,968	38,216	39,449	39,278	31,704
Financial Position (millions)						
Total Assets	2,348.0	1,936.5	1,708.0	1,672.7	1,509.5	1,089.8
Long-Term Debt	789.6	482.7	436.4	581.5	501.6	244.2
Shareholders' Equity	1,024.5	1,039.6	943.0	772.4	708.0	624.5
Depreciation of Property and Equipment	110.8	94.3	85.0	78.5	66.3	48.2
Capital Expenditures	419.7	343.9	267.4	191.2	490.4	209.6
Current Ratio	.8	.7	.9	.9	.8	1.4
Financial Ratios						
Return on Sales—Continuing	7.4%	7.8%	6.8%	7.3%	6.0%	7.4%
Return on Average Invested Capital	9.5%	9.1%	8.7%**	12.0%	10.6%	8.7%*
Return on Average Equity	12.8%	12.5%	11.3%**	18.5%	16.1%	12.1%*
Statistical Summary as of Year End						
Average Occupancy for Year (Company-Owned Holiday Inn Hotels)	70.6%	70.2%	69.2%	69.2%	71.5%	73.8%
Average Room Rate for Year (Company-Owned Holiday Inn Hotels)	49.10	44.40	41.78	40.79	36.80	32.65
Number of Holiday Inn Hotels						
Company-Owned or -Managed	211	218	230	229	240	246
Licensed	1,485	1,489	1,514	1,522	1,515	1,495
Total System	1,696	1,707	1,744	1,751	1,755	1,741
Number of Holiday Inn Hotel Rooms						
Company-Owned or -Managed	54,570	55,124	56,576	55,285	56,141	55,821
Licensed	259,462	255,213	255,726	252,828	247,437	240,430
Total System	314,032	310,337	312,302	308,113	303,578	296,251
Square Feet of Casino Space***	282,000	213,000	201,000	184,000	179,000	15,000
Number of Table Games***	612	453	483	463	445	45
Number of Slot Machines***	8,624	6,816	6,313	5,857	5,596	467
Number of Perkins Restaurants						
Company-Owned	96	94	94	101	106	94
Licensed	216	215	217	242	269	270
Total System	312	309	311	343	375	364

*Excludes the $15.1 million loss on disposition of the bus operations. Inclusion of the loss results in a return on average invested capital of 7.1% and a return on average equity of 9.5%.
**Excludes the $25.9 million loss on disposition of the steamship operations. Inclusion of the loss results in a return on average invested capital of 7.0% and a return on average equity of 8.4%.
***Includes company-owned and -managed casinos.

1978	1977	1976	1975	1974	5-Year Compound Growth Rate	10-Year Compound Growth Rate
					1979 Base	1974 Base
780.8	711.3	655.3	626.7	628.1	16.1 %	10.9 %
130.4	96.9	72.2	61.7	63.2	17.1 %	18.2 %
45.3%	46.3%	43.8%	48.8%	62.5%	—	—
50.7	32.0	21.2	17.0	5.3	16.3 %	37.8 %
12.1	18.3	17.6	24.5	21.6	—	—
62.8	50.3	38.8	41.5	26.9	18.6 %	17.2 %
—	—	—	—	—	20.6 %	—
1.64	1.04	.69	.55	.17	13.1 %	35.7 %
.40	.60	.58	.80	.70	—	—
2.04	1.64	1.27	1.35	.87	15.3 %	15.2 %
.56	.465	.40	.35	.325	6.4 %	10.7 %
17.81	16.37	15.22	14.37	13.38	8.9 %	8.0 %
32¾-14⅛	16⅛-11⅛	20-10⅝	16½-5⅛	18⅜-4¼	—	—
30,854	30,762	30,657	30,606	30,802	2.9 %	1.7 %
1,003.0	894.0	830.9	836.9	851.6	16.6 %	10.7 %
228.5	223.8	230.0	269.1	308.5	26.5 %	9.9 %
550.1	502.5	467.4	440.2	410.3	10.4 %	9.6 %
43.5	42.7	40.6	39.6	43.1	18.1 %	9.9 %
99.6	77.0	57.0	32.4	65.3	14.9 %	20.4 %
1.4	1.1	1.2	1.5	1.4	—	—
6.5%	4.5%	3.2%	2.7%	.9%	—	—
8.5%	7.8%	6.4%	6.8%	5.2%	—	—
11.9%	10.9%	8.6%	9.8%	6.7%	—	—
74.3%	71.2%	68.4%	65.4%	68.3%	—	—
27.81	24.56	22.17	20.86	18.38	8.5 %	10.3 %
270	276	289	305	309	(3.0)%	(3.7)%
1,448	1,424	1,424	1,409	1,379	(.1)%	.7 %
1,718	1,700	1,713	1,714	1,688	(.5)%	—
58,495	58,536	58,332	59,384	59,898	(.5)%	(.9)%
228,034	220,421	219,732	215,585	207,134	1.5 %	2.3 %
286,529	278,957	278,064	274,969	267,032	1.2 %	1.6 %
—	—	—	—	—	79.8 %	—
—	—	—	—	—	68.5 %	—
—	—	—	—	—	79.2 %	—
—	—	—	—	—	.4 %	—
—	—	—	—	—	(4.4)%	—
—	—	—	—	—	(3.0)%	—

Stock Data

Stock Listings (Ticker Symbol-HIA)

Holiday Inns, Inc., common stock and Special Stock-Series A are listed on the New York Stock Exchange. The common stock also is listed on the Midwest, Philadelphia and Pacific regional stock exchanges.

Market Prices

	1984 High	1984 Low	1983 High	1983 Low
Common Stock				
1st Quarter	51¾	40½	41⅝	34¼
2nd Quarter	45½	38¼	59	38½
3rd Quarter	45½	37¼	57⅝	48⅛
4th Quarter	43⅛	35¼	55¾	45¾
Special Stock-Series A				
1st Quarter	65	63¼	61	52⅞
2nd Quarter	65	60	84	60¼
3rd Quarter	60	55½	81½	77
4th Quarter	64½	64½	80	73⅜

Source: As reported in *The Wall Street Journal.*

Dividends Paid Per Share

	Common Stock 1984	Common Stock 1983	Special Stock-Series A* 1984	Special Stock-Series A* 1983
1st Quarter	$.21	$.20	$ —	$ —
2nd Quarter	.225	.21	.85	.85
3rd Quarter	.225	.21	—	—
4th Quarter	.225	.21	.85	.85
	$.885	$.83	$1.70	$1.70
Shareholders of Record	24,620	26,008	1,444	1,546

*Dividends on Special Stock-Series A are paid semi-annually in common stock.

Balance Sheets
Holiday Inns, Inc., and Consolidated Subsidiaries

(In thousands, except share amounts)	December 28, 1984	December 30, 1983
Assets		
Current Assets		
Cash	$ 51,063	$ 44,024
Temporary Cash Investments, at cost	14,100	9,657
Receivables, including Notes Receivable of $14,526 and $13,234, less Allowance for Doubtful Accounts of $21,242 and $19,338	127,376	85,619
Supplies, at lower of average cost or market	41,310	30,062
Deferred Income Tax Benefits	1,540	18,247
Prepayments	18,217	6,044
Other Current Assets	16,097	13,770
Total Current Assets	269,703	207,423
Investments in Nonconsolidated Affiliates, at equity	136,440	111,409
Notes Receivable Due after One Year and Other Investments	110,925	55,917
Property and Equipment, at cost		
Land, Buildings, Improvements and Equipment	2,129,000	1,846,835
Accumulated Depreciation and Amortization	(455,570)	(403,354)
	1,673,430	1,443,481
Excess of Cost over Net Assets of Businesses Acquired, amortized evenly over 40 years	94,152	95,658
Deferred Charges and Other Assets	63,358	22,648
	$2,348,008	$1,936,536
Liabilities and Shareholders' Equity		
Current Liabilities		
Accounts Payable	$ 92,435	$ 89,599
Long-Term Debt Due within One Year	102,670	46,765
Accrued Expenses	155,489	155,197
Total Current Liabilities	350,594	291,561
Long-Term Debt	789,586	482,736
Deferred Credits and Other Long-Term Liabilities	52,584	36,634
Deferred Income Taxes	130,787	86,043
Commitments and Contingency—See pages 43, 44, 45 and 47		
Shareholders' Equity		
Capital Stock		
Special Stock, Authorized—5,000,000 shares		
Series A-$1.125 par value		
Convertible into 1.5 shares of common stock		
Outstanding-370,529 and 388,165 shares (Excluding 92,342 and 82,342 shares held in Treasury)	417	437
Common Stock, $1.50 par value		
Authorized—120,000,000 shares		
Outstanding-34,786,931 and 37,421,649 shares (Excluding 5,673,353 and 2,992,230 shares held in Treasury)	52,180	56,133
Capital Surplus	271,004	287,012
Retained Earnings	710,909	703,948
Cumulative Foreign Currency Translation Adjustments	(8,645)	(6,298)
Restricted Stock	(1,408)	(1,670)
Total Shareholders' Equity	1,024,457	1,039,562
	$2,348,008	$1,936,536

Subsequent to December 28, 1984, the company purchased 6.3 million shares of its common stock tendered pursuant to an offer dated January 14, 1985. See page 48 for further explanation and the pro forma effects of this transaction.

The Financial Comments on Pages 42 through 49 are an integral part of these balance sheets.

Statements of Income
Holiday Inns, Inc., and Consolidated Subsidiaries

	Fiscal Year Ended		
(In thousands, except per share)	December 28, 1984	December 30, 1983	December 31, 1982
Revenues			
Hotel	$1,003,730	$ 881,633	$ 840,698
Gaming	644,098	591,778	472,792
Restaurant	106,996	105,764	100,584
Other	4,994	5,905	11,224
	$1,759,818	$1,585,080	$1,425,298
Operating Income			
Hotel	$ 195,573	$ 167,845	$ 150,205
Gaming	124,442	115,746	74,595
Restaurant	10,151	5,414	5,029
Other	6,360	2,571	4,999
	336,526	291,576	234,828
Corporate Expense	(20,195)	(23,692)	(24,487)
Interest, Net of Interest Capitalized	(86,550)	(41,703)	(50,965)
Income from Continuing Operations before Income Taxes	229,781	226,181	159,376
Provision for Income Taxes	98,806	101,782	62,157
Income from Continuing Operations	130,975	124,399	97,219
Discontinued Operations			
Income from Operations, Net of Income Taxes	—	—	4,671
Loss on Disposition, plus Income Taxes Payable of $5,505	—	—	(25,910)
Net Income	$ 130,975	$ 124,399	$ 75,980
Income (Loss) per Common and Common Equivalent Share			
Continuing Operations	$ 3.59	$ 3.28	$ 2.50
Discontinued Operations	—	—	(.56)
	$ 3.59	$ 3.28	$ 1.94
Average Common and Common Equivalent Shares Outstanding	36,487	37,968	38,216

Subsequent to December 28, 1984, the company purchased 6.3 million shares of its common stock tendered pursuant to an offer dated January 14, 1985. See page 48 for further explanation and the pro forma effects of this transaction.

The Financial Comments on Pages 42 through 49 are an integral part of these statements.

Statements of Changes in Financial Position
Holiday Inns, Inc., and Consolidated Subsidiaries

(In thousands)	December 28, 1984	December 30, 1983	December 31, 1982
Cash and Temporary Cash Investments — Beginning of Year	$ 53,681	$ 82,489	$ 59,836
Sources of Funds			
Continuing Operations			
Income	130,975	124,399	97,219
Depreciation and Amortization	121,646	104,312	97,618
Deferred Income Taxes and Other	62,794	21,141	16,058
Proceeds from Property Dispositions, excluding net gains of $33,917,			
$6,518 and $2,582 included in income above	105,895	48,904	28,630
Net Working Capital Changes from Operations	(48,680)	18,717	25,062
Funds from Continuing Operations	372,630	317,473	264,587
Net Additions to Debt	273,266	22,541	—
Common Stock Issued for Conversion of Debentures	216	2,505	143,042
Funds from Discontinued Operations	—	—	74,114
Other Sources, net	13,202	4,545	(2,036)
Total Sources	659,314	347,064	479,707
Applications of Funds			
Capital Expenditures			
Acquisitions, net of funds acquired	134,155	69,471	—
Property and Equipment Additions	268,729	268,948	209,585
Investments in Nonconsolidated Affiliates	16,770	5,468	57,828
Total Capital Expenditures	419,654	343,887	267,413
Net Retirements of Debt	—	—	144,827
Purchases of Treasury Stock	115,868	850	16,876
Increase in Notes Receivable Due after One Year and Other Investments	80,169	205	(150)
Cash Dividends Paid	32,141	30,930	28,088
Total Applications	647,832	375,872	457,054
Cash and Temporary Cash Investments — End of Year	$ 65,163	$ 53,681	$ 82,489
Working Capital Changes from Operations			
Trade Receivables, net of allowance	$ (14,627)	$ (11,899)	$ 18,774
Supplies and Other Assets	(22,280)	(6,706)	(6,271)
Trade Accounts Payable	(3,737)	5,885	11,492
Accrued Expenses	(8,036)	31,437	1,067
Net Working Capital Changes from Operations	$ (48,680)	$ 18,717	$ 25,062

Fiscal Year Ended

The Financial Comments on Pages 42 through 49 are an integral part of these statements.

Statements of Shareholders' Equity
Holiday Inns, Inc., and Consolidated Subsidiaries

(In thousands, except per share)	Shares Outstanding Special— Series A	Common	Capital Stock Special— Series A	Common	Capital Surplus	Retained Earnings	Restricted Stock	Cumulative Foreign Currency Translation Adjustment
Balance-January 1, 1982	504	30,470	$567	$45,705	$149,098	$578,970	$(1,963)	
Net Income						75,980		
Cash Dividends Declared, $.80 per Common Share						(29,886)		
Treasury Stock Acquired		(655)		(982)	(4,021)	(11,873)		
Conversion of Debentures to Common		7,148		10,723	132,319			
Special Stock-Series A Dividends and Conversions to Common	(85)	158	(95)	236	655	(795)		
Shares Issued or Returned under Incentive Compensation Plans		61		92	1,666	(13)	383	
Cumulative Effect of Change in Method of Accounting for Foreign Currency Translation								$(1,085)
Current Year Foreign Currency Translation Adjustment (net of $2,300 of Income Taxes)								(2,719)
Balance-December 31, 1982	419	37,182	472	55,774	279,717	612,383	(1,580)	(3,804)
Net Income						124,399		
Cash Dividends Declared, $.84 per Common Share						(31,354)		
Treasury Stock Acquired	(10)		(11)	(1)	(76)	(762)		
Conversion of Debentures to Common		71		107	2,398			
Special Stock-Series A Dividends and Conversions to Common	(21)	48	(24)	72	636	(684)		
Shares Issued or Returned under Incentive Compensation Plans		121		181	4,337	(34)	(90)	
Foreign Currency Translation Adjustment (net of $2,125 of Income Taxes)								(2,494)
Balance-December 30, 1983	388	37,422	437	56,133	287,012	703,948	(1,670)	(6,298)
Net Income						130,975		
Cash Dividends Declared, $.90 per Common Share						(32,114)		
Treasury Stock Acquired	(10)	(2,764)	(11)	(4,146)	(20,482)	(91,229)		
Conversion of Debentures to Common		6		9	207			
Special Stock-Series A Dividends and Conversions to Common	(7)	26	(9)	39	621	(659)		
Shares Issued or Returned under Incentive Compensation Plans		97		145	3,646	(12)	262	
Foreign Currency Translation Adjustment (net of $1,999 of Income Taxes)								(2,347)
Balance—December 28, 1984	371	34,787	$417	$52,180	$271,004	$710,909	$ (1,408)	$ (8,645)

Subsequent to December 28, 1984, the company purchased 6.3 million shares of its common stock tendered pursuant to an offer dated January 14, 1985. See page 48 for further explanation and the pro forma effects of this transaction.

The Financial Comments on Pages 42 through 49 are an integral part of these statements.

Financial Comments

Consolidation

The consolidated financial statements include the accounts of the company and its majority-owned subsidiaries. Investments in less than majority-owned companies in which Holiday Inns, Inc., has a 20 percent or more voting interest or exercises significant control are recorded on an equity basis. The company reflects its share of income before interest expense of these nonconsolidated affiliates as revenues and operating income in the consolidated statements of income. The company's proportionate share of the interest expense of such nonconsolidated affiliates is included in interest expense. (See page 47 for combined summarized financial information regarding the company's nonconsolidated affiliates.)

On March 30, 1984, the company acquired the Granada Royale all-suite hotel system for approx-imately $106 million in cash and notes, plus the assumption of $63.6 million of certain liabilities. In connection with this acquisition, which was accounted for under the purchase method of accounting, the company obtained ownership interests ranging from 29 percent to 100 percent in 11 Granada Royale hotels as well as management and franchise contracts and commitments of the Granada Royale System. The consolidated financial statements include the accounts of Granada since the date of acquisition.

On January 4, 1983, the company acquired the remaining 60 percent interest in River Boat Casino, Inc., owner of the Holiday Casino in Las Vegas. The consolidated financial statements include the accounts of River Boat since the date of the acquisition.

Fiscal Year

The company's fiscal year ends on the Friday nearest to December 31.

Income Per Share

Income per share is computed based on the weighted average number of shares outstanding during each quarter, adjusted for common stock equivalents. The principal common stock equivalent is the Special Stock-Series A.

Franchisee Receivables

The company administers certain marketing funds for the benefit of the Holiday Inn franchise system. In this capacity, the company in 1984 advanced approximately $83 million to one of these funds to pay costs related to the Priority Club frequent traveler program. This amount is expected to be reimbursed to the company through assessments from Holiday Inn franchisees over the next 3 to 4 years. At December 28, 1984, the accompanying consolidated balance sheets reflected approximately $25.5 million as current receivables and $57.5 million as notes receivable due after one year related to these expected reimbursements.

Treasury Stock

Shares of the company's common and special Series A stock which have been reacquired and are being held in treasury have been reflected in the accompanying consolidated balance sheets and statements of shareholders' equity as if they had been formally retired. Certain amounts in prior period financial statements were reclassified to conform with this presentation.

Property and Equipment

(In thousands)	1984	1983
Owned Property		
Land and Land Rights	$ 239,328	$ 237,353
Buildings, Improvements and Other	1,228,446	1,011,502
Furniture, Fixtures and Equipment	609,150	545,743
	2,076,924	1,794,598
Accumulated Depreciation and Amortization	(434,383)	(382,724)
	1,642,541	1,411,874
Property under Capital Leases		
Land	—	1,852
Buildings, Improvements and Other	42,302	45,338
Furniture, Fixtures and Equipment	9,774	5,047
	52,076	52,237
Accumulated Amortization	(21,187)	(20,630)
	30,889	31,607
	$1,673,430	$1,443,481

Land held for future development or disposition is included in the land account and amounted to $54,842,000 and $53,132,000 in 1984 and 1983, respectively.

A portion of property and equipment is pledged as security for certain long-term debt.

Depreciation and amortization are calculated on the straight-line method. Lease amortization is included in depreciation expense.

Interest capitalized during construction in 1984, 1983 and 1982 was $15,424,000, $22,180,000 and $8,401,000, respectively.

Foreign Currency Translation

Financial data of operations outside the U.S., except for operations in highly inflationary economies, are translated into U.S. dollars at the current exchange rate with resulting gains or losses reflected in shareholders' equity. Translation gains and losses applicable to highly inflationary economies and transaction gains and losses are included in net income; these amounts are not material.

Accrued Expenses

(In thousands)	1984	1983
Taxes, including Income Taxes	$ 19,625	$ 25,180
Payroll and Other Compensation	35,715	39,683
Insurance Claims	17,792	16,861
Deposits and Customer Funds	14,312	14,097
Interest	18,558	11,594
Other Accruals	49,487	47,782
	$155,489	$155,197

Long-Term Debt

(In thousands, except per share)	1984	1983
Mortgages, 5⅝%-13¾%, Maturities to 2013	$204,738	$155,558
Notes Payable-Unsecured		
14⅛%, Maturity 1992	74,770	74,740
12%, Maturities 1985 to 1988	38,657	45,100
8⅝%, Maturity 1985	37,500	40,000
9%, Maturities to 2005	70,575	—
13¼%, Maturities to 1999	99,258	—
7%-15%, Maturities to 2001	26,192	19,356
Notes Payable-Secured		
5%-11¼%, Maturities to 2008	2,921	4,298
Subordinated Debentures		
8%, Convertible into Common Stock at $35 per share, Sinking Fund Payments to 1985	2,109	2,322
Revolving Credit and Term Loan Agreement-Unsecured		
Prime-related, 9%-9¾% at December 28, 1984, Maturities to Four Years after Demand	174,000	74,000
Commercial Paper, 8⅖%-11⅕% at December 28, 1984	123,900	70,100
Capital Lease Obligations, 6½%-17⅘%, Maturities to 2005	37,636	44,027
	892,256	529,501
Long-Term Debt Due within One Year	(102,670)	(46,765)
	$789,586	$482,736

As of December 28, 1984, annual principal requirements for the four years subsequent to 1985 were: 1986, $108,216,000; 1987, $107,273,000; 1988, $121,139,000; and 1989, $56,412,000. In January 1985, the company repaid the 8⅝% unsecured notes payable with proceeds drawn under its unsecured revolving credit and term loan agreement.

At December 28, 1984, the company had $102 million of unused, prime-related, intermediate-term revolving credit facilities and $28 million in unused short-term credit facilities. The short-term credit facilities generally are available to the company at a negotiated rate not to exceed the prime interest rate, with extensions provided on an annual basis. The revolving credit facilities require annual commitment fees of .375 percent of the available credit. Compensating balances required by credit facilities are not material.

The company's various loan and credit agreements require certain defined current ratio levels and restrict both the amount of retained earnings available for dividends and the borrowing capacity of the company and its subsidiaries. Under the most restrictive of these agreements, at December 28, 1984, $358,000,000 was available for dividends.

Leases

The company has entered into leases for both real estate and equipment. In addition to a specified minimum rental, many leases provide for contingent rentals based on percentages of revenue. The average remaining term for these leases, which generally contain renewal options, extends approximately 11 years. No material restrictions or guarantees exist in the company's lease obligations.

Leases which transfer substantially all of the benefits and risks incident to the ownership of property have been capitalized. The assets are amortized over a period not in excess of the lease term.

Rental expense included in continuing operations was as follows:

(In thousands)	1984	1983	1982
Operating			
Noncancelable			
Minimum	$17,916	$17,236	$16,843
Contingent	25,864	23,111	21,959
Sublease	(249)	(463)	(616)
Other	14,450	10,808	10,755
Capital Contingent	1,735	1,349	1,298
	$59,716	$52,041	$50,239

Leases (Continued)

The future minimum rental commitments as of December 28, 1984, were as follows:

(In thousands)	Capital Leases	Non-cancelable Operating Leases
1985	$ 7,080	$ 20,064
1986	6,816	16,052
1987	6,751	13,911
1988	6,387	11,701
1989	6,204	9,876
After 1989	37,954	148,162
Total Minimum Lease Payments	71,192	$219,766
Amounts Representing Interest	(33,556)	
Total Obligations under Capital Leases	37,636	
Obligations under Capital Leases Due within One Year	(3,347)	
Long-Term Obligations under Capital Leases	$34,289	

Minimum payments have not been reduced by noncancelable sublease rentals of $2,816,000 for capital leases and $5,777,000 for operating leases. Minimum payments exclude contingent rentals which may be paid under certain leases based on a percentage of revenues in excess of specified amounts.

Income Taxes

The provision for income taxes for continuing operations was comprised of the following:

(In thousands)	1984	1983	1982
Current			
Federal	$29,111	$ 68,240	$38,841
State and Foreign	7,169	13,431	7,322
Deferred, resulting from:			
Marketing Costs	41,640	(3,415)	2,822
Accelerated Depreciation	18,648	12,357	9,126
Capitalized Interest, Taxes and Rent	5,878	11,083	4,224
Disposition of Properties	(5,306)	798	(251)
Other Timing Differences	1,666	(712)	73
	$98,806	$101,782	$62,157

Deferred taxes resulting from marketing costs in 1984 represent the effect of reporting as expenses for income tax purposes amounts which the company advanced to fund certain Holiday Inn franchise system marketing programs, principally the Priority Club frequent traveler program.

The difference between the statutory Federal income tax rate and the effective tax rate applicable to continuing operations was as follows:

(Percent of pre-tax income)	1984	1983	1982
Statutory Tax Rate	46.0	46.0	46.0
Increases (Decreases) in Tax Resulting from:			
Investment Tax Credit Available	(5.0)	(3.6)	(5.8)
State and Foreign Taxes, net of Federal Tax Benefit	1.9	3.4	2.5
Capital Gains Benefit	(2.9)	(.6)	(1.1)
Tax Basis in Excess of Financial Basis for Donation of Antique Autos	—	—	(2.2)
Other	3.0	(.2)	(.4)
Effective Tax Rate	43.0	45.0	39.0

Discontinued Operations

On December 22, 1982, the company sold Delta Steamship Lines, Inc., its wholly-owned steamship subsidiary, for $96 million in cash.

The following summarizes the 1982 results of steamship operations through December 22, 1982:

(In thousands)	
Revenues	$330,051
Costs and Expenses	(323,618)
Income Taxes	(1,762)
Income	$ 4,671

Pension Plans

Certain of the company's employees are covered under various pension plans. Pension expense includes normal cost and amortization of prior service cost/surplus over a 10 year period. The plans are funded in accordance with the Employee Retirement Income Security Act of 1974. Provisions applicable to continuing operations of $1,938,000, $5,843,000 and $6,153,000 were made in 1984, 1983 and 1982, respectively.

In 1984 the company changed certain actuarial methods and assumptions related to its principal plan. The more significant of these changes included

a change in the actuarial cost method, a decrease in the period over which prior service cost/surplus is amortized from 30 years to 10 years and an increase in the actuarial investment rate of return assumption from 6% to 8%. The effect of these changes was to reduce 1984 pension expense by $4,130,000 and increase net income by $2,354,000 ($.06 per share).

A comparison of actuarial present value of accumulated plan benefits (January 1, 1984, for the principal plan) with net assets available for benefits follows:

(In thousands)	1984	1983
Actuarial Present Value of Accumulated Plan Benefits		
Vested	$12,186	$14,854
Nonvested	4,396	4,588
Net Assets Available for Benefits	37,607	30,455

Stock Options

Under the company's stock option plan, options have been granted to key management personnel to purchase the company's stock at a price equal to the market value at the date of grant. The plan also provides for the grant of stock appreciation rights exercisable for cash and/or stock in lieu of

the options. A stock appreciation right's value equals the difference between the market value of the share under option at the date of exercise and the grant price.

A summary of stock option transactions during the year follows:

	Number of Common Shares
Options Outstanding at December 30, 1983	90,495
Granted	277,938
Exercised	(31,944)
Cancelled	(7,385)
Options Outstanding at December 28, 1984	329,104

There were 57,601 options exercisable at December 28, 1984. The option exercise price range was $12.63-$29.13 for options exercised during 1984 and $12.63-$45.13 for options outstanding at December

28, 1984. There were 60,713 and 328,113 shares available for the granting of options at December 28, 1984, and December 30, 1983, respectively.

Operating Segment Information

Holiday Inns, Inc., is a hospitality company with interests in hotels, casino gaming and restaurants. The hotel segment consists of operating results of company-owned hotels, related product services and hotel management and licensing activities. Harrah's, the company's hotel/casino subsidiary, operates gaming facilities in each of the four major U.S. gaming markets. The restaurant segment consists of operating results of Perkins Restaurants, Inc.'s company-owned free-standing family restaurants and licensing operations.

Revenues and operating income by segment for the three fiscal years ended December 28, 1984, are summarized on page 39.

The following table reflects identifiable assets, capital expenditures, and depreciation and amortization of property and equipment for the operating segments. Capital expenditures include additions to property and equipment, investments in nonconsolidated affiliates and acquisitions, net of funds acquired.

(In thousands)	1984	1983	1982
Identifiable Assets			
Hotel	$1,403,106	$1,004,257	$ 836,501
Gaming	784,261	773,308	631,275
Restaurant	78,129	80,246	83,340
Other	82,512	78,725	156,891
	$2,348,008	$1,936,536	$1,708,007
Capital Expenditures			
Hotel	$ 370,557	$ 221,929	$ 173,468
Gaming	41,597	111,171	85,616
Restaurant	5,766	3,076	695
Other	1,734	7,711	7,634
	$ 419,654	$ 343,887	$ 267,413
Depreciation and Amortization			
Hotel	$ 78,768	$ 63,110	$ 56,003
Gaming	26,613	25,363	20,663
Restaurant	4,210	4,762	4,410
Other	1,225	1,066	3,957
	$ 110,816	$ 94,301	$ 85,033

Operating Segment Information (Continued)

Supplemental hotel segment operating data for the three fiscal years ended December 28, 1984, were as follows:

(In thousands)	1984	1983	1982
Revenues			
Rooms	$ 540,677	$467,575	$449,341
Food and Beverage	174,219	167,113	172,415
Product Services	95,355	70,803	56,786
Other	193,479	176,142	162,156
	1,003,730	881,633	840,698
Costs and Expenses			
Departmental Direct Costs			
Rooms	137,459	113,590	113,749
Food and Beverage	149,227	140,880	144,867
Product Services Cost of Sales	73,619	53,625	41,535
Other, including Undistributed Operating Expenses and Fixed Charges	447,852	405,693	390,342
	808,157	713,788	690,493
Operating Income	$ 195,573	$167,845	$150,205

The consolidated financial statements include the following amounts applicable to hotel segment operations outside the U.S.:

(In thousands)	1984	1983	1982
Assets	$178,487	$134,475	$141,769
Equity	129,704	112,114	112,911
Revenues	141,849	131,432	130,836
Operating Income	25,544	20,448	22,334

Operating income of hotel segment operations outside the U.S. for 1983 and 1982 included net gains (losses) from disposition of properties and investments of ($722,000) and $2,100,000, respectively.

Supplemental gaming segment operating data for the three fiscal years ended December 28, 1984 were as follows:

(In thousands)	1984	1983	1982
Revenues			
Casino	$498,203	$464,122	$366,552
Food and Beverage	125,502	116,048	98,244
Rooms	55,177	50,065	35,269
Other	29,023	19,824	24,031
Promotional Allowances	(63,807)	(58,281)	(51,304)
	644,098	591,778	472,792
Costs and Expenses			
Departmental Direct Costs			
Casino	197,622	177,708	150,790
Food and Beverage	99,433	90,045	71,249
Rooms	19,742	17,387	12,040
Other, including Undistributed Operating Expenses and Fixed Charges	202,859	190,892	164,118
	519,656	476,032	398,197
Operating Income	$124,442	$115,746	$ 74,595

Quarterly Results of Operations (Unaudited)

(In thousands, except per share)	First Quarter	Second Quarter	Third Quarter	Fourth Quarter	Fiscal Year
1984					
Revenues	$402,506	$453,912	$473,948	$429,452	$1,759,818
Net Income	$ 25,976	$ 34,748	$ 49,713	$ 20,538	$ 130,975
Income per Common and Common Equivalent Share	$ .69	$ .94	$ 1.37	$ .59	$ 3.59
1983					
Revenues	$349,268	$396,574	$446,240	$392,998	$1,585,080
Net Income	$ 22,390	$ 38,878	$ 47,692	$ 15,439	$ 124,399
Income per Common and Common Equivalent Share	$ .59	$ 1.02	$ 1.25	$ .42	$ 3.28

Nonconsolidated Affiliates

Combined summarized balance sheets and income statements of less than majority owned nonconsolidated affiliates accounted for on the equity basis as of December 28, 1984 and December 30, 1983 and for the three years ended December 28, 1984 were as follows:

(In thousands)

	1984	1983	1982
Balance Sheets			
Current Assets	$ 42,883	$ 30,377	
Property and Equipment, net	440,232	288,396	
Other Assets	31,973	10,555	
Total Assets	$515,088	$329,328	
Current Liabilities	$ 38,762	$ 27,385	
Long-Term Debt	316,417	177,391	
Other Liabilities	1,568	2,092	
Total Liabilities	356,747	206,868	
Net Assets	$158,341	$122,460	
Company's Investments in and Advances to Less Than Majority Owned Nonconsolidated Affiliates	$127,928	$104,106	
Income Statements			
Revenues			
Hotel	$ 85,600	$ 61,511	$ 77,612
Gaming	146,988	175	63,994
	$232,588	$ 61,686	$141,606
Operating Income			
Hotel	$ 11,104	$ 5,456	$ 4,264
Gaming	13,541	161	14,615
	24,645	5,617	18,879
Interest Expense	(24,873)	(7,745)	(9,098)
Income Taxes	(50)	—	(5,278)
Net Income (Loss)	$ (278)	$ (2,128)	$ 4,503
Company's Share of Operating Income (Included as Revenues and Operating Income in the Consolidated Statements of Income)	$ 10,529	$ (225)	$ 2,662

The company performs hotel management services for certain nonconsolidated affiliates; the related management fees of $4,069,000, $2,758,000 and $2,272,000 for 1984, 1983 and 1982, respectively, are included in the company's consolidated statements of income.

In 1982 the company entered into a 50/50 partnership to build and operate the Trump Plaza hotel/casino on the Atlantic City Boardwalk. This property began operations in May 1984. In connection with its partnership investment, the company has agreed to fund partnership cash shortfalls, if any, including shortfalls in debt service on a loan of up to $170 million. This commitment is effective for the first five years of operations or until the date at which 50 percent of the loan has been amortized, if later. If the loan balance outstanding at the end of that period exceeds $75 million, the company has agreed to fund 50 percent of the excess up to a maximum of $5 million.

Related Party Transactions

Effective December 31, 1983, Roy E. Winegardner retired as chairman of the board of the company and resigned as a director. Prior to becoming an officer and director of the company in 1974, Mr. Winegardner had ownership interests in corporations and partnerships (the "related entities") that (at December 30, 1983) owned 10 Holiday Inn hotels, managed 19 Holiday Inn hotels owned by the company, provided additional services to hotels owned by the company, and purchased products from and paid license fees to the company. The company also leased land from the related entities. In 1979, Mr. Winegardner placed his related entity interests in a trust to insulate him, to the extent possible, from specific information about, and decisions affecting, the related entities. In accordance with its terms, the trust agreement terminated upon Mr. Winegardner's retirement from the company.

During 1983 and 1982, payments made to the company by the related entities, primarily license fees, totaled $1,437,000 and $1,194,000, respectively. Payments made by the company to the related entities, primarily management fees, for the same periods totaled $4,194,000 and $3,957,000, respectively. The company does not believe its transactions with the related entities, taken as a whole, were material to the overall business of the company.

Subsequent Event

On January 10, 1985, a subsidiary of the company and Hotel Corporation, a privately held company based in Wichita, Kansas, formed a 50/50 joint venture which acquired the rights and license agreements of the Brock Residence Inn franchise system from the Brock Hotel Corporation. These rights and agreements were acquired for $20 million in cash and assumption of $2.1 million in existing notes payable; no other obligations or liabilities of either Brock Residence Inns or Brock Hotel Corporation were assumed in connection with this transaction. The company advanced the cash to the joint venture to make the acquisition.

Self-Tender for Company's Common Stock

On January 14, 1985, the company made a tender offer to its shareholders for the purchase of up to 8 million common shares at a price of from $46 to $49 per share. At the close of the offer on February 5, 1985, approximately 6.3 million shares were purchased by the company at $49 per share. The total cost of shares purchased pursuant to the offer, including fees and expenses, was approximately $309 million. The stock repurchase was financed from borrowings under a credit agreement with a group of major commercial banks. The total commitment under the credit agreement is $500 million, of which $400 million is restricted to the repurchase of shares.

The company presently plans to repay the borrowings under the credit agreement principally with proceeds generated from the disposition of certain of its hotel properties. Minimum annual payments under the agreement are: 1985,

$150,000,000; 1986, 1987 and 1988, $100,000,000 in each year; and 1989, $50,000,000. The agreement provides for additional mandatory repayments if certain levels of cash proceeds from disposition of hotel properties are exceeded. Borrowings bear interest at floating rates related to certain prime, certificate of deposit or Eurodollar rates.

The pro forma effects of the stock repurchase and related borrowings under the credit agreement as of and for the year ended December 28, 1984, are summarized below. Pro forma balance sheet information is presented as though the purchase and borrowings occurred on December 28, 1984, while the pro forma income statement information is presented as though these transactions occurred on the first day of fiscal year 1984. The pro forma information does not reflect proceeds anticipated to be generated from the disposition of hotel properties.

(In thousands, except per share)	As Reported	Pro Forma (Unaudited)
Balance Sheet		
Current Assets	$ 269,703	$ 269,703
Property and Equipment, net	1,673,430	1,673,430
Other Assets	404,875	404,875
Total Assets	$2,348,008	$2,348,008
Current Liabilities	$ 350,594	$ 500,594
Long-Term Debt	789,586	948,586
Other Liabilities	183,371	183,371
Shareholders' Equity	1,024,457	715,457
Total Liabilities and Shareholders' Equity	$2,348,008	$2,348,008
Income Statement		
Revenues	$1,759,818	$1,759,818
Operating Income	$ 336,526	$ 336,526
Corporate Expense	(20,195)	(20,195)
Interest, net of Interest Capitalized	(86,550)	(122,456)
Income before Income Taxes	229,781	193,875
Provision for Income Taxes	98,806	83,366
Net Income	$ 130,975	$ 110,509
Earnings Per Share	$ 3.59	$ 3.66
Average Common And Common Equivalent Shares Outstanding	36,487	30,224

Pro forma net income reflects the effect of additional interest expense on the $309 million of borrowings made to finance the stock repurchase. Interest was calculated at an average rate of 11.6% which is the average rate that would have been in effect during fiscal year 1984 under the credit agreement.

If the purchase and borrowings had occurred on the first day of fiscal year 1984, return on average equity for 1984 would have been 15.4%.

Effects of Inflation on Selected Financial Data (Unaudited)

Current accounting rules require the disclosure of certain effects of inflation on the conventional "historical dollar" financial statements. The required disclosures are intended to reflect the effects of general inflation and changes in specific prices. However, the information required to be disclosed is imprecise and should not be expected to portray either completely or accurately the effects of inflation.

The current cost method revalues property and equipment to reflect the current cost of acquiring the same assets at the related balance sheet date, then restates that current cost into average 1984 dollars for comparison. Current cost data do not reflect specific plans for the replacement of property nor consider efficiencies and other ben-

efits that may be gained by replacing existing facilities. Also, the current cost method does not purport to represent the fair market value of the company or the financial statement items considered in the calculations.

Current cost data for buildings and improvements, furniture, fixtures and equipment were calculated by utilizing published construction indices. Under the current cost method, the revalued amounts are used to calculate revised depreciation and amortization expense using the same methods applied in calculating the historical amounts. In accordance with the accounting rules, revenues and all other costs and expenses were assumed to have occurred proportionately in relation to the changing level of prices. No adjustments were made

Effects of Inflation on Selected Financial Data (Unaudited) (Continued)

for the effects of inflation on various other non-monetary items. Therefore, net assets were adjusted for the revised property and equipment amounts only. In accordance with the guidelines, provision for income taxes was unchanged from the historical statements, recognizing that there are no permitted tax deductions for the consequences of inflation.

The company's monetary liabilities (amounts owed that are fixed in terms of dollars) were substantially in excess of its monetary assets (cash and claims to cash which are fixed in terms of dollars). During periods of inflation, as the purchasing power of the dollar decreases, a net monetary liability position results in a purchasing power gain because less purchasing power will be required to satisfy these obligations.

The company's revenue, cash dividends declared per common share and market price per common share have been revalued in 1984 dollars using the Consumer Price Index to adjust for the effects of general inflation.

Five-Year Comparison of Selected Supplementary Financial Data Adjusted for Effects of Changing Prices

	1984	1983	1982	1981	1980
Revenues (In thousands)					
As Reported	$1,759,818	$1,585,080	$1,425,298	$1,351,775	$1,156,615
In 1984 Dollars	1,759,818	1,652,542	1,533,761	1,543,822	1,457,954
Income from Continuing Operations (In thousands)					
As Reported	130,975	124,399	97,219	98,706	69,892
At Current Cost in 1984 Dollars	83,507	79,171	54,970	64,709	40,882
Income per Common and Common Equivalent Share-Continuing					
As Reported	3.59	3.28	2.50	2.68	1.94
At Current Cost in 1984 Dollars	2.29	2.09	1.39	1.85	1.24
Net Assets at Year End (In thousands)					
As Reported	1,024,457	1,039,562	942,962	772,377	707,961
At Current Cost in 1984 Dollars	1,633,636	1,792,704	1,712,725	1,602,700	1,585,154
Increase in General Price Level Over (Under) Increase in Specific Prices in 1984 Dollars (In thousands)	31,820	(11,626)	6,718	16,045	21,705
Gain from Decline in Purchasing Power of Net Amounts Owed in 1984 Dollars (In thousands)	28,953	22,604	21,913	39,332	55,998
Cash Dividends Declared per Common Share					
As Reported	.90	.84	.80	.74	.70
In 1984 Dollars	.90	.88	.86	.85	.88
Market Price per Common Share					
At Year End	43.13	47.50	36.63	28.00	26.75
In 1984 Dollars	42.52	48.69	38.97	30.94	32.21
Average Consumer Price Index	311.1	298.4	289.1	272.4	246.8

Income from Continuing Operations for Fiscal Year 1984 Adjusted for Effects of Inflation

(In thousands)

Income from Operations, as Reported	$ 130,975
Adjustment for Depreciation	(47,468)
Income from Operations, adjusted for Effects of Inflation	$ 83,507
Increase in Current Cost of Net Property and Equipment During the Year from Changes in General Price Level	$ 77,337
Effect of Changes in Specific Prices	45,517
Excess of Increase in General Price Level Over Increase in Specific Prices	$ 31,820
Current Cost of Net Property and Equipment at Year End	$2,305,714

Management's Report on Financial Statements

The company is responsible for preparing the consolidated financial statements and related information appearing in this report. Management believes that the financial statements fairly present its financial position and results of operations in conformity with generally accepted accounting principles. In preparing its financial statements, the company is required to include amounts based on estimates and judgments which it believes are reasonable under the circumstances.

The company maintains accounting and other control systems designed to provide reasonable assurance that financial records are reliable for purposes of preparing financial statements and that assets are properly accounted for and safeguarded.

Compliance with these systems and controls is reviewed through a program of audits by an internal auditing staff. Limitations exist in any internal control system, recognizing that the system's cost should not exceed the benefits derived.

The board of directors pursues its responsibility for the company's financial statements through its audit committee, which is composed solely of directors who are not company officers or employees. The audit committee meets from time to time with the independent public accountants, management and the internal auditors. The independent public accountants have direct access to the audit committee, with and without the presence of management representatives.

Auditors' Report

To the Shareholders and Board of Directors of Holiday Inns, Inc.:

We have examined the balance sheets of Holiday Inns, Inc. (a Tennessee corporation), and consolidated subsidiaries as of December 28, 1984, and December 30, 1983, and the related statements of income, shareholders' equity and changes in financial position for each of the three fiscal years in the period ended December 28, 1984. Our examinations were made in accordance with generally accepted auditing standards and, accordingly, included such tests of the accounting records and such other auditing procedures as we considered necessary in the circumstances.

In our opinion, the financial statements referred to above present fairly the financial position of Holiday Inns, Inc., and consolidated subsidiaries as of December 28, 1984, and December 30, 1983, and the results of their operations and the changes in their financial position for each of the three fiscal years in the period ended December 28, 1984, in conformity with generally accepted accounting principles applied on a consistent basis.

Arthur Andersen & Co.

Memphis, Tennessee,
February 7, 1985.

Letter to Shareholders

At our July meeting, the board of directors elected Richard J. Goeglein as president and chief operating officer, effective September 1, 1984. Dick joined Holiday Inns, Inc. in 1978. He guided our entry into the gaming business in 1979 and has successfully led us to becoming the largest casino gaming company in the world in 1983. He brings excellent operating experience from within our company to this position.

We made substantial progress during the second quarter toward the implementation of our strategy to strengthen our established businesses and expand into profitable new markets with distinctive, new products.

Development activities associated with our core Holiday Inn hotel brand remain impressive. More than 60 Holiday Inn hotels will open this year, with approximately the same number of older hotels being removed from the Holiday Inn system.

Three Crowne Plaza hotels, representing the top of the Holiday Inn brand, opened in the second quarter. These hotels in Stamford, Connecticut and New Orleans, along with our first international property in Santiago, Chile, brought the total number of Crowne Plaza hotels open to 10.

Our first Embassy Suites hotel, which opened in May in Overland Park, Kansas, already has achieved high customer ratings. As the leader in the all-suite hotel business, we are committed to enhancing our position within this emerging market segment.

In establishing a major presence in the limited-service hotel market, our Hampton Inn division is well on its way to achieving its plan of having 300 hotels open or under construction within five years. More than 60 franchise applications have been received, and six hotels currently are under construction. The first Hampton Inn hotel will open in Memphis in August.

We strengthened our leadership position in the casino gaming business with the May opening of our 50 percent-owned Harrah's at Trump Plaza hotel/casino on Atlantic City's Boardwalk. It became profitable in June, and we expect excellent results from this facility. We also opened in May a 107-slip yacht marina at our Harrah's Marina hotel/casino in Atlantic City, enhancing that property's resort appeal.

Our restaurant operations also are expanding, as 12 franchise units opened during the first six months. Two company-owned Perkins restaurants will open in August.

While the expenses related to many of the above activities resulted in a decline in second quarter earnings per share to $.94 from $1.02, we are confident that our innovative marketing programs and investments in new hotels, gaming properties, and restaurants will add to the success of each of our businesses and broaden our earnings base over the long-term. Our confidence is reflected in the company's purchase of 694,000 shares of our common stock during the second quarter. As of July 27, 1984, we have purchased a total of 2.8 million shares of the 5 million share repurchase plan authorized by the Board of Directors in 1982.

Our hospitality businesses remain healthy, and our development activities will enhance our industry leadership position in the future.

[signature]

Michael D. Rose
Chairman of the Board,
President and Chief Executive Officer

July 27, 1984

Condensed Statements of Income (Unaudited)

Holiday Inns, Inc., and Consolidated Subsidiaries

(In thousands, except per share amounts)	Second Quarter Ended		First Half Ended	
	June 29, 1984	July 1, 1983	June 29, 1984	July 1, 1983
Revenues				
Hotel	$267,943	$228,292	$499,954	$430,739
Gaming	160,502	143,943	307,231	268,537
Restaurant	24,978	22,885	47,818	44,348
Other	489	1,454	1,415	2,218
	$453,912	$396,574	$856,418	$745,842
Operating Income				
Hotel	$ 57,420	$ 53,143	$ 98,996	$ 90,583
Gaming	27,757	28,885	48,748	46,745
Restaurant	3,001	1,975	4,411	1,393
Other	565	1,318	(187)	2,195
	88,743	85,321	151,968	140,916
Corporate Expense	(5,348)	(5,813)	(10,336)	(10,757)
Interest, Net of Interest Capitalized	(20,216)	(10,084)	(31,225)	(20,752)
Income from Operations before Income Taxes	63,179	69,424	110,407	109,407
Provision for Income Taxes	28,431	30,546	49,683	48,139
Net Income	$ 34,748	$ 38,878	$ 60,724	$ 61,268
Income per Common and Common Equivalent Share	$ .94	$ 1.02	$ 1.63	$ 1.61
Average Common and Common Equivalent Shares Outstanding	36,686	37,937	37,230	37,915

Note

Income per share is computed based on the weighted average number of shares outstanding during each quarter, adjusted for common stock equivalents.

Principal common stock equivalents include the Special Stock-Series A.

Condensed Statements of Changes in Financial Position (Unaudited)
Holiday Inns, Inc., and Consolidated Subsidiaries

(In thousands)	Second Quarter Ended		First Half Ended	
	June 29, 1984	July 1, 1983	June 29, 1984	July 1, 1983
Cash and Temporary Cash Investments-Beginning of Period	$ 59,539	$ 67,997	$ 53,681	$ 82,489
Sources of Funds				
Net Income	34,748	38,878	60,724	61,268
Depreciation and Amortization	38,858	29,082	75,706	56,507
Property Dispositions, excluding net gains of $8,273, $2,633, $8,243 and $2,260	14,119	8,681	28,934	16,774
Working Capital Changes from Operations	12,645	898	(16,180)	3,998
Funds from Operations	100,370	77,539	149,184	138,547
Net Additions to Debt	49,152	13,419	220,066	83,491
Total Sources	149,522	90,958	369,250	222,038
Applications of Funds				
Capital Expenditures				
Acquisitions	7,749	3,772	104,687	58,171
Property and Equipment Additions	85,058	64,539	149,818	140,781
Total Capital Expenditures	92,807	68,311	254,505	198,952
Advances to Joint Venture	5,436	17,429	6,584	27,236
Purchases of Treasury Stock	29,053	850	72,390	850
Cash Dividends Paid	8,313	7,810	16,172	15,247
Other Applications, Net	576	1,346	404	(967)
Total Applications	136,185	95,746	350,055	241,318
Cash and Temporary Cash Investments-End of Period	$ 72,876	$ 63,209	$ 72,876	$ 63,209

Condensed Balance Sheets (Unaudited)
Holiday Inns, Inc., and Consolidated Subsidiaries

(In thousands)	June 29, 1984	December 30, 1983
Assets		
Current Assets	$ 266,574	$ 207,423
Net Property and Equipment	1,622,548	1,443,481
Other Assets	336,698	285,632
Total Assets	$2,225,820	$1,936,536
Liabilities and Shareholders' Equity		
Current Liabilities	$ 354,127	$ 291,561
Long-Term Debt	718,128	482,736
Deferred Credits and Other Long-Term Liabilities	140,969	122,677
Shareholders' Equity	1,012,596	1,039,562
Total Liabilities and Shareholders' Equity	$2,225,820	$1,936,536

NINETEEN EIGHTY-FOUR
REPORT TO SHAREHOLDERS

MANAGEMENT'S DISCUSSION AND ANALYSIS

The following discussion should be read in conjunction with Chrysler's 1984 consolidated financial statements, including Note 16 regarding inflation accounting.

RESULTS OF OPERATIONS

Reflecting 1984's brisk economic expansion, the combined U.S. car and truck market grew 18 percent, to 14.5 million units, and Chrysler's unit sales in the U.S. and Canada increased to two million cars and trucks, up 36 percent over 1983. Chrysler's share of the combined U.S. car and truck market rose to 11.1 percent for 1984, compared with 9.9 percent for 1983 and 9.9 percent for 1982. The success of Chrysler's products in this growing market, led by the Plymouth Voyager and Dodge Caravan miniwagons, was unusually well-balanced across market segments, and required production at capacity levels in all U.S. and Canadian facilities. These production levels resulted in a much needed increase in dealer stocks, permitting dealers to keep pace with the expanding market.

The operating profit of $2,430 million in 1984 reflects an increase of $1,503 million over 1983 results on an increase of 524 thousand units in U.S. and Canadian sales. Operating profit in 1983 was more than $900 million above the 1982 level on an increase of 346 thousand unit sales in the U.S. and Canada.

Chrysler's 1984 earnings from continuing operations of $1,496 million were more than four times the previous record level of 1976. 1983 earnings from continuing operations were $302 million, an increase of $371 million from the loss of $69 million in 1982.

1984 net earnings of $2,380 million were more than three times the previous record of $701 million in 1983. 1982 net earnings were $170 million. 1983 results included the effect of a $224 million writedown of Chrysler's investment in Peugeot S.A., and 1982 results included the effect of a $239 million profit on the sale of Chrysler Defense, Inc.

Chrysler's breakeven point for U.S. and Canadian operations has been held under 1.2 million units for the last three years by containing increases in fixed costs to levels approximating the rate of inflation and steady improvements in unit profitability resulting from improved quality, increased sales of upscale products and productivity gains. Programs designed to improve quality, increase productivity and control cost will continue to receive the highest priority. These programs and the successful negotiation by late 1985 of a new UAW contract with competitive labor costs are essential if Chrysler is to maintain a satisfactory breakeven level and reduce its vulnerability to future economic downturns.

Selected Comparisons of Elements of Revenue and Costs

1984 vs. 1983. Chrysler's net sales of $19.6 billion in 1984 represented a 48 percent increase over 1983. This resulted from an increase in world-wide unit sales of 36 percent year-to-year, improvement in product mix and moderate price increases. Chrysler Financial Corporation's pre-tax U.S. earnings, which are included in equity in earnings of unconsolidated subsidiaries, increased $36 million over 1983. In 1983, other income included proceeds of $20 million from the sale of tax attributes ("safe harbor leases"). There were no such sales in 1984. Depreciation expense increased $88 million as a result of both major new and modernized facilities being placed in service and additional provision for obsolescence of older facilities that will be modernized or replaced. Selling and administrative expenses rose 23 percent in 1984 reflecting increased deferred compensation and aggressive new product marketing and advertising programs, as well as the effects of inflation. The year-to-year improvement of $133 million in interest (income) expense–net reflects the combined effect of lower debt levels and increased portfolio interest income resulting from both higher rates of return and higher levels of liquidity.

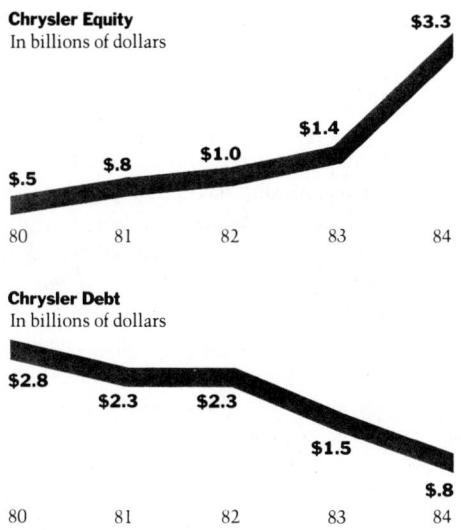

Chrysler Equity
In billions of dollars

$.5 $.8 $1.0 $1.4 $3.3

80   81   82   83   84

Chrysler Debt
In billions of dollars

$2.8 $2.3 $2.3 $1.5 $.8

80   81   82   83   84

of 46 percent because of carryforward investment tax credits of $220 million and additional investment tax credits that will be earned in 1985.

Chrysler Profit/Loss
In billions of dollars

0   $(1.7) $(.5) $.2 $.7 $2.4

80   81   82   83   84

Taxes on income in 1984 consisted of $884 million of taxes that were offset by operating loss carryforwards and $50 million of taxes on income that was not sheltered by loss carryforwards. The 1984 tax provision was reduced by $179 million, $101 million of investment tax credits and $78 million as a result of changes in the U.S. income tax law regarding the treatment of Domestic International Sales Corporations. This resulted in an effective rate for the year of 38 percent. In 1983, income tax expense reflected, for the most part, only taxes offset by loss carryforwards. Losses resulting from the writedown of the investment in Peugeot S.A. and from Mexican operations were not tax affected, resulting in an effective rate of 57 percent for 1983.

Chrysler used its remaining U.S. and Canadian loss carryforwards in 1984. Chrysler's 1985 federal income tax expense will be at a level below the statutory rate

1983 vs. 1982. Net sales for 1983 increased 32 percent to $13.3 billion from the 1982 level of $10.1 billion. Worldwide unit factory sales rose 26 percent from 1982. Most of the increase in net sales reflects the increase in unit sales. Improvement in product mix and, to a lesser extent, price increases also contributed to the increase. The year-to-year increase in equity in earnings of unconsolidated subsidiaries in 1983 resulted principally from the $63 million increase in Chrysler Financial Corporation's pre-tax U.S. earnings over 1982. The balance resulted from improved earnings of other unconsolidated subsidiaries, primarily dealership operations. Other income includes proceeds from the sale of tax attributes of $20 million in 1983, compared with $10 million in 1982. The increase in selling and administrative expenses in 1983 over 1982 resulted from increased levels of advertising and merchandising effort for Chrysler's new product offerings, as well as deferred compensation and year-to-year economic cost increases. The level of interest (income) expense-net was reduced in 1983 compared with 1982 as portfolio investment interest income remained strong and the government-guaranteed loans were repaid.

MANAGEMENT'S DISCUSSION AND ANALYSIS (continued)

LIQUIDITY

Funds provided by operations in 1984 totaled $3,271 million. This performance, which was $1,150 million better than 1983, resulted from 1984's increased sales volume and profitability. Capital expenditures for new model tooling and equipment rose $190 million from 1983 to a record $1,247 million. Cash and marketable securities increased $631 million in 1984.

In December 1984, Moody's and Standard and Poor's upgraded Chrysler's long-term debt ratings to investment grade. For the last two years, Chrysler has moved aggressively to regain access to credit and capital markets. In 1984, Chrysler retired its $250 million of $2.75 preferred stock, purchased the remaining warrants held by private lenders for $58 million, and prepaid long-term debt of approximately $350 million. In addition, Chrysler entered into bank revolving credit agreements totaling approximately $1.4 billion in the U.S. and Canada. In December 1984, Chrysler announced its plan to purchase up to 25 million shares of Chrysler common stock. As of February 21, 1985 2.9 million shares had been acquired at a cost of $81 million.

Chrysler Common Stock
Year end stock prices

$4⅞ $3⅜ $17¾ $27⅝ $32

80   81   82   83   84

Actions taken in 1983 included repayment of the $1.2 billion of government-guaranteed loans, reclassification of $1.1 billion of preferred stock held by private lenders into 29.2 million shares of common stock, and exchange of 6.2 million shares of common stock for 10.6 million warrants held by these lenders.

In addition, Chrysler paid $311 million for the 14.4 million warrants issued to the federal government in connection with the loan guarantee program. The company also paid the dividend arrearage on its $2.75 cumulative preferred stock and resumed regular quarterly preferred dividend payments.

The cumulative effect of the above actions and record capital expenditures for Chrysler's aggressive product programs has been to depress working capital which, despite the high level of profits, stood at a negative $136 million at year end 1984, compared with a negative $700 million at year end 1983. Chrysler's working capital position was significantly improved in March 1985 with the sale, in an underwritten public offering, of $350 million of 12¾% notes due 1992, and $300 million of 13% debentures due 1997.

Looking ahead, Chrysler expects to continue to generate sufficient liquidity to finance its operations and expenditure programs. In the 1985 through 1989 period, Chrysler plans to spend $10.5 billion for new product and facility modernization, of which $6.3 billion represents capital expenditures for new model tooling and facilities.

Chrysler Financial Corporation (CFC)

CFC successfully reentered the public debt market in December 1983 with a $300 million fixed-rate term debt issue. Keeping pace with Chrysler's growing sales, CFC issued $1.9 billion of new long-term debt in 1984, including $200 million of subordinated debt. At the same time, CFC reduced its reliance on bank borrowings by increasing its commercial paper outstanding to $2.9 billion at year end 1984. Chrysler supported CFC's financing efforts with capital contributions of $203 million early in 1984 and an additional $100 million in January 1985. In January and February 1985, CFC issued additional term debt of $636 million, including $100 million of subordinated debt.

CONSOLIDATED STATEMENT OF EARNINGS

Chrysler Corporation and Consolidated Subsidiaries   (In millions of dollars)

	Year Ended December 31		
	1984	1983	1982
Net sales	$ 19,572.7	$ 13,263.8	$ 10,056.5
Equity in earnings (loss) of unconsolidated subsidiaries	126.1	90.8	(5.8)
Other income	18.4	32.9	19.6
	19,717.2	13,387.5	10,070.3
Costs, other than items below	15,528.2	10,861.2	8,606.2
Depreciation of plant and equipment (Note 4)	271.6	183.3	195.9
Amortization of special tools (Note 4)	282.8	273.9	236.7
Selling and administrative expenses	987.7	804.9	669.8
Pension plans (Note 11)	267.3	254.7	271.7
Interest (income) expense–net (Note 9)	(50.7)	82.1	158.0
	17,286.9	12,460.1	10,138.3
Operating Earnings (Loss)	2,430.3	927.4	(68.0)
Writedown of investment in Peugeot S.A. (Note 3)	—	223.9	—
Earnings (Loss) from Continuing Operations			
before Taxes and Extraordinary Item	2,430.3	703.5	(68.0)
Taxes on income (Note 12)	934.2	401.6	.9
Earnings (Loss) from Continuing Operations	1,496.1	301.9	(68.9)
Gain on sale of Chrysler Defense, Inc.			
(Net of $66.9 million of taxes)	—	—	172.1
Earnings before Extraordinary Item	1,496.1	301.9	103.2
Extraordinary item–effect of utilization			
of tax loss carryforwards (Note 12)	883.9	399.0	66.9
Net Earnings	$ 2,380.0	$ 700.9	$ 170.1

		(In dollars)	
Per Share Data (Note 15):			
Primary:			
Earnings (loss) from continuing operations	$11.75	$ 2.35	$(1.28)
Earnings before extraordinary item	11.75	2.35	0.97
Net earnings	18.88	5.79	1.84
Average number of shares of common stock			
used in primary computation (in thousands)	123,841	116,039	76,700
Fully Diluted:			
Earnings (loss) from continuing operations	$11.68	$ 2.34	$(1.28)
Earnings before extraordinary item	11.68	2.34	0.97
Net earnings	18.77	5.73	1.84
Average number of shares of common stock			
used in fully diluted computation (in thousands)	124,693	117,750	77,696
Common Stock Dividends Declared	$ 0.85	$ —	$ —

See notes to financial statements.

CONSOLIDATED BALANCE SHEET

Chrysler Corporation and Consolidated Subsidiaries

(In millions of dollars)

ASSETS

	December 31	
	1984	1983
Current Assets:		
Cash and time deposits	$ 75.2	$ 111.6
Marketable securities–at lower of cost or market (Note 13)	1,624.9	957.8
Accounts receivable (less allowance for doubtful accounts: 1984–$13.8 million; 1983–$25.5 million)	332.2	291.2
Inventories (Note 2)	1,625.9	1,301.4
Prepaid pension expense (Note 11)	243.0	—
Prepaid insurance, taxes and other expenses	78.7	91.8
Total Current Assets	3,979.9	2,753.8
Investments and Other Assets:		
Investments in associated companies outside the United States (Note 3)	128.5	128.5
Investments in and advances to unconsolidated subsidiaries (Notes 3 and 13)	1,112.4	733.8
Other noncurrent assets	128.7	101.2
Total Investments and Other Assets	1,369.6	963.5
Property, Plant and Equipment: (Note 4)		
Land, buildings, machinery and equipment	5,163.8	4,469.8
Less accumulated depreciation	2,534.5	2,334.0
	2,629.3	2,135.8
Unamortized special tools	1,083.9	919.2
Net Property, Plant and Equipment	3,713.2	3,055.0
Total Assets	$9,062.7	$6,772.3

See notes to financial statements.

	(In millions of dollars)	
	December 31	
LIABILITIES AND SHAREHOLDERS' EQUITY	**1984**	1983
Current Liabilities:		
Accounts payable	$2,323.0	$1,579.1
Short-term debt	6.7	361.1
Payments due within one year on long-term debt	42.8	55.7
Employee compensation and benefits	588.4	618.8
Taxes on income	13.6	3.1
Other taxes	180.7	178.7
Interest payable	36.2	33.5
Accrued expenses	893.6	623.9
Dividends payable	30.7	—
Total Current Liabilities	4,115.7	3,453.9
Accrued Employee Benefits (Note 11)	362.3	417.6
Other Noncurrent Liabilities	497.0	431.5
Deferred Taxes on Income	21.7	—
Long-Term Debt (Note 5)	760.1	1,104.0
Commitments (Note 6)		
Preferred Stock–No par value; authorized 20,000,000 shares; 10,000,000 $2.75 cumulative shares issued of which 125,000 shares were held as treasury stock at December 31, 1983 (Redemption value of $250.0 million less unamortized issue costs and value of warrants to purchase common stock) (Notes 7 and 10)	—	222.2
Shareholders' Equity: (Note 10)		
Common stock–No par value; authorized 170,000,000 shares; issued at $1 per share stated value: (Note 8)		
123,890,674 shares	123.9	—
121,811,855 shares	—	121.8
Additional paid-in capital	2,325.3	2,276.4
Retained earnings (deficit)	921.2	(1,255.1)
Treasury stock–2,418,652 common shares, at cost	(64.5)	—
Total Shareholders' Equity	3,305.9	1,143.1
Total Liabilities and Shareholders' Equity	$9,062.7	$6,772.3

CONSOLIDATED STATEMENT OF CHANGES IN FINANCIAL POSITION

Chrysler Corporation and Consolidated Subsidiaries

(In millions of dollars)

	Year Ended December 31		
	1984	1983	1982
Funds Provided by Operations:			
Earnings (loss) from continuing operations	$ 1,496.1	$ 301.9	$(68.9)
Depreciation and amortization	554.4	457.2	432.6
Equity in (earnings) loss of unconsolidated subsidiaries	(126.1)	(90.8)	5.8
Contribution to employee stock ownership plan (Note 8)	20.3	40.6	40.6
Deferred taxes on income	21.7	—	—
Other, including writedown of investment in Peugeot S.A. in 1983	(15.8)	241.5	(19.2)
	1,950.6	950.4	390.9
Changes in working capital affecting operations:			
(Increase) decrease in inventories and other current assets	(595.4)	(212.5)	491.6
Increase (decrease) in accounts payable and accrued expenses	1,029.1	1,024.9	(30.5)
	433.7	812.4	461.1
Extraordinary item–utilization of tax loss carryforwards	883.9	399.0	66.9
Net change in noncurrent assets and liabilities	3.0	(40.8)	(47.2)
Funds Provided by Operations	3,271.2	2,121.0	871.7
Funds Provided by (Used in) Investment Activities:			
(Increase) decrease in investments and advances (Note 3)	(252.5)	243.0	(184.9)
Sale of Chrysler Defense, Inc., net of related taxes	—	—	268.1
Purchase of ABKO Properties, Inc.	—	—	(65.6)
Sale of property, plant and equipment	40.3	9.2	62.3
Expenditures for property, plant and equipment	(799.5)	(642.5)	(146.8)
Expenditures for special tools	(447.4)	(414.5)	(227.0)
Other	(.1)	(12.0)	(2.3)
Funds Used in Investment Activities	(1,459.2)	(816.8)	(296.2)
Funds Provided by (Used in) Financing Activities:			
Net (payments) borrowings on short-term debt	(354.4)	281.7	(24.4)
Proceeds from long-term borrowing	103.4	220.2	11.0
Payments on long-term borrowing	(450.3)	(1,269.4)	(69.9)
Purchase of warrants held by financial institutions (Note 8)	(58.0)	—	—
Purchase of U.S. Government held warrants, including related expenses (Note 8)	—	(313.9)	—
Proceeds from sale of common stock (exercise of public warrants)	—	63.1	—
Purchase of treasury stock (Notes 8 and 10)	(64.5)	(2.8)	—
Retirement of $2.75 preferred stock (Notes 7 and 10)	(250.0)	—	—
Other changes in common stock	13.2	6.0	.6
Funds Used in Financing Activities	(1,060.6)	(1,015.1)	82.7
Dividends:			
Preferred stock	(16.2)	(116.9)	—
Common stock	(104.5)	—	—
Funds:			
Increase during year	630.7	172.2	492.8
Cash, time deposits and marketable securities at beginning of year	1,069.4	897.2	404.4
Cash, time deposits and marketable securities at end of year	$ 1,700.1	$ 1,069.4	$ 897.2

See notes to financial statements.

NOTES TO FINANCIAL STATEMENTS

Chrysler Corporation and Consolidated Subsidiaries   Three Years Ended December 31, 1984

NOTE 1
Summary of Significant Accounting Policies

Principles of Consolidation
The financial statements of Chrysler Corporation and its consolidated subsidiaries (Chrysler) include the accounts of majority-owned and controlled subsidiaries except those engaged primarily in financing, insuring, and retail selling activities. Investments in unconsolidated subsidiaries, as well as investments in associated companies representing 20% or more of the voting stock and pursuant to which some degree of management control is exercised, are accounted for on the equity basis. Other investments are carried at cost or less.

Depreciation and Tool Amortization
Property, plant and equipment are carried at cost less accumulated depreciation. For assets placed in service beginning in 1980, depreciation is provided on a straight-line basis. For assets placed in service prior to 1980, depreciation is generally provided on an accelerated basis.

The weighted-average service lives of assets are 30 years for buildings (including improvements and building equipment), 12 years for machinery and equipment and 13 years for furniture.

The cost of special tools is amortized on a basis designed to allocate the cost to operations during the years in which the tools are used in the productive process.

Employee Benefit Plans
Accounting policies for pension plans and other benefit plans are discussed in Note 11 to the financial statements on pages 31 and 32.

Taxes on Income
Taxes on income are based upon pre-tax accounting earnings which include the effect of timing differences between pre-tax accounting earnings and taxable earnings. Investment tax credits are recognized on the flow-through method.

Product Warranty
Estimated lifetime costs of product warranty are accrued at the time of sale.

Inventories
Inventories are valued at the lower of cost or market. Effective January 1, 1984, Chrysler changed its method of accounting from First-In, First-Out (FIFO) to Last-In, First-Out (LIFO) for substantially all of its domestic productive inventories. The change to LIFO was made to more accurately match current costs with current revenues. The cost of the remaining inventories is determined substantially on a FIFO basis.

NOTE 2
Inventories

As stated in Note 1, effective January 1, 1984, Chrysler changed to the LIFO inventory method. The change to LIFO, in 1984, did not have a material effect on net earnings. Additionally, there is no effect on prior years' earnings resulting from the change to LIFO, and accordingly, prior years' earnings have not been restated.

Had the inventory, at December 31, 1984, been valued on the FIFO basis, it would have been $29.7 million higher than reported.

Inventories are summarized by major classifications as follows:

	(In millions of dollars) December 31	
	1984	1983
Finished products, including service parts	$ 557.1	$ 415.3
Raw materials, work in process and finished production parts	1,008.5	842.1
Supplies	60.3	44.0
Total	$1,625.9	$1,301.4

Raw materials and work in process inventories are combined because segregation is not practical.

In accordance with industry practice, the entire service parts inventory has been included in current assets, although in many instances parts are carried for estimated requirements during the serviceable lives of products sold and are, therefore, not expected to be sold within one year. Adequate provision has been made for obsolescence of service parts.

NOTES TO FINANCIAL STATEMENTS (continued)

NOTE 3

Investments and Advances

Detail of investments and advances included in the financial statements is as follows:

	(In millions of dollars)	
	December 31	
	1984	1983
Investments in Associated Companies Outside the United States:		
Peugeot S.A.	$ 100.0	$ 100.0
Mitsubishi Motors Corporation	28.5	28.5
Total	$ 128.5	$ 128.5
Investments in and Advances to Unconsolidated Subsidiaries: Chrysler Financial Corporation and Subsidiaries	$1,094.7	$ 708.1
Retail sales outlets	16.8	27.2
Other	.9	(1.5)
Total	$1,112.4	$ 733.8

In 1983, Chrysler reduced the carrying value of its Peugeot S.A. investment to $100 million. This adjustment was necessary to reflect the significant decline in value of Chrysler's interest in Peugeot S.A.

NOTE 4

Property, Plant and Equipment and Capitalization of Leases

A summary, by major classification, of property, plant and equipment follows:

	(In millions of dollars)	
	December 31	
	1984	1983
Land	$ 153.1	$ 120.4
Buildings	1,432.9	1,223.3
Machinery and equipment	3,012.9	2,633.3
Furniture and fixtures	82.7	77.4
Construction in process	482.2	415.4
	5,163.8	4,469.8
Less accumulated depreciation	2,534.5	2,334.0
	2,629.3	2,135.8
Unamortized special tools	1,083.9	919.2
Net Property, Plant and Equipment	$3,713.2	$3,055.0

Chrysler sold the tax benefits of certain of its depreciation deductions and investment tax credits during 1983 and 1982. The proceeds of $19.8 million in 1983 and $10.1 million in 1982 have been recorded as other income.

Chrysler conducts certain of its operations from leased facilities and leases certain dealership properties and manufacturing, transportation and data processing equipment. The amortization of assets recorded under capital leases is not material and has been included with depreciation expense in the consolidated statement of earnings.

At December 31, 1984, the future minimum lease payments under noncancelable capital leases and operating leases are as follows:

	(In millions of dollars)	
	Capital Leases	Operating Leases
1985	$ 7.0	$ 89.6
1986	6.4	76.5
1987	5.9	60.6
1988	5.2	50.2
1989	4.8	42.7
Thereafter	25.7	300.7
Total	55.0	$ 620.3
Less amount representing interest	21.7	
Present value of minimum lease payments	33.3	
Less current portion	3.5	
Long-term obligations under capital leases	$ 29.8	

Future minimum sublease rentals to be received under noncancelable subleases, principally for dealership properties, total $169.5 million as of December 31, 1984.

Rental expense for operating leases, with original expiration dates beyond one year, for the years ended December 31, 1984, 1983, and 1982 was $104.5 million, $83.8 million and $61.3 million, respectively. Sublease rentals of $21.1 million were received in 1984.

NOTE 5
Long-Term Debt

Long-term debt less payments due within one year is as follows:

		(In millions of dollars)
		December 31
	1984	1983

Non-Convertible Long-Term Debt:

	1984	1983
Chrysler Corporation		
Peugeot S.A. variable rate term loan due 1986	$ —	$ 40.0
8.875% sinking fund debentures due 1986 through 1995	64.1	74.0
8% sinking fund debentures due 1986 through 1998	172.4	187.0
11% State of Michigan Secured Notes due 1995	100.0	145.0
10.5% State of Indiana Secured Note due 1986	32.0	32.0
15.75% State of Illinois Secured Note due 1988	—	18.5
10% Volkswagen of America, Inc. Secured Note due 1995	184.7	184.7
Obligations on variable rate Pollution Control Revenue Bonds due 1999	31.7	—
Other	9.0	4.2
Total Chrysler Corporation	593.9	685.4
United States Subsidiaries		
Chrysler Realty Corporation		
8% to 14% mortgage and other loans due 1986 through 2009	69.5	44.2
Other Subsidiaries	—	.6
Total United States Subsidiaries	69.5	44.8
Subsidiaries Outside the United States		
Chrysler Canada Ltd. 12.5% Secured Notes due 1986 through 1991	—	195.7
Chrysler de Mexico S.A.		
Variable rate Secured Bonds due 1986 through 1988, payable in Mexican Pesos	10.4	—
Other	20.5	21.1
Total Subsidiaries Outside the United States	30.9	216.8
Total Non-Convertible Long-Term Debt	694.3	947.0
Convertible Long-Term Debt:		
Chrysler Corporation 12% subordinated debentures due 1991 and convertible to 8% Cumulative Preferred Stock	—	76.8
Chrysler Overseas Capital Corporation		
5% debentures due 1986 through 1988 and convertible to Chrysler Common Stock at $42.46 per share	18.0	24.0
4.75% debentures due 1986 through 1988 and convertible to Chrysler Common Stock at $48.68 per share	18.0	24.0
Total Convertible Long-Term Debt	36.0	124.8
Obligations under Capital Leases (Note 4)	29.8	32.2
Total Long-Term Debt	$ 760.1	$1,104.0

The aggregate annual maturities of consolidated long-term debt are as follows for the years ending December 31 (in millions): 1986–$111.0; 1987–$74.2; 1988–$76.7; 1989–$62.9.

Chrysler Corporation entered into a $1.1 billion revolving credit agreement dated as of July 1, 1984. Additionally, on October 5, 1984, Chrysler Canada Ltd. and its subsidiary, Chrysler Leasing Ltd., entered into $220 million (Canadian or U.S.) and $30 million (Canadian) revolving credit agreements, respectively. The full amounts of these credit lines remain unused as of December 31, 1984.

NOTES TO FINANCIAL STATEMENTS (continued)

NOTE 6
Commitments, Guarantees and Contingent Liabilities

Chrysler and its subsidiaries are parties to various legal proceedings, including some purporting to be class actions, and some which assert claims for damages in large amounts. Chrysler believes each proceeding constitutes routine litigation incident to the business conducted by Chrysler and its subsidiaries, and will not result in ultimate liability that is material in amount.

During the 1980 and 1981 model years, Chrysler Canada Ltd. failed to meet certain production versus sales ratios required by Canada pursuant to the Automotive Trade Pact. In that regard Chrysler Canada Ltd. has requested from the Canadian Federal Government a concession, similar to that obtained in the past, to utilize the excess generated during the 1982 model year to offset these deficits. Chrysler believes the Canadian Federal Government will grant the request.

At December 31, 1984, Chrysler has guaranteed approximately $25.4 million of 8% notes due 1991 of an unrelated entity, Koch Properties, Inc. (formerly debt of Chrysler Realty Corporation). Chrysler has also guaranteed securities approximating $9.4 million at December 31, 1984 of associated companies primarily outside the United States.

NOTE 7
Redeemable Preferred Stock

The terms of the Certificate of Designations, Preferences and Rights for the $2.75 cumulative preferred stock provided for both optional and mandatory redemption of the shares. On September 6, 1984, Chrysler Corporation's Board of Directors authorized the redemption, on October 31, 1984 (the redemption date), of the outstanding $2.75 cumulative preferred stock. The redemption price of the outstanding shares was composed of the redemption value of the shares ($25.00 per share) and a sum equal to all dividends accrued and unpaid to the redemption date ($.3475 per share).

Additionally, the Board of Directors authorized the retirement of the $2.75 cumulative preferred stock consisting of the redeemed shares and shares held in treasury. The unamortized issue costs and the value assigned to the warrants issued with the $2.75 cumulative preferred stock were charged directly to retained earnings. The excess of the redemption value over the purchase price of the treasury shares has been credited to additional paid-in capital.

NOTE 8
Common Stock, Employee Stock Ownership Plan, Warrants, Stock Options and Incentive Compensation

Common Stock

Of the 170,000,000 shares of authorized common stock at December 31, 1984, 3,509,926 shares were reserved for the Chrysler Salaried Employees' Savings Plan, 4,087,950 shares were reserved for stock options for officers and key employees under the Chrysler Corporation Stock Option Plan, 1,784,053 shares were reserved for issuance upon conversion of debentures, 748,109 shares were reserved for the Chrysler Corporation Employee Stock Ownership Plan and 123,628 shares were reserved for issuance upon exercise of public warrants.

In December 1984, Chrysler Corporation's Board of Directors authorized management, at its discretion, to purchase up to 25 million shares of Chrysler common stock before December 6, 1986. As of December 31, 1984, 2,418,652 shares have been acquired at a cost of $64.5 million.

Employee Stock Ownership Plan

The Chrysler Corporation Loan Guarantee Act of 1979 required Chrysler to establish an Employee Stock Ownership Plan (the Plan) and to make contributions to the Plan in the form of newly issued Chrysler common stock in four equal annual installments of $40.6 million at the then current market price. In June 1984, Chrysler made the fourth and final contribution to the Plan.

Pursuant to the Economic Recovery Tax Act of 1981, Chrysler established a payroll based tax credit Employee Stock Ownership Plan (PAYSOP). In October 1984, Chrysler contributed $10.4 million to the PAYSOP which was used to purchase on the market 330,918 shares of Chrysler common stock.

Warrants

In March 1984, Chrysler Corporation purchased for $58.0 million 2.6 million warrants held by certain financial institutions. In September 1983, Chrysler Corporation purchased for $311 million 14.4 million warrants held by the United States Government. Each warrant entitled the holder to purchase, until December 31, 1990, at a price of $13.00, one share of Chrysler common stock.

Stock Options

The Chrysler Corporation Stock Option Plan was initially adopted in 1972 and most recently amended on December 8, 1983. Outstanding options, consisting of ten year nonqualified stock options and incentive stock options, have exercise prices of not less than 100% of fair market value at date of grant. Options generally become exercisable on up to 40% of the shares after one year from the date of grant, 70% after two years and 100% after three years. Options may be exercised to purchase stock, or the right to purchase the stock may be forfeited for stock appreciation rights (SAR's) on up to a specified number of shares for payment to the holder, in cash or shares at the sole discretion of the Stock Option Committee, of the aggregate difference between the option price and the then current market price of the shares. Information with respect to options is summarized as follows:

| | Number of Shares Under Options Outstanding | Shares Issuable on Exercise of Options | | Number of Shares Available for Granting of Options |
| | | Option Price | | |
		Per Share	Total	
Balance at January 1, 1982	2,672,125	$6.25 - $30.88		43,975
Shares Reserved for Granting Options				3,500,000
Options Granted	1,105,500			(1,105,500)
Options Exercised	(18,250)	6.25 - 15.07	$ 147,867	
Options Forfeited for SAR's	(7,025)	6.25		
Options Terminated	(154,500)			136,699
Balance at December 31, 1982	3,597,850	6.25 - 26.63		2,575,174
Options Granted	1,344,000			(1,344,000)
Options Exercised	(600,725)	6.25 - 18.63	4,194,918	
Options Forfeited for SAR's	(292,450)	6.25 - 18.63		
Options Terminated	(40,875)			20,250
Balance at December 31, 1983	4,007,800	6.25 - 30.38		1,251,424
Options Granted	631,250			(631,250)
Options Exercised	(400,775)	6.25 - 16.88	2,687,762	
Options Forfeited for SAR's	(797,425)	6.25 - 27.00		
Options Terminated	(24,250)			4,750
Balance at December 31, 1984	3,416,600			624,924

At December 31, 1984, 1,895,175 options were not yet exercisable under the terms of the Stock Option Plan.

NOTES TO FINANCIAL STATEMENTS (continued)

Incentive Compensation

Incentive compensation is awarded to officers and key employees of Chrysler who have contributed significantly to its success. The awards are authorized by a resolution adopted by the stockholders (Stockholders' Resolution). The formula in the Stockholders' Resolution, as amended in 1984, limits the provision out of earnings for any fiscal year for incentive compensation to 8% of the sum of the consolidated net earnings plus the provision for incentive compensation for that year, after deducting $1.00 per share times the average number of shares of common stock outstanding during the year.

The Board of Directors has not determined the amount that will be set aside out of 1984 earnings for incentive compensation purposes, the amount that will be awarded for 1984, or the amount to be awarded to each person eligible for incentive compensation. However, the Incentive Compensation Committee has determined that it intends to recommend to the Board of Directors that the Board authorize to be set aside out of 1984 earnings for incentive compensation purposes approximately two-thirds of the maximum amount permitted by the Stockholders' Resolution. Accordingly, the consolidated statement of earnings for 1984 includes a charge of $135.0 million for incentive compensation. The Committee also has determined that it intends to recommend to the Board that the cash awards for 1984 should, in general, be larger than the cash awards for 1983, but in total significantly less than the amount set aside. Any amount set aside that is not awarded will be carried forward and may be used to make awards in the future.

NOTE 9
Interest (Income) Expense—Net

Total interest charges are as follows: 1984–$184.3 million, 1983–$267.4 million, and 1982–$338.6 million of which $52.3 million in 1984, $57.6 million in 1983, and $43.7 million in 1982, was capitalized and is included in property, plant and equipment. Interest income totaled $182.7 million in 1984, $127.7 million in 1983, and $136.9 million in 1982.

NOTE 10
Preferred Stock, Common Stock, Additional Paid-In Capital, and Retained Earnings

(In millions of dollars)

Year Ended December 31	1984	1983	1982
$2.75 Cumulative Preferred Stock (See Note 7):			
Balance at beginning of year	$ 225.0	$ 223.5	$ 221.9
Shares retired (1984–10,000,000; 1983–None; 1982–None)	(250.0)	—	—
Amortization of preferred stock discount	25.0	1.5	1.6
	—	225.0	223.5
Treasury Stock–$2.75 Cumulative Preferred Stock:			
Balance at beginning of year	(2.8)	—	—
Shares purchased for treasury (1984–4,936,800; 1983–125,000; 1982–None)	(113.8)	(2.8)	—
Shares redeemed (1984–4,938,200; 1983–None; 1982–None)	(123.5)	—	—
Shares retired (1984–10,000,000; 1983–None; 1982–None)	240.1	—	—
	—	(2.8)	—
Balance at end of year	$ —	$ 222.2	$ 223.5
1981 Series Preferred Stock:			
Redemption value at beginning of year	$ —	$ 1,097.4	$ 1,097.4
Reclassification of 1981 Series Preferred Stock to Common Stock	—	(1,097.4)	—
Balance at end of year	$ —	$ —	$ 1,097.4
Additional Paid-In Capital:			
Balance at beginning of year	$ 2,276.4	$ 692.5	$ 692.5
Excess of market value of newly issued shares over $1.00 per share	40.7	—	—
Reclassification of excess of $1.00 per share of Common Stock to Additional Paid-In Capital	—	1,583.9	—
Excess of the redemption value over the cost of $2.75 Preferred Stock retired	8.2	—	—
Balance at end of year	$ 2,325.3	$ 2,276.4	$ 692.5

(In millions of dollars)

Year Ended December 31

	1984	1983	1982
Common Stock:			
Balance at beginning of year	$ 121.8	$ 501.4	$ 460.2
Newly issued shares sold under provisions of the Chrysler Salaried Employees' Savings Plan, Employee Stock Ownership Plan and the Stock Option Plan (1984–2,062,466; 1983–1,966,325; 1982–6,342,616)	2.1	44.8	41.2
Reclassification of 1981 Series Preferred Stock to, and exchange of Warrants, 1980 Issue for, Common Stock (shares issued 1984–None; 1983–35,403,724; 1982–None)	—	1,097.4	—
Shares issued on exercise of Warrants (1984–16,353; 1983–4,860,019; 1982–None)	—	63.1	—
Recapitalization of Debt (shares issued 1984–None; 1983–106,500; 1982–None)	—	4.5	—
Issue costs for reclassification of 1981 Series Preferred Stock to Common Stock	—	(5.5)	—
Reclassification of excess of $1.00 per share of Common Stock to Additional Paid-In Capital	—	(1,583.9)	—
Balance at end of year	$ 123.9	$ 121.8	$ 501.4
Retained Earnings (Deficit):			
Balance at beginning of year	$(1,255.1)	$(1,523.7)	$(1,692.2)
Net earnings	2,380.0	700.9	170.1
Dividends	(120.7)	(116.9)	—
Amortization of Preferred Stock Discount	(25.0)	(1.5)	(1.6)
Purchase of Warrants from financial institutions	(58.0)	—	—
Purchase of U.S. Government held Warrants	—	(313.9)	—
Balance at end of year	$ 921.2	$(1,255.1)	$(1,523.7)
Treasury Stock–Common Stock:			
Balance at beginning of year	$ —	$ —	$ —
Shares purchased for treasury (1984–2,418,652; 1983–None; 1982–None)	(64.5)	—	—
Balance at end of year	$(64.5)	$ —	$ —

NOTE 11
Employee Benefit Plans

Pension Plans

Chrysler Corporation and certain of its consolidated subsidiaries have pension plans covering substantially all of their employees. The actuarial cost method used in the determination of funding and pension expense for the major pension plans, which are non-contributory, is Entry Age Normal with Frozen Initial Liability. The actuarial assumptions involved in the computation include: an annual total investment return of 9% for each of the years presented; mortality from group annuity tables; and turnover and election of retirement options consistent with company experience.

Annual payments to the pension trust fund are determined in compliance with the Employee Retirement Income Security Act (ERISA). All pension trust fund assets and income accruing thereon are used solely to administer and pay pension benefits. Generally, accrued costs are funded in the following year. However, certain costs accrued in 1979 were not funded in 1979 but are being funded over a future period of up to 30 years. Additionally, in December 1984, Chrysler contributed $243 million towards a prepayment of the estimated 1985 pension cost. The actuarial assumptions are regularly reviewed by Chrysler and its independent actuaries to assure that funding will be sufficient to cover pension benefits payable.

Current service costs of pension plans are accrued on a current basis and past service costs are accrued based on amortization periods not exceeding 30 years from the later of January 1, 1982 or the date such costs are established. Chrysler believes that the actuarial cost method and actuarial assumptions stated above provide for a systematic and rational allocation of pension costs over time periods.

NOTES TO FINANCIAL STATEMENTS (continued)

Pension expense for Chrysler's pension plans is as follows:

(In millions of dollars)

Pension Expense–	1984	1983	1982
U.S. and Canada	$267.3	$254.7	$271.7
Percentage of Payroll	8.5%	10.5%	15.8%

The net increase in pension costs of $12.6 million in 1984 from 1983 resulted principally from scheduled increases in benefits under the 1979 collective bargaining agreement which more than offset the decrease in pension costs resulting from a reduction of interest cost on pension contribution deferrals.

The net decrease in pension costs of $17.0 million in 1983 from 1982 resulted principally from decreases in pension costs due to a change in the estimate regarding future service of inactive employees which more than offset increases in pension costs due to scheduled increases in benefits under the 1979 collective bargaining agreement and an increase in employment.

The accumulated plan benefits and the plan net assets for U.S. pension plans are as follows:

(In millions of dollars)

	December 31 1984	January 1 1983	January 1 1982
Actuarial present value of accumulated plan benefits:			
Vested	$2,856.1	$3,021.8	$2,849.4
Nonvested	376.6	458.8	424.1
Combined	$3,232.7	$3,480.6	$3,273.5
Net assets available for benefits including Chrysler's accrued pension liability of 1984–$561.2; 1983–$784.6; 1982–$777.7	$2,511.4	$2,075.2	$1,948.2
Actuarial present value of accumulated vested plan benefits in excess of net assets available for benefits	$ 344.7	$ 946.6	$ 901.2

Chrysler changed to a year end information date in 1984 to present more current information for its pension plans.

The weighted-average assumed rate of return used in determining the actuarial present value of accumulated

plan benefits stated above was 12.70%, 9.75% and 10.25% for 1984, 1983 and 1982, respectively. The rate of return for 1984 is based upon the effective market interest rate as of December 31, 1984 for the pension trust fund's dedicated bond portfolio. Approximately 80% of the funds of the pension trust were invested in a dedicated bond portfolio in 1984. The rates of return for 1983 and 1982 are based on rates published by the Pension Benefit Guaranty Corporation.

Chrysler's foreign pension plans are not required to report to certain government agencies pursuant to ERISA and do not otherwise determine the actuarial value of accumulated benefits or net assets available for benefits as calculated and disclosed above. For those plans, the value of pension funds and balance sheet accruals exceeded the actuarially computed value of vested benefits as of December 31, 1984, January 1, 1983 and January 1, 1982 by $2.2 million, $21.6 million and $37.4 million, respectively.

Scheduled changes in benefits under pension plans resulting from current collective bargaining agreements will increase pension costs in 1985 by approximately $15.7 million.

Other Postretirement Benefits

Chrysler Corporation and Chrysler Canada Ltd. currently provide health insurance and life insurance benefits to their employees. Upon retirement, employees may become eligible for continuation of these benefits.

Health insurance cost for active employees and retirees and life insurance cost for active employees are charged to income as premiums are paid. The cost of life insurance provided to retirees after age 65 is accrued in a manner similar to pension costs, but is not funded.

The cost of providing these benefits to retired and active employees for Chrysler Corporation and Chrysler Canada Ltd. are as follows:

(In millions of dollars)

	1984	1983	1982
Retired Employees	$149.7	$145.8	$131.6
Active Employees	296.3	268.7	238.3
Total	$446.0	$414.5	$369.9

NOTE 12

Taxes on Income

Income tax expense shown in the consolidated statement of earnings includes the following:

(In millions of dollars)

	1984	1983	1982
Taxes on income that are offset by operating loss carryforwards:			
United States	**$801.6**	$366.7	$ —
Foreign	**82.3**	32.3	—
	883.9	399.0	—
Currently Payable:			
United States	**10.0**	—	—
Foreign	**2.8**	2.6	.9
State and Local	**15.8**	—	—
	28.6	2.6	.9
Deferred:			
United States	**6.9**	—	—
Foreign	**1.0**	—	—
State and Local	**13.8**	—	—
	21.7	—	—
Total Taxes on Income	**$934.2**	$401.6	$ .9

$883.9 million in 1984 and $399.0 million in 1983 of tax expense is computed by applying the applicable statutory rates to such pre-tax income as is sheltered by the tax loss carryforwards. The extraordinary item reflects the elimination of these tax provisions through the utilization of tax loss carryforwards.

At December 31, 1984, Chrysler had investment tax credit carryforwards of approximately $220 million, which may be used until the expiration dates occurring between 1989 and 1999.

A reconciliation of income tax expense to the U.S. statutory rate of 46% follows:

(In millions of dollars)

	1984		1983		1982	
	Amount	Percent	Amount	Percent	Amount	Percent
Tax at U.S. statutory rate	**$1,117.9**	**46.0%**	$ 323.6	46.0%	$(31.3)	(46.0%)
Writedown of investment in Peugeot S.A.	**—**	**—**	72.3	10.3	—	—
Rate differential–foreign tax rates lower than U.S. rate	**(5.0)**	**(.2)**	(5.7)	(.8)	—	—
Losses for which no income tax credits were available	**—**	**—**	16.9	2.4	31.3	46.0
Effect of the Tax Reform Act of 1984 relating to DISC	**(77.9)**	**(3.2)**	—	—	—	—
Investment tax credits	**(101.4)**	**(4.2)**	—	—	—	—
State and local taxes net of federal tax benefit	**16.0**	**.6**	—	—	—	—
Other	**(15.4)**	**(.6)**	(5.5)	(.8)	.9	1.3
Total Taxes on Income	**$ 934.2**	**38.4%**	$ 401.6	57.1%	$ .9	1.3%

NOTES TO FINANCIAL STATEMENTS (continued)

NOTE 13

Relationship with Chrysler Financial Corporation (CFC)

CFC is a wholly-owned unconsolidated subsidiary of Chrysler Corporation. CFC's primary function is to provide wholesale, retail and lease financing to Chrysler-franchised dealers. Chrysler Corporation and CFC are parties to an Income Maintenance Agreement, expiring December 31, 2000, requiring Chrysler Corporation to pay a fee to maintain CFC's ratio of income before taxes available for fixed charges at no less than 125% of fixed charges on an annual basis. No payments were required from Chrysler Corporation during 1984 or 1983 under the Income Maintenance Agreement. Payments of $63.1 million were made pursuant to the agreement in 1982. The effect of this fee was eliminated in the consolidated statement of earnings.

On January 4, 1984, Chrysler Corporation made an investment in CFC of $100 million in the form of a capital note. The note and interest accrued thereon were contributed to CFC's equity on April 1, 1984. Additionally, Chrysler Corporation contributed $100 million on March 1, 1984 and $100 million on January 2, 1985, to CFC's equity. The contribution on January 2, 1985 has been reflected in the consolidated financial statements as of December 31, 1984. At December 31, 1983, Chrysler Corporation had approximately $200 million of CFC commercial paper included in its balance sheet under the heading "Marketable Securities."

In accordance with certain legal covenants associated with CFC's debt restructuring, the private lenders to CFC were granted an option expiring on December 31, 1985 to purchase 51% of CFC at a price equal to 51% of the shareholder's investment or a fair value to be determined by an investment banking firm. No negotiations are currently underway for such a sale nor are any expected by Chrysler in the future.

The retained earnings of Chrysler include net accumulated earnings of CFC of $483.6 million at December 31, 1984 which cannot be paid to Chrysler in dividends due to CFC's loan covenants.

Pro forma condensed financial information for CFC adjusted for the January 2, 1985 capital contribution from Chrysler Corporation is as follows:

Condensed Balance Sheet (In millions of dollars)

	December 31	
	1984	1983
Cash and cash equivalents	$ 199.2	$ 114.7
Finance receivables-net	6,793.3	3,359.8
Amounts due and deferred from receivable sales-net	100.9	689.7
Assets other than above	155.2	118.0
Total Assets	**$7,248.6**	**$4,282.2**
Debt due within one year	$2,994.4	$ 575.3
Accounts payable, accruals and other liabilities (including affiliates: 1984–$15.3 and 1983–$197.2)	375.5	395.3
Long-term debt	2,784.2	2,603.7
Shareholder's investment	1,094.5	707.9
Total Liabilities and Shareholder's Investment	**$7,248.6**	**$4,282.2**

Condensed Statement of Earnings (In millions of dollars)

	Year Ended December 31		
	1984	1983	1982
Total Revenues	$792.7	$559.4	$546.1
Operating Income	129.9	92.7	38.9
Net Earnings	83.1	47.4	52.2
Effect on Net Earnings of Income Maintenance Agreement	—	—	32.0

NOTE 14

Information about Chrysler Corporation and its Subsidiaries Operating in Different Geographic Areas

	United States	Canada	Other Principally Mexico	Adjustments and Eliminations	Consolidated
Year ended December 31, 1984					
Unit Sales:					
Sales to unaffiliated customers	1,736,469	229,558	68,321	—	2,034,348
Transfers between geographic areas	188,250	333,196	4,489	(525,935)	—
Total Unit Sales	1,924,719	562,754	72,810	(525,935)	2,034,348
Dollar Sales:			(In millions of dollars)		
Sales to unaffiliated customers	$17,239.7	$1,852.2	$ 480.8	$ —	$19,572.7
Transfers between geographic areas	2,706.9	3,075.9	405.6	(6,188.4)	—
Total Dollar Sales	$19,946.6	$4,928.1	$886.4	$(6,188.4)	$19,572.7
Earnings (Loss) from Continuing Operations before Taxes and Extraordinary Item	$ 2,187.1	$ 230.4	$ 12.8		$ 2,430.3
Identifiable Assets at December 31, 1984	$ 7,673.3	$ 837.8	$ 551.6		$ 9,062.7
Year ended December 31, 1983					
Unit Sales:					
Sales to unaffiliated customers	1,263,350	178,572	52,039	—	1,493,961
Transfers between geographic areas	148,114	226,048	—	(374,162)	—
Total Unit Sales	1,411,464	404,620	52,039	(374,162)	1,493,961
Dollar Sales:			(In millions of dollars)		
Sales to unaffiliated customers	$11,665.5	$1,321.5	$ 276.8	$ —	$13,263.8
Transfers between geographic areas	2,078.6	2,209.3	230.6	(4,518.5)	—
Total Dollar Sales	$13,744.1	$3,530.8	$ 507.4	$(4,518.5)	$13,263.8
Earnings (Loss) from Continuing Operations before Taxes and Extraordinary Item	$ 642.6	$ 96.8	$(35.9)		$ 703.5
Identifiable Assets at December 31, 1983	$ 5,548.2	$ 770.6	$ 453.5		$ 6,772.3
Year ended December 31, 1982					
Unit Sales:					
Sales to unaffiliated customers	969,106	126,592	86,028	—	1,181,726
Transfers between geographic areas	94,059	225,004	—	(319,063)	—
Total Unit Sales	1,063,165	351,596	86,028	(319,063)	1,181,726
Dollar Sales:			(In millions of dollars)		
Sales to unaffiliated customers	$ 8,508.9	$ 892.2	$ 655.4	$ —	$10,056.5
Transfers between geographic areas	1,795.9	2,086.6	127.4	(4,009.9)	—
Total Dollar Sales	$10,304.8	$2,978.8	$ 782.8	$(4,009.9)	$10,056.5
Earnings (Loss) from Continuing Operations before Taxes and Extraordinary Item	$(32.7)	$ 20.3	$(55.6)		$(68.0)
Identifiable Assets at December 31, 1982	$ 4,949.8	$ 537.2	$ 776.5		$ 6,263.5

Transfers between geographic areas are based on prices either negotiated between buying and selling locations or on a formula established by the parent company.

Chrysler operates principally in one segment, automotive operations. Chrysler's automotive operations are engaged primarily in the manufacture, assembly and sale in North America of passenger cars, trucks and related automotive parts and accessories. Purchases of vehicles, component parts and service parts from Mitsubishi Motors Corporation, an associated company of Chrysler, for resale aggregated $943.5 million in 1984, $892.6 million in 1983, and $644.8 million in 1982.

NOTES TO FINANCIAL STATEMENTS (continued)

NOTE 15
Per Share Data

For 1984, primary earnings per share were computed by dividing net earnings, less the preferred stock dividends ($16.2 million) and the write-off of all unamortized preferred stock issue costs and discount ($25.0 million) by the average number of common shares outstanding plus the common stock equivalents which would arise from the exercise of stock options and warrants. Fully diluted earnings per share were determined on the assumption that the average number of common shares assumed outstanding for primary earnings per share was further increased by the conversion of the 5% debentures and 4.75% debentures, and that the related interest expense and amortization of issue costs were eliminated.

For 1983 and 1982, primary earnings per share amounts were computed by dividing the net earnings, adjusted for the preferred stock dividend requirement and amortization of discount and issue costs, by the average number of common shares outstanding plus the common stock equivalents which would arise from the exercise of stock options and warrants, if dilutive. Shares assumed to be issuable upon the conversion of the 5% debentures and 4.75% debentures have not been included in the 1982 computation of fully diluted earnings per share because the effect would be anti-dilutive.

NOTE 16
Inflation Accounting (Unaudited)

Chrysler's financial statements are prepared on a historical cost basis in accordance with generally accepted accounting principles and, therefore, do not fully reflect the effect of changing prices. Financial Accounting Standards Board Statement No. 33, as amended by Statements No. 70 and No. 82, approaches the problem of changing prices by determining the effect of specific price changes on the financial statements by using indices that measure the changes in the cost of identical assets over time. This approach is referred to as "current cost."

The effect of specific price changes on net income is measured by adjusting those components of the balance sheet that have a material effect upon the income statement, which in the case of Chrysler are inventories and fixed assets. For inventories valued on a LIFO basis, cost of sales in the historical cost income statement largely reflects current cost. Cost of sales for inventories valued on a FIFO basis was restated to a current cost basis. Fixed assets are adjusted by applying indices to their historical cost for changes in prices for each category of asset since acquisition. Depreciation and amortization are recalculated based on the revised cost using the original method of depreciation and amortization. These recalculated amounts replace the historical amounts.

Other items in the income statement are assumed to be realized or incurred evenly throughout the year and, therefore, do not require adjustment. Where there is evidence that material components of the income statement do not occur evenly throughout the year, an adjustment to average dollars for the year is made.

The impact of general inflation is also measured on selected items using the Consumer Price Index for all Urban Consumers (CPI-U). This method is referred to as "constant dollars."

The supplementary inflation data required by FASB Statement No. 33, as amended, are shown in the following schedules.

Schedule of Earnings from Continuing Operations Adjusted for the Effects of Changing Prices (Unaudited)

(In millions of dollars)

	As Reported in the Financial Statements (Historical Cost)	Adjusted for Changes in Specific Prices (1984 Current Cost)
Net sales, change in equity and other income	$19,717.2	$19,717.2
Costs, other than items below	15,528.2	15,537.8
Depreciation of plant and equipment	271.6	464.7
Amortization of special tools	282.8	335.9
Selling and administrative expenses	987.7	987.7
Pension plans	267.3	267.3
Interest (income) expense-net	(50.7)	(50.7)
	17,286.9	17,542.7
Earnings from Continuing Operations before Taxes on Income	2,430.3	2,174.5
Taxes on Income	934.2	934.2
Earnings from Continuing Operations	$ 1,496.1	$ 1,240.3
Earnings per Common Share from Continuing Operations	$ 11.75	$ 9.68
Unrealized Gain from Decline in Purchasing Power of Net Amounts Owed		$ 129.5
Difference in Specific Prices (Current Cost) of Inventories and Property, Plant and Equipment over Increase in the General Price Level		$ 271.8

At December 31, 1984, current cost of inventory was $1,655.6 million and current cost of property, plant, equipment and tooling net of accumulated depreciation and amortization was $5,616.6 million. These amounts do not represent appraised value or any other measure of market value.

Comparison of Selected Supplementary Financial Data Adjusted for the Effects of Changing Prices (Unaudited)

(In millions of dollars)

	1984	1983	1982	1981	1980
NET SALES:					
As reported	$19,572.7	$13,263.8	$10,056.5	$ 9,971.6	$ 8,600.1
In constant dollars	19,572.7	13,828.3	10,821.8	11,388.2	10,840.7
EARNINGS (LOSS) FROM CONTINUING OPERATIONS:					
As reported	$ 1,496.1	$ 301.9	$(68.9)	$(555.1)	$(1,771.6)
In current cost	1,240.3	23.9	(340.4)	(936.0)	(2,615.8)
EARNINGS (LOSS) PER SHARE FROM CONTINUING OPERATIONS:					
As reported	$ 11.75	$ 2.35	$(1.28)	$(8.31)	$(26.93)
In current cost	9.68	(0.05)	(4.85)	(13.79)	(39.67)
NET ASSETS AT YEAR END:					
As reported	$ 3,305.9	$ 1,365.3	$ 991.1	$ 779.8	$ 459.2
In current cost	5,239.0	3,349.3	2,879.6	2,992.9	2,931.6
Gain from Decline in Purchasing Power of Net Amounts Owed	129.5	115.2	295.5	590.8	705.3
Differences in Specific Prices (Current Cost) of Inventories and Property, Plant and Equipment over Increase in the General Price Level	271.8	519.4	443.6	(72.9)	(329.0)
CASH DIVIDENDS PER COMMON SHARE:					
As reported	$0.85	$ —	$ —	$ —	$ —
In constant dollars	0.85	—	—	—	—
MARKET PRICE PER COMMON SHARE AT YEAR END:					
As reported	$ 32	$ 27⅝	$ 17¾	$ 3⅜	$ 4⅞
In constant dollars	31½	28⅜	18⅞	3¾	5⅞
Average Consumer Price Index	311.1	298.4	289.1	272.4	246.8

ACCOUNTANTS' REPORT

Shareholders and Board of Directors
Chrysler Corporation
Detroit, Michigan

We have examined the accompanying consolidated balance sheet of Chrysler Corporation and consolidated subsidiaries at December 31, 1984 and 1983, and the related consolidated statements of earnings and changes in financial position for each of the three years in the period ended December 31, 1984. Our examinations were made in accordance with generally accepted auditing standards and, accordingly, included such tests of the accounting records and such other auditing procedures as we considered necessary in the circumstances.

In our opinion, the accompanying financial statements present fairly the financial position of Chrysler Corporation and consolidated subsidiaries at December 31, 1984 and 1983, and the results of their operations and changes in their financial position for each of the three years in the period ended December 31, 1984 in conformity with generally accepted accounting principles applied on a consistent basis.

TOUCHE ROSS & CO.
Certified Public Accountants

200 Renaissance Center
Detroit, Michigan   48243
February 14, 1985

FINANCIAL RESPONSIBILITY

Management is responsible for the preparation of Chrysler's financial statements. This responsibility includes maintaining the integrity and objectivity of financial data and the presentation of Chrysler's results of operations and financial position, in accordance with generally accepted accounting principles.

Chrysler maintains a system of internal controls to ensure that its records reflect the transactions of its operations in all material respects and to provide protection against significant misuse or loss of assets. The internal control system is supported by a staff of internal auditors and financial management personnel, and is augmented by written policies and guidelines.

Chrysler's financial statements have been examined by Touche Ross & Co., independent certified public accountants. Their examination was made in accordance with generally accepted auditing standards and included a review of the internal control system and tests of transactions.

The Board of Directors, acting through its Audit Committee composed solely of non-employee directors, is responsible for determining that management fulfills its responsibilities in the preparation of financial statements and financial control of operations. The Audit Committee recommends independent public accountants to the Board of Directors for appointment by the shareholders. The Audit Committee meets regularly with management, the internal auditors, and the independent public accountants. Both the independent accountants and the internal auditors have full and free access to the Audit Committee, without management representatives present, to discuss the results of their examinations and their opinions on the adequacy of internal controls and the quality of financial reporting.

Report To Shareholders

For The Year Ended
December 31, 1980

Chrysler Corporation and Consolidated Subsidiaries

Consolidated Statement of Operations

	Year Ended December 31		
	1980	**1979**	**1978**
	(In millions of dollars)		
Net sales	$ **9,225.3**	$ 12,001.9	$ 13,618.3
Equity in net earnings (loss) of unconsolidated subsidiaries	(**56.5)**	2.4	22.1
Net earnings from European and certain South American operations	**—**	—	29.4
	9,168.8	12,004.3	13,669.8
Costs, other than items below	**9,132.5**	11,631.5	12,640.1
Depreciation of plant and equipment (Note 6)	**261.5**	180.6	154.0
Amortization of special tools (Note 6)	**305.8**	220.0	198.2
Selling and administrative expenses	**561.3**	598.5	572.1
Pension plans (Note 12)	**302.4**	260.6	262.3
Interest expense—net (Note 11)	**275.5**	215.4	128.9
	10,839.0	13,106.6	13,955.6
LOSS BEFORE TAXES ON INCOME	(**1,670.2)**	(1,102.3)	(285.8)
Taxes on income (credit) (Note 13)	**39.5**	(5.0)	(81.2)
NET LOSS	$(**1,709.7)**	$(1,097.3)	$(204.6)
Loss per share of Common Stock (Note 18)	**$(26.00)**	$(17.18)	$(3.54)
Average number of shares of Common Stock outstanding during the year (in thousands)	**66,871**	65,552	61,679

See notes to financial statements.

Chrysler Corporation and Consolidated Subsidiaries

Consolidated Balance Sheet

	December 31	
	1980	**1979**

Assets

Current Assets: (In millions of dollars)

	1980	1979
Cash	$ **101.1**	$ 188.2
Time deposits	**2.6**	120.8
Marketable securities—at lower of cost or market	**193.6**	165.3
Accounts receivable (less allowance for doubtful accounts: 1980-$40.3 million; 1979-$34.9 million)	**476.2**	610.3
Inventories (Note 4)	**1,916.0**	1,873.8
Prepaid insurance, taxes and other expenses	**101.6**	102.3
Income taxes allocable to the following year (Note 13)	**70.1**	60.0
TOTAL CURRENT ASSETS	**2,861.2**	3,120.7

Investments and Other Assets:

	1980	1979
Investments in associated companies outside the United States (Note 5)	**353.3**	353.3
Investments in and advances to 20% to 50% owned companies (Notes 1 and 5)	**30.5**	58.1
Investments in and advances to unconsolidated subsidiaries (Notes 1 and 5)	**702.3**	702.9
Other noncurrent assets	**150.5**	69.2
TOTAL INVESTMENTS AND OTHER ASSETS	**1,236.6**	1,183.5

Property, Plant and Equipment (Note 6):

	1980	1979
Land, buildings, machinery and equipment	**3,877.9**	3,733.1
Less accumulated depreciation	**2,158.7**	2,097.1
	1,719.2	1,636.0
Unamortized special tools	**800.8**	712.9
NET PROPERTY, PLANT AND EQUIPMENT	**2,520.0**	2,348.9
TOTAL ASSETS (Note 3)	**$6,617.8**	$6,653.1

See notes to financial statements.

	December 31	
	1980	**1979**

Liabilities and Shareholders' Investment

Current Liabilities:

(In millions of dollars)

	1980	**1979**
Accounts payable	**$1,179.6**	$1,079.8
Short-term debt	**150.5**	600.9
Payments due within one year on long-term debt	**166.2**	275.6
Employee compensation and benefits	**616.6**	349.8
Taxes on income (Note 13)	**12.3**	16.8
Other taxes	**113.3**	100.8
Interest payable	**44.6**	40.6
Accrued expenses	**746.2**	767.3
TOTAL CURRENT LIABILITIES	**3,029.3**	3,231.6
Other Liabilities and Deferred Credits:		
Deferred employee benefit plan accruals	**353.0**	301.4
Deferred taxes on income (Note 13)	**71.6**	83.0
Unrealized profits on sales to unconsolidated subsidiaries	**31.0**	47.7
Other noncurrent liabilities	**190.4**	188.6
TOTAL OTHER LIABILITIES AND DEFERRED CREDITS	**646.0**	620.7
Long-Term Debt (Note 3):		
Notes and debentures payable	**2,321.4**	880.7
Convertible sinking fund debentures	**83.9**	96.0
12% Subordinated debentures ($32.1 million issued, $45.9 million subscribed but not issued)	**78.0**	—
TOTAL LONG-TERM DEBT	**2,483.3**	976.7
Commitments (Note 7)		
Preferred Stock—No par value, Authorized 20,000,000 shares:		
10,000,000 $2.75 shares issued and outstanding (Redemption value of $250.0 million less unamortized issue costs and value of warrants to purchase common stock) (Note 8)	**220.3**	218.7
171,473 8⅛% 1981 Preferred shares issued and outstanding as of February 27, 1981 having a redemption value of $548.7 million (Note 3)	**342.9**	—
Common Stock—Par value $6.25 a share:		
Authorized 120,000,000 shares; issued and outstanding 66,972,683 shares at December 31, 1980 and 66,703,605 shares at December 31, 1979 (Note 9)	**418.6**	416.9
Additional Paid-In Capital	**692.4**	692.2
Net Earnings Retained (Deficit) (Note 1)	**(1,215.0)**	496.3
TOTAL LIABILITIES AND SHAREHOLDERS' INVESTMENT	**$6,617.8**	$6,653.1

See notes to financial statements.

Chrysler Corporation and Consolidated Subsidiaries

Consolidated Statement of Additional Paid-In Capital

	Year Ended December 31		
	1980	**1979**	**1978**
	(In millions of dollars)		
Balance at beginning of year	**$ 692.2**	$ 683.1	$ 648.7
Excess of market price over par value of newly issued shares of common stock sold to the thrift-stock ownership programs (265,690 in 1980; 3,058,012 in 1979; 3,330,517 in 1978)	**.2**	9.0	16.2
Excess of option price over par value of shares of common stock issued under the stock option plans (3,388 in 1980; 11,300 in 1979; 14,151 in 1978)	—	.1	.1
Proceeds from sale of warrants to purchase 5,000,000 shares of common stock	—	—	18.1
Balance at end of year	**$ 692.4**	$ 692.2	$ 683.1

Chrysler Corporation and Consolidated Subsidiaries

Consolidated Statement of Net Earnings Retained

	Year Ended December 31		
	1980	**1979**	**1978**
	(In millions of dollars)		
Balance at beginning of year	**$ 496.3**	$ 1,628.7	$ 1,899.1
Net loss	**(1,709.7)**	(1,097.3)	(204.6)
	(1,213.4)	531.4	1,694.5
Cash dividends paid:			
Preferred stock (none in 1980; $2.0625 a share in 1979; $1.2757 a share in 1978)	—	20.6	12.8
Common stock (none in 1980; $0.20 a share in 1979; $0.85 a share in 1978)	—	12.9	52.2
Amortization of preferred stock discount	**1.6**	1.6	.8
Balance at end of year	**$(1,215.0)**	$ 496.3	$ 1,628.7

See notes to financial statements.

Chrysler Corporation and Consolidated Subsidiaries

Consolidated Statement of Changes in Financial Position

| | Year Ended December 31 | | |
	1980	1979*	1978*
Additions to (uses of) working capital:		(In millions of dollars)	
From operations:			
Net loss	$(1,709.7)	$(1,097.3)	$(204.6)
Depreciation and amortization	567.3	400.6	352.2
Depreciation and amortization—European and			
South American operations	—	—	46.5
Changes in deferred income taxes—noncurrent	(11.4)	(24.1)	26.0
Equity in net (earnings) loss of unconsolidated subsidiaries	56.5	(2.4)	(22.1)
(Gain) loss on translation of long-term debt	(5.4)	2.6	2.5
Funds provided by (used in) operations	(1,102.7)	(720.6)	200.5
Effect of June 24, 1980 debt restructuring (Note 3)	910.4	—	—
Proceeds from long-term borrowing (Note 3)	1,145.1	123.7	347.4
Proceeds from sale of common stock	1.9	28.3	37.2
Proceeds from sale of $2.75 preferred stock and warrants	—	—	234.4
Conversion of debt to 1981 preferred stock (Note 3)	342.9	—	—
Proceeds from sale of European operations	—	—	230.0
Retirement of property, plant and equipment	89.8	17.3	9.8
Increase (decrease) in other liabilities	36.7	264.4	(4.0)
Other	6.4	4.7	(8.7)
TOTAL ADDITIONS (USES)	1,430.5	(282.2)	1,046.6
Dispositions of working capital:			
Cash dividends paid	—	33.5	65.0
Increase (decrease) in investments and advances	28.3	(234.1)	32.2
Increase (decrease) in other noncurrent assets	81.3	18.7	(23.6)
Expenditures for property, plant and equipment	439.9	406.6	337.9
Expenditures for special tools	394.7	341.9	332.8
Reduction in long-term borrowing (Note 3)	543.5	338.1	49.2
Deconsolidation of European and			
South American operations	—	—	240.0
TOTAL DISPOSITIONS	1,487.7	904.7	1,033.5
Increase (decrease) in working capital during the year	$(57.2)	$(1,186.9)	$ 13.1

| | Increase (Decrease) in Working Capital | | |
	1980	1979	1978
Changes in components of working capital:			
Cash and marketable securities	$(177.0)	$(48.5)	$ 114.0
Accounts and notes receivable	(134.1)	(277.7)	(48.7)
Current and deferred taxes on income	14.6	(16.1)	79.7
Inventories	42.2	(107.0)	(641.8)
Accounts payable and accrued expenses	(362.0)	84.7	262.3
Short-term debt (Note 3)	450.4	(551.7)	200.7
Payments due within one year on long-term debt (Note 3)	109.4	(263.2)	78.4
Other	(.7)	(7.4)	(31.5)
	$(57.2)	$(1,186.9)	$ 13.1

*Restated to conform to 1980 classifications.

 See notes to financial statements.

Notes to Financial Statements

Note 1. Summary of Significant Accounting Policies

Principles of Consolidation

The consolidated financial statements include the accounts of Chrysler Corporation and majority-owned and controlled subsidiaries except those engaged primarily in leasing, financing, insuring, and retail selling activities. Investments in unconsolidated subsidiaries, as well as investments in associated companies representing 20% or more of the voting stock and pursuant to which some degree of management control is exercised, are carried at acquisition cost plus changes in equity in net assets from date of acquisition. Other investments are carried at cost or less.

All intercompany accounts, transactions, and earnings between the Corporation and consolidated subsidiaries have been eliminated.

Net earnings retained for use in the business by Chrysler Corporation and consolidated subsidiaries includes net accumulated earnings of Chrysler Financial Corporation, an unconsolidated subsidiary, of $360 million at December 31, 1980 of which $341 million cannot be paid in dividends. Total net accumulated earnings of unconsolidated subsidiaries were $218 million at December 31, 1980 and $203 million at December 31, 1979.

Depreciation and Tool Amortization

Property, plant and equipment are carried substantially at cost less accumulated depreciation. Depreciation is generally provided on an accelerated basis. The cost of special tools is amortized rateably on a basis designed to allocate the cost to operations during the years in which the tools are used in the productive process.

Pension Plans

Current service costs of pension plans are accrued on a current basis and past service costs are accrued based on amortization periods not exceeding 30 years. Prior to 1979, these costs were funded currently. Certain costs accrued in 1979 were not funded but will be over a future period of 30 to 40 years. Effective January 1, 1980, accrued costs are generally funded in the following year.

Other Retirement Benefits

The cost of continuing life insurance provided upon retirement is accrued in a manner similar to pension costs, but is not funded. Health insurance cost for retirees is charged to income as premiums are paid.

Cost of Investments in Consolidated Subsidiaries in Excess of Equity

To the extent that the cost of the investments in majority-owned and controlled subsidiaries exceeds the equity in net assets of the subsidiaries at dates of acquisition, such differences, if incurred after October 31, 1970, are amortized over periods not exceeding twenty years. Such amounts incurred prior to October 31, 1970 are not amortized.

Investment Tax Credit

Reductions in taxes resulting from the investment credit provisions of the United States Internal Revenue Code are being taken into income at the time the related assets are placed in service.

Inventories

Inventories are stated at the lower of cost or market, with cost determined substantially on a first-in, first-out basis.

Product Warranty

Estimated lifetime costs of product warranty are accrued at the time of sale.

Note 2. 1980 Developments and Future Risk and Uncertainties

Chrysler incurred losses of $1,097.3 million in 1979 and $1,709.7 million in 1980. Chrysler's 1980 loss significantly exceeded the loss projected in the December 17, 1979 Operating Plan submitted to the United States government, primarily due to the depressed conditions that existed in the automotive industry during 1980. Although certain of the financing risks that existed at December 31, 1979 were resolved as Chrysler restructured most of its institutional debt (see Note 3) and obtained a commitment from the United States government for loan guarantees of up to a maximum of $1.5 billion, providing certain conditions are met, significant financing and other risk and uncertainties still exist.

Through December 31, 1980, the Chrysler Corporation Loan Guarantee Board ("the Board") had authorized guarantees totaling $800.0 million and Chrysler issued notes for that amount which are due in 1990 unless certain prepayment options are exercised (see Note 3). On February 27, 1981, the Board authorized an additional $400.0 million of guarantees and additional long-term debt was incurred by the issuance of notes due in 1990 with basically the same prepayment options as those in the earlier notes. Therefore, the total amount of federally guaranteed debt now outstanding is $1.2 billion. In accordance with the Chrysler Corporation Loan Guarantee Act ("the Act"), the Board is required to make periodic determinations as to Chrysler's present and future viability and the Board has the power to accelerate the maturity of outstanding guaranteed loans and terminate the commitment to guarantee future loans, under certain circumstances if such determinations cannot be made.

In conjunction with the authorization of the additional $400.0 million of guarantees, the Board required that certain concessions be finalized between Chrysler and its lenders, suppliers, and employees. The agreed to concessions include the conversion of approximately $686 million of long-term debt to preferred stock, the option to liquidate approximately $623 million of long-term debt at 30 cents per dollar, price concession objectives from suppliers totaling $72 million, and wage and other benefits concessions from employees totaling $783 million through September, 1982. The effects of these concessions were reflected in revised (January 14, 1981) Operating and Financing Plans ("the Plans") submitted to the Board. The Board made the determination that the Plans meet the requirements of the Act. In addition, the Board has received satisfactory assurances that the Plans are realistic and feasible.

The Plans project a significant improvement in operating results for 1981 over 1980, and profits for the subsequent years. The 1981 projection assumes a U.S. car industry of 9.6 million units and Chrysler achieving 9.1% penetration. The 1981 projection also assumes U.S. truck retail sales of 2.5 million units and Chrysler achieving 9.0% penetration. Capital expenditures for 1981 have been projected to be substantially below 1980 levels and the Plans indicate an ability to finance these expenditures without any additional federally guaranteed loans.

The Corporation's long-term viability is predicated on a return to sustained profitable operations. The Plans project that improvement in earnings will be achieved through increased automotive industry sales; improvements in vehicle profit margins; reduced fixed costs; and reduced advertising and dealer incentives from 1980 levels. Achievement of the objectives in the Plans is dependent on other basic assumptions, including improved general economic conditions and consumer acceptance of Chrysler's vehicle offerings. If the current economic recession continues, this and other factors beyond the Corporation's control could have a substantial effect on the ability of Chrysler to achieve the objectives outlined in the Plans.

Note 3. Government Loan Guarantees, Pledged Assets, and Restructuring of Debt

On June 24, 1980, the Chrysler Corporation Loan Guarantee Board ("the Board") gave final approval to Chrysler's application for $1.5 billion in loan guarantees. The Agreement to Guarantee between the United States government and Chrysler provides that if certain conditions are met, the United States government may issue guarantees up to a maximum of $1.5 billion with no guarantee being issued after December 31, 1983. Chrysler is obligated to pay a guarantee fee equal to one percent of the outstanding principal of the guaranteed indebtedness. The amount of guaranteed indebtedness outstanding as of December 31, 1980 was $800 million and as of February 27, 1981 was $1.2 billion.

Before issuing loan guarantees, the Board must determine that (a) credit is not otherwise available to Chrysler, (b) a reasonable assurance of repayment of the loan exists, (c) the loan to be guaranteed bears a reasonable interest rate, (d) Chrysler continues to comply with the submitted operating plan as revised on an annual basis, and (e) the aggregate amount of nonfederally guaranteed commitments and concessions that have accrued to Chrysler are at least equal to the principal amount of guaranteed loans outstanding, taking into account the guarantee being issued.

Also, the Chrysler Corporation Loan Guarantee Act ("the Act") requires that loans guaranteed under the Act must be paid in full by December 31, 1990 and that the Board shall require security for the loans to be guaranteed at the time the commitment is made. Accordingly, Chrysler and Manufacturers National Bank of Detroit entered into an Indenture of Mortgage and Deed of Trust whereby substantially all of Chrysler's U.S. assets are subject to the lien of the United States government. Major exceptions are Chrysler's stock in Peugeot S.A. which has been pledged to secure a $100.0 million loan from that company and certain facilities pledged to the states of Michigan, Delaware and Indiana to secure loans obtained from these states with respect to which the United States government has a second lien. Chrysler has agreed to maintain a value of collateral available to the United States equal to at least $2.4 billion.

The Agreement to Guarantee contains numerous affirmative and negative covenants including net income, working capital, ratio of debt to net worth, and fixed charges coverage covenants. However, the latter three do not become applicable until January 1, 1984.

Restructuring of Debt

Substantially all of Chrysler's institutional debt was initially restructured on June 24, 1980, the date on which the United States government issued its first loan guarantees under the Chrysler Corporation Loan Guarantee Act of 1979. The total amount of debt affected by this restructuring was $910.4 million. In February 1981, in connection with the United States government issuing the additional loan guarantees of $400.0 million, the majority of Chrysler's institutional debt was again restructured.

The first restructuring involved conversion of the following borrowings into term loans:

	(In millions of dollars)
(a) Revolving credit agreement with U.S. banks	$408.6
(b) U.S. regular lines of credit	63.8
(c) Eurodollar revolving credit agreements (Total facility of $305.0 million of which $55.0 million was long-term debt at December 31, 1979)	250.0
(d) Letter of credit agreement under which Chrysler financed its purchases of Mitsubishi products	156.1
(e) Chrysler Canada Ltd.'s lines of credit	28.3
	$906.8

and the reclassification of $3.6 million of the debt of Chrysler Overseas Capital N.V. which was shown in current liabilities at December 31, 1979. The borrowings of Chrysler Overseas Capital N.V. were restructured to defer principal installments due in the 1980-83 period.

The second restructuring involves Chrysler's lenders under the Amended and Restated U.S. Credit Agreement, the U.S. Line Bank Agreement, the Eurodollar Credit Agreement, and the Japanese Letter of Credit Agreement and debt under agreements with The Prudential Insurance Company of America, Aetna Life Insurance Company and Blue Cross and Blue Shield of Michigan. Also included are the borrowings of Chrysler Overseas Capital N.V. The total amount of debt involved in the restructuring is $1,309.0 million of which $685.9 million is being converted in two installments into preferred stock having a redemption value of $1,097.4 million. Half of the $685.9 million was converted on February 27, 1981, the date on which the United States government issued the additional $400.0 million of loan guarantees. The shares issued in February are reflected on the December 31, 1980 balance sheet as preferred stock. The dividend rate on the shares is 8⅛% per annum noncumulative until the government guaranteed loans are paid in full and thereafter cumulative. The shares will be redeemed in 10 equal annual installments commencing at the later of one year after (a) government guaranteed

loans are paid in full and (b) all dividend arrearages on all outstanding series of preferred stock have been paid. The remaining half of the $685.9 million will be converted in June, 1981 or sooner if all the debt covered by the purchase option described below is repurchased or if the company requires additional equity to maintain a minimum of $100.0 million of net worth.

Chrysler has the option to redeem the remaining debt ($623.1 million) with these lenders at 30 cents per dollar. The options must be exercised during four consecutive periods of approximately three months, (the first of which begins on February 27, 1981 and ends 106 days thereafter). Chrysler may redeem 100% of the debt during the first redemption period. However, if 25% of the debt is not redeemed in each of the four periods, the option for that 25% cannot be carried to future periods. In conjunction with obtaining the additional $400.0 million of loan guarantees, Chrysler agreed to redeem 37.5% of the debt on March 31, 1981.

Until Chrysler exercises these redemption options, the debt ($623.1 million) will be secured by a second lien on the company's U.S. assets. Two issues of Chrysler's outstanding public debentures ($293.5 million) will be equally and rateably secured during this period of time.

The accounting effect of the second restructuring is as follows:

	(In millions of dollars)
Total debt subject to restructuring	$1,309.0
Less: Preferred shares issued February 27, 1981	342.9
Amount reflected as debt, December 31, 1980	966.1
Amount to be credited to preferred stock at the time of the second conversion	343.0
Remaining debt	623.1
Debt to be liquidated	190.0
Discount on debt extinguishment	$ 433.1[1]

[1]$411.5 million to be recorded as preferred stock to attain redemption value and $21.6 million to be credited to operations.

The portion of the debt to be liquidated in 1981 has been classified as "Payments due within one year on long-term debt" on the December 31, 1980 balance sheet.

The aggregate annual maturities of consolidated long-term debt are as follows for the years ending December 31 (in millions): 1982—$79.1, 1983—$32.1, 1984—$64.6, 1985—$87.5.

During 1980, Chrysler issued notes aggregating $800.0 million which are fully guaranteed as to principal and interest by the United States of America. The first issue occurred on June 24th and consisted of $500.0 million of 10.35% Secured Notes Due June 1, 1990. The Notes are not subject to redemption prior to June 1, 1983 but after that date may be redeemed at the option of the company and with the written consent of the Chrysler Corporation Loan Guarantee Board

("the Board"). The second issue occurred on July 31st and consisted of $300.0 million of 11.40% Secured Notes Due July 15, 1990. These Notes are not subject to redemption prior to June 15, 1983 but after that date may be redeemed at the option of the company and with the consent of the Board.

On February 27, 1981, Chrysler issued $400.0 million of 14.90% Secured Notes Due October 15, 1990.

Long-term debt included in the financial statements, less payments due within one year and the $342.9 million converted to preferred stock on February 27, 1981, is as follows:

Note 3. Government Loan Guarantees, Pledged Assets, and Restructuring of Debt—continued

	December 31	
	1980	**1979**
	(In millions of dollars)	
Non-Convertible Long-Term Debt:		
Chrysler Corporation		
The Prudential Insurance Company of America—		
9.30% promissory note due 1982 through 1993	$ —	$ 175.0
Aetna Life Insurance Company—		
8.875% promissory note due 1982 through 1993	—	56.5
8.875% sinking fund debentures due 1982 through 1995	93.5	100.0
8% sinking fund debentures due 1984 through 1998	200.0	200.0
7% debentures due 1982 through 1984	7.5	9.0
7% Deutsche Mark Bonds due 1982 through 1984	19.4	28.9
13% Blue Cross and Blue Shield of Michigan note due 1984	—	50.0
12.6875% promissory notes due 1981	—	10.0
10.35% United States Government Guaranteed Notes Due 1990	500.0	—
11.4% United States Government Guaranteed Notes Due 1990	300.0	—
15.5% State of Michigan Notes due 1995	150.0	—
15.5% State of Delaware Note due 1994	5.0	—
15.5% State of Indiana Note due 1985	32.0	—
All other	13.7	30.8
TOTAL CHRYSLER CORPORATION	1,321.1	660.2
Subsidiaries Outside the United States		
Chrysler Overseas Capital N.V.	—	22.6
Chrysler Canada Ltd.	168.5	134.3
Chrysler Australia Limited	—	14.8
Chrysler de Mexico S.A.	4.6	7.0
Other	1.3	1.8
TOTAL SUBSIDIARIES OUTSIDE THE UNITED STATES	174.4	180.5
Long-Term Debt Under Revolving Credit Agreements—		
Chrysler Corporation	—	40.0
TOTAL LONG-TERM DEBT— NOTES AND DEBENTURES PAYABLE	1,495.5	880.7
Convertible Long-Term Debt:		
Chrysler Corporation 12% subordinated debentures due 1991	78.0	—
Chrysler Overseas Capital Corporation		
5% debentures due 1982 through 1988 and		
convertible to Chrysler Common Stock at $62.00 per share	41.9	48.0
4¼% debentures due 1982 through 1988 and		
convertible to Chrysler Common Stock at $73.50 per share	42.0	48.0
TOTAL CONVERTIBLE LONG-TERM DEBT	161.9	96.0
Restructured debt—$343.0 million to be converted to		
8⅛% 1981 Preferred shares: $190.0 million to be		
paid in four quarterly installments; and $433.1 million		
representing discount on debt extinguishment:		
The Prudential Insurance Company of America	136.5	—
Aetna Life Insurance Company	44.1	—
Blue Cross and Blue Shield of Michigan	37.5	—
Bank debt under the following agreements:		
Amended and Restated U.S. Credit Agreement	318.6	—
U.S. Line Bank Agreement	50.4	—
Eurodollar Credit Agreement	242.1	—
Japanese Letter of Credit Agreement	117.2	—
Chrysler Overseas Capital N.V. Agreement	19.7	—
	966.1	—
Less: Portion of the $190.0 million due within one year	140.2	—
TOTAL RESTRUCTURED DEBT	825.9	—
TOTAL LONG-TERM DEBT	**$2,483.3**	$ 976.7

Note 4. Inventories

Inventories are summarized by major classifications
as follows:

| | December 31 | |
| | 1980 | 1979 |
	(In millions of dollars)	
Finished products, including service parts	$ 645.1	$ 801.3
Raw materials, work in process and finished production parts	1,426.4	1,106.9
Progress payments—defense contracts	(207.1)	(81.3)
Supplies	51.6	46.9
TOTAL	$1,916.0	$1,873.8

Inventories are stated at the lower of cost (substantially first-in, first-out) or market. The practice of Chrysler Corporation to take physical inventories at some time during each year and to adjust the books to the physical inventories was followed in 1980 and 1979.

Raw materials and work in process inventories are combined because segregation is not practical.

In accordance with trade practice, the entire service parts inventory has been included in current assets, although in many instances parts are carried for estimated requirements during the serviceable lives of products sold and are, therefore, not expected to be sold within one year. Adequate provision has been made for obsolescence of service parts.

Note 5. Investments and Advances

Detail of investments and advances included in the
financial statements is as indicated below:

| | December 31 | |
| | 1980 | 1979 |
	(In millions of dollars)	
Investments in Associated Companies Outside the United States		
Peugeot S.A.	$ 323.9	$ 323.9
Mitsubishi Motors Corporation	28.5	28.5
Other	.9	.9
TOTAL	$ 353.3	$ 353.3
Investments in and Advances to 20% to 50% Owned Companies		
Chrysler Motors do Brasil Limitada	$ —	$ 32.3
Sigma Motor Corporation (Pty.) Ltd.	30.5	24.6
Other	—	1.2
TOTAL	$ 30.5	$ 58.1
Investments in and Advances to Unconsolidated Subsidiaries		
Chrysler Financial Corporation and Subsidiaries	$ 668.0	$ 646.1
Retail sales outlets	22.6	38.2
Other	11.7	18.6
TOTAL	$ 702.3	$ 702.9

Chrysler's investment in Peugeot S.A. ("Peugeot") is valued on the balance sheet at $323.9 million, representing the net assets of the Chrysler companies sold to Peugeot, less the cash consideration received net of costs related to the transaction. At the time of acquiring the shares, Chrysler obtained an independent valuation on a long-term investment basis indicating a value greater than $323.9 million and significantly greater than the aggregate market price on the Paris Stock Exchange on August 10, 1978, the date on which the agreement to sell the companies to Peugeot was announced. Chrysler believes there has not been a permanent impairment in the value of the shares as a long-term investment.

In February 1980, Peugeot arranged for Chrysler to obtain a $100.0 million non-recourse short-term loan from a bank which is a member of the Peugeot group. As part of the loan arrangement, Chrysler agreed to pledge the Peugeot shares it owns as collateral. The two companies also signed a Memorandum of Intent whereby they agreed to pursue certain commercial and industrial cooperation arrangements which resulted in the signing of a commercial cooperation agreement on May 30, 1980. However, an industrial cooperation agreement has not been signed although discussions are continuing between the companies to determine whether they can arrive at a basis for industrial cooperation. If an industrial cooperation agreement had been entered into by October 30, 1980, the $100.0 million demand loan would have been converted into a medium-term loan. In light of present circumstances, the two companies amended the February, 1980 loan agreement to reflect that the $100.0 million loan will continue as a demand loan and the 1.8 million shares of Peugeot stock owned by Chrysler will continue to be pledged as security for the loan. Peugeot has indicated that it has no present intention of demanding payment of the $100.0 million loan. If the loan is repaid and the shares are released from the pledge, Peugeot will have the option to purchase the shares during the seven-month period beginning on the date of repayment at a price to be determined by the President of the French Association of Bankers. However, if industrial cooperation agreements are signed and become effective within 30 days after signature, the option to purchase becomes null and void. If Peugeot exercises its option and purchases the shares, Chrysler could receive an amount substantially less than the current carrying value.

Note 6. Property, Plant and Equipment, Depreciation and Amortization Policies, and Capitalization of Leases

A summary, by major classification, of property, plant and equipment follows:

	December 31	
	1980	1979
	(In millions of dollars)	
Land	**$ 91.7**	$ 117.6
Buildings	**1,147.0**	1,146.1
Machinery and equipment	**2,226.9**	1,976.3
Furniture and fixtures	**78.0**	78.6
Construction in process	**296.3**	377.9
Other	**38.0**	36.6
	3,877.9	3,733.1
Less accumulated depreciation	**2,158.7**	2,097.1
	1,719.2	1,636.0
Unamortized special tools	**800.8**	712.9
NET PROPERTY, PLANT AND EQUIPMENT	**$2,520.0**	$2,348.9

The Corporation conducts certain of its operations from leased facilities and also leases certain manufacturing, transportation and data processing equipment. The amortization of assets recorded under capital leases is included with depreciation expense in the Consolidated Statements of Operations. The capitalization of leases is not significant.

The majority of the Corporation's leases are operating leases. Minimum rental payments under these operating leases that have initial or remaining noncancelable lease terms in excess of one year are as follows for the years ending December 31 (in millions): 1981—$21.0, 1982—$17.1, 1983—$12.7, 1984—$10.6, 1985—$9.4, and averaging $8.4 per year for 1986 through 1988, and $3.5 for 1989 through 2006, or an aggregate of $154.9. Many of these leases contain options allowing the Corporation to renew the leases for various periods or to purchase the property. Rental expense for operating leases for the years ended December 31, 1980 and 1979 was $23.7 million in each year, and in 1978 was $19.8 million.

The Corporation and its consolidated subsidiaries generally follow the policy of accelerating depreciation in the early years of use by means of a declining balance method which results in accumulated depreciation of approximately two-thirds of the depreciable cost during the first half of the estimated lives of the property. The weighted average depreciation lives of assets are as follows:

Buildings (including improvements and building equipment)	30 years
Machinery and equipment	12 years
Furniture	13 years

Costs of tools, dies, jigs, patterns and fixtures have been amortized on the basis of anticipated production of particular products, with such adjustments as may be necessary to amortize fully the cost of such items upon completion of production.

Note 7. Commitments, Guarantees and Contingent Liabilities

Commitments for investments and the acquisition of property, plant and equipment excluding special tools, at December 31, 1980 and 1979 amounted to approximately $112.6 million and $151.4 million, respectively, for Chrysler Corporation and consolidated subsidiaries.

The Corporation and its subsidiaries are parties to various legal proceedings, including some purporting to be class actions, and some which assert claims for damages in large amounts. The Corporation believes each proceeding constitutes ordinary routine litigation incident to the business conducted by the Corporation and its subsidiaries, or will not result in ultimate liability that is material in amount.

At December 31, 1980, Chrysler Corporation has guaranteed approximately $74.6 million of 6% notes due January 1, 1995 of an unrelated entity, ABKO Properties, Inc. (formerly Chrysler Realty Corporation). Chrysler Corporation and consolidated subsidiaries have also guaranteed securities approximating $31.7 million at December 31, 1980 of associated companies outside the United States. Chrysler Corporation has other contingent liabilities, substantially applicable to short-term credit facilities, amounting to approximately $9.5 million.

During the 1980 model year, Chrysler Canada Ltd. failed to meet the production versus sales ratios required by Canada pursuant to the Automotive Trade Pact. The Canadian government has indicated that it is their intent not to levy any duties against Chrysler Canada Ltd. provided certain conditions are met, including making up the 1980 deficiency by the end of the 1985 model year. Chrysler feels all conditions will be met and that no liability will materialize.

Note 8. Redeemable Preferred Stock

The 10,000,000 shares of $2.75 Cumulative Preferred Stock issued and outstanding at December 31, 1980 are redeemable, at the option of the Board of Directors, at any time on or after July 1, 1983, in whole or in part at a price of $25 per share plus accrued dividends. In addition, so long as any shares of the $2.75 Cumulative Preferred Stock remain outstanding,

Chrysler Corporation must redeem 300,000 shares on June 15 in the years 1984 through 2015 and 400,000 shares on June 15, 2016. Cash dividends at the rate of $.6875 per quarter were paid on the $2.75 Cumulative Preferred Stock each quarter from the date such stock was issued on June 20, 1978, until the Board of Directors, on November 1, 1979, voted to omit the fourth quarter dividend. The $2.75 Cumulative Pre-

ferred Stock is non-voting, except that when six quarterly dividends, whether consecutive or not, are in arrears, the holders of the Preferred Stock are entitled to elect two directors to the Board of Chrysler Corporation. As of December 31, 1980, dividends applicable to the $2.75 Cumulative Preferred Stock were five quarters in arrears.

At December 31, 1980, 400,000 shares of 8% Cumulative Preferred Stock were reserved for issuance upon the conversion of Chrysler Corporation's 12% Subordinated Debentures Due 1991.

For a discussion of the redeemable preferred shares issued in conjunction with the February, 1981 debt restructuring, see Note 3—Government Loan Guarantees, Pledged Assets, and Restructuring of Debt.

Note 9. Common Stock, Warrants to Purchase Common Stock, Stock Options and Thrift-Stock Ownership Programs

Of the 120,000,000 authorized shares of common stock at December 31, 1980, 3,769,680 shares were reserved for the thrift-stock ownership programs, 2,716,100 shares were reserved for stock options for salaried officers and key employees under the Chrysler Corporation Qualified and Nonqualified Stock Option Plans, 1,784,053 shares were reserved for issuance upon conversion of debentures, 5,000,000 shares were reserved for issuance upon exercise of warrants, and 26,000,000 shares were reserved for the Chrysler Corporation Employee Stock Ownership Plan.

The 5,000,000 warrants are each exercisable at $13.00 per share ($65,000,000 aggregate amount) to

purchase one share of Chrysler Corporation Common Stock, and are applicable to the sale of 10,000,000 shares of $2.75 Cumulative Preferred Stock of Chrysler Corporation. The warrants were first exercisable on September 21, 1978 and expire on June 15, 1985, or under certain circumstances, Chrysler may accelerate the expiration date of the warrants to a date as early as July 1, 1983.

Chrysler has issued warrants to the United States government and certain lenders shown below to purchase shares of common stock of Chrysler at the price of $13 per share. The warrants may not be exercised so long as any United States government guaranteed loan or commitment for loan guarantee continues to be outstanding. The warrants ex-

pire on December 31, 1990; however, if any United States government guaranteed loan or commitment for loan guarantee continues to be outstanding at January 1, 1984, the exercise period shall be extended (for unreserved shares) by a period equal to the number of days elapsed between January 1, 1984 and the date when all loans that have been guaranteed by the United States government have been paid in full and all

commitments for loan guarantees have been fulfilled or have expired. Chrysler has agreed to submit to the holders of its common stock an amendment of Chrysler's certificate of incorporation to increase the authorized number of shares of common stock to 170,000,000 which will be more than sufficient to cover shares to be reserved for these warrants. The warrants issued as of February 27, 1981 are as follows:

	Number of Warrants
United States government	14,400,000
Participating lenders—Amended and Restated Credit Agreement	4,086,000
Participating lenders—Eurodollar Credit Agreement	1,525,000
Participating lenders—Line Bank Agreements	637,500
The Prudential Insurance Company of America	4,375,000
Aetna Life Insurance Company	1,412,500
Blue Cross and Blue Shield of Michigan	1,250,000
TOTAL	27,686,000

Note 9. Common Stock, Warrants to Purchase Common Stock, Stock Options and Thrift-Stock Ownership Programs—continued

At January 1, 1980, options for 1,609,663 shares were outstanding. During 1980, options were granted as to 1,172,000 shares, exercised as to 3,388 shares, forfeited for cash pursuant to stock appreciation rights as to 3,387 shares,

and terminated as to 369,688 shares. At December 31, 1980, options for 2,405,200 shares were outstanding at prices ranging from $6.25 to $30.88 a share, the average being $10.12. Options for 927,200 shares were exercisable at December 31, 1980.

Information with respect to options which became exercisable and options exercised during the three years ended December 31, 1980 is summarized as follows:

Options That Became Exercisable During The Three Years Ended December 31, 1980

Year Ended	Number of Shares	Option Price Per Share	Total	Market Price on Date First Exercisable Per Share	Total
1980	333,325	$6.25 to $20.25	$3,697,665	$ 5.13 to $10.19	$2,484,744
1979	410,976	9.07 to 20.25	5,348,564	5.94 to 11.13	3,460,680
1978	286,875	8.82 to 20.25	4,182,363	11.00 to 13.31	3,643,078

Options Exercised During The Three Years Ended December 31, 1980

Year Ended	Number of Shares	Option Price Per Share	Total	Market Price on Date of Exercise Per Share	Total
1980	3,388	$8.82 to $9.07	$ 30,054	$10.06 to $10.69	$ 34,814
1979	11,300	8.82	99,666	9.63 to 11.38	114,063
1978	14,151	8.82	124,812	10.13 to 13.38	170,115

All outstanding options were granted at prices not less than 100% of fair market value at dates of grant, but in no case less than the par value of the common stock. Options become exercisable on and after the first anniversary to the extent of not more than 40% of the number of shares under option, on and after the second anniversary to the extent of not more than 70% of the number of shares under option, and after the third anniversary to the extent of 100% thereof. Options granted in 1972 were concurrent options consisting of qualified options which expire not more than five years after the date of grant and nonqualified options which expire not more than ten years after the date of grant, and to the extent either option is exercised, the other is reduced. Options granted in 1973 through 1980 were ten-year nonqualified options. Upon exercise of a nonqualified option, the holder may forfeit the option on up to an equal number of shares and receive an amount in cash or shares or any combination thereof, at the sole discretion of the Stock Option Committee, equal to the aggregate difference between the option price and the current market value of shares forfeited. Amounts paid in cash or shares are charges

to compensation expense. No other charges or credits are made against income in accounting for exercise of options.

Under the Chrysler Corporation Loan Guarantee Act, Chrysler is obligated to establish an Employee Stock Ownership Plan (ESOP). A trust has been established and shares of common stock will be issued by June 30, 1981, 1982, 1983 and 1984. The contributions to the trust equal $40,625,000 in each of the four years ended June 30, 1981, 1982, 1983 and 1984.

Note 10. Dividend Restrictions

Under the Chrysler Corporation Loan Guarantee Act of 1979, the Corporation may not pay any dividends on its common or preferred stock during the period beginning on the date of the enactment of the Act and ending on the date on which loan guarantees issued under the Act are no longer outstanding. In addition, Chrysler's agreements with its institutional lenders prohibit the payment of dividends until such time as the company achieves consolidated net worth of $3.5 billion. Chrysler's consolidated net worth as of December 31, 1980 was $459.2 million.

Note 11. Interest Expense and Capitalized Interest

Total interest charges are as follows: 1978—$166.2 million, 1979—$275.4 million and 1980—$404.8 million, of which $72.0 million was capitalized in conformance with Statement of Financial Accounting Standards No. 34, "Capitalization of Interest Cost".

Note 12. Pension Plans

Chrysler Corporation and certain of its consolidated subsidiaries have pension and retirement plans covering substantially all of their employees. The cost of these pension plans, which includes amortization of the prior service costs over periods not exceeding thirty years, was $302.4 million during 1980, $260.6 million during 1979 and $262.3 million during 1978. The net increase in pension cost of $41.8 million in 1980 from 1979 resulted from the cost of increases in benefits under the 1979 collective bargaining agreements which more than offset a reduction in employment. The net decrease in pension cost of $1.7 million in 1979 from 1978 resulted from a reduction in employment which more than offset higher salary levels

and the cost of increases in benefits under the 1973 and 1976 collective bargaining agreements. Employees of Chrysler Financial Corporation, an unconsolidated subsidiary, were covered under the Corporation's pension and retirement plans during 1978 and 1979 and under separate similar Chrysler Financial Corporation pension and retirement plans during 1980.

The accumulated plan benefits, calculated by using January 1, 1982 benefit levels (the last increase under the current collective bargaining agreements), and plan net assets as of January 1, 1980 for U.S. pension plans are as follows (in millions of dollars):

Actuarial present value of accumulated plan benefits:	
Vested	$3,022.5
Nonvested	603.5
Combined	$3,626.0
Net assets available for benefits	$1,747.2
Actuarial present value of accumulated vested plan benefits in excess of net assets available for benefits	$1,275.3

The weighted average assumed rate of return used in determining the actuarial present value of accumulated plan benefits was 8.25%. The assumed rate used was based on those published by the Pension Benefit Guaranty Corporation, which is under the U.S. Department of Labor. The company's foreign pension plans are not required to report to certain governmental agencies pursuant to ERISA and do not otherwise determine the actuarial value of

accumulated benefits or net assets available for benefits as calculated and disclosed above. For those plans, the actuarially computed value of vested benefits as of January 1, 1980 exceeded the value of pension funds and balance sheet accruals by $93.5 million.

Changes in benefits under the pension plans resulting from current collective bargaining agreements will increase pension expense in 1981 by approximately $19.2 million.

Note 13. Taxes on Income

Income tax expense (credit) as shown in the consolidated statement of operations includes the following:

	1980	1979	1978
	(In millions of dollars)		
United States Federal Income Taxes:			
Current	$ —	$(14.4)	$(102.9)
Deferred	—	(2.8)	—
	—	(17.2)	(102.9)
Other Income Taxes:			
Current	**61.0**	8.8	21.8
Deferred	**(21.5)**	3.4	(.1)
Total Taxes on Income (Credit)	**$ 39.5**	$(5.0)	$(81.2)

Chrysler Corporation and Chrysler Canada Ltd. have unused operating loss carryforwards, expiring in 1983 through 1987, providing approximately $1.0 billion of potential tax benefits. In addition, as of December 31, 1980, the company has U.S.

investment tax credits of approximately $194 million, expiring in 1981 through 1987, available as carryforwards. U.S. tax has not been provided on permanently reinvested net earnings of approximately $108 million of subsidiaries outside the U.S.

Note 13. Taxes on Income—continued

A reconciliation of 1979 and 1978 income tax credits to the U.S. statutory rate follows:

		Percent	
	1980	1979	1978
Tax at U.S. statutory rate	N	(46.0)%	(48.0)%
Effect of net earnings of unconsolidated subsidiaries which are net of tax	O T	(1.3)	(8.6)
Effect of net earnings of European and certain South American operations which are net of tax	A P	—	(6.8)
Effect of U.S. and Canadian losses for which no tax carrybacks are available	P L	47.7	—
Investment tax credit	I	—	20.3
State income taxes	C	(.3)	(.4)
Foreign earnings subject to aggregate tax expense greater (less) than statutory rate	A B	(.6)	2.8
Effect of overseas losses for which no tax credits are available	L E	—	12.3
TAXES ON INCOME		(.5)%	(28.4)%

In 1980, income tax expense of $39.5 million was provided on losses before tax of $1,670.2 million, of which $1,590.8 million represents losses of corporations subject to U.S. tax. Tax expense in 1980 is primarily attributable to taxes on income of subsidiaries outside the U.S. and Canada and the absence of tax credits for losses in the U.S. and Canada.

Note 14. Foreign Currency Exchange Losses

The combined effect of the foreign currency translation and conversion, the margin reduction on inventory turnover, and the inventory write-down was a decrease of after tax earnings of $50 million in 1980, $68 million in 1979, and $27 million in 1978 as follows:

	1980	1979	1978
		(In millions of dollars)	
Gain (loss) from translation and conversion	$ 1	$(2)	$(3)
Aggregate decrease in operating margins as inventories were sold subsequent to changes in foreign currency values	(50)	(64)	(14)
Write-down of inventories to market caused by declines in foreign currency values	(1)	(2)	(10)
TOTAL EFFECT ON OPERATIONS[1]	$(50)	$(68)	$(27)

[1] The effect on operations in all years is primarily attributable to Canadian operations.

Note 15. Information about the Corporation's Operations by Segment

Chrysler Corporation operates principally in two segments, automotive operations and nonautomotive operations. The Corporation's automotive operations are engaged primarily in the manufacture, assembly and sale in North America of passenger cars, trucks and related automotive parts and accessories. Purchases of vehicles from Mitsubishi Motors Corporation, an associated company of Chrysler Corporation, for sale to Chrysler dealers aggregated $688.4 million in 1978, $541.2 million in 1979 and $742.8 million in 1980.

Defense operations constitute the major portion of the Corporation's nonautomotive operations and the remainder is comprised of the manufacture and sale of outboard motors, inboard marine engines and industrial engines. The defense operations produce combat vehicles, fire control components and other military equipment under government contracts.

Operating profit consists of revenue less operating expenses. In computing operating profit, none of the following items has been added or deducted: general corporate expenses, interest expense—net, income taxes and equity in net earnings of unconsolidated subsidiaries.

Identifiable assets are those assets that are used in the Corporation's operations in each segment. Corporate assets are principally cash and time deposits, marketable securities, investments in and advances to unconsolidated subsidiaries (principally Chrysler Financial Corporation), investments in associated companies outside the United States and certain net property, plant and equipment. Substantially all depreciation, amortization and capital expenditures for the three years ended December 31, 1980 were for automotive operations.

	Automotive Operations	Non-automotive Operations	Adjustments and Eliminations	Consolidated
		(In millions of dollars)		
Year ended December 31, 1980				
Sales to unaffiliated customers	$ 8,540.0	$685.3	$ —	$ 9,225.3
Intersegment sales	8.9	2.9	(11.8)	—
TOTAL REVENUE	$ 8,548.9	$688.2	$(11.8)	$ 9,225.3
Operating profit (loss)	$(1,250.3)	$ 39.4		$(1,210.9)
Share of net loss of unconsolidated subsidiaries				(56.5)
General corporate expenses				(127.3)
Interest expense—net				(275.5)
Loss Before Taxes				$(1,670.2)
Identifiable assets	$ 4,424.5	$203.7		$ 4,628.2
Corporate assets				1,989.6
Total Assets at December 31, 1980				$ 6,617.8
Year ended December 31, 1979				
Sales to unaffiliated customers	$11,289.6	$712.3	$ —	$12,001.9
Intersegment sales	7.8	2.3	(10.1)	—
TOTAL REVENUE	$11,297.4	$714.6	$(10.1)	$12,001.9
Operating profit (loss)	$(828.3)	$ 37.6		$(790.7)
Equity in net earnings of unconsolidated subsidiaries				2.4
General corporate expenses				(98.6)
Interest expense—net				(215.4)
Loss Before Taxes				$(1,102.3)
Identifiable assets	$ 4,299.2	$183.6		$ 4,482.8
Corporate assets				2,170.3
Total Assets at December 31, 1979				$ 6,653.1
Year ended December 31, 1978				
Sales to unaffiliated customers	$12,938.8	$679.5	$ —	$13,618.3
Intersegment sales	12.0	16.8	(28.8)	—
TOTAL REVENUE	$12,950.8	$696.3	$(28.8)	$13,618.3
Operating profit (loss)	$(144.6)	$ 40.3		$(104.3)
Net earnings from European and certain South American operations				29.4
Equity in net earnings of unconsolidated subsidiaries				22.1
General corporate expenses				(104.1)
Interest expense—net				(128.9)
Loss Before Taxes				$(285.8)
Identifiable assets	$ 4,494.4	$243.8		$ 4,738.2
Corporate assets				2,243.0
Total Assets at December 31, 1978				$ 6,981.2

Note 16. Information About the Corporation and Its Subsidiaries Operating in Different Geographic Areas

	United States	Canada	All Other Areas	Adjustments and Eliminations	Consolidated
Year ended December 31, 1980					
Unit Sales:					
Sales to unaffiliated customers	935,384	144,181	145,358	—	1,224,923
Transfers between geographic areas	114,584	99,728	—	(214,312)	—
TOTAL UNIT SALES	1,049,968	243,909	145,358	(214,312)	1,224,923
			(In millions of dollars)		
Dollar Sales:					
Sales to unaffiliated customers	$ 7,149.4	$ 923.5	$1,152.4	$ —	$ 9,225.3
Transfers between geographic areas	1,327.4	807.5	23.3	(2.158.2)	—
TOTAL DOLLAR SALES	$ 8,476.8	$ 1,731.0	$1,175.7	$(2.158.2)	$ 9,225.3
Net Earnings (loss)	$(1,573.3)	$(161.8)	$ 25.4		$(1,709.7)
Identifiable Assets at December 31, 1980	$ 5,137.0	$ 536.6	$ 944.2		$ 6,617.8
Year ended December 31, 1979					
Unit Sales:					
Sales to unaffiliated customers	1,351,038	200,722	244,705	—	1,796,465
Transfers between geographic areas	166,324	151,424	—	(317,748)	—
TOTAL UNIT SALES	1,517,362	352,146	244,705	(317,748)	1,796,465
			(In millions of dollars)		
Dollar Sales:					
Sales to unaffiliated customers	$ 9,367.2	$ 1,150.3	$1,484.4	$ —	$12,001.9
Transfers between geographic areas	1,693.1	1,125.3	53.1	(2,871.5)	—
TOTAL DOLLAR SALES	$ 11,060.3	$ 2,275.6	$1,537.5	$(2,871.5)	$12,001.9
Net Earnings (loss)	$(1,072.3)	$(81.3)	$ 56.3		$(1,097.3)
Identifiable Assets at December 31, 1979	$ 4,597.8	$ 918.2	$1,137.1		$ 6,653.1
Year ended December 31, 1978					
Unit Sales:					
Sales to unaffiliated customers	1,732,142	224,431	254,962	—	2,211,535
Transfers between geographic areas	205,210	216,930	—	(422,140)	—
TOTAL UNIT SALES	1,937,352	441,361	254,962	(422,140)	2,211,535
			(In millions of dollars)		
Dollar Sales:					
Sales to unaffiliated customers	$ 11,066.0	$ 1,156.3	$1,396.0	$ —	$13,618.3
Transfers between geographic areas	1,849.0	1,421.6	70.1	(3,340.7)	—
TOTAL DOLLAR SALES	$ 12,915.0	$ 2,577.9	$1,466.1	$(3,340.7)	$13,618.3
Earnings (loss) other than below	$(219.9)	$(38.2)	$ 24.1		$(234.0)
Net earnings from European and certain South American operations					29.4
Net Loss					$(204.6)
Identifiable Assets at December 31, 1978	$ 5,299.5	$ 705.7	$ 976.0		$ 6,981.2

Transfers between geographic areas are based on prices either negotiated between buying and selling locations or on a formula as established by the parent company.

Identifiable assets are those assets that are identified with the activities in each geographic area.

Note 17. Income Maintenance Agreement with Chrysler Financial Corporation

Chrysler Corporation and Chrysler Financial Corporation (a wholly-owned unconsolidated subsidiary) have an Income Maintenance Agreement, expiring December 31, 2000, to maintain Chrysler Financial Corporation's ratio of income before taxes available for fixed charges at no less than 125% of fixed charges on an annual basis.

Payments of $106.4 million were made pursuant to the agreement in 1980, $52.8 million in 1979, and no payments were required under the agreement in 1978. The effect of this fee on both selling and administrative expense and equity in net earnings of unconsolidated subsidiaries is eliminated upon consolidation of the statement of operations of Chrysler Corporation and its consolidated subsidiaries.

Note 18. Per Share Data

Losses per share of common stock are computed using the average number of shares outstanding during the period. The net loss is adjusted for the dividend requirement on preferred shares in making the loss per share of common stock calculation.

Note 19. Inflation Accounting

Pursuant to Standard No. 33, "Financial Reporting and Changing Prices" of the Financial Accounting Standards Board, refer to page 28 of this report for supplementary disclosure of certain information intended to measure the impact of changing prices due to inflation.

Accountants' Report

Shareholders and Board of Directors
Chrysler Corporation, Detroit, Michigan

We have examined the accompanying consolidated balance sheet of Chrysler Corporation and consolidated subsidiaries at December 31, 1980 and 1979, and the related consolidated statements of operations, additional paid-in capital, net earnings retained, and changes in financial position for each of the three years in the period ended December 31, 1980. Our examinations were made in accordance with generally accepted auditing standards and accordingly included such tests of the accounting records and such other auditing procedures as we considered necessary in the circumstances.

The Corporation has incurred substantial losses in 1979 and 1980, and as more fully described in Note 2, the continuation of the Corporation is dependent upon a return to sustained profitable operations and availability, if needed, of additional financing or concessions. The Corporation's ability to achieve sustained profitability will be affected by many factors which are beyond its control, such as the automobile market conditions, actions of competitors, availability of consumer financing, interest rates, other economic conditions and government regulation. Although the Corporation has been able to fund its losses through liquidation of assets, federally guaranteed loans and concessions from its lenders, employees, and suppliers (which activities are characteristic of a company being restructured), deterioration in the Corporation's financial condition during 1980 has diminished its ability to absorb losses without further restructuring. As the Corporation further develops and executes strategies for a return to sustained profitable operations, and as a special committee of the Board of Directors reviews alternative methods for obtaining infusions of new capital, future actions may result in adjustments of assets and liabilities and changes in the relative interests of the Corporation's equity owners, in amounts that could be significant in relation to the accompanying financial statements. The foregoing matters raise a question as to whether or not the use of generally accepted accounting principles applicable to a going concern is appropriate in the circumstances.

In addition, the Corporation is continuing its negotiations for an industrial cooperation agreement with Peugeot S.A. (see Note 5), and accordingly continues to value its 14% ownership in Peugeot as a long-term investment. However, the carrying value of the Peugeot stock may require adjustment if the nature of this investment changes.

In our opinion, the accompanying financial statements have been prepared in conformity with generally accepted accounting principles applicable to a going concern applied on a consistent basis, except for the capitalization of interest in 1980 with which we concur (see Note 11). The financial statements do not purport to give effect to adjustments, if any, that may be appropriate should the Corporation be unable to operate as a going concern and therefore be required to realize its assets and liquidate its liabilities, contingent obligations and commitments in other than the normal course of business and at amounts different from those in the accompanying financial statements.

In view of the uncertainties and the ongoing restructuring described in the preceding paragraphs, we are unable to express an opinion as to whether or not the accompanying financial statements are presented fairly because we are unable to determine whether or not the use of generally accepted accounting principles applicable to a going concern is appropriate in the circumstances.

TOUCHE ROSS & CO.
Certified Public Accountants

February 27, 1981, Detroit, Michigan

APPENDIX B
TIME VALUE OF MONEY

We have seen earlier that interest is the payment made for the use of money. As such, interest is the measure of the time value of money. A dollar expected sometime in the future is not equivalent to a dollar held today, because of the time value of money. The dollar available today can be invested to earn interest, so it will increase in value to more than one dollar in the future. Consequently, we would rather receive a dollar now than receive the same amount in the future, even if we are certain of receiving it at the later date. Businesses often invest and borrow large sums of money, so the time value of money is an important topic. The dramatic increase in interest rates in recent years has had a corresponding impact on the time value of money. For example, the average interest rates on short-term bank loans between 1965 and 1970 ranged from 5% to 9%. By the middle part of the 1970s, the rate averaged as much as 14%. In the early 1980s, the interest on short-term bank loans exceeded 20% at times. We begin the examination of the time value of money with a discussion of simple and compound interest.

SIMPLE AND COMPOUND INTEREST

Simple interest is interest earned on an original amount invested (the ***principal***). The amount of principal and the interest payments remain the same from period to period, since interest is computed on the amount of principal only as:

Interest (in dollars) = Principal (in dollars) × Rate (% per year) × Time (in years)

To illustrate the computation of simple interest, assume that the Brown Supply Company sells merchandise in exchange for a $2,000 two-year note receivable, bearing simple interest of 12% per year. The amount of interest due Brown Supply Company at the end of two years is:

$$\text{Interest} = \text{Principal} \times \text{Rate} \times \text{Time}$$

$$= \$2,000 \times .12 \times 2$$

$$= \$480$$

Compound interest is interest earned on the original amount invested (principal) plus previously earned interest. As interest is earned during any period, it is added to the principal; interest is computed on the new balance (often called the compound amount) during the next period. Interest can be compounded in a number of ways, such as daily, monthly, quarterly, semiannually, or annually. As an illustration of compound interest, assume that the note receivable held by the Brown Supply Company is the same as that described earlier, except that the interest is compounded annually. The total interest for the two-year period can be computed.

(1) Year	(2) Beginning Balance	(3) Compound Interest [Column (2) × .12]	(4) Ending Balance
1	$2,000.00	$240.00	$2,240.00
2	2,240.00	268.80	2,508.80

In the second case, the total interest is $508.80, compared with the $480.00 computed earlier. The difference of $28.80 represents interest earned in the second year on the first year's interest ($240 × .12) and is the product of using compound, rather than simple, interest. In most cases involving the time value of money, compound interest is applicable, so we will consider only compound interest in the discussion that follows.

The time value of money is used in a wide variety of accounting applications, including the valuation of bonds, valuation of notes receivable or payable, determination of amounts to contribute to a pension plan, accounting for installment contracts, valuation of leases, and capital budgeting. Four cases must be considered in developing an understanding of the time value of money.

Case I   —Future value of a single amount
Case II   —Future value of an ordinary annuity
Case III —Present value of a single amount
Case IV   —Present value of an ordinary annuity

As we have seen earlier, an amount of money invested today will have a higher future value than the original principal because of interest earned. The *future value of a single amount* invested today can be computed as follows.

$$FV = PV \, (1 + i)^n$$

where:

FV = Future value
PV = Present value of single amount invested (principal)

i = Interest rate per period

n = Number of periods

Schematically, the future-value computation can be shown as:

Present value (principal invested) $\longrightarrow$ Compounded at i interest rate for n periods $\longrightarrow$ Future value (accumulated amount)

The interest rate is normally expressed as an annual rate. However, interest is often compounded more frequently—daily, monthly, quarterly, or semi-annually. In such cases, the interest rate and number of periods must coincide with the compounding schedule. For example, if 12% per year interest is earned over a two-year period with quarterly compounding, the interest rate and number of periods used in the future value formula are 3% and 8, respectively. This means that the annual interest rate (12%) is divided by the number of times compounding takes place (4) within a year, giving 3%, and the number of years (2) is multiplied by the number of compounding periods (4), giving 8 periods.

To illustrate the use of the future value formula with annual compounding, consider again the Brown Supply Company case with compound interest. The future value of the note receivable is found as follows.

$$FV = \$2,000 \ (1 + .12)^2$$

$$= \$2,508.80$$

As we see, the total amount due Brown Supply Company at maturity ($2,508.80) is the same as we computed earlier by adding the compound interest to the principal. If the note receivable involves quarterly compounding, we must revise the formula by dividing the 12% interest rate by 4 and multiplying 2 years by 4 as:

$$FV = \$2,000 \ (1 + .03)^8$$

$$= \$2,533.60$$

The amount of interest earned with quarterly compounding will be $24.80 more than it was with annual compounding. Note that the mathematics involved with the future value formula become more tedious as we increase the number of periods involved. Fortunately, tables have been developed for various combinations of interest rates and periods to avoid the necessity of using the formula each time a future value of a single amount of money must be computed. Table B–1 shows the future value of $1 for various interest rates and various periods.

Suppose we want to know how much a dollar invested today at 12% interest compounded annually will be worth 10 years from now. We simply find the amount (called a *factor*) in the 12% column and 10 periods row of Table B–1—3.1058. Thus, the dollar invested now will become approximately $3.11 in 10 years, because of the compound interest earned. Note that the left-hand column of Table B–1 (and the other tables discussed later) refers to periods instead of years. This enables us to use the table even if interest is compounded more frequently than once a year. As we noted earlier for such cases, the

Periods	2%	3%	4%	5%	6%	8%	10%	12%	16%	20%
1	1.0200	1.0300	1.0400	1.0500	1.0600	1.0800	1.1000	1.1200	1.1600	1.2000
2	1.0404	1.0609	1.0816	1.1025	1.1236	1.1664	1.2100	1.2544	1.3456	1.4400
3	1.0612	1.0927	1.1249	1.1576	1.1910	1.2597	1.3310	1.4049	1.5609	1.7280
4	1.0824	1.1255	1.1699	1.2155	1.2625	1.3605	1.4641	1.5735	1.8106	2.0736
5	1.1041	1.1593	1.2167	1.2763	1.3382	1.4693	1.6105	1.7623	2.1003	2.4883
6	1.1262	1.1941	1.2653	1.3401	1.4185	1.5869	1.7716	1.9738	2.4364	2.9860
7	1.1487	1.2299	1.3159	1.4071	1.5036	1.7138	1.9487	2.2107	2.8262	3.5832
8	1.1717	1.2668	1.3686	1.4775	1.5938	1.8509	2.1436	2.4760	3.2784	4.2998
9	1.1951	1.3048	1.4233	1.5513	1.6895	1.9990	2.3579	2.7731	3.8030	5.1598
10	1.2190	1.3439	1.4802	1.6289	1.7908	2.1589	2.5937	3.1058	4.4114	6.1917
11	1.2434	1.3842	1.5395	1.7103	1.8983	2.3316	2.8531	3.4785	5.1173	7.4301
12	1.2682	1.4258	1.6010	1.7959	2.0122	2.5182	3.1384	3.8960	5.9360	8.9161
13	1.2936	1.4685	1.6651	1.8856	2.1329	2.7196	3.4523	4.3635	6.8858	10.6993
14	1.3195	1.5126	1.7317	1.9799	2.2609	2.9372	3.7975	4.8871	7.9875	12.8392
15	1.3459	1.5580	1.8009	2.0789	2.3966	3.1722	4.1772	5.4736	9.2655	15.4070
16	1.3728	1.6047	1.8730	2.1829	2.5404	3.4259	4.5950	6.1304	10.7480	18.4884
17	1.4002	1.6528	1.9479	2.2920	2.6928	3.7000	5.0545	6.8660	12.4677	22.1861
18	1.4282	1.7024	2.0258	2.4066	2.8543	3.9960	5.5599	7.6900	14.4625	26.6233
19	1.4568	1.7535	2.1068	2.5270	3.0256	4.3157	6.1159	8.6128	16.7765	31.9480
20	1.4859	1.8061	2.1911	2.6533	3.2071	4.6610	6.7275	9.6463	19.4608	38.3376
25	1.6406	2.0938	2.6658	3.3864	4.2919	6.8485	10.8347	17.0001	40.8742	95.3962
30	1.8114	2.4273	3.2434	4.3219	5.7435	10.0627	17.4494	29.9599	85.8499	237.3763

Table B–1
Future Value of $1

number of years is multiplied by the number of times compounding occurs to determine the number of periods that must be considered. In addition, an annual interest rate is divided by the number of compounding periods to convert it to the appropriate interest rate. For example, assume the dollar invested earlier will earn 12% interest compounded semiannually instead of annually. We need to multiply 10 years by 2 (20 periods) and divide 12% by 2 (6 percent) to determine the appropriate factor in Table B–1. The factor is 3.2071— located in the 6% interest rate column and 20 periods row. Therefore, the dollar will grow to approximately $3.21 over the 10-year period. This same adjustment is required with the later tables whenever interest is compounded more frequently than once a year.

The factors in Table B–1 were determined by using the future value formula with a principal of $1. By multiplying a specific factor found in the table for the appropriate combination of interest rate and number of periods by the single amount of money involved, the future value of that amount can be calculated. To illustrate the use of Table B–1 when the amount involved is more than $1, assume again that the two-year note receivable of Brown Supply Company has a 12% interest rate compounded annually. The factor in Table B–1 for 12% interest and two years is 1.2544, so the note's future value is:

$$FV = \$2,000 \, (1.2544)$$

$$= \$2,508.80$$

This is the same result we obtained earlier with the future value formula. If interest is compounded quarterly, the factor from the table is 1.2668 (3% and 8 periods), so the future value is:

$$FV = \$2,000 \, (1.2668)$$
$$= \$2,533.60$$

Again, the future value is the same as the one computed earlier with the formula approach.

CASE II (FUTURE VALUE OF AN ORDINARY ANNUITY)

In contrast to the single amount of money considered in Case I, an ***annuity*** consists of a series of payments over a specified number of periods, with compound interest on the payments. An ***ordinary annuity*** is a series of equal payments that occur at the end of each time period involved. Here we will consider only ordinary annuities and defer the subject of annuities due (in which the payments occur at the beginning of the time periods) to more advanced accounting courses.

The future value of an ordinary annuity is the sum of all payments, plus the compound interest accumulated on each. For example, if a business makes a deposit of $5,000 to a savings program at the end of three consecutive years, with each payment earning 12% interest compounded annually, the total amount accumulated over the three-year period is the future value of an ordinary annuity. One way to calculate the future value of the series of payments would be to treat each payment separately and determine the amount of interest earned.

(1) Year	(2) Beginning Balance	(3) Annual Interest [Column (2) × .12]	(4) Payment	(5) Ending Balance
1			$5,000	$ 5,000
2	$ 5,000	$ 600	5,000	10,600
3	10,600	1,272	5,000	16,872

It can be seen from these calculations that interest is earned for only two periods, even though three payments were made. As the number of payments increases, this approach obviously becomes more time-consuming.

A formula can be used also to calculate the future value of an ordinary annuity. The formula is more complicated than the one used for the future value of a single amount, however, so it is not normally utilized. Instead, a table, such as Table B–2, is used, because it contains factors for various combinations of interest rates and number of periods as computed with a *future value of an ordinary annuity* formula when payments of $1 are involved.

To illustrate the use of Table B–2, consider again that the company makes three annual payments of $5,000 at the end of each year and earns 12% interest, compounded annually. The factor for 12% interest and three periods in Table B–2 is 3.3744. Since the factor represents the future value of three

Periods	2%	3%	4%	5%	6%	8%	10%	12%	16%	20%
1	1.0000	1.0000	1.0000	1.0000	1.0000	1.0000	1.0000	1.0000	1.0000	1.0000
2	2.0200	2.0300	2.0400	2.0500	2.0600	2.0800	2.1000	2.1200	2.1600	2.2000
3	3.0604	3.0909	3.1216	3.1525	3.1836	3.2464	3.3100	3.3744	3.5056	3.6400
4	4.1216	4.1836	4.2465	4.3101	4.3746	4.5061	4.6410	4.7793	5.0665	5.3680
5	5.2040	5.3091	5.4163	5.5256	5.6371	5.8666	6.1051	6.3528	6.8771	7.4416
6	6.3081	6.4684	6.6330	6.8019	6.9753	7.3359	7.7156	8.1152	8.9775	9.9299
7	7.4343	7.6625	7.8983	8.1420	8.3938	8.9228	9.4872	10.0890	11.4139	12.9159
8	8.5830	8.8923	9.2142	9.5491	9.8975	10.6366	11.4359	12.2997	14.2401	16.4991
9	9.7546	10.1591	10.5828	11.0266	11.4913	12.4876	13.5795	14.7757	17.5185	20.7989
10	10.9497	11.4639	12.0061	12.5779	13.1808	14.4866	15.9374	17.5487	21.3215	25.9587
11	12.1687	12.8078	13.4864	14.2068	14.9716	16.6455	18.5312	20.6546	25.7329	32.1504
12	13.4121	14.1920	15.0258	15.9171	16.8699	18.9771	21.3843	24.1331	30.8502	39.5805
13	14.6803	15.6178	16.6268	17.7130	18.8821	21.4953	24.5227	28.0291	36.7862	48.4966
14	15.9739	17.0863	18.2919	19.5986	21.0151	24.2149	27.9750	32.3926	43.6720	59.1959
15	17.2934	18.5989	20.0236	21.5786	23.2760	27.1521	31.7725	37.2797	51.6595	72.0351
16	18.6393	20.1569	21.8245	23.6575	25.6725	30.3243	35.9497	42.7533	60.9250	87.4421
17	20.0121	21.7616	23.6975	25.8404	28.2129	33.7502	40.5447	48.8837	71.6730	105.9306
18	21.4123	23.4144	25.6454	28.1324	30.9057	37.4502	45.5992	55.7497	84.1407	128.1167
19	22.8406	25.1169	27.6712	30.5390	33.7600	41.4463	51.1591	63.4397	98.6032	154.7400
20	24.2974	26.8704	29.7781	33.0660	36.7856	45.7620	57.2750	72.0524	115.3797	186.6880
25	32.0303	36.4593	41.6459	47.7271	54.8645	73.1059	98.3471	133.3339	249.2140	471.9811
30	40.5681	47.5754	56.0849	66.4388	79.0582	113.2832	164.4940	241.3327	530.3117	1181.8816

Table B–2
Future Value of an Ordinary Annuity of $1

payments of $1 at 12% interest, it is used to determine the future value of the actual payments made as:

$$FV = \$5,000 \ (3.3744)$$
$$= \$16,872$$

This is the same answer we found earlier by treating each payment separately. The three payments of $5,000 each (total of $15,000) will increase in value to $16,872 over the three-year period. The difference between the $16,872 future value and the payments totaling $15,000 is interest amounting to $1,872. If semiannual payments of $2,500 had been involved during the three-year period, the appropriate factor from Table B–2 would be for six periods and 6%. Again, this adjustment is required because of semiannual compounding. The factor for six periods and 6% from Table B–2 is 6.9753, so the future value of the ordinary annuity is:

$$FV = \$2,500 \ (6.9753)$$
$$= \$17,438.25$$

As we see, the future value of $17,438.25 with semiannual compounding is higher than the $16,872.00 computed with annual compounding, because additional interest is earned.

CASE III (PRESENT VALUE OF A SINGLE AMOUNT)

In Case I, we were concerned with the determination of the future value of a single amount of money. Many accounting applications of the time value of money involve the reverse of the future value consideration, the concern with computing the present value of some future amount of money. As noted earlier, money held today is worth more than the same amount of money received in the future because of the time value of money. Consequently, the present value of a given amount to be received in the future will be less than the future value. To determine the present value of a specific future amount, the future value must be discounted with an appropriate interest rate to the present. The interest rate involved is also called a **discount rate.** Future value and present value have a reciprocal relationship, as can be seen by comparing the formulas for the future value and the present value of a single amount of money. Recall that the future value is computed as:

$$FV = PV (1 + i)^n$$

In contrast, the **present value of a single amount** of money is calculated as:

$$PV = \frac{FV}{(1 + i)^n}$$

where:

PV = Present value
FV = Future value of amount to be accumulated
i = Interest rate per period
n = Number of periods

Schematically, the present value computation can be shown as:

Present value   Discounted at i Future value
(amount to be ⟵ interest rate   ⟵ (amount to be
invested now)   for n periods   accumulated)

To illustrate the use of the present value of a single amount of money formula, consider again the note receivable held by Brown Supply Company. We determined earlier that the future value of the note was $2,508.80 when interest was compounded annually. By discounting the $2,508.80 for two years at 12%, we can determine its present value, which should be $2,000, as:

$$PV = \frac{\$2,508.80}{(1 + .12)^2}$$

$$= \$2,000.00$$

If the interest is compounded quarterly, we learned earlier that the future value of the note is $2,533.60. However, the present value of the note should remain at $2,000 when it is discounted for eight periods at 3% interest per period, or:

$$PV = \frac{\$2,533.60}{(1 + .03)^8}$$

$$= \$2,000.00$$

As another example of calculating the present value of a single amount of money, assume that the Holmes Company has a liability of $23,958, which must be paid in three years. The company wants to know how much it must invest today to have $23,958 in three years if the amount earns 10% interest, compounded annually. The amount to be invested would be determined as:

$$PV = \frac{\$23,958}{(1 + .10)^3}$$

$$= \$18,000$$

Consequently, the $18,000 (present value) will increase in value to $23,958 (future value) by the end of the third year, because interest amounting to $5,958 will be earned. Like the future value formulas, the math involved with the computation of present value with a formula can be tedious, so a table is normally used. Table B–3 shows factors for various combinations of interest rates and number of periods when the present value of $1 is computed. By multiplying an appropriate factor from the table by the single amount of money involved, its present value can be determined. For example, in the Brown Supply Company case with annual compounding, a value of .7972 is found in Table B–3 for 12% interest and two periods. Thus, the present value of the note receivable is:

$$PV = \$2,508.80 \ (.7972)$$

$$= \$2,000$$

With quarterly compounding, the value in Table B–3 is found for 3% interest and eight periods (.7894) and used as follows.

$$PV = \$2,533.60 \ (.7894)$$

$$= \$2,000$$

Table B–3 can also be used to determine the amount that the Holmes Company must invest today to have $23,958 three years later with the same factors discussed earlier. The factor in Table B–3 for 10% interest and three periods is .7513, so the present value of $23,958 is:

$$PV = \$23,958 \ (.7513)$$

$$= \$18,000$$

Note that each of the factors shown in Table B–3 for a particular combination of interest rates and number of periods is one divided by the corresponding factor found in Table B–1. This must be true because of the reciprocal relationship between the formulas for future value and present value of a single amount. For example, the factor in Table B–3 for 12% interest and 2 periods is .7972, which is the same as one divided by 1.2544 (Table B–1). Consequently, you can always determine the appropriate Table B–3 factor from Table B–1 and vice-versa if both tables are not available.

Periods	2%	3%	4%	5%	6%	8%	10%	12%	16%	20%
1	0.9804	0.9709	0.9615	0.9524	0.9434	0.9259	0.9091	0.8929	0.8621	0.8333
2	0.9612	0.9426	0.9246	0.9070	0.8900	0.8573	0.8264	0.7972	0.7432	0.6944
3	0.9423	0.9151	0.8890	0.8638	0.8396	0.7938	0.7513	0.7118	0.6407	0.5787
4	0.9238	0.8885	0.8548	0.8227	0.7921	0.7350	0.6830	0.6355	0.5523	0.4823
5	0.9057	0.8626	0.8219	0.7835	0.7473	0.6806	0.6209	0.5674	0.4761	0.4019
6	0.8880	0.8375	0.7903	0.7462	0.7050	0.6302	0.5645	0.5066	0.4104	0.3349
7	0.8706	0.8131	0.7599	0.7107	0.6651	0.5835	0.5132	0.4523	0.3538	0.2791
8	0.8535	0.7894	0.7307	0.6768	0.6274	0.5403	0.4665	0.4039	0.3050	0.2326
9	0.8368	0.7664	0.7026	0.6446	0.5919	0.5002	0.4241	0.3606	0.2630	0.1938
10	0.8203	0.7441	0.6756	0.6139	0.5584	0.4632	0.3855	0.3220	0.2267	0.1615
11	0.8043	0.7224	0.6496	0.5847	0.5268	0.4289	0.3505	0.2875	0.1954	0.1346
12	0.7885	0.7014	0.6246	0.5568	0.4970	0.3971	0.3186	0.2567	0.1685	0.1122
13	0.7730	0.6810	0.6006	0.5303	0.4688	0.3677	0.2897	0.2292	0.1452	0.0935
14	0.7579	0.6611	0.5775	0.5051	0.4423	0.3405	0.2633	0.2046	0.1252	0.0779
15	0.7430	0.6419	0.5553	0.4810	0.4173	0.3152	0.2394	0.1827	0.1079	0.0649
16	0.7284	0.6232	0.5339	0.4581	0.3936	0.2919	0.2176	0.1631	0.0930	0.0541
17	0.7142	0.6050	0.5134	0.4363	0.3714	0.2703	0.1978	0.1456	0.0802	0.0451
18	0.7002	0.5874	0.4936	0.4155	0.3503	0.2502	0.1799	0.1300	0.0691	0.0376
19	0.6864	0.5703	0.4746	0.3957	0.3305	0.2317	0.1635	0.1161	0.0596	0.0313
20	0.6730	0.5537	0.4564	0.3769	0.3118	0.2145	0.1486	0.1037	0.0514	0.0261
25	0.6095	0.4776	0.3751	0.2953	0.2330	0.1460	0.0923	0.0588	0.0245	0.0105
30	0.5521	0.4120	0.3083	0.2314	0.1741	0.0994	0.0573	0.0334	0.0116	0.0042

Table B–3
Present Value of $1

CASE IV (PRESENT VALUE OF AN ORDINARY ANNUITY)

In Case II, we considered how to determine the future value of an ordinary
annuity—a series of equal payments made at the end of each time period
involved. Our final concern with the time value of money is the reverse of
Case II—that is, the present value of a series of equal future payments representing an ordinary annuity. The present value of an ordinary annuity is the
amount that would have to be invested today at a certain compound interest
rate to enable the investor to receive the series of future payments over a
specified period of time. Assume that the Briden Corporation has obligations
of $6,000 that must be repaid at the end of each of the next three years,
including the current one. The firm wants to know how much it would have
to invest today to repay each of the obligations if the amount invested earns
10%, compounded annually. One way to determine the amount of the required
investment would be to treat each $6,000 payment as a single amount. Each
payment would be discounted to its present value (using Table B–3), and the
results would be added to determine the total amount needed to be invested.
If this approach is taken, the following calculations are necessary.

(1)	(2)	(3)	(4)
Year	Payment	Factor	Present Value
		(Table B–3—10%)	[Column (2) × Column (3)]
1	$6,000	.9091	$ 5,454.60
2	6,000	.8264	4,958.40
3	6,000	.7513	4,507.80
Total present value			$14,920.80

The firm would have to invest $14,920.80 today to have the money available to make payments of $6,000 at the end of each of the next three years. If numerous payments are involved, this approach will obviously be quite time-consuming. Since the $6,000 payments can be viewed as an annuity, an easier way to discount them to their present value is to use Table B–4. The factors in Table B–4 have been derived from a formula representing the **present value of an annuity of $1.** In the table, factors for various combinations of interest rates and number of periods are presented for the determination of the present value of an annuity of $1. Again, a given factor must be multiplied by the actual amount of each payment involved. The factor is 2.4869 for 10% and

Table B–4
Present Value of an Ordinary Annuity of $1

Periods	2%	3%	4%	5%	6%	8%	10%	12%	16%	20%
1	0.9804	0.9709	0.9615	0.9524	0.9434	0.9259	0.9091	0.8929	0.8621	0.8333
2	1.9416	1.9135	1.8861	1.8594	1.8334	1.7833	1.7355	1.6901	1.6052	1.5278
3	2.8839	2.8286	2.7751	2.7232	2.6730	2.5771	2.4869	2.4018	2.2459	2.1065
4	3.8077	3.7171	3.6299	3.5460	3.4651	3.3121	3.1699	3.0373	2.7982	2.5887
5	4.7135	4.5797	4.4518	4.3295	4.2124	3.9927	3.7908	3.6048	3.2743	2.9906
6	5.6014	5.4172	5.2421	5.0757	4.9173	4.6229	4.3553	4.1114	3.6847	3.3255
7	6.4720	6.2303	6.0021	5.7864	5.5824	5.2064	4.8684	4.5638	4.0386	3.6016
8	7.3255	7.0197	6.7327	6.4632	6.2098	5.7466	5.3349	4.9676	4.3436	3.8372
9	8.1622	7.7861	7.4353	7.1078	6.8017	6.2469	5.7590	5.3282	4.6065	4.0310
10	8.9826	8.5302	8.1109	7.7217	7.3601	6.7101	6.1446	5.6502	4.8332	4.1925
11	9.7868	9.2526	8.7605	8.3064	7.8869	7.1390	6.4951	5.9377	5.0286	4.3271
12	10.5753	9.9540	9.3851	8.8633	8.3838	7.5361	6.8137	6.1944	5.1971	4.4392
13	11.3484	10.6350	9.9856	9.3936	8.8527	7.9038	7.1034	6.4235	5.3423	4.5327
14	12.1062	11.2961	10.5631	9.8986	9.2950	8.2442	7.3667	6.6282	5.4675	4.6106
15	12.8493	11.9379	11.1184	10.3797	9.7122	8.5595	7.6061	6.8109	5.5755	4.6755
16	13.5777	12.5611	11.6523	10.8378	10.1059	8.8514	7.8237	6.9740	5.6685	4.7296
17	14.2919	13.1661	12.1657	11.2741	10.4773	9.1216	8.0216	7.1196	5.7487	4.7746
18	14.9920	13.7535	12.6593	11.6896	10.8276	9.3719	8.2014	7.2497	5.8178	4.8122
19	15.6785	14.3238	13.1339	12.0853	11.1581	9.6036	8.3649	7.3658	5.8775	4.8435
20	16.3514	14.8775	13.5903	12.4622	11.4699	9.8181	8.5136	7.4694	5.9288	4.8696
25	19.5235	17.4131	15.6221	14.0939	12.7834	10.6748	9.0770	7.8431	6.0971	4.9476
30	22.3965	19.6004	17.2920	15.3725	13.7648	11.2578	9.4269	8.0552	6.1772	4.9789

three periods. Therefore, the present value of the $6,000 payments can be calculated as:

$$PV = \$6,000 \ (2.4869)$$
$$= \$14,921.40$$

As we see, the results are essentially the same as those obtained by discounting each payment and adding the individual present values. If semiannual payments of $3,000 were made to satisfy the firm's obligations, the present value calculation would require an adjustment of the number of periods and the annual interest rate. Six periods (three years $\times$ 2) and an interest rate of 5% (10% $\div$ 2) would be used to determine the factor of 5.0757 from Table B–4, and the present value of the annuity would be:

$$PV = \$3,000 \ (5.0757)$$
$$= \$15,227.10$$

Note that the present value with semiannual payments is more than it was with annual payments. The reason for this is that the amount invested will not have as much time to earn interest because payments are made every six months rather than at the end of the year.

EXERCISES

Exercise B-1 Compute Simple Interest
The Hinkle Company has agreed to take a note receivable in exchange for an overdue account receivable from the Pay-Late Company. Simple interest, at 16%, is payable beginning March 1 (the date of the exchange) and the note receivable is for a three-year term. The amount of the note receivable is $4,000 and interest will be paid at the maturity of the note.

Required:
Calculate the amount of interest due at the end of three years.

Exercise B-2 Compute Compound Interest
Refer to Exercise B-1. How much interest would be due if compound interest were involved?

Exercise B-3 Compute the Future Value of a Single Amount
Using Table B–1, compute the following future values.

1. $10,000 invested at 12% for 5 years, compounded annually.
2. $10,000 invested at 12% for 5 years, compounded semiannually.
3. $10,000 invested at 12% for 5 years, compounded quarterly.

Exercise B-4 Compute the Future Value of a Single Amount
An investor wants to know how much a $5,000 investment made today will amount to in 15 years if it earns 10% interest, compounded annually.

Exercise B-5 Compute the Future Value of an Annuity
Using Table B–2, determine the following future values.

1. $10,000 invested at the end of each year for five years at 12%, compounded annually.
2. $5,000 invested at the end of each six months for five years at 12% per year, compounded semiannually.
3. $2,500 invested at the end of each three months for five years at 12% per year, compounded quarterly.

Exercise B-6 Compute the Future Value of an Annuity

An investor wants to know how much she will have if she makes annual payments of $5,000 at the end of the year for 10 years, assuming that the money will earn 10%.

Exercise B-7 Compute the Present Value of a Single Amount

Using Table B–3, determine the present values of the following situations.

1. $10,000 in five years at 12%, compounded annually.
2. $10,000 in five years at 12%, compounded semiannually.
3. $10,000 in five years at 12%, compounded quarterly.

Exercise B-8 Compute the Present Value of a Single Amount

Don Clarkson wants to establish a college fund for his only daughter, who is currently eight years old. He wants to know how much he must invest today for it to accumulate to be $50,000 in 10 years at 10%. Ignore income taxes.

Exercise B-9 Compute the Present Value of an Annuity

Using Table B–4, compute the present values of the following situations.

1. $10,000 to be paid at the end of each year for five years, assuming 12% interest and annual compounding.
2. $5,000 to be paid at the end of each six months for five years, assuming 12% annual interest and semiannual compounding.
3. $2,500 to be paid at the end of each three months for five years, assuming 12% annual interest and quarterly compounding.

Exercise B-10 Compute the Present Value of an Annuity

An investor wants to receive $5,000 at the end of each year for the next five years (including the current year). How much must she invest today to achieve this objective, assuming that the money earns 10%?

PROBLEMS

Problem B-1 Computing the Future Value of $1

Patricia Rogers wants to invest $10,000 for a five-year period and receive the largest amount of interest possible. A local bank has offered her 8% interest compounded quarterly and a savings and loan association has offered her 10% interest compounded annually.

Required:

Which of the two investments will provide Patricia with the most money at the end of the five-year period?

Problem B-2 Calculating the Future Value of an Annuity

The Johnson Company recently issued bonds totaling $535,000, and must establish a fund with which the bonds will be repaid at the end of 20 years. Annual payments of $10,000 will be made to the fund at the end of each of 20 years. A local bank has agreed to pay the company 8% for each of the first 10 years and 10% for each of the second 10 years on all funds invested if the money is deposited in the bank.

Required:

Will Johnson Company be able to accumulate enough money with this arrangement to retire the bonds at the end of 20 years?

Problem B-3 Computing the Present Value of $1

Bill Mack, a Vice President with the Brown Company, is retiring. Under the terms of his salary agreement, he has the option of receiving a $60,000 bonus now or a deferred bonus of $90,000 in five years.

Required:

Assuming that Mr. Mack can earn 10% on his investments, which option should he choose? Ignore income taxes.

Problem B-4 Computing the Present Value of an Annuity

Anne Kelly is considering retirement at age 50. She has accumulated a significant amount of cash, which is currently invested in a bank money market fund. Her accountant estimates that Ms. Kelly will need $30,000 per year to live on, for the next 15 years, until she qualifies for social security and receives an inheritance from her uncle. Her banker has guaranteed an interest rate of 10% compounded annually.

Required:

A. How much must Anne Kelly invest now to be able to receive $30,000 annually for 15 years?

B. How much interest income will she receive during the 15 years?

Problem B-5 Combining Future Value and Present Value

Robert Perry loaned his sister $12,000, so that she could buy a new car. In return, Perry received a note due in four years, with interest at 8% compounded semiannually. After one year, Perry found himself in need of cash. The sister could not repay the loan at the time, so Perry discounted the note at the bank for cash at 12% compounded quarterly.

Required:

A. How much cash did Perry receive from the bank?

B. Did Perry have interest income or interest expense from the transaction?

PHOTO CREDITS

Part 1 The Port Authority of New York

Part 2 Tom Ebenhoh/Black Star

Part 3 Jim Ayres/Black Star

Part 4 Georg Gerster/Photo Researchers

Part 5 Georg Gerster/Photo Researchers

Part 6 Wheeler Pictures/Cameramann Int'l. Ltd.

Part 7 Joan Liftin/Archive Pictures

Part 8 Van Bucher/Photo Researchers

INDEX

Numbers in **boldface color** refer to pages in the glossary.

Government Accounting Standards Board (GASB), 13
Governmental accounting, 11
Gross earnings, 471–472, **485**
Gross income, 1092, **1112**
Gross invoice method, 205, 221, **226**
Gross profit (gross margin) on sales, 202, **226**, 826–827
Gross profit method:
  defined, 387, **394**
  illustrated, 387–389

Hardware, 271, **274**
Head of household, 1097
High-low method, 1012
Historical costs, 976, 978
Horizontal analysis:
  defined, 778, **795**
  illustrated, 778–781

Ideal standards, 978–979, **991**
Idle capacity, 989
Importing transactions, 715–717
Imputing interest, 413, **430**
Inadequacy, 415, **430**
Income statement:
  consolidated, 710–712
  constant dollar, 513
  current value, 515
  defined, 17, **27**
  departmental contribution to indirect expenses, 836
  departmental gross profit, 826–827
  departmental net income, 829
  manufacturing firm, 867
  merchandising firm, 202, 217, 867
  multiple step, 216
  preparation from trial balance, 111–113
  preparation from worksheet, 154
  single-step, 112
  special items, 616–621
Income summary, 158
Income tax allocation:
  defined, 671, **675**
  depreciation timing difference, 670
  illustrated, 670–674
  Permanent differences, 669
  Timing difference, 670
Income taxes:
  cash basis vs. accrual basis, 1090–1091
  choice of business, 1108–1110
  choice of financing methods, 1111
  classification of taxable entities, 1080–1089
  corporations, 1106–1112
  income tax allocation, 669–674
  individuals, 1086–1105
  installment method, 504
  merchandise inventory, 378
  operating the business, 1111
  plant assets, 421
  reporting income tax expense, 618, 670–673

tax planning, 1089
tax shield effect, 1066–1069
timing difference, 670
trade-in of plant asset, 448
Incorporators, 574, **593**
Incremental analysis, 1048–1054
Incremental costs, 1048
Indenture, 642, **675**
Indirect cost (expense), 830, **842**, 863–864
Indirect labor, 863, 900–901
Indirect materials, 863, 897–900
Inflation:
  accounting for, 509–516
  constant dollar, 510–513
  current value, 514–516
  defined, 508, **517**
  FASB requirements, 516
Information processing system, 4–5
Installment method, 504, **517**
Installment notes, 665–666
Intangible asset:
  copyright, 453
  defined, 117, **122**, 451, **458**
  franchises, 455
  goodwill, 456–458
  leasehold, 453–455
  patent, 452
  trademarks, 453
Interest:
  compound, B2
  computing, 348
  defined, 347, **357**
  future value:
    of ordinary annuity, B5–B6
    of single amount, B2–B5
  imputing interest, 413, 430
  itemized deduction, 1095
  present value:
    of ordinary annuity, 1060, B9–B11
    of single amount, 1059–1060, B7–B9
  simple, B1
Interim statements:
  defined, 42, **74**, 172
  preparation without closing, 172
Internal accounting, 818
Internal auditing:
  defined, 11, **27**
  part of internal control, 250
Internal control:
  accounting controls, 246–247, **273**
  accounting system, 246, **273**
  administrative controls, 246, **274**
  control of cash disbursements, 297–298, 313–321
  control of cash receipts, 295–297
  defined, 246, **274**
  design of, 247–250
  payroll, 469–470
Internal Revenue Code, 1087, 1112
Internal rate of return, 1064–1065, **1071**
Internal transactions, 5, 40